THE

SECOND PART

OF THE

Institutes of the Laws of England;

CONTAINING

THE EXPOSITION OF MANY ANCIENT AND OTHER STATUTES.

Jurisperito dixit, In lege quid scriptum est? quomodo legis? Luc. x. 26.

Quod non lego, non credo. *August.*

Jurisprudentia est juvenibus regimen, senibus solamen, pauperibus divitiæ & divitibus securitas.

AUTHORE EDWARDO COKE, MILITE, *J. C.*

HÆC EGO GRANDÆVUS POSUI TIBI, CANDIDE LECTOR.

THE LAWBOOK EXCHANGE, LTD.
Clark, New Jersey

ISBN 9781584772002

Lawbook Exchange edition 2002, 2012

The quality of this reprint is equivalent to the quality of the original work.

THE LAWBOOK EXCHANGE, LTD.
33 Terminal Avenue
Clark, New Jersey 07066-1321

Please see our website for a selection of our other publications and fine facsimile reprints of classic works of legal history:
www.lawbookexchange.com

Library of Congress Cataloging-in-Publication Data

Coke, Edward, Sir, 1552-1634.
The second part of the institutes of the laws of England containing the exposition of many ancient and other statutes / authore Edwardo Coke.
p. cm.
Chiefly English; some French and Latin.
Originally published: London: W. Clarke and Sons, Law Booksellers, 1817.
Includes bibliographical references.
ISBN 1-58477-200-X (cloth: alk. paper)
1. Law—England. 2. Law—Great Britain—History—Sources. I. Title.

KD600 .C642 2001
349.42—dc21 2001045981

Printed in the United States of America on acid-free paper

THE

SECOND PART

OF THE

Institutes of the Laws of England;

CONTAINING

THE EXPOSITION OF MANY ANCIENT AND OTHER STATUTES.

Jurisperito dixit, In lege quid scriptum est? quomodo legis? Luc. x. 26.

Quod non lego, non credo. *August.*

Jurisprudentia est juvenibus regimen, senibus solamen, pauperibus divitiæ & divitibus securitas.

AUTHORE EDWARDO COKE, MILITE, *J. C.*

HÆC EGO GRANDÆVUS POSUI TIBI, CANDIDE LECTOR.

LONDON:

PRINTED FOR W. CLARKE AND SONS, LAW BOOKSELLERS,

PORTUGAL-STREET, LINCOLN'S INN.

1817.

A TABLE

Of the ſeveral Statutes treated of in this Second Part of the INSTITUTES.

DEO,

DEO,

PATRIÆ,

TIBI.

A PROEME

TO THE

SECOND PART *of the* INSTITUTES.

IN the firſt part of the Inſtitutes, following Littleton our guide, we have treated of ſuch parts of the common laws, ſtatutes, and cuſtomes, as he in his three books hath left unto us. We are in this ſecond part of the Inſtitutes to ſpeak of *Magna Charta*, and many ancient and other ſtatutes, as in the table precedent doe appeare.

It is called *Magna Charta*, not that it is great in quantity, for there be many voluminous charters commonly paſſed, ſpecially in theſe later times, longer then this is; nor comparatively in reſpect that it is greater then Charta de Foreſta, but in reſpect of the great importance, and weightineſſe of the matter, as hereafter ſhall appeare: and likewiſe for the ſame cauſe *Charta de Foreſta*, is called *Magna Charta de Foreſta*, and both of them are called *Magnæ Chartæ libertatum Angliæ*.

Marlb. cap. 5. Inſpex. 25 E. 1. 12 H. 3. *Sententia lata ſuper chartas* Bract. lib. 3. fol. 291. & lib 5 fol. 414. Mirror, cap. § Regiſtr. 8 E. 3. Itin' Pick. Rot. 43. Atons caſe. Rot. Pat. 20. Marcii 1 E. 3. de perambulatione for' in com' Eſſex. Rot. Parl. 22 E. 3. nu. 36.

King Alexander was called Alexander Magnus, not in

respect of the largenesse of his body, for he was a little man, but in respect of the greatnesse of his heroical spirit, of whom it might be truly said,

Mens tamen in parvo corpore magna fuit;

so as of this great charter it may be truly said, that it is *magnum in parvo*.

And it is also called *Charta libertatum regni*; and upon great reason it is so called of the effect, *quia liberos facit*: sometime for the same cause, *communis libertas*, and *le chartre des franchises*.

The Ends. *Sapiens incipit à fine*.

There be four ends of this great charter, mentioned in the preface, *viz.* 1. The honour of Almighty God, &c. 2. The safety of the kings soule; 3. The advancement of holy church; and 4. The amendment of the realme: foure most excellent ends, whereof more shall be said hereafter.

By what authority, and when.

By charter bearing date the 11. day of February, in the 9 yeare of king H. 3. and secondly, by that charter established by authority of parliament then sitting, and so entred into the parliament roll; the witnesses to the said charter were 31. lords spirituall, *viz.* Stephen Langton archbishop of Canterbury, E. bishop of London, I. B. of Bath, P. of Winchester, H. of Lincoln, Robert of Salisbury, W. of Rochester, W. of Worcester, I. of Ely, H. of Hereford, R. of Chicester, William of Exeter, bishops. The abbot of S. Edes, the abbot of S. Albons, the abbot of Battaile, the abbot of S. Augustines in Canterbury, the Abbot of Evesham, the abbot of Westminster, the abbot of Burghe S. Peter, the abbot of Reading, the abbot of Abindon, the abbot of Malmesbury, the abbot of Winchcombe, the abbot of Hyde, the abbot of Certesey, the abbot of Shernborn, the abbot of Cerne, the abbot of Abbotebury, the abbot of Middleton, the abbot of Selbie, the abbot of Cirencester; and 33. of the nobility, *viz.* Hubert de Burgo chiefe justice of England,

land, and 32. earles and barons, *viz.* Randall earle of Chester and Lincoln, William earle of Salisbury, William earle Warren, Gilbert of Clare earle of Glocester and Hertford, William de Ferrars earle of Derby, William Mandevile earle of Essex, H. de Bigod earle of Norffolk, William earle of Albemarle, H. earle of Hereford, John Constable of Chester, Robert de Ros, R. Fitzwalter, Robert de Vipount, William de Bruer, R. de Mountfitchet, P. Fitzherbert, William de Aubeine, Robert Gresly, Reignald de Brehus, John de Movenne, J. Fitz-Alen, Hugh de Mortimer, Walter de Beauchamp, William de S. John, Peter de Mololacu, Brian de Lisle, T. de Multon, Richard de Argentein, Jeffrey de Nevill, William Maudint, John de Baalim, and others.

There were many of the great charters, and *Charta de Foresta*, put under the great seale, and sent to archbishops, bishops, and other men of the clergie, to be safely kept, whereof one of them remain at this day at Lambeth, with the archbishop of Canterbury. The great providence and policy for preservation of it.

Also the same was entred of record in a parliament roll.

And after king E. 1. by act of parliament did ordain that both the said charters should be sent under the great seale, as well to the justices of the forest, as to others, and to all sheriffes, and to all other the kings officers, and to all the cities through the realm, and that the same charters should be sent to all the cathedrall churches, and that they should be read and published in every county four times in the yeare in full county, *viz.* the next county day after the feast of S. Michael, and the next county day after Christmas, and the next county day after Easter, and the next county day after the feast of S. John. 25 E. 1. cap. 1. 25 E. 1. cap. 3. 28 E. 1. ca. 2. & 17.

It was for the most part declaratory of the principall grounds of the fundamentall laws of England, and for the residue it is additionall to supply some defects of the common law; The quality.

Mat. Par. fo. 246, 247, 248.

law; and it was no new declaration: for king John in the 17 yeare of his raigne had granted the like, which alſo was called *Magna Charta*, as appeareth by a record before this great charter made by king H. 3.

Paſch. 5 H. 3. tit' Mordaunc' f. 53.

Home ne ſuer' mordanc' apud Weſtmonaſterium des terres in auter countie, car ceo ſer encont' leſtatut de Magna Charta ſinon que illa aſſiſa ſemel interminata fuit coram juſtic'.

Stat. 25 E. 1. Confirm. Chart.

Alſo by the ſaid act of 25 E. 1. (called *Confirm' Chartar'*) it is adjudged in parliament that the great charter, and the charter of the foreſt ſhould be taken as the common law.

How and upon what grounds it hath been impugned.

Soon after the making of this great charter, the young king by evill counſell fell into great miſlike with it, which *Hubert de Burgo ſummus juſticiarius Angliæ* perceiving (who in former times had been a great lover, and well deſerving patriot of his country; and learned in the laws (for *Rot. clauſ.* 11 *H.* 3. *membr.* 44. I finde that he, and many others were juſtices itinerant in 5 H. 3. and I have ſeen a fine levied before him, and ſixe other judges, between Stephen de Wamceſle, and the abbot of Hales) yet meaning to make this a ſtep to his ambition (which ever rideth without reines) perſwaded and humored the king that he might avoid the charter of his father king John by dureſſe, and his own great charta, and *Charta de Foreſta* alſo, for that he was within age when he granted the ſame, whereupon the king in the 11 yeare of his raign, being then of full age, got one of the great charters, and of the foreſt into his hands, and by the counſell principally of this Hubert his chiefe juſtice, at a councell holden at Oxford, unjuſtly cancelled both the ſaid charters, (notwithſtanding the ſaid Hubert de Burgo was the primier witneſſe of all the temporall lords to both the ſaid charters) whereupon he became in high favour with the king, inſomuch as he was ſoon after (*viz.* the 10 of December, in the 13 yeare of that king, created to the higheſt dignity that in thoſe times any ſubject had) to be an earle, *viz.* of

Rot. clauſ. 11 H. 3. membr. 44. 5 H. 3.

Kent.

Kent. But ſoon after (for flatterers and humoriſts have no ſure foundation) he fell into the kings heavy indignation, and after many fearfull and miſerable troubles, he was juſtly, and according to law ſentenced by his peeres in open parliament, and juſtly degraded of that dignity which he unjuſtly had obtained by his counſell for cancelling of *Magna Charta*, and *Charta de Foreſta*. And the king by his charter granted, *Quod nos firmiter & integre tenebimus judicium de Huberto de Burgo per barones dictum*; he was buried in the Frier Predicants where Whitehall is now built, ſo as no monument remains of him at this day.

Rot. clauſ. 17 H. 3. m. 1. & 2. Rot. Pat. 17 H. 2. m. 1. à tergo & 12.

In this advice Hubert de Burgo either diſſembled his opinion, or groſly erred (as ever ambitious flattery bedazles the eye, even of them, that be learned) firſt, for that a king cannot avoid his charter, albeit he make it when he is within age, for in reſpect of his royall and politique capacity as king, the law adjudgeth him of full age. Secondly, it being done by authority of parliament, and enrolled of record, it was ſtrange that any man ſhould think that the king could avoid them in reſpect he was within age. Thirdly, it was to no end to cancell one where there were ſo many, or to have cancelled all, when they were of record in the parliament roll, or to have cancelled roll and all, when they were, for the moſt part, but declaratories of the ancient common laws of England, to the obſervation, and keeping whereof, the king was bound and ſworn. What ſucceſſe thoſe potent and opulent ſubjects, Hugh Spencer the father, and ſon had, for giving raſh and evill counſell to king E. 2. *enconter la forme de la grand chartre*, I had rather you ſhould read then I ſhould declare.

Exilium turgonis la Spencer pais & filii.

After the making of *Magna Charta*, and *Charta de Foreſta*, divers learned men in the laws, that I may uſe the words of the record, kept ſchooles of the law in the city of London, and taught ſuch as reſorted to them, the laws of the realme, taking their foundation of *Magna Charta*, and *Charta de Foreſta*,

Rot. clauſ. anno 19 H. 3. m. 22.

Foresta, which as you have heard, the king by ill advice sought to impeach.

19 H. 3. ubi supra.

The king in the 19 year of his raign, by his writ, commanded the maior and sheriffes of London, *Quod per totam civitatem London clamari faciant & firmiter prohiberi, ne aliquis scholas tenens de legibus in eadem civitate de cætero ibidem leges doceat, & si aliquis ibidem fuerit hujusmodi scholas tenens, ipsum sine dilatione cessare fac'; Teste Rege, &c. 11 die Decembris, anno regni sui decimo nono.* But this writ took no better effect then it deserved, for evill counsell being removed from the king, he in the next yeare, *viz.* in the 20 yeare of his raigne compleat, and in the one and twentieth yeare current, did by his charter under his great seale confirme both *Magna Charta*, and *Charta de Foresta*, he being then 29 years old. And after in the 52 yeare of his raigne established and confirmed both the same by act of parliament, with the clause, *Quod contravenientes per dominum regem, cum convicti fuerint, graviter puniantur.* Hereby shall some opinions and resolutions in our books be the better understood, which speak of alienations without licen[s]e before or after 20 H. 3. which yeare was named for that the king then confirmed the said great charter, and in like manner did king E. 1. by act of parliament in the 25 year of his raign: and the said two charters have been confirmed, established, and commanded to be put in execution by 32 severall acts of parliament in all.

Marlb. cap. 5. 15 E. 4. 13.

20 Ass. p. 17. 14 H. 4. 2, & 3. Br. Alien. sans license. 10.

Of what high estimation it hath been.

This appeareth partly by that which hath been said, for that it hath so often been confirmed by the wise providence of so many acts of parliament.

And albeit judgements in the kings courts are of high regard in law, and *judicia* are accounted as *juris dicta*, yet it is provided by act of parliament, that if any judgement be given contrary to any of the points of the great charter, or *Charta de Foresta*, by the justices, or by any other of the kings

Confirm. Chart. 25 E. 1. ca. 1. & 2. Vet. Mag. Chart. 2. part, fol. 35.

kings miniſters, &c. it ſhall be undone, and holden for nought.

And that both the ſaid charters ſhall be ſent under the great ſeale to all cathedrall churches throughout the realm there to remain, and ſhall be read to the people twice every yeare. 25 E. 1. ubi ſupra.

The higheſt and moſt binding laws are the ſtatutes which are eſtabliſhed by parliament; and by authority of that higheſt court it is enacted (only to ſhew their tender care of *Magna Charta*, and *Charta de Foreſta*) that if any ſtatute be made contrary to the great charter, or the charter of the foreſt, that ſhall be holden for none: by which words all former ſtatutes made againſt either of thoſe charters are now repealed; and the nobles and great officers were to be ſworn to the obſervation of *Magna Charta*, and *Charta de Foreſta*. 42 E. 3. cap. 1. 25 E. 1. ubi ſupra.

Magna fuit quondam magnæ reverentia chartæ.

We in this ſecond part of the Inſtitutes, treating of the ancient and other ſtatutes have been inforced almoſt of neceſſity to cite our ancient authors, Bracton, Britton, the Mirror, Fleta, and many records, never before publiſhed in print, to the end the prudent reader may diſcerne what the common law was before the making of every of thoſe ſtatutes, which we handle in this work, and thereby know whether the ſtatute be introductory of a new law, or declaratory of the old, which will conduce much to the true underſtanding of the text it ſelfe. We have alſo ſometime in this and other parts of the Inſtitutes, cited the Grand Cuſtumier de Normandy, where it agreeth with the laws of England, and ſometime where they diſagree, *ex diametro*, being a book compounded as well of the laws of England, which king Edward the Confeſſor gave them, as he that commenteth upon that book teſtifieth (as elſewhere we have noted) as of divers cuſtomes of the duchie of Normandie, which book was com-

poſed

posed in the raign of king H. 3. *viz.* about 40 yeares after the coronation of king Richard the first, 3 *Septembris anno* 1 of his raign, *anno Dom.* 1189. about 138 yeares after the conquest. See that book cap. 22. fo. 29. a. and the comment upon the same, & cap. 112. In which Custumier a great number of the courts of justice, of the originall writs, and of many other of the titles of the laws of England, are not so much as named or mentioned. And seeing we have in these, and other parts of our Institutes, cited the laws and statutes of divers kings before the conquest, and in the Conquerors time, we have thought good for the ease of the reader, to set down the times wherein those kings lived, and deceased. *Inas* began to raign *anno Dom.* 689. and deceased 726. *Aluredus, alias Alfredus, alias Elfredus,* began to raign *anno Dom.* 872. and deceased 901. Of this *Alured* it is thus written, *Aluredus acerrimi ingenii princeps per Grimbaldum & Johannem doctissimos monachos tantum instructus est, ut in brevi librorum omnium notitiam haberet, totumque novum & vetus Testamentum in eulogiam Anglicæ gentis transmutaret (cujus translationis pars nobis feliciter accidit.)* This learned king in advancement of divine and humane knowledge, by the perswasion of those two monks founded the famous university of Cambridge. *Edwardus,* son of the said *Alured,* began to reign *anno Dom.* 901. and deceased 924. [a] *Ethelstanus,* alias, *Adelstane* eldest son of the said Edward began to raign *anno Dom.* 924. and deceased 940 [b] *Edmundus* began to raign *anno Dom.* 940. and deceased 946. [c] *Edgarus* began to raign *anno Dom.* 959. and deceased 975. [d] *Ethelaredus* began to raign *anno Dom.* 979. and deceased 1016. [e] *Canutus* began to raign *anno Dom.* 1016. and deceased 1035. [f] *Edwardus* began to raign *anno Dom.* 1042. and deceased 1066. [g] *Willielmus Bastardus* began to raign *anno Dom.* 1066. and deceased 1087.

In Historia Eliensi fol. 38. lib. 2.

Cl: Caius D. m. Cant.

[a] *Fortis, sapiens, & fortunatus: Danos expulit & Angliam in monarchiam reduxit.*

[b] *Martir apud Hoxon olim Hegilsdon.*

[c] *Pacificus, rex excellentissimus.*

[d] Named in Domesday. Glouc' Ecclesia de Evesham. Adelredus.

[e] In Domesday he is ever written *Cnut' Rex.*

[f] He is ever called in Domesd. *Episcopus S. Edw. Cestr: Rex Edwardus dedit regi Griffino terram quæ jacebat trans aquam quæ De vocatur.*

[g] He is in Domes. written Willielmus Rex, *vel* Willielmus, *vel* W. Rex.

Some fragments of the statutes in the raigns of the abovesaid

ſaid kings doe yet remain, but not onely many of the ſtatutes, and acts of parliament, but alſo the books and treatiſes of the common laws both in theſe and other kings times, and ſpecially in the times of the ancient Brittons (an ineſtimable loſſe) are not to be found.

It is to be obſerved that in Domeſday Haroldus, who uſurped the crown of England, after the deceaſe of king Edward the Confeſſor, is never named *per nomen regis, ſed per nomen Comitis Haroldi, ſeu Heraldi*; and therefore we have omitted him.

In citing of the aboveſaid laws originally written in the Saxon tongue, we have referred you to M. Lambard, who accurately and faithfully tranſlated the ſame into Latin, one page containing the Saxon, and next the Latin, and is in print (for our manner is not to cite any thing, but ſo to referre the reader, as he may eaſily finde it;) *ſed ut unicuique ſuus tribuatur honos*, all thoſe ſtatutes in the raigns of all the aboveſaid kings were of ancient time plainly and truly tranſlated into Latin, (whereof we have a very ancient, if not the firſt manuſcript) which no doubt did not a little abbreviate M. Lambards pains.

Upon the text of the civill law, there be ſo many gloſſes and interpretations, and again upon thoſe ſo many commentaries, and all theſe written by doctors of equall degree and authority, and therein ſo many diverſities of opinions, as they do rather increaſe then reſolve doubts, and incertainties, and the profeſſors of that noble ſcience ſay, that it is like a ſea full of waves. The difference then between thoſe gloſſes and commentaries, and this which we publiſh, is, that their gloſſes and commentaries are written by doctors, which be advocates, and ſo in a manner private interpretations: and our expoſitions or commentaries upon Magna Charta, and other ſtatutes, are the reſolutions of judges in courts of juſtice in judiciall courſes of proceeding, either related and reported in our books, or extant in judiciall records, or in both, and

therefore

therefore being collected together, ſhall (as we conceive) produce cer:·inty, the mother and nurſe of repoſe and quietneſſe, and are not like to the waves of the ſea, but

Regula. *Statio bene fida peritis:* for *Judicia ſunt tanquam juris dicta.*

Finis Procemii.

But now let us peruſe the Text it ſelfe.

MAGNA

MAGNA CHARTA.

EDITA *Anno nono* H. III.

HENRICUS Dei gratia rex Angliæ (1), *dominus Hiberniæ, dux Normaniæ, et Aquitaniæ, et comes Andegaviæ, archiepiſcopis, epiſcopis, abbatibus, prioribus, comitibus, baronibus* (2), *vicecomitibus, præpoſitis, miniſtris, et omnibus ballivis, et fidelibus ſuis, præſentem chartam inſpecturis, ſalutem. Sciatis quod nos intuitu Dei, et pro ſalute animæ noſtræ, &c. et ad exaltationem ſanctæ eccleſiæ, et emendationem regni noſtri* (3), *ſpontanea et bona voluntate noſtra* (4), *dedimus et conceſſimus archiepiſcopis, epiſcopis, abbatibus, prioribus, comitibus, baronibus, et omnibus liberis de regno noſtro, has libertates ſubſcript', tenend' in regno noſtro Angliæ inperpetuum.*

HENRY by the grace of God, king of England, lord of Ireland, duke of Normandy and Guyan, and earl of Anjou, to all archbiſhops, biſhops, abbots, priors, earls, barons, ſheriffs, provoſts, officers, and to all bailiffs, and other our faithful ſubjects, which ſhall ſee this preſent charter, greeting. Know ye that we, unto the honour of Almighty God, and for the ſalvation of the ſouls of our progenitors and ſucceſſors kings of England, to the advancement of holy church, and amendment of our realm, of our meer and free will, have given and granted to all archbiſhops, biſhops, abbots, priors, earls, barons, and to all free-men of this our realm, theſe liberties following, to be kept in our kingdom of England for ever.

(1 Inſt. 81. Statutes of Confirmation. 52 H. 3. c. 5. 25 Ed. 1. c. 1, 2, 3, & 4. 28 Ed. 1. ſtat. 3. c. 1. 1 Ed. 3. ſtat. 2. c. 1. 2 Ed. 3. c. 1. 4 Ed. 3. c. 1. 5 Ed. 3. c. 1, 9. 10 Ed. 3. ſtat. 1. c. 1. 14 Ed. 3. ſtat. 1. c. 1. 15 Ed. 3. c. 1. 28 Ed. 3. c. 1. 31 Ed. ſtat. 1. c. 1. 36 Ed. 3. c. 1. 37 Ed. 3. c. 1. 38 Ed. 3. ſtat. 1. c. 1. 42 Ed. 3. c. 1. 45 Ed. 3. c. 1. 50 Ed. 3. c. 2. 1 Rich. 2. c. 1. 2 Rich. 2. c. 1. 5 Rich. 2. c. 1. 6 Rich. 2. c. 1. 7 Rich. 2. c. 2. 8 Rich. 2. c. 1. 12 Rich. 2. c. 1. 1 Hen. 4. c. 1. 2 Hen. 4. c. 1. 4 Hen. 4. c. 1. 7 Hen. 4. c. 1. 9 Hen. 4. c. 1. 13 Hen. 4. c. 1. 4 Hen. 5. c. 1.)

(1) *Henricus Dei gratia Rex Angliæ,* &c.] Concerning the ſtyles of the kings of England, both before and after this king, and how often they altered the ſame, ſee in the firſt part of the Inſtitutes, *Sectione prima.*

The firſt Part of the Inſtitutes, *Sect.* 1.

Note not onely the preamble of this Charter, & of the foreſt, but the bodies of the Charters themſelves are contained in the Charter of King *Iohn*, An. 17. of his reign, *Mat. Par. pag.* 246. *Quæ ex parte maxima leges antiquas & regni conſuetudines continebant. p.* 244.

(2) *Archiepiſcopis, epiſcopis, abbatibus, prioribus, comitibus, baronibus,* &c.] This or the like particular direction, this king and his progenitors before him uſed; and ſo did E. 1. E. 2. and E. 3. King R. 2. in his letters patents uſed a more generall, and compendious direction, viz. *Omnibus ad quos præſentes literæ pervenerint,* &c. which direction is uſed to this day, ſaving in charters of creation of dignities, the directions to this day, are *archiepiſcopis, epiſcopis, ducibus, marchionibus,* &c. and *hiis teſtibus,* in the end.

(3) *Nos intuitu Dei, pro ſalute animæ noſtræ, ad exaltationē ſanctæ eccleſiæ, et emendationem regni noſtri.*] Here bee foure notable cauſes of the making of this great charter rehearſed. 1. The honour of God.

God. 2. For the health of the king's ſoul. 3. For the exaltation of holy church; and fourthly, for the amendment of the kingdome.

These be thoſe excellent laws contained in this great charter, and digeſted into 38. chapters, which tend to the honour of God, the ſafety of the king's conſcience, the advancement of the church, and amendment of the kingdome, granted and allowed to all the ſubjects of the realme.

[2] (4) *Spontanea, et bona voluntate noſtra.*] Theſe words were added, for that king John, as hath been ſaid, made the like charter in effect, and ſought to avoid the ſame, pretending it was made by dureſſe.

This great charter is divided into 38. chapters.

CAP. I.

IMPRIMIS, conceſſimus Deo (1), *et hac præſenti charta noſtra confirmavimus pro nobis et hæredibus noſtris inperpetuum* (2), *quod eccleſia Anglicana* (3), *libera ſit* (4), *et habeat omnia jura ſua integra* (5), *et libertates ſuas illæſas* (6). *Conceſſimus etiam, et dedimus omnibus liberis hominibus regni noſtri* (7), *pro nobis et hæredibus noſtris inperpetuum, has libertates ſubſcriptas* (8). *Tenend' et habend' eis et hæredibus,* (9) *ſuis, de nobis,* (10) *et hæredibus noſtris imperpetuum.*

FIRST, we have granted to God, and by this our preſent charter have confirmed, for us and our heirs for ever, that the church of England ſhall be free, and ſhall have all her whole rights and liberties inviolable. We have granted alſo, and given to all the free-men of our realm, for us and our heirs for ever, theſe liberties underwritten, to have and to hold to them and their heirs, of us and our heirs for ever.

(2 Inſt. 1. 52 H. 3. c. 5. & 42 Ed. 3. c. 1.)

* Inter Leges ſeu Inſtitutiones Regis, H. 1. cap. 1.

*Sanctam * Dei, inprimis, eccleſiam liberam facio, ita quod nec vendam, nec ad firmam ponam, nec mortuo archiepiſcopo ſive epiſcopo, vel abbate aliquid accipiam de dominio eccleſiæ, ſeu de hominibus ejus, donec ſucceſſor in eam ingrediatur, et omnes malas conſuetudines, quibus regnum Angliæ injuſte opprimebatur, inde auſero.*

(1) *Conceſſimus Deo.*] We have graunted to God: when any thing is graunted for God, it is deemed in law to be graunted to God, and whatſoever is graunted to his church for his honour, and the maintenance of his religion and ſervice, is graunted for and to God; *Quod datum eſt eccleſiæ, datum eſt Deo.*

See the firſt part of the Inſtitutes. Sect. 1.

And this and the like were the formes of ancient acts and graunts, and thoſe ancient acts and graunts muſt be conſtrued and taken as the law was holden at that time when they were made.

Here in this charter, both in the title and in divers parts of the body of the charter, the king ſpeaketh in the plurall number, *conceſſimus.* The firſt king that I read of before him, that in his graunts wrote in the plurall number, was king John, father of our king

king *H.* 3. other kings before him wrote in the ſingular number, they uſed *Ego*, and king John, and all the kings after him, *Nos*.

(2) *Pro nobis et hæredibus noſtris inperpetuum.*] Theſe words were added to avoid all ſcruples, that this great parliamentary charter might live and take effect in all ſucceſſions of ages for ever. More of this word (heires) hereafter in this chapter: When *Pro nobis, hæredibus et ſucceſſoribus noſtris* came in, ſhall be ſhewed in his fit place.

(3) *Quod eccleſia Anglicana*, &c.] This at the making of this great charter, extended not to Ireland, nor to any of the king's foraign dominions; but by the law of Poynings, made by the authority of parliament in Ireland, in anno 11. H. 7. all the laws and ſtatutes of this realm of England before that time had or made do extend to Ireland, ſo as now Magna Charta doth extend into Ireland.

(4) *Quod eccleſia Anglicana libera ſit.*] That is, that all eccleſiaſticall perſons within the realm, their poſſeſſions, and goods, ſhall be freed from all unjuſt exactions and oppreſſions, but notwith- [3]
ſtanding ſhould yeeld all lawfull duties, either to the king or to any of his ſubjects, ſo as *libera* here, is taken for *liberata*, for as hath been ſaid, this charter is declaratory of the ancient law and liberty of England, and therefore no new freedom is hereby granted, (to be diſcharged of lawfull tenures, ſervices, rents and aids) but a reſtitution of ſuch as lawfully they had before, and to free them of that which had been uſurped and incroached upon them by any power whatſoever; and purpoſely, and materially, the charter ſaith *eccleſia*, becauſe *eccleſia non moritur*, but *moriuntur eccleſiaſtici*, and this extends to all eccleſiaſticall perſons of what quality or order ſoever.

(5) *Et habeat omnia jura ſua integra.*] That is, that all eccleſiaſticall perſons ſhall enjoy all their lawful juriſdictions, and other their rights wholly without any diminution or ſubſtraction whatſoever; and *jura ſua* prove plainly, that no new rights were given (Rot. Parliam. 4 R. 2. Nu. 13.) unto them, but ſuch as they had before, hereby are confirmed; and great were ſometimes their rights, for they had the third part of the poſſeſſions of the realme, as it is affirmed in a parliament roll.

(6) *Et libertates ſuas illæſas.*] *Libertates* are here taken in two ſenſes. 1. For the laws of England ſo called, becauſe *liberos faciunt*, as hath been ſaid. 2. They are here taken for priviledges (Regiſt. fol. 19. & 262. F. N. B. fo. 229.) held by parliament, charter or preſcription more then ordinary; and in this ſenſe it is taken in the writ *De libertatibus allocandis*, and in another writ *De libertatibus exigendis in itinere*, but it is but *libertates ſuas*, ſuch as of right they had before; *jura eccleſiæ publicis æquiparantur*. (*Regula.*)

Every archbiſhoprick and biſhoprick in England are of the king's foundation, and holden of the king *per baroniam*, and many abbots and priors of monaſteries were alſo of the king's foundation, and did hold of him *per baroniam*, and in this right the archbiſhop and biſhops, and ſuch of the abbots and priors as held *per baroniam*, and called by writ to parliament, were lords of parliament; and this is a right of great honour that the church, viz. the archbiſhop and biſhops now have. *Eccleſia eſt infra ætatem, et in cuſtodia Domini Regis, qui tenetur jura et hæreditates ſuas manutenere et defendere*; and in other records it is ſaid, *Eccleſia quæ ſemper eſt infra ætatem fungitur ſemper vice minoris, nec eſt juri con-* (Glanv. l. 7. c. 1. Bract. lib. 3. fol. 226. l. 5. fo. 427. Tr. 22. E. 1. in com.)

Banc. Rot. Fleta lib. 2. *sonum quod infra ætatem existentes, per negligentiam custodum suorum exhæredationem patiantur seu ab actione repellantur.*

See hereafter c. 21. 14 E. 3. cap. 12. stat. 2. 18 E. 3. cap. 4. 1 R. 2. cap. 3. 8 E. 3. fol. 26. Regist. 289. vid. 27. H. 8. c. 24. vid. *postea.* c. 21.

They are discharged of purveyance for their own proper goods.

And this was the ancient common law, and so declared by divers acts of parliament, and there is a writ in the register for their discharge in that behalfe: and this is not restrained by the said act of 27. H. 8. for thereby it is provided that the purveyor shall observe the statutes for them provided, so as where the purveyor is prohibited to purvey by any statute, the said act of 27 H. 8. setteth him not at liberty.

And true it is, that ecclesiasticall persons have more and greater liberties then other of the king's subjects, wherein, to set down all, would take up a whole volume of it self, and to set down no example, agreeth not with the office of an expositor; therefore some few examples shall be expressed, and the studious reader left to observe the rest as he shall reade them in our books, and other authorities of law.

Regist. 58. F. N. B. 175.

If a man holdeth lands or tenements, by reason whereof he ought (upon election, &c.) to serve in a temporall office, if this man be made an ecclesiasticall person within holy orders, he ought not to be elected to any such office, and if he be, he may have the king's writ for his discharge, and the words of the writ are observable, *Rex,* &c. *cum secundum legem et consuetudinem regni nostri Angliæ clerici infra sacros ordines constituti ad tale officium eligi non debeant, nec hactenus consueverunt,* &c. and the reason thereof is expressed in the writ, *Quia juri non est consonum, quod hii qui salubri statu animarum,* &c. *(in tali loco,* &c.) *deserviunt, alibi extra (eundem locum) secularibus negotiis compellantur.*

[4]

2 Timot. c. 2.

By this writ it appeareth that this was the ancient common law, and custome of England, and had a sure foundation, *Nemo militans Deo, implicet se negotiis secularibus, ut ei placeat cui se probavit.* Ecclesiasticall persons have this priviledge that they ought not in person to serve in warre. Also ecclesiasticall persons ought to be quit and discharged of tolles and customes, avirage, pontage, paviage, and the like, for their ecclesiasticall goods, and if they be molested therefore, they have a writ for their discharge, by which writ it appeareth that this was the ancient common law of England. *Rex,* &c. *cum personæ ecclesiasticæ secundum consuetudinem hactenus in regno nostro usitatam, et approbatam; ac ad telonium, paviagium et muragium,* &c. *de bonis suis ecclesiasticis alicubi in eodem regno præstand' nullatenus teneantur,* &c.

Litt. fol. 20. Regist. fol. F. N. B. 227.

F. N. B. 29. Regist. 289.

If any ecclesiasticall person be in feare or doubt that his goods or chattells, or beasts, or the goods of his farmor, &c. should be taken by the ministers of the king, for the businesse of the king, he may purchase a protection *cum clausula nolumus.*

See the exposition of the statute of Artic. Cler. cap. 9.

Distresses shall not be taken by sheriffs or other of the king's ministers in the inheritance of the church wherewith it was anciently endowed, but otherwise it is of late purchase.

Regist. 300. F. N. B. 266. a. 16. E. 3. proces 165. Regist. judi. 22.

If any ecclesiasticall person knowledge a statute merchant or statute staple, or a recognizance in the nature of a statute staple, his body shall not be taken by force of any processe thereupon, and for more surety thereof the writ thereupon to take the body of the connusor is *si laicus sit.*

If a person bee bound in a recognizance in the chancery or in any

any other court, &c. and he pay not the ſum at the day, by the common law, if the perſon had nothing but eccleſiaſticall goods, the recognizee could not have had a *levari fac'* to the ſheriffe to levie the ſame of theſe goods, but the writ ought to be directed to the biſhop of the dioces to levie the ſame of his eccleſiaſticall goods.

[a] In an action brought againſt a perſon (wherein a *capias* lieth) for example, an account, the ſheriffe returns *quod clericus eſt beneficiatus, nullum habens laicū feodum,* in which he may be ſummoned, in this caſe the plaintiffe cannot have a *capias* to the ſheriffe to take the body of the perſon, but he ſhall have a writ to the biſhop to cauſe the perſon to come and appeare. But if he had returned *quod clericus eſt nullum habens laicum feodum,* then is a *capias* to be granted to the ſheriffe, for that it appeared not by the returne that he had a benefice, ſo as he might bee warned by the biſhop his dioceſan, and no man can be exempt from juſtice. See more of this matter *Artic. Cleri. cap.* 9.

[a] 18. E. 2. Proc. 205. 9 E. 3. 30. 24 E. 3. 44. 25. E. 3. 44. 29. E. 3. 44. 32. E. 3. Proces 58. 34. E. 3. *Scir fac.* 153. 45 E. 3. 6. 47 E. 3. 14. 21 H. 6. 16. Regiſ. judic. 62. *Artic. Cler. c.* 9.

Secundum legem et conſuetudinē regni Angliæ clerici in decenna, &c. *poni non debeant, vel ea occaſione diſtringi vel inquietari non conſueverunt:* and eccleſiaſticall perſons are not bound to appeare at tournes or viewes of frankpledge.

Marlebr. c. 10. Briton. f. 19. B. Fleta. li. 2. c. 45. Rot. brevi. an. 2. R. 2. part 2. m. 8.

But hereof this little taſte ſhall in this place ſuffice, with this, that as the overflowing of waters doe many times make the river to loſe his proper chanell, ſo in times paſt eccleſiaſticall perſons ſeeking to extend their liberties beyond their true bounds, either loſt or enjoyed not that which of right belonged to them.

(7) *Conceſſimus etiam et dedimus omnibus liberis hominibus regni noſtri,* &c.] Theſe words *(omnibus liberis hominibus regni)* doe include all perſons eccleſiaſticall and temporall incorporate politique or naturall, nay they extend alſo to villeines, for they are accounted free againſt all men ſaving againſt the lords.

Litt. ſect. 189.

(8) *Has libertates ſubſcriptas.*] Here it is to be obſerved that the aforeſaid clauſe that concerned the church onely, is in favour of the church generall without any reſtraint, but this clauſe that concernes all the king's ſubjects hath a reſtraint by reaſon of this word *(ſubſcriptas)* which reſtraineth *libertates* to the 38. chapters of this great Charter.

See the ſtatute of 34. E. 1. de tallagio non conc. cap. 4. which is more general.

[5]

(9) *Hæredibus.*] At this time *hæredes* were taken for *ſucceſſores,* and *ſucceſſores* for *hæredes.*

(10) *De nobis.*] In this place theſe words are not inſerted to make a legall tenure of the king, but to intimate that all liberties at the firſt were derived from the crowne.

[a] Mich. 17. E. 1. in Com. banc. rot. 221. leic. ſee the firſt part of the Inſtitut. ſect. 1.

[a] Note that courts of juſtice are alſo called *libertates,* becauſe in them the lawes of the realme *quæ liberos faciunt,* are adminiſtred.

CAP. II.

SI quis comitum, vel baronum (1) *nostrorum, sive aliorum tenentium de nobis in capite* (2) *per servitium militare* (3), *mortuus fuerit, et cum decesserit, hæres ejus plenæ ætatis* (4) *fuerit, et relevium nobis debeat, habeat hæreditament' suum per antiquum relevium* (5), *scilicet, hæres, vel hæredes* (6), *comitis, de com' integro, per centum libras, hæres vel hæredes baronis, de baronia integra, per centum marcas, hæres vel hæredes militis, de feodo militis integro, per centum solidos ad plus* (7). *Et qui minus habuerit, minus det, secundum antiquam consuetudinem feodorum* (8).

IF any of our earls or barons, or any other, which hold of us in chief by knights service, die, and at the time of his death his heir be of full age, and oweth to us relief, he shall have his inheritance by the old relief; that is to say, the heir or heirs of an earl, for a whole earldom, by one hundred pound; the heir or heirs of a baron, for an whole barony, by one hundred marks; the heir or heirs of a knight, for one whole knights fee, one hundred shillings at the most; and he that hath less, shall give less, according to the old custom of the fees.

(7 Rep. 33. 9. 124. 40 Ed. 3. f. 9. 1 Inst. 76. a. 83. b. 106. a. 3 Bulst. 325. Bract. 84. a. altered by 12 Car. 2. c. 24. which takes away Knight's Service, &c.)

Rot. Parliam. anno 11 E. li. 5. fo. 1. in casu principis.

(1) *Si quis comitum vel baronum.*] At this time there was never a duke, marquesse, or viscount in England, for if there had been, they had (no doubt) been named in this chapter: the first duke that was created since the conquest, was Edward the Black Prince, in 11 E. 3. Robert de Vere earle of Oxford, was in the 8. year of Richard the second, created marquesse of Dublin in Ireland, and he was the first marquesse that any of our kings created.

Rot. Pat. 8 R. 2.

Rot. Pat. 18 H. 6. 12 Febr.

The first viscount that I finde of record, and that sate in parliament by that name, was John Beaumont, who in the 18. yeare of H. 6. was created viscount Beaumont.

Bract. lib. 1. fol. 5. b. Fleta lib. 1. cap. 5. Briton 68. b.

Comites.] *Dicuntur comites, viz. quia in comitatu sive à societate nomen sumpserunt, qui etiam dici possunt consules à consulendo: Reges enim tales sibi associant ad consulendum et regendum populum Dei, ordinantes eos in magno honore, et potestate, et nomine, quando accingunt eos gladiis, ringis gladiorum,* &c. *gladius autem significat defensionem regni et patriæ.*

Bract. *ubi supra.*

Barones.] *Sunt et alii potentes sub rege qui dicuntur barones, hoc est, robur belli:* and where some have thought that *baro* is no Latin word, we find it in Tullies Epistles, *apud patronem, et alios barones te in maxima gratia posui. Galfridus Cornwall tenet manerium de Burford de rege, per servitium barniæ,* but it is to be understood, that if the king give land to one and his heirs, *tenend' de rege per servitium baroniæ,* he is no lord of parliament untill he be called by writ to the parliament. These which are earls and barons have offices and duties annexed to their dignities of great trust and confidence, for two purposes. 1. *Ad consulendum tempore pacis.* 2. *Ad defendendum regem et patriam tempore belli.* And prudent antiquity hath given unto them two ensignes to resemble, and to put them

Ad. Attic. Ep. 5. Inquis. 40. E. 3.

Inter record. in Turri 27 Aug. 5 H. 4. the Earle of Northumb. Case, &c.

them in minde of their duties; for first they have an honourable and long robe of scarlet resembling counsell, in respect whereof they are accounted in law, *de magno consilio regis*. 2. They are girt with a sword that they should ever be ready * to defend their king and country: and it is to bee observed that in ancient records the barony (under one word) included all the nobility of England, because regularly all noblemen were barons, though they had a higher dignity, and therefore of the charter of king E. 1. in the exposition of this chapter hereafter mentioned, the conclusion is, *testibus archiepiscopis, episcopis, baronibus,* &c. So placed, in respect that *barones* included the whole nobility: and the great councell of the nobility, when there were besides earles and barons, dukes and marquesses, were all comprehended under the name *de la councell de baronage.*

Glanv. l. 9. c. 4.

5 H. 4. *ubi sup.*

(2) *Sive aliorum tenentium in capite.*] It is worthy of observation, with what great judgement this statute concerning reliefe is penned; for by the act of parliament called, The Assise of Clarendon, anno 10 H. 2. *Anno Domini* 1164, it is thus enacted; *archiepiscopi, episcopi, et universæ personæ regni, qui de rege tenent in capite habeant possessiones suas de rege, sicut baroniam, et inde respondeant justiciariis et ministris regis, et sicut cæteri barones debent interessè curiæ regis cum baronibus,* &c. Therefore this chapter beginneth, *Si quis comitum, vel baronum*; So as (as to reliefe of an earle or baron) it is not materiall that he hath *baroniam,* unlesse he be noble, that is, earle or baron, and others being not noble, but holding in *capite,* shall pay reliefe according to the knights fees which he hath. See hereafter *Cap.* 31. who shall be said to hold in *capite.*

(3) *Per servitium militare.*] For this see the first part of the Institutes, Sect. 103, 112, 154, 157, 126, 127. whereunto you may adde this record following.

Per assisam Iohannes de Moyse, qui est infra ætatē, implacitat Thom' de Weylaund & Marg' ux' ejus pro uno Messuag. ii. molendinis, iiii. acris prati, & xlii. s. red. in Eastsmithfield ext' Algate. Ipsi voc' ad war' Rad' de Berners, qui war' & dic' quod nihil clamat nisi custod. eo quod Iohannes pater dicti Iohannis tenuit de eo prædicta ten' per homag' & servic' vi. d. & inveniendi quendam hominem pro eo in turri London. cum arcubus & sagittis per quadraginta dies tempore guerræ. Iohannes dic' quod tenet ten' præd. per homagium & servitium quorundam calcariorū vel vi. d. pro omni servic'. Et sic omittendo multa ex utraq' parte manifeste patebit per verd' Iur' & per Iud' Cur' quid in hac ass. terminatum fuit. Iur' dic' quod prædicta ten' tenent' de prædicto Radulpho per homagium & servic' unius paris calcariorū deauratorū vel sex den' [a] *& inven' quend' hominē pro ipso Radulpho in turri Lond. cum arcub' & sagit' per xl. dies tempore guerræ in boreal' Angulo turris prædictæ pro omni servic'.* [b] *Et quiaompertū est, &c. quod Radulphus cognoscit in responc' quod prædict' herestenere debet eadem ten' per prædict' homag' & servic' prædict' calcar' vel sex denar' & per serjantiā inveniendi unū hominē pro eo in præd' turri per xl. dies, & manifestè liquet quod huōdi minores serjantiæ quæ debent fieri pro Dominis suis de quibus tenent tenementa sua per alios quā seipsos nullā inde dabunt custodiā eisdē Dominis, nec dare debent licèt iidem Domini infra ætatem hæredū per negligentiam propinquorum parentū hujusmodi custodias occupaverint, & iste Radulphus non potest dedicere quod unquā aliquā habuit seisinam de prædict' custod' nisi per occupationem suam & negli-*

Hil. 8. E. 1. in Banc. Rot. 86. Midd. Which Record is cited in the first part of the Instit. Sect. 157. in marg.

Veredictum.

[a] Tr. 17. E. 1. in Banc. Rot. 29. Salop. Waalt. de Hoptons Case. Acc.

[b] The Judgement.

negligentiam parentum prædicti hæredis antecessoris sui dum infra ætatem fuit, & non alio jure. Considerat' est quod prædict' Iohannes rec' inde seis. &c. & damn' Cx.l. iv.s. vii.d. &c. Valor terr' per annum xx.l. x.d.

See 11 H. 4. 72. & 24. E. 3. 32.

See the first part of the Institutes, sect. 155. & 157. and note the diversitie between such a tenure of the king, for in that case it should be a tenure by grand-serjanty, and that grand-serjanty, for the greatest part, is to be done within the realme, and knights [7] service out of the realme, as Littleton there saith.

(4) *Plenæ ætatis.*] See the first part of the Institutes, sect. 104.

(5) *Antiquum relevium scilicet, &c.*] Concerning the word *relevium, vide* 1. part Institut. sect. 103. It appeareth that the reliefe here set down, is the ancient relief, and was certain at the common law; but there had been of long time an heavy incroachment of an incertain reliefe at will and pleasure, which under a fair term was called *rationabile relevium,* and this act had just cause to say, *per antiquum relevium,* for in the raign of H. 2. grandfather to H. 3. the king exacted an incertain reliefe, for so Glanvill saith, who wrote in his time, *De baroniis verò nihil certum statutum est, quia juxta voluntatem et misericordiam Domini Regis solent baroniæ capitales de releviis suis Domino Regi satisfacere.* And Glanvill under the name of baronies doth include earledomes also, so the reliefe of all the nobility was taken as incertain at that time, and therefore how necessary it was that the ancient reliefe should be restored is evident.

Glanv. l. 9. c. 4. Ockham cap. *Quod non absolvitur. Custummer de Norm. cap.* 34. and the Comment thereupon.

(6) *Scilicet hæres vel hæredes.*] Of this word *(heire)* see the first part of the Institutes, sect. 1. whereunto you may adde that which was there omitted, concerning the antiquity of descents, which the Germanes had agreeable with the ancient laws of the Britons, continued in England to this day, out of that faithfull and learned historian, who of the ancient Germanes saith; *Hæredes successoresq; sui cuique liberi, et nullũ testamentum: si liberi non sunt, proximus gradus in possessione, fratres, patrui, avunculi, &c.* Wherein we observe three things. 1. That for default of children and brethren, the uncle, &c. and not the father, or any in the right line ascendent should inherit, but the collaterall onely. 2. That by the common law no testament or last will could be made of land. 3. That of ancient time *successores* were *synonyma* with *hæredes.* But in this ancient statute it is pertinently said, *hæres,* and not successor, for every bishop of England hath a barony, and so had many abbots and priors (in respect whereof they were lords of parliament) and yet they paid no reliefe, because their successors came to it by succession and not as heire by inheritance; and this act saith, *Habeat hæreditatem suam,* and they are seised in *jure episcopatus monasterii, &c. de comitatu integro et de baronia integra.* The barons in Domesday are accounted amongst the tenants in chiefe. Vide Glanv. lib. 9. cap. 6. Magna Charta cap. 31.

Tacitus de moribus Germanorum.

It is to be understood that of ancient time (as it evidently appeareth by this chapter, and by our books) every earledome and barony were holden of the king in *capite,* which proveth that both the dignities of the earle and the baron, and the earldome and barony were derived from the crown. [a] And is to be known that the fourth part of the yearly value of an earledome, a barony, and the living of a knight, was the ancient reliefe that this chapter speaketh

Bract. lib. 2. fol. 76. a. 84. 16 E. 3. eschaunge 2. 20 E. 3. Assise. 122. & tit. avowr. 126. 22. E. 3. 18. 18. Ass. Pl. ult. 24. E. 3. 66.

ſpeaketh of. And for that of ancient time, [b] a knights living was eſteemed at 20l. per ann. (which in thoſe days was ſufficient to maintain the dignity of a knight) his ancient [c] relief was 5l. which is the fourth part of his living by one year.

The yearly value of a barony was to conſiſt of 13 knights fees, and a quarter, which by juſt account amounted to 400 marks by the year, therefore his relief was as is here ſet down 100 marks.

See an ancient manuſcript intituled, *De modo tenendi parliamentum, &c. tempore Regis Edwardi filii Regis Etheldredi, qui quidem modus fuit per diſcretiores regni corā Willielmo Duce Normannorū et Conqueſtore et Rege Angliæ ipſo conqueſtore hoc tempore præcipiente recitat' et per ipſum approbat', &c.* Of the authority and antiquity whereof you may reade in the fourth part of the Inſtitutes, cap. of the Court of Parliament, *Et hic infra.*

nontenure 16. 46 E. 3. forfeit 18. 10 H. 7. 19 a.

[a] See the firſt part of the Inſtitutes, ſect 95. Cambden Brit. 122. Acc.

[b] 1 E. 2. cap. 1. 7 H. 6. 15. M. 2 Jac. lib. 11. Metcalf's Caſe, fol. 33, 34.

Now every earledome conſiſted of the value of an entire barony and an halfe, which amounted to 20. knights fees amounting to 400l. per annum, and therefore his ancient reliefe here called *Antiquum relevium*, being the fourth part of the yearly value of his earledome was 100l. In that excellent charter which king H. I. made on the day of his coronation, *Communi concilio et aſſenſu baronum regni Angliæ*, amongſt other things it is thus contained, *Omnes malas conſuetudines, quibus regnum Angliæ opprimebatur, inde auſero, quas malas conſuetudines exinde ſuppono. Si quis baronum meorum, comitum, ſive aliorum, qui de me tenet, mortuus fuerit, hæres ſuus non redimet terram ſuam, ſicut faciebat tempore fratris mei, ſed legitima et juſta relevatione relevabit eam, ſicut homines baronum meorum legitima et juſta relevatione relevabunt terras ſuas a dominis ſuis, &c. Legem * regis Edw. vobis reddo cum illis emendationibus, quibus pater meus emendavit conſilio baronum ſuorum.* [8]

* i. Edw. filii Etheldredi.

By this charter it appeareth, 1. that there was a lawfull and juſt reliefe, to bee paid by the earle, and baron, which implyeth á proportionable reliefe according to the value of the living, by reaſon of this word (*Juſta*) which cannot be intended of an uncertaine reliefe, but of the juſt reliefe, upon the computation of ſo many knights fees contained in the *Modus*, whereunto this charter hath relation. 2. It appeareth that there was an unjuſt reliefe, in the time of William Rufus his brother, which upon ſearch we haue found in an ancient manuſcript in the librarie of arch-biſhop Parker, which we have ſeene, and will tranſcribe, in that language that we finde it.

De releefe al cunte que al Roy afert 8. *chivals enfrenees, & enſebees, &* 4. *Hauberts &* 4. *Hawmes &* 4. *eſcues, &* 4. *launces, &* 4. *eſpees les aultres, &* 4. *chaceurs &* 4. *palefrees à freins et a cheveſtre.*

De reliefe a barùn 4. *chivals les* 2. *enfrenes & enſeeles &* 2. *hauberts &* 2. *hawmes &* 2. *eſcus, &* 2. *eſpees &* 2. *launces, & les autres* 2. *chivals un chaceur & un palfrey a freins & a cheveſtres.*

De reliefe a vavaſſur a ſon lige ſenior doit eſtre quite per le chival ſon pier, tiel come il avoit jour de ſon mort, & per ſon hawme, & per ſon eſcu & per ſon haubert, & per ſon lance, & ſil fuit diſaparoile, que il nouſt chival ne arme juſte quite per C. ſol.

Le relief al villain le meliour avoir que il averad 2. *chivals,* 2. *boefs,* 2. *vaches durrad a ſon ſeignior, & puis ſont touts les villains in frankpledge.*

In K. Canutus time, *Relevatio comitis fuit* 8. *equi,* 4. *ſellati,* 4. *inſellati,*

Inter leges Canuti. cap. 97.

* CC. mar.
* i. Baronis.

4. *insellati, & galeæ 4. & loricæ. 4. cum 8. lanceis, & totidem scutis, et gladii. 4. et * CC. mancæ auri.*

*Postea * thani regis, qui ei proximus sit, 4. equi, 2. sellati, 2. non sellati. 2. gladii. 4. lancee, et totidem scuta, et galea cum lorica sua, et 50. mancæ auri.*

Et mediocris thani equus cum apparatu suo et arma sua et halstang in West-sexa, &c.

Lastly, this chapter of Magna Charta is but a restitution and declaration of the ancient common law, and that *antiquum relevium* of the earle, and baron was certaine, so now joyning both together, this certaine reliefe here set downe is *legitimum, justum & antiquum relevium*, mentioned in the *Modus, &c.*

It is said that there be ancient precedents in the exchequer, that he that held by a dukedome, which being valued at two earles livings, should pay according to the proportionall and just fourth part of his living by yeare, 200. li. And a marques that held by a marquesdome, who should have two baronies, should pay for his reliefe 200. marks. What the value of the living of a viscount should be, I have not heard, but certaine it is he should pay the fourth part of the yeerely value of his viscountesdome.

But all this is to be intended, where the king granteth a Dukedome, marquesdome, earledome, viscountesdome, or barony to hold, as here it is spoken, *de nobis in capite per servitium militare, viz. De comitatu integro & de baronia integra, & qui minus habuerit, minus det secundum antiquam consuetudinē feodorū.*

[9]

Com. Mich. 14. E. 3. rot. 8. ex pte rem. Thes. Com. Hil. 25. E. 3. rot 4. ex pte rem. Thes. Com. Hil. 7. H. 4. rot. 2. rot. cart. 36 E. 3. nu. 8. the Earle of Cambridge's case.

But in some cases the heire of an earle, or a baron may pay the reliefe expressed in this statute, albeit he hath not so many knights fees, as is abovesaid: for if upon the creation of the earle the king did grant any mannors, lands, or annuity *per comitatum, & nomine comitis*, or *sub nomine & honore comitis*, or the like, he should pay, C. li. for reliefe, and so of the baron, *mutatis mutandis*, for a speciall reservation may derogate from the common law.

But otherwise it is, if the mannors, lands, or annuity be granted unto the earle, *ut idem comes statum & honorem comitis melius manutenere & supportare possit*, or *ad sustinendum nomen et onus*, or the like; for then the earle holdeth not *per comitatum*, or *nomine comitis.*

6. H. 8. Dier. 2.

17. E. 2 prer. regis cap. 3.

But now the ancient manner of creation is altered, for now, when the king creates a duke, a marques, an earle, a viscount, or baron, he seldome creates a dukedome, marquisdome, earledome, &c. *ad sustinendum nomen et onus, viz.* to grant him mannors, lands, tenements, &c. to hold of him in chiefe, for commonly upon creations the king grants to them created an annuity; and therefore at this day noblemen doe pay such reliefes, as other men use to doe, in respect of their tenures, for as the heire of a knight shall not pay reliefe, unlesse he have a knights fee, &c. so the heire of an earle, or baron, shall not pay reliefe by this great charter, unlesse he hath an earledome, or baronie, as is aforesaid.

Glanvil lib. 9. cap. 4. lib. 9. fol. 124 Antony Lowe's case. Stat. 1. E. 2. de militibus. 1. part of the Institut. sect. 103. 112. 113.

(7) *Ad centum solidos ad plus.*] And this was the ancient reliefe for a knights fee, and so it was holden in the reigne of H. 2. for Glanvil saith, *dicitur autem rationabile relevium alicujus juxta consuetudinem regni de feodo unius militis per centum solidos*, so as the fee of a knight at that time was certaine, viz. the fourth part of his living *per annum*, and so ought, as appeareth, the relief of the nobility to have beene in certainty, though they were not permitted to have it so,

ſo, which ſavored of the power of a conqueror to keepe the nobility under, or to make himſelfe the more amiable to them. 154. 157. *vide* Bracton *ubi ſupra.* Britton cap. 69. Fleta, l. 3. c. 17.

(8) *Secundum antiquam conſuetudinem feodorum.*] This is obſervable, that theſe certaine and proportionable rates are according to the ancient cuſtome of reliefes.

* A knight holds land by grand ſerjantie, he is not within this ſtatute, and therefore ſhall not pay the reliefe of a knight declared by this act, but the heire being of full age at the deceaſe of his anceſtor, ſhall pay the value of his lands for one yeere which is his *primer ſeaſin.* * 11. H. 4. 72. b. 1. part of the Inſtitut. ſect. 154 157. Litt. ſect. 156.

But here it is demanded, ſeeing Littleton ſaith, that tenure by cornage, if it be of any other lord then the king, is knights ſervice, what releeſe the heir of ſuch a tenant ſhall pay, or whether he ſhall pay any reliefe at all. Littleton in the ſame place ſaith, that tenure by cornage draweth unto it ward, and mariage, and ſpeaketh nothing of reliefe, and by this act reliefe is to be payed according to the quantity of the knights fee, viz. *De feodo militis integro per centum ſolidos & qui minus habuerit, minus:* but a tenure by cornage hath no ſuch quantities, *nec ſuſcipit majus & minus*, and therefore tenure by cornage, though it be knights ſervice, is not within this ſtatute; hereof you may read a record to this effect. Mich. 18. E. 1. in Banco rot. 84. Weſtmerl. *& eodem anno.* rot. 158. Cumberland. Io. Swinborne caſe *acc. cornagium.*

Inter Iohannem Craiſtoke querentem verſus Idoneam de Leybourne quæ diſtrinxit ipſum per averia pro relevio dando, pro terris in Dunſton Brampton yanene which Eſeclyve, *et* Boulton, *quæ valent* C. li. per ann. *quæ tenet de ea per homagium et cornagium. Et ipſe dicit quod talis eſt conſuetudo patriæ de Weſtm. quod hæredes poſt mortem anteceſſorum ſuorum debent relevare terras ſuas dominis de quibus,* &c. *ſcilicet ſolvendo pro relevio quantum terræ valent per annum, quæ de ipſis dominis tenentur, niſi de minori ipſis dominis poſſunt ſatisfacere, unde ipſa advocat captionem pro relevio ſecundum prædictam conſuetudinem, &c.*

Iohannes negat talem eſſe conſuetudinem, ſed concedit, quod tenet tenementa prædicta per cornag' xxv. s. vi. d. et dicit quod anteceſſores ſui prius duplicarunt anteceſſor. ipſius Idoneæ ſolvendo Li. s. Ipſa dicit quod cum Iohannes cogn', quod ipſe tenet prædicta ten' de ipſa per cornagiū, ad quod hujuſmodi relevium mere eſt acceſſor,' ratione conſuet' prædictæ. Et dic' quod idem Iohannes exigit tale relevium verſus tenentes ſuos in eadem patria à tempore quo non, &c. Et de conſuet' uterq', pon' ſe ſuper patriam. Ideo ven' Iur' in Cra. S. Iohannis Baptiſtæ, &c. Inſuper Idonea dic' quod duplex eſt tenura in Com' Weſtmerl. ſcilicet, una per Albā firmā, et alia per Cornagium. Et quod tenentes per Albam firmam poſt mortem anteceſſorum ſuorum debent duplicare firmam ſuam tantum. Et tenentes per Cornagium poſt mortem anteceſſ. ſuorum tenentur reddere valorem terrarum ſuarum unius anni. Et Iohannes è contra dic' quod conſuetudo patriæ eſt quod hæredes non ſolvant niſi duplicando Cornagium, &c. [10] *Alba firma Cornagium.*

Bracton li. 2. fo. 84. cap. 36. nu. 2. *Et imprimis de feodo militari quale ſit rationabile relevium antiquum de feodo militari diſtinguitur in carta libertatum, cap. 2. &c.* And in the ſame chapter, nu. 7. ſaith thus, *De ſerjantiis vero nihil certum exprimitur, quid vel quantum dare debeant hæredes ideò juxta voluntatem Dominorum Dominis ſatisfaciant pro relevio, dum tamen ipſi Domini rationem & menſuram non excedant.* Bract. l. 2. fo. 84. vide Glanv. l. 7. cap. 9. Flet. li. 3. cap. 17. Brit. fo. 177, 178, &c.

Certain it is, that he that holdeth by caſtle-guard ſhall pay no eſcuage, for eſcuage muſt be rated according to the quantity of the knights fees, Lit. ſect. 111.

Lit. sect. 97. Lit. sect. 111. fees, as for a whole knights fee or half a knights fee, &c. and of that nature is not castle-guard. Littleton treating of castle-guard, saith, that in all cases where a man holdeth by knights service, such service draweth to it ward and marriage, and speaks not there of relief.

CAP. III.

SI autem hæres (1) alicujus talium fuerit infra ætatem, dominus ejus non habeat custodiam ejus, nec terræ suæ, antequam homagium ceperit (2); et postquam talis hæres fuerit in custodia, cum ad ætatem pervenerit (scilicet xxi. annorum) habeat hæreditatem suam sine relevio, & sine fine, ita tamen quod si ipse (dum infra ætatem fuerit) fiat miles (3), nihilominus terra remaneat in custodia dominorum suorum (4), usque ad terminum prædictum.

BUT if the heir of any such be within age, his lord shall not have the ward of him, nor of his land, before that he hath taken of him homage. And after that such an heir hath been in ward (when he is come to full age) that is to say, to the age of one and twenty years, he shall have his inheritance without relief, and without fine; so that if such an heir, being within age, be made knight, yet nevertheless his land shall remain in the keeping of his lord unto the term aforesaid.

(Hob. 46. Fitz. Gard. 136, 142, 156. 15 Ed. 4. f. 10. Plowd. f. 267. 6 Rep. 73. 8 Rep. 173. 12 Rep. 81. F. N. B. fo. 269. Altered by 12 Car. 2. c. 24. which takes away wardship &c. by reason of tenure.)

35 H. 6. 52. (1) *Hæres.*] This statute is onely to be intended of an heire male, whereof *hæres* is derived: and who shall be *hæres*, &c. See the first part of the Institutes, lib. 1. sect. 1, 2, 3. *Custumier de Norm.* 99. and the expositions upon the same.

See the Custumier de Norm. cap. 29. and the Comment upon the same. & cap. 32. & le Latine Com. fol. 48. b. (2) *Antequam homagium ceperit.*] For homage see the first part of the Institutes, sect. 85. and it is to be observed that in England and France it is called *Homage, Homagium,* and in Italy *Vassalagium.*

Some have thought that these words are to be understood that the heire within age shall not be in ward untill the lord hath taken the homage of some of the auncesters of the ward, so as the auncester of the heire may die in the homage of the lord: for in a writ of ward brought by the lord, it is a good plea to say that the auncester died not in his homage, and the statute saith not *Antequam homagium suum ceperit*, but *homagium* generally; and, say they, if the lord should receive homage of the heire, he should not be in ward at all.

[11] 16 E. 3 Relief 6. & 10.

But this is not the right intendment of these words, but the statute meant that the homage should be taken of the heire himselfe, and that for the benefit of the heire, and so doth it appear by [a] our old books that wrote soone after this statute, and *contemporanea expositio est fortissima in lege*, and so do the words themselves of this law import, and the reason thereof is notable, which was, that before the lord should have benefit of wardship, he should be bound to two things; [b] 1. To warrant the land to the heir, and to that end the heir might have a writ, *De homagio capiendo*; 2. To acquit him from

[a] Brac. l. 2. fo. 41, 71, 81, 89, 252. Brit. fol. 171. Fleta, li. 1. ca. 9. Mirror, ca. 9. § 2. Glanv. lib. 9.

from ſervice and other duties to be done and paid to all other lords, both which the lord was bound to do ([c] as the law was then holden) if the lord accepted homage *de droit* of his tenant, (in ſuch ſort as the lord is, if he receiveth homage *aunceſtrel* at this day) but otherwiſe it is of homage in fait; [d] *Homagium eſt juris vinculum, quo quis aſtringitur ad warrantizandum, defendendum, & acquietandum tenentem ſuum in ſeiſina verſus omnes per certum ſervitium in donatione nominatum & expreſſum; & etiam vice verſa, quo tenens aſtringitur ad fidem Domino ſuo ſervand. & ſervitium debitum faciend.* [e] We have an ancient manuſcript of a caſe adjudged in a writ of cuſtomes and ſervices betweene Alexander of Poulton, and Robert de Norton, that homage is of an higher nature to divers purpoſes then eſcuage. 1. [f] For that homage bindeth to warranty, which eſcuage doth not. 2. Homage is ſo ſolemne as that it cannot be done again as long as the tenant that made it liveth, but eſcuage may be given every other year. [g] And Littleton ſaith that homage is the moſt honourable ſervice, and humble ſervice of reverence, and yet it is true that eſcuage taking it for ſervice, draweth to it homage.

[h] But at the common law, if a man holding land by knights ſervice, had made a gift in frank-marriage, and the donee had died his heir within age, the heir ſhould be in ward before any homage received, *Quia dominus non poteſt capere homagium uſque ad tertium hæredem*, and this ſtatute is to be intended where homage was to be received by law, yet did the tenant in judgement of law die in the homage of the lord, or otherwiſe he could not be in ward, a caſe worthy of great conſideration.

[i] But after when it was reſolved for law, and ſo held to this day, that homage of it ſelfe doth not binde the lord to any warranty or acquitall, unleſſe it were homage aunceſtrell, which either is worne out, and very rare in England at this day; then according to the old rule, *Ceſſante ratione legis ceſſat ipſa lex*; the heir cannot binde the lord to receive homage in this caſe, but if the tenure be by homage aunceſtrell there the lord ſhall not have the cuſtody of body or land before he receiveth homage of the heire, for that homage bindeth him to warranty and acquittall, and conſequently within the reaſon of this law.

[k] Here is to be noted that one within age may doe homage, but he cannot do fealty becauſe that is to be done upon oath, *Hoc obſervato, quod ſi minor homagium fecerit nullum tamen juramentum fidelitatis, antequam ad ætatem pervenerit, præſtabit.* See more concerning this matter 1. part. Inſtitut. lib. 2. cap. Homage and Fealty.

(3) *Fiat miles.*] Be made a knight; and his tenure of ſervice is called *Servitium militare*, knights ſervice, [l] and therefore if the king create the heire within age, a duke, a marqueſſe, an earle, a viſcount or a baron, yet he ſhall remain in ward for his body, but if the heire of a duke, or of any other of the nobility be made a knight, he ſhall be out of ward for his body. If the heire in ward be created a knight of the garter, a knight of the bathe, a knight banneret, or a knight bachelor, he ſhall be out of ward for his body for that he is a knight, and ſomewhat more, and the ſtatute ſpeaketh generally, unleſſe a knight, and therefore within the words and meaning of this law, and the ſoveraigne of chivalry hath adjudged him able ſo doe knights ſervice.

cap. 1. & 6. 13 E. 1. gard. 136. 31 E. 1. gard. 155.

[b] Trin. 4 E. 2. fo. 65. b. *in libro meo.* William St. Quintin's caſe. Homage aunceſtrel only bindeth to warranty, but homage *in fait* bindeth to acquitall.

See the firſt part of the Inſtitutes, ſect. 143, fol. 101. Verb & ad receive homage.

[c] Tr. 9. E. 2. *Ubi ſupra.*

[d] Bract. fol. 78. Britt. & Fleta *ubi ſupra.* 47 E. 3. gar. 99. Temp. E. 1. garr. 90.

[e] M.S. in temp. E. 1.

[f] See the firſt part of the Inſtitutes, ſect. 149.

[g] Lit. ſect. 85. ſect. 99.

[h] 13 H. 3. gar. 42.

[i] 35 H. 6. gard. 72. 14 H. 7. 11. Lit. ſect.

[k] Brac. l. 2. fo. 79.

See the firſt part of the Inſtitutes. Lit. lib. 2. cap. Homage & Fealty.

[l] Lib. 6. fol. 73. Sir Drue Druries caſe. 15 E. 4. 10. Pl. Com. Ratcliffe's caſe. See hereafter *verbo remaneat.*

And

And this word *Fiat*, be made, proveth that knighthood ought to be by creation or making, and cannot be by descent.

m See Sir Drue Druries case, *ubi supra*.

m But albeit the heir be made a knight within age, yet is he not freed of the value * of his marriage, for that was vested before in the king, or other lord, and the king being soveraigne of chivalry hath adjudged him of full age, that is, able to doe knights service, to this intent, to free his body from custody, but neither to barre the king or other lord of the value of the marriage, no more then if he had attained to his full age of 21 years.

Lib. 8. fol. 171. Sir Henry Constable's case. 15. E. 4. 10. Pl. Com. 267. 2 E. 6. tit gard. Br. Sir Anthony Brown's case; Sir Drue Druries case. *Ubi supra*. Pl. Com. Ratcliff's case

(4) *Remaneat in custodia dominorum suorum.*] This word (*remaneat*) implieth that this statute is to be understood onely, where the heir after he be in ward is made knight within age, for when the heire apparent is made knight within age in the life of the auncester, and the auncester dieth, his heir within age, he shall be out of ward both for body and land, because the soveraign of chivalry hath adjudged him of full age, and able to do knights service in the life of his auncester, so as in that case no title of wardship did ever accrew, and there can be no *remanere* or residue, but of that thing that had his essence or beeing.

CAP. IV.

CUSTOS (1) *terræ hujusmodi hæredis, qui infra ætatem fuerit, non capiat de terra hæredis, nisi rationabiles exitus* (2), *et rationabiles consuetudines* (3), *et rationabilia servitia* (4), *et hoc sine destructione, et vasto hominum et rerum* (5). *Et si nos commiserimus* (6) *custodiam alicujus talis terræ vic', vel alicui alii, qui de exitibus terræ illius nobis debeat respondere, et ille de custodia illa, destructionem, vel vastum fecerit: nos ab eo capiemus emend'* (7), *et terra committatur duobus legal' et discretis hominibus de feodo illo, qui de exitibus terræ illius nobis respondeant, vel illi cui nos illam assignaverimus. Et si dederimus, vel vendiderimus custod' alicujus* (8) *talis terræ, et ille inde destructionem fecerit, vel vastum, amittat illam custod'* (9), *et tradatur duobus discret' et legal' hominibus de feodo illo, qui similiter nobis respondeant, sicut prædict' est.*

THE keeper of the land of such an heir, being within age, shall not take of the lands of the heir, but reasonable issues, reasonable customs, and reasonable services, and that without destruction and waste of his men and his goods. And if we commit the custody of any such land to the sheriff, or to any other, which is answerable unto us for the issues of the same land, and he make destruction or waste of those things that he hath in custody, we will take of him amends and recompence therefore, and the land shall be committed to two lawful and discreet men of that fee, which shall answer unto us for the issues of the same land, or unto him whom we will assign. And if we give or sell to any man the custody of any such land, and he therein do make destruction or waste, he shall lose the same custody; and it shall be assigned to two lawful and discreet men of that fee, which also in like manner shall be answerable to us, as afore is said.

(Rast. pl. 693. Fitz. Wast. 15, 24, 138, 146. 1. Inst. 54. a. 12 H. 4. f. 53. 6 Ed. 1. c. 5. 28 Ed. 1. stat. 3. c. 18. 14 Ed. 3. stat. 1. c. 13. 36 Ed. 3. c. 13. See 12 Car. 2. c. 24. which renders obsolete the three last mentioned acts restraining eschetors from waste.)

(1) *Custos*

(1) *Custos.*] A keeper, some derive the word *à cura & sto, quia custos est is cui cura rei stat custodiend.*; and thereupon sometime he is called *curator*, in French he is called a *gardien*, so as his name *custos* doth put him in minde of his office and duty, that is not onely to keep and preserve the lands and tenements of the ward committed to his custody in safety, but also to educate and bring up his ward vertuously, and to advance him in marriage without disparagement. Vide 1. part Institut. Sect. 103. of the cause and end of wardship; and see the 4. part of the Institut. cap. Court of Wards and Liveries.

(2) *Rationabiles exitus.*] *Exitus* is derived *ab exeundo*, and signifieth the rents and profits issuing out or comming of the lands or tenements of the ward, which must be taken by the gardien in reasonable manner, and therefore to *exitus, rationabiles* is added, for that nothing that is unreasonable is allowed by law. Bract. lib. 7. fol. 87. W. 2. ca. 39. Flet. li. 6. ca. 61. 5 E. 3. 6. 24 E. 3. 28, 29.

(3) *Rationabiles consuetudines.*] That is, things due by custome or prescription, and appendant or appurtenant to the lands or tenements in ward, as advowsons, commons, waife, straie, wreck, and the like; also the reasonable customes, fines, &c. of tenants in villenage, or by copy of court-roll where fines be incertain: for though the customes, duties, fines, or the like be incertaine, yet if that which is exacted or demanded be unreasonable, it is against the common law. For this word (*consuetud.*) and the divers significations thereof, see hereafter cap. 30. Brac. li. 2. fo. 87. [13]

(4) *Et rationabilia servitia.*] This also, as appeares by Glanvill that wrote in the reigne of H. 2. was the common law of England, that incertain services and aides ought to be reasonable; for, saith he, the lord may *rationabilia auxilia de hominibus suis inde exigere, ita tamen moderate secundum quantitatem feodorum suorum et secundum facultates, ne minus gravari inde videantur, vel suum contenementum amittere*; and that which he speaketh there of aids, is to be applied to all incertain services, customes, fines, or duties. Glanv. li. 9. c. 8. W. 1. cap. 31. 25 E. 3. cap. 11. *Contenementū.*

But it may be demanded, how and by whom shall the said reasonablenesse in the cases aforesaid be tried? this you may reade in the first part of the Institutes, sect. 69.

(5) *Et hoc sine destructione et vasto hominum et rerum.*] For these words, destruction and waste, see the first part of the Institutes, sect. 67. and the statute of Gloc. cap. 5. Marleb. cap. 17. Mirror. cap. 5. § 2. li. 4. fol. 57.

(6) *Et si nos commiserimus,* &c.] For this word *commiserimus*, vide the first part of the Institutes, sect. 58. & 531. Here the committee of the king is taken for him to whom the king committeth the custody of the land to one or more; by this word *commisimus*, reserving a rent, *Quamdiu quis alius plus dare voluerit*, and there the king remain gardien.

(7) *Nos ab eo capiemus emenda.*] And this may be upon an office found, or by writ directed to the sheriffe to this effect, *Quia datum est nobis intelligi, &c.* Reg. fo. 72, 73. Brac. li. 2. fo. 47. lib. 4. fol. 317. 20 H. 3. Waste 138. 40 Assis. Pl. 22. lib. intrat. Rast. 616.

(8) *Et si dederimus vel vendiderimus alicui custodiam,* &c.] In this case the king graunteth, or selleth the very custody it selfe, so as the grauntee or vendee becommeth guardian in fact: and that this distinction betweene the committee and grauntee was by the common law, hear what Glanvill saith, *Si verò Dominus Rex aliquam custodiam alicui commiserit, tunc distinguitur utrum ei custodiam pleno jure commiserit ita quod nullum inde reddere computum oportet ad Scaccarium, aut aliter: si* Glanv. li. 7. c. 10.

si vero plene ei custodiam commiserit, tunc poterit, &c. negotia sicut sua recte disponere. King H. 7. graunted a ward to the dutches of Buckingham, *quam diu in manibus suis fore contigerit*; and afterwards the king made a speciall livery, as by law he might, to the heir within age, and it was adjudged, as justice Frowick reported, that the duches was without remedy; but otherwise it had been if the graunt were *durante minore ætate hæredis*, or *durante minore ætate et quamdiu in manibus nostris, &c.*

7 E. 3. 12, 13. 3 E. 2. Waste 3. Registr. 72.

But here it may be materially demaunded, what if the committee or grauntee doth waste, and the king during the minority taketh no amends, what remedy hath the heire after his full age? The answer is, that he shall have an action of waste, and that by order of the common law: and then it is further doubted and demanded, what shall the heire then recover, for the wardship cannot be lost, seeing the heire is of full age, neither by this statute nor by the statute of Gloc. To this the answer is very observable, that seeing that the wardship cannot be lost, and the waste, being to the heirs disherison, ought not to remain unpunished, that the heire shall recover treble damage, for that penalty is annexed to the action of waste; and therefore if an action of waste were given against tenant in *tail apres possibilitie*, generally the plaintife shall recover treble damages, because they are annexed to this suit. But if the king doe take amends, then the heire at full age shall have no action of waste.

12 H. 4. 3. F. N. B. 59. e. & 60. c. Vide *notabile recordum*, M. 32 E 1 Coram Rege. Rot. 76. Dublin. See hereafter in the Exposition upon the Statute of Gloc. c. 5.

[14]

(9) *Amittat custodiam.*] This is understood of the land, and not of the body, for the words be *tradatur duobus, &c. qui de exitibus terræ nobis inde respondeant.*

Bracton lib. 4. fol. 285. 316, 317. Gloc. cap. 5. Dier 28 H. 8. fol. 25. Britt. fo. 33, 34. * W. 1. cap. 21. Gloc. cap. 5. Artic. sup. cart. cap. 18. 14. E. 3. cap. 13. 36. E. 3. cap. 13.

* *Nota*, since this statute of *Magna Charta* divers other statutes against wasts and destructions in the lands of wards have been made.

At the making of this statute, the king had not any prerogative in the custodie of the lands of idiots during the life of the idiot, for if he had had, this act would have provided against wast, &c. committed by the committee, or assignee of the king to be done in their possessions, as well as in the possessions of wards, but at this time the gardianship of idiots, &c. was to the lords and others accordihg to the course of the common law. And idiots from their nativity were accounted alwayes within age, and therefore the custodie of them was perpetuall so long as they lived, for that their impotencie was perpetuall. And the lord of whom the land was holden, had not a tenant that was able to doe him service. And therefore within the reason of a custodie of a minor or of an heire within age in case of wardship. And this appeareth by Fleta, *Solent tutores idiotarum et stultorum cum corporibus eorum perpetuo, quod licitum fuit et provisum, eo quod se ipsos regere non noverint, * nam semper judicabantur infra ætatem: vel quia verumq; plures per hujusmodi custodiam exhæredationes compatiebantur, provisum fuit, et cōmuniter concessum quod Rex corporū et hæreditatū hujusmodi idiotarum et stultorum sub perpetuis custodiam obtineret, dum tamen a nativitate fuerint idiotæ et stulti; secus autē si tardæ a quocunque Domino tenuerint, et ipsos maritaret et ex omni exhæredatione salvaret hoc cum adjecto quod dominis feodorum et aliis quorum interfuerit ut servitiis, redditibus et custodiis usque ad legitimam ætatem secundum conditionem feodorum, releviis et hujusmodi nihil juris deperiret.*

Fleta. lib. 1. cap. 10. § Solent. * Nota, the cause of alteration by act of parliament. Mirror cap. 1. c. 9. § *En auter maner acc.* Britton. cap. 66. fol. 167. b. acc.

But then it is demanded, when was this prerogative given to the king? Certaine it is, that the king had it before statute of

17 E.

17 E. 2. *de prærogativa regis*, for it appeareth in our bookes, that the king had this prerogative, *anno* 3 E. 2. And before that, it is manifest that the king had it before Britton wrote in the raigne of E. 1. as you may read in his booke.

Britton, cap. 66. fol. 167. b.
Brac. l. 5. 421. a.
Stanf. Prerog. ca 9. fol. 33, 34.

And it is as cleare, that when Bracton wrote (who wrote about the end of the reigne of H. 3. that the king had not then this prerogative.

And therefore it followeth, that this prerogative was given to the king E. 1. before that Britton wrote, by some act of parliament, which is not now extant. And it appeareth by the Mirror of Justices agreeing with Fleta, that this prerogative was granted by common assent, vide lib. 4. Beverley's case, fol. 126.

CAP. V.

CUSTOS autem quamdiu custodiam terræ hujusmodi habuerit, sustentet domos, parcos, vivaria, stagna, molendina, &c. ad terram illam pertinentia, de exitibus terræ ejusdem, et reddat hæredi cum ad plenam ætatem pervenerit, terram suam tot' instauratam de carucis, et omnibus aliis rebus, ad minus, sicut illam recepit. Hæc omnia observentur de custodiis archiepiscopatuum (1), *episcopatuum, abbatiarum, prioratuum, ecclesiarum, et dignitatum vacantium, quæ ad nos pertinent, except' quod custod' hujusmodi vendi non debent.*

THE keeper, so long as he hath the custody of the land of such an heir, shall keep up the houses, parks, warrens, ponds, mills, and other things pertaining to the same land, with the issues of the said land; and he shall deliver to the heir, when he cometh to his full age, all his land stored with ploughs, and all other things, at the least as he received it. All these things shall be observed in the custodies of archbishopricks, bishopricks, abbeys, priories, churches, and dignities vacant, which appertain to us; except this, that such custody shall not be sold.

(10 H. 7. f. 30. 3 Ed. 1. c. 21. 36 Ed. 3. c. 13.)

[15]

That this was the common law appeareth by Glanvile, who saith, *Restituere autem tenentur custodes hæreditates ipsis hæredibus instauratas et debitis acquietatas juxta exigentiam temporis custodiæ et quantitatis hæreditatis.*

Glanvil, lib. 7. cap. 9.
Fleta, li. 1. c. 11.
10 H. 7. 6. & 30.

(1) *Hæc omnia observantur de custodiis archiepiscoporum,* &c.] The custodie of the temporalties of every arch-bishop and bishop within the realme, and of such abbeyes, and priories, as were of the king's foundation, after the same became voide, belonged to the king during the vacation thereof by his prerogative: for as the spiritualties belonged during that time to the deane and chapter *de cōmuni jure*, or to some other ecclesiasticall person by prescription, or composition, so the temporalties came to the king as founder, and this doth belong to the king, being *patronus et protector ecclesiæ*, in so high a prerogative incident to his crowne, as no subject can claime the temporalties of an arch-bishop, or bishop, when they fall by grant or prescription.

See the 1. part of the Institutes, sect. 67.
See prer. regis, cap. 14.
W. 1. cap. 21.
Fleta, li. 1. c. 11.
14 E. 3. ca. 4, 5.
vide cap. 33.
adjudged 21 E. 1.

Regula. But as, *in omni re nascitur res quæ ipsam rem exterminat*, unlesse it bee timely prevented (as the worme in the wood, or the mothe in the cloth, and the like) so oftentimes no profession receives a greater blow then by one of their owne coat: for Ranulph an ecclesiasticall person, and king William Rufus his chaplain, a man *subacto ingenio*, and *profunda nequitia*, was a factor for the king in making merchandize of church livings, in as much, as when any archbishopricke, bishopricke, or monastery became void, first he perswaded the king to keepe them voide a long time, and converted the profits thereof sometime by letting, and sometime by sale of the same, whereby the temporalties were exceedingly wasted, and destroyed. Secondly, after a long time no man was preferred to them *per traditionem annuli et baculi*, by livery of season, freely, as the old fashion was, but by bargain and sale from the king to him, that would give most, by meanes whereof the church was stuffed with unworthy, and insufficient men, and many men of lively wits, and towardlinesse in learning despairing of preferment turned their studies to other professions. This Ranulph, for serving the kings turnes, was advanced, first, to be the kings chancellour, and after to be bishop of Duresme, who after his advancement to so high dignities, made them servants to his sacrilegious and simoniacall designes. King Henry the first seeing this mischiefe, and foreseeing the great inconvenience that would follow thereupon, was contented for his owne time to binde his owne hands, to the end the church now naked and bare might receive some comfort, and have meanes to provide things necessary for their profession, and calling. He thereupon at his coronation made a charter to this effect, *Quia regnum oppressum erat injustis exactionibus, ego in respectu dei et amore quem erga vos omnes habeo, sanctā Dei ecclesiam imprimis liberam fac' ita quod nec vendam, nec ad firmam ponam, nec mortuo archiepiscopo, sive episcopo vel abbate, aliquid accipiam de dominio ecclesiæ vel hominibus ejus, donec successor eam ingrediatur, et omnes malas consuetudines, quibus regnum Angliæ opprimebatur, inde aufero.* He committed the said Ranulph then bishop of Durham to prison for his intolerable misdeeds, and injuries to the church, where he lived without love, and died without pity, saving of those, that thought it pity, he lived so long.

See this charter at large in Mat. Par. See *libr. rubeū in principio.*

Flet. *ubi supra.* 14 E. 3. ca. 4, 5. F. N. B. 59. b.

Vendi non debent.] Fleta, *ubi supra*, saith, *vendi non debent nec legari*; yet the king may commit the temporalties of them during the vacation, as by the statute of 14 Ed. 3. appeareth.

CAP. VI.

HÆREDES autem maritentur absque disparagatione.

HEIRS shall be married without disparagement.

(1 Inst. 80. 20 H. 3. c. 6.)

This is an ancient maxime of the common law: see more hereof in the first part of the Institutes, sect. 107, 108, 109.

CAP.

CAP. VII.

VIDUA post mortē mariti sui statim et sine difficultate aliqua, habeat maritagiū suū et hæreditatē suam: nec aliquid det pro dote sua, nec pro maritagio suo, vel pro hæreditate sua habenda, quā hæreditatē maritus suus, et ipsa tenuerunt simul, die obitus ipsius mariti sui: et maneat in capitali messuagio mariti sui, per quadraginta dies (1) *post obitū mariti sui* (2), *infra quos dies assignetur ei dos* (3) *sua, nisi prius ei assignata fuerit, vel nisi domus illa sit castrū* (4): *et si de castro recesserit, statim domus ei competens provideatur, in qua possit honeste morari* (5), *quousq; dos sua ei assignetur, secundū quod prædictum est: et habeat rationabile estoverium suum interim de communi* (6). *Assignetur autem ei, pro dote sua, tertia pars totius terræ mariti sui* (7), *quæ fuit sua in vita sua, nisi de minori fuerit dotata ad ostium ecclesiæ. Nulla vidua distringatur ad se maritandam* (8) *dummodo voluerit vivere sine marito: Ita tamen quod securitatem faciat, quod se non maritabit sine assensu nostro, si de nobis tenuerit, vel sine assensu domini sui, si de alio tenuerit* (9). [*Prærogativa Regis, cap.* 4.]

A Widow, after the death of her husband, incontinent, and without any difficulty, shall have her marriage, and her inheritance, and shall give nothing for her dower, her marriage, or her inheritance, which her husband and she held the day of the death of her husband, and she shall tarry in the chief house of her husband by forty days after the death of her husband, within which days her dower shall be assigned her (if it were not assigned her before) or that the house be a castle; and if she depart from the castle, then a competent house shall be forthwith provided for her, in the which she may honestly dwell, until her dower be to her assigned, as it is aforesaid; and she shall have in the mean time her reasonable estovers of the common; and for her dower shall be assigned unto her the third part of all the lands of her husband, which were his during coverture, except she were endowed of less at the church-door. No widow shall be distrained to marry herself; nevertheless she shall find surety, that she shall not marry without our licence and assent (if she hold of us) nor without the assent of the lord, if she hold of another.

(Hobart 153. Dyer, f. 76. Plow. 32. Bro. Dower, 101. Regist. fol. 175. Co. Lit. 32. b. 19 H. 6. f. 14. 17 Ed. 2. c. 4. Fitz. Dower, 194, 196. 20 H. 3. c. 1.)

It appeareth by Bracton of ancient time, that a woman being heire, *sine dominorum dispositione et assensu, hæreditatem habens, maritari non potest, nec etiam in vita antecessorum de jure sine assensu domini capitalis, quod si olim fecissent, hæreditatem amitterent sine spe recuperandi, nisi solum per gratiam: hodie tamen aliam pœnam incurrunt, sicut inferius dicetur, et hoc ideo ne cogatur dominus homagium capere de capitali inimico, vel de alio minime idoneo.*

Bracton, li. 2. fol. 88. Fleta, li. 5. cap. 23. 35 H. 6. 52. Mat. Par. 407.

Also it appeareth by the same author, *quod si mulier dotem habens pro voluntate sua alicui nuberet, præter assensum warranti sui de dote, olim ex tali causa dotem amitteret, nunc tamen non amittet.*

Mirrour, cap. 1. § 3. See the 1. part of the Institutes sect. 36.

 Item

Item cum semel legitime maritatæ fuerint, et postea viduæ, iterum non custodientur sub custodia dominorum, licet teneantur assensum eorum requirere maritandi se, &c. And herewith agreeth Glanvile, who wrote before this statute.

Glanvil, lib. 7. cap. 12. Fleta, lib. 3. cap. 23.

Hereby you may see what had beene used of ancient time in these cases: but at this day widowes are presently after the decease of their husbands, without any difficulty to have their marriage (that is, to marrie where they will without any licence, or assent of their lords) and their inheritance, without any thing to be given to them; but in this branch the king is not included, as hereafter in the end of this chapter shall appeare.

Bract. li. 2. c. 40. Britton, c. 103. Fleta, li. 5. c. 23.

(1) *Et maneat in capitali messuagio mariti sui per quadraginta dies post obitum mariti sui.*] And this is called her quarentine, and if the widow be witholden from her quarentine, she shall have her writ, *De quarentena habenda* to the sherife, which reciting this statute, is in nature of a commission to him, *Quod vocatis coram vobis partibus prædictis, et auditis inde earum rationibus, eidem B. C. viduæ plenam et celerem justitiam inde fieri faciatis juxta tenorē cartæ prædictæ, ne pro defectu justitiæ querela ad nos perveniat iterata.* By force of which writ, the sherife may make processe against the defendant, retournable within two or three dayes, &c. and may, and ought (if no just cause may be shewed against it) speedily to put her in possession; and the reason why such speed is made, is for that her quarentine is but for forty dayes.

Register. 175. F. N. B. 161.

[17]

1 Mar. Br. Dower 101.

Vidua, &c. *maneat,* &c.] Therefore if she marry within the forty dayes, she loseth her quarentine, for then her widow-hood is past, and she hath provided for her selfe, and the quarentine is appropriate to her widowes estate.

Britton, ca. 103.

(2) *Infra quos dies assignetur ei dos.*] Here it appeareth how speedily dower ought to be assigned, to the end the widow might not be without livelihood.

Dier, 7 E. 6. fo. 76. 4 & 5 Phil. & Mar. fol. 161.

(3) *Post obitum mariti sui.*] The day wherein the husband dieth, shall be accounted the first day, so as she shall have but thirty nine after.

Bract. li. 2. fol. 46. Britton, ca. 103. Fleta, lib. 5. ca. 23. 30 E. 3. Dow. 81. 30 E. 1. vouch. 298. 8 H. 3. Dower 196. 8 H. 3. Dower 194. 17 H. 3. ibid. 192. Rot. pat. part 1. nu. 17. Escheat, 4 E. 1. m. 88.

(4) *Nisi domus illa sit castrum.*] This is intended of a castle, that is warlike, and maintained for the necessary defence of the realm, and not for a castle in name maintained for habitation of the owner, but hereof see more in the first part of the Institutes, sect. 36. & 242. *De ædibus kernelatis.* *Kernellare,* or *cernellare,* by some is derived from the French word *kerner,* or *cerner,* to fortifie, inviron, or inclose round about: and by others, from *karnean* or *carnean,* a battlement of a wall; or from *karnele* or *carnele,* imbatteled, or having imbattlements; and the truth is, it beareth all these significations in the lawes of England, and the use of it in castles and forts was to defend himselfe by the higher place, and to offend the assailants at the lower.

Britton ubi supra.

Brittons words be, *Si le chief mees soit chief del countee, ou del barony, ou castle, &c.* So as it appeareth by him that she is not to have her quarentine of that, which is *caput comitatus, seu baroniæ,* and with him, agreeth Fleta, but Bracton only speaketh *de castro.* The ancient law of England had great regard of honour and order.

Ubi supra.

Britton ubi supra.

(5) *Statim domus ei competens provideatur, in qua possit honestè morari.*] But this must be of a house, whereof she is dowable, for she

ſhe muſt have her quarentine of that, whereof ſhe may be endowed.

(6) *Et habeat rationabile eſtoverium interim de communi.*] Britton faith, *Que eux eient des iſſues del intier de les terres lour covenable ſuſtenance,* &c.

Britton ubi ſupra.

Fleta ſaith, *Ubi inveniantur ei neceſſaria honeſtè de hæreditate communi, donec rationabilis dos fuerit ei aſſignata.*

Fleta ubi ſupra.

So as *eſtoverium* here is taken for ſuſtenance: there is an opinion in our books, that the widow cannot kill any of the oxen of the huſbands, whiles ſhe remain in the houſe; but the Regiſter ſaith, *Quod interim habeant rationabilia eſtoveria de bonis eorundem maritorum,* which ſeemeth to be an expoſition of this branch.

19 H. 6. 14. b. Regiſtr. 175.

In the ſtatute intituled, *De catallis felonum,* it is ſaid, *Cum ibidem captus coram juſticiariis noſtris fuerit convictus de felonia, tunc reſid. catallorum ultra eſtoverium ſuum ſecundum regni conſuetudinem nobis remaneant;* where *eſtoverium* ſignifieth ſuſtenance, or aliment, or nouriſhment. This word *eſtoverium* commeth of the French verb *eſtover, id eſt, alere,* to ſuſtain, or nouriſh, and this agreeth with the ſaid old books, and in this ſenſe it is taken in the ſtatute of *Gloc. Trover eſtovers in viver et veſture,* that is, things that concern the nouriſhment, or maintenance of man in *victu et veſtitu,* wherein is contained meat, drink, garments, and habitation. *Alimentorum appellatione venit victus, veſtitus, et habitatio.*

Vet. Mag. Chart. 2. pt. fol. 66. Bract. li. 3. fo. 137.

Gloc. ca. 4.

[18]

When *eſtovers* are reſtrained to woods, it ſignifieth houſebote, hedgebote, and ploughbote.

(7) *Aſſignetur autem ei pro dote ſua tertia pars totius terræ mariti ſui,* &c.] See for this in the firſt part of the Inſtitutes, ſect. 37.

(8) *Nulla vidua diſtringatur ad ſe maritandam,* &c.] This is to be underſtood of widowes tenants in dower of lands holden of the king by knights ſervice in chiefe, and thereupon ſhe is called the kings widow, and if the kings widow marry without licenſe, ſhe ſhall pay a fine of the value of her dower by one year.

Prer. Regis, cap. 4. Stamford prer. 17. F. N. B. 265. c. Britton, fol. 28. a. & 29. b.

And the reaſon of this law is yeelded wherefore they ſhould not marry without the kings licenſe, *Ne forte capitalibus inimicis domini regis maritentur.*

Rot. pat. 4 E. 1. m. 31. Bract. ubi ſupra. Fleta, lib. 1. ca. 12.

And old readers have yeelded this reaſon, leſt they ſhould marry unto ſtrangers, and ſo the treaſure of the realme might be carried out, and others ſay that the reaſon is for that upon the aſſignement of her dower ſhe is ſworn in the chancery, *Que el ne marier ſans licenſe, et pur ceo ſi el fait encont. ſon ſerement el ferra fine.*

35 H. 6. 52. Forteſ.

Others ſay that it is a contempt to marry without the kings licenſe, and againſt this ſtatute, and therefore for this contempt ſhe ſhall make a fine.

If the kings tenant in *capite* dye ſeiſed, his heire female of full age, if ſhe marry without the kings licenſe, ſhe ſhall pay no fine, for ſhe is no widow, and the words be *nulla vidua diſtringatur,* &c.

35 H. 6. 52. 15 E. 4. 13.

If the queene being the widow of a king be endowed, and marry without the kings licenſe, becauſe ſhe is endowed of the ſeiſon of the king himſelfe, ſhe is out of this ſtatute: but at the parliament holden in *anno* 6 H. 6. it is enacted by the king, the lords temporall, and the commons, that no man ſhould contract with, or marry himſelfe to any queen of England, without the ſpeciall licenſe or aſſent of the king, on pain to loſe all his goods, and lands;

Rot. Parl. anno 6 H. 6. nu. 41.

to which act the bishops, and other lords spirituall gave their consent, as farre forth, as the same swerved not from the law of God, and of the church, and so as the same imported no deadly sin.

See the first part of the Institutes, sect. 174.

(9) *Si de alio tenuerit.*] This is to be understood, where such a license of marriage in case of a common person was due by custome, prescription, or speciall tenure, the words being *si de alio tenuerit*; and this exposition is approved by constant and continual use and experience, *Et optimus interpres legum consuetudo.*

CAP. VIII.

*NOS vero (1), vel ballivi nostri (2), non seisiemus terram aliquam, vel redditum (4) pro debito aliquo, quamdiu catalla debitoris præsentia sufficiunt ad debitum reddendum (3), et ipse debit' paratus sit inde satisfacere. Nec pleg' ipsius debitoris (5) distringuntur, quamdiu ipse capitalis debitor sufficiat ad solutionem ipsius debiti. Et si capitalis debitor defecerit in solutione debiti, non habens unde solvat, aut reddere noluerit cum possit (6), plegii * de debito respondeant, et si voluerint, habeant terras et reddit' debitoris (7), quousque si eis satisfact' de debit', quod antea pro eo solverint, nisi capitalis debitor monstraverit, se esse quietum versus eosdem plegios.*

*[19]

WE or our bailiffs shall not seise any land or rent for any debt, as long as the present goods and chattels of the debtor do suffice to pay the debt, and the debtor himself be ready to satisfy therefore. Neither shall the pledges of the debtor be distrained, as long as the principal debtor is sufficient for the payment of the debt. And if the principal debtor fail in payment of the debt, having nothing wherewith to pay, or will not pay where he is able, the pledges shall answer for the debt. And if they will, they shall have the lands and rents of the debtor, until they be satisfied of that which they before payed for him, except that the debtor can shew himself to be acquitted against the said sureties.

(Pl. Com. 457. in Sir Tho. Wrothes case. Pl. Com. in the Lord Berklies case, &c. Plow. 440. Regist. 158. Infra, c. 18. 33 H. 8. c. 39.)

(1) *Nos vero.*] These words being spoken in the politique capacity doe extend to the successors, for in judgement of law the king in his politique capacity dieth not.

See the first part of the Institutes; and hereafter, cap. 28.

(2) *Vel balivi nostri.*] In this place the sheriffe and his underbailiffes are intended and meant, and to this day the sheriffe useth this in his returns, *Infra balivam meam,* for *Infra comitatum,* &c.

See Artic. super Cart. cap. 12. li. 3. fol. 12. b. Sir William Herbert's case. 5 Eliz. Dier 224. Walter de Chirton's case. 24 E. 3. Pl. Com. 32. *Debet semper principalis excuti*

(3) *Non seisiemus terram aliquam, vel redditum pro debito aliquo, quamdiu catalla debitoris præsentia sufficiunt ad debitum reddendum.*] By order of the common law, the king for his debt had execution of the body, lands, and goods of the debtor: this is an act of grace, and restraineth the power that the king before had.

(4) *Redditum.*] For the severall kinde of rents, see the first part of the Institutes; Lit. lib. 2. cap. 12. whereunto you may adde, 1. *Redditus assisus,* or *redditus assisæ:* vulgarly rents of assise are the certain rents of the freeholders, and ancient copiholders, because

they

they be aſſiſed, and certain, and doth diſtinguiſh the ſame from *redditus mobiles*, farm rents for life, years, or at will, which are variable and incertain. 2. *Redditus albi*, white rents, blanch farmes, or rents, vulgarly and commonly called quitrents; they are called white rents, becauſe they were paid in ſilver, to diſtinguiſh them from work-dayes, rent cummin, rent corn, &c. And again theſe are called, 3. *Redditus nigri*, black maile, that is, black rents, to diſtinguiſh them from white rents; ſee Rot. clauſ. 12 H. 3. m. 12. *Rex conceſſit hominibus de Andevor maneria de M. F. A, &c. Reddendo per annum ad Scaccar. Regis* Lxxx. li. blanc, *de Antiqua firma*. 4. *Redditus reſoluti* be rents iſſuing out of the manors, &c. to other lords, &c. *Feodi firma*, fee farm, for this kinde of rent, vide infra Gloc. cap. 8.

antequā perveniatur ad fidei juſſores. An act of grace, ſee W. 2. ca. 10. & 29. 18 E. 1. Stat. de quo warranto optime. Art. ſuper Cart. ca. 12. & 14. Cuſtumier de Norm. cap. 60. Vide 43. El. c. 13.

After the ſtatute of 33 H. 8. cap. 39. was made for levying of the kings debts the uſuall proceſſe to the ſheriffe at this day, is, *Quod diligenter per ſacramentum proborum et legalium hominum de baliva tua, &c. inquiras quæ et cujuſmodi bona et catalla, et cujus precii idem (debitor) habuit in dicta baliva tua, &c. Et ea omnia capias in manus noſtras, ad valentiam debiti prædict', et inde fieri fac' debitum prædict', &c. Et ſi forte bona et catalla prædict' (debitoris) ad ſolutionem debiti prædict' non ſufficerent, tunc non omittas propter aliquam libertatem, quin eam ingrediaris, et per ſacramentum præfat. proborum, et legalium hominum diligenter inquiras, quas terras et quæ tenementa, et cujus annui valoris, idem (debitor) habuit, ſeu ſeiſitus fuit in dicta baliva tua, &c. Et ea omnia et ſingula in quorumcunque manibus jam exiſtunt, extendi fac', et in manus noſtras capias, &c. Et capias prædict' debitorem, ita quod habeas corpus prædict' (debitoris) ad ſatisfac' nobis de debito prædict'.*

Whereby it appeareth, that if the goods and chattels of the kings debtor be ſufficient, and ſo can be made to appeare to the ſheriffe, whereupon he may levy the kings debt, then ought not the ſheriffe to extend the lands, and tenements of the debtor, or of his heire, or of any purchaſer, or terre-tenant. To conclude this point with the authority of old and auncient Ockham.

See cap. 18. Glanv. li. 10. ca. 3. Britton, cap. 28. Fleta, lib. 2. ca. 62. F. N. B. 137. f. Pl. Com. 440. Pepy's caſe, lib. 3. fol. 13. Sir William Herbert's caſe, lib. 7. fol. 17, 18, 22. 50. aſſ. p. 5. 21 E. 4. 21.

[20]

Terræ et tenementa debitoris regis, ad quaſcunq; manus quocunq; titulo devenerunt, poſt debitum regis inceptum regi tenentur, ſi non aliunde ſatisfacere poſſit.

(5) *Nec plegii ipſius debitoris.*] As pledges, or ſureties to keepe the peace, pledges for a fine to the king upon a contempt, &c. are within this branch, but otherwiſe it is of mainperners, and this appeareth by Glanvile, to be the common law before the making of this act.

Ockham, cap. quod vicecomes a fundis ejus, &c. Cuſtumier de Nor. cap. 60. fol. 73, &c. 76. Glanvil. lib. 10. cap. 3.

And the author of the Mirror ſaith, *ceux ſont pleges queux pleviſher aut' choſe que corps de home, car ceux ne ſont propment pledges, mes ſont mainperners pur ceo que ils ſuppoſont pleviſhables ſont liver a ceux per baille corps pur corps.*

(6) *Et ſi capitalis debitor defecerit in ſolutione, &c. aut reddere noluerit cum poſſit.*] Some have thought that this branch hath taken away the next precedent, concerning pledges, but both doe ſtand well together, for *reddere noluerit cum poſſit* muſt be underſtood, when the principall is able, and yet his ability cannot bee made to appeare, being in money, treaſure or the like, or in debts owing to him, which he conceales, and will not *reddere*, ſo as *de non apparentibus, et non exiſtentibus eadem eſt lex*, and in that caſe, *plegii de debito reſpondeant*, and yet the former branch concerning pledges

[a] Britton, cap. 28. Fleta, lib. 2. c. 56. F. N. B. 137. Reg. 158. 43 E. 3. 11. a. 44. E. 3. 21. 48 E. 3. 28. 32. E. 3 trans. des faitz, 179. 1 E. 46. Dyer. 22. Eliz. 170.

[b] Glanvil. lib. 10. cap. 4, 5.

[c] Regist. 158. Mat. Parif. 247 a. Wendov. Walf. 40. Vide postea Stat. de Tallagio concedendo. 34 E. 1.

doth ſtand, where the pledges can make it appeare to the ſheriffe, that he may levie the kings debt: ſee in the ſtatute of *articuli ſuper cartas*, cap. 11.

(7) *Et ſi voluerint, habeant terras, et redditus debitoris*, &c.] [a] Upon theſe words ſome have ſaid that the writ *de plegiis acquietandis* is grounded, and ſeeing no mention is made in this ſtatute of any deed, the pledges ſhall have that writ without any deed. And if the pledges have any deed, covenant, or other aſſurance for their indemnitie, then may they take their remedie at the common law; [b] but it appeareth by Glanvile that this was the common law, for he ſaith, *Soluto vero eo quod debetur ab ipſis plegiis, recuperare inde poterint ad principalem debitorem, ſi poſtea habuerit unde eis ſatisfacere poſſit per principale placitum*, and ſet downe the [c] writ *de plegiis acquietandis*.

Note here is a chapter omitted, viz. *nullum ſcutagium, vel auxilium ponam in regno noſtro niſi per commune couciliū regni noſtri*, which clauſe was in the charter, anno 17 *regis Johannis*, and was omitted in the exemplification of this great charter, by Ed. 1. vide *cap.* 30.

CAP. IX.

CIVITAS London' habeat omnes libertates ſuas antiquas, et conſuetudines ſuas. Præterea volumus, et concedimus, quod omnes aliæ civitates, burg', et villæ, et barones de quinque portubus, et omnes alii portus, habeant omnes libertates, et liberas conſuetudines ſuas.

THE city of London ſhall have all the old liberties and cuſtoms, which it hath been uſed to have. Moreover we will and grant, that all other cities, boroughs, towns, and the barons of the five ports, and all other ports, ſhall have all their liberties and free cuſtoms.

(Cro. Car. 251. 45 Ed. 3. f. 26. 5 H. 7. f. 10, 19. 11 H. 7. f. 21. 5 Rep. 63. 8 Rep. 125. 3 Bulſtr. 2. Mirror, 311.)

[d] Mirror, ca. 5. § 2. Flet., lib. 2. cap. 48. Pl. Com. fol. 400. 5 H. 7. 10. 19. 8 H. 7. 4. 11 H. 7. 21. 28 Aſſiſ 24. 45 E. 3. 26 See acts of parliament. Art. ſuper chartas c. 7. W. 3. cap. 9. 7 R. 2. nient imprimee. 9 H. 4. cap. 1. 2 H. 6 cap. 1. &c. See the firſt of the Inſtit. ſect. 7. 31. 8 H. 7. 4. b.

[d] This chapter is excellently interpreted by an ancient author, who ſaith, *In pointe que demaunde, que le Citie de Londres eit ſes auncient franchiſes, et ſes frank cuſtomes, eſt interpretable in ceſt maner, que les citizens eient lour fraunchiſes, dont ils ſont inherit per loyall title, de dones, et confirmements des royes, et les queux ilz ne ont forfelts per nul abuſion, et que ilz eient lour franchiſes, et cuſtomes, que ſont ſufferable per droit, et nient repugnant al ley: Et le interpretation que eſt dit de Londres ſoit intendu de les cinque ports, et des autres lieus*; and this interpretation agreeth with divers of our later books.

It is a maxime in law, that a man cannot claim any thing by cuſtome or preſcription * againſt a ſtatute, unleſſe the cuſtome, or preſcription be ſaved by another ſtatute; for example: they of London claim by cuſtome, to give lands without licenſe to mortmain becauſe this cuſtome is ſaved, and preſerved, not onely by this chapter of *Magna Charta*, but by divers other ſtatutes, *et ſic de cæteris*. See more in particular concerning London, in the fourth part of the Inſtitutes, *cap.* Of the Courts of the City of London.

CAP.

* [21]

CAP. X.

NULLUS distringatur ad faciendum majus servitium de feodo militis, nec de alio libero tenemento, quam inde debetur.

NO man shall be distrained to do more service for a knights fee, nor any freehold, than therefore is due.

(Custumier de Norm. cap. 114. fol. 132. b. 1 Roll, 164. 2 Roll, 182. 10 Rep. 108. Fitz. Avowry, 96, 157, 200. Plow. 243. 14 H. 7. f. 14. Fitz. Brief, 661, 881, 882. Fitz Prærog. 28. V. N. B. f. 15.)

That this was the auncient law of England, appeareth by Glanvill, and also that the writ of *Ne injuste vexes*, was not grounded upon this act, appeareth also by him, for he saith, *Et alia quædam placita, veluti, si quis conqueratur se curiæ de domino suo, quod consuetudines, et indebita servitia, vel plus servitii exigit ab eo, quā inde facere debeat:* and setteth down the form of the writ of *Ne injuste vexes; Rex N. salutem. Probibeo tibi, ne injuste vexes, vel vexari permittas H. de libero tenemento suo, quod tenet de te in tali villa, nec inde ab eo exigas, aut exigi permittas consuetudines vel servitia, quæ tibi inde facere non debet, &c.*

Glanv. li. 12. ca. 9, 10. Reg. fol. 4. & 59. b. Bracton, fo. 329. Fleta, li. 5. cap. 38. lib. 2. c. 60. Brit. c. 27. fo. 60. b.

And another ancient author which wrote of the ancient laws long before this statute, maketh mention of the writ of *Ne injuste vexes.*

Mirror, cap. 2 § 19. & cap. 5. § 1.

Hereby it appeareth how they are deceived, that hold that this writ is grounded upon this act, and how necessary the reading of ancient authors is, to give the ancient common law his right, as hereby it appeareth.

F. N. B. 10. e. Pl. Com. 243. b.

The words of the statute be, *nullus distringatur,* therefore if the lord incroach more rent of the same nature, by the voluntary payment of the tenant, he shall not avoid this incroachment in an avowry, but in an assise *cessavit,* or *ne injuste vexes,* the tenant shall avoyd the incroachment; this rule holdeth not in case of a successor, or of the issue in taile, for they shall avoyd it in an avowry, but if the service incroached be of another nature, the tenant shall avoyd that season in an avowry, for *majus servitium* implieth a greater exaction of the same nature: if the incroachment of the same nature be gotten by cohertion of distresse, there the tenant shall avoyd that season in an avowry, for *nullus distringatur ad faciendum majus servitium.* But if an incroachment be made upon a tenant in tail, or tenant for life, or any other, who cannot maintain a writ of *ne injuste vexes,* nor a *contra formam collationis,* nor other remedy, he shall have an action upon this statute; for this statute intendeth to relieve those, which had no remedy by the common law.

Pl.Com. 94. 243. 10 H. 7. 11. b. 30 H. 6. 5. b. 22. ass. 68. 28. ass. 33. 12 E. 4. 7. b. 8 E. 4. 28. b. 4 E. 2. Avow. 202. 18 E. 2. ibidem. 217. 20 E. 3. ibid. 131. 5 E. 4. 2. 16 E. 4. 11. 20 E. 4. 11. 12 H. 423. F. N. B. 10. h. See the first part of the Inst. sect.

CAP. XI.

COMMUNIA placita (1) *non sequantur* (2) *curiam noſtram* (3), *ſed teneantur in aliquo certo loco.*

COMMON Pleas ſhall not follow our court, but ſhall be holden in ſome place certain.

(Mirror, cap. 5. § 2. 1 Inſt. 71. a. Plow. 244. 12 Rep. 59. Regiſt. 187. 28 Ed. 1. c. 4. 4 Inſt. 99. 11 Rep. 75.)

Before this ſtatute, common pleas might have been holden in the kings bench, and all originall writs retournable into the ſame bench: and becauſe the court was holden *coram rege*, and followed the kings court, and removable at the kings will, the retourns were [22] *ubicunque fuerimus*, &c. whereupon many diſcontinuances enſued, and great trouble of jurors, charges of parties, and delay of juſtice, for theſe cauſes this ſtatute was made.

Mirror, ca. 1. § 4. Stamf. Pl. cor. fo. 1. Vide cap. 17.

(1) *Communia placita.*] Here it is to be underſtood, a diviſion of pleas, for *placita* are divided in *placita coronæ*, and *communia placita: Placita coronæ* are otherwiſe, and aptly called *criminalia*, or *mortalia*, and *placita communia* are aptly called *civilia: Placita coronæ* are divided into high treaſon, miſpriſion of treaſon, petit treaſon, felony, &c. and to their acceſſories, ſo called, becauſe they are *contra coronam et dignitatem*; and of theſe the court of common pleas cannot hold plea; of theſe you may reade at large in the third part of the Inſtitutes. Common or civill pleas are divided into reall, perſonall, and mixt.

Vide cap. 17.

They are not called *placita coronæ*, as ſome have ſaid, becauſe the king *jure coronæ* ſhall have the ſuite, and common pleas, becauſe they be held by common perſons. For a plea of the crown may be holden between common perſons, as an appeale of murder, robbery, rape, felony, mayhem, &c. and the king may be party to a common plea, as to a *quare impedit*, and the like.

Now as out of the old fields muſt come the new corne, ſo our old books do excellently expound, and expreſſe this matter, as the law is holden at this day, therefore Glanvill ſaith, *Placitorum aliud eſt criminale, aliud civile*; where *placitum criminale*, is *placitum coronæ*; and *placitum civile, placitum commune*, named in this ſtatute.

Glan. li. 1. cap. 1.

Bracton, lib. 3. fol. 101. b. Fleta, li. 2. cap. 58.

And Bracton that lived when this ſtatute was made, ſaith, *Sciendum quod omnium actionum ſive placitorum (ut inde utatur æquivoce) hæc eſt prima diviſio, quod quædam ſunt in rem, quædam in perſonam, et quædam mixtæ; item earũ quæ ſunt in perſonam alia criminalia et alia, civilia, ſecundum quod deſcendunt ex maleficiis vel contractibus; item criminalium, alia major, alia minor, alia maxima, ſecundum criminum quantitatem.*

Fleta, li. 1. cap. 15.

Fleta ſaith, *Perſonalium injuriarum quædam ſunt criminales, et quædam civiles; criminalium quædam ſententialiter mortem inducunt, quædam vero minime.*

Britton

Britton calleth them pleas *de la corone,* and common pleas, and the court taketh his name of the common pleas. Britton, fol. 3. &c.

To treat of the jurisdiction of this court, doth belong to another part of the Institutes, but a word or two of the antiquity of the court of common pleas, which is the lock and the key of the common law.

Glanvill saith, *placita in superioribus,* &c. *sicut et alia quælibet placita civilia,* &c. *solet autem id fieri corā justiciariis domini regis in banco residentibus,* &c. And in another place, *coram justic' in banco sedentibus.* Glanv. lib. 11. c. 1. & lib. 2. cap. 6.

Bracton in divers places cals the justices of the court of common pleas, as Glanvill did, *justiciarii in banco residentes,* so called for that the retourns in the kings bench, are *coram rege ubicunque fuerimus in Anglia,* as hath been said, because in ancient time it was, as hath been said, removable, and followed the kings court. Bract. li. 3. fol. 105. b. & 108. b.

And therefore all writs retournable, *coram justiciariis nostris apud Westm.* are retournable before the judges of the common pleas, and all writs retournable, *coram nobis ubicunque tunc fuerimus in Anglia,* are retournable into the kings bench. Artic. super Cart. cap. 5. Fleta, lib. 2. cap. 2. F. N. B. 69. m.

Britton speaking of the court of common pleas, saith, *Ouster ceo voilloms que justices demurgent continualment a Westm. ou ailours, ou nous voudrous ordinaire* a pleader common pleas, &c. Britton.

Fleta saith, *Habet et (rex) curiam suam et justiciarios suos residentes qui recordum habent in hiis quæ coram eis fuer' placitata, et qui potestatem habent de omnibus placitis, et actionibus realibus, personalibus, et mixtis,* &c. Fleta, li. c. 28. & 54 & cap. 13.

It is manifest that this court began not after the making of this act, as some have thought, for in the next chapter, and divers others of this very great charter mention is made *de justiciariis nostris de banco,* which all men know to be the justices of the court of common pleas, commonly called the common bench, or the bench, and Doct. and Stud. saith, that it is a court created by custome. 7 E. 4. 53. D. & St. 12. b. [23]

The abbot of B. claimed conusans of plea in writs of assise, &c. in the times of king Etheldred, and Edward the Confessor, and before that time, time out of minde, and pleaded a charter of confirmation of king H. 1. to his predecessor, and a graunt, &c. so that the justices of the one bench, or of the other should not intermeddle. 26 Ass. p. 24.

It appeareth by our books that the court of common pleas was in the reign of H. 1. 4 E. 3. 49 39 E. 3. 21.

That there was a court of common pleas in anno 1 H. 3. which was before this act; *Martinus de Pateshull* was by letters patents constituted chiefe justice of the court of common pleas in the first yeare of H. 3. Rot. pat. 1 H. 3.

It is resolved by all the judges in the exchequer chamber, that all the courts viz. the kings bench, the common place, the exchequer, and the chancery, are the kings courts, and have been time out of memory, *Issint que home ne poet scaver que est plus auncient.* 9 E. 4. 53.

(2) *Non sequantur curiam nostram.*] Divers speciall cases are out of this statute. 21 H. 3. brief. 883. Tr. 26 E. 1. coram rege Northampton.

1. The king may sue any action for any common plea in the kings bench, for this generall act doth not extend to the king. Tr. 18 E. 1. coram rege Rot. 62. 31 E. 3. prer. 28.

* 2. If any man be in *custodia mareschalli* of the kings bench, any other may have an action of debt, covenant, or the like personall action 17 E. 3. 50. * 31 H. 6. fo.

10, 11. Artic. super cart. cap. 4. Pl. Com. 208. b. 38 aff. p. 20. fimil.

action by bill in the kings bench, becaufe he that is in *cuftodia marefchalli* ought to have the priviledge of that court, and this act taketh not away the priviledge of any court, becaufe if he fhould be fued in any other court, he fhould not in refpect of his priviledge anfwer there, and fo it is of any officers, or minifters of that court: the like law is of the court of chancery, and efchequer.

3. Any action that is *Quare vi et armis*, where the king is to have a fine, may be purchafed out of the chancery, retournable into the kings bench, as *ejectione firmæ trns. vi et armis*, forcible entry and the like.

9 H. 7. 10. 19 E. 3. affife 84. 1 H. 7. 12. Reg. F. N. B. 177. 14 H. 7. 14. 16 E. 3. bre. 661.

4. And a replevin may be removed into the kings bench, becaufe the king is to have a fine, and fo it is in an affife brought in the county where the kings bench is.

5. Albeit originally the kings bench be reftrained by this act to hold plea of any real action, &c. yet by a mean they may. As if a writ in a real action be by judgment abated in the court of common pleas, if this judgment in a writ of error be reverfed in the kings bench, and the writ adjudged good, they fhall proceed upon that writ in the kings bench, as the judges of the court of common pleas fhould have done, which they doe in the default of others, for neceffity, left any party that hath right fhould be without remedy, or that there fhould be a failer of juftice, and therefore ftatutes are alwayes fo to be expounded, that there fhould be no failer of juftice, but rather then that fhould fall out, that cafe (by conftruction) fhould be excepted out of the ftatute, whether the ftatute be in the negative, or affirmative.

Stat. de Mirton, cap. 10.

6. In a *rediffeifin*, or the like.

(3) *Curia noftra.*] Are words collective, and not onely extend to the kings bench, but into the court of efchequer, vide artic. fuper Cart. cap. 4.

F. N. B. 190. 224. 246.

When judgment is given before the fheriffe, and the tenant hath no goods, &c. in that county, he may have a *certiorare* to remove the record into the kings bench, and there have execution, for that is not *placitum*. See more hereof in the fourth part of the Inftitutes, cap. Of the Court of Efchequer.

[24]

CAP. XII.

RECOGNITIONES de nova diffeifina, et de morte anteceſſoris (2), *non capiantur nifi in fuis comitat'* (1), *et hoc modo; Nos vero fi extra regnum fuerimus, capital' juftic' noftri* (3) *mittent jufticiar' noftros per unumquemque comitatum, femel in ann', qui cum militibus eorund' in com', capiant in com' illis affif. prædict'. Et ea quæ in adventu fuo in illo comitat' per juftic' noftr' prædict' ad dictas affifas capiend' miffos, terminari non poffunt, per eofdem terminent' alibi in itinere fuo* (4). *Et ea quæ*

ASSISES of novel diffeifin, and of mortdancefter, fhall not be taken but in the fhires, and after this manner: if we be out of this realm, our chief jufticers fhall fend our jufticers through every county once in the year, which, with the knights of the fhires, fhall take the faid affifes in thofe counties; and thofe things that at the coming of our forefaid jufticers, being fent to take thofe affifes in the counties, cannot be determined, fhall be ended by them in fome other place in their circuit; and thofe things, which

quæ per eosdem, propter difficultatem aliquorum articulorum terminari non possunt, referant' ad justiciar' nostros de banco, et ibi terminentur.

which for difficulty of some articles cannot be determined by them, shall be referred to our justicers of the bench, and there shall be ended.

(12 Rep. 31, 52. 13 Rep. 8. Fitz. Assize, 21. 8 Rep. 57. Fitz. Mortdanc. 2, 21, 53. 24 Ed. 3. f. 23. 1 Anderson, 230. 2 H. 4. f. 1, 20. Regist. 197. 13 Ed. 1. stat. 1. c. 30.)

Before the making of this statute, the writs of assise of *novel disseisin*, and *mordanc'* were retournable, either *coram rege*, or into the court of common pleas, and to be taken there, and this appeareth by Glanvill, *Coram me, vel coram justiciartiis meis.* But since this statute, these writs are retournable, *Coram justiciariis nostris ad assisas, cum in partes illas venerint*; by force of these words, *Mittent justiciarios nostros per unumquemque comitat' nostrum semel in anno, qui cum militibus eorundem comitatuum capiant in comitat' illis assisas prædict'.* Glanv. li. 13. ca. 3. & 33. F. N. B. 177. f. Registrum.

(1) *Nisi in suis comitatibus.*] This tended greatly to the ease of the jurors, and for saving of charges of the parties, and of time, so as they might follow their vocations, and proper businesse, and the rather, for that the assise of *novel disseisin* was *frequens et festinum remedium* in those dayes, and so was the assise of *mordanc'* also. It is a great benefit to the subject to have justice administered unto him at home in his owne country. Mirror, ca. 5. § 2. See W. 2. ca. 30.

For an assise of *novel disseisin*, and assise of *mordanc'*, see the first part of the Institutes. See the first part of the Institutes, sect. 234.

And where Bracton saith, *Succurritur ei (1. disseisito) per recognitionem assisæ novæ disseisinæ multis vigiliis excogitatam, et inventam recuperandæ possessionis gratia, quam disseisitus injuste amisit, et sine judicio, ut per summariam cognitionem absq; magna juris solemnitate quasi per compendium, negotium terminetur.* See the *Custumier de Normand'*, (composed, as hath been said, in 14 H. 3.) sect. 91. & 93. of the assise of *novel disseisin*, which being invented and framed in England, as Bracton and others have testified, must of necessity be transported into Normandy. Bract. l. 4. fo. 164.

But where we yeeld to Bracton, that the assise of *novel disseisin* was so invented, so he must yeeld to us, that it was a very auncient invention, for Glanvill maketh mention thereof, and of the assise of *mordaunc'*, as hath been said, and by the Mirror also the antiquity of assise *de novel disseisin* doth appeare, who saith, that this writ of assise of *novel disseisin*, was ordained in the time of *Ranulph de Glanvil.* See the preface of the 2d part of the Institutes. Glanv. lib. 13. ca. 3. & 33. Custumier de Norm. ubi supra. Mir. ca. 2. § 15.

But the case of 26. *assise* before touched, doth prove that the writs of *assise* are of farre greater antiquity, for there it appeareth that in an *assise* of *novel disseisin*, claimed to have conusans of plea, and writs of *assise*, and other originall writs out of the kings courts by prescription time out of minde of man, in the times of S. Edmond, and S. Edward the Confessor, kings of this realme before the conquest, and shewed divers allowances thereof; but true it is, as the ancient authors affirme, that a new forme of writs of assise, for the more speedy recovery of possession, which were called *festina remedia*, was invented in England since the conquest, and were called *brevia de assisa novæ disseisinæ*; which writs so altered continue so until this day, and according to the alteration is cited in the *Custumier*, cap. 93. fol. 107. b. 26 Ass. p. 24. [25]

24 E. 3. 23. 2 E. 3. 23. 1. 1 E. 4. 1. If an assise be taken in *proprio comitatu*, and the tenant pleade, and after the assise is discontinued by the *non venu* of the justices, this act extends to the assise, but not to a reattachment thereupon, for that the assise was first arraigned and examined in the proper county, neither doth this act extend to a writ of attaint, brought 6 E. 3. 55, 56. Britton, cap. 97. fol. 240. F. N. B. 181. upon the verdict of the recognitors of the assise: and herewith agreeth Britton, who saith, *Et tout conteine la grand Chre. des franchises, que ascuns assises soient prises in counties, pur ceo ne intent nul que certifications, et attaints auter foitz estre pledes*, &c.

Bracton, lib. 4. fol. 291. And Bracton saith, *Et si ad hoc se habeat communis libertas, quod assisæ extra comitatum capi non debeant, non sequitur quod propter hoc remaneant juratæ in com' capiendæ; aliud enim habet privilegium assisa, et aliud jurata.*

6 E. 3. 55, 56. 19 E. 3. ass. 84. An assise is brought in the kings bench, then being in the county of Suff. (as it may be, as hath been said) of lands lying in that county, the tenant plead in barre, the pl' reply and pray the assise, the kings bench is removed to Westm. and there the pl' prayed the assise, this statute is, that the assise shall not be taken but in the county, and now the kings bench is in another county, and the originall cannot goe out of this place, for when a record is once in this court, here it must remaine, wherefore by th'advise of all the judges, the assise was awarded at large, *quia nihil dicit*, and a *nisi prius* granted in the county of Suff. that there might the assise be taken. A case worthy of observation, how by this exposition both the parties sute was preserved, and the purvien of this statute observed.

18 E. 2. assise 382. 13 E. 3. Jurisd. 23. Rot. Parliam. de anno 18 E. 1. inter petitiones. 28 E. 3. cap. 2. Yet in some case notwithstanding this negative statute, the assise should not have been taken in his proper county. And therefore if a man be disseised of a commote or lordship marcher in Wales, holden of the king in *capite*, as for example of *Gowre*, the writ of assise should have been directed to the sherife of Gloc. within the realme of England, and albeit the land of *Gowre* was out of the power of the sherife of Gloc. being out of his county within the dominion of Wales, and this statute saith that the assise shall not be taken but in his proper county, yet was the assise taken in the county of Gloc. and judgment thereupon given and affirmed in a writ of error: and the reason is notable, for the lord marcher though he had *jura regalia*, yet could not he doe justice in his owne case, and if he should not have remedy in this case by the kings writ out of the chauncery in England, he should have right and no remedy by law given for the wrong done unto him, which the law will not suffer, and therefore this case of necessity is by construction excepted 20 H. 3. tit. brev. 881. out of the statute. And it was well said in an old booke, *Quamvis probibetur quod communia placita non sequantur curiam nostram, non sequitur propter hoc, quin aliqua placita singularia sequantur dominum regem*, and the like in this negative statute.

Hereby it appeareth (that I may observe it once for all) that the best expositors of this and all other statutes are our bookes and use or experience.

More shall be said hereof in the exposition of the statute of W. 2.

(2) *De morte antecessoris.*] See the first part of the Institutes, sect. 234. *Custumier de Norm.* cap. 98. fol. 115.

(3) *Nos vero si extra regnum fuerimus, capitales justitiarii nostri.*] This *capitalis justitiarius* (when the king is *extra regnum*, out of the

the realme) is well described by Ockham, *Rege extra regnum agente, bria. dirigebantur sub nomine præsidentis justitiarii et testimonio ejusdem.* This is he that is * constituted by letters patents when the king is out of the kingdome, to be *custos sive gardianus regni,* keeper of the kingdome, and *locum tenens regis,* and for his time is *prorex,* Rot. Parliament such as was Edward duke of Cornewall 13 E. 3. Lionell duke of 13 E. 3. nu. 11. Clarence 21 E. 3. And the *teste* to all originall writs, were *teste* 5 H. 5. nu. 1. *Lionello filio nostro charissimo custode Angliæ, &c.* John duke of Bedford 3 E. 4. nu. 14. 5 H. 5. Richard duke of Warwick 3 E. 4. and many others: before 21 E. 3. fol. 37. whom as keepers of the kingdome, parliaments have been holden, and as hath been said, the *teste* of originall writs are under the name of the keeper, which no officer can doe when the king is within the realme. In 8 H. 5. a great question arose whether if the kings lieutenant, or keeper of his kingdome under his *teste,* doth summon a parliament, the king being beyond sea, and in the meane time the king returne into England, whether the parliament so summoned might proceed: it was doubted that in *præsentia ma-* 8 H. 5. cap. 1. *joris cessaret potestas minoris,* and therefore it was enacted that the parliament should proceed, and not be dissolved by the kings returne. Now that this statute is to be intended of such a lieutenant or keeper of the kingdome, it is proved by this act itselfe, *capitales justitiarii nostri mittent justitiarios nostros,* that is, they shall name and send justices by authority under the great seale under their owne *teste,* which none can doe but the king himselfe if he be present, or his lieutenant, or the keeper or guardian of his kingdome, if he be, as this act speaketh, *extra regnum:* and this exposition is made *ex verbis et visceribus actus.* But then it is demanded, whether this *locum tenens regis, seu custos regni,* was called *capitalis justitiarius* before the making of this act, and this very name you shall read in Glanvile, who saith *Præterea sciendum, quod secundum consuetudines regni, nemo tenetur respondere in curia domini sui de aliquo libero tenemento suo sine præcepto domini regis vel ejus capitalis justitiarii,* where *capitalis justitiarius* is taken for *custos regni.*

It is to be observed, that before the raigne of king Ed. 1. the kings Glanvil, lib. 12. chiefe justice was sometime called *summus justitiarius,* sometimes, cap. 25. *præsidens justitiarius,* and sometimes *capitalis justitiarius.* In *anno* Rot. Pat. an. 1 *primo* E. 1. his chiefe justice was called *capitalis justitiarius ad placita* E. 1. *coram rege tenenda,* and so ever since; and this chiefe justice is cre- Hereof you may ated by writ, and all the rest of the justices of either bench, by reade more in the letters patents. 4. part of the Institut. cap. of the Court of King's Bench.

In Glanviles time, and before, the kings justices were called *justiciæ,* the returnes of writs being *coram justiciis meis,* so as the Glanvil, lib. 2. kings justices were antiently called *justitiæ,* for that they ought not c. 6. to be only *justi* in the *concrete,* but *ipsa justitia* in the abstract. Hovend. fol. Since that time, as by this great charter in many places it appeareth, 413. they are called *justitiarii a justitia.* The honourable manner of Fortescu, cap. the creation of these justices you may read in Fortescue. 51.

(4) *Alibi in itinere suo.*] This is taken largely and beneficially, 12 H. 4. 20. for they may not only make adjournement before the same justices 29 Ass. 1. in their circuite, but also to Westm. or to Serjeants Inne, or any 27 Ass. 5. 60. other place out of their circuite, by the equity of this statute, and 4 E. 3. 41. according as it had been alwaies used: for constant allowance in many cases doth make law.

[a] The statute speaking only of an adjournment in assise of [a] 12 H. 4. 9. *novell disseisin,* &c. and yet a certificate of an assise is within this statute.

[b] *Regula.*

[b] *Sed rerum progressus ostendunt multa, quæ initio prævideri non possunt.*

[c] 48. E. 3. 7. 47. aff. 1. 39 E. 3. 6. 32 aff. 9. 21 E. 3. 3. 42 E. 3. 11. * 7 H. 6. 9. 3 E. 3. 16 8 aff. 15. 15 E. 3. aff. 96 17 E. 3. 28. 14 E. 3. aff. 110. 20 E. 3. aff. 123. 22 E. 3. 5. 29 aff. 7. 34 aff. 3. 43 aff. 1. 3 H. 4. 18. 22 H. 6. 19.

[c] Time found out, that because the justices of assise came not but once in the yeare, and that any adjournement could not have beene made by this act, unles the jurors had given a verdict, for this act saith *propter difficultatem aliquorum articulorum*, and not upon demurrer, doubtfull plea, *Estoppel*, &c. * or for preservation of the kings peace, and no provision was made by this act, if the ten. in the assise of *mordaunc.* had made a foreine vowcher, or pleaded a foreine plea: all these are holpen by the statute of W. 2. cap. 30. as shall appeare when we come thereunto.

[27]

CAP. XIII.

ASSISÆ de ultima præsentatione semper capiantur coram justitiariis de banco, et ibi terminentur.

ASSISES of darrein presentment shall be alway taken before our justices of the bench, and there shall be determined.

(Regist. 30. 13 Ed. 1. stat. 1. c. 30.)

Glanvil, lib. 13. cap. 16. 18, 19. Bracton, lib. 4. fol. 238, &c. Britton, cap. 90. fol. 222. Fleta, lib. 5. c. 11. Regist. fol. 30. F. N. B. fol. 30. W. 2. cap. 30. 5 Mar. Dier. 135. 9 Eliz. Dier. 260.

It appeareth by Glanvil, that before this statute the writ of *darrein presentment* was retornable *coram me vel justic. meis.* And the reason of this act was for expedition, for doubt of the laps.

By the statute of W. 2. it is provided, that justices of *nisi prius* may give judgement in an assise of *darrein presentment*, and *quare impedit.*

CAP. XIV.

LIBER homo (1) *non amercietur* (2) *pro parvo delicto, nisi secundum modum illius delicti, et pro magno delicto secundum magnitudinem delicti, salvo sibi contenemento suo* (3): *et mercator eodem modo, salva merchandisa sua* (4), *et villanus alterius quam noster, eodem modo amercietur:* (5) *salvo wainagio suo* (6), *si inciderit in misericordiam nostram. Et nulla prædictarum misericordiarum ponatur, nisi per sacramentum proborum et legalium hominum de vicineto. Comites et barones non amercientur, nisi* (7) *per*

A Free man shall not be amerced for a small fault, but after the manner of the fault; and for a great fault after the greatness thereof, saving to him his contenement; and a merchant likewise, saving to him his merchandise; and any other's villain than ours shall be likewise amerced, saving his wainage, if he fall into our mercy. And none of the said amerciaments shall be assessed, but by the oath of honest and lawful men of the vicinage. Earls and barons shall not be amerced but by their peers, and after the

pares (8) *suos, et non nisi secundum modum delicti. Nulla ecclesiastica persona* (9) *amercietur secundum quantitatem beneficii* (10) *sui ecclesiastici, sed secundum laicum tenementum suum, et secundum quantitatem delicti.*

the manner of their offence. No man of the church shall be amerced after the quantity of his spiritual benefice, but after his lay-tenement, and after the quantity of his offence.

(Mirror, 312. 3 Ed. 1. c. 6. Regist. 184, 187. 1 Roll, 74, 446. Br. Amercement, 2, 25, 32, 33, 53, 65. 10 H. 6. fo. 7. 7 H. 6. fo. 13. 19 Ed. 4. fo. 9. 2 Bulstr. 140. 3 Bulstr. 279. 21 Ed. 4. fo. 77. 8 Co. 38, 59.)

(1) *Liber homo.*] A free man hath here a speciall understanding, and is taken for him, *qui tenet libere*, for a free-holder, as it is taken in the *venire fac.* where *duodecim liberos*, &c. *homines*, are taken for free-holders, and this appeareth by this act, which saith, *salvo contenemento suo*, whereof more shall be said in this chapter. The words of this act being *liber homo*, it extendeth as well to sole corporations, as bishops, &c. as to lay men, but not to corporations aggregate of many, as major and commonalty, and the like, for they cannot be comprehended under these words *liber homo*, &c.

Vide W. 1. cap. 6.

(2) *Amercietur.*] This act extends to amerciaments, and not to fines imposed by any court of justice: what amerciaments be, and whereof this word amerciament cometh, see the 8. book of my reports, see also there, that this statute is in some cases of amerciaments, to be intended of private men, and not of amerciaments of officers, or ministers of justice, so as *liber homo* is not intended of officers, or ministers of justice. And how, and in what cases the afferment shall be, you shall also read there, together also with the ancient authors, and many other authorities of law, concerning these matters.

W. 1. cap. 18. 11 H. 4, 5. Lib. 8. fol. 39, 40. Greyslie's case. Glanvil, lib. 9. cap. 11. Fleta, lib. 2. c. 60. 10 E. 2. action sur le statut. 84. Regist. 86. 184. 187.

It appeareth by *Glanvile* that this act was made in affirmance of the common law, as hereafter shall appeare, but yet the writ *de moderata misericordia*, is grounded upon this statute, for it reciteth the statute and giveth remedy to the partie that is excessively amercied.

[28]

(3) *Salvo contenemento suo.*] First for the word, you shall read it in Glanvile, *Est autem misericordia domini regis, qua quis per juramentum legalium hominum de viceneto eatenus amerciandus est, ne quid de suo honorabili contenemento amittet.*

Glanvil. ubi sup.

And Bracton, *Salvo contenemento suo.*

Bracton, lib. 3. fol. 116.

Fleta, *continentia.*

Fleta, lib. 1. c. 43. W. 1. cap. 6.

2. For the signification, contenement signifieth his countenance, which he hath, together with, and by reason of his free-hold, and therefore is called contenement, or continence, and in this sense doth the statute of 1 E. 3. and old Nat. Brev. use it, where countenance is used for contenement: the armor of a souldior is his countenance, the books of a scholler his countenance and the like.

1 E. 3. cap. 4. Stat. 2. Vet. N. B. fol. 11.

(4) *Et mercator eodem modo salva merchandisa sua.*] For trade and traffique is the livelihood of a merchant, and the life of the commonwealth, wherein the king and every subject hath interest, for the merchant is the good bayliffe of the realme to export and vent the native commodities of the realme, and to import and

 bring

bring in the neceſſary commodities for the defence and benefit of the realme.

See the firſt part of the Inſtitutes, ſect. 172. 189. (5) *Et villanus alterius quam noſter eodem modo amercietur ſalvo wainagio ſuo.*] Here *villanus* is taken for one that is a bondman, *nativus de ſanguine* or *ſervus*.

A villein is free to ſue, and to be ſued, by and againſt all men, ſaving his lord.

(6) *Salvo wainagio ſuo.*] Wainagium, is the contenement or countenance of the villen, and cometh of the Saxon word *wagna*, which ſignifieth a cart or waine, wherewith he was to doe villein ſervice, as to carry the dung of the lord out of the ſcite of the mannor unto the lords land, and caſting it upon the ſame, and the like, and it was great reaſon to ſave his wainage, for otherwiſe the miſerable creature was to carry it on his back; it is ſaid here *wainagio ſuo*, but yet the lord may take it at his pleaſure.

See the firſt part of the Inſtitutes, ſect. 172.

But hereby it appeareth, that albeit the law of England is a law of mercy, yet is it a law, which is now turned into a ſhadow, for where by the wiſdome of the law, theſe amerciaments were inſtituted to deterre both demaundants and plaintiffs from unjuſt ſuits, and tenants, and defendants from unjuſt defences, which was the cauſe in ancient times of fewer ſuits, but now we have but a ſhadow of it. *Habemus quidem ſenatus-conſultum, ſed in tabulis reconditum, et tanquam gladium in vagina repoſitum.*

Cicero.

Mirror, cap. 1. ſect. 3. 38 E. 3. 31. 4 H.6, 7. 9 H.6. 2. 19 E. 4. 9. 21 E. 4. 77. b. Mirror, cap. 4. de amerciam. 3 E. 3. Coron. 370. Stanf. pl. cor. fol. 35. b. Mirror, ubi ſup. Britton, fol. 17. b. & 34. b.

(7) *Comites et barones non amercientur niſi per pares*, &c.] Although this ſtatute be in the negative, yet long uſage hath prevailed againſt it, for the amerciament of the nobility is reduced to a certainty, *viz.* a duke 10l. an earle 5l. a biſhop, who hath a baronie 5l. &c. in the Mirror it is ſaid that the amerciament of an earle was an Cl. and of a baron an C. marks.

It is ſaid that a biſhop ſhall be amercied for an eſcape 100l. A gayler ſhall be amercied for a negligent eſcape of a felon attaint 100l. and of a felon indited only 5l.

If a noble man and a common perſon joyne in an action, and become nonſute, they ſhall be ſeverally amercied: *viz.* the noble man at C s. and the common perſon according to the ſtatute, therefore when a noble man is plaintife, it is policy rather to diſcontinue the action, then to be non-ſuite.

(8) *Per Pares.*] By his peeres, that is, by his equalls.

[29] Britton, cap. 2. fol. 36.

The generall diviſion of perſons by the law of England, is either one that is noble, and in reſpect of his nobility of the lords houſe of parliament, or one of the commons of the realme, and in reſpect thereof, of the houſe of commons in parliament: and as there be diverſe degrees of nobility, as dukes, marqueſſes, earles, viſcounts, and barons, and yet all of them are comprehended within this word, *pares*, ſo of the commons of the realme, there be knights, eſquires, gentlemen, citizens, yeomen, and burgeſſes of ſeverall degrees, and yet all of them of the commons of the realme, and as every of the nobles is one a peer to another, though he be of a ſeverall degree, ſo is it of the commons; and as it hath been ſaid of men, ſo doth it hold of noble women, either by birth, or by marriage, but ſee hereof cap. 29.

Bracton, lib. 3. fol. 116. b. Brit. fol. 2. b. Fleta, lib. 1.

Bracton ſaith, *Comites vero vel barones, non ſunt amerciandi, niſi per pares ſuos, et ſecundum modum delicti, et hoc per barones de ſcaccario, vel coram ipſo rege. Nulla eccleſiaſtica perſona amercietur ſecundum*

secundum quantitatem beneficii sui ecclesiastici, sed secundum laicum tenent. suum. cap. 43. & lib. 2. c. 60.

(9) *Ecclesiastica persona.*] For ecclesiasticall persons, and their diversities, and degrees, see the first part of the Institutes, *ubi sup.* Vide lib. nigr. Scaccarii parte 1. cap. 4. Of ancient time the barons of the exchequer were barons and peers of the realme. See the first part of the Institutes, sect. 133.

(10) *Beneficium.*] Benefice. *Beneficium* is a large word, and is taken for any ecclesiasticall promotion or spirituall living whatsoever.

Here appeareth a priviledge of the church, that if an ecclesiasticall person be amercied (though amerciaments belong to the king) yet he shall not be amercied in respect of his ecclesiasticall promotion, or benefice, but in respect of his lay fee, and according to the quantity of his fault, which is to be afferred: and Bracton setteth downe the oath of the afferers of amerciaments, *et ad hoc fideliter faciend. affidabunt amerciatores, quod neminem gravabunt per odium, nec alicui deferent propter amorem, et quod celabunt ea quae audierunt.* Bracton, lib. 3. fol. 116. Fleta, lib. 1. c. 43.

CAP. XV.

NULLA villa, nec liber homo distringatur facere pontes, aut riparias (1), nisi qui ab antiquo, et de jure facere consueverunt tempore Henrici regis avi nostri.

NO town nor freeman shall be distrained to make bridges nor banks, but such as of old time and of right have been accustomed to make them in the time of king Henry our grandfather.

Here it is to be observed, that in the raigne of king John, and of his elder brother king Richard, which were troublesome and irregular times, divers oppressions, exactions, and injuries, were incroached upon the subject in these kings names, for making of bulwarks, fortresses, bridges, and bankes, contrary to law and right.

But the raigne of king H. 2. is commended for three things, first, that his privy counsell were wise, and expert in the lawes of the realme. Secondly, that he was a great defender and maintainer of the rights of his crowne, and of the lawes of his realme. Thirdly, that he had learned and upright judges, who executed justice according to his lawes. Therefore for his great and never dying honour, this and many other acts made in the raigne of H. 3, doe referre to his raigne, that matters should be put in ure, as they were of right accustomed in his time, so as this chapter is a declaration of the common law, and so in the raignes of H. 4. and H. 5. the parliaments referre to the raigne of king E. 1. who was a prince of great fortitude, wisedome and justice. See cap. 35. 37. See Chart. de Foresta, cap. 1 & 3. Rot. Parl. nu. 82. 13 R. 2. c. 5. 4 H. 4. cap. 2. 3 H. 5. cap. 8.

And divers statutes referre to king Edw. 3. who was a noble, wise, and warlike king, in whose raigne, the lawes did principally flourish. 27 H. 6. cap. 2.

Riparia.] Is here taken for *ripa*, which is *extrema et eminentior terrae ora, quam fluvius utrinque alluit.* [30]

But the making of bulwarks, fortresses, and other things of like kinde, were not prohibited by this act, because they could not be erected, but either by the king himself, or by act of parliament. 4 H. 8. cap. 1. 2 & 3 Phil. & Mar. 3. Phil. &

CAP. XVI.

NULLÆ ripariæ defendantur de cætero, nisi illæ quæ fuerunt in defenso tempore Henrici regis avi nostri, et per eadem loca, et eosdem terminos, sicut esse consueverunt tempore suo.

NO banks shall be defended from henceforth, but such as were in defence in the time of king Henry our grandfather, by the same places, and the same bounds, as they were wont to be in his time.

That is, that no owner of the banks of rivers shall so appropriate, or keep the rivers severall to him, to defend or barre others, either to have passage, or fish there, otherwise, then they were used in the raigne of king H. 2.

Mirror, ca. 5. § 2.

This statute, saith the Mirror, is out of use, *Car plusors rivers sont ore appropries et engarnies, et mise in defence, que soilount estre commons a pisher et user en temps le roy Henry 2.*

CAP. XVII.

NULLUS vicecomes (1), *constabularius* (2), *coronator* (3), *vel alii balivi nostri teneant placita coronæ nostræ.*

NO sheriff, constable, escheator, coroner, nor any other our bailiffs, shall hold pleas of our crown.

(Mirror, 313.)

One of the mischiefes before this statute was, that none of them here named, could command the bishop of the diocesse to give the delinquent his clergy, where he ought to have it, for as Bracton saith, *Nullus alius, præter regem, possit episcopo demandare,* &c. And therewith agreeth our other old, and later books, that the bishop is not to attend upon any inferiour court, nor that any inferiour court can write unto, or command the bishop, but the king (that is) the kings great courts of record, and such, as since that time have authority by act of parliament.

Bract. li. 3. fo. 106. Brit. c. 104. fo. 248. Fleta, li. 5. ca. 24. 8 E. 3. 59. 40 E. 3. 2. 14 H. 4. 27. 15 E. 3. conusans 41. 14 H. 7. 26. 21 H. 7. 34, 35. *Regula.* Pasch. 30 E. 1. Coram Rege Kanc. The mayor and barons of the 5. Ports. compl. in parliament.

Another cause was, that the life of man, which of all things in this world, is the most precious, ought to be tried before judges of learning, and experience in the laws of the realme: for *ignorantia judicis est sæpenumero calamitas innocentis. Et cum ex quo magna charta de libertatibus Angliæ alias concessa (quam quidem chartam dominus rex in parliamento suo apud Westm. an. regni sui 28. ad requisitionem omnium prælatorum, comitum, baronum, et communitatis totius regni, de novo concessit, renovavit, et confirmavit) placita coronæ ipsi domino regi specialiter reservantur, per quod nullus de regno hujusmodi placita tenere potest, seu habere, sine speciali concessione, post confirmationem chartæ prædictæ factæ.* In the same yeare, and terme, *coram rege,* a complaint by the abbot of Feversham, both cases

cases adjudged in the kings bench, whereunto they were referred by the parliament. See Michael. 17 Edw. 1. in Banco. Rotulo. 33. Southampton.

The chapter of *Magna Charta* here intended, and in both the said records expressed, is this 17 chapter of *Magna Charta* now in hand. [31] By these records two things are to be observed. 1. That this is a generall law, by reason of these words, *Vel alii balivi nostri*, under which words are comprehended all judges or justices of any courts of justice. 2. Albeit it be provided by the ninth chapter of *Magna Charta*, *Quod barones de quinque portubus, et omnes alii portus habeant omnes libertates, et liberas consuetudines suas*; that these generall words must be understood of such liberties, and customes onely, as are not afterwards in the same charter by expresse words taken away, and resumed to the crown. And therefore if the maior and barons of the cinque ports had power before this act to hold pleas of the crown, yet by this act of the seventeenth chapter, they are abrogated, and resumed; a notable and a leading judgement. Both these records being within two years after the confirmation of king E. 1. of *Magna Charta*, are worthy to be read and observed.

See Pasch. 33 E. 1. coram Rege. The prior of Tinemouth's case. Northumberl.

(1) *Vicecomes.*] See for his name, office, and antiquity in the first part of the Institutes, sect. 234.

1 part Institutes, sect. 234. 248.

(2) *Constabularius.*] Is here taken for *castellanus, a castellein*, or constable of a castle, for so doth the Mirror interpret. And *castellanus est qui custodit castellum, aut est dominus castelli*; and so doth Bracton; *Debet*, &c. *ostendere castellano, sicut constabulario turris*, &c. And therewith agreeth Fleta, *Item nullæ prisæ capiantur de aliquo per aliquem constabularium, castellanum, præterquam de villa, in qua situm est castrum.*

Mirror, cap. 5. § 2. Bracton, lib. 5. fo. 363. li. 2. fo. 69. Vide cap. 19. Fleta, lib. 2. ca. 43.

And the statute of W. 1. agreeth herewith, *Des prises, des constables, ou castelleins, faits des autres*, &c.

W. 1. ca. 7. & 31.

And *castellani* were men in those dayes of account, and authority, and for pleas of the crown, &c. had the like authority within their precincts, as the sheriffe had within his bailiwick before this act, and they commonly sealed (which I have often seen in many, and have cause to know, that some of the auncient family of *de Sperham* in *Norff.* did) with their portraiture on horseback.

Now for the number of castles, in ancient time, within this realme, *Certum est regis Henrici secundi temporibus castella* 1115. *in Anglia extitisse.*

And it is to be observed, that regularly every castle containeth a mannor: so as every constable of a castle, is constable of a mannor, and by the name of the castle the mannor shall passe, and by the name of the mannor the castle shall passe.

See the first part of the Institutes, fol. 5. verbo Holme.

For this word, *constabularius*, his office, and antiquity, see the first part of the Institutes, sect. 379.

Lamb. leg. Ed. c. 26.

And albeit the franchises of infangthiefe, and outfangthiefe, to be heard and determined within court barons belonging to mannors, were within the said mischiefe, yet we finde, but not without great inconvenience, that the same had some continuance after this act. But either by this act, or *per desuetudinem*, for inconvenience, these franchises within mannors are antiquated and gone.

Bract. li. 3. fo. 154. Brit. ca. 15. fo. 90. Fleta, li. 1. ca. 47. Hovend. pte. posterior. fol. 345. Mat. Par. anno 1259. 44 H. 3.

(3) *Coronator.*] His name is derived *a corona*, so called, because he is an officer of the crown, and hath conusance of some pleas, which are called *placita coronæ*.

Pl. Parl. 18 E. 1. Rot. 11. 2 R. 3. 10.

Mirror, cap. 1. § 3.

For his antiquity, see the Mirror, who (treating of articles established by the ancient kings, Alfred, &c.) saith, *Auxi ordains fuer coronours in chescun county, et viscounts a garder le peace, quant les countees soy demisterent del gard, et bayliffes in lieu de centeners* (that is) coroners in every county, and sheriffes were ordained to keep the peace, when the earles dismist themselves of the custody of the counties, and bailiffes in place of hundreders.

Brit. ca. 3. fol. 3. Stam. Pl. Cor. 48. c. [32]

For his dignitie and authority, Britton saith in the person of the king, *Pur ceo que nous volons, que coroners sont in chescun county principals gardens de nostre peace, a porter record des pleas de nostre corone, et de lour views, et abjurations, et de utlagaries, volons que ilz sont eslieus solonque ceo, que est contein in nous statutes de lour election*, &c.

Rot. brevium. 5 E. 3. nu. 38. Registr. 177. W. 1. cap. 10. * Registr. 177.

And a common merchant being chosen a coroner, was removed, for that he was *communis mercator*.

* By the auncient law, he ought to be a knight, honest, loyall, and sage, *Et qui melius sciat, et possit officio illi intendere.* For this was the policy of prudent antiquity, that officers did ever give a grace to the place, and not the place only to grace the officer.

Videa postea, c. 35. Glanv. li. 1. cap. 2. & lib. 14. cap. 8. W. 2. cap. 13. 22 E. 4. fol. 22.

But what authority had the sheriffe in pleas of the crown before this statute? this appeareth by Glanvill, that the sheriffe in the tourn (for that is to be intended) held plea of theft, for he saith; *Excipitur crimen furti, quod ad vicecomitem pertinet, et in comitatibus placitatur*; but he may enquire of all felonies by the common law, except the death of man.

Mirror, cap. 1. § Coroners. & cap. 5. § 2. Bracton, lib. 3. fol. 121. Brit. c. 1. fol. 3. Fleta, li. 1. cap. 18. 25. 22 Ass. 97, 98. &c. 3 H. 7. cap. 3. Stamf. Pl. co. 64. 116, 117.

And what authority had the coroner? the same authority he now hath, in case when any man come to violent, or untimely death, *super visum corporis*, &c. Abjurations, and out-lawries, &c. appeales of deaths by bill, &c. This authority of the coroner, viz. the coroner solely to take an indictment, *super visum corporis*; and to take an appeale, and to enter the appeale, and the count remaineth to this day. But he can proceed no further, either upon the indictment, or appeale, but to deliver them over to the justices. And this is saved to them by the statute of W. 1. cap. 10. And this appeareth by all our old books, book cases, and continuall experience.

19 H. 6. fol. 47.

And for the further authority of the coroner in case of high treason, see the book of 19 H. 6. fol. 47. and consider well thereof.

W. 2. c. 13. 1 E. 3. Stat. 2. ca. 17. 1 E. 4. 3 1 R. 3. cap. 4.

But the authority of the sheriffe to heare and determine theft, or other felonies, by the common law (except the death of man) in the tourn is wholly taken away by this statute, howbeit his power to take indictments of felonies, and other mis-deeds within his jurisdiction, is not taken away by this act.

CAP. XVIII.

SI quis tenens de nobis laicum feodum moritur, et vic', vel balivus noster ostendat literas nostras patentes de summonitione [nostra] de debito, quod defunctus nobis debuit: liceat vic', vel balivo

IF any that holdeth of us lay-fee do die, and our sheriff or bailiff do shew our letters patents of our summon for debt, which the dead man did owe to us; it shall be lawful to our sheriff

balivo noſtro attachiar', et imbreviare omnia bona et catalla defuncti inventa in laico feodo ad valentiam ipſius debiti, per viſum et teſtimonium legalium hominum, ita tamen quod nihil inde amoveatur, donec perſolvat nobis debit', quod clarum fuerit, et reſiduum relinquatur executoribus ad faciendum teſtamentum defunct'. Et ſi nihil nobis debeatur ab ipſo, omnia catalla cedant defunct': ſalvis uxori ejus, et liberis pueris ſuis, rationabilibus partibus ſuis.

ſheriff or bailiff to attach and inroll all the goods and chattles of the dead, being found in the ſaid fee, to the value of the ſame debt, by the ſight and teſtimony of lawful men, ſo that nothing thereof ſhall be taken away, until we be clearly paid off the debt; and the reſidue ſhall remain to the executors to perform the teſtament of the dead; and if nothing be owing unto us, all the chattles ſhall go to the uſe of the dead (ſaving to his wife and children their reaſonable parts).

(Raſt. Ent. f. 541. Co. Ent. f. 564. Fitz. Detinue, 52, 56, 58, 60. Bro. Ration. 2, 5, 6. Supra, cap. 8. 33 H. 8. c. 39.)

By this chapter three things are to be obſerved; firſt, that the king by his prerogative ſhall be preferred in ſatisfaction of his debt by the executors, before any other: ſecondly, that if the executors *have ſufficient to pay the kings* debt, the *heire that is to beare the countenance, and ſit in the ſeate of his anceſtor,* or any purchaſer of his lands ſhall not be charged. Thirdly, if nothing be owing to the king, or any other, all the chattells ſhall goe to the uſe of the dead, that *is, to his executors,* or adminiſtrators, *ſaving to his wife and children their* reaſonable parts, *which is conſilium, and not præceptum*; and *the nature of a ſaving regularly* is, to ſave a former right, and not to give, or create a new, and therefore, where ſuch a cuſtome is, that the wife and children ſhall have the writ *de rationabili parte bonorum,* this ſtatute ſaveth it. And this writ doth not lye without a particular cuſtome, for that the writ in the Regiſter is grounded upon a cuſtome, which (as hath been ſaid) is ſaved by this act.

* But that it was never the common-law (though there be great variety in books) heare what Bracton ſaith, who wrote ſoone after this act, *Neq; uxorem, neq; liberos amplius capere de bonis defuncti patris vel viri mobilibus, quam fuerit eis ſpecialiter relictum, niſi hoc ſit de ſpeciali gratia teſtatoris, utpote ſi bene meriti in ejus vita fuerint, &c. vix enim inveniretur aliquis civis, qui in vita magnum quæſtum faceret, ſi in morte ſua cogeretur invitus bona ſua relinquere pueris indoctis, vel luxurioſis, et uxoribus male meritis: et ideo neceſſarium eſt valde, quod illis in hac parte libera facultas tribuatur. Per hoc enim tollet maleficium, animabit ad virtutem, et tam uxoribus, quam liberis bene faciendi dabit occaſionem, quod quidem non fieret, ſi ſe ſcirent indubitanter certam partem obtinere etiam ſine teſtatoris voluntate.*

But the adminiſtrators of a man that die inteſtate, or *executor of any, that make no diſpoſition of his whole perſonall eſtate, goods, debts, and chattells,* the adminiſtrators or executors after the debts paid and will performed, ought not to take any thing to his or their owne uſe, but ought, though there be no particular cuſtome, to divide them, according to this ſtatute: and the ſaid ancient, and latter authorities (then which there can be no better direction) may guide them therein: and this right doth this ſtatute of *Magna*

Ockham Regiſt. 281. b.
17 E. 3. 73.
27 E. 3. 88.
[33]
29 E. 3. 13.
41 E. 3. 15.
41 E. 3. execut. 38.
4 E. 4. 16. F.N.B. 28. b.
33 H. 8. c. 39.
See before cap. 8.
Mirror, cap. 5. § 2.
Glanv. lib. 12. c. 20.
Bracton, l. 2. fol. 60. b.
Fleta, l. 2. cap. 50.
Regiſt. 142.
34 E. 1. detinew 60.
1 E. 2. ib. 56.
17 E. 2. ib 58.
30 E. 3. 2. 26.
31 E. 3. rn'der. 6.
39 E. 3. 6. 10.
17 E. 3. 17.
40 E. 3. 38.
3 E. 3. det. 156.
1 E. 4. 6.
7 E. 4. 21.
13 H. 4.
Sever. 30.
31 H. 8. Rationab. parte Bro. 6.
Bract. l. 2. fol. 61. Note the reaſon hereof maketh againſt perpetuities.

Charta save by these words, *salvis uxori, et liberis suis, rationabilibus partibus suis.* So as though the statute doth give no action, yet their parts are saved hereby, which by *Glanvile,* and other ancient authors appear to belong to them; and the executor, or administrator shall be allowed of this distribution, according to this statute, upon his account before the ordinary.

CAP. XIX.

NULLUS constabularius, vel ejus balivus capiat blada, vel alia catalla alicujus, qui non sit de villa, ubi castrum suum situm est, nisi statim reddat denarios, aut respectum inde habere possit de voluntate venditoris: Si autem de villa illa fuerit, infra quadraginta dies precium redd'.

NO constable, nor his bailiff, shall take corn or other chattles of any man, if the man be not of the town where the castle is, but he shall forthwith pay for the same, unless that the will of the seller was to respite the payment; and if he be of the same town, the price shall be paid unto him within forty days.

(Mirror, 313. 3 Ed. 1. c. 7. Altered by 13 Car. 2. stat. 1. c. 8.)

See W. 1. cap. 7. & 31. Here also it appeareth, that in this chapter *constabularius* is taken for *castellanus:* and this taking by *castelleins,* though the castell was kept for the defence of the realme, was an unjust oppression of the subject, and this expresly appeareth by the Mirror, Mirror, cap. 5. § 2. *Ceo que est defendu a constables a prender le autre, defend droit a touts gents de cy que nul difference parenter prise dautrui maugre soen, et robbery, lequel cel prise soit de chivalls, de vitaille, de marchandise, de cariage, de ostiels, ou des autres manners de biens.* And this appeareth also by Fleta, l. 2. cap. 43. *Quia multa gravamina multis inferuntur per diversas districtiones, quæ quidem sub colore prisarum advocantur, &c. inhibetur in Magna Charta de libertatibus,* &c. no purveyance [34] 36 E. 3. cap. 2. 23 H. 6. cap. 2. shall be taken, but only for the houses of the king, and queene, and for no other person: so as the grievance before this, and other like acts, is wholly taken away.

CAP. XX.

NULLUS constabularius distringat aliquem militem ad dandum denarios pro custodia castri, si ipse eam facere voluerit, in propria persona sua, vel per alium probum hominem faciat, si ipse eam facere non possit, propter rationabilem causam. Et si nos abducerimus, vel miserimus eum in exercitum, sit quietus de custodia castri, secundum

NO constable shall distrain any knight for to give money for keeping of his castle, if he himself will do it in his proper person, or cause it to be done by another sufficient man, if he may not do it himself for a reasonable cause. And if we do lead or send him in an army, he shall be free from castleward

cundum quantitatem temporis, quo per nos fuerit in exercitu, de feod' pro quo fecit ſervitium in exercitu.

ward for the time that he ſhall be with us in fee in our hoſt, for the which he hath done ſervice in our wars.

(1 Inſt. 70. a. 12 Car. 2. c. 24.)

Here *conſtabularius* is taken in the former ſenſe: ſee the firſt parte of the Inſtitutes, Sect. 96.

See this act in Fleta: and note, this act (conſiſting upon two branches) is declaratory of the common law, for firſt, that he, that held by caſtle gard, that is, to keepe a tower, or a gate, or ſuch like of a caſtle in time of warre might doe it, either by himſelfe, or by any other ſufficient perſon for him, and in his place. And ſome hold by ſuch ſervice, as cannot doe it in perſon, as major and comminalty, deane and chapter, biſhops, abbots, &c. Infants being purchaſers, women, and the like, and therefore they might make a deputy by order of the common law. If two joyn-tenants hold by ſuch ſervice, if one of them performe, it is ſufficient.

Fleta, lib. 2. ca. 43.

See the 1. part of the Inſtit. 96.

For the ſecond; if ſuch a tenant be by the king led, or ſent to his hoſt, in time of warre, the tenant is excuſed and quit of his ſervice for keeping of the caſtle, either by himſelfe, or by another during the time, that he ſo ſerve the king in his hoſt, for that when the king commandeth his ſervice in his hoſt, he diſpenceth with his ſervice, by reaſon of his tenure, for that one man cannot ſerve in perſon in two places, and when he ſerves the king in perſon in one place, he is not bound to finde a deputy in the other, for he is not bound to make a deputy, but at his pleaſure, and this is alſo declaratory of the ancient common law. See the firſt part of the Inſtitutes, 111. 121.

CAP. XXI.

*NULLUS vicecomes, vel balivus noſter, vel aliquis alius, capiat equos, vel carectas alicujus pro cariagio faciendo, niſi reddat liberationem antiquitus ſtatutam, ſcilicet pro una carecta ad duos equos decem denarios per diem, et pro carecta ad tres equos quatuordecim denarios per diem. Nulla carecta dominica alicujus perſonæ eccleſiaſticæ, vel militis, vel alicujus * domini, per balivos noſtros capiatur, nec nos, nec balivi noſtri, nec alii, capiemus boſcum alienum ad caſtra, vel ad alia agenda noſtra, niſi per voluntatem illius, cujus boſcus ille fuerit.*

NO ſheriff nor bailiff of ours, or any other, ſhall take the horſes or carts of any man to make carriage, except he pay the old price limited, that is to ſay, for carriage with two horſe, x. d. a day; for three horſe, xiv. d. a day. No demeſne cart of any ſpiritual perſon or knight, or any lord, ſhall be taken by our bailiffs; nor we, nor our bailiffs, nor any other, ſhall take any man's wood for our caſtles, or other our neceſſaries to be done, but by the licence of him whoſe the wood is.

* [35]

(W. 1. c. 1. verb. & que nul face, &c. Artic. ſuper cart. cap. 2. Regiſt. fol. 98. Bracton lib. 3 fol. 177. Britton fol. 33. 36. 38. Fleta, lib. 1. c. 20. ſee cap. Itineris. 3 Bulſtr. 4. 14 Ed. 3. ſtat. 2. c. 19. 25 Ed. 3. ſtat. 5. c. 6. 13 Car. 2. ſtat. 1. c. 8.)

This chapter consisteth of three branches, the first setteth down the auncient hire or allowance for the carriage for the king; the second setteth down, who are exempted from that carriage; the third, concerning purveyance of wood.

W. 1. cap. 1. & 32. 36 E. 3. cap. 2. 38 H. 6. cap. 2. Fleta, lib. 2. ca. 1. & 24.

For the first, the carriage must be taken for the king, and queen onely, and for no other, implied in these words, *Nullus vicecomes vel balivus noster*, and this is explained by divers other statutes, and by our books.

32 E. 3. Barre 259. 7 H. 3. tit. Waste.

The hire or allowance is certainly expressed, as aunciently due, *Reddat liberationem antiquitus statutam*; so as this also is declaratory of the auncient law, and the hire or allowance ought to be paid in hand, for the statute saith, *Nullus capiat*, &c. *nisi reddat*, &c.

And this *liberatio antiquitus statuta*, is (as it appeareth by this act) *per diem*, by the day.

Rastall * i. carragiis cum averiis.

Aver-penny, and *averagium*, are words common in auncient charters, and signifie to be free from the kings carriages, *cum averiis*, and this is meant where it is said, *Aver-penny, hoc est, quietum esse de diversis denariis pro * averagiis domini regis*.

W. 1. cap. 1. 14 E. 3. cap. 1. 1 R. 2. cap. 3. 10 E. 2. Vet. Mag. Chart. pt. 2 fo. 46. Fleta, lib. 3. cap. 5.

For the second branch: no demean, or proper cart for the necessary use of any ecclesiasticall person, or of any knight, or of any lord, for or about the demean lands of any of them, ought to be taken for the kings carriage, but they are exempted by the auncient law of England from any such carriage.

This statute extendeth not to any person ecclesiasticall, of what estate, order, or degree soever: and this was an auncient priviledge belonging to holy church.

Also it extendeth to all degrees, and orders of the lesser, and greater nobility, or dignity, as of knighthood, dukes, marquesses, earles, viscounts, and barons, for albeit there were no dukes, marquesses, or viscounts within England at the making of the statute, yet this statute doth extend to them, for they are all *domini*, lords of parliament, and of the barony of England; and this also was an ancient priviledge belonging to these orders and dignities: and all this concerning the ecclesiasticall and temporall state was (amongst other things for the advancement and maintenance of that great peacemaker, and love-holder, hospitality) one of the auncient ornaments, and commendations of the kingdome of England.

W. 1. cap. 1. & 32. See 25 E. 3. ca. 6. 35 H. 8. cap. 17. 5 Eliz. cap. 8. 7 H. 3. tit. Wa. 141. 11 H. 4. 28 Pl. Com. 322. 42 E. 3. cap. 1. Mic. 2. Ja. resolved 11 H. 4. fo. 28. No purveyance of gravell, because it is part of the inheritance. See 47 E. 3. fo. 18. Issue taken upon the sale of timber for reparation of Calais.

The third branch is, that neither the king, nor any of his baylies, or ministers, shall take the wood of any other, for the kings castles, or other necessaries to be done, but by the license of him whose wood it is. And all statutes made against this branch (amongst others) before the parliament of 42 E. 3. are repealed: and this branch, amongst others, hath (as hath been said) been confirmed, and commanded to bee put in execution at 32 sessions of parliament. And so it was resolved by all the judges of England, and barons of the exchequer, Mich. 2 Jac. Reg. upon mature deliberation; and that the kings purveyor could take no timber, growing upon the inheritance of the subject, because it was parcell of the inheritance, no more then the inheritance it selfe. Whereof the king, and counsell being informed, the king by his proclamation, by advise of his counsell, under the great seale, 23 *Aprilis*, *anno* 4. declared the law to be in these words: first, when we were informed, that some inferiour ministers had presumed to goe so farre beyond their commission, as they have adventured, not onely

[36]

to take timber trees growing, which being parcell of our subjects inheritance,

inheritance, was never intended by us to be taken without the good will, and full consent of the owners, but have accustomed also to take greater quantities of provisions for our house, and stable, then ever came, or were needfull, to our use, &c. As by the said proclamation bearing date 23 *Aprilis*, *anno* 4 Jac. Reg. appeareth. And divers purveyors were according to the said resolution of the judges punished in the starchamber, for purveying of timber growing, without the consent of the owners.

Boscus is an ancient word used in the law of England, for all manner of wood, and the Italian useth the word *bosco* in the same sense, and the French, *boys*, accordingly. *Boscus* is divided into two sorts, *viz.* high wood, *haut-boys*, or timber, and coppice-wood (so called, because it is usually cut) or under wood. High-wood is properly called *Sultus, quia arbores ibi exiliunt in altum.* It is called in Fleta, *maeremium.* Fleta, ubi supra.

The common law hath so admeasured the prerogative of the king, as he cannot take, nor prejudice the inheritance of any, and (as hath been said) a man hath an inheritance in his woods. Pl. Com. 236.

And see the statute of Marlebridge, *anno* 52. H. 3. *Magna Charta in singulis teneatur, tam in hiis, quae ad regem pertinent, quam ad alios,* and 31 other statutes. So as all pretence of prerogative against *Magna Charta* is taken away. Marlebr. cap. 5.

See hereafter the exposition of the statute *De tallagio, anno* 34 E. 1. & *de prisis, anno* 18 E. 2. *vet. Magna Charta.* fol. 125. 1 part. 34 E. 1. Vet. Magna Charta. fol. 37. 2. Part.

CAP. XXII.

NOS non tenebimus terras (1) *illorum, qui convicti fuerint* (2) *de felonia* (3), *nisi per unum annum, et unum diem, et tunc reddantur terrae illae dominis feodorum.*

WE will not hold the lands of them that be convict of felony but one year and one day, and then those lands shall be delivered to the lords of the fee.

(Mirror, 313.)

This appeareth by Glanvill, to be due to the king by his auncient prerogative, for he saith, *Sin autem de alio, quam de rege tenuerit is, qui utlagatus est, vel de felonia convict. tunc quoque omnes res suae mobiles regis erunt, terra quoq; per unum annum remanebit in manu domini regis, elapso autem anno, terra eadem ad rectum dominum, scilicet ad ipsum de cujus feod. est, revertetur, veruntamen cum domorum subversione, et arborum extirpatione.* Glanv. li. 7. ca. 17. fol. 59.

This chapter of *Magna Charta* doth expresse that, which doth belong to the king, viz. the yeare, and the day, and omit the waste, as not belonging to him, and this is notably explained by our auncient books with an uniforme consent: Bracton treating of the yeare, and the day in this case due to the king, saith, *Sed quae sit causa, quare terra remanebit in manibus domini regis? Videtur quod talis est, quia revera, cum quis convictus fuerit de aliqua felonia, in potestate domini regis erit, prosternendi aedificia, extirpandi gardina, et arandi prata, et quoniam hujusmodi verterentur in grave damnum dominorum,* Bracton lib. 3. fol. 129. & 137.

norum, pro communi utilitate provisum fuit, quod hujusmodi ædificia, gardina, et prata remanerent, et quod dominus rex propter hoc haberet commoditatem totius terræ illius per unum annum, et unum diem, et sic omnia cum integritate reverterentur in manus dominorum capitalium, nunc autem petitur utrumque, s. finis pro termino, et similiter pro vasto, et non video rationem quare, &c.

Nota. Provisum fuit.

Britton, cap. 5. fol. 14.

And Britton treating of this very matter, saith, *Lour biens mobles sont les nous, et lour heires disherit. et voilons aver lour tenements de qui que unques sont tenus le an, et le jour, issint que lour heritages, demourgent un an et un jour in nostre maine, si que nous ne faisons estre perie les tenements, ne gaster les boys, ne arer les prees, sicome lensoloit faire in remembrance des felons attaints,* &c.

[37]

Fleta, li. 1. cap. 28.

Fleta saith, *Si autem utlagati, vel alii convicti terram liberam habuerint, illa statim capienda est in manus regis, et per unum annum, et unum diem tenend. ad capitales dominos post illum terminum reversura, et hoc habetur ex statuto Magnæ Chartæ, quod tale est, nos non tenebimus terras illorum, qui convicti fuerint de felonia, nisi per unū annū, et unum diem, et tunc reddantur terræ illæ dominis feodorū, causa vero talis termini regis, quia in signum feloniæ olim provisum fuit, quod ædificia tal.um prosternenentur in terram, extirpentur gardina, ararentur prata, truncarentur bosci, et quoniam hujusmodi verterentur in grave dammum dominorum feodorum, pro communi utilitate provisum fuit, quod hujusmodi dura, et gravia cessarent, et quod rex propterea per annum et diem totius terræ commoditatem perciperet, secus autem, si terra non esset eschaeta dominorum, post quem terminum dominis proprietariis integre absque vasto vel destructione reverterentur.*

Nota.

Nota.

Mirror, cap. 5. § 2.

The Mirror speaking of this chapter, saith, *Le point des terres aux felons tener per un an, est desusie, car p. la ou le roy ne duist aver q. le gast de droit, ou lan in nosme de fine, pur salver le fief de lestripment, preignont les ministers le roy ambideux.* Upon all which it appeareth, that the king originally was to have no benefit in this case, upon the attainder of felony, where the free-land was holden of a subject, but onely in detestation of the crime, *ut pœna ad paucos, metus ad omnes perveniat,* to prostrate the houses, to extirpe the gardens, to eradicate his woods, and to plow up the medows of the felon, for saving whereof, *et pro bono publico,* the lords, of whom the lands were holden, were contented to yeeld the lands to the king for a year, and a day, and therefore not only the wast was justly omitted out of this chapter of *Magna Charta,* but thereby it is enacted, that after the year and day, the land shall be rendred to the lord of the fee, after which no waste can be done.

And where the treatise of *Prerogativa Regis,* made in 17 Ed. 2. saith, *Et postquam dominus rex habuerit annum, diem, et vastum, tunc reddatur tenementum illud capitali domino feodi illius, nisi prius faciat finem pro anno, die, et vasto.* Which is so to be expounded, that forasmuch, as it appeareth in the said old books, that the officers, and ministers, did demaund both for the waste, and for the year, and day, that came in lieu thereof, therefore this treatise named both, not that both were due, but that a reasonable fine might be paid for all that, which the king might lawfully claim. But if this act of 17 E. 2. be against this branch of *Magna Charta,* then is it repealed by the said act of 42 E. 3. cap. 1.

Vide Stamford. Pl. Cor. 190, 191. Vide 3 E. 3. coron. 327. 3 E. 3. ibid. 58. 3 E. 3. ibid. 310.

Hereby it also appeareth, how necessary the reading of auncient authors is for understanding of auncient statutes. And out of these old books, you may observe, that when any thing is given to the king

king in lieu, or satisfaction of an auncient right of his crown, when once he is in possession of the new recompence, and the same in charge, his officers and ministers will many times demand the old also, which may turn to great prejudice, if it be not duly, and discreetly prevented. Pasc. 31 E. 1. Cor. Rege Norff. Wil. de Ormesby.

(1) *Non tenebimus terras.*] If there be lord, mesne, and tenant, and the mesne is attainted of felony, the lord paramount shall have the mesnalty presently. For this prerogative belonging to the king extends onely to the land, which might be wasted, in lieu whereof the yeare and day was granted.

And this is to be understood when a tenant in fee-simple is attainted, for when tenant in taile, or tenant for life is attainted, there the king shall have the profits of the lands, during the life of tenant in taile, or of the tenant for life.

(2) *Convicti fuerint.*] Here *convicti* in a large sense is taken for *attincti*, for the nature, and true sense of both these words, see the first part of the Institutes, and likewise for this word felony there. See the first part of the Institutes, sect. 745.

(3) *De felonia.*] Must be understood of all manner of felonies punished by death, and not of petit larceny, which notwithstanding is felony. [38]

CAP. XXIII.

OMNES kidelli (1) *deponantur de cætero penitus per Thamesiam et Medewein per totam Angliam nisi per costeram maris.*

ALL wears from henceforth shall be utterly put down by Thames and Medway, and through all England, but only by the sea-coasts.

(25 E. 3. cap. 4. 1 H. 4. cap. 12. 12 E. 4. cap. 7. 10 Rep. 138. 13 Rep. 35. 12 Ed. 4. c. 7.)

Rex, &c. Noveritis nos pro communi utilitate civitatis nostræ London' et totius regni nostri concessisse, et firmiter præcepisse, ut omnes kidelli qui sunt in Tamisia, vel Medeweia, ubicunque fuerint in Tamisia, vel in Medeweia, amoveant', et non de cætero kidelli alicubi ponant' in Tamisia, vel in Medeweya, super forisfactur' decem libr' sterlingorum: quietum etiam clamavimus omne id, quod custodes turr' nostræ London' annuatim percipere solebant de prædictis kidellis: Quare volumus et firmiter præcipimus, ne aliquis custos præfat' turr' aliquo tempore post hoc, aliquid exigat ab aliquo, nec aliquam demandam, aut gravamen, sive molestiam alicui inferat occasione prædictorum kidellorum, satis enim nobis constat, et per fideles nostros sufficienter nobis datum est intelligi, quod maximum detrimentum, et incommodum prædictæ civitati London', nec non et toto regno nostro occasione prædictorum kidellorum perveniebat; quod ut firmum, et stabile perseveret imperpetuum, præsentis paginæ inscriptione et sigilli nostri appositione communimus, sicut carta domini regis Johannis patris nostri quam barones nostri London' inde habent rationabilit' testat'. Rot. cart. 18 Feb. Anno 11 H. 3.

(1) *Kidelli.*] Kidels is a proper word for open weares whereby fish are caught. Lib. 10. fo. 138, in the case of Chester Mill. Keylw. 15 H. 7. 15.

It was specially given in charge by the justices in eire, that all juries should enquire, *De hiis qui piscantur cum kidellis et skarkellis.* Cap. Itineris, nu. 5. Tr. 5 E. 2. Coram Rege. Rot. 18.

And

Glanv. li. 9. ca. 11.

And it appeareth by Glanvill, that this *pourpresture* was forbidden by the common law, for he saith, *Dicitur autem purprestura, vel porprestura proprie, quando aliquid super dominum regem injuste occupatur, ut in dominicis regis, vel in viis publicis obstructis, vel in aquis publicis transversis a recto cursu, vel quando aliquis in civitate super regiam plateam aliquid ædificando occupaverit, et generaliter, quoties aliquid fit ad nocumentum regii tenementi, vel regiæ viæ, vel civitatis,* and every publique river or streame, is *alta regia via*, the kings high-way.

Pourpresture commeth of the French word *pourprise*, which signifieth a close, or inclosure, that is, when one encroacheth, or makes that severall to himselfe, which ought to be common to many.

[39]

CAP. XXIV.

BREVE (1) quod dicitur præcipe in capite, de cætero non fiat alicui de aliquo libero tenemento, unde liber homo perdat curiam suam.

THE writ that is called præcipe in capite shall be from henceforth granted to no person of any freehold, whereby any freeman may lose his court.

(Mirror, cap. 5. §. 2. Bracton lib. 5. fol. 328. & 414 b. Registr. 4. 3 E. 3. 23. 6 E. 3. 15. 38 E. 3. 13. 39 E. 3. 26. F. N. B. 5. e. 38 Ed. 3. f. 13. 13 Rep. 42. F. N. B. fol. 5, 12, 39. h.)

This is for reformation of an abuse, and wrong offered to the lord, of whom the land was holden, and yet upon this statute, the tenant cannot pleade, that the lands are not holden of the king in chiefe, for two causes, first for that this act was made for the benefit of the lord, of whom this land is holden, and he cannot pleade it, because he is an estrang', and if one claiming to be lord should be admitted, another might come in and pretend the like, and so infinite. Secondly, this act extends to the chancery, for the words be *Breve, &c. non fiat,* so in that court the writ is made: and therefore when the writ is granted in the chancery, and returned into the court of common pleas, that which is by this act prohibited in the chancery, extendeth not to the court of common pleas; and therefore they cannot admit of such a plea: now the tenant, least he be concluded, must take the tenure by protestation, and the king, though he be not party to the record, yet shall he take advantage of the estoppel, for he is ever present in court.

20 E. 3. estoppel. 187. 22 E. 3. 17. 40 E. 3. 30.

And since this statute, no man ought to have this writ out of the chancery upon a suggestion, but oath must be made, before the granting thereof, that the land is holden of the king in *capite*.

Mic. 7. E. 1. in banco rot. 65. Lanc'. acc'. Peter Grellyes case.

See Mich. 4 E. 1. *de banco* Rot. 114. Norff. Barth. de Redhams case, *pro terris in curia comitis warren apud Castleacre, notabile recordum super hoc statutum. Per breve præcipitur justiciariis quod inquirant, si terræ tenentur de rege in capite.* See the writ in the Register, 4. b. by which writ power is given to the justices, that if it may appeare to them, that the land is not holden in *capite*, then that the plea be holden in the lords court, according to this statute. And for that the demandant Peter Grellye confessed that the

* lands

lands were not holden of the king in *capite*, but of Edmond brother of the king, thereupon the entrie was, *Ideo Petrus perquirat sibi per breve de recto pat' in curia ipsius Ed. versus R. si voluerit.* Mich. 14. E. 1. Rot. 48. Som. acc. Regist. fo. 4. b. & 6. a.

And the lord, of whom the land is holden, shall upon this statute, have his writ of disceit against the demandant, which have recovered by default, and recover his damages, but the record of the judgement shall stand in force; and concerning the conclusion of the tenure, the lord shall have remedy against the king by petition of right. But if the recovery be given upon triall against the tenant, then the tenant hath concluded himself: for the tenure, because his protestation cannot availe him, when his plea is found against him: but the lord may have in that case, his action against the tenant, and his petition of right to the king, to be restored to his seigniorie, and by that meanes the tenant himselfe may be relieved. 8 E. 4. 6. 6 E. 3. 15. Vet. N.B. 13. a. F.N.B. 98. n. See the first part of the Institutes, sect. 192. 17 E. 3. 31. 36. 37. 59. 32 E. 3. Avowry 113. 46 E. 3. petition 9.

(1) *Breve.*] *Dicitur ideo breve, quia rem de qua agitur, et intentionem petentis paucis verbis breviter enarrat, sicut faciat regula juris, quæ rem, quæ est, breviter enarrat.* Bract. lib. 3. f. 112. cap. 12. nu. 2. & lib. 5 fol. 413. c. 17. nu. 2.

Breve quidem cum sit formatum ad similitudinem regulæ juris, quia breviter et paucis verbis intentionem proferentis exponit et explanat, sicut regula juris rem quæ est breviter enarrat. Fleta, lib. 2. c. 12. § dicuntur etiam brevia.

And Fleta defines a writ, *totidem verbis*, as Bracton hath done.

There is a great diversity betweene a writ, and an action (although by some they are often confounded) which will best appeare by their severall definitions. [40]

Actio nihil aliud est, quam jus prosequendi in judicio quod alicui debetur.

And with Bracton agreeth Fleta. Bracton, lib. 3. fol. 98. b. cap. 1.

Actio nihil aliud est, quam jus prosequendi in judicio quod alicui debetur, et quod nascitur ex maleficio, vel quod provenit ex delicto, vel injuria. Fleta, lib. 1. cap. 16. § actio & § 3. Actors.

And the Mirror saith, *Action nest aut' chose que loiall demand de son droit. Actors sont queux suont lour droit per pleint,* &c. Mirror, cap. 2. § 1. nest.

So as the first diversity between an action, and a writ is, that an action is the right of a suite, and the writ is grounded thereupon, and the meane to bring the demandant or pl' to his right.

The second diversity, a writ grounded upon right of action is ever in *foro contentioso*, but so are not all writs, for that writs are much more large, then actions are, as shall appeare by the division of writs.

Of writs grounded upon rights of action, some be criminall, and some be civill or common. Bracton, lib. 3. fol. 101. cap. 3. nu. 1. Fleta lib. 1 cap. 16.

Of criminall, some be in *personam*, to have judgement of death, as writs of appeale, of death, robberie, rape, &c. and some to have judgement of dammage to the partie, fine to the king, and imprisonment, as writs of appeale of mayhem, &c.

Of writs civill or common, some be reall, some personall, and some mixt. And of these, some be originall, and all they goe out of the chancery, and some judiciall, and they issue out of the court, where the plea depended. Some conditionall, as writs of error, redissin, &c. some without condition, some retornable, and some not retornable. And all these are warranted, either by the common law, or grounded upon some act of parliament. Which are so well knowne, as this little touch shall suffice. Glanvil. lib. 1. c. 1. Bracton ubi sup. Fleta ubi sup. Mirror ubi sup. Plowd. Com. 73. &c. Regist. 187.

Of originall writs, some be *brevia formata*, and some *ex cursu*, some *magistralia, et sæpius variantur.* Bract. l. 5. 413. b. Fleta, lib. 2. cap. 12.

Regularly

[a] Dier, 23. Fitz. 377. a.
[b] F.N.B. 28, 29.

Regularly the kings writs are, *ex debito justitiæ*, to be granted to the subject, which cannot be denied; and some be *ex gratia*, as [a] speciall liveries, and [b] writs of protections for the safegard of the subject, being in the kings warre out of the realme.

[c] Regist. 227.
[d] Ibid. 267.
[e] Regist. 133. b. Fitz. N.B. 185. Regist. 206. F.N.B. ib.

In nature of commissions; as writs of error, of oier, and terminer, of election of knights and burgesses of the parliament, of election of a coroner, or of discharging of him, of election of verderers, [c] *de ventre inspiciendo.* [d] *De viis et venellis mundandis*, Regist. 267. Of the surety of the good behaviour, or of the peace. [e] *De odio et atia.* Association of *de admittendo in socium*, of *si non omnes*, and the like. Writs of *justicies.*

Of writs of *præcipe*, some be, *quod reddat*, as writs of right, &c. debt, &c. Some be *quod permittat*, as writs *de quod permittat*. Some be *quod faciat*, as *de consuetudinibus et servitiis. De domo reparanda.* And of writs of *præcipe*, some containe severall precepts, and some joynt, and some are sole.

Regist. 295. F.N.B 170. Regist. 294. F.N.B. 165. a. F.N.B. 85. a. Regist. 58. b. Artic. sup. cart. c. 6. Regist. 187. b. ibid. 179. a. F.N.B. 240. d.

Writs mandatory, and extrajudiciall, whereof some be affirmative, and some negative. Affirmative, as calling of men to the upper house of parliament to be peers of the realme. *De comitat' commissis.* Regist. 295. Of *conge de eslier*, licence to choose a bishop. Regist. 294. b. *De regio assensu.* Regist. *ibid.* To call one to be chiefe justice of England. To call apprentices of law to be serjants. *De brevibus et rot. deliberandis.* Regist. 295. *De restitutione spiritualium.* Regist. 294. b. Negative, as *de non ponendis in assisis, et juratis. De securitate invenienda, quod se non divertat ad partes exteras sine licentia. De non residentia clerici regis. De clerico infra sacros ordines constituto non eligendo in officium. Ne fines capias pro non pulchre placitando.*

[41]

[a] F.N.B. 153. b. 2 E. 3. ca. 8. 5 E. 3. ca. 9. 14 E. 3. cap. 14. Regist fo. 186. F.N.B. 153. Regist. 18, F.N.B. 20.

Of writs, some are for furtherance of justice, and for ousting of delayes, and to proceed. As the writ *de procedendo ad judicium*, that the justices shall not surcease to doe common right, for no commandement under the great seale, petit seale, or message from the king. Or [a] if the judges of themselves delay judgement, there lyeth also a *procedendo ad judicium.* Againe, there is a *procedendo in loquela, et ad judicium*, after aid of the king. A writ *de executione judicii.*

[b] Regist. 124, 125. revocat brevis de audiendo &c. All Writs of supersedeas.

[b] Some for advancement of justice not to proceed.

[c] Pl. com. fol. 73. &c. See 12 H. 4. 24. in debt not cited in that case. Regist. 114, 115. Writs of audita querela &c. prohibitions ad jura regal.
[d] Regist. 267. a.
[e] ib. 126. b.
[f] Ib. 192. b. 193. a. b.

[c] Regularly writs are directed to the sheriffes, or coroners, but in speciall cases to the partie, or others. To the partie, as writs of prohibitions, *ne exeat regnum.* To others, as to judges temporall, ecclesiasticall, and civill. To serjeants at armes. To the [d] party that hath the custody of an idiot. To the [e] major, and bailiffes, &c. *ad amovendum eos ab officio, quousq; inquisitio fo' et de eorum gestu.* [f] *Liberate thesaurario, et camerariis, thesaurario et baronibus.*

Note of writs of right (whereof the *præcipe in capite* is one) some be close, and some be patent.

Writs of right retornable into the court of common pleas be patent, and writs directed into auncient demesne, are close; and the reason wherefore in other courts of the lords, the writs shall be patent, is, because there is a clause in those writs, *et nisi feceris, vicecomes N. hoc faciat, ne amplius clamorem audiamus pro defectu recti*: which clause is not in the other writs, and necessary it is that such writs should be patent, that the sheriffe might take notice thereof.

CAP.

CAP. XXV.

UNA mensura vini per totum regnum nostrum, et una mensura cervisiæ, et una mensura bladi, scilicet, quarterium Lond', et una latitudo pannorum (1) tinctorum, russatorum, et haubergettarum, scilicet duæ ulnæ infra listas. De ponderibus vero sic sicut de mensuris.

ONE measure of wine shall be through our realm, and one measure of ale, and one measure of corn, that is to say, the quarter of London: and one breadth of dyed cloth, russets, and haberjects, that is to say, two yards within the lists. And it shall be of weights as it is of measures.

(14 Ed. 3. stat. 1. c. 12. 27 Ed. 3. stat. 2. c. 10. 8 H. 6. c. 5. 11 H. 7. c. 4. 16 Car. 1. c. 19.)

This act concerning measures and weights, that there should be one measure and one weight through England, is grounded upon the law of God. *Non habebis in sacculo diversa pondera, majus, et minus, non erit in domo tua modius major et minor, pondus habebis justum et verum, et modius æqualis erit tibi, ut multo vivas tempore super terram,* &c. And this hath often by authority of parliament been enacted, but never could be effected, so forcible is custome concerning multitudes, when it hath gotten an head, therefore good lawes are timely to be executed, and not in the begimming to be neglected.

Stat. de 31 E. 1. 14 E. 3. cap. 12. 27 E. 3. cap. 10. See the Custum. de Norm. cap. 16. Deutr. 25. v. 13, 14.

For weights and measures, there are good lawes made before the conquest: *in dimensione, et pondere nihil esto iniquum, ab iniquitate vero deinceps quisq; temperet: per commune concilium regni statuimus, quod habeant per universum regnum mensuras fidelissimas, et signatas, et pondera fidelissima, et signata, sicut boni prædecessores statuerunt.*

Int' leges Canut. cap. 9. Int' leges Will. Regis conq.

(1) *Una latitudo pannorum,* &c.] True it is that broade cloathes were made, though in small number, at the time, and long before this statute, but in the beginning of the raigne of Edward 3. the same came to so great perfection, as in the 11. yeare of his raigne, all men were prohibited to bring in privilie, or apertly by himselfe, or any other, any clothes made in any other places, &c. And this is the worthiest and richest commoditie of this kingdome, for divide our native commodities exported into tenne parts, and that which comes from the sheepes back, is nine parts in value of the tenne, and setteth great numbers of people on worke. For the breadth, and length of clothes, see many statutes made after this act.

Mirror, cap. 5. § 2. Vet. Mag. Cart. cap. Itin. f. 151. 11 E. 3. cap. 3.

[42]

CAP. XXVI.

NIHIL de cætero detur pro brevi inquisitionis (1) *ab eo, qui inquisitionem petit de vita, vel de membris, sed gratis concedatur, et non negetur.*

NOTHING from henceforth shall be given for a writ of inquisition, nor taken of him that prayeth inquisition of life, or of member, but it shall be granted freely, and not denied.

(3 Ed. 1. c. 11. 13 Ed. 1. stat. 1. c. 29. Mirror, 314. Regist. 133, 134.)

Mirror, cap. 5. § 2. Regist. fol. 133. Glanv. lib. 14. c. 3. Bract. l. 3. f. 121. Fleta, lib. 1. c. 23. 25 W 1. cap. 11. Gloc. c. 9. W. 2. cap. 29. Hill. 32 E. 1. coram Rege Rott. 71. & 79. 5 H. 7. 5.

(1) *Brevi inquisitionis.*] That is the writ *de odio et atia,* anciently called *breve de bono et malo,* and here, of life, and member, which the common law gave to a man, that was imprisoned, though it were for the most odious cause, for the death of a man, for the which, without the kings writ he could not be bayled, yet the law favouring the liberty, and freedome of a man from imprisonment, and that he should not be detained in prison, untill the justices in eire should come, at what time he was to be tried, he might sue out this writ of inquisition directed to the sherife, *quod assumptis tecum custodibus placitorum coronæ in pleno comitatu per sacramentum proborum, et legalium hominum de* &c. *inquiras (inde appellatur breve inquisitionis) utrum A. captus, et detentus in prisona* &c. *pro morte W. unde rettatus (1. accusatus existit) rettatus sit odio, et atia* &c. *nisi indictatus vel appellatus fuerit, coram justitiariis nostris ultimo itinerantibus in partibus illis, & pro hoc captus, et imprisonatus,* for by the common law, *in omnibus autem placitis de felonia, solet accusatus per plegios dimitti, præterquam de placito de homicidio, ubi ad terrorem aliter statutum est.* In this writ, fower things are to be observed.

Glanv. lib. 14. c. 1.

First, though the offence, whereof he was accused, were such, as he was not bayleable by law, yet the law did so highly hate the long imprisonment of any man, though accused of an odious, and heynous crime, that it gave him this writ for his reliefe.

Secondly, If he were indited, or appealed thereof, before the justices in eyre, he could not have this writ, because this writ was grounded upon a surmise, which could not be received against a matter of record.

Thirdly, Upon this writ, though it were found, that he was accused *de odio et atia,* and that he was not guilty, or that he did this act *se defendendo, vel per infortunium,* yet the sherife by this writ had no authority to bayle him, but then the party was to sue a writ *de ponendo in ballium,* directed to the sherife, whereby he was commanded, *quod si prædictus A. invenerit tibi* 12. *probos, et legales homines de comitatu tuo &c. qui eum manucapiant habere coram justiciariis nostris ad primam assisam, &c. Standum, &c. tunc ipsum A. &c. prædictis duodecim tradas in ballium.*

Hill. 32 E. 1. ubi sup.

Lastly, that there was a meane by the common law, before inditement, or appeale, to protect the innocent against false accusation, and to deliver him out of prison.

Odium, signifieth hatred, and *atia* or *acia* in this writ signifieth

fieth malice, becaufe that malice is *acida,* that is, eager, fharpe and cruell.

And this branch, for further benefit, and in favour of the prifoner, doth enact, that he fhall have it gratis, without fee, and without delay, or deniall, of which the Mirror faith thus, *le defence que se fait del breife de odio, et atia, que le roy ne son chancelor ne preignont pur le breife granter se doit extend a touts breifs remedials, et le dit breife ne doit solement extender a felonies de homicide, mes a touts felonies, et ne solemt. in appeles, mes en inditement.* Regift. f. 133, 134. Mirror, c. 5. § 2.

But this writ was taken away by a later ftatute, viz. in 28 E. 3. becaufe as fome pretended, it became unneceffary, for that juftices of affife, juftices of oyer and terminer, and juftices of gaole delivery came at the leaft into every county twice every yeare; but within 12 years after this ftatute, it was enacted, as often hath been faid, that all ftatutes made againft *Magna Charta* (as the faid act of 28 E. 3. was) fhould be voyd, whereby the writs of *odio et atia, et de ponendo in balium* are revived, and fo in like cafes upon all the branches of *Magna Charta.* And therefore the juftices of affife, juftices of oyer and terminer, and of gaole delivery, have not fuffered the prifoner to be long detained, but at their next comming have given the prifoner full and fpeedy juftice, by due triall, without detaining him long in prifon: nay, they have been fo farre from allowance of his detaining in prifon without due triall, that it was refolved in the cafe of the abbot of S. Albon by the whole court, that where the king had graunted to the abbot of S. Albon, to have a gaole, and to have a gaole delivery, and divers perfons were committed to that gaole for felony, and becaufe the abbot would not be at coft to make deliverance, he detained them in prifon long time without making lawfull deliverance, that the abbot had for that caufe forfeited his franchife, and that the fame might bee feifed into the kings hand. [43] 28 E. 3. ca. 9. Stamf. Pl. Cor. 77. F.N.B. 92. 42 E. 3. ca. 1. See the Statute of Gloc. ca. 9. 8 H. 4. 18. 20 E. 4. 6. Bro. tit. Forfeiture.

For his committing to prifon is onely to this end, that he may be forth comming, to be duly tried, according to the law and cuftome of the realme. The abbot of Crowland had a gaole, wherein divers men were imprifoned, and becaufe he detained fome that were acquited of felony after their fees paid, the king feifed the gaole for ever. 20 E. 4. 6.

And it is provided by the ftatute of 5 H. 4. that none be imprifoned by any juftice of peace, but in the common gaole, to the end they might have their triall at the next gaole delivery, or feffions of the peace. *Vide cap.* 29. 5 H. 4. cap. 10. lib. 9. fol. 119. Seignior Zanchars cafe.

And fome fay, that this ftatute extendeth to all other judges, and juftices for two reafons. 1. They fay, that this act is but declaratory of the common law. 2. *Ubi lex est specialis, et ratio ejus generalis, generaliter accipienda est.* See the Statute of Gloc. cap. 9.

Breve regis de bono et malo is fo called of the words, *de bono et malo,* contained in the writ. This writ lay when A. B. was committed to prifon for the death of a man, the king did write to the juftices of gaole delivery; *quod si A. B. captus, et detentus in gaola prædicta pro morte C. D. de bono et malo super patriam inde ponere voluerit, et ea occasione (et non per aliquod speciale mandatum nostrum) detentus sit in eadem, tunc eandem gaolam de prædicto A. B. secundum legem, et consuetudinem Angliæ, deliberetis.* So as without queftion the writ *de bono et malo,* is not the writ *de odio et atia,* as fome have imagined. Hil. 32 E. 1. Coram Rege Eboru. Roger le Wildes Cafe. See the forme of this Writ at large in this record.

Note, in thofe dayes the juftices of gaole delivery would not

proceed in case of the death of a man, without the kings writ: for in the same record it appeareth, that *R. W. indictatus de morte W. E. non tulit breve regis de bono, et malo, ideo retornatur gaolæ, et sic de aliis.*

CAP. XXVII.

SI aliqui teneant de nobis per feodi firmam (1), *vel per socagium* (2), *vel burgagium* (3), *et de alio teneant terram per servitium militare* (4), *nos non habebimus custodiam hæredis, nec terræ suæ, quæ est de feodo alterius, occasione illius feodi firmæ, vel socagii, vel burgagii. Nec habebimus* * *custodiam illius feodi firmæ, vel socagii, vel burgagii, nisi ipsa feodi firma nobis debeat servitium militare. Nos non habebimus custodiam hæred', vel alicujus terræ, quam tenet de aliquo alio per servitium militare, occasione alicujus parvæ serjantiæ, quam tenet de nobis per servitium, reddend' nobis cultellos, sagittas, vel hujusmodi.*

* [44]

IF any do hold of us by fee-ferm, or by socage, or burgage, and he holdeth lands of another by knights service, we will not have the custody of his heir, nor of his land, which is holden of the fee of another, by reason of that fee-ferm, socage, or burgage. Neither will we have the custody of such fee-ferm, or socage, or burgage, except knights service be due unto us out of the same fee-ferm. We will not have the custody of the heir, or of any land, by occasion of any petit serjeanty, that any man holdeth of us by service to pay a knife, an arrow, or the like.

(Bro. Tenures, 69. Fitz. Gard. 145. 12 Car. 2. c. 24.)

See the Statute of Gloc. cap. 4. F.N B. 210. 45 E. 3. 15.

(1) *Per feodi firmam.*] Fee farme properly taken is, when the lord upon the creation of the tenancy reserve to himselfe, and his heires, either the rent, for the which it was before letten to farme, or at least a fourth part of that farme rent.

Brit. fol. 164. b. Bract. li. 2. fo. 35. Fleta, lib. 1. ca. 10. Mirror, ca. 2. § 17.

But Britton saith, *Fee farmes sont terres tenus in fee, a rendre pur eux per ann. le veray value, ou plus, ou meins,* and is called a fee farme, because a farme rent is reserved upon a graunt in fee. And regularly, as it appeareth by this act, lands graunted in fee farme are holden in socage, unlesse an expresse tenure by knights service be reserved, as it appeareth hereafter in this chapter.

See the first part of the Institutes. sect. 117. * Rot. claus. 12 H. 3. m. 12.

(2) *Vel per socagium.*] * *Tenere per firmam albam est tenere libere in socagio. Vide in libro nigro scaccarii, capite De officio clericorum de firma blanca.* It is commonly called blanch farme, *Lucubrat. Ockham, firma blanca, et vide ibi antiquum verbum* [*dealbari.*]

Litt. sect. 162.

(3) *Burgagium.*] See the *Custumier de Normandie, cap.* 32. and the commentaries upon the same.

Ib. sect. 103.

(4) *Per servitium militare.*] See *le Custumier de Norman. cap.* 33. *De gard de orphelines,* fol. 49. and the comment upon the same.

Glanv. li. 7. ca. 9.

This act, as well concerning tenures in fee farme, socage, and burgage, as by little serjanty, is declaratory of the common law, and constantly in use to this day, and needeth no further explanation.

CAP. XXVIII.

NULLUS balivus de cætero ponat aliquem ad legem manifestam, nec ad juramentum simplici loquela sua, sine testibus fidelibus ad hoc inductis.

NO bailiff from henceforth shall put any man to his open law, nor to an oath, upon his own bare saying, without faithful witnesses brought in for the same.

(Fitz. Ley, 78. Bro. Ley, 37.)

The Mirror treating of this chapter saith, *Le point que defend, que nul bayliffe met frank home a serement sans sute present, est interpretable en cest manner, que nul justice, nul minister le roy, ne auter seneschall, ne bailif ne eit power a mitter frank home a serement faire, sans le commaundement le roy, ne puit resceive ascuns testmoignes, que testmoignent le monstrance estre veray.* Mirror, cap. 5. § 2. Fleta li. 2. cap. 56 W. 2. ca. 35. des hauts homes. Fleta ubi supra. Vide Vet. Magna Charta, pt 2. in stat. Hibern. 68. b. See the first part of the Institutes, sect. 248.

By this it appeareth, that under this word *balivus*, in this act is comprehended every justice, minister of the king, steward and bayliffe.

Simplici loquela sua.] For as Bracton saith, *vox simplex nec probationem facit, nec præsumptionem inducit; item non per sectam, quæ, fieri* * *potest per domesticos, et familiares, secta enim probationem non facit, sed levem inducit præsumptionem, et vincitur per probationem in contrarium, et per defensionem per legem.* Brac. l. 5. fo. 400. b. * [45]

It appeareth by Glanvill, that the defendant ought to make his law, 12. *manu.* And so it appeareth by a judgement in the same yeare, and term, that this great charter was made, for there, in debt the defendant waged his law, *ideo consideratum est per curiam, quod defendens se duodecima manu venit cum lege.* Glanv. li. 1. ca. 9. Mich. 9. H. 3. tit. Ley 78.

Every wager of law doth countervaile a jury, for the defendant shall make his law, *de duodecima manu, viz.* an eleven, and himself. And it should seeme, that this making of law was very auncient, for one writing of the auncient law of England saith, *hujus purgationis non omnis evanuit vetustate memoria, nam per hæc tempora de pecunia postulatus, debitum nonnunquam duodecima, quod aiunt, manu dissolvit.* 33 H. 6. 8.

How much, and for what cause the law respecteth the number of 12. see the first part of the Institutes. See the first part of the Institutes, sect. 234.

The party himselfe, when he maketh his law shall be sworne *de fidelitate*, that is, directly or absolutely, and the others *de credulitate*, that is, that they beleeve that he saith true.

To make his law, is as much as to say, as to take his oath, &c. and it is so called, because the law giveth him that meane by his owne oath, to free himselfe.

And the reason, wherefore in an action of debt upon a simple contract, the defendant may wage his law, is, for that the defendant may satisfie the party in secret, or before witnesse, and all the witnesses may die, so the law doth allow him to wage his law for his discharge: and this, for ought I could ever reade, is peculiar to the law of England, and no mischiefe insueth hereupon, for

for the plaintiffe may take a bill or bond for his money, or if it be a ſimple contract, he may bring his action upon his caſe upon his agreement or promiſe, which every contract executory implieth, and then the defendant cannot wage his law.

CAP. XXIX.

NULLUS liber (1) *homo* (2) *capiatur, vel impriſonetur* (3), *aut diſſeiſietur de libero tenemento ſuo, vel libertatibus* (4), *vel liberis conſuetudinibus* (5) *ſuis, aut utlagetur, aut exuietur, aut aliquo modo deſtruatur, nec ſuper eum ibimus, nec ſuper eum mittemus, niſi per legale judicium* (6) *parium ſuorum* (7), *vel per legem terræ* (8). *Nulli vendemus* (9), *nulli negabimus, aut differemus* (10) *juſtitiam, vel rectum* (11).

NO freeman ſhall be taken, or impriſoned, or be diſſeiſed of his freehold, or liberties, or free cuſtoms, or be outlawed, or exiled, or any otherwiſe deſtroyed; nor will we not paſs upon him, nor condemn him, but by lawful judgment of his peers, or by the law of the land. We will ſell to no man, we will not deny or defer to any man either juſtice or right.

(5 Rep. 64. 10 Rep. 74. 11 Rep. 99. Regiſt. 186. Mirror, 314. 1 Anderſ. 158. 2 Bulſtr. 328. 3 Bulſtr. 47. Wood's Inſt. 613, 614. 2 Ed. 3. c. 8. 5 Ed. 3. c. 9. 14 Ed. 3. ſtat. 2. c. 14. 25 Ed. 3. ſt. 5. c. 4. 28 Ed. 3. c. 3. 42 Ed. 3. c. 3. 11 R. 2. c. 10. 37 Ed. 3. c. 18. 4 H. 7. c. 12. 16 Car. 1. c. 10. 1 Roll. 208, 209, 225. 12 Rep. 50, 63, 93.)

See the Statute anno 34 E. 1. de tallagio, &c. an excellent Law.

(1) *Nullus liber,* &c.] This extends to villeins, ſaving againſt their lord, for they are free againſt all men, ſaving againſt their lord. See the firſt part of the Inſtitutes, ſect. 189.

20 H. 6. cap. 9. Stamf. Pl. Cor. 152. b. 25 E. 3. 43. b. li. 6. fol. 52. The Counteſſe of Rutlands caſe 11 H. 4. 15. 3 H. 6. 58. 48 E. 3. 30. 35 H. 6. 46.

(2) *Nullus liber homo.*] Albeit *homo* doth extend to both ſexes, men and women, yet by act of parliament it is enacted, and declared, that this chapter ſhould extend to ducheſſes, counteſſes, and baroneſſes, but marchioneſſes, and viſcounteſſes are omitted, but notwithſtanding they are alſo comprehended within this chapter.

*[46]

* Upon this chapter, as out of a roote, many fruitfull branches of the law of England have ſprung.

And therefore firſt the genuine ſenſe hereof is to be ſeene, and after how the ſame hath been declared, and interpreted. For the firſt, for more perſpicuity, it is neceſſary to divide this chapter into ſeverall branches, according to the true conſtruction and reference of the words.

This chapter containeth nine ſeverall branches.

See W. 1. ca. 15.

1. That no man be taken or impriſoned, but *per legem terræ*, that is, by the common law, ſtatute law, or cuſtome of England; for theſe words, *per legem terræ*, being towards the end of this chapter, doe referre to all the precedent matters in this chapter, and this hath the firſt place, becauſe the liberty of a mans perſon is more precious to him, then all the reſt that follow, and therefore it is great reaſon, that he ſhould by law be relieved therein, if he be wronged, as hereafter ſhall be ſhewed.

2. No man ſhall be diſſeiſed, that is, put out of ſeiſon, or diſpoſſeſſed of his free-hold (that is) lands, or livelihood, or of his liberties,

liberties, or free-customes, that is, of such franchises, and freedomes, and free-customes, as belong to him by his free birth right, unlesse it be by the lawfull judgement, that is, verdict of his equals (that is, of men of his own condition) or by the law of the land (that is, to speak it once for all) by the due course, and processe of law.

3. No man shall be out-lawed, made an *exlex,* put out of the law, that is, deprived of the benefit of the law, unlesse he be outlawed according to the law of the land.

4. No man shall be exiled, or banished out of his country, that is, *nemo perdet patriam,* no man shall lose his country, unlesse he be exiled according to the law of the land.

5. No man shall be in any sort destroyed *(destruere, i. quod prius structum, et factum fuit, penitus evertere et diruere)* unlesse it be by the verdict of his equals, or according to the law of the land.

6. No man shall be condemned at the kings suite, either before the king in his bench, where the pleas are *coram rege* (and so are the words, *nec super eum ibimus,* to be understood) nor before any other commissioner, or judge whatsoever, and so are the words, *nec super eum mittemus,* to be understood, but by the judgement of his peers, that is, equalls, or according to the law of the land.

7. We shall sell to no man justice or right.

8. We shall deny to no man justice or right.

9. We shall defer to no man justice or right.

The genuine sense being distinctly understood, we shall proceed in order to unfold how the same have been declared, and interpreted. 1. By authority of parliament. 2. By our books. 3. By precedent.

(3) *Nullus liber homo capiatur, aut imprisonetur.*] Attached and arrested are comprehended herein.

1. No man shall be taken (that is) restrained of liberty, by petition, or suggestion to the king, or to his councell *, unlesse it be by indictment, or presentment of good, and lawfull men, where such deeds be done. This branch, and divers other parts of this act have been notably explained by divers [a] acts of parliament, &c. quoted in the margent.

2. No man shall be disseised, &c.

[b] Hereby is intended, that lands, tenements, goods, and chattells shall not be seised into the kings hands, contrary to this great charter, and the law of the land; nor any man shall be disseised of his lands, or tenements, or dispossessed of his goods, or chattels, contrary to the law of the land.

[c] A custome was alledged in the town of C. that if the tenant cease by two yeares, that the lord should enter into the freehold of the tenant, and hold the same untill he were satisfied of the arrerages, and it was adjudged a custome * against the law of the land, to enter into a mans freehold in that case without action or answer.

King H. 6. graunted to the corporation of diers within London, power to search, &c. and if they found any cloth died with logwood, that the cloth should be forfeit: and it was adjudged, that this charter concerning the forfeiture, was against the law of the land, and this statute: for no forfeiture can grow by letters patents.

[a] 5 E. 3. cap. 9. 25 E. 3. ca. 4. 37 E. 3. ca. 8. 38 E. 3. ca. 9. 42 E. 3. ca. 3. 17 R. 2. cap. 6. Rot. Parl. 43 E. 3. Sir Jo. a Lees case. nu. 21, 22, 23, &c. lib. 10. fol. 74. in case del Marshalsea.

* See W. 1. ca. 15.

[b] See 43 Ass. p. 21. where this branch of Magna Charta, and other statutes are cited, *nota bene,* the usurpation to an advowson is within this act. 5 E. 3. cap. 9. 25 E. 3. cap. 4.

[c] 43 E. 3. 32.

Lib. 8. Tr. 41. El. fol. 125. Case de Londres.

* [47]

No man ought to be put from his livelihood without anſwer.

2 & 3 Ph. et Mar. Dier. 114, 115. 3. No man outlawed, that is, barred to have the benefit of the law. Vide for the word, the firſt part of the Inſtitutes.

Note to this word *utlagetur*, theſe words, *niſi per legem terræ*, do refer.

(4) *De libertatibus.*] This word, *libertates*, liberties, hath three ſignifications:

1. Firſt, as it hath been ſaid, it ſignifieth the laws of the realme, in which reſpect this charter is called, *charta libertatum.*

Tr. 41 Eliz. Coram Rege. Rot. 92. in trns. int. Davenant & Hurdes. 2. It ſignifieth the freedomes, that the ſubjects of England have; for example, the company of the merchant tailors of England, having power by their charter to make ordinances, made an ordinance, that every brother of the ſame ſociety ſhould put the one half of his clothes to be dreſſed by ſome clothworker free of the ſame company, upon pain to forfeit x. s. &c. and it was adjudged that this ordinance was againſt law, becauſe it was againſt the liberty of the ſubject, for every ſubject hath freedome to put his clothes to be dreſſed by whom he will, *et ſic de ſimilibus*: and ſo it is, if ſuch or the like graunt had been made by his letters patents.

3. Liberties ſignifieth the franchiſes, and priviledges, which the ſubjects have of the gift of the king, as the goods, and chattels of felons, outlawes, and the like, or which the ſubject claim by preſcription, as wreck, waiſe, ſtraie, and the like.

Tr. 44 Eliz. Coram Rege, lib. 11. fol. 84, 85, &c. Edw. Darcies caſe. So likewiſe, and for the ſame reaſon, if a graunt be made to any man, to have the ſole making of cards, or the ſole dealing with any other trade, that graunt is againſt the liberty and freedome of the ſubject, that before did, or lawfully might have uſed that trade, and conſequently againſt this great charter.

Generally all monopolies are againſt this great charter, becauſe they are againſt the liberty and freedome of the ſubject, and againſt the law of the land.

(5) *Liberis conſuetudinibus.*] Of cuſtomes of the realme, ſome be generall, and ſome particular. Of theſe reade in the firſt part of the Inſtitutes. And *liberis* is added, for that the cuſtomes of England bring a freedome with them.

4. No man exiled.

Rot. Parliam. 19 E. 1. Rot. 12. Boilands caſe. 31 E. 1. Cui in vita 31. 18 E. 3. 54. Matravers caſe. Parliam. 15 E. 2. Exilium Hugonis. * Rot. Parliam. 13 R. 2. nu. 28. Stam. Pl. Cor. 116, 117. 35 E. 1. cap. 1.

By the law of the land no man can be exiled, or baniſhed out of his native countrey, but either by authority of parliament, or in caſe of abjuration for felony by the common law: and ſo when our books, or any record ſpeak of exile, or baniſhment, other then in caſe of abjuration, it is to be intended to be done by authority of parliament:* as Belknap and other judges, &c. baniſhed into Ireland.

This is a beneficially law, and is conſtrued benignly, and therefore the king cannot ſend any ſubject of England againſt his will to ſerve him out of this realme, for that ſhould be an exile, and he ſhould *perdere patriam*: no, he cannot be ſent againſt his will into Ireland, to ſerve the king as his deputy there, becauſe it is out of the realme of England: for if the king might ſend him out of this realme to any place, then under pretence of ſervice, as amballadour, or the like, he might ſend him into the furtheſt part of the world, which being an exile, is prohibited by this act. And albeit it was accorded in the upper-houſe of parliament, anno 6

[48] E. 3. nu. 6. that ſuch learned men in the law, as ſhould bee ſent, as juſtices, or otherwiſe, to ſerve in Ireland, ſhould have no excuſe, yet

yet that being no act of parliament, it did not binde the subject. And this notably appeareth by a record, in 44 E. 3. Sir Richard Pembrughs case, who was warden of the cinque ports, and had divers offices, annuities, and lands graunted to him for life, or in fee by the king under the great seale, *pro servitio impenso, et impendendo,* the king commanded Sir Richard to serve him in Ireland, as his deputy there, which he absolutely refused, whereupon the king by advice of his councell, seised all things graunted to him, *pro servitio impendendo* (in respect of that clause) but he was not upon that resolution committed to prison, as by that record it appeareth; and the reason was because his refusall was lawfull, and if the refusall was lawfull to serve in Ireland parcell of the kings dominions, *a fortiori,* a refusall is lawfull to serve in any forein country. And it seemeth to me, that the said seisure was unlawfull, for *pro servitio impenso et impendendo,* must be intended lawfull service within the realme. Rot. claus. anno 44 E. 3. Sir Richard Pembrughs Case.

5. No man destroyed, &c. 5 E. 3. cap. 9.

That is, fore-judged of life, or limbe, disherited, or put to torture, or death. 28 E. 3. cap. 3. Fortescue cap. 22.

The Mirror writing of the auncient laws of England, saith, *soloient les roys faire droit a touts, per eux, ou per lour chiefe justices, et ore les faits les royes per lour justices comissaries errants assignes a touts pleas: en aid de tiels eires sont tornes de viscounts necessaries, et views de frankpl. et quant que bones gents a tiels inquests inditerent de peche mortel, soloient les royes destruere sans respons, &c. Accord est, que nul appelee, ne enditee soit destroy sans respons.* Mirror, cap. 2. § 3.

Thomas earle of Lancaster was destroyed, that is, adjudged to die, as a traitor, and put to death in 14 E. 2. and a record thereof made: and Henry earle of Lancaster his brother, and heire, was restored for two principall errors in the proceeding against the said Thomas Earle, 1. *Quod non fuit araniatus, et ad responsionem positus tempore pacis, eo quod cancellaria, et aliæ curiæ regis fuer' apertæ, in quibus lex fiebat unicuique, prout fieri consuevit.* 2. *Quod contra cartam de libertatibus, cum dictus Thomas fuit unus parium, et magnatum regni, in qua continetur* (and reciteth this chapter of Magna Charta, and specially, *quod dominus rex non super eum ibit, nec mittet, nisi per legale judicium parium suorum tamen per recordum prædictum, tempore pacis absq; aranamento, seu responsione, seu legali judicio parium suorum, contra legem, & contra tenorem Magnæ Chartæ)* he was put to death: more examples of this kinde might be shewed. Pas. 39 E. 3. Coram Rege, John of Gaunts case. Rot. Parl. 4 E. 3. nu. 13. Countee de Arund. case. Rot. Parl. 42 E. 3. nu. 23. Sir Jo. of Lees case.

Every oppression against law, by colour of any usurped authority, is a kinde of destruction, for, *quando aliquid prohibetur, prohibetur et omne, per quod devenitur ad illud:* and it is the worst oppression, that is done by colour of justice. Lib. 10. fol. 74. In the case of the Marshalsea. *Regula.*

It is to be noted, that to this verb *destruatur,* are added *aliquo modo,* and to no other verb in this chapter, and therefore all things, by any manner of meanes tending to destruction, are prohibited: as if a man be accused, or indicted of treason, or felony, his lands, or goods cannot be graunted to any, no not so much as by promise, nor any of his lands, or goods seised into the kings hands, before attainder: for when a subject obtaineth a promise of the forfeiture, many times undue meanes and more violent prosecution is used for private lucre, tending to destruction, then the quiet and just proceeding of law would permit, and the party ought to live of his own untill attainder. Rot. Parl. 15 E. 3. nu. 6. &c.

(6) Per

11 E. 3. breve. 173. 6 R. 2. proces. Pl. ultimo. 20 E. 4. 6. 20 Eliz. Dier, 360. Lib. 9. fol. 117. Seignior Zanchars case.

(6) *Per judicium parium suorum.*] By judgement of his peers. Onely a lord of parliament of England shall be tried by his peers being lords of parliament: and neither noblemen of any other country, nor others that are called lords, and are no lords of parliament, are accounted *pares*, peers within this statute. Who shall be said *pares*, peeres, or equalls, see before cap. 14. § *per pares.*

[49]

1 H. 4. 1. 13 H. 8. 1.

10 E. 4. 6.

Here note, as is before said, that this is to be understood of the kings sute for the words be, *nec super eum ibimus, nec super eum mittemus, nisi per legale judicium parium suorum.* Therefore, for example, if a noble man be indicted for murder, he shall be tried by his peeres, but if an appeale be brought against him, which is the suite of the party, there he shall not be tried by his peeres, but by an ordinary jury of twelve men: and that for two reasons. First, for that the appeale cannot be brought before the lord high steward of England, who is the only judge of noble men, in case of treason, or felony. Secondly, this statute extendeth only to the kings suite.

And it extendeth to the kings suite in case of treason, or felony, or of misprision of treason, or felony, or being accessary to felony before, or after, and not to any other inferior offence. Also it extendeth to the triall it selfe, whereby he is to be convicted: but a nobleman is to be indicted of treason, or felony, or of misprision, or being accessary to, in case of felony, by an inquest under the degree of nobility: the number of the noble men that are to be triers are, 12. or more.

19 H. 7. Edm. de la Pole Earle of Suff. case. Hil. 13. Jacob. the Lord Norrice case coram rege.

And a peer of the realme may be indicted of treason, or felony, before commissioners of oier & terminer, or in the kings bench, if the treason or felony be committed in the county where the kings bench sit: he also may be indicted of murder, or manslaughter, before the coroner, &c. But if he be indicted in the kings bench, or the indictment removed thither, the noble man may plead his pardon there before the judges of the kings bench, and they have power to allow it, but he cannot confesse the indictment, or plead not guilty before the judges of the kings bench, but before the lord steward; and the reason of this diversity, that the triall or judgement must be before or by the lord steward, but the allowance of the pardon may be by the kings bench, is because that is not within this statute.

Stamf. pl. cor. 130.

If a noble man be indicted, and cannot be found, proces of outlawrie shall be awarded against him *per legem terræ*, and he shall be outlawed *per judicium coronatorum*, but he shall be tried *per judicium parium suorum*, when he appeares and pleads to issue.

Pasch. 26. H. 8. in the case of the L. Dacres of the north, resolved by all the judges of England as justice Spelman reports. See the 3 part of the Institutes, cap. Treason.

(7) *Per legale judicium.*] By this word *legale*, amongst others, three things are implied. 1. That this manner of triall was by law, before this statute. 2. That their verdict must be legally given, wherein principally it is to be observed. 1. That the lords ought to heare no evidence, but in the presence, and hearing of the prisoner. 2. After the lords be gone together to consider of the evidence, they cannot send to the high steward to aske the judges any question of law, but in the hearing of the prisoner, that he may heare, whether the case be rightly put, for *de facto jus oritur*; neither can the lords, when they are gone together, send for the judges to know any opinion in law, but the high steward ought to demand it in court in the hearing of the prisoner. 3. When all the evidence is given by the kings learned councell, the high steward cannot collect

collect the evidence against the prisoner, or in any sort conferre with the lords touching their evidence, in the absence of the prisoner, but he ought to be called to it; and all this is implied in this word, *legale*. And therefore it shall be necessary for all such prisoners, after evidence given against him, and before he depart from the barre, to require justice of the lord steward, and of the other lords, that no question be demanded by the lords, or speech or conference had by any with the lords, but in open court in his presence, and hearing, or else he shall not take any advantage thereof after verdict, and judgement given: but the handling thereof at large and of other things concerning this matter, belongs to another treatise, as before I have shewed, only this may suffice for the exposition of this statute. See the 3 part of the Institutes, cap. Treason.

And it is here called *judicium parium*, and not *veredictum*, because the noble men returned, and charged, are not sworne, but give their judgement upon their honour and ligeance to the king, for so are all the entries of record, separately beginning at the *puisne* lord, and so ascending upward.

[50]

Rot. Parliam. 4 E. 3. nu. 6.

And though of ancient time the lords, and peeres of the realme used in parliament to give judgement, in case of treason and felony, against those, that were no lords of parliament, yet at the suite of the lords it was enacted, that albeit the lords and peeres of the realme, as judges of the parliament, in the presence of the king, had taken upon them to give judgement, in case of treason and felony, of such as were no peeres of the realme, that hereafter no peeres shall be driven to give judgement on any others, then on their peeres according to the law.

Anno 8 Will. conq.

This triall by peeres was very auncient, for I reade, that William the Conqueror, in the beginning of his raigne, created William Fitzosberne (who was earle of Bretevil in Normandy) earle of Hereford in England, his sonne Roger succeeded him, and was earle of Hereford, who under colour of his sisters marriage at Exninge, neare Newmarket in Cambridge shire, whereat many of the nobility, and others were assembled, conspired with them to receive the Danes into England, and to depose William the Conqueror (who then was in Normandy) from his kingdome of England: and to bring the same to effect, he with others rose. This treason was revealed by one of the conspirators, viz. Walter earle of Huntingdon an English man, sonne of that great Syward earle of Northumberland: for which treason this Roger earle of Hereford was apprehended, by Urse Tiptoft then sheriffe of Worcester shire, and after was tried by his peeres, and found guilty of the treason *per judicium parium suorum*, but he lived in prison all the daies of his life. You have heard in the exposition of the 14 chapter, who are to be said peeres, somewhat is necessary to be added thereunto. It is provided by the statute of 20 H. 6. that dutchesses, countesses, and baronesses, shall be tried by such peeres as a noble man, being a peere of the realme ought to be; which act was made in declaration, and affirmance of the common law: for marquesses, and viscountesses not named in the act shall be also tried by their peeres, and the queene being the kings consort, or dowager, shall also be tried, in case of treason, *per pares*, as queene Anne, the wife of king Henry the eight was *termino Pasch. anno* 28 H. 8. in the towre of London before the duke of Norff. then high steward.

Anno 8. W. 1.

20 H. 6. cap. 9.

Pasch. 28 H. 8. Spelmans report.

If

If a woman that is noble by birth, doth marry under the degree of nobility, yet shee shall be tried by her peeres, but if she be noble by marriage, and marry under the degree of nobility shee loseth her dignity, for as by marriage it was gained, so by marriage it
22 H. 6. 47. is lost, and shee shall not be tried by her peers. If a dutchesse by
11 H. 6. 51. marriage doe marry a baron, shee loseth not her dignity, for all degrees of nobility, as hath been said, are *pares*. If a queene dowager marry any of the nobility, or under that degree, yet looseth shee not her dignity, as Katherine queene dowager of England, married Owen ap Meredith ap Theodore esquire, and yet shee by the name of Katherine queene of England, maintained an action of detinew, against the bishop of Carlile,

Rot. Parliam. And the queene of Navarra marrying with Edmund the brother
26 E. 1. Rot. 1. of E. 1. sued for her dower by the name of queene of Navarra and recovered.

(8) *Nisi per legem terræ.*] But by the law of the land. For the true sense and exposition of these words, see the statute of 37 E. 3. cap. 8. where the words, by the law of the land, are rendred without due proces of law, for there it is said, though it be contained in the
25 E. 3. cap. 4. great charter, that no man be taken, imprisoned, or put out of his free-hold without proces of the law; that is, by indictment or presentment of good and lawfull men, where such deeds be done in due manner, or by writ originall of the common law.

Without being brought in to answere but by due proces of the common law.

28 E. 3. cap. 3. No man be put to answer without presentment before justices, or
37 E. 3. cap. 8. thing of record, or by due proces, or by writ originall, according to
42 E. 3. cap. 3. the old law of the land.

Wherein it is to be observed, that this chapter is but declaratory of the old law of England. Rot. Parliament. 43 E. 3. nu. 22, 23. the case of Sir John a Lee, the steward of the kings house.

[51] *Per legem terræ.*] i. *Per legem Angliæ*, and hereupon all commissions are grounded, wherein is this clause, *facturi quod ad justitiam pertinet secundum legem, et consuetudinem Angliæ, &c.* And it is not said, *legem et consuetudinem regis Angliæ*, lest it might be thought to bind the king only, nor *populi Angliæ*, lest it might be thought to bind them only, but that the law might extend to all, it is said *per legem terræ*, i. *Angliæ*.

19 H. 6. 7. And aptly it is said in this act, *per legem terræ*, that is, by the law of England: for into those places, where the law of England runneth not, other lawes are allowed in many cases, and not prohibited by this act. For example: if any injury, robbery, felony, or other offence be done upon the high sea, *lex terræ* extendeth not to it, therefore the admirall hath conusance thereof, and may proceed, according to the marine law, by imprisonment of the body, and other proceedings, as have been allowed by the lawes of the realme.

13 H. 4. 5. And so if two English men doe goe into a foreine kingdome, and fight there, and the one murder the other, *lex terræ* extendeth not hereunto, but this offence shall be heard, and determined before the constable, and marshall, and such proceedings shall be there, by attaching of the body, and otherwise, as the law, and custome of that court have been allowed by the lawes of the realme

11 H. 7. cap. 3. Against this ancient, and fundamentall law, and in the face thereof, I finde an act of parliament made, that as well justices of assise, as justices

justices of peace (without any finding or presentment by the verdict of twelve men) upon a bare information for the king before them made, should have full power, and authority by their discretions to heare, and determine all offences, and contempts committed, or done by any person, or persons against the forme, ordinance, and effect of any statute made, and not repealed, &c. By colour of which act, shaking this fundamentall law, it is not credible what horrible oppressions, and exactions, to the undoing of infinite numbers of people, were committed by Sir Richard Empson knight, and Edm. Dudley being justices of peace, throughout England; and upon this unjust and injurious act (as commonly in like cases it falleth out) a new office was erected, and they made masters of the kings forfeitures.

But at the parliament, holden in the first yeare of H. 8. this act of 11 H. 7. is recited, and made voide, and repealed, and the reason thereof is yeelded, for that by force of the said act, it was manifestly known, that many sinister, and crafty, feigned, and forged informations, had been pursued against divers of the kings subjects to their great dammage, and wrongfull vexation: and the ill successe hereof, and the fearefull ends of these two oppressors, should deterre others from committing the like, and should admonish parliaments, that in stead of this ordinary, and pretious triall *per legem terræ*, they bring not in absolute, and partiall trialls by discretion. 1 H. 8. cap. 6.

If one be suspected for any crime, be it treason, felony, &c. And the party is to be examined upon certaine interrogatories, he may heare the interrogatories, and take a reasonable time to answer the same with deliberation (as there the time of deliberation was tenne houres) and the examinate, if he will, may put his answere in writing, and keepe a copie thereof: and so it was resolved in parliament by the lords spirituall and temporall, in the case of justice Richill. See the record at large. Rot. pl. 1 H. 4. memb. 2. nu. 1.

And the Lord Carew being examined, for being privy to the plot, for the escape of Sir Walter Rawleigh attainted of treason, desired to have a copy of his examination, and had it, as *per legem terræ* he ought. Anno 16. Jacobi regis.

Now here it is to be knowne, in what cases a man by the law of the land, may be taken, arrested, attached, or imprisoned in case of treason or felony, before presentment, indictment, &c. Wherein it is to be understood, that proces of law is two fold, viz. By the kings writ, or by due proceeding, and warrant, either in deed, or in law without writ.

As first, where there is any witnesse against the offendor, he may be taken and arrested by lawfull warrant, and committed to prison. * [52] 7 E. 4. 20. 8 E. 4. 3.

* When treason and felony is committed, and the common fame and voice is, that A. is guilty, it is lawfull for any man, that suspects him, to apprehend him. 9 E. 4. 27. 11 E. 4. 2. 2 H. 7. 15. b. 4. 4 H. 7. 18.

[a] This fame Bracton describeth well, *fama quæ suspicionem inducit, oriri debet apud bonos, et graves, non quidem malevolos, et maledicos, sed providas et fide dignas personas, non semel, sed sæpius, quia clamor minuit, et defamatio manifestat*. 5 H. 7. 5. a. 26 H. 8, 9. 27 H. 8. 23. [a] Bracton. fo. 143.

[b] So it is of hue and cry, and that is by the statute of Winchester, which is but an affirmance of the common law: likewise if A. be [b] 29 E. 3. 9. 30 E. 3. 39. 26 E. 3. 71. W. 1. cap. 9.

be suspected, and he fleeth, or hideth himselfe, it is a good cause to arrest him.

c 11 H. 4. 4. b. 20 E. 4. 6. b. 14 H. 8. 16. 27 H. 8. 23.

[c] If treason or felony be done, and one hath just cause of suspition, this is a good cause, and warrant in law, for him to arrest any man, but he must shew in certainty the cause of his suspition: and whether the suspition be just, or lawfull, shall be determined by the justices in an action of false imprisonment brought by the party grieved, or upon a *habeas corpus*, &c.

29 E. 3. 39. A felony is done, and one is pursued upon hue and cry, that is not of ill fame, suspicious, unknown, nor indicted; he may be by a warrant in law, attached and imprisoned by the law of the land.

4 H. 7. 2. A watchman may arrest a night walker by a warrant in law.

5 H. 7. 5. 10 H. 7. 20. If a man woundeth another dangerously, any man may arrest him by a warrant in law, until it may be known, whether the party wounded shall die thereof, or no.

26 E. 3. 71. a. If a man keep the company of a notorious thiefe, whereby he is suspected, &c. it is a good cause, and a warrant in law to arrest him.

38 H. 8. faux imprisonment, Br. 6. If an affray be made to the breach of the kings peace, any man may by a warrant in law restrain any of the offenders, to the end the kings peace may be kept, but after the affray ended, they cannot be arrested without an expresse warrant.

See now the statutes of 1 & 2 Phil. & Mar. cap. 13. & 2 & 3 Phil. & Mar. cap. 10.

Now seeing that no man can be taken, arrested, attached, or imprisoned but by due processe of law, and according to the law of the land, these conclusions hereupon doe follow.

First, that a commitment by lawfull warrant, either in deed or in law, is accounted in law due processe or proceeding of law, and by the law of the land, as well as by processe by force of the kings writ.

2. That he or they, which doe commit them, have lawfull authority.

3. That his warrant, or *mittimus* be lawfull, and that must be in writing under his hand and seale.

4. The cause must be contained in the warrant, as for treason, felony, &c. or for suspition of treason or felony, &c. otherwise if the mittimus contain no cause at all, if the prisoner escape, it is no offence at all, whereas if the mittimus contained the cause, the escape were treason, or felony, though he were not guilty of the offence; and therefore for the kings benefit, and that the prisoner may be the more safely kept, the mittimus ought to contain the cause.

13 H. 7. Kelway 34. b. See more before hereof in the exposition upon the statute of 1 E. 2. de frangentibus prisonam.

5. The warrant or mittimus containing a lawfull cause, ought to have a lawfull conclusion, viz. and him safely to keep, untill he be delivered by law, &c. and not untill the party committing doth further order. And this doth evidently appeare by the writs of *habeas corpus*, both in the kings bench, and common pleas, eschequer and chancery.

Out of the kings bench, though there be not any priviledge, &c.

Rex vicecom. London. salutem. Praecipimus vobis, quod corpus A. B. in custodia vestra detent. ut dicitur, una cum causa detentionis suae, quocunq; nomine praed. A. B. censeatur in eisdem, habeatis coram nobis apud Westm. die Jovis prox' post octabis S. Martini, ad subjiciend. et recipiend. ea, quae curia nostra de eo adtunc, et ibidem ordinar. contigerit

contigerit in hac parte, et hoc nullatenus omittatis, periculo incumbente, et habeatis ibi hoc breve, teste Edw. Coke 20 Nov. anno regni nostri 10.

This is the usuall forme of the writ of habeas corpus in the kings bench, *vide* Mich. 5 E. 4. Rot. 143. coram Rege, Kesars case, under the teste of Sir John Markham. [53]

In the common pleas, for any man priviledged in that court, and the like in the eschequer.

Rex vicecom. London. salutem. Præcipimus' vobis, quod habeatis coram justiciariis nostris, apud Westm. die Jovis prox' post quinque septiman. Pasche, corpus A B. quocunque nomine censeatur, in prisona vestra, sub custodia vestra detent. ut dicitur, una cum die, et causa captionis et detentionis ejusdem, ut iidem justiciar. nostri, visa causa illa, ulterius fieri fac', quod de jure, et secundum legem, et consuetudinem regni nostri Angliæ foret faciend. et habeatis ibi hoc breve, teste, &c.

Out of the chancery generally, though there be not any priviledge, &c.

The like writ is to be graunted out of the chancery, either in the time of the terme (as in the kings bench) or in the vacation; for the court of chancery is *officina justitiæ*, and is ever open, and never adjourned, so as the subject being wrongfully imprisoned, may have justice for the liberty of his person as well in the vacation time, as in the terme.

4 E. 4.

By these writs it manifestly appeareth, that no man ought to be imprisoned, but for some certain cause: and these words, *ad subjiciend. et recipiend. &c.* prove that cause must be shewed: for otherwise how can the court take order therein according to law?

Act. Apost. ca. 25. ver. ult.

And this doth agree with that which is said in the holy history, *Sine ratione mihi videtur, mittere vinctum in carcerem, et causas ejus non significare.* But since we wrote these things, and passed over to many other acts of parliament; see now the petition of right, *anno tertio Caroli regis*, resolved in full parliament by the king, the lords spirituall, and temporall, and the commons, which hath made an end of this question, if any were.

Imprisonment doth not onely extend to false imprisonment, and unjust, but for detaining of the prisoner longer then he ought, where he was at the first lawfully imprisoned.

Hil. 32 E. 1. coram rege. Rot. 71. & 79. So it was holden Pasch. 34 Eliz. by all the justices. 8 H. 4. 18. 20 E. 4. 6.

If the kings writ come to the sheriffe, to deliver the prisoner, if he detain him, this detaining is an imprisonment against the law of the land: if a man be in prison, a warrant cannot be made to the gaoler to deliver the prisoner to the custody of any person unknown to the gaoler, for two causes; first, for that thereby the kings writ of habeas corpus, or delivery, might be prevented. 2. The mittimus ought to bee, as hath beene said, till hee bee delivered by law.

If the sheriffe, or gaoler detain a prisoner in the gaole after his acquittall, unless it be for his fees, this is false imprisonment.

In many cases a man may be by the law of the land taken, and imprisoned, by force of the kings writ upon a suggestion made.

Regist. 64. Rot. Pat. 21 E. 3. pt. 1. impugnatores jurium regis.

Against those that attempt to subvert, and enervate the kings lawes, there lieth a writ to the sheriffe in nature of a commission, *ad capiendum impugnatores juris regis, et ad ducendum eos ad gaolam de Newgate*; which you may reade in the Register at large. *Ubi supra.* And this is *lex terræ*, by processe of law, to take a man without answer, or summons in this case: and the reason is, *merito beneficium legis amittit, qui legem ipsam subvertere intendit.*

Regist. 24. & 191.

If a souldier after wages received, or prest money taken, doth absent

absent himself, or depart from the kings service; upon the certificate thereof of the captain into the chancery, there lieth a writ to the kings serjeants at armes, if the party be vagrant, and hideth himselfe, *ad capiendum conductos proficiscend. in obsequium nostrum, &c. qui ad dictum obsequium nostrum venire non curaverint*. And this is *lex terræ*, by processe of law, *pro defensione regis, et regni*, or for the same cause, a writ may be directed to the sheriffe, *de arrestando ipsum, qui pecuniam recepit ad proficiscendum in obsequium regis, et non est profectus*.

Regist. fol. 267. F. N. B. 233, 234. 20 E. 2. Cor. 233. 6 E. 3. 17. 22 E. 3. 2.

If a man had entered into religion, and was professed, and after he departed from his house, and became vagrant in the country against the rules of his religion, upon the certificate of the abbot, or prior thereof into the chancery, a writ should be directed to the [54] sheriffe, *de apostata capiendo*, whereby he was commanded in these words; *præcipimus tibi quod præfatum, &c. sine dilatione arrestes, et præfat. abbat. &c. liberes secundum regulam ordinis sui castigand'*; and this was *lex terræ*, by processe of law, *in honorem religionis*.

Registr. 59, 60. F. N. B. 54. 15 R. 2. ca. 2.

If any lay men with force and strong hand, doe enter upon, or keep the possession either of the church, or of any of the houses, or glebe, &c. belonging thereunto, the incumbent upon certificate thereof of the bishop, or without certificate upon his own surmise may have a writ to the sheriffe, *de vi laica amovenda*, by which the sheriffe is commanded in these words; *præcipimus tibi quod omnem vim laicam seu armatam, quæ se tenet in dicta ecclesia, seu domibus eidem annexis, ad pacem nostram in com. tuo perturband. sine dilatione amoveas, et si quos in hac parte resistentes inveneris, eos per corpora sua attachias, et in prisona nostra salvo custodias, &c.* and this is *lex terræ*, by processe of law, *pro pace ecclesiæ*.

Vide Regist. 284. 289, 290. for the arresting of purveyors, which make purveyance of the men of the church.

Registr. 89. F. N. B. 85. 31 H. 8. Dier 43. 1 Mar. 92. 1 Eliz. 165.

Also a writ of *ne exeas regnum* may be awarded to the sheriffe, or justices of peace, or to both, that a man of the church shall not depart the realme; the effect whereof is; *quia datum est nobis intelligere, quod A. B. clericus versus partes exteras, ad quamplurima nobis, et quamplurima de populo nostro præjudicialia, et damnosa, ibidem prosequend. transire proponit, &c. tibi præcipimus, quod prædict' A. B. coram te corporaliter venire facias, et ipsum ad sufficientes manucaptores, inveniend. &c. Et si hoc coram te facere recusaverit, tunc ipsum A. B. proximæ gaolæ committas salvo custodiend. quousque hoc gratis facere voluerit.* And there is another writ in the Register directed to the party either of the clergy or laity. And this is *lex terræ*, by processe of law, *pro bono publico regis et regni*; whereof you may reade more at large in the third part of the Institutes, cap. Fugitives.

Regist. 267. F. N. B. 234. Bract. li. 5. fo. 421. Brit. fo. 39. 88. Fleta, li. 6. ca. 39. Hil. 7 H. 5. coram rege. Rot. 7. Rot. claus. 22 E. 3. in dors. 20. pte. m. 14.

Upon a surmise that a man is a leper, one that hath *morbum elephantiacum*, so called, because he hath a skin like to an elephant, there may be a writ directed to the sheriffe, *quia accepimus quod I. de N. leprosus existit, et inter homines comitatus tui communiter conversatur, &c. ad grave damnum homin' præd. et propter contagionem morbi præd. periculum manifestum, &c. tibi præcipimus quod assumptis tecum aliquibus discretis et legalibus hominibus de comitat. præd. non suspect', &c. ad ipsum I. accedas, &c. et examines, &c. et si ipsum leprosum inveneris, ut prædict' est, tunc ipsum honestiori modo, quo poteris a communione hominum prædict' amoveri, et se ad locum solitarium ad habitand' ibidem, prout moris est, transferre facias indilate, &c.* And this is *lex terræ*, by processe of law, for saving of the people from contagion and infection.

Lib. 10. fo. 74. in the case of the Marshalsea.

But if any man by colour of any authority, where he hath not any

any in that particular case, arrest, or imprison any man, or cause him to be arrested, or imprisoned, this is against this act, and it is most hatefull, when it is done by countenance of justice. Rot. Parl. 42 E. 3. nu. 23. Sir John a Lees case.

King Edw. 6. did incorporate the town of S. Albons, and granted to them to make ordinances, &c. they made an ordinance upon paine of imprisonment, and it was adjudged to be against this statute of *Magna Charta*; so it is, if such an ordinance had been contained in the patent it selfe. Lib. 5. fol. 64. Clarks case.

All commissions that are consonant to this act, are, as hath been said, *secundum legem, et consuetudinem Angliæ*.

A commission was made under the great seale to take I. N. (a notorious felon) and to seise his lands, and goods: this was resolved to be against the law of the land, unlesse he had been endicted, or appealed by the party, or by other due processe of law. 42 Ass. pl. 5. Rot. Parliam. 17 R. 2. nu. 37.

It is enacted, if any man be arrested, or imprisoned against the forme of this great charter, that he bee brought to his answer, and have right. Rot. Parliam. 2 H. 4. nu. 60.

No man to be arrested, or imprisoned contrary to the forme of the great charter.

See more of the severall lawes allowed within this land, in the first part of the Institutes, sect. 3.

The philosophicall poet doth notably describe, the damnable and damned proceedings of the judge of hell, [55]

Gnosius hic Radamanthus habet durissima regna,
Castigatque, auditque dolos, subigitque fateri. Virgil.

And in another place,

------ *leges fixit precio atque refixit.*

First he punisheth, and then he heareth: and lastly, compelleth to confesse and make and marre lawes at his pleasure; like as the centurion in the holy history, did to S. Paul: For the text saith, *Centurio apprehendi Paulum jussit, et se catenis ligari et tunc interrogabat, quis fuisset, et quid fecisset:* but good judges and justices abhorre these courses. Act. Apost. c. 22. v. 24. 27.

Now it may be demanded, if a man be taken, or committed to prison *contra legem terræ*, against the law of the land, what remedy hath the party grieved? To this it is answered: first, that every act of parliament made against any injury, mischiefe, or grievance doth either expresly, or impliedly give a remedy to the party wronged, or grieved: as in many of the chapters of this great charter appeareth; and therefore he may have an action grounded upon this great charter. As taking one example for many, and that in a powerfull, and a late time. Pasch. 2 H. 8. *coram rege* rot. 538. against the prior of S. Oswin in Northumberland. And it is provided, and declared by the statute of 36 E. 3. that if any man feeleth himselfe grieved, contrary to any article in any statute, he shall have present remedy in chancery (that is, by originall writ) by force of the said articles and statutes. 36 E. 3. cap 9.

2. He may cause him to be indicted upon this statute at the kings suite, whereof you may see a precedent Pasch. 3 H. 8. Rott. 71. *coram rege*. Rob. Sheffields case.

3. [a] He may have an *habeas corpus* out of the kings bench or chancery, though there be no priviledge, &c. or in the court of common

[a] See the resolution of all the judges of Eng-

land in the answere to the articles of the clergy hereafter at large in the exposition of the statute of artic. Cler. to the 21. and 22. artic. Of the writ of *habeas corpus* see more in the exposition upon the stat. of W. 1. cap. 15.

common pleas, or eschequer, for any officer or priviledged person there; upon which writ the gaoler must retourne, by whom he was committed, and the cause of his imprisonment, and if it appeareth that his imprisonment be just, and lawfull, he shall be remaunded to the former goaler, but if it shall appeare to the court, that he was imprisoned against the law of the land, they ought by force of this statute to deliver him: if it be doubtfull and under consideration, he may be bailed.

In 5 E. 4. *coram rege* Rot. 143. John Keasars case, a notable record and too long here to be recited.

10 Eliz. Rot. Leas case.

In 1 & 2 Eliz. Dier. 175. Scrogs case.

In 18 Eliz. Dier. 175. Roland Hynds case *in margine*.

4. He may have an action of false imprisonment, 10 H. 7. fol. 17. but it is entred in the court of common pleas Mich. 11 H. 7. Rot. 327. Hilarie Warners case, and it appeareth by the record, that judgement was given for the plaintife: a record worthy of observation.

[b] Regist. 77. F. N. B. 66. Bract. l. 3. f. 185.

5. [b] He may have a writ *de homine replegiando*.

Vide Marlebridge, cap. 8.

[c] Regist. 83. 268. F. N. B. 249. 258. Bract. l. 3. f. 154. [d] W. 2. c. 29. Gloc. cap. 9.

6. [c] He might by the common-law have had a writ *de odio, et atia*, as you may see before, cap. 26. but that was taken away by statute, but now is revived againe by the statute of 42 E. 3. cap. 1. as there it also appeareth. It is said in [d] W. 2. *Sed ne hujusmodi appellati, vel indictati diu detineantur in prisona, habeat breve de odio et atia, sicut in Magna Charta, et aliis statutis dict' est*: and by the said act of 42 E. 3. all statutes made against Magna Charta are repealed.

[e] Mirror, c. 1. §. 5. cap. 2. § 13. cap. 5. § 1, 2. Fleta, l. 2. c. 12. Ocham, cap. quid sponte offerentibus F. N. B. 96.

(9) *Nulli vendemus, &c.*] [e] This is spoken in the person of the king, who in judgement of law, in all his courts of justice is present, and repeating these words, *nulli vendemus, &c.*

Rot. Parliam. 8 E. 3. nu. 7. 38 E. 3. n. 23. 45 E. 3. n. 19. 51 E. 3. n. 58. 5 H. 4. nu. 32. 20 R. 2. fines 134. 34 H. 6. 38. 2 E. 3. c. 10. 1 E. 4. cap. 1. 26 H. 8. cap. 3. 27 H. 8. cap. 11.

And therefore, every subject of this realme, for injury done to him in *bonis, terris, vel persona*, by any other subject, be he ecclesiasticall, or temporall, free, *or bond, man, or woman, old, or young, or be he outlawed, excommunicated, or any other without exception, may take his remedy by the course of the law, and have justice, and right for the injury done to him, freely without sale, fully without any deniall, and speedily without delay.

Hereby it appeareth, that justice must have three qualities, it must be *libera, quia nihil iniquius venali justitia*; *plena, quia justitia non debet claudicare*; *et celeris, quia dilatio est quædam negatio*; and then it is both justice and right.

*[56]

2 E. 3. c. 8. 14 E. 3. c. 14. 20 E. 3. 1, 2. 11 R. 2. cap. 11. Rot. Parl. 2 R. 2. nu. 51. Rot. Parl. 2 H. 4. nu. 64. Regist. 186. 1 E. 3. f. 25. 2 E. 3. 3. 14 E. 3. tit. Jour. 24.

(10) *Nulli negabimus, aut differemus, &c.*] These words have beene excellently expounded by latter acts of parliament, that by no meanes common right, or common law should be disturbed, or delayed, no, though it be commanded under the great seale, or privie seale, order, writ, letters, message, or commandement whatsoever, either from the king, or any other, and that the justices shall proceede, as if no such writs, letters, order, message, or other commandement were come to them. *Judicium redditum per defaltum affirmatur, non obstante breve regis de prorogatione judicii.*

That the common lawes of the realme should by no meanes be delayed, for the law is the surest sanctuary, that a man can take, and the strongest fortresse to protect the weakest of all; *lex est tutissima cassis*, and *sub clypeo legis nemo decipitur*: but the king may

stay

ſtay his owne ſuite, as a *capias pro fine*, for the king may reſpite his fine and the like.

All protections that are not legall, which appeare not in the Regiſter, nor warranted by our books, are expreſly againſt this branch, *nulli differemus*: as a protection under the great ſeale granted to any man, directed to the ſherifes, &c. and commanding them, that they ſhall not arreſt him, during a certaine time at any other mans ſuite, which hath words in it, *per prærogativam noſtram, quam nolumus eſſe arguendam*; yet ſuch protections have beene argued by the judges, according to their oath and duty, and adjudged to be void: as Mich. 11 H. 7. Rot. 124. a protection graunted to Holmes a vintner of London, his factors, ſervants and deputies, &c. reſolved to be againſt law, Paſch. 7 H. 8. Rot. 66. ſuch a protection diſallowed, and the ſherife amerced for not executing the writ. Mich. 13 & 14 Eliz. in Hitchcocks caſe, and many other of latter time: and there is a notable * record of auncient time in 22 E. 1. John de Merſhalls caſe, *non pertinet ad vicecomitem de protectione regis judicare, imo ad curiam*.

(11) *Juſtitiam vel rectum.*] Wee ſhall not ſell, deny, or delay juſtice and right. *Juſtitiam vel rectum*, neither the end, which is juſtice, nor the meane, whereby we may attaine to the end, and that is the law.

Rectum, right, is taken here for law, in the ſame ſenſe that *jus*, often is ſo called. 1. Becauſe it is the right line, whereby juſtice diſtributative is guided, and directed, and therefore all the commiſſions of oier, and terminer, of goale delivery, of the peace, &c. have this clauſe, *facturi quod ad juſtitiam pertinet, ſecundum legem*, and *conſuetudinem Angliæ*, that is, to doe juſtice and right, according to the rule of the law and cuſtome of England; and that which is called common right in 2 E. 3. is called common law, in 14 E. 3. &c. and in this ſenſe it is taken, where it is ſaid, *ita qd. ſtet recto in curia, i. legi in curia*. 2. The law is called *rectum*, becauſe it diſcovereth, that which is tort, crooked, or wrong, for as right ſignifieth law, ſo tort, crooked or wrong, ſignifieth injurie, and *injuria eſt contra jus*, againſt right: *recta linea eſt index ſui, et obliqui*, hereby the crooked cord of that, which is called diſcretion, appeareth to be unlawfull, unleſſe you take it, as it ought to be, *diſcretio eſt diſcernere per legem, quid ſit juſtum*. 3. It is called right, becauſe it is the beſt birthright the ſubject hath, for thereby his goods, lands, wife, children, his body, life, honor, and eſtimation are protected from injury, and wrong: *major hæreditas venit unicuiq; noſtrum à jure, et legibus, quam à parentibus*.

4. Laſtly, *rectum* is ſometime taken for the right it ſelfe, that a man hath by law to land: as when wee ſay there lieth *breve de recto*, in ſo much that ſome old readers have ſuppoſed, that *rectum* in this chapter, ſhould be underſtood of a writ of right, for which at this day no fine in the hamper is paid. As the goldfiner will not out of the duſt, threds, or ſhreds of gold, let paſſe the leaſt crum, in reſpect of the excellency of the metall: ſo ought not the learned reader to let paſſe any ſyllable of this law, in reſpect of the excellency of the matter.

18 E. 3. 47. 39 E. 3. 7. L. 5 E. 4. 132. Paſch. 3 H. 4. coram rege Rot. 16. Warwik. Rot. Parl. 5 H. 4. nu. 33. 22 aſſ. pl. 9. 9 H. 6. 50. b. Forteſc. cap. 51. F. N. B. 237. 240. 11 H. 4. 76. 31 E. 3. quare imp. 161. Mich. 11 H. 7. Rot. 124. in com. banc. Paſch. 7 H. 8. Rot. 66. in com. banc. Mich. 13. & 14. Eliz. in com. banc. Hitchcocks caſe. 11 H. 4. 57. 39 H. 6. 38. * Paſ. 22 E. 1. Rot. 39. coram rege Eſſex. W. 1. cap. 1. 1 E. 3. cap. 14. 2 E. 3. cap. 8. 7 H. 4. cap. 14. 1 H. 4. cap. 1. 2 H. 4. cap. 1. 4 H. 4. cap. 1. 7 H. 4. cap. 1. See the 1. part of the Inſtitut. ſect. 234. Injuria eſt in, ſeu contra jus.

Cicero.

[57]

CAP. XXX.

OMNES mercatores (1), *nisi publice antea prohibiti fuerint, habeant salvum et securum conductum, exire de Anglia, et venire in Angliam, et morari, et ire per Angliam, tam per terram, quam per aquam, ad emendum, vel vendendum, sine omnibus malis tolnetis* (2) *per antiquas et rectas consuetudines* (3), *præterquam in tempore guerræ. Et si sint de terra contra nos guerrina, et tales inveniantur in terra nostra in principio guerræ, attachientur sine dampno corporum suorum, vel rerum, donec sciatur à nobis, vel a capitali justitiario nostro, quomodo mercatores terræ nostræ tractantur, qui tunc inveniantur in terra illa contra nos guerrina. Et si nostri salvi sint ibi, alii salvi sint in terra nostra.*

ALL merchants (if they were not openly prohibited before) shall have their safe and sure conduct to depart out of England, to come into England, to tarry in, and go through England, as well by land as by water, to buy and sell without any manner of evil tolts, by the old and rightful customs, except in time of war. And if they be of a land making war against us, and be found in our realm at the beginning of the wars, they shall be attached without harm of body or goods, untill it be known unto us, or our chief justice, how our merchants be intreated there in the land making war against us; and if our merchants be well intreated there, theirs shall be likewise with us.

(12 Rep. 33. 2 Roll. 115. 1 Bulstr. 134. 9 Ed. 3. stat. 1. c. 1. 14 Ed. 3. stat. 1. c. 2. 25 Ed. 3. stat. 4. c. 2. 2 R. 2. stat. 1. c. 1. 11 R. 2. c. 7.)

(1) *Omnes mercatores.*] This chapter concerneth merchant strangers.

First it is to be considered, what the auncient lawes, before this statute, were concerning this matter.

Mirror, cap. 1. § 3. — By the auncient kings (amongst whom king Alfred was one) *defendu fuit que nul merchant aliē ne hantast Angleterre forsque aux 4 foires, ne que nul demurrast in la terre ouster 40. jours. Mercatorū navigia, vel*

Int. leges Ethel. cap. 2. — *inimicorum quidem, quæcunq; ex alto (nullis jactata tempestatibus) in portum aliquem invehentur, tranquilla pace fruuntor; quin etiam si maris acta fluctibus ad domicilium aliquod illustre, ac pacis beneficio donatum navis appulerit inimica, atq; istuc nautæ confugerint, ipsi et res illorum omnes augusta pace potiuntor.*

2. It is to be seene what this statute hath provided.

1. That before this statute, merchant strangers might be publiquely prohibited, *publice prohibeantur.* And this prohibition is intendable of merchant strangers in amitie, for this act provideth afterward for merchant strangers enemies; and therefore the prohibition intended by this act, must be by the common or publique councell of the realme, that is, by act of parliament, for that it concerneth the whole realme, and is implyed by this word *(publice.)*

2. That all merchant strangers in amity (except such as be so publiquely prohibited) shall have safe and sure conduct in 7 things. 1. To depart out of England. 2. To come into England. 3. To tarry here. 4. To goe in and through England, as well by land

as by water. 5. To buy and to sell. 6. Without any manner of evill tolles, 7. By the old and rightfull customes.

Now touching merchant strangers, whose soveraigne is in warre with the king of England.

[58]

There is an exception, and provision for such, as be found in the realme at the beginning of the warre, they shall be attached with a priviledge, and limitation, viz. without harme of body, or goods, with this limitation, untill it be knowne to us, or our chiefe justice (that is our guardien, or keeper of the realme in our absence) how our merchants there in the land in warre with us shall be intreated, and if our merchants be well intreated there, theirs shall be likewise with us, and this is *jus belli. Et in republica maxime conservanda sunt jura belli.*

But for such merchant strangers as come into the realme after the warre beginne, they may be dealt withall as open enemies: and yet of auncient time three men had priviledge granted them in time of warre. *Clericus, agricola, et mercator, tempore belli. Ut oretq; colat, commutet, pace fruuntur.*

[a] The end of this chapter was for advancement of trade, and traffique; the meanes for the well using, and intreating of merchant strangers in all the particulars aforesaid, is a matter of great moment, as appeareth by many other acts of parliament, for as they be used here, so our merchants shall be dealt withall in other countries.

Regist. 129. de arest fact. super bonis mercator. alienig. Rot. Parliam. Mich. 18 E. 1. coram rege fol. 7. reprisel. Tr. 33 E. 1. coram rege rot. 127. 27 E. 3. stat. 2. cap. 17. lawe of marke. Rot. parl. 11 H. 4. nu. 66. 4 H. 5. c. 7. 14 H. 6. c. 7. 18 H. 6. c. 9. Mat. Par. 966. [a] 2 E. 3. c. 5. 9 E. 3. c. 1. 14 E. 3. c. 2. 25 E. 3. cap. 2. 11 R. 2. c. 7. 14 R. 2. cap. 9. 16 R. 2. cap. 1.

(2) *Mala tolneta.*] [b] Evill tolles.

This word *tolnetum*, and *telonium*, and *theolonium* are all one, and doe signify in a generall sense, any manner of custome, subsidie, prestation, imposition, or summe of mony demanded for exporting, or importing of any wares, or merchandizes, to be taken of the buyer. In both these senses it is here taken of severall kind of tolles: more shall be said hereof, in the exposition of the statutes of W. 1. and W. 2. In the meane time see John Webbes case, lib. 8. fol. 46.

[b] Lib. 8. fol. 46. John Webbs case. See the exposition of W. 1. c. 31. 46 E. 3. barre 215. 30 E. 3. 13. b. F. N. B 227. d. West. 1. c. 30. W. 2. cap. 25.

[c] They are called *mala tolneta*, when the thing demanded for wares or merchandizes, doe so burden the commodity, as the merchant cannot have a convenient gaine by trading therewith, and thereby the trade it selfe is lost or hindered. And in divers statutes *maletout* for *maletot*, or *maletout* is a French word, and signifieth an unjust exaction.

[c] See Rot parlia. 17 E. 3. nu. 27, 28. and 21 E. 3 nu. 29. Maletot taken in good part.

Now this act after it hath dealt privatively, *sine omnibus malis tolnetis*, it goeth on for more surety affirmatively.

(3) *Per antiquas et rectas consuetudines.*] That is, by auncient and right duties, due by auncient and lawfull custome, which hath been the auncient policy of the realme to encourage merchants strangers, they have a speedy recovery for their debts and other duties, &c. *per legem mercator.*; which is a part of the common law.

See the expositio of W. 1. cap. 31.

This word *consuetudo*, hath in law divers significations. 1. For the common law, as *consuetudo Angliæ*. 2. For statute law, as *contra consuetudinem communi concilio regni edit.* 3. For particular customes, as gavelkind, borough English, and the like. 4. For rents services, &c. due to the lord, as *consuetudines et servitia*. 5. For customes, tributes, or impositions, as *de novis consuetudinibus levatis in regno, sive in terra, sive in aqua.* 6. Subsidies, or customes granted by common consent, that is, by authority of parliament, *pro bono publico*, and these be *antiquæ, et rectæ consuetudines* intended by

Glanvil. lib. 9. c. 7. lib. 12. cap. 9. 10. Regist. 4. 159. F. N B 10. 151. cap. Itineris. cap. Eschea-tre. See before c. 4. cap. Itineris.

by this act, this agreeth with that, which hath been ſaid before in the end of the expoſition upon the eight chapter.

See the ſtatute of Carlile. 35 E. 1. for this word impoſition, and from whom it came.

Hereby it appeareth that the king cannot ſet any new impoſt upon the merchant, and therefore this act provideth not only affirmatively, viz. *per antiquas, et rectas conſuetudines*, but privately alſo, *ſine omnibus malis tolnetis*, within which words new impoſitions are included, and are here called *mala tolneta*, as oppoſite to ancient and rightfull cuſtomes, or ſubſidies graunted by authority of parliament.

Dier, 31 H. 8. 43. 1 Mar. 92. 1 Eliz. Dier, 165.

And where ſome have ſuppoſed, that there was a cuſtom due to the king by the common law, as well of the ſtranger, as of the Engliſh, called *antiqua cuſtuma*, viz. for wools, wooll-fells, and leather, that is to ſay, for every ſack of wooll containing 26 ſtone, and every ſtone

[59]

14 pound, vj. s. viij. d. and for a laſt of leather, xiij. s. iiij. d. Certain it is, that thoſe cuſtomes had their beginning by common conſent by act of parliament, for king E. 1. by his letters patents reciteth, *cum prælati, magnates, et tota communitas quandam novam conſuetudinem nobis et hæredibus noſtris de lanis, pellibus, et coriis, viz. de ſacco lanæ dimid' marc' de 300. pellibus dimid' marc', et de laſto corii xiii. s. iiii. d. &c.* Herein foure things are to be obſerved. 1. That theſe cuſtomes had their creation by authority of parliament, and were not by the common law, appearing by theſe words, *quandam novam conſuetudinem*, ſo as it was new, and not old. 2. That this new cuſtome was graunted to king Edw. 1. proved by this word *nobis*. 3. That it was graunted at the parliament holden 3 E. 1. commonly called W. 1. (though the record thereof cannot be found) for the ſaid patent bears date 10. Nov. anno 3 E. 1. which was neare the ending of that yeare, and the parliament was holden in *Clauſo Paſch*, before. 4. That here *conſuetudo* ſignifieth a cuſtome, or ſubſidie graunted by common conſent by parliament, and in that ſenſe it is here taken, and likewiſe in the ſtatute of 51 H. 3. *ſtatutum de ſcaccario*, for in 48 H. 3. proclamation was made, *contra ſuggerentes, &c. Regem velle exigere tallagia inconſueta, et introducere extraneos*.

Rot. Pat. 3. E. 1. m. 1. rot. finium. 3 E. 1. m. 24. Mich. 26 E. 1. int' retorn. brevium. ex pte. remem. Theſaur' in Scac.

Rot. Pat. anno 48 H. 3. a tergo.

Anno 25 E. 1. See more in the expoſition of that ſtatute.

And herewith agreeth the act of parliament commonly called *confirmationes cartarum* (which is but an explanation of this branch of *Magna Charta*) wherein it is enacted, that for no occaſion any aide, taſks, or takings ſhall be taken by the king, or his heires, but by the common aſſent of the realme, ſaving the auncient aides, and takings due and accuſtomed.

Rot. Parliam. 13 H. 4. nu. 18. A new office graunted with a fee in charge of the ſubject, is againſt this act of 25 E. 1. and of 34 E. 1. hereafter following.

And whereas the moſt of the whole comminalty of the realme finde themſelves hardly grieved of the maletout (or ill toll) of woolls, that is to ſay, of every ſack of wooll 40. s. and prayed the ſaid king to releaſe the ſame, thereupon the ſaid king did releaſe the ſame, and graunted further for him and his heires, that no ſuch thing ſhould be taken without their common aſſent, and their good will; and in that act there is a ſaving, *ſauve a nous, et nous heires la cuſtume de laynes, pealx, et quiures avant grante per la comminaltie avandit*; So as this act of parliament proveth that the ſaid cuſtome of vj. s. viij. d. for wooll, and xiij. s. iiij. d. for leather was graunted by parliament.

Anno 34 E. 1. See more in the expoſition of this ſtatute.

By the ſtatute *de tallagio non concedendo* (which is but an explanation of this branch of the ſtatute of *Magna Charta*) it is provided; *Nullum tallagium vel auxilium per nos vel hæredes noſtros in regno noſtro ponatur, ſeu levetur ſine voluntate et aſſenſu archiepiſcoporum, epiſcorum, comitum,*

mitum, baronum, militum, burgensium, et aliorum liberorum comit' de regno nostro; so as E. 1. in conclusion added the effect of the clause concerning this matter, which in his exemplification he had omitted out of *Magna Charta*.

See *cap. itineris de novis consuetudinibus levatis in regno, sive in terra, sive in aqua, &c.* where *consuetudines* are taken for customes. Cap. itineris.

Upon grant to merchant strangers of divers priviledges, liberties, and immunities they graunted to the king and his heirs, *de quolibet sacco lanæ* 40 *d. de incremento ultra custumam antiquam dimid' marc' quæ prius fuerit persoluta et sic pro lasto coriorum dimid' marc', et de trescentis pellibus lanatis* 40 *d. ultra certum illud, quod et antiqua custuma fuerit prius datum.* Note here the custome which was graunted 3 E. 1. is here called *antiqua custuma*, and this new custome is called *nova custuma*, and sometime the one is called *magna custuma*, and the other *parva custuma*. Rot chartarum. 31 E. 1. nu. 44. Charta Mercatoria.

2. Here it appeareth that merchants strangers paid the former custome.

Moreover by that charter, poundage of three pence upon the pound was graunted to the king, and his heires by the merchant strangers, *et de quolibet vini nomine custumæ duos solidos, &c.* and this at this day is called butlerage, and is paid onely by merchant strangers; but prisage is paid by the English onely, except the citizens of London, and this is an auncient duty: for I finde it accounted for in the raigne of H. 3. by the kings butler, and is called *certa prisa*, which at the first was graunted in lieu and satisfaction of purveyance for wines. And lastly, by that charter it is graunted, *quod nulla exactio, prisa, vel præstatio, aut aliquod aliud onus super personas mercatorum alienorum prædict', seu bona eorundem aliquatenus imponatur contra formam expressam superius concessam*: So as no imposition can be set without assent of parliament upon any stranger. Rot. Pat. anno 40 H. 3. [60] Fleta, lib. 2. ca. 21.

It was ordered and resolved by divers prelates, earls, and barons, by force of the kings commission, that no new customes could be levied, nor auncient increased, without authority of parliament, for that should be against the great charter, *anno* 6 E. 3. Rot. Parliament, nu. 4. that no tallage shall be assessed but in such manner as it hath been in time of his auncestors, and as it ought to be, and disannull all others. Rot. ordinationum. anno 5 E. 2. in Scaccario.

In *anno* 11 E. 3. it was made felony to carry wooll out of the realme, the end whereof was, that our wooll should bee draped into cloth. But the king wanting made this use of this act: in the 12 and 13 years of his raigne he made dispensations of that statute in consideration of money paid: but that statute lived not long. In 13 E. 3. a great imposition was set upon woolls, and it is called a great wrong, *cum populus regni nostri variis oneribus, tallagiis, et impositionibus hactenus prægravetur, quod dolentes referimus*, and there doth excuse himselfe. 11 E. 3. cap. 1. Rot. parl. 13 E. 3. nu. 12. licence, &c. & 14 E. 3. nu. 3. licence. Rot. alinance. 12 E. 3. memb. 23. in dorf.

Note here is the word *impositiones* first used, imposed by any king, in any record that I have observed, and doe remember.

Anno 14 E. 3. cap. 21. A subsidie graunted to the king of wooll, woolfells, and leather, &c. by parliament, for a certain time in respect of the warres, for which the king graunteth, that 14 E. 3. cap. 21.

after that time, he nor his heires would take more then the old custome.

Rot. parliam. 17 E. 3. nu. 28. 25 E. 3. nu. 22. 36 E. 3. nu. 26.

After this time ended, the king entred into a new device to get money, viz. that by agreement and consent of the merchants, the king was to have 40 s. of a sack of wooll, &c. but hereof the commons (that in troth were to beare the burden, for the merchant will not be the loser) complained in parliament, for that the graunt of the merchants did not binde the commons, and that the custome might be taken according to the old order, which in the end was graunted, and that no graunt should be made but by parliament.

Rot. parliam. 21 E. 3. nu. 16.

No charge shall be levied of the people, if it were not graunted in parliament.

Rot. parliam. 21 E. 3 Dier, 1 Eliz. 165. Int' origin. Scac. 24 E. 3. Rot. 13.

In 21 E. 3. by authority of parliament, a custome was graunted of cloth, for that the wooll was for the most part converted into cloth, which you may see in Orig. Scaccar. 24 E. 3. Rot. 13.

27 E. 3. cap. 4.

By the statute of 27 E. 3. cap. 4. in print, a subsidie of every cloth to take of the seller (over the customes thereof due, that is, such as then endured for a time, and were graunted by parliament) that is to say, of every cloth of assise, wherein there is no grain, 4. d. &c.

And here it is worthy of observation, that there were two causes of the making of this statute. 1. For that for cloth no custome was due other then by the act of 21 E. 3. 2. For that wooll being converted to a manufacture, and made into cloth, the ancient custome of *dimid.* mark for a sack of wool was not by law payable, because the wooll was turned into another kinde, albeit the cloth was made of the wooll; and this doth notably appeare by the records of the exchequer, one of them in the same yeare that the act of 27 E. 3. was made.

Int. original. de Scaccar. anno 24 E. 3. Rot. 4. Vide simile, ibid. 24 E. 3. Rot. 13. See the first part of the Institutes, fol. 49. b.

Ac jam magna pars lanæ dicti regni nostri eodem regno pannificetur, de qua custuma aliqua nobis non est soluta; and there it appeareth that that was the cause, of giving to the king a subsidie for cloth by the said act of parliament, of 27 E. 3. And yet if in any case the king by his prerogative might have set any imposition, he might have set in that case, because as it appeareth by the record by making of cloth hee lost the custome of wooll.

[61]

Rot. parliam. 45 E. 3. nu. 42.

Rot. parliam. 45 E. 3. No imposition or charge, &c. shall be set without assent of parliament.

Rot. parliam. 50 E. 3. nu. 17, 28. Nu. 163. et vide ibidem, 191.

50 E. 3. Richard Lions, a merchant of London punished for procuring new impositions, and so was the lord Latimer, the kings chamberlaine. And in the same parliament, nu. 163. upon complaint that new impositions were set, the king in parliament assented that the ancient custome should be holden, and no new imposition set.

Rot. pat. anno 25 E. 3. created duke of Aquitaine.

In the raigne of E. 3. the black prince of Wales having *Aquitaine* granted to him, did lay an imposition of fuage or focage, *à foco*, upon the subjects of that dukedome, viz. a shilling for every fire called harth silver, which was of so great discontentment, and odious to them, as it made them to revolt.

Rot. Parl. 8 H. 6. nu. 29. & Rot. Par. 28 H. 6. nu. 35.

And no king since this time imposed by pretext of any prerogative, any charge upon marchandises imported into, or exported out of this realme, untill queen Maries time. See the statute of 11 R. 2. cap. 9. & Rot. Parliament. 8 H. 6. num. 29.

Rot. parl. 3 H. 5. nu. 50. Stat. 2.

And in 3 H. 5. the subsidie of tunnage and poundage was graunted

graunted to king H. 5. during his life, in respect of the recovery of his right in France (which was the first graunt for life of that kinde) yet therein was a *proviso*, that the king should not make a graunt thereof to any person, nor that it should be any precedent for the like to be done to other kings afterwards; but yet all the kings after him have had it for life, so forcible is once a precedent fixed in the crown, adde what *proviso* you will.

See in the fourth part of the Institutes, cap. of the high court of parliament, more of the subsidy of tunnage.

And this graunt by parliament of the subsidy of tunnage and poundage to the king is an argument, that the king taking it of the gift of the subject had no power to impose it himselfe.

The lords and commons cannot be charged with any thing for the defence of the realme, for the safeguard of the sea, &c. unlesse it be by their will in parliament, that is, in the graunt of a subsidy, whereunto the king assented.

Rot. Parliam. 13 H. 4. nu. 10.

Non potest rex subditum renitentem onerare impositionibus.

Fortesc. c. 9. & 18.

King Philip and queen Mary, graunted by letters patents to the major, bayliffes, and burgesses of Southampton, and their successors, that no wines called Malmeseyes to be imported into this realme by any denizen, or alien, should be discharged or landed at any other place within this realme, but onely at the said town and port of Southampton, with a prohibition, that none should doe to the contrary upon pain to pay treble custome to the king and queen, &c. And for that Anthony Donate, Thomas Frederico, and other merchant strangers bought divers buts of Malmesey, &c. and landed them at Goore, and in Kent, Gilbert Gerard the attourney generall, informed in the exchequer, against the said merchant strangers for the said treble custome, &c. Upon which information, as to the said treble custome, the said Anthony Donat demurred in law, &c. And this case was argued in the exchequer chamber by counsell learned on both sides, and upon conference had, two points were resolved by all the judges. 1. That the graunt made in restraint of landing of the said wines was a restraint of the liberty of the subject, against the lawes and statutes of the realme. 2. That the assessement of treble custome was meerly void, and against the law. As it appeareth by the report of the lord Dier under his hand (which I have in my custody.) But after by act of parliament, in *anno* 5 Eliz. the said charter is established as to merchant strangers onely, but not against subjects.

Int' communia de termino S. Trin. anno 1 Eliz. Rot. 73.

Mag. Charta, ca. 30. 9 E 3. c. 1. 14 E. 3. 25 E. 3. cap. 2. 27 & 28 E. 3. of the staple. 2 R. 2. cap. 1.

And where imposts, or impositions, be generally named in divers acts of parliament, the same are to be intended of lawfull impositions, as of tunnage, and poundage, or other subsidies imposed by parliament, but none of those acts or any other doe give the king power at his pleasure to impose. See the first part of the Institutes, sect. 97.

23 H. 6. cap. 18. 14 H. 8. ca. 4. 13 El. c. 4. 1 Jac. ca. 13. 3 Jac. ca. 6.

It is then demaunded, by what law custome is paid for kerseyes, whites, plaine, straits, and other new draperies, made of wooll; for it appeareth by acts of * parliament, and common experience, that all these pay custome to the king. To this it is answered, that a proportionable subsidy, or custome is paid for them within the equity of the said statute of 27 E. 3. cap. 4. and likewise a proportionable alnage is also due for them by that act.

Int' decreta in camera Scac. Mich. 3 & 4 El. Mich. 32 & 33 Eliz. Mic. 39 & 40 Eliz.

* [62]

Hil. & Pasch. *anno 2 Jacobi regis*, great questions were moved, whether frisadoes, bayes, northern cottons, northern dozens, cloth-rash, durances, perpetuanoes, tuft-mocadoes, sackcloth, fustians, worsteds, stuffes made of worsted yarne, &c. were within the said act

of

of 27 E. 3. as concerning the subsidy, and alnage: and if they were not, whether the king by his prerogative might not impose a reasonable subsidy, or custome upon them proportionably to the cloth mentioned in the statute of 27 E. 3. And this being questioned before the lords of the councell, they wrote to the judges to be certified what the law was in these cases, who upon mature deliberation, the 24 of June 1605, resolved, and so certified the lords by their letters under all their hands, that all frisadoes, bayes, northern dozens, northern cottons, cloth-rash, and other new drapery made wholly of wooll, of what new name soever made, as new drapery for the use of mans body, are to yeeld subsidy, and alnage according to the statute of 27 E. 3. and within the office of the auncient alnager, as may appeare by severall decrees in that behalfe in the exchequer, in the time of the late queen: but as touching fustians, canvas, and such like made meerly of other stuffe then wooll, or being but mixed with wooll, it was resolved by all the judges, that no charge could be imposed for the search or measuring thereof, but that all such letters patents so made are voyd, as may appeare by a record of 11 H. 4. wherein the reason of the judgement is particularly recited, which the judges thought good in their letters to set downe as followeth.

Note this.

King H. 4. graunted the measuring of woollen cloth, and canvas, that should be brought to London, to be sold by any stranger or denizen (except he were free of London) taking an ob. of every whole peece of cloth so measured of the seller, and one other ob. of the buyer, and so after that rate for a greater or lesser quantity, and one penny for the measuring of an C. ells of canvas of the seller, and so much more of the buyer; and though it were averred that two other had enjoyed the same office before with the like fees, viz. one Shearing by the same kings graunt, and one Clithew before by the graunt of R. 2. (and the truth was, Robert Pooley in 5 E. 3. and John Mareis, in 25 E. 3. had likewise enjoyed the same) yet amongst other reasons of the said judgement, it was set downe, and adjudged that the former possession was by extortion, cohertion, and without right, and that the said letters patents were in *onerationem, oppressionem, et depauperationem subditorum domini regis, &c. et non in emendationem ejusdem populi*; and therefore the said letters patents were voyd. And as touching the narrow new stuffe made in Norwich, and other places of worsted yarn, it was resolved that it was not grauntable, nor fit to be graunted, for there was never any alnage of Norwich worsteds, and for these stuffes, if after they be made, and tucked up for sale by the makers thereof, they should be again opened to be viewed, and measured, they will not well fall into their old plights, &c. as by the said letters it more at large appeareth. These letters were openly read at the councell table, and well approved by the whole councell, and the lords commanded the same to be kept in the council chest to be a direction for them to answer suitors in these cases.

13 E. 3. ex pte Remem. Thesaurar. Rot. parliam. 25 E. 3. enacted according to this resolution. 30 E. 3. Compot. Forinseco, in Scaccar. compot. Joh. Mareis.

But three judgements in the exchequer have been cited for proofe, that the king hath power to set impositions upon merchandizes exported, and imported.

Pasch. 1 Eliz. in Scacc. ex pte. remem. regis.

1. A judgement given in the exchequer in an information against Germane Cioll for 40. s. set by queen Mary upon every tun of wine, of the growth of France to be brought into the realme. But the case there was this, the attourney generall informed, that where king

king Philip and queen Mary by their proclamation 30 *Martii*, in the 4 and 5 yeares of their raigne, did will and straitly command, that no wines of the growth of France, should be brought into this realme, without speciall licence of the said king and queene, under paine of forfeiture of such wine to the king and queene, *cumq; etiā dict' nuper rex et regina de advisamento concilii sui ad tunc ordinaver' et decreverunt, quod quælibet persona, quæ in hoc regnum Angliæ induceret hujusmodi vina contra formam proclamationis prædict', solveret pro quolibet dolio hujusmodi vini* 40. s. *vocat impost. &c.* and that German Ciol, against the forme and effect of the said proclamation, had brought into the realme 338. tunnes of wines of the growth of France, and had not paid 40 s. for each and every tunne: the defendant pleaded a licence from the said king and queene, dated the 9. of Decemb. *anno* 1 & 2, to bring into the realme 1500. tunnes of wine, of the growth of Fraunce, in strangers bottoms, with a *non obstante* of any law, statute, or proclamation made or to be made to the contrary, whereupon the demurrer was joyned. [63]

In this record these things are to be observed, first that a proclamation prohibiting importation of wines upon paine of forfeiture, was against law: for it appeareth not, that any warre was betweene the realmes. 2. The proclamation was made of purpose to set an imposition, for the 40s. is imposed upon them only, and upon such as should bring in wines against the said proclamation, so as the proclamation was the ground of this information. 3. The king and queene by advice of their councell, did order, and decree, &c, and sheweth not how, or by what meanes this order and decree was made: the pleading of such a former licence so insufficiently sheweth, that it was by agreement and consent.

2. The executors of customer Smith, were charged in a speciall information for receiving an imposition of iii. s. iiii. d. set by queene Elizabeth, under her privy signet, upon every hundred weight of allome made within the dominions of the pope, and judgement in the exchequer was given against them: the reason of this judgement was, for that customer Smith received the same as due to the queene, and the issue was joyned, *quod prædicti executores non tenebantur ad computum, &c.* and the validity of the imposition was never questioned.

Mich. 38 & 39 Eliz. in Scaccario Rot. 319.

3. A judgement was given in the exchequer, for an imposition set upon currants, but the common opinion was, that that judgement was against law, and divers expresse acts of parliament; and so by that which hath been said, it doth manifestly appeare.

To conclude this point, with two of the *maximes* of the common law. 1. *Le common ley ad tielment admeasure les prerogatives le roy, que ilz ne tolleront, ne prejudiceront le inheritance dascun*, the common law hath so admeasured the prerogatives of the king, that they should not take away, nor prejudice the inheritance of any: and the best inheritance that the subject hath, is the law of the realme. 2. *Nihil tam proprium est imperii, quam legibus vivere.*

In mem. Scaccar. int. com. Pasc. 4 Jacob. Rot. 32. in inform. vers. John Bate de London mercat. Pl. com. 236. in the B. Barkleys case. Fortesc. sepe.

Upon this chapter, as by the said particulars may appeare, this conclusion is necessarily gathered, that all monopolies concerning trade and traffique, are against the liberty and freedome, declared and graunted by this great charter, and against divers other acts of parliament, which are good commentaries upon this chapter.

2 E. 3. c. 9. 9 E. 3. c. 1. 25 E. 3. c. 2. 2 R. 2. c. 1. 11 R. 2. cap. 7. 6 R. 2. cap. 1. 12 H. 7. cap. 6.

Mirror, c. 5. § 5. 4 E. 4. c. 15. 5 H. 4. c. 9. 27 H. 6. cap. 3. 17 E. 4. cap. 1. 3 H. 7. cap. 8. * See hereafter the expofition upon the ftatutes of imployments.

Le point del conge del demurrer des merchants aliens eſt iſſint interpretable, que ceo ne ſoit in prejudice des villes, ne des merchants dangleterre, et il ſoient ſerements al roy et plevyes ſilz demurront pluis que 40 jours.

For the well intreating and ordering of merchant ſtrangers and denizens, and for * due imployment of their money upon the native commodities of this realme, many ſtatutes have beene made ſince this great charter, and have been excellently expounded in the raigne of queene Elizabeth, but that matter belongs not to this place.

[64]

CAP. XXXI.

SI quis tenuerit de aliqua eſcaeta, ſicut de honore Wallingford, Notting. Bolon. et de aliis eſcaetis (1) *quæ ſunt in manu noſtra, et ſint baroniæ, et obierit hæres ejus, non det aliud relevium, nec faciet nobis aliud ſervitium, quam faceret baroni, ſi baronia eſſet in manu baronis, et nos eodem modo eam tenebimus, quo baro eam tenuit. Nec nos occaſione talis baroniæ, vel eſcaetæ habebimus aliquam eſcaetam, vel cuſtodiam aliquorum noſtrorum hominum, niſi de nobis alibi tenuerit in capite ille qui tenuit baroniam, vel eſcaetam illam.*

IF any man hold of any eſchete, as of the honour of Wallingford, Nottingham, Boloin, or of any other eſchetes which be in our hands, and are baronies, and die, his heir ſhall give none other relief, nor do none other ſervice to us, than he ſhould to the baron, if it were in the baron's hand. And we in the ſame wiſe ſhall hold it as the baron held it; neither ſhall we have, by occaſion of any barony or eſchete, any eſchete or keeping of any of our men, unleſs he that held the barony or eſchete otherwiſe held of us in chief.

(Bro. Livery, 58. Bro. Tenures, 57, 61, 94, 99. 26 H. 8. pl. 3. 2 Inſt. 14. Regiſt. 184. 1 Ed. 3. ſtat. 2. c. 13. 1 Ed. 6. c. 4.)

By this chapter it is declared, and enacted, that if any man hold of any eſcheate, as of any honour, or of other eſcheats, which are baronies, and were in the kings hands; firſt, if he die, his heire being of full age, his heire ſhall give no other reliefe to the king then he did to the baron. 2. Nor doe none other ſervice to the king, then he ſhould have done to the baron. 3. That the king ſhall hold the honour or baronie as the baron held it, that is, of ſuch eſtate, and in ſuch manner and forme, as the baron held it. 4. The king ſhall not have by occaſion of any barony, or eſcheate, any eſcheate but of lands holden of ſuch baronie. 5. Nor any wardſhip of any other lands then are holden by knights ſervice of ſuch baronie, unleſſe he, which held of the baronie, held alſo of the king by knights ſervice in *capite*.

All this is meerely declaratory of the common law, and here it appeareth that he that holdeth of the king, muſt hold of the perſon of the king, and not of any honor, barony, mannor or ſeigniory; and it appeareth farther in our books, that he that holdeth of the king in chiefe, muſt not only hold of the perſon of the king, but the tenure muſt be created by the king, or ſome one of the progenitors,

See the firſt part of the Inſtitutes, ſect. 103. 47 E. 3. 21. F. N. B. 5.

or predeceſſors kings of this realme, to defend his perſon and crowne, otherwiſe he ſhall have no prerogative by reaſon of it, for no prerogative can be annexed to a tenure created by a ſubject. Note here is not named the honour of Lanc. which was an auncient honour ever ſince the conqueſt, which E. 3. raiſed to a count palatine, as in the 4. part of the Inſtitutes, cap. Duch. of Lancaſtre appeareth. See 28 H. 6. 11. *per touts les juſtices.* 1 E. 6. Bro. trav. 53. Stamford Prerog. 29. b.

(1) *De aliis eſcheatis.*] Some queſtion hath been made of theſe words, for ſome have ſaid that theſe words are to be underſtood of common eſcheats, as where the lord dieth without heire, or where he is attainted of felony: but where the lord is attainted of high treaſon, there the king hath the land by forfeiture of whomſoever the land is held, and not in reſpect of any eſcheate by reaſon of any ſeigniorie: and therefore where William Riparave a Norman, held lands in fee of the king, as of the honour of Peverell, and Riparave forfeited his ſaid land for treaſon, and the king ſeiſed it as his eſcheate of Normandy, in this caſe the land ſo forfeited was no part of the honour, as it ſhould have been, if it had come to the king, as a common eſcheate, for it cometh to the king by reaſon of his perſon, and crowne, and therefore if he graunt it over, &c. the patentee ſhall hold it of the king in chiefe, and not of the honour. And all this is to be agreed, but yet the tenants that held before of the honour by knights ſervice, cannot hold of the king in chiefe. 1. For that they hold not of the perſon of the king, but of the honour. 2. Becauſe the tenure was not created by the king, or any of his progenitors, as hath been ſaid.

[47 E. 3. 21. Riparaves caſe.]

[65]

And ſo doth Bracton, who wrote ſoone after the ſtatute, expound this great charter to extend to forfeiture of baronies for treaſon, as of the Normans.

And yet to make an end of all ambiguities and queſtions, the ſtatute of 1 E. 6. was made, which is, as the words be, a plain declaration and reſolution of the common law. Likewiſe the ſtatute of 1 E. 3. which provideth, that where the land, that is holden of the king, as of an honour, is aliened without licence, no man ſhall be thereby grieved, is alſo a declaration of the common law.

By this chapter it appeareth, that a ſubject may have an honour.

[Bracton, l. 2. fol. 87. b. 30 H. 8. tenures. Br. 44. 29 H. 8. livery. 28 Br. 36 H. 8. Dier 58. 1 E. 6. cap. 4. 1 E. 3. cap. 13. See the 1. part of the Inſtitutes, ſect. 1.]

CAP. XXXII.

NULLUS liber homo det de cætero amplius alicui, vel vendat [alicui] de terra ſua, quam ut de reſiduo terræ ſuæ poſſit ſufficienter fieri domino feodi ſervitium ei debitum, quod pertinet ad feodum illud.

NO freeman from henceforth ſhall give or ſell any more of his land, but ſo that of the reſidue of the lands the lord of the fee may have the ſervice due to him, which belongeth to the fee.

Tr. 1. E. 1. coram rege. Not. & Derb. a declaration made of this act. Bract. l. 1. Britton. fol. 88. Fleta. l. 3. cap. 3. Mirror, c. 5. § 2. Cuſtumier de Norm. cap. 116. (1 Inſt. 43. a. 18 Ed. 1. ſtat. 1. c. 2.)

1 Firſt it is to be ſeene, what the common law was before this ſtatute.

2 What is wrought by this ſtatute, where the lands are holden of the king.

10 H. 7. 11.

3 What this ſtatute hath provided in caſe where lands are holden of a ſubject.

Before this ſtatute, in caſe where the tenure was of a common perſon, the tenant might have made a feofment of a parcell of his tenancy to hold of him, for the ſeigniory remained intire as it was, and the lord might diſtreine in the tenancy paravaile for his rent, and ſervice; but at the common law, he could not have given a part of his tenancy to be holden of the lord, for the tenant by this act could not divide the ſeigniory of the lord which was intire, for at the beginning the lord reſerved his ſeigniory out of the whole tenancy, and might diſtreine in every part thereof for his ſeigniory, but if the tenant might have made a feofment of part to hold of the lord, then had he ſecluded the lord of his liberty to diſtreine for the whole ſeigniory in every part thereof.

At the common law the tenant might have made a feofment of the whole tenancy to be holden of the lord, for that was no prejudice at all to the lord.

a 29 Aſſ. p. 19. 20 Aſſ. p. 17. 26 Aſſ. p. 37. 20 E. 3. avowry. Rot. parl. 29 E. 3. nu. 18.
b Rot. par. 18 E. 1.
c 34 E. 3. c. 15. See the Stat. of W. 3. de quia emptores terr. an. 18 E. 1. F. N. B. 143. b. & 235. c. 13 Eliz. Dier. 299. b.
d Rot. pat. an. 21 H. 3. nu. 4 H. 3. confirmed this chart. made 9 H. 3.
e 20 Aſſ. p. 17. 26 Aſſ. p. 37. 14 H. 4. 2, 3. 15 E. 4. 13. Stamf. prer. cap. 6. fo. 27, 28. 9 E. 3. 36. Hil. 13 E. 3. coram rege Norff. in Turri.

a But in the kings caſe it was doubted, whether his tenant might have given part of the tenancy to hold of himſelfe, becauſe the land, and the profit that might come to the king thereby, was removed farther off from him, and the meſnalty was ever of leſſe value, then the land, and for that cauſe the tenancy was called paravaile: b and in 18 E. 1. the king anſwered to a petition in parliament, *rex non vult aliquem medium, &c.* and this queſtion remained after this ſtatute about the ſpace of 133. years, viz. till the c ſtatute of 34 E. 3. was made, whereby it is provided, that alienations of lands made by tenants, which held of H. 3. or of other kings before him, to hold of themſelves, that the alienations ſhould ſtand in force, ſaving to the king his prerogative of the time of his great grandfather, his father, and his own, whereby it appeareth that this prerogative to have a fine for alienation, d began in the raign of H. 3. which was by this act, and therefore he beginneth with H. 3. his great grandfather.

e To the ſecond point by this act, where lands are holden of the king, as king, in *capite*, be it by knights ſervice, or in ſocage in *capite*; and aliened without licence, there * groweth, as hath been ſaid, to the king a fine: for by the common law it was againſt the nature and purity of a fee-ſimple, for the tenant to be reſtrained from alienation.

* [66]

But ſome did hold, that upon this act the land ſo aliened without licence was forfeite to the king, by reaſon of theſe words, *nullus liber homo det, &c.* and others did hold the contrary, that upon theſe words, the land was not forfeited, but that it ſhould be ſeiſed in the name of a diſtreſſe, and a fine to be paid for the treſpaſſe, which I take to be the better opinion; and the reaſon why our books ſpeake, that no fine was due before 20 H. 3. is, for that about that yeare H. 3. being of full age (as hath been ſaid) did eſtabliſh and confirme this great charter, but in truth it was in 21 H. 3. as by the charter it ſelfe appeareth.

1 E. 3. c. 12. See the ſtatute of quia emptores

But this queſtion depended about the ſpace of 100 years, &c. and was not determined untill the ſtatute made in 1 E. 3. whereby it

it is enacted, that the king ſhall not hold them as forfeite in ſuch caſe, but that of lands ſo aliened there ſhall be from thenceforth, a reaſonable fine taken in the chancery, by due proces, which act was but an expoſition of this chapter of *Magna Charta* as to lands holden of the king *in capite* aliened without licence, and extendeth to lands holden of the king by grand ſerjantie aliened without licence.

terrarum. ubi ſup. Hill. 2 E. 3. coram rege wilteſ. Prerog. regis, c. 6. F. N. B. 175. 14 E. 3. quare Imp. 54. Br. Alienation ſans licence 34. Hill. 43 Eliz. l. 2. fol. 80, 81. Seign. Cromwels caſe.

To the 3. the great doubt upon this act was, that in as much as this act was a prohibition generall, and impoſed no paine or penalty, what paine the tenant, or his feoffee ſhould incurre, if he did the contrary; and by the common opinion this act was thus interpreted: that when a tenant of a common perſon did alien parcell contrary to this act, the feoffor himſelfe during his life ſhould not avoide it, *quia nemo contra factum ſuum proprium venire poteſt*, but that his heire after his deceaſe might avoid it by the intendment of this act, to the end that men ſhould not purchaſe ſuch parcell, for feare of loſing the ſame after the death of the feoffor: but if the heire apparant had joyned with his aunceſter in the feoffment, or after had confirmed it, and thereby had given his aſſent thereunto, he or his heires ſhould never have avoided it, whether he ſurvived his father or no: and if the heire entred upon this ſtatute, the alienee of part might plead that the ſervice, whereby the land was holden, might be ſufficiently done of the reſidue, and thereuppon iſſue might be taken. And I have ſeene divers ſuch precedents betweene this act of *Magna Charta*, and 18 E. 1.

Then came the ſtatute of 18 E. 1. which enacteth, *quod de cætero liceat unicuiq; libero homini terras ſuas, ſeu tenemēta ſua, ſeu partē inde ad voluntatem ſuam vendere, ita tamen quod feoffatus teneat terram illam, ſeu tenementum illud de capitali domino per eadem ſervitia, et conſuetudines, per quæ feoffator ſuus illa prius de eo tenuit, et ſi partem aliquam earundem terrarum, ſeu tenementorum alicui vendiderit, feoffatus ille partem illam immediate teneat de domino.*

18 E. 1. de quia emptores terrarum.

Many excellent things are enacted by this ſtatute, and all the doubts upon this chapter of *Magna Charta* were cleered, both ſtatutes having both one end (that is to ſay) for the upholding and preſervation of the tenures, whereby the lands were holden; this act of 18 E. 1. being enacted *ad inſtantiam magnatum regni.*

1 Firſt this ſtatute of 18 E. 1. doth begin with a *de cætero liceat*, which proveth that before it was not lawful to alien part, unles ſufficient were left, and this approveth the aforeſaid common opinion, that in that caſe, the heire might enter, otherwiſe this chapter of *Magna Charta*, had been in vaine and this *de cætero liceat*, had not needed.

2 That by this ſtatute of 18 E. 1. the prohibition and penalty by this chapter of *Magna Charta*, to avoide the ſtate of the feoffee is taken away; *de cætero liceat, &c.*

3 The point aforeſaid of the common law, that the tenant could not alien parcell to hold of the lord, is by this act of 18 E. 1. altered.

4 Another point of the common law is by this act altered, that where by the common law, he hath aliened parcell to hold of himſelfe, this is taken away, and the alienee ſhall hold of the lord *pro particula*.

5 Where the tenant had liberty, and election by the common law [67]

law to make a feoffement of the whole, to hold either of himselfe, or of the lord, now this liberty and election is taken away, for by this act the land must be immediately holden of the lord.

Registr. 268. F.N.B. 234. 6. That the king is bound by this act, and this appeareth by the Register, that the king cannot charge the feoffee of part with the entire rent, but there lieth a writ *de onerando pro rata portione*; but the king may graunt lands to hold of himselfe, for he is not restrained by this act, for hereby no man is restrained, but he which holds over of some lord, and the king holdeth of none.

But then here riseth a question, if by this chapter of *Magna Charta*, a fine for alienation accrued to the king upon an alienation of the kings tenant in *capite*, and now this restraint (as hath been said) being taken away; how can that prerogative stand when the foundation, whereupon it is built faileth?

But hereunto it is answered. 1. The restraint of *Magna Charta, secundum quid*, as to the avoydance of the state of the feoffee by the heire, is taken away, as hath been said, but not *simpliciter*, for in respect of the king, the fine for alienation remains due, and herewith agreeth constant and continuall usage. 2. The statue of 1 E. 3. enacteth, *que desormes de tielz terres et tenements alien soit reasonable fine prise in le chauncery*, and though it saith *(desormes)* from henceforth, that was not, that any fine was due before, but, as hath been said, to take away the question of the forfeiture.

17 E. 2. ca. 7. 1 E. 3. ubi supra.

After this act out of the office of the remembrancer of the exchequer, writs of *quo titulo ingressus est*, to help the king to his reasonable fine, issued out of the exchequer, to know how the feoffee came to the whole, or part of the land, and of what estate, whereupon the feoffee was driven to plead to his great charge and trouble, and therefore upon conference had with the kings officers, and the judges, it was ordained, that seeing the kings tenant could not alien without licence, for if he did, he should pay a fine, that for a licence to be obtained, the king should have the third part of the value of the land, which was holden reasonable, and the feoffee should pay the same because his land was otherwise to be charged, and he rid of the trouble and charge by the writ of *quo titulo ingressus est*; and if the alienation was without licence, then a reasonable fine by the statute, was to be paid by the alienee, which they resolved to be one yeares value, which ever since constantly and continually hath beene observed and paid.

This fine was to be paid by the alienee, as hath been said, or by those that claimed by or under him, and if the fine be not paid, the land shall be seised into the kings hands; and the intent of a parliament is always intended just, and reasonable; and therefore if a disseisor of lands in *capite* make an alienation without licence; and the disseisee enter, the land shall not be seised for the fine, for the disseisee is in by a title before the alienation, and so in other like cases. If he in the reversion levy a fine of lands holden in *capite* without licence, the lessee for life shall not bee charged with the fine, because that estate was before the alienation, but yet in a *quid juris clamat*, the lessee shall not be compelled to attorne, because the court will not suffer a prejudice to the king in like manner, as if the reversion had been aliened in mortmain without the kings licence.

45 E. 3. ca. 6. 27 E. 3. 6.

I have been the longer in explaining this chapter, because it seemed so obscure to some readers in former times, that they passed it over without any explanation.

CAP.

CAP. XXXIII.

OMNES patroni abbatiarum, qui habent chartas regum Angliæ de advocatione, vel antiquam tenuram, vel possessionem, habeant earum custodiam cum [vacaverint] sicut habere debent, sicut superius declaratum est, cap. 5.

ALL patrons of abbies, which have the king's charters of England of advowson, or have old tenure or possession in the same, shall have the custody of them when they fall void, as it hath been accustomed, and as it is afore declared.

(25 Ed. 3. stat. 3. c. 1.)

This statute is intended where the patron, or founder of abbeyes, or priories by speciall reservation, tenure or custome, ought to have the custody of the temporalties of the same, during the vacation, as many patrons and founders in times past had. But if the king be founder, he ought to have the temporalties during the vacation, of common right by his prerogative. Mirror, ca. 5. § 2. F. N. B. 34. 44 E. 3. 24. 38 Ass. 22. 50 Ass. p. 6.

If the king and a common person joyn in a foundation, the king is the founder, because it is an entire thing. 44 E. 3. 24.

If a common person found an abbey, or priory, with possessions of small value, and the king after endow it with great possessions, yet the common person is founder. If a common person found a chauntery, and after the king translate it, and make it a monastery, and endow it with possessions, yet the common person is in law the founder, because he gave the first living; so if the translation be from regular to secular, *vel e contra*.

CAP. XXXIV.

NULLUS capiatur, aut imprisonetur propter appellum fœminæ (1), de morte alterius quam viri sui.

NO man shall be taken or imprisoned upon the appeal of a woman for the death of any other, than of her husband.

(Bro. Appeal, 5, 17, 60, 68, 104, 112. Rast. Ent. 43.)

For this word, Appeale, see the first part of the Institutes. At the common law before this statute, a woman, as well as a man might have had an appeale of death of any of her auncestors, and therefore the son of a woman shall at this day have an appeale, if he be heire at the death of the auncestor, for the son is not disabled, but the mother onely, for the statute saith, *propter appellum fœminæ*. *Vide* more of this in the first part of the Institutes. See the first part of the Institutes, sect. 500. Glanv. lib. 14. c. 3. 15 E. 2. Coro. 385. 17 E. 4. 1. 20 H. 6. 43.

* Fleta saith, *Fœmina autem de morte viri sui inter brachia sua interfecti, et non aliter poterit appellare*; and therewith agreeth the Mirror, Britton, and Bracton. Stamf. Pl. Cor. 58, 59. Bract. li. 4. fol. 148. Brit. fo. 55. Flet. l. 1. ca.

33. See the first part of the Institutes, sect. 24. * Fleta ubi supra, Mirror, ca. 5. § 2. & ca. 2, § 7. 50 E. 3. 14. 28 E. 3. 91. 3 E. 3. Coron. 357. 20 H. 6. 46.

By *inter brachia* in these auncient authors, is understood the wife, which the dead had lawfully in possession at his death, for she must be his wife both of right and in possession, for in an appeale, *unques accouple in loiall matrimony*, is a good plea.

A woman at this day may have an appeale of robbery, &c. for she is not restrained thereof.

This writ of appeale of the death of her husband, is annexed to her widowhood, as her quarentine is.

If the wife of the dead marry again, her appeale is gone, albeit the second husband die within the yeare; for shee must before any
[69] appeale brought, continue *fœmina viri sui*, upon whose death she brings the appeale.

11 H. 4. 46. So if she bring the appeale during her widow-hood, and take husband, the appeale shall abate, and is gone for ever.

So likewise, if in her appeale she hath judgement of death against the defendant, if after she take husband, she can never have execution of death against him.

35 H. 6. 63. Albeit the husband be attainted of high treason, or felony, yet if he be slain, his wife shall have an appeale, for notwithstanding the attainder he was *vir suus*, but the heire cannot have an appeale, for the blood is corrupted betweene them.

(1) *Appellum fœminæ.*] A hermophrodite, if the male sex be predominant, shall have an appeale of death as heire, but if the female sexe doth exceed the other, no appeale doth lie for her as heire.

CAP. XXXV.

NULLUS comitatus (1) de cætero teneatur nisi de mense in mensem, et ubi major terminus esse solebat, major sit (2). Nec aliquis vicecomes, vel balivus suus faciat turnum suum per hundredum, nisi bis in anno; et non nisi in loco debito et consueto, viz. semel post Pasch', et iterum post festum S. Michaelis (3), et visus francipleg' tunc fiat ad illum terminum Sancti Michaelis sine occasione. Ita scilicet quod quilibet habeat libertates suas quas habuit, vel habere consuevit tempore regis Henrici avi nostri, vel quas postea perquisivit. Fiat autem visus de frankpleg' sic (4): videlicet, quod pax nostra teneatur, et quod tithinga teneatur integra (5), sicut esse consuevit, et quod vicecomes non quærat occasiones (7), et contentus sit de eo, quod vicecomes habere consuevit (8) de visu suo

NO county court from henceforth shall be holden, but from month to month; and where greater time hath been used, there shall be greater: nor any sheriff, or his bailiff, shall keep his turn in the hundred but twice in the year; and no where but in due place, and accustomed; that is to say, once after Easter, and again after the feast of Saint Michael. And the view of frankpledge shall be likewise at the feast of Saint Michael without occasion; so that every man may have his liberties which he had, or used to have, in the time of king Henry our grandfather, or which he hath purchased since. The view of frankpledge shall be so done, that our peace may be kept; and that the tything be wholly kept as it hath been accustomed; and that the sheriff seek no

suo faciendo, tempore H. reg. avi nostri (6).

no occasions, and that he be content with so much as the sheriff was wont to have for his view-making in the time of king Henry our grandfather.

(Fitz. Leet, 11. 8 H. 7. f. 4. 1 Roll, 201. Cro. El. 125. 2 Leon. 74. Regist. 175, 187. F. N. B. 161. 31 Ed. 3. stat. 1. c. 15.)

(1) *Comitatus.*] *Quod modo vocatur comitatus, olim apud Britones temporibus Romanorum in regno isto Britanniæ vocabatur consulatus; et qui modo vocantur vicecomites, tunc temporis vice-consules vocabantur; ille vero dicebatur vice-consul, qui consule absente ipsius vices supplebat in juris foro.* Inter leges R. Ed. Lamb. 129. a. b. Idem verbo Conventus.

Curia comitatus, in Saxon, ðcypegemote, *i. comitatus conventus.* 12 H. 7. 18.

Ejus duo sunt genera, quorum alterum hodie le countie court, alterum le tourne del viscount, olim folkmote, vulgo nuncupatur; so as many times *turn' vicecomitis* is expressed under the name of *curia comitatus*, because it extended through the whole county: and therefore in the red book of the exchequer, amongst the laws of king H. 1. cap. 8. *de generalibus placitis comitatuum*, it is thus contained, *viz.* Lamb. 135. Britton, ca. 27. Flet. l. 2. ca. 36, 37. In libro rubro, in Scaccario, ca. 8.

Sicut antiqua fuerat institutione formatum, salutari regis imperio vera est recordatione firmatum, generalia * *comitatuum placita certis locis, et vicibus, et definito tempore per singulas anni provincias convenire debere, nec ullis ultra fatigationibus agitari, nisi propria regis necessitas, vel commune regni commodum sæpius adjiciant. Intersint autem episcopi, comites, vicedomini, vicarii, centenarii, aldermanni, præfecti, præpositi, barones, vavassores, tingrevii, et cæteri terrarum domini diligenter intendentes, ne malorum impunitas, aut gravionum pravitas, vel judicum subversio solita miseros laceratione conficiant: agantur itaque primo, debita veræ christianitatis jura, secundo, regis placita, postremo, causæ singulorum, &c. debet enim Sheryfmote,* (i. the sheriffes tourne) *bis; hundreda, et wapentachia,* (i. the county courts) *duodecies in anno congregari.* [70] * i. Turnorum placita. Regis placita. i. The pleas of the crown holden in the sheriffes tourn also.

And truly did H. 1. say, *sicut antiqua fuerat institutione formatum*: for these courts of the tourn, and of the county, and of the leete or view of frankpledge mentioned hereafter in this chapter were very auncient; for of the tourn you shall reade amongst the lawes of king Edw. *Statutum est quod ibi (scilicet apud le folkmote) debent populi omnes, &c. convenire, et se fide et sacramento non fracto ibi in unum et simul confederare, &c. ad defendendum regnum, &c. una cum domino suo rege, et terras suas, et honores illius omni fidelitate cum eo servare, et quod illi, ut domino suo regi intra et extra regnum universum Britanniæ fideles esse velint, &c. Hanc legem invenit Arthurus (qui quondam fuit inclytissimus rex Britonum) et ita consolidavit et confederavit regnum Britanniæ universum semper in unum, hujus legis authoritate expulit Arthurus prædictus Saracenos et inimicos a regno, lex enim ista diu sopita fuit, donec Edgarus rex Anglorum qui fuit avus Edwardi regis, illam excitavit, et erexit in lucem et per totum regnum firmiter observari præcepit: et hujus legis authoritate rex Etheldred. subito uno et eodem die per universum regnum Danos occidit.* Lamb. fol. 135. The oath of allegeance in the tourn or leet.

By the lawes of king Edward, before the conquest the first, which succeeded king Alured, it is thus enacted:

Præpositus quisque, i. vicecomes Saxonice geresa, Anglice sheriffe, ad quartam circiter septimanam frequentem populi concionem celebrato, cuique jus dicito æquabile, litesque singulas cum dies condicti adveniant dirimito. Inter leges Edw. regis. ante conq. 1. cap. 11. fol. 51.

Hereby it appeareth that common pleas between party and party were holden in the county court every month, which agreeth with *Magna Charta*, and other statutes and continuall usage to this day.

Inter leges Edgari regis, ca. 5. fo. 80.

And amongst the laws of king Edgar it is thus concerning the sheriffes tourn provided.

Celeberrimus ex omni satrapia bis quotannis conventus agitor, cui quidem illius diœcesis episcopus, et senator intersunto, quorum alter jura divina, alter humana populum edoceto; which also agreeth with *Magna Charta*, and other statutes and continuall usage.

By that which hath been said, it appeareth that the law made by king H. 1. was (after the great heat of the conquest was past) but a restitution of the auncient law of England: and forasmuch as the bishop with the sheriffe did goe in circuit twice every yeare, by every hundred within the county (which also appeareth by this chapter of *Magna Charta* in these words, *turnum suum per hundreda, &c.*) it was called tour, or tourn, which signifieth a circuit, or perambulation.

Britton. cap. 29. Fleta, lib. 2. cap. 45. Marlebr. ca. 10. 31 H. 6. Leet 11. F. N. B. 169. a.

Now let us peruse the severall branches of this chapter.

(2) *Nullus comitatus de cætero teneatur nisi de mense in mensem, et ubi major terminus esse solebat, major sit.*] This (as hath been said) is an affirmance of the common law, and custome of the realme.

Comitatus.] Here *comitatus* is taken in the common sense for the county court.

[71]

That the realme was divided into counties long before the raigne of king Alured, viz. in the time of the auncient Britons. See the first part of the Institutes, sect. 248.

2 E. 6. cap. 25.

Et ubi major terminus, &c.] This is altered by the statute of 2 E. 6. whereby it is provided that no county court shall be longer deferred, but one month from court to court, and so the said court shall be kept every month, and none otherwise.

By which act every county of England, concerning the time of the keeping of the county court is governed by one and the same law.

And there is to be accounted 28 dayes to the legall month in this case, and not according to the month of the kalender.

(3) *Nec aliquis vicecomes, vel balivus suus faciat turnum suum per hundredum, nisi bis in anno, et non nisi in loco debito et consueto, viz. semel post Pasch. et iterum post festum S. Michaelis.*] Where this branch saith, *semel post Pasch. &c.* The statute of 31 E. 3. explaineth it, viz. one time within the month after Easter, and another time within the month after S. Michael, and if they hold them in any other manner, then they should lose their tourn for that time, which is as much to say, as the court so holden for that time, shall be utterly void, and the sheriffe shall lose the profits thereof.

31 E. 3. ca. 15. 38 H. 6. fol. 7. 6 H. 7. 2. Stamf. pl. Cor. 84.

Nisi in loco consueto.] This remaineth to this day.

42 E. 3. 4, & 5. Dier, 4, & 5. Phil. & Mar. 151.

Per hundreda.] How hundreds, and the courts of the hundreds first came, see hereafter in this chapter.

Et visus franciplegii tunc fiat ad illum terminum Sancti Michaelis, &c.] It hath appeared before, that of auncient time the sheriffe had two great courts, viz. the tourne, and the county court: afterwards for the ease of the people, and specially of the husbandman, that each of them might the better follow their businesse in their severall degrees, this court here spoken of, viz. view of frank-pledge,

pledge, or leet was by the king divided, and derived from the tourn, and graunted to the lords to have the view of the tenants, and resiants within their mannors, &c. So as the tenants, and resiants should have the same justice, that they had before in the tourn, done unto them at their own doores without any charge or losse of time, and for that cause came the duty in many leets to the lord *de certo lete*, towards the charge of obtaining the graunt of the said leet.

11 H. 4. 89. 13 H. 4. 9. lib. 11. fo. 45. Godfreyes case.

So likewise, and for the same reason were hundreds, and hundred courts, divided and derived from the county courts, and this the king might doe, for the tourn and leet both are the kings courts of record: and as the king may graunt a man to have power *tenere placita* within a certain precinct, &c. before certain judges, and in a manner exempt it from the jurisdiction of his higher courts of justice, so might he doe in case of the tourne, and hundred courts: so as the courts and judges may be changed, but the lawes and customes, whereby the courts proceed, cannot be altered. And as the county court, and hundred court are of one jurisdiction, so the tourne, and leet be also of one and the same jurisdiction; for *derivativa potestas est ejusdem jurisdictionis cum primitiva*.

Regula.

The style of the tourn is *curia franc. plegii domini regis tent apud L. coram vicecomite in turno suo tali die, &c.* And therefore in some books it is called the leete of the tourn. And therefore where the sheriffe styled his court, *turn. viccom. tent. tali die apud L. &c.* it was resolved that it was insufficient for that this word tourn is but the perambulation of the sheriffe, but by the right style of the tourn, it appeareth that the tourn and leet have but one style, and the same jurisdiction.

31 H. 6. Leet 11. 8 H. 7. 11. 6 H. 7. 2. 8 H. 7. 1.

[72]

Mirror, ca. 1. § 16.

But for want of the knowledge of antiquity it was *obiter*, in 18 H. 6. denied that the tourn, and the leet were of one jurisdiction, and two instances are there put, viz. that the leet hath conusance of bread and ale, that is, of the assise of bread and ale, and the tourn hath not conusance thereof; and the other is, that in the leet they have authority *de presenter ceux, queux ne sont lies*, abridged by Fitzh. *a presenter ceux, que ne sont mises in le decennarie.*

18 H. 6. abbr. by F. Leet. 1.

To the first it is cleare, that the breach of the assise of bread and ale is presentable in the tourn, as a common nusance, and therewith agreeth constant and continuall experience, and reason proveth, that the derivative cannot have conusance of that which the primitive had not, unlesse it be given by some act of parliament; and herewith agreeth the style of the tourn, and the authority of later books.

4 E. 4. 31. 22 E. 4. 22. 12 H. 7. 18. 28 H. 8. Dier 13. b.

As to the second, it is ill reported in the book itselfe; but if it be intended as Fitzh. abridgeth it, then it is cleare that in the tourn they that be not put into the decennary may be inquired of, for, as hath been often said, the style of the tourn is, *curia visus frankpleg'*; and the derivative cannot of common right have more then the primitive.

But both of the tourn and the leete, this may be truly said,

Tempora mutantur, & nos mutamur in illis;

Quodque vera institutio istius curiæ evanuit, et velut umbra ejusdem ad huc remanet: habemus quidem senatus consultum, sed in tabulis repositum, et tanquam gladium in vagina reconditum.

Pasch. 5. Jac. lib. fo. 78. Buleins case. Cicero.

But now let us return to our *Magna Charta.*

Mirror, ca. 1. § 17. & ca. 5. § 2. 6 H. 7. 2. & 3.

Et visus de franc' plegio tunc fiat ad illum terminum Sancti Michaelis, &c.] It is to be obferved that the precedent branch is, that *vicecomes non faciat turnum per hundredum nisi bis in anno*, as hath been faid, viz. *semel post Pasch' et iterum post festum Sancti Michaelis*; this claufe extendeth to the enquiry of felonies, common nufances and other mifdeeds, the view of frankpledges, and to all things inquirable in the tourn. Now by this claufe it is provided that the article of the tourn concerning the view of frankpledge, being here underftood in a particular fenfe, fhall be dealt withall by the fheriffe in his tourne but once in the year, viz. at the tourn holden after Eafter, and fo it hath been formerly expounded: and therefore it was well refolved in 24 H. 8. that this claufe of the ftatute of *Magna Charta*, is to be underftood of the leet of the tourn, and not of other leets, and fo without queftion is the law holden at this day, that he that claimes a leet by charter, muft hold it at the fame dayes which are contained in the charter, and he that claimes it by prefcription may claime to hold it once or twice every yeare, at any fuch dayes as fhall upon reafonable warning be appointed, if the ufage hath been fo, fo that it hath been kept at uncertain times, or elfe it ought to be kept at fuch certain dayes and times, as by prefcription hath been certainly ufed; and the next words to this claufe bee, *ita scilicet quod quilibet habeat libertates suas, quas habuit, &c.* doe explaine the meaning of this chapter, that it extended not to the leets of the fubjects, but they fhould have their liberties, as before they had; and this alfo appeareth by the conclufion of this chapter, *et quod vicecomes, &c. contentus sit de eo quod vicecomes habere consuevit de visu suo faciendo*; fo as it muft be *visus suus*, the fheriffes view, which of neceffity muft be parcell of the tourn; and it is faid in the Mirror, that this view of frankpledge (parcell of the tourn) fhould be made once every yeare.

30 H. 6. Leet 11. 24 H. 8. Br. Leet 23. 22 H. 6. 14. 8 H. 7. 4. 12 H. 7. 15. 38 H. 6, 7. Dier, 7 Eliz. 233, 234.

(4) *Fiat autem visus de franc' pleg' sic, &c.*] Here it appeareth that the view of frankpledge fhould have two ends. 1. *Quod pax nostra teneatur.* 2. *Quod trithinga teneatur integra.*

[73]

For the firft, that the kings peace might be kept; the right inftitution of the view of franke pledge, and whereon the name came is to be confidered, which is as followeth.

Franci plegii. i. Liberi fidejussores, free fureties or pledges; and here it is faid *fiat visus de francis plegiis, ita scilicet quod pax nostra teneatur*, that is, let the view of pledges or fureties for free-men be made, fo that our peace may be holden: now the inftitution hereof, for the keeping of the kings peace, was, that every free-man, at his age of 12 years, fhould in the leet (if he were in any) or in the tourne, (if he were not in any leet) take the oath of alleageance to the king, and that pledges or fureties fhould be found, in manner hereafter expreffed, for his truth to the king, and to all his people, or elfe to be kept in prifon: this franke pledge confifted moft commonly of ten houfholds, which the Saxons called *Theothung*, in the north parts they call them *Tenmentale*, in other places of England *Tithing*, here in this chapter *Trithinga. i. decemvirale collegium*, whereof the mafters of the nine families (who were bound) were of the Saxons called *Freoborgh*, which in fome places is to this day called *free Barrowe*. i. Free furety, or *frankepledge*, and the mafter of the tenth houfhould was by the Saxon called by divers names, viz. *Theothungmon*, to this day in the weft called *Tythingman*, and *Tienheofod* and *Freoborker. i. Capitalis plegius*, chiefe pledge: and thefe

Bract. lib. 3. f. 124. int. leges Canuti fol. 108. 19. Int. leges Edw. regis fol. 132. cap. de friborgis. Bract. ubi sup. Lamb. verbo centuria & decuria.

Bract. fol. 19. b.

these ten masters of families, were bound one for anothers family, that each man of their severall families should stand to the law, or if he were not forth coming, that they should answere for the injury or offence by him committed, *de eo autem qui fugam ceperit, diligenter inquirend' si fuerit in franco plegio, et decenna, tunc erit decenna in misericordia coram justitiariis nostris, quia non habent ipsum malefactorem ad rectum.* Brit. ubi. sup. Bract. l. 3. f. 124.

Hereby it appeareth, that the precinct of this frank pledge was called *decenna*, because it consisted most commonly, as hath been said, of tenne housholds, and every man of these several housholds, for whom the pledge or surety was taken were called *decennarii*, because every particular person in the kingdome was of one *decenna* or other, which names are continued as shadowes of antiquity to this day. *Ordeine fuit ancientment, que nul ne demurrast en le realme, s'il ne fuit en dizein et plevye de frank homes, appent aux visc' de viewer un fois per an' franke pledges et les plevys, &c.* Brit. cap. 12. Fleta, lib. 1. cap. 27. acc. Mirror, cap. 1. §. 17.

By the due execution of this law, such peace (whereof this chapter speaketh) was universally holden within this realme, as no injuries, homicides, robberies, thefts, riots, tumults, or other offences were committed; so as a man with a white wand might safely have ridden before the conquest, with much mony about him, without any weapon throughout England; and one saith truely, *conjectura est, eaq; non levis, haud ita multis statuisse prisca tempora sceleribus, quippe quibus rapinæ, furto, cædi, plurimisq; aliis sceleribus mulctæ imponebantur pecuniariæ, cum hiis hac nostra tempestate, nos omnibus merito capitis pœnam irrogamus, &c.* Lamb. verb. Æstimatio capitis.

(5) *Et quod trithinga teneatur integra.*] *Trithinga* or *Tithinga* is expounded for *Theothinga*, which signifieth the frankpledge of tenne housholds, as hath been said, and it is notably expounded by Fleta, which there you may read at large, the sense hereof is, *quod trithinga, sive theothinga. i. decemvirale collegium teneatur integrum.* i. that no man be not within some *decenna* or other, so as he may be brought forth to stand to right if he shall offend: *olim trithinga significabat tria vel quatuor hundreda, quod autem in trithinga definiri non poterat, ferebatur in scyram.* Fleta, lib. 2. c. 54. § de Trithingis. Lamb. Int. leges sanct. Edw. nu. 34. Merton, c. 10.

What persons shall come to the tourne and leete, &c. and who be exempted, see the statute of Marlebridge, and the auncient authors. Marlebridg. c. 10. Mirror c. 1. § 16. Bract. lib. 3. fol. 124. Brit. 19. b. Fleta, lib. 1. c. 29. lib. 2. cap. 45.

(6) *Tempore regis Henrici avi.*] Twice repeated in this chapter: vid. before cap. 15. 16.

* See the exposition of this statute Rot. claus. anno 18 H. 3. nu. 10. *[74]

(7) *Et quod vicecomes non quærat occasiones, &c.*] By the common law, to avoid all extortion and grievance of the subject, no sherife, coroner, goaler, or other of the kings ministers ought to take any reward for doing of his office, but only of the king; and this appeareth by our books, and is so declared and enacted by act of * parliament in the 3 E. 1. And a penalty added to the prohibition of the common law by that act: and Fortescue, cap. 24. saith, *Vicecomes jurabit super sancta Dei evangelia, inter articulos alios quod non aliquid recipiet colore, aut causa officii sui, ab aliquo alio, quam a rege.* Mirror, c. 2. § 5. Britton, fol. 3. b. 6. a. 18. b. 37. b. Fleta, lib. 1. c. 18 § Item si officium. & lib. 2. c. 39. 27 Ass. p. 14. 42 E. 3. 5. 23 H. 6. cap. 10. 17. 1 H. 8. c. 7. 33 H. 8. cap. 22. 21 H. 7. fol. 17.

But after that this rule of the common law was altered, and that the sherife, coroner, goaler, and other the kings ministers, might in some case take of the subject, it is not credible what extortions, and oppressions have thereupon ensued. So dangerous a thing it is, to * W. 1. cap. 26.

ſhake or alter any of the rules or fundamentall points of the common law, which in truth are the maine pillars, and ſupporters of the fabric of the common-wealth, as elſewhere I have noted more at large, and yet not ſo largely, as the weight of the matter deſerveth.

See the preface to the 4. part of my reports.

42 E. 3. 5. 38 H. 6, 7. 6 H. 7. 2, 3.

(8) *Contentus ſit de eo quod vicecomes habere conſuevit, &c.*] Theſe words are not to be intended of any reward, &c. (for the ſherife by law, as hath been ſaid, could take no reward for doing of his office) but of the profits of the court of the tourn, and ſuch only as were accuſtomed in the raigne of H. 2. So they muſt be very auncient, for the which the ſherife ſhould (by an auncient law) pay a certaine ſumme *de proficuis comitatus*, and ſhould be charged in the exchequer for this certain ſumme.

Regiſt. 16. 174. 175. F. N. B. 161. d. Marleb. cap. 10.

And it is to be obſerved, that if any man be grieved contrary to the purview of this act, he may, as hath been ſaid, for his reliefe therein, have an action upon this ſtatute, albeit no action be expreſly given, which in this, and many other like caſes upon the branches of *Magna Charta*, is worthy of obſervation.

CAP. XXXVI.

NEC liceat de cætero alicui, dare terram ſuam alicui domui religioſæ, ita quód illam reſumat de eadem domo tenend'. Nec liceat alicui domui religioſæ terram alicujus ſic accipere, quod tradat illam illi, a quo eam accepit tenend'. Si quis autem de cætero terram ſuam alicui domui religioſæ ſic dederit, et ſuper hoc convincatur, donum ſuum penitus caſſetur, et terra illa domino illius feodi incurratur.

IT ſhall not be lawful from henceforth to any to give his lands to any religious houſe, and to take the ſame land again to hold of the ſame houſe. Nor ſhall it be lawful to any houſe of religion to take the lands of any, and to leaſe the ſame to him of whom he received it. If any from henceforth give his lands to any religious houſe, and thereupon be convict, the gift ſhall be utterly void, and the land ſhall accrue to the lord of the fee.

Mirror, c. 5. § 2. Glanv. l. 6. c. 7. (Fitz. Mortm. 1, 3. Bro. Mortm. 36. 7 Ed 1. ſtat. 2. 13 Ed. 1. ſtat. 1. c. 32. 27 Ed. 1. ſtat. 2. 15 R. 2. c. 5. 23 H. 8. c. 10. 18 Ed. 3. c. 3. 1 & 2 Ph. & M. c. 8. 39 El. c. 5. 21 Jac. 1. c. 1. 13 & 14 Car. 2. c. 12. 9 Geo. 2. c. 36.)

3 E. 4. 12. See the 1. part of the Inſtitutes, ſect. 133. 157. ſtat. de 7 E. 1. de religioſis. 23 H. 3. Aſſ. 436. Britton, fol. 32. b. Fleta, lib. 3. cap. 5.

[75]

This chapter is excellently abridged according to the effect thereof, and notably exppounded by a parliament holden by king Edw. 1. ſonne of H. 3. the words whereof are theſe, Of late (*viz. anno* 9 H. 3. cap. 36.) it was provided that religious men ſhould not enter into the fees of any without licence, and will of the chiefe lords, of whom ſuch fees been holden immediately: whereby it appeareth, that by this chapter of *Magna Charta*, a gift of lands to any religious houſe was prohibited, notwithſtanding the religious houſe gave not the ſame back again to hold of the ſame houſe, &c. but kept the lands ſo given unto themſelves in their own hands: and in that caſe, that the land ſhould incurre to the lord of the fee, conſider well the words; and the interpretation is worthy obſervation for the interpretation of other ſtatutes in like caſes.

For the word Mortmain, ſee the firſt part of the Inſtitutes. First part of the Inſtitutes. cap. Frankalmoigne.

There were two cauſes of making of this ſtatute: one that the ſervices that were due out of ſuch fees, and which in the beginning were created for the defence of the realme, were unduly withdrawn. 2. The chieſe lords did loſe their eſcheats, wardſhips, reliefes, and the like; for which cauſes, divers provident lords at the creation of the ſeigniory had a clauſe in the deed of feoffement, *quod licitum ſit donatori rem datam dare, vel vendere cui voluerit, exceptis viris religioſis, et Judæis. Vide* Bracton, libro 1. fol. 13. Many of theſe deeds I have ſeene. Bract. li. 1. fol. 13.

But the eccleſiaſticall perſons (who in this were to be commended, that they had ever the beſt learned men in the law, that they could get, of their councell) found many wayes to creep out of this ſtatute, viz. religious men; as abbots, priors, and other eccleſiaſticall perſons regular, to purchaſe lands holden of themſelves, or take leaſes for long term for years, and many other devices they had to eſcape out of this ſtatute: and biſhops, parſons, and other eccleſiaſticall perſons ſecular took themſelves to be out of this ſtatute. Fleta, lib. 3. cap. 5.

The ſaid ſtatute of 7 E. 1. intended to provide againſt theſe devices, in theſe words, *quod nullus religioſus, aut alius quicunque* (i. other whatſoever of like quality of being, a body politique, or corporate, eccleſiaſticall, or lay, ſole, or aggregate of many) *terras aut tenementa aliqua emere, vel vendere ſub colore donationis aut termini*; and to prevent all other inventions and evaſions added theſe generall words, *aut ratione alterius tituli cujuſcunq; terras aut tenementa ab aliquo recipere aut alio quovis modo* * *arte vel ingenio ſibi appropriare præſumat, ſub foriſfactura eorundem.* 15 R. 2. cap. 5. 29 Aſſ. p. 17. Br. 29 H. 8. Mortmain, 39.

* Theſe words are notably explained. 15 R. 2. ca. 5. 19 H. 6. 56. 41 E. 3. 16. 41 E. 3. 21. 29 H. 8. Br. Mortmain 39. 17 E. 3. 59. 21 E. 3. 46. Rot. parliam. 5 R. 2. nu. 92. Quant le terre eſt per covin convey al roy.

A man would have thought that this ſhould have prevented all new devices, but they found alſo an evaſion out of this ſtatute, for this ſtatute of 7 E. 1. extended but to gifts, alienations, and other conveyances made between them and others, *arte vel ingenio, &c.* and therefore they gave over them; and they pretending a title to the land (that they meant to get) brought a *præcipe qd. reddat*, againſt the tenant of the land, and he by conſent and colluſion ſhould make default, and thereupon they ſhould recover the land, and enter by judgement of law, *et ſic fieret fraus ſtatuto.*

When this new invention was provided for, and taken away by the ſtatute of W. 2. yet found they out an evaſion out of all theſe ſtatutes, for now they would neither get any land by purchaſe, gift. leaſe, or recovery, but they cauſed the lands to be conveyed by feoffement, or in other manner to divers perſons, and their heires, to the uſe of them and their ſucceſſors, by reaſon whereof they took the profits; but this was enacted by the ſtatute of 15 R. 2. to be mortmain within the forfeiture of the ſaid ſtatute of 7 E. 1. W. 2. cap. 32. Fleta, lib. 3. cap. 5. 45 E. 3. 19. 15 R. 2. cap. 5. 8 H. 4. 16.

But the foundation of all theſe ſtatutes, was this chapter of *Magna Charta.*

CAP.

CAP. XXXVII.

SCUTAGIUM (1) *de cætero capiatur ſicut capi conſuevit tempore Henrici regis avi noſtri* (2).

ESCUAGE from henceforth ſhall be taken like as it was wont to be in the time of king Henry our grandfather.

Fleta, lib. 2. ca. 60.

(1) *Scutagium.*] *Vide* for this the firſt part of the Inſtitutes, lib. 2. cap. Eſcuage, ſect. 95.

Tempore Henrici regis avi noſtri.] Here is another reference to the raigne of king Henry the ſecond. See for this before, cap. 15. &c.

CAP. XXXVIII.

SALVÆ ſint archiepiſcopis, epiſcopis, abbatibus, prioribus, templariis, hoſpitalariis, comitibus, baronibus, et omnibus aliis, tam eccleſiaſticis perſonis, quam ſecularibus, omnes libertates et liberæ conſuetudines, quas prius habuerunt. Omnes autem iſtas conſuetudines et libertates prædictas, quas conceſſimus in regno noſtro tenend' (quantum ad nos pertinent) erga nos et hæred' noſtros obſervemus, et omnes de regno noſtro, tam clerici quam laici obſervent (quantum ad ſe pertinent) erga ſuos. Pro hac autem donatione et conceſſione libertatum iſtarum, et aliarum libertatum contentarum in charta noſtra de libertatibus foreſtæ, archiepiſcopi, epiſcopi, abbates, priores, comites, barones, milites, liberi tenentes, et omnes de regno noſtro dederunt nobis quinto-decimam partem omnium mobilium ſuorum. (vide ſtat. 7. anno 25 E. 3) Conceſſimus etiam eiſdem pro nobis et hæredibus noſtris, quod nec nos, nec hæredes noſtri, aliquid perquiremus, per quod libertates in hac charta contentæ infringantur vel infirmentur. Et ſi ab aliquo contra hoc aliquid perquiſit' fuerit, nihil valeat, et

RESERVING to all archbiſhops, biſhops, abbots, priors, templers, hoſpitallers, earls, barons, and all perſons, as well ſpiritual as temporal, all their free liberties and free cuſtoms, which they have had in time paſſed. And all theſe cuſtoms and liberties aforeſaid, which we have granted to be holden within this our realm, as much as appertaineth to us and our heirs, we ſhall obſerve; and all men of this our realm, as well ſpiritual as temporal (as much as in them is) ſhall obſerve the ſame againſt all perſons in like wiſe. And for this our gift and grant of theſe liberties, and of other contained in our charter of liberties of our foreſt, the archbiſhops, biſhops, abbots, priors, earls, barons, knights, freeholders, and other our ſubjects, have given unto us the fifteenth part of all their moveables. And we have granted unto them on the other part, that neither we, nor our heirs, ſhall procure or do any thing whereby the liberties in this charter contained ſhall be infringed or broken; and if any thing be procured by any perſon contrary to the

et pro nullo habeatur. Hiis teſtibus Bonefacio Cantuar' archiep', E. Londonenſi epiſcopo, et aliis. Datum apud Weſtm' decimo die Februarii, anno regni noſtri nono.

the premiſſes, it ſhall be had of no force nor effect. Theſe being witneſſes; lord B. archbiſhop of Canterbury, E. biſhop of London, and others.

This chapter doth conſiſt of ſixe parts.

Firſt it is enacted, that all the liberties, and free-cuſtomes, which any archbiſhop, biſhop, abbot, prior, templar, hoſpitaller, earle, baron, or any perſon either eccleſiaſticall or ſecular, have had, be ſafe, that is, whole without prejudice unto them, for the words be *ſalvæ ſint omnibus archiepiſcopis, &c. omnes libertates, &c.* all the liberties, &c. be ſafe to all archbiſhops, &c. ſo as this is no ſaving to them, but in effect, an act that they ſhould enjoy them: for regularly a ſaving in an act of parliament enlargeth not, nor extendeth to any new thing, but preſerveth a right or intereſt, that is former to things contained in the act, which by the words of the act might have been given away. But this clauſe doth enlarge, and extendeth to all other liberties, and free cuſtomes, which any ſubject eccleſiaſticall, or temporall ought to have; and therefore the Engliſh tranſlation, both in this and many other places of this great charter, is very vicious. But it is principally to be obſerved, that here is not any ſaving at all for the king, his heires, or ſucceſſors, to the end that the king, his heirs, and ſucceſſors againſt all pretences of evaſions, ſhould be bound by all the branches of both theſe charters. [77]

The ſecond is, that all the cuſtomes, and liberties, which the king had graunted to be holden within his realme, for him and his heires, the king himſelfe and his heires, as much as appertained to him or them, ſhould obſerve and keepe.

The third is, that all the men of this realme, as well of the clergy as of the laity, the ſaid cuſtomes and liberties for themſelves and their heirs, as much as to them appertained, ſhould obſerve and keepe.

This is the chiefe felicity of a kingdome, when good lawes are reciprocally of prince and people (as is here undertaken) duly obſerved.

The fourth is, that for this gift and graunt by the king, of the liberties contained in this great charter, and of others contained in the kings charter of liberties of the foreſt, the archbiſhops, biſhops, abbots, priors, earles, barons, knights, free-holders, and other the kings, ſubjects, citizens, and burgeſſes, (aſſembled in parliament) gave unto the king one fifteenth; which proveth, that as the fifteenth was graunted by parliament, ſo was this great charter alſo graunted by authority of the ſame; but ſince this time the manner of the fifteenth is altered; for now the fifteenth, which is alſo called the Taſk, is not originally ſet upon the polles, as at this time it was, but now the fifteenth is certainly rated upon every towne. And this was by vertue of the kings commiſſions into every county of England in 8 E. 3. taxations were made of all the cities, boroughes, and towns in England, and recorded in the exchequer, and that rate was at that time the fifteenth part of the value of every town, and therefore retaineth the name of the fifteenth ſtill.

Hil. 3 Jacobi. lib. 8. The Princes caſe.

Rot. pat. 6 E. 3. 2. part. nu. 26.

And after the fifteenth is graunted by parliament, then the inhabitants

bitants rate themſelves for payment thereof, and if one towne bee joyned with another in the rate of the totall, and ſubdivided on each a certain rate in that commiſſion, and the one is rated too low, and the other too high, there lieth a writ called, *ad æqualiter taxand'* to be taken out of the exchequer to rate the townes equally. The ſubſidie is uncertaine, becauſe it is ſet upon the perſon, in reſpect of his lands, or goods, which commonly doe ebb and flow.

The fift is, that the king did graunt for him, and his heires, that neither he, nor his heires, ſhall ſeeke out any thing, whereby the liberties in this charter contained may be broken, or weakned: and if by any man againſt this charter any thing ſhould be ſought out, it ſhould be of no value, and holden for nought. And all theſe doe evidently appeare in this chapter.

The ſixt and laſt is *hiis teſtibus*.

It is true, that of auncient time nothing paſſed from the king of franchiſes, liberties, priviledges, mannors, lands, tenements, and hereditaments of any eſtate of inheritance, but it was by the advice of his councell expreſſed under *hiis teſtibus*, as it was then, and continues to this day in the creation of any to any degree of nobility, for thereto *hiis teſtibus* is ſtill uſed.

This concluſion of the kings graunts with *hiis teſtibus* was uſed
[78] by king H. 3. and his progenitors kings of this realme before him, and by his ſon E. 1. and by E. 2. and E. 3. after him: afterwards, in the beginning of the raigne of R. 2. I finde the clauſe of *hiis teſtibus* was left out, and in ſtead thereof came in *teſte me ipſo* in this manner, *in cujus rei teſtimonium has literas noſtras fieri fecimus patentes: teſte me ipſo*, which ſince by all his ſucceſſors kings, and queens of this realme (except in creations) hath been uſed.

Thoſe that had *hiis teſtibus*, were called *chartæ*, as this charter is called *Magna Charta*, and ſo is *charta de foreſta*, &c. and thoſe other that be *teſte me ipſo*, are called letters patents, being ſo named in the clauſe of *in cujus rei teſtimonium has literas noſtras fieri fecimus patentes*.

See the firſt part of the Inſtitutes, ſect. 1.

And this was the auncient forme alſo of the deeds of ſubjects, concluding with *hiis teſtibus*, which continued untill, and in the raigne of H. 8. but now is wholly omitted, and now the witneſſes are ſubſcribed under the deed, or endorſed thereupon.

Now upon this occaſion to treat how theſe clauſes, *datum per manum noſtram, per manum cancellarii noſtri, per ipſum cuſtodem, et concilium*, &c. entred in, and went out: when theſe clauſes, *de gratia ſpeciali*, and *ex certa ſcientia, et mero motu* began, which continue to this day) and the cauſe and reaſon of the inſerting of the ſame; and when and wherefore theſe clauſes were ſubſcribed under the letters patents, *per ipſum regem, per breve de privato ſigillo, authoritate parliamenti*, &c. came in, (which ſtill doe continue) would aſke a ſeverall treatiſe of it ſelfe, and not pertinent to our purpoſe for the underſtanding of this charter of *Magna Charta*, and therefore purpoſely I ſpeake not of them.

Here be witneſſes to this great charter, a great number of reverend, and honourable perſonages, in all 63. of which there were of the clergy 31. whereof there were 12. biſhops, and 19 abbots, and Hugh de Burgo chiefe juſtice, and 31 earles and barons, as hath been ſaid before.

Hil. 3 Jac. in Cancellaria. The Princes caſe. Lib. 8. fol. 19.

Beſides, it was eſtabliſhed by authority of parliament, which was holden at Weſtminſter, in forme of a charter, as many others have been,

been, for which, as hath been ſaid likewiſe, by parliament the lords and commons gave a fifteenth. Of acts of parliament in form of a charter, you may reade at large in the princes caſe, and therefore need not to be recited.

STATUTUM de MERTON. [79]

EDITUM *anno* 20. H. III.

Bracton, li. 2. c. 96, ſaith it was in anno 18 H. 3.

IT is called the ſtatute of Merton, becauſe the parliament was holden at the monaſtery of the canons regular of Merton, ſeaven miles diſtant from the city of London, which monaſtery was founded by Giſlebert a noble Norman, that came in with the Conqueror. And this is that monaſtery of Merton, the prior whereof had a great caſe in law, which long depended between him and the prior of Bingham.

18 E. 4. 22. 19 E. 4. 2. 7. 20 E. 4. 16. 21 E. 4. 60.

PROVISUM eſt in curia domini regis apud Merton, die Mercurii, in craſtino Sancti Vincentii, anno regni regis Henrici filii regis Johannis viceſimo, coram W. Cantuarienſi archiepiſcopo, et coepiſcopis ſuffraganeis ſuis (1), *et coram majore parte comitum et baronum Angliæ ibidem exiſtentium, pro coronatione ipſius domini regis* (2) *et Elianoræ reginæ* (3), *pro qua omnes vocati fuerunt, cum tractatum eſſet de communi utilitate regni ſuper articulis ſubſcriptis, ita proviſum fuit et conceſſum, tam à prædict' archiepiſcopis, epiſcopis, comitibus, baronibus, quam ab ipſo rege, et aliis.*

IT was provided in the court of our lord the king, holden at Merton on Wedneſday the morrow after the feaſt of St. Vincent, the 20th year of the reign of king Henry the ſon of king John, before William archbiſhop of Canterbury, and other his biſhops and ſuffragans, and before the greater part of the earls and barons of England, there being aſſembled for the coronation of the ſaid king, and Helianor the queen, about which they were all called, where it was treated for the commonwealth of the realm upon the articles underwritten, thus it was provided and granted, as well of the foreſaid archbiſhops, biſhops, earls, and barons, as of the king himſelf and others.

(1) *Coram Cant. archiepiſcopo, et coepiſcopis ſuffraganeis ſuis.*] *Suffraganeus* properly is a vicegerent of a biſhop, inſtituted to aid and aſſiſt him in his ſpirituall office, and is ſo called *a ſuffragiis:* of theſe you may read in the ſtatutes of 26 H. 8. 1 & 2 Phil. & Mariæ. 1 Eliz. And where ſome copies have *coram Cantuar' archiepiſcopo, et coepiſcopis et ſuffraganeis*; this latter conjunction (&) is more then ought to be; for *ſuffraganeis ſuis* muſt referre to *coepiſcopis*, that is that

26 H. 8. cap. 14. 1 & 2 Ph. and Mar. ca. 8. 1 Eliz. ca. 1.

See the first part of the Institutes, Cap. Frankalmoigne. that the bishops should aide and assist the archbishop with their suffrages: for other suffragans, which were vicegerents of bishops, never had voyce in parliament, because they held not *per baroniam*, as all bishops doe, and many abbots and priors, as hath beene said, did, in respect whereof they were lords of parliament.

Pro coronatione ipsius domini regis.] The king was formerly crowned at Gloucester on the 18 of October, in the beginning of the first yeare of his raigne, then being about nine yeares old: and here it appeareth that in the twentieth yeare of his raigne, he was crowned again, then being about 29 yeares old, twice crowned as king Henry the second, and king John before him had been, and as king R. 2. after him was.

Et Elianoræ reginæ.] This Elianor was daughter, and one of the heires of Raymond Berengary earle of Province; she was sister to the earle of Province, and to Boniface, archbishop of Canterbury, and she was crowned at Westminster.

[80] She survived the king, and of a crowned queen became a professed nun in Ambresbury, and died a nun there, in the nineteenth yeare of her widowhood.

The statutes enacted at this parliament are divided into eleven chapters.

CAP. I.

De viduis primo, quæ post mortem virorum suorum expelluntur de dotibus suis, et dotes suas, vel quarentenam suam habere non possunt sine placito, videlicèt, quod quicunque deforciaverit eis dotes suas, vel quarentenam suam, de tenementis quibus viri sui obierunt seisiti, et ipsæ viduæ postea per placitum recuperaverint, si ipsi deforc' de injusto deforciamento convicti fuerint, reddant eisdem viduis damna sua, scilicet valorem totius dotis eis contingentis, à tempore mortis virorum suorum, usque ad diem quo ipsæ viduæ per judicium curiæ seisinam suam inde recuperaverint. Et nihilominus ipsi deforciatores sint in misericordia domini regis.

FIRST, of widows which after the death of their husbands are deforced of their dowers, and cannot have their dowers or quarentine without plea, whosoever deforce them of their dowers or quarentine of the lands, whereof their husbands died seised, and that the same widows after shall recover by plea; they that be convict of such wrongful deforcement shall yield damages to the same widows; that is to say, the value of the whole dower to them belonging from the time of the death of their husbands unto the day that the said widows, by judgement of our court, have recovered seisin of their dower, &c. and the deforcers neverthelesss shall be amerced at the king's pleasure.

(Dyer, 284. pl. 33. 4 Rep. 30. 14 H. 8. 25. 38 Ed. 3. 13. 11 H. 4. 39. Fitz. Dower. 24. 46. 59. 73. Fitz. Damage, 10. 83. 119. 3 Bulstr. 278. V. N. B. fo. 7. Rast. Ent. 22. 1 Inst. 32. b. 9 H. 3. c. 7.)

First part of the Institutes, sect. 36. This chapter is explained in the first part of the Institutes, in all the points thereof, which you may see there at large; whereunto you may adde (upon this word *recuperaverint*) a case in 9 E. 2. that in

in a writ of dower, the tenant plead that the husband is alive, &c. and the triall awarded by proofes, and a day therefore given, &c. at which day the demandant came with her proofes, and the tenant made default, the demandant had judgement to recover, but if the demandant had not had her proofes there, then she should have had but a *petit cape*. Hil. 9. E. 2. fo. 62. b. in libro meo, un fem, &c.

CAP. II.

ITEM omnes viduæ (1) *de cætero possint legare* (2) *blada* (3) *sua de terra sua, tam de dotibus suis, quam de aliis terris, et tenementis suis* (4); *salvis* (5) *consuetudinibus, et servitiis dominorum de feodo, quæ de dotibus, et aliis tenementis suis debentur.*

ALSO from henceforth widows may bequeath the crop of their ground, as well of their dowers, as of other their lands and tenements, saving to the lords of the fee, all such services as be due for their dowers and other tenements.

(Kel. 125. Fitz. Bar. 149. 294.)

Before the making of this statute, it was a question, whether tenant in dower might devise the corn, which she had sowen, or whether he in the reversion should have them. Some held that she could not devise them; or if she devised them not, that her executors should not have them, but he in the reversion, for that her estate was freely created by act in law; and as she when her dower was [81] assigned to her, should have the land sowen, or unsowen for her dower, so at the time of her death, he in the reversion should have the land sowen, or unsowen. And of this opinion is Bracton who saith, *antiquitus solet observari, quod sicut uxor dotem suam recipit post mortem viri sui cultam sive incultam, ita post mortem uxoris solet restitui hæredi culta seu inculta, quia de bladis et fructibus a tenemento non separatis non habuit uxor testamenti factionem, sed nova superveniente gratia, et provisione, sicut patet de provisione apud Merton.* Bracton, lib. 2. fol. 96.

And true it is, that if the husband sow the ground and die, the property of the corne is in the executors, but subject to this condition, that if the heire assigne unto her the land sowen for her dower, she shall have the corne, for she shall be in *de optima possessione viri*, above the title of the executor. 15. El. Dier. 316.

And Fleta saith, *vidua per statutum de Merton poterit disponere de rebus suis, et fructibus in dote sua existentibus, sive separati sint a solo, sive non, quod quidem olim facere non potuit.* Fleta, lib. 2. c. 50.

And they that held this opinion, relied much upon these words, *de cætero*, which imply, as they say, a new law. Now others held the contrary, and that, for advancement of tillage, and incouragement thereunto, which is so profitable for the commonwealth, and by reason of the incertainty of her estate for life they held opinion, that the executors or administrators of the wife should have, or she her selfe by her will might dispose them, as well as any other tenant for life might doe, and they vouch authority before this statute in 4 H. 3. where it is said, note that tenant in dower may devise her corne growing upon the land at the time of her death. Now to cleare this doubt, was this statute made, and *de cætero* may as well be 4 H. 3. devise 26. 19 E. 3. bar. 249. 12 H. 7. 25. Pasch. 38. El. lib. 5. fo. 85.

be applied to the clearing of a doubt from thenceforth, as for making of a new law, and so of necessity it must be taken in this chapter for such lands and tenements, as the widow hath of inheritance, &c. *quam de aliis terris et tenementis suis.*

Regula. (1) *Omnes viduæ, &c.*] *Qui omne dicit, nihil excludit.*

Regula. *Generale dictum generaliter est intelligendum.*

1 part of the Institutes, sect. 51. Custumier de Norm. cap. 102. And therefore where there are five kindes of dowers, *viz.* dower at the common law: dower by the custome: dower *ad ostium ecclesiæ:* dower *ex assensu patris:* and dower *de la pluis beale:* this chapter doth extend to them all. But if the wife be by custome endowed *durante viduitate sua,* and she sowe the ground with corne, and after take husband, hee in the reversion shall have the corne, because though her estate was incertaine, yet she hath determined it by her owne act. (Hil. 44. El. lib. 5. fol. 116. Oland's case.)

(2) *Legare.*] This word is appropriated to a last will, and signifieth to bequeath goods, chattels, and in some cases lands and tenements. *Legatum a lege dicitur, quia lege tenetur ille, cui interest perimplere.*

Bracton, lib. 4. 235. Kelw. 125. (3) *Blada* signifieth corne or graine while it groweth: It properly signifieth corne or graine while it is *in herba, dum seges in herba:* but it is taken for all manner of corne or graine, or things annuall comming by the industry of man, as hemp, flax, &c.

And of this word *blada,* an ingrosser of corne or graine is called *bladier,* but this word *blada* extendeth not by this act to grasse, or to any thing that groweth *suapte natura,* albeit it groweth by sowing of hay-seed, or the like.

(4) *Quam de aliis terris et tenementis suis.*] This is manifestly in affirmance of the common law, and extendeth to the lands, which she hath in franck-mariage, or of any other estate of inheritance, the corne or graine growing thereupon shee may lawfully dispose.

(5) *Salvis, &c.*] Here is a saving to the lords, of whom the
[82] lands in dower, or other lands been holden, such customes and services, as are due unto them, so as they shall not be barred, or prejudiced by this act for or concerning such customes, and services, as they had before, but they shall be saved to them, as if this statute had not been made: for that is the nature of a saving, as hath been said, to save a former right, and to create no new, and by this saving the lord may distreine the corne after it be reaped and put into a cart, for his rents and services, but the corne in sheafes cannot be distreined. (7 H. 7. 10. Kelw. 125.)

See the first part of the Institutes, sect. 68.

CAP. III.

SI quis fuerit disseisitus de libero tenemento suo (1), et coram justic' itinerantibus seisinam suam recuperavit (2), per assisam novæ disseisinæ (3), vel per recognitionem (4) eorum qui fecerint disseisinam: et ipse disseisitus per

ALSO if any be disseised of their freehold, and before the justices in eyre have recovered seisin by assise of novel disseisin, or by confession of them which did the disseisin, and the disseisee hath had seisin delivered

per vic' seisinam suam habuerit (5), *si iidem disseisitores postea, post iter justic', vel infra de eodem tenement' iterum eundem conquerentem disseisiverint* (6), *et inde convicti fuerint* (7), *statim capiantur, et in prisona domini regis detineantur, quousque per dominum regem per redemptionem, vel aliquo alio modo deliberentur* (8). Vide Marlb. cap. 8. *Et hæc est forma qualiter tales convicti puniri debeant, videlicet, cum conquerentes ad curiam veniant, habeant breve domini regis vic' directum, in quo contineatur eorũ narratio de disseisina facta super disseisinã. Et ideo mandetur vic. quod assumptis secũ custodibus placitorũ* (9) *coronæ domini regis, et aliis legalibus militibus in propria persona sua accedat ad tenementũ illud, vel ad pasturã illã de quibus facta fuerit querela, et corã eis per primos juratores* (10), *et per alios vicinos, et legales homines* de vicineto illo, *diligentem inde faciat inquisitionẽ. Et si ipsũ iterũ invenerint disseisitũ (sicut prædictũ est) tunc faciat secundũ provisionẽ prædictã, sin autem, tunc sit conquerens in misericordia domini regis, et alius quietus recedat. Nec debet vic' (sine speciali præcepto domini regis) hujusmodi loquelã prosequi. Eodẽ modo fiat de illis, qui seisinã recuperaverint per assisã mortis antecessoris, et similiter de omnibus terris et tenementis recuperatis per jurat'* (11) *in curia domini regis, si postea disseisiti fuerint a prioribus deforciatoribus, versus quos recuperaverint per jurat' quoquomodo.* Vide W. 2. cap. 26.

delivered by the sheriff, if the same disseisors, after the circuit of the justices, or in the mean time, have disseised the same plaintiff of the same freehold, and thereof be convict, they shall be forthwith taken and committed, and kept in the king's prison, until the king hath discharged them by fine, or by some other mean. And this is the form how such convict persons shall be punished; when the plaintiffs come into the court of our lord the king, they shall have the king's writ directed to the sheriff, in which must be contained the plaint of disseisin framed upon the disseisin. And then it shall be commanded to the sheriff, that he, taking with him the keepers of the pleas of the king's crown, and other lawful knights, in his proper person, shall go unto the land or pasture, whereof the plaint hath been made, and that he make before them, by the first jurors, and other neighbours and lawful men, diligent inquisition thereof; and if they find him disseised again (as before is said) then let him do according to the provision aforementioned; but if it be found otherwise, the plaintiff shall be amerced, and the other shall go quit; neither shall the sheriff execute any such plaint without special commandment of the king. In the same manner shall be done to them that have recovered their seisin by assise of mortdauncestor; and so shall it be of all lands and tenements recovered in the king's court by enquests, if they be disseised after by the first deforceors, against whom they have recovered any wise by enquest.

See the statute of Marlbridge, c. 8. W. 2. cap. 26. See the first part of the Institutes, 233. (18 H. 8. 1. 11 H. 4. 6. 7 H. 7. 4. Fitz. Redisseisin, 6, 8, 9. 1 Inst. 154. a. Hob. 96. 2 Bulstr. 93. 52 H. 3. c. 8. 13 Ed. 1. stat. 1. c. 25, 26. Mirror, 317. Rast. Ent. 548.)

(1) *De libero tenemento suo, &c.*] That is, of land, rent, common, or such like, whereof if a man be disseised he may have an assise *de novel disseisin*. [83]

By this chapter the writs of redisseisin and *post disseisin*, are given for the causes hereafter expressed, which lay not at

 the

the common law, and both these writs are vicountels, and not retournable, but the sheriffes shall hold the plea and give the judgement.

23 Ass. p. 7. 30 Ass. Pl. 35. Bract. li. 4. fo. 236, 237. (2) *Et coram justic' itinerantibus seisinam suam recuperaverit.*] Here justices in eyre are named, but for example, and because assises were taken most commonly before them, for though the assise be taken in the king's bench, or court of common pleas, or before justices of assise, yet is it within this statute: for though Regula. the words be speciall, yet the reason of the law is generall; *et quando lex est specialis, ratio autem generalis, generaliter lex est intelligenda.*

F. N. B. 189. d. 23 Ass. tit. redisseisin 3. 30. ass. 35. (3) *Per assisam novæ disseisinæ.*] This branch extends not to an assise of *mordauncester*, or *darrein presentment*, or of *utrum*; but if a man recover in a writ of redisseisin, upon that recovery he shall have a redisseisin, and the like, as often as he is redisseised.

14 E. 3. redisseisin 8. 14 E. 2. ibid. 9. Upon a plaint in the nature of a fresh force, according to the custome of a city, or borough, and a recovery thereupon had, a redisseisin doth not lie, for no redisseisin doth lie, but where the first plea began by writ.

See the first part of the Institutes, sect. 234. (4) *Per assisam novæ disseisinæ, vel per recognitionem.*] That is to say, by the assise, *i.* the verdict of the recognitors of the assise, or by confession of the disseisor, &c. and yet a redisseisin doth lie upon a recovery in an assise, upon the pleading of a record, and failer of W. 2. cap. 26. Fleta, li. 4. c. 29. it, or upon a demurrer, or by default, or the like; and so it is explained by a later statute.

See the first part of the Institutes. ubi supra, F. N. B. 188. (5) *Per vicecomitem seisinam suam habuerit.*] And so it is, if the plaintife in the assise doth enter and execute the recovery by entrie.

Bract. lib. 2. fol. 294, 295. (6) *Iidem disseisitores postea, &c. de eodem tenemento iterum eundem conquerentem disseisiverunt.*] For the exposition hereof see the first part of the Institutes, sect. 233.

33 E. 3. rediss. 7. 40 Ass. 23. *Et inde convicti fuerint.*] For in the writ of redisseisin the tenant may plead to the writ as joyntenancy, or the like; or in barre, as a release, or the like; or give it in evidence.

Mirror, cap. 5. § 2. Regist. 206. Marleb. ca 8. W. 2. ca. 26. Bracton, lib. 4. fol. 236. b. Fleta, lib. 4. cap. 29. Brit. fol. 24.6. (8) *Statim capiantur et in prisona regis detineantur quousque per dominum regem, per redemptionem, vel alio modo deliberentur.*] And Bracton hereupon saith this, *Talis quidem qui ita convictus fuerit, dupliciter delinquit contra regem, quia facit disseisinam, et roberiam contra pacem suam, et etiam ausu temerario irrita ea quæ in cur' domini regis rite acta sunt: et propter duplex delictum merito sustinere debet pœnam duplicatam.*

And Britton speaking of a redisseisin, *Pur ceo que il desuy de recover' per judgement chose, que il ad conquise per sa proper force in despisant la ley.*

West. 2. c. 8. 7 E. 4. 23. F. N. B. 126. And this reason holdeth in other cases, as after a judgement in an admeasurement of pasture, if there be a surcharge by the party who was admeasured, a writ *de secunda superoneratione* doth lie, and the like.

[84] And it is to be noted, that wheresoever a man did recover the seisin or possession of the land, and the tenant or defendant did after disseise or eject him, this was a contempt at the common law, because it is done against the judgement of the court, and in despite of the Regula. law, for the which the court may commit him, for *interest reipublicæ,* Regula. *ut judicia rata sint: et ea quæ in curia nostra rite acta sunt debite executioni demandari debent.*

(9) *Assumptis*

(9) *Assumptis secum custodibus placitorum.*] This is spoken in the plurall number, therefore where there are two or more coroners, he ought to take at least two, but where there is but one, if he take him, it is sufficient within the meaning of this statute: though regularly the plurall number is not satisfied with one. 23 Ass. p. 7. F. N. B. 189.

(10) *Per primos juratores et alios.*] This must bee understood where there were *juratores* in the assise; for if there were none, then it must be tried onely *per alios:* as if the disseisor plead a record, and fail of it, or if he plead a bar, and confesse an immediate *ouster*, upon which the plaintife doth demur, and judgement is given for the plaintife, and after the plaintife is redisseised, the plaintife shall have a redisseisin, and it shall be tried onely *per alios*, because there were no jurors at all in the former assise; for the statute, (albeit it bee penal) shall not be so literally expounded, that if it cannot be tried *per primos juratores*, that it shall not be tried at all, for *verba intelligi debent cum effectu*. But where there were any jurors, it shall be tried by them and others, and where there were none, then by others alone; but if there were jurors in the assise, and they all die, and after he which recovered is redisseised, there (by the act of God) the redisseisin faileth. And so it is, if all the jurors be dead saving one, because the words of the statute be, *per primos juratores, et alios:* and so note a diversity where there were never any *juratores* at all, for there the statute could by no possibility have wrought, but upon others onely, but where there were once *juratores*, and the party neglecteth his time, and by the act of God they faile, there the redisseisin failes, because it cannot be tried *per primos juratores*, (which sometimes were in *esse*) *et alios*, as the statute speaketh. *Regula.* 8 H. 5. 1. F. N. B. 189. h.

(11) *Eodem modo fiat de illis, qui seisinam recuperaverunt per assisam mortis antecessoris, et similiter de omnibus terris et tenementis recuperatis per juratam, &c.*] Here is the *post disseisin* given, where the recovery in a *mordaunc'*, or in any other reall action is by verdict, and in this case the recoveror shall have a *post disseisin* against the former tenant being deforceour, that disseised him after the recovery; but if the recovery be by reddition or default, &c. he shall have a *post disseisin* upon the statute of W. 2. cap. 26. *Nota*, here *eodem modo* are words of great operation, for they imply, that there must be *idem conquerens de eodem tenemento, et idem tenens*, against whom the recovery was had after the same manner, as is before said in case of a redisseisin. Post disseisin. Marlebr. c. 8. W. 2. ca. 26. F. N. B. 190. Regist. 206. b.

CAP. IV.

*[85]

ITEM quia multi magnates Angliæ, qui feoffaverunt milites et alios libere tenentes (2) *suos de parvis tenementis in magnis maneriis suis, questi fuerunt, quod commodum suum facere non potuerunt* (1) *de residuo maneriorum* (3) *suorum* *, *sicut de vastis, boscis, et pasturis* communibus, *cum ipsi feoffati habeant*

ALSO because many great men of England (which have infeoffed knights and their freeholders of small tenements in their great manors) have complained that they cannot make their profit of the residue of their manors, as of wastes, woods, and pastures, whereas the same feoffees have sufficient

habeant ſufficientem paſturam, quantum pertinet ad tenementa ſua; ita *proviſum eſt, et conceſſum, quod quicunque hujuſmodi feoffati aſſiſam novæ diſſeiſinæ deferant de communia paſturæ ſuæ, et coram juſtic' recognit' fuerit* (7), *quod tantam paſturam habeant, quantum ſufficit ad tenementa ſua, et quod habeant liberũ ingreſſum* (4), *et egreſſum, de liberis tenementis ſuis, uſque ad paſturam ſuam: tunc inde ſint contenti, et illi de quibus conqueſti fuerint recedant quieti* (6), *de hoc quod commodũ ſuum de terris, vaſtis, boſcis, et paſturis fecerint* (5). *Si autem dixerint, quod ſufficientem paſturã non habeant, vel ſufficientem ingreſſum, vel egreſſum, quantum pertinet ad tenementa ſua: tunc inquiratur veritas per aſſiſam. Et ſi per aſſiſam recognitum fuerit* (8), *quod per eoſdem deforciatores, in aliqua fuerit impeditus eorum ingreſſus, vel egreſſus, vel quod non habeant ſufficientem paſturã, et ſufficientem ingreſſum, et egreſſum, ſicut prædictum eſt: tunc recuperent ſeiſinam ſuam, per viſum juratorum, ita quod per diſcretionem et ſacramentum eorum habeant conquerentes ſufficientem paſturam, et ſufficientẽ ingreſſũ et egreſſũ in forma prædict', et diſſeiſitores ſint in miſericordia domini regis, et dampna reddant, ſicut reddi ſolent ante proviſionẽ iſtã. Si autẽ recognitũ fuerit per aſſiſam, quod querentes ſufficientẽ habeant paſturam, cum libero et ſufficienti ingreſſu et egreſſu, ſicut præd' eſt: tunc licitè* & libere *faciant* dom' *commodum ſuum de reſiduo, et recedant de ill' aſſiſa quieti. Weſt.* 2. *cap.* 48.

ſufficient paſture, as much as belongeth to their tenements; it is provided and granted, That whenever ſuch feoffees do bring an aſſiſe of novel diſſeiſin for their common of paſture, and it is knowledged before the juſticers, that they have as much paſture as ſufficeth to their tenements, and that they have free egreſs and regreſs from their tenement unto the paſture, then let them be contented therewith; and they on whom it was complained ſhall go quit of as much as they have made their profit of their lands, waſtes, woods, and paſtures; and if they alledge that they have not ſufficient paſture, or ſufficient ingreſs and egreſs according to their hold, then let the truth be inquired by aſſiſe; and if it be found by the aſſiſe, that the ſame deforceors have diſturbed them of their ingreſs and egreſs, or that they had not ſufficient paſture (as before is ſaid) then ſhall they recover their ſeiſin by view of the inqueſt: ſo that by their diſcretion and oath the plaintiffs ſhall have ſufficient paſture, and ſufficient ingreſs and egreſs in form aforeſaid; and the diſſeiſors ſhall be amerced, and ſhall yield damages, as they were wont before this proviſion. And if it be certified by the aſſiſe, that the plaintiffs have ſufficient paſture, with ingreſs and egreſs, as before is ſaid, let the other make their profit of the reſidue, and go quit of that aſſiſe.

Mirror, cap. 5. § 2. Bract. li. 4. fol. 222. Britton, cap. 58. Fleta, li. 4. ca. 20. (1 Roll. 365. 8 Ed. 3. 39. 7 Ed. 3. 67. Mirror, 318. Enforced by 3 & 4 Ed. 6. c. 3. 13 Ed. 1. ſtat. 1. c. 46. 2 Vern. 290. 322.)

(1) *Quod commodum ſuum facere non potuerunt.*] Hereby it appeareth, that the lord could not approve by the order of the common law, becauſe the common iſſued out of the whole waſte, and of every part thereof, and yet ſee Tr. 6 H. 3. where the lord approved two acres, and left ſufficient, the tenant brought an aſſiſe, and the ſpeciall matter being found, the plaintife *retraxit ſe.*

Tr. 6 H. 3. tit. Common 26.

(2) *Libere*

(2) *Libere tenentes.*] The purview of this ſtatute extends onely for the lord to make an approvement againſt his tenant, and not againſt any ſtranger, nor where the lord had common appendant in the tenancy, as he may have; but the ſtatute of W. 2. provideth, *De cætero quod ſtatutum de Merton, proviſum inter dominos et tenentes ſuos locum habeat de cætero inter dominos vaſtorum boſcorum, et paſturarum, et vicinos, &c.*

W. 2. ca. 46. Bract. lib. 4. fol. 228. Fleta, lib. 4. ca. 20. 18 Aſſ. p. 4. 18 E. 3. 43. 19 E. 3. tit. Aſſ. 18 Aſſ. p. 4.

(3) *De reſiduo maneriorum.*] By this recitall a point of the auncient common law appeareth, that when a lord of a mannor (wherein was great * waſte grounds) did enfeoffe others of ſome parcells of arable land, the feoffees *ad manutenend. ſervitium ſocæ*, ſhould have common in the ſaid waſts of the lord for two cauſes. 1. As incident to the feoffement, for the feoffee could not plough, and manure his ground without beaſts, and they could not bee ſuſtained without paſture, and by conſequence the tenant ſhould have common in the waſtes of the lord for his beaſts, which doe plough and manure his tenancy, as appendant to his tenancy, and this was the beginning of common appendant. The ſecond reaſon was for maintenance and advancement of agriculture, and tillage, which was much favoured in law; like as when a man gives the land to a parſon and his ſucceſſors, whereupon a church is built for the ſervice of God, to hold of him in *frankalmoigne*, the land is holden, and by conſequent, and operation of law, the advowſon, which the law doth give to the founder, that is, the giver of the land, is alſo holden, for that the advowſon doth in a manner adhere to the church, and as the tenant had made a feoffement before the ſtatute of *quia emptores terrarum*, to hold of himſelfe by fealty, and xij. d. this meſnalty by operation of law had been holden of the lord paramount.

F. N. B. 179. e. W. 2. ca. 46. 18 Aſſ p. 4. 18 E. 3. 43. and above cited.

* [86]

Temps E. 1. Common 24. 17 E. 2. ibid. 23. 18 E. 3. 30. 20 E. 3. Admeaſurement 8. Mich. 26 & 27 Eliz. lib. 4. fol. 37. Tirringham's caſe. Pl. Com. 498. b.

(4) *Tantam paſturam habeant, quantum ſufficit ad tenementa ſua, et quod habeant liberum ingreſſum.*] The lord may approve againſt a tenant that hath * common of paſture appendant, but if the lord graunt common of paſture within his waſts, there is no approvement by this act againſt a common in groſſe, for the words of the ſtatute be *quantum pertinet ad tenementa ſua, &c.*

* See the firſt part of the Inſtitutes, ſect. 184.

And ſo was the law taken and adjudged ſoon after the making of this act, and latter authorities agree with the ſame; and albeit the common appendant be without a certain number, as to have ſufficient paſture for beaſts, *quantum pertinet ad tenementa ſua,* which may be reduced to a certainty, for, *id certum eſt quod certum reddi poteſt,* and therefore this act doth extend to it. And the writ of admeaſurement of paſture doth lie only for and againſt ſuch commoners, as have common appendant, for the words of the writ be, *et ad ipſos pertinet habendum ſecundum liberum tenementum ſuum, &c.* ſo as common appendant, be it certain or incertain, is within this ſtatute; and ſo is common appurtenant certaine or incertaine, for *pertinet* extendeth as well to common appurtenant as appendant.

W. 2. cap. 46. 31 E. 1. Common. 26. 32 E. 1. ibid. 29. 3 E. 2. ibid. 21. 10 E. 3. 56. 34 Aſſ. 11. 22 Aſſ. p. 65. 7 H. 4. 33. 11 H. 4. 26. a. F. N. B. 125. See Bracton, li. 4. fol. 228.

Bracton treating of this chapter, ſaith, *imprimis videndum eſt qualiter conſtitutio illa ſit intelligenda, ne male intellecta trahat utentes ad abuſum:* and then expoundeth the ſame in this manner: 1. *Si ſit alienus (et non proprie tenens) non ei imponit legem conſtitutio.*

Bracton ubi ſupra.

2. *Si fuer' liberi tenentes proprii, tunc refert qualiter fuer' feoffati, &c. utrum feoffati fuer' large ſcilicet p. totū, et ubiq;, et in omnibus, locis, et ad omnimoda averia, et ſine numero, &c.* So as by his opinion

nion this ſtatute extendeth not to a common in groſſe, nor to a common ſans number; *tales*, ſaith he, *non ligat conſtitutio memorata, quia feoffamentum, (i. conceſſionem communiæ) non tollit, licet tollat abuſum.*

3. *Si autem communia fuer' ſtricta cum numero averiorum certo, &c.* (which he intendeth of common appendant) *licet uſus ſe largius et latius habuerit quam neceſſe eſſet, tales ligat conſtitutio quod coarctentur ad certum locum, et infra certum locum, dum tamen locus inde ſufficiens ſit et competens cum libero ingreſſu, et egreſſu, et competenti, quod non ſit gravis nec difficilis: competens autem debet eſſe locus ita quod non longius diſtet, ſed propinquius aſſignetur, &c. cum diſtantia inducit incommoditatem.*

4. *Item eodem modo ſi ita feoffatus fuerit quis, ſine expreſſione numeri vel generis, ſed ita, cum paſtura quantum pertinet ad tantum tenementum in eadem villa, talem ligat conſtitutio ſicut prius cum expreſſione; quia cum conſtet de quantitate tenementi, de facili perpendi poterit de numero averiorum, et etiam de genere ſecundum conſuetudinem locorum.*

[87] 5. *Item tempus ſpectandum erit cum omnis nova conſtitutio, futuris formam imponere debeat et non præteritis.*

Tr. 18 E. 1. in Banco Rot. 50. Cantabr.

Note this caſe for common, &c.

Walterus Bonde implacitat Aliciam de Bordeley, & vi. alios pro eo quod cum averiis ſuis blada ſua ad Madingle creſcentia noctanter depaſti ſunt, &c. Alic' & Nicholaus Ruſſell dic' quod placea ubi tranſgreſſio ſupponitur fieri vocatur Leylonſurlonge, quæ quidem placea ſemper fuit pratum uſque ad prædictum annum quod prædictus Walterus prædictum pratum aravit, & ſeminavit, & in quo prato ipſa Alicia habet communiam ſuam poſt fena levata: et quia prædictus Walterus, ad auferendum ei communiam ſuam in prædicto prato, ſeminavit, ſicut prædictum eſt, dicunt quod quando fena in pratis adjacentibus levata fuerunt, ipſi cum averiis ſuis communiam ſuam in prædicta placea depaſti fuerunt, ſicut eis bene licuit. Et inde ponunt ſe ſuper patriam. Walterus dic' quod in electione ſua eſt ad dimittend' prædictam placeam jacere pratum, & illud falcare, vel placeam illam arare, & ſeminare pro voluntate ſua. Et de hoc ponit ſe ſuper patriam, &c. * *Jur' dict' quod prædicta placea à tempore quo non extat memoria fuit pratum falcabile, uſq; ad prædictum annum quod prædictus Walterus illud aravit: dicunt etiam quod prædictus Walterus eſt parvus tenens ejuſdem villæ, &* * *non licet alicui tali parvo tenenti ſine licentia ipſius Aliciæ prata aliqua in eadem villa arare, & quod prædicta Alicia in eiſdem pratis poſt fena aſportata communicare debet* *: *dic' etiam quod quando fena in pratis adjacentibus levata fuerint, ipſi cum averiis ſuis communiam ſuam in prædicta placea depaſti fuerunt, ſicut bene licitum eſt eis; ideo conſiderat' eſt quod* * *prædictus Walterus nihil capiat per breve ſuum, ſed ſit in miſericordia. Et affer' per jur' ad dimid. marc.*

* Verdict.

* Note this cuſtome.

* Note this, for feeding of corn, Vide 21 E.4.41.

* Judgement.

Vide Paſch. 15 E. 1. in Banco. Rot. 6. Buck. Lib. 5. fol. 78. common of paſture, *ſub modo*, or with limitation.

Throughout all this ſtatute, *paſtura et communia paſturæ*, is named ſo as this ſtatute of approvements doth not extend to common of piſchary, of turbary, of eſtovers, or the like.

(5) *Quod commodum ſuum de terris vaſtis, &c. fecerint.*] Now it is to be ſeene how this approvement muſt be. And it muſt be divided by ſome incloſure or defence, as it may be made ſeverall, for it is lawfull to the tenant to put on his cattle into the reſidue of the common, and if they ſtray into that part,

† whereof

whereof the approvement is made, in default of incloſure, he is no treſpaſſer.

And if the lord make a feoffement of certain acres, the feoffee may incloſe, becauſe the feoffement is an approvement in his nature 31 E. 1. Common 27. 16 E. 2. Garr. de Charters 31.

(6) *Tunc inde ſint contenti, et illi de quibus conqueſti fuer' recedant quieti de hoc quod commodum ſuum de terris vaſtis, &c. fecerint.*] By the approvement of part according to this ſtatute, that part by this act is diſcharged of the common, in ſo much as if the tenant which hath the common purchaſe that part, his common is not extinguiſhed in the reſidue. 10 E. 3. 15. Dier. Mich. 16 & 17 Eliz. 339.

If the lord, &c. doe make an approvement, hee may improve eft-ſoons as oft as hee will, ſo hee leave ſufficient common, and ſo it was done in 18 E. 3. 18 Aſſ. p. 4. 18 E. 3. 30. 43.

If the tenant at the time of the approvement have ſufficient common left unto him in the reſidue, with a competent way thereunto, according to this act, and after the reſidue becommeth not ſufficient; yet the approvement remaineth good, for the words of this act be, *tantam paſturam habeant, quantum ſufficit ad tenementa ſua.* 8 Aſſ. 18. 16 E. 3. Common 9. [88]

(7) *Coram juſticiariis recognitum fuit, &c.*] And yet it may bee tried in an action of treſpaſſe: for many times he ſhall faile to have an aſſiſe. 10 E. 3. 15.

Or if the lord doth incloſe any part, and leave not ſufficient common in the reſidue, the commoner may break down the whole incloſure, becauſe it ſtandeth upon the ground which is his common. 8 E. 3. 38. 16 E. 3. Common 9. 22 Aſſ. 42. 15 H. 7. 10.

Bracton reciteth a writ deviſed upon this ſtatute by that ſage of the law William de Ralegh, one of the kings juſtices, in caſe where the lord was diſturbed to incloſe, or when hee had incloſed according to this ſtatute, and his incloſure broken downe, which you may reade there at large. Bracton, li. 4. fo. 222. a. & 227.

(8) *Et per aſſiſam recognitum fuit.*] If by the aſſiſe it ſhall be found, that the plaintiſe had not ſufficient ingreſſe and egreſſe, or not ſufficient paſture, then the plaintiſe ſhall recover ſeiſin by the view of the jurors; ſo that by the diſcretion and oath of them, the plaintiſe ſhall have ſufficient paſture, and ſufficient ingreſſe and egreſſe aſſigned to him, and that the diſſeiſors ſhall be amerced, and yeeld damages.

Upon this branch of the ſtatute, we have a notable caſe in our books, viz. a commoner brought an aſſiſe of common of paſture belonging to his freehold, the tenant ſaid, that he was lord, &c. and approved part of his waſte, and left the plaintiſe ſufficient common, &c. The plaintiſe denied that he left ſufficient common, and thereupon iſſue was taken, and Sir William Herle chieſe juſtice of the court of common pleas tooke the aſſiſe, and the aſſiſe found, that the plaintiſe had not ſufficient common; whereupon the court did award that the plaintiſe ſhould recover his common, &c. and the recognitors of the aſſiſe were going from the barre: and albeit the iſſue was found againſt the tenant, yet for his advantage the recognitors of the aſſiſe ought to come back again, and to ordaine by their diſcretion and oath ſufficient common to the plaintiſe, ſo that the defendant might approve of the remnant by this ſtatute of Merton, as Trewood affirmed: whereupon Sir William Herle peruſed this ſtatute (for no man can carry the words of a poſitive law by parliament in his head) and found the ſtatute as Trewood had ſaid, and 7 E. 3. fol. 67.

therefore was in purpofe to have caufed the jurors to come againe (the record yet being in his breft) to appoint fufficient common to the plaintife according to the ftatute, but it was prevented, for that the parties agreed.

CAP. V.

SIMILITER provifum eft, et à domino rege conceffum, quod de cætero non current ufuræ contra aliquem infra ætatem exiften' a tempore mortis anteceffo-ris fui, cujus hæres ipfe eft ufque ad legitimam ætatem fuam, ita tamen quod propter hoc non remaneat folutio debiti principalis fimul cum ufuris ante mortem anteceffo-ris fui, cujus hæres ipfe eft inde provenientibus.

LIKEWISE it is provided and granted by the king, that from henceforth ufuries fhall not run againft any being within age, from the time of the death of his anceftor (whofe heir he is) unto his lawful age; fo neverthelefs, that the payment of the principal debt, with the ufury that was before the death of his anceftor (whofe heir he is) fhall not remain.

(1 Inft. 246. b. 1 Roll. 151. 37 H. 8. c. 9.)

[89]

Inter leges Sancti Edw. Lamb. Si quis de ufura convictus. Glanvil, lib. 5. ca. 16. Ockham ca. qualiter non abfolvitur. Ca. Itineris de Chriftianis ufurariis 15 E. 3. ca. 5. Rot. parl. 50 E. 3. nu. 58. 6 R. 2. nu. 57. 14 R 2. nu. &c. [a] Sta. de Judaifmo fee hereafter the expofition of it.

This ftatute hath been diverfly expounded.

1. That this ftatute extended to the ufurious Jewes, that then were in England: for at that time and before the conqueft alfo, it was not lawful for Chriftians to take any ufury, as it appeareth by the lawes of Saint Edward, &c. and Glanville and other auncient authors and records. And by this act it is manifeft that the ufury intended by the ftatute was not unlawfull, for the ufury due before the death of the auncestor is enacted to be paid, and after the full age of the heire alfo, and no ufury was then permitted but by the Jewes only.

[a] But king Edward the firft (that mirror of princes) by authority of parliament made this law, which is worthy to be written in letters of gold: Forafmuch as the king had feene that many of the evils and difherifons of the good men of his realme had come to paffe by the ufuries which the Jewes had made in times paft, and many other mifchiefes had rifen thereupon, albeit that the faid king and his auncefters have had great profit of the Jewes: neverthelesse in honour of God, and for common weale of the people; it is ordeined and eftablifhed, that no Jewe from thenceforth fhould take any ufury, &c. But yet provideth for the time paft in fuch manner, as by the act appeareth.

[b] Rot. Pat 3 E. 1. m. 14. 17. 26.

And true it is, that great was the profit (as in that act is recited) that the crowne had by the Jewes, [b] for betweene the 50 yeare of H. 3. and the 2 yeare of E. 1. the crowne was anfwered *de exitibus Judaifmi* foure hundred and twenty thoufand pounds, and then the ounce of filver was five greats.

Pl com. 126. b. 35 H. 6. 61.

Others expound thefe words *non currant ufuræ contra aliquem infra ætatem exiftentem* in this manner, that the rent fhall not be doubled during the nonage of the heire (which in a large fenfe is called ufury, for *dicitur ufura quia datur pro ufu æris*). As if the king

king give land to another, reserving a rent payable at a feast certaine, and for default of payment, that he shall double the rent for every default, and after the grantee dieth his heire within age, he shall not double the rent to the king.

If a man by obligation bind himselfe and his heires to pay 100 l. at such a feast, and if he pay it not at that feast, that then he and his heires shall pay 10 l. for every quarter it shall be behinde, the obligor dieth and leaveth assets in fee simple his heire within age, he shall have his age, and shall not pay this 10 l. incurred during his minority after his full age; and this agreeth with the words of the statute, *Non remaneat solutio debiti principalis*, and in this case there is a *principale debitum*, but *debitum* signifieth not only debt, for the which an action of debt doth lie, but here in this ancient act of parliament it signifieth generally any duty to be yeelded or paid; for *debitum* is derived of the verb *debeo*, *id enim est, quod vel lege naturæ, vel obligatione civili debetur*, as rents and the like. 11 H. 7. 22. Mich. 26 & 27. El. lib. 3. fol. 13.

So if A. knowledge a recognizance to B. of 20l. to be paid at a certain feast, and A. doth grant, that if the 20l. be not paid at the day, then he shall pay 10 s. a weeke for every week it shalbe behind, and before the feast A. dieth seased of fee simple lands, his heire within age; in a *scire facias* upon the recognizance the heire shall have his age, as in the next case before, by the common law, and after his full age he shall be freed of the 10 s. a weeke by this statute. 11 E. 3. age 4. 15 E. 3. ibidem. 95. 29 ass. 37. 29 E. 3. 50. 42 ass. 4.

CAP. VI.

*[90]

*De hæredibus per parentes, vel per alios, contra pacem vi abductis, vel detentis, seu maritatis, ita provisũ est, qd. quicunque * laicus inde convictus fuerit* (1), *quod puerũ aliquẽ sic detinuerit, abduxerit, seu maritaverit, reddat perdenti valorẽ maritagii: et pro delicto corpus ejus capiatur, ut imprisonetur, donec perdenti emendaverit delictũ si puer maritetur: et præterea donec domino regi satisfecerit pro transgressione sua. Et hoc de hærede infra quatuordecim annos existen'* (2). *De hærede autẽ cum sit quatuordecim annorum, vel ultra, usque ad plenam ætatem, si se maritaverit sine licentia domini sui, ut ei auferat maritagiũ suum, et dominus ejus offerat* (3) *ei rationabile maritagium, ubi non disparagetur* (4), *dominus suus tunc teneat terrã* (5) *ejus ultra terminũ ætatis suæ, scilicet xxj. annorũ, per tantũ tẽpus quod inde possit percipere* (6) *duplicẽ*

OF heirs that be led away, and withholden, or married by their parents, or by other, with force against our peace, thus it is provided, that whatsoever layman be convict thereof, that he hath so withholden any child, led away, or married, he shall yield to the loser the value of the marriage; and for the offence his body shall be taken and imprisoned until he hath recompensed the loser, if the child be married; and further, until he hath satisfied the king for the trespass. And this must be done of an heir being within the age of fourteen years. And touching an heir being fourteen years old, or above unto his full age, if he marry without licence of his lord to defraud him of the marriage, and his lord offer him reasonable and convenient marriage (without disparagement) then his lord shall hold his land beyond the term of his age, that is to say,

plicē valorē maritagii, secundū æstimationē legaliū hominū (7), *vel secundū quod ei pro eodē maritagio prius fuerit oblatum, sine fraude et malitia* (8), *et secundū quod probari poterit in curia domini regis.*

say, of one and twenty years, so long that he may receive the double value of the marriage after the estimation of lawful men, or after as it hath been offered before without fraud or collusion, and after as it may be proved in the king's court.

Bracton, lib. 2. fo. 91. Fleta, li. 1. cap. 12. 3 E. 3. 3. 8 E. 3. 52. 21 E. 3. 52. 21 E. 3. 19. 29 ass. 35. 29 E. 3. 37. (1 Inst. 76. a. 4 Rep. 82. 6 Rep. 74. 9 Rep. 72. Dyer, 255. to 260. pl. 23. Bro. Forf. de Marriage, 9, 12, 13. Bro. Gar. 109. 40 Ed. 3. 6. 1 Inst. 80, a. 81. b. Hob. 94. 90.)

Before the making of this statute the law gave the lord two severall remedies, if his ward were taken away, detained, or maried, *viz.* 1. An action of trespasse, wherein he should recover damages only. 2. Or a writ of right of ward, wherein he should recover the custody of body, and lands, but if the ward were maried, then was he driven to his action of trespasse *Quare se intrusit maritagio non satisfact.* The lord had also his writ, but that lieth against the heire, when he entreth into the land before or after his full age: also the lord may have his writ *de valore maritagii* at the common law, but that lay also against the heire himselfe after his full age when he intruded not.

Tr. 9. El. lib. 9. fo. 72 Doct. Hussey's case. 7 E. 3. 58. 40 E. 3. 6. 31. ass. 26. F. N. B. 141.

The writ of *ravishment de garde* is framed by the statute of W. 2. cap. 35. whereof more shalbe said hereafter in his proper place.

This statute giveth, that in the writ of right of ward the plaintife should recover *Valorem maritagii, et pro delicto corpus ejus capiatur, ut imprisonetur donec perdenti emendaverit delictum, si puer maritetur: et præterea donec domino regi satisfecerit pro transgressione sua.*

8 E. 3. 52. Regist. 161.

(1) *Si laicus inde convictus fuer'.*] The Mirror saith, that this point is reprovable, insomuch as the statute extends not to clerks, *car est nient pluis droit que clerke peche sans payne, que lay home.*

Mirror, ca. 5. § 3.

(2) *Et hoc de hærede infra* 14. *annos existen'.*] Upon these, and the words subsequent this statute doth not extend to the heire female, for the age of consent to mariage of a male is 14, and of a woman 12, and after 14 (at the making of this statute) the female was to be out of ward.

35 H. 6. 53. See the first part of the Institutes, § 104. Custumier de Norm. cap. 33. & les comentaries superinde.

But note albeit the mariage within the age of consent be voydable, yet the gardein shall recover the value, and albeit the heire at the age of consent disagree, so as the gardein shall have the mariage again, yet there is no remedy for the ravisher.

Now what alterations the statute of W. 1. cap. 22. and W. 2. cap. 35. have made, doe at large appear in Docter Husseys case abovesaid, and in the first part of the Institutes.

7 H. 6. 12. 21 E. 3. 19. 20. 27 H. 6. gard. 18. 1. part of the Institutes, sect. 103.

(3) *Si se maritaverit sine licentia domini, &c. Et dominus ejus offerat.*] Here the statute provideth remedy when the heire male, after the age of 14 yeares (when he may, as is aforesaid, consent to mariage) after tender made marieth himselfe without the licence of his lord, and giveth a writ of forfeiture of mariage, so called, because the lord shall thereby recover the double value of the

[91]

the mariage; as if the mariage were worth one hundred pounds, he ſhall recover two hundred pounds. But this forfeiture of mariage is not due by this ſtatute, but where the gardein after 14, and before 21, had tendered a covenable mariage to him, and he refuſed her, and of himſelfe maried (as it were in deſpite of him) another within age; and ſo is this ſtatute to be conſtrued, that the ward maried himſelf without licence, &c. after the lord had tendered unto him a covenable mariage; for if the ward firſt marie himſelfe after the age of 14, a tender of mariage to him that is ſo maried is void, and the ſtatute muſt be intended of a lawfull tender. And this ſtatute that only giveth the forfeiture of mariage not extending to an heire female, there is no forfeiture of mariage of an heire female.

18 E. 3. 18. 14 E. 3. Action ſur leſtatute 16. F. N. B. 241. g. Regiſt.

1. part of the Inſtitutes, § 103. Bro. forfeiture de marriage 12. 4 Jacobi, lib. 6. fo. 70, 71. Seignor Darcies caſe. 19 E. 3. Judgement 123. W. 1. c. 22. No forfeiture of marriage of an heire femal.

But if a ward be taken away and maried *infra annos nubiles*, at the age of ten yeares, there, for that he may diſagree, the lord may tender to him after his age of fourteen, which if he refuſe, and after diſagree, and mary elſewhere within age, the gardein ſhall have the forfeiture.

(4) *Ubi non diſparagetur.*] Vide Magna Charta cap. 6. and ſee the next chapter following.

(5) *Dominus ſuus tunc teneat terrã,* &c.] The lord ſhall have election either to waive the land, and to take his action of forfeiture of mariage, (for perhaps the land may be of ſmall value, and the mariage of great value,) or to enter into the land, and take the profits, till of the ſame he be ſatisfied thereby of the double value: for the words of the ſtatute be *per tantum tempus quod inde poſſit percipere duplicem valorem,* ſo as the taking of the profits in that caſe ſhall goe in ſatisfaction of the double value; but if the heire ouſte the gardein before he be fully ſatisfied of the forfeiture, the gardein ſhall recover the whole forfeiture againſt him, becauſe the heire ſhall not take advantage of his owne wrong, and the double value is caſual.

18 E. 3. 182. E. 2. action ſur leſtatute 23. 16 E. 3. ibidem 14.

43 E. 3. 20. 13 H. 7. 7. 40 E. 3. 6. 4 Jac. li. 6. fo. 70. Dier 9 El. 260. b.

The king ſhall have the forfeiture of the mariage, albeit he be not particularly named, but then the king muſt purſue the ſtatute, and make a tender, for in caſe of the forfeiture there muſt be a tender, but not for the ſingle value.

The grauntee of the body only either by the king or a common perſon ſhall not retaine the land, but he may have upon a tender and mariage elſewhere within age a forfeiture of mariage.

If the gardein entereth into the land for the double value, he cannot have a writ of forfeiture of mariage, although he waive the poſſeſſion of the land.

Temps E. 1. action ſur leſtat. 36.

(6) *Quod inde poſſit percipere,* &c.] If the gardein entereth into the land, and after ſuffer others to take the profits, ye he ſhall hold it no longer then he might have levied the double value, and his negligence ſhall be his own damage.

Mich. 41 & 42. El. li. 4. 82. Sir Andrew Corbets caſe. 15 E. 4, 5.

Although the ſtatute ſaith, *Dominus teneat terram,* yet if he die, his executors or adminiſtrators ſhall hold the land, or have a writ of forfeiture of mariage, for this act had veſted an intereſt therein in the lord, which after his death goeth to his executors, or adminiſtrators, as it doth to the ſucceſſors of an abbot.

7 H. 6. 12. 11 H. 6. 8. 15 H. 7. 14. See the 1. part of the Inſtitutes, ſect. 110.

But if the heire in ward die either within age, or of full age before the value or the forfeiture (as the caſe require) be yeelded or paid, there the lord hath no remedy by action for this incertaine perſonall

27 H. 8. 3. 28. aſſ. 7. 11 H. 4. 82. Dier 14. El. 306. 41. aſſ. p. 15.

7 H. 4. 6. 18 E. 3. 18 Dier ubi supra. personall duty against his heires, executors or administrators, no more then an action of debt lyeth against executors upon an escape made by the gardien upon the statute of W. 2. and yet Thirning chiefe justice held opinion, that if I give lands in tayl to hold of me by knights service, and the donee *devie son issue deins age, et ieo tender a luy mariage, et il ceo refuse, et luy marie sans ma volunt, uncore esteant*
[92] *deins age, et puis morust in cest case ieo retiendra la terre pur la forfeiture del double value accordant al statute de Merton, et le procheine heire in tayle navera remedy,* whereby it appeareth that by his opinion the gardein after the death of the heire might hold the land by this statute for the double value.

Wherein it is to be observed that the lord, or donor shall have nothing but the land holden of him, and which moved from him, until he be satisfied with the profits of that land of the double value by the words and meaning of this statute, the words whereof be, *teneat terram per tantum tempus quod inde possit percipere duplicem valorem.* But otherwise it is of the single value, for there the profits taken by the lord goe not in satisfaction of the value, as shall be said in the next chapter.

14 El. Dier. 306. And the grantee of the body only is without remedy, if the heire dieth.

And albeit the statute saith *teneat terram,* yet it extendeth to the holding of the mesnalty by the lord paramount, and in many cases the measne shall be supposed to hold the land.

(7) *Secundum æstimationem legaliū hominum.*] That is, by a jury of twelve men in an action to be brought: concerning the forfeiture or value of the marriage consideration must not only be had of that land that is holden, but of all other lands, leases, goods, and chattels, and other personall estate which may advance the estimation of the ward, and yet the value of the marriage ought to be so moderate, as the heire may well undergoe the same.

(8) *Vel secundum quod ei pro eodē maritagio prius fuerit oblatū sine fraude,* &c.] And herein the gardein hath the election either to have so much, as an indifferent jury will give him, or so much as for the marriage have *bona fide* been offered unto him.

CAP. VII.

DE dominis qui maritaverint illos quos habent in custod' villanis, vel aliis, sicut burgens. ubi disparagent': si talis hæres fuerit infra 14. annos, et talis ætatis quod consentire non possit matrimonio: tunc si parentes conquerantur de illo domino, dominus ille amittat custodiã usque ad ætatem hæredis, et omne commodũ quod inde perceptũ fuerit, convertatur in commodũ ipsius hæredis, qui infra ætatem est, secundum dispositionem et provisionẽ parent' suorũ, propter dedecus ei factum. Si autẽ fuerit 14. annorũ et ultra, qd. consentire poterit, et tali maritagio consenserit, nulla sequatur pœna. Si quis hæres, cujuscunque fuerit ætatis, pro domino suo se noluerit maritare, non compellatur hoc facere, sed cum ad ætatẽ pervenerit, det domino suo, et satisfaciat ei de tanto, quantum inde percipere posset ab aliquo pro maritagio suo (1), *antequam terrã suã recipiat, et hoc sive se voluerit maritare, sive non: quia maritagiũ ejus, qui infra ætatem est, de mero jure pertinet ad dominum feodi* (2).

AND as touching lords, which marry those that they have in ward to villains, or other, as burgesses where they be disparaged, if any such an heir be within the age of fourteen years, and of such age, that he cannot consent to marriage, then, if his friends complain of the same lord, the lord shall lose the wardship unto the age of the heir; and all the profit, that thereof shall be taken, shall be converted to the use of the heir being within age, after the disposition and provision of his friends, for the shame done to him; but if he be fourteen years, and above, so that he may consent, and do consent to such marriage, no pain shall follow. If an heir (of what age soever he be) will not marry at the request of his lord, he shall not be compelled thereunto; but when he cometh to full age, he shall give to his lord, and pay him as much as any would have given him for the marriage before the receipt of his land, and that whether he will marry himself, or not; for the marriage of him that is within age of meer right pertaineth to the lord of the fee.

(9 H. 3. c. 6. Regist. 161, &c. 3 Ed. 1. c. 22. 13 Ed. 1. stat. 1. c. 35. Kel. 133. Dyer, 25. 260. 306. Fitz. Brief. 937. Fitz. Gard. 68. 128. 131. 138. 153, 156. 6 Rep. 70. 73. 5 Rep. 126. b. Co. Ent. 396. Cro. El. 469.)

[93]

Sicut burgensibus, &c.] Hereof see the first part of the Institutes: and albeit the statute of 5 R. 2. cap. 4. doth rank divers degrees that are to come to parliament, as dukes, earles, barons, banerets, knights of shires, citizens, and burgesses; yet this act of Merton doth extend also to citizens, because all cities were first burroughs, and with the Saxon and Germane burgh signifieth a city. See the first part the Institutes, sect. 107, 108.

This statute concerning disparagement doth not extend to heires females, but onely to heires males, therefore the forfeiture given by this statute onely extends to the case of the heire male, but by other statutes the disparagement of the heire female is forbidden. Magna Charta, cap. 6. W. 1. c. 22. 1 pt. Inst. sect. 107.

(1) *Det domino, et satisfaciat ei de tanto quantum inde percipere possit de aliquo pro maritagio suo antequam terram suam recipiat.*] Note the severall pennings of this clause concerning the single value, and the clause in the chapter next before concerning the double value, 43 E. 3. 20. 31 Ass. 26. 27 H. 8. 4.

Mich. 41 et 42 El. lib. 4. fol. 82. Sir Andrew Corbet's case. See the first part of the Institutes, sect. 110. Mich. 4. E. 1. in Banco Rot. 118. Lincolne, a notable case for holding the land for the forfeit of the marriage.

value, and for the single value the guardein shall hold the land untill the heire satisfie him of the value, so as in this case the taking of the profits shall not be accounted as parcell of the value, but as a penalty to cause the heire to pay it the sooner.

* Keylw. 133, 134.

* But note, that neither in the writ *De valore maritagii*, nor for forfeiture of marriage, the lord shall not recover the land, but damages, for this act giveth no action for the land.

And the words of this branch are to be observed, *Cum (hæres) ad ætatem pervenerit, det domino suo*, whereby it appeareth that the paiment of the single value is personally appropriated to the heire, and therefore if he dieth, it is lost, but the clause concerning the double value is otherwise penned, as hath been observed.

Hil. 4 Jac. li. 6. fol. 70, 71. Pasch. 3 Jac. li. 5. fol. 126, 127.

(2) *De mero jure pertinet ad dominum feodi.*] See for the exposition of this branch, and where a tender is requisite, and concerning the differences between the case of the heire male, and of the heire female, the lord Darcies case, and Palmers case, and the first part of the Institutes, sect. 107. Hereunto may be added a case, where the lord cannot at any time seise the ward, or tender a marriage to him, and yet he shall have the wardship.

Casus in Cur. Wardorum. Tr. 29 Eliz.

Edward Hampden holding lands of the queen by knights service in capite had issue a daughter, who *post annos nubiles* (viz. at twelve yeares) contracted matrimony with William Ditton, and after married with John Croke, and then the father died seised in fee of the land in capite, his daughter being of the age of thirteen yeares, and after the daughter had passed the age of sixteen yeares, her marriage with Croke was dissolved by divorce, *causa præcontractus*: and it was resolved by both the chiefe justices upon hearing of councell learned on both sides, that in this case (or the lord in the like case) shall have the wardship of the daughter, albeit never any seisure could be made of her, nor tender of marriage to her, because the marriage was never lawfull, and was after dissolved by divorce, as it had never been, and she shall take no advantage of her own wrong, to barre the queene or other lord of that which by law is due to them, notwithstanding the opinion of Laicon, 35 H. 6. 40. b. that if one hold land of another by knights service, and the tenant hath issue a daughter, which entreth into religion, and is professed, and after the tenant dieth, his daughter being in religion, and within fourteen yeares, and when she is of the age of fourteen she is deraigned, that shee shall not be in ward. *Nota*, he sheweth not for what cause she was deraigned: But by the divorce, *causa præcontractus*, there is a nullity of the mariage, *ab initio*, and the children between them are meere bastards.

35 H 6. 40. b.

[94]

CAP. VIII.

De narratione discensus in brevi de recto (1) *ab antecessore a tempore H. regis senioris anno et die, provisum est, quod de cætero non fiat mentio de tam longinquo tempore, sed a tempore H. regis avi nostri, et locum habeat ista provisio*

TOUCHING conveyance of descent in a writ of right from any ancestor from the time of king Henry the elder, the year and day, it is provided, that from henceforth there be no mention made of so long time,

visio ad Pentecosten, anno regni domini regis nunc 21. et non antea: et brevia prius impetrata procedant. Brevia mortis antecessoris, de nativis, et de ingressu, non excedant ultimum redit' domini regis Johannis de Hibern' in Angliam (2), *et locum habeat ista provisio, &c. ut supra. Brevia novæ disseisinæ non excedant primam transfretationem domini regis qui nunc est in Vascon'* (3), *et locum habeat ista provisio a tempore prædict', et brevia prius impetrata procedant* (4). *Vide West.* 1. *cap.* 38. *et* 32 *H.* 8. *cap.* 2.

time, but from the time of king Henry our grandfather; and this act shall take effect at Pentecost, the one and twentieth year of our reign, and not afore, and the writs before purchased shall proceed. Writs of mortdauncestor, of nativis, and entre, shall not pass the last return of king John from Ireland into England; and this act shall take effect as before is declared. Writs of novel disseisin shall not pass the first voyage of our sovereign lord the king, that now is, into Gascoine. And this provision shall take his effect from the time aforesaid; and all writs purchased before shall proceed.

(1 Inst. 114. b. 115. b. 3 Ed. 1. c. 39. 21 Jac. 1. c. 16.)

(1) *De narratione discensus in breve de recto.*] It appeareth by Glanvill, that in the raigne of H. 2. the limitation in an assise of novel disseisin, was *post ultimam transfretationem regis in Normaniam*, which was in the yeare of his raigne. Glan. li. 13. c. 33. Custumier de Norm. cap. 22. 110, 111. 125.

But of this limitation he saith, *Infra tempus à domino rege de consilio procerum ad hoc constitutum, quod quandoque majus, quandoque minus censetur*, &c. Idem eodem lib. cap. 32.

The limitation in the assise of mordaunc', was *post primam coronationem* H. 2. which was 20 Octob. 1154. Eodem libro, c. 3.

The limitation in a writ of right before this statute of Merton, was *à tempore regis* H. 1. and now by this statute of Merton, *à tempore regis* H. 2. Note H. 1. began his raigne the first of August 1100. and H. 2. began his raigne 1154. so as this statute of Merton did abridge the limitation in a writ of right 54 yeares, whereof Bracton speaketh thus, *Quia breve de recto sicut alia brevia infra certū tempus limitatur, non enim excedit tempus regis Henrici avi domini regis (*1 *H.* 2.*) et est ratio, quia ultra tempus illud (quod inter initium regni H.* 2. *et statutum de Merton, anno* 20 *H.* 3. *est circiter nonaginta annos) non poterit quis aliquid probare, licet jus habeat in re: cum nullus aliquid probare possit ultra tempus illud, ex quo loqui non poterit de visu suo proprio, vel de visu patris suo, qui ei injunxit quod testis esset si inde audiret loqui; et unde si quis loqueretur de tempore Henrici regis senis, (*1 *H.* 1. *quod fuit circiter* 125. *annos) amittere possit propter defectum probationis.* Bract. li. 4. fo. 373. Fleta, lib. 4. c. 5. & lib. 2. c. 38.

(2) *Brevia mortis antecessoris, de nativis, et de ingressu non excedant ultimum reditum domini regis Johannis de Hibernia in Angliam.*] King John went first into Ireland in the second yeare of his raigne, and returned in the third yeare: In the 12 yeare of his raigne he went into Ireland againe, and returned the same yeare into England, and this was *ultimus reditus*, that this act speaketh of, so as betweene the twelfth yeare of king John, and 20 H. 3. were about twenty five yeares.

(3) *Brevia novæ disseisinæ non excedant primam transfretationem domini regis qui nunc est, viz. H.* 3. *in Vasconiam.*] [95]

King

King H. 3. firſt paſſage into Gaſconie, was in the fiſt yeare of his raigne, ſo as there exceeded not the fifteen yeares between that transfretation and this ſtatute.

Bract. l. 2. fol. 179.

It appeareth by Bracton, that before this ſtatute of Merton, the limitation in a writ of aſſiſe, was *Poſt ultimum reditum domini regis de Britannia in Angliam.*

W. 1. c. 38. W. 2. c. 2. & 46.

But theſe times of limitations were altered in the raigne of king Edw. 1.

Tr. 7 E. 1. in Banco Rot. 71. Hunt.

And then the limitation in a writ of right was from the time of king R. 1. betweene the beginning of R. 1. and 3 E. 1. there had paſſed about eighty eight yeares.

Mich. 7 E. 1. ibid. Rot. 50. Cantab.

And that the writ of aſſiſe of *novel diſſeiſin* and the writ of purparty, which is called the *nuper obiit,* ſhould have the terme of the firſt transfretation of H. 3. into Gaſcony, which as hath been ſaid, was in anno 5 H. 3.

And the writs of *Mordaunc', de Coſinage, de Aiel, de Entre, et bre. de Nieſte eyent le terme de coronement meſme le Henry, 1 H.* 3. which between that and this ſtatute of W. 1. was about 58 years: Note (as hath been ſaid) this king was twice crowned, firſt the 28 day of October, in the firſt yeare of his raigne, and the ſecond time on Whitſonday, in the fourth yeare of his raigne: but this ſtatute of W. 1. ſpeaking indefinitely, is to be underſtood of the firſt coronanation, for *quod prius eſt tempore potius eſt jure;* And by the ſtatute of W. 2. cap. 2. in an avowry the like limitation for ſeiſin ſhall be accounted, as in the aſſiſe, which, as is aforeſaid, is *poſt primam transfretationem Regis Henrici* 3. *in Gaſconiam.*

Regula.

But albeit theſe times of limitations were reaſonable, when theſe ſtatutes were made, yet in proceſſe of time (there being ſet times appointed in former kings raignes) the times of neceſſity grew too large, whereupon many ſuits, troubles, and inconveniences did ariſe, and therefore the makers of the ſtatute of 32 H. 8. took another, and more direct courſe which might indure for ever, and that was to impoſe diligence and vigilancy in him that was to bring his action, ſo that by one conſtant law certaine limitations might ſerve both for the time preſent, and for all times to come, *viz.* That the demandant ſhould alledge ſeiſin in a writ of right not above ſixty yeares next before the teſte of his writ. In *mordaunc', coſinage, aiel, entry ſur diſſeiſin,* or other poſſeſſary action upon the ſeiſin or poſſeſſion of any of his aunceſtors or predeceſſors, of a ſeiſin within fifty years: In any action upon his or their own poſſeſſion within thirty years: In an avowry, or conuſance for any rent, ſute, or ſervice within 40 years; In a *formedon* in reverſion or remainder, or *ſcire facias* upon fines within fifty yeares; and yet this ſtatute prefixing a certain time extended not to divers caſes, which were within the auncient ſtatutes, as to accidentall ſervices, as hereafter ſhall appeare. See the firſt part of the Inſtitutes, ſect. 170.

32 H. 8. cap. 2. 1 Mar. cap. 5.

Bract. l. 4 fo. 228. Tr. 7 E. 1 Rot. 71. in Banco. Hunt. Bract. l. 2. fo 228. 1 pt. Inſt. ſect. 170. lib. 4. fol. 10. 11. lib. 7. fol. 40. lib. 8. fol. 65 & 126.

(4) *Brevia prius impetrata procedant,* &c.] For the rule is, *Omnis nova conſtitutio futuris formam imponere debet, et non præteritis.* See a caſe upon this branch in 7 E. 1. Tho. de Redberwes caſe.

And albeit Bracton ſaith, that *omnes actiones in mundo infra certa tempora limitationem habent;* and in another place he ſaith, *Omnis querela et actio injuriarum limitata eſt infra certa tempora;* yet ſome actions

actions were not limited by any ſtatute, as by divers authorities quoted in the margent appeareth. lib. 9. fol. 36. li. 11. fol. 68.

But ſomewhat more is neceſſary to be added to the former reports, and booke caſes before quoted in the margent, for the ſaid act of 32 H. 8. extends only concerning avowries to rent, ſute, or ſervice, ſo as reliefe is not within the purview of the law, for it is no ſervice but a duty, by reaſon of the tenure and ſervice*, and albeit homage, fealty, and eſcuage, and other accidentall ſervices (being ſervices) are within the letter of the law, yet they and all other accidentall ſervices, as heriot ſervice, or to cover the lords hall, and the like, for that they may not happen within the times limited by that act, are by conſtruction out of the meaning of this ſtatute of 32 H. 8. as it appeareth by the caſes quoted before: but albeit reliefe be not within this ſtatute, yet in avowry for reliefe, the avowant muſt alledge a ſeiſin of the ſervices within the auncient ſtatute, *viz. Poſt primam transfretat. regis Henrici in Gaſconiam*, and the ſeiſin of the ſervices is traverſable. 17 E. 3. 11. 20 E. 4. 14. Fleta, lib. 2. ca. 28. 7 E. 6. Br. avowry 96. gard 69. Bract. li. 2. fo. 52. & lib. 4. fol. 314. *[96] 13 H. 4. fol. 6. Edw. Latimer's caſe adjudged.

And ſo it is of homage, and fealty, and eſcuage; albeit they be out of the ſtatute of 32 H. 8. yet are they within the auncient ſtatute.

And it is to be noted, that where the tenure is by homage, fealty, and eſcuage incertain, and by ſuite of court, or rent, or any other annuall ſervice, the ſeiſin of the ſute or rent, or any other annuall ſervice is a good ſeiſin of the homage, fealty, or eſcuage, or other accidentall ſervices, as wardſhip, heriot ſervice, or the like: and hereby (if you ſhall heedfully peruſe over the reports and book caſes before quoted) you ſhall underſtand the ſame the better. 7 E. 6. tit. gard. Br. 69. Avowr. 96. 31 E. 3. gard. fol. 118.

By this act it is declared, that the ſaid act of 32 H. 8. ſhall not extend to writs of right, of advowſon, *quare impedit*, aſſiſe of *darrein preſentment*, or *jure patronatus*, nor to any writ of right of ward, writ of raviſhment of ward, for the body or land holden by knights ſervice, but that theſe actions may be maintained, as they might have been before the making of the ſaid act of 32 H. 8. 1 Mar cap. 5. 17 E. 3. fol. 11. a. in Quare imped.

And ſeeing perſonall actions are at this day more frequent, then they have been in times paſt, it were to be wiſhed for eſtabliſhment of quiet, and avoiding of old ſuits, that Bractons rules by ſome new proviſion extended to them alſo, and that they were limited within ſome certain time.

Since we wrote this commentary, there is a good ſtatute made concerning certain perſonall actions, in *anno* 21 *Jacobi regis*, ca. 16. and therein a limitation ſet down in the formedon in diſcender, formedon in remainder, and formedon in reverter.

CAP. IX.

AD breve regis de baſtardia, utrum aliquis natus ante matrimonium habere poterit hæreditat', ſicut ille qui natus eſt poſt matrimonium, reſponderunt omnes epiſcopi, quod nolunt nec poſſunt ad iſtud breve reſpondere, quia hoc

TO the king's writ of baſtardy, whether one being born before matrimony may inherit in like manner as he that is born after matrimony, all the biſhops anſwered, that they would not, nor could not, anſwer

hoc esset contra communem formam ecclesiæ (1). *Et rogaverunt omnes episcopi magnates, ut consentirent quod nati ante matrimonium essent legitimi, sicut illi qui nati sunt post matrimonium, quantum ad successionem hæreditariam, quia ecclesia tales habet pro legitimis. Et omnes comites et barones una voce responderunt, quod nolunt leges Angliæ mutare, quæ hucusque usitatæ sunt et approbatæ* (2).

swer to it; because it was directly against the common order of the church. And all the bishops instanted the lords, that they would consent, that all such as were born afore matrimony should be legitimate, as well as they that be born within matrimony, as to the succession of inheritance, forsomuch as the church accepteth such for legitimate. And all the earls and barons with one voice answered, that they would not change the laws of the realm, which hitherto have been used and approved.

See the first part of the Institutes, sect. 399, 400. & 188. (Fitz. Bastardy, 21, 22. 25. 27, 28. 30, 33. 1 H. 6. 3. 11 H. 4. 84. 39 Ed. 3. 14 44 Ed. 3. 12. 12 Rep. 72.)

Vide Decret. Gregorii 9. fol. 260. col. 1.

(1) *Contra communem formam ecclesiæ,* &c.] For the better understanding of this branch, it is to be known, that in the time * of pope Alexander the third, (who lived *anno Domini* 1160, which was *anno* 6 H. 2.) this constitution was made, that children borne before solemnization of matrimony, where matrimony followed, should be as legitimate to inherit unto their auncestors, as those that were borne after matrimony, and thereupon the statute saith, *Ecclesia tales habet pro legitimis.*

*[97]

Glanv. li. 7. c. 15.

Of this canon, or constitution Glanvill writeth thus, *Orta est quæstio, si quis antequam pater matrem suam desponsaverat fuerit genitus vel natus, utrum talis filius sit legitimus hæres, cum postea matrem suam desponsaverat: Et quidem licet secundum canones et leges Romanas talis filius sit legitimus hæres, tamen secundum jus et consuetudinem regni nullo modo tanquam hæres in hæreditate sustinetur, vel hæreditatem de jure regni petere potest.*

Bract. li. 5. fo. 416, 417. Fleta, lib 6. c. 38. Fortescue c. 39. 11 Ass. p. 20.

And herewith doe agree not onely other auncient authors, but the constant opinion of the judges in all succession of ages ever since, of the auncient law of England. Hereupon these two conclusions doe follow:

1. That any forein canon or constitution made by authority of the pope, being (as Glanvill saith) *Contra jus et consuetudinem regni,* bindeth not untill it be allowed by act of parliament, which the bishops here prayed it might have beene; for no law, or custome of England can be taken away, abrogated, or adnulled, but by authority of parliament.

4 E. 1. Stat. de Bigamis, c. 9. simile.

2. That although the bishops were spirituall persons, and in those dayes had a great dependency on the pope, yet in case of generall bastardy, when the king wrote to them to certifie, who was lawfull heire to any lands, or other inheritance, they ought to certifie according to the law, and custome of England, and not according to the Romane canons, and constitutions, which were contrary to the law, and custome of England, wherein the bishops sought at this parliament to be relieved.

Glanv. ubi supra.

See the first part of the Institutes, sect. 399, & 400. and adde thereunto:

Assisa venit, &c. Si Nicholaus de Lewkenor pat' Thom' de Lewke-

nor

*nor fuit seisitus, &c. de manerio de Southmyms quod Rogerus de Lewkenor tenet, qui dicit quod ipse est frater ipsius Thomæ antenatus de eodem patre, & eadem matre, & est seisitus de prædictis tenementis, & clamat per eundem discensum, et petit judiciū. Thom' dic' quod Rogerus non potest clamare per eundē descensum, quia dicit quod idem Rogerus natus fuit extra sponsalia, &c. Et quia idem Tho' non potest didicere, quin idem Rogerus sit frater ipsius Tho' antenatus de eodem patre, & eadem matre, & post mortem prædicti Nicholai patris, &c. intravit in eisdem tenementis ut filius ejus & hæres, * consideratum est quod prædictus Rogerus ind' sine die. Et Tho. Nich. cap' per assisam, et sit in misericordia, &c.*

Pasch. 18 E. 1. in Banco Rot. 80. Mid. in Ass. de Mordaunc'. Vide Mic. 15 E. 1. in Banc. Rot. 129. Hertf. Tr. 15 E. 1. ibid. Rot. 60. Not. * Judgement.

Note by this judgment, that the bastard eigne to this intent is accounted heire, and of the blood with the mulier puisne, as the mulier puisne cannot have an assise of mordaunc' against him.

We remember not that we have read in any book of the legitimation, or adoption of an heire, but onely in Bracton, lib. 2. cap. 29. fol. 63. b. and that to no little purpose; but the surest adoption of an heire, is by learned advice, to make good assurance of the land, &c.

(2) *Et omnes comites, et barones, una voce responderunt quod nolunt leges Angliæ mutare quæ hucusque usitatæ sunt et approbatæ.*] The nobility of England have ever had the laws of England in great estimation and reverence, as their best birth-right, and so have the kings of England as their principall royalty and right belonging to their crown and dignity: this made king H. 1. that noble king sirnamed Beauclerk, to write to pope Pascall, *Notum habeat sanctitas vestra, quod me vivente (auxiliante Deo) dignitates et usus regni nostri Angliæ non imminuentur, et si ego (quod absit) in tanta me dejectione ponerem, optimates mei et totus Angliæ populus id nullo modo pateretur.*

See the first part of the Institutes, sect. 400.

Chart. Hen. 1.

[98]

And it is worthy the observation, how dangerous it is (as elsewhere hath been often noted) to change an ancient maxime of the common law.

Some have written, that William the Conquerour being borne out of matrimony, Robert his reputed father did after marry Arlot his mother, and that thereby he had right by the civil and canon law, but that is *contra legem Angliæ*, as here it appeareth. And during this parliament in the 20 yeare of H. 3. it may be collected by the 23. and 24. epistles of Robert Grostead then bishop of Lincoln, directed to William Rawleighe (priest) then one of the kings justices, that this matter to bring the *nati ante matrimonium* to be made legitimate was vehemently laboured by the clergie: and in the 26. epistle to the bishop of Canterbury, he findeth fault with the arch-bishop, for that the king and his councell had resolved that the law and custome of the realme in this point should continue still: whereby it appeareth, that not onely the nobles, but the king himselfe was against it.

William Malmsb. lib. 3. circa initiū Ingulphus, lib. 6. cap. 19. See the Custumer de Nor. ca. 27. fo. 42 & 44.

And in the letters, which all the nobilitie of England by assent of the whole cominalty assembled in parliament at Lincoln wrote to pope Boniface, it is thus conteyned, *Ad observationem et defensionem libertatum, consuetudinum, et legum paternarum ex debito præstiti sacramenti astringimur, quæ manutenebimus toto posse, totisque viribus cum dei auxilio defendemus, nec etiam permittimus aut aliquatenus permittemus, sicut nec possumus nec debemus præmissa tam insolita, indebita, præjudicialia, et alias inaudita dominum nostrum regem, etiam si vellet, facere,*

Rot. Par. 28 E. 1. apud Lincoln.

Jus coronæ. *cere, seu quomodolibet attemptare:* (and there the inconveniences are set down,) *præcipue cum præmissa cederent manifeste in exheredationem juris coronæ regis Angliæ et regiæ dignitatis, ac subversionem status ejusdem regni notoriam, nec non in præjudicium libertatum, consuetudinum, et legum paternarum.* Sealed by the severall seales of armes of 104. earles and barons, and in the name of all the comminalty of England. And to that effect king E. 1. wrote also to the pope.

Leges Angliæ.] Here our common lawes are aptly and properly called the lawes of England, because they are appropriated to this kingdome of England as most apt and fit for the government thereof, and have no dependancy upon any forreine law whatsoever, no not upon the civill or cannon law other then in cases allowed by the laws of England, as partly hath been touched before: and therefore the poet spake truly hereof, *Et penitus toto divisos orbe Brittannos:* so as the law of England is *proprium quarto modo* to the kingdome of England; therefore forrein precedents are not to be objected against us, because we are not subject to forrein lawes.

And it is a note worthy of observation, that where at the holding of this parliament in *anno* 20 H. 3. and before, and some time after, many of the judges and justices of this realme were of the clergy, as bishops, deanes, and priests, and all the great officers of the realme, as lord chancellor, treasuror, privy seale, president, &c. were for the most part of the clergy; yet even in those times the judges of the realme, both of the clergy and laity, did constantly maintaine the lawes of England, so as no incroachment was made upon them or breach unto them by any forreine power, as partly hath been shewed in Caudries case: and many more judgements and authorities in law might be produced for the manifestation thereof: see the first part of the Institutes, many of the clergy judges and justices of the realme of ancient time.

Lib. 5. fo. 1. &c. Caudries case. 1 part of the Institutes, § 534.

Et rogarunt omnes episcopi magnates ut consentirent, &c.] Here was the motion and request, but Bracton saith, *Rogarunt regem et magnates: et omnes comites et barones una voce responderunt, Nolumus leges Angliæ mutare, &c.* for so it is in ancient manuscripts.

Bracton, lib. 5. fo. 416, 417.

[99]

This is the first of this kind, that we remember, that hath been printed, for it is to be understood that by the parliamentary order all motions and petitions made (as this was) though they were denied, and never proceeded to the establishment of a statute, yet the same were entered into the parliament roll together with the aunswers thereunto: but this is the first of this kinde (as hath been said) that hath been printed.

See the last cha. of Merton the like. 12 Ass. p. 20.

And yet in our books this is called a statute, for Sir Galfred le Scrope chiefe justice saith, before the statute of Merton the party pleaded not general bastardy, but that he was borne out of espousals; and the bishop ought to certifie whether he were borne before espousals or not, and according to that certificate to proceed to judgement according to the law of the land: and the prelates answered that they could not to this writ answer, and therefore ever since special bastardy (viz. that the defendant, &c. was borne before espousals) have been tried in the kings courts, and generall bastardy in court christian; and herewith agreeth our old books and the constant opinion of the judges ever since.

Bract. li. 5. fo. 416. Fleta, li. 6. cap. 38. 47 E. 3. 14. 21 E. 3. 49. 28 ass. 46. 46 E. 3. 3.

Now for that this point was resolved in parliament, it is here in a large sense called a statute.

CAP.

CAP. X.

PROVISUM est insuper, quod quilibet liber homo (4), qui sectam debet (1) ad comitatum, trithingum (2), hundredum et wapentagium (3), vel ad curiam domini sui, libere possit facere attornatum (5) suum, ad sectas illas pro eo faciendas (6).

IT is provided and granted, that every freeman, which oweth suit to the country, trything, hundred, and wapentake, or to the court of his lord, may freely make his attorney to do those suits for him.

(Fitz. Attorney, 106. Regist. 172. F. N. B. 156, &c.)

(1) *Sectam debet.*] *Nota,* There be two kinds of suits, viz. suit reall, that is, in respect of his resiance to a leet or tourne: and suit service, that is, by reason of a tenure of his land of the county, hundred, wapentake, or mannor whereunto a court baron is incident: before this act every one that held by suit service ought to appeare in person, because the suiters were judges in those courts, otherwise he should be amercied, which was mischievous, for it might be, that he had lands within divers of those seigniories, and that the courts might be kept in one day, and he could be but in one place at one time: but this statute extends not to suit reall, because he cannot be within two leets, &c. 41 E. 3. Avowry 77. Vid. Gloc. c. 8. W. 2. cap. 10.

(2) *Trithingum or trithinge.*] Here it signifieth a court which consisteth on three or foure hundreds, and doth not here signifie a leet or view of frankpledge. Lamb. int. leges Ed. regis, nu. 34. Magna Cart. c. 35. Temps E. 1. Attorn, 106. Regist. 172.

(3) *Wapentagium.*] That, which in some countries is called a hundred court, in some countries is called a wapentake. * *Quod Angli vocant hundredum supradicti comitatus vocant wapentagium.* Now the reason of the name was this: when any on a certaine day and place took upon him the government of the hundred, the free suiters met him with launces, and he descending from his horse, all rose up to him, and he holding his launce upright, all the rest, in signe of obedience, with their launces touched his launce or weapon: for the Saxon word *wapen,* is weapon, and *tac,* is *tactus,* or touching: and thereof this assemblie was called wapentake, or touching of weapon. 23 E. 3. cap. 4. F. N. B. 156. * Lam. verbo centuria int. leges Ed. regis, nu. 33. Bracton, lib. 3.

Now albeit he that holdeth by suit service may make an attorney, yet that attorney cannot sit as judge, as the free suiter himselfe might doe, for he cannot depute another in his judiciall place; and the words of the statute be, *Libere possit facere attornatum ad sectas illas pro eo faciendas.* Mirror, cap. 5. § 3. [100]

(4) *Liber homo.*] This doth extend to free-holders in ancient demesne, but not to copie-holders. Temps E. 1. Attorny 106.

(5) *Facere attornatum.*] He must make a letter of attorney under his seale, which the steward ought to allow; and if he doe not, the suiter may have a writ out of the chancery for the allowance of him: or if he doubted that he should not be allowed, he might have a writ before-hand to receive him as attorney: and such a writ shall serve during the life of the tenant, &c. for the words of another writ be, *Et quia virtus brevium nostrorum de hujusmodi attornato* F.N.B. 156. E. W. 1. cap. 33. F.N.B. 157.

attornato faciendo terminum non capit, nec terminus limitatur durantibus personis, &c.

W. 1. cap. 33. Custumier de Norm. cap. 65.

What such an attorney may doe, and who cannot be attorney, see the statute of W. 1.

(6) *Ad sectas illas pro eo faciendas.*] So as by force of this act he may doe such suit, as the free-holder ought to doe.

See the Register 19. This act extendeth to justices in eire.

CAP. XI.

DE malefactoribus in parcis, et vivariis (1) nondum est discussum, quia magnates petierunt propriam prisonam (2) de illis, quos caperent in parcis, et vivariis suis. Quod quidem dominus rex contradixit, et ideo differtur.

CONCERNING trespasses in parks and ponds it is not yet discussed; for the lords demanded the proper imprisonment of such as they should take in their parks and ponds, which the king denied; wherefore it was deferred.

(1) *Vivarium.*] Is a word of a large extent, and *ex vi termini* signifieth a place in land or water, where living things be kept. Most commonly in law it signifieth parks, warrens, and pischaries or fishings; here it is taken for warrens and fishings, for that parks were named before.

(2) *Propriam prisonam.*] This petition of the lords in parliament stood upon three branches: 1. That they might imprison such as they should take in their parks or vivaries, which seemed to be against the 29 chapter of *Magna Charta.* 2. That they should have *propriam prisonam*, a prison of their owne, which no subject can have; for all prisons or gaoles are the kings prisons or gaoles, but a subject may have the custodie or keeping of them. 3. That they should not be imprisoned in the common gaole. All which *dominus rex contradixit.*

See the like before, cap. 9.

STATUTUM DE MARLEBRIDGE.

Editum 52 H. III. Anno gratiæ 1267.

Marlebridge.] Now called *Marleborough*, a town in Wiltſhire, the greateſt fame whereof is the holding of this parliament there. *Henricus vero, &c. Concilium convocavit Marlebrigium, quod eſt pagus celebris comitatus Wilceriæ, qui in eo conventu primum leges ab ſe latas, & præſertim Magnæ Chartæ de concilii ſententia approbandas, deinde alias condendas curavit, quæ ad ſtatum et commodum regni maxime conducerent.* Polyd. Virg. p. 314, 10.

This towne in our books is called a citie, and the freemen thereof citizens. 39 E. 3. fo. 15.

52 H. 3.] This king raigned longeſt of any king ſince the conqueſt, or before, that we remember; for he raigned 56 yeares. But the great and famous queene Elizabeth was of greater yeares then any of her progenitors, for ſhe attained neere to 70 yeares. So king H. 3. raigned longeſt, and queen Eliz. lived longeſt. She raigned the yeares of the emperour Auguſtus, and lived the yeares of king David.

ANNO gratiæ M. CC. LXVII. regni autem domini Henrici filii regis Johannis quinquageſimo ſecundo, in octabis S. Martini, providente ipſo domino rege, ad regni ſui Angliæ meliorationem, et exhibitionem juſtitiæ (prout regalis officii expoſcit utilitas) pleniorem, convocatis diſcretioribus ejuſdem regni, tam majoribus quàm minoribus: proviſum eſt et ſtatutum, ac concordatum et ordinatum, ut cum regnum Angliæ multis tribulationibus et diſſentionum incommodis nuper eſſet depreſſum, reformatione legum et jurium (quibus pax et tranquillitas incolarum conſervetur) indigeat, ad quod remedium ſalubre per ipſum regem et ſuos fideles oportuit adhiberi: proviſiones, ordinationes, et ſtatuta ſubſcripta, ab omnibus regni ipſius incolis, tam majoribus quàm minoribus, firmiter et inviolabiliter temporibus perpetuis ſtatuerit obſervari.

IN the year of grace, one thouſand two hundred ſixty ſeven, the two and fiftieth year of the reign of king Henry, ſon of king John, in the Utas of St. Martin, the ſaid king our lord providing for the better eſtate of his realm of England, and for the more ſpeedy miniſtration of juſtice, as belongeth to the office of a king, the more diſcreet men of the realm being called together, as well of the higher as of the lower eſtate: it was provided, agreed, and ordained, that whereas the realm of England of late had been diſquieted with manifold troubles and diſſenſions; for reformation whereof ſtatutes and laws be right neceſſary, whereby the peace and tranquillity of the people muſt be obſerved: wherein the king, intending to deviſe convenient remedy, hath made theſe acts, ordinances, and ſtatutes underwritten, which he willeth to be obſerved for ever firmly and inviolably of all his ſubjects, as well high as low.

This generall preamble to all the statutes of Marlebridge doth consist on foure parts.

1. The end wherefore these statutes were made, for *sapiens incipit a fine*, and that is two fold; 1. *ad meliorationem regni Angliæ*. 2. *Ad exhibitionem justitiæ (prout regalis officii exposcit utilitas) pleniorem.*

2. Of what numbers this parliament consisted, *convocatis discretioribus ejusdem regni, tam majoribus, quàm minoribus.*

3. What was the cause of calling this parliament, *cum regni Angliæ multis tribulationibus et dissentionum incommodis nuper esset depressum.* The many fearfull and dangerous troubles and dissentions [102] between the king and his barons, which I had rather you should reade in history, then I should relate, grew originally out of this root, that the king sometimes allowed, and sometimes disallowed *Magna Charta*, and *Charta de Foresta.*

4. What should be the remedy that peace and tranquillity might ensue. *Ut cum regnum &c. reformatione legum et jurium quibus pax et tranquillitas incolarum conservetur indigeat, ad quod remedium salubre per ipsum regem et suos fideles provisiones, ordinationes, et statuta subscripta, ab omnibus regni suis incolis tam majoribus quam minoribus firmiter et inviolabiliter temporibus perpetuis statuerit observari.*

This remedy that should for ever in all future times be inviolably observed, consisted upon two parts.

1. For establishing of *Magna Charta*, and *Charta de Foresta*, whereof more shall be said when we come to the first chapter. In the meane time, this is to be observed, that after this parliament neither *Magna Charta*, nor *Charta de Foresta*, was ever attempted to be impugned or questioned: whereupon peace and tranquillity, whereof this preamble speaketh, have ever since ensued.

2. For enacting of new lawes, or declaring of old, with addition of great punishment.

CAP. I.

CUM autem tempore turbationis nuper in regno Angliæ subortæ, et deinceps multi magnates et alii justitiam indignati fuerint recipere per dominum regem, et curiam suam, prout debuerunt, et consueverunt temporibus prædecessorum ipsius domini regis, et etiam tempore suo: sed de vicinis suis, et aliis per seipsos graves ultiones fecerint, et districtiones, quousque redemptiones reciperent ad voluntatem suam. Et præterea quidam eorum, se per ministros domini regis justiciari non permittant, nec sustineant quod per ipsos liberentur districtiones, quas authoritate propria fecerint

WHEREAS at the time of a commotion late stirred up within this realm, and also sithence, many great men, and divers other, refusing to be justified by the king and his court, like as they ought and were wont in time of the king's noble progenitors, and also in his time; but took great revenges and distresses of their neighbours, and of other, until they had amends and fines at their own pleasure; and further, some of them would not be justified by the king's officers, nor would suffer them to make delivery of such distresses as they

fecerint ad voluntatem suam. Provisum est, concordatum et concessum, quod tam majores, quam minores, justitiam habeant et recipiant (1), *in curia domini regis* (2). *Et nullus de cætero ultiones, aut districtiones faciat per voluntatem suam* (4), *absque consideratione curiæ domini regis* (3), *si forte dampnum vel injuria sibi fiat, unde emendas habere voluerit de* aliquo *vicino suo, sive majore sive minore. Super articulo autem supradicto provisum est et concessum, quod si quis de cætero ultiones hujusmodi capiat per voluntatem suam* propriam *absque consideratione curiæ domini regis (ut prædictum est) et inde convincatur, puniatur per redemptionem* (5), *et hoc secundum quantitatem delicti. Et similiter* * *si vicinus super vicinum suum faciat districtionẽ sine consideratione curiæ domini regis, per quod dampnum habeat, puniatur eodem modo, et hoc secundum quantitatem delicti. Et nihilominus fiant emendæ plene et sufficienter eis, qui dampna sustinuerunt per hujusmodi districtionem.*

they had taken of their own authority: it is provided, agreed, and granted, that all persons, as well of high as of low estate, shall receive justice in the king's court; and none from henceforth shall taken any such revenge or distress of his own authority, without award of our court, though he have damage or injury, whereby he would have amends of his neighbour either higher or lower. And upon the foresaid article it is provided and granted, that if any from henceforth take such revenges of his own authority, without award of the king's court (as before is said) and be convict thereof, he shall be punished by fine, and that according to the trespass. And likewise if one neighbour take a distress of another without award of the king's court, whereby he hath damage, he shall be punished in the same wise, and that after the quantity of trespass. And nevertheless sufficient and full amends shall be made to them that have sustained loss by such distresses.

* [103]

(Mert. cap. 11. 12 Rep. 13. 11 H. 4. 2. 17 Ed. 3. 9. 2 Inst. 162.)

This first chapter consisteth of a preamble, and the body of the act.

The preamble shews the mischiefs, which were foure.

1. That in the time of the late troubles, great men and others refused to be justified by the king and his court, as they ought, for here it is said, *multi magnates et alii indignati fuerint recipere justitiam per dominum regem, et curiam suam.*

2. *Sed graves ultiones fecerint,* That they (refusing the course of the kings lawes) tooke upon them to be their owne judges in their owne causes, and to take such revenges as they thought fit, untill they had ransomes at their pleasures. *Aliquis non debet esse judex in sua propria causa.* *Regula.*

3. That some of them would not be justified by the kings officers.

4. Nor would suffer them to make delivery of such distresses, as they had taken of their owne authority at their pleasure. Here you may see the defects of a disordered and troubled state.

The body of the act consisteth of divers branches.

First, a remedy in generall for all the said mischifes.

(1) *Provisum est, concordatum, et concessum, quod tam majores quam minores, justitiam habeant et recipiant in curia domini regis.*] This is the golden met wande, that the law hath appointed to measure the cases

cases of all and singular persons, high and low, to have and re-
8 H. 4. 19. Gasc. ceive justice in the kings courts; for the king hath distributed his
24 H. 8. cap. 12. judiciall power to severall courts of justice, and courts of justice
25 H. 8. cap. 21. ought to determine all causes, and that all private revenges bee avoided.

Upon this generall law, foure conclusions doe follow.

1. That all men, high and low, must be justified, that is, have and receive justice in the kings courts of justice.

See cap. Itineris, Artic. ult. 2. That no private revenge be taken, nor any man by his owne arme or power revenge himselfe: and this article is grounded upon the law of God, *vindicta est mihi et ego retribuam*, saith Almighty God. All revenge must come from God, or from his lieutenant the king, in some of his courts of justice.

3. That all the subjects of the realme ought to be justified, that is, submit themselves to the kings officers of justice according to law.

4. That they ought to suffer replevies to be made according to the law, to the end that men may possesse their horses, beasts, and other cattle and goods in peace, whereof they have so great and continuall use. See hereafter cap. 4.

(2) *In curia domini regis.*] These words are of great importance, for all causes ought to be heard, ordered, and determined before the judges of the kings courts openly in the kings courts, whither all persons may resort; and in no chambers, or other private places: for the judges are not judges of chambers, but of courts, and therefore in open court, where the parties councell and attorneys attend, ought orders, rules, awards, and judgements to be made and given,
[104] and not in chambers or other private places, where a man may lose his cause, or receive great prejudice, or delay in his absence for want of defence. Nay, that judge that ordereth or ruleth a cause in his chamber, though his order or rule be just, yet offendeth he the law, (as here it appeareth) because he doth it not in court.
Seneca. And the opinion is good, and agreeable to this law, *qui aliquid statuerit parte inaudita altera, æquum licet statuerit, haud æquus fuerit:* Neither are causes to be heard upon petitions, or suggestions and references, but *in curia domini regis.*

(3) *Et nullus de cætero ultiones aut districtiones faciat per voluntatem suam absque consideratione curiæ domini regis.*] The first clause was affirmative: this clause, for the more surety, is in the negative.

(4) *Districtiones faciat per voluntatem suam.*] That is, taking distresses not according to the law, as for services, rents, or for damage fesaunt, or for other lawfull cause, but for revenge without cause, of his owne head and will, that is, to be his owne judge and carver, to satisfie himselfe without any lawfull meane or course of law, and so it is to be understood through this whole chapter: for this chapter is to be understood *de ultionibus*, of revenges, which are of two natures, 1. personall, as by combat, imprisonment, and the like: 2. By distresses, that is, revengefull taking of goods. Concerning takings in nature of distresses, provision is made in the next three chapters.

1 part Institutes, sect. 194. Here, cap. 4. (5) *Puniatur per redemptionē.*] For this word *(redemptio)* and the signification thereof, see the first part of the Institutes, sect. 194.

CAP. II.

NULLUS insuper major (1) *vel minor distringat aliquem ad veniendum ad curiam suam, qui non sit de feodo suo, aut super ipsum non habeat jurisdictionem per hundredum,* wapentagium, *vel balivam* (2), quæ sua sit *nec districtiones faciat extra feodum suum, seu locum ubi balivam habeat, vel jurisdictionem. Et qui contra hoc statutum fecerit, puniatur eodem modo, et hoc secundum delicti quantitatem, et etiam qualitatem.*

MOREOVER, none (of what estate soever he be) shall distrain any to come to his court, which is not of his fee, or upon whom he hath no jurisdiction, by reason of hundred, or bailiwick; nor shall take distresses out of the fee or place where he hath no bailiwick or jurisdiction: and he that offendeth against this statute, shall be punished in like manner, and that according to the quantity and quality of the trespass.

(Fitz. Barre, 281.)

(1) *Nullus insuper major, &c.*] This chapter concerning distresses enacteth three things: 1. That no man shall distreine any to come to his court but such as be within his fee: this is intended of suit service in respect of a seigniory, and not of suit reall in respect of resiance. 2. Or that he hath jurisdiction by hundred, wapentake, or bayliwick. 3. That he shall not take distresses out of his fee or place where he hath a bailiwick or jurisdiction.

Fleta, li. 2. ca. 40. W. 1. cap. 16. Here, cap. 15. Artic. cler. c. 6. Artic. super cart. cap. 12.

This chapter is a declaration of the common law, saving for the penaltie hereby inflicted; and therefore if A. distreine B. and in a replevie A. avow as lord for rent or service, B. plead *hors de son fee,* and it is found for B. A. shall not in this replevy be punished by ransome, &c. according to this act, but hee must have an action upon this statute, *et sic de similibus.*

41 E. 3. 26. 47 E. 3. 7.

[105]

Regist. 97. 4 E. 3. 1.

(2) *Infra balivam.*] Here *baliva* is well expounded by the statute it selfe, for it signifieth here jurisdiction, and therefore it is here said, *infra balivam seu jurisdictionem.*

19 E. 3. Barre 281. 19 E. 2. breve 842.

11 R. 2. Avow. 87. 18 E. 2. Action sur le stat. 85. F.N.B. 89, 90.

CAP. III.

SI quis autem major vel minor permittere noluerit liberari per ministros domini regis, secundum legem et consuetudinem regni, districtiones quas fecerit: aut etiam sustinere noluerit summonitiones, attachiamenta, executiones judiciorum curiæ domini regis fieri secundum legem et consuetudinem regni ut prædict' est *puniatur modo prædicto,*

IF any, of what estate soever he be, will not suffer such distresses as he hath taken, to be delivered by the king's officers, after the law and custom of the realme, or will not suffer summons, attachments, or executions of judgments given in the king's court, to be done according to the law and custom of the realm, as is aforesaid,

prædicto, tanquam se justiciari non permittens, et hoc secundum delicti quantitatem. Et si quis major vel minor districtiones faciat super tenentem suum pro servitiis et consuetudinibus, quæ sibi deberi dicat, vel pro re altera, unde ad dominum feodi pertineat districtiones facere, et postea convincat', quod tenens ea sibi non debeat: non ideo puniatur dominus per redemptionem, ut in supradictis casibus, si permittat districtiones deliberari secund' legem et consuetudin' regni, sed amercietur, velut hactenus consuetum est, et tenens dampna sua recuperet versus eum.

aforesaid, he shall be punished in manner aforesaid, as one that will not obey the law, and that according to the quantity of the offence. And if any, of what estate soever he be, distrain his tenant for services and customs being due unto him, or for any other thing, for the which the lord of the fee hath cause to distrain, and after it is found that the same services are not due, the lord shall not therefore be punished by fine, as in the cases aforesaid, if he do suffer the distresses to be delivered according to the law and custom of the realm; but shall be amerced as hitherto hath been used, and the tenant shall recover his damages against him.

W. 1. cap. 17. (Bro. Trespass, 16, 384. 5 H. 7. c. 9.)

This chapter consisteth on three branches.

Regist. 97. 1. That all of what estate soever, shall suffer such distresses as have been taken to be delivered by the kings officers after the law and custome of the realme. But if any will not suffer them to be delivered, it is no good returne for the sheriffe to say, that he was resisted, for he may take *posse comitatus*.

2. That all shall suffer summons, attachments, or executions of judgements in the kings court, &c.

44 E. 3. 20. li. 4. fol 11. Bevils case. li. 9. fo. 76. Combes case. 3. If the lord distrein his tenant for customes, services, or any other duty, which the lord alledged to be behinde, if it be found that it is not behinde, *non puniatur dominus per redemptionem, &c.* But at the common law an action of trespasse *vi et armis* in that case did lie.

This branch is interpreted that the lord shall pay no fine, and therefore since this act by a consequent no action of trespasse *quare vi et armis* lieth against the lord in this case, for then he should pay a fine.

41 E. 3. 26. 44 E. 3. 13. 28 E. 3. 97. 8 E. 4. 15. 10 E. 4. 7. 20 E. 4. 3. 21 E. 4. 3. 2 H. 4. 4. 11 H. 4. 78. 1 H. 6. 6. 9 H. 7. 14. Combes case. ubi supra. 9 H. 6. 20. 44 E. 3. 13. 19 R. 2. Heriot 5.

The former chapters inflict punishment, where the distresse is unlawfull, for that he that distrained had no seigniory or jurisdiction at all, or distrained out of his fee or jurisdiction, &c. But in this last branch, he which distrained had a lawfull seigniory, and distrained within his fee and seigniory, and so this case differeth from the other, (although in truth nothing was behinde.) But this * is to be intended where the lord himselfe doth distrain; for if his baylie take a distresse, where nothing is behinde, there an action of trespasse, *quare vi et armis* lieth against him, because the baylie is not *dominus*; and so it is against a guardien in socage. And if the lord himselfe doth cut any wood, or break the house, or feed the ground of his tenant, or the like, which he doth not in respect of his seigniory, there an action of trespasse, *quare vi et armis* lieth against him, for he doth not these things as *dominus*.

* [106]

And

And *(dominus)* in this act is extended to the lessor upon a lease for life, or for yeares made, for the lessee for yeares shall doe fealty also; but if the lessor put out the lessee for yeares, or disseise the tenant for life, or doe any act, not as *dominus*, the lessee shall have an action of trespasse against him, *vi et armis*. 48 E. 3. 5, 6. 28 E. 3. 97. 38 E. 3. 33. 5 H. 7. 10.

CAP. IV.

NULLUS de cætero faciat ducere districtiones quas fecerit extra comitatum in quo captæ fuerint. Et si vicinus hoc fecerit super vicinum suum, et per voluntatem suam, et sine judicio, puniatur per redemptionem ut supra, veluti de re facta *contra pacem. Veruntamen si dominus hoc super tenentem suum facere præsumpserit, castigetur per gravem misericordiam. Districtiones insuper sint rationabiles, et non nimis graves. Et qui districtiones fecerint irrationabiles, et indebitas, graviter amercientur propter excessum* (1) *districtionum ipsarum.* Vide statut. anno 1 & 2 Phil. & Mar. cap. 13.

NONE from henceforth shall cause any distress that he hath taken, to be driven out of the county where it was taken; and if one neighbour do so to another of his own authority, and without judgement, he shall make fine (as above is said) as for a thing done against the peace: nevertheless, if the lord presume so to do against his tenant, he shall be grievously punished by amerciament. Moreover, distresses shall be reasonable, and not too great. And he that taketh great and unreasonable distresses, shall be grievously amerced for the excess of such distresses.

W. 1. c. 16. (Fitz. Bar. 120, 275. 29 Ed. 3. c. 23. Kel. 50. 1 & 2 P. & M. c. 12. 28 Ed. 1. stat. 3. c. 12.)

This chapter emptieth itselfe into five parts, viz.

1. That none shall drive any distresse out of the county, where he hath taken it.

2. If one neighbour doe so to another, (as for damage fesant, or rent charge) of his owne authority, he shall make ransome, that is a fine, as of a thing done against the peace. 22 E. 4. 11.

3. If the lord presume to doe it against his tenant, he shall be punished by a great amerciament.

At the common law a man might have driven the distresse to what county he would, which was mischievous for two causes: 1. Because the tenant was bound to give the beasts being impounded in an open pound sustenance, and being carried into another county, by common intendment he could have no knowledge where they were. Another cause, he could not know where to have a replevy, but the party was before this statute driven to his action upon his case; and albeit this statute be in the negative, yet if the tenancy be in one county, and the mannor in another county, the lord may drive the distresse which he taketh in the tenancy to his mannor in the other county, for that the tenant is out of both the said mischiefes; for the tenant by doing of suite and service to the mannor, by common intendment may know what is done there, and therefore may give his beasts sustenance; and to know where to have his 6 H. 3. Avow. 242. Temps E. 1. ibid. 192. 30 Ass. 38. 29 E. 3. 13. 1 H. 6. 9. 22 E. 4. Barre 120. F.N.B. 89. Pl. Com. 9. b.

his replevy, the bayliffe of the mannor usually drive the cattell distrained to the pound of the mannor; and this act extends as well to goods as to beasts: note here by a case out of the mischiefs is out of the meaning of the law, though it be within the letter.

Registr. 97. 1. pt. Inst. sect. 69. 29 E. 3. 23. 42 E. 3. 26. 11 H. 4. 2. 8 H. 4. 16. 29 E. 23.

4. That distresses be reasonable, and not too great: vide the first part of the Institutes, what shall be said reasonable, and by whom it shall be tried in this and in all other cases: some say that for homage, or fealty, for the expences of the knights of the parliament an excessive distresse cannot be taken; but this statute is generall, and extendeth unto all.

5. He that takes unreasonable and undue distresses, shall be grievously amerced for the excesse of those distresses.

Stat. 51 H. 3. W. 1. c. 16. 28 E. 1. c. 12. 1 & 2 Phil. & Mar. c. 12.

It is worthy of observation, how provident the makers of these and other statutes be, that mens beasts, cattell, or other goods be not unjustly or excessively distrained; and if they be, that deliverance be speedily made of them by replevy, otherwise the husbandry of the realme, and mens other trades might be overthrowne or hindred: and this agreeth with the reason of the common law.

7 E. 3. 8. b. 20 Ass. 38. 13 H. 4 17. 14 H. 4. 4. Lib. 8. fol. 147. le 6. Carpenters case. li. 5. fo. 76. Pilkingtons case.

And therefore if the lord or his bayliffe come to distraine the beasts or goods of his tenant for his rent behinde, before the distresse the tenant (that he may keep and use his beasts or other goods) may upon the land tender the arrerages, and if after that a distresse be taken, it is wrongfull: and if the lord have distrained, if the tenant before the impounding of them tender the arrerages, the lord ought to deliver the distresse, and if he doth not, the detainer is unlawfull: even so it is in case of a distresse for damage feasant, the tender of amends before the distresse, maketh the distresse unlawfull, and after the distresse, and before the impounding, the detainer unlawfull. But if a man bring an action of trespasse for taking away his beasts or other goods, there tender of such sufficient amends before the action brought is no barre, because he that tendred the amends is not the owner of the goods; as in the other cases, but a trespasser, whom the law favoureth not: and further, if the avowant hath retourned irreplegiable, yet if the owner of the beasts or goods tender to him all that is due upon the judgement in the avowry (whereby the certainty doth appeare) he may have an action of detinue for the detainer afterward, or upon satisfaction made in court, have a writ for their delivery.

21 H. 7. 30. a. But this is now holpen by the Statute of 21 Jac. cap. 13 H. 4. 4. a. 33 H. 6. 27. a. 45 E. 3. 9.

51 H. 3. distr. de Scaccar. acc.

(1) *Districtiones sunt insuper rationabiles et non minus graves, &c. propter excessum, &c.*] *Quicquid in excessu actum est, lege prohibetur.*

Regist. 97. 22 E. 4. 26. 11 H. 4. 2. 8 H. 4. 16. F.N.B. 89.

For example, if the lord distraine two or three oxen for xij. d. or the like small summe, and the owner bring a replevy of the oxen, and the lord avow the taking of them for the twelve pence, &c. of his owne shewing hee shall make fine, &c. or the party may have his action upon the statute.

If the lord distraine an oxe, or horse for a penny, if there were no other distresse upon the land holden, the distresse is not excessive, but if there were a sheepe or swine, &c. then the taking of the oxe or horse is excessive, because he might have taken a beast of lesse value.

CAP.

CAP. V.

MAGNA Charta (1) *in ſingulis ſuis articulis teneatur, tam in his quæ ad regem pertinent, quam quæ ad alios* (2), *et hoc coram juſticiariis itinerantibus* (3) *in ſuis itineribus, et vicecomes in comitatibus ſuis, cum opus fuerit demandetur, et brevia verſus eos qui contravenerint gratis concedantur* (4) *coram rege* (5), *vel coram juſticiariis de banco*, (6), *vel coram juſticiariis itinerantibus, cum in partes illas venerint. Similiter Charta de Foreſta in ſingulis ſuis articulis teneatur* (7), *et contravenientes per dominum regem, cum convicti fuerint graviter puniantur modo ſupradicto.*

THE great charter ſhall be obſerved in all his articles, as well in ſuch as pertain to the king, as to other; and that ſhall be enquired afore the juſtices in eyre in their circuits, and afore the ſheriffs in their counties, when need ſhall be. And writs ſhall be freely granted againſt them that do offend, before the king, or the juſtices of the bench, or before juſtices in eyre, when they come into thoſe parts. Likewiſe the charter of the foreſt ſhall be obſerved in all his articles, and the offenders when they be convict, ſhall be grievouſly puniſhed by our ſovereign lord the king in the form above mentioned.

(15 E. 4. 13)

This, as hath beene ſaid, was one of the principall cauſes of the ſummons of this parliament, and after this enſued great and conſtant peace and tranquility.

And where ſome have thought, that *Magna Charta* had not the ſtrength of a parliament before this act, how they miſtake it, you may reade before in *Magna Charta*, cap. 32, and 38. Magna Charta, c. 32, 38.

(1) *Magna Charta.*] By this time this charter had got the name of *Magna Charta*, and by that name onely is here confirmed.

(2) *Tam in hiis quæ ad regem pertinent quam ad alios.*] Theſe be ſhort and effectuall words, and to avoid all ſcruples, the king is expreſly named, and it hath not words of confirmation, but words of eſtabliſhment, *Quod Magna Charta in ſingulis ſuis articulis teneatur*, which is the ſureſt way.

(3) *Coram juſticiariis itinerantibus.*] Vide cap. *itineris*, the articles of *Magna Charta* eſpecially given in charge, and enquired of, &c. by juſtices in eyre, and by this act they had their authority therein. Cap. Itineris. Vet. Mag. Cart. 150. b.

(4) *Brevia gratis concedantur.*] Writs againſt the breakers of *Magna Charta* ſhall be freely graunted, to encourage ſuch as would purſue againſt them. Mag. Cart. c. 29.

(5) *Coram rege.*] That is, in the kings bench.

(6) *Coram juſticiariis de banco.*] That is, in the court of common pleas.

(7) *Similiter charta de foreſta, in ſingulis ſuis articulis teneatur, &c.*] This was another of the principall cauſes of the ſummons of this parliament, as hath been ſaid.

CAP.

CAP. VI.

DE his autem qui primogenitos, et hæredes (1) *suos infra ætatem existentes* (2) *feoffare solent de hæreditate sua* (3), *ut per hoc amitterent domini feodorum custodias suas, provisum est, concordatum, et concessum, quod occasione hujusmodi* falsi *feoffamenti, nullus capitalis dominus amittat custodiam suam. De his insuper qui de terris suis* (4), *quas tradere voluerint ad terminum annorum* (5), *ut per hoc domini feodorum amittant custodias suas, falsa fingunt feoffamenta continentia, quod eis satisfactum est de summa servitii in illis contenti usque ad terminum aliquem: ita quod si ad dictum terminum solvere tenentur hujusmodi feoffati summā aliquam ad valorem terrarum illarum, vel in multo excedentem, ut sic post terminum illum terra eorum revertatur ad ipsos vel ad hæredes suos, eo quod nemo eam pro tanto tenere curaret: provisum est, concordatum, et concessum, ut per hujusmodi fraudem nullus capitalis dominus amittat custodiam* (6) *suam: veruntamen non licebit eis hujusmodi feoffatos sine judicio disseisire* (7): *sed breve habeant de hujusmodi custodia sibi reddenda* (8), *et per testes in chartis* (9) *ne hujusmodi feoffamento contentos, una cum aliis liberis et legalibus hominibus de patria, et per quantitatem et valorem tenement', et per quantitatem summæ, quæ inde reddi debeant post terminum* prædictum *attingatur, utrum hujusmodi feoffamenta bona fide facta sint, an in fraudem, ad auferendum capitalibus dominis feodorum custodiam suam. Si vero capitales domini per judicium curia in hujusmodi casibus recuperaverint custodiam suam, salva sit nihilominus hujusmodi feoffatis actio sua, quo ad terminum, seu ad feodum recuperandum, quam inde habuerint cum hæredes ad legitimam ætatem per-*

AS touching them that use to infeoff their eldest sons and heirs, being within age, of their heritage, for to defraud the lords of the fee of their wardships, it is provided, accorded, and agreed, that by occasion of any such feoffment no chief lord shall leese his ward. Moreover, touching them that fain false feoffments of their lands, which they will lease for term of years, for to defraud the chief lords of their wards, wherein it is contained, that they are satisfied of the whole service due unto them until a certain term; so that such feoffees are bound at the said term to pay a certain sum to the value of the same lands, or far above; so that after such term the land shall return unto them, or to their heirs, because no man will be content to hold it upon the price; it is provided and agreed, that by such fraud no chiefe lord shall leese his ward. Neverthelefs, it shall not be lawful to them to disseise such feoffees without judgement, but they shall have a writ for to have such a ward restored unto them; and by the witnesses contained in the deed of feoffment, with other free and lawful men of the country, and by the value of the land, and by the quantity of the sum payable after the term, it shall be tryed whether such feoffments were made bona fide, or by collusion, to defraud the chief lords of the fee of their wards. And if the chief lords in such cases recover their wards by judgement, the feoffees shall neverthelefs have their action to recover such term or fee, which they had therein, when the heirs come to their lawful age. And if any chief lords do maliciously implead such feoffees, faining this case

pervenerint. Et si aliqui capitales domini feoffatos aliquos malitiosè implacitaverint, fingentes casum istum, maximè ubi feoffamenta legitimè et bona fide facta fuerint (11), *tunc adjudicentur feoffatis dampna sua, et misæ suæ* (10), *quas fecerint occasione præd' placiti, et ipsi actores per misericordiam graviter puniantur.*

case, namely, where the feoffments were made lawful, and in good faith, then the feoffees shall have their damages awarded, and their costs which they have sustained by occasion of the foresaid plea, and the plaintiffs shall be grievously punished by amerciament.

(34 & 35 H. 8. c. 5. 1 Roll 91. 2 Roll 106, 134. Godbolt 78. pl. 92. Fitz. Gard. 79, 102, 155. 6 Rep 76. Dyer 9. 27 H. 8. 7. Fitz. Gard. 33. Fitz. Collusion, 12, 14, 29, 36, 47. 11 Rep. 77. Fitz. Gard. 119. Fitz. Brief, 779. 19 H. 6. f. 30. Ejectione custodiæ, Co. Ent. 183. Regist. 161. 4 H. 7. c. 17.

Robert Walrand penned and preferred this act, and by aid and common assent of the great lords of the realme, obtained to passe it for a statute. This Robert Walrand was learned in the lawes of the realme, and soone after this statute, died: his son and heire conveyed his lands holden by knights service to his son and heire apparent, being within the age of 21 yeares, rather trusting his land in his son within age, then in himselfe, and died, his son being still within age; and this statute which Robert Walrand the grandfather had penned and preferred, took first effect in the heire of his heire, as Britton reporteth. [110] Brit. c. 36. fo. 95. b.

The mischiefe before this first branch of this statute was, that such a feoffment as well in the kings case, as in the case of a common person, did take away the wardship of the heire, as it appeareth by the preamble, and our books, because by the common law the heire could not be in ward, unlesse he were in by descent, and tenaunt by knights service to prevent the lord of the wardship, would enfeoffe him or her to whom the land should descend by the common law. And upon this statute collusion of this kind was divided into two branches; the first was called collusion apparent, upon this first branch, *qui primogenitos feoffare solent*; the second was called collusion averrable, that is to be proved upon issue thereupon to be taken upon the second branch, *De hiis insuper qui de terris suis, &c.* 9 H. 4. 6. 33 H. 6. 15. b. Lib. 6. fo. 76. Sir Geo. Cursons case. 17 E. 3. reliefe 3. 33 H. 6. 16. Pl. com. 82.

(1) *Qui primogenitos et hæredes.*] Albeit the heire be not *primogenitus*, but an heire female, or male lineall or collaterall, yet every of them is within the same mischiefe; and therefore the auncient sages of the law (that I may say it once for all) did ever apply the remedy to the mischief; and therefore here this *(et)* a conjunctive, was by construction taken for a disjunctive, *viz. qui primogenitos vel hæredes, &c.* Rot. claus. an. 2. E. 1. m. 14. Pl. com. ubi sup. Hil. 16 E. 1. in Banco. Rot. 51. Norf. Johannes de Brampton. 9 H. 4. 6.

If a tenant by knights service of land of the nature of borough-english infeoffe his youngest sonne, he is within this statute; for *hæres dicitur ab hæreditate, et sic se similibus.* See the stat. of 34 H. 8. c. 15. versus finem. 13 Eliz. cap. 5.

(2) *Infra ætatem existentes.*] This branch extends not to give remedy for reliefes which is due when the tenant dieth, his heire of full age; but by divers statutes of later time provision is made for reliefe. And thus much concerning the person to be infeoffed within this first branch. 17 E. 3. 63. relief 3. 31 E. 3. tit. collusion 29. 7 E. 3. tit. rel. 11. 4 E. 3. 22.

(3) *Feoffare solent de hæreditate sua.*] 1. [a] This word *feoffare* implyeth a fee-simple, and therefore if the auncestor had made a lease [a] 1. Part Instit. 1. sect. 1. for this word *feoffare*. 33 H. 6. 14. 27 H. 8. 10.

leafe for life, or a gift in taile to his heire apparent with a remainder or without a remainder over of the eftate in taile, it was out of this ftatute.

[b] 31 E. 1. collu. 29. 33 H. 6. 14.

2. [b] This act fpeaketh of a feoffement made folely to the heire; and therefore if a feoffement had beene made to the heire and an eftranger, though the fee-fimple were limited to the heires of the heire, yet it was out of this act.

[c] 33 H. 6. ubi fup.

3. [c] And this is to be underftood of an immediate gift to the heire apparent; for if a leafe for life be made, the remainder to the heire apparent in fee, this is no collufion.

4. Though it was not a feoffment, but inured by way of graunt; as if the mefne had graunted his mefnaltie to his heire, or if the tenant or mefne had levied a fine, or fuffered a recovery by confent, or had made a leafe and releafe, or confirmation, or the like, fuch conveyances had beene in equall mifchiefe, and therefore within the remedy.

27 H. 8. 8. b.

5. This act extended not to a feoffment to the ufe of his heire, or to the ufe of himfelfe and his heires; for at the common law the lord fhould not have the wardfhip but of the heire of his tenant, that died in his homage, and therefore the ftatute of 4 H. 7. cap. 17. was made to remedy this mifchiefe.

33 H. 6. 16. Lib. fo. Ham. Stranges cafe, and Porriges cafe.

6. If the eldeft fon within age purchafe of his father the lands holden by knights fervice for valuable confideration, *bona fide*, by feoffment or other conveyance, this is within the letter, but not within the meaning of this ftatute, no more then if he had fold the land to any other.

[111]

13 H. 7. 7. 27 H. 8, 9.

7. If *ceftuy que ufe* after the ftatute of 4 H. 7. cap. 17. and before the ftatute of 27 H. 8. cap. 10. of ufes, had enfeoffed his eldeft fon, this was taken within the equitie of this ancient act.

33 H. 6. 16.

8. When fhall this feoffment be upon this act deemed to be by collufion? The anfwer is, after the deceafe of the auncefter, for then the title of wardfhip accrues, and not in his life time.

33 E. 3. gar. 12. 31 E. 1. ibid. 155. 32 E. 3. ibid. 33. 33 H. 6 16.

9. If the lord accept homage of the heire apparant (after the feoffment made to him by his auncefter) in the life of the auncefter, he fhall not have the wardfhip, becaufe he allowed him to be his tenant.

Tr 7 Jac. li. 8. fo. 164. Mights cafe.

10. But at this day, albeit the father infeoffe his eldeft fon, or any of his children, though it be found to be made upon collufion, to defeat the king or other lord of wardfhip, yet the king or other lord fhall not have but a third part by the ftatutes of 32 and 34 H. 8. of Wills. So note this ftatute altered in part. And thus much of the manner of the feoffment.

(4) *De hiis infuper qui de terris fuis*, &c.] This is the fecond branch of this act concerning collufion averrable, when feoffments are made to ftrangers, whereof here is an example fet downe in this act.

Briton, 95. b. 32 E. 3. gard 33. 4 E. 2. gard. 119.

(5) *Qui tradere voluerint ad terminum annorum.*] This is to be underftood of a feoffment in fee referving no rent, for that they fuppofe they are fatisfied for a certaine terme, which fhould end when the heire fhould come to full age, and then it was conditioned that the feoffee fhould pay more then the land was worth, and thereupon the heire entred, for that none would give fo great a price.

47 E. 3. 19. 32 E. 3. gard. 33. 8 R. 2. collus. 47.

(6) *Per hujufmodi fraudē nullus capitalis dominus amittat cuftodiam.*] By fuch fraud, that is, fuch in mifchiefe, or fuch in inconveniencie,

conveniencie, and therefore all other fraudulent feoffments tending to the ſame end are within this ſtatute, whatſoever colourable pretext they have, and ſo is this word [ſuch] oftentimes taken in other ſtatutes. It is the opinion of Huls juſtice, and of Gaſcoine chiefe juſtice of England, that by the words and purview of this ſtatute, it holdeth only betweene lord and tenant; and therefore if a man hold land by knights ſervice in *capite* of the king; and other land of a ſubject by knights ſervice, and maketh a feoffment by colluſion of the land holden of the ſubject, and dieth, his heire within age, the king ſhall not take advantage of this ſtat. for he is not *dominus* of this land; but in this caſe the king is relieved by the ſtat. of 34 H. 8. c. 5. *verſus finem ejuſd. actus*. 9 H. 4. 6.

(7) *Veruntamen non liceat hujuſmodi feoffatos ſine judicio diſſeiſire.*] *Hujuſmodi feoffatos*, ſuch feoffees. And yet the feoffees of the feoffees upon the ſame colluſion are taken to be within this ſtatute; but if the feoffees in the life of the auncester make a feoffment in fee *bona fide*, and then the tenant dieth, his heire within age, the lord ſhall not have any action upon this ſtatute, for that the colluſion continued not untill the death of the tenant; but if the tenant had died, his heire within age, and then the feoffees had infeoffed others *bona fide*, yet the lord ſhall recover the wardſhip, becauſe the lord by the death of his tenant was once intitled to his action; but yet in ſome caſes the lord ſhall enter upon the feoffee. 33 H. 6. 16. 31 E. 3. gard. 29.

If the tenant infeoffe a ſtranger upon colluſion, and that ſtranger infeoffe the heire in the life of the tenant, and then the tenant dieth, the lord may enter upon the heire, becauſe no writ of right of ward lyeth againſt the heire; and therefore the lord ſhall enter upon the heire, being feoffee: for otherwiſe he ſhould be without remedy, the words of the writ of ward being *Præcipe A. quod reddat B. cuſtodiam terræ et hæredis C. quæ ad ipſum B. pertinet, &c.* ſo as this writ is ever brought againſt a ſtranger. 33 H. 6. 16. F.N.B. 139.

If the tenant infeoffe the villein of the lord upon colluſion, and dieth, his heire within age, the lord ſhall enter upon this feoffee; for if the lord ſhould be driven to his action againſt the villein, it ſhould amount to an enfranchiſement; and ſtatutes muſt be ſo conſtrued, as no collaterall prejudice grow thereby. [112]

Alſo the heire of the feoffee is within this ſtatute; and if the feoffee dieth, his heire within age, the lord ſhall have his writ of ward againſt the heire, who ſhall not have his age, but the lord ſhall recover againſt him by this act. 18 E. 3. covenãt 7.

The ſtatute ſaith, *feoffatos*, and yet conuſees of fines, and all other conveyances are within this ſtatute. 7 H. 4. 15. 12 H. 4. 16.

And here it appeareth, that the ancient law did ever favour him that came by title, and put him that right had to his action. 1 Part Inſtit. ſect. 472.

If the father had made a feoffment for the maintenance and livelihood of his wife, preferment of his daughters, or of his younger ſons, or for the payment of his debts, and after had infeoffed his heire apparent, this was holden no colluſion; for every man by the law of God and nature, ought to provide for his wife and children, and he is worſe then an infidell that doth not provide for his family: and by the law of God and of nations debts ought to be paid: *Nemini quicquam debeatis, niſi quod invicem diligatis*. 33 H. 6. 14. Dier 10 El. 260. 3 Eliz. 193. 20 Eliz. 361. 19 Eliz. 276. 5 Mar. 158. Lib. 6. fo. 76. Sir Geo. Curſons caſe.

* Now by the ſaid ſtatutes of 32 and 34 H. 8. where the tenant by knights ſervice doth infeoffe others to any of theſe three intents, * See Sir Geo. Curſons caſe *ubi ſupra*.

tents, *viz.* for the livelihood of his wife, preferment of his children, or payment of his debts, the heir shal be in ward for his body, and for the third part of his lands so conveyed, whereby the common law was changed in that behalfe.

27 H. 8. 10. 4 H. 7. c. 10. Of lands holden by knights service deviseable by custome, no collusion could have been averred upon a devise by will; the same law, if *cestuy que use* had devised the use by will; but now that is altered by the statute of 34 H. 8. c. 5.

39 E. 3. 33, 34. (8) *Breve habeat de hujusmodi custodia reddenda.*] This writ is a writ of right of ward, and when the lord hath recovered the wardship against the feoffee, the freehold and inheritance is left 4 E. 2 gard. 119. 32 E. 3. ibid. 33. 12 H. 4. 13. b. 4 H. 7. 10 F.N.B. 143. k. in the feoffee, and not restored to the heire, and therefore if the gardein commit waste, the same is dispunishable, for the feoffee cannot have an action of waste against the gardein in this case. And the lord upon this statute could not seise the body of the heire, or have a ravishment of ward, before he had recovered the land 34 H. 8. c. 5. versus finem. 13 El. c. 5. in a writ of right of ward, for therein ought the collusion be first tryed, because unlesse that were found according to this statute, there is no cause of wardship by this act.

12 E. 2. c. 2. 1. Part Instit. sect. 1. (9) *Et per testes in cartis.*] Note, the deed is not here denyed, and yet proces to be awarded against the witnesses. For this see the first part of the Institutes. *Vide postea, cap.* 14.

(10) *Adjudicentur feoffatis damna sua et misæ suæ.*] This is the first statute that gave the defendant damages and costs if it were found for him, and the lord to be grievously amercied, and many other statutes have followed this example: and where this statute saith *(malitiose) implacitaverint*, if the matter be fained, and without just ground, the law implyeth malice in this case.

(11) *Fingentes casum istum maximè ubi feoffamenta legitima et bonæ facta fuer'.*] There is no greater injustice, then when under colour of justice injury is done.

Regula. *Multi litigant in foro, non ut aliquid lucrentur, sed ut vexent alios.* Therefore justly did this act, which gave an action in a new case, give dammages and costs to the defendant, if he were maliciously vexed thereby without good cause.

[113]

CAP. VII.

IN placito vero communi de custodiis (1), *si ad magnam districtionem non venerint deforciatores* (3), *tunc bis vel ter iteretur breve prædictum ad terminos quibus fieri poterit, infra medietatem anni sequentis, ita quod singulis vicibus legat' breve in pleno comitatu nisi al' ubi prius inventus fuerit deforciator. Et ibi publicè denuncietur, ut veniat ad diem sibi præfixum. Quod si ipse extunc se subtraxerit, ita quod infra medietatem anni prædict' responsurus non venerit, nec vicecomes eum invenire*

IN a plea of communi custodia, if the deforceors come not at the great distress, then the said writ shall be renewed twice or thrice, at such terms as it may be done within the half year following, so that every time the writ shall be read in the open county (if the deforceor be not found before) and there openly be proclaimed, that he may come at the day limited: so that if he absent himself then, and come not to answer within the said half year, nor the sheriff cannot get his

invenire possit (5), *per quod corpus suum habere non possit* (4), *coram justiciariis* (6), *ad respondendum secundum legem et consuetudinem regni, tunc (tanquam rebellis, et se justiciari non permittens) amittat seisinam hujusmodi custodiæ* (2), *salva sibi alias actione sua, si fortè jus habeat ad eandem. In casibus autem ubi custodiæ pertinent ad custodes* (7), *hæredum infra ætatem existentium versus custodes ill'* petatur custodia quæ accidit hæredibus illis *tanquam pertinens ad eorum hæreditates: et non amittant hujusmodi hæredes infra ætatem existentes, hæreditatem suam per negligentiam, vel rebellionem suorum custodum, sicut in casu prædicto, sed currat lex communis eodem modo quo prius currere consuevit.*

his body, to have it before our justices to answer according to the law and custom of the realm, then as a rebel, and such a one as will not be justified, he shall leese the seisin of his ward; saving to him his action at another time, if he have any right to the same. But in such cases, where the wardships belong to the guardians of wards being within age, and where the guardians demand a wardship which belongeth to the heir, or as appertaining to their inheritance, such heirs within age shall not leese their inheritance by the negligence or rebellion of their guardians, as in the case afore rehearsed; but let the common law run in like manner as it hath been accustomed to do.

(13 Ed. 1. stat. 1. c. 35. 12 Car. 2. c. 24.)

(1) *In placito communi de custodiis.*] In the common plea of ward, that is, in a writ of right of ward, or in an *ejectment de gard.* 30 E. 3. 10. 24 E. 3. 33. 2 H. 4. 1.

In the chapter going before, remedy was given to the lord for wardship, where there was none due to him by the common law: in this chapter more speedy remedy is given to the lord, as well when the lord hath right by the common law, as by the next precedent chapter.

Before the making of this statute, the proces in the writ of ward was summons, attachment, and distresse infinite, and the sheriffe would many times returne small issues, and so the lord was greatly delayed, and if the heire came to full age, hanging the writ, the writ abated, which was mischievous. 9 E. 4. 50. 18 E. 3. scire fac. 10.

Now this statute provideth, that if the deforceours come not at the grande distresse, that after the returne thereof a distresse with proclamation shall be made in the county by sixe moneths, and if hee appeare not, judgement shall be given against him, saving to him his right at another time, *si inde loqui voluerit:* Westminst. 2. cap. 35. prescribeth but three moneths. 9 E. 3. 15. 3 H. 4. 45. 16 E. 3. Proclam. 4. 30 E. 3. 10. 14 E. 3. Procl. 8. 16 E. 3. gard 138.

In a resummons of gard upon the statute of W. 2. a proclamation shall be awarded upon this statute, for it is in equall mischiefe, but in a ravishment * of gard, no proclamation shall be awarded, for that action is formed, and given by the statute of W. 2. cap. 35. which was but trespasse at the common law. 2 H. 4. 1. 30 E. 3. 10. 22 E. 3. 8. 14 E. 3. Proclam. 7. * [114]

(2) *Amittet seisinam hujusmodi custodiæ.*] If the defendant in a writ of ward make default at the returne of the distresse with a proclamation, judgement shall be given for the plaintife against the deforceour to recover the ward and damages, and have a writ to enquire of the damages; and yet this act saith, that he shall lose the seisin of custody, and speaketh not of damages, but in this action the plaintife should recover damages at the common law. 7 E. 3. 22. 5 E. 3. Damages 115. 13 E. 3. Judgement 138. 24 E. 3. Damages 5. 24 E. 33. 4 E. 3. 26.

17 E. 3. 70.
14 [illegible] 4. 37.
19 E. 3. Pro-clam. 5. & 10.

In a writ of ward against two, at the grand distresse one of them appeared, and the other made default, the plaintife prayed a distresse with a proclamation, and it was denied, for the body is not severable, and therefore the plaintife cannot have judgement to recover the moity of the body, otherwise it is of the land, for that is severable.

29 E. 3. 38.
13 E. 3. Proclam. 9.
33 E. 3. ibid. 19.

(3) *Non venerint deforciatores.*] If in a writ of ward, the defendant vouch, no proclamation shall be awarded against the vouchee for two causes. 1. The statute extendeth onely to the suite of the plaintife, and this is the suite of the defendant against the vouchee. 2. The statute provideth that proclamation shall be awarded against the deforceors, and the vouchee is not deforceor.

(4) *Quod corpus suum habere non possit.*] This is to be understood, that there is no default in the sheriffe in retourning of good issues, so as by that meanes he might have his body to appeare, for the sheriffe cannot arrest him.

17 E. 3. 70, 71.

(5) *Nec vicecomes eum invenire non poterit.*] This must be understood of the sheriffe in that county, where the originall is brought, for no other sheriffe in another county upon a *testatum*, *&c.* shall make proclamation, but there processe lieth, as it was at the common law.

3 E. 3. Procl. 17.

(6) *Coram justiciariis.*] This is before the justices of the court of common pleas, and that court being particularly named, this act extended not to justices in eyre, as it is said in our books.

(7) *In casibus ubi custodiæ pertinent ad custodes.*] If one demand a ward against me, which I claime by cause of ward, he shall not have processe upon this statute, lest by negligence or collusion of the gardien, the heire within age may be prejudiced, but therein the processe shall be at the common law.

* [115]

CAP. VIII.

ILLI autem qui pro iterata disseisina (1) *capti fuerint et detenti, non deliberentur sine speciali præcepto domini regis, et hoc per finem cum domino rege inde faciend' pro hujusmodi transgressione sua. Et si compertum fuerit* (2) *quod vicecomes aliter eos deliberaverit, propter hoc graviter * amercietur, et nihilominus illi qui per vicecomitem sine præcepto domini regis, sic deliberantur, pro sua transgressione graviter puniantur.* Merton cap. 3. Westminst. 2. cap. 26.

THEY which be taken and imprisoned for redisseisin, shall not be delivered without special commandment of our lord the king, and shall make fine with our lord the king for their trespass. And if it be found, that the sheriff delivereth any contrary to this ordinance, he shall be grievously amerced therefore; and nevertheless, they which are so delivered by the sheriff without the king's commandment, shall be grievously punished for their trespass.

(1 H. 8. f. 1. Rast. 10. 548. V. N. B. 108. F. N. B. 188, 189. 20 H. 3. c. 3. Regist. 206. 13 Ed. 1. stat. 1. c. 26.)

The ſtatute of Merton, cap. 3. as hath been ſaid, gave the rediſſeiſin, and poſt diſſeiſin, the words of which ſtatute being, *In priſona domini regis detineantur, quouſque per dominum regem, vel aliquo alio modo deliberentur.* Upon theſe words, *vel aliquo alio modo deliberentur*; they were delivered by the common writ *de homine replegiando*, for the liberty of a free-man is ſo much favoured in law, as there is ever a benigne interpretation made for the benefit thereof. Now this ſtatute doth enact that they ſhall not be delivered *ſine ſpeciali præcepto domini regis*, that is, by the kings writ reciting the ſpeciall matter, and for a fine with the king therefore to be made. And he that is attainted in a rediſſeiſin, and in priſon, this fine that this act ſpeaketh of, as ſome have ſaid, ought to be aſſeſſed in the chancery, to which end he muſt have a *certiorari* to remove the record thither, and out of the chancery to have his writ to diſcharge him: for *ſine ſpeciali præcepto domini regis*, is intendable by writ (ſay they) in the chancery.

Merton, cap. 3. Regiſt. 206. Mirror, cap. 5. § 3.

Bracton, lib. 3. fo. 154. F.N.B. 66.

Dier 36. H. 8. 60, 61.

18 H. 8. 1.

18 H. 8. ubi ſupra.

And therefore if one be attainted in a rediſſeiſin, and is at large, the party may have a *certiorari* to remove the record into the court of common pleas, and by *capias* out of that court he may be taken; and ſome doe hold, that this court cannot aſſeſſe the fine, nor make the ſpeciall writ.

But certain it is, if a man be attainted before the ſheriffe in a rediſſeiſin, and taken in execution, becauſe he cannot be delivered by this act without a ſpeciall commandement of the king, he may ſue a *certiorari* to remove the record before the king in his bench, in which court after he hath made fine, he is thereupon to have a writ for his delivery, reciting the ſpeciall matter, which is the ſpeciall commandement that this act ſpeaketh of, which appeareth in the Regiſter, and F. N. B.

Regiſt. F.N.B. 190. f. & 242 b.

(1) *Pro iterata diſſeiſina.*] This doth extend as well to the poſt diſſeiſin, as rediſſeiſin.

(2) *Et ſi compertum fuerit,* &c.] That is, by way of indictment and conviction of the ſheriffe. and ſo it is of the party, that procureth himſelſe to bee delivered in that manner alſo: but no action can be grounded upon this act.

CAP. IX.

De ſectis (1) vero faciendis ad curiam magnatum, vel ad curiam aliorum dominorum ipſarum curiarum, de cætero ſic obſervandum eſt, quod nullus qui per chartam feoffatus eſt, diſtringatur de cætero ad hujuſmodi ſectam faciendam ad curiam domini ſui, niſi per formam feoffamenti ſui *ſpecialiter teneatur ad ſectam illam faciendam* (2). *His autem exceptis quorum anteceſſores, vel ipſiment, hujuſmodi ſectam facere conſueverunt ante primam transfreta-*

FOR doing ſuits unto courts of great lords, or of meaner perſons, from henceforth this order ſhall be obſerved, that none that is infeoffed by deed, from henceforth ſhall be diſtrained to do ſuch ſuit to the court of his lord, without he be ſpecially bound thereto by the form of his deed: theſe only except, whoſe anceſtors, or they themſelves, have uſed to do ſuch ſuit before the firſt voyage of the ſaid king Henry into Britain, ſithence which

fretationem prædicti domini regis Henrici in Britanniam (3), *a tempore cujus transfretationis elapsi sunt xxxix. anni et medietas unius anni ad tempus quo hujusmodi constitutiones fuerunt statutæ. Similiter nullus feoffatus a tempore conquestus* sine charta *vel aliquo alio antiquo feoffamento distringatur ad hujusmodi sectam faciendam; nisi ipsemet, vel antecessores sui eam facere consueverunt ante primam transfretationem prædictam* (4): *qui autem per chartam pro certo servitio* (5), *veluti pro libero servitio tot solidorum annuatim pro omni servitio solvend' feoffati sunt, ad hujusmodi sectam vel ad aliud, contra formam feoffamenti sui, de cætero non teneantur. Et si hæreditas aliqua* (6), *de qua tantum unica secta debeatur, ad plures hæredes participes ejusdem hæreditatis devolvatur, ille vero qui habet enitiam partem* (7) *hæreditatis illius, unicam faciet sectam pro se et participibus suis, et alii participes sui pro portione sua, contribuant ad sectam illam faciendam. Et si plures feoffati fuerint de hæreditate aliqua, de qua tamen unica secta debeatur, dominus illius feodi unicam sectam inde habeat* (8), *nec possit de prædicta hæreditate nisi unicam sectam exigere, sicut prius inde fieri consuevit. Et si feoffati warrantum, vel medium non habeant* (9), *qui inde eos acquietare debeat, tunc omnes illi feoffati, contribuant* pro portione sua *ad sectam illam pro eis faciendam. Si autem contingat, quod domini* (10) *curiarum tenentes suos contra hanc constitutionem, pro hujusmodi secta distringant, tunc ad querimoniam tenentium illorum attachientur eorum domini, quod ad curiam regis veniant ad brevem diem, inde responsuri, et unicum inde habeant essonium si fuerint in regno, et incontinenter deliberentur conquerenti averia sua, sive aliæ districtiones, hac occasione factæ, et deliberatæ, remaneant, donec placitum inde inter eos terminetur. Et si domini curiarum, qui hujusmodi districtiones fecerint,*

which nine and thirty years and an half are passed, unto the time that these statutes were enacted. Likewise from henceforth none that is infeoffed without deed, from the time of the conquest, or any other ancient feoffment, shall be distrained to do such suits, unless that he or his ancestors used to do it before the said voyage. And they that are infeoffed by deed to do a certain service, as, for service of so many shillings by year, to be acquitted of all service, from henceforth shall not be bounden to such suits, or other like contrary unto the form of their feoffment. And if any inheritance, whereof but one suit is due, descend unto many heirs, as unto parceners, whoso hath the eldest part of the inheritance, shall do that one suit for himself and his fellows, and the other coheirs shall be contributaries, according to their portion, for doing such suit. And if many feoffees be seised of an inheritance, whereof but one suit is due, the lord of the fee shall have but that one suit; and shall not exact of the said inheritance, but that one suit, as hath been used to be done before. And if those feoffees have no warrant or mean which ought to acquit them, then all the feoffees, according to their portion, shall be contributaries for doing the suit for them. And if it chance that the lords of the fee do distrain their tenants for such suits, contrary to this act, then, at the complaint of the tenants, the lords shall be attached to appear in the king's court at a short day, to make answer thereto, and shall have but one essoin therein, if they be within the realm; and immediately the beasts, or other distresses taken by this occasion, shall be delivered to the plaintiff, and so shall remain, until the plea betwixt them be determined. And if the lords of the courts which took distresses, come not at the day that they were

*fecerint, ad diem, ad quem attachiati fuerint, non venerint, vel diem per essonium sibi datum non observaverint, tunc mandetur vicecomiti, quod eos ad alium diem venire faciat, ad quem diem si non venerint, tunc mandetur vicecomiti, quod distringat eos per omnia catalia, quæ habent in baliva sua, ita quod vicecomes respondeat domino regi de exitibus dicti hæredis, et quod habeat corpora eorum ad certum diem sibi præfigendum * coram justitiariis. Ita quod si ad diem illum non venerint, eat pars conquerens inde sine die, et averia sua, sive aliæ districtiones hac occasione factæ, deliberata remaneant, donec ipsi domini sectam illam recuperaverint* (11) *per considerationem curiæ regis, et cessent interim hujusmodi districtiones, salvo dominis curiarum jure suo de sectis illis recuperandis in forma juris, cum inde loqui voluerint.*

Et cum domini curiarum inde venerint responsuri conquerentibus de hujusmodi districtionibus, et super hoc convincantur, tunc per considerationem curiæ domini regis recuperent versus ipsos conquerentes dampna sua quæ sustinuerunt occasione districtionis prædictæ. Simili autem modo si tenentes, post hanc constitutionem, subtrahunt (12) *dominis [feodorum] sectas quas facere [debeant] et quas ante tempus prædictum transfretationis, et hactenus facere consueverunt, tunc per eandem justitiam, et celeritatem quo ad dies præfigend', et districtiones adjudicand', consequantur domini curiarum justitiam de sectis illis perquirendis, una cum dampnis suis quemadmodum tenentes dampna sua recuperarent. Et hoc scilicet de dampnis recuperandis, intelligatur de subtractionibus sibi factis, et non de subtractionibus factis prædecessoribus suis. Veruntamen domini curiarum versus tenentes suos seisinam de hujusmodi sectis recuperare non poterunt per defaltam, sicut prius fieri consuevit. De sectis autem quæ ante tempus supradictum subtractæ fuerunt, currat lex*

were attached, or do not keep the day given to them by essoin, then the sheriff shall be commanded to cause them to come at another day; at which day, if they come not, then he shall be commanded to distrain them by all their goods and chattles that they have in the shire, so that the sheriff shall answer to the king of the issues of the said inheritance; and that he have their bodies before our justices at a certain day limited. So that if they come not at that day, the party plaintiff shall go without day, and his beasts, or other distresses taken by that colour, shall remain delivered, until the same lords have recovered the same suit by award of the king's court; and in the mean time such distresses shall cease, saving to the lords of the court their right to recover those suits in form of law, when they will sue therefore.

And when the lords of the courts come in to answer the plaintiffs of such trespasses, and be convict thereupon; then, by award of the king's court, the plaintiffs shall recover against them the damages that they have sustained by occasion of the said distress. Likewise if the tenants, after this act, withdraw from their lord such suits as they were wont to do, and which they did before the time of the said voyage, and hitherto used to do; then by like speediness of justice, as be to limiting of days, and awarding of distresses, the lords of the court shall obtain justice to recover their suits, with their damages, in like manner as the tenants should recover theirs: and this recovering of damages must be understood of withdrawing from themselves, and not of withdrawing from their ancestors. Nevertheless, the lords of the court shall not recover seisin of such suits against their tenants by default, as they were wont to do. And touching suits withdrawn before the time aforementioned,

lex communis (13), *sicut prius currere consuevit.* | mentioned, let the common law run as it was wont before time.

Regist. 176. F. N. B. 159. 45 E. 3. 23. (6 Rep. 1. Stat. Hiberniæ. 14 H. 3. par. 7. Particion 1. Fitz. Avowry, 15 42. 48. 51. 60. 66. 68. 89. 99. Fitz. Avowry, 86. 92.)

This chapter hath nine branches. The first is,

Regist. 176. F.N.B. 159. 45 E. 3. 23. (1) *De sectis.*] This is understood of suit service to courts baron, hundreds, and the like, and not to suit reall in respect of resiance, nor to suit to the mill, for the words be, *de sectis fac' ad curiam, &c.*

(2) *Nullus qui per cartam feoffatus est, distringatur de cætero ad hujusmodi sectam faciendam ad curiam domini sui nisi per formam feoffamenti sui specialiter teneatur ad sectam illam faciendam.*] There is another clause in this chapter concerning this matter, *Qui autem per cartam pro certo servitio, veluti pro libero servitio tot solidor' annuatim pro omni servitio solvend' feoffati sunt ad hujusmodi sectam, vel ad aliud, contra formam feoffamenti sui, de cætero non teneantur.* Mag. cart. c. 10.

3 E. 2. acc' sur le stat. 23, 24. 4 E. 3. avow. 202. 6 E. 2 avow. 210. 3 E. 3. 27, 28. 22 E. 3. 18. b. 19 E. 3. avow. 122. 28 ass. 33. 32 E. 3. avow. 114. 14 H. 4, 5. 30 H. 6, 7. 10 H. 7. 11. Dier 25 H. 8. 51. F.N.B. 163. d. ‡[118] * Fleta, lib. 3. c. 14. F.N.B. 162, 163.

At the common law, before the making of this statute, if the lord had made a feoffment by deed, and reserved certaine services, as for example, fealtie, and 2 s. rent, or 2 s. rent generally, which had implyed fealtie; in this case if the lord had distreined for homage, or suit, or any other rent or service, then was reserved in the deed, not onely the tenant and his heires, but his ‡ assignes also, or any other tenant of the land might have rebutted the lord, his heires, or assignes, by the deed, and this doth hold betweene partie and partie, privie and privie, privie and estranger, and estranger and estranger. * But this act giveth the tenant or his heires a more speedy remedy, for hereby is given to the tenant against the lord and his heires a writ of *contra formam feoffamenti*, wherein six things are worthy of observation.

1. When any act doth prohibit any wrong or vexation, though no action be particularly named in the act, yet the party grieved shall have an action grounded upon this statute, which in this case is a prohibition to the lord or his bailiffes, and reciteth this act, the forme whereof you may reade in the Register, and F. N. B.

Regist. F.N.B. 163. b. 16 H. 3. avow. 243.

Now where it may be objected, that in Mich. 16 H. 3. reported by F. *tit. avowrie*, 243, that upon a confirmation a writ of *contra formam feoffamenti* doth lie, and by that book it should seeme, that a writ of *contra formam feoffamenti* did lie at the common law before this statute, which was made in 52 H. 3. To this it is answered, that the said case is mis-printed, for where it is Mich. 16 H. 3. it should be 56 H. 3. when the case was so resolved, and in which terme, *viz.* the 16 day of Novemb. Hen. 3. died, so as that opinion was after our statute: and that the writ was given by this statute, the writ (as hath been said) doth recite it. And where in this clause the statute saith (*distringatur*) all this chapter is to be understood of suit service, because for suit reall no distresse can be taken, but for the amerciament in default thereof. Regist. F.N.B. 163. b. 8 H. 4. 16. 12 H. 7. 15.

46 H. 3. avow. 243. 11 E. 3. ibid. 100. 30 E. 3. 13. 27 E. 3. 92.

2. Where the statute saith, *contra formam feoffamenti*, yet if the lord confirme the estate of the tenant to hold by certaine services, upon this confirmation he shall have a *contra formam feoffamenti*, for that it is within one and the same reason.

3. Pro

3. *Pro certo servitio.* Upon these words if one give land in frankalmoigne, or in frank-mariage, he cannot have a writ of *contra formam feoffamenti*, because there is no certaine service contained in the feoffment or gift, and therefore out of this act, but he may rebut. 4 E. 3. avow. 201. 15 E. 3. confir. 8. F.N.B. 163. g. P. 10 E. 3. per Parning.

4. If the lord distreine either for suite, or for any other service, or rent not contained in the deed, the tenant shall have this writ of *contra formam feoffamenti*, for the words of this act be, *ad hujusmodi sectam, vel ad aliud, &c.* F.N.B. 163. f.

5. The statute saith, *contra formam feoffamenti*; hereupon exposition hath been made, that this writ lyeth onely betweene privies, *viz.* by the tenant and his heires, against the lord and his heires, for they be included in privitie of the feoffment, but so are not the assignes on either side. 14 H. 4, 5. 22 H. 6. 50. 30 H. 6, 7. 10 H. 7. 11. F.N.B. 163. c. Li. 4. fo. 121. Bustards case. Ibid. fo. 11. Bevils case. Li. 9. fo. 34. Bucknals case.

* If the feoffment be without deed, the feoffee is driven to his writ of *Ne injustè vexes.* * Mag. Car. c. 10.

(3) *Hiis autem exceptis quorum antecessores vel ipsi hujusmodi sectam facere consueverunt ante primam transfretationem prædicti domini regis Henrici in Britanniam*, &c. The law doth ever favour possession as an argument of right, and doth incline rather to long possession without shewing any deed, then to an ancient deed without possession; and therefore this act doth except long possession: but in respect of the great troubles that did arise in this realm after the cancellation, which H. 3. made of the charters of *Magna Charta*, and *Charta de Foresta* in the 11 yeare of his raigne, this act doth give reliefe against any seisin since his first going over into Britaine, which was in the 14 yeare of his raigne, but the seisin before that time, when the times were regular and peaceable, this act doth except. 2. *Branch.*

How, and in what manner seisins by incroachments shall be avoided, you may reade in Bevills case, in Bucknalls case, *ubi supra*, and in the first part of the Institutes, sect. Li. 4. fo. 11. Bevills case. Lib. 9. fo. 34. Bucknals case.

[119]

(4) *Similiter nullus feoffatus à tempore conquestus sine carta vel aliquo alio antiquo feoffamento distringatur ad hujusmodi sectam faciend', nisi ipsemet seu antecessores sui eam facere consueverunt ante primam transfretationem prædictam.*] Here he beginneth with feoffments without deed; in the next branch with feoffments by deed, wherein is to be observed the great antiquity of feoffments by deed or without deed of ancient time before the conquest. 3. *Branch.* Fleta, li. 2. cap. 60.

Secondly, the reason in those troublesome times, since the first going over of the king (as hath been said) is not allowed of, but a seisin is required before that time, when times were regular and peaceable.

(5) *Qui autem per cartam pro certo servitio*, &c.] This branch is repeated before, and coupled with the first, being both to one effect. 4. *Branch*

(6) *Et si hæreditas aliqua*, &c.] For parceners, see the first part of the Institutes, sect. 241, & le Custumier de Norm. cap. 30. fol. 46. tenure per parage, i. per coparcenarie, & cap. 36. fo. 55. 5. *Branch.*

(7) *Ille qui habet enitiam partem.*] This is to be understood after partition, for before that the eldest hath not *enitiam partem*, and therefore before partition this act extends not to it, and before partition there can be no contribution, as hereafter shall be said, but in the kings case all the coparceners shall doe suit as well after partition as before, and so shall their severall feoffees, for this act extendeth 24 E. 3. 34, 73. 14 H. 3. Stat. de Hibernia. Vet. Mag. Char. fo. 110.

F.N.B. 159. extendeth not to the king, for the words be, *ad curiam magnatum, &c.*

If the eldest after partition will not doe the suit, in the case of a common person the lord may distreine the other parceners, as well as the eldest for the suit, and the other parceners may have upon this act a writ against the eldest to compell her to do the suit, and if the eldest doth the suit, and the residue refuse to con-
Regist. 174. tribute to her charge, she shal have upon this act a writ *De contri-*
F.N.B. 160. *butione facienda* to compell them to contribute.

F.N.B. 159. *Qui habet enitiam.*] And yet this act extendeth to the feoffee of him that hath *enitiam partem*, and so it is of the tenant by the curtesie.

Note, a woman may be a free suiter to the courts of the lord, but though it be generally said, that the free suiters be judges in these courts, it is intended of men, and not of women.

6. *Branch.* (8) *Et si plures feoffati fuerint de hæreditate aliqua de qua unica secta debeatur, dominus unicam sectam habeat.*] This is to be understood, either when the tenant holdeth by suit, and enfeoffeth others severally, one of one part, and another of another part, &c. in
F.N.B. 159. certaine; there the lord shall have but one suit, and he that doth
Regist. 174. the suit shall have a writ *de contributione facienda* against the
176, 177. others: or where the tenant that holdeth by one suit infeoffeth
Li. 6. fo. 1. many jointly, they shall make but one suit; as they shall deliver
Bruertons case. but one hawke, or other intire service; and if one of them doth
F.N.B. 162. d. the suit, he shall not have a writ *de contributione facienda* by this
Bruertons case ubi sup. act, for when the possession is individed, and intire, there can be no contribution; but if one of the joynt feoffees make a feoffment in fee, the feoffee shall doe a severall suit, and the rest of the joynt feoffees shall doe but one. And if one of the severall feoffees
Regist. 174. doth the suit, if the other feoffees be distrained for the suit, they
176, 177. shall have a writ against the lord to discharge them of the suit, wherein it is to be noted (as before hath beene observed) what actions are grounded upon this and other the like statutes, though no mention be made of them in the acts, all which appeare in the Register.

[120] If parcell of the land holden by suit come to the hands of the
40 E. 3. 5. lord, all the suit is gone, for he neither can receive, nor make
34 ass. 15. contribution.
24 E. 3. 73.
Bruertons case *ubi supra.* (9) *Et si feoffati illi warrantum, vel medium non habeant.*] That is to say, if they have neither one to warrant by speciall graunt,
7. *Branch.* nor any mesne by tenure which ought to acquit them, *tunc omnes*
For warranty & acquitall, see the 1. part of the Instit. sect. 142. *illi feoffati pro portione sua contribuant, &c.* This clause is to be understood of severall tenants, as hath been said before: and no provision is made by this act concerning contribution, where the parties are provided for by graunt or tenure.

8. *Branch.* (10) *Si autem contingat quod domini, &c.*] Here is a remedy given to the tenant against the lord, if he distraine contrary to this statute.

7 E. 4. 14. (11) *Donec domini sectam suam recuperaverint, &c.*] Nota, the suit
9 H. 7. that is past cannot be recovered, but damages for the same.
12 H. 7. 15.
9. *Branch.* (12) *Simili autem modo si tenentes post hanc constitutionem subtrahant, &c.*] Here is remedy given to the lord against his tenant that shall withdraw his suit.

(13) *Currat lex communis.*] See before, cap. 7.

CAP.

CAP. X.

De tournis vicec' (1) *provisum est, quod necesse non habeant* (2) *ibi venire archiepiscopi, episcopi, abbates, priores, comites, barones, nec aliqui viri religiosi* (3), *seu mulieres, nisi eorum præsentia ob aliquam causam specialiter exigatur sed teneatur tournus, sicut temporibus prædecessorum domini regis teneri consuevit* (4). *Et qui in* [*diversis*] *hund' habeant tenementa, non habeant necesse ad hujusmodi tournos* (6) *venire, nisi in balivis* (7) *ubi fuerint conversantes* (5). *Et teneantur tourni secundum formam Magnæ Chartæ, et sicut temporibus regum Richardi et Johannis teneri consueverunt.* Vide Mag. Char. cap. 35.

FOR the turns of sheriffs, it is provided, that archbishops, bishops, abbots, priors, earls, barons, nor any religious men or women, shall not need to come thither, except their appearance be especially required thereat for some other cause; but the turn shall be kept as it hath been used in the times of the king's noble progenitors. And they that have hundreds of their own to be kept, shall not be bound to appear at any such turns, but in the bailiwicks, where they be dwelling. And the turns shall be kept after the form of the great charter, and as they were used in the times of king Richard and king John.

(Regist. 174, 175.)

De tournis vicecomitis provisum est quod necesse non habent ibi venire archiepiscopi, episcopi, abbates, priores, comites, barones, nec aliqui viri religiosi, seu mulieres, nisi eorum præsentia ob aliquam causam specialiter exigatur.] Mirror, cap. 1. § 16. F. N. B. 160. c. Mag. Cart. c. 35. & hic ca. 18. 24.

This is the first branch of this chapter.

Before the making of this statute, the sheriffe in his tourne, and the lords of leets did use to amerce archbishops, priors, earles, barons, religious men, and women, if they came not to the tournes, or to the leets of others, because for suite reall no distresse can be taken, but for the amerciaments for default of suit, which this act doth remedy; for now, seeing it is hereby provided that the persons above named shall not need to come to tournes, &c. therefore for their not coming they cannot bee amercied. 8 H. 4. 15. 12 H. 7. 15. [121]

First, heare what the Mirror saith of this matter: *Abusion est de suffer ascun deins le realme ouster 40 jours, que il soit del age de xiij. ans, insuis Anglois ou alien, sil ne soit jure al roy per serement del fealti & plevise, & in decenne; abusion est que clerks & fems sont exempt de faire al roy le dit serement, de sicome le roy prent lour homage, & lour fealty pur terre.* Mirror, cap. 5. § 1.

Now this oath is well expressed in Britton, *Voillons nous que trestouts ceux de xiij. ans, desouth nous facent le serement que ilz serr' foiall & loiall, & que ilz ne serr' felons ne aux felonies assentants.* Brit ca. 12. fo. 19. Lib. 7. fo. Calvins case.

And it is worthy of observation, that by the common law, parsons of churches, that had *curam animarum*, the better to performe their function, were not compellable to come to tournes, or leets; and if they were distrained to come thither, they might have a writ, *Cum secundum consuetudinem regni nostri personæ ecclesiasticæ, ra-* Regist. 175, 176. F.N.B. 160.

tione terrarum et tenementorum suorum ecclesiis suis annexorum ad veniend. ad visum franc' pleg' in cur. nostra, vel aliorum quorumcunque, &c. Whereby it appeareth that this writ is grounded upon the common law, being the generall custome of the realme; but other clerks (that be no parsons of churches with cure) under which name all ecclesiasticall parsons regular and secular are contained, if they be distrained to come to tourne or leet, they shall have a writ reciting this statute to be discharged thereof. Which writ Regist. ubi supra. beginneth, *Cum de communi consilio provisum sit quod viri religiosi non habeant necesse venire ad tournum vicecom. &c.*

Regist. ubi supra. F.N.B. 161. 3 H. 5. tit. ulagar. Statham. So likewise women shall have the like writ, *Cum de communi consilio, &c. provisum sit quod mulieres non habeant necesse venire ad tournum, &c.*

And it is a rule of law, that whensoever a writ doth recite a statute, there the statute doth introduce a new law.

Now albeit the abovesaid persons be exempted from their personall comming to the tourne and leet, and many other persons never tooke the said oath of allegiance, yet are all subjects of what quality, profession, or sex soever, as firmly bounden to their allegiance, as if they had taken the oath, because it is written by the finger of the law in every one of their hearts, and the taking of the corporall oath, is but an outward declaration of the same.

In the chapter next before, provision was made for doing of suite service, now in this chapter a law is made concerning suite reall, by reason of resiancie.

Mag. Chart. c. 35. F.N.B. 159, 160, 161. Regist 175, 176. (1) *De tournis vicecom'.*] This tourne of the sheriffe is *curia vicecom' franci plegii* (as it hath been said) and therefore this act extendeth to all leets and views of frankpledge, of all other lords and persons.

(2) *Necesse non habeant.*] That is, they are not compellable to come, but left to their owne liberty, *nisi eorum præsentia ob aliquam causam specialiter exigatur,* as to be a witnesse or the like.

See the first part of the Institutes, sect. 133. (3) *Nec aliqui viri religiosi.*] *Religiosi* in the proper sense are taken for those that be regulars; but ecclesiasticall persons, that be seculars are also within this act, and that doth notably appeare by a writ in the Register, *Cum personæ ecclesiasticæ non habeant necesse venire ad tournum vicecom. vel ad visum franci plegii, &c. juxta formam provisionis de communi consilio regni nostri in consimili casu pro viris religiosis factæ, &c.* Whereby it appeareth, that ecclesiasticall persons secular, are in *consimili casu* with them that be *religiosi*, and consequently within this act. In consimili casu.

[122] Mag. Chart. c. 35. (4) *Sed teneatur tournus sicut in temporibus prædecessorum domini regis teneri consueverunt, et teneantur tourni secundum formam Magnæ Chartæ et sicut temporibus regis Richardi et Johannis teneri consueverunt.*] In this 52 yeare of H. 3. so long it was by effluxion of time since the raigne of H. 2. mentioned in *Magna Charta*, that this act had just cause to have reference to the times of R. 1. and king John.

F.N.B. 160. Mag. Chart. c. 35. (5) *Et qui in diversis hundredis habeant tenementa, non habeant necesse ad hujusmodi tournos venire nisi in balivis ubi fuerint conversantes.*] Here *hundredum* is taken *pro visu franci plegii:* so as the sense is, that he which hath tenements in the tourn, and in some other view of frankpledge of some other lord, or in divers views of frankpledge, he shall not need to come to any other but where

he

he is converſant, and hundreds here are named, becauſe ſheriffes (as hath been ſaid) kept their tournes in every hundred.

(6) *Ad hujuſmodi tournos.*] Here *tournus* is taken not only for the kings view of frankpledge, but for the views of frankpledge of other lords.

(7) *In balivis.*] Here *baliva* is taken for the tourn or leet where he is converſant.

If a man hath a houſe within two leets, he ſhall be taken to be converſant where his bed is, for in that part of the houſe he is moſt converſant, and here converſant ſhall be taken for moſt converſant.

If a man hath a houſe and family in two hundreds, ſo as he is in law converſant or commorant in both hundreds, yet he ſhall doe his ſuit to the tourne or leete where his perſon is commorant. 33 H. 6. fol. 9. 19 H. 6. fol. 1. a.

Laſtly, if any man be grieved in any thing contrary to the purview of this ſtatute, he ſhall have an action grounded upon this ſtatute (as often in other caſes hath been obſerved) for his remedy, and relief therein, which actions appear in the Regiſter. Mag. Chart. c. 35. & hic, cap. 9. Regiſt. 174, 175. F.N.B. 160, 161. d. 36 E. 3. cap.

CAP. XI.

PROVISUM eſt etiam, quod nec in itinere juſtic', nec in comitat', in hundred', nec in curia baron' de cætero capientur fines ab aliquibus pro pulchre placitand' (1), *neque [pro eo] quod non occaſionentur* (2). *Et ſciendum eſt, quod per iſtam conſtitutionem non tolluntur fines certi* (3), *ſeu præſtationes arrentatæ à tempore quo dominus rex primum transfretavit in Britanniam uſque nunc.*

IT is provided alſo, that from henceforth neither in the circuit of juſticers, nor in counties, hundreds, and court barons, any fines ſhall be taken of any man for fair-pleading, nor ſo that any occaſion ſhall be. And it is to be known, that by this act fines certain, or loans aſſeſſed ſince the time that our lord the king firſt paſſed into Britain, are not taken away.

W. 1. ca. 8. 1 E. 3. cap. 8. ſtat. 2. Britton, fol. 32. Fleta, li. 2. ca. 60. (1 Ed. 3. ſtat. 2. c. 8. 3 Ed. 1. c. 6. Regiſt. 179.)

Before the making of this ſtatute, juſtices in eyre, the ſuitors in the courts of the county, hundred, and court baron did uſe to ſet fines at their pleaſure upon the defendant or plaintiſe, tenant or demandant, and not upon the councell learned for vicious pleading; and the reaſon thereof was, for that it was in delay of juſtice, and ſo a contempt to the court, and then he had leave to amend it, and to make it perfect, which is called *Beaupleder*. [123] This act conſiſteth upon two branches: by the firſt all fines incertain for vicious pleading, and for amendment thereof, are wholly taken away.

By the ſecond, fines certain for vicious pleading, and amendment thereof aſſeſſed ſince the firſt going of H. 3. into Britain, which was in the 14 yeare of his raigne, are not taken away by this ſtatute.

(1) *Pro pulchre placitando.*] In truth it was, as hath been ſaid, as

as well in respect of the vicious pleading, as of the faire pleading by way of amendment.

This extended to pleadings, and not unto counts, and pleints, neither doth it extend to the kings higher courts of justice, but to these foure here named, for in the higher courts there were faire and good pleadings; whereof the English poet (speaking of the serjant at law) saith,

Chaucer.

Thereto he could indite and make a thing,
There was no wight could pinch at his writing,

(2) *Neque pro eo quod non occasionentur.*] That is, that for that cause they should not be occasioned or troubled.

Regist. 179. F.N.B. 270. 13 E. 1. Attachment 8.

If any man be grieved contrary to the purview of this statute, he may have an action in nature of a prohibition upon this statute.

(3) *Non tolluntur fines certi.*] And the reason of this was, for that fines certaine grew by consent, and therefore this act tooke them not away, for *omnis consensus tollit errorem*; and I have seene, and doe know in divers court barons, &c. fines certain for *beaupleder* paid to this day.

*[124]

CAP. XII.

*IN placito vero dotis, quod dicitur unde nihil habet (1), dentur de cætero quatuor dies per annum ad minus, et plures si commodè fieri poterit, ita quod habeant quinque vel sex dies ad minus per annum. In assisis [autem] ultimæ præsentationis, et in placito quare impedit (2) de ecclesiis vacantibus, dentur dies de quinden' in quinden' (3), vel de tribus septimanis in tres septimanas, prout locus fuerit propinquus, vel remotus. Et in placito quare impedit, si ad primum diem ad quem summonitus fuerit (5), non venerit (4), nec essonium miserit impeditor, tunc attachietur ad alium diem, quo die si non venerit, nec essonium miserit (6), distringatur per magnam districtionem superius datam. Et si tunc non venerit per ejus defaltam scribatur episcopo illius loci quod reclamatio impeditoris illa vice conquerenti (8) non obsistat (7), salvo impeditori alias jure suo, cum inde loqui voluerit. Eadem lex * de attachiamentis (9) faciendis in omnibus brevibus ubi attachiamenta jacent de cætero (quoad districtiones faciendas) firmiter observetur:*

IN a plea of dower, that is called unde nihil habet, from henceforth four days shall be given in the year at the least, and more if conveniently it may be, so that they shall have five or six days at the least in the year. In assises of darraine presentment, and in a plea of quare impedit, of churches vacant, days shall be given from fifteen to fifteen, or from three weeks to three weeks, as the place shall hap to be near, or far. And in a plea of quare impedit, if the disturber come not at the first day that he is summoned, nor cast no essoin, then he shall be attached at another day; at which day if he come not, nor cast no essoin, he shall be distrained by the great distress above given; and if he come not then, by his default a writ shall go to the bishop of the same place, that the claim of the disturber for that time shall not be prejudicial to the plaintiff; saving to the disturber of his right at another time, when he will sue therefore. The same law, as to the making of attachments, shall from henceforth be observed

obſervetur: ita tamen quod ſecundum attachiamentum fiat per meliores plegios, et poſtmodum ultima diſtrictio. [Vide artic' ſuper chartas cap. 15.]

obſerved in all writs where attachments lie, as in making diſtreſſes, ſo that the ſecond attachment ſhall be made by better pledges, and afterwards the laſt diſtreſs.

Vide 51 H. 3. Dies Communes in Banco, in placito dotis. (32 H. 8. c. 21. Fitz. Jour. 18, 19. 32. 11 H. 6. 4. 33 H. 6. 1. Fitz. Brief, al. Eveſque, 14. 21, 22. 27. 32 H. 8. c. 21.)

The miſchiefe before this act was, that in a writ of dower, *unde nihil habet,* there were dayes of common retourn, as in other reall actions, which was miſchievous to the woman, in reſpect of the long delay, ſhe claiming but an eſtate for her life, which miſchiefe this ſtatute, as by the letter thereof appeareth, doth remedy.

And this ſtatute in favour of dower is alſo extended againſt the vouchee, for this act ſaith, *in placito dotis,* and the vouchee is in *placito dotis.*

(1) *Unde nihil habet.*] This act extends not to a writ of right of dower, but the ſtatute of 32 H. 8. extends to it, neither doth this act extend to a writ of dower *ad oſtium eccleſiæ,* or *ex aſſenſu patris,* unleſſe it be *unde nihil habet,* but the ſaid act of 32 H. 8. extends to every writ of dower. 32 H. 8. cap. 21.

(2) *In aſſiſis ultimæ præſentat' et in placito quare impedit.*] This act extendeth not to a writ of *quare non admiſit,* nor to an *incumbravit,* but onely to the aſſiſe of *darrein preſentment,* and *quare impedit,* and the reaſon thereof is, for feare of the laps. 26 E. 3. 75. 17 E. 3. 21. 18 E. 3. jour 19.

(3) *Dentur dies de quindena in quinden.'*] By aſſent of parties a longer day may be given then is preſcribed by this act, but that aſſent muſt be entred of record. 11 H. 6. 23.

And it is to be obſerved, that by the common law great delayes bee diſallowed in foure kindes of actions, *viz.* in all writs of dower, *quare impedit,* aſſiſe of *darrein preſentment,* and aſſiſe of *novel diſſeiſin,* and therefore no protection ſhall be allowed, or *eſſoine de ſervitio regis* ſhall be caſt in any of them. 44 E. 3. 5. 39 H. 6. 40. Artic. ſuper Chartas, cap. 15.

(4) *In placito quare impedit ſi ad primum diem ad quem ſummonitus fuerit non venerit,* &c.] At the common law in a *quare impedit,* the proces was ſummons, attachment, and diſtreſſe infinite, which was miſchievous in reſpect of the laps, now it is provided that if he appeare not at the graund diſtreſſe, judgement ſhall be given for the plaintife, and a writ to the biſhop awarded. Bract. l. 4. fo. 246, 247. Fleta, lib. 5. c. 16. Brit. 233. 11 H. 6. 4.

(5) *Summonitus fuerit.*] Put the caſe that upon the ſummons, the defendant is retourned *nihil,* and at the attachment and diſtreſſe, *nihil* alſo, this caſe is out of the letter of the ſtatute, for the defendant was never ſummoned, but it is ſaid, * that when there be two miſchiefes at the common law, and the leſſer is provided for by expreſſe words, the greater ſhall be included within the ſame remedy; this caſe when *nihil* is returned is the greater miſchiefe, for he by his default ſhall loſe nothing, but in the caſe provided, the defendant by his default ſhall loſe iſſues, and the law intends that he will rather appeare then loſe iſſues. 14 E. 3. Default 17. 11 H 6. 4. 5. 21 H. 6. 56. Lib. 5. fol. 41. * *Regula.*

A *quare impedit* is brought againſt two, upon the diſtreſſe one doth appeare, and the other makes default; in 7 E. 3. it was reſolved that the plaintife ſhould not preſently have a writ to the biſhop againſt him that makes default, for that it might be, that 7 E. 3, 4.

[125]

the other that appeares shall have against the plaintife a writ to the bishop; and it was there said, that it was not reasonable, that upon one originall the plaintife should have one writ to the bishop for him, and another against him; but this notwithstanding the plaintife by this act ought to have against him that makes default a writ to the bishop; and it is not against reason, if the other defendant can barre the plaintife, for him to have a writ to the bishop against the plaintife by the common law, and so bee the later bookes, and common experience at this day.

14 H. 7. 19 b. F.N.B. 39. b. 13 E. 3. bre. al Evesque 21. 8 H. 4. 2. 10 H. 6. 4. Vide hic c. 2. & 13.

(6) *Tunc attachietur ad alium diem, quo die si non venerit nec essonium miserit.*] *Essonium*, or *exonium* is derived of the French verb *essonier*, or *exonier*, which signifieth to excuse, so as an essoine in legall understanding is an excuse of a default by reason of some impediment, or disturbance, and is as well for the plaintife as the defendant, and is all one with that which the civilians call *excusatio*. * Of essoines, there have been (as we reade in our bookes) five kindes, *viz.* 1. *De servitio regis.* 2. *In terram sanctam.* 3. *Ultra mare.* 4. *De malo lecti*, in our old bookes called *essonium de resiantisa.* 5. *Et de malo veniendi*, and this last is the common essoine, which is intended in this act.

Glanv. li. 1. c. 10, 11, &c. Bract. l. 5. fo. 334, 335, &c. Brit. cap. 122, 123, &c. Fleta, lib. 6. ca. 7, 8. &c. Mirror, c. 2. § 20. De Essoines, & cap. 5. § 1.

* 27 H. 6. 1. 26 H. 6 Essoine 107. 10 H. 4. 6. 8 H. 3. Essoine 195. W. 2. cap. 17.

In a *quare impedit*, or *darrein presentment*, an essoine *de service le roy, ad terram sanctam*, or *ultra mare* lyeth not for doubt of the laps, but a common essoine lieth, and of essoines the Mirror said well, *Abusion est que faux causes de essoines sont resceivable de cy que droit ne allowe fauxime in nul case, & abusion est dallower essoine in personel action*; for the same author treating *De articles per viels roys ordein*, saith, *Ordein fueront essoines in mixt actions, & realls, & ne in personels*; and I finde, not in Glanvill any essoines, but in reall and mixt actions, but before the making of this act, essoines were allowed in personall actions.

Mirror ubi supra. Mirror ubi supra.

Non jacet essonium, quia summonitio testificata non est, vel par non attachiatur, eo quod vicecomes mandavit quod non est inventus.

Vide 12 E. 2. Stat. de essonio calumniando.

(7) *Per ejus defaltam scribatur episcopo quod reclamatio impeditoris illa vice conquerenti non obsistat.*] Upon these words of this act the plaintife shall have a writ to the bishop without making of any title.

34 H. 6. 28. 2 H. 4. 1. b. 22 H. 6. 45. 33 H. 6. 1. a. F.N.B. 38. n.

The statute saith only, *Scribatur episcopo*, and yet the plaintife shall have both a writ to the bishop, and besides a writ to enquire of damages; if the bishop be out of the realme, a writ to the bishop may be awarded to his vicar generall, for he is in place of the bishop.

2 H. 4. 1. 24 E. 3 37. 38 E. 3. 12.

If the defendant appeare at the grand distresse, and take a day by *prece partium*, and after make default, no writ shall be awarded to the bishop, for this case in respect of his appearance is out of the statute, but a new distresse shall be awarded.

13 E. 3. bre. al Evesque 19.

(8) *Conquerenti.*] The king shall take the benefit of this statute.

24 E. 3.

(9) *Eadem lex de attachiamentis*, &c.] This is the last clause of this chapter, and is to be understood according to the letter, and needeth not any exposition.

CAP. XIII.

ET sciendum est [quod] postquam aliquis posuerit se in inquisitionem aliquam (1), quæ emerserit, vel emergere poterit in hujusmodi brevibus, non habebit nisi unicum essonium (2), vel unicam defaltam (3), ita quod si ad diem sibi datum per essonium suum non venerit, aut secundo die defaltam fecerit, tunc inquisitio illa per ejus defaltam capiantur, secundum inquisitionem illam ad judicium procedatur. Si vero inquisitio illa capta fuerit in comitatu (4) coram vicecom' vel coronatore, ad justiciarios domini regis ad certum diem est remittend'. Et si pars rea non venerit ad diem illum, tunc propter defaltam ipsius assignetur et alius dies, secundum discretionem justiciariorum, et mandetur vicecomiti, quod ad diem illum faciat eum venire ad audiendum judicium (si velit) secundum inquisitionem illam. Ad quem diem si non venerit, propter defaltam suam procedatur ad judicium. Eodem modo fiat, si non veniat ad diem sibi datum per essonium suum.

AND it is to be known, after that a man hath put himself upon any enquest, the which hath or must pass in such manner of writs, he shall have but one essoin, or one default; so that if he come not at the day given to him by the essoin, or make default the second day, then the enquest shall be taken by his default, and according to the same enquest they shall proceed to judgement. And if such enquest be taken in the county, before the sheriff or coroners, it shall be returned unto the king's justices at a certain day; and if the party defendant come not at that day, then, upon his default, another day shall be assigned to him after the discretion of the justices; and it shall be commanded to the sheriff, that he cause him to come to hear the judgement, if he will, according to the enquest; at which day, if he come not, upon his default they shall proceed to judgement. In like manner it shall be done, if he come not at the day given unto him by his essoin.

Dier, 5 Eliz. 224. 15 Eliz. 324. (Fitz. Essoin, 21. 33, 34. 38. 100. 130. 159. Godbolt 236. pl. 327. Salk. 216.)

The mischiefe before this statute was for the great delay that might come to the plaintife in any personall action. 2 R. 2, Esso. 159.

(1) *In inquisitionem aliquam.*] That is, when issue is joyned, and the defendant *ponit se super patriam, et prædict' querens similiter.*

This statute extendeth not to a demurrer in law.

In an action of debt *un custome de London fuit alledge & denie per le pl':* this issue shall not be tryed by inquest, but by the certificate of the maior by the mouth of the recorder, *proces issuist al maior a certifier a quel jour le def. pria destre essoine,* and was essoined by the opinion of the whole court, for this tryall was not *per patriam.* 21 E. 4. 74, 78.

(2) *Nisi unicum essonium.* Here *essonium* is taken for a common essoine, and extendeth not the essoine *de servitio regis, &c.* 19 E. 3. essoine 21.

This is to be understood where an essoine doth lie, for this act restraineth delaies, and giveth not any, where none was before. And therefore after issue in a *scire fac',* the defendant shall not be essoined, because no essoine lyeth in that case, *et sic de similibus.* 19 H. 6. 51. 25 E. 3. 8.

2 E. 4. 19. But if there be divers tenants in a *præcipe*, or divers defendants in a personall action, albeit in law they be but one tenant, or one defendant, yet each of them shall have one essoine; and so hath
20 E. 3. Esso. 30. this act been expounded.
22 E. 3, 4. 7. 2 R. 2. essoine 159. (3) *Vel unicam defaltam*, &c.] Upon consideration of these words, and of these words subsequent, *tunc inquisitio illa per defal-*
14 H. 6. 1. *tam capiatur*, two conclusions are collected. 1. That this act ex-
Dier, 5 Eliz. 224. tendeth to the defendant, and not to the plaintife, because the de-
15 Eliz. 324. fendant maketh default, and on the plaintifes side it is called a non-
[127] suit: also the enquest is awarded by the default of the defendant. And lastly, the mischiefe was for the delay of the plaintife by the defendant, and therefore the delay which the plaintife maketh himselfe is out of the mischiefe, and remains at the common law.

14 H. 6. 19. 9 H. 5. 12, 13. Dier, ubi sup. The second conclusion is, that this act is to be understood in an action personall, for that no enquest in any action reall can be taken by default.

(4) *Si verò inquisitio capta fuerit in comitatu*, &c.] The meaning of this clause is, that if after issue joyned in a base court, the defendant hath had his essoine, yet if the plea be removed before the kings justices, he shall have another essoine before the justices, for the proceeding in the base court is not of record above.

CAP. XIV.

DE chartis vero exemptionis, et libertatis (1), *ne ponantur impetrantes in assisis, juratis, vel recognitionibus aliquibus: provisum est, quod si adeo necessarium sit eorum juramentum, quod sine eis justitia exhiberi non poterit (veluti in magnis assisis, et in perambulationibus, et in chartis vel scriptis conventionum, uti fuerunt testes nominati* (2), *aut in attinctis, vel aliis consimilibus) jurar' cogantur, salva sibi aliàs libertate, et exemptione sua prædicta* (3).

CONCERNING charters of exemption and liberties, that the purchaser shall not be impannelled in assises, juries, and enquests; it is provided, that if their oaths be so requisite, that without them justice cannot be ministred, as in great assises, perambulations, and in deeds or writings of covenants, (where they be named for witnesses) or in attaints, and in other cases like, they shall be compelled to swear; saving to them at another time their foresaid liberty and exemption.

W. 2. cap. 28. 29 H. 6. c. 3. (34 H. 6. 25. 18 H. 8. 5.)

34 H. 6. 25. per Moyle. 21 E. 4. 47. b. (1) *De chartis vero exemptionis et libertatis*, &c.] Hereby it appeareth that this act is in affirmance of the common law, for every charter of any franchise or liberty whatsoever, by reason whereof there should be a failer of justice, is void and of none effect in law, as in the case of conusans, and this case of exemption.

39 E. 3. 15. 12 E. 4. 17. 35 H. 6. 42. Broke exempt 6. In this act there be foure examples set downe, *viz.* the grand assise in the writ of right, in the writ of *rationabilibus divisis*, here called *in perambulationibus*, in deeds where witnesses be named, and in attaints.

Rationabilibus

Rationabilibus divisis.]

*Magna assisa inter Priorem de Tynemuwe petentem, & Simonem de Rucestre tenentem, de eo quod idem Simon permittet rationabiles divisas fieri inter terras ipsius Prioris in Weiham, & terras ipsius Simonis in Rucestre, sicut esse debet & solet. Et unde idem Simon qui tenens est posuit se magnam assisam illam, & petit recogn' fieri, utrum ipse majus jus habet in quindecim acris terrae, & quindecim acris morae, cum pertin' in Rucestre * per metas & divisas subscriptas, scil. incipiendo apud altam viam quae extendit se ultra Swalnspotleche, & sic descendendo per Swalnspotleche versus austrum usq. Rysdenburne, ubi Swalnspotleche & Rysdenburne conjungunt, & sic ascendendo in Rysdenburne versus boream usque Aldewylumway, & sic adhuc per Rysdenburne versus boream usque le Redeford, ubi alta via transit versus novum Castrum super Tynam sicut illas tenet, An praedictus Prior per metas & divisas subscriptas, viz. incipiendo apud Redeford, & sic per altam viam versus occidentem usq. * Munleshened, & sic versus occidentem per altam viam usq. Swalnspotleche, & sic de Swalnspotleche versus austrum usque Rysdenburne, & sic de Rysdenburne versus boream ascendendo usq. Redeford praedict' sicut illas exigit: ven' recogn' in forma praedict. per Willielmum de Haulton, Robertum de Insula, Nicholaum de Punchardon, Iohannem de Oggeill, Iohannem de Eslington, Richardum de Horsele, Hugonem Gobion, Walterum de Egloythenebam, David de Coupland, Franconem Tyeys, Henricum de Dytheend, & Robertum du Maner, & modo veniunt praedict' Simon & Prior per attorn' suos: Et praedicti milites super sacramentum suum dicunt, quod praedictus Simon majus jus habet in praedictis tenementis per praedictas divisas per quas illa tenet, quam praedictus Prior per divisas per quas illa exigit. Ideo consideratum est, quod praedictus Simon eat inde sine die, & teneat praedictum tenementum sibi & haeredibus suis per praedictas divisas, scil. incipiendo apud Swalnespotleche ubi alta via extendit se ultra Swalnespotleche, & sic descendendo per Swalnespotleche versus austrum usq. Rysdenburne ubi Swalnespotleche & Rysdenburne conjungunt, & sic ascendendo per Rysdenburne versus boream usq. Aldewylumwey, & sic adhuc per Rysdenburne versus boream usque le Redeford ubi alta via transit versus novum Castrum super Tynam, quietè de praedicto Priore & successoribus suis, et ecclesia sua de Tynemuwe imperpetuum, & Prior in misericordia, &c.*

Pasch. 18 E. 1. rot. 65. in Banc. Northumb. de rationabilibus divisis.

Magna Assisa utrum ipse majus jus, &c.

* Per metas & divisas.

Vide Mich. 3 E. 1 in Banc. rot. 26. Sur'Int' Priorem de Berm. & Priorem de Hidawint. Pasch. 6 E. 1. in Banc. rot. 57. Salop. Int. Episc. Hereford & Petr. Corbet perambulatio. Vide Pasc. 8 E. 1. in banc. rot. 58.

Veredictum.

Judicium.

*[128]

Finale.

Magna assisa inter Priorem de Tynemuwe petentem, & Richardum Turpin tenentem de eo, quod idem Richardus permittet rationabiles divisas fieri inter terras ipsius Prioris in Wylum, & terras ipsius Richardi in Hoghton, sicut esse debent & solent, et unde idem Richardus, qui tenens est posuit se in magnā assisam illam, et petit recogn' fieri, utrum ipse majus jus habet in medietate decem acrarum morae, viginti acrarum terrae, et sexaginta acrarum bosci, cum pertin' in Hoghton, per metas et divisas subscriptas, videl. incipiendo ex parte boreali de le Thwertonerdike, et sic versus boream usq. ad cursum aquae quae currit inter le Strother de Hoghton, et le Strother de Rucestre, et sic sicut cursus illius aquae se extendit versus occidentem usque Redeford, et sic descendendo versus austrum usq. le Holleford, et sic del Holleford descendendo versus austrum usq. Rysdenburne, usque ad terram arabilem de Wylum, et sic per fossatum ejusdem terrae usque lel Longhing quod venit de bosco de Wylum, et sic descendendo versus austrum sicut Sygpethway se extendit inter boscum de Hoghton, et boscum de Wylum, et usq. Wylum Halugh, et sic per fossatum quod se extendit versus orientem inter Wylum Halugh et boscum de Hoghton usq. Alberystrother in parte occidentali, et sic per partem occidentalem de Alberystrother versus austrum usque les Pullys per partem

Pasch. 18 E. 1. in Banco. rot. 72. Northumb. Mich. 18 E. 1. in Banc. rot. 76. Northumb.

partem occidentalem, et sic de les Pullys versus occidentem per quoddam fossatum usq. quoddam Run quod se extendit usque aquam de Tyne salva communia pasturæ eidem Priori et successoribus suis in prædicta mora de Hoghton usque le Thwertonerdike per partem occidentalem, et sic per partem occidentalem de le Br-hill, et de Hyndeschawe, et sic versus austrum descendendo per le Greneleghe, et sic usque Sygpethway sicut ea tenet, an prædictus Prior per metas et divisas subscriptas, videlicet incipiendo in parte boreali in Wylummore descendendo versus austrum per le Thwertonerdike usque Thornrawe, et sic de Thornrawe usque Martinpol versus austrum, et sic de Martinpol usque Aldehewey et sic descen-
[129] *dendo per le Haldeheyway versus austrum ultra Raveneshurne, et sic de Raveneshurne versus austrum et iterum ultra Raveneshurne, et sic de Raveneshurne versus austrum usq. Standandestan, et sic de Standandestan versus austrum usq. le Fisherewey usq. aquam de Tyne sicut illum exigit. Venit recogn' in forma prædicta per Willielmum de Hauleton Robertum de Insula, Nichol' de Punchardon, Iohannem de Oggill, Iohannem de Eslington, Robertum de Glantingdon, Richardum de Horslee, Hugonem Gobyon, Walterum de Egleyntham, David de Coupeland, Francione Tyeis,*
Veredictum. *& Henric' de Dycheend. Et modo veniunt prædict' Richardus, & Prior per atturnatos suos, & prædicti milites super sacrum suum dicunt quod prædictus Richardus majus jus habeat tenendi medietat' prædictorum ten' per easdem metas & divisas, per quas idem Richardus superius clam', quam prædictus Prior. Ideo considerat' est quod prædictus Richardus eat inde sine die, & teneat medietat. prædictorum ten' cum pertinen' per*
Judicium finale *prædictas metas & divisas, per quas illam clam' sibi & hæred' suis quiete de prædicto Priore & successoribus suis, & ecclesia sua de Tynemuwe imperpetuum. Et Prior in misericordia.*

Vide Mich. 18 E. 1. in Banco Rot. 76. Northumb. a notable record. For this writ de rationabilibus divisis, and the writ de perambulatione fac', vide Regist. 157. b. Glanvill, lib. 9. cap. 14. Bracton, lib. 4. fol. 207. a. 211. b. De perambulatione fac.' lib. 5. 372. a. & 444. De rationabilibus divisis. Fleta, lib. 4. cap. 15. lib. 5. cap. 9,39. 31 E. 1. Droit, 70. 5 E. 3. fol. 12. 28 E. 3. fo. 43 14 E. 3. tit. Aid 23. 29 E. 3. 45. 45 E. 3. 4. 3 E. 4. 10. F. N. B. 128. m. &c. 133. d. &c. Vet. 73, 74. Coke, lib. intr. 565, 566. lib. intrat. Rast. 541. 495.

Upon all these records and books, the learning of these two writs standeth thus;

1. This writ of *rationabilibus divisis* is a writ of right in his nature, wherein battaile, and the graund assise lieth, and judgement finall shall be given: in this writ the view and voucher is to be graunted, and esples are to be laid, and this writ *est breve adversarium.*

2. The writ *de perambulatione facienda,* is no writ of right in his nature, and is *breve amicabile,* and had by consent of parties.

3. The perambulation may be made as well by commission to certain persons as by writ; but the proceeding, *de rationabilibus divisis,* is by writ onely.

4. This is common to them both for a division to be made between severall townes or hamlets.

5. If it be for a division between two counties, for the better directions of sheriffes, coroners, and other the kings officers, and ministers, it must be done by the kings commission under the great seale, but the division hereby made shall not estoppe or conclude the parties interessed in the land.

Upon

Upon the verdict in any of the four examples before mentioned, no writ of attaint doth lie; then followeth these words, *Et in aliis casibus consimilibus:* these by the letter of this statute, must be such, as thereupon no attaint doth lie; as in the *partitione fac'*, and other inquests of office, as hath been said: but all charters tending to the failer of justice, are void by the common law, without any aide of this act: as if there be not sufficient hundreders, besides those that have charters of exemption, for triall of an issue in an action, wherein an attaint doth lie, there charters shall be disallowed, because *sine eis justitia exhiberi non potest*, and so in all other like cases: so if the king graunt an exemption to all the freeholders in one county, and to all the citizens in a city, this is void.

(2) *In chartis, &c. ubi testes fuerint nominati.*] Hereby it appeareth, that by the common law, the witnesses named in the deed should joyne with the enquest, or else the charter of exemption, *De assisis juratis et recognitionibus aliquibus*, should not have freed them. Vide the first part of the Institutes, and see before cap. 6. [130] 1 Part of the Institutes, sect. 1.

In attinctis.] Hereby appeareth that the writ of attaint, which by our old books and auncient records is called *breve de convictione*, was given by the common law, and the forme of the writ is set downe in our auncient authors at the suite of the party grieved: and it appeareth by the Register that no writ of attaint reciteth any statute, and the judgement in the writ of attaint is fearfull and penall, and given by no statute, and this is proved by this act, which nameth attaints, and is before any act of parliament in print made concerning attaints.

And it seemeth by our old bookes and auncient records, that by the common law, it lay as well in plea reall as personall. Vide Regist. 122. Mirror, cap. 3. De Attaints. & cap. 2. § 4. De Loiers. Glanville, lib. 2. cap. 19. Bracton, lib. 4. fol. 289. Fleta, lib. 5. cap. 21. 34. Britton, cap. 97. fol. 237. 6 H. 3. tit. Attaint, 72, & 73. 15 H. 3. ib. 74. Temps E. 1. ibid. 70. 12 E. 1. ib. 71. 30 Ass. 24. 28 E. 3 91. 44 E. 3. 2. b. Temps R. 2. Conusans, 88. 3 H. 4. 15. Fortescue, ca. 26. F. N. B. 107. k. W. 1. cap. 38. 47. 1 E. 3. cap. 6. 5 E. 3. cap. 6, 7. 28 E. 3. cap. 8. 34 E. 3. cap. 7. 23 H. 8. cap. 3. See the first part of the Institutes. Sect. 514. Verb. en Attaint.

But some say the writ could not be obtained without difficulty (because he had other remedy to try it in an action of higher nature) and therefore the statutes were made. See the statute of W 1. cap. 38. and the exposition thereupon, and a judgement given. Mich. 5 E. 1. Of an attaint heare what the Mirror saith, *En temps le roy Henry le primer estoit ordein & communement assentu que jurors in enquests, &c. in attaints, et tiels autres ne prendront rien de loiers, &c.* See the other ancient authors and books above cited; by them it appeareth how necessary the reading of auncient authors and records be for the knowledge of the common law, and how the statutes concerning attaints are but in affirmance of the common law, for the plaintife may have upon them the penall and severe judgement given by the common law. Vide 40. Ass. 23. See W. 1. cap. 38. 40 Ass. 23.

If a man have a charter of exemption, and sheweth it to the sheriffe, yet notwithstanding he may retourne him, for the sheriffe is not to judge of his charter, nor to allow, or disallow thereof; but if he will have the effect of his charter, he must sue out a writ of allowance of his charter, and deliver the writ to the sheriffe, and F.N.B. 165, 166 Act D. 39 E. 3. 15. 40 E. 3. 30. 18 H. 8. 5.

ſhew his charter to him, and then if the ſheriffe retourne him, he may have his action upon his caſe againſt the ſheriffe, and ſo muſt our old and other books be intended.

28 H. 8. 5. After the ſheriffe hath retourned him, if a full jury doe appeare, then he may ſhew forth his charter, and if the plaintiffe confeſſe it, he ſhall be diſcharged, but if the plaintiffe ſaith that he is not the ſame perſon, it ſhall be preſently tried, and ſo in the like caſe; but he cannot plead his charter for his diſcharge before a full jury doe appeare, for if any anſwer bee made thereunto the jury muſt try it.

41 E. 3. exemption 4. 42 Aſſ. 25. 25 H. 6. exemption 5. Such generall charters of exemption *in aſſiſis, juratis, et recognitionibus*, as in this act are mentioned, ſhall not be allowed where the king is either ſole party, or where the ſuite is *tam pro domino rege quam pro ſeipſo*, without theſe or the like words, *licet tangat nos*.

18 E. 3. 20. 3 H. 6. 14. 36 H. 6. 32. *Salva ſemper alias libertate et exemptione prædict'.*] And ſo it is in caſe of conuſance, and of a protection, the party may waive the benefit of it in one action, and yet take the advantage of it in another: and ſo if a *non omittas* be awarded within a franchiſe that hath retourn of writs, yet he ſhall in other ſuits enjoy it.

[131]

CAP. XV.

NULLI de cætero liceat (1) ex quacunque cauſa diſtrictiones facere (3) extra feodum ſuum, nec in via regia, aut in communi ſtrata (2) niſi domino regi et miniſtris ſuis (4) ſpecialem authoritatem ad hoc habentibus.

IT ſhall be lawful for no man from henceforth, for any manner of cauſe, to take diſtreſſes out of his fee, nor in the king's high-way, nor in the common ſtreet, but only to the king or his officers having ſpecial authority to do the ſame.

Fleta, lib. 2. ca. 41. W. 1. c. 16. Artic. Cleri, cap. 9. Artic. ſuper Cart. ca. 12. 51 H. 3. Diſt. de Scaccar. (8 Rep. 60. 7 H. 7. 1. 22 Ed. 4. 49. Fitz. Bar. 281. Fitz. Treſpaſs, 188. Fitz. Brief, 511, 842. Fitz. Avowry, 87, 232. Raſt. 226. Regiſt. 98. 183. 9 Ed. 2. ſtat. 1. c. 9. 2 Inſt. 131. Cro. El. 710.

13 E. 4. 6. The miſchiefe before this ſtatute was, that whereas the king by his prerogative might diſtrein for his rent in any other lands of his tenant, being in his owne actuall poſſeſſion, though they were out of his fee, and ſeigniory, divers lords tooke upon them alſo to diſtrein out of their fee, which was wrong and oppreſſion: and whereas all the kings ſubjects ought to have free paſſage in *via regia, et communi ſtrata*, as well to faires and markets, as about their other affairs, the lords uſed to diſtrein in the high-wayes, both which miſchiefs this ſtatute doth remedy.

(1) *Non liceat.*] This is divided into three branches: the firſt branch is, *Non liceat ex quacunque cauſa diſtrictiones facere extra feodum.*

34 E. 1. Avowry 232. 41 E. 3. 26. 2 H. 4. 24. 1. This is to be underſtood of diſtreſſes, by reaſon of a ſeigniory, and not for diſtreſſes for rent charges, &c. or by reaſon of a leet.

2. This

2. This branch is but in affirmance of the common law, for regularly no ſubject can diſtrein out of his fee and ſeigniory, and therefore if the lord doe diſtrein out of his fee, the tenant may either have an action of treſpaſſe at the common law, or an action upon this ſtatute, but in ſome ſpeciall caſe the lord by the common law may diſtrein out of his fee and ſeigniory, as if the lord come to diſtrein, and the tenant, or any other ſeeing the lord come to diſtrein them, drive them to a place out of the fee of the lord, yet in this caſe the lord may diſtrein them out of his fee, becauſe the lord had a view of them within his owne fee, by reaſon whereof the lord ſhall be adjudged in a kinde of poſſeſſion of them; but if the beaſts goe out of the tenancy of themſelves without enchaſement before the lord can diſtrein them, there the lord cannot diſtrein them, though he had the view of them within his fee, and ſeigniory.

2 E. 2. Avow. 182. 44 E. 3. 20, 21. 6 R. 2. Reſcous. 11. 33 H. 6. 51. 2 E. 4. 6. 9 E. 4. 35. 16 E. 4. 10.

The ſecond branch is,

(2) *Nec in via regia, aut in communi ſtrata.*] See what ſhall be ſaid, *regia via,* and what *communis ſtrata,* in the firſt part of the Inſtitutes, ſect. 69.

First part of the Inſtitutes, ſect. 69. F.N.B. 173, 174.

This law had the foundation of the auncient law of England before the conqueſt, *Alia, s. immunitas, quam habent quatuor chemini (i. viæ regiæ) Watlingſtreet, Foſſe, Hilkenildſtreet, et Erminſtreet, quorum duo in longitudinem, alii duo in latitudinem deſcendunt.*

Inter leges Edw. Regis. Lamb. fol. 129. Flet. l. 2. cap. 42. Artic. Cler. cap. 42. Regiſt. fol. 97.

In this branch, *non liceat* ſhall be taken not *ſimpliciter,* to make it utterly unlawfull, as to take advantage thereof in barre to an avowry, but *ſecundum quid,* that is to this purpoſe, that if the lord diſtrein in the high ſtreet, or in the common way, the tenant may have an action againſt the lord upon this ſtatute: and the reaſon hereof is, that whenſoever any thing is prohibited by a ſtatute, the party grieved ſhall have his action upon the ſtatute, and the offender ſhall be for his contempt fined and impriſoned; and ſo it is declared by act of parliament, as hath been often obſerved. Now if the tenant ſhould plead it in barre of the avowry, the king ſhould loſe his fine; for in that nature of ſuite hee cannot bee fined, and therefore the tenant is to take * his remedy by action upon the ſtatute, wherein the king ſhall have his fine, &c.

19 E. 2. bre. 842. 21 E. 3. 11. 30 E. 3. 20. 41 E. 3. 6. 43 E. 3. 30. 11 R. 2. Avowry 87. 36 E. 3. c. 9. 19 H. 6. 4. 35 H. 6. 6. 9 E. 4. 26. F.N.B. 90. 173.

(3) *Diſtrictiones facere.*] A heriot cuſtome the lord may ſeiſe in the high-way, for that is no diſtreſſe but a ſeiſure, but he cannot diſtrein for a heriot ſervice there.

Lib. 8. fol. 60. Bechers caſe. 11 R. 2. Avow. 87.

If the lord come to diſtrein, and ſee the beaſts within his fee, and before he can diſtrein them, the tenant enchaſe them into the high-way, the lord may, as hath beene ſaid, diſtrein them there, for the cauſe above expreſſed.

* [132]

The writ upon this ſtatute ſhall be *contra pacem,* and not *vi et armis.* 17 E. 3. 1.

The third branch:

(4) *Niſi domino regi et miniſtris ſuis,* &c.] Here is an exception of the kings prerogative (which by this act appears to be auncient) as well to diſtreine for his rent, or ſervice out of his fee, and ſeigniory, as in the high-way, or common ſtreet. But where it is ſaid that the king may diſtrein out of his fee, that is, in the other lands of his tenant; it muſt be underſtood in ſuch other lands as his tenant hath in his owne actuall poſſeſſion, and manured with his own beaſts, and not in the poſſeſſion of his leſſee for life, yeares, or at will, for their beaſts are not ſubject to ſuch diſtreſſe.

44 Aſſ. 32. 5 E. 3. 6. 13 E. 4. 6.

There

Artic. super Cart. cap. 12.

There was a statute made in a parliament holden at Westminster in 51 H. 3. the yeare next before this parliament holden at Marlebridge, concerning distresses, consisting on two branches.

1. *Que nul home de religion ne auter soit distreine per ses beasts, queux gainont son terre, ne per ses barbits pur la det le roy, ne pur la det de auter home, ne pur auter encheson per les bailiffes le roy, ne per autres, tanque come ils trove auters chateux sufficient dont ilz poient lever le det, ou que suffist sa demaund (forspris emparkement des beasts queux homes trove feasants damage solonque le ley, usage, & le manner de la terre.)*

Artic. super Cart. ca. 12. 27 l. Ass. 52. 28 Ass. p. 50. 29 E. 3. 23. 8 H. 4. 16. 11 H. 4. 2. Lib. 11. fo. 44. Godfreyes case. Flores Histor. Polyd. Virg. 22. b. Regist. Lucubr. Ockham.

2. *Et que distresses soient reasonable a la mountaince de la det, ou de la demaunde solonq; bone value, & per estimation ne pas outragious des vicines, & nemi per estrangers.* Of both these shall be spoken together, because divers of the authorities extend to both.

Beasts queux gainont son terre & ses berbits.

This law had his foundation of the auncient law before the conquest, *Dunvallo Mulmutius* prohibited that the beasts of the plough should be distreined, &c. and gave priviledges to temples and ploughs: and Ockam, that wrote before this statute of the kings debts, saith, *Bobus tamen arantibus, per quos agricultura solet exerceri, quantum poterint parcant, ne ipsa deficiente debito amplius in futurum egere cogatur, quod si nec sicquidem summa quæ requiritur exurgit, nec arantibus parcendum est.*

Bracton, lib. 4. fo. 217. Fleta, li. 2. c. 42.

Bracton treateth of both these branches notably, and hee divideth *animalia* into *laboriosa et otiosa*, and saith, *Fit districtio injuriosa ordine non observat', si fiat districtio per oves, et sunt quæ ad minus damnum distringantur animalia otiosa; item ordine non observat' si fiat districtio per boves, ut culturam auferant vel impediant, cum sint aliæ res et animalia otiosa quæ sufficiant ad districtionem; item si subsit causa et observetur ordo, adhuc potest esse injuriosa, si fuerit nimia, et districtio modum excedat in qualibet specie.*

Lib. 2. cap. 42.

And Fleta saith, *Quod pro communi utilitate communitatis regni inhibitum fuer' ne quis distringeret alium per oves suas vel per averia sua carucarum, quamdiu alia sufficiens districtio inveniri possit.*

Districtiones sint rationabiles et non nimis graves. See before Chapter 4.

[133]

Brit. fo. 35. & 133. b.

And Britton saith, *Ou si ascun viscount eit pur malice fait prendre plus des avers pur nostre det, ou pur autre, que a la vailance de le det, ou sil eit prist beasts des carues, ou motons, ou berbis, ou vessel, ou mounture, ou robes, ou deins meson la ou auter distres poet trover sufficientment et hors de meason.* And in another place he saith, *Si ascun distreine auter per que gainage est disturbe, &c.*

29 ass. pl. 49.

Lege Executores & Auten.

And this agreeth with the civill law, *Executio fieri non potest in boves, aratra, aliáve instrumenta rusticorum quatenus alia bona habent.*

W. 2. cap. 18. Fleta, lib. 2. c. 55.

The statute of W. 2. which giveth the *elegit*, doth absolutely except the beasts of the plough in these words, *Exceptis bobus et afris carucæ.*

Regist. 97. temps E. 1. avowry 230. 18 E. 2. acc' sur lestat. 35. 4 E. 3. 1. 29 E. 3. 16, 17. P. 17 H. 6. Rot. 93, in com. banco. F.N.B. 174. b. 14 El. Dy. 312.

This statute doth not extend onely to distresses betweene lord and tenant, but also to all other distresses whatsoever, as well at the kings suit, as at the suit of the subject, so there be other goods sufficient; also to all manner of executions, as well at the suit of the king, as of the subject, with the like caution as is aforesaid.

And an action upon this statute doth lie, as well after deliverance, as before, for the cause of the distreining may be lawfull, and yet notwithstanding if he take the beasts of the plough where he might

might find others, the distresse is wrongfull. And albeit the tenant after such a distres taken pay the rent, and thereby affirme the cause of distres lawfull, notwithstanding this doth not purge the offence against this statute.

And the statute is to be construed, that at the time of the distres, &c. there must be other cattell sufficient, and it is not materiall what was before or after. 29 E. 3. 17. 4 H. 7. 8. b.

The writ upon this statute also shall be *contra pacem, et non vi et armis.* 17 E. 3. 1.

Now where the statute speaks of the beasts of the plough, and not of the plough itselfe: by the common law alwayes used the plough or any thing belonging to it was not distreinable, so long as any other distres might be taken.

This statute of 51 H. 3. being of record and in print, I thought to touch specially so much thereof as concerne distresses, whereof our statute of Marlebridge hath treated both in the fourth, and this fifteenth chapter. See Art. super cart. cap. 12.

And it appeareth by the Mirrour, that many other beasts and living things, and other goods were not distreinable by the common law, if there were other goods sufficient. As for mort goods, a covenable distresse is not of armour, or vessell, or apparell, or jewels, so long as there are other sufficient or covenable; nor of sheep, saddle horse, beasts of the plough, poultry, fish, or salvagne, *ut supra.* Mirror cap. 2. § 16. Vee de Name.

CAP. XVI.

*[134]

*SI hæres aliquis post mortem antecessoris (1) sui infra ætatem extiterit, et dominus suus custodiam terrarum, et tenementorum suorum habuerit, si dominus ille dicto hæredi, cum ad legitimam ætatem pervenerit, terram suam sine placito reddere noluerit, hæres ille terram suam per assisam mortis antecessoris recuperabit, una cum dampnis suis, quæ sustinuerit propter detentionem illam à tempore quo fuit legitimæ ætatis. Et si hæres aliquis tempore mortis antecessoris sui plenæ ætatis fuerit (2), et ille hæres apparens, et pro hærede cognitus et inventus sit in hæreditate illa, capitalis dominus * eum non ejiciat, nec aliquid sibi capiat, vel amoveat, sed tamen inde simplicem seisinam habeat pro recognitione dominii sui ut pro domino cognoscatur (3). Et si capitalis dominus hujusmodi hæredem (4) extra seisinam malitiose teneat, propter quod breve mortis antecessoris, vel consanguinitatis*

IF any heir after the death of his ancestor be within age, and his lord have the ward of his lands and tenements, if the lord will not render unto the heir his land (when he cometh to his full age) without plea, the heir shall recover his land by assise of mortdauncestor, with the damages that he hath sustained by such withholding, since the time that he was of full age. And if an heir at the time of his ancestor's death be of full age, and he is heir apparent, and known for heir, and be found in the inheritance, the chief lord shall not put him out, nor take, nor remove any thing there, but shall take only simple seisin therefore for the recognition of his seigniory, that he may be known for lord. And if the chief lord do put such an heir out of the possession maliciously, whereby he is driven to purchase a writ of mortdauncestor, or of cousenage,

sanguinitatis oporteat ipsum impetrare, tunc dampna sua recuperet sicut in assisa novæ disseisinæ. De hæredibus autem, qui de domino rege tenent in capite (5), *si observandum est, ut dominus rex primam inde habeat seisinam, sicut prius inde habere consuevit* (6). *Nec hæres nec aliquis alius in hæreditatem illam se intrudat, priusquam illam de manibus domini regis recipiat* (7), *prout hujusmodi hæreditas de manibus ipsius et antecessorum suorum recipi consueverit temporibus elapsis. Et hoc intelligatur de terris et feodis, quæ ratione servitii militaris* (8), *vel serjantiæ, sive juris patronatus in manibus domini regis esse consueverunt.* Vide Prærogativa cap. 3. Et Glanvil. lib. 7. cap. 9. fol. 4.

senage, then he shall recover his damages as in assise of novel disseisin. Touching heirs, which hold of our lord the king in chief, this order shall be observed, that our lord the king shall have the first seisin of their lands, like as he was wont to have before time: neither shall the heir, nor any other, intrude into the same inheritance, before he hath received it out of the king's hands, as the same inheritance was wont to be taken out of his hands and his ancestors in times past. And this must be understood of lands and fees, the which were accustomed to be in the king's hands by reason of knights service, or serjeanty, or right of patronage.

(17 Ed. 2. stat. 1. c. 3. 12 Car. 2. c. 24.)

Abridg. ass. 120, b. F.N.B. 196. f. Glanv. li. 7. c. 9. Bract. li. 4. fo. 252, 253. Brit. fo. 178. b. Fleta, li. 5. ca. 1. 10 E. 4. 9, 10. per Curiam. 8 E. 3. 63. 10 E. 3. 41. 11 E. 3. ass. 87. 12 E. 3. ass. 86. 12 ass. p. 21. 13 E. 3 tit. Assise 92. 28 ass p. 11. 34 ass. p 10. 39 E. 3. 28. 2 E. 4. 38. 18 E. 4. 25. Temps H. 8. Br. tit. ten' à volunt. 15. *46 E. 3 fo. 20.

(1) *Si hæres aliquis post mortem antecessoris,* &c.] This act is but a declaration of the common law, for in this case when a gardein in chivalrie holdeth over, he is an abator, which is manifestly proved by this act, whereby it is declared that the assise *de mord'* doth lie against him. Also it is so resolved in our books, wherein this diversitie is to be observed, that where a man commeth to a particular estate by the act of the partie, there if he hold over, he is a tenant at sufferance; but where he commeth to the particular estate by act in law, as the gardein in our case doth, there he is no tenant at sufferance, but an abator. *Vide* 1. part of the Instit. sect. 461.

And yet for the benefit of the heire to some purpose, the possession of the gardein is the actuall seisin of the heire, for if the gardein be ousted, and he disseised, he shall have an assise, as it is holden in 2 E. 4. 5. b.

* If a woman bring a writ of dower against a gardein, and recover without title, the heire shall have an assise of *mord'* at his full age at the common law, notwithstanding the possession of the gardein.

(2) *Et si hæres aliquis tempore mortis antecessoris plenæ ætatis fuerit.*] This is the second clause of this chapter, and is also a rehearsall of the common law.

Glanvil, Bracton, Britton, Fleta } ubi supra.

(3) *Simplicem seisinam habeat pro recognitione dominii sui, ut pro domino cognoscatur.*] This is understood of the payment of reliefe, whereby he putteth the lord in seisin, and doth acknowledge him for his lord, so as of ancient time, and in ancient books, reliefe is called *simplex seisina*.

(4) *Et si capitalis dominus hujusmodi hæredis.*] This is the third clause, and is evident.

[135] (5) *De hæreditatibus autem quæ de domino rege tenentur in cap.* &c.] This is the fourth clause of this chapter, and is also a rehearsall

hearsall of the common law, in which clause are these words, *Sicut prius inde habere consuevit*, and these words, *prout hujusmodi hæreditas de manibus ipsius et antecessorum suorum recipi consueverit.*

(6) *Ut dominus rex primam inde habeat seisinam, sicut prius habere consuevit.*] Note, in the former clause concerning the tenure of subjects, the lords should have *simplicem seisinam, i. relevium:* but in this clause where the tenure is of the king *in capite*, and his tenant dieth, his heire of full age, he saith not that he shall have *simplicem seisinam*, but *primam liberam seisinam*, whereof you may reade at large in Stamford Prerog. 11. b.

(7) *Priusquam illam de manibus domini regis recipiat.*] That is, before he sueth his livery out of the kings hands, albeit he be of full age at the death of his auncester, whereof you may reade at large in Stamford, *ubi supra.*

(8) *Et hoc intelligatur de terris et feodis quæ ratione servitii militaris, &c.*] *i. Servitii militaris in capite*, serjantiæ. *i. magnæ serjantiæ*, sive juris patronatus. *i. fundationis episcopatuum, monasteriorum, &c.* Prerog. regis, c. 3.

CAP. XVII.

PROVISUM est insuper, quod si terra quæ tenetur in socagio, sit in custodia parent' hæred', eo quod hæres infra ætatem extiterit, custod' illi vastum facere non possunt (1), *nec venditionem nec aliquam destructionem de hæreditate illa, sed salvo eam custodiant ad opus dicti hæredis, ita quod cum ad legitimam ætatem pervenerit, sibi respondeant* (2) *de exit' dictæ hæreditatis, per legalem computationem, salvis ipsis custodibus rationabilibus misis suis. Nec etiam possunt dicti custodes maritagium dicti hæredis dare* (3) *vel vendere, nisi ad commodum dicti hæredis: sed parentes dicti hæredis propinquiores, qui hujusmodi custodiam habuerint, à toto tempore illo à quo brevia non conceduntur implacitandi, hujusmodi custodias habeant ad commodum hæredum, ut prædictum est, sine vasto, vel exilio, vel destructione facienda.*

IT is provided, that if land holden in socage be in the custody of the friends of the heir, because the heir is within age, the guardians shall make no waste, nor sale, nor any destruction of the same inheritance; but safely shall keep it to the use of the said heir, so that when he cometh to his lawful age, they shall answer to him for the issues of the said inheritance by a lawful accompt, saving to the same guardians their reasonable costs. Neither shall the said guardians give or sell the marriage of such an heir, but to the advantage of the foresaid heir; but the next friends which had the ward, for all that time that writs of impleading did not lie, shall have such wardship unto the advantage of the heir, as is said before, without waste, sale, or destruction making.

(Fitz. Wast. 1. 9. 100. 107. Fitz. Present. 10. Fitz. Brief, 847. Fitz. Gard. 159. 166. Plowd. 293. Fitz. Accompt. 35. 59, 60. 77. 107. 1 Inst. 87. a. Lib. Ent. 47. Rast. 21.)

(1) *Vastum facere non possunt.*] The heire within age shall have an action of wast against the gardein in socage, but he shall not be punished for waste made by strangers. 2 E. 2. Wast. 1. 16 E. 3. Wast. 100. 28 H. 6. Wast. 9.

(2) *Cum ad legitimam ætatem pervenerit, sibi respondeat.*] This F.N.B. 59, g. second

Vide Mag. Ch. c. 4. & Glouc. c. 5
See the first part of the Institutes, sect. 124.

second clause is a declaration of the common law: the lawfull age of * the heire of a tenant in socage is the age of 14 yeares, and at that age he shall have an action of account against his gardein; all which you may reade at large in the first part of the Institutes, sect. 104. See also there the severall ages of men and women.

(3) *Nec etiam possunt dicti custodes maritagium dicti hæredis dare, &c.*] This is the third clause of this act, in affirmance also of the common law. Vide the first part of the Institutes for this clause, sect. 124.

CAP. XVIII.

NULLUS escaetor, vel inquisitor (1), *aut justiciar' ad assisas aliquas specialiter capiendas assignatus, vel ad querelas aliquas audiendum et terminandum, de cætero habeant potestatem aliquam amerciandi pro defalta communis summonitionis, nisi capitales justiciarii, vel justic' itinerantes* (2) *in itineribus suis.*

NO escheator, commissioner, or justicer specially assigned to take assises, or to hear and determine matters, from henceforth shall have power to amerce for default of common summons, but the chief justices, or the justices in eyre in their circuits.

Glanv. li. 9. c. 10. Fleta, li. 1. cap. 43.

(1) *Inquisitor.*] Enquiror, that is to say, sheriffe, coroner *super visum corporis*, or the like, that have power to enquire in certaine cases.

The mischiefe before this statute was, that the eschaetor, sheriffe, coroner, speciall justices of assise, and justices of oier and terminer, in speciall cases (whom Britton calls simple enquirors) would upon the common summons amerce such as made default. Now this statute takes away their power to amerce, *Nullus, &c. habeant potestatem amerciandi pro defalta.*

Britton, fo. 4.

But this extendeth not to sheriffes in their tournes, nor to stewards in leets, notwithstanding that they be inquirors, for that they deale with common nusances, or matters concerning the publique, and not in private causes, and therefore are not restrained by this statute.

Vide hic c. 24.
Brit. fol. 4.
Glanv. li. 9. c. 11.
10 E. 3. fol. 9.
2 H. 4. 24.
8 H. 4. 16.
11 H. 4. 8.

(2) *Nisi capitales justiciarii, vel justiciarii itinerantes.*] That is, justices of general assises, whose authority increasing by divers acts of parliament, and comming twice every yeare where the justices in eire came but from seaven years to seaven years, the authority of justices in eire by little and little vanished.

So as if any amerciament is to be made for default upon common summons, upon due certificate made thereof to the justices of assise (here called *capitales justiciarii*, in respect that speciall justices of assise were named before) they may amerce upon such defaults, but the escheator dealing *virtute officii*, did after this statute certifie the defaults into the exchequer, and there was the amerciament imposed; which is worthy of observation.

Britton, fo. 1. cap. 4.
Fleta, l. 1. c. 43.

And this exposition agreeth with Britton, who wrote soone after this statute, *(et contemporanea expositio est fortissima in lege)* and saith, *Et*

Et ceux que avoient estre summons, et ne viendront a cels enquests des coroners, volons q. ils soient in nostre mercie, a la venue de nous justices as primiers assises en cel countie, si tielz defaults trovant entres en rol de coroner. Issint que nous coroners, ne nous escheators, ne simples enquirers, ne eient poer de nulluy amercier pur nul defaute.

CAP. XIX.

DE essoniis (1) *autem provisum est, quod in comitatu, hundred', aut in curia baronis, vel aliis curiis* (2), *nullus habeat necesse jurare pro essonio suo warrantizando* (3). Vide Glanv. lib. 1. cap. 12. fol. 4.

TOUCHING essoins, it is provided, that in counties, hundreds, or in courts barons, or in other courts, none shall need to swear to warrant his essoin.

Fleta, lib. 6. ca. 10. (Fitz. Essoin, 119. Rast. 297.)

By the order of the common law, for that essoines which were first instituted upon just and necessary cause, should not be used upon feigned causes for delay, he that cast the essoine ought to be sworne, that the cause thereof was just and true, and this held in all the five essoines before mentioned, cap. 12. and this appeareth in Glanvill, *Essoniator probabit quodlibet essonium jure jurando propria et unica manu, &c.* But yet at the common law an oath was not alwayes required in that case; *Non autem omnes essoniatores ad diem recipiend. affidabunt, sed illi tantum qui sunt baronibus inferiores, barones vero et baronissæ et eorum superiores, sicut comites et eorum attornat' non affidabunt, sed plegios invenient, &c. Ratio vero hujus diversitatis talis esse potest, quod ita nobiles et dignæ personæ in warrantizatione essonii non per se jurabunt, sed per procuratores, scilicet plegios suos, &c.* And herewith agreeth other auncient authors.

Vide hic. ca. 12. & 13. Glan. l. 1. ca. 12. Bract. li. 5. fol. 351, 352. Fleta, li. 6. c. 10. Britton, fo. 282. cap. 122. See the third part of the Institutes, cap. Perjury.

(1) *De essoniis.*] This act speaketh generally of essoines, and yet it is particularly to be understood of one of the five essoines, and that is, of the common essoine *de malo veniendi*; so as in the essoine *de service le roy*, and the rest, he that cast the essoine must be still sworne; and this law hath beene thus interpreted for two reasons. 1. For that in the essoine *de service le roy*, and the rest, the delay is great, *viz.* a yeare and a day, &c. and therefore those essoines ought to be more precisely proved. 2. *Ad ea quæ frequentius accidunt jura adaptantur*: in those dayes those other essoines were very rare, and therefore the judges of the law, that ever hated delayes, interpreted this act to extend to common essoines only, that had the least delay in it.

12 H. 4. 14. 2 E. 4. 16. l. 5 E. 4. 70. Vide Gloc. c. 8.

(2) *Vel in aliis curiis.*] These generall words are interpreted to extend to the kings courts of record at Westminster, and other courts of record, although the act beginneth with inferiour courts, as it is manifest by common experience; and the cause is, for that otherwise these generall words should be void, for it cannot according to the generall rule extend to inferiour courts; for none be more inferiour or lower than these, that be particularly named, and so note a just exception out of the generall rule.

12 H. 4. 24. per Hankford. Fleta, lib. 6. cap. 10. Lib. 2. fol. 46. Levesque de Cant. case. Vide hic ca. 28. W. 1. c. 3. 15, 26.

(3) *Warrantizando.*]

Bracton, li. 4. fo. 352. 12 H. 4. 15, 24. (3) *Warrantizando.*] *Est autem warrantizare, jurare quod ita detentus fuit ægritudine in veniendo versus curiam, quod venire non potuit.* This was the oath of him that cast the essoine at the common law before this act.

[138]

CAP. XX.

NULLUS de cætero (excepto domino rege) teneat placitum in curia sua de falso judicio facto in curia tenentium suorum; qui hujusmodi placita specialiter spectant ad coronam et dignitatem domini regis.

NONE from henceforth (except our lord the king) shall hold in his court any plea of false judgement, given in the court of his tenants; for such plea specially belongeth to the crown and dignity of our lord the king.

(Fitz. Faux Judgement, 7, 8, 10. 14. 1 Ed. 3. stat. 1. c. 4. Regist. 15. Rast. 342. Co. Ent. 305.)

Before the making of this statute, if a false judgement had been given in a court baron, this should have been redressed in the court baron of the lord next above him, and so upward of the lords paramount, which both was an occasion of long delayes, and the king had also many times prejudice thereby, for that those base courts could assesse no fine or amerciament to the king; which is so to be understood, that if the next immediate mesne had no court baron, the false judgement could not be redressed in the court of
Regist. fol. 15. the lord next above, for default of privity, but then the false judgement was to be redressed in the court of common pleas, or before the justices in eyre: hereby shall appeare, how necessary it is to know what the common law was before the making of any, and especially of this statute, for without that this act could not be understood.

This act consisteth on two branches, the first is negative, the other affirmative.

1. That none from henceforth (except the king) shall hold plea in his court of false judgement in the court of his tenants.

Hereby is implied that by the common law, the false judgement in a court baron was to be redressed in the courts of the lords above.

2. The affirmative is, because such pleas (of false judgment) specially belong to the crowne and dignity of our lord the king; this is a reason of the taking away of the jurisdiction of the superiour lords: and the effect of the reason is this, that in such proceedings, many times fines and amerciaments to the king were to be imposed, which did belong to the kings crowne and dignity,
Dier, 9 Eliz. 263. that is, to the kings courts of record, and not to inferiour courts of lords, that were not of record: and besides, if the judgment were reversed in the lords court, the suitors that gave the false judgement were to be amercied to the king, which the inferiour court could not doe.

And for that at the common law, for default of courts of superiour lords, the false judgement was to be redressed in the court of

of common pleas, therefore though the words be *excepto domino rege*, and *hujusmodi placita spectant ad coronam et dignitatem domini regis*, which might give a countenance to the kings court, *coram rege*, yet this statute taketh away no jurisdiction from the court of common pleas, that it had before this statute. And this doth Britton, who wrote soone after this statute, grounding himselfe upon this act, notably expresse in these words:

Et si faux judgement, ou faux proces soit trove in le record, et la parol soit in counte, de ceo ne voilons nous my que le visc' ne les suiters eient conusans: mes plein soy, que greve se sentira, & face vener le proces & le record devant nous justices in banke, & illonques soit redresse le error si poient issint trove. Britton, fol. 59.

And the rule in the Register is, Regist. fol. 15.

Si faux judgement soit done en county, court baron, ou auter court nient enfranchise (i. nient de record) que ont conusans de plea, celuy contre que judgement est done poet aver bre. de recorder la parole devant justices in banke on in eire. Et cest rule extend auxi bien in autre bre. come in bre. de droit, et la ou la parole est per bre. ou sans bre. [139]

And now the justices in eyre being (as hath been said) worn out, the originall writ of false judgement is retournable, *coram justiciariis nostris apud Westm'*: which are the justices of the court of common pleas. Regist. ubi supra.

CAP. XXI.

PROVISUM est etiam, quod si averia alicujus capiantur, et injuste detineantur, vicecomes post querimoniam inde sibi factam (1), ea sine impedimento (3) vel contradictione ejus qui dicta averia ceperit, deliberare possit, si extra libertates capta fuerint. Et si infra libertates capta fuerint hujusmodi averia, et balivi libertatis ea deliberare noluerint (2), tunc vicecom' pro defectu ipsorum balivorum ea faciat deliberari.

IT is provided also, that if the beasts of any man be taken, and wrongfully withholden, the sheriffe, after complaint made to him thereof, may deliver them without let or gainsaying of him that took the beasts, if they were taken out of liberties. And if the beasts were taken within any liberties, and the bailiffs of the liberty will not deliver them, then the sheriff, for default of those bailiffs, shall cause them to be delivered.

Glanv. li. 12. c. 12. 15. Mirror, c. 2. § 16. Fleta, lib. 2. ca. 39. 1 E. 3. 11. b. Vide W. 1. c. 17. (Dyer, f. 245. Bro. Riots, 2, 3. Bro. Parliament, 108. Fitz. Retorn. de Viscont. 17. 1 Inst. 145. b. 13 Rep. 31. 3 Ed. 1. c. 17. Regist. 82, &c.)

The mischiefes before this statute were first when a mans beasts or other goods were distreined and impounded, the owner of the goods had no remedy but a writ of replevin, by which delay the beasts or other goods were long detained from the owner to his great losse and damage. 21 H. 6. tit. retorn. del Visc. 17. Dier Mich. 7&8. Eliz. 246.

Secondly, when the beasts or other goods were distreined and impounded within any liberty that had retourn of writs, the sheriffe was driven to make a warrant to the baylie of the liberty to 29 E. 3. 23. F.N.B. 58. b.

make deliverance, and that wrought a longer delay, for at the common law he could not enter into the liberty in that case.

A third mischiefe was when the distresse was taken out of the liberty, and impounded within: Now this statute doth apply cures to all these three mischiefes.

Mirror, c. 2. § 16. 8 E. 4. 14. 9 E. 4. 48. 14 H. 7. 9. 16 H. 7. 16. 21 H. 7. 23. F.N.B. 69. First part of the Institutes, sect. 219. & 237. * 21 E. 4. 66.

(1) *Post querimoniam inde sibi fact',* &c.] That is, the sheriffe upon a pleint made unto him without writ may either by paroll, or by precept, command his bayly to deliver them, that is to make replevin of them, and by these words *post querimoniam sibi fact'*, the sheriffe may take a pleint out of the * county court, and make replevin presently (which he ought to enter in the county court) for it should be inconvenient, and against the scope of this statute, that the owner for whose benefit the statute was made, should tarry for his beasts to the next county court, which is holden from moneth to moneth.

And in a replevin by pleint, the sheriffe may hold plea in his county court, although the value be of 20 l. or above, by force of this statute, but in other actions he shall hold plea under 40 s.

30 E. 3. 23.

The usage of the county of Northampton is, that in the absence of the sheriffes baylie the frankpledge may make deliverance; note this.

Regist. 81. b.

If J. S. be sheriffe, and the distresse was taken by him, the writ or pleint shall be in common forme, naming the sheriffe by his christen name and sirname, *quæ* J. S. *cepit,* and not *quæ tu ipse cepisti,* and the sheriffe in that case ought to make deliverance.

[140]

(2) *Et si infra libertates, &c. balivi libertatis ea deliberare noluerint.*] Hereby it appeareth that when the distresse is taken and impounded within a liberty that hath retourne of writs, whether the matter be before the sheriffe by writ or by pleint, the sheriffe ought to make a warrant to the baylife of the liberty to make deliverance; whereunto if he make no answer, or retourn that he will make no deliverance, or the like, the sheriffe may by force of this statute, and the statute of W. 1. enter into the liberty, and make deliverance; and herewith agreeth Fleta.

W. 1. cap. 17. F.N.B. 68. f.

Fleta, li. 2. c. 39. § si balivus. Regist. 82.

Et si balivus alicujus habentis libertatem retorn' brevium postque vicecom' sibi precept' reg', vel aliud mandatum ex officio suo dependens averia, ut prædictum est, detenta non deliberet, vicecom' extunc habet ingressum, et faciat quod suum est, &c. Et eodem modo fiat deliberatio licet sine brevi suscepta securitate de prosequendo, &c.

And if the distresse be taken without the franchise, and impounded within, the sheriffe may upon pleint made, presently enter and make deliverance (without any precept to the bayly of the liberty) for the statute provideth that he shall replevy, *Si extra libertates capta fuer,' et si infra libertates capta fuerint hujusmodi averia, &c.* So as there is no precept to be directed to the bayly of the liberty, but where the distresse was taken within the liberty; and where the distresse was taken out of the liberty, there by the expresse words of the statute the sheriffe may enter and make deliverance presently.

31 E. 3. gager deliverance. 15.

(3) *Sine impedimento,* &c.] A man by deed makes a lease for yeares, reserving a rent with a clause of distresse, and to detaine the distresse against gages and pledges untill gree be made, yet the sheriffe, or bayly of the liberty, as the case requires, ought to make deliverance of such a distresse.

Note

Note the original writ of *repleg'* is in nature of a *justicies*, and is not retournable; and in a *justicies* no conusance can be demanded, because none can demand conusance, but he that hath a court of record, and of a plea in a court of record; but the county court, though the plea be holden therein by a *justicies* the kings writ, yet is it no court of record, for of a judgement therein there lieth a writ of false judgement, and not a writ of error: also if the sheriffe should graunt the conusance, he could not award a resummons, and the lord of the franchise can demand no conusance in a replevin. 34 H. 6. 48.

And yet divers lords of hundreds, and court barons have power to hold plea, *de vetito namio*, in old books called *de vee*: for the better understanding of this act, and of divers auncient acts of parliament, books, and records, it is good to know what the genuine sense of *vetitum namium* is, wherein many have erred. *Namium* signifieth a taking, or distresse, and *vetitum* i. forbidden, and properly it signifieth when the bayly of the lord distreineth beasts or goods, and the lord forbiddeth his bayly to deliver them when the sheriffe comes to replevy them, and to that end to drive them to places unknowne, or to take such a course as they should not be replevied: but it is also called a distresse, that is forbidden *vetitum namiũ*, when without any words they are eloigned, or so handled by a forbidden course, as they cannot be replevied, for then they are forbidden in law to be replevied. F.N.B. 73. b. Reg. Orig. 12 H. 7. 8, 9. See W. 2. ca. 2. F.N.B. 73.

Now by this it appeareth how they erre, that take it, that beasts or goods taken in withernam should be beasts or goods taken in *vetito namio*, for *vetitum namium*, or *vetitum namii* is unlawfull, for whether the distresse were lawfully taken or no, yet the forbidding of them against gages and pledges to be replevied, out of question is unlawfull. But the beasts in withernam are lawfully taken by authority of law, in lieu of those that were distreined and forbidden to be replevied, and the writ or precept of withernam reciteth, *Quod postquam predict' B. averia predict' A. cepit, et in comit' tuo ea fugavit, &c. per quod ea eidem A. replegiari non potuisti, nos malitiæ ipsius B. obviare volentes in hac parte tibi præcipimus quod averia prædict' B. in baliva tua cap' in withernam, et ea detineas donec eidem A. averia sua prædict' secundum legem et consuetudinem regni nostri replegiar' possis, &c.* So as the taking in withernam is a lawfull taking by authority of law, and therefore cannot be termed a taking forbidden, for that it is expresly commanded to be done, and this agreeth with our old bookes. Hereof Bracton saith, *Si autem averia capiantur per servientem domini (sine judicio curiæ) et postea petita fuerint ab ipso domino, cum præsens fuerit, et ipse ea vetuerit per vadium et plegium, uterque tenebitur, ut videtur, unus de captione, et alter de vetito namio; et licet dominus ipse advocaverit captionem servientis, servientem non liberat sed onerat seipsum, et uterque tenetur de facto servientis, serviens quia cepit, et dominus dupliciter, quia advocat factum servientis, et quia vetat: item sunt qui dicunt, quod non tenetur quis respondere de vetito, antequam convincatur captio injusta, ad quod dico, quamvis captio justa, vel injusta, tamen vetitum semper erit injustum.* Bracton, lib. 3. fol. 155. b. Regist. 82, 83, 79, 80. F.N.B. 73. [141] Bract. li. 3. 158. 155. b. 157. a. sect. 6. Withernã.

And in W. 2. *placita de vetito namio*, is intended a power to hold plea of taking of distresses, and forbidding of them to be replevied, as clearly appeareth by the words of that act, and cannot be intended of pleas of withernam. W. 2. cap. 2.

Mirror, ca. 2. § 16. De vee de naam.

De vee sont 2. manners, lun quant un vee vive naam, &c. contre gages, & pledges suffisant, lauter quant lun ne suffer my soy estre distrein a droit, & lun & lauter sont personel trespasses contre la peace.

Vee is an old French word, and is as much to say, as *vetitus*, or forbidden.

Naam nest autre chose que reasonable distresse; it commeth of the Saxon word *nemmen*, or *nammen*, to take hold on, or distrein, whereof comes *namium*, *i. captio*, and so *vetitum namium* signifieth in law a distresse, or taking forbidden to be replevied.

Now seeing withernam hath been mentioned, you shall finde that the true sense of the word is a proofe of the aforesaid matter, for it is compounded of two old Saxon words, *viz. weder*, which common speech hath turned to *oder*, or *other*; and *naam*, that signifieth, as hath been said, a caption, or taking, and therefore is as much as a taking, or a reprisall of other goods in lieu of them that were formerly taken and eloigned or withholden, and this is *capere in withernam'*, whereof the Register speaketh, and well expoundeth, which now you see clearly is just and lawfull.

Lambard verbo Withernam.

And therefore one speaking of withernam, and condemning the aforesaid error, saith, *Verum maximam mihi admirationem movet introducta nominis depravatio, quæ withernam vetitum (cum potius iteratum sonat) namium dicit.*

F.N.B. 89. u. Regist. Vide Bract. ubi supra.

And albeit the distresse were lawfull, yet by matter, *ex post facto*, it may be called *vetitum namium*, a wrongfull taking: for when (for example) he that destreineth them eloigneth them, so as they cannot be replevied, the owner shall have an action of tresspasse, *quare vi et armis, averia ipsius A. cepit et ea ad loca ignota fugavit ita quod averia illa eidem A. secundum legem et consuetudinem regni nostri replegiand. inveniri non poterit:* whereby it appeareth, that by the matter subsequent, the first distresse is in this sense, and to this effect, termed unlawfull.

[142]

CAP. XXII.

NULLUS de cætero possit distringere libere tenentes suos ad respondendum de libero tenemento suo, nec de aliquibus ad liberum tenementum suum spectantibus (1), *nec jurare faciat libere tenentes* (2) *suos contra voluntatem suam, quia hoc nullus facere potest sine præcepto domini regis.*

NONE from henceforth may distrain his freeholders to answer for their freeholds, nor for any things touching their freehold, without the king's writ: nor shall cause his freeholders to swear against their wills; for no man may do that without the king's commandment.

15 R. 2. cap. 2. 16 R. 2. cap. 2. (15 R. 2. c. 12.)

Rot. claus. 18 H. 3. m. 10. in Havering.

This act is confirmed and enlarged by the statute of 15 and 16 R. 2.

Before this statute, lords would distraine their free tenants to come and shew the deeds, specially the originall deed, whereby they might know by what rent and services the tenancie was holden of them, and obliquely many times perusing the deeds (which are the secrets and sinews of a mans land) brought in question the title of the

the free-hold it selfe. Another mischiefe was, that the lords of court barons, hundreds, &c. where the suitors were judges, would constraine them to sweare betweene partie and partie, both which mischiefes are taken away by two severall branches of this act.

(1) *Ad liberum tenementum suum spectantibus.*] By these words are intended the charters or tenure of their lands, for they doe properly belong to the free-hold; and if the freeholder be distrained contrary to the purview of this statute, he shall have a writ of prohibition grounded upon this act, *Cum de communi consilio regni nostri Angliæ statutum sit, quod nullus distringere possit libere tenentes suos ad respondendum de libero tenemento suo, nec de aliquibus ad liberum tenementum suum spectantibus, &c. Tibi præcipimus quod non distringas ad respondendum, &c.*

And it appeareth by the Register, that this act doth bind the king, for there is a writ directed to the kings bailiffes of his mannor of N. the words whereof be, *Vobis præcipimus, quod non distringatis A. ad respondendum coram vobis in curia nostra prædict' de libero tenem' suo, nec de aliquibus ad liberum tenementum suum spectantibus.* And if the kings bailiffe doth not obey this writ, the tenant shall have an attachment against him, which also appeares in the Register. Regist. 171.

(2) *Nec jurare facit libere tenentes.*] This is to be understood betweene partie and partie; but to enquire for the lord of all the articles belonging to the court baron or hundred, they may be sworne, and so are the books to be understood. Hereof you may reade a notable record in 14 E. 1. in Banco, &c. 27 aff. p. 6. 20. 39 E. 3. 20. 12 H. 4. 8. b. F.N.B. 75. e.

*Gilbertus de Pincebek & Richardus filius Guilielmi de Spalding implacitaver' Priorem de Spalding pro eo quod cum sint liberi homines, & terras & tenementa sua tenent liberè, ipse Prior distringit eos ad corporale sacramentum præstand' sibi sine præcepto regis, contra legem & consuet' regni regis, & contra * prohibitionem, &c. Prior dicit quod habet libertatem & regalitatem, quod si quis captus fuerit cum latrocinio, quod ipse per balivos suos in curia sua inde habet cogn'. Et quod super captionem furis cum manuopere dictum fuit dictis Gilberto & Richardo, quod ad rei veritatem inde inquirend' præstarent sacramentum, qui illud facere recusarunt, unde dic' quod per considerationem curiæ præd' fuerunt ipsi districti propter contemptum prædict' judic'. Et quia in casu hujusmodi liber homo in curia domini sui corporale debet sacramentum præstare, si per consuetudinem ejusdem curiæ ad hoc electus fuerit, & idem Gilbertus & Richardus non possunt dedicere, quin per consuetud' ejusdem curiæ ad hujusmodi corporale sacramentum electi fuerunt. Considerat' est, quod Prior sine die, & hab' return' averiorum, & ipsi Guilielmi & Richardi in misericordia.* M. 14. E. 1. rot. 19. Lincoln. * That is this statute. A freeholder refuse to present for the lord. [143] The custome of the court.

But in the leet or tourne, the suitors may be compelled to be sworne as well for the king, as betweene partie and partie; for they are not *liberè tenentes*, as this statute speaketh, in respect of tenure, but doe their suit in respect of resiance; also the leets and tournes are the courts of the king and of record; and the court baron and hundred court of other lords are not courts of record. 39 E. 3. 35. 44 E. 3. 19. F.N.B. 75 E.

The rule of law is, that whensoever any man hath any thing of common right and by course of law, the same may well be enlarged by custome and prescription; as the lord of a manour that hath a court baron, of common right and by course of law all pleas therein are determinable by wager of law, and yet by prescription the lord may prescribe to determine them by jurie. And this branch doth 12 H. 7, 8, 9. Regist. 171. b.

doth binde the king in his court baron, hundred or countie court.

Bract. li. 3. fo. 106. Of both these articles Bracton saith thus, *Non potest aliquis baro, vicecomes, vel alius de liberis tenementis cognoscere, nec tenens tenetur respondere sine praecepto vel warranto domini regis, nec etiam possunt aliquem ad sacramentum sine warranto compellere.*

Glanv. li. 12. c. 2, 3. &c. Bract. li. 5. fo. 328. Brit. cap. 120. Fleta, li. 6. c. 3. Regist. fo. 1. F.N.B. fo. 1. In a writ of right patent directed to the lord of the manour, plea shall be holden of freehold, and the court in that case may give an oath, for there is the kings writ of *praecipe quod reddat*, which is *praeceptum domini regis*. Of this you shall reade plentifully in our old books, and it properly belongeth to another treatise. And note these words in our act, *Sine praecepto domini regis*, doe refer to both clauses.

CAP. XXIII.

PROVISUM est etiam, quod si balivi (1), qui compotum suum dominis suis reddere tenentur, se subtraxerint, et terras vel tenementa non habuerint (2), per quae distringi possunt, tunc per eorum corpora attachientur, ita quod vicecomes in cujus baliva inveniantur, eos venire faciat ad compotum suum reddend'.

IT is provided also, that if bailiffs, which ought to make account to their lords, do withdraw themselves, and have no lands nor tenements whereby they may be distrained; then they shall be attached by their bodies, so that the sheriff, in whose bailiwick they be found, shall cause them to come to make their account.

(Fitz. Brief, 791, 806. Fitz. Process, 203. Fitz. Exigent, 12. 1 Roll. 182.)

The mischiefe before this statute was, as it appeareth by the letter thereof, that the last proces in an action of accompt was distres infinite, and the accomptants seeking subterfuges did withdraw themselves and become vagrant, flying to secret places, sometimes in foreine counties, and had no lands or tenements whereby they might be distrained, so as the lords were in a manner remedilesse.

Regist. 72. 136. F.N.B. 117. h. Fleta, li. 2. c. 64. Brit. fo. 163. b. Mirr. c. 2. § 17. de contracts, & c. 5. § 3. This act doth give to the lord a writ of account, founded upon this statute, which of the words of the writ is called a *monstravit de compoto*, and beginneth thus: *Monstravit nobis A. quod cum B. balivus suus, &c.* Of which writ you may reade in the Register, in Fleta, and other ancient books and records, and lyeth in any county where the accountant may be found.

[144] Britton ubi sup. 17 E. 2. Proc. 203. 18 E. 2. avow. 220. 17 E. 3. 59. Regist. 137. (1) *Balivi.*] This statute extends not onely to bailiffes according to the letter, but to gardeins in socage, receivers, and other accountants: but the statute of W. 2. c. 11. extends only to bailifes and receivers, and not to a gardein in socage; for a capias lyeth against him by this statute, but no exigent by the statute of W. 2.

W. 2. cap. 11. Regist. 136. F.N.B. 118. And where some have supposed, that the statute of W. 2. which giveth proces of utlagary in an action of account, hath taken away either the effect or the use of this act, the contrary appeareth in that

that caſe, and in other caſes in our books, as hereafter ſhall appeare.

(2) *Et terras et tenementa non habuerint.*] If the accomptants have any lands or tenements, whereby they might be diſtrained, though it be not to the value of the account, yet it ſufficeth to exempt them out of this ſtatute, but they muſt have lands and tenements for terme of life at the leaſt, and ſo is this act to bee underſtood.

For proof whereof; after this ſtatute, and after the ſaid ſtatute of W. 2. cap. 11. *viz.* in 4 E. 2. one brought a writ of *monſtravit de compoto* upon this ſtatute, and counted that he was his receiver of C. l. &c. In which action foure points were reſolved. 1. That our ſtatute extendeth to a receiver as well as to a bailife. 2. That if the accountant hath any lands or tenements, though they be not ſufficient to render the account, yet he is exempted out of the ſtatute. 3. By theſe words [lands and tenements] is intended an eſtate of freehold; and therefore where it was there found that the accountant had a houſe of the yearly value of vi. s. in the right of his wife, who had the inheritance thereof, but for that it was the freehold of his wife, and not his freehold, it was adjudged no ſufficiencie within the ſtatute. 4. Laſtly, it was reſolved, that if the huſband had iſſue by his wife, ſo as he had a franktenement for his life, he had beene exempted out of the ſtatute. And the like caſe was in 6 E. 2. in caſe of a receiver, and many other authorities and records there be to that effect, whereby it appeareth that both this act hath ſtill his effect, and that it was in uſe after the ſtat. of W. 2. cap. 11. And herewith agreeth Fleta, which wrote ſoone after the ſtatute of W. 2. and that ſtatute doth confirme this act, *Et ſi diffugerit, et gratis compotum reddere noluerit, ſicut in aliis ſtatutis alibi continetur:* by which words this ſtatute is meant.

4 E. 2. breve 791.

6 E. 2. breve 806. 17 E. 2. Proc. 203. 17 E. 3. 59. F N.B. 118. Flet. li. 2. c. 64. Britton ubi ſup.

And good uſe may be made of this writ of *monſtravit de compoto,* if the plaintife can learne in what place or countie he lurketh, but he cannot have this writ *ſed per fidem, quam præſtare debet in cancellaria, &c.*

F.N.B. 118. Regiſt. 136, 137.

But if any ſue out this writ of *monſtravit de compoto,* and attache the accountants body, where he hath lands and tenements, contrary to this act, *in deceptionem curiæ contra formam ſtatuti, &c.* the party grieved ſhall have a writ for his reliefe, which appeareth in the Regiſter.

Regiſt. 137.

CAP. XXIV.

ITEM firmarii (1) tempore firmarum ſuarum vaſtum, venditionem, vel exilium (2) non facient (3) de domibus, boſcis, vel hominibus, nec de aliquibus ad tenementa quæ ad firmam habent ſpectantibus (4), niſi ſpecialem inde habuerint conceſſionem (5), per ſcriptum conventionis mentionem faciens quod hoc facere poſſunt. Quod ſi fecerint,

ALSO fermors, during their terms, ſhall not make waſte, ſale, nor exile of houſe, woods, and men, nor of any thing belonging to the tenements that they have to ferm, without ſpecial licence had by writing of covenant, making mention, that they may do it; which thing if they do, and thereof be convict, they ſhall

rint, et super hoc convincantur, dampna plena restituant, et per misericordiam graviter puniantur (6).	shall yield full damage, and shall be punished by amerciament grievously.

See the statute of Glouc' c. 8. (Mirror, 320. 5 Rep. 18. Dyer, f. 281. Fitz. Wast. 12. 22. 30. 32. 37. 42, 43, 46, 47, 48. 53. 68, 69. 76. 78. 82. 88. 4 Rep. 63. Rast. 689. 6 Ed. 1. stat. 1. c. 5.)

The mischiefe before this statute was, that against lessees for life or years, there lay no prohibition of waste at the common law, because they came in by the act of the lessor, and he might have provided upon the making of the lease, against waste to be done, and he that might and would not provide for himself, the common law would not provide for: otherwise it is of estates created by law, as tenant in dower, and the gardien; but seeing waste and destruction is hurtfull to the common-wealth, this act provideth remedy for waste done by lessee for life, or lessee for yeares, and it is the first statute that gave remedy in those cases: for the rule of the Register is, that there are five manner of writs of wastes, *viz.* two at the common law, as for waste done by tenant in dower, or by the gardien; and three by statute, or speciall law, as against tenant for life, tenant for yeares, and tenant by the courtesie.

Regist. 72. Bract. li. 4. fo. 355, 356, 357.

(1) *Firmarii.*] For the word *firma,* whereof *firmarius* commeth, see the first part of the Institutes, sect. 1.

Here *firmarii* doe comprehend all such as hold by lease for life, or lives, or for yeares, by deed or without deed; *large se habet hæc dictio firmarius ad terminum vitæ, et ad terminum annorum*; and so much Fleta saith, *de termino.*

Fleta, lib. 5. ca. 34.

Regist. 72.

Albeit the Register saith, *Sciend',* that *per statutum de Marlebridge, cap.* 23. *data fuit quædam prohibitio vasti versus tenentem annorum,* which is true, though the statute doth extend to farmers for life also, but this act extended not to tenant by the courtesie, for he is not a farmer, but if a lease be made for life or yeares, he is a farmer, though no rent be reserved.

First part of the Inst. sect. 67.

(2) *Vastum, venditionem, vel exilium.*] Of these you shall reade in the first part of the Institutes. But a reason is required, that seeing as well the estate of the tenant by the courtesie, as the tenant in dower are created by act in law, wherefore the prohibition of wast did not lie as well against the tenant by the curtesie, as the tenant in dower at the common law; and the reason is this, for that by having of issue the state of tenant by the courtesie is originally created, and yet after that he shall doe homage alone in the life of his wife, which proveth a larger estate; and seeing at the creation of his estate he might doe waste, the prohibition of waste lay not against him after his wives decease, but in the case of tenant in dower, she is punishable of waste at the first creation of her estate: the prohibition of waste lay not against tenant in taile *apres possib.* (whose state was created by act in law) because the originall estate was not punishable of waste.

Dier 11 Eliz. 281. b.

(3) *Non faciant.*] To doe or make waste, in legall understanding in this place, includes as well permissive waste, which is waste by reason of omission, or not doing, as for want of reparation, as waste by reason of commission, as to cut downe timber trees, or prostrate houses, or the like; and the same word hath the statute of Glouc. cap. 5. *que aver fait waste,* and yet is understood as well of

of passive, as active waste, for he that suffereth a house to decay, which he ought to repaire, doth the waste: and therefore if a man maketh a lease for yeares by indenture of a house and lands, upon condition, that if it happen the lessee to doe any waste, that the lessor shall reenter, in this case if the lessee suffer the houses to be wasted, the lessor shall re-enter, so as this word *facere*, hath not onely this signification in a penall statute, but in a condition also.

This act prohibiteth that farmers shall not doe waste, and yet if they suffer a stranger to doe waste, they shall be charged with it, for it is presumed in law, that the farmer may withstand it, *Et qui non obstat quod obstare potest, facere videtur.* [146] Secondly, the law doth give to every man his proper action, so as none of them be without due remedy: and therefore in this case the lessor shall have his action of waste against the lessee, and the lessee his action of trespasse against him that did the waste, and so the losse, as reason requireth, in the end shall lie upon the wrong doer, and if the lessor should not have his action of waste, hee should bee without remedy.

21 H. 7. 37. a.

First part Inst. sect. 67.

(4) *Nec de aliquibus ad tenementa quæ habent ad firmam spectantibus.*] There were before particularly named *de domibus, boscis, et hominibus*; these words doe comprehend lands and meadowes belonging to the farme.

Also these generall words have a further signification, and therefore if there had been a farmer for life, or yeares of a mannor, and a tenancy had escheated, this tenancy so escheated did belong to the tenements that he held in farm, and therefore this act extended to it, and the lessor shall have generally a writ, and suppose a lease made of the lands escheated by the lessor, and maintain it by the speciall matter.

(5) *Nisi habeant specialem concessionem.*] This graunt ought to be by deed, for all waste tendeth to the dis-inheritance of the lessor, and therefore no man can claime to be dispunishable of waste without deed.

3 E. 3. fol. 34. 24 E. 3. 37.

[a] In Lewis Bowles case you may reade plentifully of this matter. This speciall graunt is intended to be *absque impetitione vasti*, without impeachment of waste. Impeachment commeth of the French word *empeshement*: [b] the sages of the law have used the word *impetitio*, derived of *in* and *peto*, and that *sine impetitione vasti*, is as much to say, as without impeachment, that is, without any demand or challenge for doing of waste; but if the clause be either *sine impedimento*, or *impeditione vasti*, it amounteth in judgement of law to as much as *sine impetitione vasti.*

(6) [c] *Damna plena restituant et per misericordiam graviter puniantur.*] [d] And this must be understood in such a prohibition of waste upon this statute, as lay against tenant in dower at the common law, and single damages was given by this statute against lessee for life, and lessee for yeares.

This statute of Glouc'. cap. 5. gave treble damages, and the place wasted against lessee for life, lessee for yeares, and tenant by the courtesie, &c.

[a] Lib. 11. fo. 82, 83. Vide lib. 4. fo. 63. lib. 9. fol. 9.
[b] Vide l. 11. fo. 82. b. Lewys Bowls case. See the first part of the Inst. sect. 354 verb. sans Impeachment de Waste. Adjudg. Tr. 6 Jac. in Com. Banco. Lib. intrat. Co. 664, 665.
[c] Fleta, li. 1. ca. 11.
[d] Regist. 72.

But after this statute, and the statute of Glouc'. *Consuevit fieri breve de prohibitione vasti, per quod breve multi fuerunt in errore, credentes quod illi qui vastum fecerint non habuerunt necesse respondere nisi tantum de vasto facto post prohibitionem eis directam; dominus rex (ut*

W. 2. cap. 14.

hujusmodi

hujusmodi error de cætero tollatur) statuit quod de vasto quocunque, &c. non fiat de cætero breve de prohibitione sed breve de summonitione, quod ille, de quo queritur, respondeat de vasto facto quocunque tempore, &c.

Whereupon the prohibition of waste was abrogated, and the Regist. fol. 72. action of waste framed upon the act of Westm. 2. as in the Register appeareth.

[147]

CAP. XXV.

JUSTICIARII itinerantes de cætero non amercient villatas in itinere suo, pro eo quod singuli xii. annorum (1) *non venerint coram vicecomitibus et coronatoribus, ad inquisitiones de roberiis* (2), *incendiis domorum* (3), *vel aliis ad coronam spectantibus* (4) *faciend'. Dum tamen de villatis illis veniant sufficientes* (5), *per quos inquisitiones hujusmodi plene fieri possunt, exceptis inquisitionibus de morte hominis* (6) *faciend', ubi omnes xii. annorum, venire debent, nisi rationabilem causam habeant absentiæ suæ.*

THE justices in eyre from henceforth shall not amerce townships in their circuits, because all being twelve years old came not afore the sheriffs and coroners, to make inquiry of robberies, burnings of houses, or other things pertaining to the crown; so that there come sufficient out of those towns, by whom such enquests may be made full: except enquests for the death of man, whereat all being twelve years of age, ought to appear, unless they have reasonable cause of absence.

Magna Chart. ca. 35. Hic. ca. 10. & 8. (Fitz. Wast. 11. 39. 53. 66. 72, 73. 101. 103. 120.)

Two mischiefes were before the making of this statute.

First, that if the sheriffe did present before the justices in eyre, that those of the age of twelve yeares came not to the tourn, that the townships where they dwelt should be amercied, for that every one above twelve years appeared not at their tourns, where they should be sworne, (as hath been said) amongst other things, that they should doe no felony, nor assent to any, and therefore albeit they could not be present *ad inquisit' faciend'*, being under age of 21, yet they ought to be there to take the oath, and to discover felonies, if any they knew, according to their oath.

Another mischiefe, that when any robbery, burning of houses, homicide, or other felony was done, the sheriffe, for so much as pertained to him, or the coroner in case of the death of man, would summon many townships, and sometime a whole hundred, where twelve would serve to make enquiry: and if all did not appear according to the summons, they would present the same before the justices in eyre, where the whole townships or hundred were amercied, albeit many times a sufficient number to make enquiry did appeare. Now this statute provideth remedy, that when there commeth out of the townships so summoned, a sufficient number by whom inquisitions may be fully made, that no amerciaments shall be set upon the townships or hundred by the justices in eyre, which was one remedy for both the two mischiefes.

(1) *Singuli*

(1) *Singulii xii. annorum.*] Where old bookes mention ſometime 14 years, it is but miſprinted; for the time for one to come to the tourn or leet, and to take his oath, as is aforeſaid, is twelve yeares, and ſo it is provided by this act. Mag. Chart. c. 35.

(2) *De roberiis.*] See for this word in the firſt part of the Inſtitutes, ſect. 501. Vide W. 1. c. 15.

(3) *Incendiis domorum.*] By this it appeareth, that burning of houſes was felony by the common law, for otherwiſe he could not have enquired of the ſame in his tourn. Bract. l. 2. fol. Brit. fol. 16. Fleta, lib. 2. ca. 35.

This is to be underſtood not onely of a dwelling houſe, but of the barne or ſtable belonging thereunto. Stamf. Pl. Cor. fol. 36. a. 11 H. 7. 1.

The Mirror goeth further, for he reckoning the ſame amongſt the higheſt offences, ſaith, *ardours ſont que ardent city, ville, maiſon, beaſt, ou autres chateux de lour felony in temps de peace pur haine, ou vengeance.* Mirror, c. 1. § 8. de Ardours et § 13.

Les appeales de arſons ſe ſont in tiel manner, cedde icy appeal Harding illonque (ove les ſurnoſmes) de ceo q. come meſme ceſti cedde avoit un maiſon ou pluſors, ou un taſſe de blee, ou un mollein de feyne, ou auter manner de biens in tiel lieu, &c. la vient meſme celuy Harding, et en le dit meaſon miſt fewe, &c. felonIouſment, &c. Cap. 2. § 11. de Appeal de Arſon & cap. 1. § 13. [148]

And Fleta ſaith, *Si quis ædes alienas nequiter ob inimicitiam vel prædæ cauſa tempore pacis combuſſerit, et inde convict' fuer' per appellum vel ſine, capitali debet ſententia puniri.* But this belongeth to another treatiſe. Fleta ubi ſupra.

(4) *Vel aliis ad coronam ſpectantibus.*] Here is meant other felonies at the common law, which are called *placita coronæ*, either enquirable before the ſheriffe in his tourne, or the coroner, of whom the ſtatute here ſpeaketh.

(5) *Dum tamen de villatis illis veniunt ſufficientes.*] But if there appeare not ſufficient, as if there appeare under 12, then all that were ſummoned ſhall be amercied, and this doth follow the reaſon of the common law, for where for triall of any iſſue, there ſhall be ſummoned 24, if there 12 onely appeare, and are ſworne, the others that made default ſhall not be amercied; but if any of them that doe appeare be challenged and tried out, ſo that 12 remain not to try the iſſue, then all the reſt ſhall be amercied, as if there had under 12 originally appeared: and it is a good expoſition of a ſtatute, when the reaſon of the common law is purſued: see before cap. 18. concerning amerciaments.

(6) *Exceptis inquiſitionibus de morte hominis, &c.*] The law hath ſo great reſpect to the puniſhment of homicide or murder, that at that inquiſition before the coroner, all above 12 muſt appeare (to the end the truth may be found out and puniſhed, and the horrible crime of murder detected) unleſſe they have a reaſonable excuſe to the contrary. Britton, ca. 6.

CAP.

CAP. XXVI.

MURDRUM (1) *de cætero non adjudicetur coram justiciariis, ubi infortunium tantummodo adjudicatum est, sed locum habeat murdrum de interfectis per feloniam* (2) *tantum, et non aliter.*

MURTHER from henceforth shall not be judged before our justices, where it is found misfortune only, but it shall take place in such as are slain by felony, and not otherwise.

Bracton, lib. 1. fol. 120, 121. Britton, cap. 6. Fleta, lib. 1. cap. 23. (Keyling, 123. Co. Ent. 354. 2 Roll, 120.)

Britton, cap. 7. 3 E. 3. Coron. 354. 3 E. 3. ibid. 322. The mischiefe before this statute was, that he that killed a man by misadventure, *per infortunium*, as by doing any act that was not against law, and yet against his intent the death of a man ensued, this was adjudged murder: as if a man had cast a stone over an house, or shot at a mark, and by the fall of the stone, or glaunce of the arrow a man was slain, the party should suffer death. And so 21 E. 3. 17. b. it was at the common law, if a man had killed a man *se defendendo*, he should be hanged, and forfeit in both cases, as in case of murder; so tender a regard had the law to the preservation of the life of man. Numb. 35. 9. Deut. 29. 2. Joshua 20, 21. &c. And with the common law was agreeable the judiciall law, before the cities of refuge were appointed; he that killed a man by misadventure, &c. was put to death, to the end that men should be so provident and wary of their actions, as no death of man, woman or child might ensue thereupon.

[149] See the statute of Glouc' c. 9. 2 H. 4. 18. 11 H. 7. 23. 3 E. 3. coron. 302. This statute doth remedy both points, for the latter clause is generall, that it shall not be murder, but where it is done *per feloniam, i. felleo animo*, and by malice prepensed. And albeit his life in neither of these cases is now lost, yet the forfeiture of his goods and chateux remained in both cases. And so if a man kill a man by misadventure, if he escape, the towne shall be amercied, &c. is also a mark of the common law.

(1) *Murdrum.*] For this word, see the 1 part of the Instit. sect. 500. To speak of the parts of homicide, doth belong to another treatise; this onely shall suffice for the understanding of this act.

See the first part of the Inst. sect. 745. (2) *Per feloniam.*] For this word, and the signification thereof, see the first part of the Institutes at large.

CAP. XXVII.

PROVISUM est, quod nullus qui coram justiciariis itinerantibus vocatur ad warrantum in placito terræ, vel tenement', amercietur de cætero, pro eo quod præsens non fuerit quando vocatur ad warrantum (excepto primo die

IT is provided, that none, being vouched to warranty before our justices in eyre, in plea of land or tenement, shall be amerced from henceforth, because he was not present when he was vouched to warranty, except the

die adventus justiciar' ipsorum) sed si warrantus *ille fuerit infra comitatum, tunc injungatur vicecom', quod ipsum infra tertium diem, vel quartum (secundum locorum distantiam) faciat venire, sicut in itinere justiciar' fieri consuevit. Et si extra comitat' maneat tunc rationabilem habeat summonitionem xv. dierum ad minus, secundum discretionem justiciar' et legem communem.*

the first day of the coming of the justices: but if the party vouched be within the shire, then the sheriff shall be commanded to cause him to come within the third or fourth day, according to the distance of the place, as it was wont to be done in the circuit of the justices. And if he dwell without the shire, then he shall have reasonable summons of fifteen days at the least, after the discretion of the justices, and the common law.

Bract. l. 3. fo. 115, 116. Brit. c. 2. fo. 7. Fleta, li. 1. cap. 9. Mirror, cap. 4. cap. Itineris.

By the common law, all the men of the county ought to appeare before the justices in eire *per breve de generali summonitione vic' direct', quod præmoneat omnes de com' quod sint coram talibus justiciariis ad certum diem et locum per quadraginta dies,* as well that every man should be ready to answer to any matter, wherewith he was to be charged, or commenced against them, as to serve the king and his country, as need should require, and to heare and learne the lawes and customes of the realme, under which they lived. Now the mischiefe was, that if the * vouchee appeared not at the first day, he was amercied, for that he ought to be present. Now this statute enacteth, that he shall not be amercied at the first day, but proces shall be awarded against him, as by this act is limited; and if he come not then, he shall be amercied: wherein it is to be observed how the common law provideth for expedition of justice, and how necessary it is for understanding of old statutes, to reade old bookes.

* For this word Vouchee, see the first part of the Inst. § 145. verb. Et il vouche, &c. Custumier de Norm. cap. 50. fo. 64. b.

CAP. XXVIII. [150]

SI clericus aliquis (2) pro crimine aliquo, vel retto, quod ad coronam pertineat (3), arrestatus fuerit, et postmodum per præceptum domini regis in ballium traditus fuerit *vel replegiatus extiterit (1), ita quod hii, quibus traditus fuerit in ballium, eum habeant coram justiciariis, non amercientur de cætero illi quibus traditus fuerit in ballium, nec alii pleg' sui, si corpus suum habeant coram justiciar', licet coram eis propter privilegium clericale respondere noluerit, vel non potuerit propter ordinarios suos.*

IF a clerk, for any crime or offence touching the crown, be arrested, and after, by the king's commandment, let to bail, or replevied, so that they, to whom he was let to bail, have him before our justices; the sureties from henceforth, nor they to whom he was let to bail, shall not be amerced (if they have his body before our justices) although he will not answer before them, by reason of a clerk's privilege, nor cannot by reason of his ordinary.

(Bro. Coron. 111. 28 H. 8. c. 1. 32 H. 8. c. 3.)

(1) In

Vide W. 1. c. 15. Stam. pl. cor. 72. Regist. 77.

(1) *In ballium traditus fuerit, vel replegiatus extiterit.*] Here note a difference betweene baile, and replevie; for the one is by the higher courts at Westminster, and the other, viz. replevie, by the sheriffe, by force of the writ of *homine replegiando*.

For the understanding of this act, it is to be knowne, that at the common law when any man was appealed or indicted of felony, if he were bayled, the bayle was, that he should appeare at a certaine day before such justices to answer to the felony. Now the mischiefe was, that if a man were bailed, or delivered by plevin, albeit he did appeare, yet if he claimed the benefit of his clergie, the persons that bailed him, or his pledges were amercied, because he refused to answer to the felony, but tooke himselfe to his clergie; this statute doth provide, that if in that case the clerk doth appeare before the kings justices, his baile or pledges shall not be amercied, although he will not answer before them by reason of his clerks priviledge.

(2) *Si clericus aliquis.*] If he were no clerk at the time of the baile, or deliverie by plevin, but learned to reade before his appearance, yet he was within this statute, and yet a clerk was not bailed nor delivered by plevin.

(3) *De aliquo crimine vel retto quod ad coronam pertineat.*] [a] Where it is printed *rectum*, it must be amended after the originall, and made *rettum*: this is derived of an old word *rette*, or *reatte*, *à reatu*, and signifieth in our legall understanding an offence or fault.

[b] *Crimen* and *rettum* are here taken for such offences wherefore a man should lose life or member, because for no other offence he can have his clergie, or the priviledge of a clerk. But *in crimine læsæ majestatis* he was not to have his clergie, and therefore this act extendeth not to persons let to baile for high treason, and so it is in case of sacriledge, and the like.

And thus is this dark statute cleerly expounded.

[c] Now to set down in what cases one shall be bailed, or delivered by plevin, and where a man shall have the benefit of his clergie, and where he is barred thereof by act of parliament, doe belong to another treatise: in the meane time somewhat you shall reade of clergie in Alex. Powlters case, *ubi supra*, and lib. 4. fo. 44, 45, 46.

[a] W. 2. cap. 2. Regist. in homine replegiand. F.N.B. fo. 66.

[b] Al. Powlters case, li. 11. 29, 30. Art. cler. cap. 14. Mich. 31 E. 3. coram rege rot. 138. in Thesau. Abbas de Misfenden. 17 E 2. rot. Rom. m. 6. Adam Evesq; de Heref. 20 E. 2. coro. 283. 19 H. 6. 47. 25 E. 3. c. 4, 5. 18 E. 3. c. 1. Vide Powlters case ubi sup.

[c] Mirror, c. 3. de except. de Clergy. Bract. li. 3. 123, 124. Flet. l. 1. c. 28. Brit. ca. 4. fo. 11. lib. 6. cap. 36.

[151]

CAP. XXIX.

PROVISUM est, quod si deprædationes, vel rapinæ aliquæ fiant abbatibus, prioribus, vel aliis prælatis ecclesiasticis (1), *et ipsi jus suum de hujusmodi deprædationibus prosequentes morte præveniantur* (2), *antequam judicium inde fuerint assequuti, successores eorum habeant actiones ad bona* (4) *ecclesiæ suæ*

IT is provided, that if any wrongs or trespasses be done to abbots, or other prelates of the church, and they have sued their right for such wrongs, and be prevented with death before judgement given therein; their successors shall have actions to demand the goods of their church out of the hands

suæ (5) de manibus hujusmodi transgressoris repetend' (3). Similem insuper habeant actionem successores de hiis quæ domui suæ et ecclesiæ [recenter] ante obitum (6) prædecessorum suorum per hujusmodi violentiam fuerint subtracta, licet prædicti prædecessores sui jus suum prosecuti non fuerint in vita sua. Si autem in terris et tenementis hujusmodi religiosorum, de quibus eorum prælati obierint seisit', ut de jure ecclesiæ suæ, aliqui se intrudant tempore vacationis, successores sui breve habeant de seisina recuperand', et adjudicētur eis dampna sua (7), sicut in nova disseisina adjudicari consuevit.

hands of such trespassers. Moreover, the successors shall have like action for such things as were lately withdrawn by such violence from their house and church, before the death of their predecessors, though their said predecessors did not pursue their right during their lives. And if any intrude into the lands or tenements of such religious persons in the time of vacation, of which lands their predecessors died seised as in the right of their church, the successors shall have a writ to recover their seisin. And damages shall be awarded them, as in assise of novel disseisin is wont to be.

(Fitz. Trespass, 205. 211. 237. 242. Fitz. Brief, 176. 296. 359. 623. 828. 2 H. 4. 4. Regist. 72. 125. F. N. B. 112.)

There were two mischiefs at the common law (as many did hold) that in the case of abbots, priors, and other regular and religious persons, if the goods of the monastery were taken away in the life of the predecessor, that after his death his successor had no remedy for such trespasses: the other mischief was, that if in time of vacation, when there was no abbot, or prior, or other regular or religious soveraigne, any intrusion were made, the successor had no remedy to recover the land with damages, though thereof his predecessour died seised, and both these are remedied by this act.

(1) *Abbatibus, prioribus, vel aliis prælatis ecclesiasticis.*] This act extendeth onely to abbots, priors, and other prelats that be religious and regular, and not to bishops and other persons ecclesiasticall being secular: for in the second clause of this act, *hujusmodi religiosorum* is mentioned for the distinction betweene religious and secular. See the first part of the Institutes, sect. 133. And the reason of this diversitie is, that the abbots, priors, and other religious and regular persons are dead persons in law, and have capacity to have lands and goods onely for the use and benefit of the house; 42 E. 3. 22. and cannot make any testament; and therefore the church or religious house is holden alwayes one, in respect whereof the succeeding abbot shall have an assise for a disseisin done in the life of the predecessour, and an action of waste for waste done in his predecessors time; but so shall not a bishop, archdeacon, dean, parson, or the like, that are ecclesiasticall secular, because the church by their death hath an alteration, and is not alwayes one, and they may make their testament, for that they may have goods and chattels to their own use.

2 H. 4. 2, 3. 19. 21 H. 6. 46. 4 E. 4. 8. 9 E. 4. 33. 18 E. 4. 16. 1 E. 5. 4, 5. li. 2. fo. 46. Hic c. 19. W. 1. c. 3. 15. 26.

Also the bishop is of an higher degree then the abbots and priors with which this act begins.

(2) *Morte præveniant'.*] So it is if an abbot or prior be deposed, the successor shall have an action upon this act, although the predecessour be alive, as well as if he had died, for as to that house he is *civiliter mortuus.* Temps E. 1. trns. 242.

(3) *Successores habeant actionem ad bona ecclesiæ suæ de manibus hujusmodi transgressoris repetend'.*] Some have thought in respect of this word *repetenda*, that this must be intended of an action of detinue, or the like action, wherein the thing it selfe is to be recovered; but *de manibus hujusmodi transgressoris* make it evident, that it must be intended of a trespasse *quare vi et armis*, for thereof was the doubt at the common law: for it is holden, that for goods taken from the predecessour of an abbot or prior, no action was given to the successor at the common law before this act, for by the taking the property was divested. But an action of account, debt, detinue, replevin, and the like action, which affirmes the property to continue, the successor shall have an action at the common law.

12 H. 4. tit. Account 124. 4 E. 3. 11. 17. 25 E. 3. 45. 9 H. 6. 25. 17 E. 3. tit. Execut. 106. 11 E. 3. Account 57. 47 E. 3. 23.

3 E. 3. 31. 4 E. 4. 8. 18 E. 4. 16. 7 H. 4, 5. 11 H. 4. 55. semble.

(4) *Bona.*] 1. If an obligation be taken from the predecessour, it is within this statute. 2. The successor shall have by the equitie of this statute an action of trespasse of cutting downe of trees, and carrying them away: wherein it is to be observed, that acts that give remedy for wrongs done, shall be taken by equitie.

7 E. 4. 15. a. 9 E. 4. 33. 9 H. 6. 25, 26. Regist. 96.

(5) *Ecclesiæ suæ.*] The action that the successor shall bring upon this statute, shall be *bona et catalla domus et ecclesiæ suæ tempore I. prædecessoris sui*, which without question a bishop, deane, or other ecclesiasticall secular cannot say.

16 E. 3. trns 211.

(6) *Recenter ante obitum.*] Yet if the taking of the goods were long before the death of the abbot or prior, his successor shall have an action of trespasse by this statute.

18 E. 2. trns 237. 2 H. 4. ubi sup. 18 E. 4. 16. F.N.B. 89. i.

(7) *Si autem in terris et tenementis hujusmodi religiosorum, &c. aliqui se intrudant tempore vacationis, &c. breve habeant de seisina sua, et adjudicentur eis damna.*] This branch is also taken by equitie, for by these words, the successor of an abbot, prior, or any other religious soveraigne shall have an action of trespasse for trees cut downe and carryed away in the time of vacation.

Regist. 125. F.N.B. 112 h. & 113.

But a bishop shall not have an action of trespasse in that case, 1. as hath been said, for that this act extends not to him; 2. the king hath the temporalties during the vacation, and therefore he cannot have an action of trespas: but in the Register there is in that case an oier and terminer to be granted to heare the trespasses done in time of vacation of the bishoprick, as thereby appeareth, which seemeth in favour of the church to be granted by the common law, for it is not grounded upon this act, and therefore I leave the marginall notes in the Register that are newly added, and are not warranted by ancient manuscripts, to the judicious reader.

4 E. 4. 8.

And the writ of intrusion lieth not for the successor of the bishop, for an intrusion in time of vacation for the kings possession (which he hath without office) preserveth the inheritance of the bishop, but it lyeth by this statute, where one intrudes after the decease of an abbot or prior. Vide the first part of the Institutes sect. 443. for this manner of intrusion, while the freehold and inheritance is in consideration of law.

CAP. XXX.

PROVISUM est etiam, quod si alienationes (1) illæ, de quibus breve de ingressu (2) dari consuevit, per tot gradus fiant (3), per quot breve illud in forma prius usitata fieri non possit, habeant conquerentes breve ad recuperandum seisinam suam, sine mentione graduum (4), ad cujuscunque manus per hujusmodi alienationes res illa devenerit (5), per breve originale, et per commune consilium domini regis inde providendum (6), &c.

IT is provided also, that if those alienations (whereupon a writ of entry was wont to be granted) hap to be made in so many degrees, that by reason thereof the same writ cannot be made in the form beforetimes used, the plaintiffs shall have a writ to recover their seisin, without making mention of the degrees, into whose hands soever the same thing shall happen to come by such alienations, and that by an original writ to be provided therefore by the council of our lord the king.

Bract. l. 4. fo. 318. &c. Brit. ca. 114. Fleta, lib. 1. ca. 11. lib. 4 cap. 1. Pasch. 18 E. 1. in Banco Rot. 4. Eborum, John de Hodlestons case. (Fitz. Cui in vita 23. Fitz. Entre, 9. 11. 49. 56. Fitz. Brief, 438. 469. 693. 812. 1 Inst. 238. b. 239. a. Regist. 228. F. N. B. 191. D. K. 192. 201. 203. Rast. 283.)

It is to be observed, that the common law provided for the quietnesse of mens freehold and inheritance, and that they should not be disturbed from manurance of their grounds; in so much as he that right had could not enter upon him that came in by descent or lawfull conveyance, but was driven to his writ of entry; and the common law for the safety of mens possessions further provided, that if the land were conveyed out of the degrees, so as the demandant could not have his writ of entry in *le per*, or in the *per et cui*, the demandant (to the end that suits might have an end) was driven to his writ of right, a long and finall remedy, and that he which right had should take his remedy by writ of entry before there were above two descents, or two conveyances, and also within the time of prescription.

See the 1. part of the Institutes, sect. 473.

14 H. 4. 39, 40.

This statute in cases of descents and conveyances, after the degrees past, doth give a writ of entry in the *post*, which in those cases lay not at the common law. But in other cases, then in case of alienation and descent, there was a writ of entry in the *post* at the common law: as where one entred by disseisin, intrusion, abatement, judgement, succession, or as tenant by the curtesie, in these cases a writ of entry in the *post* did lie at the common law, but if the wife recover her dower by judgement, yet is she in the [*per*] by her husband, and if the second alienee be disseised, and he recover in a reall action, yet lieth the writ against him in the *per et cui*, because the alienation to him is the ground of his title, *et sic de cæteris*.

F.N.B. 192. f. Fleta, lib. 5. c. 34.

(1) *Si alienationes*, &c.] Hereby it appeareth that this act extendeth where the lands were aliened from one to another, either by lawfull conveyance, or by descent; and by construction this act extendeth as well to alienations, &c. made before the statute as

5 E. 2. Cui in vita 23.
7 E. 3. 12.

after, for ſtatutes, that give remedy to them that right have, are ever favourably expounded; obſerve well the words of this act: if the diſſeiſee doth releaſe to the diſſeiſor, this doth amount to an alienation, and maketh a degree, but a ſurrender of an eſtate for life maketh no degree, yet is it an alienation.

19 H. 6. 17. 21 H. 6. 8. 9 E. 4. 16. 1 H. 6. 1.

(2) *Breve de ingreſſu.*] This is underſtood of writs of entry, *ſur diſſeiſin in le poſt, in le quibus, ſine aſſenſu capit', cui in vita, ſur cui in vita, non compos mentis, dum fuit infra ætatem, ad term' qui præteriit, in caſu proviſo, in conſimili caſu ad communem legem,* of intruſion, *cauſa matrimonii prælocuti.*

(3) *Per tot gradus fiant.*] *Gradus dicitur à gradiendo,* becauſe the ſtate paſſeth by degrees from one to another, and in the law it ſignifieth, a conveyance, or a deſcent from one to another, and there be but two degrees, viz. in the *per,* and in the *per* and *cui,* if it proceed any further either by conveyance, or deſcent, it is out of the degrees: if a gift in taile, or a leaſe for life be made the remainder over, the firſt eſtate, and all the remainder make but one degree.

[154] 50 E. 3. 21.

* And theſe alienations that make degrees ought (as hath been ſaid) to be ſo lawfull, as the alienee may be in by title; and therefore a feoffement by a garden in chivalry, ſocage, or by nurtur, a termer for yeares, tenant at will, or bayliffe, or tenant in villenage doe make no degree, becauſe they amount to a diſſeiſin, and ſome hold the feoffee was a diſſeiſor at the common law; and where the words of the ſtatute be *quod alienationes,* thoſe muſt be intended lawfull alienations, ſuch as by the auncient law ſhould have taken away an entry.

* 15 H. 3. brē. 878. 20 H. 3. Aſſ. 432. 19 E. 2. Aſſ. 450. 4 E. 2. brē. 790. 8 E. 3. 63. 8 Aſſ. 28. 7 E. 3. 69 50 E. 3. 22. 43 Aſſ. 14. 3 E. 4. 17. 10 E. 4. 18 W. 2. cap. 25.

[a] Regularly a man ſhould not have a writ of entry in the *poſt,* where he may have a writ within the degrees, and the cauſe thereof is to ouſte falſe vowchers, yet in ſome caſes a man may have election either to have a writ of entry in the *poſt,* or a writ of entry in the *per et cui;* [b] as if I may have a writ of entry in the *per et cui* againſt B. who aliens, ſo as now it is out of the degrees, yet if B. take back an eſtate again, I may chooſe either a writ of entry in the *per et cui* or in the *poſt,* but *prima facie,* the writ of entry in the *per et cui* is more beneficiall, becauſe the tenant in the writ of entry in the *poſt* may vowch at large, and ſo he cannot doe in the other writ, but onely within the degrees.

Bract. fo. 318. 323, 324. 326. Brit. cap. 11. Fleta, li. 1. c. 11. lib. 4. cap. 1. [a] W. 1. c. 40. 7 E. 3. 25. 11 E. 3. brē. 472. 22 E. 3. 1. b. 5 E. 3. 216. 24 E. 3. 70. 39 E. 3. 25. 14 H. 4. 39. 27 H. 6. ent. 23. F.N.B. 192. [b] 31 E. 1. brē. 875. 39 E. 3. 33.

[c] But if the tenant take back an eſtate to him, and to another, then I am driven to my writ of entry in the *poſt,* ſo it is if the ſtate be made to the heire of B.

44 E. 3. 45. 9 E. 4. 47. 5 H. 7. 6.

A woman ſeiſed of a rent taketh huſband, the huſband purchaceth the land where out, &c. and after alieneth the land in fee, by which he includedly paſſeth the rent and dieth, the wife in a *cui in vita,* ſhall ſuppoſe the alienee to be in the *per* or *poſt.* And yet in ſome caſe one ſhall have a writ of entry in the *poſt,* when the degrees be not paſt, (note well the words of this act.)

21 H. 6. 8. Br. tit. Entry 19. [c] 5 E. 3. 31. 3 H. 6. 38. 7 H. 4. 17. 7 E. 3. 53.

If a diſſeiſor hath iſſue two daughters, and the one daughter hath iſſue and dieth, in this caſe the aunt is in the *per,* and the niece is in the *per et cui,* and one writ muſt be brought againſt them both, which muſt be in the *poſt,* becauſe one writ cannot be brought both in the *per* as to one, and in the *per et cui* as to the other.

Howbeit

Howbeit in some cases a writ of entry in the *per* shall lie, although there be many alienations or disseisins; as if the husband be seised in fee and die, and twenty alienations or disseisins be made, now doth the writ of entry in the *post* lie but if the wife be endowed, the entry of the wife shall be supposed by her husband; but otherwise it is of the tenant by the courtesie, for the law worketh by issue had without any assignement, and therefore meerely in the *post*.

30 E. 1. brẽ. 884. 4 E. 3. fo. 24. E. 3. 32. 36 H. 6. Dower 30. Vide first part of the Inst. sect. 393.

(4) *Sine mentione graduum.*] This is intended a writ of entry in the *post*, so called of this word used in the writ, *in quod idem A. non habet ingressum nisi post disseisinam quam C. injuste, &c. fecit prædict' B, &c.*

As the writ of entry, which writ is *sine mentione graduum*, as our act speaketh: as the writ of entry in the *per*, is so called of this word [*per*] in the writ, *in quod idem A. non habet ingressum nisi per C. qui illud ei dimisit:* and in the *per et cui*, of those words in the writ, *in quod idem A. non habet ingressum nisi per C. cui D. illud dimisit, qui inde injustè, et sine judicio disseisivit, &c.*

But for as much as the law is never knowne untill the reason thereof be apprehended; wherefore should not the successors of a bishop, deane, abbot, prior, &c. be as well in the *per*, as the heire by descent? And the reason thereof is, for that the heire commeth in by his auncester, and therefore a descent shall take away an entry, and the warranty of the auncester shall barre the heir, but in case of succession, a dying seised taketh not away an entry, nor the warranty of the predecessour doth binde the successor; and therefore the Register delivereth it for a rule, with the reason thereof, *breve de ingressu debet impetrari versus successorem semper in le post, quia successor per prædecessorem non ingreditur.* And herewith agreeth Bracton who saith, *item quæritur, &c. an faciunt gradum de abbate in abbatem, sicut de hærede in hæredem; et videtur quod non, magis quam in computatione descensus, quia etsi alternatur persona, non propter hoc alternatur dignitas, sed semper manet.*

[155]

Regist. 230. See the first part of the Institutes, § 386. 534. 5 Ed. 3. 13.

(5) *Res illa devenerit.*] This is intended of lands, tenements, rents, and other things whereof a præcipe doth lie.

(6) *Per consilium domini regis inde providendum.*] Which was done accordingly, and the writ set downe in the Register. Regist. 130.

STATUTUM DE WESTMINSTER PRIMER.

Editum anno 3 Edw. I.

CEUX sont les establishments (1) *le roy Edward fits le roy H. faits a Westminst. a son primer parliament general* (2) *apres son coronement* (3), *lendemaine de la cluse de Pasche* (4), *lan de son raigne* 3. (5), *per son counsell* (6), *et per lassentments des archievesques, evesques, abbes, priors, countes, barons, et tout le comminalty de la terre illonques summones* (7): *pur ceo que nostre seignior le roy ad graund volunt et desire del estate de son realme redresser en les choses ou mestier est damendment, et ceo pur le common profit de saint esglise, et de* son *realme, et pur ceo que lestate de son realme, et de saint esglise ad este malement garde, et les prelates et religious de la terre en mults des manners grieves, et le people auterment treit que estre duist, et la peace meines garde, et les leyes meins uses, et les misfesants meins punies, que estre duissent, per quoy les gents de la terra doubteront meins a misfaire: cy ad le roy ordeine et establie les choses southscripts, les queux il entende destre profitables et covenables a tout le realme.*

THESE be the acts of king Edward, son to king Henry, made at Westminster at his first parliament general after his coronation, on the Monday of Easter Utas, the third year of his reign, by his council, and by the assent of archbishops, bishops, abbots, priors, earls, barons, and all the commonalty of the realm being thither summoned, because our lord the king had great zeal and desire to redress the state of the realm in such things as required amendment, for the common profit of holy church, and of the realm: and because the state of the holy church had been evil kept, and the prelates and religious persons of the land grieved many ways, and the people otherwise intreated than they ought to be, and the peace less kept, and the laws less used, and the offenders less punished than they ought to be, by reason whereof the people of the land feared the less to offend; the king hath ordained and established these acts under-written, which he intendeth to be necessary and profitable unto the whole realm.

The preface of the statute of W. 1.

(1) *Ceux sont les establishments.*] *Stabilimina*, or *stabilimenta*, establishments, or assurances comming of *stabilis*, and that againe *à stando*, of standing; and justly may not onely these chapters challenge that name, but all other the statutes made in the raigne of this king may be styled by the name of establishments, because they are more constant, standing, and durable laws, then have been made ever since: so as king E. 1. who (as sir William Herle chiefe justice of the court of common pleas, that lived in his time, said, *Fuit le pluis sage roy que unques fuit*) may well bee called our Justinian.

5 E. 3. 14.

(2) *A son parliament generall.*] So called, because all the laws then

then made were generall, and that great and honourable assembly were not entangled with private matters, but with such onely, as were for the generall good of the common-wealth, for the end of this parliament, is, as hereafter in the preface is expressed, *pour le common profit de saint esglise, & del realme.*

(3) *Apres son coronement.*] He began his raigne the 16 day of November, *anno Dom.* 1272. he then being in the land of Palestine; and after his returne into England, was crowned the 19 day of August, in the 2 yeare of his raigne (and not the 9 day of December, in the 1 yeare of his raigne, as some have mistaken) as evidently appeareth by this preface, and by ancient records hereafter remembred. [157]

Vet. Mag. Chart. fo. 144.

(4) *Lendemaine de la cluse de Pasche.*] That is, *in crastino clausi Paschæ,* or *in crastino octabis Paschæ,* which is all one: in English, the morrow of the utas of Easter. It is called *utas* of *huit,* which signifieth eighth, *viz.* the eighth day after, including Easter day itselfe for one.

Glanv. li. 1. c. 6.

Note, this parliament was summoned to be holden at London *in quindena* of the purification after his coronation, and prorogued from thence untill the morrow after the utas of Easter to be holden at Westminster. And the number of eight was much respected in the ancient lawes, as amongst the lawes of king Edward the Confessor, *Pax regis die qua coronatus est, quæ dies tenet octo, in die natali domini dies octo, in Paschate dies octo, in Pentecoste dies octo, &c.* Now the eighth day, accounting the feast day for one, is *clausum festi,* that is, the closing up of the feast for many purposes.

(5) *L'an de son raigne* 3.] This proveth that he was crowned in *anno* 2. for if he had been crowned in *anno* 1. of his raigne, then this parliament should have been holden in the 2 yeare: and this is proved by other matter of record. But the truth is, that the 19 day of December, in *anno* 1. of his raigne, he was not returned into England.

Vide vet. Mag. Char. 1 part, fo. 144. b.

Rex venerabili in Christo patri, Roberto Cant' archiepiscopo, totius Angliæ primati, salutem. Quia generale parliamentum nostrum, quod cum prælatis et magnatibus regni proposuimus habere London' ad quindenam purificationis beatæ Mariæ proxim' futur', quibusdam certis de causis prorogavimus usque in crastinum clausi Paschæ proxim' sequen'; vobis mandamus rogantes quatenus eidem parliamento ibidem in eodem crastino clausi Paschæ intersitis ad tractandum et ordinandum una cum prælatis et magnatibus regni nostri de negotiis ejusdem regni, et hoc nullatenus omittatis. Teste rege apud Woodstock, 27 die Decembris.

Dors. claus. an. 3 E. 1. m. 21.

Rex in primo generali parliamento suo post coronationem suam in crastino octabis Paschæ, anno regni sui 3. de voluntate sua, et consiliariorum suorum consilio, et communitatis regni sui ibidem convocat' consensu, ad honorem Dei, &c. ordinavit et statuit quod, &c.

Rot. pat. an. 4 E. 1. m. 9. 14.

Rex Edw. tenuit primum generale parliamentum suum post coronationem suam in crastino octabis Paschæ, anno 3. regni sui.

Rot. pat. an. 10 E. 1.

(6) *Per son counsell.*] This proveth that this king and other kings before him had a privie councell, which appeareth by the writs of parliament, that parliaments are ever summoned to be holden *de advisamento consilii nostri.* Of this see more in this first chapter.

(7) *Per lassentments des archevesques, evesques, abbes, priors, countes, et barons, et tout la comminaltie de la terre illonq; summones.*] Here is a compleat parliament for the making or enacting of

 lawes,

lawes, the king, the lords spirituall and temporall, and the commons: for if an act be made by the king, and the lords spirituall and temporall, or by the king and the commons, this bindeth not,
See the 4. part of the Instit. cap. of the high court of parliament. for it is no act of parliament; for the parliament concerning making or enacting of lawes consisteth of the king, the lords spirituall and temporall, and the commons; and it is no act of parliament, unlesse it be made by the king, the * lords and commons.
11 H. 7. 27. And where it is said, by all the commonalty, all the commons of
* [158] the realme are represented in parliament by the knights, citizens, and burgesses.

The purpose of this parliament is to redresse the state of the church and of the realme in those things that need amendment. The end is twofold, *Pur le common prosit de saint esglise, & de son realme.*

There were five things that needed amendment.

1. For that the state of the realme and of holy church (which are ever like Hipocrates twins) had been ill governed.

2. That the prelates and other men of the church many wayes had been grieved, and the people otherwise entreated then they ought to have been.

3. The peace had not been well kept, which was against a maine maxime of law, *Inprimis interest reipublicæ, ut pax in regno conservetur, et quæcunq; paci adversentur, providè declinentur:* which
3 E. 6. cap. 12. 1 Mar. cap. 12. maxime hath been repeated and affirmed by authority of parliament.

4. That the lawes had not been put in execution against another principle of the common law, *Nihil infra regnum subditos magis conservat in tranquilitate et concordia, quàm debita legum administratio.*
32 H. 8. cap. 9. Affirmed also in parliament.

5. Offendors seldome punished, *Et impunitas continuum affectum tribuit delinquendi*; for this statute saith, By reason whereof the people of the land feare lesse to offend.

The remedy hath two excellent qualities, which ought to be inseparable to every act of parliament, *viz.* to be profitable, and convenient.

Here shall you see the effects of the writs of parliament, as they be at this day: First, the writ is, *Nos de advisamento concilii nostri*; and this act saith, *Le roy per son councel.*

2. The writ is, *Pro quibusdam arduis et urgentibus negotiis nos, statum et defensionem regni nostri Angliæ concernentibus:* and it is expressed in this act, *Que nostre seigniour le roy ad graunt volunt, et desire del estate de son realme redresser, en les choses ou mestier est damendement, & ceo pur le common profit de saint esglise & de son realme, & pur ceo que lestate de son realme & de saint esglise ad estre malement gard, &c.*

And here it is to be observed, that this noble and wise king E. 1. was contented in a free and generall parliament to heare of the misgovernment of the state of the realme and of the church,
Rot. Parl. 50 E. 3. nu. 10. 15, 16, 17, 18, &c. Rot. Parl. 5 H. 4. nu. 8. 7 H. 4. nu. 30, 41. 9 H 4. indemnitie des Seigniors, &c. 1 H. 5. nu. 8. &c. and never sought to cover those irregular proceedings, either in his fathers time, or his owne; and thought it should be greater honour for him to rip up these grievous ulcers both in the church and common-wealth, and to cure them by wholsome rules and lawes, then to cover them, lest it should be vainly feared they should reflect upon his fathers, or his owne misgovernment, where in truth all the fault should rest upon great counsellors, and officers, and ministers

miniſters of juſtice, and other the kings officers and miniſters · and ſo it hath falne out in divers other kings times. This pr ᴀble to all the ſtatutes is worthy of due and deliberate conſideration.

Of this worthy king we have ſpoken in other places; this we will adde out of an approved author, *Nemo in conſiliis illo argutior, in eloquio torrentior, in periculis ſecurior, in proſperis cautior, in adverſis conſtantior.*

Now this parliament holden at Weſtminſter, is called Weſtminſter the firſt for excellencie.

CAP. I. [159]

EN primes voit le roy et commaunde, que la peace de ſaint eſgliſe, et de la terre, ſoit bien garde et mainteign' en touts points, et que common droiture ſoit fait a touts, auxybien as povers, come as riches, ſans regard de nulluy (1). *Et pur ceo que les abbies, et les meaſons de religion de la terre, ont eſte ſurcharges et greves malement, per le venue des graundes gents et dauters, que lour biens ne ſuffiſont a eux meſmes, per que les religious ſont ci abates et impovers, que ilz ne poient eux meſmes ſuſteign', ne la* charge de *charitie quils ſoilent faire. Purview eſt que nul ne veigne manger, herberger, ne giſer a meaſon de religion* (2) *dauter avowſon, que de la laine, al coſtages de la meaſon, ſi ne ſoit prie et requiſe ſpecialment per le governour de la meaſon, avant que il veigne. Et que nul a ſes coſtages demeſne, ne entr', ne veign' giſer encounter la volunt ceux de la meaſon. Et per cel eſtatute nentend' pas le roy, que grace de hoſpitality ſoit ſuſtreit as beſoignes* (3), *ne que les avowes des meaſons lez puiſſent per lour ſovent venues ſurcharger ne deſtruer* (4). *Purview eſt enſement, que nul graund ne petit, per colour de parent', ou deſpecialtie, ou per auter affiance, ne per auter encheſon, ne courge en auter parke, ne peſhe en auter viver* (5), *ne veign' manger ne herberger en meaſon, ne en manour, ou en meaſon de prelate, ne de home de religion, ne dauter encounter la volunt le ſeignior,*

FIRST the king willeth and commandeth, that the peace of holy church and of the land, be well kept and maintained in all points, and that common right be done to all, as well poor as rich, without reſpect of perſons. And becauſe that abbeys and houſes of religion of the land have been overcharged, and ſore grieved, by the reſort of great men and other, ſo that their goods have not been ſufficient for themſelves, whereby they have been greatly hindred and impoveriſhed, that they cannot maintain themſelves, nor ſuch charity as they have been accuſtomed to do; it is provided, that none ſhall come to eat or lodge in any houſe of religion of any other's foundation than of his own, at the coſts of the houſe, unleſs he be required by the governor of the houſe before his coming thither. And that none, at his own coſts, ſhall enter and come to lie there againſt the will of them that be of the houſe. And by this ſtatute the king intended not, that the grace of hoſpitality ſhould be withdrawn from ſuch as need, nor that the founders of ſuch monaſteries ſhould overcharge, or grieve them by their often coming. It is provided alſo, that none high nor low, by colour of kindred, affinity, or alliance, or by any other occaſion, ſhall courſe in any park, nor fiſh in any pond, nor come to eat or lodge in the houſe or manor

seignior, ou le bailife, de costages le seignior, ne a son cost demesne. Et sil veigne, ou enter per le gree, ou sans le gree le seignior ou le bailife nul sarure, huis, ne fenestre, ne nul maner de ferme ne faire overer, ne de pecher per soy, ne per auter, ne nul maner de vitail' ne auter chose preigne per colour de achate, ne auterment. Et que nul face barter blee, ne prender blee (6), *ne nul maner de vitaile, ne les auter biens, de nulluy prelate, home de religion, ne de auter, ne de clerke, ne de lay, per colour de achate, ne auterment enconter la [bone] volunt, et le conge de celuy, a que la chose serra, ou de gardein, deins ville merchandise, ou dehors. Et que nul preigne chivals, boses, chares, ne charets, neefes, ne bateux, ne auter choses affaire cariage* (7), *sans le bone volunt * de celuy, a que les choses serront. Et si il per la bone volunt de celuy le face, lors maintenant face son gree solonque le covenant fait enter eux. Et ceux que viendront enconter les establishments avantdits, et de ceo soient attaints* (8), *soient adjudges a la prison le roy, et dillonques soient rentes, et punies solonque la quantity et le maner du trespas, et solonque ceo que le roy en sa court veier que bien soit. Et soit assaver, que si ceux a que le trespasse fuit fait, voillent suer les damages, que ils avera resceux, lour serra agarde et restore au double. Et ceux que le trespas averont fait, soient ensement punies in le maner avantdit. Et si nul ne voile suer, eit le roy la suit, come de chose fait enconter son defence, et encounter sa peace. Et le roy ferra enquire de an en an, sicome il quidra que bien soit, queux gents eyent tiel trespas fait. Et ceux queux serront endites per ceux enquests, serront attaches et distreign' per la grand distresse, de vener a certain jour, que conteigne le space du moys en la court del roy, la ou luy plerra. Et si ceux ne veigne a cel jour, ils serront auterfoits de recheffe distreigne per mesme distr', de vener a un auter jour, que conteigne le space de vi. semaignes. Et si ceux adonques ne veignent, soient adjudges*

* [160]

manor of a prelate, or any other religious person, against the will or leave of the lord, or his bailiff, neither at the cost of the lord, nor at his own. And if he come in, or enter with the good-will, or against the will of the lord or his bailiff, he shall cause no door, lock, nor window, nor nothing that is shut, to be opened or broken, by himself, nor any other, nor no manner of victual, nor other thing, shall take by colour of buying, nor otherwise; and that none shall thresh corn, nor take corn, nor any manner of victual, nor other goods of a prelate, man of religion, nor any other clerk, or lay-person, by colour of buying, or otherwise, against the will and licence of him to whom the thing belongeth, or of the keeper, be it within market-town, or without. And that none shall take horses, oxen, ploughs, carts, ships, nor barges, to make carriage, without the assent of him to whom such things belong; and if he do it by the assent of the party, then incontinent he shall pay according to the covenant made between them. And they that offend against these acts, and thereof be attainted, shall be committed to the king's prison, and after shall make fine, and be punished according to the quantity and manner of the trespass, and after as the king in his court shall think convenient. And it is to be known, that if they to whom such trespass was done, will sue for damages, they shall be thereto received, and the same shall be awarded and restored to the double; and they that have done the trespass, shall be likewise punished in the manner abovesaid; and if none will sue, the king shall have the suit, as for a thing committed against his commandment, and against his peace: and the king shall make enquiry from year to year, what persons do such trespasses, after as he shall think necessary and convenient; and they that be indicted by such inquests shall be attached and distrained by the great

adjudges come attaints, et rendent le double (per le suit del roy) a ceux queux le dammages averont resceux, et soient grevement rentes, solonque le maner del trespas. Et le roy defende et commande, que nul desormes ne face male (9), *damm', ne grevance a nul home de religion, person de saint esglis, ne a auter, per encheson de ceo que ils eyent deny lhostelle, ou le manger a nulluy, ou per encheson de ceo que ascun soy pleint ou court, de ceo que il soit greve des ascuns choses avantdits, et si ascun le face, et de ceo soit attaint, soit incurre le peine avantdit. Et est purview que ces points avantdits lient auxibien nous counsellors, justices del forest, et auter nous justices, come auters gents* (10): *et que les points avantdits soient mainteignes* (11), *gardes, et tenus. Cy defende le roy sur sa grieve forfeiture, que nul prelate, abbe, prior, home de religion, ou bailife dascun de eux, ou del auter, ne resceive nul home enconter la forme avantdit. Et que nul envoy au meason* (12), *ne au manor de religion, ne de auter home, gents, chivalx, ne chiens a sojourn', ne nul lez. resceive. Et que le ferra, pur ceo que est enconter le * defense et le commandement le roy, il serra punish grevement. Uncore est purview, que les vic' ne herbergent ove nulluy* (13), *ovesque plus que v. ou vi. chivalx, ne que ils ne grevevent la gentes de religion, ne auter per lour sovent vener, ou giser a lour measons, ne a lour manors.*

* [161]

great distress, to come at a certain day, containing the space of a month, into the king's court, or where it shall please the king; and if they come not at that day, they shall be distrained again of new by the same distress, for to come at another day, containing the space of six weeks at the least; and if they come not then, they shall be judged as attainted, and shall yield double damages (at the king's suit) to such as have taken hurt or damage, and shall make grievous fine after the manner of the trespass. And the king forbiddeth and commandeth, that none from henceforth do hurt, damage, or grievance to any religious man, or person of the church, or any other, because they have denied meat or lodging unto them, or because that any complaineth in the king's court that he hath been grieved in any of the things above mentioned; and if any do, and thereof be attainted, he shall incur the pain aforesaid. And it is further provided, that the points aforesaid shall as well bind our counsellors, justicers of forests, and other our justices, as any other persons; and that the aforesaid points be maintained, observed, and kept. Likewise the king forbiddeth upon grievous forfeitures, that no prelate, abbot, man of religion, or bailiff of any of them, or of other, receive any man contrary to the form aforesaid. And that none shall send to the house or manor of a man of religion, or of any other person, his men, horse, or dogs, to sojourn, nor none shall them receive; and he that doth (seeing the king hath commanded the contrary) shall be grievously punished. Yet it is further provided, that the sheriff from henceforth shall not lodge with any person, with any more than five or six horses; and that they shall not grieve religious men, nor other, by often coming and lodging, neither at their houses nor their manors.

(14 Ed. 3. stat. 2. & 3. c. 1. 18 Ed. 3. stat. 3. & 4. c. 4. 1 R. 2. c. 3. Regist. 98. 9 Ed. 2. stat. 1. c. 11.

This

This chapter doth spread itselfe into thirteen branches.

1. Branch. (1) *En primes voet le roy, et commaund, que le peace de saint eglise, et de la terre soit bien gard, et mainteine en touts points, et que common droiture soit fait a touts, auxibien as poures, come as riches, sans regard de nulluy,* &c.]

Observe well this law. *Imprimis rex vult, et præcipit, quod pax sacrosanctæ ecclesiæ, et regni solide custodiatur, et conservetur in omnibus, quodque justicia singulis tam pauperibus, quam divitibus administretur, nulla habita personarum ratione.*

Inter leges Edgari Regis. This is an auncient maxime of the common law repeated and affirmed amongst the lawes of king Edgar: *Primum ecclesia Dei jura et immunitates suas omnes habeto, publici juris beneficio quisque fruitor, eique ex æquo et bono (sive is dives, sive inops fuerit) jus redditor.*

Fleta, lib. 1. c. 29. Fleta reciteth this fundamentall law in few words, *Quod pax ecclesiæ, et terræ inviolabiliter observetur, ita quod communis justicia singulis pariter exhibeatur.*

1 R. 2. cap. 2. 1 H. 4. cap. 1. 2 H. 4. cap. 1. 4 H. 4. cap. 8. 7 H. 4. cap. 1. &c. And this law hath been explained and affirmed by divers other acts of parliament.

Britton, fol. 1. saith, *Peace ne poet my bien estre sans ley*; therefore this law as a meane, that peace may be kept and maintained, provideth that common *droiture (i. justice selonque le ley, & customs d'angliterre) soit fait a touts, &c.*

But this auncient law had great need at this time to be rehearsed, and commanded to be put in execution, for that, by reason of the often insurrections, tumults, and intestine warres in the raigne of king Hen. 3. the peace of the church, and of the land was for a long time miserably disturbed, and in a manner overthrown, for of those intestine warres the poet said truly,

Nulla fides pietasve viris, qui castra sequuntur.

And of these seditious subjects, another in the person of the poore ploughman in the like case said;

Virgill.

Impius hæc tam culta novalia miles habebit?
Barbarus has segetes? en quo discordia cives
Perduxit miseros!

Another mischiefe was, that during these tumults and intestine warres, law and justice lay asleep, for *Silent leges inter arma*; but the rule is good, and doth ever hold, *Dormiunt aliquando leges, moriuntur nunquam.*

By all which it appeareth, *quòd ex malis moribus bonæ leges oriuntur.*

2. Branch. (2) *Purview est que nul ne veigne manger, herberger, ne giser al meason de religion,* &c.] The mischiefe is at large set downe in this act, wherein it is to be observed, that over and above their owne competent maintenance, the residue ought to be expended in works of charity.

Vide le statute de Carlile, anno 35 E 1. Lib. 8. fo. 130. the case of Thetford schole.

Fleta, li. 3. c. 5. Britton, fol. 37. Hereof Fleta saith, *Et ne religiosi per onerationes indebitas supervenientium depauperentur, per quod eleemosynas et servitia subtrahere cogantur, vel terras suas vendere, vel alienare, ex principis constitutione prohibitum est, quod nullus hospitari præsumat in domibus religiosorum de aliena advocatione, nisi specialiter rogatus, nec sumptubus domus nec suis propriis contra tutorum domuum voluntatem.*

[162]

(3) *Et per ceſt ſtatute nentend' pas le roy, que grace de hoſpitalitie ſoit ſuſtreit as beſoignes.*] Here it appeareth that the grace of hoſpitality conſiſteth in diſtributing to them that have neede. 3. *Branch.*

(4) *Ne que les avowes des meſons les puiſſent per lour ſovent venues ſurcharger ne deſtruer.*] This is evident. 4. *Branch.*

(5) *Purview eſt enſement que nul graund ne petit, per colour de parent', ou deſpecialtie, ou per auter affiance, ne per auter encheſon, ne courge en auter parke, ne peſhe en auter viver,* &c.] Hereof Fleta ſaith, *Nec etiam præſumat quis temere illicentiatus currere in parco alieno, nec in alterius vivario piſcari, veruntamen ſi contingat aliquis in hujuſmodi domibus per licentiam magiſtri domus vel ejus balivi, quod non aperiat feneſtras inhibitas, vel aliquas frangat ſeruras, et victualia vel alia bona violenter capiat, vel extrahat ſub colore emptionis, vel alio quoquo modo, &c.* 5. *Branch.* Fleta ubi ſupra.

Here note that *vivarium*, vivary is here taken for waters where fiſhes are nouriſhed and kept. Vide hic. cap. 20.

(6) *Et que nul face barter blee ne prender blee,* &c.] This branch againſt purveiors doth extend as well to lay, as eccleſiaſtical perſons, and is well explained and confirmed by divers and many ſtatutes. 6. *Branch.* Mag. Chart. c. 21. Artic. Cler. c. 1?.

(7) *Et que nul preigne chivals, boefs, chares, ne charets niefs, ne bateux, ne auter choſe a faire carriage,* &c.] And by the ſtatutes abovesaid, and many other, this branch concerning cariage is alſo well explained and confirmed. 14 E. 3. cap. 3. 18 E. 3. c. 3. Regiſt. 92. 7. *Branch.*

(8) *Et ceux queux viendront encontre les eſtabliſhments avandits, & de ceo ſoient attaints.*] Here is contained the puniſhments of ſuch as doe offend againſt any of theſe eſtabliſhments, as well at the kings ſuit, as at the ſuit of the party grieved. 8. *Branch.*

And herewith agreeth Britton, for he ſaith, *Et auxi des viſcounts & des touts nous auters miniſters, juſtices, & coroners, & auters que gents de religion, & auters gents greveront per ſurcharges de lour venues pur herberger oveſque eux ſovent a auter coſtages, oveſq; trope de frap de gents & per ſojourners de lour gents, & de lour chivaux, ou de cheines, ou auterment per emprompts de lour chivaux ou de cariage, ou de deniers, ou per begger merime, ou fees, ou auter choſe a eux ou a aſcun de lour meyne, ou de lour amys, & in ceo caſe ſoient puny per fyns.* Brit. fol. 37.

(9) *Et le roy defend, & commaund que nul deſormes face male damage,* &c.] This clauſe extends as well to lay as eccleſiaſticall perſons. 9. *Branch.*

(10) *Et eſt purview que ceux points liont auxibien nous counſellors, juſtices de foreſts, et auters juſtices, et auters gents.*] Of theſe two branches Fleta ſaith thus, *Item nec graventur viri religioſi, perſonæ eccleſiaſticæ, vel alii, pro eo quod vetuerunt hoſpitium, vel victualia alicui, vel pro eo, quod queſti fuerunt de aliquo gravamine eis illato in prædictis articulis contento, quod ſi quis fecerit, et inde convincatur, puniatur per pœnam ſupradictam, nec excipiantur in præmiſſis conſiliarii regis nec juſtic' de foreſta, vel alii quicunque juſticiarii vel miniſtri regis, non magis quam mediocres, vel minores.* 10. *Branch.* Fleta ubi ſupra. [163] Conſiliarii Regis.

(11) *Et que les points avandits ſoient mainteynes,* &c.] This branch extends as well to lay, as eccleſiaſticall perſons. 11. *Branch.*

(12) *Et que nul envoie a meaſon,* &c.] This is alſo as generall as the former. 12. *Branch.*

Note it is an article, *inter capitula itineris de hiis qui miſerunt*

ad domus vel maneria religioſorum homines, equos, vel canes perhendinando ad cuſtum eorum.

13. *Branch.* Fleta ubi ſupra. (13) *Uncore eſt purview que viſcounts ne herbergent ove nulluy,* &c.] Of this Fleta ſaith, *De vic' proviſum eſt quod non hoſpitentur alicubi niſi propriis ſumptibus, veruntamen conceſſum eſt, quod in domibus religioſorum viciſſim per unam noctem tantum cum ſex equis, et non pluribus ſumptibus alienis in ſuis balivis hoſpitentur, dum tamen frequenter non venerint.* See cap. *Itineris de vicecomitibus venientibus ad hoſpitandum cum pluribus quam* 5. *vel.* 6. *equis in balivis ſuis, vel qui per frequentes adventus ultra quoſcunque oneraverint.*

Here is to be obſerved that often in Fleta, and other old authors and ſtatutes this word *perhendinare* is uſed, which ſignifieth to ſojourne, and *perhendinationes* ſignifieth ſojourning.

36 E. 3. cap. Itin. Vet. Magna Cart. 154. And that we may note once againe for all, whenſoever an act of parliament doth generally prohibit any thing, as in this chapter it doth, the party grieved ſhall not have his action onely for his private reliefe, but the offender ſhall be puniſhed at the kings ſuit for the contempt of his law; and therefore upon this ſtatute it ſhall be inquired at the kings ſuit, *De hiis qui miſerunt ad domos vel maneria religioſorum vel aliorum homines, equos, vel canes perhendinando ad cuſtum eorum, et de vicecomitibus venientibus ad hoſpitandum cum pluribus quam quinque vel ſex equis in balivis ſuis, vel qui per frequentes adventus ultra quoſcunque oneraverint.*

CAP. II.

PURVIEW eſt enſement, que quant clerke eſt priſe pur rette de felony, et il ſoit demande per lordinary, il luy ſoit liver, ſolonque le priviledge de ſaint eſgliſe, en tiel peril come ils appent (1), *ſolonque le cuſtome avant ſes heures uſe. Et le roy amoniſt les prelates, et eux enjoine en la foy que ils luy doient, et pur la common profit de la peace de la terre, que ceux que ſont endites de tiel rette per ſolempne queſtes des probes homes fait en la court del roy, en nul manner ne les deliverent* (2) *ſans due purgation* (3), *iſſint que le roy neit meſtier de mitter auter remedy.*

IT is provided alſo, that when a clerk is taken for guilty of felony, and is demanded by the ordinary, he ſhall be delivered to him according to the privilege of holy church, on ſuch peril as belongeth to it, after the cuſtom aforetimes uſed. And the king admoniſheth the prelates, and enjoineth them upon the faith that they owe to him, and for the common profit and peace of the realm, that they which be indicted of ſuch offences by ſolemn inqueſt of lawful men in the king's court, in no manner ſhall be delivered without due purgation, ſo that the king ſhall not need to provide any other remedy therein.

Marlb. cap. 27. (18 El. c. 7. Hob. 288. Chart. de Pardon, Br. 21. 23 H. 8. c. 11.)

The miſchiefes before this ſtatute were three: 1. That the ordinary would often challenge one for a clark that was none. [164] 2. That when any that were or had ability to be of the clergy, were endicted of felony, the ordinary would preſently demaund them, and the court would deliver them without inquiſition. But alwayes

alwayes after this statute, the court took an inquisition of office, *Ut sciatur qualis ordinario deliberari debeat.* 3. That the ordinaries would often deliver them without due purgation, whereby the king lost his forfeiture, and offences remained unpunished.

(1) *En tiel peril come il appent.*] The perill was, that if the ordinary should demand any man for a clark that was none, his temporalties should be for that contempt seised, and some have holden that he should lose that franchise or priviledge to demaund clarks for him and his successors for ever; but see the statute of 25 E. 3. cap. 6. for since that statute it hath been holden but finable. 20 E. 2. Coro. 233. 26 Ass. 19. 7 H. 4. 36. 9 E. 4. 28. 25 E. 3. cap. 6.

(2) *Que ceux queux sont endites de tiel rette per solemne enquest des probes homes en la court le roy in nul manner ne deliveront sans due purgation.*] Before this statute if any clark had been arrested for the death of a man, or any other felony, and the ordinary did demaund him before the secular judge, he was delivered without any inquisition to be made of the crime; and this appeareth by Bracton, who writing before this statute saith, *Cum verò clericus, &c. captus fuer' pro morte hominis, vel alio crimine, et imprisonatus, et de eo petatur curia christianitatis ab ordinario loci, &c. imprisonatus ille statim ei deliberetur sine aliqua inquisitione facienda.* Lestatute de Bigamis, cap. 6. & Artic. Cler. ca. 15. Bract. l. 3. fo. 123. Artic. Cler. c. 15.

But after this statute, to the end that the ordinary might have more care of purgation to be duly done according to the provision of this act, when any clark was indicted of any felony, and refused to answer to the felony, but claimed *privilegium clericale*, and was demaunded by his ordinary, yet before he was delivered to the ordinary, all the records say, *Sed ut sciatur qualis ei (s. ordinario) liberari debeat, inquiratur inde rei veritas per patriam:* and thereupon an inquisition was taken whether he were guilty of the fact or no, and if he were found guilty, his goods and chattels were forfeit, and his lands seised into the hands of the king.

Britton, that wrote after this statute, saith, *Si le clerk encoupe de felony (i. indite ou appeale de felony) alledge clergie, & est tiel trove (s. q. est un clerke) & p. lordinary demaund, donques serra inquise coment il est mescrue (i. culpable) & sil soit nient mescrue, &c. donques il serra aroge touts quits, & sil soit mescrue si soient ses chateux taxes, & ses terres prises in nostre maine, & son corps deliver al ordinarie:* so as by the one author, who wrote a little before this statute, and the other who wrote presently after (together with the continuall practise thereof) the diversity doth appeare. Brit. c. 4. fo. 11.

Monachus indictatus de felonia, petiit privilegium clericale, abbas præsens petiit eum tanquam suum professum, et ad hoc fuit admissus loco ordinarii, inquisitio capta ex officio dixit quod non culpabilis, ideo quietus recessit, et si culpabilis inventus fuisset, ad huc dicto abbati liberaretur, &c. 8 E. 2. Coro. 417. 17 E. 2. ibid. 386. 3 H. 7. 12.

But of the allowance of the benefit of clergy upon the arraignment, it was very prejudiciall to the prisoner, for that he lost his challenges to the inquest, that found him guilty, and yet upon the inquest of office formerly used, *ut sciatur qualis ordinario liberari debet*, he forfeited all his goods, and chattels, and the profits of his lands untill he had made his purgation: and therefore that thrice reverend and learned judge sir John Prisot chiefe justice of the court of common pleas, studying how to relieve the poore prisoners that were destitute of counsell, with the advice of the rest of the judges in the raigne of H. 6. for the safety of the innocent, 3 H. 7. fo. 1. 12.

would

would not allow the prisoner the benefit of clergy before he had pleaded to the felony, and having had the benefit of his challenges and other advantages, had beene convicted thereof: which just
[165] and charitable course hath been generally observed ever since.

(3) *Sans due purgation.*] Before this statute, purgations were unduly made, more for favour, then for furtherance of justice, whereby malefactors were encouraged to offend; wherefore the king admonished and enjoyned by this act of parliament the prelates upon the faith which they ought unto him, &c. to deliver no clerks, that were indicted, without due purgation, as they tendred the common profit of the peace of the land. But this royall admonition and injunction (and many other in succeeding ages, as it by parliament rolls appeareth) tooke little effect, but the abuses in making purgations in the end became so intollerable, as queene
18 Eliz. cap. 6. Elizabeth, by assent of the lords spirituall and temporall, and the commons in parliament assembled, as matter unreformable, tooke it quite away; but yet, what the law was therein before that statute, is good to be knowne, and therefore somewhat shall be said thereof in the treatise of the pleas of the crowne, being the proper place for the same.

CAP. III.

PURVIEW est ensement, que nul rien desormes soit demande, ne prise, ne levie per viscount, ne per auter, pur escape de laron, ou felon, jesque a tant que lescape soit adjudge per justices errants (1). *Et que auterment le ferra, cy rendra a celuy, ou a ceux que tiel averont pay, quant que il avera prise et resceive, et au roy au tant.*

IT is provided also, that nothing be demanded nor taken from henceforth, nor levied by the sheriff, nor by any other, for the escape of a thief or a felon, until it be judged for an escape by the justices in eyre. And he that otherwise doth, shall restore to him or them that have prayed it, as much as he or they have taken or received, and as much also unto the king.

Regist. 184. cap. Itineris. Vet. Mag. Chart. 154. (21 Ed. 3. f. 54.)

18 E. 2. Stat. de visu Franc'. The mischiefe before this statute was, that sheriffes in their tournes, and lords in their leets, who had jurisdiction to enquire of escapes of theeves and felons, upon presentment before them of such escapes, would levie fines or amerciaments for such escapes, for that they pretended that the said presentment was not traversable: now forasmuch as it required judgement in law to discerne betweene a voluntary escape and a negligent in case of felony, and also what should be judged an escape, and what not, they might enquire onely, and the judgement thereupon belonged to the justices in eire.

This statute doth declare, that nothing should be demanded, taken, or levied by any sheriffe, or other, untill the escape be adjudged by the justices in eire, and addeth a penalty if any such thing be done.

For

For proof whereof, we find before the making of this statute, *Quod evasiones latronum secundum legem et consuetudinem regni coram justiciariis regis itinerantibus, et non alibi, debeant et consueverunt judicari, et amerciamenta inde provenientia per summonitionem scaccarii sunt levand'.* We find also in the same yeare, that before this act of 3 E. 1. was made another record, *Quia evasiones latronum coram justiciariis regis itinerantibus, et non alibi judicari debent, mandatum est vicecomiti quod restituat 8. l. W. C. quas ab eo cepit pro evasione cujusdam hominis, &c.* Now that the common law, the mischiefe before the statute, and the purview of the statute be understood, let us peruse the words of the act. Rot. claus. 2 E. 1. m. 11. Mirror, ca. 2. sect. 9. Rot. claus. 3 E. 1. m. 15.

(1) *Per viscount, ne per auter, &c. jesque a tant que lescape serra adjudge per justices errants.*] By these words the court of the kings bench, which is holden *coram rege*, is not excluded, but presentment of such escapes may be made there: First, for that this prohibition beginneth with sheriffes, and therefore the generall words [or by any other] shall be intended of leets, being inferiour courts, and not of the justices of the kings bench, being the highest of any ordinary court of justice in England. Secondly, for that the court of the kings bench is an eire (the returnes there being *ubicunq; fuerimus in Anglia)* and more than an eire; for if the kings bench had come into a county where the eire had sit, the eire had ceased, for *in præsentia majoris cessat potestas minoris.* [166] Lib. 2. fol. 46. Marleb. c. 19. 28. Hic cap. 15. 21 E. 3. 54. b. 21 ass. 12. 27 ass. p. 2. *Regula.*

But by the statute of 31 E. 3. it is enacted, that escapes of theeves and felons, &c. from henceforth to be judged before any of the kings justices shall be levied from time to time as they shall fall, as well in the time past, as in the time to come. 31 E. 3. cap. 14. stat. 1. 1 R. 3. cap. 3.

CAP. IV.

DE wreck de mere (1) est accorde, que la ou home, chien, ou chat (2) escape vive hors de la niefe, la niefe ou batell', ou nul rien, que la eins fuit, ne soit [adjudge] wreck, mes soient les choses saves et gardes pur le vieu del vicont, coroner (3), ou al', ou del baillife le roy, et bailes en les mains ceux de la ville, ou les choses sont troves, issint que si nul sue les biens, et puit prover que ils soient, ou a son seigniour, ou en sa garde peris, deins lan et le jour (4), sans delay luy soient rendus: si non, remaigne au roy. Et soient prises per le vic' et coroners, et bailes a la ville pur respoign' devant justices de wrecke que appent a roy (5). Et la ou wrecke appent a auter que au roy (6), ci le eit per mesme le maner. Et que auterment fra, et de ceo soit attaint, soit agarde

CONCERNING wrecks of the sea, it is agreed, that where a man, a dog, or a cat escape quick out of the ship, that such ship nor barge, nor any thing within them, shall be adjudged wreck: but the goods shall be saved and kept by view of the sheriff, coroner, or the king's bailiff, and delivered into the hands of such as are of the crown, where the goods were found; so that if any sue for those goods, and after prove that they were his, or perished in his keeping, within a year and a day, they shall be restored to him without delay; and if not, they shall remain to the king, and be seised by the sheriffs, coroners, and bailiffs, and shall be delivered to them of the town, which shall answer before the justices of the wreck belonging

garde al prison, et rent al volunt le roy (7), et rendra les dammages ensement. Et si le bailife le face, et soit disavow de son seigniour, et le seigniour ne ottrie de ceo a luy, respoign' le bailife, sil eit de quoy, et sil neit de quoy, rendra le seigniour le corps du bailife au roy.

belonging to the king. And where wreck belongeth to another than to the king, he shall have it in like manner. And he that otherwise doth, and thereof be attainted, shall be awarded to prison, and make fine at the king's will, and shall yield damages also. And if a bailiff do it, and it be disallowed by the lord, and the lord will not pretend any title thereunto, the bailiff shall answer, if he have whereof; and if he have not whereof, the lord shall deliver his bailiff's body to the king.

Custumier de Norm. cap. 17. (5 Rep. 106. 5 Ed. 3. 3. Bro. Wreck, 1. 17 Ed. 2. stat. 1. c. 11. 12 Ann. stat. 2. c. 18.)

Doct. & Stud. cap. 51. fo. 156.

Many have doubted what the common law was before the making of this statute; and some have holden, that the common law was, that the goods wrecked upon the sea were forfeited to the king, and that they be forfeited also since the statute, unlesse they be saved by following this statute. To this I answer with Macrobius, *Multa ignoramus, quæ nobis non laterent, si veterum lectio nobis esset familiaris*: for Bracton, who wrote before this statute, proveth, that this act is but a declaration of the common law, *Magis propriè dici poterit wreccum, si navis frangatur, et de qua nullus vivus evaserit, et maxime si dominus rerum submersus fuerit, et quicquid inde ad terram venerit, erit domini regis, &c. et quod hujusmodi dici debeant wreccum, verum est, nisi ita sit, quod verus dominus aliunde veniens per certa indicia et signa docuerit res esse suas, ut si canis vivus inveniatur, &c. Et eodem modo si certa signa apposita fuer' mercibus et aliis rebus.*

Bract. li. 3. fo. 120. Brit. fo. 7. 26. 85. Flet. li. 1. c. 41.

[167]

Mirr. c. 1. § 13. & c. 3. § de wrecks.

The Mirrour saith, *A lour view, (s. les coroners) de wrecks a les appent denquirer ou les wrecks vient a terre, quel les choses, combien & la value distinctment per parcells. Et si home, beste, oisell, ou auter chose vivant vint avecq; ou non, & essint per divident soit livre a la prochein ville, un ou plusors pur ent responder al verey seigneur (i. proprietarie) si la vient challenger, & defresuer de deins lan.*

And albeit this author wrote after this statute, yet he wrote of the ancient lawes before the same, and is more large then the words of the act: for therein is named onely of a man, a dog, and a cat, that escapeth alive; and this author speaketh generally of any beast, hawke, or other living thing, so as he pursueth not this act, but treateth of the common law.

Rot. cart. an. 20 H. 3. Rot. claus. 14 H. 3. m. 6. Vide li. 5. fo. 107. Sir Henry Constables case.

Rex pro salute animæ suæ, et ad malas consuetudines abolendas, concessit, quod bona in mari periclitata non perdantur nomine wrecci, quando aliquis homo, aut bestia vivus de navi evaserit. And now having cleared this point, let us peruse the words of our act.

Custumier de Norm. c. 17.

(1) *De wreck de mere.*] Wrecke or shipwrecke is an English word, in French, *naufrage*, in ancient French, *varech*, in Latine, *naufragium*, legally *wreccum maris*, wrecke of the sea in legall understanding is applyed to such goods as after shipwreck at sea are by

by the sea cast upon the land, and therefore the jurisdiction thereof pertaineth not to the lord admirall, but to the common law.

5 E. 3. 3. 11 H. 4. 16. F.N.B. 112. e. Sir Hen. Const. case, ubi sup.

Although this statute speaketh onely of wrecke, yet this statute extendeth to flotsam, jetsam, and lagan: for which see sir Henry Constables case, lib. 5. *ubi supra.*

The cause wherefore originally wrecke was given to the crowne, stood upon two maine maximes of the common law; First, that the property of all goods whatsoever must be in some person. Secondly, that such goods, as no subject can claime any property in, doe belong to the king by his prerogative, as treasure trove, strayes, wrecke of the sea, and others; because of ancient time, when the art of navigation was not so perfect, nor trade of merchandize grown to such perfection, as now it is, it was a matter of great difficulty to be proved, in whom the property of goods wrecked at sea was. Bracton saith, *Item tempore dicuntur res in nullius bonis esse, ut thesaurus. Item ubi non apparet dominus rei, sicut est de wrecco maris. Item de hiis quæ pro waivio habentur, sicut de averiis ubi non apparet dominus, quæ olim fuerunt inventoris de jure naturali, jam efficiuntur principis de jure gentium.* Others have yeelded another reason, that the king by old custome of the realme, as lord of the narrow sea, is bound to scoure the sea of the pirats and petie robbers of the sea: and so it is read of that noble king Edgar, that he would twice in the yeare scoure the sea of such pirats, &c. and because that could not be done without great charge, the law gave unto him such goods as be wrecked upon the sea towards the charge.

Bract. li. 1. fo. 8. 9 H. 6. 45.

If a ship be ready to perish, and all the men therein for safeguard of their lives leave the ship, and after the forsaken ship perisheth, if any of the men be saved and come to land, the goods are not lost.

Rot. pat. 28 E. 1. m. 23. in dorf. the Merchants of Portugals case. 46 E. 3. 15.

A ship on the sea is pursued with enemies, the men for safegard of their lives forsake the ship, the enemies take the ship, and spoile her of her goods and tackle, and turne her into sea, by the weather she is cast on land, where her men arrived, and it was resolved by all the judges of England that the ship was no wrecke, nor lost.

Rot. claus. 5 R. 2. pro Willielmo Fishlake.

(2) *Home, cheine, ou cat.*] This statute, as hath beene said, being but declaratorie of the common law, these three instances are put but for examples, for besides these two kind of beasts, all other beasts, fowles, birds, hawkes, and other living things are understood, whereby the ownership or property of the goods may be knowne: and Bracton yet goeth farther, *Si certa signa apposita fuerint mercibus, et aliis rebus, &c.*

[168]

Bract. ubi supra, fo. 120. 27 E. 3. c. 13. by his marks cart or cocket. 31 H. 6. c. 4. 2 R. 3. fo. 2. a.

(3) *Mes soient les choses saves & gardes per le vieu del visc', coroner, &c.*] Yet if the goods be *bona peritura*, the sheriffe may sell such goods within the yeare, lest they should perish, and nothing be made of them; and therefore for necessity (which is excepted out of law) the sale in that case is good within the yeare.

Pl. Com. 466.

(4) *Et poient prover, &c. deins l'an & le jour.*] Yet if the owner die within the yeare, his executors or administrators may make proofe, for that this act is but a declaration of the common law.

Doct. & Stud. fo. 118.

This yeare and day shall be accounted from the seisure made as wrecke, for that is the thing whereof the owner may take the best notice.

35 H. 6. 27. per Notingham. Sir Hen. Const. case, ubi supra.

35 H. 6. 27. But if the kings goods be wrecked, and cast upon ground, where a subject hath wreck of the sea, who seiseth the same, the king may make his proofes at any time when he will, and is not confined to a yeare and a day, as the subject is.

Regist. fo. F.N.B. 112. Now if the goods or merchandises so cast upon the land be not seised, as is aforesaid, but taken away by certaine wrong doers not knowne, the partie may have a commission of oier and terminer to enquire of them, that did the trespasse, and to heare and determine the same, and to make restitution to the partie.

Vide Rast. Pl. cor. fol. 611. 15 R. 2. cap. 3. (5) *Devant les justices del wrecke que appent al roy.*] That is, it shall not be tryed in the admirall court, but before the kings justices at the common law, because the wrecke is ever cast upon the land.

(6) *Et la ou wrecke appent al auter que au roy*, &c.] Wrecke may belong to the subject, either by graunt from the king, or by prescription.

Bract. li. 3. fo. 120. Britt. 7. 26. 85. Of ancient time, wrecke of the sea, and other casualties, as treasure trove in the land, strayes, and the like, were *primi inventoris quasi totius populi, sed postea ad regem translata fuerunt, quia non modo totius populi, sed reipublicæ etiam caput est:* but if treasure be found in the sea, the finder shall have it at this day.

2 R. 3. fol. 11. Vide hic ca. 9. 20. 24, 25, 26. 29. (7) *Et rent al volunt le roy.*] That is, be fined at the kings will, which is to be understood, that the kings justices, before whom the party is attainted, shall set the fine, *Et non dominus rex per se in camera sua, nec aliter coram se, nisi per justiciarios suos: Et hæc est voluntas regis, viz. per justiciarios, et legem suam, unam est dicere.*

CAP. V.

ET pur ceo que elections doient estre frankes, cy defend le roy sur la greeve forfeiture (1), *que nul haute home, ne auter, per poyar des armes, ne per malice ou manaces, ne disturbe de faire franke election.*

AND because elections ought to be free, the king commandeth upon great forfeiture, that no man by force of arms, nor by malice, or menacing, shall disturb any to make free election.

Art. super cart cap. 8. & 13. 33 H. 8. cap. 37. Dier, 8 El. 247. 14 H. 8. 2. 29. 31 Eliz. cap. 6. (Br. Amercement, 6. 13. 32. 35. 37. 9 Ed. 2. stat. 1. c. 14.)

7 H. 4. cap. 14. [169] See the statute of 7 H. 4. that knights of shires for the parliament shall be chosen *libere et indifferenter sine prece aut præcepto.*

There were two mischiefs before the making of this statute. 1. For that elections were not duly made. 2. That elections were not freely made; and both these were against the ancient maxime

Regula. of the law, *Fiant electiones rite et libere sine interruptione aliqua*; and again, *Electio libera est*; for before this act in the irregular raign of H. 3. the electors had neither their free, nor their due elections, for sometimes by force, sometimes by menaces, and sometimes by malice the electors were framed, and wrought to make election of men unworthy, or not elegible, so as their election was neither

7 H. 6. 12. due, nor free: this act briefly rehearseth the old rule of the common

mon law (for that elections ought to be free) wherein both the said points are included; 1. It must be a due election, and 2. It must be a free election.

This statute doth enact, that no man upon grievous forfeiture shall disturb any to make free election, and is excellently penned in two respects; first, for that generally it extendeth to all elections, that is to say, to every dignity, office, or place elective, be it ecclesiasticall or temporall, of what kinde or quality soever. Secondly, the act is penned in the name of the king, *viz.* the king commandeth: and therefore the king bindeth himself not to disturb any electors to make free election, as in the like case upon a statute made in the raigne of the said king; the act saying, *rex perpendens*, &c. the same bound the king. Now that electors might make free and due elections without displeasure or fear thereof, by this act of parliament, as a sure defence, the king commandeth the same upon grievous forfeiture: and this act extends to all elections, as well by those that at the making of this act had power to make them, as by those whose power was raised, or created since this act.

W. 2. 13 E. 1. c. 1. Pl. Com. The Lord Berklies case. 14 H. 4. 20, 22. Stamf. Pl Cor. 168. c. d. 12 E. 2. Coro. 381. 22 E. 3. ibid. 275. Dier 12 El, 289. semble.

(1) *Greve forfeiture.*] That is, the disturbers to be punished by grievous fines and imprisonment.

What offices and places be eligible, see Artic. super Chart. cap. 8. and this act extendeth to all elections in counties, universities, cities, corporations, and other places.

Art. super Chart. ca. 8. & vide hic. ca. 10.

And thus much shall suffice for the understanding of this excellent and necessary act. See hereafter cap. 10.

CAP. VI.

ET que nul city, borough, ne ville, ne nul home soit amerce sans reasonable encheson, et solonque le quantity del trespasse (1), *s. franke home savant son contenement, merchant savant son merchandise, et villein savant son gainage, et ceo per lour peeres.*

AND that no city, borough, nor town, nor any man be amerced, without reasonable cause, and according to the quantity of his trespass; that is to say, every free-man saving his freehold, a merchant saving his merchandise, a villain saving his waynage, and that by his or their peers.

Cap. Itin. Vet. Mag. Chart. fol. 164. b. (Regist. 187. 9 H. 3. stat. 1. c. 14.)

One mischiefe before this statute was, that seeing the words of the statute of Magna Charta were *Liber homo non amercietur*, &c. it extended not onely to naturall and singular men, but to sole bodies politique or corporate, and not to corporations, or companies aggregate of many, as cities, boroughs, and towns. Another mischiefe was, that many times not onely cities, boroughs, and townes, but private men also were amercied without cause. Lastly, that the said statute of Magna Charta extended but to him that was *liber homo*.

Mag. Chart. ca. 14. 13 E. 1. Attachment 8. F.N.B. 170.

For all these three this statute provideth, *viz.* that no city, bo-

 rough

rough or town, nor any man shall be amercied without reasonable cause, and according to the quantity of his trespasse, and upon this statute the party grieved may have an attachment without any prohibition precedent; for this act is a prohibition of it selfe.

Mirror, c. 5. § 4. And yet the Mirror doth take it, that all this was contained in the graund charter.

Stat. voc. Ragman anno 4 E. 1. (1) *Quantity de trespasse.*] Here trespasse, *transgressio* signifieth offence, fault or default, and so it is taken in many auncient records, as taking one example for many: the statute, that is called Ragman, ordaineth that justices shall goe through the land, to enquire, heare, and determine the plaints and querels of trespasses, as well of the bayliffes and ministers of the king, as of the bayliffes of others, and of other people whatsoever they be, except appeales of felony, &c. which was understood as well of outragious takings, as of all manner of trespasse, contempt, neglect, default, or offence to the king or any other, &c.

Fleta, lib. 2. c. 1. And in that sense the apostle saith, *Ubi non est lex, ibi non est transgressio.* Fleta describing it saith, *Transgressio autem est, cum modus non servatur nec mensura, debet etenim quilibet in facto suo modum habere et mensuram.*

CAP. VII.

DES prises des constables, ou castelcins, faits des auters que des gents de la ville, ou la castles sont assise. Purview est, que nul constable ne castelein desormes nul manner de prise ne face dauter home que de la ville ou son castle est assise, et ceo soit paie, ou gree fait deins xl. jours, si ceo ne soit auncient prise due au roy, ou a castle, ou al seignior del castle.

OF prises taken by constables, or castellains, upon such folk as be not of the town where the castle is; it is provided, that no constable, nor castellain, from henceforth exact any prise, or like thing, of any other than of such as be of their town or castle; and that it be paid, or else agreement to be made within fourty days, if it be not an antient prise due to the king, or to the castle, or to the lord of the castle.

Cap. Itineris vet. Mag. Chart. fol. 154. b. (9 H. 3. stat. 1. c. 19. Altered by 13 Car. 2. stat. 1. c. 8.)

Fleta, lib. 2. ca. 43. Of this chapter Fleta saith thus, *Nullæ prisæ capiantur de aliquo per aliquem constabularium castellanum, præterquam de villa, in qua situm sit castrum, et illis satisfact' sit infra 40 dies, nisi sint prisæ antiquæ debit' regi aut domino castri aut castro debend'.*

Mag. Chart. c. 19. Upon the statute of Magna Charta, and this act, there were two articles amongst others, that the justices in eyre enquired of, *viz. De prisis factis per vicecomites, vel constabularios, vel alios balivos contra voluntatem eorum quorum catalla fuerint: item de prisis domini regis sive in terra, sive in mari, sive in aqua dulci, sive in libertatibus spectantibus ad castra sua, sive ad civitates suas, sive ad burgos suos, vel in aliis locis, quæ sunt, et quantum valeant, vel quis eas occupaverit, celaverit, vel suffocaverit, et quis eas ceperit, constabularius, vel alius, et quid valent.*

Bracton

Bracton treating of the articles of the justices in eyre saith thus, *De prisis domini regis in terra, sive in aqua dulci, sive salsa, et libertatibus spectantibus ad castella sua, sive ad comitatum, sive ad burgos suos, quæ sunt, et quantum valeant per annum.* Bract. li. 3. fo. †17.

And Britton writing of the same matter saith, *Et auxi des prises faits, per nous castellans, & autres que sont perners de vittaile, ou de autre chose, per queux tiels prises ount estre faits, & a queux damages, & de quels gents, & en tiel case, voillons nous que nul ne soit garrant per continuance de seisin in damage.* Brit. fol. 27. [†71]

And Fleta hath it thus, *De prisis factis per vicecom. constabularios, vel alios contra voluntat' eorum quorum catalla illa fuerint: item de prisis constabulariorum castrorum factis de bonis aliorum, quam eorum, qui sunt de villis, ubi castra sita sunt, et de bonis eorum, &c. si non satisfact' fuer' infra 40 dies, &c.* Fleta ubi supra.

It is to be observed, that in the raigne of this king, and in most of the succeeding kings, there have been many other statutes made concerning purveyors, yet never did any reporter publish any case, that I have seene, and remember, that may serve for the exposition of any of them, and many proceedings have beene judicially upon many of them against purveyors, which doe appeare of record. *Vide* Magna Charta, cap. 19. and the exposition thereof, and the third part of the Institutes, cap. Purveyors.

CAP. VIII.

ET que nul fine soit prise pur beaupleder, sicome auterfoits fuit defendu en temps le roy Henry, pier le roy que ore est.

AND that nothing be taken for fair pleading, as hath been prohibited heretofore in the time of king Henry, father to our lord the king that now is.

(52 H. 3. c. 11. 1 Ed. 3. stat. 2. c. 8. Regist. 179.)

That is to say, by the statute of Marlebridge, anno 52 H. 3. where this matter is explained. Marleb. cap. 11.

CAP. IX.

ET pur ceo que la peace de la terre ad estre feeblement garde avant ces heures, pur defalt de bone suit fait sur les felons solonque due manner (1), et nosment per encheson des franchises ou les felons sont resceves: purview est, que touts communement soient prestes, et aparailes, au commandement et a les summons des viscounts (2), et au crie de pays (3), de suer et arrester les felons (4), quant,

AND forasmuch as the peace of this realm hath been evil observed heretofore for lack of quick and fresh suit making after felons in due manner, and namely because of franchises, where felons are received; it is provided, that all generally be ready and apparelled, at the commandment and summons of sheriffes, and at the cry of the country, to sue and arrest felons, when

quant meſtier ſerra, auxibien deins franchiſes come dehors (5). *Et ceux que ceo ne ferront, et de ceo ſoient attaintes, le roy prendra a eux grevement* (6). *Et ſi le default ſoit trove en le ſeignior de la franchiſe, le roy ſe prendra meſme le franchiſe* (7). *Et ſi le default ſoit trove en le bailife, eit lenpriſonment dun an*(8), *et puis ſoit grevement rente, et ſil neit de quoy, eit lenpriſonment de ii. ans. Et ſi viſcount, coroner, ou auter bailife deins franchiſe, ou dehors* (9), *per lower, ou per prier, ou* **per poies, ou per nul manner daffinity, concelent, conſentent, ou procurent de conceler les felonies faits en lour bailies, ou auterment, ſe teignont attacher, ou arreſter les misfeſants per la ou ils purra, ou auterment ſe feignont de faire lour office, en nul maner de ſavour des misfeſants, et de ceo ſoient attaintes, que ils eient lenpriſonment dun an* (10), *et puis ſoient greevement rentes a le volunt le roy* (11), *ſils eient de quoy, ſinon, eient lenpriſonment de iii. ans.*

*[172]

when any need is, as well within franchiſe as without; and they that will not ſo do, and thereof be attainted, ſhall make a grievous fine to the king: and if default be found in the lord of the franchiſe, the king ſhall take the ſame franchiſe to himſelf; and if default be in the bailiff, he ſhall have one year's impriſonment, and after ſhall make a grievous fine; and if he have not whereof, he ſhall have impriſonment of two years. And if the ſheriff, coroner, or any other bailiff within ſuch franchiſe, or without, for reward, or for prayer, or for fear, or for any manner of affinity, conceal, conſent, or procure to conceal, the felonies done in their liberties, or otherwiſe will not attach nor arreſt ſuch felons there, as they may, or otherwiſe will not do their office for favour born to ſuch miſdoers, and be attainted thereof; they ſhall have one year's impriſonment, and after make a grievous fine at the king's pleaſure, if they have wherewith; and if they have not whereof, they ſhall have impriſonment of three years.

(4 Ed. 1. ſtat. 2. *Officium Coronat.* 13 Ed. 1. ſtat. 2. c. 1, 2. & 6. 28 Ed. 3. c. 11. 7 R. 2. c. 6. 27 El. c. 13. 39 El. c. 25.)

(1) *Pur default de bone ſute fait ſur les felons in due manner.*] Some have thought that hue and cry have been grounded upon this ſtatute, but this act proveth that hue and cry for the apprehenſion of felons was before this ſtatute, for it findeth fault that good ſuit, that is, freſh ſuit, was not duly made; and it appeareth that hue and cry in thoſe caſes hath been by the auncient laws of this realme.

Mirror, ca. 1. § 3. The author of the Mirror writing of the auncient laws before the conqueſt under the title *Des articles des viels royes ordeines*, ſaith, *Ordeine fuit que cheſcun del age de xiiii. ans, & ouſtre de mortels pechєors enſuivre de ville, & ville a hue and cry.*

Inter leges Regis Canuti. *Si quis latroni obviam dederit, eumque nullo edito clamore abire permiſerit, quanticunque fuerit latronis vita æſtimata, extremum ſolvat denariolum, aut pleno et perfecto jurejurando de facinore nihil habuiſſe cogniti confirmato. Sin quis proclamantem audierit, neque vero fuerit inſecutus, ſuæ in regem contumaciæ (ni omnem criminis ſuſpicionem diluerit) pœnas dato.*

Glanv. li. 14. c. 3. Glanvill calleth hue and cry *clamor popularis juxta aſſiſam (i. ſtatutum) ſuper hoc proditam.* But this ſtatute is not now extant.

Bract. l. 3. fo. 121. Bracton of hue and cry ſaith, *Statim et recenter inveſtiganda ſunt veſtigia malefactorum, et ſequenda per ductum carectæ, paſſus equorum,* et

et vestigia hominum, et alio modo, secundum quod consultius et melius fieri possit.

And it is one of the articles of that auncient court of the view of frankpledge (of whose antiquity we have spoken before) to enquire of hue and cries levied and not pursued. Mag. Chart. c. 35.

All these authorities were before the making of our act, and therefore it was truly said, whosoever said it, *Pervetusta Anglorum lege sancitum est, ut si quis damnum ex furto passus, aut qui ipsum spoliatum viderit, sontem per acclamationem insequatur, constabularius ejus villæ cujus opem implorat, auxilia ciere furemque perquirere debeat; quod si furem illic non deprehenderit, in proximam commigrare, et constabularium ad ferendas suppetias iterum invocare, &c.*

Of this hue and cry our auncient authors since our statute have also written, and divers acts of parliament have since been made, concerning hue and cry, as the statute *De officio coronatoris*, made the next yeare after our act, where it is said, *Et omnes sequantur hutesium, et vestigium, si fieri potest; et qui non fecerit, et super hoc convictus fuerit, attachietur, quod sit coram justiciariis de gaola, &c.* 28 E. 3. & 27 Eliz. Brit. fol. 19, 20. Fleta, lib. 1. c. 24. Anno 4 E. 1. 4 E. 1. De Offic. Coro. Vid. 13 E. 1. Stat. de Winch. 28 E. 3. ca. 11. 27 Eliz. ca. 13.

(2) *Au commandement et a les summons des viscounts*, &c.] Men ought to be in these cases at the commandement of the sheriffe, for he hath *custodiam comitatus* committed to him; and he that goeth not at the commandement of the sheriffe or constable at the cry of the country, that is, upon hue and cry, shall be grievously fined and imprisoned. Cap. Itin. Vet. Mag.Chart. 155. W. 2. cap. 29. 5 H. 7. 5. a. 2 H. 7. 15. b.

[173]

(3) *Ou a crie de pais.*] Note, in legall understanding hue and crie is all one; in ancient records they are called *hutesium et clamor*, and here crie is used for both. And this hue and crie may be by horne and by voice, *avec hue & crie de corne & de bouche*. Now the hue and crie shall be made, and all incidents thereunto, you shall reade in the abovesaid statutes, and in our reports you shall find how the same have been expounded. Mirr. cap. 2. Britt. ubi sup. Lib. 7. fo. 6, 7. Dier 23 El. 370.

(4) *De suer & arrester les felons.*] By these words it is holden, that there must be a felonie done, or else the arresting of the party, though it be upon hue and cry, is unlawfull, because it wanteth a foundation; but if a felonie be done, and the hue and cry is against one, that is neither indicted, nor of ill fame, nor suspicious, nor unknowne, yet the arrest of him is lawfull, though he be not guilty; for the hue and cry of it selfe is cause sufficient, where there is a foundation of a felonie committed. And he that levieth hue and crie upon another without cause, shall be attached and punished for disturbance of the kings peace. 29 E. 3. 39. 11 E. 4. 4. b. 5 H. 7. 5. 2 H. 7. 15.

(5) *Auxibien deins franchises come dehors.*] This was not intended of sanctuaries, but of lords, and others, that had franchises of infangthefe, outfangthefe, and the like.

(6) *Le roy prendra eux grevement.*] That is, at the kings suit they shall be fined grievously, and imprisoned.

(7) *Et si le default soit trove in le seigniour de la franchise, le roy se prendra a mesme le franchise.*] It seemeth hereby, that the franchise is lost for ever, for the words be, that the king shall take to himselfe the franchise (*viz.* as forfeit.)

(8) *Et si le default soit trove en le bailife, eit lenprisonment dun an, &c.*] And this is according to the old rule, *Qui non habet in ære, luet in corpore.*

(9) *Et si viscount, coroner, ou auter bailife de franchise, ou de hors, &c.*] Note here five things are rehearsed, as causes wherefore sheriffes, and other the kings officers and ministers of justice doe neglect their duties. 1. By prayer, *prece* (by letters, messages, or word of mouth.) 2. Reward, *precio* (sordid bribery.) 3. Feare, *metu* (the basest, and yet the most forcible of all affections.) 4. *Sanguine*, any manner of consanguinitie or affinitie: under which word (affinitie) in this act is included as well neerenesse of bloud, as alliance by marriage. Lastly, *favore*, favour, in respect of friendly affection, for men may be corrupted, not onely by reward, but in respect of the other foure also, all tending to one and the same end, to suppresse truth; as here to conceale, consent, or procure to conceale the felonies done within their severall precincts or bayliwicks.

Præce. Precio. Metu. Sanguine. Favore.

(10) *Ils eyent lenprisonment dun an*, &c.] Note here the punishment for concealement of felonies, or consenting to, or procuring the concealment of the same; for all this make not them accessarie to the felony, for then they were to have been punished in another manner, but it is called misprision, or concealement of felonie. Observe well the punishment of this misprision, but the learning thereof appertaines to the treatise of the pleas of the crowne, and therefore this little touch here shall suffice. See the 3. part of the Institutes, cap. Misprision.

(11) *Al volunt le roy.*] See here cap. 4. 20. 25.

[174]

CAP. X.

ET pur ceo que petits gents meins sages soient eslieus (1) *ore de novel communement al office de coroner: et mestier serroit que probes homes loialx et sages se intermellent de cel office: purview est, que per touts les counties soient eslieus suffisant* (3) *homes coroners* (2), *des plus loyals et plus sages chivallers* (4), *queux melius sachent, puissent, et voilent a cel office entender* (5), *et que loyalment attachent et representent les plees de la corone* (6). *Et que le vicont eit conter-rolles ove les coroners, auxybien des appeales, come des enquests, de attachments, ou des auters choses, que a cel office appendent. Et que nul coroner riens demande, ne preign' de nulluy pur faire son office, sur paine de la greeve forfeiture al roy* (7). [14 E. 1. Stat. Exon.]

AND forasmuch as mean persons, and undiscreet, now of late are commonly chosen to the office of coroners, where it is requisite that persons honest, lawful, and wise, should occupy such offices; it is provided, that through all shires sufficient men shall be chosen to be coroners, of the most wise and discreet knights, which know, will, and may best attend upon such offices, and which lawfully shall attach and present pleas of the crown; and that sheriffs shall have counter-rolls with the coroners, as well of appeals, as of enquests, of attachments, or of other things which to that office belong; and that no coroner demand nor take any thing of any man to do his office, upon pain of great forfeiture to the king.

Cap. Itin. fo. 155. (28 Ed. 3. c. 6, 1 H. 8. c. 7. 4 H. 6. 15. 4 Ed. 1. stat. 2. *Officium Coronat.* 3 H. 7. c. 1.)

The

The miſchiefe before doth appeare in the preamble, *viz.* That men of ſmall value and little underſtanding, of late times were choſen to the office of a coroner, where it ſhould be needfull that a coroner ſhould have five qualities: 1. That he ſhould be *probus homo:* 2. Lawfull, *i. legalis homo:* 3. Of ſufficient underſtanding and knowledge: 4. Of good ability and power to execute his office according to his knowledge: 5. and laſtly, Of diligence and intendance for the due execution of the ſaid office. And reaſon required it ſhould ſo be, for that coroners were in thoſe dayes the principall gardeins of the peace, and therefore the common law did not onely require expert men to be coroners, but men of ſufficient ability and livelihood for three purpoſes: 1. The law preſumes that they will do their duty, and not offend the law, at the leaſt for feare of puniſhment, whereunto their lands and goods be ſubject. 2. That they be able to anſwer to the king all ſuch fines and duties as belong to him, and to diſcharge the country thereof, wherewith the country being their electors were chargeable, as hereafter ſhall be touched. 3. That they might execute their office without bribery. And theſe five properties are neceſſary to every officer. *Vide* the laſt clauſe of this act.

(1) *Soient eſlieus.*] It is to be knowne, that the office of a coroner ever was, and yet is eligible in full county by the freeholders, by the kings writ *De coronatore eligendo:* and the reaſon thereof was, for that both the king and the country had a great intereſt and benefit in the due execution of his office, and therefore the common law gave the freeholders of the county to be electors of him. And for the ſame reaſon of ancient time the ſheriffe called *vicecomes,* who had *cuſtodiam comitatus,* was alſo eligible; for firſt, the earle himſelfe of the county had the office of the ſheriffe of the county, and when he gave it over, the *vicecomes* (as the word ſignifieth) came in ſtead of the earle, and was eligible by the freeholders of the county: and moreover, for the ſame cauſe were conſervators of the peace in like manner choſen, and ſo were, and yet are elected the verderors of the foreſt, and all theſe for the time of peace: for the time of war, there were likewiſe leaders of the counties ſouldiers, of ancient time choſen by the freeholders of the county. Vide devant, c. 5.

Erant et aliæ poteſtates et dignitates per provincias et patrias univerſas, et per ſingulos comitatus totius regni prædict' conſtitutæ, qui Heretoches apud Anglos, vocabantur, ſcilicet barones, nobiles, et inſignes ſapientes, et fideles et animoſi: Latinè verò dicebantur ductores exercitus, apud Gallos, capitales conſtabularii, vel mareſchalli exercitus. Illi verò ordinabant acies denſiſſimas in prœliis, et alas conſtituebant prout decuit, et prout eis viſum fuit, ad honorem coronæ, et ad utilitatem regni. Iſti verò viri * *eligebantur per commune concilium pro commune utilitate regni, per provincias et patrias univerſas, et per ſingulos comitatus in pleno Folkemote, ſicut et* * *vicecomites provinciarum et comitatuum eligi debent, &c.* [175] Inter leges Edw. regis, cap. de Heretochiis. * Nota. * Nota.

The Mirrour ſpeaking of the articles by old kings ordained, ſaith, *Auxi fuer' ordeines coroners in cheſcun countie, et viſcounts a garder le pais, quant les countes ſoy demiſteront del gard, &c.* And the ſheriffe was choſen by writ directed to the coroners. Mirr. cap. 1. § 3.

And ſo were the conſervators of the peace eligible alſo, by writ directed to the ſheriffe, Rot. pat. an. 5 E. 1.

For

For the verderor, he is still chosen by the freeholders of the county by the kings writ.

Art. super cart. an. 28 E. 1. c. 8. 13. Vide supra.

Our king in the 28 yeare of his raigne restored to his people the ancient election of sheriffes in these words, *Le roy ad grant a son people, que ils eint election de lour viscount en chescun countie, ou viscount nest my de fee, silz voilliont.*

12 R. 2. cap. 2. Vide Stat. 9 E. 2. De Vic'. 14 E. 3. 7.

But now by the statute of 12 R. 2. the chancellor, treasurer, keeper of the privy seale, steward of the kings house, the kings chamberlaine, clerke of the rolls, justices of the one bench and of the other, barons of the exchequer, and all other that shall be called, are to ordaine, name or make sheriffes, shall be firmly sworne that they shall not ordaine, name, or make any sheriffe, for any gift or brocage, favour or affection, but that they shall be of the most lawfull men, and sufficient, to their estimation and knowledge.

Dier, 1 El. fo. 165.

It is holden in our books, that albeit the king dieth, yet the coroner, because he is elected by the freeholders of the county by writ, and retourned of record in the chancery, which is a judiciall act, remained, and so of the verderor: otherwise it is of judges and justices, that hold their places by writ, commission, letters patents, or otherwise at will, which might be a reason wherefore the sheriffe of ancient time was eligible, for that he had *custodiam comitatus*, and a principall conservator of the peace; and therefore his authority should not cease by the death of the king, no more then that of the coroner.

In Scaccar. inter præcept. Term. Hill. anno 14 E. 3. ex parte Rememb. Regis. 20 H. 9.

Respondeat superior.

Now seeing that coroners are elected by the county, if they be insufficient, and not able to answer such fines and other duties in respect of their office, as they ought, the county as their superiour shall answer the same: as for example, the county of Kent made election, by force of the kings writ, of William Herlizon to be one of the coroners for the same county, who after was amercied *pro falso retourno* 40 *s.* whereupon processe went out to the sheriffe to levie it; the sheriffe upon his oath said, that the said William Herlizon *non habet terras vel tenementa, bona seu catalla in baliva sua, nec habuit, unde dict' denarii levari possint:* now saith the record, *Et quia ipse coronator electus fuit per comitatum, &c. ita quod in defectu ejusdem coronatoris totus comitatus ut elector et superior, &c. tenetur regi respondere; præceptum fuit nunc vicecomiti, quod de terris et tenementis hominum totius comitatus in baliva sua fieri fac' prædict'* 40 *s.* And the like law was of the sheriffe, and other the said officers, when they were eligible. But now let us returne to the purview of our act.

23 ass. p. 7. 14 H. 4. 34. 39 H. 6. 40. F.N.B. 163. k.

(2) *Homes coroners.*] The number of coroners are not set down by law: in most counties there are foure, in some counties sixe, in some fewer, and in some counties one.

For the word *coronator*, see Mag. Cart. cap. 17.

[176]

Li. 8. fo. 41. Greislies case. F.N.B. 163. n.

(3) *Sufficients.*] *Sufficiens* is a large word, and implyes as much as *idoneus*, and it hath two of the attributes mentioned in the preamble, that is lawfull, and sage.

4 E. 1. de offic' Coronat'. 14 E. 3. cap. 7. Brit. 3. b. Flet. lib. 1. cap. 18. 25. 23 ass. p. 7. Mag. Char. c. 17. F.N.B. 164.

(4) *Chivaliers.*] In ancient times none were chosen under the degree of knighthood to be coroners. But some say, that this word *(chivaliers)* was put into this statute, to the end that the party to be chosen might have sufficient in the county, which may serve for interpretation of divers other statutes, being accompanied with use and experience.

(5) *Queux*

(5) *Queux melius ſachent, puiſſent, et voilent a cel office entender,* &c.] *Qui melius ſciant, poſſint, et velint officio illi intendere, &c.* Note well theſe three qualities.

Now what cauſes there be to remove a coroner, *vide* Regiſt. & F. N. B.

See the next chap. & chap. 36. See hereafter Stat de milit. Regiſt. 177. b. F.N.B. 163. m.

(6) *Que les coroners loialment attachent et repreſentent les plees del coron,* &c.] By this it appeareth, that the coroner is judge of the cauſe, and not the ſheriffe; and this agreeth with our old and latter books, onely the ſheriffes have counter-rolls with the coroners by force of this act, and therefore a *certiorari* may be directed to the ſheriffe and coroner to remove an appeale by bill before the coroner, becauſe the ſheriffe hath a counter-roll: but if the *certiorari* be directed to the ſheriffe onely in caſe of appeale or indictment of death, it is not ſufficient to remove the record, becauſe he is not judge of the cauſe, but hath onely a counter-roll. *Vide* Magna Chart. cap. 17. many authorities cited there concerning this matter.

Regiſt.& F.N.B. ubi ſup. Mirr. lib. 1. cap. de office de Coroner. Bract. li. 3. fo. 121. Britt. fol. 3. Flet. lib 1. ca. 18. & 25. 4 E. 1. Stat. de officio. Coronat. Regiſt. jud. 16. 22 aſſ. 98. 4 H. 6. 16. Mag.Char. c. 17. Hic cap. 14. 4 H. 6. ubi ſupra.

(7) *Et que nul coroner riens demaund, ne preigne de nulluy pur faire ſon office, ſur peine de la greve forfeiture al roy.*] And this was the ancient law of England, that none having any office concerning adminiſtration of juſtice, ſhould take any fee or reward of any ſubject for the doing of his office, to the end he might be free and at liberty to doe juſtice, and not to be fettered with golden fees, as fetters to the ſuppreſſion or ſubverſion of truth and juſtice: and therefore this ſtatute was made in affirmance of the common law; this onely is added, *ſur paine de greve forfeiture al roy.*

14 E. 1. Stat. de Exonia. 3 H. 7. cap. 1. Vide hic c. 26. See 5 E. 6. c.

A coroner received 1 d. of every viſne when they came before the judges in eire, as belonging to his office, which was neither againſt the common law, nor this ſtatute; for he tooke it not for doing of his office, but a right due to his office, which might have a reaſonable beginning, *viz.* for and towards his travaile, attendance, and charges.

3 E. 3. coron. 372.

And this ſtatute ſtood in force untill the ſtatute made in 3 H. 7. ca. 1. which gave him a fee of xiii. s. iiii. d. upon the view of the body, of the goods of the murderer, &c.

3 H. 7. cap. 1.

But if the coroner ſit upon the view of any ſlaine by miſadventure, he ſhall have nothing. More ſhall be ſaid hereof hereafter, cap. 26.

1 H. 8. cap. 7.

CAP. XI.

E T pur ceo que pluſors reintes de mort de home, et que ſont culpables de meſme la mort ſont (per favorables enqueſts, priſes per viſconts et per bre' le roy que eſt appelle odio et atia*) replevies, jeſques a la venue des juſtices errants: purview eſt, que tiel enqueſts ſoient deſormes priſes per probes homes eſlieus per ſerement, dount les deux ſoient a meines chivalers' que per nul affinitie,*

AND foraſmuch as many being indicted of murther, and culpable of the ſame, by favourable inqueſts taken by the ſheriff, and by the king's writ of *odio et atia*, be replevied unto the coming of the juſtices in eyre; it is provided, that from henceforth ſuch inqueſts ſhall be taken by lawful men choſen out by oath (of whom two at the leaſt ſhall be knights) which by no affinity

affinitie, touchent a les priſoners, ne auterment ne ſoient ſuſpectious. [Gloc. c. 9. Weſt. 2. c. 29.]

affinity with the priſoners, nor otherwiſe, are to be ſuſpected.

(5 H. 7. f. 5. Regiſt. 133. 9 H. 3. ſtat. 1. cap. 26. 6 Ed. 1. ſtat. 1. c. 9.)

Mag. Cart. ca. 26.

See the 26 chapter of Magna Charta where this matter is handled at large, and need not here to be repeated, and how this writ *De odio et atia* was taken away, and ſince revived by a later ſtatute, as there it appeareth.

CAP. XII.

PURVIEW eſt enſement, que les felons (1) eſcries, et queux ſont apertement de male fame (2), et ne ſ'y voilent mitter en enqueſts des felonies (3), que homes met ſur eux devant juſtices a la ſuit le roy (4), ſoient miſes en la priſon forte et dure (5), come ceux queux refuſent eſtre al common ley de la terre. Mes ceo neſt mye a entender pur priſoners que ſont priſes per legier ſuſpection.

IT is provided alſo, that notorious felons, and which openly be of evil name, and will not put themſelves in enqueſts of felonies, that men ſhall charge them with before the juſtices at the king's ſuit, ſhall have ſtrong and hard impriſonment, as they which refuſe to ſtand to the common law of the land. But this is not to be underſtood of ſuch priſoners as be taken of light ſuſpicion.

(Dyer, 205. Kel. 70. 8 H. 4. 2. 4 Ed. 4. 11. 14 Ed 4. 7. 21 Ed. 3. 8. Fitz. Coron. 233. 283. 359.)

15 E. 4. 32. Stam. pl. cor. 150.

(1) *Que les felons.*] This ſtatute extendeth not to treaſon, which is the higheſt offence, nor to petit larceny, which is of all felonies the loweſt.

Tr. 40. El coram Rege, Rot. 4. Jane Wiſemans caſe.

This act doth extend as well to women as to men, and ſo it doth appeare by divers auncient and late precedents, and to that end the makers of this act did uſe this generall word, felons.

(2) *Eſcries et apertement de male fame.*] No perſon ſhall be put to this puniſhment unleſſe the matter be evident or provable, which is the duty of the judge to look unto.

(3) *Ne ſoy voilent mitter en enqueſts des felonies.*] This act ſpeaketh onely of indictments at the ſuit of the king. But the judgement of *paine forte et dure* was at the common law, both in appeales, and in indictments.

43 Aſſ Pl. 30. 8 H. 4. 1. 4 E. 4. 11. 7 E. 4. 29. 14 E. 4. 7.

A man may ſtand mute two manner of wayes; firſt, when he ſtands mute without * ſpeaking of any thing, and then it ſhall be inquired, whether he ſtood mute of malice, or by the act of God; and if it be found, that it was by the act of God, then the judges of the court (who ever are to be of counſell with the priſoner, to give him law and juſtice) *ex officio* ought to inquire whether he be the ſame perſon, and of all other pleas which hee might have pleaded, if hee had not ſtood mute.

* [178]

And note well the aboveſaid words of our books [whether of malice, or by the act of God] for it may be, the priſoner in truth cannot

cannot ſpeake, and yet being not mute by the act of God, he ſhall be forthwith put to his penance, as if the delinquent cut out his owne tongue, and thereby become mute.

Another kinde of mute is, when the priſoner can ſpeake, and perhaps pleade Not guilty, or pleade a plea in law, and will not conclude to the enqueſt according to this act; or ſpeake much, but doe not directly anſwer, &c. for *idem eſt nihil dicere, et inſufficienter dicere:* to be ſhort, when in the end he will not put himſelfe upon the enqueſt, that is, *de bono et malo* to be tried by God and the countrey, then this act is ſufficient warrant, if the cauſe be evident or probable, to put him to his penance; but if he demurre in law, and it be adjudged againſt him, he ſhall have judgement to be hanged: and though by his demurrer he refuſe to put himſelfe upon the enqueſt according to the letter of this act, yet for as much as he is out of the reaſon of this act, for that he refuſeth not the triall of the common law, the demurrer being allowed to him by law, and to be tried by the judges, he ſhall not be put to his penance, but have judgment to be hanged; and ſo it is if he challenge above the number of 36. he ſhall be hanged, and not have *paine fort et dure.*

4 E. 4. 11. 7 E. 4. 29. 14 E. 4. 7. 3 H. 7. 2. & 12.

(4) *Al ſute le roy.*] This act extends not to the ſuit of the party by appeale, becauſe the judgement of *paine fort et dure* was both in appeale and indictment at the common law, as hath been ſaid, and hereafter ſhall be ſaid and proved.

(5) *Soient myſes en la priſon fort et dure.*] Upon theſe words there have beene divers opinions; firſt that the puniſhment of *paine fort et dure* was given by this act. Stamf. Pl. Cor. 149. f.

Some other have holden, that at the common law for felony the priſoner ſtanding mute ſhould upon a *nihil dicit* be hanged, as at this day it is in caſe of high treaſon, and, as they ſay, in caſe of appeale. Others have holden that at the common law, in favour of life he ſhould neither have *paine fort et dure,* nor have judgement to be hanged, but to be remaunded to priſon untill he would anſwer.

8 H. 4. 2. Stamf. Pl. Cor. ubi ſupra. 21 E. 3. 18.

For the finding out of the truth herein, let us firſt ſee, what the judgement, which our act calleth *fort et dure* is, and then what the reaſon ſhould be, that ſo ſevere a judgment is given in that caſe.

The judgement is, that the man or woman ſhall be remaunded to the priſon, and laid there in ſome low and dark houſe, where they ſhall lie naked on the bare earth without any litter, ruſhes, or other clothing, and without any garment about them, but ſomething to cover their privy parts, and that they ſhall lie upon their backs, their heads uncovered and their feet, and one arme ſhall be drawne to one quarter of the houſe with a cord, and the other arme to another quarter, and in the ſame manner ſhall be done with their legges, and there ſhall be laid upon their bodies iron and ſtone, ſo much as they may beare, and more, and the next day following they ſhall have three morſels of barly bread without any drink, and the ſecond day they ſhall drinke thrice of the water that is next to the houſe of the priſon (except running water) without any bread, and this ſhall be their diet untill they be dead.

8 H. 4. 1. 4 E. 4. 11. Tr. 40 El. ubi ſup.

So as upon the matter they ſhall die three manner of wayes, *viz. Onere, fame, et frigore,* by weight, famine, and cold, and therefore this puniſhment (if it were executed according to the ſeverity of

of the law) fhould be of all other the moft grievous and fearfull. But what fhould be the reafon of this fo terrible a judgement? This act anfwereth, becaufe he refufeth to ftand to the common law of the land, that is, lawfull and due triall according to law, and therefore his punifhment for this contumacy without comparifon is more fevere, lafting, and grievous, then it fhould have beene for the offence of felony it felfe; and for the felony it felfe, it cannot be adjudged without anfwer.

Now let us examine the opinions abovefaid, and we hold, that none of them are confonant to law; for as to the firft, we hold that this heavy punifhment was not given, that is, firft inflicted by this act: for what court, or judges upon thefe words [have ftrong and hard imprifonment] could frame fuch a judgement as is abovefaid, confifting upon fo many divers particulars? and therefore it muft neceffarily follow, that the faid punifhment which this ftatute calleth *fort et dure* imprifonment, becaufe the penance was to be done in prifon, was before this act, but fufficiently fignified (as it hath beene ever fince) by thefe two epithets, *fort et dure*; fo as this act fetteth forth the quality of the judgement, and not the judgement it felfe.

2. This act defcribeth what perfons fhall be punifhed by *paine fort et dure, viz.* notorious felons, and which be openly of ill name, but fetteth not downe (as hath been faid) what the punifhment is, but provideth it fhall not be for legier fufpition.

Mirror, cap. 5. § 4. 41 Aff. p. 30. 8 H. 4. 1. 4 E. 4. 11. 14 E. 4. 7. 3 H. 7. 2. Fleta, li. 1. c. 32. Britton, fo. 40. Fleta ubi fupra.

3. All books, that held with great authority, that in cafe of appeale the prifoner upon ftanding mute fhould have judgement *de paine fort et dure,* do prove that fuch a judgement was before the making of this act, for this ftatute extends not to appeales, which are the fuit of the fubject, but onely to the fuit of the king, which is by way of indictment: and herein the words of Fleta are very remarkable, *Si autem appellatus nihil refpondere velit, &c. et appellans inde petierit judicium, indefenfus remanebit, morti tamen non condemnabitur, fed gaolæ committetur, &c.* And there fetteth downe the penance, which of neceffity muft be (as hath been faid) by the common law. And herewith agreeth Britton that wrote foone after this act; fo as the penance in cafe of appeale, is both by auncient and found authority.

Britton ubi fupr.

To the fecond opinion, if the prifoner ftanding mute fhould be hanged by the common law; the aunfwer to the firft doth anfwer this alfo, and if he fhould be hanged by the common law, this ftatute taketh it not away, but ordaineth that he fhall have ftrong and hard imprifonment. And therefore by their opinion, the felon ftanding mute might be hanged at this day, which is againft all our books, and againft conftant and continuall experience.

To the third, let no man imagine that the common law, which is the abfolute perfection of reafon, could fofter fo unreafonable and unjuft a meane of encouragement of felons, that they by their owne contumacy againft the common law fhould fuffer onely one of the loweft punifhments, *viz.* imprifonment untill they would anfwer; and the anfwers to the firft are anfwers to this alfo.

Now let us fee what our auncient authors (who as you have often perceived, have heretofore beene our good guides) fay in this behalfe.

Britton, fo. 11. a. & 40. b.

You have already heard Fleta; and Britton alfo mentioneth this penance in two feverall places, both upon the indictment, and in the

the appeale, and voucheth no ſtatute therefore, as no doubt in this caſe he would, as in other like caſes he had done, and ſpecially, ſeeing he wrote ſoone after this ſtatute, hee would have mentioned the act that had inflicted ſo ſtrange and ſtupendious a puniſhment, if the ſtatute had not beene made in affirmance of the common law.

And the Mirror ſaith, *In peche de homicide chient mortalment ceux* Mirror, c. 1. § 9.
que occiont home in priſon per ſurcharge de peine en caſe quant aſcun eſt
judge al penance. And in another place writing upon our very Mirror, c. 5. § 4.
chapter, hee ſaith, *Le point de mitter gents rettes de felony, que ſe ne*
voillent mitter in paiis, a penance, eſt cy diſuſe que ben les tue ſans aver [180]
regard as conditions des perſons, &c. This author, as hath been ſaid, writeth of the auncient law long before this act, as he himſelfe teſtifieth in the beginning of his booke. He calleth this puniſhment of *paine forte et dure* (the penance) becauſe it is the greateſt and moſt ſevere penance, and paine of all other, and ſo it is commonly called in our books.

CAP. XIII.

ET le roy defende, que nul ne raviſe ne preigne a force (1) damaſelle deins age (2), ne per ſon gree, ne ſans ſon gree, ne dame ne damaſelle de age, nauter feme mauger le ſoen. Et ſi ul le face, a le ſuit celuy que ſuera deins les 40 jours, le roy luy fra common droiture. Et ſi nul commence la ſuit deins les 40 jours, le roy ſuera, et ceux queux il trovera culpables, ils averont la priſonment de ii. ans, et puis ſerront rentes, a la volunt le roy, et ſils neient dont eſtre rentes, ſoient punies per plus longe priſonment, ſolonque ceo que le treſpaſſe demande.

AND the king prohibiteth that none do raviſh, nor take away by force, any maiden within age (neither by her own conſent, nor without) nor any wife or maiden of full age, nor any other woman againſt her will; and if any do, at his ſuit that will ſue within fourty days, the king ſhall do common right; and if none commence his ſuit within fourty days, the king ſhall ſue; and ſuch as be found culpable, ſhall have two years impriſonment, and after ſhall fine at the king's pleaſure; and if they have not whereof, they ſhall be puniſhed by longer impriſonment, according as the treſpaſs requireth.

Cap. Itineris. 155. 4 E. 1. Offic. Coronatoris. Vide Paſc. 6 E. 1. Rot. 4. in Banco Lanc. W. 2. 13 E. 1. ca. 34. 6 R. 2. ca. 6. 4 & 5 Ph. & Mar. ca. 18. 18 Eliz. c. 6. Regiſt. fo. 97. (22 Ed. 4. 22. 1 Inſt. 123. b. 2 Inſt. 180. 2 Rep. 37. Hob. 91. 13 Ed. 1. ſtat. 1. c. 34. 6 R. 2. c. 6.)

For the better underſtanding of this and other ſtatutes concerning rapes, it is firſt to be ſeene, what this word [rape] doth ſignifie, and ſecondly, what offence rape was at the common law before this ſtatute.

This is well deſcribed by the Mirror, *Rape ſolonque le volunt del* Mirror, ca. 1.
eſtatute eſt priſe pur un proper mote done pur cheſcun afforcement de fem, § 12.
de quelle condition q. el ſoit; but better in another place, rape is, See the firſt part
when a man hath carnall knowledge of a woman by force, and of the Inſtitutes,
againſt her will; and, as the Mirror ſaith, it is a proper word; and ſect. 190.
rapere to raviſh legally ſignifieth as much, as *carnaliter cognoſcere,* Third part Inſt. cap. Rape. 9 E. 4. 26.

and cannot be expressed in legall proceeding by other words, as elsewhere hath been said.

The offence is called *raptus*, and the offender *raptor*. This offence was felony at the common law, but had a punishment under such a condition as no other felony had the like, that I have read of; for first, divers of our auncient authors, that wrote before our statute, agree, that of old time rape was felony, for which the offender was to suffer death, but before this act the offence was made lesser, and the punishment changed, *viz.* from death, to the losse of the members whereby he offended, *viz.* his eyes, *propter aspectum decoris, quibus virginem concupivit. Amittit etiam testiculos, qui calorem stupri induxerunt*; so as it was no felony at the making of this act: and in those dayes if the offender in the appeale brought by her, that was ravished, had been condemned by the country, without any redemption he should lose his eyes and his privy members, unlesse she that was ravished before judgement demaunded him for her husband; for that was onely in the will of the woman and not of the man: for if (say they) it should have been in the will of the man, this inconvenience might have followed, that a ribaud, or a rascall slave might ravish a noble-woman, and by occasion of one shamefull pollution, perpetually to defile her, and to the dishonour of her house to take her to wife.

Glan. li. 1. c. 2. lib. 14. ca. 6. Mirror, c. 4. de homicide. Bracton, lib. 3. fo. 147. Brit. fo. 3. 7. 39. 45. Fleta, l. 1. c. 25. 33.

[181] But admit that the ravisher had been a nobleman, and the woman ravished base and ignoble, it might be thought that the like inconvenience might follow, if in that case the woman should have the election. *Responsio*; *quod sive vir nobilis, sive ignobilis sit, voluntas semper erit fœminæ, et electio*; *quia quod est in fœmina voluntarium, in viro erit necessarium, ut membra sua redimat ex necessitate: cum igitur mulier habeat electionem, et spreto judicio petit eum in virum, conceditur ei de gratia domini regis ob favorem matrimonii.*

Mirr. cap. 4. de homicide.

And herewith agreeth the Mirrour; that before the time of our king Edw. the 1. the punishment was by castration and putting out of the eyes of the offender, &c. but of ancient time at the common law it was death at the election of the single woman ravished.

Li. 2. controversiarum, contr' 5. and 24.

And that also was the law amongst the Romans, for Seneca saith, *Rapta raptoris aut mortem, aut indotatas nuptias optet*: upon which law there arose this case, *Una nocte quidam duas rapuit, altera mortem optat, altera nuptias*: there the case is largely and doubtfully disputed, which in our law would make but little question; for though the one for the offence done to her might take him to her husband, yet shall he suffer death according to the law for the offence done to the other.

Inter leges regis Canuti. Int. leges Aluredi regis.

Now let us heare what the law was herein before the conquest, *Qui viduam per vim stuprarit proprii capitis æstimatione compensato, nec mitiori conditione qui virgini vim intulerit. Qui per vim pagani hominis ancillam stuprarit, pagano sol' senos numerato, et 60 præterea sol' mulctator: servus autem si servulam stuprarit, virga virilis ei præciditor; qui teneræ ætatis virginem stuprarit, eadem lege tenetor, qua is qui adultam compresserit.*

See the 1. part of the Inst. sect. 190.

And if the lord had ravished his niefe or bondwoman, she might have had an appeale of rape against her lord, as at this day she may.

Bract. ubi supra, & li. 3. fo. 123.

And the punishment abovesaid, *viz.* the losse of the said members in such sort, as Bracton expressed the same, continued untill the

the making of this act; the purpoſe of which act was once againe to change the puniſhment, and yet to make it leſſer, that is, to make it puniſhable by fine and impriſonment at the kings ſuit, if ſhe purſued not her remedy within forty dayes, as by this act appeareth.

But it is not credible what ill ſucceſſe this act, that mitigated the former puniſhment, had; for many ill diſpoſed perſons taking upon this occaſion encouragement to follow the heat of luſt, did many ſhameleſſe and ſhamefull rapes in barbarous and inhumane manner: as taking one example for all, Warren de Henwicke raviſhed openly in the high way Matild the daughter of Syward de Warton, and after he came and deſired to have her to his wife, which was granted by the juſtices, and was affianced to her in open court. Hil. 6 E. 1. in com. banc. Rot. 4. Lanc'.

This crying ſin daily increaſing, our noble king, ten yeares after this act, made rape by authority of parliament felony, as by the ſtatute in that caſe provided, appeareth. W. 2. 13 E. 1. c. 34.

Now this that hath been ſaid doth agree with our books, and therefore it is *benedicta expoſitio*, when our ancient authors, and our yeare books, together with conſtant experience doe agree: for if rape had not been made felonie by the ſtatute of W. 2. but had been felony when that act was made, then ſhould the court of the leet have enquired of it, as of a felonie by the common law; but ſeeing it was made felonie by that ſtatute, it hath been often adjudged, that the leet cannot inquire thereof: for albeit it was once felonie, yet the nature of the offence being changed, as is aboveſaid, to be no felonie, when another act made it felonie againe, yet could not the leet enquire thereof, as of a felonie, which is worthy of obſervation. 18 E. 2. Stat. de viſu franc'. 9 E. 4. 26. 22 E. 4. 22. 1 R. 3. 1. 6 H. 7. 4. 11 H. 7. 22. Dier, 3 El. 201.

More ſhall be ſaid of rape in the treatiſe of the pleas of the crowne, and when we come to the ſaid ſtatute of W. 2. cap. 34.

(1) *Ne preigne a force.*] The taking away by force of a woman whatſoever * againſt her will, albeit there be no rape, &c. is generally prohibited by this act, upon the penalty herein expreſſed. Regiſt. fo. 97. 22 E. 4. 22. Raſt. pl. 496. Dier, 9 El. 256.

Deins age.] Here it ſhall be taken for her age of conſent, that is 12 yeares old, for that is her age of conſent to mariage; and the taking her away within that age, whether ſhe conſent or no, is prohibited by this act. Whereof, notwithſtanding all the aboveſaid ſtatutes, good uſe may be made, becauſe it is generall, and not bound with ſo many fetters as ſome of them be. See more hereof in the third part of the Inſtitutes, cap. Rape. * [182]

CAP. XIV.

ET pur ceo que home ad uſe en aſcun pays de utlager les gentes appeales de commandement (1), *force* (2), *aide* (3), *ou de receiptment* (4), *deins meſme la terme, que home doit utlager celuy que eſt appelle de fait: purview eſt et commaunde per le roy, que null' ne ſoit utlage*

AND foraſmuch as it hath been uſed in ſome counties to outlaw perſons being appealed of commandment, force, aid, or receipt within the ſame time that he which is appealed for the deed, is outlawed; it is provided and commanded by the king, that

utlage pur appele de commandement, force, aide, ou de receiptment, jesque a taunt que lappellee del fait (5) *soit attaint* (6), *issint que un mesme ley soit de ceo per tout la terre* (7), *mes celuy que voit appeller, ne lessa pas pur ceo de attacher son appele, al procheine countie* (8) *vers ceux, auxibien come vers les appelles du fait: mes lexigent de eux demurge* (9) *tanque les appellees de fait soient attaints per utlagarie, ou auterment.*

that none be outlawed upon appeal of commandment, force, aid, or receipt, until he that is appealed of the deed be attainted, so that one like law be used therein through the realm: nevertheless he that will so appeal, shall not, by reason of this, intermit or leave off to commence his appeal at the next county against them, no more than against their principals, which be appealed of the deed; but their exigent shall remain until such as be appealed of the deed be attainted by outlawry, or otherwise.

Utlage, utlagatus, exlex. Utlagaria, exlegalitas. Vide Lam. inter leges Ed. Confess. cap. 38. 3. Part of the Inst. ca. Appeals. Un mesme ley. (9 Rep. f. 119. Plowd. 97. 2 R. 3. 21. 9 H. 7. 19. 20 Ed. 4. 7. 7 H. 4. 36. Fitz. Coron. 10. 12. 33. Rast. pla. f. 42. 47, 48.)

3. Part of the Inst. ca. Principall et Acc.

Here are accessaries divided into two parts, *viz.* to accessaries before the fact, and to accessaries after the fact.

Againe, accessaries before the fact are divided into three branches: *De commandement, force, et aid*; accessaries after the fact is only by recitement.

(1) *Commandement.*] *Præceptum.* Under this is understood all those that incite, procure, set on, or stir up any other to doe the fact, and are not present when the fact is done.

(2) *Force.*] *Fortia,* is a word of art, and properly signifieth the furnishing of a weapon of force to doe the fact, and by force whereof the fact is committed, and he that furnisheth it is not present when the fact is done: for these two words, *præceptum, et fortia,* heare what Bracton saith, *Ubi factum nullum, ibi fortia nulla, nec præceptum nocere debet.* And againe, *Vulnus, fortia, et præceptum, generant unicum factum; non esset vulnus forte, si non adfuisset fortia; nec vulnus, nec fortia, nisi præceptum præcessisset:* and sometimes in a large sense is taken for any that is accessary before the fact.

Bract. li. 3. fo. 139. Britt. li. 5. b. Mirr. ca. 1. § 13. 40 ass. 25.

Fleta, li. 1. c. 23.

Et potest quis corporaliter occidi, facto, et lingua.

(3) *Aide.*] *Auxilium.* Under this word is comprehended all persons counselling, abetting, plotting, assenting, consenting, and encouraging to doe the act, and are not present when the act is done; for if the party commanding, furnishing with weapon, or aiding, be present when the act is done, then is he principall.

[183]

Brit. ubi supra.

(4) *Resceitment.*] This is understood after the fact done, that is, when one knowing the felonie doth receive the felon, and not onely conceale his offence, but favour and aid him, that he be not knowne.

In the preamble the mischiefe is recited, that before this act in some countries it had been used to outlaw accessaries within the same time, that the principall was outlawed. Here it is to be understood, that in those dayes most appeals of death, &c. were sued by bill in the county before the coroner, in which bill of appeale the appellant doth make a distinction betweene the principall and the accessary. And therefore this act is intended of appeales commenced

43 E. 3. 17. 18. 34.

commenced by bill, for in the appeale by originall writ, both principalls and accessaries are generally charged alike, without any distinction, who be principalls, and who be accessaries, untill the plaintife maketh his counte, and therein he must distinguish them; but if the defendants in such an appeale, where some be principals, and some accessaries, make default, the appellant before the exigent ought to declare, to the end it may be knowne who be principals, and who be accessaries, and to take the exigent onely against the principals, and continue the plea against the accessaries, untill the principals be attainted; for if the plaintife should pray an exigent against them all, he is concluded afterward to charge any of them as accessaries. The difference between an appeal by bill and by writ. 7 H. 4. 31. Nota. Declare before any appearance.

This act was made in affirmance of the common law, and it doth not hold onely in appeals at the suit of the party, but in indictments also at the suit of the king: for it is an ancient and fundamentall maxime of the common law, *juri non est consonum, quod aliquis accessorius in curia regis convincatur, antequam aliquis de facto fuer' attinctus*: yet if the accessary will, he may pray proces against the enquest before the principall be attainted, for *quilibet potest renunciare juri pro se introducto*. *Regula.*

(5) *Jesque lappellee del fait soit attaint.*] If the principall wage battaile, and is slaine in the field, yet he is not attainted, but the judgement must be, that he was vanquished in the field, *Ideo consideratum, quod sus' per coll'*, &c. And this was agreed by the justices, for otherwise in this case the lord should have no escheat, nor any outlawrie could be sued by the appellant against the accessarie. 8 E. 3. judgm. 225. 3. part of the Instit. Hic cap. 14. fo. 353.

Our act speaketh *appellee* in the singular number; yet in an appeale brought against two as principals, and against another as accessarie to them, in this case both of them must be attainted before the accessary be outlawed; and if one of the principals be found not guilty, the accessarie is discharged, for the plaintife made him accessary to two, and therefore he cannot be found accessary to one. But where there be divers principals, the appellant may have his appeale against any one of them, and make the accessary accessary to him only, if he will, for the felonie is severall, but the appellant cannot have severall appeals of one death. 40 ass. 25. 7 H. 4. 30. Pl. com. 99. Li. 4. fo. 47. Waits case, & fo. 44, 45. Vaux case.

In case of poysoning, albeit the delinquent be not present when the poison is received, yet is he principall, and so the principall and accessarie may be both absent. Vaux case, ubi supra.

It is to be observed, that in the highest offence, and lowest injury, there are no accessaries, but all be principals; as in treason, petit larcenie, and trespasse.

And in one case of felonie all be principals as well before as after, though they be absent at the doing of the felonie; but that is specially provided by the statute of 3 H. 7. cap. 2. of taking of women against their wils, &c. 3 H. 7. cap. 2. 2 E. 3. 27. 5 lib. ass. 5. 13 ass. 14. 22 E. 3. coro. 260. 7 H. 4. 16. 36. 10 H. 4. 5. 11 H. 4. 93. 3 H. 7. 1. 3 H. 7. coron. 53. 4 E. 6. coron. Br. 184. Li. 4. fo. 43, 44. Eyres case, & Bibithes case.

(6) *Soit attaint.*] That is, have judgement in case of felonie for the felonie; for if the principall be convict by verdict, and prayeth his clergie; or if the principall upon his arraignment confesse the felonie, and before judgement obtaine a pardon, the accessarie is thereby discharged, because the principall was never attainted, as our statute speaketh; and so it is if the principall * die before judgement, or upon his arraignment stand mute. And these cases have been according to this declaratorie act well resolved, wherein there had been great variety of opinions. * [184]

 If

2 R. 3. fo. 21, 22. If the principall be erroniouſly attainted, yet this erronious attainder is within this act, for the acceſſary ſhall not take advantage of the error, but the principall onely.

And note, that the attainder of the principall muſt be in the ſame ſuit where the acceſſary is alſo to be put to anſwer; and therefore if the principall be attainted of murder at the kings ſuit, and after the wife bring an appeale againſt the principall and acceſſary, the principall plead the former attainder, the acceſſary ſhall not be put to anſwer, and yet the principall is attainted. 7 H. 4. 47. 9 H. 7. 19. b.

40 aſſ. p. 8. 7 H. 4. 30. 9 H. 4. 2. Li. 9. fo. 19. Seig. Zanchars caſe. The experience and courſe at this day is, and warranted by good authority and reaſon, that if the principall plead not guilty, the acceſſary ſhall plead not guilty alſo, and may be tryed by one inqueſt; but the charge of the jury is, that if they find the principall not guilty, they ſhall find the acceſſary not guilty alſo; and this is for advancement of juſtice; for if there were no procurers before, nor any receivers after, there would be fewer principals.

9 H. 7. 19. But if the principall plead not directly to the felonie a plea to bar the plaintife, as *auterfoits attaint*, or *unques accouple*, or the like; there the acceſſary ſhall not plead untill that plea be determined: and ſo if the principall plead a plea to the writ, the acceſſary ſhall not be driven to anſwer untill the plea be determined. 50 E. 3. 15, 16.

For this word [attaint] and of attainders in deed and in law, ſee the firſt part of the Inſtitutes, ſect. 747.

(7) *Iſſint que un meſme ley ſoit de ceo per tout la terre.*] This is the honour of the law, when all the courts of juſtice through the whole land, in all caſes pronounce the law *tanquam uno ore*, which this branch doth aime at in this particular caſe, and ought to be obſerved in all other caſes; *lex uno ore omnes alloquitur*.

(8) *Dattacher ſon appeale al procheine countie.*] That is, to commence his appeale before the coroner at the next countie.

Raſt. pl. 42. 47, 48. (9) *Lexigent de eux demurge*, &c.] So much hath been ſaid as may ſerve for the expoſition of this act, the reſidue ſhall be handled in the treatiſe of the pleas of the crowne. See the third part of the Inſtit. *ubi ſupra*.

CAP. XV.

ET pur ceo que viſcounts, et auters (1), queux ount priſes et retenus en priſon gents retties de felonie (2) [et] meint foits ount leſſe per replevin les gents, queux ne ſont my repleviſables, et ont detenus en priſon ceux queux ſont repleviſables, per encheſon de gaign' des uns, et de grever les auters, et pur ceo que avant ces heures ne fuit my determine (3) [certainment] queux gentes fuiſſent repleviſables (4), et queux non, forſpris ceux queux fuiſſent priſes (5), pur mort de home (6), ou per commandement le roy (7), ou de les juſtices (8), ou

AND foraſmuch as ſheriffs, and other, which have taken and kept in priſon perſons detected of felony, and incontinent have let out by replevin ſuch as were not repleviſable, and have kept in priſon ſuch as were repleviſable, becauſe they would gain of the one party, and grieve the other; and foraſmuch as before this time it was not determined which perſons were repleviſable, and which not, but only thoſe that were taken for the death of man, or by commandment of the king, or of his juſtices, or for the foreſt;

ou pur la foreſt (9): *purview eſt, et per le roy commande, que les priſoners queux ſont avant utlages* (10), *et ceux queux eyent forjure la terre* (11), *provours* (12), *et ceux queux ſont priſes ove mainer* (13), *et ceux queux ount debruſe la priſon le roy* (14), *larons apertment eſcries et notories* (15), *et ceux que ſont appelles des provours tanque come les provours ſont en vie (ſils ne ſoient de bone fame)* (16) *et ceux queux ſont priſes pur arſon feloniouſment fait* (17), *ou pur faux money* (18), *ou fauxer le ſeale le roy* (19), *ou excommenge priſe per prier' leveſque* (20), *ou pur appiert melveiſt* (21), *ou pur treaſon que touche le roy* (22) *meſme, ne ſoient en nul maner repleviſables per le common briefe, ne ſans briefe* (23): *mes ceux queux ſont endites de larceny* (24), *per enqueſts des viſconts, ou des bailifes* (25) *priſes de lour offices, ou per legier ſuſpection, ou pur petit larceny, que namount ouſter le value de xii. deniers, ſils ne ſoient rettes dauter larceny devant cel heure, ou rettes de receiptment des larons, ou des felons, ou de commaundement, ou de la force, ou del aide de le felony fait, ou rettes dauter treſpaſſe, pur le quel un ne doit perdre vie ne member, et home appell' de provour puis la mort le provour, ſil ne ſoit apert laron eſcrie, ſoit deſormes leſſe per ſuffiſant plevin, devant le vicont* (26), *dont le vicont voile reſpondre* (27), *et ceo ſans rien doner* (28) *de lour biens pur la plevin. Et ſi le vicont ou auter leſſent per plevin ul', que ne ſoit repleviſable* (29), *ſi ceo ſoit vicount, conſtable, ou auter bailiſe de fee que eit gard de priſons* (30), *et de ceo ſoit attaint, perdr' le fee et baillie a touts jours. Et ſi ſoit ſouth-vicount* (31), *conſtable, ou bailiſe, ou celuy que ad tiel fee pur garder les priſons, et ait ceo fait ſans la volunt ſon ſeignior, ou auter bailiſe que ne ſoit de fee, eit lenpriſonment de 3. ans, et ſoit rent a le volunt le roy. Et ſi ul' deteigne les priſoners repleviſables, puis que le priſoner eit offre ſuffiſant ſuerty, il*

foreſt; it is provided, and by the king commanded, that ſuch priſoners as before were outlawed, and they which have abjured the realm, provors, and ſuch as be taken with the manour, and thoſe which have broken the king's priſon, thieves openly defamed and known, and ſuch as be appealed by provors, ſo long as the provors be living (if they be not of good name) and ſuch as be taken for houſe-burning feloniouſly done, or for falſe money, or for counterfeiting the king's ſeal, or perſons excommunicate, taken at the requeſt of the biſhop, or for manifeſt offences, or for treaſon touching the king himſelf, ſhall be in no wiſe repleviſable by the common writ, nor without writ: but ſuch as be indicted of larceny, by enqueſts taken before ſheriffs or bailiffs by their office, or of light ſuſpicion, or for petty larceny that amounteth not above the value of xii d. if they were not guilty of ſome other larceny aforetime, or guilty of receipt of felons, or of commandment, or force, or of aid in felony done; or guilty of ſome other treſpaſs, for which one ought not to loſe life nor member, and a man appealed by a provor after the death of the provor (if he be no common thief, nor defamed) ſhall from henceforth be let out by ſufficient ſurety, whereof the ſheriff will be anſwerable, and that without giving ought of their goods. And if the ſheriff, or any other, let any go at large by ſurety, that is not repleviſable, if he be ſheriff or conſtable or any other bailiff of fee, which hath keeping of priſons, and thereof be attainted, he ſhall loſe his fee and office for ever. And if the under-ſheriff, conſtable, or bailiff of ſuch as have fee for keeping of priſons, do it contrary to the will of his lord, or any other bailiff being not of fee, they ſhall have three years impriſonment, and make fine at the king's pleaſure. And if any

il serra en le greve mercy le roy (32). *Et s'il prent loure pur luy deliverer* (33), *il rendra le double au prisoner, et ensement serra en le greve mercy le roy.* De Finibus levatis. 27 E. 1. cap. 13.

any with-hold prisoners replevisable, after that they have offered sufficient surety, he shall pay a grievous amerciament to the king; and if he take any reward for the deliverance of such, he shall pay double to the prisoner, and also shall be in the great mercy of the king.

Cap. Itin. Vet. Mag. Char. 155. 27 E. 1. cap. 3. 23 H. 6. cap. 10. Pl. com. 67. (1 Roll, 134. 192. 268. Bro. Mainprise, 11. 56. 78. Fitz. Mainprise, 1. 39, 40. Bro. Mainprise, 54. 57. 59, 60. 75. 78. 91. 11 Rep. 29. Bro. Main. 6. 9. 19. 22. 30. 48. 50, 51. 53. 58. 63, 64. 73. 91. 94. 97. 2 Bulstr. 328. 3 Bulstr. 113. 27 Ed. 1. stat. 1. c. 3. 3 H. 7. c. 3. 1 & 2 Ph. & M. c. 13.)

(1) *Viscounts et autres.*] That is to say, sheriffes and gaolers that have custody of gaoles, so as this act extends not to any of the kings justices, or judges of any superiour courts of justice; first, for that they being superiours are not comprehended in the generall words, as often have been observed. 2. *Queux ount prises ou reteynus prisoners*, which judges doe not. 3. Because in those dayes prisoners were commonly bailed by the kings writ *de homine repleg'*, and then also by the writ *de odio et atia*, both which were directed to the sheriffe.

[186] Lib. 2. fol. 46. Marleb. c. 19. 28.

And here it is proved, that it is an offence as well to baile a man not bailable, as to deny a man baile, that ought to be bailed; and the reason is yeelded wherefore the sheriffes and others did so offend, because they would gaine of the one, and grieve the other, *viz.* either for avarice, or for malice.

Brit. fol. 34. b.

(2) *Gents rets de felony.*] In those dayes felony comprehended in it as well treason (as in this chapter it appeareth) as homicide, rape, or burglary, robbery, arsons, and all larcenies and thefts; for the word and signification, see the first part of the Institutes, sect. 745.

For the word replevisable, see Marleb. cap. 28. Stamf. Pl. Cor. 72. Regist. 77.

(3) *Avant ces heures ne fuit determine, &c.*] Here is another mischiefe recited, that it was not certainly determined, what people were replevisable, and what not, within the generall words of the writ *de homine repleg'*, *viz. Pro aliquo alio retto, quare secundum consuetudinem regni non sunt replegiabiles.*

(4) *Et queux homes fuer' replevisables.*] This word [replevisable] proveth, that this act intendeth what persons were to be replevied by the common writ *de homine replegiando*, which was directed to the sheriffe under whose custody the prisoners are, and of whom this act speaketh, and so it appeareth by the Register: and replevy, or plevy is applied to the sheriffe to take pledges, and baile to the highest courts of record. And the writ *de manucaptione* directed to the sheriffe is grounded upon this act, in which writ not onely *replegiar'* but *manucapere* also is used.

Marlb. ca. 28. Regist. F.N.B. 249.

(5) *Forspris ceux queux fuer' prises pur mort de home.*] Here our act first setteth downe what persons were not baileable for certain offences by the common writ *de homine repleg'*, and they be in number foure. But by the auncient law of the land in all cases of felony, if the party accused could finde sufficient sureties, he was not to be committed to prison, *quia carcer est mala mansio*; but afterwards it was provided by parliament that in case of homicide

Regist. 77. & 133. Brac. l. 3. 121. 154. Fleta, lib. 2. cap. 2. Britton, fo. 73. Hil. 43 E. 3. Coram Rege. Rot. 110.

micide the offender was not bailable, for ſo Glanvill ſaith, *In omnibus autem placitis de felonia ſolet accuſatus per plegios dimitti, praeterquam in placito de homicidio, ubi ad terrorem aliter ſtatutum eſt.* Glanv. l. 14. c. 1. 3. Bract. l. 3. fo. 123.

(6) *Pur mort de home.*] The death of man is ſo odious in law, that, (as is aboveſaid) by the common writ *de homine repleg'*, neither principall nor acceſſary was repleviſable. 25 E. 3. 42. 28 E. 3. 94. 40 E. 3. 42. 44 E. 3. 38.

(7) *Per maundement le roy.*] *Per praeceptum regis.* 43 E. 3. 17.

1. [a] The king being a body politique cannot command but by matter of record, for *rex praecipit, et lex praecipit* are all one, for the king muſt command by matter of record according to the law. 29 Aſſ. 44. 37. 12. 43 Aſſ. 49. 41 Aſſ. 14. 7 H. 4. 27. 21 E. 4. 84. F.N.B. 250. b.

2. [b] When any judiciall act is by any act of parliament referred to the king, it is underſtood to be done in ſome court of juſtice according to the law. And the opinion of Gaſcoine chiefe juſtice is notable in this point, that the king hath committed all his power judiciall to divers courts, ſome in one court, ſome in another, &c. And becauſe ſome courts, as the kings bench, are *coram rege*, and ſome *coram juſticiariis*, therefore the act ſaith, *per maundement le roy*, and the next words be, *ou de ſes juſtices.* a Pl. Com. 234. Seign. Berkleyes caſe. & 217. le Duchy caſe. Stamf. Pl. Cor. 72, 73. b See before c. 4. 2 R. 3. fol. 11.

Huſſey chiefe juſtice reported, that ſir John Markham ſaid to king E. 1. that the king could not arreſt any man for ſuſpition of treaſon, or felony, as any of * his ſubjects might, becauſe if the king did wrong, the party could not have his action: if the king commaund me to arreſt a man, and accordingly I doe arreſt him, he ſhal have his action of falſe impriſonment againſt me, albeit he was in the kings preſence; reſolved by the whole court in 16 H. 6. which authority might be a good warrant for Markham to deliver his ſaid opinion to E. 4. 1 H. 7. 4. See hereafter at this mark †. Paſch. 18 E. 3. Coram Rege. Rot. 33. Jo. de Bildeſtons caſe. optime. 16 H. 6. tit. Monſtrans des faits 182. Stamf. Pl. Cor. 72. e.

The words of the ſtatute of 1 R. 2. cap. 12. are, *Si non que il ſoit per brieſe ou auter maundement le roy*; and it was reſolved by all the judges of England, that the king cannot doe it by any commandement, but by writ, or by order, or rule of ſome of his courts of juſtice, where the cauſe dependeth, according to law. Dier 4 & 5. Ph. & Mar. 162. b. 10 Eliz. 275. Mich. 12 & 13 Eliz. 297.

Dominus rex de aliquo contemptu ſibi illato, alium judicem in regno, quam in curia ſua, habere non debet. Vide Marleb. cap. 1. Tr. 21 E. 3. Norf. Coram Rege. Rot. 170. Marlb. cap. 1.

And Forteſcue ſpeaking to the prince to inſtruct him againſt he ſhould be king, ſaith, *Melius enim per alios, quam per teipſum judicia reddes, quo, proprio ore nullus regum Angliae uſus eſt, et tamen ſua ſunt omnia judicia regni, licet per alios ipſa reddantur, ſicut et judicum olim ſententias Joſaphat aſſeruit eſſe judicia Dei.* Forteſc. cap. 8. *[187]

And Bracton ſaith, *Nihil aliud poteſt rex, &c. quam quod de jure poteſt.*

So, as, *maundement le roy* is as much as to ſay (as ſome affirme) as by the kings court of juſtice; * for all matters of judicature, and proceedings in law are diſtributed to the courts of juſtice, and the king doth judge by his juſtices, 8 H. 4. fol. 19. & 24 H. 8. cap. 12. and regularly no man ought to be attached by his body, but either by proces of law, that is (as hath beene ſaid) by the kings writs, or by indictment, or lawfull warrant, as by many acts of parliament is manifeſtly enacted and declared, which are but expoſitions of *Magna Charta*; and all ſtatutes made contrary to *Magna Charta*, which is *lex terrae*, from the making thereof untill 42 E. 3. are declared and enacted to be void, and therefore if this act of W. 1. concerning the extrajudiciall commandement of the king be againſt *Magna Charta*, it is void, and all reſolutions of Mag. Char. c. 29. 5 E. 3. c 9 28 E. 3. ca. 3. 38 E. 3. ca. 9. 42 E. 3. c. 3. 2 E. 3. fo. 2 & 3. See Mag. Chart. ca. 29. verb. per legem terrae. * 8 H. 4. 19 Gaſc. & 24 H. 8. ca. 12. 42 E. 3. ca. 1.

judges concerning ths commandement of the king are to be understood of judiciall proceeding.

Britton, fo. 73. 2 R. 3. 11. (8) *Ou de les justices,*] Upon any cause, whereof they are judges, appearing to them.

1 E. 3. ca. 9. (9) *Ou par la forest.*] And all these foure are particularly excepted out of the common writ *de homine replegiando*, that the sheriffe in his county court, which is not a court of record, shall not replevy any of these foure that are committed; for example, though the party be committed by the personall commandement of the king, albeit the commitment be unlawfull, yet the sheriffe shall not deal therein by the writ *de homine replegiando*, but the superiour courts at Westm. upon a *habeas corpus*, &c. shall doe justice to the party in all those foure causes; so as Stamford, being well considered, impugneth not in any sort this opinion, for his opinion extendeth only to the county court upon the writ *de homine replegiando*, and not to the superiour courts.

But since we had written thus much, and passed over; see the Petition of Right, *anno* 3 *Caroli regis*, resolved by the king, the lords spirituall, and temporall, and the commons in full parliament.

Now this act doth provide, that these prisoners hereafter following shall not be replevisable neither by the common writ (that is the writ *de homine repleg'*, nor *ex officio* (without writ) by the sheriffe or other gaoler, and they be 13 in number, and all these 13 are excepted out of the said common writ by the said generall words, *viz. Vel pro aliquo alio retto, quare secundum consuetudinem regni non sunt replegiabiles.*

Bract. l. 3. 154. 2 Eliz. Dier 179. 15 H. 7. 9. Britton, fol. 73. *[188] (10) 1. *Persons utlages.*] Persons outlawed are attainted in law, and therefore * are not replevisable or to be bailed: for if a man be arraigned of homicide, and plead not-guilty, and is found guilty, and for difficulty of clergy is reprieved, it was resolved by the justices, that he was not bailable, for the intendment of the law in bails is, *Quod stat indifferenter*, whether he be guilty or no; but when he is convict by verdict or confession, then he must be deemed in law to be guilty of the felony, and therefore not bailable at all, *à fortiori*, when the party is attainted in law.

Bract. l. 3. 121. b. 5 H. 7. 14. 9 H. 6. fo. 2. And herewith agreeth Bracton, *Nec sunt illi qui culpabiles inveniuntur, per plegios dimittendi*, &c. And yet if the party upon the *cap. utlag'* plead misnomer, or alledge error, &c. he may be bailed.

(11) 2. *Queux eient forjure.*] They be also attainted upon their owne confession, and therefore not bailable at all by law.

Brac. l. 3. fo. 153. b. (12) 3. *Provours.*] The reason wherefore provours or approvours be not bailable is, for provours doe first confesse the felony to be done by themselves, and therefore they are not bailable, because it appeareth that they be guilty of the fact.

(13) 4. *Ceux queux sont prises ove le mainer.*] For in this case *non stat indifferenter*, as hath been said, whether he be guilty or no, being taken with the mainer, that is with the thing stolne, as it were

Bract. li. 3. fo. 154. Brit. fo 22. b. & 72. b. in his hand, auncientl y called handhabbend; the like is auncientl y called backberend, as a bundle or fardle at his back, which Bracton useth for manifest theft, *furtum manifestum*, and so doth Britton.

Bract. l. 3. 153. b. (14) 5. *Ceux queux ont debruse la prison le roy.*] Here be two offences: 1. His breaking of the prison; for it is presumed, that he

he that is innocent will never break priſon: and 2. his flying *Quia fatetur facinus, qui judicium fugit.*

(15) 6. *Larons apertment eſcries et notories.*] Felons openly known and notorious are not bailable. 16 E. 4. 5.

(16) 7. *Ceux queux ſont appelles des provours tanque come les provours ſont en vie (ſilz ne ſoient de bone fame.)*] The appeale of the approver is forcible againſt the appellee, becauſe the approver confeſſeth himſelfe guilty of the ſame felony, and therefore it ſerveth in nature of an indictment againſt the appellee, ſo long as the approver liveth, unleſſe the appellee be of good fame. But yet the generall words doe receive qualification, for albeit the prover be alive, yet if the approver waive his appeale, the appellee ſhall bee bailed, if no other appeale bee againſt him. 25 E. 3. 42.

(17) 8. *Ceux queux ſont priſes pur arſon, feloniouſment fait.*] Burning of houſes, &c. was felony by the common law, as it appeareth by this act, and by our auncient authors, *viz.* Glanvill, the Mirror, Bracton, Britton: and Fleta ſaith, *Si quis ædes alienas nequiter et ob inimicitiam vel prædæ cauſa tempore pacis combuſſerit, et inde convictus fuerit, &c. capitali debet ſententia puniri.* And this ſeemeth to be the law before the conqueſt: [a] *Incendiariis capitis pœna eſto.* And againe, [b] *Sanè quidem tectorum exciſiones et incendia, apertæ compilationes, cædes manifeſtæ, dominorumque proditores ſcelera ſunt jure humano inexpiabilia.* Lib. 11. fo. 29. Alex. Powtlers caſe. Glanv. li. 14. & 1. cap. 2. Mirror, ca. 1. § 8. De Ardours. Bract. l. 3. fo. 118. Brit. fo. 16. 39. Fleta, li. 1. c. 35. 10 E. 4. 14. 11 H. 7. 1.

(18) 9. *Ou pur faux money.*] This appeares to be treaſon by the common law. Glanvill, lib. 14. cap. 7. Bracton, lib. 3. fo. 118. Britton, fol. 16. Fleta, lib. 1. cap. 22. Mirror, cap. 6.

[a] Inter leges Ethelſtani.

[189]

Præterea autem ſtatuimus, ut unus per omnem ditionem noſtram atque idem ſit nummus, eumque nemo extra oppidum cudito, atqui ſi monetariorum quiſq; nummos corruperit, ei manus ſcelere violata præciditor. See the third part of the Inſtitutes, in the expoſition upon the ſtatute of 25 E. 3. c. 1. of Treaſon.

[b] Int' leges Canuti.

Int. leges Ethelſtani regis.

(19) 10. *Ou fauxer le ſeale le roy.*] This was alſo treaſon by the common law, as it appeareth by the ſaid ancient authors.

And both theſe were declared to be high treaſon at the common law, by the ſtatute of 25 E. 3. cap. 1. See more hereof in the third part of the Inſtit. *ubi ſupra.*

(20) 11. *Ou excommenge priſe per prier del eveſque.*] That is, he that is certified into the chancery by the biſhop to be excommunicated, and after is taken by force of the kings writ of *excommunicato capiendo* (which is ſo called of words in the writ called a *Significavit*) is not baileable, for in ancient time men were excommunicated but for hereſies, *propter lepram animæ*, or other hainous cauſes of eccleſiaſticall conuſance, and not for ſmall or petie cauſes; and therefore in thoſe caſes the partie was not baileable by the ſheriffe, or gaoler without the kings writ: but if the party offered ſufficient caution *de parendo mandatis eccleſiæ in forma juris*, then ſhould the party have the kings writ to the biſhop to accept his caution, and to cauſe him to be delivered. And if the biſhop will not ſend to the ſheriffe to deliver him, then ſhall he have a writ out of the chancery to the ſheriffe for his delivery: or if he be excommunicated for a temporall cauſe, or for a matter whereof the eccleſiaſticall court hath no conuſaunce, he ſhall be delivered by the kings writ without any ſatisfaction. Bract. l. 5. f. 408, 409. Flet. li. 6. cap. 44. Regiſt. F.N.B. 63. &c. Doct. & Stud. li. 2. cap. 32.

(21) 12. *Ou pur apert malveiſt.*] Or for open or manifeſt offences.

fences. For, as hath beene said, baile is *quando stat indifferenter*, and not when the offence is open and manifest.

Brit. fo. 73. (22) 13. *Ou pur treason que touche le roy.*] Britton, who wrote after this statute, saith, *Queux son replevisables, et queux non, avons dit in nous statutes. Et ouster ceo ne sont my replevisables endites ou appeales de compassement de nostre mort, sicome desuis est dit, ne ceux que sont prises per judgement de nous justices, &c.*

For by the common law a man accused or indicted of high treason, or of any felonie whatsoever, was bayleable upon good surety; for at the common law the gaole was his pledge or surety that could find none. And this appeareth by Glanvill, who saith, *Is qui accusatur, ut prædiximus, per plegios salvos et securos solet attachiari, aut si plegios non habuerit, in carcerem detrudi:* so as a man by the common law was baileable for any offence, untill he were convicted: and this seemeth to be the old law of the land before the conquest, *viz. Ingenuus quisque fidejussores, qui enim (si quando in crimen vocetur (jus suum cuique tribuere quam paratissimum fore præstent, fidissimos adhibeto.*

Glanv. li. 14 c. 1. & 3. 40 ass. p. 33.

Int. leges Etheldred. regis.

(23) *Ne soient in nul manner replevisables per le common briefe, ne sauns briefe.*] That is, the sheriffe shall not replevie them by the common writ *de homine replegiando*, nor without writ, that is, *ex officio:* but all or any of these may be bailed in the kings bench, &c.

(24) *Mes ceux queux sont endites de larcenie.*] *Latrocinium, larcinium, i. furtum,* theft: and this act divideth larcenie into two kinds: *sc.* grand and petit; grand larcenie is when the thing stolne is above the value of xii. d. *ouster le value de xii. d.* as our act speaketh: and petit larcenie is when it is of the value of xii. d. or under. And the things stolne are to be reasonably valued, for the ounce of silver at the making of this act was at the value of
[190] xx. d. and now it is of the value of v. s. and above.

Regist. 269. Flet. li. 1. c. 36. Bract. lib. 3. fo. 150, 151. Britt. fo. 22. 45. Fortescue ca. 46. 8 E. 2. coro. 404, 406. 415. 18 ass. 14. 22 ass. p. 39. Tr. 21 E. 3. Coram rege Rot. 42. 10 E. 4. 14.

Est enim furtum de re magna, et re parva: pro minimo tamen latrocinio 12. denariorum, et infra, nullus morte condemnetur, &c. ex pluralitate tamen et cumulo modicorum delictorum poterit capitalis sententia generari: And this is good law at this day, and approved by many authorities.

(25) *Per enquests des viscounts ou des bailiffes,* &c.] That is, of sheriffes in their tournes, or lords in their leets, or those that have infangthiefe and outfangthiefe, &c.

Here our act setteth downe seaven kinds of offenders that may be bailed.

1. Persons indicted of larceny before the sheriffe, &c. yet this
Regist. 83. 268. is so expounded by the Register, that they be of good fame.

2. Imprisoned for light suspicion. Here is added also, *dum tamen bonæ famæ sunt.*

3. For petit larceny, which doth not amount above the value of xii. d. if they be not charged with other larceny.

Regist ubi sup. F.N.B. 249, 250.

4. Accused for the receiving of thieves or felons.

5. Or of commandement, force, or aid of the felonie done.

6. Or accused for other trespasse, for which a man ought not to lose life or member.

Regist. ubi sup. F.N.B. ubi sup.

7. Or the appellee of an approver after the death of the approver; and upon our act is the writ *de manucaptione* grounded, which maketh mention thereof.

(26) Soit

(26) *Soit deſormes leſſé per ſuffiſant plevin devant le viſcount.*] That is to be underſtood where the indictment was taken before the ſheriffe in his tourne, for there he was judge of the cauſe, for other priſoners could not be bayle without writ: and if the ſheriffe having ſufficient ſurety offered unto him, refuſed to bayle him, he ſhould have a writ *de manucaptione* directed to the ſheriffe to take pledges of him; and if the bailiffe of a hundred (which is intended of a ſteward in a leet) refuſed to take pledges of one indicted before him, the priſoner ſhould have had a writ *de manucaptione* to the ſheriffe to take pledges of him; and all this appeareth by the writ *de manucaptione*. But ſince this time (to ſpeak once for all) this writ of *manucaptione* is taken away by the ſtatute of 28 E. 3.

Bract. li. 3. fo. 154. Regiſt. 83. 268. 291. F.N.B. 249, 250. F.N.B. ubi ſup.

The ſtatute of 1 & 2 Phil. & Mar. concerning baylement by juſtices of peace, hath relation to our act, which hath made me the longer in explaining hereof. And ſee the ſtatute of 2 & 3 Phil. & Mar. concerning that matter.

1 & 2 Ph. & M. c. 13. 2 & 3 P. & M. ca. 10.

(27) *Per ſufficient plevin dont le viſcount voille reſponder.*] They which take pledges, ought to take ſufficient pledges, for which they will anſwer.

Vide ca. 10. & 26.

(28) *Et ceo ſans riens doner.*] For neither the ſheriffe, nor other of the kings officers could take any thing for doing his office. *Vide* cap. 26.

(29) *Et ſi le viſcount ou auter leſſent per plevin ul que ne ſoit plevìſablè.*] *Ou auter.* This is expounded by the words following.

(30) *Si ceo ſoit viſcount, conſtable, ou auter bailiſe de fee que eit gard de priſoners.*] So as at this time there were ſheriffewickes in fee, and conſtables and bailiwicks in fee, which had the keeping of priſons: theſe being attainted of letting to baile of any priſoner not baileable, ſhould loſe the fee and bayliwicke for ever: and upon office found, the king ſhould have the inheritance of the office in him to be grantable over.

(31) *Et ſi ſoit ſouth viſcount,* &c.] Here it appeareth, that under-ſheriffes are of greater antiquity, then ſome have ſurmiſed. [191]

Note, the act of the under-ſheriffe or other under baylie without the aſſent of his ſuperiour is no forfeiture of the fee, or bayliwick of his ſuperiour, though in many other caſes the ſuperiour ſhall anſwer for his deputie.

39 H. 6. 32. For this ſee the ſtat. of 26 E. 1. intituled, *Contra Vic' & Clericos.*

(32) *Et ſil deteine les priſoners replevìſables puis que le priſoner eit offre ſuffiſant ſuretie, il ſerra en le greve mercy le roy.*] Here it appeareth, that to deny a man plevin that is plevìſable, and thereby to detaine him in priſon, is a great offence, and grievouſly to be puniſhed.

Vet. Mag. Chart. 159, 160. Vet. N.B. fo. 40.

(33) *Et ſi il priſt louer pur luy deliverer.*] And if the ſheriffe, &c. take any reward for his deliverance, the party ſhall recover double the value, and alſo he ſhall be in the great mercy of the king. *Vide* cap. 26.

There be many ſtatutes made ſince our act, that doe prohibite baile or mainpriſe in very many caſes, and alloweth the ſame in many other, which tend not to the expoſition of our act, and doe belong to another treatiſe, and therefore we omit to ſpeak of them any farther in this place.

See the ſtatute of 1 E. 4. cap. 2. that upon all preſentments and indictments taken before any ſheriffe or other in their tournes, leets,

2 E. 4. ca. 2.

leets, or law-dayes, they ſhall have no power to attach, arreſt, or put in priſon any perſon ſo preſented or indicted, but that the ſheriffe ſhall deliver all ſuch preſentments and indictments to the juſtices of peace at their next ſeſſions.

CAP. XVI.

EN droit de ceo que aſcun gents parnount, et prendre fount les avers des auters, et les chaſent hors del countie ou les avers fueront priſes: purview eſt, que nul deſormes ne le face. Et ſi ul le face, ſoit grevement rente ſolonque ceo que eſt contenue en les eſtatutes de Marleb. cap. 4. *faits en temps le roy H. pier le roy que ore eſt. Et per meſme le maner ſoit faits de ceux, queux parnont les avers a tort, et queux font diſtres en auter fee, plus grevement ſoient punies, ſi le maner de treſpas le demaund.*

IN right thereof, that ſome perſons take, and cauſe to be taken, the beaſts of other, chaſing them out of the ſhire where the beaſts were taken; it is provided alſo, that none from henceforth do ſo; and if any do, he ſhall make a grievous fine, as is contained in the ſtatute of Marlebridge, made in the time of king Henry, father to the king that now is. And likewiſe it ſhall be done to them which take beaſts wrongfully, and diſtrain out of their fee, and ſhall be more grievouſly puniſhed, if the manner of the treſpaſs do ſo require.

Vide Flet. lib. 2. c. 40. 30 aſſ. 28. (1 H. 5. 3. 7 H. 7. f. 1. 52 H. 3. c. 4. 1 & 2 Ph. & M. c. 12. Regiſt. 183.)

This ſtatute conſiſteth upon two branches: the firſt is a confirmation of the ſtatute of Marlebridge, cap. 4. and the ſecond branch is a confirmation of the ſtatute of Marlebridge, cap. 2. & 15. where you may reade the expoſition of them: Onely theſe differences I obſerve betweene them, that Marlebridge, ca. 4. ſpeaketh onely of diſtreſſes, and our act ſpeaketh of all manner of takings. Marlebridge prohibiteth diſtreſſes generally; our act, of beaſts, and goeth no farther. Marlebridge ſpeaketh of diſtreſſes which he hath taken; our act which he hath taken, or cauſed to be taken. Marlebridge, cap. 15. excepteth the king and his miniſters, &c. which our act doth not, but yet by conſtruction of law they are excepted, becauſe the king might doe it by his prerogative.

Vide Cap. Itin. Vet. Mag. Char. fo. 155.

13 E. 4. 6.

Fleta ubi ſup.

This act Fleta reciteth in this manner: *Proviſum eſt quod nullus averia aliena capiens per ſe, vel per ſuos notos vel ignotos extra com', in quo capta fuerint, fugare præſumat, &c.*

[192]

CAP.

CAP. XVII.

PURVIEW eſt enſement, que ſi ul deſormes preigne les avers des auters, et les face chaſe en chaſtell, ou en forcelet (1), *et illonques dedeins le cloſe du chaſtell, ou de forcelet les deteign' encounter gage et pledge, pur que les avers ſerront ſolempnement demandes per viſc', ou per auter bailiſe le roy a la ſuit del pl', le viſc' ou le bailiſe priſe ove luy poyar de ſon countie* (2), *ou de ſa bail', et voile aſſaier de faire de ceo repl'* (3) *des avers a celuy que les aver' priſe, ou a ſon ſeigniour, ou as auters des homes ſon ſeigniour quicunque queux ſont troves en le lieu, ou les avers fueront enchaſes. Et ſi home luy deſorce adonques de la deliverance des avers, ou quel ne trove home pur le ſeigniour, ou pur celuy que les aver' priſe que reſpoign' et face le deliverance, apres ceo que le ſeigniour, ou parnour, per viſc' ou per bailiſe, ſerra admoniſt de faire la deliverance, ſi ſoit en pays, ou pres, ou la ou il purra per le parnour, ou per auters des fees covenablement eſtre garnie de faire le deliverance, ſil fuit hors de cel pays quant le priſe fuit fait, et ne face adonques maintenant les avers deliver, que le roy pur le treſpas et pur le deſpite, face abate le chaſtell, ou le forcelet ſans recoverie*(4) *: et touts les dammages que le plaintiſe avera reſceve de ſes avers, ou de ſon gainage diſturbe* (5), *ou en auter maner puis le primer demaund des avers fait per le vic', ou per le bailiſe, luy ſoient reſtores au double, de ſeigniour ou de celuy que les avers aver' priſe, ſil eit de quoy, et ſil neit de quoy, reſpoign' le ſeigniour quel heure, et en quel maner deliverance ſoit fait apres ceo que le vicount ou le bailiſe ſerra venue pur la deliverance faire. Et ſoit aſcavoire, que la ou le vic' dever' faire returne del briefe le roy ou bailiſe le ſeigniour du chaſtell, ou le forcelet, ou*

IT is provided alſo, that if any from henceforth take the beaſts of other, and cauſe them to be driven into a caſtle or fortreſs, and there within the cloſe of ſuch caſtle or fortreſs do withhold them againſt gage and pledges, whereupon the beaſts be ſolemnly demanded by the ſheriff, or by ſome other bailiff of the king's; at the ſuit of the plaintiff, the ſheriff or bailiff, taking with him the power of the ſhire or bailiwick, do aſſay to make replevin of the beaſts from him that took them, or from his lord, or from other, being ſervants of the lord (whatſoever they be) that are found in the place whereunto the beaſts were chaſed; if any deforce him of the deliverance of the beaſts, or that no man be found for the lord, or for him that took them, for to anſwer and make the deliverance, after ſuch time as the lord or taker ſhall be admoniſhed to make deliverance by the ſheriff or bailiff, if he be in the countrey, or near, or there whereas he may be conveniently warned by the taker, or by any other of his to make deliverance; if he were out of the countrey when the taking was, and did not cauſe the beaſts to be delivered incontinent, that the king, for the treſpaſs and deſpite, ſhall cauſe the ſaid caſtle or fortreſs to be beaten down without recovery; and all the damages that the plaintiff hath ſuſtained in his beaſts, or in his gainure, or any otherwiſe (after the firſt demand made by the ſheriff or bailiff) of the beaſts, ſhall be reſtored to him double by the lord, or by him that took the beaſts, if he have whereof; and if he have not whereof, he ſhall have it of the lord, at what time, or in what manner the deliverance be made, after that the ſheriffe or bailiff ſhall come

ou a auter a que returne de briefe le roy appent, si le bailife de cel franchise ne face le deliverance, puis que le vicount aver' le return' a luy fait, face le vicount son office sans delay (6), *et sur lavantdit peine. Et per mesme le maner soit fait la deliverance* per attachment de pleint fait sans briefe, et sur mesme la peine* (7). *Et ceo face a entender per tout la, ou le briefe le roy court. Et si ceo soit en le marche de Gales* (8), *ou ailors, la ou le briefe le roy ne court mye, le roy que est soveraigne seigniour ent fra droit* (9) *a ceux queux pleindre se voudront.*

* [193]

come to make deliverance; and it is to wit, that where the sheriff ought to return the king's writ to the bailiff of the lord of the castle or fortress, or to any other, to whom the return belongeth, if the bailiff of the franchise will not make deliverance after that the sheriff hath made his return unto him, then shall the sheriff do his office without further delay, and upon the foresaid pains: and in like manner deliverance shall be made by attachment of plaint made without writ, and upon the same pain. And this is to be intended in all places where the king's writ lieth. And if that be done in the marches of Wales, or in any other place where the king's writs be not current, the king, which is sovereign lord over all, shall do right there unto such as will complain.

(52 H. 3. c. 3. 13 Ed. 1. stat. 1. c. 39. Regist. 85. 52 H. 3. c. 21.)

Vide Marlb. 52 H. 3. ca. 1.

The mischiefe before this act was, that in the irregular time of H. 3. great men, when they took a distresse of the beasts of their tenants or neighbours, that served for their tillage or husbandry, to prevent the speedy course of justice, and to enforce the owners of the beasts for necessity to yeeld to their desire, would drive the beasts into a castle or fortresse, and there detaine and keepe them against gages and pledges, so as no replevy could be made according to the ordinary course of law; for that in case of a subject he could not break the castle or fortresse, but the sheriffe was to retourne *averia elongata*, and thereupon the owner was to lose the use of his beasts of long time. But this act giveth remedy, that the sheriffe taking with him the power of the county may make replevin, as by the body of the act appeareth.

Vide 52 H. 3. c. 3. Britton, 54. b. Fleta, li. 2. c. 40. W. 2. ca. 39. lib. 5. fo. 91, 92. Semaines case. Vet. N B. 43, 44. Regist. 83. 85. 8 H. 4. 17. in Repl.

(1) *Chase in castel ou en forcelet.*] And so it is, if he that distrain chase the distresse into any other house, park, or other place of strength, the sheriffe to make replevin may by force of this act break the house, castle, or fortresse, park, or other place of strength by force of this act, at the suite of a subject.

(2) *Pur que les avers serront solempnement demandes per viscont, ou auter bailife le roy a la sute del plaintife, le viscont ou le bailife prise ove luy poyar de son county,* &c.] Nota, every man is bound by the common law to assist not only the sheriffe in his office for the execution of the kings writs (which are the commandements of the king) according to law; but also his baily, that hath the sheriffes warrant in that behalfe, hath the same authority, which his master the sheriffe hath, for the sheriffe cannot doe all himselfe, and if they doe it not being required, they shall be fined and imprisoned; but this is so to be understood, where the sheriffe may lawfully do it, and that before the sheriffe doth use any force, he ought (as

our

our act teacheth) to demand according to the law the goods to be delivered, so as replevy might be thereof made, for *sequi debet potentia mandatum legis, non praecedere,* force ought to follow, and not to precede the commandement of the law.

Bracton who wrote before this act saith, *Et si [vicecomes] aliquem invenerit resistentem, assumptis secum (si opus fuerit) militibus et liberis hominibus de com' ad sufficientiam capiat corpora hominum resistentium, et illos in prisona salvo custodiat, donec dominus rex inde praeceperit voluntatem suam, &c.* Bract. li. 5. 442. b. Fleta, li. 2. c. 62.

And our statutes of W. 1. W. 2. and Marlebridge are all in affirmance of the common law in that point, saving for breaking of the castle, fortresse, house, &c. in case of the subject; in which case our act giveth remedy. W. 1. c. 9. & 17. W. 2. ca. 29. Marlb. ca. 21. Semaines case. ubi supra.

If any man, how great soever, might have resisted the sheriffe in executing of the kings writs, then had it been a good retourn for the sheriffe to have retourned such resistance, but as the statute of W. 2. saith, *Quod hujusmodi responsio multum redundat in dedecus domini regis et coronae suae*; and that which is in *dedecus domini regis, &c.* is against the common law, therefore of necessity, if need be, for the due execution of the kings writs, the sheriffe may by the common law take *posse comitatus* to suppresse such unlawfull force, and resistance. 3 H. 7. 2. 10. 12 H. 7. 17. b. W. 2. ca. 39.

[194]

R. did graunt and render lands by fine to I. I. sued the kings writ to the sheriffe to deliver seisin, the sheriffe retourned, that he could not execute the kings writ for resistance of B. and others unknown; and because the sheriffe tooke not the power of the county in aid of the execution, as the statute willeth, he was amercied at xx. marks, and an attachment awarded against B. and the rest, &c. 19 E. 2. tit. Execution 24.

And it is holden for a maxime of law, that it is not lawfull for any man to disturb the ministers of the king in the due execution of the kings writs, or processe of law. 8 E. 2. tit. Execution 252.

Now besides the warrant of the common law, the sheriffe hath his letters patents of assistance, whereby the king commandeth, that all arch-bishops, bishops, dukes, earles, barons, knights, freemen, and all other of that county be to the sheriffe thereof in *omnibus quae ad officium illud pertinent, intendentes, auxiliantes, et respondentes*; so as no man ecclesiasticall or temporall is exempted from this service being above 15. and under 70. for so it is by construction of law.

(3) *Et voille assaier de faire plevin.*] By force of this clause he ought by the power of the county to make replevin, and it is no retourn for him to say, that the beasts be in a castle, &c. whereof you shall reade more hereafter in this chapter. Fleta, li. 2. c. 40.

(4) *Que le roy pur le trespasse & pur le dispite face abater le castel ou le forcelet sans recovery.*] But this totall prostrating or demolishing of the castle, &c. cannot be done upon the retourne of the sheriffe, but upon a suit on the kings behalf, wherein the parties interested may be called to answer, and upon judgement given against them processe to be made to the sheriffe to prostrate and demolish the castle and fortresse, and so is the book that speaks thereof to be intended. Semaines case. ubi sup. fo. 93. a.

(5) *De ses avers, ou son gainage disturbe.*] For the law doth ever favour tillage, and the husbandry of the realme, as by this clause

clause appeareth, and therefore gives the party grieved double damages.

(6) *Et soit assavoir, que la ou le viscount dever' faire retourne del briefe le roy au bailife, le seignior del castel, ou de forcelet, ou a auter a que retorne del briefe le roy appent, si le bailife del franchise ne fait deliverance, &c. face le viscont son office sans delay.*] This doth give some light to the former branch, that if the beasts be detained in a castle or fortresse, the sheriffe must doe his office without delay, that is, forthwith to replevy the beasts; and if he ought to doe it in this case of the franchise, the same he ought to doe in the other case.

Regist. 83. It appeareth by the Register, that if the constable of the castle upon a mandat to him to make replevin, *nihil inde curavit*, or if he make no retourne, &c. at all, upon retourne hereof, a *non omittas*
F.N.B. 68. shall be awarded, &c. But such retournes were permitted before
47 E. 3. 33. this act, but now by this act the sheriffe in that case ought presently to enter, and make deliverance of the beasts.

(7) *Et per mesme le manner soit fait la deliverance per attachment*
Marleb. ca. 21. *de pleint fait sans briefe & sur mesme la paine.*] See the statute of Marlebridge that provideth to the same effect, where you shall reade more of this matter.

[195] (8) *Et si ceo soit en le marches de Gales.*] The marches of Wales
18 E. 2. Ass. 382. were the commots, great seigniories, and baronies in Wales, which
1 E. 3. 14. 3 E. were holden of the king in chiefe, and out of every county of
3. 82. 8 E. 3. England: if any distresse were driven into a castle or fortresse in
427. 13 E. 3. the marches of Wales, and detained, a writ should be directed to
Jurisdict. 23. the sheriffe of the county of England next adjoyning to the castle,
15 E. 3. ib. 24. or fortresse, where the beasts be so detained, to make replevy.
24 E. 3. 42.
47 E. 3. 6. 50 E. (9) *Le roy que est soveraigne seigniour ent fra droit.*] At this time,
3. 26. 6 H. 4. 9. *viz.* in 3 E. 1. Lluellen was a prince, or king of Wales, who held
6 H. 5. Juris- the same of the king of England as his superiour lord, and ought
diction 34. him liege, homage, and fealty; and this is proved by our act, *viz.*
35 H. 6. 30. that the king of England was *superior dominus*, *i.* soveraigne lord of the kingdome or principality of Wales.

Polydor Virg. King H. 3. after prince Edward had married Elianor daughter
37 H. 3. p. 306. of Spaine, perceiving him (to use the words of mine author) *Ita*
Pl. Com. 126. b. *suapte natura tanta indole praeditum, ut maturius ad res gerendas ido-*
Cambden in *neum redderet, primo Walliae principatu donavit, deinde Aquitaniae et*
Flintsh. p. 525. *Hiberniae praeposuit; hinc natum, ut deinceps unusquisque rex, qui secutus est, filium majorem natu principem Walliae facere consueverit.*

Lluellen prince of Wales, by the incitation of David his brother, in the 9 year of E. 1. rebelled against their soveraigne lord; in which rebellion Lluellen was slaine, and the king brought all Wales under his subjection: the said David being brother and heire of Lluellen for his rebellion and treason against his soveraigne lord was after the death of his brother at a parliament
Rot. Parl. anno holden in the 11 yeare of E. 1. attainted of high treason; of
11 E. 1. whose judgement and execution heare what Fleta saith, *Et unico*
Fleta, li. 1. c. 16. *malefactori plura poterunt infligi tormenta, prout meruerit, sicut contigit de Davide principe Walliae cum per recordum quinque judiciis mortalibus torquebatur, suis namque meritis exigentibus, detractus, suspensus, decollatus, dismembratus fuit et combustus, cujus caput principali civitati, quatuorque quarteria ad quatuor partes regni in odium traditorum deferebantur suspendenda.* By reason whereof, where Wales was before holden of the king, as of his soveraigne lord, as is aforesaid,

aforesaid, now king Edw. 1. became king of the same in possession, which appeareth by the statute of Snowdon in these words; *Edwardus Dei gratia, &c. divina providentia (quæ in sua dispositione non fallitur) inter alia suæ dispensationis munera, quibus nos et regnum nostrum Angliæ decorari dignata est, terram Walliæ cum incolis suis prius nobis jure feodali subjectam, jam sui gratia in proprietatis nostræ dominium, obstaculis quibuscunque cessantibus, totaliter et cum integritate convertit, et coronæ regni prædict' tanquā partem corporis ejusdem annexuit et univit:* by which act it further appeareth, that king E. 1 had considered, and perused all the laws of Wales, and some of them hee utterly abrogated, some of them hee permitted, some hee corrected, and some he newly added to the others. Rot. Parllam. anno 12 E. 1. Pl. Com. 126. that this is a statute.

We have been, above our usuall manner, the more copious herein, because our desire is, that truth might prevaile. See the statutes of 27 H. 8. and 34 and 35 H. 8. concerning Wales. See the fourth part of the Institutes, cap. Of the Courts, &c. of Wales. 27 H. 8. ca. 27. 34 & 35 H. 8.

CAP. XVIII. [196]

PUR ceo que la common fine et amerciament (1) de tout le county en eyre des justices pur faux judgements (3), ou pur auter trespas, est assesse (2) per vicount et barretors (4) des counties malement, issint que la summe est meintfoits encrue, et les parcels auterment assesse que estre ne duissent, au damage du people, et plusors foits sont paies as viconts et barretors, que ne poient les acquitent. Purview est, et voit le roy, que desormes en eyre des justices devant eux devant lour departure soit tiel summe assesse per serement de chivalers et des probes homes, sur touts yceux que escoter deveront (5), et les justices facent mitter les parcels en lour estreats que ils liverent al eschequer (6), et non pas la summe totall (7).

FORASMUCH as the common fine and amerciament of the whole county in eyre of the justices for false judgements, or for other trespass, is unjustly assessed by sheriffs and baretors in the shires, so that the sum is many times increased, and the parcels otherwise assessed than they ought to be, to the damage of the people, which be many times paid to the sheriffs and baretors, which do not acquit the payers; it is provided, and the king will, that from henceforth such sums shall be assessed before the justices in eyre, afore their departure, by the oath of knights and other honest men, upon all such as ought to pay; and the justices shall cause the parcels to be put into their estreats, which shall be delivered up unto the exchequer, and not the whole sum.

(8 Rep. 39.)

There were foure mischiefes, or rather grievances before this act.

1. That this common fine and amerciament before justices in eyre was promiscuously assessed by the sheriffe and barretors of the county (for so our act speaketh) upon the faultlesse, as well as

upon

upon the faulty, and that after the justices in eyre were departed and gone.

2. That the same was many times by them increased.

3. That the parcells were otherwise, then they ought to be, to the damage of the people.

4. That the said amerciament was paid to the sheriffe, and barretors, that could not acquite them, and therefore were often doubly charged.

The remedy by the body of the act consisteth on two parts.

1. That such summes shall be assessed by the oath of knights, and other honest men before the justices in eyre, upon such as ought to pay the same.

2. That the justices shall cause the parcels to be put in their estreats, which shall be delivered up in the exchequer, and not the whole summe.

Lib. 8. fo. 39. Greislies case.

(1) *Common fine et amerciament.*] Here fine and amerciament are all one, for, as by this act appeareth, it ought to be afferred, which a fine in his proper sense ought not: this is parcel of the green wax, so called, because the estreats to the sheriffe for levying of them are sealed with green waxe.

42 E. 3. ca. 9. 7 H. 4. ca. 3.

This common amerciament was a great grievance to the people, for that the faultlesse, as well as the faulty, were (as hath been said) thereby charged; and this was *disperdere innocentem cum delinquente*, much like the abuse of the clark of the market, who used to take a common fine, untill it was remedied by act of parliament.

23 R. 2. ca. 4.

Greislies case. ubi supra.

(2) *Est assise.*] That is, is afferred.

9 Eliz. Dier 263.

(3) *Pur faux judgements.*] The suitors in a base court for false judgements shall be amercied, to the end they may be the more wary, and take better advice to doe justice.

Li. 8. fo. 36, 37. First part of the Inst. sect. 701.

(4) *Per barretors.*] For the signification of this word, see Pasch. 30 Eliz. the case of barretry, and the first part of the Institutes.

[197]

Mirr. li. 4. § de amerciaments leviable.

(5) *Sur touts ceux queux escoter deveront.*] This is a law of great equitie, that such as be faulty should onely be contributory to the payment of fine and amerciament.

See hereafter cap. 45.

(6) *Al eschequer.*] For that court is the true center, into which all the kings revenue and profit ought to fall, and by this meanes the toll shall come to the right mill.

See hereafter cap. 45.

(7) *Et non pas le totall.*] But particularly, and by parcell, upon every one that ought to contribute.

Rot. Parl. an. 17 E. 3. nu. 37.

The commons petitioned, that no common fine of any county from thenceforth should be made, but that every man may be particularly punished. Whereunto the kings answer was,

The king willeth the same.

CAP.

CAP. XIX.

*EN droit des vic', ou auters queux respoign' per lour maines al eschequer, et queux ount resc' de les dets le roy (1) pier le roy que ore est, ou les dets le roy mesme avant ceux heures, et queux ne ount my acquites de ceo les dettours al eschequer : purview est, que le roy envoiera bones gentes per touts les counties, a oyer touts iceux, queux de ceo pleine se voudront et a terminer issint la besoign', que ceux que purront monstrer que ils eient issint avant paies, a touts jours (ent) serront quites, le quel que les viconts ou auters serront morts ou vives, en certaine forme que lour serr' baill'. Et ceux que issint naver' fait, silz soient en vies, serront punies grevement; et sils soient morts, lour heires respoign' (2), et soient charges de la dette. Et commaund le roy, que les viconts, et les auters avantdits desformes loialment acquitent les dettors a prochin accompt (3), puis que ils averont le dette resceive : et donque soit le det allowe al eschequer, issint que jammes ne veign' en summon'. Et si le vic' auterment face, et de ceo soit attaint, cy rendra al plaintife le treble de ceo que il aver' de luy resceive, et soit rent a le volunt le roy. Et bien se garde chescun vicont, que il eit tiel resceivor, pur que il voudra responder (4), car le roy se prendra del tout as viscont, et a lour heires. Et si auter que respoign' per sa maine al eschequer le face, il rendra le treble al plaintife, et soit rent en mesme le maner. Et que les vic' facent tayles a touts iceux, queux paieront * le det le roy. Et que la summons deschequer a touts les debtors, queux demander voudront la view, facent monstrer sans denier les a nuiluy, et ceo sans rien prender de louer, et sans rien don' (5), et*

* [198]

IN right of the sheriffs, or other, which answer by their own hands unto the exchequer, and which have received the king's father's debts, or the king's own debts before this time, and have not acquitted the debtors in the exchequer; it is provided, that the king shall send good and lawful men through every shire, to hear all such as will complain thereof, and to determine the matters there, that all such as can prove that they have paid, shall be thereof acquitted for ever (whether the sheriffs or other be living or dead) in a certain form that shall be delivered them; and such as have not so done (if they be living) shall be grievously punished; and if they be dead, their heirs shall answer, and be charged with the debt. And the king hath commanded, that sheriffs and other aforesaid, shall from henceforth lawfully acquit the debtors at the next accompt after they have received such debts; and then the debt shall be allowed in the exchequer, so that it shall no more come in the summons; and if the sheriff otherwise do, and thereof be attainted, he shall pay to the plaintiff thrice as much as he hath received, and shall make fine at the king's pleasure. And let every sheriff take heed, that he have such a receiver, for whom he will answer; for the king will be recompensed of all, of the sheriffs and their heirs. And if any other, that is answerable to the exchequer by his own hands so do, he shall render thrice so much to the plaintiff, and make fine in like manner. And that the sheriffs shall make tallies to all such as have paid their debt to the king; and that the summons of the exchequer be shewed to all debtors that

et que ne le fra, le roy prendra a luy grevement.

that demand a sight thereof, without denying to any, and that without taking any reward, and without giving any thing; and he that doth contrary, the king shall punish him grievously.

(51 H. 3. stat. 4. 42 Ed. 3. c. 9. 7 H. 4. c. 3.)

W. 1. ca. 32. (1) *Detts le roy.*] Under this word [*debitum*] are all things due to the king comprehended; and not onely debts in their proper sense, but duties or things due, as rents, fines, issues, amerciaments, and other duties to the king received, or levied by the sheriffe: for debt in his large sense signifies, whatsoever any man doth owe, and *debere dicitur, quia de st habere: debitori enim deest quod habet, cum sit creditoris, maxime in casu domini regis.*

(2) *Lour heires responderont.*] That is to be understood, *quoad restitutionem, sed non quoad pœnam*; that is, for the civill, but not for the criminall part: for it is a maxime in law, *pœna ex delicto defuncti hæres teneri non debet*: and againe, *in restitutionem, non in pœnam hæres succedit.*

(3) *Au prochein account.*] See for this the statute of 51 H. 3. Statutum de Scaccario, and the statute of W. 4. Vet. Mag. Chart. fo. 33, 34.

(4) *Et tiel receivor pur quoy il voet responder.*] For the rule of this, and like cases of the king, is, *respondeat superior.*

(5) *Et que la summons deschequer a touts les debtors, queux demander vouduront la view, facent monstrer sans denier les a nulluy, et ceo sans rien prender de louer, et sans riens don', &c.*] That is, the proces, together with the estreats under the scale of the exchequer shall be
42 E. 3. ca. 9.
7 H. 4. ca. 3.
shewed to the party presently without denyall, and freely without any thing to be given therefore, upon pain of grievous fine and imprisonment.

CAP. XX.

PURVIEW est ensement de misfeasors (2) en parkes (1), et en vivers (3), que si ul de ceo soit attaint per le fait del plaintife (4), soyent agardes bones et hautes amendes (5), solonque le maner del trespas, et eit la prisonment de trois ans (6), et dillonq; soit rent a le volunt le roy (7), sil ad de quoy poit estre rent, et lors trova bon suertie que il jammes ne misface (8). Et sil neit dont poit estre issint rente, apres la prisonment de trois ans, trova mesme le suertie (9), et sil ne puisse trover

IT is provided also for trespassers in parks and ponds, that if any be thereof attainted at the suit of the party, great and large amends shall be awarded according to the trespass, and shall have three years imprisonment, and after shall make fine at the king's pleasure (if he have whereof) and then shall find good surety, that after he shall not commit like trespass; and if he have not whereof to make fine, after three years imprisonment, he shall find like surety; and if he cannot find

trover la suerty, for jur' la realme (10). *Et si ul de ceo rette soit fugitive, et neit terre, ne tenement suffisant pur quoy il poit estre justifie, cicourt * come le roy avera ceo trove per bone enquest, soit demaund de countie en countie. Et sil ne veigne, soit utlage. Purview est ensement et accorde, que si ul ne suist dedeins an et le jour pur le trespas fait, le roy avera le suit, et ceux queux il trova de ceo rettes per bon enquest, serront punies per mesme le maner en touts points, sicome desuis est dit. Et si ul tiel misfeisour soit attaint, quil eit prise en ses parkes beasts domestes* (11), *ou auter chose en le maner de robberie* (12) *en venant, ou demurrant, ou en returnant, soit fait de luy common ley, que affiert a celuy que est attaint de apert robberie et larceny, auxibien a la suit le roy come dauter.*

find like surety, he shall abjure the realm; and if any being guilty thereof be fugitive, and have no land nor tenement sufficient (whereby he may be justified) so soon as the king shall find it by enquest, he shall be proclaimed from county to county; and if he come not, he shall be out-lawed. It is provided also and agreed, that if none do sue within a year and a day for the trespass done, the king shall have the suit; and such as be found guilty thereof by lawful enquest, shall be punished in like manner in all points as above is said. And if any such trespasser be attainted, that he hath taken tame beasts, or other thing, in the parks, by manner of robbery, in coming, tarrying, or returning, let the common law be executed upon him, as upon him that is attainted of open theft and robbery, as well at the suit of the king, as of the party.

Capt. Itin. Vet. Mag. Chart. 155. Rot. Claus. 17 H. 3. m. 9. (Regist. 80. 111. Rast. 651, &c. Kel. 39. 202. Dyer 238. 47 Ed. 3. 10. 9 H. 6. 2. 5 H. 5. 1. 19 H. 8. 9. 18 H. 6. 21. 21 H. 7. 21. 13 H. 7. 10. 12. Fitz. Barre, 83. Keilw. 114. b. 2 Ed. 4. 4. b. 9 H. 3. stat. 2. c. 10, 11. 1 Ed. 3. stat. 1. c. 8. 1 H. 7. c. 7.)

The cause of the making of this statute was, that at the common law, the plaintife in an action of trespas, should, as in other cases, recover no other dammages, but according to the quantity of the trespasse: which the plaintife for trespasses in parks and vivaries esteemed at a high rate; but the country commonly found the dammages very small; for the common law gave no way to matters of pleasure (wherein most men do exceed) for that they brought no profit to the common-wealth; and therefore it is not lawfull for any man to erect a park, chase, or warren, without a licence under the great seale of the king, who is *pater patriæ*, and the head of the common-wealth.

47 E. 3. 10. b. 9 H. 6.

Temps E. 2. tit. act' sur lestat. Br. 48. Li. 11. fo. 85, 87.

(1) *En parks.*] This is understood of a lawfull parke, whereunto three things are required: 1. A liberty, either by graunt, as is aforesaid, or by prescription. 2. Inclosure by pale, wall, or hedge. And 3. beasts savages of the parke, for the which, and for the name, see the first part of the Institutes.

1. Part of the Inst. sect. 378.

But this statute extendeth not to a nominative park erected without lawfull warrant, albeit it be called a park; for this statute is very penall, and therefore, as hath been said, extendeth onely to a lawfull parke. But he may have an action of trespasse at the common law, *quare clausum fregit, et unam damam cepit, &c.*

Under this word park, a chase is not included.

9 H. 6 2. 18 H. 6. 21. 19 H. 6. 6. 22 H. 6. 59. 34 H. 6. 28. 43. 10 H. 7. 6. b. 12 H. 8. 10. a. 43 E. 3. 13. 24. 38 E. 3. 10.

3 H. 6. 55. 8 E. 4. 5. See the statutes of 13 R. 2. c. 13. 19 H. 7. ca. 11. 14 H. 8. cap. 1. 3 Jac. c. 13. 7 Jac. c. 13. 21 Jac. c. 28. 3 Car. cap. 4.

* 21 H. 7. 21. * This act extends not to a forest in the hands of a subject, for the law is so penall, as it shall not be taken by equitie.

(2) *Misfesauns.*] In this act is understood when a man either chaseth in a park, or by bow, or other engine endevoureth to kil some of the game of the park against the liberty and priviledge
† 30 E. 3. f. 11. the countesse of Athols case. of the park, † and not when the lord of a park takes beasts to agistment in his park, and the owner breaks the park, and takes them away without agreement for their pasture, for it is not within these words, *de malefactoribus in parcis*, because the trespasse concerneth not the liberty of the park by chasing of the game thereof, but a collaterall trespasse, *et sic de similibus*.

(3) *Vivers* or *viviers.*] This being a French word, signifieth fish-ponds, or waters wherein fish are kept and nourished; which being a matter of profit, and increase of victuals, any man may erect; and that in legall understanding it signifieth a fish-pond, or waters where fish are kept, it appears by our ancient authors, who
Brit. fo. 34. wrote soone after this time: for Britton saith, *Auxi de wast fait per eux en parks & en vivers, de venison & de pesson, & de conies, & auter*
[200] *destruction per eux faits en garrens:* where he applyeth *venison* to parks, *pesson* to *vivers*, and *conies* to warrens. And Fleta agreeth
Flet. li. 2. c. 36. with him, for he saith, *De feris et piscibus potest fieri furtum: ex benignitate tamen principis constituitur, ne quis pro hujusmodi furto vitam perdat, neque membra: constitutio quidem talis est, provisum est de malefactoribus in parcis et vivariis, quod ad sectam querentis statim adjudicentur emendæ, &c.* and reciteth summarily this act; and so it
Vide hic cap. 1. is taken before in this very parliament, cap. 1. for fish-ponds, or places where fish are kept, in these words, *ne curge en auter parke,*
Bract. li. 3. fo. 117. *ne pische en auter viver.* And Bracton, who wrote a little before our statute, coupleth them together in the charge given by the justices in eyre, as our statute doth, *viz. De malefactoribus in parcis, et vivariis.*

F.N.B. 88. H. It appeareth in the Register, that there be divers formes of writs for fishing in his piscarie: one writ is, *quare in vivariis suis piscatus fuit:* another, *quare in separali pischaria ipsius A. piscatus fuit, &c.*

Hic c. 1. Artic. super cart. c. 18. 34 H. 6. 28. 21 H. 7. 21. F.N.B. 67. d. Therefore, as some have stretched this word too far, extending it to warrens of conies, which they might as well under the generality of the word [*vivarium*] extend it to forests and chases (for they be *loci ubi viventes custodiuntur*) whereof you have heard before; so some would restraine this word to fish-ponds onely that be in parks, which is expresly against both the letter and meaning of this act, and the fish-pond concerneth nothing the liberty and priviledge of the park, whereof also a touch hath been given before.

If a man committeth a trespasse in the fish-pond, &c. of another, by taking and carrying away of water, he is no mis-feasor within this statute; but if he let out the water, to the end to take fish, he is a mis-feasor within this statute, or he must fish there, if he be within the danger of this law, for collaterall trespasses neither in parks, nor fish-ponds, &c. are within this act.

And if one hunt in a park, or fish in a pond, &c. though he kill no deer, nor take any fish, yet this is a mis-feasauns within this statute.

Regist. 111. b. 47 E. 3. 10. b. (4) *Per le suit del plaintife.*] This suit is intended in an action of trespas, but the writ must rehearse, and be grounded upon this

statute; for it is a maxime in the common law, that a statute made 5 H. 5. 1. 2 E. 4.
in the affirmative, without any negative expressed or implyed, doth 4. 9 H. 6. 2.
not take away the common law: and therefore in this case the F.N.B. 67. d. 87. a. 7 El.
plaintife may either have his remedy by the common law, or upon Dier 238. Lib.
the statute; if he bring his action of trespasse generally without Intr. Rast. 585.
grounding the same upon the statute, then he waiveth the benefit of the statute, and taketh his remedy by the common law.

The presidents of this action are, *Ad respondendum tam domino* 7 El. Dier 238.
regi, quam parti querenti: and yet by the Register, he may have Regist. ubi sup.
this in his owne name, and that may be gathered by some of our books, quoted before in this section, in the margent.

(5) *Soient agardes bones et hautes amends.*] By these words [shall be awarded good and large amends] if the dammages be too small, the court hath power to increase the dammages, for this word [award] properly belongeth to the court.

(6) *Et eit la prisonment de trois ans.*] Both dammages and im- Dier ubi sup.
prisonment concerne the plaintife, and therefore the kings pardon 15 El. Dier 323.
cannot dispense with them: but the ransome, the finding of surety, 9 El. Dier 269.
and the forejuring of the realme are punishments exemplarie, and concerne the king, and therefore he may pardon the same.

(7) *Et dillonque soit rent a le volunt le roy.*] And after shall make fine at the kings pleasure.

See before for the exposition of these words, cap. 4. Vide hic cap. 4.

(8) *Et lors trova bone surety, que il jammes ne misface.*] And then [201]
shall finde good surety, that after he shall not misdoe.

This surety must be by recognisance to the king, and not to the Hil. 24 H. 7.
plaintife; for example, the sureties in 10 l. and the defendant in Cor. Rege. Rot. 26. Tr.
40 l. the condition must be generall, and not restrained to that park, 13 H. 8. Cor.
or vivary: for example, *Quod ipse in aliquibus parcis et vivariis contra* Rege. Rot. 480.
formam statuti prædict' amplius non malefaciet, &c.

(9) *Le roy avera le sute.*] Either by indictment, information, or action of trespasse upon this act.

(10) *Forjure le realme.*] Fleta translating this act into Latine, Fleta, l. 1. c. 36.
saith, *abjurabit regnum*, and so doth the Register; and Bracton useth Regist. 80. b. & fol. 111. b.
the same word in case of felony, *abjurabit regnum.* Bracton.

And Britton useth our word, *forjure nostre realme*, and fol. 25. in Brit. fo. 7. 25.
the same case he useth the word of abjuration.

It signifieth in law a perpetuall banishment of the defendant out of the realme, which to observe he bindeth himselfe by oath, for so much is implied in this word *forjure*, or *abjure*, which properly signifieth to forsweare the realme.

By the common law no man can be exiled, or banished out of his Mag. Chart. c.
country, but in case of abjuration for felony: in all other cases 29.
exile or banishment ought to be done by authority of parliament (as here it is) and so are our books that speak of exile or banishment to be understood.

If such a person, as hath forjured or abjured the realme, returne againe, he shall be punished at the kings suit for the perjury, and high contempt.

(11) *Beasts domests.*] This is understood of kine, oxen, sheep, and other domesticall beasts within the park.

If there be within the park tame deere, and misdoers come to 10 E. 4. 15. b.
hunt and kill venison, and they kill a tame deere, and carry Stamf. Pl. Cor.
it away, not knowing the same to be a tame deere, this is no 25. b.

 felony,

felony, for the intent maketh felony, and so are the books to be intended.

First part of the Instit. sect. 501. (12) *En le manner de robbery.*] In this act robbery is taken in a large sense; see the first part of the Institutes.

CAP. XXI.

EN droit des terres des heires deins age, queux sont en le garde lour seigniors: purview est, que les gardeins les gardent, et susteinent, sans destruction faire en tout rien: et que de tiels manners des gardes soit fait en touts points solonque ceo que est conteigne en la graund charter des franchises fait en temps le roy H. pier le roy que ore est, Magna Charta, cap. 4, 5, & 6. *Et que issint soit use desormes, et per mesme le manner soient gardes les archivesqueries, evesqueries*, abbies, esglises, et dignities en temps de vacation.* Vide Artic' super Chartas cap. 18.

*[202]

IN right of lands of heirs being within age, which be in ward of their lords; it is provided, that the guardians shall keep and sustain the land, without making destruction of any thing; and that of such manner of wards shall be done in all points, as is contained in the great charter of liberties made in the time of king Henry, father to the king that now is, and that it be so used from henceforth. And in the same manner shall archbishopricks, bishopricks, abbacies, churches, and all spiritual dignities be kept in time of vacation.

(Bro. Wast. 32. 37 40. 68. 107. 137. 1 Inst. 54. Bro. Wast. 58. Regist. 72. 9 H. 3. stat. 1. c. 4. 6 Ed. 1. stat. 1. c. 5. 13 Ed. 1. stat. 1. c. 14. 28 Ed. 1. stat. 3. c. 18. 36 Ed. 3. c. 13.)

Mag Chart. c 4, 5, 6. Artic. super Chart. ca. 18. This act both to heires in ward, and the custody of archbishopricks, bishopricks, &c. during vacation, is but a confirmation of the statute of *Magna Charta,* cap. 4, 5, 6. whereof there you may reade at large.

CAP. XXII.

DES heires maries deins age, sans le gree de lour gardeins, avant que ils averont passes lage de xiiii. ans, soit fait solonque ceo que est contenue en le purveiance de Merton, cap. 6. Et de ceux que serront maries sans le gree de lour gardeins puis que ils averont passes lage de xiiii. ans, le gardein eit le double value de son mariage, solonque le tenour de mesme le purveyance. Ouster ceo ceux queux averont sustret le mariage (1), *rendant le droit value del mariage*

OF heirs married within age, without the consent of their guardians, afore that they be past the age of fourteen years, it shall be done according as it is contained in the statute of Merton. And of them that shall be married without the consent of their guardians, after they be past the age of fourteen years, the guardian shall have the double value of their marriage, after the tenour of the same act. Moreover, such as have with-

mariage al gardein pur le treſpaſſe, et jalemeins le roy eit les amends ſolonque meſme le purveyance de celuy que le avera ſuſtret, Weſtm. 2. cap. 35. Et des heires females (2), puis que ils averont accomplies lage de xiiii. ans, et le ſeignior a que le mariage appent celes ne voudra marier, mes pur covetiſe de la terre, les voudra tener diſmarie. Purview eſt, que le ſeignior (3) ne poit aver ne tener per encheſon del mariage (6), les terres (5) a tielx heires females ouſtre deux ans apres la terme de lavantdit xiiii. ans (4). Et ſi le ſeignior deins les deux ans ne les marie, donques eiant els actions de recover lour heritage quietment ſans rien done pur le garde, ou pur la mariage. Et ſi els pur malice, ou per malveis counſel ne ſe voilent (7) pur lour chiefe ſeigniors marier, ou els nes ſont diſparages, que les ſeigniors teignent la terre, et la heritage jeſque al age del enfant male, ceſtaſcavoire, xxi. ans, et ouſter jeſque ils eiant priſes le value (8) del mariage.

withdrawn their marriage, ſhall pay the full value thereof unto their guardian for the treſpaſs, and nevertheleſs the king ſhall have like amends, according to the ſame act, of him that hath ſo withdrawn. And of heirs females, after they have accompliſhed the age of fourteen years, and the lord (to whom the marriage belongeth) will not marry them, but for covetiſe of the land will keep them unmarried; it is provided, that the lord ſhall not have nor keep, by reaſon of marriage, the lands of ſuch heirs females, more than two years after the term of the ſaid fourteen years. And if the lord within the ſaid two years do not marry them, then ſhall they have an action to recover their inheritance quit, without giving any thing for their wardſhip, or their marriage. And if they of malice, or by evil counſel, will not be married by their chief lords (where they ſhall not be diſparaged) then their lords may hold their land and inheritance untill they have accompliſhed the age of an heir male, that is to wit, of one and twenty years, and further until they have taken the value of the marriage.

(Cro. El. 469. Stat. Merton, cap. 6. Co. Ent. 262. Fitz. Gard. 59. 71. Bro. Gard. 86. 6 Rep. 71. Regiſt. 161. 13 Ed. 1. ſtat. 1. c. 35. Repealed by 12 Car. 2. c. 24.)

The ſtatute of Merton provideth (as hath been ſaid) that if any lay-man raviſh an heire, or detain him within the age of 14 yeares, that then the gardien ſhould recover the value of the marriage againſt the raviſher together with the infant and his lands, and that the defendant ſhould be impriſoned untill he hath recompenced the plaintife, &c. and further, untill he hath ſatisfied the king for the treſpaſſe. Merton, cap. 6. 21 E. 3. 19, 20. 27 H. 6. tit gard. 118. 33 E. 3. Judgement 251.

This act doth firſt confirme the ſtatute of Merton, both concerning the raviſhment, and alſo concerning the forfeiture of mariage: and provideth further, that of them that be above the age of 14 yeares (over and above the double value of the marriage after tender made according to the ſtatute of Merton to be recovered againſt the heire) the gardien ſhall recover againſt the raviſher or detainer, the heire being maried, the full value thereof, and the king ſhall have alſo like amends according to the ſaid act. [203]

(1) *Ceux que averont ſuſtret le mariage.*] That is, the raviſher or detainer of the heire, and which married the heire after 14, and before 21.

This extendeth after 14, as well to eccleſiaſticall, as lay perſons, which

which the statute of Merton of a ravishment before 14, doth not, but to lay men onely.

Brit. fol. 169. 35 H. 6. 40. 35 H. 6. Gard. 71. 39 H. 6. c. 2. F.N.B. 143. d. (2) *Et des heires females.*] The mischiefe before this act was, that whereas the heire female after her age of 14 yeares, ought of right to be out of ward, the lord for covetousnesse would not marry them, but keep their lands at their will and pleasure many yeares after their age of 14, against the which wrong this statute provideth remedy, and was made for the restraint of the wrong, and in truth for the advantage of the lords.

Bract. l. 2. fo. 86. b. And here we are occasioned to explain a place in Bracton, *Fœmina 14. vel. 15. annorum potest disponere domui suæ, et habere cone et key, &c.* Which word [*cone*] is mistaken in the impression, for it should be *cover et key*; and for *cover* we use *cofer* at this day, changing the *v* to an *f*, (which is usuall) so as at that age like a good huswife shee is able to discerne what things are in a houshold fit to bee kept in cofer under locke and key; and the reason wherefore, if the heire female of a tenant by knights service be of the age of 14 years at the death of her auncester, she shall not be in ward, is, for that she is *viri potens*, and can govern an houshold, and may marry an husband, which may doe knights service.

See the first part of the Institutes, sect. 103, 104. If a man hath two daughters and dieth, the one above the age of 14, and the other within the age of 14, the lord shall have the wardship of the body of her within age, and the moiety of the land.

35 H. 6. 52. (3) *Purview est que le seignior.*] 1. Every lord is not within the purview of this act. The heire female shall enter upon the lord by posteriority, because her marriage belongs not unto him.

35 H. 6. ubi supra. Gard. 71. 2. If the lord graunt the mariage of the heire female to one, neither the grauntor nor the grauntee shall have two years, but the heir female shall enter at her age of 14, for the grauntee cannot hold the land, and the grauntor hath not the mariage.

35 H. 6. ubi supra. 3. So it is, if the king graunteth the wardship of the body of the heire female, she shall sue her livery at her age of fourteen, for neither the king nor his grauntee can hold the land during the two yeares.

35 H. 6. 52. (4) *Per 2. ans ouster les 14. ans.*] By this is understood that the lord shall not have the 2 yeares, but where the heire female was within the age of 14, at the death of her auncester, and in ward to the lord.

(5) *Les terres.*] Here a mesnalty that is holden is understood, though this statute speak of lands onely.

35 H. 6. ubi supra. (6) *Per encheson de mariage.*] *Cessante causa cessat effectus*, and therefore if within the two yeares the lord marrieth the heire female, the heire female shall presently enter, because for that cause the two yeares are given.

[204] If the gardien marry the heire female after the age of 12 yeares, he shall not detaine her land but untill her age of 14, for the cause ceaseth.

F.N.B. 143. d. So it is if the auncester marrieth his heir female, and dieth before shee attain to her age of 14, the land shall be in ward, but the lord shall not have the 2 years.

35 H. 6. 40. tit. Gard. 71. Institutes, ubi supra. And it is to be observed, that the lord hath these two years by force of this act, and not as gardien, because his gardienship ended at her age of 14, and therefore a writ of dower doth not lie against

against him during those two yeares, because he holdeth not the land as gardien.

And for that cause if the lord tender to her a marriage, and she within the two years marry her selfe elsewhere, there lieth no forfeiture of marriage against her. 35H.6. Gard.71.

(7) *Et si els per malice ou malveis counsel ne soy voillent*, &c.] Here the act in hatred of contradiction and disobedience, *in odium contradictionis et disobedientiæ*, giveth to the lord her lands untill her age of 21, &c. but he holdeth not the same as gardien for the cause aforesaid.

Of this whole act Fleta saith thus, *de fæmellis* 14 *annos habentibus, quibus domini sui maritagium competens medio tempore non obtulerint, taliter provisum est, quod negligentia dominorum hujusmodi talibus hæredibus, non sit damnosa, sed retenta hæreditate per duos annos post* 14 *annos, eam hæredibus sine contradictione reddere non contradicant; quod si infra ætatem competenter et palam contulerint, ipsæque maritari non consenserint, tunc usque ad ætatem masculinam hæreditatem talium impune poterint retinere ulterius quam per duos annos, pro fine maritagii, et in odium contradictionis et inobedientiæ.* Fleta, l. 1. c. 12.

(8) *Ouster jesque ils eient prises le value.*] Here the profits are accounted to goe in satisfaction of the value. *Vide le statute de Merton* cap. 6.

If the lord grant over the wardship of the body onely, neither grauntor nor grauntee shall take the advantage of this branch.

CAP. XXIII.

PURVIEW est ensement, que en city, burgh, ville, faire, ne marche, ne soit nul home forein, que soit de cest realme (1), *distreine pur dette* (2), *dont il nest dettour ou pledge, et que le fra, serra grevousement punie, et sans delay soit le distresse deliver per les bailifes due lieu, ou per auter bailifes le roy, si mestier soit.*

IT is provided also, that in no city, borough, town, market, or fair, there be no foreign person (which is of this realm) distrained for any debt wherefore he is not debtor or pledge; and whosoever doth it, shall be grievously punished, and without delay the distress shall be delivered unto him by the bailiffs of the place, or by the king's bailiffs, if need be.

27 E. 3. Sta. 2. c. 17.

The mischiefe before this statute was, that divers cities, the cinque ports, boroughs, towns corporate, &c. within this realme, did claime such a custome, that if any of one city, society, or merchant guild were indebted to any of another city, society, or merchant guild, if any other of the same city, society, or merchant guild that the debtor was of, came into the city, society, or merchant guild whereof the creditor was, that he would charge such a foreiner for the debt of the other; which customes are taken away by this statute, whereof Fleta teacheth in these words; *solent plerique homines in feriis, mercatis, civitatibus, burgis, et feodis, et in jurisdictionibus suis aliquos transeuntes de feodis, vel jurisdictionibus suis nullatenus existentes ad querimoniam alicujus invenientis plegios de prosequendo impedire,* Fleta, li. 2. c. 56. Cap. Itin' in Vet. Mag. Cart. fo. 155.

impedire, distringere et gravare pro alieno debito, cujus non fuerit plegius nec debitor, imponentes ei quod erat tali debitori affinis, ut de una societate vel civitate, et hujusmodi et impune: propter quod provisum est, et inhibitum, ne quis aliquem forinsecum, dum plegius non fuerit nec debitor, pro aliquo debito alieno alicubi distringat, nec ad aliquam solutionem compellat, et qui fecerit graviter punietur.

Mirror, cap. 5. sect. 4. And it seemeth by the Mirrour, treating of this chapter, that such customes were against the common law, for there it is said, *le point de tortiousnes distresses duist conteine le paine de roberie.*

(1) *Que soit de cest realme.*] These are materiall words: for if a merchant of England be either wrongfully imprisoned in the parts beyond the sea, or have his merchandises or goods taken from him there wrongfully, he shall have the kings letter to the king, prince, or lord of that territorie, where the wrong is done, wherein the wrong is briefly recited, and request made, *quod satisfactionem debitam ac justitiæ complementum fieri faciat, &c.* which letters of divers
Regist. fo. 129. formes appeare in the Register. Now if he be destitute of justice there, then may he either have the kings writ *de arresto facto super bonis mercatorum alienigen' pro transgressione facta mercatoribus Angliæ*, or
27 E. 3. Stat. 2. cap. 17. 4 H. 5. c. 7. else according to the law of marque, he shall have from the king letters of marque or reprisall under the great seale, whereby he may redresse himselfe of the goods of any of the men of that territorie taken within this realme. And it is called the law of marque, of a Saxon word, which signifieth a limit or bound; because seeing he cannot obtaine justice within the limits of the foreine country, he may be redressed of the men of that country within the limits of his owne: which appeareth by the statute of 27 E. 3. in these
27 E. 3. ubi sup. words, "No merchant stranger be impleaded for anothers trespasse, "or for anothers debt, whereof he is not debtor, pledge, nor main-"pernor. Provided alwayes, that if our liege people, merchants, "or other be endamaged by any lords of strange lands, or their "subjects, and the said lords (duly required) faile of right to our "said subjects, we shall have the law of marque, and of taking "them againe, as hath beene used in times past, without fraud or "deceit." Wherein many things are worthy of observation; and (amongst them) that this law of marque extends not onely to merchants, but to all other the kings subjects. And this law of marque in some records is called the kings right, *jus regium*, because thereby he doth his subjects right: as taking one example for many, in the
Rot. Parl. an. 11 H. 4. parliament holden in 11 H. 4. John Kowley of Bridgwater, in his petition prayed the king that he might take marque and reprisall of all French-mens goods, (having no safe conduct of the king) to a certaine value, for certaine his ships and other goods taken by the French in the time of the truce: the answer of the king was, that upon suit made to the king, he should have such letters requisitory as are needfull, and if the French king refuse to doe him right, the
Norf Tr. 33 E. 1. Coram rege rot. 18. Mat. Paris fo. 966 b. king will then shew his right. This letter of marque or reprisall was anciently called *litera mercatoria*, (because most commonly merchants obtained it) *litera mercatoria conceditur mercatoribus Anglis contra mercatores Heynon, Holland, Zealand, et Frisland.* So as if those words [which is of this realme] had been omited, and the statute had been generall in the negative, that no foreine persons should be distrained for any debt, wherefore he is not debtor or pledge, this had taken away the ancient law of marque or reprisall; and therefore necessarily were added the said words [which is of

this

this realme] whereby the law of marque or repriſall is implyed and ſaved.

(2) *Diſtreine pur dett.*] At this time a capias did not lie in an action of debt, but is given by the ſtatute of 25 E. 3, but yet this ſtatute doth extend to the capias, becauſe the capias commeth in lieu of the diſtres. 25 E. 3. cap. 7.

CAP. XXIV. [206]

PURVIEW eſt enſement, que nul eſchetor, viſcount, ne autre bailiſe le roy (1), *per colour de ſon office* (2), *ſans eſpeciall garrant* (3), *ou commandement* (4), *ou certaine authoritie que appent a ſon office* (5), *ne diſſeiſe nul home de ſon franktenement, ne de choſe que appent a ſon franktenement. Et ſi aſcun le fait, ſoit a le volunt le diſſeiſee, que le roy de ſon office le face amend' a ſon pleint, ou que il eit la common ley per briefe de* novel diſſeiſin (6). *Et celuy que ſerra de ceo attaint, rendr' les dammages a double a meſme le plaintiſe, et ſerra en le grevous mercie le roy.*

IT is provided alſo, that no eſcheator, ſheriff, nor other bailiff of the king, by colour of his office, without ſpecial warrant, or commandment, or authority certain pertaining to his office, diſſeiſe any man of his freehold, nor of any thing belonging to his freehold; and if any do, it ſhall be at the election of the diſſeiſee, whether that the king by office ſhall cauſe it to be amended at his complaint, or that he will ſue at the common law by a writ of novel diſſeiſin; and he that is attainted thereof ſhall pay double damages to the plaintiff, and ſhall be grievouſly amerced unto the king.

(1 R. 2. c. 9.)

The miſchiefe before this ſtatute was, that eſchaetors, ſheriffes, and other of the kings bailiffes, would, *colore officii*, ſeiſe into the kings hands the freehold of the ſubject, and thereby diſſeiſe the partie, who thereupon to his intolerable vexation and delay, was put to his ſuit to the king by petition, for which this ſtatute provideth remedy.

(1) *Bailiffe le roy.*] Here by bailiffe is underſtood any other officer or miniſter of the kings.

(2) *Per colour de ſon office.*] *Colore officii* is ever taken *in malam partem*, as *virtute officii* is taken *in bonam:* and therefore this implyeth a ſeiſure unduly made againſt law. Pl. com.

And he may do it *colore officii* two manner of wayes: either when he hath no warrant at all, or when he hath a warrant, and doth not purſue it.

(3) *Eſpecial warrant.*] That is, to the eſchaetor, &c. a *diem clauſit extremum, mandamus,* or any other of the kings writs, and office thereupon found for the king.

Likewiſe to the ſheriffe the kings writ, as an *habere facias ſeiſinam,* or the like. 5 E. 6. Br. 55. tit. Office Li. 8. fo. 168. Paris Stoughtons caſe.

By this act no ſeiſure can be made of lands or tenements into the kings hands before office found, and ſo is the common experience at this day. See the ſtatute of *articuli ſuper cart, cap.* 19. & 29 *E.* 1. *leſtat. de Lincolne.* Art. ſuper cart. ca. 19. 29 E. 1. Stat de Lincoln.

(4) *Ou*

* 17 E. 2. ass. 371. 32 E. 1. ibid. 378. 4 E 2. disseis. 10. 8 E. 2. coron. 390. 3 E. 3. coron. 347. & 300. 8 E. 3. 38. 15 E. 3 extent 17. 31 ass. 28. 10 E. 3. 47. 17 E. 3. 66. 22 ass. 96, 81. 44 ass. 14. 43 E. 3. 24. 26 ass pl. 32. 7 H. 4. 41. 13 H. 4. 13. Stamf. pl. cor. 192, 193. Pl. com. Morgans case, 12, 13. 4 E. 1. officium coronat.

(4) *Ou commandement.*] Under these words are comprehended not onely the king's commandements by his writs, as hath been said, but also the commandement of the justices of the kings courts of justice.

* A man was indicted before the sheriffe in his tourne of felonie, upon which indictment his lands and chattels were by the sheriffe seised for the king: afterward before justices assigned he was acquitted, and sued out a *certiorari* to remove the record into the kings bench; which being removed, he prayed there to have restitution of his lands and goods; and it was resolved that the sheriffe had not warrant to seise the lands, (before he were attainted) and therefore that he should sue his assise against the sheriffe upon this statute. It was further resolved, that if the sheriffe seise lands by the commandement of the justices, then is the sheriffe excused, though the justices therein did erre; and if he did it of his owne head, then had the party remedy by an assise; therefore * the partie was required to sue out a writ to the justices to certifie if the seisure were made by their commandement.

1 R. 3. cap. 3. Stamf. prærog. regis, 83, 84.

* [207]

(5) *Ou certain authoritie que appent a son office*] That is, *ex officio*, without any writ or commandement: for example, when the eschaetor taketh an office *virtute officii*, he may seise the land; for this, as our act saith, doth belong to his office; but if of his owne head (as hath beene said) he seiseth the land without any office, that seisure is *colore officii*, and therefore the assise upon this statute is maintainable against him in that case, *et sic de cæteris*.

(6) *Per briefe de novel disseisin.*] This is put for an example, for he may have any other writ, or action against him.

Bract. lib. 3. fo. 121. b. Brit. fo. 3, 4. Flet. li. 1. c. 18. 25. Mirr. ca. 1. § 5.

This statute is made in affirmance of that, which ought to have been done by the common law, and is the foundation as well of our book-cases above-said, as of the acts of parliament, that after have been made concerning undue seisures by escheators, sheriffes, and other bailifes, as coroners, and the rest.

And if it doth appeare to the court, that the kings officer doth seise for the king any lands without warrant against the law, in an action brought against the officer, he ought not to have any aid of the king; neither doth the writ *de domino rege inconsulto* lie in that case, because that which is done by him is void; and where the cause of aid faileth, there no aid is to be granted. It were against reason, that the king, who is the head of justice, should aid him in his wrong; and therefore this act for doing of wrong in the kings name, doth give the party grieved an assise against him, wherein the plaintife shall recover his land, and double dammages, and besides the kings officer shall be in the grievous mercy of the king, for doing injury in his name to the subject.

28 E. 3. 94. Mortimers case. Rot. Parl. 8 R. 2. nu. 14. the Prior of Mountegues case adjudged in parliament. 4 H. 6. 29, 30.

9 H. 7. 10. 30 ass. p. 5.

Therefore in a reall action, if the eschaetor (of whom this statute speaketh) be examined, and upon his examination saith generally, that he hath seised the lands in demand into the kings hands; this is not good, and the action shall proceed, for he must shew the cause of the seisure, (as is implyed in this act) which cause, if it appeare to be against the law, the judges of the law ought to disallow the same.

CAP.

CAP. XXV.

NUL miniſter le roy (1) *ne maintaine* (2) *per luy, ne per auter, les plees, parols, ou beſoignes queux ſont en la court* (3) *le roy* (4), *des terres, tenements, ou des auters choſes* (7), *pur aver part de ceo* (5), *ou auter profit* (6) *per covenant fait* (8). *Et que le fra, ſoit punie a le volunt le roy* (9). Vide Champertie 11 Ed. 1.

NO officer of the king by themſelves, nor by other, ſhall maintain pleas, ſuits, or matters hanging in the king's courts, for lands, tenements, or other things, for to have part or profit thereof by covenant made between them; and he that doth, ſhall be puniſhed at the king's pleaſure.

(9 H. 7. 18. 15 H. 7. 2. Regiſt. 182. Raſt. 119. 13 Ed. 1. ſtat. 1. c. 49. 28 Ed. 1. c. 11. 33 Ed. 1. ſtat. 3.)

(1) *Nul miniſter le roy.*] Fleta in rehearſing this ſtatute, ſaith, *nullus miniſter regis cujuſcunque fuerit officii, &c.* and another ſtatute provideth againſt all others. *Miniſter regis* was taken in this kings time to extend to the judges of the realme; for in the caſe of juſtice Heigham for a ſcandall, and reproachfull words ſpoken unto him, the record ſaith, *ſicut honor* * *et reverentia, quæ miniſtris domini regis attribuuntur, ipſi regi attribuuntur; ita dedecus et infamia, quæ miniſtris domini regis inferuntur, ipſi regi inferuntur:* in which record and many other of that time [*miniſtri regis*] extend to the judges of the realme, as well as to them, that have miniſteriall offices.

Flet. li. 1. ca. 30. Brit. fo. 37. b. Art. ſuper cart. ca. 11. 20 H. 6. 30, 31. M. 33 & 34 E. 1. Corã rege. See hereafter the 29. and 35 chapters.

* [208]

(2) *Ne mainteine,* &c.] Of maintenance ſhall be ſpoken in the expoſition upon the 28 and 29 chapters of this parliament.

(3) *Queux ſont en la court.*] By theſe words it is declared, that regularly champerty is *pendente placito,* and therefore a feoffement after judgement is not within this ſtatute.

(4) *En la court le roy.*] That is, in ſome of the kings courts of record.

Regiſt. 183. 30 Aſſ. p. 15. 19 R. 2. Champerty 15. 3 H. 6. 54. 8 E. 4. 13.

(5) *Pur aver part de ceo.*] Here is champerty forbidden by this act: firſt, therefore it is to be ſeene what champerty is; and ſecondly, whether it were not prohibited by the common law before this act; and laſtly, what was the cauſe of the making of the ſame.

Champerty is derived from two Latin words, *campo et parte,* and therefore champerty is a bargaine with the demandant or tenant, plaintife or defendant, to have part of the thing in ſuit, if he prevaile therein, for maintenance of him in that ſuit; it is called *campi pars,* becauſe he ſhall have a part of the field or land, &c. in demand, in the ſtatute called *definitio conſpirat',* champertors are called *campi participes,* and are thus deſcribed, *campi participes ſunt, qui per ſe, vel per alios placita movent, vel moveri faciunt, et ea ſuis ſumptibus proſequuntur, ad campi partem vel pro parte lucri habend'.*

Flet. l. 2. ca. 30. Britton, fo. 37. 47 E. 3. 9. 31 H. 6. 9. F.N.B. 171. f.

33 E. 1. Vet. Mag. Char. fo. 9. & 111.

Every champerty is maintenance, but every maintenance is not champerty, for champerty is but a ſpecies of maintenance, which is the genus.

It

It was an offence against the common law; for the rule of law is, *culpa est se immiscere rei ad se non pertinenti*. And, *pendente lite nihil innovetur*.

Bract. l. 3. f. 117. Flet. li. 1. c. 20. Brit. ubi supra. Cap. Itineris. Vet. Mag. Chart. 152.

Bracton, who wrote before this statute, rehearsing the articles enquirable by the justices in eyre, saith, *de excessibus vic', et aliorum balivorum, si quam litem suscitaverint, occasione habendi terras vel custodias, vel perquirendi denarios, vel alios profectus, per quod justitia et veritas occultetur, vel dilationem capiat*; and Fleta agreeth with him, where it is said, *per quod justitia et veritas occultetur*; it appeareth that the end of champerty and maintenance is to suppresse justice and truth, or at least to work delay, and therefore it is *malum in se*, and against the common law.

Mirror, c. 1. § 5.

And the Mirror saith, *en perjurie chiont, &c. touts ceux ministers le roy, que mainteinont faux actions, faux appeales, ou faux defences a escient.*

11 H. 6. fo. 11.

An action of maintenance did lie at the common law, and if maintenance *in genere* was against the common law, *à fortiori* champerty, for that of all maintenances is the worst.

8 H. 5. 8. 15 H. 7. 2. in Sub pœna.

And our act and other acts concerning champerty prohibite maintenance, and champerty *en le court le roy*, yet an action of maintenance in the nature of an action of trespasse doth lie in ancient demesne, and other base courts at the common law.

11 H. 6. ubi supra.

As it is said in our books, this act and other statutes concerning champerty and maintenance doe give a greater punishment against them, that offended in maintenance and champerty then was at the common law; by this act he shall be punished at the will of the king, i. by his justices, so as champerty is both *malum in se*, by the common law, and *malum prohibitum*, by this act.

[209]

And for that the kings ministers or officers within his courts, were in place to doe more mischiefe therein to the subverting of justice and truth then others, therefore this act provideth onely against the kings ministers and officers of his courts.

Regist. 182. 4 E. 2. Champerty 12. 21 E. 3. 10. 52. 22 E. 3. 10 30 ass. p. 15. 50 ass. 3. 32 E. 3. Champ. 6. 19 R. 2. ibid. 15. 12 H. 4. 26. 13 H. 4. 16, 17. 8 E. 4. 1. 9 H 7. 18 F.N.B. 172. Regist. Judic. 57. F.N.B. 172. k.

Note it is provided by this act that no minister of the king should maintain to have part, so that hereby it appeareth that it is no champerty unlesse the state, &c. be made for maintenance; note the words of the writ of champerty be *assumpsit manutenend.* or *manucepit, &c.* But see after the 29 chapter, some persons prohibited to purchase at all *pendente placito*.

(6) *Ou auter profit.*] * If the tenant in a reall action graunt a rent, common, or other profit apprender out of the land to maintaine, &c. this is champerty, and yet the rent, common, &c. is not in demand, but they are profits out of the land.

(7) *Ou auters choses.*] Within these words are included leases for yeares; and other goods and chattels, debts and duties.

F.N.B. 171. i.

(8) *Per covenant fait.*] That is, by agreement, either by word or writing; for albeit in the common sense a covenant is taken for an agreement by writing, yet *conventio* in his large sense is taken (as here it is) for an agreement by writing, or by word.

(9) *Il serra puny a la volunt le roy.*] See before cap. 4, 9, 20. and hereafter cap. 26, 29.

This act concerning champerty is the foundation of all the acts and book cases that ensued.

Vide

Vide Vet. Mag. Chart. 11 E. 1. *stat. de champerty. Artic. super chart. cap.* 11. 33 E. 1. *Definitio conspiratorum.* 1 E. 2. cap. 14. 20 E. 3. cap. 4. 1 R. 2. cap. 4. And thus much for the understanding of this first act which is enlarged by divers of the acts abovesaid.

CAP. XXVI.

ET que nul viscount, ne auter minister le roy (1) ne preigne reward pur faire son office (2) mes sont paies de ceo que ilz purnont del roy, et que le fra rendre le double al plaintife, et serra puny a la volunt le roy.

AND that no sheriff, nor other the king's officer, take any reward to do his office, but shall be paid of that which they take of the king; and he that so doth, shall yield twice as much, and shall be punished at the king's pleasure.

Cap. itineris Vet. Mag. Cha. fo. 155. Marlb. ca. 19. 28. W. 1. ca. 3. 15. (1 Inst. 308. 23 H. 6. c. 10. 28 H. 6. c. 5.)

(1) *Minister le roy.*] Under these words, the law beginning with *nul viscount*, are understood escheators, coroners, bailiffes, gaolers, the kings * clerk of the market, aulnager, and other inferiour ministers and officers of the king, whose offices do any way concerne the administration or execution of justice, or the common good of the subject, or for the kings service; that none of the kings officers or ministers doe take any reward for any matter touching their offices, but of the king. And some doe hold that the kings heraulds are within this act, for that they are the kings ministers, and were long before this statute.

Fleta, li. 2. c. 18. & 39. 27 Ass p. 14. Stamf. Pl. Coron. 49. a.
* See the fourth part of the Inst. Cap. Court of the Clerk of the Market.
Rot. Parl. 50 E. 3. nu. 11.

(2) *Ne preigne reward pur faire son office.*] See before cap. 10. *versus finem*; and Fortescue saith, *Quod vicecomes jurabit super sancta Dei evangelia inter articulos alios quod bene, fideliter, et indifferenter exercebit, et faciet officium suum toto illo anno, neque aliquid recipiet colore, aut causa officii sui ab aliquo alio, quam à rege*; and note it is not said, that he shall take no reward generally, but no reward to doe his office. *Vide devant*, cap. 10.

W. 1. cap. 10. Fort. c. 24. f. 28.

[210]

The sheriffe, or any other minister of the king cannot prescribe to take a reward or fee for doing of his office: but the fee of 20. d. called barre fee time out of minde taken by the sheriffe of every prisoner that is acquited, is not against this statute or any other, for it is not taken for doing his office.

42 E. 3. fol. 5. 21 H. 7. 17.

This statute is made in affirmance of a fundamentall maxime of the common law, which is *non capiant vicecomites, vel alii ministri regis præmium, vel mercedem, vel aliquid pro officio suo faciendo, sed tantum de feodis suis à domino rege sint contenti.*

Mag. Chart. c. 29. 28 E. 1. ca. 18. 36 E. 3. ca. 15.

It is a certain and true observation, that the alteration of any of those maximes of the common law is most dangerous, whereof you shall elsewhere reade some instances; whereunto you may adde this ancient maxime affirmed by our act of parliament: for whiles sheriffes, escheators, coroners, and other ministers of the king, whose offices any way did concerne the administration or execution of justice, or the good of the common weale, could take no fee at all for

See the preface to the 4th part of my Reports, and the third part of the Institutes, Cap. Of the high court of parliament. Verb. See here ca. 42.

for doing their office, but of the king, then had they no colour to exact any thing of the ſubject, who knew, that they ought to take nothing of them.

Vide 4 E. 3. c. 10. 27 E. 3. cap. 4. 8 Eliz. cap. 12. 23 H. 6. ca. 10. 34 H. 8. cap. 28 Eliz. cap. 4. 3 H. 7. cap. 12. 1 H. 8. cap. 7. 11 H. 7. cap. 4. 12 H. 7. cap. 5. 8 H. 6. cap. 5. 13 R. 2. c. 4. &c. See before ca. 4. 9, &c.

But when ſome acts of parliament changing the rule of the common law, gave to the ſaid miniſters of the king fees in ſome particular caſes to be taken of the ſubject, whereas before without any taking at all their office was done, now no office at all was done without taking: but at this day they can take no more for doing their office, then have been ſince this act allowed to them by authority of parliament.

This ſtatute doth adde a greater penalty then the common law did give, for by this act the plaintiffe ſhall recover his double damages, and beſides they ſhall be puniſhed at the will of the king, that is, by the kings juſtices, before whom the cauſe depends.

CAP. XXVII.

ET que nul clerke de juſtice, deſchetor, ou denquiror (1), *nul rien ne preigne pur liverer chapiters* (2), *forpris ſolement clerks des juſtices errants en lour eyres, et ceo ii. s. et nient plus de cheſcun wapentake, hundred, ou ville, que reſpoigne per xii. ou per vi.* (3) *ſolonque ceo que auncientment fuit uſe. Et que auterment le fra, rendra le treble de ceo quel avera priſe* (4), *et perdra la ſervice de ſon ſeigniour per un an.*

AND that no clerk of any juſticer, eſcheator, or enquiror, ſhall take any thing for delivering chapiters, but only clerks of juſtices in their circuits, and that ii s. and no more, of every wapentake, hundred, or town, that anſwereth by twelve, or by ſix, according as it hath been uſed of old time; and he that doth contrary ſhall pay thrice ſo much as he hath taken, and ſhall loſe the ſervice of his maſter for one year.

Mirror, c. 4. des Artic. des Eires, Bract. l. 3. fo. 115, 116. Brit. ca. 2. fo. 9, 10. Flet. li. 1. c. 20. Mirror, cap. 2. § 13. See the fourth part of the Inſtitutes, cap. Juſtices in Eire.

*[211]

For the better underſtanding of this act, the manner of the proceeding by the juſtices in eyre in their eyre is to be known. Firſt, they had their authority and power by writs, which writs were at their ſeſſions firſt read, *Quibus auditis, quidam major eorum et diſcretior publice coram omnibus propoſuit quæ ſit cauſa adventus eorum, quæ ſit utilitas itinerationis, et quæ commoditas, ſi pax obſervetur, &c.* The charge being given, then were the bayliffes of the hundreds * called, and their names enrolled, and every of them ſworn that out of every hundred they ſhould chooſe four knights, who forthwith ſhould come before the juſtices, and ſhould be ſworn, that they ſhould chooſe twelve knights, or free and lawfull men, if knights could not be found, &c. by whom the buſineſſe of the king the better, and with greater profit might be expedited; who being returned and ſworn, then ſhould be read to them the chapters or articles of their charge in writing indented, the one part whereof was delivered to them, and the other part remained with the juſtices: and commandement was given to them by the juſtices, that to every chapter or article they ſhould

... ſwer

answer in their verdict severally and by it selfe, sufficiently, distinctly, and openly.

Capitula verò quæ illis duodecim proponenda sunt, quandoque variantur, secundum varietatem temporum et locorum, et quandoque augentur, quandoque minuuntur. Bract. ubi supra. Brit. c. 3. fo. 10. Flet. li. 1. c. 20.

But the ordinary chapters or articles, as it appeareth by *capitula itineris*, amounted to the number of 138, or thereabouts. Cap. Itin' Mag. Chart. fo. 150.

(1) *Enquiror.*] Presently after the making of this statute, there was added to the chapters of the eyre the effect of this act to be inquired of, viz. *De clericis justiciariorum, eschaetorum, vel aliorum ministrorum capientibus denarios pro capitulis deliberand. &c.* Where enquirors or inquisitors are included under the name of *ministri.*

Before this statute, not onely the clerks of the justices, but of escheators and other ministers and officers, that followed the eyre, did use to write them, who would doe it readily, sufficiently, and with lesse charge, which was born by the twelve of every hundred. This liberty that the subject had, could not be restrained but by act of parliament, and therefore two things are hereby provided. 1. That no clerks, &c. but onely the clerks of the justices errants in their eyres, should deliver the chapters. 2. When this act of parliament had drawn it to the hands of the clerks of the justices in eyre, it was necessary to set down in certain, what they should take, and that was but 2. s. of every hundred, which they well deserved, and the county thereby much eased.

(2) *Pur liverer chapters.*] *Capitula* are derived *à capite*, the highest and principall part of man, so when matters are distributed into principall articles, they are said to be digested into heads, which thereupon are called *capitula*: what is intended here by chapters, is declared before. Cap. Itin' ubi sup.

(3) *Que responde per 12. ou per 6.*] For some hundreds were so decayed, as they used to answer to the chapters or articles by 6. as before time had been anciently used.

Now how this chapter could be understood without reading of the ancient authors and old records, let the indifferent reader judge.

(4) *Et que auterment le fra rendr' le treble value de ceo que il aver prise.*] That is to say, if any clerk, but the clerks of the justices in eyre, did for reward deliver the chapters, or if the clerks of the justices in eyre for the delivery of them did take above 2. s. they should render to them of whom they tooke treble so much as they received, and besides lose the service of their master for one yeare.

CAP. XXVIII. [212]

ET que nul clerk le roy ne des justices resceive disformes presentment del esglise, dont plea ou conteke soit en la court le roy, sans speciall conge le roy, et ceo defende le roy sur paine de perdre lesglise

AND that none of the king's clerks, nor of any justicer, from henceforth shall receive the presentment of any church, for the which any plea or debate is in the king's court,

lesglise et son service. Et que nul clerke de justice, ne de vicont (2), *ne mainteine parties* (1) *en quarels, ne besoignes queux sont en la court le roy, ne fraud ne face* (3) *pur common droiture delayer, ou disturber* (4). *Et si ull' le fait, il serra punie per la paine procheinment avantdit, ou per pluis grievous, si le trespasse le requiert.*

court, without special licence of the king; and that the king forbiddeth, upon pain to lose the church, and his service: and that no clerk of any justicer, or sheriff, take part in any quarrels of matters depending in the king's court, nor shall work any fraud, whereby common right may be delayed or disturbed; and if any so do, he shall be punished by the pain aforesaid, or more grievously, if the trespass do so require.

(Regist. 182. 189. Rast. 119. 427, &c. 28 Ed. 1. c. 11. 1 Ed. 3. stat. 2. c. 14. 4 Ed. 3. c. 11. 20 Ed. 3. c. 4. 1 R. 2. c. 4.)

1. This act is divided into foure branches, first, that no clerk of the king, nor of any justice receive any presentment to any church, whereof any plea was depending in the kings court; the mischiefe before this act was, that depending a suit for a church in the kings court, the one party or the other would present the chaplain of the king, or of some of the judges, the more to countenance the one party, and discourage the other, and the mischiefe was the greater for that at this time, *cum aliquis jus præsentandi non habens præsentaverit ad aliquam ecclesiam; cujus præsentatus sit admissus (i. institutus) ipse qui verus est patronus per nullum aliud breve recuperare poterit advocationem suam quam per breve de recto.*

Brit. fo. 37. b. W. 2. 13 E. 1. c. 3. 45 E. 3. Quar. Imp. 139.

2. The second branch containeth the punishment, viz. that if he doth it without the kings license, he shall lose the church, that is, that the church shall be void as unto him, and that he shall lose his service, that is, that he be not after chaplain to the king during one yeare. And at this time divers ecclesiasticall persons were not onely clerks in the chancery, and other the kings courts, but also stewards of houshold to noble men, justices, and other great men.

Regist. fo. 58. F.N.B. 44. g.

3. The third branch is, that no clerk of any justice or sheriffe shall maintain any party in any querels, or businesse depending in the kings courts.

(1) *Ne mainteine parties, &c.*] *Ne manuteneas,* whereof commeth the word of art *manutenentia,* or *manutentio,* derived *à manu et tenere: manus* doth not onely signifie power or help by word or countenance, but *manus* is herein used, for that most usually maintenance is done by the hand, either by delivery of money, or other reward, or by writing on the behalfe of one of the parties in a suit depending.

It is in the Register thus coupled, *manutenuit et sustentavit,* and *sustentare* is properly to underprop any thing that is likely to fall.

Maintenance is an unlawfull upholding of the demandant or plaintife, tenant or defendant in a cause depending in suit, by word, writing, countenance, or deed.

This maintenance (as hath been said) is *malum in se,* and against the common law, and that is notably proved by this act, for hereby main enance

maintenance is branded with this quality that thereby common right is delaied, or disturbed, and consequently against the common law.

And it is to be understood, that *manutenentia est duplex*, that is to say, *curialis*, that is, in courts of justice, *pendente placito*, and of this the said description is given; and *ruralis*, that is, to stir up and maintaine querelas, that is, complaints, suits, and parts in the country, other then their owne, though the same depend not in plea, and this is punished with great severity, as by the acts therefore provided appeareth. [213] 1 E. 3 c. 14. 4 E. 3. c. 11. 20 E. 3. ca. 4. 1 R. 2. ca. 4.

Manutenentia curialis is divided into lawfull, and unlawfull, and into generall, and speciall, as shall be shewed in his proper place, *viz.* in the exposition of the act of 28 Ed. 1. *Art. super cart'.* Art. super cart. cap. 11.

(2) *Nul clerke de justice ne de viscount*] These were prohibited by this act, because they were in place, as before hath been said, to do more mischiefe, that is, by their maintenance to disturbe or delay common right. See cap. 24.

(3) *Ne fraude ne face.*] This fraud is worthy of the punishment inflicted by this act, for that it tendeth to delay, or disturbe common right, that is, the due proceeding of law.

(4) *Pur common droit delayer ou disturber.*] These words refer as well to maintenance, as to fraud.

4. The fourth branch is the punishment, which evidently appeareth by the act.

CAP. XXIX.

PURVIEW est ensement, que si ul serjeant, counter (1) ou auter (2) face ul maner de disceit (3), ou de collusion en la court le roy, ou consent de faire la, en disceit de la court, pur engin' (4) le court, ou la partie, et de ceo soit attaint, lors puis eit la prisonment dun an et un jour, et ne soit oye en la court le roy a counter pur nulluy (5). Et si ceo soit auter que count', per mesme le maner eit la prison dun an en dun jour a tout le meins. Et si le trespas demande greinder paine, soit a volunt le roy (6).

IT is provided also, that if any serjeant, pleader, or other, do any manner of deceit or collusion in the king's court, or consent unto it, in deceit of the court, or to beguile the court, or the party, and thereof be attainted, he shall be imprisoned for a yeare and a day, and from thenceforth shall not be heard to plead in that court for any man; and if he be no pleader, he shall be imprisoned in like manner by the space of a year and a day at least; and if the trespass require greater punishment, it shall be at the king's pleasure.

(8 R. 2. c. 4. 10 H. 6. c. 4. 18 H. 6. c. 9. Rast. 2. 11 Ed. 4. 3. b. Palmer, 288. Salk. 517.

Before this statute, in the irregular raigne of H. 3. serjeaunts, apprentices, attorneys, clerks of the kings courts, and others did practise and put in ure unlawfull shifts and devises so cunningly contrived (and specially in the cases of great men) in deceit of the kings courts, as oftentimes the judges of the same were by such crafty and finister shifts and practises invegled and beguiled, which

which was against the common law, and therefore this act was made in affirmance of the common law; onely it added a greater punishment: for heare what the Mirrour saith of the serjeant at law, what his office and duty was: *Chescun serjeaunt counter est chargeable per serement que il ne maintenera, ne defendera tort ne faixime a son scient, eins guerpera son client, a quel heure que il puit son tort a perceiver. Auxi que il ne mitter in court faux delaies, ne faux tesmoignes ne movera, ne profera, ne aux corruptions, deceits, menjonges, ne aux fauxes lies ne consentera, mes loialment maintenera le droit de son client, que il ne chiet per follie, negligence, ne default de luy, ne de resonne que a luy appendroit de pronouncer et per mesterie, leding, despiser, coup, polie, tenson, manace, noise, ne villanie, ne disturbera judge, party, serjeaunt, ne auter in court per quoy il disturbe droit ou audience.* In former times learned and grave apprentices of law came not to this state and degree *per ambitum*, but contrariwise when they were called thereunto, they assayed all means to avoid it, taking the degree of an apprentice to be the more permanent place: as taking one example for many; in the 5 yeare of H. 5. John Martine, William Babington, William Pole, William Westbury, John June, and Thomas Rolfe, six grave and famous apprentices, having writs delivered unto them to take the state and degree of serjeaunts retournable in Michaelmas terme, when all the meanes which they had used could not prevail, they at the returne thereof in chancery absolutely refused the same; whereupon they were called into the parliament then sitting, and there charged to take the state and degree upon them, which in the end they did, and divers of them afterwards did worthily serve the king in the principall offices of the law, as by our books appeareth.

Mirr. c. 2. § 5. des counters.

[214]

Rot Parl. an. 5. H. 5.

(1) *Serjeaunt counter.*] Of his antiquity and calling *ad statum et gradum servientis ad legem*, I have spoken in another place. In ancient books he is called, *counter*, or *narrator* of the count or declaration, being grounded upon the originall writ, the foundation of the suit: and serjeaunt being a generall word, *counter* is added to it, to restraine it to a serjeaunt at law. *Vide* ca. 30. And untill this day, when serjeaunts proceed, every of them counteth, that is, reciteth count in an action appointed to him by the judges before them.

1. part of the Instit. sect.

Flet. li. 2. c. 21. Cust. de Norm cap. 64. Mirr. ubi sup.

The Mirrour saith, *Counters sont serjeaunts sachants le ley del realme, que servent al common del people a pronouncer & defender les actions en judgement, pur ceux que mitteront pur loier, &c.*

Mirr. ubi supra.

(2) *Ou auter.*] This extendeth to apprentices, attornies, clerks of courts, or any other.

For the better understanding of this act, it is necessary to set downe the oath of the serjeaunt at law.

This oath consisteth on foure parts.

The oath of the serjeaunt at law.

1. That he shall well and truly serve the kings people, as one of the serjeaunts of the law.

2. That he shall truly counsell them, that he shall be retained with, after his cunning.

3. That he shall not defer, tract, or delay their causes willingly, for covetousnesse of money, or other thing that may tend to his profit.

4. That he shall give due attendance accordingly.

This oath consisteth on six parts.

The oath of the kings serjeaunt at law.

1. That he shall well and truly serve the king and his people, as one of the kings serjeaunts at law.

2. That

2. That he shall truly counsell the king in his matters when hee shall be called.

3. And duely and truly minister the kings matters after the course of the law, to his cunning.

4. He shall take no wages or fee of any man for any matters, where the king is party, against the king.

5. He shall as duly, as hastily speed such matters, as any man shall have to do against the king in the law, as he may lawfully doe, without delay, or tarrying the party of his lawfull proces in that belongeth to him.

6. He shall be attendant to the kings matters when hee shall be called thereto.

The apprentice at law is not sworne.

Concerning attorneys, it is provided by the statute of 4 H. 4. cap. 18. that they that be good and vertuous, learned, and of good fame, shall be received, and their names put into the roll, and shall be sworne well and truly to serve in their offices, and specially that they make no suit in a forein county. [215] 4 H. 4. ca. 18. The Roll of Attorneys.

Newton, chiefe justice of the court of common pleas, gave judgement of an attourney of that court, that had sued out a *capias* without an originall, that his name should be drawne out of the roll of attorneys, and that he should never be attorney in this court, nor in any other court of the king, and that he should not meddle in them in the law; and to perform all this, he in those days was sworne on a book. And Newton said to him, The king hereafter, when you shall have better grace, may pardon you by his letters patents, &c. and then you may be restored againe. 20 H. 6. fo. 37.

(3) *Face ul maner de disceit.*] This must be a mis-fesauns, and not a non fesauns; for the words be doe, *i. faciat aliquam deceptionem seu collusionem, &c.* And to illustrate this matter, it is good to put some examples,

A writ of *habere facias seisinam* did falsly recite a recovery in a reall action (where in truth there was no recovery at all) by colour of which writ a man was put out of his freehold; [a] this was a collusion in deceit of the court, and the delinquent was by this statute awarded to prison, &c.

[b] So it is to sue out a *capias* without an originall.

[c] Also to bring a *præcipe* against a poore man, knowing that he hath nothing in the land, of purpose to get the possession of the land against the tenant who is in possession.

[d] To procure an attourney to appeare for a man, and plead without warrant.

If a serjeaunt, or an apprentice of the law in pleading a matter of fact issuable for his client, alledge the same to be done at a towne in such a county, where in deed he knoweth there is no such towne, of purpose to delay justice, *et a enginer la court*, this is a deceit within this statute, and so it hath beene holden.

[e] A. H. in execution in the counter of London, and because that prison is a strait prison, devised a shift (in deceit of the court) to be removed from thence to the Fleet, and his device was this: He made an obligation of xx. l. to S. and caused the obligation to be put in suite against himselfe in the name of S. and judgement in the court of common pleas was given against him upon his confession, and procured a *habeas corpus cum causa*, and thereupon he was brought into the court of common pleas, and there one in the

[a] 17 E. 3. 51. F.N.B. 98. o. Hil. 16. E. 1. in Banc. 58. deceit, & collusion sur recovery, &c. Radulphus Paymel, &c. Hil. 22 E. 1. Rot. 70. in com. Banc. Allan Prats case.
[b] 20 H. 6. 37.
[c] 39 E. 3. fo. 15. 3 E. 3. 49, 50. semble. 4 E. 3. 37. F.N.B. 103. a.
[d] 41 E. 3. 1. Die 20 El. 361.
[e] Dier 8 El. 249

name of S. prayed that he might be committed in execution to the Fleet; and the court being beguiled, and knowing nothing of this deceit, and subtill and false practise, committed him to the Fleet, where S. never had such a debt, nor ever was privie to any of the said proceedings, A. H. and his counsellors, &c. are within this statute.

10 E. 4. 9. b. F.N.B. 98. 1. This act is also in affirmance of the common law, for fraud and falshood is against the common law: and therefore if the client would have the attourney to plead a false plea, he ought not to doe it, for he may plead *quod non sum veraciter informatus, et ideo nullum responsum, &c.* and that shall be entred into the roll to save him from dammages in a writ of disceit: and if an attorney ought not wittingly to plead a false plea, *á fortiori*, a serjeaunt or an apprentice ought not to doe the same.

(4) *Pur enginer* (ou engingner) *le court ou la partie.*] That is, to beguile the court, or the partie, as by the examples before expressed have appeared.

And this artificiall deceit is of all other the worst, for hereby the matter is so tricked, shadowed, and heightned by colour of painted art, as thereby the judges themselves are abused and beguiled.

[216] (5) *Eit la prisonment dun an, & ne soit oye en la court le roy a counter pur nulluy.*] This punishment extends as well to the apprentice, as to the serjeaunt.

(6) *Soit a volunt le roy.*] These words are before expounded, cap. 4. &c.

Tr. 18 E. 1. in Bi. Rot. 168. warr'. William de Wasthill plaintife against Matthew of the exchequer, in an action of deceit, and declared, that where he had demised to the said Matthew certain lands in Wyrlingscote in the county of Worcester, and Blakgreve in the county of Warwick for the terme of twelve yeares, and covenanted by fine to assure the same, the said Matthew other lands in the said fine fraudulently did insert, to have and to hold to him in fee, to the disherison of the plaintife, &c. This matter was treated of, and examined by all the judges of England, and the treasurer and barons of the exchequer in the presence (saith the record) of Henry de Lacy earle of Lincolne, master William de bishop of Ely, and Robert of Tipetet, and others: and, to use the words of the record, *Super examinationem tam ipsius Matthæi quam recordorum, compertum est, quod hæc et alia perpetravit in deceptionem curiæ:* and thereupon judgement is given, *Quod committatur gaolæ ibidem moratur' per unum annum et unum diem secundum * statutum, et finis † cassetur.*

* W. 1. ca. 29. † Nota hoc. The quashing of the fine was by force of these words in this statute, *Et si le trespas demand greinder paine, soit a volunt le roy*, that is, of the kings court, where the plea dependeth.

Hæc est finalis concordia facta in curia domini regis apud Westm' a die Sancti Michaelis in xv. dies, anno regni regis Edwardi filii regis Henrici tricesimo tertio, coram Radulpho de Hengham, Willielmo de Bereford, Elia de Bekingham, Petro Malore, Willielmo Howard, & Lamberto de Trykingham justic', & aliis domini regis fidelibus tunc ibi præsentibus. inter Rogerum de Gamages, & Ceciliam uxorem ejus querentes, & Iohannem filium Iohannis de Ballingham deforc' de duabus mesuagiis, quinquaginta & duabus acris terræ, & una acra bosci, & dimid' un' acræ pasturæ, & medietate unius acræ prati, cum pertinentiis in Ballingham, unde placitum conventionis summonitum fuit inter eos

Nota. Six judges in the court of Common Pleas. Mich. 33 E. 1.

Placit' convent'.

eos in eadem curia, scilicet quod prædictus R. recogn' prædicta tenementa cum pertinentiis esse jus ipsius Iohannis. Et pro hac recognitione, fine & concordia, idem Iohannes concessit prædictis Rogero & Ceciliæ prædicta tenementa cum pertinentiis, & illa eis reddidit in eadem curia. Habend' & tenend' eisdem Rogero et Ceciliæ, & hæredibus ipsius Ceciliæ de capitalibus domini feodi illius per servitia quæ ad tenementa pertinent imperpetuum. Et præterea idem Iohannes concessit pro se & hæredibus suis, quod ipsi warrant' eisdem Rogero & Ceciliæ, & hæredibus ipsius Ceciliæ, prædicta tenementa cum pertinentiis contra omnes homines imperpetuum. Et pro hac recognitione, redditione, warrant', fine & concordia iidem Rogerus & Cecilia dederunt prædicto Iohanni viginti libr' sterlingorum. A render to Cecilie, which was not party to the conusans.

This fine being removed *coram rege*; the heires of John Ballingham, *viz.* Cecilie the wife of Roger Burghull, and her husband, and Sibyl and Cecilie daughters and heires of Margerie, brought a writ of deceit, &c. for the avoiding of the fine: *asserentes* (saith the record) *prædictum finem minus ritè esse levatum in deceptionem curiæ regis, et in exhæredationem hæredum prædict', eo quod prædicta tenementa in prædict' fine contenta sunt de manerio de Ballingham, quod est de antiquo dominico coronæ Angliæ.* Afterwards Roger and Cecilie his wife upon their default were severed, and Sibill and Cecilie sued forth, and prayed that the fine for the cause aforesaid, *revocetur et penitus adnulletur*, and the court in this case resolved thus, *Et quia videtur curiæ quod præd. Sibilla et Cecilia filiæ præd. Margeriæ ad breve suum præd. respondere' non debent, eo quod prædict' Johannes filius Johannis antecessor earundem, &c. si modo vixisset ad præd. finem adnulland. admitti non debuit:* and yet the record proceedeth for the punishment of the deceit to the court in these words, *Quæsitum est à præfatis Rogero de Gamages, et Cecilia uxore ejus, quia respondeant ad deceptionem et collusionem curiæ domini regis præd. &c. qui dicunt quod præd. tenementa in prædicto fine contenta sunt ad communem legem placitabilia, et semper à tempore, quo non extat memoria hucusque, &c. et non per breve clausum de recto, &c. eo quod non sunt de antiquo dominico, &c. et de hoc pon' se * super patriam, &c. Ideo ven' inde jurata coram rege à die Paschæ in quindecim dies ubicunque, &c.*

Hil. 7 E. 2. coram rege. rot. 93. Hereford.

[217]

Vid. 17 E. 3. 31. 30 E. 3. 22. 8 Ass. 35. 8 H. 6 11. The writ of Deceit is to bee brought by the lord for the adnulling and revoking of the fine, but the court may punish the deceit to the court, at the suit of the party or his heires.

* 17 E. 3. 31.

There is a chapter added amongst the acts made in W. 2. anno 13 E. 1. the last chapter saving one in these words, *chauncellor, treasurer, justices, ne nul del councel le roy, ne clerk de la chauncery, ne del eschequer, ne de justice, ne dauter minister, ne nul del hostle l' roy ne clerk, ne lay, ne puit receiver esglise, ne advowson de esglise, ne t're ne tenement en fee per done, ne per achate, ne a farme, ne a champerty, ne en auter maner, tanque come le chose est en plea devant nous, ou devant ul de nous ministres, ne nul lower ent soit prise, &c.*

It is certain that this chapter was not enacted in 13 E. 1. therefore it is to be seen when it was made a law.

First, Fleta coupleth the 25 chapter of this parliament of W. 1. and the said chapter inserted into W. 2. together; whereby it seemeth that it was made at this parliament. Fleta ubi supra.

2. It is enacted in the French tongue, as this statute of W. 1. is, and all the rest of the statute of W. 2. is in Latine.

3. It hath the same phrase and manner of penning that the 25. 28. and 29. chapters of this act of W. 1. hath.

4. The statute of champerty made in the 11 yeare of E. 1. (which was before the statute of W. 2.) reciteth the effect of this chapter, Stat. de Champ. anno 11 E. 1. Vet Mag. Cha. fo. 80. b.

chapter, and the 29 chapter of the parliament of W. 1. for by the said act of 11 E. 1. it is recited, *Come contenue soit in nostre estatute, que nul de nostre court preigne plea a champerty per art ne per engin'*; which is a summary recitall of the said act inserted, as is aforesaid, amongst the statutes of W. 2. for the chauncellor, treasurer, justices, &c. are all of the kings courts, and it was fitter to rehearse them generally, then by particular names.

And further, the said act of 11 E. 1. reciteth this 29 chapter concerning counters, attourneyes, and apprentices, and others, as Fleta doth, rather by way of explanation, then in the same words.

5. There is no one act in W. 1. so general as this rehearsall in the 11 E. 1. is, for the 25 chapter is *nul minister*, and this is *nul generalment* without limitation.

6. Mention is made in the recitall of the said act of 11 E. 1. of officers *à hauts homes & auters de la terre*, and in no statute before that, any mention is made *des hauts homes*, that is, of the chauncellor, treasurer, the kings counsellors, &c. but onely in this act, which is inserted amongst the statutes of W. 2.

7. And where by the 28 chapter, provision was made against the clerks of the king, and of the justices, and by the 29 chapter against serjeants, apprentices, attournies, and others, it had been a great omission and defect in the makers of these laws, to have left out the great officers and justices themselves of the kings courts, and others recited in this act inserted in W. 2. against whom it was more necessary to provide, then against the other, because they had more power to offend; and the law had not seemed equall, if provision had not been made as wel against the majorities, as the minorities, the great, as the small.

[218] 8. The said act inserted into W. 2. inflicteth punishment *(a la volunt le roy)* the act of 11 E. 1. doth adde hereunto three years imprisonment, for *dignitas personæ auget pœnam.*

En fee.] That is, in fee simple.

Per done.] That is, by a gift in taile.

Ne per achate.] That is, by purchase for mony or other consideration.

30 Ass. 15. *Ne a farme.*] That is, by lease for life, or for yeares.

30 E. 3. 3. *Ne a champerty.*] This hath beene explained before, chap. 25.

8 E. 4. 13. *Ne en auter manner.*] These be generall words, and forbid all purchases *pendente placito* by the persons named in this act; which is worthy of observation, to make a diversity between these persons herein named, and others: see before cap. 25. and note well the books there quoted.

A volunt le roy.] This is explained before cap. 4. &c.

Vide W. 2. cap. 49. Stat. de. 33 E. 1 De conspiracy, Vet. Mag. Cart. fo. 111. b. *Auxibien celuy que purchase come celuy que le fra.*] Note the punishment lieth by this act equally, as well upon the giver as the taker.

CAP.

CAP. XXX.

ET pur ceo que multz des gents ſe pleignent des ſerjeaunts (1), criours de fee (2), et les marſhals des juſtices (3) en eire, et [dauters juſtices] quelles pernent a tort deniers de ceux queux recoveront ſeiſin del terre, ou queux gaignont lour quereles, et de fine levie, et des jurors, villes, priſoners, et des auters attaches en plees de la corone, auterment que faire ne duiſſent, en muts des manners, et de ceo quil ad plus grand number de ceux que eſtre ne duiſt (4), per que le people eſt malement greve; le roy defende, que ceſt s choſes ne ſoient diſormes faits. Et ſi ull' ſerjeant de fee le face, office ſoit priſe en le maine le roy. Et ſi marſhals des juſtices le facent, ſoient punis grevement a la volunt le roy. Et a touts les plaintiſes lun et lauter rendre le trebie de ceo quels aver' priſe en cel maner.

AND foraſmuch as many complain themſelves of officers, cryers of fee, and the marſhals of juſtices in eyre, taking money wrongfully of ſuch as recover ſeiſin of land, or of them that obtain their ſuits, and of fines levied, and of jurors, towns, priſoners, and of others attached upon pleas of the crown, otherwiſe than they ought to do, in divers manners; and foraſmuch as there is a greater number of them than there ought to be, whereby the people are ſore grieved; the king commandeth that ſuch things be no more done from henceforth; and if any officer of fee doth it, his office ſhall be taken into the king's hand; and if any of the juſtices marſhals do it, they ſhall be grievouſly puniſhed at the king's pleaſure; and as well the one as the other ſhall pay unto the complainants the treble value of that they have received in ſuch manner.

Vide Mirror, c. 5. § 4. Britton 37. b. (11 Ed. 4. 3. b. 4 Inſt. 101.)

(1) *Serjants.*] Fleta rendreth theſe words thus, *virgatores ſervientes*, they were called *virgatores à virgis*, of white rods, which they carried in their hands before the juſtices in eyre and other juſtices. Flet. li. 2. c. 32. de Virgatoribus. [219]

(2) *Criors de fee.*] It appeareth by Fleta that theſe are comprehended under the generall name of *virgatores*, and therefore carried rods alſo, he rendreth theſe words *clamatores de feodo.* Fleta ubi ſupra.

(3) *Et les marſhals des juſtices.*] *Juſticiariorum mareſchalli.* Fleta ubi ſupra.

(4) *Et de ceo que il ad pluis nombre que eſtre ne duiſt.*] Hereby it appeareth, that the over-great number of theſe virgers, criers, and marſhals, was a meanes of extortion, or grievance of the people; and ſo it is in all other caſes of what profeſſion or place ſoever, *Multitudo imperatorum perdidit cariam:* beſides it taketh away the eſtimation and credit of the ſame.

CAP.

CAP. XXXI.

DE ceux queux parnent outragious tolnet' (1), enconter common usage du realme en la ville merchandie (2): purview est, que si ull' le face en la ville le roy mesme, que soit bail' a fee farme, le roy prendra le franchise (4) del marche (3) en sa maine. Et si soit auter ville, et ceo soit fait per le seigniour de mesme la ville (5), le roy le fra per mesme le maner. Et sil soit fait per le bailife sans le commandement le seigniour, il rendra al plaintife au tant pur le outragious prise, come il avoit prise de luy, sil ust import son tolne: et il avera prison del xl. jours. Des citizens, et des burgesses a que le roy ou son pere ad grant murage pur lour villes encloser (6), et que tiel murage parnent auterment que lour est grante, et de ceo soient attaintes: purview est, que ils pardent cel grant de touts le temps (6) que serra a vener, et serront en le grievous mercy le roy.

TOUCHING them that take outragious toll, contrary to the common custom of the realm, in market-towns; it is provided, that if any do so in the king's town, which is let in fee-farm, the king shall seise into his own hand the franchise of the market; and if it be another's town, and the same be done by the lord of the town, the king shall do in like manner; and if it be done by a bailiff, or any mean officer, without the commandment of his lord, he shall restore to the plaintiff as much more for the outragious taking, as he had of him, if he had carried away his toll, and shall have forty days imprisonment. Touching citizens and burgesses, to whom the king or his father hath granted murage to enclose their towns, which take such murage otherwise than it was granted unto them, and thereof be attainted; it is provided, that they shall lose their grant for ever, and shall be grievously amerced unto the king.

Mag. Chart. c. 30. W. 2. cap. 25.

In the troublesome and irregular raigne of H. 3. outragious tols were taken and usurped in cities, boroughs, towns, where faires and markets were kept, to the great oppression of the kings subjects, by reason whereof very many did refraine from the comming to faires and markets, to the hindrance of the common-wealth; for it hath ever been the policy and wisdome of this realm that faires and markets, and specially the markets, be well furnished and frequented.

Lib. 8. fol. 46. Mag. Chart. ubi sup. W. 2. ubi sup.

[220]

(1) *Tolnet.*] Toll. For the generality of the word, see Jehu Webs case, lib. 8. Magna Charta, and W. 2. whereof, and of the severall kinds thereof, more shall be said in the exposition of the statute of W. 2. for that here it is restrained, as hereafter appeareth.

Vide ca. 36. for this word.

Outragious.] That is, either where a reasonable toll is due, and excessive toll is taken, or where no toll at all is due, and yet toll is unjustly usurped, for it is an outrage to doe such a common injury and wrong; sometime it is called *superfluum, vel indebitum, vel injustum.*

Cap. Itin' Vet. Mag. Chart.

No

No toll is due either on the part of the lord, when he hath a faire or market, and not any toll; or on the part of the market-man, who ought to be diſcharged of toll, or of the thing ſold that is not tollable. Flet. li. 2. c. 43. & li. 1. ca. 20.

(2) *En la ville merchandie.*] That is, in a city, borough, or town of merchandize, where faires and open markets are kept, for merchandizing, and buying and ſelling. Bract. li. 2. 56, 57. *Forum, nundinæ, feria, mercatus, oppidum.*

This is intended of toll to the faire or market, whereof we will only ſpeak in this place.

Toll to the faire or market is a reaſonable ſumme of money due to the owner of the faire or market, upon ſale of things tollable within the fair or market, or for ſtallage, picage, or the like.

And this was at the firſt invented, that contracts might have good teſtimony, and be made openly; for of old time, privy or ſecret contracts were forbidden, and the Mirror ſaid truth, for the auncient law was, *Negotiator in vulgo ſi quid mercatus fuerit in eam rem teſtimonia habeto; nemo extra oppidum, niſi præſente præpoſito aliiſve fide dignis hominibus, quicquam emito.* And another, *Ne quis extra oppidum quid emat*; in theſe laws *oppidum* is taken for faire or market. Cap. 1. § 3. Inter leges Inæ regis. Inter leges Ethelſtani regis.

And again the ſame king, *Si quis teſtatò rem aliquam mercatus fuerit, quam alius deinceps quiſque ſuam eſſe contenderit, eam venditor præſtet, atque in ſe recipiat, ſive is ſervus ſive ingenuus fuerit: die autem dominico nemo mercaturam facito; id quod ſi quis egerit, et ipſa merce, et 30. præterea ſolidis mulctator.*

Here note by the way two things, firſt, the antiquity of the law for changing of property, according to theſe auncient laws, and therefore to this day it is called, *apertum forum*, or *apertus mercatus*, an open market, or market overt; and ſecondly, that no merchandizing ſhould be on the Lords day.

Bonorum (ſine fidejuſſione, et teſtimonio) emptio, aut permutatio non eſto. Inter leges Etheldredi regis.

Si quis teſtibus non adhibitis quicquam fuerit mercatus, idemque alter uti ſuum ipſius proprium vendicaret, emptori nulla fiat advocandi poteſtas, verum is domino rem reddito, &c. Which I have recited for the confirmation of the Mirror, and for the honour of venerable antiquity. Inter leges Canuti regis.

Every one, that hath a faire or market, ought to have it by graunt or preſcription; if the king graunt to a man a faire or market, and graunt no toll, the patentee ſhall have no toll, for toll being a matter of private for the benefit of the lord is not incident to a faire or market ſo graunted without a ſpeciall graunt, as it was adjudged in the caſe of Northampton, for ſuch a faire or market is accounted a free faire or market; and there it was alſo reſolved, that after ſuch a graunt made the king cannot graunt a toll to ſuch a free faire or market without *quid pro quo*, ſome proportionable benefit to the ſubject. Laſtly, it was there reſolved, that if the toll graunted with the faire or market bee outragious or unreaſonable, the graunt of the toll is void, and that the ſame is a free market or faire. Mich. 39 & 40. Eliz. Cor. Rege.

But if the king graunt unto one a faire or market, he ſhall have without any graunt a court of record, called a court of pipowdres *, as incident thereunto, for that is for advancement and expedition of juſtice, and for the ſupporting and maintenance of the faire or * [221] Bract. l. 5. c. 334. 17 E. 4. c. 2. 1 R. 3. c. 6. 7 E. 4. 23. 13 E. 4. 8.

7 H. 6. 18, 19. 13 H. 7. 19. b. Dier 3 Mar. 132, 133. * 9 H. 6. fo. 45. tit. toll 7.

or market; and so note a diversity between the private and the publique.

* No toll for any thing tollable brought to the fair or market to be sold, shall be paid to the owner of the faire or market before the sale thereof, unlesse it be by custome time out of mind used, which custome none can challenge that claime the faire or market by graunt within the time of memory, *viz.* since the raigne of king R. 1. which is a point worthy of observation for the suppression of many outragious and unjust tolls incroached upon the subject to be punished within the purview of this statute. So note, it is better to have a faire by prescription, then by graunt.

2 & 3 P. & M. c. 7. 31 Eliz. ca. 12. 9 H. 6. 45.

Also if the lord or owner of the faire or market doe take toll of the seller of horses, &c. he is to be punished within this statute, for he ought to take it of the buyer onely. *Vide* 2 & 3 Ph. & Mar. & 31 Eliz. And so *de communi jure* no toll shall be paid for things brought to the faire or market, unlesse they be sold, and then toll to be taken of the buyer; but in ancient faires and markets toll may be paid for the standing in the faire or market, though nothing be sold.

Bract. li. 2. f. 57. 3 E. 3. ass. 445. 14 E. 3. Barr. 177. 16 E. 3. grant 53. 39 E. 3. 13. b. 41 E. 3. 24. 43 E. 3. 29. 44 E. 3. 20. F.N.B. 94. f. & 227.

If the king or any of his progenitors have granted to any to be discharged of this toll either generally or specially, this grant is good to discharge him of all tolls to the kings owne faires or markets, and of the tolls, which together with any faire or market have been granted after such grant of discharge, but cannot discharge tolls formerly due to subjects, either by graunt or prescription.

Bract. fo. 56. a. & 57. b.

Hereof Bracton said, *In omni libertate concessa, &c. erit prioritas præferenda.* And againe, *Esse enim poterit libertas, ut si quis teneatur ad dandum ex servitute, sicut theolonium et consuetudines, ex libertate defendi poterit ad non dandum, item si ex servitute teneatur quis ad non capiendum, ex libertate concessa capere possit consuetudines et theolonia.*

7 H. 4. 4. 9 H. 6. 25. F.N.B. 228. d. Regist.

Tenants in ancient demesne, for things comming of those lands shall pay no toll, because at the beginning by their tenure they applyed themselves to the manurance and husbandry of the kings demeans, and therefore for those lands so holden, and all that came or renewed thereupon, they had the said priviledge: but if such a tenant be a common merchant for buying and selling of wares or merchandises, that rise not upon the manurance or husbandry of those lands, he shall not have the priviledge for them, because they are out of the reason of the priviledge of ancient demesne, and the tenant in ancient demesne ought rather to be a husbandman then a merchant by his tenure, and so are the books to be intended. And herewith agreeth an ancient record, the effect whereof is,

Hil. 14 E. 1. corã rege rot. 41. Devon.

Quod hii qui clamant esse immunes de theolonio præstando, ut tenentes in antiquo dominico, vel per chartas regum, non debent distringi pro aliquo theolonio pro merchandizis ad usus suos proprios emptis; imo pro merchandizis qu' emerint vel vendiderint ut mercatores, debent solvere pro eis.

Rot. Parl. an. 18 E. 1. fo. 2. int. Abbatem loci sancti Edw, & Balivos de Southampton.

King H. 3. did grant to the abbot of L. and his successors, *Quod ipsi et homines sui sint quieti ab omni theolonio in omni foro et in omnibus nundinis, &c.* And there it is resolved, that the abbot should have this priviledge by force of this generall graunt in this manner, *Quod ipsi et homines sui sint quieti à præstatione theolonii in venditionibus*

ditionibus et emptionibus pro suis necessariis, ut in victu, vestitu, et similibus, et hoc ad opus proprium ipsius abbatis et hominum suorum. Mich. 2 E. 2. coram rege pro mercato de Brimmingham acc'.

* The king shall not pay toll for any of his goods, and if any be taken, it is punishable within this statute.

(3) *Marche.*] This word doth here include as well a faire as a market; for *forum*, from whence faire is derived, signifieth both: and a mart is a great faire holden every yeare, derived *à merce*, because merchandises and wares are thither abundantly brought: and *mercatus* is derived *à mercando*. * 35 H. 6. 57.

(4) *Prendra le franchise.*] That is, shall seise the franchise of the faire or market untill it be redeemed by the owner: but this is intended upon an office to be found, for in statutes incidents are ever supplyed by intendment. [222]

(5) *Seignior de mesme la ville.*] That is, the owner of the faire or market.

Fleta collecteth the effect of this former part of the act in these words, *Inhibitum est ne quis in villis regis merchandiis, quæ dimissæ sunt et commissæ ad feodi firmam, indebita et injusta capiat theolonia; quod si quis fecerit, extunc eo ipso capiet rex libertatem mercati in manum suam; eodem modo facit rex, licet in alterius villa præmissa fieri contigerit, si balivus hoc fecerit sine voluntate domini sui, reddet tantum querenti, quantum cepisset balivus ab eo, si tolnetum asportasset, et nihilominus habeat prisonam 40. dierum.* Flet. li. 2. c. 43. versus finem.

Here I perswade my selfe some would desire to know, what is due for toll to the faire or market: to which I answer, that I can tell what was due of old, and what was ordained in times past by ancient kings to be paid: for the Mirrour saith, *Que faires et markets se fissent per lieus, et que achators de blee, et beasts donassent toll a les bailifes des seigniours de markets, ou de faires, cestascavoire maile de dixe soux de biens, et de meynes, meynes, et de pluis, pluis al afferant, issint que nul tol passast un denier de un maner de merchandize, et cest tolle fuit trove pur testmoigner les contracts, car chescun privie contract fuit defendue.* But at this day there is not one certaine toll to the market taken, but if that which is taken be not reasonable, it is punishable by this statute, and what shall be deemed in law to be reasonable, shall be judged, all circumstances considered, by the judges of the law, if it come judicially before them Mirror, c. 1. § 3. Cap. Itin. ubi sup. 3 E. 3. ass. 445. 13 H. 4. 17. a. Rot. pat. 12 E. 3. 1. part. m. 30. Harwich. Rot. pat. 8 R. 2. 1. part. m. 35. Salop. m. 38. Yarmouth.

(6) *Murage pur lour villes incloser.*] *Muragium, à muro*, as our act doth explaine it, to wall in, or inclose with wall a towne, under which word is here included a city and burghe.

Murage is a reasonable toll to be taken of every cart, wayne, horse laden comming to that towne, for the inclosing of that towne with walls of defence, for the safegard of the people in time of war, insurrection, tumults, or uprores, and is due either by grant or by prescription. * Flet. li. 1. c. 42. [a] 3 E. 3. & 13 H. 4. ubi sup. Rot. pat. 1 E. 2. m. 17. de transeuntibus subtus pontem Londō. Rot. pat. 12 H. 6. m. 18. 1. part, Reg. 259. F.N.B. 227.

But if a wall be made, which is not defensible, nor for safegard of the people, then ought not this toll to be paid, for the end of the graunt or prescription is not performed.

* He that hath burghbote granted to him, is discharged of murage granted afterwards: and although murage be here particularly named, yet are graunts of like nature within the purview of this statute: as, [b] Rot. pat. 10 E. 3. m. 32. Henley 2. part. Rot. Pat. 1 E. 2. 1. part. m. 1. Gainsburgh. F.N.B. 227. Regist. 259. [c] Rot. Pat. 1 E. 3. m. 10.

[a] Pontage.
[b] Paviage.
[c] Keyage, &c.

(6.) *Pardent*

(6) *Pardent cel graunt de touts temps.*] Here the whole franchise is forfeited, and so note a diversity betweene *prendra la franchise, &c.* and *pardent cel graunt*, the one implying a seisure, as hath been

d 22 ass. p. 34. said, and the other a forfeiture for ever, [d] for it is a misuser, or
39 H. 6. 32. abuser: [e] and thereof Bracton saith, *Hujusmodi autem libertates,*
20 E. 4. 6. *&c. statim quasi transferuntur, et quasi possidentur, &c. donec amiserit*
2 H. 7. 11.
e Bract. l. 2. f 56. *per abusum, vel non usum.*

Lib. 3. fo. 117. It is to be observed, that *consuetudines* hath severall significations
Flet. li. 1. c. 20. in law: for sometime it signifieth custome, which doth include
Ca. Itin. ubi sup. all manner of tolls: and therefore Bracton saith, *De novis consuetudinibus levatis sive in terra, sive in aqua, quis eas levavit, et ubi:* so called, because they colour things so taken under pretext of prescription or custome, where there is none at all: and therefore

[223] here they are called *novæ consuetudines*, because they were new tolls or exactions, under the visard of antiquity.

Flet. li. 2. c. 43. Fleta rendreth this last part of this chapter in these words: *Item qui muragium ad villam claudendam gravius ceperint, quam concessum fuerit per cartam regis, perdant extunc gratiam suæ concessionis, et graviter amercientur.*

And presently after the making of this act, the effect thereof for justices in eire to enquire of it, was inserted in the chapters or ar-

Cap. Itin. ubi sup. ticles of the eire in these words: *Item de hiis qui ceperunt superflua vel indebita tolneta in civitatibus, burgis, vel alibi contra communem usum regni: item de civibus et burgensibus qui de muragio per dominum regem eis concesso, plus ceperunt quam facere deberent, secundum concessionem domini regis factam.*

Mirr. c. 5. § 4. The Mirrour saith, touching murage, thus: *Le point que voet que ceux que misusent murages les perdent ne fuit mistier daver estre, car ley voet que chescun perdra son franchise que misusera:* so as this statute was made in that point for two purposes, *viz.* to affirme the common law, and to adde a farther punishment, *viz.* to be grievously amercied.

CAP. XXXII.

DE ceux queux parnent vitaile (1), *ou nul riens al oeps le roy a creance, ou a garrison du chastell, ou aylors, et quant ils ont resceive le payement al exchequer, ou en garderobe, ou ayllors, deteignont le payment des creancers, a grand dammage de eux, et en esclander du roy: purview est, de ceux queux ont terres ou tenements, que maintenant soit ceo leve de lour terres ou de lour chateux, et paies as creancers, ove les dammages queux ils averont ewe, et soient rentes pur le trespas, et sils neient terres ne tenements, soient en le prison a la volunt le roy. De ceux que*

OF such as take victual or other things to the king's use upon credence, or to the garrison of a castle, or otherwise, and when they have received their payment in the exchequer or in the wardrobe, or otherwhere, they with-hold it from the creditors, to their great damage, and slander of the king; it is provided, for such as have lands or tenements, that incontinent it shall be levied of their lands, or of their goods, and paid unto the creditors, with the damages they have sustained, and shall make fine for the trespass; and if they have no

que pernont (2) *part des dets le roy* (3), *ou auters louers pernent des creanſors le roy, pur faire le payment des meſmes celles dets: purview eſt, quils rendent le double, et ſoient punies grevement a la volunt le roy. Et de ceux queux parnont chivals* (4), *ou charettes a faire le cariage le roy, plus que meſtier ſerroit, et parnont louers pur* [*releſſer*] *ſes chivals, ou les charettes. Purview eſt, que ſi ul de la court le face, il ſerra grevement chaſtice per les mareſchals, et ſi ceo ſoit fait hors de la court,* [*per un del court*] *ou per auter que de la court, et il* [*ent*] *ſoit attaint, il rendra le treble, et ſerra en le priſon le roy per xl. jours.*

no lands nor goods, they ſhall be impriſoned at the king's will. And of ſuch as take part of the king's debts, or other rewards of the king's creditors for to make payment of the ſame debts; it is provided, that they ſhall pay the double thereof, and be grievouſly puniſhed at the king's pleaſure. And of ſuch as take horſe or carts for the king's carriage more than need, and take rewards to let ſuch horſe or carts go; it is provided, that if any of the court ſo do, he ſhall be grievouſly puniſhed by the marſhals; and if it be done out of the court, or by one that is not of the court, and be thereof attainted, he ſhall pay treble damages, and ſhall remain in the king's priſon forty days.

(28 Ed. 1. c. 2. 21 R. 2. c. 5. 28 H. 6. c. 2.)

(1) *De ceux queux parnent vitaile.*] Concerning this point of purveiance, we ſhall refer the reader to Magna Chart. cap. 21. and ſhall ſay no more concerning that matter for three cauſes: [224]
1. For the text of this law is evident. 2. For that there have beene many excellent ſtatutes made concerning purveyours, and purveyance, in all to the number of 48, which are fully and plainly penned, one of them being a good expoſition and inlargement of another. 3. I find no book caſe, nor any report for the expoſition either of this or of any of the ſaid ſtatutes, which (to ſay the truth) had more need of execution then expoſition: and therefore either the purveyours have been ſo honeſt and juſt dealing men, as they ſeldome or never offended; or elſe they have had either ſo good friends, or ſo good hap, as their offences have beene covered, or not imputed to them.

(2) *De ceux queux parnent part des dets le roy.*] The miſchiefes before this ſtatute were, firſt, that in the raigne of king H. 3. the kings officers, that had charge of his treaſure and revenue, or their agents would, in reſpect of his troubles and expences, pretend to thoſe, to whom the king was indebted, that the kings coffers were empty, and thereupon paying part to the kings creditors, compounded for their whole debts, and took their acquitances for the whole, and converted the reſidue to their owne uſe.

The ſecond was, that ſometime they would craftily pay the whole, and take a great reward therefore, which was diſhonourable to the king, damage to the creditors, and corrupt dealing in thoſe officers, or their agents.

This act is generall againſt all thoſe that take part of the kings debts, or other reward of the kings creditors, for payment of the ſame debts. This law doth provide, that he that ſo doth, ſhall render double to the party grieved, and ſhall be puniſhed grievouſly at the kings will.

This act is in affirmance of the common law; onely it addeth a greater punishment.

Rot. Parl. 50 E. 3. nu. 17. Richard Lions merchant of London, and farmor of the kings customes and subsidies was adjudged in parliament for buying debts of divers men, due by the king, for small values, and for taking of bribes, to pay to the kings creditors their due debts, to be imprisoned at the kings will, and all his lands, tenements, and goods to be seised to the kings use, which proveth it an offence or misdemeanour against the common law, for the judgement was not given according to this act.

Rot. Parl. 50 E. 3. nu. 34. John Lord Nevill, while he was one of the kings privy councel, bought divers debts due by the king, namely, of the lady of Ravensholme, and Simon Love merchant, far under the value: the lord Nevill being herewith charged in parliament, confessed that he received of the said lady 95 l. which she gave him of her own good will for the obtaining of her debt: for this (amongst others) he had judgement of imprisonment at the kings will, and that his offices, lands and goods should be seised into the kings hands, and to make restitution to the executors of the lady (who then was deceased) of the said 95 l.

See for these words before, cap. 19. (3) *Detts le roy.*] See for the exposition of these words before, ca. 19.

Cap. Itin. Vet. Mag. Char. 155. Cap. Itineris doth render this clause thus: *Et similiter de hiis qui partem ceperunt debitorum domini regis, vel alia munera, ut de residuo creditoribus satisfacerent.*

Mirr. c. 1. § 5. Cap. 5. § 4. To conclude this point, the Mirrour saith, *In perjurie vers le roy pechent ceux ministers, queux rien de paierent des dets le roy, solonq; ceo que enjoyne lour fuit a faire, ou rendant part pur satisfaction del entier, et ne rendant au roy le remnant.*

(4) *Et de ceux queux parnent chivals,* &c.] This article concerns purveyances, and purveyors; and therefore for the causes before rehearsed, no more shall be said hereof in this place.

[225]

CAP. XXXIII.

PURVIEW est, que nul vicount ne suffer' barretors (1), ne maintainours des parols en counties (2), ne seneschalles des graundes seigniours, ne des auters (que ne soit attorney son seigniour) a [la] suit faire, ne render les judgements des counties, ne pronouncer les judgements [ou assenter de faire les justicements (3)] sil ne soit especialment prie et requise de touts les suitors, et les attornies des suitors, queux serront a la journe (4). Et si ul le face, le roy se prendra grievousement al vicount, et a luy.

IT is provided that no sheriffe shall suffer any barretors or maintainers of quarrels in their shires, neither stewards of great lords, nor other (unless he be attorney for his lord) to make suit, nor to give judgements in the counties, nor to pronounce the judgements, if he be not specially required and prayed of all the suitors, and attornies of the suitors, which shall be at the court, and if any do, the king shall punish grievously both the sheriff and him that so doth.

(8 Co. 36.)

Where

Where by the ſtatute of Merton it is provided, that every free ſuitor of the county, &c. might freely make his attourney to doe theſe ſuits for him.

Merton, ca. 10. See there the expoſition thereof.

Now by colour hereof two miſchiefes did ariſe.

1. That barretors and maintainers of querels were by the ſheriffe countenanced to be attorneys to make ſuit, and amongſt the ſuitors to give judgements in the counties, and ſometime pronounce judgement in the name of the ſuitors.

2. That ſtewards of great lords, and of others, who had no letters of attourney, according to the ſaid ſtatute of Merton would doe the like: This act doth remedy both theſe miſchiefes, as by the letter hereof appeareth.

(1) *Barretors.*] For the word and the ſenſe thereof, ſee lib. 8. fol. 36. in the caſe of barretry.

Li. 8. fo. 36. in the caſe of barretry. See the firſt part of the Inſt. 701. ſect.

(2) *En counties.*] That is, in the county court, for there the ſuitors be judges.

(3) *Juſticements.*] That is, all things belonging to juſtice.

(4) *A la journe.*] That is, at the court.

CAP. XXXIV.

PUR ceo que pluſors ſont ſovent troves in counte (1) *controvours* (2) *des novelles, dont diſcord* (3), *ou manner de diſcord* (4) *ad eſtre ſovent enter le roy et ſon people, ou* [*aſcuns de*] *les hautes homes de ſon roialme: defendu eſt pur le damage que ad eſtre* (5), *et que uncore ent purra avenier, que deſormes nulle ne ſoit cy harde de dire, ne de counter nulles faux novelles, ou controvor* (6), *dont diſcord, ou manner de diſcord* *, *ou eſclaunder puit ſurdre entre le roy et ſon people, ou les hautes homes de ſon roialme* (7). *Et qui le fra ſoit pris, et detenus in priſon jeſques a tant que il eit trove en court celuy dont la parol ſerra move* (8). 2 R. 2. cap. 5.

* [226]

FORASMUCH as there have been oftentimes found in the country deviſors of tales, whereby diſcord, or occaſion of diſcord, hath many times ariſen between the king and his people, or great men of this realm; for the damage that hath and may thereof enſue, it is commanded, that from henceforth none be ſo hardy to tell or publiſh any falſe news or tales, whereby diſcord, or occaſion of diſcord or ſlander may grow between the king and his people, or the great men of the realm; and he that doth ſo, ſhall be taken and kept in priſon, until he hath brought him into the court, which was the firſt author of the tale.

(1 Leon. 287. Dyer 155. 12 Rep. 133. 1 Roll 444. 3 Bulſtr. 225. 2 R. 2. ſtat. 1. c. 5. 12 R. 2. c. 11. 1 & 2 Ph. & M. c. 3. 1 El. c. 6)

The offences, *viz.* falſe reports and news puniſhable by this law are forbidden by the law of God:

> Thou ſhalt not have to do with any falſe report, neither ſhalt thou put thy hand to the wicked to be an unrighteous witneſſe.

Exodus 23. 1.

For they which gladly heare falſe reports and newes, will be alſo as ready to publiſh them.

Ep. Jude. ver. 8. ver. 10. Exod. 22. 28. Againſt thoſe that deſpiſe rulers, and ſpeak evill of thoſe that be in authority, and againſt thoſe that ſpeake evill of thoſe things which they know not: *judicibus non detrahes, et principi populi non maledices:* thou ſhalt not raile of the judges, nor ſpeak evill of the ruler of the people.

Before this ſtatute, in the raigne of king H. 3. two kinde of perſons were authors of great diſcord and ſcandall in two ſeverall degrees; firſt, men that did raiſe and imagine, out of their own heads, falſe bruits and rumours, and others that reported and ſpread the ſame, whereby diſcord and ſcandall was oftentimes ſo kindled, ſometime between the king and his commons, and other times between the king and his nobles, the great men of the realm, as they wrought privy diſcontentment, that produced publique diſcord and ſcandall, whereof our act ſpeaketh; which ſcandall and diſcord appeared in many parliaments between the king and his commons, and between the king and his lords of parliament, and eſpecially in thoſe two parliaments, the one in 21 H. 3. when *Magna Charta* was confirmed, and the other in 42 H. 3. holden at Oxford, which in ſtory is called *inſanum parliamentum*; and this diſcord and ſcandall did oftentimes in the raigne of that king break out into fearfull and bloody warres and rebellions according to that old obſervation, *Improbi rumores diſſipati ſunt rebellionis prodromi*, which fully appear in our hiſtories warranted by good record, and is implied in this act in theſe words; "Foraſmuch as "there hath been oftentimes found deviſors and reporters of rumors, &c. whereby diſcord hath many times ariſen between the "king (meaning H. 3.) and his people, or the great men of the "realm." And amongſt all thoſe rebellions in thoſe dayes, thoſe at Lewes in Suſſex and Eveſham in Worceſterſhire were moſt fearfull, bloody, and dangerous, for at Lewes, the king himſelf manfully fighting, *confoſſo ex utroque latere equo capitur cum Richardo* Polydor Virgil. lib. 16. p. 312. anno Dom. 1264, 1265. 48 & 49 H. 3. *rege Almanorum fratre ſuo, et Edovardo principe filio, &c.* And at Eveſham, Simon Mountford earle of Leiceſter (our Engliſh Catiline) *inſtruit aciem impedimentis ex acie remotis, ac in fronte aciei ponit Henricum regem, quem ſecum captivum ducebat, atque ſuis armis induit, ut ſi fortuna adverſa ſit, dum ille imperatoris perſonam gerens ab hoſte petitur, ipſe interim fuga ſaluti conſulere poſſit: inſtruuntur contra et hoſtes et animis et viribus ſuperiores: committitur utrinque pugna, quæ aliquandiu anceps ſtetit, Henricus inter primos hoſtium ictus non pugnat, ſed regem Henricum clamando indicat, quod ei ſaluti fuit, &c. Quod ubi Simon animadvertit, ſuos cohortans in medios hoſtes prorumpit, qui à multitudine circumventus prœliando occiditur cum Henrico filio.*

King E. 1. finding by dangerous experience the wofull effects of ſuch falſe rumors and reports, as is aboveſaid, and knowing that the ſtate of every king ſtood more aſſured by the hearty and inward love of the ſubject towards their ſoveraigne, then by the dread and feare of ſevere and rigorous laws, did therefore make this law for redreſſe both for the deviſing and ſpreading of ſuch falſe rumors and bruits in all mild and temperate manner, both for the ſtyle and the puniſhment, rather leaving the ſame to the cenſure of the common law (which all men willingly obey) then by inflict- [227] ing any new deviſed puniſhment, which moderation of our king, leaving the puniſhment to fine and impriſonment, was the greater, for that the auncient law of England before the conqueſt was much

much more ſevere, and rigorous, as by a few examples ſhall appeare.

Qui falſi rumoris in vulgus ſparſi author fuiſſe deprehendetur, leviori aliqua pœna non mulctator, verum lingua ei præciditor, ni is eam integra capitis ſui æſtimatione data redemerit. Int' leges Aluredi regis, ca. 28. Edgari, ca. 4.

Si quis alium rumoribus diſſipatis improba voce lacerarit, quam ob rem, aut corpori ejus damnũ inferatura, aut de fortunis imminuatur aliquid, tum ſi alter auditiones tanquam falſas refellere et coarguere poterit, aut is linguam data capitis æſtimatione redimito, aut ei lingua præciditor. Inter leges Edgari regis, & inter leges Canuti regis.

(1) *En counte.*] That is, in the country or realme.

(2) *Controvors.*] That is, deviſors or inventors of their owne head.

(3) *Diſcord.*] *Diſcordia.* That is, *diſſenſio cordium*, diſſention of hearts; this grew (as hath been ſaid) to ſuch an height in the raign of H. 3. as that of the philoſophicall poet might well be applied to it: (which before is remembred.)

Impius hæc tam culta novalia miles habebit? Virgil.
Barbarus has ſegetes? en quo diſcordia cives
Perduxit miſeros!———

Diſcordes, quaſi duo habentes corda.

(4) *Ou maner de diſcord.*] That is, *latens odium*, privy hatred or diſcontentment, which is occaſion of diſcord, and whereby men become malecontents.

(5) *Defendu eſt pur le damagè que ad eſtre.*] This damage or danger you have partly heard before.

(6) *De dire, de counter, ou controvor.*] Two manner of perſons are hereby prohibited, the firſt, thoſe that tell, ſpread or report falſe and feigned bruits and rumours under theſe words, *Dire ou counter*; and ſecondly, ſuch as deviſe or invent of their own head the ſame under this word *controvor:* now the perſons being deſcribed, this ſtatute doth ſet down generally what thoſe bruits and rumours ſhould be.

(7) *Faux novels, dont diſcord, ou maner de diſcord ou diſlaunder poet ſurder enter le roy, & ſon people ou les hauts homes de ſon realme.*] Of theſe falſe newes, that is, falſe bruits or rumours, there be five kindes within this act.

1. Firſt, if they be againſt the king, whereby diſcord or ſcandall may ariſe betweene the king and his commons, ſignified here by *people.*

2. Againſt the commons, whereby diſcord or ſcandall may be moved between them and the king.

3. Thirdly, againſt the king, whereby diſcord or ſcandall may grow between the king and the peeres, or lords and nobles of the realme, ſignified here by *les hauts homes de ſon realme.*

4. Fourthly, againſt the peeres, or lords, and nobles of the realme, whereby diſcord or ſlander may happen betweene them and the king.

5. Laſtly, whereby diſcord or ſcandall may ariſe between the king, his lords, and commons.

Quod narratores rumorum qui cedere poſſunt ad timorem, et tremorem populi, et in dedecus regis et regni, capiantur, et in carcere detineantur, &c. Tr. 19 E. 2. Rot. 15. Coram rege.

By this record it appeareth of what quality the rumors must be.

By commissions of oyer and terminer power is given to enquire, *De illicitis verborum propalationibus*; and to punish the same.

Britton, fo. 33. Britton speaketh of both these kinds of offenders, *viz.* the devisor, and the reporter, in these words, *De ceux que trovont, et countent mensoynes del roy, &c.*

Fleta, li. 2. c. 1. And Fleta saith, *Sunt etiam quædam atroces injuriæ, quæ prisonam voluntariam inducunt, sicut de inventoribus malorum rumorum, unde pax possit exterminari.*

5 R. 2. ca. 6. 1 E. 6. c. 12. 1 Mar. c. The statute of 5 R. 2. punished seditious rumors in an high degree, but that is repealed by 1 E. 6. & 1 Mar.

17 R. 2. c. 8. 13 H. 4. ca 7. 5 Mar. Dier 155. Oldnolles case. It was resolved by all the justices, that horrible and slanderous words spoken of queen Mary, were within this statute and punishable hereby, and not by the statutes of 2 R. 2. cap. 5. nor 12 R. 2. cap. 11. for the king or queene is an exempt person, and not included within these words [*Les hauts, ou graund homes, ou nobles, &c.*]

Some say that *Rumores dicuntur à ruendo, quia inducunt ruinam*; Cicero pro Cluentio. and true it is that another saith, *Ut mare, quod sua natura tranquillum est, ventorum vi agitatur; sic populus sua sponte placatus, hominum seditiosorum vocibus, ut violentissimis tempestatibus, attollitur.*

Dier fo. 13 H. 7. Keylway 28, 29. F.N.B. 42. g. 2 R. 3. 9. But it is to be understood, that albeit this statute, and the said act of 2 R. 2. be generall in the negative; yet doe they not extend to all manner of false newes, or horrible and false scandals and lies, &c. for they extend onely to extrajudiciall slanders, &c. And therefore if any man bring an appeale of murder, robbery, or other felony against any of the peeres or nobles of the realme, &c. and charge them with murder, robbery, or felony, albeit the charge be false, yet shall they have no action *de scandalis magnat'*, neither at the common law, nor upon either of these statutes for the bringing of his action, nor for affirming the same to his councell, attourney, or cursiter for the framing of his writ, or for speaking the same in evidence to a jury, or for using of those words for the necessary commencement or prosecution of his action judicially; and so it is in an action of forger of false deeds, or any other action F N.B. 41. g. 22 E. 3. 1[illegible]. 43 E. 3. 20. tit. faux judgment 10. 43 Ass. 40. 2 R. 3 9. 13 H. 7. Keylwey 28, 29. whatsoever: for it is a maxime in law, *Que home ne serra puny pur suer des briefes en court le roy, soit il a droit ou a tort*; and the reason thereof is, that men should not be deterred to take their remedy by due course of law; and therefore the statutes never intended to prohibit the suing out of the kings writs, and the proceeding thereupon: and so it is, if in the star-chamber a peere of the realme be charged with forgery, perjury, or the like; but if in the bill the plaintife chargeth him with felony, or any other offence not examinable in that court, that slander is within these statutes, for that the plaintife pursueth not his charge in any judiciall course, seeing the court hath no jurisdiction of the same, and so hath it been adjudged.

(8) *Soit prise & detenus in prison jesque a taunt que il eit trove en court celuy dont le parol serra move.*] It hath appeared before, that by the body of the act not onely the tellers and reporters of such false news, but the devisors and inventors thereof are prohibited: but no punishment is inflicted by this act upon the devisor or inventor. for he is left to the common law to be punished by fine and imprisonment according to the quality and quantity of the offence,

which is aggravated in reſpect that it is prohibited by this act of parliament.

And the law is grounded upon the law of God in this point, *Non maledices principi populi.* Deuter. ca. 17.

Nay, in the kings caſe the ſecret cogitation of the heart is prohibited, *In cogitatione tua regi ne detrahas:* and the ſcandals of great men are likewiſe forbidden, *Et in ſecreto cubiculi tui ne maledixeris diviti, quia aves cœli portabunt vocem tuam, et qui habet pennas annunciabit ſententiam*; that is, Almighty God will provide means, that ſuch detraction and malediction ſhall come to light, and be diſcovered. Eccleſiaſtes, c. 10. [229]

Onely this law inflicteth impriſonment upon the reporter, untill he hath found out, and brought into court the author of thoſe falſe news.

7 E. 1. the king ſent commiſſions to all the counties of England, to enquire *De ſparſoribus rumorum, &c.* 25 *E.* 1. *Declaratio regis miſſa ad omnes com' Angliæ, de rege purgand' de certis rumoribus iniquis contra ipſum ortis, &c.*

Rex mandavit maiori et vicecom' London' quod facta inquiſitione de ſparſoribus rumorum et ſedic' in civitate ipſos caperet, et in priſona de Newgate detineret, &c.

Vide lib. Intrat. Coke, fo. 302, 303. in falſe impriſonment.

Rot. Pat. 7 E. 1. m. 13. Rot. Pat. 25 E. 1. pars 2. m. 7. & Franc. m. 4. Rot. clauſ. Vaſc. anno 10 E. 3. m. 26. In dorſ. clauſ. anno 20 E 3. pt. 1. m. 18. & 26.

CAP. XXXV.

DES hautes homes, et de lour bailifes (1), *et des auters* (2) *(forſpris les miniſters le roy, as queux ſpeciall authoritie eſt done de ceo faire* (3),*) que a le pleint des aſcuns, ou per lour authoritie demeſne attachent auters ove lour biens treſpaſſantes per lour poier a reſponder devant eux des contracts, covenants, ou de treſpas faits hors de lour poier, et lour juriſdiction* (4), *la ou ils ne teignont riens de eux* (5), *ne deins le franchiſe* (6) *ou lour poier eſt, en prejudice du roy, et de ſa corone, et a damage du people: purview eſt, que nul deſormes ne le face. Et ſi aſcun le face, il rendra a celuy, que per cel encheſon ſerra attache, ſon damage au double, et ſerra en le grieve mercy le roy.*

OF great men and their bailiffs, and other (the king's officers only excepted unto whom eſpecial authority is given) which at the complaint of ſome, or by their own authority, attach other paſſing through their juriſdiction with their goods, compelling them to anſwer afore them upon contracts, covenants, and treſpaſſes, done out of their power and their juriſdiction, where indeed they hold nothing of them, nor within the franchiſe, where their power is, in prejudice of the king and his crown, and to the damage of the people; it is provided, that none from henceforth ſo do; and if any do, he ſhall pay to him, that by this occaſion ſhall be attached his damages double, and ſhall be grievouſly amerced to the king.

(Lutw. 1026. F. N. B. 45, f.)

The mischiefe before this statute was, that great men and others that had particular jurisdiction and power to hold plea of contracts, covenants, and trespasses made or done within a certaine precinct, as within a manour, citie, or borough, would attache others by their goods to answer in their courts of contracts, covenants, and trespasses made or done out of their power or franchise, pretending the same to be transitorie, and suppose the same to be done within their power and franchise, which was to the prejudice of the king and his crown in losing his fines in actions of debts and trespasses *vi et armis*, and amerciaments, and other profits upon a false supposall, not like to the generall jurisdiction, and power of the kings justices of the court of common pleas, through the whole realme; for wheresoever the contract, covenant, trespas, &c. were made, the matter being transitory, the plaintife may alledge it in what countie he will, and the king can lose nothing; and so it is in the kings bench and exchequer against priviledged persons in those generall courts: and the statute saith further, and to the damage of the party being attached and sued, as he is passing and travailing within that particular precinct, upon a false supposall, where in truth he ought not. For this mischiefe this act provideth remedy, as by the same shall appeare.

Mag. Chart. c. 28. (1) *De lour bailifes.*] Here bailifes are taken for the judges of the court, as manifestly appeareth hereby.

[230] (2) *Et des auters.*] That is, others that have particular jurisdictions and powers, as manifestly appeareth by the exception hereafter.

Regist. fol. 98. Flet. l. 2. c. 42. Cap. Itineris. (3) *Forsprise les ministers le roy, as queux especiall authoritie est done a ceo faire.*] Here is to be observed,

1. That all these words belong to the exception, as by the Register appeareth.

2. That *ministri regis* are intended here the kings justices in his generall courts of justice, and so taken in this kings time, as it hath been touched before.

(4) *Des contracts, covenants, et trespas faits hors de lour poier et lour jurisdiction.*] That is, out of the precinct of the manour, or such like particular jurisdiction, &c. where by prescription or grant they have power and jurisdiction to hold plea of contracts, covenants, and debts made or done within the manour, or such other particular jurisdiction.

(5) *La ou ils ne teignont riens de eux.*] This act beginneth, *Des*
Bract. l. 2. f. 14. Lib. 2. fol. 56. Lib. 3. fo. 228. Li. 5. fo. 328. b. *hauts homes:* and Bracton saith, *Sunt qui barones, et alii libertatem habentes, scilicet, soc et sac, &c. et isti possunt indicare, &c.* for *soc* is a power or jurisdiction to have a free court, to hold plea of contracts, covenants, and trespasses of his men and tenants; therefore materially were these words added; that if a great man or others having *soc*, should hold plea by force of that liberty of any that is not his tenant, it is *coram non judice*, and punishable within this
Mirr. c. 1. § 3. Int' leges S. Ed. fo. 23. & 132. statute. It is diversly written, *viz. soc, soca, sock, soeke, soke, sockne,* and *soknes*, and it is derived from the old Saxon word *soken, sochen,* or *suchen, i.* to enquire or find out, that is, to enquire and find out the truth of the matter in plea before him, and to determine it accordingly, which is as much to say, as *ad inquirend', audiend', et terminand'.*

Flet. li. 1. c. 42. And Fleta therewith agreeth, and saith, *Soke significat libertatem*

curiæ

curiæ tenentium, quam ſokam appellamus: and *curia* implyeth *ad audiendum et terminandum.*

The Mirrour ſaith, that *En temps le roy Alfred, perdront les ſuters de Doncaſter lour juriſdiction ouſter lauter paine, pur ceo que ils tiendront plea defendu per les uſages del realme aux judges ordinaries ſuters a tener,* which I rather vouch together with the derivation of the word *ſoc,* for the great antiquity of the law in this point. Mirr. c. 5. § 1.

(6) *Ne deins la franchiſe.*] That is, nor within any ſuch like particular power or juriſdiction, either by the graunt of the king, or preſcription.

For the reliefe of the ſubject upon this ſtatute, two originall writs are framed: the one in nature of a prohibition before the ſuit begun, commanding that the party ſhall not be arreſted contrary to the forme of this ſtatute. Regiſt. 98.

The other, after the ſuit begun, the party to recover the penalty of this act, *viz.* double dammages, and a command to deliver the goods attached or diſtrained; both which writs appeare in the Regiſter: but the party may waive the benefit of this ſtatute, and therefore if he plead to the action any barre, &c. he hath concluded himſelfe, and ſhall not have any action upon this ſtatute, therefore he muſt plead the ſpeciall matter, and by that meanes take benefit of this act.

Fleta rendreth this act in this manner: *De magnatibus et eorum balivis et aliis (exceptis miniſtris regis, quibus ad hoc authoritas data eſt) qui ad querimoniam aliquorum, vel authoritate propria attachiant alios per bona ſua, qui per eandem poteſtatem et juriſdictionem veniunt ad reſpondendum coram eis de contractibus, conventionibus, et tranſgreſſion' extra eorum poteſtatem et juriſdictionem, ubi nihil tenent de eis, nec ſunt de libertate eorum aut juriſdictione: ſtatutum eſt, quod ſi quis de hujuſmodi convictus fuer', reddat querenti damna in duplo, ac etiam graviter amercietur.* Fleta, li. 2. c. 42. 18 E. 2. tit. Teſtament. f. 6. [231]

And it is to be obſerved that at the making of this ſtatute, if a man had brought an action of debt, account, detinue, or covenant upon any contract by originall writ in the county of Norff. he might have declared of the contract in Suff. or any other county then where the originall was brought; for the rule was, that *debitum et contractus, &c. ſunt nullius loci,* and every duty is a duty in every county: but in caſe of account this diverſity is to be obſerved, that in account againſt a receiver the law was then as is aforeſaid, but if a man brought an action of account againſt one as bayly in one county, he could not charge him as bayliffe of a mannor in another county, for that is locall. 6 E. 3. 10 E. 3. 7. 12 E. 3. bre. 479. 14 E. 3. bre. 274. 30 E. 3. 26. 4 H. 6. 6. 15 E. 4. 20. 21 E. 4. li. 7. f. 3. Bulwers caſe.

But after this act it is provided by the ſtatute of 6 R. 2. cap. 2. that in pleas of debt, or account, or ſuch like, as detinue, or contract, it ſhall not be declared that the contract was made in any other county, then is contained in the originall writ. 6 R. 2. cap. 2. 13 R. 2. bre. 469.

But at the common law one that hath a particular juriſdiction to hold plea of debt, contract, detinue, covenant, or treſpaſſe within his mannor, or the like, could not hold plea of a debt, contract, account, detinue, covenant, or treſpaſſe alledged to be made out of the mannor, &c. becauſe albeit it was tranſitory, yet was it (being ſo alledged) not within his power or juriſdiction which he had by preſcription or by graunt; for all pleas holden there muſt be *infra juriſdictionem curiæ.* 3 H. 6. 30.

As

2 R. 3. Testam 4. 11 H. 7. 12. As if a lord hath probate of testaments made within the precinct of his mannor, he cannot prove a testament made out of the precinct of his mannor.

17 E. 4. c. 2. 1 R. 3. c. 6. lib. 6. fo. 20. And likewise of the court pipowders of contracts, &c. made out of the faire or market. *Et sic de cæteris.*

Michelborns case. Dier. 3 Mar. 132, 133. 7 E. 4. 19. 13 E. 4. 8. 7 H. 6. 18, 19. 13 H. 7. 19.

CAP. XXXVI.

PUR ceo que avant ceux heures ne fuit unques reasonable aid' a faire leigne fitz chivaler (1), *ne a leigne file marier* (2) *mise en certein, ne quant ceo deveroit estre prise, ne quel heure, per quoy les uns leverent outragious aide* (3), *et plus tost que ne sembleit mestier, dount la people se sentit greve: purview est, que desormes de fee de chivaler entier solement soient dones* 20. *s.* (4) *et de* 20. *l. de terre tenus per socage* 20. *s.* (5) *et de pluis, pluis, et de meins, meins, selonque lafferant. Et que nul ne puisse lever tiel aide a faire son fits chivaler, tanque que son fits soit del age de xv. ans* (6), *ne a sa file marier tanque que el soit del age de* 7. *ans* (7). *Et de ceo serra fait mention en le briefe le roy fourm' sur ceo quant home le voile demander. Et si aveigne que le pier, quant il avera tiel aide leve de les tenants, morust avant quil eit sa file marie* (8), *les executors le pier soient tenus a la file* (9), *en tant come le pier avera resceu pur cest aide. Et * si les biens le pier ne suffisent, son heire soit de ceo tenus a la file* (10).

* [232]

FOR as much as before this time, reasonable ayde to make ones sonne knight, or marrie his daughter was never put in certain, nor how much should be taken, nor at what time, whereby some leavied unreasonable aid, and more often then seemed necessary, whereby the people were sore grieved: it is provided, that from henceforth of an whole knights fee there be taken but xx. s. And of xx. pound land holden in socage xx. s. and of more, more, and of lesse, lesse; after the rate. And that none shall levie such ayde to make his sonne knight, untill his sonne be fifteene yeares of age, nor to marrie his daughter, untill she be of the age of seven yeares. And of that there shall be made mention in the kings writ, formed on the same, when any will demand it. And if it happen, that the father, after hee hath levied such ayde of his tenants, die before he hath married his daughter, the executors of the father shall be bound to the daughter, for so much as the father received for the aide. And if the father's goods be not sufficient, his heir shall be charged therewith unto the daughter. (*Rastell's Translation.*)

Fleta, lib. 2. c. 40. lib. 3. cap. 14. Brit. fo. 57. & 70. Custumier de Norm. cap. 35. fol. 53, 54. (13 Rep. 27, 28, 29. 1 Roll 157. 165. Regist. 87. F. N. B. 82. B. 122. G. 25 Ed. 3. stat. 5. c. 11. Repealed by 12 Car. 2. c. 24.)

By the common law to every tenure by knights service, and socage, there were three aides of money, called in law *auxilia*, incident and implied, without speciall reservation or mention, that is to say, reliefe when the heire was of full age, aide *pur faire fits chivalier,*

lier, and aide *pur file marier*; now the first aide, *viz.* reliefe by reason of a tenure by knights service, was certain, because he was to pay it, if he were of the age of 21 years at the death of his ancestor, as hath been said before, without regard of any circumstance; and likewise the reliefe of an heire in socage being of the age of 14 at the death of his auncestor was ever certain, *viz.* to double his rent. But the aids *pur faire fits chivalier*, and *pur file marier* were incertain at the common law, for that the lords many times would pretend their eldest son, and eldest daughter to be hopefull and forward, and therefore would exact too great an aid, and before due time, whereas by the law they ought to have reasonable aids, and in reasonable time, which in a suit therefore should be determined by the justices of that court before whom the suit depended. Now the tenants found themselves grieved in three things:

5 E. 3. fo. 11. 40 E. 3. 21. 47. Mag. Char. c. 2.

Vid. Inst. sect. 127.

1. That the said aids were outragious and excessive, *Et excessus in re qualibet jure reprobatur communi*, so as these outragious, and excessive aides were against law, whereof elsewhere you may reade at large.

Lib. 11. fo. 44. R. Godfreys case. See before cap.

2. The lords exacted those fines at what time they pleased before reasonable age apt for the paiment of those aides.

3. That he could not avoid the same but by suit in law with his lord, wherein he found by experience those old verses true:

Cum pare luctari dubium, cum procere stultum,
Cum puero pœna, cum muliere pudor.

And our act saith, *Dont le people se sentist greve.*

These three mischiefes are redressed by this act, and certainty the mother of quiet and concord established therein.

But where it is said that these aids are incidents, it is to be understood that they are incidents separable, either by speciall words at the creation of the tenure, or by discharge or release by speciall words, or speciall rehearsall afterwards.

18 E. 3. fo. 16. 40 E. 3. 22. 47. 13 R. 2. Avowry 89. 14 H. 4. 8. 5 E. 4. 41.

But if the lord at the creation of the tenure had reserved fealty, and 4 marks *per annum, pro omnibus servitiis, exactionibus et demandis quibuscunque*; or if the lord after the seigniory created had released to the tenant, *omnia servitia, exactiones et demanda quæcunque (except' fidelitate et reddit' iiij. mercarum per annum,)* yet should the tenant pay reliefe, aid *pur faire fits chivalier*, and *file marier*, which is necessary to be knowne for the understanding of auncient deeds.

(1) *A faire leigne fits chivalier.*] Lord, grandfather, father, and two sons, the father dieth, the lord shall not have aide for his eldest grandchild, for he is not his eldest son, much lesse shall he have aide for his elder brother, or his eldest cousin and heire: but if a man hath issue two sons, and the eldest die in the fathers life without issue, he shall have aide for the second son, for he is now eldest, and the statute saith eldest son, and not first-born; yet the writ grounded upon this statute is *ad primogenitum filium suum maritandum*, but he is *primogenitus* then living. But if the lord had received aide for his eldest son, he shall not have aid again for the second, for *unicum auxilium*, one aid is onely due to one and the same lord, to make his eldest son a knight: *Non tenetur quis de uno tenemento eidem domino plura dare auxilia ad filium suum militem faciend.'*

Britton 57. b. F.N.B. 82. g. Regist. 87. in the rehearsall of this act it is said, *primogenito filio et primogenitæ filiæ.*

Regist. ubi supra.

If

Mirror, ca. 1. § 3. Fleta ubi supra. F.N.B. 82.

If the lord hath issue two sonnes, the eldest son hath issue a daughter and dieth, the lord shall not have aide to make his second son a knight, for the second son is not his heir apparent (and in this case he ought to be his heire apparent) for at this time the state of all lands was fee-simple, and the lands of the lord should descend to the daughter, and therefore the law would not have the dignity of chivalry to be apparelled with poverty, and in respect thereof the son to be knighted was to be heire apparent. And this agreeth with the letter and meaning of this act, *a faire son eigne fits chivalier*, who by common intendment is heire apparent.

If the eldest son be made a knight before the age of fifteen, the lord can have no aide, because the words be a *faire leigne fits chivalier*; and none was ever due to the lord.

If the lord hath issue bastard eigne, and mulier puisne, he shall not have aide to make the bastard a knight, for he is not in judgement of law accounted his son, but he shall have it for the mulier puisne.

Vide cap. 10.

It was holden in auncient time, that the lord could not demaund aide *pur faire fits chivalier*, unlesse he himselfe were a knight, *ne filius antecederet patri*: but knights in auncient time grew so scarce, as esquires that were of ability to be knights, not onely in this case, but in many other, supplied the place of knights; *sufficiens honor est homini, qui dignus honore est.*

Hereby it appeareth that by the policy of the law, the eldest son of a knight was not only trained up in his tender years in learning and knowledge of liberal arts to adorn the minde, but when he came to convenient yeares, did for the defence of the realme learne and exercise the deeds of armes and chivalry, that he might be able to serve his country both in time of peace, and of warre.

See 35 H. 6. 40.

(2) *Ne a leigne file marier.*] By this the policy of the law appeareth, that the eldest daughter might be timely preferred in mariage, for thereby come strength and good alliance to the family, and both these are given by law without any speciall reservation: and the observation of the auncients was, that marry the eldest daughter well, and all the rest will bee preferred the better; and to that end aide was graunted for the eldest daughter.

F.N.B. fol. 82 c. d.

Pasch. 17 E. 1. in Banco Rot. 38. Northampt.

(3) *Outragious aide.*] Tenant *peravaile* shall be contributory to the aide for the mariage of the kings daughter. See for this word before cap. 31.

Mag. Chart. c. 2.

(4) *De fee de chivalier entier solement soient done 20. s.*] Here it is to be observed (as it hath been noted) that reliefe is the fourth part of a knights fee being then 20. l. is 5. l. and aide *pur faire fits chivalier*, or *pur file marier*, is the twentieth part of a knights fee, *viz*, 20. s. limited by this act.

See more hereof in the Commentary upon the statute of 1 E. 2. de militibus.

(5) *Et de 20. l. de terre tenus per socage.*] This summe is set downe because the value of a knights fee was then 20. l. (which then was sufficient to maintaine the dignity of knighthood) and so the statute maketh them equall in value; the king was not bound by this statute, but he might take such reliefe, and at such time as was due by the common law.

25 E. 3. c. 10.

But the statute of 25 E. 3. doth assesse the aides at such a rate as this statute doth, and that act doth well expound this statute,

ſtatute, that none ſhall pay theſe aides but the tenants of the land holding the ſame immediately in demeſne without any meſne. Rot. Parliam. 29 E. 3. nu. 16.

For meſne lords ought to pay no aide implied in theſe words of our act, *De ſee de chivalier, et de 20. l. terre*, and if the tenant *peravaile* by knights ſervice goeth with his lord, &c. he diſchargeth all the meſne lords. Note theſe words, *De ſee de chivalier*, doth exclude grand ſerjeanty, for he that * holdeth by that tenure ſhall pay no aide to the lord either to make his ſon a knight, or to marry his daughter; for by this act it appeareth, that none ſhall pay any aide but tenants by knights ſervice, or tenant in ſocage, and no other tenure. 6 H. 3. Avowry 242. F.N.B. 83. k. 11 H. 4. 34. 10 H. 4 Avowry 267. 10 H. 6. Aunc' demeſne 11 Rot. Par. 9 H 6. nu. 15. * [234]

(6) *Tanque le fits ſoit del age de 15 ans.*] Note no man ſhall be compelled to take knighthood upon him untill he be 21 yeares old, and have ſufficient land for maintenance of that degree, yet at the age of fifteen yeares he may begin to learn ſome things that belong to chivalry, but it is good for the lord to make what ſpeed he can after that age to recover the aide either by the writ *De auxilio ad filium' ſuum militem faciend'*, or by diſtreſſe: for if the ſon die, the lord loſeth the aide, for that by his death the finall cauſe ceaſeth, and ſo likewiſe if the father dieth, the aide is loſt, for that the duty and remedy is onely given to the father, who in reſpect of nature hath the wardſhip of his eldeſt ſon, and as a naturall father is to provide for his advancement; and ſo as a father by the law of nature is bound to provide a competent mariage for his daughter, which are therefore perſonall to the father: and ſo note the diverſity betweene reliefe, which is abſolutely due to the lord in reſpect of the ſeigniory meerly, and theſe aids, which are not abſolutely due to the lord, but for the performance of a duty of nature. 1 E. 2. ſtat. de militibus. *Jura naturalia.* Inſt. ſect. 114. Lib. 7. fo. 13 b. Calvins caſe. 1 E. 3. fo. 17. 33 H. 6. 57.

(7) *Tanque el (s. la file) ſoit de 7 ans.*] In auncient time gentlemen of good houſes, for knitting themſelves in greater bonds of amity and alliance, maried their children very young, which the law doth ſeeme to favour, for that it giveth her dower, if ſhe be of the age of nine yeares at the death of her huſband, whereof I have knowne ſome to have proſpered well, but more that have proved unfortunate.

(8) *Et moruſt avant que il avoit ſa file marie.*] Here our act giveth onely remedy to the daughter, and maketh no mention of the ſon in that caſe, and yet the ſon ſhall have the ſame remedy againſt the executors, that the daughter ſhall have, being in *æquali jure*. F.N.B. 82. i. et 83. a.

Tenant for life, or tenant in dower ſhall not have aide *pur file marier, ou pur faire fits chivalier*, but the verie lord, to whom by poſſibility they might inherit, and whom the lord by nature is bound to preferre; but tenant for life, &c. ſhall have eſcuage, ward, mariage, and reliefe. Hil. 9 E. 2 fo. 62, 63. in libro meo. Phil Leuteynes caſe.

If the father receive the aide, and after the ſon is knighted, or the daughter maried in the life of the father, neither ſon nor daughter ſhall have remedy for the aide, for the end of the law is performed. But by the whole context of this act it appeareth, that ſmall portions preferred in mariage the daughters of good families, when vertue and good blood was more eſteemed then great portions. 3 E. 3. Debt 156.

(9) *Les executors ſon pier ſont tenus al file.*] Note, the father himſelf hath time to make his eldeſt ſon a knight after his age of 15, and

and to marry his daughter after her age of 7 yeares at any time during his life, and therefore though the father receive the aides, yet have they no remedy against him, but to depend upon his paternall care, and their remedy is against the executors, or administrators of the father, if they be not preferred in his life time, as it appeareth by this act.

(10) *Et si les biens le pier ne suffisent, son heire de ceo soit tenus a le file.*] And here it is to be observed, that if the personall estate of the lord be sufficient to pay the aide, the heire (who is to maintaine the state and countenance of his father) is not to bee charged therewith.

[235] 3 E. 3. Debt 157. In an action of debt brought by the eldest daughter against the heire for an C. s. which the father received of his tenants for reasonable aide to mary her, and that she was not maried in his life time, &c. and in her declaration made no mention that the executors had no assets, and yet the count was ruled to be good, for that is the ordinary count in an action of debt, which the statute giveth, and if the executors have assets, the heire shall plead it in barre.

Although the statute be, that his heire shall be bound to the daughter, it is understood, that he shall be bound, if he hath assets in fee-simple by descent from his father.

The daughter shall not recover part against the executors, and the residue against the heire, but either all against the executors, or all against the heire, as these words doe prove.

F.N.B. ubi supra. The eldest son must have his remedy onely against the executors, for he himselfe is heire.

Mirr. c. 1. § 3. And these aides appeare by the Mirror to be very auncient, ordained by king Alfred, and other auncient kings, for he saith, *Et que escuage, reliefe et aides, se fissent per les tenants a lour seigniours de lour heritage reliever, les heires les seigniours faire chivaliers, et de lour eignesses files marier.* It is to be observed how moderate the aids be by force of this act, and therefore it is to be collected that the fees of the heralds were then (and yet ought to be) moderate also.

CAP. XXXVII.

PURVIEW est et accorde ensement, que si home soit attaint de disseisin fait en temps le roy que ore est (1), ovesque robbery (2), de ascun maner de chattel, ou de moveable (3), et soit trove vers luy per recognisance de assise de novel disseisin, le judgement soit tiel, que le plaintife recovera sa seisin et les damages, auxibien de chattel et de moveable avantdits, come de soile. Et le disseisor soit rente (4), le quel que il soit present ou non, issint que [s'il soit present] primes soit agard a la prison.

IT is provided also and agreed, that if any man be attainted of disseisin done in the time of the king that now is, with robbery of any manner of goods or moveables, and be found against him by recognisance of assise of novel disseisin, the judgement shall be such; that the plaintiff shall recover his seisin and his damages, as well of the goods and moveables aforesaid, as for the freehold, and the disseisor shall make fine, which, whether he be present or not so it be presented) shall first

priſon. Et per meſme le maner ſoit fait de diſſeiſin fait a force et armes, tout ne face home robbery (5).

firſt be awarded to priſon. And in like manner it ſhall be done of diſſeiſin with force and arms, although there be no robbery.

See Marlb. ca. 14. verb. Attinct. the firſt part of the Inſt. ſect. 514. Verb. en Attaint. (Fitz. Damages, 10. 14 H. 7. 15.)

This ſtatute is made in affirmance of the common law, as appeareth by originall writs of aſſiſe, wherein the words be, *Facias tenement' illud reſeiſiri de catallis quæ in ipſo capta fuerunt, et ipſum tenementum cum catallis eſſe in pace uſque ad primam aſſiſam*; which writ was at the common law before this ſtatute, as it appeareth by Glanvill, and by Bracton who wrote before this act. Glanv. l. 3. ca. 33, 34, &c. Bract. l. 4. f. 179.

And the judges of the aſſiſe ought to enquire of the ſame, for if goods be taken away by the diſſeiſor, it is a diſſeiſin with force, and therefore *ex officio*, the judges ought to enquire thereof. 11 H. 4, 16, 17. 11 H. 4. 16, 17.

(1) *En temps le roy que ore eſt.*] Yet this act being in affirmance of the common law doth extend to all times after, which the judges in 4 E. 2. not obſerving, nor remembring the words of the writ of aſſiſe denied to enquire of the taking away of the goods. [236.] 4 E. 2. damage 10.

(2) *Oveſque robbery.*] Here [robbery] is taken in a large ſenſe, for a wrongfull taking away of goods, as a wrong doer and treſpaſſer.

(3) *De aſcun manner de chattel, ou de moveable,* &c.] If a man be diſſeiſed, and hath goods, which he hath thereupon as executor or adminiſtrator, taken away, theſe are not accounted his goods within this ſtatute, becauſe he hath them, in *auter droit,* to the uſe of the dead, 8 E. 3. 3. 54.

A man ſeiſed of land in the right of his wife, or joyntly with his wife, and is diſſeiſed, and his goods taken away; in an aſſiſe brought by the huſband and wife, he and his wife ſhall recover ſeiſin of the land, and he alone upon that originall brought by him and his wife ſhall have damages, which is worthy of obſervation. 11 H. 4. 16. 7 H. 6. 30 b.

And ſo it is, if two joynt-tenants be diſſeiſed, and the goods of one of them taken away, both ſhall recover the land, and the one damages for his goods: theſe be the only caſes that I remember in the law, where one demandant or plaintiſe without any ſummons or ſeverance ſhall have judgement alone in one originall; for regularly the judgement ought to be given according to the originall writ: as if the huſband and wife bring an action of battery for the beating of himſelfe and his wife, the writ ſhall abate, becauſe the wife cannot joyne for the battery of her huſband, and the huſband cannot have judgement alone, becauſe his wife is joyned with him in the originall; *et ſic de ſimilibus.* 12 E. 4. 6.

But the aſſiſe is a ſpeciall caſe, for the plaintiſe making his plaint to be diſſeiſed of his free hold in ſuch a towne with the appurtenances generally, yet ſhall he recover his goods, if the diſſeiſin be found with robbery of his goods, as the ſtatute ſpeaketh, and the goods are contained in the originall, and not in the pleint; and the aſſiſe of *novel diſſeiſin* was *feſtinum remedium,* and much favoured in law for the reliefe of the diſſeiſee, both for the regaining of his poſſeſſion

session of the land, and of his stock of cattle, and goods thereupon: therefore where our act saith, that the plaintife shall recover his seisin, and his damages, as well for the goods and moveables aforesaid, as for the freehold, it is so to be understood *reddendo singula singulis*, according to that which hath been said. William Burchester, and Margaret his wife were disseised of the land which he held in the right of his wife, and dispossessed of his goods; in an assise brought by the husband and wife, judgement was given for them both, *Damna pro disseisina C. l. pro bonis C. marc'*: in a writ of error the judgement was reversed for the C. marks, because the wife had nothing in them.

Coram Reg. Tr. 4 H. 4. Rot. 24. Suff.

(4) *Et le disseisor soit rente.*] And the disseisor shall be fined, which is also in affirmance of the common law, for a disseisin with taking away of goods is a disseisin with force, and therefore finable.

(5) *Et per mesme le maner soit fait de disseisin fait a force et armes, tout ne face home robbery.*] Note the writ of assise mentioneth not a disseisin *vi et armis*, but the words thereof be *Injuste et sine judicio disseisivit*, and therefore if the jurors finde a disseisin, and no force, the judgement shall be *ideo in misericordia*, and not *quod capiatur*, but as it hath been said, the court *ex officio* ought to enquire of the force; but if they doe not, it is not error, as it hath been adjudged.

M. 25 & 26 El. Co. Reg. in bre. de Error. int' Bartlet & Baxter in Ass. de fresh force in Ipsewich.

[237]

CAP. XXXVIII.

PUR ceo que ascuns gentes de la terre doutent meins faux serement faire, que faire ne duissent, per que mults des gents son disherites, et perdent lour droit: purview est, que le roy, de son office, desormes donera attaints sur les enquests en plea de terre, ou de franktenement, ou de chose que touche franktenement, quant il semblera que besoigne soit (1).

FORASMUCH as certain people of this realm doubt very little to make a false oath (which they ought not to do) whereby much people are disherited, and lose their right; it is provided, that the king, of his office, shall from henceforth grant attaints upon enquests in plea of land, or of freehold, or of any thing touching freehold, when it shall seem to him necessary.

(44 Ed. 3. 2. Regist. 122. Rast. 84. 1 Ed. 3. stat. 1. c. 6. 5 Ed. 3. c. 6. & 7. 28 Ed. 3. c. 8. 34 Ed. 3. c. 7.)

Pasch. 32 E. 3. fo. 65. in libro meo. H. 3. graunted to the Burgesse of S. Albans, that none of them should be impleaded of no freehold in attaint, &c. *& allocatur.*

The mischiefe before this statute (which was the first concerning attaints) was, that albeit (as the common opinion is) an attaint did lie upon a false verdict given in a plea of land, yet the king many times would not graunt it without suit made to him, which turned the party grieved, not onely to great delay, but to extreame trouble, attendance, and charges. And the reason that made the difference between the plea reall, and the plea personall, was, that in the plea personall the party grieved had no other remedy, but the attaint; but in the plea reall he had other remedy in an action of higher nature, and for that cause was not granted without difficulty. And

And ſome judges held, that in a plea reall an attaint did not lie, and therefore this act provideth that the king ſhall grant it * *ex officio*, that is, *ex merito juſtitiæ*. And this act is holden to be in affirmance of the common law, whereof you ſhall reade at large, Marlebr. cap. 14. And this is the common opinion agreeable with our old bookes, as there you may reade.

* De ſon office.

Marleb. ca. 14.

That perjury in jurors was puniſhed before this act hath been ſufficiently proved already: now the preamble of this act giveth juſt occaſion to examine whether perjury alſo in witneſſes were puniſhable by the auncient lawes of England; *De pejerantibus prætерea ſtatutum eſt, ut ſi quis jusjurandum violarit, falſumve dixerit teſtimonium, fides ei in poſterum non habetor, verum is in ordalium adjudicator.*

Int' leges Edw. Regis, 43. 3.

Si quis falſum juraſſe convictus fuerit, ei poſtea non modo non creditor, verumetiam ſacra ei etiam prohibetor ſepultura.

Inter leges Ethelſtani, 67. 25.

Si quis ſacra tenens pejeraſſe convictus fuerit, ei manus præciditor, &c.

Inter leges Canuti 113. 34.

Vide inter leges W. Conq. fol. 125. b.

And the Mirror ſaith, *Que ſolonque les auncient privileges, et uſages aſcuns ſe font per perde del ponce, come eſt de faux notaries, et de ciſſers de burſes de meyns q. xii. d. et pluis que vi. d. que le roy R. 1. ſe chaunzea a la parte de oriel, aſcuns per couper des langues, come ſoloit eſtre de faux teſtmoines.*

Mirror, c. 4. de paines. 10 H. 3. Coron. 434.

And in the ſame chapter treateth further of this matter, ſaying, *Perjury eſt graund peche, &c.* whereof you may reade there more at large. Britton ſaith that it was puniſhable, and to be enquired of *De ceux queux ſe voilont perjurer pur lower.*

Britton, fo. 38. Fleta, l. 5. c. 21. & li. 2. cap. 1. Bract. l. 4. f. 289.

Fleta deſcribeth perjury thus, *Perjurium eſt mendacium cum juramento firmatum*; and further ſaith, *Et tribus modis committitur; primo, cum quis ſcit, vel putat aliquid falſum eſſe falſum, et jurat eſſe verum; ſecundo, cum quis fallitur, et credit verum eſſe quod eſt falſum, et temere et indiſcrete jurat; tertio, ſi quis credit falſum eſſe verum, et jurat quod verum eſt.*

Where you may reade further of this matter. And of ſome it is called, *crimen læſæ conſcientiæ*.

Bract. fo. 292.

Thomas Vigras and two others were found guilty, &c. of perjury.

[238]

Hil. 8 E. 1. in Communi Banc. Rot. 38. Eſſex. John of Huntingfields caſe.

18 E. 3. 53. Once forſworne, and ever forlorne.

7 H. 6. 25. Perjury puniſhed.

Vide the ſtatutes of 3 H. 7. cap. 1. 11 H. 7. cap. 25. 32 H. 8. cap. 9. 5 Eliz.

Upon all that which hath been ſaid touching this point, you may obſerve how milde the late laws have been in puniſhing of perjury in reſpect of the auncient, wherein I have been the longer, for that ſome have given out, that perjury was not puniſhed by the auncient laws of England, wherein there ſhould have been a great defect, and an encouragement to ill diſpoſed men, if jurors ſhould by the common law have been puniſhed for perjury, and witneſſes, which are great motives to them of giving their verdict, ſhould be perjured, and not be puniſhed.

(1) *Quant il ſemble que beſoigne ſoit.*] See 5 E. 1. which was within two yeares after this act, an attaint was brought upon a falſe verdict given in aſſiſe before juſtices in eyre before the making of this ſtatute: and the record ſaith, *Quod non eſt intentio domini regis, nec extitit tempore confectionis ſtatuti prædicti, quod breve de attinctu tranſiret ſuper hujuſmodi inquiſitionibus ante ſtatutum captis, prout*

Mich. 5 E. 1. in Banco Rot. 63. Midd.

Johannes de Lovet recordatur, imò post statutum concess' consideratum est quod querens nihil capiat per breve, &c. And this was the law taken then by colour of these words; but others hold, that these words are not to be so taken for the reason aforesaid, for that the party grieved in this plea reall had remedy in an action of higher nature: but later statutes quoted before in the margent have cleared this point.

CAP. XXXIX.

ET pur ceo que le temps est mult passe puis que les briefes desouth nosmes fuerent auterfoits limittes: purview est, que en count countant de descent en briefe de droit, nul ne soit ci ose de counter de la seisin son anc' de plus longe seisin que de temps le roy R. (1) *uncle le roy Henry, pier le roy que ore est. Et que le briefe de novel disseisin, et de purparty, que est appelle nuper obiit, eyent le terme puis le primer passage le roy Henry, pier le roy, que ore est en Gascoigne* (2), *mes nemy avant. Et les briefes de mortdanc', de cosinage, de ayle, de entre, et briefe de neifrie, eiant le terme del coronement mesme le roy Henry* (3), *et nemy avant. Mes que touts les briefes ore a per mesme purchases, ou a purchaser, entour cy et* [*la feast*] *S. John en un an, soient pledes de temps que avant solent estre pleades.*

AND forasmuch as it is long time passed since the writs undernamed were limited; it is provided, that in conveighing a descent in a writ of right, none shall presume to declare of the seisin of his ancestor further, or beyond the time of king Richard uncle to king Henry, father to the king that now is; and that a writ of novel disseisin, of partition, which is called nuper obiit, have their limitation since the first voyage of king Henry, father to the king that now is, into Gascoin. And that writs of mortdancestor, of cosinage, of aiel, of entry, and of nativis, have their limitation from the coronation of the same king Henry, and not before. Neverthelesss all writs purchased now by themselves, or to be purchased between this and the feast of St. John, for one year compleat, shall be pleaded from as long time, as heretofore they have been used to be pleaded.

(1 Inst. 114, 115. 20 H. 3. c. 8. 32 H. 8. c. 2. 21 Jac. 1. c. 16.)

1. Inst. sect. 170. (1) *De temps le roy R.*] That is by construction from the first day of the raigne of king Richard the first, and so hath it been resolved in parliament.

[239] 34 H. 6. 36. Instit. ubi supra. This act doth limit within what time the seisin shall be in a writ of right, and by construction the time of prescription is taken for this time.

(2) *Puis le premier passage le roy Henry, &c. in Gascoine.*] That was in *anno* 5 H. 3.

Vet Mag. Chart. 144. (3) *Del coronement mesme le roy Henry.*] H. 3. was crowned 28 *Octobris, anno Dom.* 1217. *et regni sui primo*; but others say he was crowned 16 *Junii, anno regni sui primo.*

This king was crowned again in *anno* 5. of his raign, but this act intendeth his first coronation.

These

Theſe limitations are altered by the ſtatute of 32 H. 8. as you may reade before in the expoſition upon the ſtatute of Merton, cap. 8. See the firſt part of the Inſtitutes, ſect. 170.

CAP. XL.

*PUR ceo que mults des gents ſont delayes de lour droit, per fauxment voucher a garranty: purview eſt que en briefes de poſſ (1), tout adeprimes come en briefe de mortdaunc', coſinage, del ayle, nuper obiit, de intruſion, et auters briefes ſemblables, per les queux terres ou tenements ſont demands (2), queux devoient diſcender (3), reverter (4), remainder (5), ou eſchier (6), per mortdanc', ou dauter, que ſi le tenant vouche a garrant', et le demandant luy counterpled', et voile averrer per aſſiſe, ou per pays, ou en auter maner, ſicome le court le roy agarde, que le tenant (9) ou ſon aunc' (8) que heire il eſt, fuit le primer que entra (10) apres la mort celuy de que ſeiſin il demand, ſoit le averrement del de demandant reſceve (7), ſi le tenant le voile attender, et ſi non, ſoit bote ouſter le auter reſpons (11) ſil neit ſon garrantor en preſent, que luy voile garranter de ſon gree (12), et maintainant enter en reſpons, ſalve al demandant ſes exceptions enconter luy, ſil voile voucher ouſter, come il avoit avant, enconter le primer tenant. De recheſſe en touts maners des briefes dentre, queux ſont mention des degrees: purview [eſt] que nul deformes vouche (13) hors de la line (14). Et en auters briefes dentrie, ou nul mention eſt fait de degrees (15), les queux briefes ne ſont ſuſtenus, forſque la ou les avantdits briefes de degrees ne poient giſer ne lieu tener. Et en briefe de droit (16) purview eſt; que ſi le tenant vouche a garranty, et le demandant le voile counterpleder, et ſoit priſt * de averrer per pays, que celuy que eſt vouche (17) a garranty, [ne nul] de ſes anceſters (18) ne unques avoient ſeiſin de la terre, ou del*

FORASMUCH as many people are delayed of their right by falſe vouching to warranty; it is provided, that in writs of poſſeſſion, firſt in writ of mortdaunceſter, of coſinage, of aiel, nuper obiit, of intruſion, and other like writs, whereby lands or tenements are demanded, which ought to deſcend, revert, remain, or eſcheat by the death of any anceſtor, or otherwiſe, if the tenant vouch to warranty, and the demandant counterpleadeth him, and will aver by aſſiſe, or by the country, or otherwiſe, as the court will award, that the tenant, or his anceſtor (whoſe heir he is) was the firſt that entered after the death of him, of whoſe ſeiſin he demandeth; the averment of the demandant ſhall be received, if the tenant will abide thereupon; and if not, he ſhall be further compelled to another anſwer, if he have not his warrantor preſent, that will warrant him freely, and incontinent enter into the warranty; ſaving unto the demandant his exceptions againſt him, if he will vouch further, as he had before againſt the firſt tenant. From henceforth in all manner of writs of entry, which make mention of degrees, none ſhall vouch out of the line: or in other writs of entry, where no mention is made of degrees, which writ ſhall not be maintained, but in caſes where the other writs of degrees cannot lie, nor hold place: and in a writ of right it is provided, that if the tenant vouch to warranty, and the demandant will counter-plead him, and be ready to aver by the country, that he that is vouched to warranty, nor his anceſtors, had never ſeiſin of the land

del tenement (19) demande (20), ne fee, ne ſervice per la maine le tenant, ou [aſcun] de ſes aunceſters (21), puis le temps celuy de que ſeiſin le demandant counte (22) jeſques al temps que le briefe fuit purchaſe et plee move (23), per que il poit le tenant ou ſes aunceſtors aver feoffe: adonques ſoit laverrement del demandant reſceive, ſi le tenant le voil' attender, et ſi non, ſoit le tenant bote ouſter a auter reſpons (24), ſil neit ſon garrantor en preſent, que luy voile garranter de ſon gree, et maintenant enter en reſpons, ſalve al demandant ſes exceptions enconter luy, ſicome il avoit avant encounter le primer tenant. Et lavantdit exception eit lieu en briefe de mortdaunceſtre, et en les auters briefes devant noſmes, auxibien come briefes queux touchent droit (25). Et ſi le tenant per cas eit charter de garranty de auter home de ceo choſe que ſoit oblige en nul des avantdits caſes (26) a le garranty de ſon eigne degree, ſalve luy ſoit ſon recoverer per briefe de garranty de charter de le chauncellor le roy, quant il le voudra purchaſer, mes que le plee ne ſoit pur ceo delay.

land or tenement demanded, nor fee or ſervice by the hands of his tenant, or his anceſtors, ſince the time of him, on whoſe ſeiſin the demandant declareth, until the time that the writ was purchaſed, and the plea moved, whereby he might have infeoffed the tenant, or his anceſtors, then let the averment of the demandant be received, if the tenant will abide thereupon; if not, the tenant ſhall be further compelled unto another anſwer, if he be not preſent that will warrant him freely, and incontinent enter in anſwer, ſaving unto the demandant his exceptions againſt him, as he had afore againſt the firſt tenant. And the ſaid exception ſhall have place in a writ of mortdaunceſtor, and in the other writs before named, as well as in writs that concern right. And if percaſe the tenant have a deed, that compriſeth warranty of another man, which is bound in none of theſe caſes before mentioned to the warranty of an elder degree; his recovery, by a writ of warranty of charters out of the king's chancery, ſhall be ſaved to him at what time ſoever he will purchaſe it; howbeit the plea ſhall not be delayed therefore.

(Bro. Parl. 34. Fitz. Counterplea de Voucher, 78. 81, 82, 83. 89. 96. 98. 100. Fitz. Counterplea, &c. 3, 4, 5. 7, 8, 9, 10. 17, 18. 20. 23, 24. 27. 29, 30. 40, 41, 42. 44. 48, 49. 58, 59, 60. 63. 65. 85. 88. 94. 114. 126. Fitz. Execut. 122. Fitz. Gar. de Charters, 3, 4, 5. 7, 8, 9, 10, 11, 12, 13. 19, 20, 21, 22. 26. 28, 29, 30, 31. 20 Ed. 1. ſtat. 1. De Vouchers.)

13 E. 1. counterplea de voucher. 118. 16 E. 2. ibid. 110. 8 E. 3. 61. The miſchiefe before this ſtatute was, that every tenant in a reall action was permitted to vouch any of the people, though he or any of his aunceſtors had never any thing in the land whereof he might enfeoffe the tenant or any of his aunceſtors; and againe that vowchee might vowch another in like manner, and upon every ſummons *ad warrantizandum*, there muſt be nine retourners, &c. ſo as the delay was in manner infinite, and all upon falſe vowchers; which matter being ſhewed in this parliament, *Fuit adviſe al roy que ceſt ley fuit malveis*, for it is a maxime in law, that *Lex dilationes* 22 H. 6. 40. per Markham. *ſemper exhorret*; whereupon this act of parliament for remedy was made.

Inſtit. ſect. 143. *Vouchee a garranty.*] For this word [vouchee] ſee Lit.

Glanv. l. 13. c. 9, 10. & alibi ſæpe. Vide Glanv. of this matter.

Bract. l. 5 f. 380. Vide Bracton, a whole tractate of vowching to warranty.

Britton, c. 75. Vide Britton, a chapter of the ſame.

Fleta

Fleta saith, *Sunt autem nonnulli lites protrahere nitentes, minores falso vocant ad warrant', et de quibus provisum est* (summing up the principall part of this statute in few words) *quod si petens replicando offerat verificare quod vocatus nec aliquis antecessorum vocati nunquā seisinam habuit de re petita, feodum nec servitium per manus tenentis vel alicujus antecessoris ejus à tempore ejus ex cujus seisina petit usque ad tempus impetrationis brevis et placiti moti, per quod potuit verificare tenentem vel ejus antecessores inde feoffatos fuisse, admittatur verificatio illa si tenens voluit hoc expectare, alioquin ulterius respondere compellatur, salvis petenti talibus replicationibus, quales versus principalem tenentem obtineret: et si tenens chartam habuerit alicujus extraneæ personæ qui se ad warrantiam obligaverit, vel per antecessorem obligatus fuerit qui gratis warrantizare voluerit, tunc competit tenenti remedium per breve de warrantia chartæ, sed propterea non capiat placitum jam motum dilationem.*

Fleta, lib.

[241]

In ancient time it seemed strange when the originall *præcipe* was brought against the tenant of the land, that the court upon that originall should hold plea between the tenant and the vowchee, but it is more strange to make a question of that, which hath received an ancient, continuall, and constant allowance, and the vowchee commeth in *in loco tenentis*, and in judgement of law is a tenant to the demandant, and our act doth allow of true vowchers, but provideth against false vowchers, as our act speaketh, for delay onely.

Mirror. 8 E. 3. 61.

(1) *En briefes de possession.*] So called, because either the auncestor, of whose seisin he demands, was in possession the day he died, or the demandant himselfe was in possession, as *mortdaunc'*, *cosinage*, *aiel*, *nuper obiit*, *intrusion* and other like writs, as *besaile*, &c.

8 E. 3. 57. b. 32 E. 3. Count. de vowcher 82. 21 E. 3. 11. 46 E. 3. 2.

The diversity between the actions *auncestrel droiturel*, and the actions *auncestrel possessorie*, you shall reade at large in my reports in Markals case, and is necessary to be observed for the understanding of this act, which maketh the same distinction of actions.

Li. 6. fo. 34, 35, &c. Markals case.

(2) *Per les queux terres ou tenements sont demaundes.*] In a writ of right of ward of body and land, the defendant vowched, and the plaintife counterpleaded the vowcher by this first branch of this act, that the defendant was the first that abated after the death of his tenant, and the same continued till the vowcher, and adjudged a good counterplea; for albeit it is named a writ of right, and so in letter is out of this branch, yet is it in nature of a writ of possession, and the words are *per mort dauncester ou dauter*, and though no lands or tenements be demaunded, which regularly is intended of an estate of freehold, yet this case being within the same mischiefe is taken within the remedy.

8 E. 3. 57. 61. 21 E. 3. 11. 22 E. 3. 6. 25 E. 3. 39. 32 E. 3. Count. de vow. 83.

In dower the tenant vowch T. cosine & heire; A. the demandant said that her husband died seised, and the vowchee was the first that abated; and a good counterplea within these words, *autres briefes sembles*, but that plea is not in case of the heire.

2 E. 3. 31. 22 E. 3. 3. 32 E. 3. 75. a. in libro meo.

(3) *Discender.*] A *formedon* in the descender is out of this branch, for it is a writ of right in his nature, and not a writ of possession, and he demandeth not the land of the seisin of his auncestor, as the statute speaketh, but of the gift.

4 E. 3. 56. 39 E. 3. 36. b.

32 E. 3. infra †.

(4) *Reverter.*] A *formedon* in the reverter is not within this branch, for that it is a writ of right in his nature.

4 E. 3. Count de vowcher. † See 32 E. 3. fol. 74, 75. in libro meo. Lopinion del Court al contrary. vide 32 E. 3. tit. counterplea de vowcher. 82.

(5) *Remainder.*] A *formedon* in the remainder is not within this branch, for it is no writ of possession, but a writ of right in his nature, and the demandant doth not demand the land of the seisin of his auncester, as the statute speaketh, but by the remainder.

4 E. 3. 33. 32 E. 3 count-de vow. 82.

(6) *Eschier.*] This is in the English translation turned to escheate, which ought not to be, but *eschier* signifieth to fall, and a writ of escheat is not within this branch, for that it soundeth in the right, and reverter, remainder, or eschier is to be intended after the death of his auncester, or tenant for life, tenant in dower, or by the curtesie.

3 E. 3. vowch. 199. 26 H. 6. tit. count. de vowcher 5. 21 H. 6. 50.

An assise of *novel disseisin,* and in assise of *darrein presentment* are within this branch, if the tenant vowch any named in the writ, and the demandant may counterplead the vowcher, as well when the tenant is present in court, as when he is absent.

[242]

The first counterplea given by this act.

46 E. 3. 2. 4 E. 3. Count de Voucher 96.

(7) *Que le tenant ou son auncester que heire il est fuit le primier que entra apres la mort celuy de que seisin il demaund, soit laverment del demaundant resceive.*] A. dieth seised in fee, B. abateth, and maketh a lease for life, and graunteth the reversion to C. in fee, and dieth, C. graunteth the reversion to D. the heire of B. tenant for life is impleaded in a writ of cosinage, and makes default after default, D. is received and vowcheth to warranty C. the demandant counterplead the vowcher, for that B. was the first that abated after the death of his auncester, of whose seisin he makes his demand: and two objections were made, that this counterplea was not within this statute. 1. That D. claimed the reversion by purchase, and so B. was not his auncestor within this statute, for he claimed not the land as heire. 2. That this statute speaketh of the tenant, which must be understood of the tenant for life, who is the tenant to the *præcipe* in deed, and not of the tenant by receit, who is tenant in law: as to the first it was answered and resolved, that in as much as the abatement is confessed, albeit that divers states be made, yet for that D. is heire to the abator, and B. his auncester within the letter of the statute, and *injuria per circuitum non tollitur,* and so within the meaning. But if the state of the abator had been avoided by a title paramount, and the heire of the abator had been enfeoffed, there the heire had not claimed under the abatement, and therefore although he were within the letter of this act, yet had he been out of the meaning.

40 Ass. 22.

(8) *Auncestre.*] And where it is said here auncester, predecessor is taken by equity; for acts of parliament made for suppression of falshood practised for delay, as these false vouchers be, shall have a benigne interpretation.

Hil. 9. E. 2. fo. 63. in lib. meo. en Cosinage.

(9) *Tenant.*] To the second, albeit tenant by receit be but tenant in law, yet is he in lieu of the tenant, and so within this branch, for otherwise the abator may make a lease for life, and by his default after default be received, and so by covin between them make this branch of none effect, which should be against reason, *et in fraudem legis*; and tenant in law by warranty is within this act, albeit he be not present in court.

(10) *Primier que entra.*] A. and B. doe abate to the use of B. the whole state is in B. if B. infeoffe A. this coadjutor is within this act, and yet he gained no freehold, but this statute saith, *Le primer*

que

que enter, and though he entred not at the firſt ſolie, yet is he within this ſtatute.

But if the abator maketh a feoffement in fee, and taketh back an eſtate to him and a ſtranger, and they both be impleaded in a writ of *aiel*, and vouch their feoffor for the benefit of the ſtranger (who is out of the ſtatute) the vowcher cannot be counterpleaded within this branch.

But if the ſtranger releaſe to the abator, and he be impleaded, and vowch, this vowcher may be counterpleaded by force of this branch.

(11) *Et ſi non, ſoit bote ouſter al auter reſpons.*] So as this clauſe giveth no benefit to the tenant unleſſe he giveth over his vowcher, and then he ſhall be received to anſwer, but if he ſtand to his vowcher, and demurre in law upon the counterplea, and it be adjourned to another terme, it is peremptory to the tenant in reſpect of the delay, in ſuch ſort, as if iſſue had been taken, and a triall had: By theſe words [*Soit bote a auter reſpons*] he may as well vowch as plead in chiefe. Note the words be, *Soit bote a auter reſpons, et ne dit en chiefe*, ſo as any anſwer ſufficeth, and therefore the vowchee may plead outlawry in the plaintife in an action of debt, after the laſt continuance. 45 E. 3. 16. 8 H. 7. 5. 40 E. 3. 14. Br. tit. Coun. de vouch 5. 21 E. 4. 54.

[243]

But if the counterplea be adjudged for the demandant in the ſame term, he may plead in bar, but he cannot vouch. 22 H. 6. 40.

A demurrer in law upon a voucher adjourned to another term is peremptory; for the demurrer is in lieu of an anſwer, otherwiſe in caſe of counterplea the ſame term, as hath been ſaid. 11 H. 4. 22. 42 E. 3. 16. 10 H. 7. 22.

(12) *Sil neit ſon garantor en preſent, que luy voille garrant' de ſon gree*, &c.] In a writ of right of ward, the defendant vouch, and for that the vouchee was preſent in court, and entred into warranty, the plaintife could not counterplead. Hil. 9 E. 2. fol. 63. in lib. meo en Coſinage. Temps. E. 1. Count. de Vouch. 116.

(13) *Des recheiſe in touts maners des briefes des entries queux ſont mention des degrees; purvieu eſt que nul diſormes vouchera hors del lien.*] A diſſeiſor makes a leaſe for life, the remainder in fee, the diſſeiſee brings a writ of entry *ſur diſſeiſin* in the *per* againſt the leſſee, who makes default after default; he in the remainder is received, he ſhall vouch out of the line, becauſe he is not within the degrees mentioned in the writ. See the ſtatute de Vocat. ad Warr. 20 E. 1. The ſecond counterplea given by this act. 16 H. 7. 5.

And there is no ſuch miſchief in this caſe, as ſhould follow, if the law were ſo taken in the firſt branch, as before it appeareth. 9 E. 3. 16. ſimile.

But of the vouchee, in caſe of the *per et cui*, Fleta ſaith, *Fiat vocatio de perſona in perſonam, et de warranto in warrantum de perſonis in brevi nominatis uſque ad ipſum diſſeiſitorem*; and the reaſon may be, becauſe it appeareth that the vouchee is within the degrees mentioned in the writ: and the words of the ſtatute are generall, *Nul vouchera hors de lien*; in which words, the vouchee is included. Laſtly, it had been to little purpoſe, to reſtrain the tenant in the *per*, and to let the vouchee in the *cui* at large; ſo as this branch hath (as you ſee) his ſpeciall reaſon. Fleta, li. 5. c. 37.

If a writ of entry in the *per* be brought againſt the huſband and wife, and upon the default of the huſband the wife is received, ſhe ſhall not vouch out of the line, becauſe ſhe is party to the writ.

So it is, if a writ of entry in the *per* be brought againſt the tenant

for life, and he pray in ayd of him in the reversion, and he joyn in ayd, he must joyn in plea with the tenant, and therefore shall not vouch out of the degrees.

(14) *Hors del lien.*] Lien is properly the binding of the vouchee by force of the warranty; for the vouchee saith, *Que aves a vous a lier a garranty*; and then the tenant sheweth the *lien*, that is, the deed or fine, &c. that bindeth him to warranty: here it is taken for the degrees; of which you have heard before, in the exposition of the last chapter of Marlebridge.

12 E. 3. Count. de Vouch. 92. 27 H. 6. 1.

In a writ of entry in the *per* and *cui* against B. of the feoffment of A. A. dyeth, B. shall vouch the heir of A. for the heir is within the intention and meaning of this law, lest he should lose his warranty (so much favoured in law) by the act of God, *viz.* the death of A.

(15) *Et in autres briefes dentre ou nul mention est fait de degrees.*] That is, writs of entry in the *post*; whereof, and of this whole clause, somewhat hath been spoken in exposition of the said statute of Marlebridge.

(16) *Et in briefe de droit.*] This is not onely understood of a writ of right right, but of all writs of right in his nature, or which touch the right, as this law hereafter speaketh, as the writ of escheat, writs of formdon in reverter, remainder, discender, &c.

[244]

The third counterplea given by this act. 12 E. 3. Count. de Voucher. 42. [a] 21 E. 3. 9. 31 E. 3. Count de Vouch. 88. Dyer. 13 El. 290. [b] 10 E. 3. 30. 18 E. 3. 3. 26. 38 E. 3. 22. 40 E. 3. 14. 23. 43 E. 3. 19. 27 H. 6. 1. 35 H. 6. 34. 22 E. 4. 10. 20 H. 7. ibid. [c] 40 Ass. 22. 19 E. 2. Count. de Vouch. 114. 6 E. 2. Vieu. 162. Temps, E. 1. ib. 171. [d] 22 Ass. 30. 48 E. 3. 28. 18 E. 3. 53, 54. 47. 39 E. 3. 30. 32. 16 H. 7. 13. 20 H. 7. ibid. [e] Temps. E. 1. tit. Count de Vouch. 126 50 E. 3. ibid. 124. 16 E. 3. Count de Garr. 36, 37. 18 E. 3. Issue 36. 40 E. 3. 12, 13. 44 E. 3. 27. 13 E. 3. Count. de Vouch. 36. 8 H. 7. 5. 21 H. 6. Count. de Vouch. 3. 14 H. 6. 10.

(17) *Que celuy que est vouche.*] If the tenant vouch A. as assignee to B. the demandant may counterplead the seisin of B. within the meaning of this branch, for that overthrows the voucher, which is the end of this law.

[a] If an infant be vouched as heir to A. it is not sufficient to counterplead the seisin of A. the ancestor, for that the infant cannot make a feoffment; but he must counterplead the seisin of the infant and his ancestors, and the infancie shall come upon the lien.

(18) *Ne nul de ces auncesters.*] [b] Here is implyed (whose heir he is) but yet this doth extend aswell to the speciall heir of the possession (as the heir in borough English, and in gavelkinde) as to the generall heire at the common law.

[c] Where a bishop or an abbot be vouched, the counterplea must not be of the bishop or abbot and his ancestors, according to the letter of the law; but of him and his predecessors, according to that capacitie whereby the land is demanded: and so it is of other bodies politique and corporate.

[d] If a baron and feme be vouched, the seisin of the feme and her ancestors may be counterpleaded, unlesse speciall matter be shewed to the contrary: and so it is, if two others be vouched, it is a good counterplea to counterplead the seisin of one of them, for ousting of delay by essoine, protection, death, and his heir within age, &c.

(19) *Ne unques avoient seisin de la terre out tenement, &c. per que il poet aver, &c. feoffe.*] [e] Yet if he hath but an estate for yeers, it is sufficient; for by the livery he gaineth seisin, and both the feoffments *de jure* and *de facto* are within this statute, but otherwise it is of an estate at will.

If the vouchee hath but an estate for life, so as his feoffment should be a surrender, yet hath he such an estate, as is within this statute.

Husband

Husband *cesti que use* in the right of his wife, or seised in the right of his wife, hath a seisin *dont il poet feoffment faire*, a feoffment for maintenance, though the statute of 1 R. 2. make it void, yet seeing it is not void untill entry, it is a sufficient seisin to make a feoffment.

[f] One joyntenant cannot enfeoff another, yet hath he such a seisin as is within this act; for [*feoffment faire*] is spoken but for example; but a fine, release, or any other conveyance which giveth an estate, is within this law.

If a vouchee or any of his ancestors had any seisin, though it were avoided or determined, it is sufficient.

(20) *En demaunde.*] [g] If a rent be demanded, and the tenant vouch by reason of a feoffment of the land discharged of the rent with warranty, the demandant may counterplead the seisin of the vouchee, &c. of the land, albeit the rent is onely in demand.

(21) *Ne fee, ne service per la maine le tenant, ou ascun de ses auncesters*, &c.] [h] For in respect of some tenure and service, the tenant may vouch to warranty; as frankalmoigne, homage, auncestrel, reversion, &c.

(22) *Puis le tẽps celuy de que seisin le demand' coũte.*] [i] Here [seisin] is taken for the title of the demandant in his writ, for it is a maxime in counterpleas, that the demandant is not to counterplead any seisin, but after the title of his writ; and where the seisin is in the title, there the counterplea must be after that seisin: as for example, in a writ of right, after the seisin of him of whose seisin he demand.

Here is implyed (and before the writ purchased) for if it be *pendente brevi*, it ought not to be allowed. [245]

(23) *Iesq; le temps que le briefe fuit purchase & plea move.*] * For no warranty, created after the purchase of the writ, shall delay the plaintife, unlesse upon that conveyance the writ be made good; as if a *præcipe* be brought against A. of land whereof B. is seised, and B. infeoffe A. hanging the writ, he shall vouch by force of this warranty, otherwise not.

(24) *Soit le tenant bote oust' al aut' respons.*] Of this sufficient hath been said before.

(25) *Lavantdit exception eyt lieu en briefe de mordanc', & en les autres briefs devant nosmes auxy bien come in briefs queux touchant droit.*] By this clause, the demandants in writs of possession, as the *mortdauncester, cosinage, aiel, nuper obiit, intrusion*, and the like, have a greater privilege and advantage, then demandants in actions which touch the right; for this act gives the demandants in writs of possession, not onely the first counterplea, that is, that the tenant or his ancestor was the first that entered, &c. but also the last counterplea, which is given in writs touching the right, *viz.* that neither the vouchee, nor any of his auncestors had ever any seisin, &c.

(26) *Et si le tenant per case eyt charter de garrantie de auter home, que soit oblige in nul des avantdits cases*, &c.] If any man be ousted of his voucher by this statute, yet if he hath a charter of warranty, he may have his writ of *warrantia chartæ*; as if a man that never had any thing in the land, nor any of his ancestors before him, releaseth to the tenant of the land with warranty, if the tenant vouch him, and the demandant counterplead the voucher, by the last

[f] 44 E. 3. Count. de Vouch. 45 E. 3. 16. 14. 35 H. 6. 10. 9 H. 6. 49. 8 H. 7. 5. 50 E. 3. tit. Count. de Vouch. 124.

[g] 3 E. 3. 36. 5 E. 3. 16. 37. 10 E. 3. 20. 26 H. 6. Count de Vouch. 5. 12 R. 2. ibid. 34. 35 H. 6. 30. 21 E. 4. 26.

[h] Fleta, li. 6. c. 23. 13 E. 1. Count. de Vouch. 118. 47 H. 3. Vouch. 270, 271. 9 H. 3. ibid. 277. 1. part. Instit. sect. 143.

[i] 13 E. 3. Count. de Vouch. 118. 6 E. 3. 21. 38 E. 3. 28. 39 E. 3. 36. 41 E. 3. 15. 46 E. 3. 32. 48 E. 3. 2. 11 H. 4. 19. 22 H. 6. 42. 21 E. 4. 20. 21 E 3. 20. 21 E. 4 26. 12 H. 7. 2.

* 8 E. 3. 40. 28 E. 3. 90. 41 E 3. 5. 12 R. 2. Count. de Vouch. 33. 18 E. 4. 27. a simile. 12 H. 7. 2 b. per Wood & 3. per Brian.

Instit. 1. part. sect. 743. More of this matter.

last branch of this act, *viz.* that the vouchee, nor any of his ancestors had ever any seisin, &c. and the vouchee is not there present, to enter into warranty; in that case the tenant shall be ousted of his voucher, but may have his writ of *warr' chartæ.* So if a man after the death of my ancestor abate, and make a feoffment in fee, and after purchase the land again with warranty, and after is impleaded in an assise of *mortdancester*, he shall be ousted of his voucher by the first branch of this act, because he was the first that entred, &c. but he may have his *warrantia chartæ.* So if a disseisor make a feoffment in fee to A. who infeoffeth B. and after repurchaseth the land of B. with warranty, against whom the disseisee brings a writ of entry in the *per*, as he may do, he cannot vouch B. by the second branch of this statute, but the disseisor onely, and is driven to his writ of *warrantia chartæ* against B.

It is to be known, that there are counterpleas to the voucher, and that this statute giveth to the demandant, against the tenant in three cases, as hath been said.

And there is a counterplea to the warranty, or to the lien (which is all one) and that is between the tenant and vouchee, whereof there is no occasion given to treat at this time; for this act deals not in any sort with it.

There were at the common law divers counterpleas of the voucher, to prevent or to oust the demandants delay, whereof it is not impertinent to say somewhat.

7 E. 3. 27. 7 Ass. 4. 28 E. 3. 96. It was a good counterplea at the common law, to say, that there was *nul tiel*, as the vouchee; and that the statute of 14 E. 3. cap. 18. was in affirmance of the common law.

* 14 H. 6. 10. 48 E. 3. 17. 14 E. 3. Count. de Vouch. 67. * So it is, if one be vouched as heir within age, and that the parol may demur, to say, that he is a bastard; so it is, to say that the vouchee is villein to the demandant.

[246]

40 E. 3. 36. 25 E. 3. 43. 17 E. 3. 41. 21 E. 3. 36. 7 E. 3. 27. 5 E. 3. 35. It was a good counterplea at the common law, to say that the vouchee was dead, but upon this distinction, that the demandant shew the same before any processe awarded; for after processe awarded, it must come in by the retourn of the sherife: and that the statute of 14 E. 3. ca. 18. was made but in affirmance of the common law, for it was adjudged in 5 Edw. 3. a good counterplea.

39 E. 3. 32. And so it is, if two be vouched, it is a good counterplea, to say, that one of them is dead for preventing of delay.

18 E. 3. 55. In dower, it is a good counterplea, to say, that the tenant entred by her husband.

3 E. 3. 38. 6 E. 3. 18 E. 3 Vouch. 7. It is a good counterplea of the voucher, to say, that the tenant hath formerly prayed in aid of him, in respect of the delay.

32 E. 3. ibid. 99. 7 H. 4. 11 H. 4. 21. 22 H. 6. 19. In all cases, where one doth vouch out of common course, there the tenant ought to shew cause.

And whensoever the tenant cannot be admitted to his voucher without shewing of cause, there by the common law the demandant may counterplead the cause.

21 E. 3. 37. 25 E. 3. 53. 40 E. 3. 14. 41 E. 3. 21. 44 E. 3. 38. 38 E. 3. 4. 29 E. 3. 29. 32 E. 3. Vouch. 96. When one voucheth himself, for saving of his estate tail; or when he voucheth himself as heir, and his brother as tenant in borough English, because it is out of common course, the tenant must shew cause, and the demandant shall have a counterplea to the cause.

10 H. 7. 21, 22. 10 H. 7. 13. 43 E. 3. 19. In a *præcipe*, the tenant vouched two brethren as one heir, and that the youngest was within age; and because it was out of common

mon course, he was ruled to shew cause; and shewed, that the father was seised of lands in gavelkinde, and that the same descended to them, and the demandant counterpleaded the cause.

So it is, if a *præcipe* be brought by four, and two be summoned and severed, the tenant cannot vouch them that be summoned and severed, without shewing cause for the reason aforesaid; and the cause being shewed, the demandant shall counterplead the same. 4 E. 3. 13. 11 H. 4. 16. 21. 48.

In a *præcipe* against two they cannot vouch severally without shewing of cause, because it is out of common course, that jointenants should vouch severally without shewing of cause: which cause the demandant shall counterplead by the common law: and so in all other cases, whereof there are plentifull authorities in our books. 42 E. 3. 16. 3 E. 3. 8. 12 H. 7. 2, 3. 3 E. 3. 38. 8 E. 3. 61. 17 E. 3. 61, 62. 25 Ass. Pl. ult. 31 E. 3. Vouch. 24. 44 E. 3. 18. 14 H. 6. 10.

See more of this matter in the first part of the Institutes, cap. Garrantie.

CAP. XLI.

DE serements des champions (1), *est issint purview: pur ceo que rarement avient que le champion le demandant ne soit perjure en ceo quil jure, que il ou son pier veist la seisin son seigniour, ou de son auncestour, et que son pier luy commande a faire la darreign'* (2), *que desormes ne soit le champion le demandant constreint a ceo jurer* (3), *mes soit le serement garde en touts ses auters points.*

TOUCHING the oaths of champions, it is thus provided, because it seldom happened, but that the champion of the defendant is forsworn, in that he sweareth, that he or his father saw the seisin of his lord, or his ancestor, and that his father commanded him to dereign that right; that from henceforth the champion of the demandant shall not be compelled so to swear: nevertheless his oath shall be kept in all other points.

At the common law none could be a champion for the demandant, but such an one, as either himself saw, or heard his father say, that he saw the seisin of the demandant or his ancestor, and that his father commanded him to testifie the right, and that this was true, he took a corporall oath: but oftentimes the demandants seisin was so ancient, as seldome any man could take that oath, and yet in these cases, champions in those times took the oath, though they knew it not, either *ex visu*, or *ex auditu*, &c. and therefore as this act saith, were perjured. Glan. li. 2. c. 3. [247]

(1) *Des serements des champions.*] Champion, *campio dicitur à campo*, because the combat was strucken in the field, and therefore is called campfight, and he must be *liber homo*, a free man.

This triall by champion in a writ of right hath been anciently allowed by the common law, and the tenant in a writ of right hath election either to put himselfe upon the grand assise, or upon the triall by combat by his champion with the champion of the demandant, which was instituted upon this reason, that in respect the tenant had lost his evidences, or that the same were burnt or imbezeled, or that his witnesses were dead, the law permitted him to try Bract. l. 5. f. 344. 9 H. 3. Flet. l. 6. cap. 9. in fine.

try it by combat between his champion, and the champion of the demandant, hoping that God would give victory to him that right had, and of whose party the victory fell out, for him was judgement finally given, for seldome death ensued hereupon (for their weapons were but batounes) victory only sufficed.

Brac. l. 3. f. 141. b. 4 E. 3. 41. 17 E. 3. 2. 29 E. 3. 12. 30 E. 3. 20. 9 H. 4. 3. 1 H. 6. 6. 9 E. 4. 35. 19 H. 6. 35. 21 H. 6. 4. 14 E. 4. 7. 13 El. Dier 301. See the first part of the Inst. sect. 489 & 514.

Now concerning the oath of the champions, and the solemne manner and order of proceeding therein, and between what parties triall by battell should be joyned, you may reade in the statute of W. 2. cap. 41. and at large in our books; and the oath of the champion, as well of the tenant as of the demandant continued since this statute, followeth in these words:

> Heare this you judges, that I have this day, neither eate, drunke, nor have upon me either bone, stone, ne grasse, or any inchauntment, sorcery, or witchcraft, where through the power of the word of God might be * inleased or diminished, and the Devils power increased, and that my appeale is true, so helpe mee God and his Saints, and by this booke.

* Of the French word, enlasse. i. intangled, or ensnarled.

Brac. l. 3. f. 138. b. Mirror, c. 1. § 3. Flet. l. 1. c. 32. Bract. l. 3. f. 141, 142.

The law doth allow a triall by battell in another case, and that is in case of life in an appeale of felony, the defendant may choose either to put himselfe upon the country, or to try it by body to body, that is by combate between him and the plaintiffe, but there the parties themselves shall fight.

Brit. 41. fo. Fleta ubi supra. Mir. c. 3. ordinatio pugnantium.

And it appeareth by our auncient authors, *Quod si appellatus se defenderit contra appellantem tota die usque horam qua stellæ incipiunt apparere, tunc recedat appellatus quietus de appello.*

And in case of the writ of right, the champions are not bound to fight but untill the starres appeare, and if the champion of the tenant can defend himselfe untill the starres appeare, the tenant shall prevaile, for they shall combat but once, and it is sufficient for the tenant to defend being in possession.

Mirror, Bracton, Britton, Fleta — ubi supra.

The judges of the court of common pleas are judges of the battell in a writ of right, and the judges of the kings bench in an appeale of felony. But if the cause of appeale be not determinable by the common law, but before the constable and the marshall according to the civill law, there the constable and marshall are judges.

37 H. 6. 26. Rot. Vasc. 9 H. 4. m. 14. 19 E. 2. Cor. 385. 13 R. 2. c. 2. 5 Mar. tit. Batt. Br. 15. Dier 13 El. ubi supra. * 20 E. 4. 6.

But this triall in an appeale at the common law of later times seldome come in use, for that the appellant procures the appellee to be indicted, and then he cannot try it by battell: * but if the indictment be insufficient, then the defendant may try it by battell.

Mirror, ca. 3. ordinatio pugnantium.

Now the auncient law was, that the victory should be proclaimed, that he that was vanquished, should acknowledge his fault in the audience of the people, or pronounce the horrible word of *cravent* in the name of recreantise, &c. and presently judgement was to be given, and after this the recreant should *amittere liberam legem*, that is, he should become infamous, and should not be accounted in that respect *liber et legalis homo*, and therefore could not be of any jury, nor give testimony as a witnesse in any case, because he is become infamous, and of no credit: and this doth notably appeare in an ancient record, where the case was, that battell being joyned in a writ of right of advowson, in *anno* 55 H. 3. before the justices in eyre in the county of Northampton, and the champions combating, Philip le Pugil champion for one of the parties was vanquished, and thereupon proclamation made accordingly:

[248]

Rot. Pat. anno 55 H. 3. m. 3. *Pugil* a champion.

ingly: the king by advice of his councell reciting under his great seal the joyning of battell in the said writ of right of advowson, and the proceeding thereupon did signifie, *Quod in duello prædicto coram justiciariis prædictis percusso, irruerit in eundem Philippum tanta multitudo hominum, unde oppressus se defendere non potuit, qui homines perpetuam defamationem sibi imposuerunt, et in eodem duello creantiam proclam': rex inde certior factus, &c. statuit quod prædictus Philippus propter creantiam prædict' liberam legem non amitteret, &c.*

Vide Mic. 15 E. 1. Rot. 8. in Banco Norff. *Duellum percussum, & serviens Abbatis de Bury, tenentis devictus & interfectus.* Vide Mich. 3 E. 1. Rot. 19.

Of this triall by battell, Fleta saith thus, *Duellum singularis pugna inter duos ad probandam veritatem litis, et qui vicerit probasse intelligitur; et quamvis judicium Dei expectetur ibidem, quicunque tamen monomachiam, i. singularem pugnam, sponte susceperit, vel obtulerit, homicida est, et mortale contrahit peccatum.*

Flet. li. 1. c. 32. See li. 9. f. 32. b. Le case del Abbot de Strata Marcella. Deuter. cap. 18. ver. 10.

(2) *Son pier luy commande a faire la dereign'.*] And these words are well explained by Glanvill, *Cui pater suus injunxit in extremis agens, in fide qua filius tenetur patri, quod si aliquando loquelam de terra illa audiret, hoc dirationaret, sicut id quod pater suus vidit et audivit.*

Glanv. ubi supra. Bract. li. 5. fo. 373.

(3) *Ne soit le champion le demandant constreint a ceo jurer.*] Hereby it appeareth that preventing justice is better then punishing justice, *melior est justitia verè præveniens, quàm severè puniens*; for when it is punished, yet the offence is committed, but when it is prevented, then there is neither offence nor punishment: this law preventeth perjury, which taketh away that part of the oath which seldome or never was or could be kept.

CAP. XLII.

PUR ceo que en briefe dassise, dataints (1), et de juris utrum (2), les jurors sont sovent travels per essoines des tenants: purview est, que del heure que le tenant (3) un foits apparust en court, jammes ne puisse le tenant se essoine (4), mes faire son attourney a suer pur luy (5), sil voile. Et si non, soit lassise, on le jurie prise per son default.

FORASMUCH as in a writ of assise, attaints, and juris utrum, the jurors have been often troubled by reason of the essoins of tenants; it is provided, that after the tenant hath once appeared in the court, he shall be no more essoined, but shall make his attorney to sue for him, if he will; and if not, the assise or jury shall be taken through his default.

(Fitz. Essoin, 52. 55, 56. 63, 64. 13 Ed. 1. stat. 1. c. 28.)

The mischiefe doth appeare by the preamble, and that the rather, for that in these actions here rehearsed there is a jury retourned the first day, and therefore the delay of the jurors was the greater, but of two mischiefes, one onely remedy was provided; for as great delay had the jurors where the demandant, as where the tenant was essoigned, and here provision is made for the essoine of the tenant which was the greater mischiefe, for commonly the tenant seeks delay, and the plaintifes expedition; *petens præsumitur desiderare potius instantiam litis, quam dilationem.*

Bract. li. 5. fo. 342.

This

Britton, f. 164. Flet. li. 6. c. 9. 10 H. 6. 22. 14 H. 6. 22. 8 Aff. 22. 22 Aff. 79. 30 Aff. 51. 34 Aff. 6. 6 E 3. 25.

This act is not understood of a writ of assise *de novel disseisin*, for that in that writ, the tenant shall not be essoined, neither before, nor after appearance, *locum non habet essonium in persona disseisitoris, vel redisseisitoris*; but this is intended of an assise of *mordauncester*, and it is said, that the justices of the kings bench will not allow an essoine for the plaintiffe in no manner of assise, nor for the tenant in assise of *mordaunc'*.

44 E. 3. 5. 44 Aff. 24.

But albeit no essoine for the tenant doth lie in assise of *novel disseisin*, yet if the same be discontinued by the *non venu* of the justices, or by the demise of the king, in a reattachment the tenant shall be essoined, and so shall the tenant be in a resummons after a discontinuance in assise of *mord.*

30 Aff. p. 5. 8 Aff. p. 22.

An assise of *mord.* was brought in Chester, the tenant vowched a foreiner to warranty, whereupon the record was removed into the court of common pleas, 15 Pasch. at which day (though it be in an assise of *mord.*) the tenant may be essoined, for the plea in bank is not the plea of assise, but the plea there is onely upon the warranty, for the assise shall not be taken in bank.

W. 2. ca. 28. 26 Aff. p. 35. 45 Aff 2. 30 H. 6. 1. 16 Aff. 10.

The statute of W. 2. doth provide for the other mischiefe in the case of assise of *mord. attaint*, and *juris utrum*, *viz.* that the demandant therein after appearance shall not be essoined; but that statute extendeth not to the assise of *novel disseisin*.

26 Aff. p. 25. 34 Aff. p. 6.

(1) *Dattaints.*] This statute is intended of the tenant in an attaint as well in a plea personall, or mixt, as upon a plea meerly in the reality.

6 E. 3. 25.

(2) *Juris utrum.*] See the statute of W. 2. abovesaid.

22 Aff. p. 79. 23 Aff. p. 15.

(3) *Que le tenant.*] This doth extend as well to the tenant in law, as the vowchee, and tenant by receipt, as to the tenant in deed, for it is to oust delay for expedition of justice, and for the ease and benefit of the jurors, and therefore being in equall mischiefe shall be within the same remedy.

Hereby it appeareth that this statute provideth onely against the tenant after appearance, and leaveth the essoine of the plaintiffe (as hath been said) at large.

12 E. 1. essoin 175. 4 E. 3. 34. 6 E. 3. essoine 55.

(4) *Se essoine.*] Though here essoine be spoken indefinitely, yet is it to be taken in a common sense, and therefore is it to be understood of a common essoine, and not of an essoine *de service le roy*, for *statuta per regem, dominos, et communitatem regni ordinata in communi, et vulgari sensu intelliguntur.*

F.N.B. 25. Brit. 285, 286, 287, &c. Merton, ca. 10. Gloc. cap. 8. W. 2. ca. 10. 27 E. 1. de terris. amortisand. Stat. de York. 12 E. 2. cap. 1. 15 E. 2. Stat. de Carlile. 3 H. 7. c. 1. 23 H. 8. cap. 3, &c. In the preface to the fourth book, and here before, cap. 26.

(5) *Mes fait son attourney a suer pur luy.*] By the policy of the common law, that suits might not encrease and multiply, *cum lites potius restringendæ sunt, quam laxandæ*, both plaintife, and defendant, demandant, and tenant in all actions reall, personall, and mixt did appeare in person, as well in courts of record, as not of record, because the writs doe command the tenant or defendant to appeare, which was alwayes taken in proper person; and the entry in every action for the demandant or plaintife is, *et prædictus petens*, or *querens obtulit se 4. die*, which was ever understood in proper person: but when this and other statutes had given way to appeare by attourney, it is not credible how (with attourneys and their multiplication) suits in law (for the most part unnecessary and for trifling causes) when the parties themselves might sit quiet at home, increased and multiplied: so dangerous and ill successe have ever had the breach of the maximes and auncient rules of the common law, as elsewhere hath been observed.

It

It appeareth in Glanvils time, that the juſtices admitted the parties, *per reſponſalem loco ſuo ad lucrandum vel perdendum*, but then onely when the parties themſelves were preſent, for he ſaith, *Verum oportet eum eſſe praeſentem in * curia, qui reſponſalem ita in loco ſuo ponit: et nota differentiam inter reſponſalem et attornatum.* Glan. li. 11. c. 1. Bract. lib. 5. fo. 353, 360. Mirr. c. 2. § 21. Des Attornies. See the firſt part of the Inſtitutes, ſect. 196.

And the Mirror ſpeaking of the auncient law before the ſtatute ſaith, *Abuſion eſt a receiver attourney, ou nul poier eſt a ceo done per briefe en la chauncery: et abuſion eſt a receiver attourney, ou le parol neſt my attaine per preſence des parties, &c.*

After this in divers parliaments it was thought good to decreaſe the number of attourneys, finding them to be the cauſes of multiplication of ſuits. But though divers good laws have been made therein, yet the number of them daily increaſeth, to great inconvenience in the common-wealth, and to the no ſmall blemiſh and diſcredit of that auncient and neceſſary vocation. Rot. Parl. 20 E. 1. De Attournatis. 4 H. 4. ca. 14. 33 H. 6. ca. 7.

CAP. XLIII.

PUR ceo que les demandants (2) ſont ſovent delayes de tout droit, pur ceo que ou ſont pluſors parceners tenants (3), dont nul puit reſpoign' ſans auter, ou quil ad pluſours tenants jointment feoffes (4), ou nul ne ſciet ſon ſeveral, et ceux tenants ſovent forchient per eſſoine (1), iſſint que cheſcun eit un eſſoine: purview eſt deſormes, que ceux tenants neient eſſoigne, forſque a un jour, nient pluis que un ſole tenant naveroit, iſſint que jammes ne puiſſent forcher, forſque tant ſolement aver un eſſoine.

FORASMUCH as demandants be oftentimes delayed of their right, by reaſon that many parceners be tenants, of which none may be compelled to anſwer without the other, or there may be many jointly infeoffed (where none knoweth his ſeveral) and ſuch tenants oftentimes fourch by eſſoin, ſo that every of them hath a a ſeveral eſſoin; it is provided, that from henceforth ſuch tenants ſhall not have eſſoin, but at one day, no more than one ſole tenant ſhould have; ſo that from henceforth they ſhall no more fourch, but only ſhall have one eſſoin.

(Hob. 8. 46. Fitz. Eſſoin, 82. 119. Fitz. Fourcher, 3, 4. 10. 13, 14. Bro. Fourcher, 20. 6 Ed. 1. ſtat. 1. c. 10.)

(1) *Forchient per eſſoine.*] The true underſtanding, what it is to fourch by eſſoin, doth open both what was the miſchiefe before, and what is remedied by this ſtatute.

Fourcher by eſſoine, on the part of the tenant, is when a *praecipe* is brought againſt two or more tenants, and after each of them have had one eſſoine, which is due to them by law, they over again delay the demandant by ſucceſſive eſſoines. Bract. l. 5. f. 342. 33 H. 6. 25. 2 E. 4. 19.

For example, a *praecipe* is brought againſt A. and B. A. is eſſoined, and B. appears, and hath *idem dies* given him; at which day A. appears, and B. is eſſoined, this is lawfull, but then at that day B. is eſſoined again, and C. appears, *et ſic viciſſim et alternis vicibus*, this is called fourcher by eſſoine, and ſo it is explained in our books. 39 H. 6. 28, 29. See hereafter verbo Tenants.

This

Fleta, li. 6. c. 9. Britton, f. 184. This doth Fleta comprehend in few words, and rendreth to fourch by essoine *essoniare vicissim:* for he saith, *Si autem plures fuerint tenentes pro indiviso provisum est, quod non essonientur vicissim, sed simul ad unicum diem, sicut fuissent unum corpus ratione unitatis juris, et hæreditatis.*

To fourch in one of the significations is to divide, and because they divide themselves in delay of the demandants by essoines and appearances interchangeably, it is called *fourcher per essoine.*

2 E. 4. 19. Now this mischiefe was not that every one of the tenants should not have one essoine, but that there should be a fourcher, a vicissitude of essoines after each of them have had one essoine. So as this act doth onely prohibite the fourcher by essoine, which was used for delay, and not one onely essoine, as hath beene said, which is lawfull and necessary.

[251]

20 E. 2. Fourcher 1. 16 E. 3. ibid. 9. 38 E. 3. 1. 12 H. 4. 14 H. 4. 37. 3 H. 6. 36. 8 H. 6. 15. (2) *Demandants.*] This act doth extend onely to reall actions in respect of this word *demandant,* which is proper to reall actions; and the words be also, Where be divers parceners tenants, or tenants joyntly infeoffed, and those tenants fourch by essoine; so as this act extendeth to actions in the realty.

But this statute extends not to an action of debt upon an obligation, covenant, or other like personall actions.

9 H. 6. 21. 44. 22 E. 3. 5. 38 E. 3. 12. 18. 48 E. 3. 20. Gloc'. ca. 20. (3) *Tenants.*] This act is to be understood after apparance, and so doth the statute of Gloc' recite it, for there is no fourcher but after former essoins and reciprocall apparance, as hath been said; and this doth also prove what fourcher is.

3 H. 6. 36. F. tit. Fourcher 3. 44 E. 3. 38. Dyer 28 H. 8. 26. This statute being made for expedition of justice, and for ousting of delays is benignly interpreted; for in a writ of annuity against a parson, he prayeth in aid of the patron and ordinary, and they, after each of them have had one essoin, would have fourched by essoin, and could not by the rule of the court; and yet the priee in aid is no party to the writ.

Bract. ubi supra. 33 H. 6. 25. And this statute is made against the fourcher by essoin of the tenants, and not of the demandants.

Flet. ubi supra. Gloc' ca. 10. 6 E. 1. (4) *Parceners et jointment feoffes.*] This statute speaking expresly of parceners and jointenants, extends not to baron and feme seised in the right of the wife, which is remedied by the said statute of Glouc': but where baron and feme be joyntly infeoffed, they are within the purview of this statute: all jointenants are within this statute, although their estate be created by any other conveyance then by feoffment.

CAP. XLIV.

PUR ceo que multes des gentes se font fauxment essoine (1) de oustre le mere (2), la ou ils fuerent en Engleterre le jour de le summons: purview est desormes, que cel essoine ne soit pas de tout allow, si le demaundant le challenge, et soit prist daverrer (3) quil fuit en Engleterre le jour que le summons fuist

FORASMUCH as divers persons cause themselves falsly to be essoined (for being over the sea) where indeed they were within the realm the day of the summons; it is provided from henceforth, that this essoin be not always allowed, if the demandant will challenge it, and will be ready to aver

fuist fait, et iii. semaignes apres (4): *mes soit ajourne en cest forme, que si le demandant sue a tiel jour averment per pais, ou sicome la court le roy agardre et soit attaint que le tenant fuist deins le quater meres Dengleterre* (5) *le jour que il fuit summons, et trois semains apres, issint que il puit estre reasonablement garny de la summons* (6), *soit lessoine turne en un default* (7), *et ceo fait a entend' tantsolement devant les justices le roy.*

aver that he was in England the day of summons and three weeks after; but shall be adjourned in this form: that if the demandant be ready at a certain day, by averment of the country, or otherwise as the court shall award, to prove that the tenant was within the four seas the day that he was summoned, and three weeks after, so that he might be reasonably warned by the summons, the essoin shall be turned into a default; and that is to be understanden only before justices.

Of the diversity of essoins, and amongst them, of this essoin, called here *ultra mare*, you have heard before in the exposition of the statute of Marlebridge: for the better understanding of the mischief before this act, and of the purview thereof, it is necessary to understand the diversity of essoins *ultra mare*; some of which, ancient authors call *essoines de servitio regis æterni*: and some, *de servitio regis temporalis*: of the first sort were, *viz. ad terram sanctam.* And this was two-fold, *viz. Cum peregrinatio vel passagium generale fuerit ad terram sanctam, et tunc recedant partes sine die, quousque essoniatus redierit, vel obierit, &c. Semper tamen non habet locum istum essonium, quia non nisi tempore transfretationis alicujus regis cum peregrinatione publica et generali, aut cum simplex fuerit, dabitur essoniato terminus unius anni et unius diei.* Marlebridge, cap. 12. [252] Bract. lib. 5. fo. 338, 339. Fleta, lib. 6. cap. 8. Brit. cap. 123. Bracton, Britton, Fleta ubi supra. 3 E. 3. 29 Acc.

Et si simplex sit peregrinatio, et ultra annum et diem moram fecerit ultra mare, excusatur ejus absentia secundum quosdam per essonium simplex de ultra mare, et sic habebit spacium 40. dierum et unius flud et unius ebbe; et si adhuc moram longiorem protraxerit, habet essonium simplex de malo veniendi citra mare, per quod habebit ad minus spacium 15. dierum quod verum est ad minus habebunt essoniati tantum tempus et ex causa majus tempus secundum discretionem justiciariorum. Et quid si tunc non venerit? procedatur ad defaltam contra eum, nisi forte contingat talem essoniari de morte ad cautelam. Si quis autem essoniatus fuerit essonio de ultra mare citra mare Græcorum quod profectus sit in servitio domini regis æterni in peregrinatione alia quam ad terram sanctam, sicut apud Sanctum Jacobum, vel alibi, datur dilatio ad minus quadraginta dierum et unius flud et unius ebbe ad excusationem essoniati de simplici essonio de ultra mare, &c. And after he saith, *In hoc casu induciæ sunt arbitrariæ dum tamen ad minus quadraginta dierum ut supra.* And Fleta further saith, *Essonia autem ultra mare Hiberniæ et Scotiæ vertenda sunt in essonium de malo veniendi* 1. *per* 15. *dies.* Mirror, cap. 2. § 20. de Essoins. Mirror, Bracton, Britton, Fleta ubi supra. Fleta ubi supra. 7 E. 4. 27.

And Glanvile, who wrote before all these, saith, *Est aliud genus essoniandi et necessarium, cum quis essoniat se de ultra mare, et tunc si recipiatur essonium, dabuntur ipsi essoniato ad minus quadraginta dies, &c.* And speaking of essoins, by reason of peregrination, he saith, *Si versus Jerusalem iverit is qui se essoniare facit, tunc solet ei dari respectus unius anni et unius diei ad minus, &c.* Glanv. li. 1. c. 25. Idem li. 1. c. 29.

By these ancient authors it appeareth, what delay this *essoine de ultra mare* wrought to the demandant; and by the law no averment could be had against it, no more then in a protection, or in

the *essoine de service le roy*, which (specially in those dayes when such *essoines de ultra mare* were so frequent) was vere mischievous; for some fained such a passage or peregrination, and some went of purpose after the purchase of the *præcipe*, which is well expressed by Fleta: *Sunt tamen quidam, qui cum fuerint brevia super ipsos impetrata, extra regnum se divertunt, ne summonitione sint præventi ut sic jus petentis per essonium de ultra mare deferri possit, et unde provisum est, quod si petens offerat verificare, quod tenens fuerit in Anglia die summonitionis, et per tres septimanas sequentes, adjournetur essonium, et irrotuletur calumnia petentis, et si alia die constare possit justitiariis per inquisitionem, vel alio modo, quod tenens fuit in Anglia die summonitionis, et per tres septimanas sequentes, ita quod potuit rationabiliter præmuniri, vertatur illud essonium in defaltam, sed hoc observetur tantummodo coram justitiariis.*

Ubi supra.

Mirror, ca. 5. § 1. & 4.

(1) *Font fauxment essoine.*] All falshood is abhorred in law, and therefore the Mirrour said well, *Abusion est que faux causes de essoine sont de cy que droit ne allowe fauxime en ascun case*; the law alloweth no falshood in any case, which is a maxime of the common law, *contra veritatem lex nunquam aliquid permittit.*

21 H. 6. 20.

(2) *Essoine de oustre mere.*] This act doth extend onely to the *essoine de ultra mare*, whereof we have spoken at large, and not to the *essoine de servitio regis, &c. Vide* 21 H. 6. fol. 20.

[253]

Stat. de 33 E. 1. de prot. 28 H. 6. 3. 21 H. 6. 20. 39 E. 3. 35. 47 E. 3. 6. 1 H. 6. 6. 34 H. 6. 62. 35 H. 6. 5. 8. 19 H. 6. 35. 5 E. 4. 2. 21 E. 4. 20. [a] Regist. fol. 18. F. N. B. 17. H. [b] Gloc. cap. 8.

(3) *Et soit prist daverrer*, &c.] This averment, as hath been said, could not be taken by the common law, no more then in case of a protection before the statute of 33 E. 1. which giveth an averment in case of protection; of which statute you shall read in our books, and how the protection may be repealed; and in the common *essoine de malo veniendi*, or *de service le roy*, no such averment can be taken against it. [a] But if the tenant be essoined in any action *de servitio regis*, where in truth he is not in the kings service, then the demandant or plaintife may sue a [b] speciall writ out of the chancery directed to the justices, rehearsing, that he is not in the king service, and commaunding them to proceed; then the essoin shall not be adjourned, but shall be quashed presently.

And so before this statute in the *essoine de ultra mare*, if the party were in England, the demandant might have purchased the like writ, as is abovesaid; but for that many times that could not be obtained without great difficulty, this averment was given for avoiding of falshood.

(4) *Jour que le somons fuist fait, et per tres semaignes apres.*] For the summons alwayes is made upon the land by two sumners, whether the tenant, or any for him, be there or no.

The day of the summons is not counted parcell of the three weeks, but it must be three weeks after that day; otherwise had it been, if the words had been, three weeks after the summons made.

(5) *Deins le quater meres d'Angleterre.*] Within the four seas, is as much to say, as within the jurisdiction of the king of England; for all within the four seas was either part or holden of the crown of England, as by many ancient records appeareth.

(6) *Que il puit estre reasonablement garny de la summons.*] The three weeks after the day of the summons were given as a reasonable time, wherein by common intendment he might have notice of the summons made upon his land.

(7) *Soit lessoine turne en un default.*] This is the remedy given by this act, for the benefit of the demandant, who was unjustly delayed by this essoin.

A woman tenant in a writ of entre, &c. was essoined, for that she was in *terra sancta, viz.* from the time of the essoin, for a yeer and a day; and it was said, that the tenant should lose her land, if it be found by inquest, that she was in England the day of the essoin; and there it is said, that at the day that the parties have by the essoin, the demandant shall be received to aver his challenge. Consider well this book, and the book also of 28 H. 6. which expounds the statute of 33 E. 1. *Vide* Rast. Pl. fol. 297. See more for the antiquity of essoins, and great variety of matter, both of this essoin and of all other, in the Mirrour.

3 E. 3. 29.

28 H. 6. 3.

Mirror, cap. 1. §. 3. cap. 2. §. 20. de Essoins. cap. 5. §. 1.

And though this kinde of essoin is this day out of use, yet have I spoken of the same thus much for two causes: first, for that mine endeavour hath been, to explain these ancient laws, and to make every word of them so to speak, as they may be understood. Secondly, the severall points of learning that do rise out of this law (though the particular case be out of use) may serve to good purposes, you shall observe in this and many others of this nature, in this second part of mine Institutes.

Where the text is evident, it were losse of time to make any exposition.

CAP. XLV.

De delayes en touts maners des briefes, et des attachments (1) *est purview, que si le tenant ou le defendant, apres le primer attachment tesmoign', face default, maintenant soit le grand' distresse* (2) *agarde. Et si visc' ne respoigne sufficientment au jour, soit grevousment amercie. Et sil maunde que il ad fait lexecution en due maner, et les issues bailes as mainpernors, adonques soit maunde au viscount, que il al auter jour face venir les issues devant justices. Et si lattachee veigne a ceo jour a saver ses defaults, eit il ses issues* (3). *Et sil ne veigne, eit le roy les issues* (4). *Et les justices le roy* (5) *les facent liverer a la gardrobe* (6), *et justices del banke a Westminster* (7) *les facent liver' al exchequer, et justices en eyre, au viscount de cell' countie* (8) *ou ils pledent, auxybien de cel countie, come des forreine counties, et de ceo soient charges*

CONCERNING delays in all manner of writs and attachments, it is thus provided, that if the tenant or defendant, after the first attachments returned, make default, that incontinent the great distress shall be awarded; and if the sheriff do not make sufficient return by a certain day, he shall be grievously amerced; and if he return, that he hath done execution in due manner, and the issues delivered to the sureties, then the sheriff shall be commanded, that he return issues at another day before the justices; and if the party being attached come in at his day to save his defaults, he shall have the issues; and if he come not, the king shall have them; and the king's justices shall cause them to be delivered in the wardrobe; and the justices of the bench at Westminster shall deliver them

char es en summons per rolles des justices (9).

them in the exchequer; and the justices in eyre unto the sheriff of that shire where they plead, as well of that shire, as of foreign shires, and shall be charged therewith in summons by the rolls of justices.

The mischief appeareth by this short preamble, to be delay, &c.

27 H. 6. 2. 7 H. 6. 9. Brit. ca. 26. de attachments.

(1) *Attachment.*] The attachment must be made by moveable goods, and meer personall, which may be forfeited by outlawry, and not by goods which he hath as executor or administrator, nor by a clod of the earth, nor by any chattell reall, as wardship, or the like.

Regist. judic' fol. 1. Brit. fol. 50. b. 48 E. 3. 26.

(2) *Grand distresse.*] *Districtio magna,* it is so called, not for the quantity, for it is very short; but for the quality, for the extent is very great: for thereby the sherife is commanded, *Quod distringat tenentem, ita quod ipse, nec aliquis per ipsum ad ea manum apponat, donec habuerit aliud præceptum, et quod de exitibus eorundem nobis respondeat, et quod habeat corpus ejus, &c.*

This writ lyeth in two cases, either when the tenant or defendant is attached, and so retourned, and appeareth not, but makes default, then by this act a grand distresse is to be awarded; or when the tenant or defendant hath once appeared, and after makes default, then this writ lyeth by the common law in lieu of a *petit cape.*

Brit. ubi supra.

Britton speaketh of distresses personall, which he intendeth of personall goods upon the attachment, and distresses reall, which concern the realty; and a third may be added, *viz.* distresses which do concern both the realty and personalty, as this grand distresse doth.

18 E. 3. judgement. 120. f. 6 E. 2. ibid. 230. 14 E. 3. Default. 17.

In a *secta ad molendinum,* after apparance the defendant made default, whereupon a grand distresse was awarded, and the defendant made default again, and thereupon the plaintife had judgement.

(3) *Et si latachee veigne a ceo jour a saver ses defaults, eit il ses issues.*] Here the *lattachee* is taken for him that is distrained, and appeareth upon the grand distresse.

[255]

(4) *Et sil ne veigne eit le roy les issues.*] For then judgement is to be given against the defendant, as hath been said before, and the king to have the issues.

(5) *Et les justices le roy.*] That is, the justices of his bench, so called, for that all the pleas there are *coram rege.*

Ockham. 51 H. 3. stat. de Scacc. Artic. super Chart. 28 E. 1. cap. 2. Fleta, l. 2. cap. 6.

(6) *Les facent liver a le gardrobe.*] There hath been an ancient officer of the kings houshold of old time, called *custos magnæ gardrobæ,* warden or keeper of the great wardrope or wardrobe, of later times called master of the wardrobe, so called, because he hath the keeping and charge of the royal robes of former kings and queens, and for providing of robes, &c. of the king: he hath also the charge of keeping and providing of hangings, bedding, &c. in standing wardrobes in the kings houses, and the delivery of velvet and scarlet allowed for liveries, &c. And many other things belong to his office, which are not necessary to be here repeated: he is accountable in the exchequer.

De

De articulis porrectis coram domino rege per comitem mareſchallum pro hiis quæ ad officium ſuum in curia regis clamabat pertinere, dominus rex vult quod dicti articuli irrotulentur in garderoba, et quod tranſcriptum eorundem liberetur præfato comiti, et quod nec ipſe nec miniſtri, ſui aliquid habeant, ſeu ſibi attrahant ultra ea quæ ibidem inveniuntur, &c. Rot. Parl. Paſch. 21 E. 1. Rot. 14

Vide in the exchequer, *de anno* 19 E. 2. a privy ſeale bearing date 30 *Junii, anno* 19 E. 2. concerning his account amongſt others. Int' communia in Scac. de anno 19 E. 2.

But here it may be demanded wherefore theſe iſſues were to be delivered into the wardrobe; for the anſwering hereunto, it muſt be underſtood, that the kings juſtices of his bench did in thoſe dayes follow the court (the retourne of the proceſſe of which court to this day is *coram rege ubicunque fuerimus in Anglia)* therefore it was fitteſt for them to make delivery of theſe iſſues to this officer of court. Art. ſuper Chart. cap. 5. Fleta, l. 2. ca. 2.

(7) *Les juſtices del banke al Weſtm'.*] That is, the juſtices of the court of common pleas ſhall make their eſtreats, and theſe iſſues are part of the green waxe.

(8) *Al viſcount de cel countie.*] In this particular caſe of iſſues the juſtices in eyre delivered the eſtreats to the ſheriffe, *vide* before ca. 18. which extendeth to fines and amerciaments. W. 2. ca. 18.

(9) *Per rolles des juſtices.*] That is, particularly, and not a totall. W. 2. ca. 18.

Vide more for eſtreats the ſtatutes of 51 H. 3. W. 2. cap. 8. 42 E. 3. cap. 9. 7 H. 4. cap. 3.

CAP. XLVI.

*PURVIEW eſt enſement, et per le roy commaunde, que les juſtices de banke le roy, et juſtices de banke a Weſtminſter (1) deſormes per pledant les plees a terminer a un jour (2), avant que rien ſoit arraine, ou commence des plees del jour * enſuant, forſpris que lour eſſoines ſoient entres, judges, et rendus, et per encheſon de ceo nul home ſe affie, que il ne veigne au jour que don' luy eſt.*

IT is provided alſo, and commanded by the king, that the juſtices of the king's bench at Weſtminſter from henceforth ſhall decide all pleas determinable at one day, before any matter be arraigned, or plea commenced the day following, ſaving that their eſſoins ſhall be entered, judged, and allowed; yet, by reaſon hereof, let none preſume to abſent himſelf at the day to him limited.

* [256]

Firſt, in ſome impreſſions both in French and Engliſh of this act, theſe words [*Et juſtices de bank al Weſtm'*] be omitted, and towards the end theſe words [*forpriſe lour eſſoines*] be likewiſe omitted, both which without queſtion ought to be inſerted as parcell of this excellent law.

The miſchiefe before this ſtatute was, in reſpect of prepoſterous or diſorderly hearing of cauſes; for many times the judges of the kings bench, and of the court of common pleas would by importunacy of great men and others in the irregular time of H. 3.

 put

put off matters to be heard at one day untill another, and at that time heare some other matters appointed to be heard on a day following, whereby the parties, whose causes were then disappointed, were not onely delayed, and put to further charges, but many times, when their cause came to be heard, either were disappointed of their councell which they had instructed, or the day appointed not being come, had no councell instructed at all; and besides where witnesses were requisite, they many times failed of them: this law therefore is made to remedy these preposterous and disorderly proceedings, and to give judges a just cause of deniall of any such requests, though never so powerfully, or importunately made, and that this law may serve for their buckler and shield, which Fleta rendreth in these words:

Fleta, li. 2. c. 29. *Et provisum est, quod justiciarii de utroque banco placita ad unum diem adjournata persiniant, antequam placita diei sequentis quicquam placitare incipiant, hoc tamen excepto, quod essonium illius diei supervenientis admittatur, adjudicetur, et reddatur.*

And hereby it appeareth that both the said clauses so omitted, as is aforesaid, ought to be inserted. Of this kinde of hearing of causes it is truly said, *Merito hæc dicuntur præpostera, quia in hiis præsunt posteriora.*

(1) *Que justices de banke le roy, & del banke al Westm'*, &c.] This statute being made in affirmance of common right doth extend to the court of chauncery, court of exchequer, and to all other courts of justice, for that all are within the same mischiefe, and therefore ought to be within the same remedy.

(2) *A terminer a un jour.*] Upon this act this auncient conclusion of law doth follow, *Judicis officium est opus diei in die ipso perficere.*

Mag. Chart. c. 29. And this agreeth with that excellent law of *Magna Charta*, *Nulli vendemus, nulli negabimus, aut differemus justitiam, vel rectum.*

CAP. XLVII.

*PURVIEW est ensement, que si ul desormes purchase briefe de novel disseisin (1), et celuy sur que le briefe vient, come principal disseisor mourge avant que lassise soit passe, que le pl' eit son briefe dentre foundus sur disseisin, sur le heire, ou sur les heires les disseisors (2), de quel age que ils soient. En mesme le maner eit le heire, ou les heires le * disseisee lour briefes dentre sur les disseisors lour auncestre, ou lour heires (3), de quel age que ils soient. Et si paraventure le disseisee mourge avant que il eit son purchase fait (4), issint que pur les nonages des heires dun part ne dauter (5) ne soit le briefe*

* [257]

IT is provided also, that if any from henceforth purchase a writ of novel disseisin, and he against whom the writ was brought as principal disseisor, dieth before the assise be passed, then the plaintiff shall have his writ of entrie upon disseisin against the heir or heirs of the disseisor or disseisors, of what age soever they be. In the same wise the heir or heirs of the disseisee shall have their writs of entrie against the disseisors, or their heirs, of what age soever they be, if peradventure the disseisee die before that he hath purchased his writ; so that for the nonage of the heirs of the one

briefe abatus, ne le plee delay (6), *mes en quant que lhom' poit fans ley offender, foit hafte pur la frefh fuit apres le diffeifin* (7). *Et en mefme le maner foit en ceo point gard' en droit des prelates, gents de religion, et auters* (8), *as queux terres et tenements en nul maner puiffent devener apres auter mort, le quel que ils foient diffeifees, ou diffeifours. Et fi les parties en pledant difcendont en enqueft, et lenqueft paffa encounter le heire deins age, et nofmement encounter le heire le diffeifee, que il en ceo cafe eit lattaint* (9) *de la grace le roy fans rien doner.*

one party, nor of the other, the writ fhall not be abated, nor the plea delayed; but as much as a man can without offending the law, it muft be hafted to make frefh fuit after the diffeifin. And in like manner this fhall be obferved in all points for the right of prelates, men of religion, and other to whom lands and tenements can in no wife defcend after others death, whether they be diffeifees or diffeifors. And if the parties in pleading come to an inqueft, and it paffeth againft the heir within age, and namely, againft the heir of the diffeifee, that in fuch cafe he fhall have an attaint of the king's fpecial grace.

Mirror, ca. 5. § 4. (Dyer 137. 6 Rep. 4. 17 Ed. 3. 16. 12 Ed. 4. 17. 8 Ed. 3. 71. 21 Ed. 3. 27. 27 H. 6. 1. Fitz. Age, 71. 3 Bulftr. 137. Regift. 229, 230. 13 Ed. 1. ftat. 1. c. 15.)

The mifchiefe before this ftatute was, that if a man had been diffeiffed, and either the diffeifee, or the diffeifor had died, their heire being within age, in a writ of *entre fur diffeifin* brought by the heire of the diffeifee being within age, or by the diffeifee or his heire againft the heire of the diffeifor being within age, the paroll had demurred untill the full age of the heire refpectively, which was a great delay, and is remedied on both parts by this act. See the Cuftum. de Norm. ca. 43.

(1) *Purchafe briefe de novel diffeifin.*] Albeit the diffeifee purchafed no writ of affife of *novel diffeifin*, yet the heire or heires of the diffeifor are within this ftatute; for feeing in this cafe here put by the makers of this law, true it is, that notwithftanding the purchafe of the writ in a writ of *entre fur diffeifin* brought by the diffeifee againft the heire of the diffeifor, the heire fhould have had his age to the great delay of the demandant, this is fhewed for a mifchiefe in this particular cafe, to perfwade that the law might be generall, though no writ was brought, as by the body of the act appeareth. 3 E. 3. age 71. 8 E. 3. 71.

(2) *Briefe de entry foundus fur diffeifin, fur le heire ou heires les diffeifors.*] This is to be underftood of a writ of entry in the *per*, and not in the *poft*, for the words of the ftatute be *fur le heire le diffeifor*, which is a writ of entry in the *per*, and therefore if the heire of the diffeifor make a feoffment in fee, and the feoffee dieth, his heire within age, in a writ of entry againft the heir, he fhall have his age, for this act extends but to the heir of the diffeifor, who fitteth in his fathers feat, and commeth to the land without confideration; but otherwife it is of him that purchafeth the land of the heir, for he and his heires are out of the letter and meaning of this act: the fame law is of the vowchee and priee in aide within age. 12 E. 4. 17. 5 E. 3. age 70. 6 E. 3. 3. 21 E. 4. 15. 27 H. 6. 1. Dier 4 Mar. 137.

If the fem' heire of the diffeifor taketh hufband, and hath iffue within age, and dieth, the diffeifee bring a writ of entry againft the tenant by the curtefie, he pray in aide of the heir within age, he 17 E. 3. 61. 27 H. 6. 1.

he ſhall have his age, for this is a writ of entry in the *poſt*, being brought againſt the tenant by the curteſie, and ſo out of the ſtatute.

24 E. 3. 25. b. 46, 47. If there be two brothers, and a ſiſter, the elder brother diſſeiſeth one, and dieth, and the land deſcendeth to his brother, and he enters and dieth ſeiſed, and the land deſcendeth to the ſiſter within age: in a writ of entry brought by the diſſeiſſee againſt the ſiſter, ſhe ſhall be ouſted of her age by this ſtatute: wherein three things are to be obſerved. Firſt, that the mediate heire on the part of [258] the diſſeiſor is within this ſtatute. 2. That though the ſiſter is to make herſelf ſiſter and heire to the younger brother, and not to the diſſeiſor, for that her younger brother entred, yet is ſhe heire within the meaning of this ſtatute to the diſſeiſor, and therefore to be ouſted of her age. 3. That a writ of entry in the *per* and *cui* in this ſpeciall caſe is within this act.

Speciall heires, as in gavelkinde, borough Engliſh, and the ſiſter of the whole blood are on both ſides within this ſtatute, for though they be not heires by the common law, yet are they heires within the intention of this law, which is to be taken benignly, being made for expedition of juſtice, and to ouſt delay.

8 E. 3. 71. 10 E. 3. 58. 21 E. 3. 27. 6 E. 3. 31. (3) *En meſme le maner eit le heire, ou les heires le diſſeiſee lour briefes dentre ſur les diſſeiſors ou lour heires.*] This is to be underſtood as well of the mediate as of the immediate heire of the diſſeiſor; and therefore if there be grandfather, father, and ſon, and the grandfather is diſſeiſed and dieth, and the father of full age likewiſe dieth, the ſon is within age, and brings his writ of entry againſt the diſſeiſor, he is an heire within this ſtatute, for he maketh himſelfe heire to the grandfather, who was the diſſeiſee.

(4) *Et ſi peraventure le diſſeiſee murge avant que il eit ſon purchaſe fait.*] Here by expreſſe words proviſion is made, though the diſſeiſee die before the purchaſe of his writ, whereof ſomwhat hath been ſaid before.

(5) *Iſſint que pur les nonages des heires dun part ne daut'*, &c.] Where the demandant or the tenant ſhall have his age at the common law, you may reade at large in Markals caſe abovesaid: it is there reſolved, that the heire as well of the demandant as the tenant, ſhould have had his age in this caſe.

(6) *Ne ſoit le briefe abatus ne le plea delay.*] Here abatement is taken for putting off the writ and plea without day untill full age, but the writ is not abated, that is, overthrown, *non cadit breve*, for Bract. li. 5. fo. & lib. 4. f. 218. b. ſo Bracton ſaith, *Minor ante tempus agere non poteſt infra ætatem, maxime in cauſa proprietatis, nec etiam convenire, ſed differetur uſque ætatem, ſed non cadit breve.*

8 E. 3. 71. Dier 4 Mar. ubi ſupra. (7) *Pur la freſh ſuit apres le diſſeiſin.*] *Statutum de W. 1. habetur intelligi, ubi hæres diſſeiſiti facit recentem ſectam, aliter non.*

24 E. 3. 25. 46, 47. Lib. 6. fol. 4. Markals caſe. 10 E. 3. 58. 6 E. 3. 11. 9 E. 2. age 141. 24 E. 3. 25. 46. This freſh ſuit is not to be underſtood between the diſſeiſor and the diſſeiſee, although the diſſeiſor continue in poſſeſſion by the ſpace of 30 or 40 yeares, &c. But when the diſſeiſor dies, then is the freſh ſuit to be made, and that is regularly within a yeare and a day after the death of the diſſeiſor, for within that time continuall claim may be made, which is in law *recens et continuum clameum*, and within that time an appeale of death may be brought, which is *recens inſecutio*, and *ſic in multis aliis ſimilibus.*

(8) *En droit des prelats, gents de religion, et auters*, &c.] This clauſe is to be underſtood of eccleſiaſticall perſons, that be regular, and not of eccleſiaſticall perſons, that be ſecular, for the regular are dead

dead perſons in law, to whom no lands (as this ſtatute ſpeaketh) can deſcend after the death of any other: but to the ſecular, as to biſhops, parſons, vicars, and the like lands may deſcend, and therefore they are not within this clauſe, but within the former branches of this act for ſuch lands as they are ſeiſed of to them and their heirs in their naturall capacity.

(9) *Eit lattaint.*] Of the writ of attaint, ſee before the ſtatute of Marlebridge, cap. 14, and here cap. 37.

CAP. XLVIII.

[259]

SI gardein ou chiefe ſeignior enfeoffe (1) *ul home de la terre que eſt del heritage del enfant (que eſt deins age et en ſa garde) a le diſheritance del heire: purview eſt, que le heire eyt maintenant ſon recoverie per briefe de novel diſſeiſin vers ſon gardein, et vers le tenant* (2). *Et ſoit la ſeiſin baille per juſtices (ſi el ſoit recover') al prochein amy lenfant, a que le heritage ne purra my diſcend'* (3), *pur approver al oeps lenfant, et a reſponder des iſſues al heire quant il viendre a ſon pleine age. Et le gardein perde a tout ſa vie la garde* (4) *de meſme la choſe recover', et tout la remainder del heritage, quel tient en noſme del heire. Et ſi auter gardein que chiefe ſeigniour* (5) *le face, perde le garde de tout cel choſe* (6) *a cel foits et ſoit en grieve peine envers le roy. Et ſi lenfant ſoit eſloigne, ou diſturbe per le gardein, ou per le feoffee, ou per auter, per que il ne puiſſe ſa aſſiſe ſuer, ſue pur luy* (7) *un de ſes prochein amies* (8) *que voudra, et ſoit a ceo reſceve.* W. 2. cap. 15.

IF a guardian, or chief lord, infeoff any man of land, that is the inheritance of a child within age, and in his ward, to the diſheritance of the heir; it is provided, that the heir ſhall forthwith have his recovery by aſſiſe of novel diſſeiſin againſt his guardian, and againſt the tenant; and the ſeiſin ſhall be delivered by the juſtices (if it be recovered) to the next friend of the heir (to whom the inheritance cannot deſcend) for to improve to the uſe of the heir, and to anſwer for the iſſues unto the heir, when he ſhall come unto his full age; and the guardian, during his life, ſhall loſe the cuſtody of the thing recovered, and all the inheritance that he holdeth by reaſon of the heir. And if another guardian than the chief lord do it, he ſhall loſe the wardſhip of all together, and be grievouſly puniſhed by the king. And if the infant be carried away, or diſturbed by the guardian, or by the feoffee, or by other, by reaſon whereof he cannot ſue his aſſiſe, then may one of his next friends (that will) ſue for him, which ſhall be thereto admitted.

(Fitz. Aſſiſe, 105. Bro. Aſſiſe, 491. 2 Ed. 3. 16. 8 Aſſ. pla. 22. 27 H. 8. 1. 40 Ed. 3. 16. 13 Ed. 1. ſtat. 1. c. 15. Raſt. 366, 367.)

The miſchief before this ſtatute was, that when the gardein in chivalry made a feoffment in fee, the judges, for the ſaving of the warranty between the feoffor and the feoffee, and that the right of each might be ſaved, allowed that a writ of entry in the *per* did lye for the heir before this ſtatute, as it appeareth by Bracton, and 15 H. 3. Bract. l. 5. fo. 324. 15 E. 3.
nay,

Bre.878. 19 E. 2. Ass. 400. 4 E. 2. Bre. 790. nay, the judges in ancient time did allow a writ of entry in the *per*, as it appeareth by the old Register, of a feoffment made by a baillie: but this opinion, or errour rather, was holpen by the resolution of the judges; and the alienation of the gardein (after this act) to be made is holpen by this act, by enacting and declaring, that an assise of *novel disseisin* doth lye against the gardein and his feoffee; therefore of a feoffment made by the gardein after the statute, no writ of entry in the *per* doth lye, but an assise of *novel disseisin*: and the statute hath adjudged the feoffment a *disseisin*; but of an alienation by the gardein before this statute, a writ of entry in the *per* doth lye after this act, because this act doth extend to feoffments made afterwards, as appeareth by the letter thereof; but if the tenant alien, and the gardein and his feoffee dye, or if the heir dye, so as no assise can lye by this act, then of such an alienation after this act a writ of entry doth lye: and all this is approved by the authority of our books, and upon these diversities all the books are reconciled.

19 E. 2. Ass. 400. 7 E. 3. 69. 8 E. 3. 63. 8 Ass. 28. 14 E. 3. Feoffmts. 67. 10 E. 4. 18. Vid. W. 2. c. 25.

This statute speaketh onely of a gardein in chivalry, therefore tenant for yeers, tenant by *elegit*, statute merchant, &c. shall be reserved till we come to the statute of W. 2. cap. 25.

West. 2. ca. 25.

(1) *Enfeoffe.*] The feoffment at these times was the generall assurance of the realm, but a fine is within this act, for that is a feoffment of record.

[260]

(2) *Maintenant son recoverie per briefe de novel disseisin vers son gardein, et vers le tenant.*] Here two things are to be observed, 1. upon this word *maintenant*, that is, presently without any delay: and this is the 7. act made at this parliament for expedition of justice, and for the ousting of delayes; for as it is commonly said, the devill deviseth delayes: wherein this noble king followed the steps of that good king Alfred, in whose time the law of England was as followeth; *En son temps puissoit chescun pl' aver commission, ou briefe a son visc' al seigniour de fee, ou a certein justices assignes sur chescun tort; en son temps se hasta droit de jour en jour, issint que ouster* 15 *jours nestoit nul default, ne nul essoine adjornable.*

Mirror, cap. 5. § 1.

2. By this act, not onely the gardein is a disseisor, but the feoffee also; and so doth Fleta render it, *Et apud Westm' fuit provisum quod custos, qui alienat terras hæredis, habeatur pro disseisitore, &c.* and soon after he saith, *Habeantur pro disseisitoribus tam custos, quam emptor.*

Fleta, li. 1. c. 11. 10 E. 4. 18. W. 2. cap. 25.

(3) *Et soit le seisin baille per justices, &c. al prochein amy del infant, a que le heritage ne purra my discend'.*] This clause Fleta rendreth in this manner, *Et cum terra fuerit recuperata, tradatur propinquiori amico, cui hæreditas descendere non debeat, qui respondeat puero de exitibus, cum ad ætatem suam pervenerit.*

Fleta ubi supra.

And where the statute saith, *Soit, &c. baille per justices,* the meaning is no more but this, that the justices before the recovery was had, shall charge the next of the kin, to whom the land cannot descend, to take according to this act the custody of the lands, and to yeeld a true account to the heir at his full age, and to enter an order of court thereof accordingly.

And he is neither a gardein in chivalry, nor in socage, but a statute gardein in lieu of the gardein in chivalry by force of this act.

And if this gardein dye before the full age of the heir, his executors shall not have the custody, but the next of kin, to whom the land

land cannot deſcend; for this act hath annexed it to the next of blood, to whom the land cannot deſcend.

(4) *Et le gardein perde a tout ſa vie la garde*, &c.] This branch is to be underſtood of a gardein in *droit*, that is to ſay, of the chief lord, for he is not onely to loſe the cuſtody of the land aliened, and of all the reſidue of the heritage which he had in ward; but alſo to loſe all benefit of wardſhip of that tenancie, by the letter of this law, during his life, for that againſt the office and duty of a gardein, he hath ſought the diſheriſon of the heir which he had in his cuſtody: and Fleta tranſlateth this clauſe in theſe words, *et ſi ſit capitalis do-* Fleta, li. 1. c. 11.
minus qui hoc faciat, amittat cuſtodiam tota vita ſua tam de reſiduo, quam de terra alienata; but in this caſe the lord by his feoffment Vide 1. part Inſtit. ſect. 968.
of the tenancie, or any part thereof hath extinguiſhed his ſeigniority for ever, whether the feoffment be made of all the tenancie, or but of part, by the common law: and theſe words (during his life) being in the affirmative, reſtraineth not the operation of the common law in this caſe.

(5) *Et ſi auter gardein que chieſe ſeigniour.*] This is intended of a gardein *in fait*: as where the lord aſſigneth over the cuſtodies to another, he is called a gardein *in fait*; hereof Fleta ſaith, *et ſi alius* Fleta ubi ſupra.
fuerit cuſtos, quam capitalis dominus feodi illius, amittat cuſtodiam rei recuperatæ, &c.

(6) *Perde le garde de tout cel choſe.*] The feoffment made by the gardein *in fait* is a forfeiture of his eſtate by the common law of the whole, if the feoffment were made of the whole; and if of part, then of that part onely by the common law; but this ſtatute giveth the forfeiture of the whole land in ward: but it ſeemeth in this, the wardſhip of the body is not loſt, becauſe this branch extendeth to [261]
the land onely; no more then upon the ſtatute of Glouc' in caſe of Gloc'. cap. 5.
waſte done to the diſheriſon of the heir, the ſtatute ſaith, *perdra le garde*, yet ſhall he not loſe the cuſtody of the body: and in both Mich. 28 H. 8.
theſe caſes, the ſeigniory, which is the cauſe of the wardſhip, con- Benloes.
tinueth; but where the ſeigniory is extinct, there the heir ſhall be out of ward, both for body and land.

(7) *Sue pur luy un de ſes prochein amies.*] Before the making of this act, the gardein or his feoffee, or ſome other would eſſoigne or diſturb the infant, ſo as he could not take his remedy by law, and See before, c. 42.
by attorney he could not appear, therefore this act in this particu- 40 E. 3. 16.
lar caſe doth give the infant to purchaſe and follow his writ of W. 2. ca. 15.
aſſiſe upon this act by *prochein amy*, albeit he be not preſent in court; and ever ſince the ſtatute of Weſtm. 2. which is generall, the common rule is holden, that an infant ſhall ſue by *prochein amy*, and defend by *gardein*.

(8) *Prochein amy.*] *Amicus propinquior*; in our books the names of *gardein* and *prochein amy* are ſometimes taken the one for the other becauſe the *gardein* and *prochein amye* are oftentimes all one, as the gardien in ſocage is alſo *prochein amy, &c.* And now as well the *gardein*, as the *prochein amy* are allowed by the judges to be ſome of the officers of the court, and both in reſpect of their place and ſkill are in troth the beſt *prochein amyes* for the good and furtherance of the infants cauſe.

Fleta rendreth this clauſe in theſe words, *Et ſi hæres impeditus* Fleta ubi ſupra.
fuerit ad ſequendum, ſequatur unus de propinquioribus amicis, et admit- 40 E. 3. 16.
tatur; and this admiſſion is by the order of the court, but the gardein 48 E. 3. 10.
muſt put in a warrant. 33 E. 3. Attorney 94. 19 Aſſ. 10. 27 Aſſ. 53.

In

34 Aſſ. 5. 28 Aſſ. 2. 29 Aſſ. 67. 35 H. 6. 12. 20 E. 4. 2. 16 H. 7. 5. F.N.B. 27. I. 13 E. 3. Attorney 76.

In an action of waſte, brought by an infant againſt the abbot of R. as gardein in chivalry, *quas tenet*, the infant came not in perſon, but one came as *prochein amy* by the ſtatute, which is intended by the ſaid ſtatute of Weſt. 2. and prayed to be received to ſue, for that the infant was eſſoined; againſt which this objection was made, that it appeared not judicially to the court that the infant was eſſoined, and that ſuch a ſuggeſtion in the caſe of aſſiſe and mordanceſter had uſed to be made, becauſe the eſſoyning, which is the cauſe that the ſtatute ſetteth down, might be enquired of, being a jury, the firſt day, but otherwiſe it was in the caſe at the barre being an action of waſte; but it was reſolved, that the *prochein amy* ought to be admitted upon the ſaid ſuggeſtion in this caſe, for that the writ is brought againſt the *gardein*, which peradventure had eſſoined the infant, and he of his own wrong ſhall not take advantage, and therefore the court did award that the *prochein amy* ſhould be admitted to ſue, &c. Which caſe I have remembred here, becauſe it may ſerve for an expoſition as well of this act of Weſtm. 1. as of the ſaid act of Weſtm. 2.

CAP. XLIX.

EN briefe de dower dont dame riens nad, ne ſoit le briefe abatus per exception del tenant (1), *pur ceo que el avera reſceive ſon dower de auter home avant ſon briefe purchaſe, ſil ne puit monſtre que el eit reſceive part de ſa dower de luy meſme* (2), *et en meſme la ville* (3) *avant ſon briefe purchaſe* (4).

IN a writ of dower called *unde nihil habet*, the writ ſhall not abate by the exception of the tenant, becauſe ſhe hath received her dower of another man before her writ purchaſed, unleſs he can ſhew that ſhe hath received part of her dower of himſelf, and in the ſame town, before the writ purchaſed.

(Regiſt. 170, 171. Fitz. Voucher, 196. Fitz. Dower, 75, 76. 86. 89. 114. Kel. 128.)

[262]

Bract. li. 4. fo. 311. b.

The miſchief before this act doth notably appear by Bracton, who treating of this writ, *Unde nihil habet*, ſaith, *ad hoc autem quod dicit mulier in intentione ſua (et unde nihil habet) ſi quidem partem dotis habuerit, licet minimam, ſi hoc dedicere non poſſit, vel cum hoc probatum fuerit, cadit breve, nec de reſiduo quod ei defuerit poterit ſibi proſpicere niſi per breve de recto de dote, nihil igitur recipiat de dote ſua ante brevis impetrationem, ita quod breve contineat omnes deforcientes ubicunq; fuerint in uno comitatu, vel in diverſis. Et cum omnes contineantur, tunc primo recipiat, et ſi recipiat ante judicium, etiam ſine judicio non obſtabit ei exceptio, quod aliquid habuerit, quia reſpondere poterit, quod ſatisfactum eſt ei ante judicium, &c. ſi petens dicat quod exceptio, &c. ei nocere non debet, quia nihil habet in tali villa, vel in alia tali villa, non valebit talis ſua replicatio, quia id quod dicitur (unde nihil habet) non debet referri ad villas, ſed ad dotem:* hereby doth the miſchiefe before this act manifeſtly appear.

Fleta, li. 5. c. 25.

And Fleta rehearſing the effect of this ſtatute, ſaith, *in brevi autem de dote unde mulier petens nihil habet, non cadit breve per exceptionem tenentis petentis judicium de brevi, deſicut ſuppoſuit eam nihil habere,*

cum

cum aliquid habeat, vel dotem ſuam de aliquo receperit pro parte ipſam contingente, niſi partem dotis receperit a ſeipſo in eadem villa ante brevis impetrationem.

(1) *Per exception del tenant.*] Regularly tenant is taken for him that is tenant of the free hold, but in the caſe of dower, it lyeth againſt gardein in chivalry, becauſe in that caſe he is to anſwer for the heir, but not againſt the gardein in ſocage. See hereafter in this chapter, where this exception ſhall lye in the mouth of the vouchee being tenant in law. Brit. fo. 258. 13 E. 1. Bre. 863. 8 E. 2. ibid. 809. 18 E. 2. ibid. 833. 6 E. 3. 257. 7 E. 3. 308. 8 E. 3. 384.

(2) *De luy meſme.*] Firſt, it muſt be of the ſame tenant, and not of another, though it be in the ſame town; as if the huſband infeoffeth A. of Whiteacre, and B. of Blackacre, both in Dale, and the wife receiveth dower of A. ſhe notwithſtanding ſhall have a writ of dower *(unde nihil habet)* againſt B. by the expreſſe purview of this act, for he is not the ſame tenant of whom ſhe received her dower. 10 E. 3. 509. 11 E. 3. Bre. 475. 13 E. 3. ibid. 242. 16 E. 3. ibid. 657. 4 E. 3. 42.

Secondly, if A. having a wife doth infeoffe the huſband of one acre, and the wife of another, and both in Dale; A. dyeth, the huſband aſſigneth dower of his acre, yet doth the writ of dower *(unde nihil habet)* lye againſt the huſband and wife, for they are not the ſame tenant. Brit. fol. 257. 12 E. 3. Dower 89.

Thirdly, if the baron be ſeiſed of Blackacre and Whiteacre in Dale, and after the coverture maketh a leaſe for life of Blackacre, and granteth Whiteacre and the reverſion of Blackacre to A. and his heirs, to whom attornment is made, and dyeth; the wife receiveth dower of A. of Whiteacre, and after the leſſee for life dyeth, the wife ſhall have a writ of dower *(unde nihil habet)* to be endowed of Blackacre; for albeit it be againſt the ſame tenant, and in the ſame town, and before the writ purchaſed, which are the three points required by this act, yet is there another property neceſſarily implyed, and that is, that he be ſuch a tenant of both the one land and the other, at the time of the receit of dower, as ſhe might have had her writ of dower *(unde nihil habet)* againſt him, of both which ſhe could not have in this caſe, in reſpect the leſſee for life was tenant of the free-hold at that time, and ſo no default in her. 2 E. 2. Dower 124. 12 E. 3. Dower 86.

The baron is ſeiſed of a carue of land holden by knights ſervice, and of Whiteacre in Dale, and after the coverture infeoffeth A. of Whiteacre with warranty, and dyeth, his heir within age, the gardein aſſigneth dower of the carue of land, and then the wife brings her writ of dower againſt A. who voucheth the heir in the cuſtody of the gardein, the gardein pleads the receit of dower of the ſaid carue in the ſame town, and adjudged a good plea and the writ of dower *(unde nihil habet)* abated. 3 E. 3. Dower 76. 3 E. 3. Voucher 196. Kelw. 128.

The ſame law it is, if the gardein that aſſigned the dower dyed, and the heir had been vouched in the guard of his executors, his executors in the caſe aboveſaid ſhould plead the ſame plea.

And ſo if the heire in that caſe had been vowched of full age, he might have pleaded as vowchee, as an aſſignement of dower by himſelfe in the ſame towne. [263] First part of the Inſt. ſect. 39.

(3) *En meſme la ville.*] A writ of dower, *unde nihil habet*, doth lie in an hamlet, but yet if the demandant have received dower out of the hamlet, and in the ſame town, the writ ſhall abate: otherwiſe it is, though it be in the ſame pariſh, if it be 18 E. 2. bre 829. 4 E. 3. ibid. 745. 4 E. 3. 52. 8 E. 4. 6.

be in another town, for the words of the statute be, *en mesme la ville.*

Fleta ubi supra. Bracton ubi supr. 3 E. 3. Vowch. 196. 12 E. 3. Dower 86, Regist. 171.

(4) *Avant son briefe purchase.*] Of this clause Fleta saith thus, *Si partem dotis suæ receperit post breve impetratum, quamvis ab ipso tenente, non propter hoc cadit breve mulieris, cum dicere poterit ante judicium, quod de residuo, vel omissione est ei satisfactum,* and so it appeareth by Bracton, it was, as to this point, at the common law.

CAP. L.

ET pur ceo que le roy ad fait cel chose (1) al honour de Dieu, et saint esglise, et pur le common profit de people, et pur le allegeance de ceux queux sont greves (2), il ne voit my que auterfoits puissent turner a prejudice de luy, ne de sa corone: mes que les droits, que a luy apperteign' (3), luy soient saves en touts points.

AND forasmuch as the king hath ordained these things unto the honour of God and holy church, and for the commonwealth, and for the remedy of such as be grieved, he would not that at any other time it should turn in prejudice of himself, or of his crown; but that such right, as appertains to him, should be saved in all points.

This is a saving to the king of the rights of his crowne.

(1) *Cel chose.*] That is, that this statute of W. 1. which hath been made to foure excellent ends, *viz.* the honour of God, the honour of the church, for the commonwealth, and for the remedy, disburdening, and ease of them, that be grieved, should not be prejudicial to him, or to his crown, but that the rights, which to him appertain, should be saved.

(2) *Allegeance de ceux queux sont greves.*] This should be *alleviance de ceux, &c.* That is, disburdening, remedying, and easing of such as be grieved.

Regist. fol. 61. Bracton.

(3) *Mes que les droits queux a luy appertain.*] That is to say, the kings rights, or the kings rights of his crowne, or the rights of the crown, for so these, which since are called prerogatives, before this time were called *jura regia,* or *jura regia coronæ,* or *jura coronæ*; Bracton cals them *privilegia regis,* and Britton, *droit le roy.*

Britton, fol. 1.

17 E. 2. Prærog. Regis. 26 E. 3. Quar. Imp. 95. 18 E. 3. Scire fac' 10. 8 H. 4. 2. 9 H. 4. 6. 15 E. 4. 12, 13.

But since this act *jus regni, &c.* hath been commonly called *prærogativa regis,* which is all one with this, that this act calls *droit le roy.*

See the first part of the Institutes, sect. 3. *Lex coronæ.*

CAP.

CAP. LI.

ET pur ceo que graund charitie serra de faire droit a touts en tout temps (1), *ou mestier serroit: purview est per assentment des prelates* (2), *que assises de novel disseisin, mortdauncester, et de darrein presentment* (3) *fuissent prises en le Advent* (4), *en Septuagesime* (5), *et en Quaresme* (6), *auxibien come le home prent lenquests, et ceo pria le roy as evesques* (7).

AND forasmuch as it is great charity to do right unto all men at all times (when need shall be) by the assent of all the prelates it was provided, that assises of novel disseisin, mortdauncester, and darrain presentment, should be taken in Advent, Septuagesima, and Lent, even as well as enquests may be taken, and that at the special request of the king, made unto the bishops.

The cause of the making of this statute doth manifestly appeare by Britton, who being B. of Hereford, and expert both in the common and canon law in his chapter *De challenge de jurors*, saith thus, Britton, ca. 53. *Et sils ysoient assets des jurors uncore purrount ascuns estre removables per verie challenges des parties, et auxi pur le temps en case: car heures ne sont pas meures: car per canon est defendu de saint esglise sur peyne de excommengement, que de la Septuagesme jesque al utas de Pasche, ne del commencement de Advent jesque al utas de la Epifayne, ne en jours del quatre temps, ne en jours de major letanies, ne en jours de roveysouns, ne en le semaigne de Pentecost, ne en temps de scier blees, ne de vendenges que durent de la S. Margaret jesque al 15. de saint Michael, ne en solemne jours de fesaints de saints, nulluy ne jurge sur le evangelies, ne nul secular plea ne teigne, ne summons ne face en temps avandits, issint que touts cest temps soit done a Dieu prier, et de peser contekes, et de accorder ceux, que sont a discord, et pur coiller les biens del terre, dont le people doit vivre.*

Which in respect of some difficulty I have thought good to translate; "and if sufficient jurors appeare, some are removeable for "just challenges of the parties, and also for the time in case; for "all houres are not fit for all seasons: for it is forbidden by the "canon of holy church upon paine of excommunication, that from "the Septuagesme untill eight days after Easter, and from the begin"ning of Advent untill eight days after the Epiphany, (or twelfe day) "or in the dayes of the foure times (that is, the ember dayes ap"pointed for publike fasts foure times in the yeare) or in the dayes "of the great letanies, or in rogation or gange dayes, or in the "week of Pentecost, or in time of harvest, or of vintage which Harvest, *Arviveslis.* "dureth from the feast of S. Margaret (which is the thirteenth of "July) untill 15 dayes after the feast of S. Michael the arch"angell, or in the solemne feasts of the acts of saints, no man be "sworne upon the holy evangelists, nor any secular plea be holden "in the times aforesaid, but that all these times be given for "prayer to God, and to appease debate, and to accord them that "be at discord, and to gather the fruits of the earth, whereof the "people may live, which were works of piety and charity."

This act beginneth with a maxime of law, *Summa charitas est facere*

facere justitiam singulis in omni tempore, quando opus fuerit, and therefore provideth that the three assises, *viz.* of *novel disseisin, mordaunc'*, and of *darrein presentment* should be taken in Advent, Septuagesme, and Quaresme.

Int' leges Edw. regis, anno Dom. 924. (1) *Tout temps.*] Here is understood *covenable in ley*, for in the common law there be *dies juridici, et dies non juridici*; *dies non juridici sunt dies dominici*, the lords dayes throughout the whole yeare, so called, because the Lord and Saviour of the world did arise again on that day: and this was the ancient law of England, and extended not onely to legall proceedings, but to contracts, &c. [265] 27 H. 6. c. 5. *Dacus si die dominico quicquam fuerit mercatus, re ipsa, et oris praeterea duodecim mulctator, Anglus triginta solidos numerato*; and it is truly said, *reges, qui serviunt Christo, faciunt leges pro Christo.* 2. In Easter terme the day of the ascension of the Lord Jesus Christ. 3. Before the statute of 32 H. 8. Trinity terme extended into the time of harvest, and then in that terme the day of the nativity of S. John Baptist was not *dies juridicus*, but by that statute that terme is so abbreviated, as that day fals not within the same, onely *dies dominici* are not *dies juridici* in that terme. In Michaelmasse terme the day of All Saints, and the day of All Soules; and in Hilary terme, the day of the Purification of the blessed Virgin Mary, are not *dies juridici.*

Fortescu, c. 51. fol. 66. b. And it should seem by Fortescue, that there be also *horae juridicae*, for he dedicating his book to the prince saith, *Scire te etiam cupio, quod justiciarii Angliae non sedent in curiis regis, nisi per tres horas in die, scilicet ab hora octava ante meridiem, usque horam undecimam completam, quia post meridiem curiae ille non tenentur, sed placitantes tunc se divertunt ad pervisum, et alibi consulentes cum servientibus ad legem, et aliis consiliariis suis. Quare justiciarii postquam se refecerint, totum diei residuum pertranseunt studendo in legibus; sacram legendo scripturam, et aliter ad eorum libitum contemplando, ut vita ipsorum plus contemplativa videatur, quam activa, &c.*

Mirror, c. 5. § 1. And the Mirror saith, *Abusion est que tient pleas per Dimenches* (i. sabbath dayes) *ou per auters jours defendus, ou devant le soleil levie, ou noctantre, ou in dishonest lieu.*

(2) *Purview est per assentment des prelates.*] Which is expressed, not that the prelates assented alone, but that it was enacted by the king with the whole assent of parliament, which is implied by these words, *purview est*, and this act is entred into the parliament roll with the rest made in this parliament. But *per assent des prelates* is added to manifest that this act concerning the crossing of a canon of the church was enacted by their assents.

See the first part of the Institutes, sect. 524. And here it is worthy of observation, that albeit divers judges of the realme were men of the church, as Britton, Martin de Patteshull, William de Raleighe, Robert de Lexinton, Henricus de Stanton, and many others; and that the honourable officers of the realme, as lord chauncellor, lord treasurer, lord privie seale, master of the rolls, &c. were in those dayes men of the church, yet they ever had such honourable and true-hearted courage, as they suffered no incroachment by any forein power upon the rights of the crowne, or Li. 5. fo. 1. Cawdries case. the lawes and customes of the realme, as in Cawdryes case in the fifth part of my Reports is partly shewed, and much more (if it were requisite) may be said in that behalfe.

(3) *En assise de novel disseisin, mordauncester, et darrein presentment.*]

Brit. ubi supra. Hereof Britton saith, *Les evesques nequident et prelats de saint esglise*

fount

ſount diſpenſations que aſſiſes, et juries ſont priſes en tiels temps per reaſonable encheſons.

(4) *Advent.*] *Adventus Domini in carne, et incipit die dominica* 7 aſſ. p. 7.
proxim' ante feſtum Sancti Andreæ, vel ipſa die Sancti Andreæ, ſi in 14 aſſ. 4.
dominica venerit; and endeth eight dayes, after twelfe-tide, or the Epiphany.

(5) *Septuageſime.*] *Septuageſima* beginneth on the third Sunday before Shroveſunday, and endureth till eight dayes after Eaſter.

(6) *Quareſme.*] *Quadrageſima* beginneth the firſt Sunday in Lent, [266]
and endureth all Lent.

(7) *Et ceo pria le roy as eveſques.*] Faire and good words many times further, but never hinder any good work.

How the canon abovesaid tooke no place in other actions not named in this act (if you obſerve the times forbidden by the canon) is maniſeſt by our bookes, and common experience in all ages ſince the making thereof.

STATUTUM DE BIGAMIS. [267]

Editum anno 4 Edw. I.

IT is called *Statutum de Bigamis* of the fift chapter of this parliament, wherein thoſe that be *bigami*, are barred of the privilege of clergie.

IN præſentia venerabilium patrum quorundam epiſcoporum Angliæ, et aliorum de conſilio regis, recitatæ fuerunt conſtitutiones ſubſcriptæ, et poſtmodum coram domino rege et conſilio ſuo auditæ et publicatæ, quia omnes de conſilio, tam juſticiarii, quam alii concordaverunt (1), *quod in ſcripturam redigerentur ad perpetuam memoriam, et quod firmiter obſerventur.*

IN the preſence of certain reverend fathers, biſhops of England, and others of the king's council, the conſtitutions under-written were recited, and after heard and publiſhed before the king and his council, foraſmuch as all the king's council, as well juſtices as other, did agree that they ſhould be put in writing for a perpetual memory, and that they ſhould be ſtedfaſtly obſerved.

Here may you obſerve the ancient order of proceeding in parliament for paſſing of bills; firſt a ſelect committee of certain biſhops, barons, and ſome of the commons, with the judges aſſiſtants (who after are expreſly named) expreſſed here under theſe words, *et aliorum de conſilio regis* (for at this time the lords and commons ſate together) and after the committee of both houſes had reſolved hereupon, then to report it to the whole councell here expreſſed

expressed under these words [*auditæ et publicatæ:*] which order in the severall houses is continued to this day.

30 Ass. 5. 8 E. 2. Dower 169. 5 E. 3. 65. 9 E. 3. 33. 10 E. 3. 26. 39 E. 3. 12, 13. 2 H. 7. 7. 4 H. 7. 1. 2. tit. Aide le roy 33.

Shard beholding the manner of the penning of this act, was of opinion that it was no act of parliament; but the contrary is holden by many expresse authorities both before, and after him. And these words in the first chapter [*Concord' est per justiciarios et alios sapientes de consilio regni*] do prove it to be by authority of parliament, for *consilium regni*, is the lords and commons, legally called *commune consilium regni.*

(1) *Quia omnes de consilio, tam justiciarii, quam alii concordaverunt,* &c.] And because this was done by the advice of the justices, and was but a declaration of the common law concerning *aid prier* of the king, and warranties, as by the words of the act it appeareth, therefore they are inserted into the act with this addition, *Qui consuetudines et usum judiciorum hactenus habuerint*; and sir Ralph de Hengham was chiefe justice of the kings bench, and sir Thomas de Weyland chiefe justice of the court of common pleas at this parliament.

[268]

CAP. I.

De placitis ubi tenens excipit, quod sine rege respondere non possit: concordatum est per justiciarios, et alios sapientes de consilio regni domini regis (1), *qui consuetudines et usum judiciorum hactenus habuerunt* (2), *quod ubi feoffamentum factum fuerit per regem, et charta super hoc confecta, tantum se habeat, quod si alia persona per consimile feoffamentum et consimilem chartam teneretur ad warrantiam, justiciarii ulterius procedere non potuerunt* (3), *nec hucusque processerunt, nisi super hoc præceptum à rege habuerint* (4), *nec videre possunt quod procedere possint.*

Concerning pleas where the tenant excepteth, that he cannot answer without the king; it is agreed by the justices, and other learned men of our lord the king's council of the realm, which heretofore have had the use and practice of judgement, that where a feoffment was made by the king with a deed thereupon, that if another person by a like feoffment and like deed be bounden to warranty, the justices could not heretofore have proceeded any further, neither yet do proceed without the king's commandment had therefore, neither can it be thought that they may proceed.

(2 H. 7. 11. 5 H. 7. 16. 9 H. 7. 15. 15 H. 7. 10. Fitz. Proced. 5, 6. Fitz. Traverſ. 41. 1 Roll 288.)

(1) *Per justiciarios, et alios sapientes de consilio regni domini regis.*] Here was used the ancient forms of parliaments, when the acts were *Rex ex consilio sapientum,* &c.

Inter leges Inæ, an. Dom. 727.

At a parliament holden by king Inas, *anno domini* 727. the statutes began thus, *Ego Inas Dei beneficio rex suasu et instituto Ceneredi patris mei, Heddæ et Erkenwaldi episcoporum meorum, omnium senatorum meorum, et natu majorum sapientum populi mei in magna servorum Dei frequentia,* &c. Here is the parliament expressed, as it continueth to this day.

Hac

Has ego Aluredus rex sanctiones in unum collegi, &c. multa tamen quæ nobis minus commoda videbantur ex consulto partim antiquanda, partim innovanda curavi. Inter leges Aluredi regis, anno dom. 900.

And again, *Hæc sunt senatus consulta ac instituta, &c. quæ à sapientibus recitata sæpius, atque ad communem regni utilitatem amplificata sunt.*

Decreta actaque sunt hæc omnia in celebri Grantaleano concilio, cui Walstunus interfuit archiepiscopus, et cum eo optimates et sapientes ab Æthelstano evocati frequentissimi; this is that Grandcestier in Cambridge-shire, of which the poet said, Inter leges Æthelstani, anno dom. 940.

Olim Granta fuit multis urbs inclyta rebus,
Nunc etenim magnum nil nisi nomen habet.

And that great parliament which Etheldred held, is called *sapientum consilium:* and more of this kinde might be remembred. Inter leges Etheldredi, anno dom. 1016.

(2) *Qui consuetudines et usum judiciorum hactenus habuerunt.*] For of ancient, and at this time many of the nobility and of the clergie were expert in the laws and customes of the realm, and had judiciall places, as partly hereby, and more at large may appear in the first part of the Institutes. See the first part of the Institutes, sect. 534.

(3) *Tantum se habeat, quod si alia persona per consimile feoffamentum et consimilem chartam teneretur ad warrantiam, justic' ulterius procedere non potuerunt.*] By this branch, if the king give lands with clause of an expresse warranty, yet the patentee, &c. shall not have or recover in value against the king, without speciall words that the king shall yeeld lands in value upon eviction, &c. and neverthelesse, in that case he shall have aid of the king by the generall purview of this law, for it is for the honour of the king, that he aid the patentee with any records or evidence that he hath for maintenance of the estate which he hath granted and warranted to him. [a] But if the king exchange lands with another by this warranty in law, the king is bound to warranty, and to yeeld in value, and so it was adjudged, Hil. 6 E. 1. *in communi banco* Rot. 2. William Brewses case, Wallia. 3 H. 6. 56. sic adjudicatur tempore E. 1. [269] [a] 17 E. 3. 12. H. 6 E. 1. Rot. 2. in banc' Wallia.

[b] If the king give lands to one in fee, by this word *dedi*, this bindeth not the king to warranty, and yet the patentee shall have aid of the king by the letter of this branch, because in that case another person should be bound to warranty by this word *dedi:* and so it is, albeit the tenure by the patent is to hold of the chief lords. [b] 8 E. 3. 10. 18 E. 3. tit. Aide. 31 & 142. 2 H. 7. 7. & 15 H. 7. 10.

[c] If it appear to the court, that the letters patents, or other causes of *aide prier* be void, against law, or insufficient in law, no aid shall be granted, for the law will not suffer those things to be aided or maintained by the countenance of law, which appear to the court to be void, against law, or insufficient; *ubi lex aliquem cogit ostendere causam, necesse est quod causa sit justa et legitima.* [c] 28 Ass. 19. 39. 28 E. 3. 94. b. 24 E. 3. 34. b. 26 E. 3. 58. 31 Ass. 2. 7 E. 3. 7. 39 E. 3. 12. 7 H. 4. 43. 11 H. 4. 86. 13 H. 4. 14. 4 H. 6. 29. 7 H. 6. 36. 8 H. 6. 25. 11 H. 6. 12. 8 H. 7. 9. 11.

[d] And according to former authorities of law, so was it adjudged 43 Eliz. in Foxleys case, and that *aid prier* ought not to be used for delay of justice, see notable and ancient records; and where *feoffamentum* and *charta* mentioned in this chapter must be taken for lawfull feoffments and charters, as in other cases. [d] Lib. 5. fo. 106. 111. Foxleys case. Tr. 18 E. 1. Coram rege Rot. 43. Wiltsh. 27 E. 1. Coram Just. ad Ass. in Com' de Suff. Radulphus de Mounthering comes Gloc.

[e] And as it hath been said in the case of *aid prier*, so it holdeth in all points, in the case when the tenant or defendant prayeth not in aid, but a writ *de domino rege inconsulto* is brought and directed to the judges; if it appear to the court, that the cause is not [e] Pasch. 10 E. 3. Corā rege Rot. 86. Wiltsh.

Tr. 11 E. 3. Coram rege Rot. 101. South. 21 E. 3. 24. 44. 22 E. 3. 6. 25 E. 3. 48. 2 R. 3. 13. tit. Aide le roy 33. 9 H. 7. 15. 4 H. 7. 1. F.N.B. 153. f. & 154. d. e. Regist. 220, 221. 227. lib. 9. fol. 16. Anna Bedingf. case.

not available or sufficient in law, the court ought to disallow the writ, and to proceed in the cause; and if the cause appear to the court to be just and lawfull (as in our books it appeareth to be, and not brought for delay) then the judges ought to surcease, &c. and so it was resolved, Mich. 34 & 35 Eliz. *in communi banco*, between Giles Blofeild pl' *in ejectione firmæ* of the demise of Reighnold earl of Kent plaintife, and Thomas Havers farmor of the earl of Arundell defendant, of the mannour of Winfarthinge in Suffolk.

[f] Upon the *aide prier*, or writ, the award is *quod tenens sive defendens sequatur penes dominum regem,* and the tenant or defendant ought to remove the record into the chancery, and in case of the *aide prier* the plea is not put without day.

[f] Lib. 9. fo. 16. Anna Bedingf. case. 10 E 3. 61. 22 Ass. p. 5. [g] Regist. 220, &c. F.N B. 153, &c. 26 E. 3. 58. 12 H. 4. 18. 11 H. 4. 72. 13 H. 4. 3. 9 H. 6. 40. 12 H. 6. Proc. 9. Dier 1. Mar. 101. 4 Eli. 209. 9 Eliz. 256. 15 Eliz. 320.

(4) *Nisi super hoc præceptum à rege habuerint.*] This *præceptum* is by the kings writ of *procedendo,* whereof there be two sorts, *viz. in loquela et ad judicium*; for the kings commandments in judiciall proceedings are ever by writ, according to the course of the common law, whereof you may read in the [g] Register, F. N. B. and our books; and which writs the king, *ex merito justiciæ,* in due time ought to grant; for the king himself by the great charter is presumed in law to sit in court, and to say *Nulli vendemus, nulli negabimus, vel differemus justiciam, vel rectum*; but if a title doth appear for the king to the possession, then no *procedendo* shall be granted.

[270]

CAP. II.

IN certis autem casibus, utpote ubi rex confirmaverit, vel ratificaverit (1) *factum alicujus in rem alienam, vel rem aliquam alicui concesserit, quantum in ipso est* (2), *vel ubi charta profertur, quod rex tenement' aliquod reddiderit, nec clausula aliqua in ea contineatur, per quam warrantizare debeat* (3), *et in consimilibus casibus, non erit supersedendum occasione confirmationis, ratificationis, concessionis, seu redditionis, aut aliorum consimilium, quin postquam hoc regi fuerit ostensum, sine dilatione procedatur* (4).

AND it seemeth also, that they could not proceed in certain cases, as where the king hath confirmed or ratified any man's deed to the use of another, or hath granted any thing as much as in him is, or where a deed is shewed, and clause contained therein, whereby he ought to warrantize: and in like cases they shall not surcease by occasion of a confirmation, grant, or surrender, or other like, but, after advertisement made thereof to the king, they shall proceed without delay.

(Rast. 27.)

30 Ass. p. 5. 8 E. 3. 33. 39 E. 3. 12. 35 H. 6. 56. 9 H. 6. 50, &c.

(1) *Ubi rex confirmaverit, vel ratificaverit.*] Here be three cases where aid, &c. ought not to be granted of the king, nor the court surcease by force of a writ *de domino rege inconsulto:* whereof the first is, when the king confirms or ratifies, &c. which must so be understood, when the confirmation giveth no estate, and if it giveth any estate, where no rent or service is reserved, or where in like case

case (as hath been said) another person were not bound to warranty; but if a rent or service be reserved, and by the action brought (if the demandant prevail) the rent or service should be defeated, then there is good cause of *aide prier*, &c. or if a common person were in that case bound to warranty, then is the confirmation in nature of a feoffment, and within the first chapter: what hath been said in case of confirmation, the same holdeth in case of release.

(2) *Alicui concesserit, quantum in ipso est.*] Here is the second case where no aide ought to be granted, for the king granteth but his own estate without any warranty.

(3) *Quod rex tenementum aliquod reddiderit, nec clausula aliqua in ea contineatur, per quam warrantizare debeat,* &c.] This is the third case where no aide shall be granted, in case of a restitution.

(4) *Postquam hoc regi fuerit ostensum, sine dilatione procedatur.*]
Here some have supposed, that in these three cases aide should be 2 H. 7. 7, 8.
granted, but by force of these words, that no search should be 39 E. 3. 12, 13.
granted, wherein two errours be committed: 1. That aide should be granted, which is against the expresse letter of the statute, *non erit supersedendum, &c.* and against the book of 39 E. 3. *ubi supra.* 2. That in case of *aide prier* of the king, or of the writ *de domino*
rege inconsulto, no search ought to be granted, but onely in a pe- 14 E. 3. ca. 14.
tition of right. 9 E. 4. 32. Dier. 15 Eliz. 320.

And if aid had been in any of these three cases erroniously granted, the tenant or defendant should have a *procedendo sine dilatione,* that is, without delay, and of course, which is the sense of these words.

CAP. III.

[271]

DE dotibus mulierum ubi aliqui custodes hæreditat' maritorum suorum custodias habent ex dono vel concessione regis, sive custodes rem petitam teneant, sive hæredes dictorum tenementorum vocentur ad warrant', si excipiant, quod sine rege respondere non possint, non ideo supersedeatur, quin in loquela prædict', prout justum' fuerit, procedatur.

CONCERNING the endowment of women, where the guardians of their husbands inheritance have wardship by the gift or grant of the king, or where such guardians be tenants of the thing in demand; or if the heirs of such lands be vouched to warranty, if they say that they cannot answer without the king: they shall not surcease upon the matter therefore, but shall proceed therein according to right.

(Fitz. Aid de Roi, 11, 12. 17. 30. 34. 37, &c.)

This statute having not been put in print untill towards the lat- 8 E. 3. 15. 18 E.
ter part of the raigne of H. 8. and thereby, as it seemeth, not 3. 38. 19 E. 3.
commonly known; there have divers aide prayers been graunted aide le Roy 64.
directly against both the points of the purview of this statute, as 39 E. 3. 8.
well when the writ of dower hath been brought against the kings 46 E. 3. 19.
grauntee 13 R. 2. bre. 646. 11 H. 4. 39. 5 H. 5. 13 F.N.B. 154 d.

4 H. 7. 1, 2. 8 E. 2. Dower 169. Li. 9. fo. 15, 16. Anna Bedingfields case. Ad Parliam. tent' post festum S. Hil. 18 E. 1. fo. 6.

grauntee or committee, as where the heire came in as vowchee in his custody; and the like rule Brian gave in 4 H. 7. but when justice Townesend remembred him of this statute of Bigamis, the aide was over-ruled.

And at the parliament holden in 18 E. 1. an act is in the parliament roll thus entred, *Quod viduæ recipiant dotem de terris in custodia regis existentibus, dominus rex præcepit justiciariis de banco, quod viduæ post mortem virorum suorum petant dotem suam, &c. et quod in placitis illis procedant secundum communem legem regni, et quod partibus faciant debitum justiciæ complementum.*

So as seeing the letter of this chapter of 4 E. 1. extends but where the king hath graunted the custody over, or where the heire came in as vowchee, this act of 18 E. 1. made about fourteen yeares after, addeth, that these widowes shall recover dower against the heire in the custody of the king, where the king graunteth not the custody to any, but keepeth the lands in his owne hands. And I am verily perswaded, that seeing the graunting of aide, where no aide was grauntable, was not any error (whereby the judgement might be reversed) some judges either for that cause, or for feare, have graunted aide of the king in many cases, where it was not to be graunted by law, and the rather, for that in ancient times aides of the king were little or no delay at all; for writs of *procedendo* were speedily graunted, whereas of later times aides prayers, and specially writs *de domino rege inconsulto* are used meerly for delay of justice, and that for no small time.

CAP. IV.

DE purpresturis (1), *seu occupationibus* (2) *quibuscunque factis super regem, sive in libertatibus, sive alibi* (3). *Concordatum est quod tempore regis H. diffinitum erat et concordat', quod ubi occupatores superstites fuerint* (4), *rex de plano resumat* * (5) *sibi rem taliter occupatam de manibus occupantium, quod etiam de cætero in regno observetur. Et si aliquis de hujusmodi resumptionibus conqueratur* (6), *prout justum fuerit, audiatur.*

* [272]

CONCERNING purprestures, or any manner of usurpations, made upon the king within franchises, or elsewhere, it was agreed and determined in the time of king Henry, that where such usurpers were living, the king should reseise of new the land so usurped out of the hands of the usurpers; the which thing also shall be from henceforth observed in the realm; and if any do complain upon such reseisers, he shall be heard like as right requireth.

17 E. 2. cap. 13. (9 Rep. 16. Fitz. Dower, 169. 17 Ed. 2. c. 13.)

This act is but a confirmation of a former statute made in the raigne of king H. 3.

(1) *De purpresturis.*] *Purprestura* commeth of the French word *purprise*, or *pourpris*, which signifieth an inclosure or building, and in legall understanding signifieth an incrochment upon the king, either upon part of the kings demesne lands of his crown, which are

are accounted in law as *res publicæ, et ſemper favorabile fuit in omni republica principis patrimonium*; or in the high-wayes, or in common rivers, or in the common ſtreets of a city, or generally when any common nuſans is done to the king and his people, endeavouring to make that private, which ought to be publique, which Glanvill very aptly deſcribeth in theſe words, *Dicitur autem purpreſtura, vel porpreſtura proprie, quando aliquid ſuper dominum regem injuſte occupatur, ut in dominicis regis, vel in viis publicis obſtruct', vel in aquis publicis tranſverſis à recto curſu, vel quando aliquis in civitate ſuper regiam plateam aliquid ædificando occupaverit, et generaliter quoties aliquid fit ad nocumentum regii tenementi, vel regiæ viæ, vel civitatis.* Glanv. li. 9. cap. 11.

It was an article of the eyre before this act to enquire *De purpreſturis factis ſuper dominum regem, ſive in terra, ſive in mari, ſive in aqua dulci, ſive infra libertatem, ſive extra.* Cap. Itineris.

It appeareth alſo by Glanvill, that there be alſo purpreſtures done to ſubjects, but this chapter treateth onely of purpreſtures done to the king and his people.

(2) *Seu occupationibus.*] Here *occupationes* are taken for uſurpations upon the king, and it is properly, when one uſurpeth upon the king by uſing of liberties and franchiſes, which he ought not to have: and as an unjuſt entry upon the king into lands or tenements is called an intruſion, ſo an unlawfull uſing of franchiſes or liberties is ſaid an uſurpation, but *occupationes* in a large ſenſe are taken for purpreſtures, intruſions, and uſurpations.

(3) *Seu in libertatibus, ſive alibi.*] That is to ſay, within liberties, or places that have franchiſes, or priviledges, or without.

(4) *Ubi occupatores ſurperſtites fuerint.*] This was a law of great equity, for it extended not but to the wrong doers themſelves.

(5) *Rex de plano reſumat.*] That is, may clearly reſeiſe. But this is to be intended upon due conviction, for ſo ſaith Glanvill, *Et qui per juratam ipſam aliquam hujuſmodi feciſſe purpreſturam convictus fuerit, in miſericordia domini regis remaneat, &c. et quod occupavit, reddet.* Glanv. ubi ſupra.

(6) *Et ſi aliquis de hujuſm' reſumptionibus conqueratur, &c.*] And yet ſuch reſeiſures ſhall not be finall, but the party grieved may complaine of ſuch reſeiſures, *Et prout juſtum fuerit, audiatur.*

CAP. V.

[273]

De bigamis (1) quos dominus papa in concilio ſuo Lugdunenſi (2) omni privilegio clericali privavit, per conſtitutionem inde editam, et unde quidam prælati (3) illos qui effecti fuerant bigami ante prædictam conſtitutionem, quando de felonia rectati fuerunt, tanquam clericos exegerunt ſibi liberandos: concordatum eſt et declaratum coram rege et concilio ſuo, quod conſtitutio illa intelli-

CONCERNING men twice married, called *bigami*, whom the biſhop of Rome, by a conſtitution made at the council of Lions, hath excluded from all clerks priviledge, whereupon certain prelates (when ſuch perſons have been attainted for felons) have prayed for to have them delivered as clerks, which were made *bigami* before the ſame conſtitution; it is agree

intelligenda ſit (4), *quod ſive effecti fuerint bigami ante prædictam conſtitutionem, ſive poſt, de cætero non liberentur prælatis, immo fiat eis juſticia ſicut de laicis.*

agreed and declared before the king and his council, that the ſame conſtitution ſhall be underſtood in this wiſe, that whether they were *bigami* before the ſame conſtitution, or after, they ſhall not from henceforth be delivered to the prelates, but juſtice ſhall be executed upon them, as upon other lay people.

(Altered by 1 Ed. 6. c. 12. Raſt. 106. 1 Jac. 1. c. 11.)

Mirror, ca. 3. de except. de Clergy. Britton, fo. 11. b. Fleta, li. 1 c. 32. 11 H. 4. 10. 18 E. 3. ca. 3. 2 E. 6. c. 12. Stam. Pl. Co. 135. Per decret. Epiſtol' Gregor. 9. lib. 6. decretal. a Bonifacio 8. in Lugdunenſi conc' edit.

(1) *De bigamis.*] *Bigamus* is he that either hath maried two or more wives, or that hath maried a widow, as it appeareth in the ſtatutes of 18 E. 3. cap. 2. 1 E. 6. cap. 12.

(2) *Concilium Lugdunenſe,* &c.] The conſtitution here mentioned is in theſe words, *Altercationis antiquæ dubium præſentis declarationis oraculo decidentes bigamos omni privilegio clericali declaramus eſſe nudatos, et coertioni fori ſecularis addictos, conſuetudine contraria non obſtante; ipſis quoque anathemate prohibemus deferre tonſuram, vel habitum clericalem.*

This conſtitution is hereafter in this chapter explained.

This councell was holden at the city of Lyons in France, Bonifacius the eight being pope.

Britton, fo. 225. Fleta, li. 1. c. 32. Bract. l. 4 fo. 247.

At the councell of Lyons, Britton and Fleta ſay, at Lateran ſaith Bracton, the pope endeavoured to take away the preſentations from princes and lay patrons to preſent by laps, for that the conſtitution ſaith, *Quod collatio beneficii eſt res ſpiritualis, et aliter credentes eſſent hæretici,* &c. and the common law ſaith, that a preſentation to a benefice is temporall, and ſo it is declared by divers acts of parliament.

Regiſt. 18 E. 3. 21. 38 E. 3. 2. 27 E. 3. 8. 5 E. 3. 26. 11 H. 4. 80. 13 E. 4. 3. Doct. et Stud. 116. F.N.B. 38. f. & 35. a. See W. 2. ca. 5. verbo ſemeſtre.

At this councell after ſixe moneths the dioceſan ſhall preſent: the Regiſter ſaith, that to preſent by laps was *dioceſanis ſpecialiter indultum* after ſixe months, and yet if after the ſixe moneths the patron preſent before the dioceſan collate, he ought to receive his clerk, notwithſtanding the generall councell.

But when the kings turn came to preſent *jure coronæ* by laps, the Regiſter ſaith, *Nullum tempus occurrit regi ex conſuetudine hactenus obtent' in regno Angliæ,* ſo as the councell did not binde the right of the king, nor could the dioceſan preſent by laps untill it was *ei indultum*; that is, untill it was allowed to him by conſent of the realme with ſuch limitations and reſtrictions, and with binding him in many caſes to give notice, as was thought juſt and reaſonable in ſubjects caſes, for the better ſervice of God and inſtruction of the people. But the king, who is *ſupremus dominus,* loſeth not his preſentation by any laps at all, the ſaid conſtitution notwithſtanding.

(3) *Unde quidam prælati,* &c.] Certain prelates did interpret the ſaid generall councell to extend onely to ſuch as became *bigami* after the councell, and they challenged ſuch clerks, as were *bigami* before that councell, when they were arraigned for felony, and required to have delivery of them.

[274]

See Art. Cler. cap. 15.

2 R. 2. cap. 6.

But hath the parliament power in theſe caſes to make declarations? yea, and in greater, for by authority of parliament it was declared,

declared, that Urban the twelfth was duly elected, and ought to be accepted pope; the truth is, that the cardinals forsook Urban, and accepted Clement the seventh, therefore it was enacted that all benefices and possessions of cardinals rebels within England should be seised, &c.

This schisme between these two popes continued 39 years, till the councell of Constance, one cursing and warring with another, in so much, that by reason of this schisme, above 200,000 Christians were miserably slain, this Urban drowned, five cardinals slew the bishop of Aquitane, gave authority to Spencer bishop of Norwich against Clement the anti-pope. Theorike Crantz.

(4) *Concordatum est et declaratum coram rege et concilio suo quod constitutio illa intelligenda sit.*] Here the king by advise and counsell of his high court of parliament doth expound and explain this constitution made at the said generall councell, and declareth where clergy should be taken away in respect of bigamy.

And this interpretation of the parliament was against the practise of the prelates, as before it appeareth, and contrary to the custome before used, as by the constitution it self appeareth.

But the true cause of this declaration by act of parliament was, that seeing the judges of the common law were judges of allowance or disallowance of clergy to him that was arraigned of felony, and that the said constitution tooke away the priviledge of clergy, and by consequent the life of man, the judges, before they allowed of the said constitution, would have it declared by authority of parliament. 12 E. 3. Cor. 117. 34 H. 6. 42. 9 E. 4. 29. 22 E. 4. Coron. 44. 15 H. 7. 9.

This law to deprive men that were *bigami* of the priviledge of their clergy was complained of in parliament, in 51 E. 3. and by king E. 6. in the first year of his raigne wholly abrogated and taken away. Rot. Parl. 51 E. 3. nu. 63. 1 E. 6. c. 12.

It fell out at this councell of Lyons mentioned in our act (as our histories report) that the popes wardrobe in that city (wherein was that detestable charter which king John made to the pope to bring the crown of England in servage to the see of Rome) then was wholly consumed with fire; a divine and fiery revocation of that most unjust and forcelesse charter, as was unanimously resolved both in parliament and elsewhere. William Thorn, Thomas Sprotte, &c. Rot. Parl. anno 40 E. 3. nu. 8. Rot. claus. 3 E. 1. memb. 9. in schedula.

CAP. VI.

IN chartis autem ubi continentur (dedi et concessi tale tenementum sine homagio (1), vel sine clausula quæ continet warrantiam, et tenend' de donatoribus et hæredibus suis (2) per certum servitium) concordat' est per eosdem justiciar' (3), quod donatores et hæredes sui teneantur ad warrantiam. Ubi autem continentur (dedi et concessi, &c.) tenendum de capitalibus dominis feodi, aut

IN deeds also where is contained *dedi et concessi tale tenementum* without homage, or without a clause that containeth warranty, and to be holden of the givers, and their heirs, by a certain service; it is agreed, that the givers, and their heirs, shall be bounded to warranty. And where is contained *dedi et concessi, &c.* to be holden of the chief lords of the fee, or of

*aut de aliis, quam de feoffatoribus, vel hæredibus suis, nullo servitio sibi retento, sine homagio *, vel sine dicta clausula warrantiæ, hæredes sui non teneantur ad warrantiam. Ipse tamen feoffator in vita sua (4) ratione doni proprii tenetur warrantizare (5). Prædict' autem constitutiones editæ fuerunt apud Westmonasterium in parliamento post festum Sancti Michaelis, anno regni regis E. filii regis H. quarto, et extunc locum habeant.*

of other, and not of feoffors, or of their heirs, reserving no service, without homage, or without the foresaid clause, their heirs shall not be bounden to warranty, notwithstanding the feoffor during his own life, by force of his own gift, shall be bound to warrant. All these constitutions aforesaid were made at Westminster, in the parliament next after the feast of St. Michael, the fourth year of the reign of king Edward, son of king Henry; and from that time forth they shall take effect.

(Dyer 15, 221. 1 Rep. 1. 1. 3 Rep. 58. 4 Rep. 81. 5 Rep. 17. 8 Rep. 51.)

There be two branches of this act, and two consequents thereupon, the first branch is, that where *dedi* is contained in a deed (albeit there be no other warranty) to hold of the donor and his heires (as at the making of this act, *viz.* in 4 E. 1. a man might have done) there the feoffor and his heires had beene bound to warranty, and this was the common law; for where *dedi* is accompanied with a perdurable tenure of the feoffor and his heirs, there *dedi* importeth a perdurable warranty for the feoffor and his heires

Glanv. l. 7. c. 2. to the feoffee and his heirs; and herewith agreeth Glanvill, *Tenentur autem hæredes donatorum donationes et res donatas sicut rationabiliter factæ sunt, illis quibus factæ sunt, et hæredibus suis warrantizare.*

Bracton, lib. 5. fol. 388. b. And Bracton herewith agreeth saying, *Et sciendum est quod ad omnes chartas de simplici donatione competit tenenti warrantizatio, et tenentur donatores et eorum hæredes ad warrantiam, si hora congrua, et modo debito cum prosecutione competenti vocati fuer' ad warrantiam, nisi forte in charta de feoffamento contrarium exprimitur.* And in those dayes regularly the donee did hold of the donor, unlesse there were a speciall limitation to the contrary. And when the

31 E. 1. Vowcher 290. feoffement was made by this word [*dedi*] to hold of the donor and his heires, then he and his heires are bound to warranty.

20 E. 3. Count. de garr. 7. 31 E. 3. Vow. 286. Li. 4. 81 Nokes case. The consequent is, that although there be an expresse warranty contained in the deed, yet that taketh not away the warranty that is wrought by force of *dedi*, but the feoffee may take advantage either of the one, or the other at his pleasure.

The second branch is, that where *dedi* is contained in the deed, to hold of the chiefe lord, and not of the feoffor, there, although there were no other warranty in the deed, the feoffor shall be bound

Britton, fo. 88. b. to warranty during life. Britton saith, *Si le purchasor soit del done challenge in sa seisin, si ert le donor tenu de garranter auter son done tant come il vivera, tout ne soit a ceo oblige per especialtie de escript tout face le purchasor de ceo homage a auter que al donor, sicome al chiefe Seigniour.*

31 E. 1. Vowcher 290. If the gift be made to hold of the chiefe lord of the fee, then *dedi* bindes none to warranty, but him that made the gift.

6 E. 2. Vowch. 258. 39 E. 3. 20 2 H. 7 7. And it is to be known that since the statute of *quia emptores*, 18 E. 1. the feoffee in fee simple doth hold of the chiefe lord, and therefore

therefore at this day in that case the feoffor is onely bound to warranty during his life; but if a man at this day give lands in taile by the word *dedi*, the donor and his heires are bound to warranty; and so it is of a lease for life, reserving a rent, though it be without deed. 6 H. 7. 2. 20 E. 3. Count. de garr. 7. 6 E. 3. 11. 22 Ass. 52. 18 E. 3. 8. 14 H. 6. 25.

The consequent hereupon is, that albeit there be in this case of the second branch an expresse warranty, the feoffee may take advantage of the one or the other, as upon the first branch hath been said. See for this Nokes case abovesaid. 6 H. 7 2. 10 H. 7. F.N.B. 134. h. 5 Eliz. Dier 121. Nokes case, ubi supra.

(1) *Sine homagio.*] The law was generally holden in those dayes, that homage being parcell of the tenure reserved to the feoffor and his heires, imported a warranty to the feoffee and his heires, and so much is implied by these words in this act, *sine homagio*, that is, without any warranty by reason of homage, but that was ever intended, so long as the tenancy continued * by descent in blood of the first purchaser, for if the tenement were transferred out of his blood by feoffment, or any other translation, in that case the tenant should vouch his feoffor or his heirs, if he had any warranty, but not in respect of the homage: and that this was the ancient law, appeareth by Glanvile, who saith, *Si aliquis alicui donaverit aliquod tenementum pro servitio et homagio suo, quod postea alius versus eum dirationaverit, tenebitur quidem dominus tenementum id ei warrantizare, vel competens excambium ei reddere. Secus est tamen de eo, qui de alio tenet feodum suum sicut hæreditatem suam, et unde fecerit homagium, quia licet is terram illam amittat, non tenebitur dominus ad eschambium*; and this is signified in the doing of homage, *Homagium si dominus recipere voluerit, tunc in signum warrantiæ acquietationis et defensionis manus tenentis infra manus suas tenere debet, dum tenens profert verba homagii.* And this day it holdeth in case of homage auncestrell. Bract. l. 5. f. 389. Fleta, li. 6. c. 23. Britton, fo. 170. The first part of the Institutes, cap. Homage Auncest. sect. 143. * [276] Glanv. li. 9. c. 4. 14 H. 6. 25. Vide the first part of the Institutes ubi sup.

(2) *De donatoribus et hæredibus suis.*] So it is if a body politique or incorporate had by deed, wherein *dedi* was contained, infeoffed another to hold of him and his successors, this had created a like warranty, as in this act is mentioned. 31 E. 1. Voucher 290.

(3) *Concordatum est per eosdem justiciarios.*] That is (as hath been said before) enacted according to the advice, and resolution of the justices.

(4) *Ipse tamen feoffator in vita sua.*] The letter of this act extends but to the feoffor upon a feoffment made, but if *dedi* doth enure by way of release or confirmation, it importeth a warranty during the life of him that makes the deed; so it is if a reversion expectant upon an estate for yeers, life, or in tail be granted by this word *dedi*, and attornment had, here *dedi* doth import a warranty, though the state passeth not by way of feoffment; so it is of a rent, of an advowson, or the like.

Bracton saith, *Si vero charta fuerit de confirmatione, non sequitur inde warrantizatio, nisi in se contineat donationem; ut si dicatur, do, et confirmo tali et hæredibus suis, &c.* If a man by *dedi* letteth land for life, by this the lessee shall vouch the lessor (though the reversion be granted away) and yet the lessor is not properly *feoffator*. Bract. ubi supra. 48 E. 3. 2. a. 14 H. 6, 25.

(5) *Ratione doni proprii tenetur warrantizare.*] Albeit in two places before in this act *dedi et concessi* are coupled together, yet these words *ratione doni proprii* do appropriate the warranty to *dedi* onely; 11 H. 6. 41. 11 H. 4. 41. 14 H. 6. 25. 6 H. 7. 2. F. 13. 4. h.

onely; and agreeable to this expoſition in our books is the common and conſtant opinion of learned men at this day.

39 E. 3. 26. Two jointenants make a feoffment in fee by this word *dedi*, the one dyes, the ſurvivour ſhall be vouched, and render in value for

11 H. 7. 13. the whole; for though the ſtate paſſed from both, and the ſtatute ſaith, *ratione doni proprii*, yet each of them did warrant the whole by this word *dedi*, otherwiſe the ſurvivour ought not to have yeelded the whole in value, as it hath been adjudged; and the reaſon is, for that the heir of the jointenant that dieth cannot be bound by the warranty created by this word *dedi*.

But if two jointenants make a feoffment in fee, with an expreſſe warranty for them and their heirs to the feoffee and his heirs, and the one of them dye, the ſurvivour ſhall not be vouched alone, but the heir alſo of the other, and the recompence in value ſhall lye equally upon them; but if the one of them have nothing, the other ſhall anſwer the whole; for it is a maxime in law, *Quando de una et cadem re duo onerabiles exiſtunt, unus pro inſufficientia alterius de integro onerabitur.* But in the ſaid caſe of *dedi*, the ſurvivour was onely chargeable with the warranty.

---

[277]

STATUTUM de GLOCESTER.

Editum Anno 6 Edw. I.

THIS parliament was holden at Glocester bordering upon Wales, for the better preſervation of peace in Wales, Lluellin prince of Wales, and the Welſh-men being a little before this parliament brought to quietneſſe.

LAN du grace M. CC. lxvii, (1) *et del raigne le roy Ed. fits le roy Henry, vi. a Glouceſtre le moys Dauguſt, purview ante meſme le roy, pur amendement de ſon roialme, et pur plus pleiner exhibition de droit* (2) *ſicome le profit doffice demaunde, appelles les pluis diſcrectes de ſon roialme, auxibien des greinders come des meinders. Eſtablie eſt et concordantment ordaine, que come meſme le roialme en pluſours divers caſes, auxibien des franchiſes, come dauters choſes, en les quels ley avant fallit, et a eſchever les treſgreves damages, et les nient numerables diſheriſons, les quels icel maner default de ley fiſt a la gent du roialme, eit meſtier de divers ſuppletions de ley, et de novels purveiances: les eſtatutes, ordeinments, et purveyances ſuis eſcriptes de tout la gent de la roialme deſormes ſoient firmement gardes, come prelates, countees, barons, et auters del roialme clament daver divers franchiſes, et les quels examiner' et judger', le roy a meſmes les prelates, countees, barons, et auters, avoit done jour. Purview eſt, et concordantment grante, que les avantdits prelates, countees, barons, et auters cel maner de franchiſe uſent, iſſint que rien ne lour accreſer per uſurpation, ou occupation, ne rien ſur le roy occupient, jeſque al prochein venue ceo roy per le countie, ou a le procheine venue des juſtices errants, as common plees en meſme le countie, ou jeſques le roy commande*

auter

auter chose : save le droit le roy come il en voudra parler, solonque ceo que il eit contenue en le briefe le roy. Et de ceo soient maundes briefes as viscontes, bailifes, ou auters pur chescun demandant. Et soit la forme del briefe change, solonq; la diversitie des franchises, les quels chescun claime daver. Et les viscontes per touts lour baillies ferront communement cryer, cestascavoire, en cities, burghes, et villes merchandes, et aylors, que touts ceux que ascuns franchises claiment aver per les charters les predecessors le roy, royes Dengleterre, ou en auter maner, soient devant le roy, ou devant justices en eire a certaine jour et lieu, a monstrer quel manner de franchises ils claimant daver, et per quel garrant. Et les visconts mesmes donques serront illonq; personalment, ou lour bailifes et ministers a certifier le roy sur les avantdits franchises, et auters choses que celles franchises touchent. Et cest crie destre devant le roy conteigne garnisement dee iij. semaignes. Et in mesme le maner ferront les viscontes crier en oyer de justices. Et in mesme le maner serront ils personalment, ou lour bailifes, et lour ministers, a certifier les justices de tiel maner de franchises, et des auters choses que celles franchises touchent. Et cest crie conteigne garnisement de quarante jours, sicome le common summons contient : issint que si la partie, que claime daver franchises, soit devant le roy, ne soit paz mis en defaut devant les justices en eyre, pur ceo que le roy de sa grace especiall ad grant, que il gardera la partie de dammage quant a cel ajornement. Et si cel party soit impled' sur tiels maners de franchises devant un payer de justices avantdits, mesmes les justices devant les queux la partie est en plee, garderent le partie de dammage devant auters justices, et devant le roy luy mesme, mesq; il sache per les justices, que le partie fuit en plee devant eux, sicome il est avantdit. Et si ceux que tiels franchises claiment aver, ne veignent paz al jour avantdit, donques soient les franchises en nosme de distresse prises en la maine le roy per le viscont del lieu, issint quils tiel manner de franchises ne usent, jesques ils veigne a receiver droit. Et quant ils veignent per cel distres, lour franchises eux soient replevies sils les demand, les quels replevies respoignent maintenant in la forme avantdit. Et peradventure les parties exceptent, quils ne debuient nient de ceo respondre sans briefe original, donques sil puisse estre sure que eux de lour proper fait, eient usurpe ou occupy ascuns franchises sur le roy, ou sur ses predecessors, dit lour soit que maintenant respoignent sans briefe, et puis resceivent judgement, sicome le court le roy agardera. Et sils diont [279] ouster, que lour ancester, ou lour ancesters de mesmes les franchises morront seisies, soient oyes, et maintenant soit le verity enquise, et solonque ceo aillent les avant en le besoigne. Et sil soit trove que lour ancesters ent morust seisie : donques eit le roy briefe original de sa chancery en forme fait de ceo. Le roy mande salute au viscount : summones per bone summonours un tiel, que il soit devant nous a tiel lieu en nostre prochein venue en cel countie, ou devant nous justices a primer assises, come ils en celles parties veindront, a monstrer per quel grant il claime daver quitance de torn' pur soy ou pur ses homes per tout nostre roialme per continuation apres la mort tiel jadis son predecessor. Et eiets les summonours et ceo briefe. Et si les parties veignont al jour, respoignent, et soit reply et judge. Et sils ne veignent, ne soy essoinent devant le roy, et si le roy demurra ouster en cel county, soit commande au viscont que il le face vener al quart jour. A quel jour sils ne veignent, et le roy demurr' ouster en cel county, soit fait sicome en eyre de justices. Et si le roy depart del countie, soient les parties ajornes a briefe jour, et eint reasonables delaies, juxte les discretions des justices, sicome en actions personal. Et les justices en eyre facent de ceo en lour oyers solonque lordeinment avantdit, et solonque ceo que tiel maner de plees debuient estre deduct. En oyer de pleints faits et affaires des bailifes le roy, et dauters bailifes, soit fait solonque lor-*

deinment

deinment avant fait de ceo, et solonque les enquests de ceo avant prises, et de ceo ferront les justices en eyre solonque ceo que le roy lour ad enjoynt, et solonque les articles que le roy lour ad livere. Vide tout ceo in Latin pluis plaine 30 E. 1. lestat° de Quo warranto, tit. Franchises 5.

[*The said statute of* Quo Warranto, *being necessary to the intelligence of our author's commentary, is here subjoined.*]

ANNO Domini M.CC.LXXVIII. regni autem domini regis E. sexto, apud Glocest. mense Augusti, providente ipso domino rege, ad regni sui Angliæ meliorationem, et exhibitionem justice pleniorem, prout regalis officii exposcit utilitas, convocatis discretioribus ejusdem regni, tam ex majoribus quam minoribus, statutum est, concordatum et ordinatum, quod cum regnum Anglie in diversis casibus, tam super libertatibus, quam in aliis in quibus prius lex deficiebat, ad evitand' incollarum damna gravissima, et exheredationes innumerabiles, quæ hujusmodi legum defectus induxerat, diversis legum suppletionibus, et novis quibusdam provisionibus indigeat, provisiones, ordinationes, et statuta subscripta ab omnibus regni sui incolis de cetero firmiter ac inviolabiliter observentur. Cum prelati, comites, barones, et alii de regno nostro diversas libertates habere clamant, ad quas examinand' et judicand' rex hujusmodi prelatis, com', baron', et aliis diem prefixerat, provis. est, et concorditer concessum (4), *quod dicti prelati, com', baron', et alii, hujusmodi libertatibus utantur* (3) *in forma brevis subscripti* (5):

THE year of our Lord M.CC. LXXVIII. the sixth year of the reign of king Edward, at Gloucester, in the month of August, the king himself providing for the wealth of his realm, and the more full ministration of justice, as to the office of a king belongeth (the more discreet men of the realm, as well of high as of low degree, being called thither) it is provided and ordained, That whereas the realm of England in divers cases, as well upon liberties as otherwise, wherein the law failed, to avoid the grievous dammages and innumerable disherisons that the default of the law did bring in, had need of divers helps of new laws, and certain new provisions, these provisions, statutes, and ordinances underwritten shall from henceforth be straitly and inviolably observed of all the inhabitants of his realm. And whereas prelates, earls, barons, and other of our realm, that claim to have divers liberties, which to examine and judge, the king hath prefixed a day to such prelates, earls, barons, and other; it is provided and likewise agreed, that the said prelates, earls, barons, and other shall use such manner of liberties, after the form of the writ here following:

Rex vic' salutem. Cum nuper in parliamento nostro apud Westmonasterium (6), *per nos et consilium nostrum provisum sit et proclamatum* (7), *quod prelati, comites, barones, et alii de regno nostro, qui diversas libertates per chartas progenitorum nostrorum regum Angliæ habere clamant, ad quas examinandas et judicandas diem præfixerimus in eodem parliamento, libertatibus illis taliter uterentur, quod nihil sibi per usurpationem seu occupationem accrescerent, nec aliquid super nos occuparent, tibi precipimus, quod omnes illos de comitatu tuo libertatibus suis quibus hucusque rationabiliter usi sunt* (8) *uti et gaudere*

gaudere permittas in forma prædicta, usque ad proximum adventum nostrum per comitatum prædictum, vel usque ad proximum adventum justiciariorum itinerantium (9) *ad omnia placita in comitatu, vel donec aliud inde præceperimus: salvo semper jure nostro cum inde loqui voluerimus. Teste, &c.*

Eodem modo et in eadem forma dirigantur brevia vic' et aliis ballivis pro quolibet petente, et mutetur forma secundum diversitatem libertatis, qua quis habere clamat, sic:

In like manner and in the same form writs shall be directed to sheriffs and other bailiffs for every demandant, and the form shall be changed after the diversity of the liberty which any man claimeth to have, in this wise:

Rex vic' salutem. Præcipimus tibi, quod per totam ballivam tuam, videlicet, tam in civitatibus, quam in burgis, et aliis villis mercatoriis, et alibi, publice proclamari facias, quod omnes illi qui aliquas libertates per chartas progenitorum nostrorum regum Angliæ, vel alio modo, habere clamant, sint coram justiciariis nostris ad primam assisam, ad ostendendum cujusmodi libertates habere clamant, et quo warranto, et tu ipse sis ibidem personaliter una cum ballivis et ministris tuis, ad certificandum ipsos justiciarios nostros super his et aliis negociis illud tangentibus.

Ista clausula de libertatibus que sic incipit. Precipimus tibi, quod publice proclamari fac', &c. ponitur in brevi de communi summ' itin' justic', et habeat premunitionem quadraginta dierum (10) *sicut communis summonitio habet: ita quod si pars aliqua, q. clamat habere libertatem, fuerit coram rege, non ponatur in defalta coram aliquibus justiciariis in suis itineribus, eo quod rex de gratia sua speciali concessit conservare partem illam indemnem, quo ad illam ordinationem. Et si pars illa sit in placito super hujusmodi libertatibus coram domino pari justic' predictorum, iidem justic', coram quibus pars illa sit in placito, conservabunt eam indemnem coram aliis justiciariis, et rex etiam coram ipso, dum tamen constiterit per justiciarios quod sic fuerit in placito coram ipsis, sicut predictum est. Et si pars predicta fuerit coram rege, ita quod ad diem coram justic' predictis in itineribus suis esse non possit, rex hujusmodi partem indemnem conservabit coram justiciariis predictis in itineribus suis ad diem illum quo fuerit coram rege. Et si ad diem illum non venerit,*

This clause of liberties, that beginneth in this wise, *Præcipimus tibi, quod publice proclamari facias, &c.* is put in the writ of common summons of the justices in eyre, and shall have a premonition by the space of forty days, as the common summons hath; so that if any party that claimeth to have a liberty, be before the king, he shall not be in default before any justices in their circuits; for the king of his special grace hath granted, that he will save that party harmless as concerning that ordinance. And if the same party be impleaded upon such manner of liberties before one or two of the foresaid justices, the same justices, before whom the party is impleaded, shall save him harmless before the other justices; and so shall the king also before him, when it shall appear by the justices, that so it was in plea before them as is aforesaid. And if the foresaid party be afore the king, so that he cannot be the same day afore the said justices in their circuits, the king shall save that party harmless before

nerit, tunc libertates ille nomine districtionis capiantur in manum domini regis per vic' loci: ita quod eis non utantur, donec venerint coram justiciariis respons. Et cum per districtionem venerint, replegientur libertates suæ, si eas petent: quibus replegiatis statim respondeant ad formam brevis predicti. Et si forte exceperint, quod non tenentur sine brevi originali inde respondere (11) *tunc si quoquo modo constare possit, quod ipsi de facto suo proprio aliquas libertates usurpaverint, vel occupuverint super regem, vel predecessores suos, dicatur eis quod statim respondeant sine brevi, et ulterius recipiant judicium, prout curia domini regis consideraverit. Et si ulterius dicant, quod antecessores sui inde obierint seisiti, statim audiantur, et statim veritas inquiratur* (12), *et secundum hoc ad judicium procedatur. Et si constiterit quod antecessores sui inde obierint seisiti, tunc habeat rex brevi originale de cancellaria sub hac forma:*

before the foresaid justices in their circuits for the day, whereas he was before the king. And if he do not come in at the same day, then those liberties shall be taken into the king's hands in name of distress, by the sheriff of the place, so that they shall not use them until they come to answer before the justices; and when they do come in by distress, their liberties shall be replevised (if they demand them) in the which replevins they shall answer immediately after the form of the writ aforesaid; and if percase they will challenge, and say that they are not bounden to answer thereunto without an original writ, then if it may appear by any mean, that they have usurped or occupied any liberties upon the king, or his predecessors, of their own head or presumption, they shall be commanded to answer incontinent without writ, and moreover they shall have such judgement as the court of our lord the king will award; and if they will say further, that their ancestors died seised thereof, they shall be heard, and the truth shall be inquired incontinent, and according to that judgement shall be given; and if it appear that their ancestors died seised thereof, then the king shall award an original out of the chancery in this form:

Rex vic' salutem. Sum' per bonos summonitores talem, quod sit coram nobis apud talem locum in proximo adventu nostro in comitatum prædictum vel coram justiciariis nostris ad primam assisam, cum in partes illas venerint, ostensurus quo warranto tenet visum francipleg' in manerio suo de N. vel sic, quo warranto tenet hundredum de S. in comitatu prædicto; vel, quo warranto clamat habere tholonium pro se et hæredibus suis per totum regnum nostrum; et habeas ibi hoc breve. Teste, &c.

Et si ad diem illum venerint, respondeant replicetur et triplicetur. Et si non venerint, nec esson' fuerint coram rege, et rex ulterius moretur in comitatu illo, precipiatur vic', quod faciat eos venire ad quartum diem.

And if they come in at the same day, they shall answer, and replication and rejoinder shall be made; and if they do not come, nor be essoined before the king, and the king do tarry longer in the same shire, the sheriff

diem. Quo die si non venerint, et rex in com' illo extiterit, fiat sicut in itiner' justic' (13). Et si rex a com' illo recesserit, adjornentur ad bres dies, et habeant dilationes competentes, juxta discretionem justic', sicut in actionibus personalibus. Etiam justic' itinerantes in itineribus suis faciant secundum ordinationem predictam, et secundum quod hujusmodi placita deduci debent in itineribus suis. De querimoniis factis et faciend' de ballivis regis et aliorum, fiat secundum ordinationem prius inde factam (14) et secundum inquisitiones prius inde captas: et ponatur clausula subscripta in brevi de communi summ' itiner' justic' ad communia placita directo vic', &c. quod tale est:

sheriff shall be commanded to cause them to appear the fourth day; at which day if they come not, and the king be in the same shire, such order shall be taken as in the circuit of justices; and if the king depart from the same shire, they shall be adjourned unto short days, and shall have reasonable delays according to the discretion of the justices, as it is used in personal actions. Also the justices in eyre in their circuits shall do according to the foresaid ordinance, and according as such manner of pleas ought to be ordered in the circuit. Concerning complaints made and to be made of the king's bailiffs, and of other, it shall be done according to the ordinance made before thereupon, and according to the inquests taken thereupon heretofore; and the clause subscribed shall be put in a writ of common summons in the circuit of the justices assigned to common pleas directed to the sheriff, &c. and that shall be such:

Rex vic' salutem. Præcipimus tibi, quod publice proclamari facias, quod omnes conquerentes, seu conqueri volentes, tam de ministris et aliis ballivis nostris quibuscunque, quam de ministris et ballivis aliorum quorumcunque, et aliis, veniant coram justiciariis nostris ad primam assisam, ad quascunque querimonias suas ibidem ostendendas, et competentes emendas, inde recipiendas secundum legem et consuetudinem regni nostri, et juxta ordinationem nostram per nos inde factam, et juxta tenorem statutorum nostrorum, et juxta articulos eisdem justiciariis nostris inde traditos (15), prout predicti justiciarii tibi scire faciant ex parte nostra. Teste meipso, &c. decimo die Decembris, anno regni nostri xxx.

(1) *L'an du grace*, 1267.] This should be 1278. for that was *anno* 6 E. 1. this parliament being holden in August, *anno* 6 E. 1. for 1267. was in 51 H. 3. Vet. Mag.Chart. fol. 130.

This chapter concerning liberties and franchises, and the *quo warranto* (and intituled *Statutum de quo warranto)* hath been supposed by many to be enacted in Latin, *anno* 30 E. 1. and therefore some have omitted to insert it in the 6. yeare; but it is utterly mistaken: for the king in the 30. yeare did publish and proclaime this act under the great seale, and doth recite it to be made *anno Dom.* 1278. and in the 6. yeare of his raigne. *Vide* 14 E. 1. *Inter original' de anno* 14 E. 1. *Breve de libertatibus allocandis*, and there is another statute made in 18 E. 1. called *Statutum de quo warranto novum*, so called, in respect of this former statute. Lib. 9 fol. 28. In the case of Strata Marcella. [280]

And besides, the statute in French differeth from the recitall thereof in 30 E. 1. which, for that it agreeth with the record, we will follow it when we come to the body of the act.

(2) *Pur amendement de son realme, & pluis plenier exhibition de droit.*] Which by the said proclamation in 30 E. 1. is rendred thus, *Ad regni sui Angliæ meliorationem, et exhibitionem justiciæ pleniorem:* two excellent ends of a parliament, *regni melioratio*, that is for the common good of the kingdome, the parliament being *commune concilium*, and *exhibitio justiciæ plenior*, for nothing is more glorious, and necessary, then full execution of justice.

And it is added, *Prout regalis officii exposcit utilitas*; and accordingly at this parliament many profitable and just laws were made, as one speaking of this parliament saith truly, *In quo quædam de regni statu decreta sunt, quæ nunc ut jura, et æquitate plena maxime usurpantur.* And that I may speak once for all, it is worthy of observation that the statutes made in this noble kings time are so agreeable to common right and equity, as few or none of them have been abrogated, but being founded upon these two pillars (the amendment of the kingdome, and the due execution of justice) remaine and continue as just and constant laws to this day.

Pol. Virgil.

Vide Vet. Magna Charta, fo. 130. Stat. de Quo Warranto. Pol. Virgil.

(3) *Hujusmodi libertatibus utantur,* &c.] For the better understanding of this act it shall be necessary out of history to shew the cause of the making hereof.

The truth is, that the king wanting money, there were some *innovatores* in those dayes, that perswaded the king, that few or none of the nobility, clergy, or commonalty, that had franchises of the graunts of the kings predecessors, had right to them for that they had no charter to shew for the same, for that in troth most of their charters either by length of time, or injury of wars and insurrections, or by casualty were either consumed, or lost: whereupon (as commonly new inventions have new wayes) it was openly proclaimed, that every man, that held those liberties, or other possessions by graunt from any of the kings progenitors, should before certain selected persons thereunto appointed shew, *quo jure, quove nomine ill' retinerent, &c.* whereupon many that had long continued in quiet possession, were taken into the kings hands, *Eo quod nulla tabella constarent:* Hereof the story saith, *Visum est omnibus edictum ejusmodi post homines natos longe acerbissimum: qui fremitus hominum?. quam irati animi? quanto in odio princeps esse repente cœpit?*

Mag. Charta. cap. 1. 9. 38.

The good king understanding hereof, and finding himselfe abused by ill counsell, and considering the statute of Magna Charta, at the parliament holden in the end of his fourth yeare by proclamation, and at the petition of the lords and of the commons now at this parliament, by authority of parliament provideth remedy, as hereafter you shall heare: this is fully agreed upon in all our histories, onely the time in some of them (as oftentimes in other cases it falleth out) is mistaken, which by this act shall be rectified according to true chronologie.

(4) *Provisum est et concorditer concessum.*] It was rightly said *concorditer concessum,* for that the said innovation was like to have beene a cause of great discord between the king and the better sort of his subjects.

(5) *Quod*

(5) *Quod dicti prælati, comites, barones, et alii hujusmodi libertatibus utantur in forma brevis subscripti.*] This * forme of a writ is more satisfactory, then any other forme is, and this was the auncient use.

(6) *Cum nuper in parliamento nostro apud Westm'.*] That is, in the last parliament holden after Michaelmas, towards the end of the fourth yeare of his raigne, and therefore the great grievances abovesaid must be before that parliament, for the cure was after the disease, and the remedy after the grievance.

(7) *Provisum sit et proclamatum.*] But this was never (that I can finde) recorded: now by this act it is provided that a writ shall be graunted.

(8) *Quibus hucusque rationabiliter usi sunt.*] See the Register 162, 163. *De libertatibus allocandis*, & F. N. B. 229, 230.

(9) *Usque ad adventum nostrum per comitatum prædictum, vel usque proximum adventum justiciariorum itinerantium*, &c.] That is, untill the court of kings bench came thither, or the next comming of the justices in eyre: so all men should quietly enjoy their franchises, which they had reasonably used, untill the court of kings bench, or untill the justices in eyre came into that county: here it is to be observed, that this good king and his councell in parliament referred the party grieved to a legall proceeding, which implieth, that a contrary course was holden before. But you will demand, What remedy was this for him, that could not produce his charter, to be left to the law? I answer, that this was a full and perfect remedy according to justice and right; for the better apprehension whereof these distinctions are to be observed: First, these franchises intended by this act be of two sorts, the one may be claimed by usage and prescription, as wreck of the sea, waife, stray, faires, markets, and the like, which are gained by usage, and may become due without matter of record: and felons goods, outlawes goods, and the like, which grow not due but by matter of record, and therefore cannot be claimed by usage in *paiis*, but by charter: and yet all these at the first were derived from the crowne.

8 E. 3. 18. 17 E. 3. 11. 26 Ass. 24. 30 Ass. 31. 34 Ass. 14. 38 Ass. 1. 1 H. 4. 3. 12 H. 4. 23. 8 H. 6. 8. 2 E. 4. 22. 7 H. 6. 33. 9 H. 7. 12. 10 H. 7. 14. 16 H. 7. 16. 20 H. 7. 7. Kelwey 189, 190. 8 H. 8.

Secondly, *Judicis officium est, ut res, ita tempora rerum quærere*; all these were graunted either before the time of memory, or after the time of memory: if before the time of memory, then for the former sort, such as might be claimed by prescription, the party grieved might prescribe, and by law he ought to be relieved. And for such as lay in point of charter graunted before time of memory, the party grieved had two remedies, either by allowance, or confirmation; by allowance in the kings bench, or before the justices in eyre, and in some case before the justices of the court of common pleas, and in the exchequer; or by confirmation of the king under the great seale: and these were sufficient for him without shewing the charter, and the equity of the law herein was notable, for that no charter before time of memory was pleadable by law.

If those franchises either of the one sort or other were graunted within memory, yet if the same had been allowed, as is aforesaid, the same might also be claimed by force of the charter and allowance, without shewing the charter, because it had been adjudged and allowed of record. And it is to be knowne that all franchises, which any man had either by prescription or by charter, ought to be

18 H. 6. prescript. 45. 2 E. 3. 29. 8 H. 8. Kelwey 189. Stat. de 18 E. 1. De quo warranto novum. Lib. 9. fo. 29. in case de Strat' Marcella.

be claimed before justices in eyre, or else for non-claime the same might bee lost, as hereafter shall bee said: so as the remedy provided by this act was plenary and perfect to give reliefe to them that right had.

[282] 34 Ass. pl. 14. 40 Ass. 21. 6 E. 3. 54, 55. 7 E. 3. 40, 41. 18 E. 3. Conus. 39. 12 H. 4. 12. 14 H. 6. 12. 33 H. 6. 22. 35 H. 6. 54. 9 H. 7. 11. 10 H. 6. 13. 16 H. 7. 9. * Regist. 158. 5 E. 3 50, 51. 6 E. 3. 18. 20 H. 6. 34. 34 H. 6. 36. Dier, 8 El. 245. a 3 E. 6. c. 4. 13 El. ca. 6. lib. 5. fo. 52, 53. Pages case.

To this for the time may be added, that ancient charters, whether they be before time of memory, or after, ought to be construed, as the law was taken when the charter was made, and according to ancient allowance. * Now what the time of memory is, see the first part of the Institutes, sect. 170.

[a] But now by the statutes of 3 E. 6. and 13 Eliz. there is further remedy given: for albeit the charters or letter patents be lost, yet the exemplification or *constat* of the roll may be shewed forth, &c. And when any claimed before the justices in eyre any franchises by an ancient charter, though it had expresse words for the franchises claimed; or if the words were generall, and a continual possession pleaded of the franchises claimed, or if the claim was by old and obscure words, and the party in pleading, expounding them to the court, and averring continuall possession according to that exposition; the entry was ever *Inquiratur super possessionem et usum, &c.* which I have observed in divers records of those eyres, agreeable to that old rule, *Optimus interpres rerum usus.*

(10) *Habeant præmunitionem per* 40. *dies.*] This was by writ of the common summons of the eyre, by the space of 40 dayes before the sitting of the justices in eyre.

Now leaving all that is evident, and needeth no exposition, let us come to the next that is worthy of observation.

Bract. li. 1. fo. 5. & 171. 6 E. 3. 50. 22 E. 3. 3. 24 E. 3. 1. 23. 43 E. 3. 22. 11 H. 4. 86. 9 H. 6. 58. * Magna Charta. cap. 29. 25 E. 3. cap. 4. Stat. 5. 28 E. 3. ca. 3. 42 E. 3. ca. 3. Stat. de 18 E. 1. de quo war' nov. 6 E. 35. 8 E. 3. 10, 11. 16 E. 4. 6. 3 H. 7. 15. Stanf. Prærog. 74. Pasch. 9 E. 1. Coram rege Rot. 17. Sussex.

(11) *Et si forte exceperint quod non tenentur sine brevi originali respondere.*] Here is an ancient maxime in the law implyed, that regularly no man ought to answer for his freehold, franchises, or other thing without originall writ *secundum legem terræ*; and that the * statutes to that end provided are but declarations of the ancient common law, as here it is to be seen in case of franchises in the kings own case.

(12) *Et si ulterius dicunt quod antecessores sui inde obierint seisiti, statim audiantur, et statim veritas inquiratur,* &c.] By this it appeareth that a descent of franchises doth put the king to his writ of *quo warranto*, which writ is here expressed; and note that the *quo warranto* is in nature of the kings writ of right for franchises and liberties, wherein judgement finall shall be given either against the king for the point adjudged, or for the king; and the *salvo jure* for the king serveth for any other title then that which was adjudged; and therefore William de Penbrugge the kings attorney, for prosecuting of a *quo warranto* against the abbot of Fischamp for franches within the mannour of Steynings *sine præcepto*, was committed to the gaole.

2 E. 3. 29. 6 E. 3. 5. 15 E. 4. 6, 7.

(13) *Et si non venerint, &c. præcipiatur vicecom' quod faciat eos venire, &c. quo die si non venerint, &c. fiat sicut in itinere justiciariorum.*] If before the justice in eyre the party came not, the franchise should be seised into the kings hands *nomine districtionis*, which the party in the same eyre might replevy; but if he did not replevy them while the eyre sate in that county, the franchises were lost and forfeited for ever.

Therefore if the party now upon the *venire facias* (which this act doth give) come not while the eyre sit in that county, the franchises be lost for ever.

And so it is in the kings bench, if the party come not in upon the *venire facias* during that term, and replevy his franchises, they be lost for ever. And therefore we concurre not with that chiefe justice that said, that non-claim of liberties before justices in eyre lost the liberties, for that (saith he) was but of the kings grace to grant a replevy of them, and not of right; for this opinion is against the authority of our books, and the continuall practice before the justices in eyre. Pl. Com. 372. in le Signior Zouches case. [283]

See the statutes of 18 E. 1. *De quo warranto novum*, and *De tallagio non concedendo.*

(14) *De querimoniis factis et faciendis de ballivis regis et aliorum fiat secundum ordinationem prius inde factam.*] That is, according to the articles of the justices in eyre called *capitula itineris* collected and authorised amongst other things, as here it appeareth, by ordinance of parliament, and entred into the parliament roll, which you may see in old Magna Charta, fol. 150, 151, &c.

(15) *Juxta articulos eisdem justic' nostris tradit'.*] The French saith, *Solonque les articles que le roy lour ad livere.* These articles were delivered by the king to the justices in eyre to be enquired of, heard, and determined by them through all the counties of England, which afterwards were encreased, as by the same may appear.

CAP. I.

COME avant ces heures damages ne fueront agardes en assises de novel disseisin forsque tantsolement vers les disseisors: purview est, que si les disseisors aliont les tenements (1), & neient dont les damages puissent estre levies (2), que ceux a que maines ceux tenements deviendront, soient charges des dammages, issint que chescun respoign' de son temps (3). Purview est ensement, que le disseisee recover' damages en briefe dentre foundue sur disseisin, vers celuy que est trove tenant apres le disseisor (4). Purview est ensement, que la ou avant ces heures damages ne fueront agardes en plee de mortdancestor (6), forsque en case (5) ou tenements fueront recoveres devers chiefes seigniors (7) [ceo fuist per statut' Marlbr. cap. 16.] que desormes damages soient agardes en touts cases (8), ou home recover per assise de mortdancestor, sicome est avantdit en assise de novel disseisin. Et in mesme le

WHEREAS heretofore damages were not awarded in assises of novel disseisin, but only against the disseisors: it is provided, that if the disseisors do aliene the lands, and have not whereof there may be damages levied, that they to whose hand such tenements shall come, shall be charged with the damages, so that every one shall answer for his time. It is provided also, that the disseisee shall recover damages in a writ of entry, upon novel disseisin against him that is found tenant after the disseisor. It is provided also, that where before this time damages were not awarded in a plea of mortdauncestor (but in case where the land was recovered against the chief lord) that from henceforth damages shall be awarded in all cases where a man recovereth by assise of mortdauncestor, as before is said in assise of novel disseisin: and likewise damages shall be recovered in

le maner recover' home damages en briefe de coſinage, ayel, & beſayel (9). *Et la ou avant ces heures damages ne fueront taxes, forſque a le value des iſſues de la terre: purview eſt, que le demandant puit recover vers le tenant les coſtages de ſon briefe purchaſe* (11), *enſemblement oveſque les damages* (12) *avantdits* (10.) *Et tout ceo ſoit tenus en touts caſes, ou home recover damages* (13). *Et ſoit deſormes cheſcun tenus a render damages, la ou home recover vers luy de ſa intruſion demeſne, ou de ſon fait demeſne* (14).

in writs of coſinage, aiel, and beſaiel. And whereas before time damages were not taxed, but to the value of the iſſues of the land; it is provided, that the demandant may recover againſt the tenant the coſts of his writ purchaſed, together with the damages aboveſaid. And this act ſhall hold place in all caſes where the party is to recover damages. And every perſon from henceforth ſhall be compelled to render damages, where the land is recovered againſt him upon his own intruſion, or his own act.

(Fitz. Damage, 14. 43. 66. 68. 82. 95. 101, 102. 104. 108. 110. 121. 123. 127. 129. Hob. 95. Godbolt, 112. 1. Inſt. 10. 116. Dyer, f. 370. Fitz. damage, 6. 19. 97.)

[284] Before this ſtatute no damages were recovered in aſſiſe of novel
See the firſt part of the Inſtitutes, 685. 37 H. 6. 35. diſſeiſin (which then was *frequens et feſtinum rem dium)* but onely againſt the diſſeiſor, and not againſt the tenant that came to the lands or tenements after the diſſeiſin, for no damages could be recovered by the common law, but againſt the wrong doer by him, to whom the wrong was done.

Now the miſchief was, that many times the diſſeiſor was inſufficient, and not able to ſatiſfie the damages, and by that means the diſſeiſee recovered damages in ſhew againſt the diſſeiſor (who was the wrong doer to him) but had not the effect thereof; now this branch doth remedy this miſchief, as by the ſame it appeareth.

(1) *Alienont les tenements.*] The letter of this law extendeth onely to them, that came in by title, as by feoffment, or fine after the diſſeiſin; but by equity it extendeth to them, that came in by wrong, and to them alſo, whoſe eſtate was before the diſſeiſin; for example, if the diſſeiſor were diſſeiſed, the ſecond diſſeiſor is with-
14 H. 7. 28. per Wood. in this ſtatute, for if he that comes in by title ſhall be within the remedy of this law, *à fortiori,* he that comes in by wrong; and ſo it is of all others, that come in under the diſſeiſor, though it be not by alienation.

10 Aſſ. p. 3. 10 E. 3. 24. Alſo if the lord diſtraineth for his rent, and a ſtranger without the privity of the tenant maketh reſcous, the ſtranger is onely the diſſeiſor, and though the tenant claim not under him, but his eſtate is before, &c. yet in aſſiſe againſt the diſſeiſor and the tenant, if the diſſeiſor be found inſufficient, the plaintife by force of this ſtatute ſhall recover damages againſt them both.

And yet in ſome caſes the tenant that claimeth under the diſſeiſor ſhall not for the inſufficiencie of the diſſeiſor be anſwerable
22 Aſſ. 28. to yeeld damages by this ſtatute; as if the diſſeiſor of lands holden in *capite* alien the ſame to another, the alienee dyeth, his heir within age, upon office found the king committeth the cuſtody to A. who taketh the whole profits, the diſſeiſor is inſufficient, the heir within age is no tenant within this ſtatute, for that he never did,

nor could take any profit: but if the disseisor alien to an infant, who taketh the profits, he is a tenant within this statute; or if the infant coming in as heir had been out of ward, and had taken the profits, he had been a tenant within this statute.

If the disseisor infeoffe the villein of the disseisee and a stranger, and the disseisor is insufficient, in this case either the disseisee must lose his damages, or infranchise his villein. 48 E. 3. 17.

No lessee for yeers, or tenant by statute staple, or merchant, or the like, that have but a chattell, shall be accounted a mean occupier within this statute, but he that hath the inheritance or free-hold at the least; otherwise he is not said to be a tenant of the land; and so much is implyed in this word alien, which cannot be intended of a lessee for yeers, &c. where he, that bringeth the assise, hath right to the inheritance or free-hold: but where tenant by statute merchant, or staple, &c. brings an assise, there lessee for yeers, or tenant by statute merchant, &c. may be a mean occupier, because the plaintife in the assise hath right but to a chattell.

(2) *Et nient dont les damages poient estre levies.*] Hereupon do follow three conclusions in law: 1. That if the disseisor be sufficient to yeeld the whole damages, he is solely to be charged therewith; for then this statute extendeth not to the tenant; and, as it appeareth by the preamble, he was not answerable by the common law.

The 2. conclusion is, that for the insufficiencie of the disseisor the tenant shall answer the damages by this act.

The 3. conclusion is, that if the disseisor be able to yeeld part, and not the whole damages, both shall be charged, and therefore judgement is ever given as well against the disseisor (though he be found insufficient) as against the tenant generally.

(3) *Chescum respondra pur son temps.*] The ground hereof is, *Quod bonæ fidei possessor in id tantum, quod ad se pervenerit, tenetur.* [285]

Hereupon seven conclusions are grounded: 16 E. 3. Damages, 82.

1. Albeit the mean occupiers are neither disseisors nor tenants, yet unlesse they be named in the assise, no judgement can be given against them, neither can they be charged for the time they take the profit.

2. Though they be named, yet, as hath been said, the disseisor must be found by the assise to be insufficient, and the mean occupiers must be found to take the profits; for if they be omitted, and none but the disseisor and tenant named, and the disseisor is found insufficient, and no further enquired of, the tenant shall be charged for the whole.

3. If the assise be brought against the disseisor and the tenant, and it is found by the assise, that the disseisor is insufficient, and that the disseisor infeoffed A. who infeoffed B. who infeoffed the tenant, and that A. had it one yeer, and B. half a yeer, and the tenant two yeers; upon this speciall finding, the tenant shall answer damages but for his time, for *chescun respondra pur son temps,* and the plaintife hath lost his damages against A. and B. for that they were not named in the writ. 35 Ass. 5.

4. If the disseisor, A. and B. and the tenant in the case before be all named, and the disseisor, A. and B. are all found insufficient, the tenant shall answer for the whole; for although the letter of this law is, where the disseisors have nothing, &c. yet these words, 35 Ass. p. 5.

chescun respondra, &c. do imply (if they have sufficient) for otherwise they cannot answer, that is, they cannot satisfy; for in that sense [answer] is here taken.

5. It shall never be inquired of the tenants insufficiencie, for against the disseisor and him must the assise of necessity be brought.

18 E. 2. tit. Execution, 14. 6 Upon these words, *chescun respondra pur son temps*, severall judgements shall not be given, but one judgement is to be given intirely against all, and so was it ever used since this statute; but the sherife upon the execution may use such indifferencie, as justice requireth.

18 E. 2. ubi sup. And it is said, that if the assise be brought against the disseisor and the tenant, and judgement given for the plaintife, and a writ issueth to the sherife, and he retourns, that the disseisor is insufficient, the plaintife shall have proces to levie it of the tenant.

West. 1. cap. 24. 34 E. 1. de plead de Io nt. 22 Ass. 1. 9 H. 6. 1, 2. 1 H. 4. ca. 8. 8 H. 6. cap. *Vide* the statutes of Westm. 1. 34 E. 1, 1 H. 4. & 8 H. 6. &c. where double and treble damages are given in assise, there also every mean tenant, that came in to be tenant of the free-hold under the disseisor, shall for the insufficiencie of the disseisor answer every one for his time the treble or double damages.

3 E. 6. cap. 3. 7. Lastly, this giveth no damages where none was recoverable in the assise at the common law, but giveth damages against the tenant for the insufficiencie of the disseisor, as hath been said.

As if he in the reversion upon a term for yeers, or tenant by statute staple, &c. be disseised, he shall have an assise to recover the state of the land, but shall recover no damages for the profits of the lands, because they belonged not to him.

12 E. 4. fol. 1. 22 Ass. p. 1. If the disseisor committed the disseisin with force, and infeoffeth A. who infeoffeth B. who infeoffeth C. an assise is brought against them all, and treble damages for the insufficiencie of the disseisor shall be levyed upon all, according to this act *chescun respondra pur son temps*, that is, what damages should be recovered against the disseisor, if he were sufficient, shall be recovered for his insufficiencie against the mean occupiers and the tenant, and for insufficiencie of the mean occupiers, against the tenant onely.

[286] (4) *Purview est ensement, que le disseisee recovera damages en briefe dentre foundue sur disseisin vers celuy que est trove tenant apres le disseisor.*] Regularly in personall and mixt actions damages were to be recovered at the common law, but in reall actions no damages were to be recovered at the common law, because the court could not give the demandant that which he demanded not, and the demandant in reall actions demanded no damages, neither by writ, nor count; *judex non reddit pluis, quam quod petens ipse requirit*, and it is a maxime in law, *que droit ne done pluis que soit demaunde*; and therefore in reall actions, where damages are given by this act, the demandant shall recover damages *pendente brevi*, because the old form of the count remaineth. The words of the act are, *Vers celuy que est trove tenant*; he may be tenant by title, by wrong, or by act in law; and of these in order.

Regula. 33 H. 6. 47. 7 E. 4. 5. 16 H. 7. 5, &c. See li. 10. fo. 117. Pilfords case.

42 E. 3. 7. 39 E. 3. Dam. 66. 20 E. 3. ib. 101. 22 E. 3. 2. 12 E. 3. Dam. 95. 3 E. 3. ib. 120. 19 E. 3. ibid. 99. If the disseisor make a feoffment in fee, and the disseisee dyeth, the heir of the disseisee shall not recover damages by this act against the alienee; for this branch of the act provideth for the disseisee, and not for his heirs.

But

'* But if a man be disseised, and the disseisee dye, his heir shall recover damages against the disseisor, but not by this branch, but by a latter branch of this act, *viz. Et soit desormes chescun tenus a render damages la ou home recover vers luy de say intrusion demesne, ou de son tort demesne:* and by this distinction the books that seemed *prima facie* to differ are well reconciled; but by the intention of this law, the heir in his writ of entry against the disseisor shall recover damages but from the death of his ancestor. *4 E. 3. 39. 40. 36. 23 Eliz. Dier, 320. 22 E. 3. 2.

The disseisee shall recover damages by this act in a writ of entry *sur disseisin* in the *post*: as if the tenant cometh to the land by disseisin, intrusion, or abatement, or when by alienation it is out of the degrees; for the words be, *Vers celuy que est trove tenant apres le disseisor,* within which words he that comes in the *post* is included. Note the writ of entry in the *post* is given by the statute of Marlebridge, *cap. ultimo*; for the disseisee was driven to his writ of right at the common law. 16 E. 3. Dam. 82. 8 E. 3. 23. 23 El. Dier, 320.

And in this second branch the tenant is onely charged with the whole damages, though there were divers mean tenants, for *chescun respondra pur son temps* is onely in the case of an assise upon the first branch; neither ought the writ of entry to be brought against any, but against him, that is the tenant of the land: but in some case another then the disseisee shall recover damages by this branch; as the successor of an abbot, but otherwise of bishops, or other sole secular bodies politique. 19 E. 3. Dam. 99. 3 E. 3. ib. 120. 39 E. 3. ib. 66. 26 Ass. p. 4.

If the tenant cometh to the land by act in law, which he cannot withstand, and where there is no act, or default in him; in that case he shall not be charged: as if the disseisor alien to A. and his heirs, and A. dyeth without heir, the law (that there may be a tenant to a strangers *præcipe*) doth cast the land upon the lord; in this case, if the lord doth not take any profits of the lands, in a writ of entry in the *post* brought against him for the land, the lord may plead the speciall matter, and how that he never took any profits of the lands, and so dicharge himself of the damages; for albeit he be a tenant of the land, yet is he no tenant against his will within the meaning of this law, because there is no wrong nor default in him.

But if the lord by escheat doth enter, and take the profits of the land, then shall he be charged as a tenant within this act, for albeit he could not withstand the escheat, which made him tenant in law, yet might he have refrained to take the profits, which in right belonged to the disseisee, but his rent or valuable services shall be recouped in damages.

And so it is in all respects, when the alienee of the disseisor dye seised, and the land descend to his heir, he may refrain from the taking of the profits, and plead the like plea, and discharge himself of the damages.

In like manner, if the disseisor make a deed of feoffment, by the which he infeoffeth A. and B. and maketh livery of seisin to A. in the name of both, B. never agreeing to the feoffment, nor taking any profit of the land, A. dyeth; in this case by the law the freehold and inheritance is vested in B. by survivor; and in a writ of entry in the *per* brought by the disseisee against B. he may, as is aforesaid, plead the speciall matter, and that he never agreed, nor took any profits, and discharge himselfe of the damages for the cause aforesaid. First part of the Institutes, sect. 685. [287]

Et

Regula. *Et sic in casibus consimilibus:* for *nemo punitur sine injuria, facto, seu defalta;* and *actus legis nemini est damnosus.*

The statute saith, *ce' que est trovetenant,* and yet if a writ of entry be brought against two joynt-tenants, and the one disclaime, and the other take the whole tenancy upon him, and plead in barre, and it is found against him, the demandant shall recover damages for the whole against him, because he tooke upon him the whole tenancy.

8 H. 4. 5. 29 E. 3. 49. 8 E. 3. 61. 9 E. 3. 30. 25 E. 3. 51. 30 E. 3. 6. A disseisor infeoffeth A. which infeoffeth B. the disseisee brings a writ of entry in the *per* and *cui* against B. which vowcheth A. who pleads and loseth; judgement for the damages shall be given against the vowchee, for he is found tenant in law.

(5) *Purview est ensement que lou avant ceux heures damages ne fuer' agardes en plea de mordauncester forsque en case,* &c.] This plea of mordaunc', and the other pleas hereafter in this act named are pleas reall, and auncestrel, and therefore no damages are recoverable (as hath been said) in them by the common law.

Lib. 6. cap. 3. Markals case. But yet it is to be observed once for all, that these actions in this act named, are actions *auncestrel possessarie,* and not actions *auncestrel droiturel.*

Glan. li. 13. c. 2. 3, 4, &c. Bract. l. 3. fol. 282, 283. 253, 254. Brit. fo. 180. Fleta, l. 5. c. 1, 2, &c. (6) *De mordaunc'.*] Of this writ you shall reade plentifully in our auncient authors, and other books.

(7) *Recoveres de vers chiefe seigniors.*] This was by the statute of Marlebridge cap. 16.

In auncient time not onely the references, as here, were ever generall, but also the citing of authorities in law were in like manner; *est tenus in nostre livres.*

(8) *Damages soient agardes en touts cases,* &c.] This purview being generall must be taken in a particular sense, that is, in all cases in the mordaunc', as in the assise, having regard to the time of the damages, *viz.* from the wrong done, for in the mordaunc' the plaintiffe shall not recover damages against the meane occupiers for the insufficiency of the abator, as in the assise for the insufficiency of the disseisor; for in construction of generall references in acts of parliament, such reference must be made onely as may stand with reason and right: and therefore seeing the writ of mordaunc' must of right be brought against the tenant of the land onely, and not against the meane occupiers (as hath been said in the former clause concerning the writ of entry) the meane occupiers cannot be charged in the mordaunc', but the tenant shall be charged for the whole damages.

If a man hath issue two sonnes, and the father dieth seised of lands in fee simple, the eldest son dieth, the second son shall have an assise of mordauncester, and he shall make himselfe heire to his 3 E. 3. damag. 121. father, and he shall recover damages, not onely from such time as the right accrued unto him from the death of his brother, but from Doct. & Stud. lib. 2. cap. 12. the death of his father, because he hath not the right of this land as heire to his brother, but as heire to his father. More shall be said hereof when we come to speake of the writ of cosinage, &c.

9 E. 3. 30. In a mordaunc', if the tenant vowch, and the vowchee plead and loose, in this case the plaintiffe shall recover against the tenant the land, and the tenant in value against the vowchee, and the plain-

tiffe shall recover his damages against the vowchee. And by this act damages shall be recovered in a *nuper obiit*. 21 E. 3. 57. 28 E. 3. damag. 61. 13 E. 3. ibidem 97.

(9) *En mesme le maner recover' home damages en briefe de cosinage, aiel, et besaiel.*] In a writ of cosinage, of the seisin of the *tresaiel, de seisina tritavi, seu atavi, &c.* it is to be seene for what time the demandant shall recover damages by force of this act, and so of the writ of *besaiel, breve de proavo*, and of the writ of *aiel de avo*. For this writ see all the auncient authors ubi sup. 6 E. 3. 34. 7 E. 3. 46, &c.

And it is a rule upon this statute, that in none of these writs the demandant shall recover damages but from the death of his next immediate auncester, whose heir he is: as if there be grandfather, father, and son, the grandfather dieth seised, an estranger abate, the father dieth, the son in a writ of *aiel* must make his resort as son and heire of the father, son and heire of the grandfather, therefore he shall in that case recover damages, but from the death of his father, because he is his next immediate auncester, and from him the right descended: and so in the writ of *besaiel*, and *cosinage*; but in the case before, if the grand father had survived the father, the son shall recover damages from the death of his grandfather, because he is his immediate auncester, and the right immediately descended to him: *Et sic de cæteris*. 2 E. 3. 9. 3 E. 3. dam. 122. 17 E. 3. 45. 2 H. 4. 13. 2 E. 3. dam. 118.

If a man hath issue two daughters, and dieth seised of lands, an estranger abate, one of the daughters hath issue and dieth, the aunt and the niece shall joyne in an assise of mordaunc', and the aunt onely shall recover damages till the death of the sister, and both of them from her death, which standeth upon the reason aforesaid. 45 E. 3. 10. 35 H. 6. 23.

If there be grandfather, father, and daughter, the grandfather dieth seised, an estranger abate, the father dieth, his wife being *privement enseint* with a son, the son is borne, he shall recover damages in a writ of *aiel* from the death of the father, for now hee is immediate heire to the father.

(10) *Vers le tenant les costages de son briefe purchase en semblement ovesque les damages avandits.*] Before this statute at the common law no man recovered any costs of sute either in plea real, personall, or mixt: by this it may be collected that justice was good cheap of auncient times, for in king Alfreds time there were no writs of grace, but all writs remedialls were graunted freely, and Fleta saith, *Ne clerici superflua petant stipendia pro scriptura sua, constitutum est, quod tam clerici justiciar', quam cancellar' de solo denario pro scriptura unius brevis se teneant contentos.* This statute was the first that gave costs. Mirror, l. 5 § 1. Glanv. li. 1. ca. 32. Fleta, li. 2. c. 12. 14 H. 6. 13.

(11) *Costages de son briefe purchase.*] Here is expresse mention made but of the costs of his writ, but it extendeth to all the legall cost of the suit, but not to the costs and expences of his travell and losse of time, and therefore *costages* commeth of the verb *coster*, and that againe of the verb *constare*, for these *costages* must *constare* to the court to be legall costs and expences.

If a writ doth abate by the act of God, in a new writ by Journies accounts, he shall have costs for the first writ and the proceedings thereupon; but if the first writ be faulty in default of the demandant or plaintiffe, in the second writ the demandant or plaintiffe shall have no costs for such an insufficient or faulty writ. 9 E. 4. 6. 13 H. 4. Execution 118. 21 H. 6. 9 Livre de entres Rast. 382. Lib. 10. fol. 10. Jentlemans case.

(12) *Ensemblement ove les damages.*] For costs are in law so coupled together, as they are accounted parcell of the damages. And

And therefore if the plaintiffe in trespasse declare to the damages
13 H. 7. 16, 17. of twenty marks, and the jury give twenty marks for damages, and twenty marks for costs, yet shall the plaintiffe recover in all but twenty marks, for damages and costs must not exceed * the damages, which the plaintiffe demaunds by his count, and the entry reciting both the damages and costs, *Quæ damna in toto se attingunt ad, &c.*

In an action reall, personall, or mixt, where double or treble, &c. damages are given by any statute, it hath been controverted in books, whether the demandant or plaintiffe shall recover costs, and whether the same shall be also doubled or trebled; which doubt and variety of opinions hath grown in respect the right reason of the diversity of the law in those cases hath not been observed, which is, that whensoever any statute doth increase damages to the double or treble value, &c. where damages before were given, there the demandant or plaintiffe shall recover his double or treble damages and costs also, and the costs also as parcell of the damages shall be trebled.

22 H. 6. 57. 14 H. 6. 13. 19 H. 6. 6, 7. 32. 27 H. 6. 10. 12 E. 4. 1. F.N.B. 248. c.

But where damages double or treble are in an action newly given, where no damages were formerly recoverable, there the demandant or plaintiffe shall recover those damages onely, and no costs. For example, in an action upon the statute of forcible entry upon the statute of 8 H. 6. which giveth treble damages, in this case the plaintiffe shall recover his damages and his costs to the treble for that he should have recovered single damages at the common law, and the statute increased them to treble.

Dier 2 Eliz. 177. • But upon the statute of 1 & 2 Phil. & Mar. for chasing of distresses out of the hundred, &c. whereby 5. l. is given and treble damages, the plaintiffe shall recover no costs, because this action and penalty is newly given.

27 H. 6. 10. And so in the *quare impedit* no costs, for that no damages were given at the common law.

30 E. 3. 27. 5 E. 3. dam. 114. 2 H. 4. 17. 9 H. 6. 66. nota 14 H. 6. 13. Mich. 29 H. 6. in Communi Banc. Rot. 103. 5 E. 4. 7. 12 E. 4. 1.

In an action of waste against tenant for life, or yeares, the plaintiffe shall recover the place wasted, and treble damages given at this parliament, cap. 6. but no costs, because no action lay against them at the common law, but the action and damages are newly given: but against the gardein, or tenant in dower, &c. there the plaintiffe shall recover treble damages and costs also, for that an action lay against them at the common law, and for the waste damages should be recovered; and so are all the books, that seeme *prima facie* to be at variance, well reconciled.

(13) *Et tout ceo soit tenus en touts cases ou home recover damages.*] Before the making of this statute no demandant recovered damages in any reall action, but onely in a writ of dower, *unde nihil habet*, by the statute of Merton cap. 1.

This clause doth extend to give costs, where damages are given to any demandant or plaintiffe in any action by any statute made after
Regula. this parliament: *Ubi damna dantur, victus victori in expensis condemnari debet.*

(14) *Soit desormes chescun tenus a render damages, la ou home recover vers luy de son intrusion demesne, ou de son fait demesne.*] This is a generall and a beneficiall branch, which we have partly expounded before in our expositions upon the second branch of this chapter; generally this branch giveth damages to him that right hath and his

his heires against the intrudor, abator, disseisor, or other wrong doer himselfe.

And *de son fait demesne*, is interpreted *de son tort demesne*, of his owne wrong. And therefore if a coparcener refuse to make partition in a writ of partition against her, the plaintiffe shall not recover damages, for this writ is a writ of right in his nature, and she hath a right *per my et per tout* to take the profits. 33 E. 3. dam. 6. 28 E. 3. ibid. 61. 13 E. 3. ibid. 97. 4 E. 3. 39, 40. 21 E. 3. 57. 7 H. 6. 35, 36. 3 E. 3. fo. 48.

If a man make a lease for life, the lessee dieth, an estranger intrudes, the lessor or his heire shall have the writ of intrusion against the intrudor himselfe, and recover damages by this act, *Et sic de similibus*. [290]

And that I may observe it here once for all concerning these auncient statutes both of those that are past, and those that are to come, how necessary it is not onely to know the law, but also the roote and reason, out of which the law deriveth his life, *viz.* whether from the common law, or from some act of parliament, lest if he taketh it to spring from the common law it may lead him into error in like cases.

CAP. II.

SI enfant deins age soit tenus hors de son heritage apres la mort son pier, cosin, ayel, ou besayel (1), per que il covient, que il purchase briefe, et son adversary veigne en court et en respoignant alleage feoffement, ou auter chose (2) dit, per que justices agardent lenquest, la ou lenquest fuit delay jesque al age lenfant, cy passa ore lenquest auxy come il fuit de pleine age (3).

IF a child within age be holden from his heritage after the death of his father, cosin, grandfather, or great grandfather, whereby he is driven to his writ, and his adversary cometh into the court, and for his answer alledgeth a feoffment, or pleadeth some other thing, whereby the justices award an enquest, there whereas the enquest was deferred unto the full age of the infant, now the enquest shall pass as well as if he were of full age.

(1 Inst. 6. f. 3. Dyer, f. 104. 3 Bulstr. 137.)

First it is good to cleare this chapter, which is a very beneficiall law made for avoyding of delay, that great enemy to justice.

Justiciam non justicium vult juris amicus,
Justicium non justiciam vult juris inimicus.

For the very text of this law in two maine points hath been falsified or mistaken.

First of auncient time some manuscripts of this chapter before printing came to us were *apres le mort son cosin, aiel, ou besaiel*, omitting these words, *son pier*; which being shewed to the judges in 8 E. 3. they were of opinion that a writ of mordauncester was not within this law. And Fleta following that error rehearsing this chapter saith, *Apud Gloc' provisum fuit, si hæres infra ætatem* 8 E. 3. 23. 8 Ass. 12.

petat

See the books in 3 E. 2. age 133. 42 E. 3. 13. 18 E. 3. 23, &c.

petat seisinam consanguinei, avi sui, vel proavi, et excipitur contra eum, &c. omitting *patris sui.*

But in the print the former error is amended, and accordeth with our latter bookes.

And it is not to be thought, that the wisdome of the parliament would provide for the seisins of them that were so farre remote, as in the writ of besaiel and cosinage, and leave unprovided the seisin that was in the next auncester of all, as of the father, &c.

And therefore the rule is good, *Satius est petere fontes, quam sectari rivulos.*

The other error, and that continueth still in the print, was, the words of the record be, *per que les justices agardent le age,* and in stead of *le age,* it is in the print *lenquest,* which is *oppositum in subjecto,* for in the writ of aiel, besaiel, and cosinage, there could be no enquest awarded before an issue joyned, neither could any enquest in those writs enquire of circumstances (as in the assise of mord', or assise) but of the issue joyned onely, and this also may well be collected by our books.

[291]

18 E. 4. 23. 8 E. 3. 23. Dier 3 & 4 Ph. & Mar. 137. Li. 6. fo. 3. Markhalls case.

And these words next following, [*ou lenquest fuit delay jesque al age lenfant*] are to be referred to the mordancester onely, because in that writ there appeareth a jury the first day, as in the assise of *novel disseisin,* but so it is not in the writ of ayel, besaiel, or cosinage, unlesse you will take enquest for triall, and then the sense is, where triall is delayed untill the age of the infant, and then it may have reference to all the writs named in this chapter..

Now these clouds being removed, we shall more cleerly peruse the text.

Before the making of this act, albeit the ancestor dyed seised of the lands, so as a free-hold in law was cast upon the heir; if an estranger abated, in a mordauncester, ayel, besaiel, or cosinage, the tenant might have shewed, that the demandant was within age, and have prayed that the paroll might demurre untill the age of the heir, as he may do when the action is auncestrell droiturell, that is when the ancestor hath but a right, and no possession, that is, no free-hold and inheritance at his death, so as no free-hold and inheritance descend to the heir, but a bare right; and so note a diversity between an action auncestrell droiturell, and an action auncestrell possessary. But at the common law, if in a mordancester, ayel, besaiel, or cosinage, the tenant did plead a feoffment, or a release from a collaterall ancestor with warranty in barre, &c. there, lest the infant for want of intelligence might receive prejudice by tryall thereof during his infancie, the law in his favour at the first gave him the benefit of his age, which when it was used for delay to his prejudice, this act was made for his relief therein.

(1) *Apres le mort son pier, cousin, ayel, ou besaiel.*] After the death of his father. By this is necessarily implyed the assise of mordancester; and the case of the father is here put for an example, for it extendeth to the cases of the mother, brother, sister, uncle or aunt, nephew or neece, after the dying seised, of all which persons a writ of mordancester doth lye; for all the said cases are in equall mischiefe with the case of the father, and therefore are within the same remedy.

Bract. fol. 253, 254. Brit. f. 180. Flet. li. 2. cap. 1, 2, 3, &c.

3 E. 2. Age 133. 33 E. 3. Age 153. 8 E. 3. 9.

But in a formedon in the descender brought by an infant, if the feoffment of his ancestor be pleaded in barre with warranty and assets,

aſſets, or a collaterall warranty without aſſets, this caſe is not within this ſtatute for two cauſes; firſt, for that is an action aunceſtrell droiturell, for nothing deſcended but a right, and therefore had not any freehold and inheritance at the time of his death, and therefore out of the letter and meaning of this act. 2. The Formedon in the deſcender is in nature of his writ of right, for the iſſue in tail can have no writ of an higher nature, and therefore not within this ſtatute; for ſeeing this act gave the infant a tryall during his minority, it gave it him in ſuch actions as he might not be for cloſed of his right; but though he were barred in any of the ſaid actions during his minority, he might at his full age have recourſe to his writ of an higher nature, ſo as he ſhould not be remedileſſe, or any finall judgement given againſt him during his infancy.

42 E. 3. 13. 34 H. 6. 3, 4. 18 E. 4. 23. Dier 3 & 4 Ph. & Mar. 137. Lib. 2. fol. 3. Markhalls caſe.

By this it appeareth, that the writ of formedon in the reverter, or remainder, *Dum non fuit compos mentis, dum fuit infra ætatem, ſur cui in vita, in caſu proviſo, caſu conſimili,* and all actions of like nature are neither within the miſchief, nor within the letter or meaning of this act, for that none of them are actions aunceſtrel poſſeſſary, as hath been ſaid.

12 E. 2. Age 145. 8 E. 3. 36. 59. 3 E. 3. Age 72. 34 H. 6. 3, 4. Markhalls caſe. ubi ſupra.

(2) *Alledge feoffment ou auter choſe.*] A feoffment with warranty from the ſame anceſtor is a barre to the aſſiſe, and no barre in the aſſiſe of mordanceſter; and therefore this is to be intended of a feoffment of a collaterall anceſtor with warranty, or a releaſe with warranty from ſuch an anceſtor, or ſuch other matter, whereunto the infant during his minority could not anſwer, as hath been ſaid, at the common law: and the rule of Glanvile is good, *Generaliter verum eſt, quod de nullo placito tenetur reſpondere is, qui infra ætatem eſt, per quod poſſit exhæredari, nec ipſi minori ſuper recto reſpondebit donec plenam habuerit ætatem.* And that of Bracton, *Quod minor ante tempus agere non poteſt maxime in caſu proprietatis, nec etiam convenire, differetur uſque ætatem, ſed non cadit breve.*

30 Aſſ. p. 25. 43 Aſſ. p. 20. 9 E. 2. Age 143. 19 E. 2. Mord. 45. 8 E. 3. 23. 8 Aſſ. 12. 6 E. 4. 11. 43 E. 3. 5. 18 E. 4. 23. Glanv. lib. 13. cap. 15.

[292]

Bract. lib. 5.

(3) *Si paſſa ore lenqueſt come il fuit de plein age.*] So as now ſuch pleading, triall and proceeding ſhall be in theſe four actions, as if the plaintife were of full age.

CAP. III.

*ESTABLIE eſt enſement, que ſi home alien tenement (1), que il tient per le * ley Dengleterre (2), ſon fits ne ſoit pas forbarre (3) per le fait ſon pier (de que nul heritage luy diſcend') (4) a demander et recoverer per briefe de mordanceſter (5) de la ſeiſin ſa mier, tout face le charter ſon pier mention que luy et ſes heyres ſont tenus a la garrant. Et ſi heritage luy diſcend' de part ſon pier, donques ſoit il forcloſe de le value del heritage, que luy eſt*

IT is eſtabliſhed alſo, that if a man aliene a tenement, that he holdeth by the law of England, his ſon ſhall not be barred by the deed of his father (from whom no heritage to him deſcended) to demand and recover by writ of mortdaunceſtor, of the ſeiſin of his mother, although the deed of his father doth mention, that he and his heirs be bound to warranty. And if any heritage deſcend to him of his father's ſide, then he ſhall be barred for

est discendus. Et si en tiel cas apres la mort son pier, heritage luy soit discendus per mesme le pier (6), *donques avera le tenant vers luy recovery de la seisin sa mier* (7), *per briefe de judgement que issera hors de rolles des justices, devant queux le plee fuit pleade, a resom' son garrantie sicome avant ad estre fait en auters cases, ou le garantie vient en court, et dit que riens ne luy est discend' de luy per que fait il est vouche. Et en mesme le maner eit lissue le fits recover per briefe de cosinage, ayel, et besaiel. Ensement et en mesme le maner ne soit l'heire la feme* (8) *apres la mort le pier et la mier barr' daction a demander le heritage sa mier* (9) *per briefe dentre* (10), *que son pier en temps sa mier aliena, dont nul fine nest levie en court le roy* (11).

for the value of the heritage that is to him descended. And if in time after any heritage descend to him by the same father, then shall the tenant recover against him of the seisin of his mother by a judicial writ that shall issue out of the rolls of the justices, before whom the plea was pleaded, to resummon his warranty, as before hath been done in cases where the warrantor cometh into the court, saying, that nothing descended from him by whose deed he is vouched. And in like manner the issue of the son shall recover by writ of cosinage, aiel, and besaiel. Likewise in like manner the heir of the wife shall not be barred of his action after the death of his father and mother, by the deed of his father, if he demand by action the inheritance of his mother by a writ of entry, which his father did aliene in the time of his mother, whereof no fine is levied in the king's court.

* Custumer de Norm. cap. 119. fol. 138. (Vaughan 366. Stat. 4 & 5 Ann. c. 16. Bro. Formedon, 73. 5 Rep. 80. 8 Rep. 52. 1 Inst. 365, 366. 381. a. 382. a. 383. a. b. Dyer, f. 148. Fitz. Garranty, 5. 9 Rep. 26. Fitz. Cui in vita, 7, 8. 32 H. 8. c. 28. Keilw. 104. b. 124, 125.)

Bract. li. 4. fo. 321, 322. Fleta, li. 5. c. 34. See the first part of the Institutes, sect. 197. 724. 726, 727. 32 E. 3. Gar 30.

Before the making of this statute, when the heir demanded inheritance on the part of his mother, the warranty of the tenant by the courtesie, whose heir he was, barred him of that inheritance without any assets. This statute doth provide, that it shall not be a barre without assets.

But at the common law, if the heir had been within age, and his entry congeable, though he had not entred in the life of the ancestor, the warranty bound him not, but that he might enter and avoid the warranty; but if he were driven to his action, the warranty had bound him, and so it was in case of a *fem covert*.

Temps E. 1. 87. 31 E. 1. ibid. 95. 7 E. 3. 53. Bract. li. 4. fol. 228.

(1) *Alien tenements.*] This extendeth to alienations made after the statute, and not before, for it is a rule and law of parliament, that regularly *nova constitutio futuris formam imponere debet, non praeteritis.*

[293]

See before ca. 1. W. 2. cap. 41. Temps E. 1. gar. 87. 27 E. 3. 80. 14 E. 4. gar. 5. 17 E. 3. 83.

This word (alien) doth properly signifie a transmutation of possession, but yet a release or confirmation of the tenant by the courtesie with warranty, where no transmutation of possession is, is within the same mischief, and therefore is within the remedy of this statute; for otherwise the statute should serve to little purpose.

Dier 4 Mar. 148. First part of the Institutes, sect. 724, 725.

(2) *Tient per la ley Dangleterre.*] If the heir demand the heritage of the part of his father, and the warranty on the part of his mother be pleaded, this case is not holpen by this statute, as in the first part

part of the Institutes it appeareth; for this act by this branch provideth onely for the case of the tenant by the courtesie, and therefore tenant for life, or tenant in dower is not within the case or classis of this act; but as concerning the case of the tenant by the courtesie, which is the case of this act, this statute is taken by equity, as heretofore hath been partly touched, and hereafter shall appear.

See the statute of 11 H. 7. c. 20. Temps E. 1. gar. 86. 12 Ass. p. 9.

(3) *Son fits ne soit pas forbarre.*] This doth not onely extend to the son, but to the daughter, and to any other heire immediate, as here the example is put, or mediate, as cosin and heire, be they never so remote.

11 E. 3. gar. 83.

(4) *De que nul heritage luy descend.*] That is to say, from whom no lands or tenements in fee simple of the yearly value of the inheritance of the part of the mother doth descend to the heire, for the warranty is no barre without such assets.

And by the equity of this statute the warranty of tenant in taile is no barre unlesse there be assets in fee simple descended.

11 E. 2. garranty. Statham.

Albeit the word heritage be generall, yet hath it in construction a speciall signification, for the assets must respect the essentiall quality of the inheritance, whereof the heire is to be barred, and that is, that it be a locall, possessary, and certaine inheritance, as lands, rents, commons, and the like: and therefore an annuity, that is a personall inheritance, and lieth in action, nor any right of action of inheritance is no heritage within this statute, untill it be reduced into possession, *Et sic de similibus.*

21 E. 3. 28. 38 E. 3. 23. Pl. Com. 110. Lib. 8. fol. 53. Syms case. Doct. & St. fo. 76. Kelwey 124, 125.

(5) *Per briefe de mordauncester.*] And after the writs of aiel, besaiel, and cosinage are also named.

11 E. 2. gar. 83. 8 E. 2. ibid. 81.

The intendment of the makers of this act is, that the warranty of him that held by the courtesie should not be a barre to the heir of his wife, unlesse he left assets; and the makers of the statute could not put all the cases that might happen, but did put the strongest cases, and by construction the lesser shall be included, and therefore in all actions, as the writ of right, the formedon in the descender, the writ of entry in the *per*, the writ of entry *ad communem legem*, and the like are within this statute.

46 E. 3. age 76. 4 E. 3. gar. 63. F.N.B. 208. b.

(6) *Heritage luy descend de mesme le pier.*] If a seigniory of homage and fealty descend to the heire, this is no assets, but if a tenancy doth escheat to the heire, although it were never in the father, this shall be accounted assets, because the seigniory that came from the father was the means to bring it to the heire, *Et sic de similibus.*

16 E. 3. age f. 41. Br. 5. 6 H. 4. 1. Kelwey 104. b. Pl. Com. Chapmans case.

(7) *Donques avera le tenant vers luy recovery de la seisin sa mere.*] By this act the warranty of a tenant by the courtesie being pleaded with assets descended is a bar to the heire of the mother; but if assets be not then descended, but after it descend from the same father, then the tenant shall have recovery of the inheritance of the mother by a writ of judgement, as this act appointeth: and by the equity of this act it is taken, that in a formedon in the descender, if the warranty of tenant in taile be pleaded, where no assets is then descended, but after assets doth descend to the issue, there the tenant shall have a *scire facias* to have the assets, and not the land in taile, for if he should have the land in taile, it was considered, that if the issue aliened the assets, his issue might recover the land tailed in a formedon: wherein is to be observed the great wisdome of the sages of the law in auncient times, ever so to resolve, and give

Hil. 9 E. 2. 62. b. in Entr. sur diss. 43 E. 3. 26. 46 E. 3. 29. Pl. Com. fo. 110.

[294]

judgement, *Ut sit finis litium.* But in none of the bookes that treat of this matter is expressed how the tenant shall demeane himselfe in pleading to take advantage upon this statute of the assets, which after descended.

Pl. Com. 110. Lib. 8. fol. 53. Syms case.

And therefore if in a mordanc', &c. the tenant plead the warranty of the tenant by the curtesie with assets (as in some of the books it is said) or in a formedon the tenant plead a lineall warranty with assets, and the demandant take issue upon the assets, and it is found that nothing descended, and thereupon the demandant recover, and after the recovery assets descend, the tenant shall never have a *scire facias* to take benefit of this act, for he that will take benefit of this act must not begin with an untruth, but must plead the warranty, and confesse the title of the demandant, and pray the advantage of this act, when assets shall descend, and upon this record when assets descend, he shall have a *scire facias*; for our act saith, *Per briefe de judgement que issera hors de rolles des justices*; and this exposition agreeth with the words of this act, *a resummon son garrantie sicome avant ad estre fait en auters cases ou le garrantee vient en court, et dit, que riens ne luy est descend' de luy, per quel fait il est vouch:* for there without question after assets shall descend, upon the record a *scire facias* shall be awarded.

(8) *Ensement et en mesme le maner ne soit le heire la fem,* &c.] This is the last branch of this act.

8 E. 2. gar. 81. Hil. 9 E. 2. ubi sup. 17 E. 3. 51. 27 E. 3. 89. Hil. 9 E. 2. ubi sup. Thomas de Mertons case.

(9) *Barre daction a demander le heritage sa mere,* &c.] By the first branch the act provideth remedy against the warranty made by tenant by the curtesie after the decease of his wife; this branch provideth remedy against the alienation of the husband with warranty during the life of his wife: upon these words some have conceived, that this warranty shall not binde, albeit assets doth descend from the father, because assets is not mentioned in this branch, as it is in the former. But these words, *ensement et en mesme le maner,* doe so couple this branch by reference to the former, as if in this case assets doth descend, by the warranty and assets the heire is barred.

If the husband make a feoffement in fee of the wives land with warranty, and hath issue by her, and they both die, in a writ of entry *sur disseisin* brought against the feoffee he vowcheth the heir of the husband, who is also the heire of the wife, he may upon this statute devolve the ten' of the warranty, for that the husband left no assets, and that he hath an action as heire to his mother to recover the land, and if he should enter into the warranty, he should forclose himselfe of his action, and therefore by the rule of the court he entred not into the warranty.

See the first part of the Institutes, cap. Gar. sæpe.

(10) *Briefe dentre.*] That is a *sur cui in vita,* but if the lands were entailed to the wife, and after the statute of *donis condic' de W.* 2. the heire brought a formedon, the collaterall warranty of the husband shall barre in that action.

27 E. 3. 89. Pl. Com. 57. First part of the Institutes, sect. 729, 730, 731.

(11) *Dont nul fine est levie en court le roy.*] This is to be understood whereof no fine is lawfully levied, that is by the husband and wife, for then her heire claiming a fee-simple is barred; but a fine levied by the husband alone was a wrong, and at that time a discontinuance, and therefore such a fine was not within the intention of this act.

CAP.

CAP. IV.

ENSEMENT si home lessa sa terre a ferme (1), *ou a trover estovers en viver, ou en vesture* (2), *que amount a la quart part de la veray value* (3) *de la terre, et celuy que la terre tient* (4) *issint charge la lessest giser fresh* (5), *issint que home ne puit trover distresse per deux ans* (6), *ou per trois, a faire le ferme render, ou a faire ceo que est contenue en lescript* (7) *ou leas: Establie est, que apres les deux ans passes eit le lessor action* (8) *a demander la terre en demeign'* (9) *per briefe que il avera en le chancery* (10). *Et si celuy vers que la terre est demande, veigne avant judgement, et render les arrerages et les damages* (11), *et trova suerty tiel come la court verra que soit suffisant* (12) *a render en apres* [*solonque*] *ceo que est contenue en lescript du leas, ci, reteign' la terre. Et sil demurr' tanque ele soit recover per judgement, soit il forclose a remnant* (13). W. 2. cap. 21. & cap. 41.

ALSO if a man let his land to ferm, or to find estovers, in meat or in cloth, amounting to the fourth part of the very value of the land, and he which holdeth the land so charged letteth it lie fresh, so that the party can find no distress there by the space of two or three years to compel the farmor to render, or to do as is contained in the writing or lease; it is established, that the two yeares being passed, the lessor shall have an action to demand the land in demean by a writ which he shall have out of the chancery. And if he against whom the land is demanded come before judgement, and pay the arrearages and the damages, and find surety (such as the court shall think sufficient) to pay from thenceforth as is contained in the writing of his lease, he shall keep the land. And if he tarry until it be recovered by judgement, he shall be barred for ever.

(7 H. 8. f. 28. Fitz. Resceit, 96. 105. Fitz. Scire fac' 154. Kel. f. 75. 132. Fitz. Cessavit. 21 10. 12. 19, 20. 23. 25. 27. 29. 32. 38, 39. 49. 52, 53. 56. Rast. pla. f. 111. Regist. 237. 13 Ed. 1. stat. 1. c. 21. 41. 10 Ed. 2.)

What the common law, or some custome was before the making of this statute, you may reade in Bracton who wrote a little before this statute; *Item poterit intervenire justum judicium ab initio, ut in districtionibus faciendis, et vertitur ex post facto in disseisinam, sicut in burgagiis, terris, tenementis, et tenuris exterioribus. Ut si dominus per considerationem curiæ suæ pro defectu servitii ceperit tenementum tenentis sui in manum suam, sicut simplex namiū, donec de redditu fuerit satisfactum; sed cum talis, cujus ten' fuerit, obtulerit de satisfaciend' de redditu et arreragiis, restitui ei debet possessio, et si dominus hoc recusaverit, tunc erit manifesta disseisina.* And afterwards in another place he saith; *Item si propter paupertatem possessionem dereliquerit, et ita quod dominus capitalis pro defectu servitii tenementum suum in manum suam ceperit et retinuerit, vel alio excolend' dederit, &c. satis moritur tenens seisitus.* Bract. lib. 4. fol. 205. b. Fol. 262.

And I reade amongst auncient records, that a *cessavit* was brought in the raigne of king John, but this act is the first statute that was made by authority of parliament concerning the *cessavit*; after this came the statutes of Westm. 2. and 10 E. 2. *De Gamletto*; Int' Record 87. Regis Johannis.

W. 2. c. 21 & 41. 10 E. 2. Stat. de gamletto. Vet. Mag. Cha. f. 122. Pasch. 17 E. 3. coram Rege. Rot. 139. London. First part of the Institutes, sect. 1. 45 E. 3. 27. 33 H. 6. 53. 13 E. 2. Cessavit 51. F.N.B. 209. g. See Mich. 9 E. 1. in Banco Rot. 39. Kanc. Hil. 13 E. 1. in Banco Rot. 7. Pasch. 16 E. 1. Rot. 5.

letto; and note that the writ framed upon this act doth recite this statute.

(1) *Lessa sa terra a ferme.*] *Lessa, demise, nota dimittere* is a good word of a feoffement, and therefore if a man let or demise lands to a man and his heires, and make livery of seisin, this is a good feoffement, and so is this word here to be intended, for a *cessavit* lieth not against tenant in taile, or tenant for life, unlesse the remainder be limited over to another in fee, so as he is tenant to the lord, as tenant by the curtesie is.

(2) *Estovers en viver ou vesture.*] That is to say, *estovers in victu et vestitu*, of this sufficient hath been said in the exposition upon the seventh chapter of *Magna Charta*.

(3) * *A la quart part de la verie value.*] *Vide* for fee ferme the exposition upon the twenty seventh chapter of *Magna Charta.* And such rent or other profit, as was answered to the owner of the land, was accounted the verie value.

* [296]

(4) *Celui que la terre tient.*] So as there must be a tenure betweene the feoffor and the feoffee in fee-simple, for a *cessavit* lieth not upon a reservation without such a tenure, and so was it adjudged in 11 E. 2.

11 E. 2. cessav. 50. 21 E. 3. 23. 45 E. 3. 15. 27. 21 H. 6. 50. 33 H. 6. 53. F.N.B. 209. 11 H. 4. 3. 27 H. 8. 28. Kel. 104, 105.

At the making of this act all estates of inheritance were in fee simple, and therefore the donor upon an estate in taile (created by a statute made after this act) shall not have a *cessavit* against the donee in taile, nor against tenant for life; neither for the cesser of the mesne a *cessavit* lieth for he holdeth not the land as this act speaketh, which ought to be overt, and sufficient to the distresse of the lord, which is a good plea in a *cessavit*.

Pasc. 16 E. 1. in Ban. Rot. 5. *Non potuit excolere propter duras districtiones.* Regist. 237. F.N.B. 210. a. 6 E. 3. 45. 8 E. 3. 46, 47. 10 E. 3. 6. 21 E. 3. 20, 21. 30 E. 3. 22. 43 E. 3. 15. 8 H. 6. 17. 33 H. 6. 8.

And in this writ the tenure between the demandant and the tenant is traversable, because this writ is grounded upon the tenure by force of this act; but in this writ the seisin is not traversable, because it is not grounded upon the seisin, neither is the quantity of the services traversable, but to be taken by protestation; for whether he hold by more, or lesse, the *cessavit* lieth; but in an avowry the seisin is traversable, for that is grounded as well upon the seisin, as the tenure: also in the *cessavit* the land is to be recovered, and not the services, and it is in his nature a writ of right, and the jury shall measure in their consciences the quantity of the service.

Neither is *hors de son fee* a good plea in a *cessavit*, because (as hath beene said) the tenure is traversable.

(5) *La lessest giser fresh.*] The tenant of the land is called tenant *per availe*, because it is presumed, that he hath availe and profit by the land, and therefore the law never expected, that he would let the land lie fresh, that in his proper sense is as much, as unmanured, or unoccupied.

Temps E. 1. cessavit 58. 10 E. 4. 1. 2. 30 E. 3. 22. 11 E. 3. cessavit 21. 35 H. 6. ibid. 7. F.N.B. 208, 209.

It is said in law to lie fresh, not onely when there is no cattle, or other thing distrainable upon the land of the value of the rent, or other profit behinde; but also, though there be a sufficient distresse to be taken, yet by construction upon this act, if the land be so immured or inclosed about, as the lord cannot come to take and carry away the distresse to the pound, it is said to lie fresh, that is, without profit as to the lord, for though it be sufficient, yet it is not sufficient to his distresse, so as the land must lie open and sufficient to the distresse of the lord: or else it is said in law to

lie

lie fresh within this statute, which construction is worthy of observation.

(6) *Per deux ans.*] *Per biennium*; so as by these words is implied, that it lieth onely for annuall services, and not for homage, fealty, or the like. And upon these words, *rien arere, &c.* is a good plea in this action.

12 E. 3. cessavit. 8 E. 3. 46, 47. 17 E. 3. 57. 27 E. 3. 17. 14 H. 4. 44. 33 H. 6. 44. 6 H. 7. 7. 8 H. 7. 2. 30 E. 3. 22. 14 E. 3. cessavit 20. 19 R. 2. surety 27. 35 H. 6. cessavit 7. F.N.B. 209.

This act saith, if the tenant let the land lie fresh, yet if a stranger wrongfully occupy the ground by putting in his cattle and feeding of it, or otherwise by manurance of the ground, this is sufficient to the distresse of the lord within this act, for the lord may distrein them, which is the end of this act; otherwise it is in this case, if cattle escape, and the owner freshly follow to take them.

(7) *Ou a faire chose que est contenue en lescript.*] By these words the *cessavit* did lie for non-payment of a fee ferme contained in the deed.

(8) *Eyt le lessor action a demaunder terre en demeign'.*]

Five doubts were conceived upon this act:

[297]

1. Whether the heires of the lord might have a *cessavit*, because the words be *eyt le lessor*. Regist. 237.

2. Upon the same words whether the grauntee of the seigniory with attornement, or tenant by the curtesie, tenant in dower, &c. might have a *cessavit*.

3. Whether against the alienee of the tenant or his disseisor, &c. a *cessavit* did lie upon this act, because the letter of this law extended but to the feoffee.

4. Whether the *cessavit* should be against the heires of the feoffee. 45 E. 3. 15.

5. Whether it extended to rents and services created without deed, for as much as this act speaketh of such onely, as were reserved by deed.

These doubts were conceived upon that notable rule delivered in our bookes in the case of *cessavit*, *Ou recoverie est done en especiall case per estatut, il coveit que home aver touts voies accord al statut.*

As to the first Britton saith, *Fee fermes sont terres tenus en fee a responder pur eux per an le verie value, ou pluis, ou meyns, de quel rent si les feoffees cessent a respondre per deux ans ensemble per tant accrest action as feoffors et lour heires a demaunder les tenements en demeane.* But notwithstanding this point and the residue of the doubts are briefly and excellently remedied by the statute of W. 2. made seven yeares after this act, as we shall shew when we shall come to it. W. 2. cap. 21.

(9) *Demaunder sa terre in demeign'.*] Upon these words it is concluded that a *cessavit* doth not lie of a mesnalty consisting of rents and services, but this writ lieth against the tenant *per availe*.

13 E. 3. gard. 38. 21 E. 3. 44. 27 H. 8. 28. 1 H. 4. 3. 12 R. 2. cessav. 46.

It is holden that a *cessavit* doth lie of an advowson, and yet it is not in demesne, and overt, and sufficient to his distresse cannot be pleaded.

5 H. 7. 37. 43 E. 3. 15. 31 E. 3. cessavit 24. 33 H. 6. 34.

(10) *Per briefe que il avera en la chauncery.*] Hereupon also great question grew for the forme of the writ, but in the end a writ was conceived upon this act, as it appeareth in the Register, and F. N. B.

Regist. 237. F.N.B. 210.

45 E. 3. 27. 29. 21 E. 3. 23. 33 H. 6. 19. 7 E. 3. 58. 13 E 3. cessavit 29. 15 H. 7. 10. (11) *Avant judgement, et tender les arrerages et damages,* &c.] After verdict and before judgement, the tenant may tender the arrerages, &c. He ought to tender the arrerages in proper person, though he be a lord of parliament, for the words of this act be, *Celuy vers que le terre est demande vient, &c.* and he ought to finde surety.

Tr. 9 E. 2. f. 65. In libro meo in cessavit. In a *cessavit* after the enquest joyned, the tenant made default, and at the retourne of the *petit cape*, the tenant appeared, and offered to pay the arrerages with damages, and to finde such surety as the court would award, which was received, because he came before judgement, and found surety, that is, three pledges, which bound their lands to the distresse of the lord in the same forme as the tenant his land is bound.

5 E. 3. 30. 7 E. 3. 58. 21 E. 3. 23. 25 E. 3. 42. 6 E. 2. cessavit 49. He ought to tender all the arrerages, for so are the indefinite words to be taken as well before as after the two yeares, and damages to be allowed of by the court, but if the demandant doe not alledge how much is behinde over and above the two yeares, &c. and that be found by the jury that findes the issue, the tenant need not tender more then for the two yeares, because it appeare not of record, or by necessary consequence as such arrerages as incurre
17 E. 3. 57. hanging the writ; and for any arrerages incurred before this tender, the lord shall not avow, because the tenant ought to have paid all.

13 E. 3. cessav. 20. The court may assesse the damages by their discretion.

13 E. 3. ubi supra. 14 H. 4. 3, 4. Where this act saith, that he shall tender the arrerages, it is to be understood of such things as may be yeelded, as rent, &c. but of suit, divine service and such like which cannot be yeelded, damages shall be paid for the same.

40 E. 3. 40. 31 E. 3. cessav. 23. F.N.B. 209. a. Mic. 31 E. 3. fo. 50 & 51. in lib. meo in cessavit. If two joyntenants be impleaded in a *cessavit*, and the one make default, &c. the other cannot tender the arrerages but for the moity, for the other joyntenant hath * power to alien and lose his moity, the words of the statute be, *Celuy vers que la terre est demaund,* and the land is demaunded against both.

*[298] But if A. and B. be seised to them and the heires of A. and B. make default, A. may tender for the whole in respect of his remainder.

6 E. 2. tit cessavit 49. In a *cessavit*, the jury in *anno* 6 E. 2. found the cesser, and that the rent was behinde by 30 yeares, part of which time was before the statute whereupon the writ was grounded, and yet the demandant shall recover all the arrerages, as is well warranted by the statute.

If the demandant in the *cessavit* be outlawed in a personall action, this outlawry may be pleaded in barre of the action, because the arrerages are due to the king.

(12) *Et trovera suertie come le court verra sufficient,* &c.] This surety is referred to the discretion of the court, for herein upon these words there is a rule conceived, *Suretie est al court d'ordeiner, et al*
25 E. 3. 42. *tenant dassent et affirme.* And therefore being referred to discretion, in divers cases severall sureties have been ordained upon due consideration had in respect of the state of every particular case.

50 E. 3. 23. 19 E. 4. 5. 17 E. 3. 57. 21 E. 3. 23. 29 E. 3. 33. Vet. N. B. 138. Sometime in respect of the quality of the demandant, as if he be a body politique or corporate, ecclesiasticall or temporall for feare of a mortmain, therefore their collaterall surety is to be found, &c.

3 *Vide*

Vide 15 *Martini, anno* 4 E. 3. *coram justic' itin' apud Dunstable*, surety was graunted to the prior of D. demandant in a *cessavit*, that he should distrain for the rent in other lands.

[a] Sometime in respect of the quality of the tenant in respect he is a body politique or corporate, or a feme covert, or an infant.

[b] Sometime in respect of the tenancy it selfe, as if it be a house, &c. lest the tenant should waste it, and so make it not sufficient to pay the rent.

[a] 10 E. 4. 5. Temps E. 1. cessavit 55, 56. 19 R. 2. surety 27. 15 E. 2. ibid. 20. 19 E. 2. ibid. 21. 4 E. 3. 42. 13 E. 3. cessavit 29. 21 E. 3. 23. Doct. & Stud. lib. 2.

Though the statute referreth the surety to the discretion of the court, yet will it be good to follow precedents of former times, for *discretio est discernere per legem quod sit justum*.

[b] 41 E. 3. 29. 19 E. 4. 5.

[c] Albeit it is for the benefit of the demandant to have surety, yet he cannot waive it, because it is made parcell of the judgement.

[c] 50 E. 3. 23. 19 E. 4. 5.

[d] But what if the surety be a judgement of the court, that if he cesse againe by one or two years, *que la t're incurgera la remnant*, that is, that he shall have judgement to hold the land, &c. for ever, wherein the tenant shall never tender any more, and his remedy, that after such cesser again, he shall have a *scire facias* upon the record, and if the tenant be warned and make default, &c. the demandant shall have judgement against him for ever.

[d] 41 E. 3. 29. 19 R. 2. Scire fac' 134.

If the tenant after a judgement given against him in a *cessavit*, that if he cease againe, *Que la terre incurgera le remnant*, in that case if the tenant alien, the alienee shall not be bound by the said surety or judgement, because it bound him that was tenant in the *cessavit* onely, and upon a new cesser a new *cessavit* must be brought. But if the surety or judgement be, that if he or his assignes doe cease again, &c. then the assignee is bound thereby, and upon a *scire facias* the matter shall come in question.

(13) *Soit forclose a remnant.*] That is, shall be forclosed or barred for ever, for this writ is a writ of right in his nature; by this act if the lord recover by defalt, judgement finall by these words, [*Soit forclose del remnant*] shall be given, and shall be a barre in a writ of right: otherwise it is of a judgement by verdict. 6 E. 3. 45. 4 E. 3. droit 41.

See more of the writ of *cessavit* in our exposition upon the statute of W. 2. cap. 21.

CAP. V. [299]

ENSEMENT est purview, que home eit desormes (1) *briefe de wast* (2) *en le chancery vers home que tient per le ley Dengleterre* (3), *ou en auter maner a terme de vie* (4), *ou des ans* (5), *ou feme que tient en dower* (6). *Et celuy que serra attaint de waste* (7), *perde le chose que il aver' waste* (8): *et ouster ceo face gree del treble de ceo que le waste serra taxe* (9). *Et*

IT is provided also, that a man from henceforth shall have a writ of waste in the chancery against him that holdeth by law of England, or otherwise for term of life, or for term of years, or a woman in dower. And he which shall be attainted of waste, shall leese the thing that he hath wasted, and moreover shall recompence thrice so much as the waste shall

Et en waste fait en gard' (10), *soit fait solonque ceo que contenue est en le graund charter, cap.* 4. *Et per la ou il est contenue en la grand charter, que celuy que avera fait waste en garde, perdr' le garde: accorde est, que il rendra al heire les damages del waste* (11), *si issint soit que la garde perdue ne suffist mie a le value des damages, avant lage del heire de mesme le garde* (12). W. 1. cap. 21. Articuli super chartas, cap. 18.

shall be taxed at. And for waste made in the time of wardship, it shall be done as is contained in the great charter. And where it is contained in the great charter, that he which did waste during the custody, shall leese the wardship, it is agreed that he shall recompense the heir his damages for the waste, if so be that the wardship lost do not amount to the value of the damages before the age of the heir of the same wardship.

(Dyer, 25. Fitz. Wast. 62. 117. 146. Bro. Parl. 17. Fitz. Judgement, 85. 134. 255 Fitz. Damage, 7. 22. 42. 52. 90. 114. 133. 1. Inst. 53. b. 54. b. 200. b. 355. b. 1. Roll, 91. 97. 156. Rast. 689, &c. Sayill, 42. 9 H. 3. c. 4. Regist. 72.

12 H. 4. 3. 21 H. 6. 28. Doct. & Stud. lib. 2. cap. 1. Regist. 72. First part of the Institutes, sect. 67.

At the common law waste was punishable in three persons, *viz.* tenant in dower, tenant by the curtesie, and the guardien, but not against tenant for life, or tenant for yeares; and the reason of the diversity was, for that the law created their estates and interests, and therefore the law gave against them remedy: but tenant for life, and for yeares came in by demise and lease of the owner of the land, &c. and therefore he might in his demise provide against the doing of waste by his lessee, and if he did not, it was his negligence and default.

7 H. 6. 35. 8 H. 6. 34. 32 H. 6.

There is also an action of waste by custome, as in London, &c.

Bract. l. 4. fo. 315. Doct. & Stud. l. 2. c. 1. F.N.B. 55. c. W. 2. cap. 14.

Now the remedy at the common law was in two degrees: first, if he that had the inheritance did feare (for example) that tenant in dower would doe waste, he that had the inheritance might before any waste done have a prohibition directed to the sheriffe, that he shall not permit her to doe waste in this forme.

Rex vicecom' salutem. Præcipimus tibi quod non permittas quod talis mulier faciat vastum, vel venditionem, vel exilium de terris, hominibus, redditibus, domibus, boscis, vel gardinis, quæ tenet in dotem de hæreditate talis in tali villa, ad exhæredationem ipsius talis ne amplius, &c.

And Bractons advice hereupon is as followeth:

Regula.

Et hoc faciat tempestive, ne per negligentiam damnum incurrat, quia melius est in tempore occurrere, quam post causam vulneratam remedium quærere.

Lib. 5. fol. 115. Foljambes case.

And the sheriffe having the warrant of this writ may, as in case of a writ of *estrepement*, take *posse comitatus*, and withstand the doing of any waste.

And this was the remedy that the law appointed before the waste done by the tenant in dower, tenant by the curtesie, or the gardien, to prevent the same, and this was an excellent law, for *præstat cautela quam medela*, and preventing justice excelleth punishing justice. And this remedy may be used at this day. Now after waste done there lay an action of waste at the common law in this forme. *Rex vicecom'. Salutem. Si talis fecerit te securum de clamore suo prosequendo, tunc pone per vad', et salvos plegios talem mulierem, &c. quod sit coram justiciariis nostris, &c. ostensura quare fecit vastum,*

Regula. Vide W. 2. c. 14.

[300]

vastum, venditionem, et exilium de terris, hominibus, redditibus, boscis, vel gardinis, quæ tenet in dotem de hæreditate talis, in tali villa, contra prohibitionem nostram, et habeas ibi nomina plegiorum, et hoc breve, teste, &c.

Where in this writ it is said *contra prohibitionem nostram,* the plaintiffe should have well maintained his writ, albeit no writ of prohibition of wast had been sued out before, for that the common law was a prohibition of it selfe, and so saith Bracton speaking of the waste done by a guardien, *Dominus vastum emendabit sic, quod damna restituet, sive vastum fecerit ante prohibitionem, sive post.* 4 H. 3. Wast, 129. ib. 140. 8 R. 2. tit. Attachment sur prohib. 15. Bract. l. 4. fo. 285. Vide W. 2. c. 14.

By this writ of waste the plaintiffe, if the waste were done in woods, *Et mulier inde per inquisitionem convincatur, talis erit ei pœna infligenda, et in tantum erit coarctanda, quod de cætero nihil capiat in bosco illo, nisi (per visum *forestariorum hæredis) rationabile estoverium suum, et talis servitus imponetur ei ad pœnam, et de forestario apponendo fiat tale breve* (which there you may reade at large) *Si custos de vasto convincatur, amittit custodiam, et restituet damna, et det domino regi misericordiam, quod non est in muliere, si de dote sua fecerit vastum, quia dotem suam non amittit, sed custos vel curator ei adjungatur, qui impediat ne faciat, et damna debet refundere.* Bract. fo. 315, 316.

* *Forestarius* in ancient authors, is taken for *custos boscorũ,* a woodward.

So as the tenant in dower (and likewise the tenant by the curtesie) had two punishments, *viz.* to yeild damages to the value of the waste, and a keeper or curate to be appointed to them, who should withstand any waste to be afterwards done by them.

And the guardien had three punishments. 1. He should lose the custody. 2. He should yeeld damages to the value of the waste: and 3. He should be fined to the king, for that contrary to the trust in him reposed by reason of his guardienship he did waste to the disherison of the heire, and this did hold as well in case of a guardien in *droit,* as a guardien in *fait.* 10 H. 3. Wast. 138. 20 H. 3. ib. 139. 34 E. 3. Wast, 146.

And the reason wherefore at the common law the action of waste did lie against the tenant in dower, or tenant by the curtesie, albeit they had assigned over their estates, was, because no action of waste by the common law lay against the assignee for wast done after the assignment, therefore the action of necessity did for such waste (after the assignement) lie against the tenant by the curtesie, or tenant in dower, which law continueth to this day. Temps E. 1. Wast, 132. 30 E. 3. 16. 38 E. 3. 23. 40 E. 3. 33. 11 H. 4. 18. Doct. & Stud. l. 2. ca. 1. F.N.B. 56.

But if the heire granted away the reversion and the tenant attourned, the action failed at the common law, as hereafter shall be shewed more at large. Hereby it appeareth how necessary it is for the understanding of this act, to know what the common law was, and the reason thereof, before the making of our statutes, whereof you shall reade more largely in Bracton both concerning the points abovesaid, and other matters concerning waste, worthy of your reading and observation. Bract. ubi supra. First part of the Instit. sect. 67. F.N.B. 56. b.

But at the common law if the guardien in *droit* had assigned over his estate and interest, the heir should have had an action of waste for waste done after the assignement against the assignee, for he was guardien in *fait,* and so within the rule of the common law.

(1) *Home eyt deformes,* &c.] Here the persons are not named who shall have the action of waste, but that is left to the common law to judge thereupon, of which matter you shall reade plentifully in our books, and it were too long to be here inserted,

neither

neither doth it tend to the exposition of this act being left to the common law.

(2) *Briefe de waste.*] *Breve de vasto.* Of this word *vastum* you may reade in the first part of the Institutes, sect. 67. onely this may be added that neither this act, nor the statute of Marlebridge
[301] doth create new kinde of wastes, but doe give new remedies for old wastes; and what is waste, and what not, must be determined by the common law.

(3) *Home que tient per la ley d'Angleterre.*] Here tenant by the curtesie is named for two causes: 1. For that albeit the common
20 H. 6. 1. 21 H. 6. 38. opinion was, that an action of waste did lie against him, yet some doubted of the same, in respect of this word *tenet* in the writ, for that the tenant by the curtesie did not hold of the heire, but of the lord paramount, and after this act the writ of waste grounded thereupon doth recite this statute.

2. For that greater penalties were inflicted by this act, then were at the common law.

37 H. 6. 26. (4) *Ou en auter maner a terme de vie.*] If a lease be made *quam diu sola fuer'*, or *quam diu se bene gesserit*, or *quousque promotus fuerit, &c.* in all these and like cases they are in judgement of law leases for life within this act.

Upon these words there be many conclusions worthy of observation.

Temps E. 1. Wast, 122. 4 E. 3. 25. 18 E. 3. 3. 30 E. 3. 16. 38 E. 3. 23. 11 H. 4. 18. F.N.B. 56. f. First, albeit the assignee of the tenant by the curtesie, or tenant in dower, is within the letter of this law, for he holdeth in some manner for life, yet no action of waste shall be brought by the heire against the assignee, but onely against the tenant by the curtesie, or tenant in dower; for in construction of statutes, the reason of the common law giveth great light, and the judges, as much as may be, follow the rule thereof.

Regist. 72. lib. 3. fol. 23. b. Walkers case, li. 11. fo. 84. Bowles case. But if the heire granteth away the reversion, and the assignee attorne, there the grauntee by this statute shall have an action of waste against the assignee, and the plaintiffe must declare upon this statute: for (as hath been said) in that case there lay no action of waste at the common law, so as in this point our act is introductory of a new law.

Regist. 72. 11 H. 4. 3. 5 H. 7. 17. Lib. 11. fol. 83. Bowles case. 2. If the heire had graunted his reversion expectant upon an estate in dower or by the curtesie, the grauntee should not have had an action of waste against tenant in dower or by the curtesie at the common law, for that the privity was destroyed, therefore the grauntee in an action upon this statute doth recite the statute.

Marlb. cap. 23. 3. A lessee for his own life, or for another mans life, is within the words and meaning of this law, and in this point this act introduceth that which was not at the common law.

33 E. 3. Wast, 144. 11 E. 3. graunt 13. 11 E. 3. receit 118. 4 E. 3. 18. 50 E. 3. 3. 10 E. 4. 9. 1. 5 E. 4. 89. Regist. F.N.B. 59. Lib. 5. fol. 76. b. Pagets case. 4. If a lease for life be made to A. the remainder for life to B. he in the reversion shall have no action of waste against the first lessee, for then the estate of him in the remainder should be destroyed, and such construction must be made to preserve the estate of an estranger, in whom there is no fault or default. But if he in the remainder for life dieth, then the waste is punishable as well before as after his death.

8 E. 3. 26. * 17 E. 3. 68. 39 E. 3. 25. 6 E. 3. 19. * 5. If a lease be made to A. for his life, the remainder to A. for the life of B. if A. doth waste, an action of waste doth lie against him, for the wrong doer hath both the states in him, and of that

that opinion was sir James Dier chiefe justice of the common pleas, Pasch. 18 Eliz.

6. If a lease for life be made, the remainder for years, an action of waste shall lie against the lessee, for the recovery therein shall not destroy the terme for yeares. 4 E. 3. 18. 3 E. 3. 18. F.N.B. 59. h.

7. Fem' lessee for life taketh husband, the husband doth waste, the wife dieth, the husband shall not be punished by this law, for the words of this act be, *home que tient, &c. pur vie*, and the husband held not for life, for he was seised but in the right of his wife, and the estate was in his wife. 46 E. 3. 32. 46. tit. Waste Statham. Lib. 10. fol. 11. Southcots case.

8. An occupant is within this law, for the words of this act (as hath been said) are *home que tient*, which are more liberall words then if the statute had spoken of a lease or demise, and certain it is that the occupant holdeth for life, so it is of the lord that entreth on his villein tenant for life. 48 E. 3. 19. l. 6. fol. 3. Le D. de Worcesters case. Lib. 10. fol. 98.

9. He that hath an estate * for life by conveyance at the common law, or by limitation of use, is a tenant within this statute. [302] * Hil. 16 E. 1. in Banco Rot. 63. Buck. & Rot. 73. Hereford.

10. A lease for life is made, the remainder over in taile or in fee, he in the remainder shall by this act have an action of waste; for the words of the statute are generall.

11. Albeit tenant in taile *apres* possibility of issue extinct doth hold but for life, and so within the letter of this law, yet is he out of the meaning thereof in respect of the inheritance which was once in him, in respect whereof his estate is by law dispunishable of waste, but his assignee shall be punished for waste by this statute. Temps E. 1. Wast, 126. 39 E. 3. 16. 45 E. 3. 25. Li. 11. fol. 83. Ewens case, 27 H. 6. Aide Statham.

12. It is to be observed that such remedy as the heire had against the tenant in dower, and tenant by the curtesie, &c. by the common law, such remedy had the lessor and his heires against the farmors for life or yeares by the statute of Marlebridge, which remaineth to this day. 29 E. 3. 1. b. Doct. & Stud. li. 2. ca. 1. Marlb. c. 23. l. 11. fol. 81. b. Bowles case.

(5) *Ou des ans.*] See before the statute of Marlebridge, cap. 23. Regist. 72.

Tenant by statute merchant, or staple, or *elegit*, are not within this act, for albeit they have but a chattell, yet are they not tenant for yeares. 16 E. 3. Wast, 100. 21 E. 3. 26. Doct. & Stud. fo. 66. b. F.N.B. 58. h. li. 6. fo. 37. First part of the Instit. sect. 67.

Although the words of the act be tenant for yeares in the plurall number, yet tenant for a yeare, or halfe a yeare, &c. is within this act.

Executors or administrators of a terme for yeares, though they hold in *auter droit*, shall be punished for waste done in their time, but not in the time of the testator, or intestate. 38 E. 3. 17. 10 E. 4. 1. 23 H. 8. Wast. Br.

Two executors be of a ward, the one doth waste, the action lieth against him onely. See more hereof hereafter, and note the diversity. 3 E. 2. Waste, 3.

Tenant for yeares graunts his estate upon condition, the lessee doth waste, the grauntee enters for the condition broken, the action of wast is to be brought against the grauntee, and so it is in case of lessee for life. 30 E. 3. 16.

Tenant by the curtesie, or other tenant for life maketh a lease for yeares, he in the reversion confirmeth it, tenant by the curtesie dieth, an action of waste lieth against the lessee. 8 E. 3. 26.

Tenant for yeares of a moity, third, or fourth part *pro indiviso* holdeth a terme for yeares, he is within this act; and so it is of a tenant by the curtesie, or other tenant for life of a moity, &c. In like 10 E. 3. 32. 44 E. 3. 34. 45 E. 3. 35. 9 H. 6. 11. 12 E. 4. 2. 21 H. 7. 40.

like manner if two be plaintiffes, and one of them is summoned, and severed, a moity shall be recovered.

Lib. 5. fol. 12. Foljambs case. Tenant for yeares or for life assignes over his lease for yeares, or estate for life, excepting the timber trees, and after waste is done in felling downe the trees, the action of waste is maintainable against the assignee, for as to the lessor they are not severed from the land.

Lib. 5. fol. 78. Booths case. Tenant for yeares, or for life assignes over his estate, and notwithstanding takes the profits, an action of waste lieth against the first lessee, and so it is of meane assignes, the action lieth against him that taketh the profits, but this is by the statute of 11 H. 6. cap. 5. for in that case the pernor of the profits did not hold the land.

33 E. 3. p. 6. 6 E. 3 54. 34 E. 3. retorn 111. Two joyntenants for yeares, or for life, one of them doth waste, this is the waste of them both, as to the place wasted, and yet the words of the act are, *(home que tient)* but treble damages shall be recovered against him that did the waste onely.

40 E. 3. 33. 41 E. 3. 27. 43 E. 3. 15. 48 E. 3. 19. F.N.B. 56. a. Temps E. 1. Waste, 126. Tenant for yeares or for life doth waste, and after assigneth over his estate, now the words be *(home que tient)*, *&c.* he that holdeth for life or for yeares, and after the assignement he holdeth not the land, yet shall the action of waste be brought against him in the *tenet*, because in the eye of the law he is tenant as to the action of waste, and against him that was the wrong doer did the action accrew, which he cannot avoid by his assignement, and against him shall the treble damages be recovered and the place wasted, and so 40 E. 3. 33. 43 E. 3. 8. 44 E. 3. 5. it is of the meane assignes; a just interpretation that he that did the wrong should answer the same, and this is the cause that generall nontenure is no plea in an action of waste, but speciall non- [303] tenure may be pleaded, as the granting over of his estate, before which graunt no waste was done.

Tr. 7 E. 1. in Communi Banco. Rot. 21. Norff. (6) *Ou feme que tient en dower.*] This is to be understood of all the five kindes of dowers whereof Littleton speaketh, *viz.* dower at the common law, dower by the custome, dower *ad ostium ecclesiæ*, dower *ex assensu patris*, and dower *de la pluis beale*, and against all these the action of waste did lie at the common law.

(7) *Et celuy que serra attaint de waste.*] As it hath beene said, if one joyntenant doe the waste, both shall be attainted of the waste, &c.

In an action of waste brought against tenant by the curtesie, tenant for life, tenant for yeares, or tenant in dower, which before hath been named in this act, the entry of the plea of the tenant is *quod predict' (talis) non fecit vastum*, and yet all these by construction of law shall answer for the waste done by any stranger, 32 E. 3. Wast, 30. 19 E. 3. ib. 30. 41 E. 3. ibid. 81. for he in the reversion cannot have any remedy but against the tenant, and the tenant shall have his remedy against the wrong doer, and recover all in damages against him, and by this meanes the losse shall light upon the wrong doer; for voluntary waste and permissive waste is all one to him that hath the inheritance. But 33 H. 6. 1. F.N.B. 59. b. Dier, 28 H. 8. 33. 29 H. 8. 36. 14 Eliz. 314. Pasch. 9 E. 2. 63. b. In libro meo, Un briefe de Waste. 19 E. 3. Wast, 31. if the waste be done by the enemies of the king, the tenant shall not answer for the waste done by them, for the tenant hath no remedy over against them. The same law it is if the waste be done by tempest, lightning, or the like, the tenant shall not answer for it. It is adjudged in 9 E. 2. that if theeves burn the house of tenant for life, without evill keeping of lessees for lives fire, the lessee

lessee shall not be punished therefore in an action of waste; *nota* the case of fire, &c.

A. seised of land in fee acknowledgeth a statute merchant, and infeoffeth B. who letteth the same for life, the land is extended upon the statute, B. bringeth an action of waste against the lessee, he may plead this execution, &c. before which execution no waste done, for the possession of the land is lawfully taken from him by course of law, which he could not withstand, and if he should be punished for waste, he should have no remedy over.

So it is if a man make a lease for yeares, and put out the lessee, and make a lease for life, the lessee enter upon the lessee for life, and doth waste, the lessee for life shall not be punished therefore for the cause aforesaid.

If tenant in dower be of a mannor, and a copiholder thereof commit wast, an action of waste lieth against tenant in dower. 32 E. 3. Wast, 104.

If an infant be tenant by the curtesie, or lessee for life, or yeares, he shall answer for the waste done by a stranger, and have his remedy over, though some have holden the contrary, for in that case also the losse shall be upon the wrong doer; and so it is in case of a feme covert, for the priviledge of infancy and coverture in this case shall not prevaile against the wrong and disherison done to him that hath the inheritance, especially when they have their remedy over, and the estate is of their owne purchace or taking. And so it is if a lease be made to the husband and wife, and the husband doth waste and dieth, if the wife agreeth to the estate, she shall be punished for the waste done by her husband in like manner, as if a stranger had done the waste, and after the death of her husband she is in from the lessor, and if the action had been brought against the husband and wife, the writ should have been *quod fecerunt vastum*, so as it was as well the waste of the wife, as of the husband.

Doct. & Stud.
Temps E. 1. Waste, 128.
3 E. 3. 13. 46.
9 E. 3. 42.
11 Ass. 11.
10 E. 3. 17.
42 E. 3. 21.
46 E. 3. 25.
2 H. 4. 3. a.
7 H. 6. 2. b.
2 H. 6. 24. b.
33 H. 6. 31.
19 E. 3. bre. 246.
10 E. 4. 18.
15 H. 3. Waste, 133.

(8) *Perdra le chose que il aver waste.*] That is, these foure tenants before named shall lose the thing which he hath wasted, but it is ever rendred *amittet locum vastatum.*

* If wast be committed in a house *sparsim* in divers severall parts, the whole house shall be recovered, although all be not wasted. In auncient time it was holden ‡ by some, that if the hall were wasted, the whole house should be recovered, for that in those dayes the hall was the place of greatest resort, and use, in so much as the whole house was called by the name of the hall, as Dalehall, &c. but the purview of this act is, that he shall lose the thing that he hath wasted.

* Temps, E. 1. Waste, 127.
8 E. 2. Waste, 112. 4 E. 3. 32.
15 E. 3. Judgement, 134.
15 E. 3. Wast, 108. 34 H. 6. 44.
15 H. 7. 11.
‡ [304]
4 E. 6. Waste Br. 136.
18 H. 8. 1.

So it is of a wood, if waste be done *sparsim*, though all the wood be not wasted, the whole wood shall be recovered: and the reason of both these cases was, for that if waste were done *sparsim* in houses or woods, that by the construction of these words, the whole should be recovered, for that otherwise the house that was for the habitation of man, or the woods that so many wayes were for mans necessary use, could not be enjoyed, neither by him that had the inheritance, nor by the tenant without continuall trespassing the one to the other, *et boni judicis est causas litium dirimere*; but if waste were done in one part of the wood that might be conveniently divided from the rest, that part only is *locus vastatus*, and shall be recovered.

And

And so it is of brook medow, if the tenant plough it up *sparsim* (as hath been before said.)

7 H. 3. Wast, 141. Pl. Com. in Case de Mines. 5 R. 2. Waste, 97. Têps E. 1. Wast, 128.

A tenant for life or yeares of a parke, vivary, warren, or dovehouse, if he destroy the deere, or the fish in the vivary or ponds, or the game in the warren, or the doves in the dovehouse, it is waste, and hee that hath the inheritance shall recover the park, vivary, warren, or dovehouse, and therefore the makers of this act meaning to include all kinde of wasts, used this generall word [*chose.*]

And so it is if the tenant kill so many of the deere, fish, game or doves, as there be not left sufficient for store having regard to the number that were there when his estate or interest was created or made, this is waste, and so it was holden, Pasch. 15 Eliz. *in communi banco, et sic de similibus.*

Exile and destruction of villeins by tallage and oppression is wast, and this act saith [*perdra le chose.*]

3 E. 2. Waste, 2. 9 E. 2. Waste, 2. 16 H. 3. ib. 135. 9 H. 6. 42. 22 H. 6. 10, 11. 11 H. 7. per Fineux, 8 E. 2. Wast, 113. 17 E. 2. ib. 118. 15 H. 3. ib. 130. 2 H. 6. 10. F.N.B. 60. o. Lib. 5. fol. 115. Foliambes case. Regist. 72.

(9) *Et ouster ceo face gree de treble de ceo que le waste serra taxe.*] Concerning costs in this action sufficient hath been spoken, ca. 1.

The plaintiffe shall not recover damages for any waste done hanging the writ, and therefore the plaintiffe may have a writ of *estrepement* in this action, *et sic de similibus.*

Lessee for yeares committeth wast, and the years doe expire, yet shall the lessor have an action of waste for the treble damages, although he cannot recover the place wasted, and though the statute be in the conjunctive, *perdra le chose, &c. et ouster ceo face gree, &c.* for as there was at the common law two forms of actions of waste, *viz.* in the *tenet*, as against tenant by the curtesie, &c. and in the *tenuit* against the gardein after full age, so upon this act the like kinde of formes is framed by equall construction, *viz.* in the *tenet* to recover the place wasted, and treble damages, and in the *tenuit* to recover treble damages only.

46 E. 3. 25. 19 E. 2. Wast, 190. 8 H. 6. 10. 45 E. 3. 9.

But this is to be understood when the terme expires by effluxion of time, as in the case of a lease for years, or when the estate determines by the act of God, as when *cesti que vie* dieth, or when the estate is ended or defeated by the act and wrong of the tenant, as when he makes a feoffement in fee, or commits any other forfeiture, and the lessor enters, yet the lessor shall have his action of waste; but when the tenant commits waste, and after surrendreth to the lessor his estate or terme, and he in the reversion agreeth thereunto, he shall not have an action of waste in the *tenuit*, for he cannot by his owne act alter the forme and nature of his action from the *tenet* to the *tenuit*, and he cannot plead, *devant quel surrender nul waste fait.*

8 H. 5. 3. 4 E. 3. 33. 14 H. 6. 14. 19 H. 6. 41. 66. 12 H. 4. 5. 3 H. 6. Waste, 35. 32 E. 3. barre 262. 12 R. 2. Wast, 99.

An action of waste is brought against the lessee for years, or against tenant *pur terme dauter vie*, and hanging the action the term expires, or *ce' que vie* dieth, yet the writ shall not abate, for that an action of waste (as hath been said) lieth onely for the damages in those cases, which he shall recover in that action then depending.

[305]

33 E. 3. Judgement, 255.

In an action of waste against a lessee for life for waste done in three acres, the defendant claimeth fee, whereupon issue is joyned, the jury findes against the defendant that he hath but an estate for life, and enquired further of the waste, and found the waste done in one acre onely, the plaintiffe cannot have judgement for the whole

whole land, in reſpect of the forfeiture and treble damages, for that judgement is not according to this act, that is to ſay, of the place waſted, and treble damages in reſpect of the place waſted, wherefore he had judgement according to the ſtatute of the one acre and treble damages.

Upon this branch it hath been received for a certain rule, that if waſte be committed, and he in the reverſion dieth, that the action of waſte faileth, for that the heire cannot recover damages for the waſte done in the life of the aunceſtor, and the waſte was not done by the diſheritance of the heire, and yet the law doth extend the action of waſte favourably as much as with convenience may be, leſt waſte which is hurtfull to the common wealth ſhould remaine unpuniſhed; and therefore if two coparceners be, and they make a leaſe for life or yeares, and the leſſee commit waſte, and one of them hath iſſue and dieth, and after the leſſee commit waſte againe, albeit the writ ſhall ſay that both the waſts were done to the diſheritance to the aunt and neece, yet ſhall the action be maintained, and the judgement ſhall be ſeverall, though the action be joynt, for judgement ſhall be given for them both for the place waſted, and the damages treble for the waſte done in their owne time, and the aunt ſhall have a ſole judgement for the whole damages for the waſte done in the time of her ſiſter by ſurvivor, which is a leading caſe, and worthy of great obſervation.

8 E. 2. Waſt, 110. 11 E. 2. ib. 115. 45 E. 3. 3. 20 E. 3. Quar. Imp. 63. 35 H. 6. 23. F.N.B. 6. r. Kelwey, 105.

(10) *Et en waſte fait en garde.*] There is gardein in chivalry, and gardein in ſocage: again gardein in chivalry is twofold, gardein in *droit*, and gardein in *fait* of the graunt of the king, or of the ſubject; alſo both theſe are either gardeins by right, or gardeins by claime and poſſeſſion without right: likewiſe gardein in ſocage is two-fold, *viz.* gardein by right, who is called *tutor proprius*, and gardein by poſſeſſion and claime, who is called *tutor alienus*.

[a] Againſt all theſe both a prohibition of waſte, and an action of waſt lie at the common law, but none of theſe gardeins ſhall be charged but for the voluntary or permiſſive waſte, and not for the waſte done by a ſtranger. But if there be two joyntenants of a ward, and the one doth waſte, this is the waſte of both, for he is no ſtranger, 3 E. 3. 18.

If the gardein ſuffereth a ſtranger to cut down timber trees, or to proſtrate any of the houſes, and according to his name of gardein doth not endeavour to keep and preſerve the inheritance of the ward in his cuſtody and keeping, nor to forbid and withſtand the wrong doer, this ſhall be taken in law for his conſent, for in this caſe, *qui non prohibet quod prohibere poteſt, aſſentire videtur.* [b] And if ſuch waſte and deſtruction be done without the knowledge of the gardein, or with ſuch number as he could not withſtand, then ought the gardein to cauſe an aſſiſe to be brought againſt ſuch wrong doers by the heire, wherein he ſhall recover the freehold and damages for ſuch wrong and diſheriſon: ſo note a diverſity between the intereſt of a gardein created by law, for there in an aſſiſe the heir ſhall recover damages, but otherwiſe it is in the caſe of a leaſe for yeares, which is the leſſors own act.

[c] The gardein doth waſte, and after aſſigneth over his intereſt, an action of waſte lieth againſt the grantor in the *tenet.*

[d] Note that the action of waſte againſt the gardein is generall, *fecit vaſtum, &c. de terris, &c. quas habet vel habuit in cuſtodia de hæreditate*

[a] Glan. l. 7. c. 9, 10. Bract. li. 4. fol. 28. & 316, 317. Britton, 33, 34. Fleta, l. 1. c. 11. 7 H. 3. Waſte, 141. 9 H. 3. ib. 136. 10 H. 3. ibid. 142. 20 H. 3. ibidem. 2 E. 2. ib. 1. 4 E. 2. Account. 107. 16 E. 3. Waſt, 100. 13 E. 3. Account, 77. 32 E. 3. ib. 59. 41 E. 3. ib. 35. 40 Aſſ. 22. 44 E. 3. 27. 5 R. 2. Waſte, 97. 11 R. 2. ib. 98. 28 H. 6. ib. 9. 10 H. 6. 7. 32 H. 6. 7. F.N.B. 59. b.

[b] 40 Aſſ. 12. Temps E. 1. Waſte, 126. 27 E. 3. 81. F.N.B. 60. g. 26 E. 3. Waſte, 10.

[c] Regiſt. 72.

[d] F.N.B. 59. c. 2 E. 2. Waſte, 1.

e Mag. Chart. c. 4. 19 E. 2. tit. Waste, 117. Temps E. 1. ib. 127. See Mich. 7 E. 1. in communi banco Essex. Picots case. Hil. 8 E. 1. ibid. Rot. 52. North Lovets case, 48 E. 3. 10. F.N.B. 60. c.

hæreditatè prædict', which writ doth extend as well to the gardein in socage as in chivalry.

(11) e *Perdra le gard, et rendra al heire les damages del waste.*] So as if the heire bring his action of waste within age, the judgement by this act is, that he shall lose the whole wardship, not *locum vastatum* onely, and * yeeld to the heire single damages, if the wardship be not sufficient to satisfie the damages; see before what the judgement was at the common law.

But then it may be demanded, What if the gardein commit waste, and the heire did not, or perhaps could not bring an action of waste, being done so neare his full age, or having no notice thereof, what remedy hath the heire after his full age, for the gardein cannot lose the wardship, for his estate is ended, and it seemeth by the letter of the law that he must bring his action upon this statute within age, for the words bee [*perdra la garde.*] To this it is answered that the heire at his full age shall have an action of waste, and recover treble damages by this act, for the wardship cannot bee lost, and the wrong and disherison done to the heire ought to be fully recompenced, and the statute hath annexed treble damages to the action of waste, as if it were enacted by parliament, that an action of waste should lie against tenant in taile *apres possess.* therein treble damages should be recovered as incident or annexed by this law to the action of waste.

3 E. 2. Waste, 3. 7 E. 3. 12, 13. 43 E. 3. 88. Regist. 72. F.N.B. 59. e. & 60. c. coram rege per bre. de errore placita apud Dublin. Coram Johanne, justic. Hibern. Pasc. 30 E. 1.

And wheresoever the common law gave single damages against any, this act doth give treble, unlesse there be any speciall provision made by this act. Also in an action of waste, the jurors shall have the view of the place wasted, &c. as an incident to the action of waste, for in the action at the common law the jurors should have had the view.

Bract. l. 4. fo. 316. F.N.B. 60. c.

The law appointeth not of what value the waste shall be, neither in the case of the foure tenants first before mentioned, nor in the case of the gardein, who is to lose all for waste done in any part. Herein the rule of Bracton is good, *Vastum erit injuriosum, nisi vastum ita modicum fuerit, propter quod non sit inquisitio faciend'*; and *de minimis non curat lex*; for waste done to the value of xx. d. (which now is v. s.) the gardein lost the whole wardship.

Bract. l. 4. fo. 316. 38 E. 3. 7. 14 H. 4. 11, 12. 8 E. 2. Wast, 111. 34 E. 3. ib. 146. 12 H. 4. 3. F.N.B. 60. p.

If a feme seignioresse take husband, the tenant holding by knights service dieth his heire within age, the husband doth waste and dieth, the action of waste lieth against the wife. So if an infant be gardein in chivalry, and doth waste, an action of waste lieth against him, for he is within the letter and meaning of this law made against waste and destruction.

Pl. Com. in Stowels case.

(12) *Si le gard' perdue ne suffist a la value des damages, avant le age de mesme le garde.*] See a notable record upon this branch in the same yeare that this statute was made.

Mich. 6 E. 1. in banco Rot. 47. Essex Petrus Picots case.

A. hath the wardship of Blackacre and the heire of B. and Whiteacre and the heire of C. *per cause de gard*, A. doth waste in Blackacre, he shall lose but Blackacre, for that waste is done onely to the disherison of that heire; and so it is if he doth waste in Whiteacre, he shall onely lose that acre for the waste done there to the disherison of that heire.

At the common law in case of tenant by the curtesie, tenant in dower, or gardein, the heire, &c. might have entred into the houses and lands to see if waste were done, to the end that if he found any waste done, he might bring his action, and to that end might

11 H. 4. 75. 12 E. 4. 10. 15 H. 7. 4. Lib. 8. fol. 146. Les Carpenters case.

might the heire or he in reversion send any other to that intent; now this act giving an action of waste against tenant for life, and tenant for years, doth impliedly give authority to him in the reversion either by himself, or by another to enter into the houses or lands so letten for life or years, to see if any waste be done, *quia quando lex aliquid concedit, concedere videtur et id, per quod devenitur ad illud*, and therefore he in the reversion may lawfully enter, to see if any waste be done, whereupon he may ground an action upon this statute.

An action of waste lieth not upon this act in the court of ancient demesne, because that court fails of the incidents to an action of waste, *viz.* to award a writ to the sheriffe to enquire of the waste, &c.

28 H. 6. 25. 7 H. 6. 35. 8 H. 6. 35. 22 H. 6. 18. 20 E. 3. Wast, 32. 38 Ass. p. 1. 42 E. 3. 22.

If a tenant for life or yeares commit waste, so as he in the reversion is intituled * to his action of waste, yet if the tenant repaire the same before any action brought, he in the reversion cannot have an action of waste, but the tenant must plead it specially: but if the tenant doth repaire it after the writ brought, and before he hath day to plead, he cannot plead it in barre of the action.

* [307]

Upon the construction of this act, whether in this mixt action the place wasted is the principall, or the damages, some question hath been made, and in divers respects the one is more principall then the other, for in respect of the antiquity against tenant in dower, and the tenant by the curtesie, the damages are the principall, as hath been before shewed; and therefore they shall be sometime preferred, *viz.* the plaintiffe to have execution of the damages before the place wasted. But in respect of the quality, the realty is ever preferred before the personalty, and therefore in waste, if the defendant confesse the action, the plaintiffe may have judgement of the land, and release his damages, which proveth the realty to be the principall, and an accord is no plea in an action of waste in the *tenet*, for *omne majus dignum trahit ad se minus*.

40 E. 3. 37. 38 E. 3. 27. 13 E. 4. 15.

34 H. 6. 7. tit. Waste, 50. 48 E. 3. 19. per Finchd. 11 H. 7. 13. 13 H. 7. 20.

And in an action of waste there shall be summons, and severance, for the writ is *ad exhæredationem*, and the action of waste is a plea reall: in an action of waste brought by two in the *tenuit*, a release of the one is a barre to both, but otherwise it is in the *tenet*, for there it barreth but himselfe.

Lib. 6. fol. 43, 44. Blaks case. 6 E. 3. 47. 9 H. 5. 15. 30 H. 6. barre 39.

Thus have we endeavoured to expound this excellent law enacted *pro bono publico*, for preservation of buildings for the habitation of mankinde, and of woods and timber, sometime one of the beautifull, and profitable ornaments of England, and generally against all waste and destruction by particular tenants, which law being very penall, and shortly and artificially penned hath beene with great wisdome and judgement expounded in our bookes, and may be a light to many other like cases. *Vide* Magna Charta, cap. 4. Marlebridge, cap. 23. W. 1. cap. 21. W. 2. cap. 14. 21. 20 E. 1. Vet. Magna Charta, 124. 28 E. 1. ca. 18. See the first part of the Institutes, sect. 67. 71. 380, 381, 382. 492. 570. 573. 574. 577. 585, 586. 666, 667, 668. 674, 675.

CAP. VI.

PURVIEW est ensement, que si home mourge (1), *& eit plusors heires* (2), *dont lun est fits ou file* (3), *frere ou soer, nephew ou niece* (4), *& les auters sont en pluis longe degree, touts les heires desormes* (5) *eyent recoverie per briefe de mortdauncester* (6).

IT is provided also, that if a man die, having many heires, of whom one is son or daughter, brother or sister, nephew or niece, and the other be of a further degree, all the heirs shall recover from henceforth by a writ of mortdauncestor.

(Fitz. Joinder, in Act 11. 31. 34, 35, 36. 1. Inst. 164. a.)

Bract. l. 4. fol 254. 283. Brit. fol. 181. b. Fleta, lib. 5. cap. 2.

It appeareth by our auncient authors that this act is made in affirmance of the common law, for Bracton saith, *Cum sit assisa mortis antecessoris conjungenda cum consanguinitate, non erit post recurrendum ad præcipe de consanguinitate, sed ad assisam mortis, quia persona quæ propinquior est, et facit assisam, et trahit ad se personam et gradum remotiorem, ut ibi potius procedat assisa, quam præcipe, quia illud quod est majus remotum non trahit ad se quod est majus junctum; sed è contrario in omni casu, et bene poterit quælibet istarum conjungi cum alia actione, quia quælibet loquitur de seisina ejus quam habuit die quo obiit, quod non est in brevi de recto, et quælibet de possessione et non de proprietate.*

[308]

So as it appeareth by Bracton that the abovesaid rule doth not hold onely in case of mordauncester, but in the writ of aiel and besaiel, which is also a proofe of the common law, for this act nameth the assise of mordaunc' onely, and his opinion is approved by our books.

Temps, E. 1. joyndre in action, 35. 32 E. 1. ib. 34. 19 E. 2. ib. 31. 13 E. 3 ib. 29. 19 E. 3. ib. 31. 12 E. 3. ib. 11. 7 E. 3. 34. 24 E. 3. 13. 28. 48 E. 3. 14. 27 E. 3. 89. 30 E. 1. joyndre en action 36. 19 E. 2. Judgement 239.

Also this act extends to dying seised after the statute, and yet like joyning shall be in the writ of mordaunc', aiel and besaiel of dying seised afore the statute, which is another proofe of the common law. And the same law it is in a formedon in the descender, and in writs of entry *sur disseisin* to the common ancestor, and in a *sur cui in vita*, writs of entry *in casu proviso, consimili casu ad communem legem*, and the like, the aunt and the neece shall joyne at the common law.

To know what the common law was before the making of any statute (whereby it may be known whether the act be introductory of a new law, or affirmatory of the old) is the very lock and key to set open the windowes of the statute, as partly appeareth by that which hath been said, and particularly in the exposition of this act shall appeare.

(1) *Si home mourge.*] Hereby it appeareth that one right must descend from one auncestor, or else the case is not within this law.

5 E. 3. 185.

If two coparceners die seised, and a stranger abate, the aunt and the neece shall not joyne in a writ of mordaunc' but have severall writs, the one a mordaunc', and the other a writ of aiel.

In like manner if two coparceners be disseised, the one hath issue and die, the aunt and the neece shall not joyne, for they have not one right, but severall, and therefore they must have severall actions, but when they have recovered they shall hold in coparcenery. 37 H. 6. 8. 35 H. 6. 23.

(2) *Plusors heires.*] Divers heires either in gavelkinde by the custome, or heirs females coparceners by the common law, for this act extends to both of them.

(3) *Dont lun est fits ou file, &c.*] By this it appears that this act extends as well to heires by the custome, as by the common law.

The aunt and the neece bring a writ of mordaunc' of the dying seised of the father, the aunt is summoned and severed, yet the neece shall proceed and recover the moity (although she alone could never have a writ of mordaunc' of the dying seised of the grandfather) because the writ was rightly and duly commenced, and when the neece hath recovered, the aunt may enter, and enjoy that moity with her; for the rule of the law is, that in all cases when coparceners, or joyntenants may joyn in action, and have one and the same remedy, there if one be summoned and severed, and the other sueth forth and recovers the moity, the other may enter with her; but when they are driven to severall actions, or where their remedies are not equal, there if one recover or continue the one moity, the other cannot enter with her, and yet when both have recovered they shall be coparceners again. 10 H. 6. 10. 19 H. 6. 45. 31 H. 6. Entry cong. 54. First part Inst. sect. 696.

(4) *Frere ou soer, nephew ou niece.*] Here is implied the uncle and aunt being relatives, and then here be all the persons that may have an assise of mordaunc', and so there be one that may have an assise of mordaunc', it maketh no matter how remote the other is. See the auncient authors, ubi sup. F.N.B. 195. c.

(5) *Desormes.*] So as this law extends to the future, and not to the time past, and yet being made in affirmance of the common law, the same law that guideth *in futuro*, ruleth also *in præterito*.

(6) *Eyent recoverie per briefe de mordaunc'.*] These words are generall, but they have a speciall intendment, for as to the damages, the aunt alone shall recover damages untill the death of her husband, and both of them damages from the death of her sister, and so it is in the writ of aiel, and besaiel, and all this is according to the course of the common law before the making of this act, see the exposition upon the first chapter of this parliament. See cap. 1. 45 E. 3. 3. 35 H. 6. 23.

[309]

CAP. VII.

ENSEMENT si feme vende, ou done en fee, ou a terme de vie (2), *tenement que el tient en dower* (1). *Establie est, que le heire, ou auter, a que la terre deveroit reverter* (3) *apres le decease la feme, eit maintenant*	ALSO if a woman sell or give in fee, or for term of life, the land that she holdeth in dower; it is ordained, that the heir, or other to whom the land ought to revert after the death of such woman, shall have present

nant (4) son recoverie per briefe dentre (5) fait de ceo en la chauncerie.

present recovery to demand the land by a writ of entry made thereof in the chancery.

Custumier de Norm. cap. 118. fol. 138. (Fitz. Entre, 7, 8. Bro. Ingress, 3. 1 Roll. 161. 11 H. 7. c. 20. Regist. 235.)

Regist. 237. Mirror, ca. 5. § 5. First part of the Instit. sect. 483.

The mischief before the making of this statute was not, where a gift or feoffement was made in fee, or for terme of life by tenant in dower, for in that case he in the reversion might enter for the forfeiture, and avoid the estate: but the mischiefe was, that when the feoffee, or any other died seised, whereby the entry of him in the reversion was taken away, he in the reversion could have no writ of entry *ad communem legem* untill after the decease of tenant in dower, and then the warranty contained in her deed (as in those dayes all deeds of feoffement for the most part comprehended warranty, and specially when she intended to barre her heire that had the reversion) barred him in the reversion, if he were her heir, as commonly he was, and for the remedy of this mischief this statute gave the writ of entry in *casu proviso* in the life time of tenant in dower, which is implied by this word [*maintenant, &c.*] The purview of this act Fleta rendreth thus, *Est autem quoddam breve provisum de ingressu, per quod habens statum, recuperabit dotem alienatam per formam statuti, quod tale est; si mulier alienet dotem suam in feodo, vel ad terminum vitae donatoris, haeres vel alius ad quem spectat reversio, statim ipso facto habeat actionem petendi dotem illam in dominico.*

Fleta, li. 5. c. 34.

(1) *Fem', &c. que tient en dower.*] The tenant by the curtesie, or the lessee for life is not within the case of this statute, but he in the reversion upon their alienation shall have a writ of entry *in consimili casu* by that excellent statute of W. 2. cap. 24. *quotiescunque evenerit in cancellaria, quod in uno casu reperitur breve, et in consimili casu cadente simili indigente remedio, &c. concordent clerici de cancellaria in brevi faciendo*, as we shall shew more at large when we come to that statute.

22 Ass. 37. 29 Ass. 54. 3 E. 2. entry 8. F.N.B. 207. f. 5 H. 7. 31. 14 H. 7. 13, 14. 33 H. 6. 3. 30. 14 H. 4. 28.

Tenant in dower taketh husband, the husband aliens in fee, he in the reversion during the husbands life may enter for the forfeiture, but he cannot have a writ of entry *in casu proviso*, for the husband hath nothing but during the coverture in the right of the wife, and our act saith, *Fem' que tient en dower vend' ou done*, so as the alienation of the husband is not within the case of the statute, and so it is *in consimili casu* when tenant for life take husband and he alien.

16 Ass. 11.

(2) *Done en fee ou a terme de vie.*] At this time all estates of inheritance were fee-simple, and here (for terme of life) is intended of a state for the terme of the life of a stranger, and not for the life of the tenant in dower her selfe, for such an estate wrought no wrong.

See the first part of the Institutes, sect. 483. 205. F.N.B. 206. g. Bract. fol. 323.

The words of the writ grounded upon this statute are generall, *Et quae post dimissionem factam ad praefatum B. reverti debet*, without expressing any estate, and doth count that the tenant in dower did alien in fee, and the tenant saith that the tenant in dower did not alien in manner and forme, &c. if it be found that the tenant in dower did alien in fee taile, or for life, the demandant shall recover, as it appeareth by Littleton, for auncient formes of writs or counts cannot be altered.

[310]

(3) *A que le terre deveroit reverter.*] If a man hath the reversion in fee, in taile, or for life, either upon his own gift or lease, or by assignation, he shall have a writ of entry upon this statute (and in like case *à consimili casu*) for the words of this act are generall (to whom the land ought to revert) and the words of the writ grounded upon this statute are, *Quam clamat esse jus et hæreditatem suam*, but yet an estate for life, as hath been said, is within this statute. And this act providing against the alienation of tenant in dower, speaketh onely of him in the reversion, because there can be no remainder limited upon her estate, otherwise it is of the writ of *consimili casu*, as we shall shew when we come to the statute of W. 2. cap. 24.

Fleta ubi supra. 31 E. 1. Entry 64. 12 E. 2. ibid. 60. 20 E. 2. bre. 149. 7 E. 3. 54. 8 E. 3. 48. 21 E. 3. 11. F.N.B. 205. n.

And this act speaketh onely of land which lieth in livery, for the feoffement or estate for life made by tenant in dower devesteth the reversion, otherwise it is of rents, and other things that lie in graunt. Pl. Com. Colthirsts case.

(4) *Eyt maintenant.*] That is, presently after the alienation made in the life of tenant in dower, which writ he could not have, as hath been said, at the common law in the life of tenant in dower.

(5) *Son recovery per briefe dentre.*] This writ of entry goeth by the name of a writ of entry *in casu proviso*, so called, because it hath the words of the writ of entry, *ad communem legem* (mentioned by Bracton) with this addition, by force of this act, *Et quæ post dimissionem per ipsum C. (viz. tenentem in dotem) præfato D. contra formam statuti de Gloc', de communi concilio regni nostri inde provisi ad præfatum B. reverti debet per formam ejusdem statuti ut dicit*, and of these words, *inde proviso*, it taketh his name of the writ of entry *in casu proviso*, and by these words this writ differeth from the writ of entry, *ad communem legem*, because this writ lieth during the life of tenant in dower by the reference it hath to this act, which giveth the writ *maintenant*, &c. as hath been said. Bract. l. 4. f. 324. Fleta ubi supra.

But the writ of entry *ad communem legem* lieth not during the life of tenant in dower, and the writ of entry *ad communem legem* doth not make mention of the death of the tenant for life, but that must be expressed in the count. 16 E. 3. bre. 661.

CAP. VIII.

PURVIEW est ensement, que les visconts pled' en counties (1) les plees de trespas, auxy come ils soilent estre pledes. Et que nul neit desormes briefes de trespasse devant justices (2), sil ne affirme per foy, que les biens emportes vailent 40. s. al meins (3). Et sil se pleint de batery affirme per foy que sa pleint est veritable. Des plaies, et des maihemes, eit home briefe sicome home soleit aver (4). Et graunt est, que les defend' puissent faire attorneies

IT is provided also, that sheriffs shall plead pleas of trespass in their counties, as they have been accustomed to be pleaded. And that none from thenceforth shall have writs of trespass before justices, unless he swear by his faith, that the goods taken away were worth forty shillings at the least. And if he complain of beating, he shall answer by his faith, that his plaint is true. Touching wounds and maims, a man shall have his

neies en tiel plees, ou appell' ne gist (5) *mie, issint que sils soient attaints* du trespas *en lour absence, soit maund' al visc', que ils soient prises* (6), *et eient adonques* * *la peine, que ils averont sils ussent estre presents quant le judgement fuit rendus. Et si les plaintiffes desormes en tiel trespas se facent essoine apres la primer apparans, soit jour done jesques a la venue des justices errants* (7), *et les def. en dementires soient en peace en tielx plees, et en auters plees, ou attachments, et distres gisent* (8). *Si le defend' se face essoine del service le roy* (9), *et ne port son garrant* (10) *au jour que done luy est per son essoine: establie est que il rendra al plaintife les damages de la tourne de xx. s. ou de pluis, solonque le discretion des justices* (11), *et jademains soit en le greve mercy le roy.*

his writ as before hath been used; and it is agreed, that the defendants in such pleas may make their attornies, where appeal lieth not; so that if they be attainted being absent, then the sheriff shall be commanded to take them, and shall have like pain as they should have had, if they had been present at the judgement given. And if the plaintiffs from henceforth in such trespasses cause themselves to be essoined after the first appearance, day shall be given them unto the coming of the justices in eyre, and the defendants in the mean time shall be in peace. In such pleas and other, whereas attachments and distresses do lie, if the defendant essoin himself of the king's service, and do not bring his warrant at the day given him by the essoin, he shall recompense the plaintiff damages for his journey twenty shillings, or more, after the discretion of the justices, and shall be grievously amerced unto the king.

(Fitz. Brief. 550. 14 H. 8. f. 15. Bro. Attorn. 64. 74. 78. 82. 88. Fitz. Essoin, 16, 17. 39. 41. 79. 116. 118. 198. Cro. El. 96. 43 El. c. 6. 21 Jac. 1. c. 16. Keilw. 106. b.)

This act is divided into two branches.

The first branch is in affirmance of the common law.

The second branch concerning the affidavit, this is new, and made in favour of the county court, but experience taught, that this course was so full of danger and trouble, that it was forborne, and the defendant left to take such exceptions as the common law gave him.

(1) *En countie courts.*] This is put for an example, for the hundred court, and the court baron being no courts of record are also within this law.

Regist. fo. 111. F.N.B. 47. a. 239. d.

(2) *Briefes de trespas devant justices.*] Writs of trespasse are here put but for an example, for debt, detinue, covenant and the like: but if the trespasse be *vi et armis*, where the king upon the conviction of the defendant shall have a fine, there the sheriffe in his county cannot hold plea of it, for no court can assesse a fine but a court of record, because a capias to take the body is incident to it: for it is a rule in law, *Quod placita de transgressione contra pacem regis in regno Angliæ vi et armis factis secundum legem et consuetudinem Angliæ sine brevi regis placitari non debent.*

Regist. 11. F.N.B. 47.

Regist. 11. F.N.B. 47.

Neither shall he hold plea of trespasse for taking away of charters concerning inheritance or free-hold, for it is a maxime in law, *Quod placita concernent' chart', seu script' liberum tenementum tangentia in aliquibus*

quibus curiis quæ recordum non habent secundum legem et consuetudinem regni Angliæ sine brevi regis placitari non debent.

(3) *Vaillent* 40. *s. al meyns.*] For as the inferiour courts which are not of record regularly cannot hold plea of debt, &c. or damages, but under 40 s. so the superior courts that are of record cannot hold plea of debt, &c. or damages regularly, unlesse the summe amount to 40 s. or above. Now the ounce of silver was at the time of making of this act but 20 d. and now it is above thrice so much; for the wisdome of the common law was, that men should not be troubled for suits of small value in the kings courts, but that they should be heard and determined in the country with small charge, and little or no travell or losse of time, for it was then accounted against the dignity and institution of those high courts, to hold plea of small or trifling causes, *Ne dignitas curiarum illarum vilesceret, et ne materiam superaret opus*; otherwise the law that was instituted for the quiet of man, and for his defence, might be abused to his charge, vexation, and offence.

Now as the superior courts ought not to incroach upon the inferiour, so the inferiour courts ought not to defraud the superiour courts of those causes that belong to them. For example, if in the county court, or other inferiour courts, they shall divide a debt of xx. l. into severall pleints under 40 s. in this case the defendant may plead the same to the jurisdiction of the court, or may have a prohibition to stay that indirect suit, for as an ancient record saith, *Contra jus commune est, petere integrum debitum excedens summam* 40 *s. per diversas querelas, per parcellas, scilicet,* 39 *s.* 11 *d. ob. q.*

Regist. 146. F.N.B. 46. [312] Pasch. 20 E. 3. Coram Rege. Rot. 164. Cestr.

The maxime of the common law is, *Quod placita de catallis, debitis, &c. quæ summam* 40 *s. attingunt, vel eam excedunt, secundum legem et consuetudinem Angliæ sine brevi regis placitari non debent.*

Regist. 146. F.N.B. 46. Brit. ca. 28. fo. 61.

And these words, *sine brevi regis* are materiall words, for by the kings writ the sheriffe in the county court may hold plea of goods, debts, &c. above the value of 40 s. and by force of the kings writ of justicies, he may hold plea of an obligation of what summe soever, for example of 1000 marks, the which writ is in nature of a commission to the sheriffe to hold plea of debt above 40 s. the words of which writ are, *Rex vicecom' salutem: Præcipimus tibi, quod justicies A. quod juste et sine dilatione reddat B. mille marcas, quas ei debet, ut dicit, &c. ne amplius inde clamorem audiamus pro defectu justiciæ.* By force of which writ he may hold plea of the same, and the proces therein is attachment by his goods, &c. but no capias, and although the power of the court by this writ is in this particular inlarged, and the words of the writ to the sheriffe are, *Quod justicies, &c.* yet is not the jurisdiction of the court as concerning the judicature thereof, altered, for those words of the writ do not, nor can make the sheriffe judge of that court in that particular case, for that were to alter the jurisdiction and judicature of the court, whereof by the common law the suitors be judges, which cannot be altered but by act of parliament: the plaintiffe may remove this plea without cause shewed, but the defendant cannot without shewing of cause.

3 H. 6. 54, 55. Glanv. l. 12. c. 18. Brit. fo. 53, 54. Fleta, l. 2. c. 55. Brac. l. 3. f. 105. b. F.N.B. hereafterwards.

Also by force of a justicies to the sheriffe, he may hold plea of a trespasse *vi et armis.* *Vide* Register, and F. N. B. divers formes of writs of justicies in many actions.

Bract. ubi supra. Brit. ubi supra. 8 E. 4. 5. 14 H. 8. 15. F.N.B.

 The

86. b. c. d. 85. g. 86. a. 7. a. 117. a. c. 119. 123. 125. 128. 132. 135. 137. 139. 148. 161. 184. 151, 152. The sheriffe may also hold plea in a replevin of goods and chattels above the value of 40 s. for if it be by writ, the words of the writ be, *Rex vicecom', &c. Praecipimus tibi quod juste, et sine dilatione replegiari facias B. averia sua, or bona et catalla sua, quae D. cepit et injuste detinet, ut dicit, &c. ne amplius inde clamorem audiamus pro defectu justiciae.* By force of which writ, which is in nature of a commission, the sheriffe may deliver the beasts, or goods and chattels of what value soever. And if the replevin be by pleint in the county court, the sheriffe by the statute of Marlebridge may hold plea of what value soever.

The like writs in the nature of a commission directed to sheriffes are the admeasurement of pasture, recaption, *nativo habendo,* and many others.

Brit. c. 28. f. 61. 19 H. 6. 8. b. The said words, *vaillent* 40 *s. al meins,* have received this construction, that the same must so appeare to be of value in the plaintiffes count, for it is not sufficient that it appeares by verdict that the summe is under 40 s. For example, if the plaintiffe count in trespasse, debt, detinew, covenant, &c. to the damage of 40 s. and the jury finde the damages under 40 s. yet the plaintiffe shall have no judgement, albeit in truth the cause *de jure* belonged to the inferiour courts.

This shall suffice for the exposition of this branch of our act, the residue shall be referred to the treatise concerning the jurisdiction of courts whereunto this matter properly belongeth.

(4) *Des playes et des mayhems eyt home briefe sicome home soiloit aver.*] This is the third branch of this act, and hereby it appeareth that the county court hath no jurisdiction to hold plea *de plagis et maihemiis,* of wounds and maihems, but those pleas must be determined in the kings higher courts, but of battery (without wounding or maiheming) this act proveth that the county court hath jurisdiction.

What in law is adjudged a maiheme, and whereof the word is derived, you shall reade in the first part of the Institutes, sect. 194.

[313] (5) *Et graunt est, que les defend' puissent faire attornies en tiels plees, ou lappeale ne gist,* &c.] See before W. 1. cap. 41. Merton cap. 10. W. 2. cap.

Regist. 19. b. this extends to justices in eyre. Some have thought that this clause concerning making of attourneys is generall, and extendeth to all actions reall and personall, but it seemeth to be particular, for in ancient manuscripts the former branch, *viz. des playes et des mayhems, &c.* is a distinct chapter by itselfe, and this branch is parcell of that chapter, so as these words,
6 H. 7. 1. *en tiels pleas,* such pleas must be referred to pleas of trespasse, battery, wounding, and mayheming, unlesse it be in appeal of mayheme,
3 H. 7. cap. 1. which being *felonice maihemavit,* the defendant should not make an attorney no more then he could at the common law: and the words subsequent *(issint que sils soient attaint de trespasse en lour absence)* prove that this branch is not generall, but referred to the clause next
40 Ass. 17. 40 E. 3. 42. 11 H. 4. 11. 8 E. 4. 3. precedent: and note that neither the plaintiffe nor defendant at the common law could make an attourny in any appeale untill triall, acquitall, judgement, &c.

But it may be objected that against this exposition the booke in
21 H. 7. 39. b. 21 H. 7. is, *Que home ferra attorney in appeale de maiheme, quod vide de common course* 16 H. 7. in Caworths case; which case is incertainly reported, for it appeareth not whether it be meant of the plaintiffe

or

or defendant; but of the defendant it cannot be intended, for that should be against our books, the true interpreters of this act. And of the plaintiffe (it seemeth it was intended) he cannot be by attourney, and that was Caworths case mentioned in the report of 21 H. 7. the record whereof being found out is against the report thereof; which very point came in question in my time in the kings bench in an appeale of mayheme brought by Hudson against Marwood, the plaintiffe appeared by attourney, and declared against the defendant, the defendant prayed that the plaintiffe might be demaunded, for that he could not appeare by attourney, and if the plaintiffe appeared not, that he might be nonsuited; against which the councell of the plaintiffe objected, that the plaintiffe in an appeale of mayheme might appeare by attourney, for that it might be, that he was so wounded as he could not appeare, and for authority cited the said booke in 21 H. 7. whereunto answer was made by the councell of the defendant, and resolved by the whole court, that the plaintiffe could not appeare by attourney, for the defendant may demand *oyer* of the mayhem, &c. which shall be peremptory to him being a tryall of the mayheme, which is a triall which the law giveth him.

8 E. 3. Attourney 93. 2 R. 3. 13. 6 H. 7. 1. F.N.B. 26, 27. Vet. N.B. 19, 20.

M. 25 & 26 Eliz. Coram Rege Rot.

And albeit it may be hard and difficult in some particular case in respect of the grievousnesse of the mayheme for the plaintiffe to appeare in person, as it was in 16 H. 7. where the mayheme was hainous and horrible, the legges of the plaintiffe being broken over a threshold, yet that must not change the law, nor take from the defendant his just defence and triall, for so upon the like surmise the defendant might be barred thereof in all cases.

And Sir Christopher Wray chiefe justice said that the record of Caworths case had been seen, and that the record thereof was against the report, and thereupon the plaintiffe was called, and by the rule of the court was non-suit, and I was of councell in this case, which I have the rather reported the more at large, for that no man should bee deceived by the said report of 21 H. 7.

(6) *Soit maund al visc' que ils sont prises.*] This is the fourth branch of this act.

Albeit this statute speaketh onely of the execution of the body, yet might he have had at the making of this act a *fieri fac'*: and afterwards by the statute of W. 2. cap. 45. he may have an *elegit*, for this branch being in the affirmative doth not restrain the plaintiffe to take any other remedy.

[314]

(7) *Si les plaintifes desormes en tiel trespas, &c. se facent essoine, &c. soit jour done tanq; al venu des justices errants*, &c.] This is the fift branch of this act, and is to be intended of an essoine *de service le roy*, and extendeth to actions of trespasse, and not actions of debt. Touching common essoines, which were used for delay onely, former provisions had been made. By matter subsequent this branch is become of no use, for seeing the authority of justices in eyre is ceased, when the plaintiffe is essoined of the service of the king, the court cannot give day before the justices in eyre, and therefore it remaineth, as it was before the making of this act.

45 E. 3. 10. b. Marleb. c. 13. 19. W. 1. c. 41, 42, 43, &c.

Note that when the demandant or plaintiffe is essoined *de service le roy*, and at the day brings not in his warrant, this shall be adjudged a non-suit.

Tr. 18 E. 3. 21 E. 3. 37. b.

(8) *En*

27 E. 3. 81. 12 H. 4. 14. per Skrene.

(8) *En tiels pleas et en auters pleas, ou attachments et distres gisont.*] That is to say, in personall actions, where the processe is by attachment and distresse. This is the sixt branch of this act.

Marl. c. 19. 12 H. 4. 14. 2 E. 4. 16. l. 5 E. 4. 70.

(9) *Essoine de service le roy.*] Herein the delay is great, *viz.* for a yeare and a day, therefore he that cast the essoine must appeare in person in court to the end he may be sworne, &c. and that day may be given to bring in the warrant for the essoine.

34 H. 6. 1. 35 H. 6. 2.

(10) *Et ne port son garrant.*] A warrant under the privy seale is not sufficient, but it must be by writ under the great seale directed to the justices; also the warrant must testifie that he is in the kings service, &c. which commonly is upon certificate made to the lord chancellor by the captaine of the host under whom he serves.

And this is the first act, that concerned the essoine *de service le roy.*

(11) *Il rendra al plaintife les damages de la journey de 20 s. ou de pluis solonque le discretion les justices.*] The statute speaketh where there is one defendant, &c. he shall pay 20 s. and if there be divers defendants, and they are essoined *de service le roy,* and at the day bring in no warrant, every one of them shall pay 20 s. for they are in law several essoins.

4 E. 2. essoine 79. 28 E. 3. 98. Kelwey 106 & 107.

29 E. 3. 13. 36.

And the court by their discretion may by force of the act increase it to a greater summe, as sometime to 40 s. &c.

29 E. 3. 36. 31 E 3. 37.

And albeit this branch doth not by expresse words determine what shall be further done, yet if the essoine were cast after issue in a personall action, and seeing the essoine for want of a warrant is turned to a default, it followeth that by the common law the enquest shall be awarded by default, and therefore in that case he shall have the * 20 s. *pur la journey* by the statute, and by the enquest recover his damages and costs by the common law; for statutes made for the ousting of delayes are ever construed liberally and beneficially.

* Hil. 16 E. 1. in Banco 75. Buck. & Rot. 73. Hereford.

In a reall action if an essoine be cast for the tenant *de service le roy,* and no warrant is brought in at the day, he shall not pay the * 20 s. &c. for this act extends not to reall actions; but a *petit cape,* or a graund *cape* shall lie as upon a default, as the case shall require.

* Hil. 16 E. 1. ubi supra. 20. s. in Action de Waste vers Tenant pur vie.

* [315]

CAP. IX.

*PURVIEW est ensement, que nul briefe ne isser' desormes de le chauncerie pur mort de home, denquirer si home occist auter per misadventure, ou soy defend', ou en auter maner * sans felony* (1), *mes celuy soit en prison jesque al venue des justices errants, ou assign' a gaole deliverie* (2), *et se mist en pais devant eux de bien et male. Et si soit trove per pais que il le fist soy defend', ou*

THE king commandeth that no writ shall be granted out of the chancery for the death of a man to enquire whether a man did kill another by misfortune, or in his own defence, or in other manner without felony; but he shall be put in prison until the coming of the justices in eyre, or justices assigned to the gaol-delivery, and shall put himself upon the

ou per misadventure (3), *donques fra les justices assavoier au roy* (4), *et le roy luy en fra sa grace, si luy pleist* (5.) W. 1. cap. 11. *Purview est ensement, que nul appell' soit abatue* (7) *ci legierment come avant ad este* (6), *mes si lappellour* (8) *counte le fait* (9), *lan* (10), *le jour* (11), *le heure* (12), *le temps le roy* (13), *et la ville* (14), *ou le fait fuist fait, et de quel arme il fuist occise* (15), *se estoia la appell', et jammes ne soit lappell' abatus per default de fresh suit* (16) *puis que home sue dedeins lan et le jour* (17) *apres le fait* (18).

the country before them for good and evil: in case it be found by the country, that he did it in his defence, or by misfortune, then by the report of the justices to the king, the king shall take him to his grace, if it please him. It is provided also, that no appeal shall be abated so soon as they have been heretofore; but if the appellor declare the deed, the year, the day, the hour, the time of the king, and the town where the deed was done, and with what weapon he was slain, the appeal shall stand in effect, and shall not be abated for default of fresh suit, if the party shall sue within the year and the day after the deed done.

(Kel. fo. 53. 108. Woods Inst. 628. 2 Ed. 3. c. 2. 1 Bulst. 80. Regist. 134. 300. 14 Ed. 3. stat. 1. c. 15.)

Before the making of this statute, for that men were detained long in prison before they were called to answer, which was ever odious in law, writs *de odio et atia* issued out of the chancery for their relief (as it appeared before in the exposition upon the statute of *Magna Charta)* specially where the fact was either by misadventure, or *se defendendo*; and therefore this act restraining those writs, doth prescribe a course for their speedy calling to answer in those two cases. But now the writ *de odio et atia* is revived by the statute of 42 E. 3. cap. 1. as it appears in the exposition upon the six and twentieth chapter of *Magna Charta*. See the Mirror, cap. 5. § 5. Magn. Chart. ca. 26. 29. See W. 2 ca. 29. Regist. 134.

And where the statute of Marlbridge had determined, that killing of a man by misadventure should not be any offence for the which the delinquent should dye, this statute maketh the killing of a man *se defend'* in the same degree, where by the common law he should have dyed for it. Marlb. ca. 26. 21 E. 1. 17. b.

Lastly, where the statute of Marlbridge took an order for the parties speedy delivery out of prison in case of misadventure, this act provideth for the same both in case of misadventure, and of *se defendendo*.

(1) *Per misadventure ou soy defendant, ou en auter manner sans felony.*] Of this matter somewhat hath been said in the exposition upon the statute of Marlbridge: an indictment or a verdict that A. killed B. *se defendendo* is not good, but the speciall matter must be set down, to the end the court may adjudge it to be upon inevitable necessity; whereof you shall read a notable record in the parliament rolls of 3 R. 2. John Imperials case; note the words here, *Sans felony, vide Marlbridge ubi supra*, and in our books it is said to be no felony; and the reason is, because neither of them is done *felleo animo*. Marlbr. ca. 25. 43 Ass. p. 3. 3 E. 3. Coron. 302. 354. 15 E. 3. ibid. 116. 2 H. 4. 18. 11 H. 7. 23. Fleta, lib. 1. cap. 31. Rot. Parliam. 3. R. 2. nu. 18. John Imperials case.

If a man kill another in his own defence, if he escape, &c. the town shall be amercied, as an ancient mark of the common law, that made it felony.

(2) *Soit*

(2) *Soit en priſon jeſque al venue des juſtices errants ou aſſign' a gaole deliverie.*] Hereby it appeareth what expedition ought to be uſed
Magn. Chart. ca. 26. & 29. for avoiding of long impriſonment, *viz.* untill the next coming of the juſtices; ſee for this *Magna Charta.*

And here it is to be obſerved, that the law of England is a law of mercie, *Lex Angliæ eſt lex miſericordiæ*, for three cauſes:

Firſt that the innocent ſhall not be worn and waſted by long impriſonment, but (as hereby, and by the ſtatute of *Magna Charta* appeareth) ſpeedily come to his triall.

Secondly, that priſoners for criminall cauſes, when they are
* *Regula.* brought to their triall, be humanely dealt withall; for * *Severos*
[316] *quidem facit juſticia, inhumanos non facit.* And therefore it is ſaid,
Bract. lib. 3. fol. 137. a. Brit. fo. 17. b. *Cum autem captus coram juſticiariis producendus fuerit, produci non debet ligatis manibus (quamvis aliquando compedibus propter periculum evaſionis) et hoc ideo, ne videatur coactus ad aliquam purgationem ſuſci-*
Fleta, li. 1. c. 31. *piendam.* And Fleta ſaith, *Cum autem capti in judicio produci debeant, non producantur armati, ſed ut judicium recepturi, nec ligati, ne videantur reſpondere coacti.*

Thirdly, the judge ought to exhort him to anſwer without fear, and that juſtice ſhall be duly adminiſtred to him.

It is to be obſerved, that juſtices of gaole delivery may take an indictment of killing of a man *ſe defend'*, becauſe their authority is generall, but juſtices of peace cannot take ſuch an indictment, becauſe their commiſſion is limited, and it is taken not to be within their commiſſion.

(3) *Et ſi ſoit trove per paiis que il ſoy fiſt ſoy defendend' ou per miſadventure*, &c.] This may be two wayes, either when he is indicted of murther or homicide, and the jury finde it *ſe defendendo*, or when he is ſpecially indicted, that he killed a man *ſe defendendo*, whereunto (for ſafeguard of his goods) he may plead not-guilty; and if he be found guilty *ſe defendendo*, he forfeiteth his goods, if not guilty, he ſaveth them.

37 H. 8. Appeal. B. 122. 26 Aſſ. 32. 29 Aſſ. 23. Stamf. Pl. Cor. 15. Pl. Com. 101. 25 E. 3. 42. 29 E. 3. 94. Here is implyed a maxime of the common law, that the life of a man is of ſo precious regard in law, that the death of a man cannot be juſtified, as in this caſe the defendant in the appeal cannot juſtifie the death *ſe defendendo*, but muſt plead not-guilty, and as our act ſpeaketh, *Si ſoit trove per paiis, &c.* the jury may finde *veritatem facti*, the truth of the fact.

And herein note a diverſity between an appeal of death, and an appeal of mayhem; for in appeal of mayhem, if the defendant plead not-guilty, he cannot give in evidence that it was *ſe defendendo*, for that he ought to have pleaded it by way of juſtification in barre of the action.

19 H. 6. 31. 21 H. 6. 27. 41 Aſſ. 21. 9 E. 4. 28. 22 H. 6. 48. There is alſo another diverſity between an appeal of mayhem, or an action of treſpaſſe for wounding, or mannas of life and member; and an action of treſpaſſe of aſſault and battery for a man in defence, or for the preſervation of his poſſeſſion of lands or goods; for in that caſe he may juſtifie an aſſault and battery; but he cannot juſtifie either mayheming, or wounding, or mannas of life and member: and ſo note a diverſity between the defence of his perſon, and the defence of his poſſeſſion or goods.

3 E. 3. Coron. 286. See Marlbr. cap. 25. If a man be indicted before the coroner of the death of a man *ſe defendendo*, and that he fled for the ſame, he ſhall forfeit his goods, which ſavoureth of the common law.

No

No man can be accessary to one that killeth another *se defendendo.* 15 E. 3. Coron. 116.

If a man be indicted for killing of a man by misadventure, or *se defendendo*, and is out-lawed thereupon, he shall forfeit no lands, but goods and chattels onely.

(4) *Ferra les justices assavoir au roy, et le roy luy ferra grace sil luy pleist.*] To the king, that is, in the court of chancery the pleas whereof be *coram domino rege in cancellaria*; and there the lord chancellor, upon the record certified to him in the chancery by force of a writ of *certiorari*, shall of course by force of this act grant him his pardon without speaking hereof to the king, for that speaking is intended judicially in court, as hath been said: and note this clause is generall, and extendeth as well to an appeal, as to an indictment; and therefore if a man be appealed of murther, and it is found that he did it *se defendendo*, or by misadventure, the king is to pardon it, for the offender cannot be put to death, which is the end of his suit, and an appeal lyeth not for such a killing; otherwise it is where the appellee is to have judgement of death, for there the king cannot pardon it. 3 E. 3. Coron. 261. 44 E. 3. 44. 2 H. 4. 18. Stamf. Pl. Cor. fol. 16.

[317]

(5) *Ferra grace si luy pleist.*] Are but words of reverence to the king, for the king is obliged *ex merito justiciæ*, to grant the pardon, albeit some opinion is to the contrary; otherwise the lord chancellor could not do it without warrant from the king. 3 E. 3. Coron. 361. ibid. 354. 29 E. 3. 42. 44 E. 3. 44. Stamf. Pl. Cor. 16. b. Kelwey 108.

(6) *Purview est ensement que nul appeale soit abatu cy ligerment come avant ad estre.*] The mischief before this branch of this act, was, that there were so many exceptions to abate the appeal, especially being ever allowed learned councell to defend them; and the mischief was the greater, for that the appeal being once abated, never any other appeal (in favour of life) could be brought afterward. Brit. fo. 40. b.

At the common law, these exceptions were allowed to the plaintife in the appeal of death:

1. That the plaintife was not present at the mortall blow given, or felony done; for Glanvile saith, *Ita ut de morte loquatur sub visus sui testimonio mulier auditur accusare aliquem de morte viri sui si de visu loquatur.* And Bracton saith, *In omni vero casu criminali, quæ sub se continet feloniam, in appello debet fieri mentio de anno, de loco, de die, de hora, loqui etiam oportet de visu et auditu.* And the conclusion of the writ of appeal then was, *Offert se disrationare, &c. sicut ille, seu illa, qui vel quæ præsens fuit, et hoc vidit.* Glanv. lib. ult. ca. 3, 4, 5, &c. Bract. li. 3. fol. 138, &c.

And in another place he saith, *Non autem habet appellum fœmina, nisi de morte viri sui inter brachia sua interfecti, &c.* And Britton saith, *Des fems volons nous que nul ne puisse appeale de felony de mort de home, forsque de mort son baron tue deins lan et jour enter ses braches.* Lib. 3. fol. 125. Brit. ubi supra.

These words, *infra brachia*, have this signification, that she must not onely be his wife *de jure*, but also *de facto*, that is, in possession; for the wife in possession without lawfull matrimony shall not have the appeal, but she must be his wife both in right and in possession without elopement from her husband, &c. or divorce, &c. Many other exceptions were before this act, as appeareth by our ancient authors, to be taken, and another manner of count made before this act, now this act hath retained all that was certain, and rejected the rest, as hereafter shall appear. Mirror, c. 2. § 7. 7 E. 4. 15. 14 E. 4. 7. 22 E. 4. 39. 50 E. 3. 15. 28 E. 3. 91. 27 Ass. 3. Ubi supra.

If

If the writ of appeal doth comprehend the speciall matter, *viz.* that the husband or ancestor was slain *se defendendo*, or by misadventure, the writ of his own shewing shall abate; for an appeal, as hath been said, lyeth not of such a killing, because the end of the appeal of death is, that the appellee may have judgement of death, *viz.* death for death.

(7) *Purview est què nul appeale soit abatu*, &c.] This clause, if it be taken by it self, is generall, and literally, as some hath taken it, extendeth to all appeals, as of death, robbery, rape, felony, mayhem, &c. but *ex antecedentibus et consequentibus fit optima interpretatio*, and all the antecedent clauses do concern the death of man; nay in this very sentence these words are contained, *et de quel arme il fuit occise*, which manifestly do prove that this act is onely intended of the appeal of the death of man. And therefore the appeals of robbery, rape, and of other felony and mayhem are not within this act; for the mischief was, as hath been said, in the case of the death of man.

See 1. part of the Instit. sect. 500, 501. Brit. f. 45, 46. 22 Ass. p. 97. 7 H. 4. 38. Stamf. Pl. Cor. 62.

(8) *Lappellour counte le fait, lan, le jour, le heure, le temps le roys et la ville ou le fait fuist fait, et de quel arme il fuit occise.*] By this act the count of the appellant must comprehend these seven things: 1. the fact, 2. the yeer, 3. the day, 4. the hour, 5. the time of the king, 6. the town where the fact was done, and lastly, with what weapon.

See the statute of 4 E. 1. de offic. coronatoris.

[318]

(9) *Le fait.*] The fact: herein must be set forth, first, whether it was by wound, or without wound; if by wound, 4. things are necessary to be rehearsed in the setting out of the fact, besides the circumstances mentioned in the act, *viz.* 1. In what part of the body the wound was: 2. of what length and depth the wound was, where the wound is of such a quality, so as it may appear to the court that the wound was mortall; but if his arm were cut off, or the like, there the length or depth cannot be shewed: 3. that the party wounded dyed of that wound; and lastly, that it may appear that he dyed of that wound within the yeer and day after the giving of the wound; if without wound, either by weapon or without; if by weapon, as by a blow or bruising, or by putting up a hot iron in the fundament or the like, then as many of the circumstances before mentioned in the declaration of the fact as do agree therewith, and the rest of the circumstances required by the act are to be set forth: if without weapon, as by poysoning, drowning, burning, suffocating, strangling, or the like, the manner of the fact must be set forth, and so many of the circumstances required by the act as agree therewith, namely, all the circumstances, saving with what weapon the felony was done, because no weapon was used in committing of this felony: but notwithstanding, this act extendeth to all homicides, though they were not done with any weapon.

Brit. fo. 7. li. 5. fo. 120. 122. Longs case. See hereafter Heydons case.

(10) *Lan.*] That is, the yeer of the raign of the king.

(11) *Le jour.*] The day here is taken for the naturall day, comprehending both the solare day, and the night also, containing 24 hours, and therefore if it be done in the night, it is said, *In nocte ejusdem diei.*

Bract. li. 5. fo. 359.

If a man be feloniously strucken the 10 day of December, &c. whereof he dyed the 10 day of January, he cannot alleage the killing the 10 day of December when the stroke was, but he may alleage the killing to be the day that he dyed; but the surest conclusion is; and so he killed him in manner and form aforesaid: for

Lib. 4. f. 41, 42. Heydons case. 22 E. 3. Coron. 244. 11 H. 4. 12. Pl. Com. 401.

for though to some purpose the death hath relation to the blow, yet this relation being a fiction in law maketh not the felony to be then committed.

(12) *Le heure.*] *Hora constat ex* 40 *momentis.* The hour, as for example to say, 10 *die Decembris, viz. in hora decima in nocte ejusdem diei.*

There are divers diversities between the alleaging of the hour, and the day, or yeer; 1. In the count upon the appeal one may say, *circa horam* 10 *ante meridiem, &c. or, inter horam decimam et undecimam ante meridiem*; but the like cannot be done either of day, yeer, or part of the body: as the fact cannot be alleaged to be done *circa* 10 *diem Decembris, &c.* or, *inter decimum et* 11 *diem Decembris*, or *circa annum sextum domini regis nunc*, or *inter sextum et septimum dicti domini regis nunc*, or alleage the wound to be given *circa* or *circiter pectus*: and the reason of this diversity is, that it is more difficult to alleage the true hour, then the true day or yeer; and yet the plaintiffe in the appeal is not bound to prove in evidence, neither the precise hour, nor the very day that he alleageth in his count: another diversity is between the appeal and the indictment, for in the indictment the hour needs not to be alleaged. Bract. ubi supra. Heydons case, ubi supra. Lib. 9. fol. 62. Seign' Zanchars case.

And although the day be alleaged, yet if the jury finde him guilty at another day, the verdict is good, but then in the verdict it is good to set down on what day it was done, in respect of the relation of the felony; and the same law is in the case of an indictment.

At the sessions of the peace holden for the county of Norff. one Syer was indicted of burglary, 1 *Augusti*, 31 Eliz. and upon not guilty pleaded, it fell out in evidence that the burglary was done, 1 *die Septembris in eodem anno*, so as *primo Augusti* there was no burglary done, and thereupon he was found not guilty, and afterwards he was indicted againe 1 *Septembris, &c.* and it was resolved by Wray and Periam justices of assise, and by the greatest part of the judges, that he ought not to be tried again, for he mought have been found guilty upon the first indictment, for the day is not materiall; but it is necessary for the jury in that case to set down the day, and so in case of appeale. Pasch. 32 Eliz. resolved by the justices. [319]

(13) *Le temps le roy.*] The yeare being already named, it might seem that the time of the king, which is the year of the raigne of the king, is needlesse, but it is here againe added, to the end, that not onely the yeare shall be alledged wherein the blow, &c. was given, but also the yeare when the death ensued thereupon, to the end that it may appeare, that he died of that blow, &c. within the yeare and day; and whensoever the yeare of the king ought to be alledged, it draweth with it time and place, that is, the day and time, when and where the death ensued. Vide Machallis case here following, and Heydons case, and Longs case ubi supra.

(14) *La ville.*] This must be understood, if the murder or homicide, were done in a town, but if it were done in a place knowne out of any towne, then may it be alledged in that place knowne in such a county.

And so in a city it may be alledged in a parish, &c. because such a parish is in lieu of a towne.

But in the country if a parish contain divers towns, the murder or homicide cannot be alledged in such a parish, for that this statute requireth, that the fact be alledged in a town.

(15) *Et*

Lib. fo. Machallis case.

(15) *Et de quel arme fuit occise.*] With what weapon the wound was given: and albeit one certaine weapon must be alledged in the count, yet upon the evidence, if it be proved that the wound were given with any other weapon, the offender shall be found guilty; as if it be alledged in the indictment that the wound was given with a dagger, and it is proved in evidence, that it was given with a sword, rapier, hooke, hatchet, bill, or any like weapon with which a wound may be made; for it were unreasonable to drive the plaintiffe in the appeale to prove the selfe same particular weapons whereof many times he cannot have notice; but upon such a count, or an indictment in evidence it cannot be proved, that the party was poysoned, or drowned, or burnt, suffocated or strangled, or the like, where no weapon at all was used; for that evidence doth not maintain the count in the appeale or the indictment, because it is murder or homicide of another kinde, and not under the same *classis* that is alledged in the count or indictment, and thereof the plaintiffe by such as viewed the body may have notice.

And albeit this statute requireth, that it be alledged in the count of the appeale, with what weapon he was killed, it is to be understood in case where he is killed with a weapon, for albeit (as hath been said) there was no weapon at all, as in case of poysoning, drowning, &c. yet doth the appeale lie for such a murder or homicide; and the weapon is in this act mentioned for example.

(16) *Pur default de fresh sute.*] At the common law if the plaintiffe in the appeale of death had not made fresh suit, he should not have maintained his appeale: for fresh suit *recens insecutio*, that is, a speedy and continuall pursuit of the felon for his apprehension and conviction, and that is for two severall purposes, one to have restitution of his goods, as in the appeale of robbery and the like, and the other for the maintenance of the appeale it selfe, as here in the case of death, where no restitution of goods is to be had, but punishment of the offender by death, and that fresh suit which the plaintiffe in the appeale of death is to make, is here intended. What this fresh suit was at the common law doth notably appeare by Bracton, *Qui appellare voluerit et bene sequi, debet ille cui injuriatum erit, statim quam cito poterit hutesium levare, et cum hutesio ire ad villas vicinas et propinquiores, et ibi manifestare scelera et injurias perpetratas, et continuo accedere debet ad servientes domini regis, si inveniri possint et deinde ad coronatores, et sic inde sine intervallo ad proximum comitatum, &c.*

Bract. l. 3. fo. 139. Brit. fol. 43. Acc'.

[320]

(17) *Deins l'an et le jour.*] Here the yeare is to be accounted for the whole yeare according to the kalender, and not according to 28 dayes to the moneth, and the day is intended of the naturall day, and by this act if the appeale of death be commenced within the yeare and the day, it is sufficient fresh suit, but after the yeare and day the appeale of death cannot be commenced.

27 E. 3. 83. 32 E. 3. age 57. 45 E. 3. 21. 13 Ass. 10. 21 Ass. 24. 21 E. 3. 23. 11 H. 4. 94. 17 E. 4. 2. b. 27 H. 8. 11. a. Stamf. Pl. Cor. fo. 60. c. d.

If the next heire of the dead be within age, he must bring his appeale of death within the yeare and the day according to this act, but it hath been holden in many books that the paroll should demurre untill his full age; and the reason yeelded therefore is, that the defendant cannot wage battell, &c. But it hath beene often adjudged and approved by continuall experience of latter times that it shall proceed during his minority, and the reason of failer of battell is of no force, for that a man above seventy yeares of age shall

ſhall have an appeale, &c. and yet the defendant ſhall be ouſted of battell, and ſo if the plaintiſe in an appeale be mayhemed, &c. the defendant ſhall be ouſted of battell, and yet the appeale ſhall proceed. 15 E. 2. Cor. 385.

(18) *Apres le fait.*] That is, after the felony by homicide committed.

If a man be mortally wounded, &c. the firſt day of May, and thereof dieth the firſt day of July, ſome doe hold that the appeale is to be brought within the yeare and day after the blow given, for that the death enſuing hath relation to it, and that is the cauſe of the death, and the offender did nothing the day of the death. Stamf. Pl. Cor. fo. 63. a.

Here the law hath made a limitation in the appeale of death: by the ancient law juſtices in eyre did ride from ſeven yeare to ſeven yeare, and before them no plea of the crown could be inquired of for any offence committed before the laſt former eyre: ſo the juſtices in eyre in the kings foreſts may hold a juſtice ſeat from three yeare to three yeare. But no offence in the foreſt can be at the juſtice ſeat inquired of before the laſt former juſtice ſeate. See the fourth part of the Inſt. cap. Juſtices in Eyre, and all the auncient authors quoted there. See the fourth part of the Inſt. cap. the Courts of the Foreſt.

* But the yeare and the day ſhall be accounted from the death, for before that time no felony was committed, and thus it hath been often reſolved and adjudged, and the reaſon aboveſaid grounded upon relation, which is a fiction in law, holdeth not in this caſe. * Heydons caſe ubi ſupra.

If an appeale of murder be brought, and hanging the ſuit, and after the year and day is run out, one become acceſſary to the appellee, the plaintiffe ſhall have an appeale againſt him after the yeare and day paſt after the death, but it muſt be brought within the yeare and day after this new felony as acceſſary, for that in this caſe [*apres le fait*] is underſtood after this new felony as acceſſary done. 26 Aſſ. p. 52.

Thus much ſhall ſuffice for the expoſition of this law, more ſhall be ſaid concerning appeales in the treatiſe of pleas of the crowne, whereunto it properly belongeth.

See the ſtatute of 3 H. 7. cap. 1.

CAP. X.

COME il ſoit contenue en leſtatute le roy que ore eſt W. 1. cap. 43. *que deux parceners, ou deux queux teigne en common, ne puiſſent fourcher per eſſoine, del heure que * ils ount un foits apparus en courte: purview eſt, que meſme ceo ſoit tenus et garde per la ou home et ſa feme ſont enpledes en la court le roy.*

* [321]

WHEREAS it is contained in the ſtatute of the king that now is, that two parceners, or two that hold in common, may not fourch by eſſoin, after that they have once appeared in the court: it is provided, that the ſame be obſerved and kept, where a man and his wife be impleaded in the king's court.

W. 1. cap. 43. (Fitz. Eſſoin, 5. 62.)

39 E. 3. 29. The mischiefe before this statute was, that notwithstanding the statute of W. 1. the husband and wife (unlesse they were joyntly enfeoffed) might fourch by essoine, for that statute extended but to parceners and joyntenants: see in the exposition upon the statute of W. 1. cap. 43.

13 E. 3. essoine 5. 3 E 3. 29. 12 H. 4 3. 38 E. 3. 18. 39 E. 3. 29. 12 H. 4. 1. 22 E. 3. 5. b. & 14. a. 2 E. 4. 1.

This statute extendeth to common essoines, and not to essoine *de service le roy*.

Also this statute extendeth onely to reall actions, and therefore in personall actions baron and feme may fourch by essoyn.

Moreover this act extendeth to essoynes after appearance, that is, that all the tenants have appeared, and therefore baron and feme may fourch by essoyne before appearance notwithstanding this act; hereby it appeared that essoynes, at the first allowed upon just cause, were afterwards used meerely for delay.

CAP. XI.

PURVIEW est ensement, que si home bailla en la citie de Londres (2) *son tenement a terme des ans* (1), *et ceuy a que le franktenement est* (3), *se face empled' per collusion* (4), *et face default apres default, ou veigne en court, et la voile render* (5) *pur faire le termour perdre son terme, et le demandant eit querele* (6), *issint que le termour puisse aver recover' per briefe de covenant, le maire et les bailifes puissent enquirer* (7) *per bone visne en la presence del termour, et del demandant, le quel le demandant movest son plee per bon droit quel avoit, ou per collusion et per fraude pur faire le termour perdre son terme. Et si trove soit per enquest, que le demaundant movest son plee per bon droit quil avoit, ci soit le judgement performe maintenant. Et si trove soit per enquest, que il luy empleda per fraud' pur toller le termour son terme, ci demurge le termor en son terme, et lexecution del judgement pur le demaundant soit suspendus* (8), *jesques apres le terme passe. Et en mesme le maner soit fait de equitie en tiel case devant justices, si le termour le challenge devant judgement* (9) *rendus.*

IT is provided also, that if any man lease his tenement in the city of London, for term of years, and he to whom the freehold belongeth, causeth himself to be impleaded by collusion, and maketh default after default, or cometh into the court, and giveth it up, for to make the termor lose his term, and the demandant hath his suit, so that the termor may recover by writ of covenant: the mayor and bailiffs may inquire by a good inquest, in the presence of the termor and the demandant, whether the demandant moved his plea upon good right that he had, or by collusion, or by fraud, to make the termor lose his term: and if it be found by the inquest, that the demandant moved his plea upon good right that he had, the judgement shall be given forthwith: and if it be found by inquest, that he impleaded him by fraud, to put the termor from his term, then shall the termor enjoy his term, and the execution of judgement for the demandant shall be suspended until the term be expired. And in like manner it shall be of equity before the justices in such case, if the termor do challenge it before the judgement.

(2 Roll, 221, 222. 245. 21 H. 8. c. 15. 1 Inst. 46. a. Rast. 81.)

The

The generall mischiefe before this statute was, that the tenant for terme of yeares was subject to the pleasure of him that had the freehold, for if he had suffered a recovery in a reall action, though in truth it were by collusion (such credit the common law gave to recoveries in reall actions) the interest of the termour was overthrown, because he could not falsifie the recovery of the freehold, for that by the common law none could falsifie a recovery of a freehold, but he that had a freehold. This act provideth a twofold remedy: 1. for the city of London by writ in nature of a commission to the mayor and baylifes grounded upon this statute, &c. 2. generally by receit before judgement, which act Fleta doth render in these words, *Constitutum est, quod si quis in hujusmodi locis (viz. civitatibus et burgis privilegiatis) tenementum dimisit ad terminum annorum, et ille cujus liberum est tenementum permiserit se implacitari per collusionem, et defaltam fecerit post defaltam,* (and so to the end) *vide* Fleta. [322] Fleta, li. 2. c. 48.

Another mischiefe was, that after such a recovery had by collusion, and the lessee ousted thereupon, he should have his action of covenant at the least upon this word *dimisit, &c.)* against the lessor, and so the termour lost his possession, and was driven to his action, which was a cause of multiplication of suits, *et boni legislatoris est lites dirimere.*

(1) *Bailla a son tenant a terme des ans.*] At the making of this statute there was neither tenant by statute merchant, nor staple, nor *elegit*, for these executions against lands were given by acts of parliament made afterwards, and yet having but chattels, they could not falsifie (as hath beene said) no more then tenant for yeares. And though in our books there be a *concessum* that tenant by statute merchant might falsifie, yet the reason yeelded there doth weaken the authority thereof, for there they give the reason, for that he was not made party, which he could not be in the *præcipe* he having but a chattell: and latter authorities are against it, and a judgement in parliament also, yet being in equall mischiefe, though they be created since our statute, yet are they within the remedy of this act, for upon the matter they are but termours. But otherwise it is holden in case of a gardein in chivalry, that he is not within this act, for he commeth not in by any contract betweene the parties, as lessee for yeares, and tenant by statute merchant, staple, or *elegit* originally doe, but meerly by act in law. 19 E. 3. Ass. 82. 10 E. 3. 46. 22 E. 3. 8. 16 E. 3. receit 100. 7 H. 4. 12. a. & b. 30 H. 6. Fauxer de recovery 9. 30 H. 6. 16. 9 E. 4. 38. 1 H. 7. 9. 7 H. 7. 12. Pl. Com. 83. Kelwey 108. F.N.B. 198. Lib. 6. fo. 135. Bredimans case. Lib. 9. 85. Ascoughs case. 21 H. 8. ca. 15. 24 E. 3. 27. 7 H. 4. 12. Kelwey 128.

This termour for yeares intended by this law must be by deed by the expresse words of the body of this act, *issint que le termour eyt recoverie per briefe de covenant*; which must be by deed, as in those dayes few were made otherwise, and so it was resolved by the court of common pleas, and this act required a deed, lest it might be used for delay. But now by the statute of 21 H. 8. cap. 15. tenant for yeares by deed or without deed may falsifie, and so by that law may tenant by statute merchant, staple, or *elegit* doe, which act being a beneficiall law is construed favourably. 33 H. 6. 41. b. Prisot. 9 E. 4. 30. 19 E. 3. receit 15. 9 Eliz. Dier. Britton, 93 b. Tr. 3 Jacobi in Communi Banco. 21 H. 8. ca. 15. Lib. 11. fo. 33. b. Powiters case.

(2) *En la citie de Londres.*] That is in the court of the hustings the greatest and highest court in London: it is called *hustingum* or *hustings* of two Saxon words, *viz. Hus. i. domus, et* Ꝥing, *i. placitum,* so *hustingum* is as much to say, as *domus placitorum,* or *forum contentiosum,* where causes are pleaded; and other cities have the like court, and so called, as York, Lincoln, Winchester, &c.

Here the city of London is named, but it appeareth by that which hath been said out of Fleta, that this act extends to such cities and boroughs Fleta ubi supra.

boroughs priviledged, that is, ſuch as have ſuch priviledge to hold plea as London hath.

But London was named for excellency, for that in thoſe dayes it excelled in freedome and fulneſſe of trade and merchandizing (with order, but without monopolizing) like the good bayliffes of the kingdome exporting our native, neceſſary, and reall commodities, and importing profitable and neceſſary commodities. And in thoſe dayes the exportation farre exceeded the importation, whereby
[323] the realme flouriſhed in all opulency and in multitude of ſhips, merchants, and mariners, aſwell in war as in peace, inſomuch as taking one example that was next my hand, in time when England was deeply ingaged in a long and chargeable war, the native commo-
28 E. 3. in Scaccar'. dities exported (as taking one yeer for example) amounted to the value of two hundred and twelve thouſand, three hundred thirty and eight pounds, the ounce of ſilver then being xx. d. and the goods imported to the ſum of thirty and eight thouſand fourſcore pounds, and nine pence; whereby it may be concluded what money was brought into the realm, and how much the exportation exceeded the importation.

And to the end, that merchants and others might enjoy the houſes which they held for yeers, for the advancement of trade and traffique, London was particularly named.

(3) *Et celuy a que franktenement eſt.*] Theſe words are ſtronger, then if the ſtatute had ſaid tenant, and yet the vouchee is taken within this, and the other branch alſo, as in the expoſition upon the ſecond branch ſhall be ſhewed.

(4) *Se face implead per colluſion.*] But the termor that is to be received by the ſecond branch, which referreth to this, muſt not onely alledge the colluſion, but alledge matter for the ſafeguard of his intereſt, as there ſhall be ſhewed.

(5) *Face default ou voille render.*] Faint pleader is not taken to be within this act; ſee the laſt clauſe of this act.

(6) *Et le demandant eyt querel'.*] That is, if the demandant have execution, and the termor ouſted, ſo as he may have his action of covenant.

Regiſt. 179. a. (7) *Le maire et les bailifes puiſſent inquirer,* &c.] And this enquiry muſt be done by writ in nature of a commiſſion grounded upon this act, directed to the maior and bailifes, reciting the leaſe, the bringing of the action by colluſion, and this ſtatute, and concluding thus, *ideo vobis mandamus, quod convocatis partibus coram vobis, et inquiſita ſuper hoc plenius veritate, eidem A.* (that is, the termor) *de prædict' meſſuagio terminum ſuum quod juſtum fuerit, ſecundum formam ſtatuti prædict' habere faciatis.* And ſo regularly, when any like authority is generally given by any act to do juſtice, it ought to be done by force of the kings writ grounded upon the act, and the writ grounded upon this act is called, *Breve de inquirendo veritatem ſuper ſtatutum Gloc'.*

17 E. 3. fo. 29. Kelw. 108. b. (8) *Execution del judgement pur le demandant ſoit ſuſpendus.*] So as the leſſor and his heirs in the mean time having the reverſion, notwithſtanding the judgement, ſhall have the rent, and ſhall puniſh waſte, &c.

4 E. 2. Receit 159. 10 E. 3. 45. 21 E. 3. 1. 17 E. 3. 29. (9) *En meſme le manner ſoit fait de equitie in tiel caſe devant juſtices, ſi le termor ceo challenge devant judgement.*] This termor muſt be by force of a leaſe by deed, as it was reſolved Trinit. 3. Jacobi *ubi ſupra.*

This

This is the first act that gave receit in any case, and by force of this act the termor before judgement may pray to be received to defend the right and interest of his term upon the default, or render, or *nient dedire* of the tenant, but not upon faint pleader: and tenant by statute merchant, staple, and *elegit* are taken within this branch, aswell as within the former branch of this act.

22 E. 3. 8. 19 E. 3. Receit 112. 9 E. 4. 30. 7 H. 7. 11, 12. 21 H. 7. 25. 14 H. 8. 4. 45 E. 3 7. 27 H. 8. 7. 19 Eliz. Dier 263. b.

And it is not sufficient for the termor to alledge collusion, but he must also traverse the point of the demandants writ, or plead some barre to his title; for this law that giveth him to be received, enableth him to plead for the safeguard of his interest.

[324]

The termor must be received before judgement, and albeit he doth defend his term, he shall not arrest judgement, but suspend execution during the term; for these words, *En mesme le manner*, maketh this branch in equipage with the former.

19 E. 3. Receit. 15.

If the tenant vouch, and the vouchee enter into warranty, and after make default, the termor shall be received; for albeit the first branch (whereunto this doth refer) is when he that hath the franktenement make default, yet in as much as the vouchee is tenant in law (this law being beneficiall for safeguard of the interest of the termor) he shall be received, for it is within the same mischief.

14 H. 8. 4. 27 H. 8. 7.

CAP. XII.

PURVIEW est ensement, que si home soit implede de tenement en mesme la citie (1), *et vouch forrein' a garrantie* (2), *quel veigne en la chancery et eit briefe de sommons* (3) *son garrantor a certe jour devant justices du banke, et un auter briefe au maire et as bailifes, que ils surcessent* (5) *en le parolle que est devant eux per briefe, jesques a taunt que le paroll' de le garrantee serra termine devant justices du bank* (4) *: et quant le parol de la garrant' serra termine devant justices du bank, donques serra dit au garrant' que il veigne en la citie de Londres a respoign' de chiefe plee. Et le demandant per sa suit eit brief de justices* (6) *de bank, au maire et as bailifes, que ils voilent avant en le plee. Et si le demandant recover vers le tenant, veigne le tenant as justices de bank, et eit briefe au maire et as bailifes, que si le tenant eit la terre perdus, que ils facient extende la terre* (7), *et retorne lextent en bank a certe jour, et apres soit*

IT is provided also, that if a man, impleaded for a tenement in the same city, doth vouch a foreigner to warranty, that he shall come into the chancery, and have a writ to summon his warrantor at a certain day before the justices of the bench, and another writ to the mayor and bailiffs of London, that they shall surcease in the matter that is before them by writ, until the plea of the warranty be determined before the justices of the bench: and when the plea at the bench shall be determined, then shall he that is vouched be commanded to go into the city, to answer unto the chief plea. And a writ shall be awarded at the suit of the demandant by the justices unto the mayor and bailiffs, that they shall proceed in the plea. And if the demandant recover against the tenant, the tenant shall come before the justices of the bench, which shall direct a writ to the mayor and bailiffs, that if the tenant have lost

soit maunde au viscount du pais ou le garrantee fuist summons, que il luy face aver de la terre le garrantor a le value. Vide Articul' Glouc, correct' anno 9 Edw. 2.

lost his land, they shall cause the land to be extended, and valued, and shall return the extent at a certain day into the bench, and after it shall be commanded to the sheriff of the shire (where the warrantee was summoned) that he shall cause him to have as much of the land of the warrantor in value.

(Rast. 240. 354. Coke pla. f. 170. 41 Ed. 3. f. 2. Kel. f. 109. Fitz. Resceit, 106. Regist. 2. 9 Ed. 1.)

Regist. 2. b. 14 H. 4. 25. See how this is corrected by the statute of 9 E. 2. intitled, *Articulos Statuti Gloc' correctos, &c.*

The mischief at the common law, when the tenant did vouch one to warranty, and prayed that the vouchee might be summoned in a forein county, was the great delay that the demandant had thereby, and specially in London, for that in London the plea could not be removed neither by *tolt* nor *pone*; but the plea was put without day, and the record removed by the kings writ into the court of common pleas, &c. and some did hold, that at the common law the inferiour court was put out of jurisdiction: but now by this statute, and that of 9 E. 2. the demandant shall sue out of the chancery a writ of *summons ad warrantizandum* against the vouchee, retornable before the justices of the court of common pleas at a certain day, and another writ out of the chancery called a *recordare* to the maior and bailifes to remove the record before the same justices at the same day, and thereupon the maior and bailifes, being required thereunto by that writ, to prefix the day of the return of that writ to the parties to appear at the return of that writ; and when the court of common pleas hath determined of the warranty, then the vouchee shall be commanded to go into London to answer to the chief plea, and by a judiciall writ the court of common pleas shall remand the record, requiring them to proceed in the same plea; and so forth, as it is contained in both these acts.

[325]

Fleta, li. 2. c. 48. Regist. 2. 7. 8 Ass. 22. 15 E. 3. Record 37. 49 E. 3. 9. 3 Ass. p. 10. 10 E. 3. 24. Record 13. 11 H. 4. 27, 28. 14 H. 4. 25. 18 H. 8. 1. 5 E. 6. Dier 69. 12 E. 3. Voucher 115. 21 E. 3. Ibid. 122. 13 E. 1. ibid. 269. 35 E. 3. ibid. 316. 8 E. 4. 10. 34 H. 6. 42. 13 E. 4. Cause de remover plea 23. Temps E. 1. Gar' de Chartres 23. 3 H. 7. 30. 27 H. 8. 12. Pasch. 15 H. 8. Rot. 343. in communi banco.

(1) *En la citie.*] That is, the citie of London specially named for the cause aforesaid, but extended by equity to all other priviledged places where a forrein voucher is made, as to Chester, Durham, Salop, &c.

Ancient demesne is (as some do hold) within this statute, because the freehold is in the tenants, and is within these words *(Soit implead de tenement)* but otherwise it is of a tenant by copy roll in a court baron, because he hath no franktenement.

(2) *Vouch forrein' a garrantie.*] *De forinsecis vocatis ad warrantiam*, that is, when one is vouched, and the tenant prayeth that the vouchee may be summoned in a forrein county.

a 46 E. 3. Voucher 223. 3 H. 4. 12. a. 32 H. 6. 26. 34 H. 6. 42. F.N.B. 6. b.

[a] This act being a beneficiall law for furtherance of justice, and for ousting of delay is taken in this point also by equity, not onely to forrein pleas in reall actions, but also to pleas although they be not forrein, yet for default of power to proceed, the same shall be removed *ut supra*, and remanded *ut supra*: as if in an action auncestrell the tenant plead bastardy in the demandant, or in a writ of dower the tenant plead *unques accouple in loyall matrimony*, neither the

[b] the court in London, or any like inferiour court cannot award a writ to the bishop for tryall thereof, for *nullus alius præter regem possit episcopo demandare inquisitionem faciendam.* And another treating of the plea of *ne unques accouple*, in barre of a writ of dower, saith, *ac si alius quam rex demandaret episcopo quod inde inquireretur, episcopus alterius mandatum quam regis non tenetur obtemperare*; and herewith agree our books in all successions of ages.

[b] Bract. l. 3. fo. 106. Brit. f. 248. b. Fleta, li. 5. c. 24. 8 E. 3. 59. 14 E. 3. Trials 63. 24 E. 3. 33. 42. 40 E. 3. 2. 44 E. 3. 28. 35 H. 6. 30. 36 H. 6. 33. 37 H. 6. 30. 14 H. 7. 21. 21 H. 7 34, 35. 14 H. 4. 26. b. Judgement cite per Hankford.

And therefore if such pleas be pleaded in London, or such other inferiour courts, the record shall be removed; and after a writ to the bishop, and certificate made by the bishop, the record shall be remanded: [c] and it appeareth that this act doth extend to reall actions wherein voucher lyeth, and not to personall actions; [d] and lest that forrein vouchers should be used for delay, they must shew a charter, &c. comprehending warranty to the court.

[c] 3 H. 4. fo. 12. 32 H. 6. 26.
[d] 35 E. 3. Voucher 316.

(3) *Veigne en la chauncerie et eit briefe de summons*, &c.] [e] This is corrected and altred by the said article upon this statute in *an.* 9 E. 2. for by that statute the maior and bailifes shall adjourn the parties before the justices of the bench at a certain day, and shall send the record thither, *Et le justices face summon le garrantee devant eux et pledent le garrantie*, and hereby the justices of the bench shall award the summons *ad auxiliandum, &c.* and [f] not fetch it out of the chancery: and by the said act of 9 E. 2. it is provided, that if at the day given in banke the tenant make default, a petit cape shall be awarded to the maior and bailifes, to give judgement upon that default, if it cannot be saved, &c.

[e] 9 E. 2. ubi supra.
[f] See a notable case, Pasch. 31 E. 3. fo. 31. a. & b. in libro meo.

In a præcipe in the hustings in London, the tenant voucheth one in London, and other forrein vouchees in the county of Norffolk, &c. In this case aswell the voucher within London as the forrein vouchers shall be removed, for although the words of this act be, *vouch forrein' a garrantie*, yet because processe must be made against all the vouchees at one time, and if processe should be made by the court of common pleas onely against the forrein vouchees, although they came in, they should not warrant, nor answer without the others before processe were determined against them in London; so as necessity requireth, that processe should be made against all at one time, and that ought to be done in the more worthy court, and when the warranty is determined in the court of common pleas, all shall be remanded.

49 E. 3. 9 & 10. 50 E. 3. Voucher 217. 29 Ass. 48.

[326]

(4) *Que le parol del garrantie serra termine devant les justices del banke.*] This is the power given to the justices of the court of common pleas, and this act is in nature of a commission to them, therefore it is good to be seen what is within their commission, the words of the said writ of *recordare* are, *Ut terminata warrantia illa coram præfat' justic' eadem recordum et process' vobis remittamus, &c.*

18 E. 3. 1. 49 E. 3. 9, 10. Pasch. 15 H. 8. Rot. 343. in communi banc. 5 E. 6. Dier 69.

If the tenant vouch a foreiner to warranty, and the record is removed into the court of common pleas to determine the warranty, the vouchee may vouch over in a forein county, and that vouchee may vouch over, and if the vouchee make default, the court may make processe against him, &c. *Quia quando lex aliquid alicui concedit, omnia incidentia tacite conceduntur*; but none of the vouchees can plead in chief, but that must be pleaded in the inferiour court, for that is not within the said commission given by this act. But if the demandant in banke appear not, the court may award

Kelw. 109. 13 E. 3. Vouch. 18. 32 E. 3. ibid. 101. 50 E. 3. ibid. 217. 41 E. 3. 31. 42 E. 3. 1. 49 E. 3. Vouch. 223. 20 E. 3. Essoin 28. 8 Ass. 22. 16 E. 3. Essoin 167. 28 H. 8. 1.

award a non-suit as incident, and so the tenant in banke may be essoined.

In dower in the hustings in London against the husband and wife, who vouch a foreiner to warranty, whereupon the plea is adjourned into the common pleas at a certain day, at which day the husband and wife sued out a writ against the vouchee; whereupon the vouchee appeared, and the baron made default, and the wife prayed to be received upon his default; and by the rule of the court she was received, and that it was within their commission, for that the default was made in this court, whereupon the land was to be lost if she were not received; for it is a maxime in law, *Necessitas sub lege non continetur, quia quod alias non est licitum, necessitas facit licitum,* but yet others are of another opinion.

18 E. 3. 1. a. b. tit. Receit 106. 31 E. 3. Receit 125.

Bract. li. 2. f. 93. 31 E. 3. Receit 125.

Regist. fo. 7.

(5) *Un auter briefe al maire et bailifes que ils surcess'*, &c.] That is, the said writ of *recordare*, whereby they are commanded *quod recordum et processum ejusdem loquelæ cum omnibus ea tangentibus justiciariis nostris de banco sub sigillo vestro mittatis, &c.* which to them is a *supersedeas* in law.

Regist. judic. fo. 73.

(6) *Et le demandant per sa sute eit briefe des justices.*] This is a *procedendo in loquela* directed to the maior, &c. to proceed, which you may read in the Judiciall Register.

(7) *Que ils facient extender la terre,* &c.] For the better performance of this act, the tenant must surmise, that execution is sued against him, and pray a *venire fac' recordum.*

By force of this act the justices of the common pleas upon that record shall award a writ of *extendi et appreciari fac'*, to the maior and bailifes, which writs grounded upon this act are sufficient expositions of the same, and will resolve many doubts that may arise thereupon.

Hil. 24 E. 3. in com. banc'. Rast. livre de Entres. 240. 354. 615. Coke Pl. f. 176. Note here the foreign Voucher.

A notable record you may read in *libro G.* in the chamber of the Guild-hall in London, fol. 7. in *anno* 24 E. 3. whereby it appeareth that Thomas Drokensfield and Emme his wife brought a writ of dower in the hustings, against Alice Colwell, to be indowed of a house in London, of the indowment of R. de Envil late her baron; the tenant appeared, and vouched to warranty Thomas son and heir of John de Colwell, and prayed that he might be summoned in the county of Middlesex, whereupon the record saith, *Dies datus est partibus coram justiciariis domini regis de banco apud Westm' in crastino purificationis, ut tunc fiat ibi juxta formam artic' Gloc', pro civibus London inde correcti.*

[327]

And there it appeareth that the justices of the common pleas awarded the summons against the vouchee, who appeared upon the grand cape, and entred into the warranty, *ideo loquela præd. remittatur in Husting' coram majore et vicecom' ut ibi ulterius fiat, prout hactenus de jure fieri consuevit:* whereupon a resummons was awarded in the hustings against Alice the tenant, *et idem dies* given to the demandant, at which day the tenant appeared and the vowchee also, and rendred dower, and thereupon judgement was given against Alice the tenant, *et dictum est per curiam dictæ Aliciæ, quoa sequatur in curia domini regis coram justiciariis de banco ad habendum de terra dict' Thomæ de Colewell tenentis per warrantiam in comitat' Midd', si sibi viderit expedire.* And after the tenant came into the court of common pleas, and prayed her remedy against the vowchee surmising that execution was sued against her, and a third part of the house delivered to the demandant, whereupon a writ issued out of

of the court of common pleas, *ad venire faciendum recordum coram justic' de banco:* by which it appeareth that in the hustings by the forein vowcher, *placitum prædict' sine die remansit, et partes prædict' secundum formam statuti coram præfatis justiciariis nostris apud Westm', ut eadem Alicia versus prædict' hæredem de warrantia sua habenda secundum formam ejusdem statuti prosequi possit, adjornat' fuissent, &c.*

I have set forth this record the more at large for that it setteth forth this statute, and that of 9 E. 2. in their lively colours, so as a man may see that (as it were) acted, which by those acts is required. And I know that many have followed that precedent; which is worthy to be seene at large: but he that is desirous to reade this whole chapter in a small map, let him reade Fleta who saith, *De warrantis vocatis extra jurisdictionem hujusmodi locorum privilegiatorum (viz. civitat' et burgorum, &c.) taliter statutum est, quod si implacitati per breve de recto aliquem forinsecum vocarunt ad warrantum, tunc perquirant sibi de cancellaria duo brevia, viz. ad summon' warrant' coram justic' de banco ad certum diem, et aliud balivis civitatis, quod placitum illud supersedeant, donec de placito warrantiæ fuerit terminat', quando terminat', dicatur warrantis, quod adeant civitatem et respondeant de placito principali, et habeant brevia judicialia ad balivos quod tenementa petita extendantur si fuerint amissa, et retornentur extentæ ad certum diem coram justic' per quos mandetur vicecom' quod faciat tenentibus habere ad valenciam eschambium.* And it is worthy the observation that at the common law in case of a forein vowcher in the hustings of London, the plea was adjorned before the justices in eyre, when they came to the tower of London; for the court of the hustings London was not derived out of the jurisdiction of the court of common pleas, as other courts that have power to hold pleas reall are, and therefore the adjornement was (as hath been said) before the justices in eyre: for the antiquity of this court of hustings amongst the laws of S. Edward, you shall reade, *Debet enim in London, quæ caput est regni et legum. semper curia domini regis singulis septimanis die Lunæ hustingis sedere, et teneri, &c.*

Fleta, li. 2. c. 48.

Int' leges Ed. Regis Lamb. 136. b.

CAP. XIII.

PURVIEW est ensement, que del heure que plee serra move (1) *en la citie de Londres per briefe, que le tenant* (2) *neit power de faire waste* (4), *ne estrepement du tenement que* * *est en demaunde* (3) *pendant le plee* (5), *et sil face, le maire et les bailifes facent garde a le suit le demandant. Et mesme le ord' et statute soit garde en auters cities, boroughs, et ailours per tout le roialme.*

* [328]

IT is provided also, that after such time as a plea shall be moved in the city of London by writ, the tenant shall have no power to make any waste or estrepement of the land in demand (hanging the plea) and if he do, the mayor and bailiffs shall cause it to be kept at the suit of the demandant. And the same ordinance and statute shall be observed in other cities, boroughs, and every where throughout the realm.

(Rast. pla. f. 317. 14 H. 7. f. 7. 10. Dyer, f. 325. 5 Rep. 115. Godbolt, 112. pl. 134. Regist. 76.)

Bract. fo. 355. 4 H. 3. Estrepement 12. 22 E. 3. 2. 21 E. 3. 51. 4 E. 3. 32. 6 H. 4. 1. 5 E. 2.

Before this statute there lay at the common law a writ of estrepement after judgement, and before execution; and so an estrepement doth lie for waste done after verdict, and before judgement.

Estrepement 11. 2 H. 6. 13. 3 H. 6. 16. 21 E. 3. 51. 34 E. 3. Estrepement 14.

There are two kindes of estrepements prohibiting waste *pendente placito*, one originall, and may be sued out of the chauncery, either together with the originall *præcipe* by which the land is demaunded, or at any time after *pendant le plea* directed to the sheriffe, the party, or both; the other is judiciall to be graunted by that court where the plea dependeth.

Lib. 5. fol. 48. Littletons case. Regist. 126. F.N.B. 61.

And some doe hold that the originall writ of estrepement did lie at the common law to prohibit any waste done *pendente placito*, for (say they) there lieth a writ *de bonis arrestandis ne dissipentur pendente placito, &c. à fortiori* in case of inheritance, wherein if waste should be done, it should be inconvenient, and against the common wealth: but certain it is, that the judiciall writ is given *pendente placito* by this statute.

Mirror, fo. 76.

(1) *Que plea serra move.*] Some doe hold that this is to be intended of reall actions, wherein no damages are to be recovered, for that in reall actions where the demandant shall recover damages, he shall recover damages *pendant le briefe*, and that is the reason, that in those cases the demandant count to no damages, and therefore in those cases the tenant might be doubly charged, once in the estrepement, and again in the principall action. To this it is by some answered. 1. That this statute is generall to reall actions. 2. There is no mischiefe, for a recovery of damages in the one is a barre to the other. 3. It is (as hath been said) inconvenient and against the common-wealth that waste should be done. But where damages are to be recovered, but not *pendente placito*, there without question the estrepement doth lie.

Lib. 5. fo. 115. Foljambes case.

Rot. Parl. 28 E. 3. nu. 19.

Amongst the petitions of the commons in the parliament holden in *anno* 28 E. 3. one was, that the writ of estrepement might lie in every action where the party should recover damages for estrepement after the writ purchased; and the answer was, the old law should be continued.

28 H. 6. 8. b. F.N.B. 61. b.

(2) *Que le tenant.*] If the tenant make a feoffement *pendente placito*, in law he remaineth tenant; and yet the demandant may have an estrepement against him and the feoffee also, and so against the tenant and the vowchee or *priee in aide*.

22 E. 3. 2. F.N.B. 61. p.

If there be two tenants, the demandant may sue an estrepement against the one of them; and after judgement a writ of estrepement lieth against the tenant and stranger by the common law.

3 H. 6. 16.

In an estrepement the tenant shall not have his age, for it is in nature of a trespasse.

12 R. 2. Estrepement 6.

In the estrepement *pendente placito*, the demandant shall not recover damages before judgement be given in the principall.

32 E. 3. ibid. 7. 3 H. 6. 17. F.N.B. 61. h.

If an estranger of his owne wrong without the privity of the tenant doth estrepement or waste after the writ sued out, the tenant shall not be punished for this waste.

2 H. 6. 13. 33 H. 6. 6. 14 H. 7. 8. b. F.N.B. 61. i. Dier. 16 Eliz. 315. 34 E. 3. Estrepement 15.

(3) *Dun tenement que est en demaund.*] In a *scire fac'* to execute a fine or a recovery (though no land be demaunded thereby) yet may the plaintiffe have a writ of estrepement, for it is in equall mischiefe, and so it is in * a *quid juris clamat*, and in an attaint an estrepement doth lie, and yet no land is demaunded.

*[329]

In an action of waste no land is demaunded, and yet an estrepement in that case lieth. 4 E. 3. 32. Foljambs case ubi supra.

In a *particione fac'* no estrepement doth lie, for both of them are in possession, and there is no reason, that one shall be restrained, and not the other. 12 R. 2. Estrep. Br. 13. Pasch. 33 H. 8. Bendloes.

If a formedon be brought of a mannor, and the demandant sue out an estrepement, and after that a tenancy escheat, the writ of estrepement extends to the land escheated, because it commeth in lieu of the services, and yet that land was not demaunded. F.N.B. 61.

(4) *Neyt power de faire waste.*] The tenant notwithstanding the prohibition in the writ of estrepement may cut down corn, or grasse, or underwood, or the like, so it be no waste or destruction. F.N.B. 61. c.

(5) *Pendant le plea.*] This is to be understood of a judiciall writ of estrepement granted out of the court of common pleas, &c. when the principall writ is retourned, for before that it is not depending there, but the demandant may have an originall writ of estrepement (as hath been said) together with the principall writ out of the chauncery. 18 H. 8. 5. 2 H. 6. 13.

This act is so construed, that by a consequent the party shall recover damages for waste done *(pendente placito)* after the writ delivered, and therefore it is good policy to purchase the writ of estrepement together with the writ. Note the writ it selfe founded upon this statute is but a prohibition, and upon the attachment the parties doe pleade, &c.

But note upon the writ of estrepement at the common law, viz. after judgement, the plaintiffe shall recover damages for the waste done before without any prohibition formerly delivered. Regist. judic. 13. 22 E. 3. Estrepement 9.

And upon a writ of estrepement grounded upon this act, the sheriffe may resist them that doe offer to doe waste; and if otherwise he cannot doe it, he may lawfully imprison them, or make a warrant to others to doe it, and if necessity require it, he may take *posse comitatus*: so odious in law is waste and destruction. Foljambs case, ubi supra.

CAP. XIV.

LE roy grant de sa grace as citizens (1) de Londres, que la ou avant ces heures ceux queux fueront disseisies de lour franktenement en mesme la citie, ne poient recover lour damages avant le venue des justices a la tower: que desormes iceux disseisies eyent lour damages per recognisans de lassise, per le quel ils recoveront lour tenements, et les disseisors soient amercies devant deux barons dexchequer, queux un foits per an veindr' en le citie a ceo faire. Et

THE king of his special grace granteth unto the citizens of London, that whereas beforetimes they that were disseised of freehold in the same city could not recover their damages before the coming of the justices to the tower, that from henceforth the disseisees shall have damages by recognizance of the same assise whereby they recovered their lands. And the disseisors shall be amerced before two barons of the exchequer,

Et ceo soit maunde a treasorer et as barons dexchequer quels le facent faire chescun an per ii. de eux a lour lever apres la chaunceleure. Et les amercements per les summons del eschequer soient levies al oeps le roy, et al eschequer deliveres.

chequer, which shall resort once a year into the city to do it. And it shall be commanded unto the barons and to the treasurer of the exchequer, that they shall cause it every year to be levied by two of them at their rising after Candlemas. And the amerciaments by summons of the exchequer shall be levied to the king's use, and be delivered at the exchequer.

[330] Fleta, li. 2. c. 48. The mischiefe before this statute was, that in London if one were disseised of his freehold, he could not in the assise of freshforce recover damages, but the land onely, because the assise of fresh-force did not lie by originall writ, but by bill; and therefore if he would recover damages, he must tarry untill the justices in eyre came Lib. intrat. Rast. F.N.B. 7. 13. into the tower, which came but once in seven yeares: and therefore this statute doth give damages in the assise of freshforce, and by equity it extendeth to Glocester, and to other cities and boroughs which by usage and custome hold plea of assise of freshforce by bill.

Bract. 164. b. Note Bracton saith, *Recognitio assisæ novæ disseisinæ multis vigiliis excogitata et inventa recuperandæ possess. gratia, ut per summariam cognitionem absque magna juris solemnitate, quasi per compendium negotium terminetur:* and it was called [*assisa novæ disseisinæ*] in respect of the delay before the justices in eyre.

(1) *Citizens de Londres.*] Note London is a corporation by prescription, and therefore may have divers names of corporation, as namely here (citizens.)

CAP. XV.

PURVIEW est ensement, que le maire et les bailifes avant le venue de ceux barons enquergent des vines vendus encounter lassise (1), *et le presentent devant eux a lour venue, et donque soient amercies, la ou ils soilent attendre, jesque a le venue des justices errants. Dones a Gloucestre le quart jour de October, lan du raigne le roy Edward fits le roy Henry*, 6.

IT is provided also, that the maior and bailiffes, before the comming of those barons, shall enquire of wines sold against the assise, and shall present it before them at their comming, and then shall be amerced where before they were wont to tary unto the comming of the justiciers in eyre. Given at Gloucester the iiij day of October, the VI. year of the reign of king Edward, the sonne of king Henry. [*Rastell's translation.*]

The like mischiefe was concerning the enquiry of the breach of assise of wines, as before in the former chapter concerning the recovery of damages: therefore this act giveth power to the mayor and bailiffes to enquire of the breach of the assise of wine, and not to tarry till the justices in eyre do come.

(1) *Des*

(1) *Des vines vendus enconter laſſiſe.*] This ſtatute here intended is limited by the ſtatute *de piſtoribus et braciatoribus.* Cap. 5.

Aſſiſa vini ſecundum aſſiſam domini regis obſervetur, ſcilicet ſixtertium ad xij.d. & ſi tabernarii illam aſſiſam exceſſerint, per majorem et balivos oſtia claudantur, et non permittant vinum vendere, donec licentiam à domino rege obtinuerint. But this act is repealed by 21 *regis Jacobi.*

---

[331]

STATUTUM de WESTMINST. SECUNDO,

Editum Anno 13 Edw. I.

The Preface of the Statute of W. 2.

CUM nuper dominus rex, in quindena Sancti Johannis Baptiſtæ, anno regni ſui ſexto, convocatis prælatis, comitibus, baronibus, et concilio ſuo apud Glouceſtre: quia plures de regno ſuo exhæredationem patiebantur, eo quod in multis caſibus, ubi remedium apponi debuit prius, non fuit per prædeceſſores ſuos, aut per ipſum remedium proviſum, quædam ſtatuta populo ſuo valdè neceſſaria et utilia edidit, per quæ populus ſuus Anglicanus et Hybernicus ſub ſuo regimine gubernatus, celeriorem juſticiam, quam prius, in ſuis oppreſſionibus conſecutus eſt, ac quidam caſus, in quibus lex deficiebat, remanſerunt indeterminati, et quidam ad reprimendam oppreſſionem populi remanſerunt ſtatuend'. Dominus rex in parliamento ſuo, poſt Paſcham, anno regni ſui tertio decimo apud Weſtminſter, multas oppreſſiones populi, et legum defectus, ad ſuppletionem dictorum ſtatutorum apud Gloceſter editorum, recitari, fecit, et ſtatuta edidit, ut patebit in ſequent'.

WHEREAS of late our lord the king, in the quinzim of Saint John Baptiſt, the ſixth year of his reign, calling together the prelates, earls, barons, and his council at Glouceſter, and conſidering that divers of this realm were diſherited, by reaſon that in many caſes, where remedy ſhould have been had, there was none provided by him nor his predeceſſors, ordained certain ſtatutes right neceſſary and profitable for his realm, whereby the people of England and Ireland, being ſubjects unto his power, have obtained more ſpeedy juſtice in their oppreſſions, than they had before; and certain caſes, wherein the law failed, did remain undetermined, and ſome remained to be enacted, that were for the reformation of the oppreſſions of the people: our lord the king in his parliament, after the feaſt of Eaſter, holden the thirteenth year of his reign at Weſtminſter, cauſed many oppreſſions of the people, and defaults of the laws, for the accompliſhment of the ſaid ſtatutes of Glouceſter, to be rehearſed, and thereupon did provide certain acts, as ſhall appear here following.

IT

IT is commonly called Westminster the second: Westminster, because this parliament was holden at Westminster; and the second, in respect of the former parliament holden at Westminster, called Westminster the first.

CAP. I.

*[332]

*IN primis, de tenementis (1), quæ multotiens dantur sub conditione (2), videlicet, cum aliquis dat terram suam alicui viro et ejus uxori, et hæred' de ipsis (3) viro et muliere procreatis, adjecta conditione expressa tali (4.) Si hujusmodi vir et mulier sine hæred' de ipsis viro et muliere procreat' obiissent, terra sic data ad donatorem, vel ad ejus hæredem revertatur. In casu etiam cum quis dat tenementum alicui in liberum * maritagium (5), quod donum habet conditionem annexam, licet not exprimatur in charta doni, quæ talis est. Quod si hujusmodi vir et mulier sine hæred' de ipsis viro et muliere procreat' obiissent, tenementum sic datum ad donatorem, vel ad ejus hæredem revertatur. In casu etiam cum quis dat tenementum alicui, et hæred' de corpore suo exeuntibus (6), durum videbatur, et adhuc videtur, hujusmodi donatoribus, et hæredibus donatorum, quod voluntas donatorum ipsorum in donis suis expressa, non fuit prius, nec adhuc est observata. In omnibus enim prædictis casibus post prolem suscitatam, et exeuntem ab ipsis quibus tenementum sic conditionaliter fuit datum, hucusque habuerunt hujusmodi feoffati potestatem alienandi (7) tenementum sic datum, et exhæredandi exitum eorum, contra voluntatem donatorum (8), et contra formam in dono expressam. Et præterea cum deficiente exitu de hujusmodi feoffatis, tenementum sic datum ad donatorem, vel ad ejus hæredes reverti debuit per formam in charta de dono (9) hujusmodi expressam, licet exitus (si quis fuerit) obiisset per factum tamen*

FIRST, concerning lands that many times are given upon condition, that is to wit, where any giveth his land to any man and his wife, and to the heirs begotten of the bodies of the same man and his wife, with such condition expressed, that if the same man and his wife die without heirs of their bodies between them begotten, the land so given shall revert to the giver or his heir. In case also where one giveth lands in free marriage, which gift hath a condition annexed, though it be not expressed in the deed of gift, which is this, that if the husband and wife die without heir of their bodies begotten, the land so given shall revert to the giver or his heir. In case also where one giveth land to another, and the heirs of his body issuing; it seemed very hard, and yet seemeth to the givers and their heirs, that their will being expressed in the gift, was not heretofore, nor yet is observed. In all the cases aforesaid, after issue begotten and born between them (to whom the lands were given under such condition) heretofore such feoffees had power to aliene the land so given, and to disherit their issue of the land, contrary to the minds of the givers, and contrary to the form expressed in the gift. And further, when the issue of such feoffee is failing, the land so given ought to return to the giver, or his heir, by form of the gift expressed in the deed, though the issue (if any were) had died: yet by the deed and feoffment of them (to whom land was so given upon condition) the donors

tamen et feoffamentum eorum, quibus tenementum sic fuit datum sub conditione, exclusi fuerunt hucusque de reversione eorundem tenementorum, *quod manifestè fuit contra formam doni: propter quod dom' rex perpendens, quod necessarium et utile est in prædictis casibus apponere remedium, statuit* (10) *quod voluntas donatoris, secundum formam in charta doni sui* (12) *manifestè expressam, de cætero observetur, ita quod non habeant illi, quibus tenementum sic fuit datum* (13) *sub conditione, potestatem alienandi tenementum sic datum, quo minus ad exitum illorum, quibus tenementum sic fuerit datum remaneat post eorum obitum, vel ad donatorem, vel ad ejus hæredem (si exitus deficiat) revertatur* (11), *per hoc quod nullus sit exitus omnino, vel (si aliquis exitus fuerit, et per mortem deficiet) hærede de corpore hujusmodi exitus deficiente. Nec habeat de cætero secundus vir* (14) *hujusmodi mulieris aliquid in tenemento sic dato per conditionem, post mortem uxoris suæ, per legem Angliæ: nec exitus de secundo viro et muliere successionem hæreditariam* (15)*: sed statim post mortem viri et mulieris, quibus tenementum sic fuit datum, post eorum obitum ad eorum exitum, vel ad donatorem, vel ad ejus hæredem (ut prædictum est) revertatur. Et quia in novo casu novum* remedium est apponendum* (16)*: fiat impetranti tale breve.*

donors have heretofore been barred of their reversion, which was directly repugnant to the form of the gift. Wherefore our lord the king, perceiving how necessary and expedient it should be to provide remedy in the aforesaid cases, hath ordained, that the will of the giver, according to the form in the deed of gift manifestly expressed, shall be from henceforth observed; so that they to whom the land was given under such condition, shall have no power to aliene the land so given, but that it shall remain unto the issue of them to whom it was given after their death, or shall revert unto the giver, or his heirs, if issue fail (whereas there is no issue at all) or if any issue be, and fail by death, or heir of the body of such issue failing. Neither shall the second husband of any such woman, from henceforth, have any thing in the land so given upon condition, after the death of his wife, by the law of England, nor the issue of the second husband and wife shall succeed in the inheritance, but immediately after the death of the husband and wife (to whom the land was so given) it shall come to their issue, or return unto the giver, or his heir, as before is said. And forasmuch as in a new case new remedy must be provided, this manner of writ shall be granted to the party that will purchase it:

* [333]

Præcipe A. quod justè, &c. reddat B. (17) *tale manerium cum pertinentiis, quod C. dedit tali viro, et tali mulieri, et hæred' de ipsis viro et muliere exeuntibus.*

Vel,

Quod C. dedit tali viro in liberum maritagium cum tali muliere, et quod post mortem prædictorum viri et mulieris prædicto B. filio eorundem viri et mulieris descendere debet per formam donationis prædictæ, ut dicit.

Vel,

Quod C. dedit tali et hæred' de corpore suo exeuntibus, et quod post mortem ipsius talis, prædict' B. filio prædicti talis descendere debet per formam donationis, &c.

Breve per quod donator habet recuperare deficiente exitu, satis est in usu in cancel-

The writ whereby the giver shall recover (when issue faileth) is common

cancellaria (18). *Et ſciendum eſt, quod hoc ſtatutum quoad alienationem tenementi contra formam doni impoſterum faciendam, locum habeat, et ad dona prius facta non extendatur* (19). *Et ſi finis ſuper hujuſmodi tenementum impoſterum levetur, ipſo jure ſit nullus* (20). *Nec habeant hæredes hujuſmodi, aut illi ad quos ſpectat reverſio, (licet fuerunt plenæ ætatis, in Anglia, et extra priſonam* (21)*) neceſſe apponere clameum ſuum.*

mon enough in the chancery; and it is to wit, that this ſtatute ſhall hold place touching alienation of land contrary to the form of the gift hereafter to be made, and ſhal! not extend to gifts made before. And if a fine be levied hereafter upon ſuch lands, it ſhall be void in the law; neither ſhall the heirs, or ſuch as the reverſion belongeth unto, though they be of full age, within England, and out of priſon, need to make their claim. *Altered by* 32 *H.* 8. *c.* 36.

(1 Leon. 212. 1 Roll 48. 153. 158. 333. 357. 385. 2 Roll 429. Godbolt, 308. 367. pl. 458. Vaughan 365. Latch. 67. Savil 67. 88. 7 Rep. 33. Fitz. Tail, 11, 12, 13, 14. 16, 17, 18. 21, 22, 23. 1 Inſt. 18. b. 19. a. 24. a. 223. b. 224. a. 12 Rep. 81. Fitz. Formed. 61. 65. Fitz. Tail, 9, 10. Fitz. Tail, 15. Hob. 293. Fitz. Garranty, 16. 46. 57. 59. 3 Co. 85. Fitz. Formed. 1. 27. 33. 35. 52. 54. 59. 62 64. Fitz. Dower, 87. 3 Rep. 8. 5. 14. 7. 32, 33. 8. 35. 86. 166. 9. 105. 11. 72. 1 Inſt. 327. b. Regiſt. 238. Co. pla. 317. 338. 341. Dyer 216. 247. Fitz. Fines 125. Fitz. Formed. 5, 6, 7. 11. 14. 22. 30. 42. 44. 46, 47. 49. 8 H. 4. f. 8. Fitz. Continual Claim, 9.)

See the firſt of the Inſtitutes, ſect. 14.

(1) *In primis de tenementis.*] What inheritances may be intailed within this act, you may read at large in the firſt part of the Inſtitutes, cap. Taile, ſect. 14.

See the firſt part of the Inſtitutes, ſect. 13.

(2) *Multotiens dantur ſub conditione.*] Before this ſtatute, all inheritances were eſtates in fee, *viz.* either fee-ſimple abſolute, or fee conditionall, or a qualified fee, whereof you may alſo read in the firſt part of the Inſtitutes, ſect. 1. And tenant of lands intailed, had before this ſtatute a fee-ſimple conditionall ſubſequent; for albeit Britton, who wrote before this ſtatute, ſaith, that if any purchaſe to him and his wife, and to the heirs of them lawfully begotten, the donees have preſently but an eſtate of free-hold for the term of their lives, and the fee accrueth to their iſſue, &c. taking the condition to be precedent, yet had the donees at the common law a fee-ſimple conditionall preſently by the gift.

Brit. cap. 36.

19 E. 2. Formd. 61. 30 E. 1. ibid. 65. Pl. come often in Lord Berkleys caſe.

For if lands had been given to a man and the heirs of his body iſſuing, and before iſſue he had before this ſtatute made a feoffment in fee, the donor ſhould not have entred for the forfeiture, but this feoffment had barred the iſſue had afterwards; which proveth that he preſently by the gift had a fee ſimple conditionall, and this agreeth with the authority of Littleton, *ubi ſupra.*

Now for the better underſtanding of this act, ſeeing that the eſtate was conditionall at the common law, it is neceſſary to be known when the condition was performed, and to what purpoſes. If the donee had iſſue, he had not thereby a fee-ſimple abſolute, for if after he had dyed without iſſue, the donor ſhould have entred as in his reverter. But after iſſue had, the condition was performed to this purpoſe, that he might have aliened, and thereby have barred the donor and his heirs from all poſſibility of reverter for default of iſſue, for the heirs of his body (he having a fee conditionall) might have barred them as well before iſſue (as hath been ſaid) as after: and to what other purpoſes the condition by having of iſſue

See the firſt part of the Inſtitutes, ca. Tail, ſect. 13.

issue was performed, *vide* the first part of the Institutes, *ubi supra.*

(3) *Et hæredibus de ipsis.*] For to a gift in tail made, this word [heirs] is requisite, unlesse it be in case of a last will, &c. See the first part of the Institutes, sect. 1. & 14.

(4) *Adjecta conditione expressa tali,* &c.] If this condition expressed had not been added, the very gift would have implyed so much.

(5) *In casu etiam cum quis dat tenementum alicui in liberum maritagium,* &c.] By this clause it appeareth that an inheritance passeth by these words frank-mariage, whereof we have in another place written at large. See the first part of the Institutes, sect. 17.

(6) *In casu etiam cum quis dat tenementum alicui et hæredibus de corpore suo exeuntibus,* &c.] This act having put two examples of estates tail speciall, *viz.* the first to a man and to his wife, and to the heirs of their bodies; the second, of a gift in frank mariage, a speciall case, and a speciall estate in tail; here he putteth a case of an estate tail generall, not that the makers of this statute meant to enumerate all the forms of estates in tail, but to put these as examples, so as all manner of estates tail, generall or speciall, are within the purview of this act. 3 E. 3. 31, 32. 18 E. 3. 46. 33 E. 3. Tail 5. Dier 1 Mar. 96.

(7) *Potestatem alienandi,* &c.] That is to say, by fine, feoffment, release, or confirmation. 8 E. 3. 379. 44 E. 3. 3.

But the tenant in tail had not onely *potestatem alienandi,* but *forisfaciendi, &c.* also; for if after issue had, he had been attainted of treason or felony, the land entailed had been forfeited, and thereby the donor barred of the possibility of reverter, and *forisfacere* is *alienum facere,* and therefore in this act is included in these words, *potestatem alienandi.* And so might the tenant in tail, before the making of this act, have charged the land with rent, common, or the like, to have bound his issue, but by this act he is restrained aswell to charge as to alien. 7 E. 3. 368. 5 E. 3. 141. 7 H. 4. 31. 3 E. 3. Formed. 46. See the first part of the Institutes, sect. 3.

But the having of issue before this act did not alter the course of descent, as in another place we have said. In the first part of the Institutes, ubi supra.

(8) *Exhæredandi exitum eorum contra voluntatem donatorum.*] Hereby it appeareth that there were two mischiefs before this act, *viz.* first, the disherison of the issues in tail; secondly, that it was *contra voluntatem donatorum, et contra formam in dono expressam,* for the donor and his heirs were barred of the possibility of reverter: and both these were wrongs, for which at the common law there lay no remedy; for disherisons, and breaking the expresse will and intention of the donor are wrongs which this act doth remedy. Pl. Com. 247. a.

(9) *Per formam in charta de dono,* &c.] It was said before, *contra formam in dono expressam,* so as whether the estate were made by deed or without deed, it is all one to the intention of this act, and the most usuall gifts in tail being of inheritance, were by deed.

(10) *Propter quod dominus rex, &c. statuit.*] Albeit here be no mention made of the assent of the lords and commons (whose assents are necessary to the making of every law) yet forasmuch as in the preface of this parliament it is said, *dominus rex in parliamento suo, &c. statuta edidit,* and that this act and the rest were entred into the roll of the parliament, and that this word [*statuit*] implyeth the assent of the lords and commons, for it cannot be *statutum* without 7 H. 7. 14. 11 H. 7. 27. 39 E. 3. 7. For the divers forms of parliaments, see lib. 8. the Princes case. Bro. tit. Parliament 76.

without their assents, therefore it hath (as many other of like form) been without question received for an act of parliament.

(11) * 1. *Quod voluntas donatoris, secundum formam in charta doni sui manifeste expressam, de caetero observetur; 2, Ita quod non habeant illi, quibus tenementum sic fuerit datum sub conditione potestatem alienandi tenementum sic datum, quo minus ad exitum illorum. quibus tenementum sic fuerit datum remaneat post eorum obitum, vel ad donatorem, vel ad ejus haeredem (sic exitus deficiat) revertatur*, &c.] Upon these two branches, *viz.* that the will of the donor should be observed, and that the donee should not have power to alien, the judges by a threefold construction did not onely remedy all the said former mischiefes, but prevent all other that might arise.

1. 1. Therefore in execution of the will of the donor, and that he should have no power to alien either lands that lay in livery, or tenements that lay in graunt, they adjudged that the donee should not have a fee-simple, but divided the estates, and created a particular estate in the donee, and a reversion in the donor, so as where the donee had a fee-simple before, by this act he had but an estate taile, and where the donor had but a possibility before, which after issue might be barred at the pleasure of the donee, now by construction upon this act the donor had the fee-simple expectant upon the estate taile, which we call a reversion; so as by this division of the estates the donee after issue, or before could not barre or charge his issue, nor for default of issue the donor or his heirs, either by alienation, forfeiture, or any charge whatsoever.

5 H. 7. 14. vide c. 4. verb. quando ux' dotata, &c. et verb. non habeant aliud recuperare, &c.

9 E. 3. 22. Sir William Herle chiefe justice of the court of common pleas said of them that made this statute, *Ilz fueront sages gents queux fieront cest statut*; and I may say as truly, *Que ils fueront sages gents queux interpretont cest act*. And in another place he saith, *Nous veiomus ceux queux fieront lestatut, & auxi en temps de quel roy lestatut fuit fait, que fuit le pluis sage roy que unques fuit, & le cause del statut fuit, a saver le heritage en le sang ceux as queux le done se fist.*

5 E. 3. 14.

2. The second construction was, that no lineall warranty should barre the issue in taile, unlesse there were assets descended in fee-simple from the same auncestor, but a collaterall warranty made by a collaterall auncestor should barre the issue in taile without assets, for that warrantry is not restrained by this act, whereof we have spoken at large in another place; and so likewise the collaterall warranty of the donee shall barre the donor, and is not restrained by this act, as well as the warranty of the donor shall barre the donee, as there also it appeareth.

See the first part of the Institutes, sect. 712.

3. The third construction was, that albeit tenant in taile was restrained from power of alienations, yet of lands and tenements that lay in livery, his fine or feoffment should worke a discontinuance, and drive the issue in taile to his action: for seeing he had an estate of inheritance, the judges compared it to the case where a man was seised in the right of his wife, or a bishop in the right of his bishoprick, or an abbot in the right of his monastery, *et sic in similibus*; and of inheritances that lay in graunt, as of rents, advowsons, and the like, tenant in taile could not make any discontinuance, no more then the others before recited might doe, which construction was made according to the rule and reason of the common law in other like cases.

(12) *Secundum formam in charta doni sui*, &c.] This holdeth, though there be no deed, as before hath been said.

(13) *Non*

(13) *Non habeant illi quibus tenementum sic fuerit datum.*] It was adjudged by Beresford, that the issues in taile should not alien no more then * they to whom the land was given, and that was the intent of the makers of this act, and it was but their negligence, that it was omitted, as there it is said. In this case by way of purchase the land is given to the donees, and by way of limitation to the issues in taile, and therefore by a benigne interpretation the purview of this extends to the issues in taile. 5 E. 2. Formedon 52. 4 E. 3. 29.

(14) *Nec habeat de cætero secundus vir*, &c.] These are but consequents to the words of the purview, and are but explanatory, and not of substance, and might well have been omitted. Pl.Co.247. Sieg's Berklies case.

Yet was it adjudged soon after the making of this act, that where lands were given in frankmarriage, and the husband died, and the wife took another husband, and had issue before this act, that the husband should be tenant by the curtesie, and the principall reason was upon this branch of the statute, *Nec habeat de cætero secundus vir, &c.* for that this restraint proved, as there it is said, that the law before was, that he should be tenant by the curtesie, and yet without question the issue should not inherit that land. 10 E. 1. Form. 66. Vide Pasc. 18 E. 1. in banco Rot. 27. in Dower.

(15) *Successionem hæreditariam.*] In auncient time if land had been given to I. S. and his successors, hee had had a fee-simple, but otherwise it is at this day, as it appeareth in the first part of the Institutes, sect. 1.

(16) *Et quia in novo casu novum remedium est apponendum.*]

Ea quæ de novo emergunt, novo indigent remedio. *Regula.*

Hereby it appeareth that a formedon in the descender lay not at the common law, but was given by this act, and the forme of the writ is here set downe. 10 E. 2. Formed. 55. 4 E. 2. ib. 50. 21 E. 3. 47. F.N.B. 211. Pl. Com. 240.

(17) *Præcipe A. quod juste reddat B*, &c.] Here is the forme of the formedon in the descender set downe, and therefore this statute need not be recited, nor any statute which giveth the forme of the writ. Fleta, li. 5. c. 34. Regist. 238, 239. 5 H. 7. 17. b.

(18) *Breve quod donator habeat recuperare deficiente exitu satis est in usu in cancellaria.*] The formedon in reverter did lie at the common law, but not a formedon in remainder upon an estate taile, because it was a fee-simple conditionall, whereupon no remainder could be limited at the common law, but after this statute a remainder may be limited upon an estate taile in respect of the division of the estates. Regist. 243. F.N.B. 217, 218.

(19) *Sciendum est quod hoc statutum quoad alienationem tenementi contra formam doni imposterum faciendam locum habeat, et ad dona prius facta non extenditur.*]

This clause ought to receive a two-fold interpretation. 1. That [*ad dona prius facta*] must be intended of feoffements or alienations made by the donee or his issues, and not to guifts made by the donor, for to them this act doth extend.

2. *Dona prius facta*, that is, *post prolem suscitatam*, for then the alienation by the tenant in taile, or his issues was good in law: so as [*dona*] here are to be intended lawfull gifts, and made in due manner, and such as could not be avoided, for law alloweth no wrong. 4 E. 2. Formed. 50. 12 H. 4. 7. 21 E. 3. 45. Pl. Com. 246. First part of the Instit. sect. 729, 730.

(20) *Et si finis super hujusmodi tenementum imposterum levetur, ipso jure sit nullus.*] This act doth not make the fine void, but *ipso jure sit nullus*, that is, it shall not binde the right, yet it shall (as hath been said) make a discontinuance. 6 E. 3. 20. 8 H. 4. 10. 33 E. 3. Estoppel, 280. 33 H. 6. 18.

But now by the statutes of 4 H. 7. cap. 24. and 32 H. 8. cap. 34. a fine levied with * proclamations doth barre the issues in taile, but a fine without proclamations is a discontinuance onely, and no barre.

See the first part of the Institutes, sect. 440. Custumier, cap. 48.

(21) *Nec habeant hæredes hujusmodi, nec illi ad quos spectat reversio, licet fuerint plenæ ætatis, in Anglia, et extra prisonam.*] Here is *non compos mentis* left out, and so is a *feme covert.*

See the first part of the Institutes, sect. 441.

4 H. 7. cap. 24. Stat. de modo levand. finis. 18 E. 1.

Hereby it may be gathered (as the law was) that a fine at the common law did not binde a stranger that was within age, in prison, or beyond the seas.

See more for the construction of this statute in the first part of the Institutes, sect. 21, 22, 23. 271. 362, 363. 441. 746, 747.

CAP. II.

QUIA domini feodorum distringentes tenentes suos (1) *pro servitiis et consuetudinibus sibi debitis multotiens gravantur per hoc, quod cum tenentes sui districtionem suam per breve, vel sine brevi replegiaverint, ac cum ipsi domini (ad querimoniam tenentium suorum) ad com', vel ad aliam curiam* (3) *habentem potestatem placitandi placita de vetito namio* (2), *per attachiament' venerint, et rationabilem et justam districtionem advocaverint, per hoc quod tenentes disadvocant* (4) *nihil tenere, nec clamant tenere de eo qui districtionem fecit, et advocavit, remansit ille qui distrinxit in misericordia, et tenentes sui quieti, quibus pro illa disadvocatione per recordum com', sive aliarum curiarum, quæ recordum non habent, pœna infligi non potest. De cætero provisum est et statutum, quod cum hujusmodi domini in com' vel hujusmodi curia justiciam de hujusmodi tenentibus suis consequi non possint, quam cito attachiati fuerint ad sectam tenentium suorum, concedatur eis breve ad ponend' loquelam* (6) *illam coram justiciariis* (5), *coram quibus et non alibi justicia hujusmodi dominis exhiberi poterit, et inseratur causa in brevi, quia talis distrinxit in feodo suo pro servic' et consuetud' sibi debitis. Nec per*

FORASMUCH as lords of fees distraining their tenants for services and customs due unto them, are many times grieved, because their tenants do replevy the distress by writ, or without writ: and when the lords, at the complaint of their tenants, do come by attachment into the county, or unto another court, having power to hold pleas of withernam, and do avow the taking good and lawful, by reason that the tenants disavow to hold ought, nor do claim to hold any thing of him which took the distress and avowed it, he that distrained is amerced, and the tenants go quit; to whom punishment cannot be assigned for such disavowing by record of the county, or of other courts having no record. It is provided and ordained from henceforth, that where such lords cannot obtain justice in counties and such manner of courts against their tenants, as soon as they shall be attached at the suit of their tenants, a writ shall be granted to them to remove the plea before the justices, afore whom, and none otherwhere, justice may be ministred unto such lords; and the cause shall be put in the writ, because such a man distrained in his fee for services and customs to him due.

per iſtud ſtatutum derogat' legi communi uſitatæ, quod non permiſit aliquod placitum poni coram juſtic' ad petitionem defendentis (7): quia licet prima facie videatur tenens actor, et dominus defendens, habito tamen reſpectu ad hoc quod dominus diſtrinxit, et ſequitur pro ſervitiis et conſ. ſibi aretro exiſten' realiter apparebit potius actor, ſive querens, quam defendens (8). *Et * ut in certo ſint juſtic'* (9) *de qua recenti ſeiſina poterint domini advocare rationabilem diſtrictionem ſuper tenentes ſuos: de cætero concordatum eſt, quod rationabilis diſtrictio poterit advocari de ſeiſina anteceſſorum vel prædeceſſorum ſuorum, à tempore quo breve novæ diſſeiſinæ currit.* Vide W. 1. cap. 38. *Et quia aliquando contingit, quod tenens poſtquam replegiaverit averia ſua, averia illa vendit vel elongat, quo minus retornum poſſit fieri domino diſtringenti, ſi adjudicetur: proviſum eſt, quod vicecomes, vel balivi de cætero non recipiant à conquerentibus ſolummodo plegios de proſequendo, antequam deliberationem faciant de averiis, ſed etiam de averiis retornandis* (10), *ſi adjudicetur retornand'. Et ſi quis alio modo plegios ceperit, reſpondeat ipſe de precio averiorum. Et habeat dominus diſtringens recuperare per breve, quod reddat ei tot averia, vel catalla. Et ſi non habeat balivus unde reddat, reddat ſuperior ſuus* (11). *Et quia aliquando contingit, quod poſtquam adjudicat' fuerit diſtringenti retornum averiorum, et ſic diſtrictus, poſtquam averia ſic retornata* (13) *iterum replegiaverit, et cum viderit diſtringent' comparentem in curia paratum ſibi reſpondere, defaltam fecerit* (12), *ob quam iterum readjudicabitur diſtringenti retornum averiorum, et ſic bis, vel ter, et in infinitum* (14) *replegiabuntur averia, nec habebunt judicia* (15) *curiæ regis in hoc caſu effectum, ſuper quo non fuit prius remedium proviſum. Ordinat' eſt in hoc caſu talis proceſſus, quod*

due. Neither is this act prejudicial to the law commonly uſed, which did not permit that any plea ſhould be moved before juſtices at the ſuit of the defendant. For though it appear at the firſt ſhew that the tenant is plaintiff, and the lord defendant, nevertheleſs, having reſpect to that, that the lord hath diſtrained, and ſueth for ſervices and cuſtoms being behind, he appeareth indeed to be rather actor, or plaintiff, than defendant. And to the intent the juſtices may know upon what freſh ſeiſin the lords may avow the diſtreſs reaſonable upon their tenants; from henceforth it is agreed and enacted, that a reaſonable diſtreſs may be avowed upon the ſeiſin of any anceſtor or predeceſſor ſince the time that a writ of novel diſſeiſin hath run. And becauſe it chanceth ſometimes that the tenant, after that he hath replevied his beaſts, doth ſell or aliene them, whereby return cannot be made unto the lord that diſtrained, if it be adjudged: it is provided, that ſheriffs or bailiffs from henceforth ſhall not only receive of the plaintiffs pledges for the purſuing of the ſuit, before they make deliverance of the diſtreſs, but alſo for the return of the beaſts, if return be awarded. And if any take pledges otherwiſe, he ſhall anſwer for the price of the beaſts, and the lord that diſtraineth ſhall have his recovery by writ, that he ſhall reſtore unto him ſo many beaſts or cattle; and if the bailiff be not able to reſtore, his ſuperiour ſhall reſtore. And foraſmuch as it hapneth ſometime, that after the return of the beaſts is awarded unto the diſtrainor, and the party ſo diſtrained, after that the beaſts be returned, doth replevy them again, and when he ſeeth the diſtrainor appearing in the court ready to anſwer him, doth make default, whereby return of the beaſts ought to be awarded again unto the diſtrainor,

quod quam cito adjudicatum fuerit retornum averiorum distringenti per breve de judicio, mandetur vicecomiti, quod retornum habere faciat distringenti de averiis, in quo brevi inseratur, quod vicecom' ea non deliberet sine brevi, in quo fiat mentio de judicio per justic' reddit': quod fieri non poterit, nisi per breve quod exeat de rotulis justic', coram quibus deduct' fuerit loquela (16). *Cum igitur districtus adierit justic', et petierit averia sua iterum sibi replegiari, fiat ei breve de judicio* (17), *quod vic' (capta securitate de prosequendo, et etiam de averiis seu catallis retornand', vel eorum precio, si adjudicetur retornum) deliberet ei averia, vel catalla prius retornata: et attachietur ille qui distrinxit ad veniend' ad certum diem coram justic', coram quibus placitum deducatur in præsentia partium. Et si iterato ille, qui * replegiaverit averia, fecerit defaltam, vel alia occasione adjudicetur retornum districtionis jam bis replegiat', remaneat districtio illa in perpetuum irreplegiabilis* (18). *Sed si de novo, et de nova causa* (19) *fiat districtio, de nova districtione servetur processus supradictus.*

* [339]

distrainor, and so the beasts be replevied twice or thrice, and infinitely, and the judgements given in the king's court take no effect in this case, whereupon no remedy hath been yet provided; in this case such process shall be awarded, that so soon as return of the beasts shall be awarded to the distrainor, the sheriff shall be commanded by a judicial writ to make return of the beasts unto the distrainor; in which writ it shall be expressed, that the sheriff shall not deliver them without writ, making mention of the judgement given by the justices, which cannot be without a writ issuing out of the rolls of the said justices before whom the matter was moved. Therefore when he cometh unto the justices, and desireth replevin of the beasts, he shall have a judicial writ, that the sheriff taking surety for the suit, and also of the beasts or cattle to be returned, or the price of them (if return be awarded) shall deliver unto him the beasts or cattle before returned, and the distrainor shall be attached to come at a certain day before the justices, afore whom the plea was moved in presence of the parties. And if he that replevied make default again, or for another cause return of the distress be awarded, being now twice replevied, the distress shall remain irrepleviable; but if a distress be taken of new, and for a new cause, the process abovesaid shall be observed in the same new distress.

(16 H. 7. f. 1. Regist. 83. Dyer, 188. 2 H. 6. 15. 8 Ed. 3. 72. 9 H. 6. 42. Fitz. Return des Avers, 35. Cro. Car. 594. Dyer, 41. 59. Kel. 92. 26 H. 8. 6. 21 H. 7. 28. 12 H. 7. 4. 14 H. 7. 6. Dyer, 280. Fitz. Return des Avers, 6. 15. 18, 19. 24. 26. 32, 33, 34, 35.

(1) *Quia domini feodorum distringentes tenentes suos,* &c.]

Fleta, li. 2. c. 37. In this preamble is the mischief set down, that was at the common law before the making of this act.

Mirror, cap. 5. § 5. The Mirror without cause doth finde great fault with this act, which you may read, and being of no use need not here to be inserted.

(2) *Ad*

(2) *Ad comitatum vel aliam curiam habentem poteſtatem placitandi de vetito namio.*] *De vetito namio,* of a forbidden or unjuſt taking, and is not underſtood of a taking in withernam, for that is a juſt and no forbidden taking, as in another place I have proved more at large. Vide Marlebr. cap. 21.

(3) *Vel aliam curiam.*] So as lords of hundreds, wapentakes, &c. may have power to hold plea of replevin, &c. Marlbr. ubi ſupra F.N.B. 73. b.

(4) *Diſadvocant,* &c.] That is diſclaim, whereof the court being no court could have no conuſans, becauſe it concerned free-hold. F.N.B. 70. b.

(5) *Quod cum hujuſmodi domini in com' vel hujuſmodi curia juſticiam de hujuſmodi tenentibus ſuis conſequi non poſſunt, &c. concedatur illis breve ad ponend' loquel' illam coram juſticiariis,* &c.] Failer of juſtice, is ever a good cauſe to remove the plea.

(6) *Ad ponend' loquelam.*] The writ of *pone* doth lye when there is a replevin depending by writ out of the chancery, the plaintife or defendant may remove the plea by a *pone*; and if the plea be depending in the county, the plaintife may remove the ſame without cauſe, but the defendant cannot remove it without cauſe, and that cauſe muſt be put in the end of the writ. And if it be upon this ſtatute, the words be, *Quia prædict' B. cepit averia prædict' in feodo ſuo pro conſuetudinibus et ſervitiis ut dicitur,* which are the very expreſſe words of this act. Fleta ubi ſupra. F.N.B. 69. in Regiſt. 84. a. Regiſt. ubi ſup.

And when the plaint is in the county by writ or without writ, or in the court of any other, the ſame may be removed by a writ of *recordari fac' loquelam.*

And if the plaint be in the county, the plaintife may remove the ſame without cauſe, as hath been ſaid; but the defendant cannot remove it (as hath been ſaid) without cauſe. But if the plaint be in the court of any other, neither the plaintife nor defendant can remove the plaint without cauſe, for the prejudice that may come thereby to the lord.

(7) *Quod non permiſit aliquod placitum poni coram juſtic' ad petitionem defendentis.*] This muſt be underſtood without cauſe ſhewed, for by the common law, the defendant for cauſe ſhewed might remove the plaint. F.N.B. 70. a. Regiſt. 83.

(8) *Potius actor ſive querens quàm defendens.*] In truth the defendant by making avowry doth become actor, and ſhall have judgement given for him, and after avowry he ſhall not have a protection caſt for him no more then a plaintife ſhall, becauſe he is become an actor, and not meerly a defendant. [340] 5 H. 5. 5.

(9) *Et ut in certo ſint juſticiarii,* &c.] It was a doubt before this act, within what limitation of time an avowry might be made, and by this act it is provided, *Quod rationabilis diſtrictio poterit advocari de ſeiſina anteceſſorum, vel prædeceſſorum ſuorum a tempore quo breve novæ diſſeiſinæ currit*; which limitation in an aſſiſe appeareth before in W. 1. cap. 38. which was *poſt primam transfretationem regis H. 3. in Vaſconiam,* in the fift yeer of his raign. But this limitation, both in the aſſiſe and in the avowry, is altered by a latter ſtatute. 5 H. 3. W. 1. cap. 38. 32 H. 8. cap. 3.

(10) *Non ſolummodo plegios de proſequendo, &c. ſed etiam de averiis retornandis, &c.*] If the ſherife retorn inſufficient pledges, they are no pledges within this ſtatute, and in that caſe the ſherife ſhall be charged by this act, as if he had taken no pledges at all. Fleta, li. 2. c. 38. Regiſt. Judic. 4. 2 H. 6. 15.

If the retorn of pledges be upon a writ of replevin, then if the plaintife be nonſute, &c. if upon the writ *de retorno habendo*, the ſherife retorn *averia elongata*, *&c.* the plaintife may have a writ to have retorn of the beaſts of the pledges. But if the deliverance were by plaint, becauſe in that caſe the pledges do not appear to the court, the plaintife can have no ſuch writ.

8 E. 3. 72. 39 E. 3. 28.

And if upon the writ to have retorn of the beaſts of the pledges, the ſherife retorn *nihil*, then may the plaintife have a *ſcire facias* againſt the ſherife, *quod reddat ei tot averia*, or *tot catalla*; and that which hath been ſaid of the ſherife, is to be intended of the bailife of a franchiſe.

2 H. 6. 15. 9 H. 6. 42. & 48.

(11) *Et ſi non habeat balivus unde reddat, reddat ſuperior ſuus.*] *Vide* Simile, 44 E. 3. 13. *Vide* 52 H. 3. Leſtatute del Eſchequer. *Vide* 2 H. 6. cap. 10.

34 E. 1. Judgement, 244. 34 H. 6. 37. 19 E. 2. Repl. 25. 6 E. 3. 37. 24 E. 3. 71. 21 E. 4. 6.

(12) *Defaltam fecerint*, &c.] At the common law, if the plaintife in the replevin had been nonſute either before or after verdict, the defendant that diſtrained ſhould have had retorn, but not irreplevisable, ſo as the plaintife after nonſute might have had as many replevins as he would, which was vexatious and miſchievous; for remedy whereof, this act doth reſtrain the plaintife from any more replevin after nonſute, but giveth a writ of ſecond deliverance, whereof we ſhall ſpeak in his proper place.

11 E. 2. Ret. des avers 31. 10 E. 2. ibid. 5. 41 E. 3. ib. 14. 21 R. 2. ib. 29. 3 H. 6. 2, 3. 27 H. 6. 3. 48 E. 3. 10. 49 E. 3. 24. 2 H. 4. 23. 4 H. 6. 8, 9. 34 H. 6. 37. 12 H. 7. 4, 5. 13 H. 7. Retorne des avers miſreport per Fitzh. See the authorities next before concerning theſe matters. Temps E. 1. Ret. des avers 33.

If the writ of replevin doth abate for want of form in default of the clerk, the defendant ſhall not have retorn at all; but if it abate for matter apparant by miſinformation, or other default of the plaintife, the defendant ſhall have retorn, but not irreplevisable.

But if the defendant doth plead a plea to the writ, and the plaintife confeſſeth it, then the plaintife ſhall have retorn, but not irreplevisable, for the plaintife may have a new writ of replevin; for this act onely giveth remedy in caſe of nonſute.

But if the plea to the writ, or any other plea be tryed by verdict, or judged upon a demurrer, retorn irreplevisable ſhall be awarded, and no new replevin ſhall be granted, nor any ſecond deliverance by this act, but (as it hath been ſaid) upon a nonſute.

(13) *Averia ſic retornata.*] Note neither court baron, nor county court, nor any court that is not the court of the king before his juſtices can award retorn irreplevisable.

(14) *In infinitum.*] *Infinitum in jure reprobatur.*

[341]

(15) *Nec habebunt judicia*, &c.] Here is a maxime of the common law implyed, *viz. Judicia ſuum effectum habere debent. Judicium non debet eſſe illuſorium.*

17 E. 2. Repl. 21. 6 E. 3. 37. 20 E. 3. Eſtopp. 186. 20 E. 3. Avowry 125. 21 E. 3. 43. 16 E. 3. Aide 131. 3 H. 6. 9. 12 H. 7. 4. 21 H. 7. 28. 26 H. 8. 6. Vide Mich. 31 E. 3. fo. 50. in lib. meo. Dier, 36 H. 8. f. 59. Regiſt. Judic. 58.

(16) *Per breve de judicio*, *&c. quod exeat de rotulis juſtic' coram quibus deducta fuerit loquela.*] The writ of ſecond deliverance given by this act is a writ judiciall, as here it appeareth, and iſſueth out of the record of the replevin in which the nonſute was; and regularly the judiciall writ ought not to vary from the record, out of which it iſſueth; and therefore if after nonſute the ſherife retorn *averia elongata*, and the defendant upon the withernam hath other beaſts delivered to him, the plaintife is to have his ſecond deliverance of the firſt beaſts mentioned in the former record.

(17) *Fiat ei breve de judicio*, &c.] The effect of the writ of ſecond deliverance is here ſet down, and appeareth in the Judiciall Regiſter.

And

And this writ is a supersedeas in law to the sherife, that he make no retorn to the defendant upon the former nonsute. 33 Avowry 256. Dyer, 30 H. 8. 41. b.

(18) *Et si iterato, ille qui replegiaverit averia, fecerit desaltam, vel alia occasione adjudicetur retornum districtionis jam bis replegiat', remaneat districtio illa in perpetuum irreplegiabilis.*] If the plaintife in the second deliverance by nonsute, or if the plea be discontinued, or the writ abate, or if he prevail not in his sute, retorn irreplevisable shall be granted. 5 E. 2. Ret. des avers 64. 10 E. 2. ib. 5. 33 E. 3. ib. 34. 8 R. 2. ib. 35. 6 E. 3. 37.

But if retorn irreplevisable be granted, the owner of the cattell or other goods distrained may come to the defendant and offer the arrerages, &c. and if the defendant refuse to deliver the distress, the plaintife may have an action of detinue, and by that means recover them, for they are in nature of a gage. 17 H. 8. Second Deliverance. Br. 15. Pl. Com. 82. b. 45 E. 3. 9. 14 H. 4. 4.

(19) *Sed si de nova causa.*] The second deliverance must be brought for the same distresse, but if the same lord distrain the same tenant for a rent, or other service behinde at another day, or for another cause, there the replevin doth lye, and such proceeding as is abovesaid. 33 H. 6. 27.

CAP. III.

IN casu quando vir amiserit (1) per defaltam (2) tenementum, quod fuit jus uxoris suæ (3), durum fuit quod uxor post mortem viri non habuerit aliud recuperare, quam per breve de recto: propter quod dominus rex statuit, quod mulier post mortem viri sui habeat recuperare per breve de ingressu, cui ipsa in vita (4) sua contradicere non potuit, quod in forma subscripta erit placitandum (5). Si contra petitionem mulieris tenens excipiat, quod habuerit ingressum per judicium, et compertum fuerit, quod per defaltam, ad quod tenens necesse habet responder', si ab eo quæratur, tunc ulterius habet necesse ostendere jus suum, secundum formam brevis, quod prius impetravit super virum et uxorem. Et si verificare poterit quod * *habuerit, vel habet jus in tenemento petito, nihil capiat mulier per breve suum. Quod si ostendere non poterit, recuperet mulier tenementum petitum: hoc observato, quod si vir absentaverit (6) se, et noluerit jus uxoris suæ defendere, vel invita uxore sua reddere voluerit, si uxor ante judicium venerit pa-*

*[342]

IN case when a man doth lose by default the land which was the right of his wife, it was very hard that the wife, after the death of her husband, had none other recovery but by a writ of right; wherefore our lord the king hath ordained, that a woman, after the death of her husband, shall recover by a writ of entry (whereto she could not disagree during his life) which shall be pleaded in form under-written. If the tenant do except against the demand of the wife, that he entered by judgement, and it be found that his entry was by default, whereto the tenant of necessity must make answer, if it be demanded of him, then he shall be compelled to make further answer, and to shew his right according to the form of the writ that he purchased before against the husband and the wife. And if he can verify that he hath or had right in the land demanded, the woman shall gain nothing by her writ; which thing if he cannot shew, the woman shall recover the land in demand; this being observed,

(7), *parata petenti respondere* (8), *et ius suum defendere* (9), *admittatur uxor. Eodem modo* (11) *si tenens in dotem, per legem Angliæ, vel aliter ad terminum vitæ* (12), *vel per donum* (13) *in quo reservatur reversio, fecerit defaltam, vel reddere voluerit* (16), *admittantur hæredes* (14), *vel illi ad quos spectat reversio* (15), *ad responsionem* (17), *si venerint ante judicium* (10). *Et si per defaltam, vel reddition' reddatur judicium, tunc habeant hæred', vel illi ad quos spectat reversio, post mortem hujusmodi tenentium, recuperare per breve de ingressu* (18): *in quo observetur idem processus, sicut prædict' est in casu ubi vir amittat per defaltam tenementum uxoris suæ. Et sic in casibus prædict' duæ concurrunt actiones* (19) *una inter petentem et tenentem, et alia inter tenentem jus suum ostendentem et petentem.* Vide 20 E 1. defensio juris, fol. 88.

observed, that if the husband absent himself, and will not defend his wife's right, or against his wife's consent will render the land, if the wife do come before judgement, ready to answer the demandant, and to defend her right, the wife shall be admitted. Likewise if tenant in dower, tenant by the law of the land, or otherwise for term of life, or by gift, where the reversion is reserved, do make default, or will give up; the heirs, and they unto whom the reversion belongeth, shall be admitted to their answer if they come before judgement; and if upon such default, or surrender, judgement hap to be given, then the heirs, or they unto whom the reversion belongeth after the death of such tenants, shall have their recovery by a writ of entry, in which like process shall be observed as is aforesaid, in case where the husband loseth his wife's land by default. And so in the cases aforesaid two actions do concur, one between the demandant and tenant, and another between the tenant shewing his right, and the demandant.

(Regist. 232. 6 Rep. 8. 8 Co. 72. 26 H. 8. 2. Fitz. Cui in vita, 7, 8, 9, 10, 11. 14. 16, 17. 19, 20. 22. 26. 28. 30. 32. 34. 1 Inst. 352. b. 353. a. 355. a. 356. a. Dyer, 298. 315. 341. Fitz. Resceit, 1. 3. 5, 6. 9. 11, 12. 19. 27. 30. 32. 139. 10 Rep. 44. 5 Ed. 3. 61. Cro. Car. 43. Keilw. 128. Regist. 133. 32 H. 8. c. 28.)

(1) *Vir amiserit.*] This is to be understood of the husband and the wife, for the husband alone is not tenant to the *præcipe*, and therefore it was the opinion of Hankford, that if the land be recovered against the husband sole, that after the death of the husband the wife shall have an assise; but Fitzh. in abbreviating this case saith, that it is hard to be proved by reason, because the wife cannot be disseised (during the coverture) but where the husband is disseised, but of such a recovery she cannot have a *cui in vita* upon this statute: but seeing the husband was not tenant to the *præcipe*, this can be no discontinuance, and therefore not like to a feoffment, for that conveyance is compleat and good, but so is not the recovery, and therefore in that case the wife may enter after the death of her husband; but when the *præcipe* is brought against the husband and wife, it may be said that *vir amiserit*, for it is principally his act or default; and therefore though the words of the statute of 32 H. 8. be (suffered by the husband onely) yet a feined recovery against the husband and wife is within that statute.

10 H. 4. Disseis. 7. 30 E. 3. 6. Resceit 128. 48 E. 3. Pl. Com. 57. b. 19 E. 2. Receit 176. 2 E. 2. ib. 148.

32 H. 8. cap. 28.

(2) *Per*

(2) *Per defaltam.*] A recovery by render is within the equity of this statute, because it is within the same mischief; but a recovery by action tryed is out of this statute.

It is said, that a recovery by default in a cessavit against the husband and wife, doth binde the wife; but I hold the law to the contrary, unlesse the cause of the action be just, and then it bindeth, as in all other cases; for this act giveth no remedy, but where the recovery is without title.

49 E. 3. 23. 50 E. 3. 7. 47 E. 3. 13. See the first part of the Institutes, sect. 675. 4 E. 2. Cui in vita. 20. F.N.B. 193. i.

In a *quid juris clam'*, *quod permittat*, assise of rent, *scire facias*, attaint, &c. the wife upon default of the husband shall be received.

36 H. 6. Fauxer Recovery 27. 2 H. 5. 1. 7 E. 3. 15. 19 E. 3. Receit 14. 34 Ass. p. 3. Pasch. 28 E. 1.

In a *quare impedit* against the husband and wife, the wife shall not be received upon the default of the husband; for the Record saith, *Inspecta causa confectionis statuti manifeste liquet, quod non est in casu consimili*; for the husband may present alone.

Coram rege. Cestria. Bract. li. fo. 367. Fleta, li. 5. c. 22. 7 E. 3. 62. Lib. 6. fol. 8. Ferrers case.

(3) * *Quod fuerit jus uxoris suæ.*] This is intended of a fee-simple, for so is *jus* regularly taken; and this act saith, that the wife had no recovery but by a writ of right, which none can have but tenant in fee-simple, and so one part of this act doth expound another; and for tenant in taile (reduced formerly (as hath been said) at this parliament to a divided and particular estate) and for tenant for life provision is made in the next chapter by a *quod ei deforceat*, as shall be declared when we come thereunto; for tenant in taile, and tenant for life are out of the letter of this statute, because they could have no writ of right; and yet if the husband and wife seised in the right of his wife for terme of her life lose in a *præcipe quod reddat* by default, and the husband die, the wife shall have a *cui in vita*, for this is, as it were, a demise made by the husband, for otherwise she should be without remedy, for she cannot have a *quod ei deforceat*, as shall be said hereafter.

* [343]

4 E. 3. 38, 39. 5 E. 3. 4. 33 E. 3. Avowry 255. 2 E. 4. 13. F.N.B. 156.

If lands during the coverture be given to the husband and wife, and their heirs, this is *jus uxoris* within this statute.

7 E. 3. 6. 4 E. 3. 19.

(4) *Cui ipsa in vita.*] Sir William Herle said, that he had seene in auncient time, that where the husband aliened the right of his wife, she had no other recovery but by a writ of right, yet I finde in Bracton and Fleta, that a *cui in vita* in their times lay upon the alienation of her husband.

5 E. 3. 58. See the first part of the Institutes, sect. 594. Bract. li. 4. 321. b. Fleta, l. 5. c. 34. 36. Custumier de Norm. cap. 10.

(5) *Quod in forma subscripta erit placitand'.*] If the tenant doth plead in barre the recovery by default, he must averre the title of his writ, whereupon if issue be taken, and found for the tenant, the demandant shall take nothing by her writ, and if it be found for her, she shall recover the land.

21 E. 4. 65. 22 E. 4. 30. 24 H. 8. Pleadings Br.

(6) *Hoc observato quod si vir absentaverit.*] This act having before given the wife a *cui in vita* after the decease of her husband, doth by this branch give her a remedy upon the default, or reddition of her husband in his life time to defend her right, so as she should not be driven to a reall action after the decease of her husband, and this receit to the wife is given by this act, which she could not have at the common law.

a Regist. F.N.B. 19. g.

a This act doth extend to courts that be not of record; as if husband and wife be sued in a court baron by writ of right, &c. upon the husbands default the wife shall be received.

Mich. 18 E. 1. in banco Rot. 222. Thomas de Maws case.

Upon *feint pleder* of the husband, the wife shall not be received by the opinion of Prisot: but it is resolved in 8 E. 2. to the contrary; yet I hold the law with Prisot; upon a *nient dedire*, and a *nihil*

33 H. 6. 21. Vide 13 R. 2. c. 17. 8 E. 2. receit 182. 4 E. 3. receit 46.

nihil dicit the feme ſhall be received within the purview of this ſtatute, 4 E. 3. receit 46.

(7) *Si uxor ante judicium venerit.*] [b] It is to be obſerved, Firſt, that the time of the receit is when judgement ſhould be given. 2. It is to be underſtood *de principali judicio*, as in an admeaſurement of paſture judgement is given that admeaſurement ſhall be made, and if after admeaſurement made and retourned the baron maketh default, the wife ſhall be received before the principall judgement given.

[c] And ſo in an aſſiſe of mordaunc' againſt the huſband and wife, if the aſſiſe be awarded by default, if after the baron make default before the principall judgement, the wife may bee received; and ſo in the aſſiſe of novel diſſeiſin.

[d] And albeit ſhe come not at the time of the default, yet if ſhe come before judgement ſhe ſhall be received, and ſo of him in the reverſion or remainder, and ſo if default be made at the *niſi prius*, receit may be prayed in bank, for the juſtices * of *niſi prius* have no power to allow the receit, but the ſafe way is to pray it there.

In an aſſiſe the huſband and wife plead a record and faile thereof, the words of an act made at this parliament, cap. 25. be, *Habeat' pro diſſeiſitore abſque ulla recognitione*, and yet the wife ſhall be received in that caſe upon the default of her huſband, for the words be *abſque ulla recognitione*, that is, of the recognitors of the aſſiſe, and not *abſque ulla receptione, &c.*

Al briefe de enquirer pur waſte le fem ſerra receive, mes apres le waſte trove ſur le briefe d'enquirer pur waſte, el ne ſerra receive, car ſerra inconvenient que le fem trier' le matter de novel,

(8) *Parata petenti reſpondere.*] And in reſpect of this word [*parata*] tenant by receit ought alway to appeare, for upon any default made, judgement ſhall be given.

Littleton ſaith, that in every caſe that the wife is received for default of her huſband, ſhe ſhall plead and have the ſame advantage in pleading to defend her right, as if ſhe were a fem ſole (ſee the firſt part of the Inſtitutes, ſect. 665. 668, 669). But ſhe cannot after receit levy a fine, for that † were not to defend, but to give away her right, but he in the reverſion that is received may confeſſe the action.

* The wife after ſhe is received ſhall have her age, or pray in aide, though the words of this act be *parata petenti reſpondere*, that is to be underſtood, that when ſhe ought to plead by law, then ſhe ſhall be ready to plead.

The wife after ſhe be received ſhall vowch and plead all manner of pleas, and take all other advantages, which ſhe and her huſband might have done, and ſpecially ſuch pleas, as trench to the miſchiefe of the warranty.

(9) *Et jus ſuum defendere.*] This right muſt be intended, which the wife had in the lands in demaund at the time when the *præcipe* was brought againſt her huſband and her, and not at the time of the receit, for if a *præcipe* be brought againſt her and her huſband, and after the huſband and wife levy a fine, and after the huſband make default after default, albeit the wife hath no right in the land at this time, yet may ſhe pray to be received for the right which ſhe had at the time of the originall purchaſed, which in judgement, and by preſervation of law, as to the demandant, ſhall be ſuppoſed to continue *in uno et eodem ſtatu* in the tenancy as tenant

*

[b] 5 E. 2. receit 165. See the firſt part of the Inſtitutes, ſect. 668, 669. 675. Lib. 11. fol. 39. Metcalfes caſe. 12 Aſſ. 31. 22 E. 3. receit 139. 17 E. 2. ibid. 173.

[c] 22 Aſſ. 11. 22. 24 E. 3. 29. 2 H. 4. 2.

[d] 10 E. 3. 27. 12 E. 3. receit 139. 14 E. 3. ib. 139. 29 Aſſ. 36. 38 E. 3. 23. 3 H. 4. 18. 34 H. 6. receit 73. 22 H. 6. 1. 2 E. 4. 16. 33 H. 6. 19. 37 H. 6. 1. 3 H. 6. 58. 20. 11 H. 6. 51. 11 H. 4. 3. 3 H. 4. 13. 22 H. 6. 1. 14 H. 6. 1.

* [344]

7 H. 4. 16. 2 H. 4. 2. 7 E. 3. 32. 28 E. 91. 20 E. 3. receit 16. 22 Aſſ. 27. 9 E. 3. 12. 20 H. 6. 37. Firſt part of the Inſtitutes, ſect. 665. 668, 669. 42 Aſſ. 4. 3 E. 3. receit 47. 19 E. 3. ib. 15. 10 E. 3. 51. 9 E. 4. 16. † 10 E. 3. 4. 12 R. 2. receit 97. 18 E. 3. 32, 33. * 5 E. 3. age 61. 24 E. 3. 68. 20 H. 6. 23. 10 E. 3. 27. 10 E. 3. 32, 33. 31 E. 3. receit 126. 11 E. 3. ib. 1. 19. 48 E. 3. 25. 2 E. 4. 27. 17 Aſſ. 41. 22 Aſſ. 13. 23 E. 3. 21. 9 E. 3. 17. 38 E. 3. 10, 11. 12 Aſſ. 41. 25 E. 3. 40. 14 E. 3. procedendo 4. 32 E. 3.

nant in law without any change or alteration of the estate, notwithstanding any act done by the tenant. Quar. Imp. 2. 9 E. 4. 16.

This also is to be understood not onely of a tenancy in deed, but also of a tenancy in law, for if the husband and wife be vowched, the wife upon the default of her husband shall be received, and yet she can have no *cui in vita* in that case according as this act limits. 5 E. 2. receit 62. 8 E. 2. ib. 181, 182, 183. 19 E. 2. ib. 176. 7 E. 3. 44. 48 E. 3. 28. b.

The words be *jus suum defendere*, and therefore she being not to all intents a feme sole cannot confesse, nor render the action, but he in the reversion that is received may confesse, or render the action. 31 E. 1. receit 186. 9 H. 5. 10. 10 E. 3. 4. 12 R. 2. receit 97. 18 E. 3. 32, 33.

(10) *Eodem modo si tenens in dotem, per legem Angliæ, vel aliter ad terminum vitæ, vel per donum in quo reservatur reversio fecerit defaltam vel reddere voluerit, admittantur hæredes vel illi ad quos spectat reversio ad responsionem, si venerint ante judicium.*] It appeareth by Bracton who wrote before this statute, that he in the reversion should be received by the common law, for he saith, *Poterit etiam quis intrare in warrantiam, et si non vocetur ad warrantum ad proprii juris tuitionem, ut si quis tenuerit ad vitam suam, sicut mulier nomine dotis, vel alio modo, vel ad terminum terram aliquam, quæ post vitam vel terminum reversura esset ad dominum proprietatis, si se in fraudem et exhæredationem ipsius permiserit implacitari ab aliquo cum possit dominum proprietatis inde vocare ad warrantum ad defensionem suam, hoc omiserit; bene poterit dominus ille proprietatis, cum sibi viderit exinde periculum imminere, comparere per se, et si non vocetur, intrare in warrantiam ad suii proprii juris defensionem; cum melius et utilius sit in tempore occurrere, quam post causam vulneratam quærere remedium, et maliciis hominum obviare.* See the first part of the Institutes, sect. 302. Bracton, lib. 5. f. 393. b. nu. 14. [345]

Upon the recovery against such a particular tenant he in the reversion was driven to his writ of right, but he in the remainder was without remedy, if he never had seisin; see the first part of the Institutes. See the first part of the Institutes, sect. 481, 482.

(11) *Eodem modo.*] Though it be said here *eodem modo*, in the same manner, yet it is not in the same manner to all purposes, for the wife upon the default of her husband shall be received without shewing any cause. But so shall not he in the reversion, and therefore it is not *eodem modo* in that respect, and the reason of the diversity is, for that the feme is party to the action, and affirmed tenant by the bringing of the *præcipe*, but he in the reversion is a meere stranger to the action, and therefore ought to shew cause how the reversion is in him. 28 E. 3. 90. 12 E. 3. issue 25. 22 E. 3. ib. 20. 10 E. 3. 10. 4 H. 6. 5. 8 H. 16. 21 H. 6. 13. 32 H. 6. 12. 33 H. 6. 39. 41. 9 H. 5. 3. 8 E. 3. 39. 18 E. 3. 32. 3 H. 6. 41. 21 H. 6. 48. 21 Ass. 17.

But as to age, he in the reversion shall have the same in the same manner, as the wife shall have it, the demandant shall count of new against the wife that is received, and *eodem modo* against them in reversion or remainder. 21 E. 3. 45. 33 H. 6. 52. 15 E. 3. receit 122, 123.

(12) *Si tenens in dotem vel aliter ad terminum vitæ.*] In a writ brought against a feme gardein in chivalry and her husband, the wife shall not be received for the default of her husband, for it is out of the words of the statute, and the husband hath power to alien, or lose the chattell. 19 E. 2. ib. 179. 8 E. 2. ib. 170. 32 Ass. 9 E. 4. 16. 2 E. 2. receit 147. 5 E. 2. ib. 161. 11 H. 4. 13.

(13) *Vel per donum.*] This is to be understood of a tenancy in taile, *apres possibilitie de issue extinct*, and not of an estate in taile generall or speciall, for upon an estate in taile no receit is given by this act, because it is an inheritance which may continue for ever. 39 E. 3. 18. 42 E. 3. 12. 20 E. 3. receit 17. 16 E. 2. ib. 104. 33 H. 6. 22. l. 10. fo. 44. Jenings case. Regist. 135.

(14) *Ad-*

(14) *Admittantur hæredes.*] * By colour of these words, the heire apparent of tenant in taile making default, &c. hath been admitted, *sed non est lex, quia nullus est hæres viventis.*

(15) *Ad quos spectat reversio.*] He must have a reversion, and not onely a condition or possibility.

A wife being tenant for life is received upon the default of her husband, and after makes default, he in the reversion shall be received; and so note a receit upon a receit; and so if a baron and feme be received, and after the baron make default, the feme shall be received.

If an infant make a lease for life, though the lease be defeasible, yet upon the default of the lessee, he shall be received, and so it is of a lease by baron and feme.

One may be received by attorney by a speciall writ affirming infirmity, and the words of the statute are generall.

In a *præcipe* the tenant maketh default, &c. he in the reversion prayeth to be received, and sheweth that he let the land to the tenant and another for life, and the demandant was driven to maintain his writ.

If tenant for life pray in aide of him in reversion, and he refuse to joyne, and after tenant for life maketh default, &c. he in reversion shall not be received, because he refused to joyne, but if he had joyned, and after the tenant make default, he should have been received.

Regularly for a reversion created hanging the writ there shall be no receit: but if the lessee make the writ good, there shall be a receit: as if a *præcipe* be brought against B. that hath nothing, and the terre-tenant make a lease for life to B. he shall be received.

[a] If tenant for life be impleaded, and surrender hanging the writ to him in reversion, he shall be received, and yet he hath no reversion in him, *et sic in similibus.*

[b] If a rent be demaunded against tenant for life, he in the reversion or remainder shall be received by the equity of this statute; albeit the words be, *ad quos spectat revertio,* yet he in the remainder upon default of tenant for life, shall be received, for he is in the same mischiefe.

The king shall not be received, for he cannot become tenant, nor be *in loco tenentis.* 4 E. 3. 38. 25 E. 3. 47.

[c] It is not necessary, that he that prayeth to be received hath the immediate reversion; for if a lease for life be made, the remainder for life, he in the reversion shall be received; so it is where the reversion is graunted for life, he in the reversion in fee may be received: but if he that hath the meane estate, and he in the reversion or remainder in fee pray to be received at one time, he that hath the immediate particular estate, in respect of the proximity shall be received, but if he be received and make default, he in the reversion in fee shall not be received.

(16) *Fecerit defaltam vel reddere voluerit.*] [d] *Feynt pleder* was not (as hath been said) within this act, but is remedied by a later statute, in case of him in reversion.

[e] But a *nient dedire,* and a *nihil dicit* are (as hath been said) within the purview of this act, both for him in the reversion, and the wife also, for they are in equall mischiefe.

* 2 E. 2. receit 147. 20 E. 3. receit 17. 8 E. 3. 3. 45 E. 3. 19. 23 H. 6. receit 156. 5 E. 3. 61. 6 E. 3. 14. 15 E. 3. receit 124. 5 H. 5. 11. 11 E. 3. receit 117. 10 H. 6. 24. 28 E. 3. 98. 33 H. 6. 52. 41 E. 3. 8. 22 H. 6. 1. 19 H. 6. 46. 40 E. 3. 12. 4 E. 2. receit 160. 18 E. 3. 13. 23 E. 3. tit. receit 156. 4 E. 4. 14. 18 E. 4. 25, 27. [a] 5 H. 4. 2. 32 H. 6. 12. 7 E. 3. 15. 18 E. 3. 13, 47. 16 H. 7. 5.

[346]

[b] 32 E. 1. receit 185. 9 E. 4. 40. 10 E. 4. 9. 13 E. 3. receit 17 E. 2. ib. 175. 24 E. 3. 33. 35. 4 E. 2. receit 160. 13 E. 3. ib. 145. 19 E. 3. ib. 111. 14 E. 3. mrans. des faits 6. 29 E. 3. 48. Rot. Parliam. 29 E. 3. nu. 11 H. 4. 15. 4 E. 3. 38. 25 E. 3. 47. [c] 11 E. 3. receit 118. 4 E. 3. ib. 160. 18 E. 2. ib. 174. 18 E. 3. 12. 42 E. 3. 12. b. 24 E. 3. 32. Lib. 10. fol. 44. Jenings case. [d] 13 R. 2. c. 17. 6 E. 3. 16. 4 E. receit 4. 22 E. 3. 10. 1 H. 6. 4. 2 H. 6. 14. 20 E. 3. receit 18, 19. [e] 4 E. 3. receit 46. 19 E. 2. ib. 184. 158. 6 E. 2. ib. 168. 14 E. 3. ib 136. 19 E. ib. 114. F.N.B. 155. i.

If

If the appearance of the tenant be recorded, and after he depart in despight of the court, he in the reversion shall be received, for judgement is to be given upon the default.

(17) *Ad responsionem.*] [f] That is, when the time come when by law he ought to answer, and therefore he shall have his age, or pray in aide, &c. [f] 19 E. 3. receit 1. 5 E. 2. ib. 163.

[g] *Vide statut. de anno* 20 E. 1. where he that prayeth to be received, before his receit shall finde surety, &c. and the statute of 13 R. 2. cap. 17. to that purpose, but those statutes extend not to a feme, that is to be received in default of her husband, because she is party to the writ, but to him in the reversion or remainder, that is a stranger to the writ, *et venit a latere.* [g] 9 H. 5. 10. 48 E. 3. 13. 29 E. 3. 48. 34 E. 3. receit 190. 11 E. 3. ib. 117. 19 E. 3. ib. 112. 6 R. 2. ibid. 94.

(18) [h] *Post mortem hujusmodi tenentium recuperare per breve de gressu,* &c.] This is understood of a writ of entry *ad communem legem,* which is a speedier remedy, then a writ of right, and the demandant shall count upon a demise according to the writ and usuall forme, and if the tenant traverse the demise, the demandant shall maintain his count by the recovery by default. [h] Vet. N.B. 136. Regist. 235.

(19) *Et sic in casubus prædictis duæ concurrunt actiones.*] For in these cases the tenant shall shew his right according to the forme of the writ, whereupon he recovered, even as the tenant shall doe in the *cui in vita,* upon the former part of this act, and therefore this branch saith, *Duæ concurrunt actiones, viz.* the writ of entry upon this action, and the former writ, whereupon the recovery was by default. Regist. ubi supra.

CAP. IV.

In casu quando vir implacitatus (1) *de tenemento reddit tenementum peritum adversario suo de plano, post mortem viri, justiciarii adjudicent mulieri dotem suam, si per breve petat. Sed in casu quando vir amittet per defaltam tenementum petitum, si mulier post mortem viri petat dotem, et compertum est, quod per aliquos justiciarios adjudicata fuit dos mulieri petenti, non obstante defalta, quam vir suus fecit, aliis justiciariis in contraria opinione existentibus, et contrarium judicantibus, ut de cætero hujusmodi ambiguitas amputetur, et sit in certo: ordinatum est quod in utroque casu audiatur mulier, quæ dotem petit. Et si excipiatur contra ipsam, quod vir suus tenementum, unde dos petita est, amisit per judicium, per quod dotem habere non debet, et si quæratur per quod judicium,*

In case where the husband, being impleaded for land, giveth up the land demanded unto his adversary by covin; after the death of the husband, the justices shall award the wife her dower, if it be demanded by writ. But in case where the husband loseth the land in demand by default, if the wife, after the death of her husband, demandeth her dower, it hath been proved, that some justices have awarded unto the woman her dower notwithstanding the default which her husband made, other justices being of the contrary opinion, and judging otherwise. To the intent that from henceforth such ambiguity shall be taken away, it is thus ordained in certain, that in both cases the woman demanding her dower shall be heard. And if it be alledged against her, that

dicium, et compertum fuerit quod per defaltam, ad quod tenens necesse habet respondere, tunc oportet tenentem ulterius respondere, et ostendere quod ipse tenens jus habuit, et habet in prædicto tenemento, secundum formam brevis, quod tenens prius super virum impetravit. Et si ostendere poterit, quod vir mulieris non habet jus in tenement', nec aliquis alius quam ipse qui tenet: recedat quietus, et uxor nihil capiat de dote. Quod si ostendere non poterit, recuperet mulier dotem suam. Et sic in casibus istis, et in quibusdam casibus subsequent'. s. quando uxor dotata amittat dotem (3) *suam per defaltam* (4), *et tenentes in libero maritagio per legem Angliæ, vel ad terminum vitæ, vel per feodum talliatum, concurrunt plures actiones* (2). *Quia hujusmodi tenentes, cum oporteat eos petere tenementa sua per defaltam amissa* (9), *et cum ad hoc pervent' fuerit, quod tenens necesse habeat* (6) *ostendere jus suum, non possunt ipsi, sine his* (7) *ad quos spectat reversio, de jure respondere: et ideo concedatur eis, quod vocent ad warrant' secundum tenorem brevis, ac si essent tenentes in priori brevi* (8) *warrant' habeant* (5). *Et cum warrantus warrantizaverit, procedat placit' inter illum qui seisitus est et warrantum, secundum tenorem brevis, quod tenens prius impetravit, et per quod recu-* [348] *paverit per defaltam. Et si ex pluribus actionibus ad ultimum perveniat ad unum judicium, videlicet ad hoc quod hujusmodi petentes recuperent petitionem suam, vel quod tenentes eant quieti. Et si actio hujusmodi tenentis, qui necesse habet ostendere jus suum, mota fuerit per breve de recto, licet magna assisa, vel duellum jungi non possunt per verba consueta, jungi tamen possunt per verba satis apta. Quia cum tenens in hoc quod ostendat jus suum, quod ei competet per breve quod prius impetravit et sit loco actoris, benè poterit*

that her husband lost the land, whereof the dower is demanded by judgement, whereby she ought not to have dower, and then it be enquired by what judgement, and it be found that it was by default, whereunto the tenant must answer; then it behoveth the tenant to answer further, and to shew that he had right, and hath in the foresaid land, according to the form of the writ that the tenant before purchased against the husband. And if he can shew that the husband of such wife had no right in the lands, nor any other but he that holdeth them, the tenant shall go quit, and the wife shall recover nothing of her dower; which thing if he cannot shew, the wife shall recover her dower. And so in these cases, and in certain other following, that is to say, when the wife being endowed loseth her dower by default, and tenants in free marriage, by the law of England, or for term of life, or in feetail, divers actions do concur for such tenants, when they must demand their land lost by default: and when it is come to that point, that the tenants must be compelled to shew their right, they cannot make answer without them to whom the reversion of right belongeth; therefore it is granted unto them to vouch to warranty, as if they were tenants, if they have a warranty. And when the warrantor hath warranted, the plea shall pass between him that is seised and the warrantor, according to the tenor of the writ that the tenant purchased before, and by which he recovered by default; and so from many actions at length they shall resort to one judgement, which is this, that the demandants shall recover their demand, or the tenants shall go quit. And if the action of such a tenant, which is compelled to shew his right, be moved by a writ of right, though that the great assise or battail cannot be joyned

terit warrant' defendere jus tenentis, qui loco petentis (ut dictum est) habet, et seisinam antecessoris sui offerre et defendere per corpus liberi hominis sui, vel ponere se in magnam assisam, et petere inde recognitionem fieri, utrum ipse majus jus habeat in tenemento petito, an prædictus talis: vel alio modo jungi poterit magna assisa, et sic talis warrantus defend' jus, &c. Et cognoscit seisinam antecessoris sui et ponit se in magnam assisam, &c. et petit recognitionem fieri, utrum ipse majus jus habeat in prædicto tenemento, ut in illo de quo feoffavit talem, vel quod talis remisit, et quietum clamavit, &c. an prædictus talis, &c. Cum aliquando contingat (10), *quod mulier non habens jus petendi dotem hæreditatis hæredis alicujus infra ætatem existen', impetret breve de dote super custodem, et custos per favorem mulieri dotem reddiderit, vel defaltam fecerit, vel placitum ita fictum per collusionem defenderit, per quod dos hujusmodi mulieri (in præjudicium hæredis) adjudicata fuerit: provisum est quod hæres, cum ad ætatem pervenerit, habeat actionem petendi seisinam antecessoris sui versus hujusmodi mulierem, qualem haberet versus quemcunque alium deforciatorem, ita tamen quod salva sit mulieri versus petentem exceptio ostendendi, quod jus habet in dote sua, quod si ostendere poterit, recedat quieta, et dotem suam retineat, et sit hæres in misericordia, et amercietur graviter secundum discretionem justiciariorum. Sin autem recuperet hæres petitionem suam. Eodem modo subveniatur mulieri, si hæres vel alius eam implacitaverit de dote sua, si dotem suam per defaltam amiserit. In quo casu sua defalta non sit ei ita præjudicialis, quin dotem suam (si jus habeat) recuperare possit, et fiat ei tale breve:*

joyned by the words accustomed, yet it shall be joyned by words convenient; for when the tenant, in that he sheweth his right which belongeth to him by the writ that he before purchased, instead of a demandant, the warrantor may well defend the right of the tenant, which is accounted in place of the demandant, as before is said, and offer to defend the seisin of his ancestors by the body of his freeman, or put himself in the great assise, and pray recognizance to be made, whether he hath more right to the land in demand, or else the party before named. Or otherwise the great assise may be joyned thus, *talis defendit jus, &c.* and so the warrantor may defend the right, and knowledge the seisin of his ancestor, and put himself in the great assise, &c. and pray recognizance to be made, whether he hath more right in the foresaid land, as in that whereof he infeoffed such a man, or that such a one released and quit claimed, &c. or else the foresaid party, &c. And where sometime it chanceth that a woman not having right to demand dower, the heir being within age, doth purchase a writ of dower against a guardian, and the guardian endoweth the woman by favour, or maketh default, or by collusion defendeth the plea so faintly, whereby the woman is awarded her dower in prejudice of the heir; it is provided, that the heir, when he cometh to full age, shall have an action to demand the seisin of his ancestor against such a woman, like as he should have against any other deforceor; yet so, that the woman shall have her exception saved against the demandant, to shew that she had right to her dower, which if she can shew, she shall go quit and retain her dower, and the heir shall be grievously amerced, according to the discretion of the justices; and

if not, the heir shall recover his demand, &c. In like manner the woman shall be aided, if the heir or any other do implead her for her dower, or if she lose her dower by default, in which case the default shall not be so prejudicial to her, but that she shall recover her dower, if she have right thereto, and she shall have this writ:

Præcipe A. quod juste * (11), *&c. reddat tali, quæ fuit uxor talis tantam terram cum pertinentiis in C. quam clamat esse rationabilem dotem suam, vel de rationabili dote sua, et quam prædictus talis ei deforceat.*

Et ad istud breve habeat tenens exceptionem suam, ad ostendendum, quod mulier jus non habet in dote (12). *Quod si verificare poterit, recedat quietus, alioquin recuperet mulier tenementum, quod prius tenuit in dote. Et cum temporibus retroactis aliquis amisisset terram suam per defaltam, non habuit aliud recuperare quam per breve de recto, quod eis competere non potuit, qui de mero jure loqui non potuerunt, veluti tenentes ad terminum vitæ, vel per liberum maritagium, vel per feodum talliatum, in quibus casibus salvatur reversio* (13). *Provisum est quod de cætero non sit eorum defalta eis ita præjudicialis, quin statum suum (si jus habeant) recuperare possint per aliud breve quam per breve de recto. De maritagio amisso per defaltam fiat tale breve:*

And to this writ the tenant shall have his exception, to shew that she had no right to be endowed; which if he can verify, he shall go quit; if not, the woman shall recover the land whereof she was endowed before. And whereas before time, if a man had lost his land by default, he had none other recovery than by a writ of right, which was not maintainable by any that could not claim of meer right, as tenants for term of life, in free marriage, or in tail, in which estates a reversion is reserved; it is provided, that from henceforth their default shall not be so prejudicial, but that they may recover their estate by another writ than by a writ of right, if they have right. For land in free marriage, lost by default, such a writ shall be made:

Præcipe A. quod justè (11), *&c. reddat B. manerium de C. cum pertinentiis, quod clamat esse jus et maritagium suum, et quod prædictus A. ei deforceat.*

Eodem modo de tenemento ad terminum vitæ per defaltam amisso, fiat tale breve:

Likewise of land for term of life, lost by default, this writ shall be made:

Præcipe A. quod juste, &c. reddat B. manerium de C. cum pertinentiis, quod clamat tenere ad terminum vitæ suæ, et quod prædictus A. ei deforceat.

Similiter,

Similiter,

Quod clamat tenere sibi et hæredibus suis de corpore suo legitimè procreatis, et quod prædictus A. ei deforceat, &c.

(14 H. 4. f. 31. 50 Ed. 3. f. 7. Fitz. Dower, 80. 140. 173. Fitz. Voucher, 46. 59. 159. 165. 186. 261. 275, 276. 300. 11 Rep. 62. Hob. 299. 6 Rep. 8. 1. Inst. 131. b. 354. b. 355. a. 356. a. Fitz. Quod ei deforceat, 1, 2, 3, 4, 5, 6. 8, 9, 10, 11, 12, 13. 17. Cro. Car. 445. F.N.B. 155. b. Regist. 171. b. 230. Rast. 491.)

(1) *In casu quando vir implacitatus,* &c.] It appeareth by the preamble of this statute, that if a recovery had been in a reall action against the husband, and the husband did render the land to the demandant, that notwithstanding this recovery, the wife should recover her dower. But if the husband had lost by default, it was a question and a doubt, whether in that case she should recover or no; and some judges would give judgement for the woman, and some were in a contrary opinion. Here is to be noted, that a recovery by reddition of the husband, is not of so great account in law as a recovery against the husband by default: but therein before this act this diversity was holden for law, that if in a writ of dower the tenant did plead the recovery in barre, the demandant might reply, *Que ceo fuit per fraud, ou per collusion, ou per gree le baron,* as Britton saith, who wrote before this statute; but if it were by default without covin, then the greater opinion was, it barred the feme. Brit. c. 109. fol. 261. Fleta, lib. 5. cap. 22.

But the reddition of the husband was holden for clear law, as it was adjudged the yeer before the making of this act, for that the wife was ready to maintain the title of her husband. 12 E. 1. dower 173. 49 E. 3. 23. 12 H. 4. 21.

[350]

All this is to be understood, where he that recovereth hath no right, for where he that recovered either by reddition or default had right, there neither the common law, nor this statute extended thereunto. 36 H. 6. Fauxer de recovery 27.

If the recovery he had by verdict, the feme shall not falsifie in the point tryed, but she may say, that he might have pleaded a better plea, or confesse and avoid the recovery. 47 E. 3. 13. 50 E. 3. 7. 36 H. 6. ubi sup. 14 H. 4. 32.

(2) *Quando uxor dotata amittat dotem suam per * defaltam, et tenentes in libero maritagio per legem Angliæ, vel ad terminum vitæ, vel per feodum talliat', concurrunt plures actiones, &c.*] By this act the writ of *quod ei deforceat* is given; at the common law there lay no writ of *quod ei deforceat,* but by custome there did, as in Wales. 4 E. 3. 52, 53. * Custumier de Norm. cap. 23. fol. 56.

If tenant in dower, tenant by the courtesie, or tenant for life had lost by default, they were without remedy, because they could not have a writ of right. Another mischief was, that seeing by the first chapter of this parliament it did alter the estate of tenant in frank-mariage, and tenant to them and the heirs of their bodies, &c. from a fee-simple to an estate tail, whereupon a reversion in point of state was in the donor expectant; by reason whereof, if a recovery by default had been against tenant in frank-mariage, or other tenant in tail, they had been also without remedy, because their estate being so changed, they could not have a writ of right no more then the other tenants for life here recited could have; therefore by this act a *quod ei deforceat* is given to them all, whereby it appeareth, that (as hath been said) the makers of the act intended a change of the estate tail, and providently made provision for tenant in tail by this act. 2 E. 4. 13. 33 H. 6. 46. 4 H. 7. 2. Lib. 5. fo. 85. li. 3. fo. 9. See the first part of the Institutes, 481, 482. 674, 675.

4 E. 3. 38. 5 E. 3. 4. 8 33 E. 3. Avowry 255. 29 E. 3 47. 41 E. 3. 30. 2 E. 4. 13. F N.B. 156. a. c.

It is agreed, that if a recovery by default be had against the husband and wife, tenants in frank-mariage, or tenants for term of their lives, that they shall have a *quod ei deforceat* upon this act; but it is holden in some books, that if the husband and the wife be seised, as in the right of the wife, for term of her life, and a recovery be had against them by default, that they shall not have a *quod ei deforceat* for three reasons:

1. That the husband is not within the words of the statute, for he is not tenant for life, but seised in the right of his wife, who is tenant for life.

2. That the husband may dispose of his wives estate, and alien the same during his life.

3. Provision is made by the next precedent chapter, that the wife in this case may have a *cui in vita* after the decease of her husband.

But I take it that in this case, if the recovery be had meerly by default without the agreement of the husband, that the husband and wife may have a *quod ei deforceat* by this act; for as to the first reason, though the husband be seised but in the right of his wife, yet the wife is tenant for life, and the husband is named but for conformity.

And if a lease be made to a feme sole, and she taketh husband, and a recovery be had by default against them, they shall have a *quod ei deforceat* by this act.

As to the second reason, the same may be said, when the husband and wife are donees in frank-mariage, or joyntenants for life; for in these cases the husband may dispose of the lands during his life.

And as to the last reason, this statute intended to give to the tenants for life a present remedy to relieve themselves, as in this case the husband and wife may during the life of the husband; for it is agreed, that after the death of the husband the wife shall have a *quod ei deforceat*.

But if the recovery be had by the agreement of the husband, then he can never bring a *quod ei deforceat*.

[351] 10 E. 4. 2.

(3) *Amittat dotem*, &c.] This statute doth also extend to courts that be not of record, as the court baron, as in a writ of right in a court baron, &c.

See the first part of the Institutes, sect. 674, 675. 46 E. 3. 21. [a] 46 E. 3. 21. F.N.B. 155. h. [b] 14 H. 7 5. b. F.N.B 155. f. 5 H. 7. Quod ei deforc' 9. [c] 15 E. . Quod ei deforc' 9. F.N.B. 155. i. Pasch. 33 Eliz. Rot. 1125. in Banco Elimers case. [d] 33 E. 3. Quod ei deforc' 17. F.N.B. 155. e. 49 E. 3. 8. 2 H. 4. 2. 21 H. 6. 56. 9 E. 4. 16.

(4) *Per defaltam.*] If A. and B. be seised of lands, and to the heires of A. a recovery is had against them by default, A. shall have a writ of right of his moity, and B. a *quod ei deforceat* upon this statute, and when they recover they shall be joyntenants again.

[a] Two coparceners in taile lose by default, they shall joyne in a *quod ei deforceat*, yet the default of the one is not the default of the other: [b] but if tenant in taile lose by default, &c. and die, the issue in taile shall not have a *quod ei deforceat* but a formedon in the descender.

[c] A departure in despight of the court (unlesse it be in a writ of right after the mise joyned) is holden to be within this act, for he makes default in that case when he is demaunded; but upon a *nihil dicit*, no *quod ei deforceat* doth lie.

[d] A tenant for term of life makes default in a *præcipe*, whereupon he in the reversion is received and plead to issue, and it is found against the tenant by receit, and judgement is given for the demandant,

demandant, the tenant shall have a *quod ei deforceat*, for albeit there is a verdict given, yet the judgement is given upon the default.

But in an assise, and in an action of waste, although the tenant make default, yet there is a verdict given, and upon that verdict the judgement is given in both cases, and therefore there no *quod ei deforceat* doth lie within this act.

A woman brings a writ of dower against tenant for life, and recover by default, the tenant brings a *quod ei deforceat*, and recover by default, the tenant in dower shall have a *quod ei deforceat* by this statute: and so note a *quod ei deforceat* upon a *quod ei deforceat*. 13 E. 1. vowcher 286.

If the tenant for life in a *præcipe* vowch, and the vowchee will not appeare, by reason whereof the tenant loseth by default, he shall have a *quod ei deforceat* by this act, albeit the judgement is not given for the proper default of the tenant, for this statute saith, *per defaltam* generally, and not *per defaltam suam*. F.N.B. 156. b.

(5) *Cum ad hoc perventum fuerit, quod tenens necesse habet ostendere jus suum, non possunt ipsi sine hiis ad quod spectat reversio de iure respondere: et ideo concedatur eis quod vocent ad warrant' secundum tenorem brevis ac si essent tenentes in priori brevi, warrant' habeant.*] For the better understanding whereof the forme and order of the entry of the record and pleading (a window which letteth in light to many cases) is herein to be known, which is, that in the *quod ei deforceat*, the demandant count that he or she was seised of the land for terme of life, or in taile, without shewing of whose lease or gift, for that the action is brought of his owne possession, and alledgeth the esples in himselfe, and that the defendant hath deforced him without making of any mention of the record. And then the tenant may defend the right of the demandant, &c. and either shew how he recovered against the demandant by formedon or other reall action, and in the purclose of his plea shall say, that *ipse paratus est ad manutenendum jus et titulum suum prædict' per donum prædict', &c. unde petit judicium*, whereby the defendant in the *quod ei deforceat* is become actor, and in effect reviveth the former action, and the demandant in the *quod ei deforceat* is become in manner of a tenant to the former action, and may vowch as if he were tenant to the former action, because if he hath but an estate for life, it is not safe for him to pleade in chiefe, but to vowch him in the reversion, therefore he can vowch no other, but him in the reversion; or if the defendant notwithstanding upon the title of the former recovery plead some other barre, then the demandant in the *quod ei deforceat* shall not vowch at all, because the former action is not revived. And if the defendant plead the former recovery, the demandant may traverse the title, or plead any thing in barre of the title. 29 E. 3. 47. 10 E. 4. 2. F.N.B. 156. d. 9 E. 3. 22. 41 E. 3. 30. 48 E. 3. 8. 2 E. 4. 11. [352]

(6) *Quod tenens necesse habet.*] It is not of necessity that the defendant in the writ of *quod ei deforceat*, doe plead the former recovery, but (as hath been said) he may plead any other barre.

(7) *Non possunt ipsi sine hiis*, &c.] By these words the demandant in the *quod ei deforceat* after the recovery pleaded cannot vowch any other but him in the reversion. 9 E. 3. 22. 33 E. 3. Count Pl de vowch. 101. 33 H. 6. 46. Lib. 11. fol. 62. D. Fosters case.

(8) *Concedatur iis quod vocent ad warrantum, &c. ac si essent tenentes in priori brevi.*] Upon these words, two conclusions are to be observed.

Firſt, that albeit the demandant in the *quod ei deforceat* after the recovery pleaded cannot vowch, yet the *quod ei deforceat* may be maintenable.

Secondly, if the recovery by default be in ſuch an action where no vowcher doth lie, yet the *quod ei deforceat* is maintenable, and theſe words are to be intended, that ſuch tenant ſhall vowch which might have vowched in the firſt writ.

14 H. 7. 9. 18 b. 41 E. 3. 30. 44 E. 3. 42. li. 11. ubi ſup. And therefore if the judgement by default be in a *ſcire facias* brought upon a recovery or fine, or in a writ of entry, or in the *quibus* brought againſt the diſſeiſor himſelfe, there lieth no vowcher, and yet a *quod ei deforceat* is given by this act upon ſuch a recovery by default. And where the vowchee ſhould not have his age in
50 E. 3. 25. the former writ, hee ſhall not have his age in this writ, for this writ is of the nature of the other.

10 H. 7. 10. The tenant in a *quod ei deforceat* may vowch, &c. and ſo both tenant and demandant (as hath been ſaid) may vowch in this act, ſeeing the ſtatute doth give a vowcher, by conſequence he ſhall recover in value.

10 H. 7. 29. a. 9 E. 3. 22. But note this act doth give but one vowcher, and therefore the vowchee ſhall not vowch over, and ſir William Herle ſaid, that they were *ſages gents queux fieront ceſt ſtatut.*

41 E. 3. 8. 30. 50 E. 3. 25. F.N.B. 155. f. (9) *Cum oportet eos petere tenementa per defaltam amiſſa.*] Hereupon it is holden, that he that loſt by default may have a *quod ei deforceat* againſt the alienee of the recoveror, becauſe the words of the ſtatute are indefinite; and unleſſe the writ did lie againſt the alienee, the demandant could not have the effect of his ſuit, *viz.* the reſtitution of the land.

See the firſt part of the Inſtitutes, ſect. 674, 675.

(10) *Cum aliquando contingat.*] By the purview of this ſtatute, if the wife having no right to be endowed, bring a writ of dower againſt the gardien in chivalry, and by favour the gardein in chivalry doe yeeld dower, or make default, or plead faintly, by
See the Statute of Marlb. c. 16. means whereof the wife recovereth her dower in prejudice of the heire, the heire after he commeth to his full age ſhall have a writ of mordaunc' againſt the wife, as he might have againſt any other deforceour.

[353] (11) *Præcipe A. quod juſte,* &c.] Here the forme of the writ of *quod ei deforceat* for tenant in dower is ſet down, and it is ſo called,
See before cap. 1. Formedon. becauſe of theſe words in the writ, *quod ei deforceat*, and ſeeing the forme of the writ is here expreſſed, the ſtatute that giveth the writ needs not to be recited, as before hath been ſaid.

Regiſt. 171. Note in none of theſe writs it is ſaid *injuſte deforceat* (as commonly in writs it is) becauſe this act giveth the forme, and *injuſte* is not in the ſtatute.

(12) *Quod mulier jus non habet in dote.*] Note, this is a good barre in a *quod ei deforceat.*

(13) *Non habuit aliquod recuperare quam per breve de recto, quod eis competere non potuit qui de mero jure competere non potuerunt veluti tenentes ad terminum vitæ vel liberum maritagium, vel per feodum talliatum, in quibus caſibus ſalvatur reverſio.*] Upon theſe words foure things are to be obſerved,

1. Firſt, that none ſhall have a writ of right, but he that hath a fee-ſimple, here called *merum jus.*

2. That tenants in taile cannot have a writ of right.

3. This

3. This is an exposition of the first chapter of this parliament, that thereby the estate taile is of an estate in fee-simple become a divided and particular estate, whereupon the reversion in fee is expectant.

4. Fourthly, albeit tenant by the curtesie be not expressely named in these former writs, yet is he within the mischiefe and purview of this statute, for he is *tenens ad terminum vitæ*. Regist. 171. b.

CAP. V.

CUM de advocationibus ecclesiarum non sint nisi tria brevia originalia videlicet breve de recto, et duo de possessione, sciz. ultimæ præsentationis, et quare impedit (1), *et hucusq; usitatum fuerit in regno, quod cum aliquis jus præsentandi non habens* (4) *præsentaverit* (3) *ad aliquam ecclesiam* (5), *cujus præsentatus sit admissus* (6), *ipse qui verus est patronus per nullum aliud breve recuperare potuit advocationem suam* (2), *quam per breve de recto* (7) *quod habet terminare per duellum, vel per magnam assisam, per quod hæredes infra ætatem existentes per fraudem et negligentiam custodum, hæredes etiam sive majores, sive minores per negligentiam vel fraudem tenentium per legem Angliæ, vel mulierum tenentium in dotem, vel alio modo ad terminum vitæ, vel annorum,* [354] *vel per feodum talliatum, multotiens exhæredationem patiebantur de advocationibus illis, vel ad minus (quod eis melius fuit) ponebantur ad breve de recto, et in casu omnino exhæredati fuerunt hucusque: statutum est quod hujusmodi præsentationes* (8) *non sint hujusmodi rectis hæredibus* (9), *aut illis ad quos post mortem aliquorum, hujusmodi* (11) *advocationes reverti debent* (10) *ita præjudiciales, quin quotiescunque aliquis jus non habens, tempore hujusmodi custodiarum præsentaverit, vel tempore t nentium in dote, per legem Angliæ, vel alio modo, ad terminum vitæ, vel annorum* (12), *vel per*

WHEREAS of advowsons of churches there be but three original writs, that is to say, one writ of right, and two of possession, which be darrein presentment, and quare impedit; and hitherto it hath been used in the realm, that when any having no right to present, had presented to any church, whose clerk was admitted, he that was very patron could not recover his advowson, but only by a writ of right, which should be tried by battail or by great assise, whereby heirs within age, by fraud, or else by negligence of their wardens, and heirs both of great and mean estate, by negligence or fraud of tenants by the courtesie, women tenants in dower, or otherwise, for term of life, or for years, or in fee-tail, were many times disherited of their advowsons, or at least (which was the better for them) were driven to their writ of right, in which case hitherto they were utterly disinherited; it is provided, that such presentments shall not be so prejudicial to the right heirs, or to them unto whom such advowsons ought to revert after the death of any persons: for as often as any, having no right, doth present during the time that such heirs are in ward, or during the estates of tenants in dower, by the courtesie, or otherwise for term of life, or of years, or in tail; at the next avoidance, when the heir is come to full age, or when after the death of the tenants before named the advow-

per feodum talliatum (13), *in proxima vacatione, postquam hæres ad ætatem pervenerit* (14), *vel advocatio post mortem tenentium in forma prædicta ad hæredem plenæ ætatis existentem revertetur, habeat eandem actionem et recuperationem per breve de advocatione possessorium* (15), *qualem haberet ultimus antecessor* (16) *hujusmodi hæredis plenam habens ætatem, in ultima vacatione tempor' suo accidente ante mortem suam, vel antequam dimissio facta fuerit ad terminum vel ad feodum talliatum* (17), *ut prædictum est. Hoc idem observetur de præsentationibus factis ad ecclesias de hæreditate uxorum* (18), *tempore quo fuerunt sub potestate virorum suorum, quibus per istud statutum subveniatur, per remedium supradictum. Viris etiam religiosis* (19), *episcopis, archidiaconis, rectoribus ecclesiarum, et aliis personis ecclesiasticis per istud idem statutum subveniatur: si aliquis jus præsentandi non habens præsentaverit ad ecclesias domus sive prælatiæ, dignitati aut personatui spectantes, tempore quo vacaverint prælatiæ, dignitates, aut personatus hujusmodi. Nec tamen ita large intelligatur istud statutum, quod personæ, ad quorum remedium statutum istud est editum, habeant recuperare supradictum, dicentes quod custodes, tenentes in dotem, per legem Angliæ, vel alias ad terminum vitæ, vel annorum, vel viri ficte defenderint* (20) *placitum per ipsos, vel contra ipso motum, quia judicia in curia regis reddita* (21) *per istud statutum non adnihilentur, sed stet judicium in suo robore, quousque per judicium curiæ regis tanquam erroneum* (*si error inveniatur*) *adnulletur, vel*
[355] *assisa ultimæ præsentationis, vel inquisitio per quare impedit si transierit per attinctam, vel per certificationem adnulletur, quæ gratis concedatur. Et de cætero una forma placitandi in brevibus ultimæ præsentationis, et quare impedit, inter justiciarios observetur, quoad hoc, quod si pars*

son shall revert unto the heir being of full age, he shall have such action by writ of advowson possessorie, as the last ancestor of such an heir should have had at the last avoidance happening in his time, being of full age before his death, or before the demise was made for term of life, or in fee-tail, as before is said. The same shall be observed in presentments made unto churches, being of the inheritance of wives, what time they shall be under the power of their husbands, which must be aided by this estatute by the remedy aforesaid Also religious men, as bishops, archdeacons, parsons of churches, and other spiritual men, shall be aided by this estatute, in case any having no right to present do present unto churches belonging to prelacies, spiritual dignities, parsonages, or to houses of religion, what time such houses, prelacies, spiritual dignities, or parsonages be vacant. Neither shall this act be so largely understanden, that such persons, for whose remedy this statute was ordained, shall have the recovery aforesaid, surmising that guardians of heirs, tenants in tail, by the courtesie, tenants in dower, for term of life, or for years, or husbands, faintly have defended pleas moved by them, or against them; because the judgements given in the king's courts shall not be adnulled by this statute, the judgement shall stand in his force, until it be reversed in the court of the king as erroneous, if errour be found; or by assise of *darrein presentment*, or by enquest by a writ of *quare impedit*, if it be passed, or be adnulled by attaint, or certification, which shall be freely granted. And from henceforth one form of pleading shall be observed among justices in writs of darrein presentment and quare impedit, in this respect, if the defendant alledgeth plenarty of the church of his own presentation, the plea shall not fail by reason

ſi pars rea excipiat de plenitudine eccleſiæ per ſuam propriam præſentationem, non propter illam plenitudinem remaneat loquela, dummodo breve (22) *infra tempus semeſtre* (23) *impetretur, quanquam infra tempus ſemeſtre præſentationem ſuam recuperare non poſſit. Et cum aliquando inter plures clamantes advocationem alicujus eccleſiæ pax fuerit formata inter partes, et irrotulata coram juſticiariis in rotulo, vel in fine ſub hac forma, quod unus primo præſentet* (24), *et in ſequente vacatione alius, et in tertia tertius, et ſic de pluribus, ſi plures ſint. Et cum unus præſentaverit, et habuerit ſuam præſentationem, quam habere debet per formam conventionis illius, et in proxima vacatione impediatur ille ad quem ſpectat ſequens præſentatio per aliquem qui fuit pars illius conventionis, vel loco ejus: ſtatutum eſt quod de cætero non habeat hujuſmodi impeditus neceſſe perquirere breve de quare impedit, ſed habeat recurſum ad rotulum, vel ad finem. Et ſi in rotulo, vel in fine comperta fuerit prædict' pax, vel conventio, mandetur vicecomiti, quod ſcire faciat parti impedienti, quod ſit ad aliquem brevem diem continentem ſpacium xv. dierum, vel trium ſeptimanarum, ſecundum quod locus eſt propinquus vel remotus oſtenſ. (ſi quid ſciat dicere) quare ſic impeditus talem præſentationem ſuam habere non debeat. Et ſi non venerit, vel forte venerit, et nihil ſciat dicere, quare ſic impeditus præſentationem ſuam habere non debeat, ratione alicujus facti poſt pacem factam, vel irrotulatam, vel chirographatam, recuperet præſentationem ſuam cum damnis ſuis. Et cum contingat quod poſt mortem anteceſſoris ſui, qui ad aliquam eccleſiam præſentavit perſonam, aſſignata fuerit illa advocatio in dotem alicujus mulieris, vel tenenti per legem Angliæ, et tenentes in dotem, vel tenentes per legem Angliæ præſentaverint, et verus hæres poſt mortem hujuſmodi tenentium per legem Angliæ, vel in dotem, impediatur præſentare,*

ſon of the plenarty; ſo that the writ be purchaſed within ſix months, though he cannot recover his preſentation within the ſix months. And ſometimes when an agreement is made between many claiming one advowſon, and inrolled before the juſtices in the roll, or by fine, in this form, that one ſhall preſent the firſt time, and at the next avoidance another, and the third time another; and ſo of many, in caſe there be many. And when one hath preſented, and had his preſentation, which he ought to have according to the form of their agreement and fine, and at the next avoidance he to whom the ſecond preſentation belongeth, is diſturbed by any that was party to the ſaid fine, or by ſome other in his ſtead; it is provided, that from henceforth they that be ſo diſturbed ſhall have no need to ſue a quare impedit, but ſhall reſort to the roll or fine; and if the ſaid concord or agreement be found in the roll or fine, then the ſheriff ſhall be commanded, that he give knowledge unto the diſturber, that he be ready at ſome ſhort day, containing the ſpace of fifteen days, or three weeks (as the place happeneth to be near or far) for to ſhew if he can alledge any thing, wherefore the party that is diſturbed ought not to preſent: and if he come not, or peradventure doth come, and can alledge nothing to bar the party of his preſentation, by reaſon of any deed made or written ſince the fine was made or inrolled, he ſhall recover his preſentation with his damages. And where it chanceth that after the death of the anceſtor of him that preſented his clerk unto a church, the ſame advowſon is aſſigned in dower to any woman, or to tenant by the curteſie, which do preſent, and after the death of ſuch tenants the very heir is diſturbed to preſent when the church is void, it is provided, that from henceforth

*sentare, cum ecclesia vacaverit: provisum est, quod de cætero sit in electione impediti, utrum * perquirere velit per breve de quare impedit, vel ultimæ præsentationis* (25). *Hoc etiam de cætero observetur de advocationibus dimissis ad terminum vitæ, vel annorum, vel ad feodum talliatum. Et de cætero in brevibus ultimæ præsentationis, et quare impedit adjudicentur dampna, videlicet, si tempus semestre transierit per impedimentum alicujus, ita quod episcopus ecclesiam conferat* (28), *et verus patronus ea vice præsentationem suam amittat, adjudicentur dampna* (26) *ad valorem ecclesiæ* (29) *de duobus annis. Et si tempus semestre* (27) *non transierit, sed disrationetur præsentatio infra tempus prædictum, tunc adjudicentur damna ad valorem medietatis ecclesiæ per unum annum. Et si impeditor* (30) *nihil habeat, unde restituere possit damna, in casu quando episcopus confert ecclesiæ per lapsum temporis, puniatur per prisonam duorum annorum. Et si advocatio disrationetur infra tempus semestre, puniatur tamen impeditor per prisonam dimidii anni. Et de cætero concedantur brevia de capellis, præbendis, vicariis, hospitalibus, abbatiis, prioratibus, et aliis domibus quæ sunt de advocationibus aliorum, quæ prius concedi non consueverunt* (31). *Et cum per breve* (32) *indicavit* (33), *impeditur rector alicujus ecclesiæ, ad petend' decimas* (34) *in vicina parochia, habeat patronus rectori sic impedit' breve ad petendum advocationem decimarum petitarum. Et cum disrationatum fuerit, procedat postmodum placitum in curia christianitatis, quatenus disrationatum fuerit in curia regis* (33). *Cum advocatio descendat participibus, licet unus bis præsentet, et usurpet super cohæredem, non propter hoc exclusus sit ille in toto qui fuit negligens, sed alias habeat turnum suum præsentandi, cum acciderit* (35).

forth it shall be in the election of the party disturbed, whether he will sue a writ of quare impedit, or of darrein presentment. The same shall be observed in advowsons demised for term of life, or years, or in fee-tail. And from henceforth in writs of quare impedit and darrein presentment, damages shall be awarded, that is to wit, if the time of six months pass by the disturbance of any, so that the bishop do confer to the church, and the very patron loseth his presentation for that time, damages shall be awarded for two years value of the church. And if the six months be not passed, but the presentment be deraigned within the said time, then damages shall be awarded to the half year's value of the church; and if the disturber have not whereof he may recompense damages, in case where the bishop conferreth by lapse of time, he shall be punished by two years imprisonment: and if the advowson be deraigned within the half year, yet the disturber shall be punished by the imprisonment of half a year. And from henceforth writs shall be granted for chapels, prebends, vicarages, hospitals, abbeys, priories, and other houses which be of the advowsons of other men, that have not been used to be granted before. And when the parson of any church is disturbed to demand tythes in the next parish by a writ of indicavit, the patron of the parson so disturbed, shall have a writ to demand the advowson of the tythes being in demand; and when it is deraigned, then shall the plea pass in the court christian, as far forth as it is deraigned in the king's court. When an advowson descendeth unto parceners, though one present twice, and usurpeth upon his coheir, yet he that was negligent shall not be clearly barred, but another time shall have his turn to present when it falleth.

(13 Rep. 6. 1 Roll. 151. 156, 157, 158. 211. 462. St. 7 Ann. c. 18. Rast. 101. 144. 496. 3 Bulst. 40. Hob. 240. Kel. 1. Fitz. Quare imp. 43. 67, 87. 92. 96. 99. 105. 127. 142. 167. 39 Ed. 3. 15. Cro.

15. Cro. El. 207. Cro. Jac. 166. 6 Rep. 61. Fitz. Quare impedit. 19. 48. 73. 96. 116. 169. Fitz. Encumbent, 1, 2. 4. Bro. Plenarty, 1, 2. 7. 11, 12. 14, 15. 16. Bro. Preſentat. 46. 58. 1 Inſt. 344. b. 5 Rep. 102. 13 Ed. 4. 3. Dyer, 29. Fitz. Quare impedit, 7. 49. 62. 196. Fitz. Darrein preſent. 21. Co. pl. 468. 479. Hob. 244. Fitz. Darrein preſent. 13. Regiſt. jud. 50. V.N.B. 25, 26. Cro. El. 31. 162. Hob. 242. Fitz. Damage, 4. 9. 17. 29. 38. 93. 106. Fitz. Quare impedit, 24. 45. Dyer, 135. 236. 241. Kel. 57. 6 Rep. 48. 2 Roll. 112. 24 Ed. 3. 26. Fitz. Quare impedit. 4. 16. 18. 27. 30. 38. 70. 82. 129. 140. 157. 183. Diſturbance by Indicavit. Regiſt. 35. 31 H. 6. 13. Bro. Droit, 8. 7 Rep. 25. 27. 35 H. 6. 60. 38 H. 6. 9. 22 Ed. 4. 8. Fitz. Quare impedit, 1. 3. 7. 8. 20. 39, 40. 51. 58, 59. 64, 65. 69. 104. 148. 196. Hob. 238. 2 & 3 Ed. 6. c. 13.)

(1) *Cum de advocationibus eccleſiarum non ſint niſi tria brevia originalia, viz. breve de recto, et duo de poſſeſſione, ſcil. ultimæ præſentationis et quare impedit.*] An aſſiſe of *darrein preſentment* no man can have, without alledging a preſentment in his own time.

A writ of right of advowſon a purchaſer cannot have, without alledging a preſentation in his own time, but a *quare impedit* a purchaſer may have, and alledge a preſentation in him, from whom he purchaſed the ſame; and to that end ſaith Britton was the *quare impedit* provided for remedy of ſuch purchaſers, but the *quare impedit* is more ancient than the time of E. 1. as appeareth by Glanvile.

Brit. c. 94. fol. 233. Bract. li. 4. 246, 247. Fleta, li. 5. c. 12, 13, 14, 15, 16. Glan. lib. 6. ca. 17. li. 13. cap. 20, 21.

[357]

In 8 E. 1. it appeareth *quod ſunt tria brevia de advocatione placitabilia, breve de recto, quare impedit, et ultimæ præſentationis*; but yet the originall writs of dower and ceſſavit, &c. do lye of an advowſon, and ſo doth the judiciall writ of *ſcire facias.*

Tr. 8 E. 1 Rot. 26. Coram Rege. Bract. li. 4. fo. 246, 247. Fleta, li. 5. c. 17. 7 E. 3. 27. 43 E. 3. 15. 14 E. 2. Quare imp. 172.

(2) *Et hucuſque uſitatum fuerit in regno, quod cum aliquis jus præſentandi non habens præſentaverit ad aliquam eccleſiam, cujus præſentatus ſit admiſſus, ipſe qui verus eſt patronus, per nullum aliud breve recuperare potuit advocationem ſuam, quā per breve de recto.*] For theſe words, *advocatio, præſentatio, eccleſia, &c.* whereof they are derived, and the ſeverall ſorts of them ſee the firſt part of the Inſtitutes.

See the firſt part of the Inſtitutes, ſect. 10. 180. 184. 643, 644, 645, 646, 647, 648.

(3) *Præſentaverit.*] By the order of the common law, if one had preſented to a church whereunto he had no right, and the biſhop had admitted and inſtituted his clerk, this incumbent could not be removed for divers reaſons.

See li. 6. fo. 50. Boſwels caſe. Bro. tit. Preſent. al eglise 46. 6 E. 3. 38, 39. See the firſt part of the Inſtitutes, ſect. 648.

1. Firſt, for that he came into the church by a judiciall act from the biſhop (who the law intended, *ſcrutatis archivis*, to do right) the incumbent could not be removed, neither by writ of right of advowſon, nor aſſiſe of *darrein preſentment*, nor *quare impedit*, onely the patron ſhould recover his advowſon in a writ of right of advowſon, which by the uſurpation was deveſted from him.

2. Secondly, that by the common law in every town and pariſh there ought to be *perſona idonea*, and this appeareth by the words of the writ of *quare impedit, &c. quod permittat præſentare idoneā perſon', &c.* And when the biſhop had admitted him able, which implyed that he was *idonea perſona*, then the law had his finall intention, *viz.* that the church ſhould be ſufficiently provided for, and then the church was ſaid to be *plena et conſulta.*

Regiſt. F.N.B. 36.

3. Thirdly, that the incumbent having *curam animarum* might the more effectually and peaceably intend ſo great charge, the common law provided, that after inſtitution he ſhould not be ſubject to any action, to be removed at the ſuit of any common perſon, without all reſpect of age, coverture, impriſonment or non-ſane memory, and without regard of title, either by deſcent or purchaſe, or of any eſtate; wherein you may (as often it hath been) obſerve what inconveniences

Bract. li. 4. fo. 244. 35 E. 1. Quare imp. 180. 1 E. 2. ibid. 41. 10 E. 2 Common 22. 6 E. 3. 52. 11 E. 3. Quare imp. 158. 39 E. 3. 24.

44 E. 3. 21.
35 H. 6. 64.

conveniences follow, when the right institution of the common law is not observed.

Lib. 6. fol. 5. Boswels case. 17 E. 3. 64. b.

By this words *præsentaverit*, it appeareth that no plenarty doth put the patron that hath title to present, out of possession, but onely plenarty by presentation; but plenarty by collation doth put him that had right to collate out of possession.

50 E. 3. 14. b.

(4) *Pari jure et ratione jus præsentandi non habens.*] If tenant for yeers, or gardein in chivalry bring a *quare impedit*, although the defendant hath a writ to the bishop against the termor or gardein, and his clerk is admitted, instituted and inducted, notwithstanding the tenant of the free-hold of the advowson is not put out of possession. Note a diversity between a meer usurpation, and him that comes in by course of law.

(5) *Ad ecclesiam.*] This is intended of a church presentative.

(6) *Cujus præsentatus sit admissus.* Albeit that *admissus* in his proper sense is, when the bishop upon examination findeth him able (that is) *idonea persona*, yet here it is taken for institution; for here is implyed *ad eandem ecclesiam*, and therefore of necessity it must [358] be here taken for institution, and the rather, for that before institution the rightfull patron is not put out of possession. And it is to be observed, that by the institution the church, as to all common persons, is *plena et consulta* as to the spiritualty, that is to say, the cure of souls: for when the bishop doth institute him, he saith, *instituo te ad tale beneficium, et habere curam animarum, et accipe curam tuam et meam*; but before induction the parson hath not the temporalties belonging to his rectory.

33 H. 6. 13. Boswels case ubi sup. Pl. Com. fo. 528. lib. 4. fo. 79. Bigby's case. 18 Eliz. Dier. Giles case, lib. 9. fol. 132. Holts case. Regist. 286. b. F N.B. 246. m. 2 H. 4. 17. 8 H. 4. 20. 14 H. 6 21. 1 H. 7. 19. 10 H. 7. 15.

But the church is not full against the king before induction, because in the kings case plenarty is to be intended of a full and compleat plenarty, aswell to the temporalties as to the spiritualty. *Nota*, present admissions and institutions, &c. are the life of advowsons; and therefore if patrons suspect that the register of the bishop will be negligent in keeping of them, he may have a *certiorari* to the bishop, to certifie them into the chancery.

25 E. 3. cap. 3. 13 R. 2. cap. 1. 4 H. 4 ca. 21. F.N.B. 36. k. 1. 3. & 34. k. 21 E. 4. 34.

And if there be an usurpation upon the king by a compleat plenarty, the king cannot present to the church, before he hath removed the incumbent by *quare impedit*, lest contentions might grow in the church between the severall claimers of the benefice, to the disturbance or hindrance of divine service, and this was by the common law.

43 E. 3. 3. b. 22 H. 6. 27. 38 E. 3. 8, 9. * Pasch. 24 E. 3. Coram Rege Cornub. Tr.

But in that case the king is onely put out of possession, as to the bringing of an action, but the inheritance of the advowson is not devested out of him: see in the fourth part of the Institutes, cap. Ireland; when an * incumbent is made a bishop, either in England or Ireland, &c. who shall present.

32 E. 1. Coram Rege Rot. 75. 17 E. 3. 40. 21 E. 3. 40. 41 E. 3. 5. 46 E. 3. 32. 6 Eliz. Dier 228. 45 E. 3. Quare Imp. 139. 43 E. 3. 15. 43 Ass. 21.

(7) *Quam per breve de recto.*] This is to be understood where the patron that had a fee simple, and that he or some of his ancestors had presented: but if the patron claimed the fee-simple of the advowson by purchase, and had never presented, there he could have no writ of right of advowson, but before this statute had lost the advowson. And likewise if tenant in tail, or tenant for life had suffered any usurpation, they had been remedilesse by the common law, because they could have no writ of right.

5 E. 3. 60. F.N.B. 34. 35 H. 6. 54, 60. 5 E. 3. 60. 19 H. 6. 40.

If a bishop, abbot or prior, &c. purchase an advowson, and suffer an usurpation before they present, they and their successors are barred for ever, unlesse by force of this act the usurpation be avoided in a *quare impedit*.

Therefore

Therefore in perusing over the severall branches of this statute, it shall appear what cases be remedied by this act, and what remain at the common law.

Per quod hæredes infra ætatem existentes per fraudem et negligentiam custodum, hæredes etiam sive majores sive minores per negligentiam, vel fraudem tenentium per legem Angliæ, vel mulierum tenentium in dotem, vel alio modo ad terminum vitæ, vel annorum, vel per feodum talliatum multotiens exhæredationem patiebantur de advocationibus illis, vel ad minus (quod eis melius fuit) ponebantur ad breve de recto, et in casu omnino exhæredati fuerunt hucusq; &c.

Here is the preamble containing the mischief, let us therefore peruse the words of the act.

(8) *Statutum est quod hujusmodi præsentationes.*] The preamble extendeth onely to heirs in ward, *per fraudem et negligentiam custodum, &c.* and the words of the body of the act are, *quod hujusmodi præsentationes,* such presentations; but these words are to be expounded, such presentations that be in the same mischief: and therefore this act extends to heirs of advowsons, though they be out of ward. 44 E. 3. 21. lib. 11. fol. 33. Powlters case. For this word *Hujusmodi,* see ca. 4. & circumspecte agatis.

(9) *Rectis hæredibus.*] This act relieveth onely infants that have advowsons by descent; for if an infant have an advowson by purchase, he remaineth at the common law, and is not remedied by this act. 35 H. 6. 64.

And this being a law that suppresseth wrong, and advanceth right, doth binde the king, though he be not named in the act. [359] 35 H. 6. ubi sup. Lib. 21. fo. 72. Magd. Colledge case.

(10) *Aut illis ad quos post mortem aliquorum hujusmodi advocationes reverti debent.*] *Nota* [*illis*] *hoc est illis hæredibus,* to those heirs that have the reversion of the advowson by descent; for the preamble saith, *hæredes etiam sive majores, sive minores, &c.* And the perclose of this branch is, *qualem haberet ultimus antecessor hujusmodi hæredis, &c.* So as this statute doth help the heir of him in the reversion, and not the lessor himself, but the heir of him in the remainder is not within the purview of this act. P. com. 58. F.N.B. 31. g. Bro. tit. Presentment al eglise 46.

(11) *Post mortem aliquorum hujusmodi.*] That is, of tenant by the courtesie, tenant in dower, or otherwise for life, or for yeers, or in fee tail.

(12) *Pro termino annorum.*] Tenant for term of half a yeer, or a yeer, and grantee of the next avoidance are within the purview and meaning of this act; tenant by statute merchant, or staple, or *elegit,* are within the purview of this statute. 34 H. 6. 30.

(13) *Vel feodum talliatum.*] Tenant in tail of a mannor, whereunto an advowson was appendant, and before this statute an estranger usurped, and then the statute of *donis condit'* and this act is made, tenant in tail dyeth, and the mannor descendeth to his issue; yet the heir in tail hath no remedy, because the advowson was severed by the usurpation: and this act extendeth not to usurpations before this act. 8 E. 2. Quare impedit. 167. 16 E. 3. ibid. 67.

But if tenant in tail suffer an usurpation after this act, and dyeth, his issue shall have remedy by *quare impedit* within the purview of this statute. 8 E. 2. ubi supra. 46 Ass. 4.

(14) *In*

(14) *In proxima vacatione poſt quam hæres ad ætatem pervenerit.*] Note, albeit the heir hath the advowſon by deſcent, yet if he ſuffereth an uſurpation, he hath no remedy by this branch, untill after he cometh of full age; this is to be intended when the heir is in ward, for ſo this act putteth the caſe: but if the heir be out of ward, he may have his *quare impedit*, or his aſſiſe of *darrein preſentment* during his minority.

16 E. 3. Quare imp. 67. F.N.B. 31. b. Boſwels caſe, ubi ſupra.

(15) *Per breve de advocatione poſſeſſorium.*] This is by *quare impedit*, or aſſiſe of *darrein preſentment.*

(16) *Qualem haberet ultimus anteceſſor*, &c.] Then put caſe, that one purchaſeth an advowſon in fee, and dieth before any preſentation made by him, and this deſcends to his heir within age, the church becomes void; if the heir be in ward, the heir may have his *quare impedit* at his full age, and if he be within age, and out of ward, he may have his *quare impedit*, and count of a preſentation made by him of whom the purchaſe was made: but he can have no writ of right of advowſon, becauſe his anceſtor, or he never preſented.

Note it is not ſaid here, *qualem habuit*, but *qualem haberet*, as the anceſtor ſhould have had if the church had become void in his time, and his title to preſent had accrued unto him, for there the right, or at leaſt the poſſibility of action doth deſcend.

2 E. 3. 10, 11.

One ſeiſed of an advowſon in fee, preſenteth to the church being void, and granteth the ſame to A. for life, and after granteth the reverſion to K. and his heirs; A. tenant for life ſuffereth an uſurpation to the church, the heir of K. having the right of this advowſon by deſcent, ſhall, after the death of A. the church becoming [360] void, preſent, and yet K. could not have had a *quare impedit*: but if A. had dyed before the uſurpation, then might K. have had a *quare impedit*, and therefore his heir ſhall have at the next avoidance that remedy which by poſſibility he might have had; and herewith agreeth the authority of the book in 2 E. 3. for there Tond taketh this exception, but durſt not demur.

(17) *Vel antequam dimiſſio facta fuerit ad terminum vel ad feodum talliatum.*] Hereof ſufficient hath been ſaid before.

(18) *Hoc idem obſervetur de præſentationibus factis ad eccleſias de hæreditate uxorum.*] If a feme covert hath an advowſon by purchaſe, ſhe is not within the remedy of this act, and that for two reaſons:

1 E. 2. Quare imp. 43. 5 E. 3. 30. 43 E. 3. 15. Thorp. F.N.B. 34. s. Bro. tit. Preſentment al egliſe 46.

Firſt, here it is ſaid, *hoc idem obſervetur*; but an infant having an advowſon by purchaſe is not holpen by this act, *et hoc idem obſervetur* in caſe of a feme covert.

Secondly, *de hæreditate uxorum*, is here intended of an advowſon by deſcent; for this word *hæreditas*, ſee the firſt part of the Inſtitutes, ſect. 9.

See the firſt part of the Inſtitutes, ſect. 443. F.N.B. 34. m. Br. Preſentment al egliſe 46. See Marlbr. ca. 28.

(19) *Viris etiam religioſis*, &c.] By this preſentation and uſurpation in time of vacation, albeit the free-hold and inheritance is *in abeiance in gremio legis*, yet the uſurper gaineth a fee-ſimple in the advowſon: like as if one entereth into lands during the vacation, and claim the ſame as his inheritance, he gaineth an inheritance by wrong; but yet as the dying ſeiſed of lands in that caſe during the vacation ſhall not take away the entry of the ſucceſſor, no more ſhall the uſurpation during the vacation take away his right of preſentation, when the church becomes void, and if he be diſturbed, he ſhall have his *quare impedit*.

(20) *Nec tamen ita large intelligatur, &c. ficte defenderint.*] So great regard the law hath to judgements, as this act provideth, that by any generall words of this act they shall not be avoided by pretence of *feint defence: quia judicia in curia regis reddita pro veritate accipiuntur, et judicia sunt tanquam juris dicta.*

(21) *Quia judicia in curia regis reddita.*] Here is one of the maximes of the common law.

" *Judicia in curia regis reddita non adnihilentur, sed stent in suo robore, quousque per errorem, aut attinctam adnullentur.*

" *Nihil tam conveniens est naturali æquitati, unumquodq; dissolvi eo ligamine, quo ligatum est.*

" *Interest reipub. res judicatas non rescindi.*

(22) *Et de cætero una forma placit' in brevib' ultimæ præsent' et quare impedit inter justic' observetur, quoad hoc, quod si pars rea excipiat de plenitudine ecclesiæ per suam propriam præsentationē, non propter illam plenitudinē, remaneat loquela, dummodo breve infra tempus semestre impetretur.* By the common law (as hath been said) plenarty before the writ of *quare impedit* brought was a good plea, but plenarty hanging the writ was no barre at the common law; but now by this statute, plenarty is no plea in a *quare impedit*, or *darrein presentment*, unlesse it be by the space of six moneths before the *quare impedit* brought; for if the rightfull patron bring his action within the six moneths, it is maintainable by this statute, which short purview doth remedy many mischiefs at the common law. Brit. fo. 234.

But this act doth not bind the king, for plenarty by the space of six moneths is no barre against him, but he may have his *quare impedit* when he will, for *nullum tempus occurrit regi.* [361]

But some have taken a diversity, when the king claimeth the advowson in his owne right *in jure coronæ*, and when he claimeth it in the right of a subject; for then he shall not be in better case then the subject was: as where the king was intitled to present in the right of a ward, and one did usurp, and the church was full by the space of six moneths, and it was adjudged within twelve yeares after the making of this act, that the king by this plenarty was barred of his *quare impedit.* But since that time the law hath been otherwise taken. Mich. 25 E. 1. rot 148. in banco. 3 H. 6. tit. coron. simil. 18 E. 3. 2.

Plenarty by six moneths against the queen is a good plea, albeit she claime the advowson by the kings indowment. 8 E. 3. 38. 43 E. 3. 13. 25 E. 3. 54. 4 E. 3. 1. 18 E. 3. 2. 24 E. 3. 76.

And yet in all cases plenarty by six moneths is no plea in a *quare impedit.* If an advowson be aliened in mortmain, and the church become void, and a stranger usurp, and his clerke is in by six moneths, yet the immediate lord shall have a *quare impedit* within the yeare, for the statute of 7 E. 1. *de religiosis*, giveth him a yeare, and the immediate lord halfe a yeare after, &c. and for that cause also no descent of lands in the meane time shall take away his entry.

(23) *Infra tempus semestre.*] *i. infra sex menses.* And because this computation doth concerne the church, it is great reason that it shall be made according to the computation of the church, which church-men do best know; and therefore the computation shall be made according to the kalender for one halfe year, and not accounting 28 daies to the moneth, and so was it resolved in the court of common pleas, *temps* E. 2. and *temps* H. 8. as in the said case it appeareth. Lib. 6. f. 61, 62. Catesbies case.

Ante

Bract. li. 4. fo. 247. nu. 5. Flet. lib. 5. c. 14. Extr. suppl. prælat negl. 3. & 4. de conc' præb. ca. 5. &c. Cap. unico. § 1. de jure patronatus. Mich. 3. E. 1. in banco 105. Stafford. prior de Lauda.

Ante concilium Lateranense nullum currebat tempus contra præsentantes, but the bishop was to provide one to serve the cure in the meane time, and the patron might present when he would. Britton fo. 225. a. calleth it the councell of Lyons in France, for the councell of Lateran in Rome. This councell of Lateran was holden under pope Alexander the third, *anno domini* 1179. 25 H. 2. But our lapse is not according to the times and persons expressed in the canons; for they do give foure moneths to a lay patron, and six moneths to an ecclesiasticall, &c. neither hath therein the king any supreme title by them to conferre by lapse. And by the councell, *tempus semestre* is to be accounted *per dies, et non per menses anni:* and therefore we hold, that the time and title to present by lapse, is *per legem Angliæ*, occasioned and established it may be by reason of the said generall councell. See lib. 6. fol. 62. in Catesbyes case.

Mich. 5. E. 1. rot. 100. in banco Lincoln. Nota. * Rot. pat. 27 E. 3. pars 1. m. 18. The councell bound not the prerogative of the king.

* In the reigne of Ed. 3. the clergy pretended that lapse should incurre against the king, whereupon it was thus resolved and published, *Rex ad agnitionem veritatis, et ad tollendum dubitationis scrupulum, quam quidem prærogativarum et jurium coronæ suæ, nescii hæredicuntur, omn' patr' voluit notitiæ, quod ab exordio nascente ecclesia in Anglia. Reges Angliæ ad omnia ecclesiastica beneficia qualitercunque vacantia, ad eorum collationem, &c. spectantia, quandocunq; placeret eis, jure suo regio præsentarunt, &c. suique præsentati, &c. admissi fuerunt, &c. non obstantibus aliquibus curriculis temporum, seu * constitutionibus de præsentationibus hujusmodi infra certū tempus fact' in contrarium edit' &c.*

* Concilium Lateran.

Regist. 42. b. Nota per lapsum, &c. est secundum legem & consuetudinem Angliæ. Pasch. 9 E. 1. in banco rot. 58. Southt' the Bishop of Canterburies case per tempus semestre. 19 E. 2. brev. 842. Regist. fo. 98. nota.

But see the Register, *rex venerabili in Christo patri R. episcopo London, &c. Quia secundum legem et consuetudinem regni nostri Angliæ, episcopi, seu alii diocesani ecclesias, seu alia beneficia de quorumcunque patronatu existunt, infra dioceseriam suam vacantia per lapsum temporis ante sex menses à tempore vacationis earundem transactas conferre non debent, &c.*

And albeit if the lapse were established by authority of some act of parliament now (as many others be in like cases) not extant, yet the writ may serve *secundùm legem et consuetudinem Angliæ*, as our bookes doe warrant.

[362]

It was well and graciously done of king James, in his generall pardon at his parliament holden *in anno* 21. of his reigne, he pardoned all titles and actions of *quare impedit*, as his majesty had or might, by reason of laps incurre above three yeares then past. A necessary branch to be contained in every generall pardon. For we have known an incumbent turned out of his benefice after 40 yeares quiet possession, by pretence of a laps upon the statute of 21 H. 8. ca. 13. yet after so long possession *omnia præsumi debent solenniter esse acta.*

22 E. 3. 9. 30 E. 3. quare imp. 49. 43 E. 3. 35. F.N.B. 36. c.

(24) *Et cum aliquando inter plures clamantes advocationem alicujus ecclesiæ pax fuerit formata inter partes quod unus primo præsentet,* &c.] This clause extendeth as well to strangers of bloud, as to coparceners that are privie in bloud, and if one of the parties or his heires, or any stranger usurp in the turne of another, the party wronged is not driven to his *quare impedit*; for so it may be, that the *quare impedit*, or assise of *darren presentment* may faile, and yet he may have remedy by this branch of the act, for albeit there be a plenarty by six moneths, yet the party may have a *scire facias* upon the roll or fine, and therein recover the presentation and damages.

(25) *Et*

(25) *Et cum contingat, &c. utrum perquirere velit breve de quare impedit, vel ultimæ præsentationis.*] Upon this branch two conclusions are to be observed.

1. First, that the heire in reversion is provided for in this case, and not the lessor himselfe, for here it is said, *verus hæres.*

2. That albeit tenant by the curtesie, tenant in dower, tenant for life or tenant in taile presented last, yet the heire, to whom the reversion falleth in possession, shall have by this branch an assise of *darren* presentment, albeit the heire or his ancester did not immediately present before.

[F.N.B. 31. g. i. Glanv. l. 13. ca. 19. Bract. lib. 4. 240, 241. &c. Brit. ca. 62. fol. 224. Flet. lib. 5 c. 11. 20 E. 3. Darr. present. 13.]

Et de cætero in brevibus ultimæ præsentationis, et quare impedit, adjudicentur damna, viz. si tempus semestre transierit per impedimentū alicujus, ita quod episcopus ecclesiam conferat, et verus patronus ea vice præsentationem suam amittat, adjudicentur damna, ad valorem ecclesiæ de duobus annis.

(26) *Adjudicentur damna.*] Before the making of this act, the plaintife in a *quare impedit* recovered no damages, lest any profit the patron should take should savour of simony, which the common law did so detest: and this is the cause that the king in a *quare impedit* recovereth no damages, because he could recover none by the common law, and the king is not within the purview of this act, for the causes shewed in Boswels case.

And forasmuch as no damages were in a *quare impedit* at the common law, and this act after the statute of Glocester giveth damages only, the plaintife shall recover no costs.

In a *quare impedit* against a prior patron, and incumbent, the prior plead in barre, and the incumbent plead the same plea, whereupon issues are joyned, the prior dyeth, the issue is found for the incumbent, he shall not recover damages by this act, for he cannot have a writ to the bishop, and he continued in possession.

[Lib. 5. f. 58, 59. Specot's case. Lib. 6. f. 49. 51. Boswels case. 14 E. 3 quare imped. 54. Temps E. 1. ibid. 181. 3 H. 6. damag 17. 34 H. 6. 51. 18 E. 1. coram rege & concilio ad parliament. fol. 2. inter dominum regem & episcopum Winton. pro custod. hospit. South.]

(27) *Si tempus semestre.*] If upon the foundation of a chauntery the composition be, that if the patron present not within a moneth, the ordinary shall collate in a *quare impedit* brought for this chauntery, if the moneth be past, the plaintife shall recover damages for two yeares within the equity of this statute, for that the patron in this case loseth the presentation, although the words of the statute be *per tempus semestre.* and this is *per tempus mensis tantum.*

[27 H. 6. 10. 9 H. 6. 30. 32. 13 E. 4. 3.]

[363]

(28) *Ita quod episcopus ecclesiam conferat,* &c.] Here *conferat* is to be taken for *legitimè conferat.*

Albeit the bishop hath not collated, yet if he hath *jus conferendi,* the plaintife shall, if he will, recover double damages within the meaning of this act.

[11 H. 4 80. lib. 9. fo. 26. Strat. mercella. 43 E. 3. 11.]

But albeit the six moneths be past, so as the bishop hath a just title to present by lapse, yet if the church doth remaine void, the plaintife at his perill may pray a writ to the bishop: but then he shall not recover double damages but for halfe a yeare only, because in that case he shall recover his presentation, so as it is in the plaintifes election in that case, either to lose his presentation, and have double damages, or to have his presentation, and single damages.

[8 E. 3. quare imped. 24. 39 E. 3. 15. 46 E. 3. 15. 13 E. 3. enquest 43. 11 H. 4. 40. 13 E. 4. 3. Dyer 3. El. 15. 7 El. 241.]

The plaintife in a *quare impedit* after appearance was non-suit, whereupon the court awarded a writ to the bishop for the defendant, and a writ to the sherife to enquire when the church became

[27 E. 3. damages 106.]

void, the yearly value thereof, and whether the church were full, &c. the sheriffe returned the time of the voidance, the yearly value, and that the bishop had collated by lapse, whereby it appeared *tempus semestre* was past before the writ could be served, yet seeing the judgement was given within the six moneths, he could recover the damages but for halfe a yeare.

And it is to be observed, that albeit the bishop doth collate, yet if his incumbent be removed by judgement within the six moneths, or after, the plaintife shall recover the damages but for halfe a yeare, for the words of this branch are, *et verus patronus ea vice præsentationem suam amittat*, so as if he lose not his presentation, the collation of the bishop is not materiall.

24 E. 3. 35. 39 E. 3. 15 Regist. 50. 54. F.N B. 52. 46 E. 3. 15 b.

(29) *Ad valorem ecclesiæ.*] This shall be accounted according to the very true value, as the same may be letten.

(30) *Et si impeditor*, &c.] No damages by this act are to be recovered but against him that is *impeditor*, a disturber.

In a *quare impedit* against the patron and incumbent, the plaintife recovers the advowson *post semestre tempus*, and because the incumbent was *impeditor*, for that he had counterpleaded the title of the plaintife, therefore he recovered the value for two yeares as well against the incumbent as the patron.

Trin. 23. H. 3. rot. 15. in turri. Bract. lib. 4. fol. 241. b. Brit. fol. 226. b. Flet. li. 5. ca. 14. 14 H. 3. quare imped. 183. 34 E 1. ibid. 187. 47 E. 3. 4. 8 H. 6. 32. 24 E. 3. ibid. 26. 45 E. 3. ibid. 128. 14 H. 4. 11. Inter. brevia 28 Maii, anno regis E. 1. 11. 6 E. 3. 5. 39. Bract. li. 4. f. 240, 241. Regist. 31. a. 19 H. 3. Dar. presentment, pl. ult. Vid. Rot. claus. 18 H. 3. m. 3.

(31) *Et de cætero concedantur brevia de capellis, præbendis, vicariis, hospitalibus, abbatiis, prioratibus, et aliis domibus quæ sunt de advocationibus aliorum, quæ prius concedi non consueverunt.*] *Ecclesia, capella.* When the question was, whether it were *ecclesia, aut capella pertinens ad matricem ecclesiam*, the issue was, whether it had *baptisterium et sepulturam:* for if it had the administration of sacraments and sepulture, it was in law judged a church, Trin. 20. E. 1. *in banco* Rot. 177. *in quare imped.* Ric' de Smithes case. Mich. 21. E. 1. *in banco* Rot. 1. Hertf. Prior de Elies case. Hill. 8 E. 1. *in banco*, Roger de Bigod, & Counte de Norff. case, Hill. 8 E. 2. *coram rege Cornub. pro capella sancti Berione. A capella venit capellania* Rot. Cart. 26. Nov. *an.* 28 H. 3. *in cart' fact' Will. Oxon' episcopo et capellan' ut patet*, Mich. 32. E. 1. *coram rege Gloc' capellania Sancti Oswaldi, prioratus Sancti Oswaldi de Gloc' quæ est de libera capellania nostra.*

It appeareth here, and by 6 E. 3. that before this act writs did not lye *de capellis, præbendis, &c.* and yet it is adjudged in 14 H. 3. which was long before this statute, that a *quare impedit* did lye of a chappell, and it was resolved in parliament, Hill. 19 H. 3. *Quod nulla assisa ultimæ præsentationis capiatur de * ecclesiis præbendatus, nec de præbendis:* but now this act hath made it cleare, and the writ shall be *ad capellam, &c.*

* [364]

47 E. 3. 4. 8 H. 6. 32.

If a patron of a chappell present unto it by the name of a church and the clerke be instituted and inducted thereunto, &c. it hath lost the name of a chappell.

(32) *Brevia.*] That is, writs of right of advowson, *quare impedit*, and assise of *darren* presentment, which in this act had been named before.

Et cum per breve de indicavit impeditur rector alicujus ecclesiæ ad petendum decimas in vicina parochia, habeat patronus rectoris sic impediti breve ad petendam advocationem decimarum petitarum. Et cum disrationatum fuerit, procedat postmodum placitum

citum in curia christianitatis, quatenus disrationatum fuerit in curia regis.

(33) *Indicavit.*] Hereby, and by the Register, and F. N. B. it appeareth where the writ of *indicavit* doth lye, and it properly appertaineth to another treatise. Regist. 35, 36.

But this is an ancient writ by the common law of England, the forme whereof appeareth in Glanvile, and other ancient authors. Glanvile, lib. 4. ca. 13. Bract. li. 5. fol. 402. b. Britt. fo. 260.

(34) * *Ad petendum decimas.*] By the common law, if the incumbent of one patron demanded tithes against the incumbent of another patron, the writ of *indicavit* did lye, for that the right of the patronage should come in question, for by the presentation of the patron, his incumbent is to have the tithes, which are the profits of the church; and in a writ of right of advowson the patron shall alledge the esplees in his incumbent in taking of the great and small tithes: and therefore if the right of tithes came in question, that concerned the right of advowson, the writ of *indicavit* did lye, and this appeareth by the writ it selfe. 31 H. 6. 14. b. Mich. 2 E. 1. in banco rot. 52. Leic' indicavit de 4. part. * 4 E. 3. 27. 7 E. 3. 42. 31 H. 6. 14. 38 H. 6. 20, 21. 12 E. 4. 13. 2 H. 7. 12.

But for subtraction of tithes against an inhabitant within the parish of the rector claiming from one patron, where the right of the advowson of the tithes never come in question, the court christian hath jurisdiction. Bract. li. 5. 402. Brit. fol. 33. 28 E. 3. 97.

The mischiefe before this statute was, that seeing the right of tithes could not be tried between the two persons after the *indicavit* granted, the person prohibited was without remedie for tryall of the right of tithes; and therefore this act doth give the patron, whose clerke is prohibited, a writ of right *de advocatione decimarum*, the forme of which writ appeareth in the Register, and if the right be tryed for the demandant, the cause shall be remaunded into the court christian. 4 E. 3. 27. 31 H. 6. 14. 38 H. 6. 20, 21.

But what if the patron hath but an estate in taile, or an estate for life, &c. so as he cannot have this writ of right of advowson, what remedy shall be had for tryall of the right of tithes in this case? It seemeth that by construction of this statute, the defendant in the *indicavit* appearing upon the attachment shall plead to the right of the tithes in the kings court, or otherwise he shall be without remedy. And this standeth well with the words of the writ of *indicavit, viz. Vobis prohibemus, ne placitum illud teneatis, donec discussum fuerit in curia nostra, ad quem illorum pertineat ejusdem ecclesiæ advocatio, &c.*

By this branch it appeareth, that the value of the tithes at the making of this act was not materiall; for of whatsoever value they were of, the right of tithes could not be determined in court christian; but by the statute of *artic' cleri*, cap. 2. the tithes must amount to a fourth part of the value of the church in that case, or otherwise the writ of *indicavit* doth not lye, but the king may have a writ of a lesser part, for he is not bound by that act. See Art. cleri ca. 2. 9 E. 2. Bract. li. 5. 402, 403. 38 H. 6. 20.

Also by this act a writ of *indicavit* was maintainable *ante litem contestatam*, that * is, when the party hath libelled in court christian, and the adverse party hath answered thereunto, but this is remedied by the statute of *conjunctim feoffatis*. Regist. 29. F. N. B. 45. b. * [365] An. 34. E. 1.

A writ of *indicavit* must be brought by the patron before sentence given in court christian, as it appeareth by the words of the writ; 31 H. 6. 13, 14. F. N B 45. b. 12 E. 4. 13.

 for

for it is but a *superſed' donec*, &c. *ne placitum illud teneatis, donec diſcuſſum fuerit*, &c. and this act ſaith, *procedat poſtmodum placitum in curia chriſtianitatis*, which could not be after ſentence.

38 E. 3. 13. a. 4 E. 3. 28. F.N.B. 45. Doct. & Stud. ca. 25. fol. 108. Rot. Parliament. 50 E. 3. nu. 203.

And albeit this ſtatute doth give the writ of right of advowſon of tithes, yet a writ may be brought *de decimis et oblationibus*; for oblations be *in conſimili caſu*.

This writ of *indicavit* is againſt the canonicall ſanction, and yet hath been ever obeyed; for all forraine ſanctions or canons againſt the law or cuſtome of the realme are of no force, and binde not here, as elſewhere hath been ſpoke more at large.

F.N.B. 45. d.

The writ of *indicavit* ſhall not mention that the tithes, &c. in ſuit amount to a fourth part of the church, but it ſhall be pleaded by the other party to have a conſultation.

31 H. 6. 14. 38 H. 6. 26. F.N.B. 45. e.

If an abbot be parſon in-parſonee of the church of D. and another abbot is parſon in-parſonee of the church of E. ſo as there be (in reſpect of the appropriations) but two parſons, yet for that each party is both patron and incumbent, an *indicavit* lyeth between them.

18 E. 2. quare Imp. 176. 19 E. 2. ibid. 177. 19 E. 3. ibid. 59. 31 E. 3. ibid. 1. 20 E. 3. ibid. 63, 64. 7 E. 3. 20. 45 E. 3. 12. 11 H. 4. 54. 5 H. 5. 10. 21 H. 6. 47. 34 H. 6. 40. 35 H. 6. 59. 38 H. 6. 8, 9. 2 H. 7. 4. 5 H. 7. 8. li. 8. fo. 22. Walkers caſe. F.N.B. 36. d. 15 E. 3. Darr. preſent. 11. 22 E. 4. 94. 33 E. 3. quare imped. 146. 30 E. 3. Statham quare imped. 21 E. 3. 32. 13 E. 3. quare imped. 58. 6 E. 3. 39. 52. 7 E. 3. 20, 21. 15 E. 3. Darr. preſent. 11. 20 E. 3. monſt' de faits 72. 13 E. 3. quare imped. 58. 17 E. 3. 30. 37. 21 E. 3. 37. 11 H. 4. 54. 27 H. 8. 11. 36 H. 8. tit. preſent. Bro. Bract. lib. 4. fol. 238. 245. Brit. fol. 224.

(35) *Cum advocatio diſcendat participibus, licet unus bis præſentet, et uſurpet ſuper cohæredem, non propter hoc excluſus ſit ille in toto qui fuit negligens, ſed alias habeat turnum ſuum præſentandi, cum acciderit.*] By the common law, if an advowſon deſcended to divers coparceners, if they cannot agree to preſent, the eldeſt ſiſter ſhall have the firſt turne, and the ſecond the ſecond turne, *et ſic de cæteris*, every one in turne according to ſeniority: and this priviledge extends not onely to their heires, but to the ſeverall aſſignees of every coparcener, whether he hath the eſtate of them by conveyance, or by act in law, as tenant by the curteſie, hee ſhall have the ſame priviledge by preſenting in turne as the ſiſters had: therefore albeit the coparceners do make compoſition to preſent by turne, this being no more then the law doth appoint, *expreſſio eorum quæ tacite inſunt nihil operatur:* therefore they remaine coparceners of the advowſon, and the inheritance of the advowſon is not divided, and notwithſtanding this compoſition they may joyne in a *quare impedit*, if any eſtranger uſurp in the turne of any of them: and the ſole preſentation out of her turne did not put her ſiſter out of poſſeſſion in reſpect of the privity of eſtate, no more then if one coparcener taketh the whole profits. If one joyntenant preſent alone, this doth not put the other out of poſſeſſion, in reſpect of the unity of the title, but the ordinary might have refuſed his preſentee, as he might the preſentee of one tenant in common, in reſpect of ſome varying opinions in old bookes: therefore this act doth declare the law, as here it appeareth.

This law doth extend to uſurpations by one coparcener upon another, as well before partition, as after.

CAP.

CAP. VI.

CUM quis petat tenementum versus alium, et implacitatus vocaverit ad warrantum, et warrantus dedicat warrantiam, et diu pendeat placitum inter tenentem et warrantum, cum ad ultimum convincatur, quod vocatus ad warrantum warrantizare tenetur per legem et cons. hactenus usitatam, non fuit antea alia pœna inflicta vocato, qui warrantiam dedixit, nisi tamen quod warrantizaret, et esset in misericordia, quia prius non warrantizavit, quod durum fuit petenti, quia multotiens per collusionem inter tenentem et warrantum magnas sustinuit dilationes. Propter quod dominus rex statuit, quod sicut tenens amitteret tenementum petitum, si vocasset ad warrantum, et warrantus se posset devolvere de warrantia: eodem modo amittat warrantus si warrantiam dedicat (1), *et convincatur quod warrantizare debeat. Et si inquisitio pendeat inter tenentem et warrantum, et petens petat per breve ad faciendum venire juratum, concedatur ei, &c.* (2).

WHEN any demandeth land against another, and the party that is impleaded voucheth to warranty, and the warrantor denieth his warranty, and the plea hangeth long between the tenant and the warrantor; and at length, when it is tried, that the vouchee is bound to warranty: by the law and custom of the realm hitherto used there was none other punishment assigned for the vouchee that denieth his warranty, but only that he should warrantize, and should be amerced, because he did not warrant before, which was prejudicial unto the demandant, because he suffered oftentimes great delays by collusion between the tenant and the warrantor. Wherefore our lord the king hath ordained, that like as the tenant should leese the land being in demand, in case where he vouched, and the vouchee could discharge himself of the warranty, in the same wise shall the warrantor leese in case where he denieth his warranty, and it be tried against him that he is bounden to warranty. And if an inquest be depending between the tenant and the warrantor, and the demandant will require a writ to cause the jury to come, it shall be granted him.

(45 Ed. 3. 26. Rast. 352. 687, &c.)

Albeit the Mirror saith of this act, *L'estatute de garranties nest forsque revocation de error usee jesque a droit ley*, yet the tenant, according as it is here recited in the preamble of this act, after the warranty tryed, could have no other judgement, but that the vouchee should warrant the land, according to the voucher of the tenant, but this was many times in great delay of the demandant by collusion or agreement between the tenant and the vouchee, for remedy whereof this statute was made.

Propter quod dominus rex statuit quod sicut tenens amitteret tenementum petitum, si vocasset ad warrantum, et warrantus se posset devolvere de warrantia, eodem modo amittat warrantus, si

si warrantiam dedicat, et convincatur quod warrantizare debeat.

Lib. 6. cap. 23. Which Fleta rendreth in these words:

Si is qui ad warrantiam tenetur warrantizare falso contradixerit, provisum est, quod sicut tenens amitteret tenementum, si vocasset ad warrantum, et warrantus se posset devolvere de warrantia, eodem modo amittat warrantus warrantizare dedicens, si convincatur quod warrantizare debeat.

Mich. 16 E. 1. in banco rot. 44. Rog. de Mowbrays case. 5 E. 3. Voucher 249. Paris case. 30 E. 3. 6. Simeons case. Liber plac' Rast' 352. 614. 6 H. 4. 3, 4.

(1) *Si warrantiam dedicat.*] This is not to be understood onely where the vouchee denieth the deed, or other cause of the warrantie, and thereupon issue is taken, and found against the vouchee: and where the vouchee entereth into the warranty, and demands of the tenant what he hath to bind him to warranty, and the tenant sheweth speciall matter to bind him to warranty, and the vouchee demurreth in law upon the lien, this is within the remedy of this act; for the words subsequent be, *si convincatur quod warrantizare debeat*, which the vouchee is in this case; and this act being made to oust delayes, which are odious in law, is to be interpreted favourably.

[367] And it is to be observed, that here is *sicut*, which is an adverb of similitude, *viz.* *Sicut tenens amitteret, si vocasset ad warrantum, et warrantus se posset devolvere de warrantia.* Under which words are included, if the vouchee can devolve him of the warranty by demurrer, or any issue whatsoever, *eodem modo* (saith this act) *amittat warrantus, &c.* which fortifieth the former exposition that hath been made; and to be short, wheresoever the judgement at the common law should have been against the vouchee upon false plea, or demurrer, &c. *quod warrantizaret*, all these cases are within the provision of this act.

(2) *Et si inquisitio pendeat inter tenentem et warrantum, et petens petat breve ad fac' venire juratum, concedatur ei.*] Here is further remedy given for the demandants expedition, that he may sue out the *venire fac'* for the tryall of any issue between the tenant and vouchee.

These things are necessary to be knowne; for at this day vouchers are most commonly used for delay.

CAP. VII.

CUSTODI (1) de cætero concedatur breve de admensuratione dotis. Nec per sectam custodis, si ficte et per collusionem sequatur (2) versus mulierem tenentem in dotem, præcludatur hæres cum ad ætatem pervenerit ad dotem admensurandam, secundum quod per legem Angliæ fuit admensuranda. Et tam in isto brevi, quam in brevi de admensuratione pasturæ, celerior quam prius de cætero sit processus (3), ita quod

A Writ of admeasurement of dower shall be from henceforth granted to a guardian; neither shall the heir, when he cometh to full age, be barred by the suit of such a guardian, that sueth against the tenant in dower feignedly, and by collusion, but that he may admeasure the dower after, as it ought to be admeasured by the law of England. And as well in this writ, as in a writ of admeasurement of pasture,

quod cum perventum fuerit ad magnam districtionem, dentur dies, infra quos duo comit. teneantur (4), ad quos publica fiat proclamatio, quod defendens veniat ad diem in brevi contentum querenti responsurus. Ad quem diem si venerit, procedat placitum inter eos, et si non venerit, et proclamatio supradicta modo per vicecomitem testificatâ fuerit, procedatur per defaltam ad admensurationem faciendam.

ture, more speedy process shall be awarded than hath been used hitherto; so that when it is come unto the great distress, days shall be given, within which two counties may be holden, at the which open proclamation shall be made, that the defendant shall come in at the day contained in the writ, to answer to the plaintiff; at which day, if he come in, the plea shall pass between them; and if he do not come, and the proclamation be testified by the sheriff in manner abovesaid, upon his default they shall make admeasurement.

Vide Mich. 10 E. 1. In banco rot. 105. Northt. Pasc. 18 E. 1. in banco rot. 15. Laurence de Oysileurs case. (Fitz. Admeasur. 3, 4, 5. 9, 10. 13. 17. 7 Ed. 4. 22. 18 Ed. 3. 30. Regist. 171. 297.)

Before this act, if the heire within age, before the garden in chivalry enter into the land, had assigned dower to the wife more then she ought to have, the garden had been without remedy: for no writ of admeasurement of dower being a reall action lay for the garden at the common law implyed by *de cætero*. Brit. cap. 113. fol. 263.

(1) *Custodi.*] Garden *in droit* or *in fait* shall have this writ by this act, if the assignement of dower be made in his owne time; but if the assignment be made by the heire in time of garden *in droit*, and after the garden *in droit* assigneth his interest over, the assignee shall not have a writ of admeasurement, for that the garden *in droit* had but a chose in action; but if the assignement had been made in the time of the garden *in fait*, he should have had a writ of admeasurement of dower by this act. 7 R. 2. tit. admeasurement 4. F.N.B. 149. a.

But this is to be understood (though the statute be generall) when the heire within age assigneth dower, as is aforesaid, or when dower is assigned in the right of the heire, or the garden assigneth more dower then he ought, the heire after his full age shall have a writ of admeasurement of dower by the common law, and he cannot have it before, because the interest of the garden (which he may give away) endureth untill that time; but if the heire within age be out of ward, and assigneth more dower then he ought within age, he may have an admeasurement of dower within age, for enter he cannot. [368] Glanv. li. 6. ca. 13. Bract. li. 2. fo. 93. lib. 4. 314, 315. Flet. li. 5. c. 22. &. 33. Brit. fo. 263.

If the garden assigneth more dower than he ought, and the heire dyeth, his heire shall have a writ of admeasurement of dower. Mirror, c. 5. § 5. 7 E. 4. 22. b. 7 E. 2. admeasur. 13. 7 R. 2. ibid. 4. 21 H 7. 43.

* And so if the heire within age assigne dower, and dyeth, his heire shall have the like writ; but if the ancester of full age, being tenant in fee-simple, assigneth dower more then he ought, his heire shall never avoid it, because he had full power to assigne as much as he would. * Brit. c. 113. fo. 263. b. 6 H. 3. admeasur. 8. 7 R. 2. tit. admeasur. 4. le Countee de Devons case.

The king is intituled by false office to the wardship of the body and lands of the heire of J. S. being within age, dower is assigned to

17 E. 3. 71. F.N.B. 149. to the wife more then she ought, the garden in chivalry traverseth the office, and avoideth it, this garden shall by this act have a writ of admeasurement of dower of the assignment made by the king, having but a defeasible title to the wardship.

By the like reason, if tenant by knight-service dyeth, his heire within age an estranger abate, and endoweth the wife of more then she ought, the garden seiseth the ward, he shall by this act have a writ of admeasurement of dower: and so if J. S. seised of lands in fee taketh wife, and is disseised and dyeth, the disseisor assigneth more in dower than she ought, the heir entreth into the residue, he shall have a writ of admeasurement by the common law, and this well agreeth with the words of the writ, *viz. Quod C. quæ fuit uxor prædict' B. plus habet in dotem de libero tenemento, quod fuit prædict' B quondam viri sui in N. quam habere debet, et ad ipsam pertinet habendam.*

14 H. 3. admeasur. 10. F.N.B. 149. c. And albeit the words of the writ be in the present time, *plus habet in dotem, &c.* yet it is to be taken, that she had more in value at the time of the assignment of dower; for if by her industry and policie it be made of greater value afterward, no writ of admeasurement lyeth for this improvement.

(2) *Nec per sectam custodis si fictè per collusionem sequatur,* &c.] Hereby is remedy given to the heire at his full age, if the garden prosecute feintly, or by collusion against the wife, so as the heire shall not be barred in his writ of admeasurement against the tenant in dower.

11 H. 4. 3. Plow. com. 55. The heire shall not be driven to shew the manner of the feint pleading, but to alledge the same generally.

9 H. 6. 5. The tenant in a *precipe* doth plead, that an estranger hath recovered against him by verdict in an assise, the plaintife against this verdict cannot generally averre, that this was by covin, but must shew some speciall matter.

(3) *Et tam in isto brevi, quam in breve de admensuratione pasturæ,*
Regist. 171. Vet. N.P. 9. & 10. F.N.B. 148. h. *celerior quam prius de cætero fiat processus.*] Whereas by the common law the processe in both these writs were summons, attachment, and distresse infinite, by this act a more speedy proceding is provided.

34 E. 3. damag. 2. 42 E. 3. 19. Regist. 171. There is great affinity between these two writs, as hereby it appeareth: amongst others there is one difference, that in a writ of admeasurement of dower the demandant shall recover damages, if the tenant appeare not the first day, and yeeld to admeasurement for the issues in the meane time: but in admeasurement of pasture no damages shall be recovered at all.

More shall be said of the processe, and proceeding in this writ of admeasurement of dower in the exposition of the next chapter,
Mirror, c. 5. § 5. onely to remember by the way what the Mirror saith, *Le' statute de admeasurement est reprovable in plusors points quant as proclamations, de sicome admeasurement, et surchage sont feasibles per juries de office.*

(4) *Ita qd' cum perventũ fuerit ad magnã districtionem, dentur dies, infra quos duo comitatus teneantur,* &c.] By reason of these words, *cum perventum fuerit ad magnam district'* the very writ of distresse
[369] shall containe, *et interim in duobus plenis comitatibus tuis publice proclamari fac', quod prædict' A. quæ fuit uxor T. veniat coram præfatis justiciariis ad respondendum, &c. si voluerit, et ad audiendum judicium suum pro pluribus defaltis.*

And

And yet I find, that after the grand distresse returned, the plaintife prayed a proclamation, and there it is taken, that he had not surcessed his time, but it was granted. 4 E. 3. admeasur. 12.

See more of admeasurement of dower in the next chapter following.

CAP. VIII.

CUM per placitum motum per breve de admensuratione pasturæ, pastura fuerit admensurata aliquando coram justic', aliquando in com' coram vicecom', multotiens contingit, quod post hujusmodi admensurat' actam, iterum ponit ille, qui primo superoneravit pasturam, pluria animalia quam ad ipsum pertinet haben'', nec super hoc hucusque provisum fuisset (1) remedium: statutum est, quod de secunda superoneratione fiat remedium conquerenti sub hac forma, quod conquerens habeat breve de judicio, si coram justic' admensurata fuerit pastura (2) quod vic' in præsentia partium præmonitarum (si interesse voluerint) inquirat de secunda superoneratione. Quæ si inventa fuerit, mandetur justic' sub sigillo vic', et sigillis juratorum, et justic' adjudicent conquerenti damna, et ponant in extractis valorem animalium quæ superonerat' post admensurationem factam posuit in pastura, ultra quod debuit, et extractas liberent baronibus de scaccario, ut inde respondeant domino regi. Si in com' facta fuerit admensuratio, tunc ad instantiam querentis exeat breve de cancellaria (3) quod vic' inquirat super hujusmodi superonerat', et de averiis positis in pasturam ultra debitum numerum, vel de pretio dom' regi ad scaccar' suum respondeat. Et ne vic' fraudem faciat domino regi (5) in isto casu, concordatum est, quod omnia hujusm' brevia de secunda superonerat' (4), quæ exeunt de cancel' irrotulentur, et in fine anni mittantur transcripta ad scaccar', sub sigillo cancellarii, ut videant thesaurius

WHEREAS by a plea moved upon a writ of admeasurement of pasture, the pasture was sometime admeasured before the justice, sometime before the sheriff in the county, and it chanced many times, after such admeasurement made, the pasture to be overcharged again by him that first did it, with more beasts than he ought to keep, whereupon no remedy hath been yet provided; it is ordained, that upon the second overcharge, the plaintiff shall have remedy in this manner: if the admeasurement were before the justices, the plaintiff shall have a writ judicial, that the sheriff in presence of the parties being summoned (if they will come) shall inquire upon the second overcharge; which if it be found, it shall be returned before the justices, under the seals of the sheriff, and the seals of the jurors; and the justices shall award the plaintiff damages, and shall put in the extreats the value of the beasts which were put into the pasture after such admeasurement more than he ought, and shall deliver the extreats unto the barons of the exchequer, whereof they shall answer unto the king. If such admeasurement were made in the county, then, at the request of the plaintiff, a writ shall go out of the chancery, that the sheriff shall inquire of such overcharge; and for the beasts put in the pasture above the due number, or for the value of them, he shall answer to the king at the exchequer. And lest the sheriff might defraud the king in this case, it is agreed,

rius et barones de scaccar' qualiter vic' respondeat de exitibus hujusmodi brevium. Eodem modo irrotulentur brevia de redisseisina, et mittantur ad scaccarium in fine anni.

agreed, that all such writs *de secunda superoneratione*, that pass out of the chancery, shall be inrolled, and at the year's end the transcripts shall be sent into the exchequer under the chancellor's seal, that the treasurer and barons of the exchequer may see how the sheriff doth answer of the issues of such writs. In the same wise writs of redisseisin shall be inrolled and sent into the exchequer at the year's end.

Glanv. li. 12. c. 13. Bract. li. 4. fo. 229. Brit. fo. 138. Flet. lib. 4. cap. 23. Mirr. cap. 5. § 5. (Rast. 22. Regist. 157.)

7 E. 4. 22. F.N.B. 225 h. & 148. f. g. It is to be observed, that the writs of admeasurement of pasture and of dower are vicountell, and are not returnable, and the parties may thereupon plead before the sheriffe in the county.

44 E. 3. 10. Both these pleas may be removed out of the county court by *pone* at the suit of the plaintife, without shewing cause in the writ, but at the suit of the defendant he ought to shew cause.

[370] Now where this statute saith, *aliquando coram justiciariis*, that is, when the plea is removed before the justices, there upon pleading, or confession before them after admeasurement made and returned, Regist. judic. fo. 36. b. & 40. a. judgement shall be given by the justices; but if the plea be not removed, the admeasurement shall be enquired of, and made before the sheriffe, and so be these words (*aliquando in comit' coram vicecom'*) to be understood.

Regist. judic. ubi supra. See the judiciall writ of admeasurement of pasture granted by the court of common pleas for making of admeasurement, which writ is returnable before the justices.

Anno 11 H. 3. in archivis turris London. (1) *Nec super hoc hucusque provisum fuisset.*] Yet I have seen a record in 11 H. 3. where a writ *de secunda superoneratione* was granted.

(2) *Statutum est, quod de secunda superoneratione fiat remedium conquerenti sub hac forma, quod conquerens habeat breve de judicio, si coram* Regist. 157. Regist. judic. 36. F.N B. 126. Flet. li. 4. c. 23. 7 E. 4. 22. Vet. N. B. fol. 72. *justiciariis admensurata fuerit pastura.*] The effect of which judiciall writ is, that the sherife in the presence of the parties, if they will be present, being warned, shall enquire by a jury of the second surcharge, and what cattell secondly surcharged, and the value of them, which if it be found, and returned under the seale of the sherife, and the seales of the jurors, the justices shall adjudge damages to the party, and the cattell which surcharged after the admeasurement made shall be forfeited to the king, and the value of them shall be estreated into the exchequer, that thereof the king may be answered.

(3) *Si in com' fact' fuerit admensuratio, tunc ad instantiam* Registr. 157. *querentis exeat breve de cancellaria.*] Which writ you may find in the Register.

Temps E. 1. admeasurement 15. 18 E. 3. 30. 7 E. 4. 23. 8 H. 6. 26. F.N.B. 126. i. (4) *De secunda superoneratione.*] And here it is to be knowne, that a writ *de secunda superoneratione* lyeth not against any that surchargeth after a former admeasurement, but onely against them, against whom the writ was brought, and which were particularly charged

charged with surcharge in the writ; for all the commoners, as well those which surcharged not, as those which surcharged, are to be admeasured; and therefore it appeareth not who surcharged, but onely they that are charged therewith, and so found: hereupon it followeth, that a writ *de secunda superoneratione* lyeth not against any but against them that were named, and thereof convicted in the first writ; for he cannot be charged with a second, that was not culpable of the first: and therefore none but such as were named in the former writ shall forfeit their cattell, &c. or yeeld damages.

(5) *Et ne vicecomes fraudem fac' domino regi.*] Here is provision made to prevent the fraud of sherifes, lest by their fraud they should prevent the king of his duty.

CAP. IX.

CUM capitales domini distringunt feodum suum pro consuetudinibus et servitiis (1) *sibi debitis, et medius sit* (2) *qui tenentem acquietare debeat* (3), *cum non jaceat in ore tenentis, postquam districtionem replegiaverit, dedicere demanda capitalis domini sui, qui advocat in curia regis justam districtionem fieri super tenentem suum, viz. super medium: multi per hujusmodi districtiones hucusque*
[371] *gravati extiterunt, per hoc quod medius (licet haberet per quod distringi posset) magnas fecit dilationes antequam ad curiam venerit ad respondendum hujusmodi tenentibus suis ad breve de medio: per hoc etiam quod durius fuit in casu quando medius nihil habuit, in casu etiam cum tenens paratus esset facere capitali domino servitia et consuetudines exactas, et capitalis dominus servitia, et consuet. sibi debitas renuebat percipere per manum alterius, quam per manum proximi tenentis sui* (4), *et sic amiserunt hujusmodi tenentes in dominico proficuum terrarum suarum aliquando ad tempus, aliquando toto tempore suo, nec fuit antea aliquod remedium in hoc casu provisum. Ordinatum est et provisum in hoc casu remedium in posterum, sub hac forma, quod quam cito hujusmodi tenens in dominico, habens medium inter ipsum et capitalem dominum, distringitur,*

WHEN chief lords distrain in their fee for customs and services to them due, and there is a mean which ought to acquit the tenant, sithence it lieth not in the mouth of the tenant, after that he hath replevied the distress, to deny the demand of the chief lord, which avoweth in the king's court, that the distress is lawfully taken upon his tenant, which is upon the mean; and many have been heretofore sore grieved by such distresses, in so much as the mean (notwithstanding that he hath whereby he may be distrained) doth make long delays before he will come into the court to answer for his tenant unto the writ of mean; and further, the case was most hard when the mean had nothing: in case also when the tenant was ready to do his services and customs unto his lord, and the chief lord would refuse to take such services and customs by the hands of any other than of his next tenant, and so such tenants in demean lost somewhiles the profits of their lands for a time, and somewhiles for their whole time, and hitherto no remedy hath been provided in this case; a remedy is provided and ordained hereafter in this form, that so soon as such tenant in demean (having a mean between him and the chief lord) is distrained, incontinent the

tringitur, statim perquirat sibi tenens breve de medio. Et si medius habens terram in eodem comitatu (6) *diffugerit usq; ad magnam districtionem* (5), *detur querenti in brevi suo de magna district' talis dies, ante cujus adventum duo comitatus teneantur, et præcipiatur vicecom', quod distringat medium per magnam districtionem, prout in brevi continetur. Et nihilominus vicecomes in duobus plenis comitatibus solemniter proclamare faciat, quod hujusmodi medius veniat ad diem in brevi contento, responsurus tenenti suo. Ad quem diem si venerit, procedat placitum inter eos modo conjuncto. Et si non venerit hujusmodi medius, amittat servitium tenentis sui, et à modo non respondeat* (7) *ei tenens in aliquo, sed (omisso illo medio) respondeat capitali domino de eisdem servitiis et consuetudinibus, quæ prius facere debuit prædictus medius. Nec habeat capitalis dominus potestatem distringendi tenentis in dominico, dum prædictus tenens offerat ei servitia debita et consueta* (8). *Et si capitalis dominus exegerit plus quam medius ei facere deberet, habeat tenens in hoc casu exceptionem versus dominum quam haberet medius* (9). *Si vero medius nihil habuerit in potestate regis* (10), *nihilominus perquirat tenens breve suum de medio ad vicecomitem illius comitatus in quo distringitur. Et si vicecomes mandaverit, quod medius nihil habet unde potest summoneri, nihilominus sequatur breve de attachiamento. Et si vicecomes mandaverit, quod nihil habet per quod potest attachiari, nihilominus sequatur breve*
[372] *de magna districtione, et fiat proclamatio in forma prædicta. Si vero medius non habeat terram in comitatu in quo fit districtio, sed habeat terram in alio comitatu* (11) *tunc exeat breve originale ad summonendum medium ad vicecomitem illius comitatus in quo fit districtio. Et cum testificatum fuerit per illum vicecomitem, quod nihil habet in comitatu suo,*

the tenant shall purchase his writ of mean. And if the mean, having land in the same county, absent himself until the great distress awarded, the plaintiff shall have such day given him in his writ of great distress, afore the coming whereof two counties may be holden, and the sheriff shall be commanded to distrain the mean by the great distress, like as it is contained in the writ, and neverthelesss the sheriff in two full counties shall cause to be proclaimed solemnly, that the mean do come at a day contained in the writ, to answer his tenant: at which day, if he come, the plea shall pass between them after the common usage; and if he do not come, then such mesne shall lose the services of his tenant, and from thenceforth the tenant shall not answer him in any thing; but the same mean being excluded, he shall answer unto the chief lord for such services and customs as before he ought to have done to the same mean; neither shall the chief lord have power to distrain, so long as the aforesaid tenant doth offer him the services and customs due. And if the chief lord exact more than the mean ought to do, the tenant in such case shall have such exceptions as the mean should. And if the mean have nothing within the king's dominion, the tenant shall neverthelesss purchase his writ of mean to the sheriff of the same shire wherein he is distrained. And if the sheriff return, that he hath nothing whereby he may be summoned, then shall the tenant sue his writ of attachment. And if the sheriff return, that he hath nothing to be attached by, he shall neverthelesss sue his writ of great distress, and proclamation shall be made in form abovesaid. And if the mean have no land in the shire where the distress is taken, but hath land in some other shire, then a writ original shall issue to summon the mean unto the sheriff of the same

exeat breve de judicio ad ſummonend' medium ad vicecomitem illius comitatus in quo teſtificatum fuerit quod habet tenem', et fiat ſecta in illo comitatu, quouſq; perveniatur ad magnam diſtrictionem, et proclamationem, ſicut dictum eſt ſupra de medio habente terram in eodem comitatu in quo ſit diſtrictio. Et nihilominus fiat ſecta in comitatu in quo nihil habet (ſicut dictum eſt ſupra de medio nihil habente) quouſq; perveniatur ad magnam diſtrictionem et proclamationem, et ſic poſt proclamationem in utroque comitatu factam adjudicetur medius de feodo et ſervitio ſuo (12). *Et cum aliquando contingat, quod tenens in dominico feoffatus eſt ad tenendum de medio per minus ſervitium, quam medius facere debuit capitali domino, cum poſt hujuſmodi proclamationem attornatus ſit tenens capitali domino, medio omiſſo, neceſſe habet tenens reſpondere capitali domino de ſervitiis et conſ. quæ medius ei prius facere debuit, et poſtquam medius venerit in curiam, et cognoverit, quod acquietare debet tenentem ſuum, vel adjudicetur ad acquietandum, ſi poſt hujuſmodi cognitionem aut judicium queremonia perveniat, quod medius non acquietat tenentem* (13), *tunc exeat breve de judicio, quod vicecomes diſtringat medium ad acquietandum tenentem, et ad eſſendum coram juſticiariis ad certum diem, ad oſtendendum quare prius eum non acquietavit. Et cum per diſtrictionem venerit, audiatur querens. Et ſi querens verificare poterit, quod ipſum non acquietavit, ſatisfaciat de damnis, et per judicium recedat* (14) *tenens quietus de ſuo medio, et attornetur capitali domino. Et ſi ad primam diſtrictionem non venerit, exeat breve de alia diſtrictione, et fiat proclamatio, et poſtquam teſtificatum fuerit, procedatur ad judicium, ſicut ſuperius dictum eſt. Et ſciendum eſt, quod per hoc ſtatutum non excluduntur tenentes, quin habeant warrantiam* (15), *ſi de tenementis ſuis implacitentur, ſuper medios ſuos,*

ſhire where the diſtreſs is taken, and when it is returned by the ſheriff that he hath nothing in his ſhire, a writ judicial ſhall iſſue to ſummon the mean unto the ſheriff of the ſame ſhire, in which it ſhall be teſtified that he hath land, and ſuit ſhall be made in the ſame ſhire until they have paſſed unto the great diſtreſs and proclamation, as above is ſaid in the mean having land in the ſame ſhire in which the diſtreſs is taken. And nevertheleſs ſuit ſhall be made in the ſame ſhire where he hath nothing, as above is ſaid of the mean that hath nothing, until the proceſs come to the great diſtreſs and proclamation; and and ſo after proclamation made in both counties, the mean ſhall be fore-judged of his fee and ſervice. And where it happeneth ſometimes, that the tenant in demean is infeoffed to hold by leſs ſervice than the mean ought to do unto the chief lord, when after ſuch proclamation the tenant hath attorned to the chief lord, and the mean being excluded, the tenant muſt of neceſſity anſwer unto the chief lord for all ſuch ſervices and cuſtoms as the mean was wont to do to him. And after that the mean is come into the court, and hath confeſſed that he ought to acquit his tenant, or be compelled by judgement to acquit, if after ſuch confeſſion or judgement it is complained that the mean doth not acquit his tenant, then ſhall iſſue a writ judicial, that the ſheriff ſhall diſtrain the mean to acquit the tenant, and to be at a certain day before the juſticers, for to ſhew why he hath not acquitted him before; and when they have proceeded unto the great diſtreſs, the plaintiff ſhall be heard; and if the plaintiff can prove that he hath not acquitted him; he ſhall yield damages, and by award of the court the tenant ſhall go quit from the mean. and ſhall attorn unto the chief lord, And if he come not at the firſt diſtreſs,

suos, et eorum hæredes, secundum quod prius habuerunt, nec etiam excluduntur tenentes (16), *quin sequi possunt versus medios suos, secundum consuetudinem prius usitatam, si viderint quod processus eorum plus valeat * per antiquam consuetudinem, quam per istud statutum. Et sciendum est, quod per istud statutum non providetur remedium quibuscunque mediis, sed solummodo in casu cum sit unus medius* (17) *tantum inter dominum distringentem et tenentem, et in casu quando medius ille est plenæ ætatis* (18), *et in casu quando tenens, sine præjudicio alterius* (19) *quam medii, attornare se potest capitali domino, quod dictum est pro mulieribus tenentibus in dotem, et tenentibus per legem Angliæ, vel aliter ad terminum vitæ, vel per feodum talliatum, quibus pro aliquibus causis nondum est provisum remedium: sed* (*Deo dante*) *alias providebitur.*

tress, a writ shall go forth to distrain him again, and proclamation shall be made, and as soon as it is returned, they shall proceed in judgement, as before is said. And it is to be understanden, that by this statute tenants are not excluded, but they shall have a warranty of the means and their heirs, if they be impleaded of their lands, as they have had before; nor the tenants shall be excluded, but that they may sue against their means, as they used heretofore, if they see that their process may be more available by the old custom, than by this statute. And it is to wit, that by this statute no remedy is provided to any means, but only in case where there is but one onely mean between the lord that distraineth and the tenant; and in case where that mean is of full age; and in case where the tenant may attorn unto the chief lord without prejudice of any other than of the mean, which is spoken for women tenants in dower, and tenants by the courtesie, or otherwise for term of life, or in fee-tail, unto whom for certain causes remedy is not yet provided, but (God willing) there shall be at another time.

(Regist. 160. Fitz. Mesne, 1. 3. 7. 11, 12. 15, 16, 17. 19, 20, 21. 24. 56. 58. Fitz. Proclamat. 20, 21. 1 Inst. 100. a. Fitz. Mesne, 3. 18. 47. 57. 66, 67. 70. Fitz. Mesne, 1. 53. Fitz. Avowry, 146. 168. Fitz. Mesne, 28, 29. Fitz. Process, 153. Fitz. Mesne, 20. 24. 38. 59. 68. 70. Fitz. Mesne, 68. 25. 35. 79. Rast. 433, &c.)

50 E. 3. 23. One mischiefe here first mentioned before the making of this statute was, the great delayes which were used in the writs of mesne, in which the processe at the common law was summons, attachment, and distresse infinite; and yet the tenant in default of the mesne was presently distrained by the lord paramount, which mischief appeareth by the preamble of this act: for remedy whereof a more speedy proceeding is given by this act in a writ of mesne.

Another mischiefe was, when the mesne had nothing within the same county; for there the tenant was without remedy, and though the mesne had sufficient in another county, the common law extended not thereunto, in both which cases remedy is given by this act.

4 E. 3. 42. F.N.B. 137. a. (1) *Pro consuetudinibus et servitiis*, &c.] The distresse must bee taken for the customes or services which the mesne by reason of his tenure ought to doe to the lord, within which, sute service to a hundred

hundred is comprehended, but not sute reall, that is, by resiancie either to hundred, leet, or tourne, for that is not by reason of his tenure.

But if the tenant be distrained for the reliefe of the mesne, or for reasonable aide, albeit they are rather improvements of services then services, yet the tenant shall have a writ of mesne, because they grow by reason of the tenure. 5 E. 3. 49. 10 H. 6. 26. 39 H. 6 31. a. 9 E. 4. 27. F.N.B. 136. m.

(2) *Et medius sit.*] If there be A. lord, B. mesne, C. mesne, D. tenant *per availe*, A. the lord paramount distrein D. for services, &c. he bringeth a writ of mesne against C. and recovereth damages against him, whereupon C. the mesne may have a writ of mesne against B. but if B. plead *nient distrein de son default*, the speciall matter must be shewed, and not to take the generall issue, and so every mesne shall have his writ against his mesne. 18 E. 3. 19. 29 E. 3. 34. 39 E. 3. 19. 39 H. 6. 31. b.

(3) *Qui tenentem acquietare debeat.*] There be two kinds of acquitals; one expresse, and the other implyed: expresse, three manner of waies: 31 E. 1. mesn. 55. 7 E. 2. ibid. 66. 20 E. 2. ibid. 59. 8 E. 3. 49. 39 E. 3. 19. 38 E. 3. 10. F.N.B. 136.

First, by fine or deed, either at the creation of the tenure, or after: secondly, by acknowledgement of acquittall: thirdly, by prescription.

Implyed, five manner of waies:

First, by owelty of services; secondly, by tenure in frankalmoigne; thirdly, in frankmarriage; fourthly, by homage auncestrell; and fifthly, in dower.

(4) *In casu etiam cum tenens paratus esset facere capitali domino servitia et consuetudines exactas, et capitalis dominus servitia et consuetudines sibi debitas renuebat percipere per manum alterius, quam per manum proximi tenentis sui*, &c.] By the common law the lord paramount might have refused his services by the * hands of the tenant *per availe*, or by the hands of tenant for life, where the reversion was over, because the mesne or he in reversion was his very tenant in privity, for the which remedy is given by this act. Lib. 6. 58. Bredimans case, lib. 9. fol. 110, 111. 21 E. 3. 49. 2 H. 6. 3. 8 H. 6. 16.

(5) *Usque ad magnam districtionem.*] This must be understood of a writ of mesne returnable into the court of common pleas, and not of a writ of mesne that is vicountell, and not returnable. * [374]

And although a writ of mesne be depending between the tenant and the mesne, yet the lord paramount may proceed, &c. for he shall not tarry till the matter be tried in the writ of mesne. F.N.B. 136. d.

But it appeareth by Fleta, *Si medius sit paratus ipsum tenentem acquietare de servitiis, quod capitalis dominus ab eo exigit, tunc secundum æquitatem juris subvenietur tenenti per breve, viz. quod capitalis dominus desistat*, and there the writ in that case appeareth. Flet. li. 2. cap. 43. Brit fol. 58. b.

(6) *Et si medius habens terram in eodem comitatu*, &c.] Here is provided a more speedy proceeding in the writ of mesne, if the mesne had land in the same county. Brit. ubi supra.

(7) *Et si non venerit hujusmodi medius, amittat servitium tenentis sui, et à modo non respondeat*, &c.] If the mesne appeare not at the grand distresse, he shall be fore-judged, that is to say, that the mesne shall lose the services of his tenant of the tenements before holden. And that the mesne being omitted, the tenant from thenceforth shall be *attendens et respondens* to the chiefe lord by the same services, as the mesne holdeth by. Flet. lib. 2. ca. 43. Brit. fol. 58. 10 H. 6. 26.

But it is to be observed, that the immediate chiefe lord must be named in the fore-judger; for albeit he be a stranger to the writ, and by his death the writ of mesne shall not abate: yet in the judgement 21 E. 3. mesn. 48. 10 H. 6. fol. 26. 4 H. 6. 28.

judgement he that is then immediate lord paramount must be particularly named.

(8) *Nec habeat capitalis dominus potestatem distringendi tenentes in dominico, dum prædictus tenens offerat ei servitia debita, et consueta.*] Here three things are to be observed.

1. That the tenant must offer and tender the rent or service due upon the land, and not be ready only, by reason of the word (*offerat.*)

2 H. 6. avowry 1. 2 H. 6. fol. 3. 21 E. 3. 49. Bredimans case, ubi supra, li. 9. fol. 110, 111.

2. This must be done at the time, when the lord comes to distraine.

3. That this act is to be understood of services, and customes which the tenant may doe, as payment of rents, delivery of heriot-service, or the like; but extendeth not to personall services annexed to the person of the mesne, as homage, fealty, &c. for he cannot say, I become your man: nor sweare to him fealty, &c. But after fore judger, then the tenant shall doe all manner of services which the mesne ought to have done, for then the mesnalty is extinct; but as long as the mesnalty remaines, the personall services remaine with the *mesne, servitia personalia sequuntur personam.*

(9) *Et si capitalis dominus exegerit plus, quam medius ei facere deberet, habeat tenens in hoc casu exceptionem versus dominum quam haberet medius.*] Hereby provision is made for the tenant to take any advantage that the mesne might do, if the chiefe lord demand other services then the mesne ought to doe, albeit he be a stranger to the avowry.

Lib. 7. in Calvins case, cap. Itineris, Vet. Magn. Chart. fol. 154.

(10) *Si vero medius nihil habuerit in potestate regis.*] Here *sub potestate regis* is taken for the power of the king to administer justice to his subjects by his writs, *potestas regia est facere justitiam.* See the first part of the Institutes, sect. 199.

And by this branch remedy is given to the tenant where the mesne had nothing, where he had no remedy by the common law.

[375]

(11) *Si vero medius non habeat terram in comitatu in quo fit districtio, sed habeat terram in alio comitatu,* &c.] Here is remedy given to the tenant, where the mesne hath land in a forraine county.

Mich. 17. E. 1. in banco rot. 147. Suff. Rich. de Rokeles case. 31 E. 1. mesn. 55. 18 E. 2. ibid. 57. 46 E. 3. 31.

(12) *Adjudicetur medius de feodo et servitio suo.*] Here also forejudger is given in the cases here mentioned, which is a better and speedier remedy then the common law gave.

(13) *Et postquam medius, &c. cognoverit, &c. vel adjudicetur ad acquietandum. &c. si post, &c. medius non acquietavit tenentem.*] Medius, the heire of the mesne shall not be fore-judged within this statute, for that this act speaketh of the mesne onely, and not of the mesne and his heires.

31 E. 1. mesn. 55. 13 E. 2. ib. 68. 46 E. 3. 31. 49 E. 3. 8.

(14) *Satisfaciat de damnis, et per judicium recedat,* &c.] This branch of the statute giveth damages and fore-judger, and the plaintife cannot take damages, and leave the fore-judger, but he must either take both according to this branch, or neither of them.

8 E. 3. 49.

(15) *Et sciendum est, quod per hoc stat' non excluduntur tenentes, quin habeant warrantiam.*] By this clause the warranty of the tenant (which was ever much esteemed in law) is saved and preserved, and many deeds comprehended both warranty and acquitall.

(16) Nec

(16) *Nec etiam excluduntur tenentes*, &c.] Here the tenant hath election either to take the benefit of this act, by taking the processe given by the same, or to take the processe at the common law, and this was *abundans cautela*; for this statute being in the affirmative, the tenant might have had election (if this clause had not been) but *abundans cautela non nocet*: and the ancient sages of the law did ever make things as plain, and leave as little to construction, as might be. 13 E.2. mesn.68. 50 E. 3. 23. F.N.B. 137. b.

(17) *Sed solummodo quando unus sit medius*, &c.] Hereby it appeareth, that no fore-judger can be, but when there is but one mesne betweene the lord paramount and the tenant.

(18) *In casu quando medius est plenæ ætatis.*] Albeit a feme covert be not here excepted, yet by good construction she is excepted. 7 E. 2. mesn. 76. 9 E. 2. ibid. 67.

(19) *Sine præjudicio alterius.*] These words were specially intended of tenant in dower, or of tenant for life, or in taile with a remainder over; for against them no fore-judger shall be given, but their extent is farre more large. 7 E. 3. fol. 41. 34 E. 3. mesn, 47. Dyer 2. mar. 104. 14 E. 2. tit. mesn. 79.

If the disseissor, or any other that hath a defeasible title in the tenancy doth fore-judge the mesne, this shall not prejudice the disseisee, or him that right hath; for they are within the remedy of these words, that every fore-judger ought to be *sine præjudicio alterius*.

But if the daughter fore-judge the mesne, and a son is borne after the fore-judgement, the son shall not avoid it; for it was *sine præjudicio alterius*, when the judgement was given.

If two joyntenants bring a writ of mesne, and the one is summoned and severed, and the other sueth forth, he cannot fore-judge the mesne, because he cannot *respondere capitali domino de eisdem servitiis et consuetudinibus, quæ prius facere debuit prædictus medius*. 14 H. 4. 37.

So it is, if there be two joynt mesnes, and the one appeare, and the other make default, no fore-judgement shall be, for the same cause necessarily collected upon the same words.

They that are seised in *auter droit*, as the bishop in right of his bishopricke, or the abbot or prior in the right of his monastery, or the like, shall neither fore-judge, nor be fore-judged, because it is to be intended, that it cannot be done *sine præjudicio alterius*, for that the consent of them is not had, which by law to the alteration of any estate is requisite, as the deane and chapter to the bishop, and the covent to the abbot, prior, &c. 19 E. 3. tit. mesn. Statham. [376]

If the mesne hanging the writ of mesne against him alien by fine, albeit the right of the mesnalty passeth to the conusee, yet the mesne may be fore-judged, and the conusee shall not take advantage of these words, *sine præjudicio alterius*, because he came to the mesnalty, *pendente brevi*, and in judgement of law the mesne (as to the plaintife) remaine seised of the mesnalty; for, *pendente lite nihil innovetur*. 34 E. 3. mesn. 47.

CAP. X.

CUM in itinere justic' proclamat' fuerit, quod omnes qui brevia liberare voluerint, ea liberent infra certum terminum (1), *post quem nullum breve recipiatur, multi de hoc confidentes, cum moram fecerint usque ad prædictum terminum, et nullum breve super eos fuerit liberatum, de licentia justic' recedunt, post quorum recessum adversarii sui ipsorum absent' percipientes, brevia sua porrigunt in cera, quæ aliquando per favorem, aliquando pro dono per vicecomitem recipiuntur, et illi, qui secure credebant recessisse, ten' sua amittunt: ut hujusmodi fraudi subveniatur imposterum, statuit dominus rex, quod justic' in itineribus suis statuant terminum quindenæ, vel mensis, minoris vel majoris termini, secundum quod comit' fuerit major vel minor, infra quem terminum publice proclametur, quod omnes qui brevia liberare voluerint, ea liberent infra terminum illum. Et in adventum illius termini certificet vicecomes capitali justic' itineranti, quot brevia habet, et quæ, et quod ultra illum terminum nullum breve recipiatur, quod si receptum fuerit, processus per illud factus pro nullo habeatur* (1): *excepto quod breve* (2) *cessatum durante toto itinere relevari poterit. Breve etiam de dote de viris qui obierint al' seisiti infra summonitionem itineris, assisæ ultimæ præsentationis, et quare impedit, de ecclesiis vacantibus, infra summonitionem præd', quocunq; tempore ante recessum justic' recipiantur in itinere. Brevia etiam novæ disseisinæ, quocunque tempore facta fuerit disseisina, recipiantur in itineribus justic'.*

Concedit dominus rex de gratia speciali (3) *quod illi qui habent tenen'* (4) *in diversis comitatibus, in quibus*

WHEREAS in the circuit of justices it was proclaimed, that all such as would deliver writs, should deliver them within a certain time, after which no writ should be received; many trusting upon the same, and tarrying until the said time, and no writ served upon them, departed by licence of the said justices; after whose departure their adversaries, perceiving their absence, delivered their writs in wax, which sometime by fraud, and sometimes for rewards, be received of the sheriff, and they, that thought to have departed quiet, lose their lands. For the remedy of such fraud from henceforth, the king hath ordained, that the justices in their circuits shall appoint a time of fifteen days, or a month, or a time more or less (after as the county shall happen to be more or less) within which time it shall be openly proclaimed, that all such as will deliver their writs, shall deliver them before the same time; and when the time cometh, the sheriff shall certifie the chief justice in eyre how many writs he hath, and what, and that no writ be received after the same time; and if it be received, the process issuing thereupon shall be of none effect; but only that a writ abated any time during the circuit may be amended; also writs of dower of men that died within the summons of the circuit, assises of darrain presentment, quare impedit, of churches vacant within the foresaid summons, shall be received at any time before the departure of the justices; also writs of novel disseisin, at what time soever the disseisin was done, shall be received in the circuit of justices.

Our lord the king of his special grace granteth, that such as have land in divers shires where the justices make

*quibus justic' itinerant, vel de quibusdam ten' in com' in quo justic' non itinerant, timent implacitar', et de aliis tenem' in comitatu, in quo justic' non itinerant, implacitentur: ut coram justic' apud Westm', vel * de banco domini regis, vel coram justiciariis ad assisas capiendas assignatis, vel in aliquo comitatu coram vic', vel in aliqua cur' baronum, facere possint generalem attornat'* (6) *ad prosequendum pro eis in omnibus placitis in itinere* (7) *justic' pro ipsis, vel contra ipsos motis vel movendis, durante itinere. Qui quidem attornatus, vel attorn', habeat potestatem in placitis motis in itinere quousque placitum terminetur* (5), *vel dominus suus ipsum amoverit, nec per hoc excusentur, quin sint in juratis, et assisis, coram eisdem justic'* (8).

make their circuit, and that have land in shires where the justices have no circuit, that fear to be impleaded, and are impleaded of other lands in shires where they have no circuit, as before the justices at Westminster, or in the king's bench, or before justices assigned to take assises, or in any county before sheriffs, or in any court baron, may make a general attorney to sue for them in all pleas in the circuit of justices moved or to be moved for them, or against them, during the circuit; which attorney or attorneys shall have full power in all pleas moved during the circuit, until the plea be determined, or that his master remove him; yet shall they not be excused thereby, but they shall be put in juries and assises before the same justices.

Regist. 19. b. (13 Ed. 2. stat. 1. c. 4.)

(1) *Cum in itinere justic. proclamat. fuerit, quod omnes qui brevia liberari voluerunt, ea liberent infra certum terminum, &c.*]

Hereby is recited the mischiefe which was before the making of this act, the remedy followeth.

Ut hujusmodi fraudi imposterum, statuit dominus rex, quod justiciarii in itineribus suis statuant terminum, quindenæ, vel mensis, minoris vel majoris termini secundum quod comitatus fuit major vel minor, infra quem terminum publice proclametur quod omnes qui brevia liberare voluerint ea liberent infra terminum illum, et in adventu illius termini certificet vicecomes capitalem justiciar' itinerant' quot brevia habent et quæ, et quod ultra illum terminum nullum breve recipiatur, quod si receptum fuerit processus per illud factus pro nullo habeatur.] Upon this purview was great question, whether the king might dispense with this law, and give a further day then hereby is prescribed, and in the end adjudged that he might for advancement and furtherance of justice: of this purview, the Mirror with too much asperity saith thus, *Lestatute de suspention de briefes en eyres est reprovable come repugnant a la grand chartre que dit nous ne veerons a nul droit, ne delaierons, & pur quoy sont briefes rebotables de audience eins pur le multitude des briefes qve adonques se font & pur le petit nombre des justices perit droit de plusors.*

Fleta, li. 1. c. 19.

Tr. 6 E. 2. in Thesaur. Regist. fo. 19. F.n.b. 17. E.

Mirror, c. 5. § 5.

(2) *Excepto quod breve, &c.*] Here followeth five exceptions:

1. The first is, that a writ abated, may, during the whole eyre, be amended.

2. Writs of dower, of the seisin of men that dyed within the summons of the heir (which is by the space of forty dayes) before the beginning of the heir.

Brit. c. 2. Fleta, lib. 1. c. 19, &c.

3. Assises of darrein presentment.

4. *Quare impedit* of churches vacant within the aforesaid summons, shall be received at any time before the departure of the justices.

5. Writs of assise of novel disseisin, at what time soever the disseisin

disseisin was done, shall be received during the eyre of the justices.

Regist. fo. 19, 20. F.N.B. 25. c. e. 26. a. c. d. 18 E. 3. 46. 8 E. 3. 20.

(3) *Concedit dom' rex de gratia speciali quod illi qui habent tenem', &c.*] Here is an act of grace, and therefore it is termed accordingly, *De * gratia speciali*; for where the king by his prerogative before this and other statutes might by letters patents, or by writ under his great seal, grant to any demandant or pl', tenant, or defendant, to make attorney in any action, and to command the judges to admit such persons to be attorneys for them: Now justly is this act stiled an act of grace, for that the king gave his royall assent to this law for the quiet and safety of his subjects, giving them power hereby to make attorneys in cases herein expressed, whereby the king lost such profit of the great seal, as he formerly received in such cases. *Statutum ex gratia regia dicitur, quando rex dignatur cedere de jure suo regio pro quiete et commodo populi sui.*

*[378]

(4) *Illi qui habent, &c.*] This act extends aswell to corporations aggregate of many, as maior and commonalty, and to sole corporations, as to private persons: and it extendeth aswell to justices in eyre of the forest, as to other justices in eyre; see the fourth part of the Institutes, cap. Justices in Eyre, & cap. the Courts of the Forests, and the Register *ubi supra* for claim of liberties.

4 E. 3. Attorney 18. 8 E. 3. 9. 32 H. 6. 1. 33 H. 6. 49. 34 H. 6. 51.

(5) *Quousque placitum terminetur.*] By the judgement against the defendant, the warranty of attorney is determined; for thereby *placitum terminatur*, but onely to sue execution (which is the fruit of the judgement) within the yeer: and if he sue out execution within the yeer, he may prosecute the same after the yeer; but if he sue out no execution within the yeer, then after the yeer is ended after judgement, his warrant of attorney is determined.

8 E. 3. 20. 18 E. 3. 47. F.N.B. 25 E. Regist. 19, 20.

(6) *Attornatum generalem.*] Of this generall attorney you shall often reade in our books.

(7) *In omnibus placitis in itinere.*] This is not understood of an assise of novel disseisin, for it is *querela*, and not *placitum assise*, whereof (as elsewhere hath been said) there is plentifull authority in our books.

Marlbr. cap. 14. 39 E. 3. 15. 34 H. 6. 25. 35 H. 6. 42.

(8) *Nec per hoc excusentur quin sint in juratis et assisis coram eisdem justic'.*] The wisdom of parliaments, and of the sages of the law hath ever been, that able and sufficient men should not (to the hindrance of justice) be exempted for service in juries and assises.

CAP. XI.

DE servientibus (1), balivis (2), camerariis (3), et quibuscunque receptoribus, qui ad compotum reddendum tenentur (4): concordatum est et statutum, quod cum dominus hujusmodi servient' dederit eis auditores (5) compoti, et contingat ipsos esse in arreragiis super compotum suum omnibus allocatis,

CONCERNING servants, bailiffs, chamberlains, and all manner of receivers, which are bound to yield accompt, it is agreed and ordained, that when the masters of such servants do assign auditors to take their accompt, and they be found in arrearages upon the accompt, all things

locatis, et allocandis (6), *arrestentur corpora eorum* (7), *et per testimonium auditorum ejusdem compoti, mittantur et liberentur proximæ gaolæ domini regis* (8) *in partibus illis, et à vic', seu custode ejusdem gaolæ recipiantur* (9), *et carceri mancipentur* * *in ferris* (10), *et sub bona custodia, et in illa prisona remaneant de suo proprio viventes* (11), *quousque dominis suis de arreragiis plenariè satisfecerint. At tamen si quis sic gaolæ liberatus conqueratur, quod auditores compoti sui ipsum injustè gravaverunt* (12), *onerando ipsum de receptis quæ non recepit, vel non allocando ei expensas aut liberationes rationabiles, et inveniat amicos, qui eum manucapere voluerint ad ducendum coram baronibus de scaccario, liberetur eis, et scire faciat vicecomes (in cujus prisona fuerit) domino, quod sit coram baronibus de scaccario* (13) *ad aliquem certum diem cum rotulis et aliis, per quos compotum suum reddiderit, et in præsentia baronum vel auditor', quos assignare voluerint, recitetur compotus, et fiat partibus justitia, ita quod si fuerit in arreragiis, committatur gaolæ de Fleete, ut supradictum est. Et si diffugerit, et gratis compotum reddere noluerit* (14), *sicut in aliis statutis alibi continetur*; Marlbridge, cap. 23. *distringatur ad veniendum coram justiciariis, ad compotum reddendum, si habeat per quod distringi possit. Et cum ad curiam venerit, dentur ei auditores compoti, coram quibus si fuerit in arreragiis, et statim arreragia solvere non possit, committatur gaolæ custodiend' in forma prædict'. Et si diffugerit, et testificatum* (15) *fuerit per vicecomit', quod non sit inventus, exigatur de comit' in comitatum, quousque utlagetur. Et sit hujusmodi incarceratus irreplegiabilis. Et caveat sibi vicecomes, vel custos ejusdem gaolæ, sive sit infra libertatem* (16) *sive extra, quod per commune breve, quod dicitur replegiare, vel alio modo sine assensu*

things allowed which ought to be allowed, their bodies shall be arrested, and by the testimony of the auditors of the same accompt, shall be sent or delivered unto the next gaol of the king's in those parts; and shall be received of the sheriff or gaoler, and imprisoned in iron under safe custody, and shall remain in the same prison at their own cost, until they have satisfied their master fully of the arrearages. Nevertheless if any person being so committed to prison, do complain, that the auditors of his accompt have grieved him unjustly, charging him with receipts that he hath not received, or not allowing him expences, or reasonable disbursements, and can find friends that will undertake to bring him before the barons of the exchequer, he shall be delivered unto them; and the sheriff (in whose prison he is kept) shall give knowledge unto his master, that he appear before the barons of the exchequer at a certain day, with the rolls and tallies by which he made his accompt; and in the presence of the barons, or the auditors that they shall assign him, the accompt shall be rehearsed, and justice shall be done to the parties, so that if he be found in arrearages, he shall be committed to the Fleet, as above is said. And if he flee, and will not give accompt willingly, as is contained elsewhere in other statutes, he shall be distrained to come before the justices to make his account, if he have whereof to be distrained. And when he cometh to the court, auditors shall be assigned to take his accompt, before whom if he be found in arrearages, and cannot pay the arrearages forthwith, he shall be committed to the gaol to be kept in manner aforesaid. And if he flee, and it be returned to the sheriff that he cannot be found, exigents shall go against him from county to county,

aſſenſu domini (17) *ipſum à priſona exire non permittat. Quod ſi fecerit, et ſuper hoc convincatur, reſpondeat domino de damnis, per hujuſmodi ſervientem ſibi illatis, ſecundum quod per patriam verificare poterit, et habeat dominus ſuum recuperare per breve de debito* (18) *verſus cuſtodem. Et ſi cuſtos gaolæ non habeat, per quod juſticietur, vel unde ſolvat, reſpondeat ſuperior ſuus qui cuſtodiam hujuſmodi gaolæ ſibi commiſit* (19), *per idem breve.*

county, until he be outlawed, and ſuch priſoner ſhall not be replevisable. And let the ſheriff or keeper of ſuch gaole take heed, if it be within a franchiſe, or without, that he do not ſuffer him to go out of priſon by the common writ called replegiare, or by other means, without aſſent of his maſter; and if he do, and thereof be convict, he ſhall be anſwerable to his maſter of the damages done to him by ſuch his ſervant, according as it may be found by the country, and ſhall have his recovery by writ of debt. And if the keeper of the gaol have not wherewith he may be juſtified, or not able to pay, his ſuperior that committed the cuſtody of the gaol unto him, ſhall be anſwerable by the ſame writ.

Fleta, lib. 2. c. 64. Brit. fol. 70. a. (1 Inſt. 295. a. 2 Inſt. 378. Fitz. Accompt, 96. 109. Fitz. Avowry, 220. Regiſt. 137. Raſt. 14, &c. Fitz. Accompt, 23. 26. 47. 74. 106. 52 H. 3. c. 23. 29 Ed. 3. f. 5. 17 Ed. 3. f. 59. 1 R. 2. c. 12. 7 H. 4. c. 4. 2 Leon. 9. Fitz. Debt. 172. Fitz. Iſſu. 160. Bro. Dett. 103. 2 Bulſtr. 321.)

3. E. 3. 8. 4 E. 3. 7. 13 E. 3. Account 76. 41 E. 3. ib. 74. 8 E. 3. 46. 2 R. 2. Account 45. 11 R. 2. ib. 48. F.N.B. b. c. d. e.

(1) *Servientibus.*] Every writ of account muſt be brought againſt one, either as bailife, receiver, or gardein in ſocage; and therefore againſt a ſervant as ſervant, or againſt an apprentice, or a controller, ſurveyor, meſſenger *, or the like, a writ of account lyeth not, unleſſe he be charged as bailife or receiver.

* [380]

17 E. 2. Procl. 203. 18 E. 2. Avowry 220. 17 E. 3. 59. 29 E. 3. 5. See the firſt part of the Inſtitutes, ſect. 124. For this *ſervientes*, ſee towards the end of this chapter.

A gardein in ſocage cannot be committed to priſon by force of this act, for a gardein in ſocage is *in loco parentis*, and this act beginneth with *ſervientibus*, and this word *ſervientibus* is to be applyed to *balivis, camerariis, et receptoribus*; for this act ſoon after this ſaith, *Cum domini hujuſmodi ſervientum dederit eis auditores, &c.* Where theſe words are to be obſerved, *viz. domini*, the lords or maſters, and *ſervientes*, ſervants, which word *ſervientes* extends to all; and therefore the gardein in ſocage being no ſervant, nor the heir lord, or maſter is not by this act to be impriſoned, &c.

(2) *Balivis.*] This word is ſufficiently known, and if gardein in ſocage occupy after the heir attain to the age of 14 yeers, he may be charged as bailife.

1. Part of the Inſtitutes, ubi ſup. 1. Part of the Inſtitutes, 153. Fleta, li. 2. c. 70.

(3) *Camerariis.*] Receivers were anciently called chamberlains, becauſe they were wont to keep the money received in chambers ſpecially provided for that purpoſe; yet cannot he be charged as chamberlain in an account, but as bailife, or receiver, for the cauſe aboveſaid.

(4) *Et quibuſcunq; receptoribus qui ad compotum reddend' teneantur.*] *Receptores* is a known word, and needeth no further explication.

43 E. 3. 31. 49 E. 3. 2. 50 E. 3. 17. 27 Aſſ. 3.

(5) *Dederit eis auditores.*] An account taken before one auditor, is not within the purview of this ſtatute; for this act is in nature of a com-

a commiſſion, and a commiſſion being made to two or more, cannot be executed by one alone.

20 H. 6. 17, 18. 41. 45. 8 H. 6. 15. 14 H. 6. 24. 22 H. 6. 35. 47. lib. 10. fol. 103. Denbauds caſe. 38 H. 6. 6.

By this act the auditors are judges of record, and therefore by conſequence in an action of debt for the arrerages of an account before two or more auditors, the defendant ſhall not wage his law.

2 H. 6. 41. 10 H. 6. 24, 25. Denbauds caſe, ubi ſupra.

And by the ſame conſequence of reaſon, if the lord be found in ſurpluſage upon the account determined by the auditors as an incident to their authority in an action of debt brought by the bailife for this ſurpluſage, the lord ſhall not wage his law, becauſe by force of this act (they being judges of record) no wage of law can be allowed againſt their record: and ſo was it adjudged in the exchequer chamber, as it is reported in 20 H. 6. But if the account be made before one auditor, this (as hath been ſaid) is out of the ſtatute, and therefore there he ſhall wage his law; but the lord cannot be committed to priſon (for the cauſe aforeſaid) by force of this act.

5 H. 4. cap. 8. 20 H. 6. 17, 18. 14 H. 6. 24. Vide infra, †.

In an action of account againſt a receiver, for 13 s. 4 d. or any other ſum under 40 s. the ſherife in his county court ſhall not hold plea of it; and the reaſon thereof is, becauſe the ſherife cannot aſſigne auditors who (as hath been ſaid) are judges of record, and the county court is no court of record.

43 E. 3. 21.

(6) *Omnibus allocatis et allocandis.*] † By theſe words, if the lord be found in ſurpluſage, it is within their authority, and therfore parcell of their record, and ſo in that caſe (as hath been ſaid) no wager of law.

But albeit the auditors do diſallow a juſt demand, yet ſhall he take no averment or advantage upon theſe words, againſt the record of the judgement of the auditors; for, *judicium pro veritate accipitur*, and *nemo poteſt contra recordum verificare per patriam*: but he hath remedy after by this act, by a writ of *ex parte talis* for his relief, whereof more ſhall be ſaid hereafter in his proper place.

(7) *Arreſtentur corpora eorum.*] Note at the common law, the proceſſe in account was ſummons, attachment, and diſtreſſe infinite; by the ſtatute of Marlbr. a writ of *monſtravit de compoto* was given; and here by this branch the body may be arreſted, and after by this act proces of outlawry is given in account, ſo as after the account determined the body of the defendant may be arreſted, &c.

Marlbr. cap. 23. lib. 3. fol. 11. Sir William Herberts caſe.

[381]

Note the words in effect be *ſuper compotum ſuum, &c. arreſtentur et liberentur*, ſo as the auditors by force of this act ought to commit him, &c. preſently after the account determined.

46 E. 3. 30. 27 H. 6. 8. li. 8. fo. 119. D. Bonhams caſe.

(8) *Proximæ gaolæ domini regis.*] This is intended of the next gaole, though it be not in the ſame county, for, as it hath been ſaid, the ſtatute is in nature of a commiſſion, and therefore this word *proximæ* muſt be purſued.

13 E. 3. barre 253. 27 H. 6. 8.

(9) *Et à vic' ſeu cuſtode ejuſdem gaolæ recipiantur.*] The auditors muſt make a warrant in writing under their ſeales to the ſheriffe upon the ſpeciall matter, and thereupon the ſheriffe ought to receive the accountant in execution.

Dier, 24 H. 8. 249. lib. 3. fol. 44. Boytons caſe. Lib. 8. fol. 100. Pl. Com. 360. a.

(10) *Carceri mancipentur in ferris.*] Hereby it appeareth that the ſheriffe ought to keep him *in ſalva et arcta cuſtodia*, and hath power by this act, if need require, to lay irons upon him for his ſafe keeping; but this the gaoler could not have done by the common law, as by all our ancient authors it appeareth.

Brac. l. 3. 105. 137. Brit. fo. 14. 17. Fleta, l. 1. ca. 26. Mirror, c. 5. § 1. 8 E. 2. Coron. 432. Vide 3. part des Inſtitutes. Cap. petit treaſ. in fine.

(11) *De suo proprio viventes.*] By this clause it appeareth, that he that is so imprisoned must live of his owne.

Britton, fol. 70. Fleta, l. 2. c. 64. Regist. 137. F.N.B. 129. f. 13 E. 3. barre 253. 14 E. 3. account 74. 2 E. 3. 12.

(12) *Auditores compoti sui ipsum injuste gravaverunt.*] By this clause is the writ of *ex parte talis* given to the accountant, if the auditors assigned by the lord either charge him *de receptis quae non recepit, vel non allocando ei expensas aut liberationes rationabiles,* and this writ is, in nature of a commission to the barons of the exchequer, for that they are the soveraigne auditors of England to heare and audite the account, *et quod fiat justicia partibus.*

But this writ lieth not, but where the account is taken before auditors assigned by the lord, for if there be a writ of account brought, and the court assigneth auditors, there lieth no writ of *ex parte talis,* for in that case he ought to shew his griefe to the justices, and they ought to doe him justice, and the writ of *ex parte talis* is grounded upon this act, where the lord assigneth auditors.

(13) *Quod sit coram baronibus de scaccario.*] The writ in the Register, and F.N.B. *ubi supra,* is *coram thesaurario et baronibus nostris de scaccario,* but it ought to be *coram baronibus de scaccario* according to this act, and that the rather, because the barons are (as hath been said) the soveraigne auditors of England, and herewith agreeth Fleta.

Fleta, l. 2. c. 64.

Dier, 36 H. 8. c. 64.

Upon sureties found he shall be at large to follow his writ of *ex parte talis,* before the barons, but if it be found that he was in arrerages, he shall be in execution again.

(14) *Et si diffugerit, et gratis compotum reddere noluerit,* &c.] *Vide* Marlebridge whereby the writ *de monstravit de compoto* is given.

Marlb. ca. 23.

Fleta, ubi supra.

(15) *Et si diffugerit et testificatum,* &c.] Here is proces of outlawry given in account.

[382]

11 H. 4. 73. See 1 R. 2. c. 12.

(16) *Et caveat sibi vicecomes vel custos ejusdem gaolae si sit infra libertatem.*] This act extends to all keepers of gaoles, and therefore if one hath the keeping of a gaole by wrong, or *de facto,* and suffereth an escape, he is within this statute, as well as he, that hath the keeping of it *de jure.*

27 H. 8. 24. b. per Curiam.

(17) *Sine assensu domini.*] And this assent may be by paroll, and shall be a sufficient barre in an action of debt brought for the escape.

14 E. 4. 3. Dier, 15 El. 322. 16 E. 3. damag. 81. 13 E. 3. barre 253. 42 Ass. Pl. 11. 45 E. 3. 1. 2 R. 2. issue 160. 9 H. 6. 19. 30 H. 6. 6. Dier, 10 Eliz. 275.

(18) *Et habeat dominus suum recuperare per breve de debito,* &c.] There was no action of debt against the gaoler for an escape at the common law, but the party was driven to his speciall action upon his case, which action was grounded upon a trespasse or wrong, and not upon any contract in deed or in law, but this act first gave the action of debt against the gaoler, which had let one to escape, which was committed to prison by auditors for arrerages of account, but it lieth not against the gaolers executors, because it is a trespasse, and before any other act of parliament by the equity of this act an action of debt did lie against the gaoler for an escape in court pipowders, and so in all other cases.

1 R. 2. cap. 12.

Afterwards the statute of 1 R. 2. for a further declaration gave the action against the gardein of the Fleet.

But albeit this act, and the statute of 1 R. 2. also doth speake *per breve,* yet a bill of debt lieth also by the equity of this and that statute, albeit it hath been holden to the contrary, but since it hath been

been often adjudged that a bill of debt is maintenable upon the said acts. 42 Aff. p. 11. 7 H. 6. 5. Pl. Com. 38. a.

Now for as much as the statutes doe give recovery by writ of debt, incidently, they do give damages also. 16 E. 3. dam. 81. 13 E. 3. ibid.

This act doth extend to feme coverts and infants, that are keepers of gaoles, to charge them in an action of debt for the escape of one in execution. Lib. 8. fol. 44. Wittinghams case.

(19) *Respondeat superior suus, qui custodiam hujusmodi gaolæ sibi commiserit.*] This is to be understood, when one that hath the custody of a gaol of freehold or inheritance, committeth the same to another that is not sufficient, his superior shall answer for the escape of the prisoner; but he shall not have the action of debt against the superior as long as the inferior is sufficient. See cap. 43. 13 E. 3. barre 253.

The mayor and citizens of London have the sherivalty of London in fee, and the sheriffes of London are gardeins under them, and removable from yeare to yeare, in this case the sheriffes of London are gardeins, and the mayor and citizens their superiors; and though the sheriffes appoint a keeper under them, yet he is not within this statute, because it is intendable when the gardein commeth in by him that hath the freehold or inheritance in the custody, for this act doth extend but unto two such degrees, for there cannot be two superiors within this act, but one superiour and one inferiour. 11 E. 2. Debt 272. 11 El. Dier, 278.

The duke of Norffolk being marshall of England of inheritance, and having authority to make a deputy doth make a deputy, who hath the custody of the gaole, he is the gardein, and the duke of Norffolk his superiour within this act. 11 El. ubi supra.

CAP. XII.

[383]

QUIA multi per malitiam (1) volentes alios gravare, procurant falsa appella (2) fieri de homicidiis, et aliis feloniis (3), per appellatores nihil habentes, unde domino regi pro falso appello, nec appellatis de damnis respondere possint: statutum est, quod cum aliquis sic appellatus de felonia sibi imposita se acquietaverit in curia regis modo debito (4), vel ad sectam appellatoris, vel domini regis: justiciarii coram quibus auditum erit hujusmodi appellum et terminatum, puniant appellatorem per prisonam unius anni, et nihilominus restituant hujusmodi appellatores damna appellatis, secundum discretionem justic', habito respectu ad prisonam vel arrestationem quam occasione hujusmodi appellorum sustinuerint appellati, et ad infamiam suam (5), quam

FORASMUCH as many, through malice intending to grieve other, do procure false appeals to be made of homicides and other felonies by appellors, having nothing to satisfy the king for their false appeal, nor to the parties appealed for their damages; it is ordained, that when any, being appealed of felony surmised upon him, doth acquit himself in the king's court in due manner, either at the suit of the appellor, or of our lord the king, the justices, before whom the appeal shall be heard and determined, shall punish the appellor by a year's imprisonment, and the appellors shall nevertheless restore to the parties appealed their damages, according to the discretion of the justices, having respect to the imprison-

quam per impriſonamentum, vel alio modo incurrerunt, et nihilominus verſus dominum regem graviter redimantur. Et ſi forte hujuſmodi appellatores non habeant, unde prædicta damna reſtituere poſſint, inquiratur per quorum abbettum (6) *formatum fuerit hujuſmodi appellum per malitiam, ſi appellatus hoc petat. Et ſi inveniatur per illam inquiſitionem, quod aliquis ſit abbettator per malitiam* (7), *per breve de judicio ad ſectam appellati diſtringatur* (8) *ad veniendum coram juſtic'. Et ſi legitimo modo convictus fuerit de hujuſmodi abbetto per malitiam, puniatur per priſonam, et teneatur ad reſtitutionem damnorum, ſicut ſuperius dictum eſt de appellatore.* Vide anno 1 R. 2. cap. 13. *Nec jaceat de cætero appellatori in appello de morte hominis eſſonium* (9), *in quacunque curia ubi appellum fuerit terminandum.*

impriſonment or arreſtment that the party appealed hath ſuſtained by reaſon of ſuch appeals, and to the infamy that they have incurred by the impriſonment or otherwiſe, and ſhall neverthelefs make a grievous fine unto the king. And if peradventure ſuch appellor be not able to recompenſe the damages, it ſhall be inquired by whoſe abetment or malice the appeal was commenced, if the party appealed deſire it; and if it be found by the ſame inqueſt, that any man is abettor through malice, at the ſuit of the party appealed he ſhall be diſtrained by a judicial writ to come before the juſtices; and if he be lawfully convict of ſuch malicious abetment, he ſhall be puniſhed by impriſonment and reſtitution of damages, as before is ſaid of the appellor. And from henceforth in appeal of the death of a man there ſhall no eſſoin lie for the appellor, in whatſoever court the appeal ſhall hap to be determined.

(12 Rep. 126. Hob. 98. Fitz. Damage, 77. Fitz. Coron. 12. 77. 98. 386. 11 Rep. 77. 1 E. 3. ſtat. 1. c. 7. Regiſt. 56. 12 Rep. 125. Cro. El. 223. 71. 14 H. 7. 2. 26 H. 8. 3. Dier, 120. 131. 8 H. 5. 6. 8 Ed. 4. 3. Regiſt. 134.)

See the Mirror, c. 4. de homicide. 48 E. 3. 22. Stamf. Pl. Cor. 167. c. F.N.B. 114. f. Regiſt. 134.

By the words hereof it appeareth, that before this ſtatute the defendant being duly acquited, ſhould recover his damages, but that is to be underſtood in a writ of conſpiracy, wherein he ſhould recover damages for ſatisfaction in regard of the infamy, impriſonment, and vexation done to him, and further that the parties convicted ſhould be fined to the king and impriſoned, which, I have read, began in this ſort before the raigne of H. 1. They which plotted, or compaſſed the death of a man under pretext of law by bringing falſe appeales, or preferring untrue indictments againſt the innocent of felony, who being duly acquited, both the appellant and his abbettors were to ſuffer death.

[384]

24 E. 3. 24. 27 Aſſ. 59. Tr. 18 E. 3. Coram rege. Rot. 148. 43 E. 3. conſpir. 11.

But king H. 1. by authority of parliament did mitigate the ſeverity of this auncient law (leſt men ſhould be deterred and afraid to accuſe) and did ordaine that if the delinquents were convicted at the ſuit of the party, they ſhould make ſatisfaction, and be fined and impriſoned; but if they were convicted by judgement at the ſuit of the king (whom they pretended to intitle to the forfeiture) then they ſhould loſe the freedome of the law, they ſhould be ſo infamous as never to be any witneſſe, or to be of any jury. That they ſhould never come in or neare the kings court, but make their attournies, that they, their wives, and their children, ſhould be caſt out of their houſes, and their houſes proſtrated, their trees eradicated

cated and subverted, their meadowes plowed up and wasted, every thing to be destroyed which nourished or comf rted them in respect of the villany, and shame done to the delinquent, all against nature and order, for that the delinquent sought the blood of the innocent under pretext and colour of law, and this in later bookes is called a villanous judgement, all which in case of conspiracy remaine a constant law to this day. But this act doth give the party a speedier remedy for his satisfaction then he had before, as hereafter shall appeare.

(1) *Per malitiam.*] These words doe open divers windowes for the better understanding and inlightening of the generall words of this statute. Pasch. 30 E. 1. Coram rege. Northampt. Joh. de Bosco, &c.

1. If the appellee be first indicted of the felony whereof he is appealed, the appeale shall not be understood to be commenced *per malitiam*, because the plaintiffe hath a foundation to build upon, *viz.* an indictment by the other of twelve or more men, so as it shall be presumed that the plaintiffe was moved to his appeale by the indictment, *et non per malitiam*; for in those dayes (as yet it ought to be) indictments taken in the absence of the party, were formed upon plain and direct proofe, and not upon probabilities or inferences: but if the indictment be insufficient, then it is in judgement of law as no indictment, and then the appeale may notwithstanding be commenced *per malitiam, et sic in similibus*, or if it be a good indictment, and found after the appeale commenced, yet may the appeale be commenced *per malitiam.* Hil. 26 E. 1. Coram rege. Leic' Will. Burnell. 22 Ass. 39. 40 Ass. p. 18. 40 E. 3. 42. 33 H. 6. 2. 14 H. 7. 2. 26 H. 8. 3, 4. First part of the Institutes, sect. 208. 9 H. 4. 2. 9 H. 5. 2. 30 E. 4. 6.

2. If one be appealed of murder, and it is found by verdict that he killed him *se defendendo*, this shall not be said to be *per malitiam*, because he had a just cause, for *quod quisque ob tutelam corporis sui fecerit, jure id fecisse videtur*; *et sic de similibus.* 22 Ass. p. 77.

3. The heire or other near of kin, may abbet the wife plaintiffe in the appeale, *Et sic adjudicatur quod pater, mater, frater, &c. non sunt in casu hujus statuti ratione propinquitatis sanguinis, et ad eos pertinet prædictam mortem ulcisci:* Hoylands case, and cannot be said to be *per malitiam.* Term. Mich. 21 E. 1. Coram rege. Rot. 276. Hoylands case. 6 E. 3. 33.

4. *Malitia* referreth onely to the procurers and abbettors, as it appeareth by the expresse words of this act.

(2) *Falsa appella.*] Soone after the making of this statute, the wife and her second husband brought an appeale for the death of her former husband, the record saith, *Non potest esse appellatrix pro morte prioris mariti, &c. ipsa pro repellend. pœna statuti pro falsis appellis advocat appellum suum esse justum nec falsum, licet sit cassatum, et licet illud prosequi non potest, quia habet virum; quæ quidem causa potius est quædam stultitia quam falsitas, ideo ex gratia curiæ concess'. est in præsent' aliorum justic' de banco, postquam prisonam 15. dierum habuerit, quod finem fac' cum rege.* Mich. 34 E. 1. Coram rege. Linc' Rot. 19. Potius stultitia quam falsitas.

(3) *De homicidio et aliis feloniis.*] This is not onely intended of such offences as were felonies at the making of this act, but of all such offences also, as have been made felonies by any act of parliament since this act.

(4) *Se acquietaverit in curia regis modo debito.*] This statute doth extend both to acquitals in deed, and to acquitals in law. [385]

Acquitals in deed, as either by verdict, or by battell, and in that case when the plaintiffe yeelds himselfe creant, or vanquished in the field, the judgement shall be that the appellee shall goe quite, and that he shall recover his damages against the appellor, but if the Regist. 34. 24 E. 3. 73. 41 E. 3. Coro. 98. 21 H. 6. Cor. 12.

the plaintiffe had been slaine, then no judgement can be given against a dead person.

Acquitals in law, as if two be appealed of felony, the one as principall, and the other as accessary, and both of them plead not-guilty, &c. and the jury doth acquite the principall, in this case by
33 H. 6. 2. law the accessary is acquited, and shall recover damages by this act
8 H. 5. 6. against the appellant, &c. or may have his writ of conspiracy at the common law.

41 Ass. 24. But if the principall be acquited by verdict, proces depending against the accessory, the accessory shall not recover damages within this statute, because no jury can be retourned to assesse them.

3 Mar. 120. Dier. If one be appealed as accessory to two principals, one of the principals is acquited, the accessory shall recover no damages untill the other principall be acquited.

41 Ass. 24. If the plaintiffe in an appeale be non-suit, and the defendant is
46 E. 3. Coro. arraigned at the suit of the king, and acquited, he shall recover his
102. 14 H. 7. 2. damages by this act, for the words be, *Vel ad sectam appellantis vel*
9 H. 5. 2. *domini regis*, but this suit of the king must be intended upon the
Stamf. Pl. Cor. 135. F.N.B. 214. appeale after non-suit, for an acquitall upon an indictment is not within this statute.

9 H. 5. 2. For *debito modo acquietatus*, see 9 H. 5. 2. that the defendant
20 E. 4. 5. being acquited by verdict, yet if his life was never in jeopardy
9 H. 4. 2. either in the originall, or proces, though it be in default of the plaintiffe himselfe, yet is he not *debito modo acquietatus* within this statute.

Pasch. 15 Eliz. Coram rege. Dier Manuscript. The wife of Copleston brought an appeale of murder against Stowell, and five of his servants as principals by being present, aiding and abetting Stowell to commit the murder, and Stowell appeared, against whom the plaintiffe declared with a *simul cum* of his five servants, and Stowell pleaded not-guilty, and processe was continued against the other five, and by verdict it was found that Stowell killed Coplestone in his owne defence, whereupon he was acquited, and had his pardon of grace; and it was resolved by all the judges of England, that this acquitall of him was in law an acquitall of all the other five that were charged as principals by being present, aiding, and abbetting, and Stowell could not upon this statute recover damages for the cause before remembred.

27 Ass. 25. If the defendant plead that there is a nearer heire, and issue thereupon taken, and found for the defendant, he is discharged of the action, but is not acquited of the felony within the purview of
17 E. 2. Coro. this statute; so it is if the defendant be discharged by clergy, he
386. is not acquited within the purview of this statute.

If the defendant wage battell, and the plaintiffe demurre upon it, and it is adjudged against the plaintiffe, the defendant is discharged of the appeale, but hee is not acquited, untill he be acquited of the fact at the suit of the king.

22 E. 3. Coro. *Damna appellatis secundum discret' justiciar' habito respectu ad pri-*
276. Artic. *sonam.*] Though this branch bee generall, yet every appellee shall
Cleri. c. 16. not upon his acquitall recover damages, for if a monke be appeal-
Lib. 9. fol. 73. ed, or a feme covert be appealed alone without her husband and
D. Husseyes case. acquited, they cannot recover any damages by this act in respect
Lib. 11. fol. 77. Magd. Coll. case. of their disability, for the generall words of this act doth not
12 R. 2. judg. enable any to recover damages that thereunto was disabled by law.
108. But if an appeale bee brought against the husband and wife, and they

they be acquitted, damages ſhall be given to the huſband alone for his damage, and to the huſband and wife for the damage of the wife.

And where ſeverall perſons be acquited, the damages muſt be ſeverall, for the words of the ſtatute be *habito reſpectu ad perſonam.*

But then may be demaunded, what remedy hath the monke or feme covert being ſolely appealed: the anſwer is, that they have no remedy by this ſtatute, but the abbot and monke, and the huſband and wife may have a writ of conſpiracy at the common law. Tr. 30 E. 1. Rot. 2. London. 8 H. 6. 5, 6. 24 E. 3. 73.

Whenſoever any is acquited by verdict, and yet his life was never in jeopardy, either by reaſon of the erronious proces, or originall, or otherwiſe, though this be within the letter of the law, yet it is out of the meaning, and therefore the defendant in that caſe ſhall recover no damages. 9 H. 5. 2. ubi ſupra.

(5) *Ad infamiam ſuam.*] For a mans fame is above all things to be repaired.

Omnia ſi perdas, famam ſervare memento:
Que ſemel amiſſa, poſtea nullus eris. Cato.

(6) *Et ſi forte hujuſmodi appellatores non habeant, &c. inquiratur per quorum abettum.*] If the defendant in an appeale be tried before juſtices of *niſi prius*, albeit they have but *delegatam poteſtatem*, yet ſhall they inquire of the inſufficiency of the plaintiffe, and of the abbettors, and the words of this act are, *Quod juſtic' coram quibus auditum fuerit appellum et terminatum*; but that great over-ruler *experientia* hath ruled, and over-ruled it by precedents, that they cannot give judgement for the damages. 3 E. 2. Action ſur leſtat. 28. 22 E. 4. 19. 10 E. 4. 14. Dier, 3 Mar. 120. Tr. 30 E. 1. Coram rege. Rot. 2. London.

This inſufficiency of the plaintiffe in the appeale muſt be found by the jury, and cannot come in by the averment of the party, and ſo it is in other like caſes.

But here it may be demanded, What if the plaintiffe in the appeale be ſufficient for part of the damages, and not for all, may not the defendant by this act recover part againſt the plaintiffe, and part againſt the abbettors? And it is reſolved that he muſt recover either all againſt the plaintiffe, or all againſt the abbettors, and not by parcels, ſo as if the plaintiffe be not ſufficient for the whole, the defendant ſhall recover the whole againſt the abbettors, for *prædicta damna et omnia damna*, are all one. 8 E. 4. 3. 8 H. 5. 6. 17 E. 2. Cor. 386. 26 H. 8. 3, 4. Tr. 30 E. 1. ubi ſup.

It is a certain concluſion upon theſe words of the ſtatute, that where damages ſhall not be recovered againſt the plaintiffe, there none ſhall bee recovered againſt the abbettors; alſo where the plaintiffe is ſufficient and ſo found by the jury, the abbettors ſhall not be inquired of.

(7) *Abbettator per malitiam.*] Abbettors were found (upon the acquitall of the defendant) by name, *Et quod procuraverunt, inſtigaverunt et abbettaverunt prædictum querentem ad capiendum et proſequendum appellum prædictum in forma prædicta*, and ſaid not *per malitiam*, and yet allowed of. But *nota* the ſurer way is to purſue the words, *falſo et per malitiam*, according to this act. 3 Mar. Dier, 120. Tr. 30 E. 1. ubi ſupra.

(8) *Per breve de judicio ad ſectam appellati diſtringatur, &c.*] This writ is given in lieu of the writ of conſpiracy at the common law, the abbettors comming in upon this proces may travers the abbetment, becauſe they were eſtrangers to the verdict, and if the Reg. 34. 8 E. 4. 3. 17 E. 2. Cor. 386. Tr. 19 E. 2. Coram rege. Rot. 82. 40 E. 3. dam. 77.

Tr. 30 E. 1. ubi supra. 22 E. 4. Coro. 45.

the defendant that sueth the distresse be non-suit, yet may he have a new writ, and it is not peremptory to him. And albeit the jury finde neither the time, nor the place where the abbetment was, yet if they finde the abbettors, it is sufficient, for when the plaintiffe appeareth, the defendant may shew time and place in good time.

[387]

46 E. 3. Coron. 102. 3 E. 2. Action sur lestatut. 28. 8 H. 6. cap. 10. F.N.B. 115. i. Kelwey, 21. Tr. 30 E. 1. Coram rege. Rot. 2. Hil. 35 E. 1. ib. Rot. 19. Tr. 19 E. 2. ibid. 82. Mich. 14 H. 7. ib. Rot. 76. Tr. 14 H. 7. ib. Rot. 74. Hil. 10 H. 7. ib. Rot. 38. Mich. 19 H. 7. ib. Rot. 27. Liure de entries. Rast. 56. & 297. Stamf. Pl. Cor. 297.

Note in 46 E. 3. the court granted first a *venire facias*, and then distresse, but it seemeth that the processe given by the statute is a distresse infinite.

But if the jury give too small damages, it being but an enquest of office, the plaintife may have an originall writ of abbetment, and count to greater damages. *Vide* 8 H. 6. cap. 10.

Note reader, that judiciall precedents, and the right entries of pleas upon this (or any other) statute are good interpreters of the same, and of questions that have been, or may be moved thereupon.

(9) *Nec jaceat de cætero appellatori in appello de morte hominis essonium.*] The defendant that is appealed of the death of man ought to have convenient expedition, and not to be detained in prison, or to live under the infamy of a murtherer longer than there is cause: and this statute was chiefly made for the benefit of the defendant.

Vide the statute of 1 E. 3. cap. 7. parliament' primo, & statut' de 1 R. 2. cap. 13.

CAP. XIII.

QUIA etiam vicecomites multotiens fingentes aliquos coram eis in turnis suis indictatos de furtis, et aliis malefactis (1), *capiunt homines non culpabiles, nec legitimo modo indictatos, et eos imprisonant, ut ab eis pecuniam extorqueant* (3); *cum legitimo modo per duodecim juratores non fuerint indictati: statutum est, quod vic' in turnis suis, et alibi, cum inquirere habeant de malefactoribus per preceptum regis* (4), *vel ex officio suo, per legales homines* (2) *ad minus duodecim faciant inquisitiones suas de hujusmodi malefactoribus, qui hujusmodi inquisitionibus sigilla sua apponant* (5), *et illos quos per hujusmodi inquisitiones invenerint culpabiles, capiant et imprisonent, secundum quod alias fieri consuevit. Et si aliquos aliter imprisonaverint, quam per hujusmodi inquisitiones indictatos, habeant hujusmodi imprisonati*

FORASMUCH as sheriffs, feigning many times certain persons to be indicted before them in their turns of felonies and other trespasses, do take men that are not culpable nor lawfully indicted, and imprison them, and do exact money from them, whereas they were not lawfully indicted by twelve jurors; it is ordained, that sheriffs in their turns, and in other places where they have power to enquire of trespassors by the king's precept, or by office, shall cause their inquests of such malefactors to be taken by lawful men, and by twelve at the least, which shall put their seals to such inquisitions; and those that shall be found culpable by such inquests, they shall take and imprison, as they have used aforetimes to do. And if they do imprison other than such as have been indicted by

imprisonati actionem suam per breve de imprisonamento (6) *versus vicecom', sicut haberent versus quamcunque aliam personam, qui eos imprisonaret sine warranto. Et sicut dictum est de vicecom' observetur de quolibet balivo libertatis* (7).

by inquest, the parties imprisoned shall have their action by a writ of imprisonment against the sheriffs, as they should have against any other person that should imprison them without warrant. And as it hath been said of sheriffs, so shall it be observed of every bailiff of franchise.

(2 Inst. 387. 1 E. 3. stat. 2. c. 7. 1 E. 4. c. 2.)

(1) *Quia etiam vicecomites multotiens fingentes aliquos coram eis in turnis suis indictatos de furtis et aliis malefactis.*] Two things are provided, or rather declared by this act. Fleta, li. 2. c. 45.

1. *Per legales homines ad minus* 12. *faciant inquisitiones.* 1.

That indictments *in tournes* ought to be found by 12. at the least.

(2) *Legales homines.*] More shall be said hereof when we come to the eight and thirtieth chapter of this parliament, and the ninth chapter of Articuli super Chartas. [388] F.N.B. 165.

(3) *Ut ab eis pecuniam extorqueant.*] This is the greatest injustice, when the innocent under colour of justice, whereby he ought to be protected, is oppressed, and wrought to give money to redeem his vexation: three things (it is said) overthrew the flourishing estate of the Roman empire, *Latens odium, juvenile consilium, et privatum lucrum.* Vide cap. Itineris.

By this act you may see that justice was pretended, and sordid lucre intended, which this act in reliefe of the innocent provideth to prevent.

(4) *Per præceptum regis.*] That is, by the kings writ or commission; but thereupon grew so many evils and mischiefes for the singular profit of the sherifes, that by a latter statute it is provided that no such writs or commissions should be granted to them; so as at this day the sherifes cannot proceed in those cases *per præceptum regis.* See hereafter how this power *ex officio* is restrained. 28 E. 3. cap. 9. F.N.B. 92. c. 144. l. 250. a.

(5) *Qui hujusmodi inquisitionibus sigilla sua apponant.*] The 2. part is, that the jurors do put their seals to the inquisitions or indictments. 2.

By a latter statute, these indictments are to be by a roll indented, whereof one part is to remain with the indictors, and the other part with him that takes the enquest. 1 E. 3. Parliam. 2. cap. 17.

This act of 1 E. 3. doth extend to presentments or indictments, not onely in tourns, but in leets also, and the like.

See the statute of 1 R. 3. of what quality, hability, and livelyhood, the indictors in tournes and leets ought to be. 1 R. 3. ca. 4.

But such corrupt and partiall proceedings upon presentments and indictments before the sherife *ex officio*, were, notwithstanding all these provisions in tourns and leets, continued, untill by the statute of 1 E. 4. the power of them, save only to take presentments and indictments, and to deliver the same to the justices of peace at the next sessions of the peace, &c. is taken away; and by that act authority is given to justices of peace, to award processe upon all such 1 E. 4. c. 2. 4 E. 4. 31. 8 E. 4. 5. lib. 9. fol. 96. Strata Marcel.a.

ſuch preſentments and indictments delivered to them, &c. which is to be intended of ſuch as be lawfull.

(6) *Per breve de impriſonament'.*] This act doth not onely preſcribe a form for the ſherife to purſue, but giveth the party remedy againſt the ſherife, if he purſueth not the form of the act; for, *Non obſervata forma infertur adnullatio actus.*

(7) *Et ſicut dictum eſt de vicecom', obſervetur de quolibet balivo libertatis.*] Every bailife of franchiſe, that is, of leets, and views of frankpledge, which are exempted out of the ſherifes tourn, and are the franchiſes here intended.

STATUTUM de WESTMINST. SECUNDO.

CAP. XIV.

CUM de vasto facto in hæreditate alicujus per custodes, tenentes in dotem, per legem Angliæ, vel aliter ad terminum vitæ, vel annorum, consueverit fieri breve de prohibitione vasti (1), *per quod breve multi fuerunt in errore, credentes quod illi qui vastum fecerint, non habuerint necesse respond', nisi tamen de vasto facto post prohibitionem eis directam, dominus rex (ut hujusmodi error de cætero tollatur) statuit, quod de vasto quocunque ad nocumentum alicujus facto, non fiat de cætero breve de prohibitione* (2); *sed breve de summonitione, ita quod ille, de quo queritur, respondeat de vasto facto quocunque tempore. Et si post summonitionem non venerit, attachietur, et post attachiamentum distringatur, et post districtionem, si non venerit, mandetur vicecom'* (3), *quod in propria persona, assumptis secum xii, &c. accedat ad locum vastatum* (4); *et inquirat de vasto facto* (5), *et retornet inquisitionem. Postquam retornata fuerit inquisitio, procedatur ad judicium, secundum quod continetur in statuto prius edito apud Glocest', cap. 5. de vasto,* 20 *E.* 1.

WHEREAS for waste done in the inheritance of any person, by guardians, tenants in dower, tenants by the courtesie of England, or otherwise for term of life, or years, a writ of prohibition of waste hath been used to be granted, by which writs many were deceived, thinking that such as had done the waste should not need to answer but only for waste done after the prohibition to them directed; our lord the king, to remove from henceforth this error, hath ordained, that of all manner of waste done to the damage of any person, there shall from henceforth be no writ of prohibition awarded, but a writ of summons, so that he of whom complaint is shall answer for waste done at any time; and if he come not after the summons, he shall be attached, and after the attachment he shall be distrained; and if he come not after the distress, the sheriff shall be commanded that in proper person he shall take with him twelve, &c. and shall go to the place wasted, and shall enquire of the waste done, and shall return an inquest, and after the inquest returned, they shall pass unto judgement, like as it is contained in the statute of Gloucester.

(Fitz. Waste, 129, 130, 131. 134, 135, 136, 137. Regist. 72, &c. 1 Brownl. 240. Dyer, 204. 3 Cro. 18. 6 Ed. 1. stat. 1. c. 5. 20 Ed. 1. stat. 2. Rast. 697.)

(1) *Cum de vasto facto in hæreditate alicujus per custodes, &c. consueverit fieri breve de prohibitione vasti,* &c.] This errour herein recited is hereby cleerly confuted, and hereof you may read more in the statute of Gloc.

Gloc. cap. 5. 4 E. 3. Waste 129. 15 H. 3. ibid. 130. Regist. 172. F.N.B. 55.

(2) *Non fiat de cætero breve de prohibitione.*] By this the prohibition of waste, whereupon an attachment did lye, &c. is taken away, and in lieu thereof an action called here a writ of summons, because the writ beginneth, *Si A. fecerit te securum, &c. tunc summoneas per bonos summonitores, &c.* is given.

(3) *Ita quod respondeat de vasto facto quocunque tempore. Et si post summonitionem non venerit, attachietur, et post attachiamentum distringatur, et post districtionem, si non venerit, mandetur vicecomiti,* &c.] If the defendant be retourned *nihil, &c.* so as peradventure he was never summoned, nor any other writ served, whereby he might have notice, yet a writ of inquiry of waste shall be awarded by this branch; for here it is not specified that issues should be retourned, &c. but generally and by the writ, the waste shall be inquired of by the oath of twelve men, where the defendant or any for him may attend if he will, and the jurors may finde against the plaintife.

21 H. 6. 56. 34 H. 6. 44. 11 H. 6. 3. 3 H. 6. 29.

[390]

7 H 4. 15. 12 H. 4. 3, 4.

Note the words here be, *et post districtionem, si non venerit, mandetur vicecomiti, &c.* So as if the defendant appear upon the distresse, and plead, and after make default, the plaintife shall not by this branch have a writ to inquire of the waste, because it is out of the words and purview of this act.

(4) *Quod in propria persona sua assumptis secum duodecim accedat ad locum vastatũ.*] Here are three things to be observed:

a Regist. judi. 23. 25. 27. 2 H. 4. 2. 3 H. 6. 29. 11 H. 6. 6. 11 H. 4. 82. lib. 4. fo. 65. Fulwoods case, lib. 8. fol. 52. Althams case.

1. [a] That the sherife ought to go in proper person, for that, though in *rei veritate* he is no judge, yet this writ is in nature of a commission unto him, and he is in *loco judicis*, and therefore he ought to go in *propria persona.* If the sherife upon this writ return *quod mandavi balivo libertatis, &c. qui mihi nullam dedit responsionem,* the return is insufficient, because by the writ (as the book saith) he is a judge, and hath power to enter into the franchise.

b F N.B. 16. 7. c. Regist. judic. ubi sup. 41 E. 3. 7. 48 E. 3. 19. 2 H. 4. 2. 3 H. 6. 29. 21 H. 6. 56. 34 H. 6. 12.

2. [b] Where some have holden, that the sherife may inquire upon this writ by the oath of 6 or 8 persons, it appeareth, that there ought not to be under 12, for the words of this branch are, *assumptis secum* 12, yet this is but an inquest of office, for it is taken *sans mise des parties*, that is without any issue joyned.

c 16 E. 3. Retorn de Viscont 82. 34 H. 6. 42. 44.

3. [c] The sherife must go *ad locum vastatum*, together with the jurors, and view the same; for, *ista cadunt potius sub visu, quam sub auditu.*

d 16 E. 3. ubi sup. 34 H. 6. ubi sup.

(5) *Et inquirat de vasto facto.*] [d] If the waste be assigned in divers towns, the sherife and the jurors must view (as hath been said) all the places wasted in every of the towns, but he may inquire thereof in any one of the towns; and this copulative doth so knit the words together, as he cannot inquire of it in a forein town.

See more of this matter in the exposition upon the statute of Gloc. cap. 5.

CAP.

CAP. XV.

IN omni casu quo minores infra ætatem implacitare possunt: concessum est, quod si hujusmodi minores elongati sint, quo minus personaliter sequi possint, propinquiores amici admittantur ad sequendum pro eis. Westminst' 1. cap. 47.

IN every case whereas such as be within age may sue, it is ordained, that if such within age be eloined, so that they cannot sue personally, their next friends shall be admitted to sue for them.

(Dyer, 104. 2 Ed. 3. 16. 40 Ed. 3. 16. Bro. Gardein, 13. 22. 24, 25, 26, 27. Regist. 78. 3 Ed. 1. c. 47.)

The act of W. 1. touching this matter was particular, but this act is generall. W. 1. cap. 47.

Upon this statute, whether the infant be esloigned or no, he shall sue by *prochein amy*, for the esloignment is put in this act, to shew what mischief may fall out in this case; and therefore when a serjeant offered, that oath should be made of the esloignment of the heir, the judge said, he would take it upon his honesty; but if the surmise that the plaintife is within age be untrue, and that the plaintife is of full age, his admittance by *prochein amy* is errour. Regist. 78. 28 Ass. 22. 2 E. 3. 16. 40 E. 3. 6. 13 E. 3. Attorney 76. 34 H. 6. 4. 20 E. 4. 2. F.N.B. 27. 27 H. 8. fol. 11.

See before in the exposition upon the 40 chapter of W. 1. where this matter is handled at large; and observe well our books, where many times a gardein is taken for a *prochein amy*, and a *prochein amy* for a gardein.

This act extends not to an ideot. 33 H. 6. 28. F.N.B. 24. g.

CAP. XVI. [391]

IN casu quo alicui minori descendat hæreditas (2) ex parte patris, qui tenuit de uno domino, et ex parte matris quæ tenuit de alio domino (1), dubitatio hucusque extitit de maritagio hujusmodi minoris, ad quem de duobus dominis pertineat. Concordatum est, quod ille dominus de cætero habeat maritagium (3), de quo antecessor suus prius fuit feoffatus, non habito respect' ad sexum, nec ad quantitatem tenementi, sed solummodo ad antiquius feoffamentum (4) per servitium militare.

IN case where inheritance descendeth to one within age of the father's side, that held of one lord, and the mother's side that held of another lord, there hath been hitherto doubt, for the marriage of such an heir, to which of the two lords it should belong; it is agreed, that the same lord shall from henceforth have the marriage of whom the child's ancestor was first infeoffed, not having respect to the sex, nor to the quantity of the land, but onely to the more ancient feoffment by knights service.

(44 Ed. 3. f. 15. Dyer, 11. 5 Ed. 3. f. 4. Bro. Gard. 114, 115, 116. Fitz. Prerog. 23, 24. Fitz. Gard. 2. 3. 16. 19. 27. 36. 46. 53. 81. 86. 115. 134. 139. Stat. 12 Car. 2. c. 24.)

4 E. 3. receit 46. Albeit this act putteth a case onely where one inheritance descends on the part of the father, and when another descends on the part of the mother, yet this statute extends to all cases of priority.

By these words in the act, [*non habito respectu ad sexum nec ad quantitatem*] the doubts at the common law are here mentioned: the first, that some did hold opinion that the part of the father being
14 E. 3. gard 37. 8 H. 3. gard 139. *digniori de sanguine*, the worthier blood should be preferred; others did hold opinion that if the lord of the land of the part of the mother, first happed or seised the ward, he should have it, and that *melior est conditio possidentis*.

Lastly, some did hold that the tenure by the greater quantity and value should be preferred: all which doubts are cleared by the purview of this act.

11 E. 2. c. 2. 21 E. 3. 41. 11 E. 3. gard. Statham. 5 E. 3. 4. 12 E 3. Prærog. 23. 24 E. 3. 31. 65. 18 E. 3. 29. 12 H. 4. 25. 14 H. 4. 9. 9 H. 4. 4. simile.

(1) *De uno domino, &c. de alio domino,* &c.] This act extendeth not to the king, because before the making of this act hee was to have the wardship of the body though the land were holden of him by posteriority; and so it is, if the king graunt that seigniory for life, the grauntee shall have the same benefit, in respect that the reversion remaine in the king: but if the king graunteth the fee-simple to another, there the lord by priority shall have the wardship, and the tenure by priority is revived, for the king had the wardship in respect of his person and prerogative.

(2) *Alicui minori descendat hæreditas.*] This act is to be understood of a descent from one auncestor to one heire, and not from divers auncestors to one heire, nor from one auncestor to divers heires, nor from one auncestor to one heire at severall times.

As if a man seised in fee of the mannor of D. of the part of the father holden of A. by knights service, and of the mannor of S. of the part of the mother holden of B. by knights service, and dieth, his heire within age, this case (as by the letter thereof it appeareth) is within the scope and purview of this statute; for if the father holdeth land by knights service, and the mother hold land also by knights service, which of them die first, the lord of whom the land
24 E. 3. 26. 45. 15 E. 4. 14. 3 H. 7. 15. is holden, albeit there be but one heire to both, shall have the wardship of the body, which being once vested, shall not after be devested in respect of any priority, no though it were in the king's case.

Vet. N.B. 97. b. The tenant maketh a feoffement in fee upon condition of the land holden by priority, and dieth seised of the land holden by posteriority his heire within age, the lord by posteriority seiseth
[392] the body, the condition is broken, the heire entreth into the land holden by priority, the lord by posteriority shall retain the wardship, for seeing that both descended not at one time, it is out of this statute.

(3) *Habet maritagium.*] The lord by priority shall have the wardship of the body, for the lord by posteriority shall have the wardship of the land holden of him, as well as the lord by priority of the land holden of him, but the wardship of the body being intire, and which both cannot have, of right belongeth to the lord
44 E. 3. 15. by priority by this act, and therefore if the lord by priority waive the wardship of the body, and refuse to take the same, yet the lord by posteriority cannot take advantage of it, for by this act the wardship of the body belongeth to the lord by priority and to no other.

(4) De

(4) *De quo antecessor suus fuerit feoffatus, habito respectu solummodo ad antiquius feoffamentum.*] Here it appeareth that the feoffement of the tenancy doth onely make the priority, and not the change of the seigniory. 14 E. 3. gard 37.

But where this statute speaketh of a feoffement, it is to be understood of any other assurance or conveyance of the tenancy.

Per antiquius feoffamentum, are not to be understood of the feoffement of the lord upon the creation of the seigniory, but of the feoffement made by the tenant of the land. 3 E. 3. gard 19.

To illustrate the meaning of this law by examples:

One holdeth Black acre of A. by knights service, and White acre of B. by knights service, *anno* 10 reg. Eliz. infeoffeth C. of Black acre, and 20 reg. Eliz. infeoffeth C. of White acre, who dieth his heire within age, B. shall have the wardship of the body, for C. had Black acre *per antiquius feoffamentum.*

So it is if the heire of C. die seised, and both acres had descended to his heire, he had holden Black acre by priority, that is *per antiquius feoffamentum* made to his auncestor, and so from heire to heire so long as both acres continue in that line by descent.

On the lords side the priority shall not onely continue as long as the seigniories continue in the lines of the lords, but also the change of the seigniory maketh no alteration, and therefore though the lord of whom Black acre is holden alien the seigniory, yet if he taketh it back to him again, Black acre shall be still holden of him by priority, the assignee of the lord by priority shall take advantage of it as well as the grauntor.

But if the tenant had aliened Black acre to another, and acquired it backe againe, yet shall he hold it by posteriority, for now he holdeth White acre, *per antiquius feoffamentum*; so as the feoffement of the land (as hath been said) doth make the priority, and that feoffement must be understood of the immediate feoffement, but the priority of the land doth attend on the seigniory, into whose hands soever it commeth. Temps E. 1. gard. 134. F.N.B. 142. f. 13 E. 1. Cor. Rege Rot. 40. Eborum. 2 E. 2. gard. 2. 7 E. 3. 11. 34, 35. 13 E. 3. gard. 39.

If there be lord, mesne, and tenant, and the mesne hold by priority, the tenant in a writ of mesne doth forejudge the mesne; in this case the mesnalty is extinct, and the tenant shall be answerable to the lord, *de eisdem serviciis et consuetudinibus quæ prius facere debuit prædictus medius*; in this case the tenant shall hold by priority: for 1. he shall hold *per antiquius feoffamentum*; 2. The mesne in supposition of law was said to hold the land. 3. The statute of W. 2. that give the forejudger, provideth that he shall hold by the same services, and customes, and in such sort, as it may be done *sine prejudicio alterius*, and this should be to the prejudice of the lord by priority, if he should lose that benefit. 18 E. 3. 29. b. 7 E. 3. 11. 63, 64. 11 E. 3. gard. 115. 14 E. 3. gard. 37. 33 E. 3. ibid. 12. F.N.B. 142. 13 E. 3. gard. 38.

In a ravishment of ward the defendant pleaded that the father of the infant held the mannor of D. of him the defendant by knights service, *et quod tenuit* * *manerium illud de ipso per antiquius feoffamentum, quam pater suus tenuit manerium de A. de modo querente*; and this was agreed to be a good plea without shewing of whose feoffement he held by priority, but generally, which is worthy of observation. 7 E. 3. 11. 34, 35. 21 E. 3. 11. 19. 4 E. 3. 37. 30 E. 3. 7. 13 E. 3. gard. 39. 30 E. 3. 7. *[393]

A. holds land of B. by priority, and other land of C. by posteriority, and in eoffeth D. of both: this case is out of this statute, because he commeth to both the lands at one time, so as he holds not 8 E. 3. 57. 18 E. 3. 29. Vet. N.B. 97. F.N.B. 142. f. Bro. gard. 115.

not either of them *per antiquius feoffamentum, sed per unum et idem feoffamentum*; and therefore if he dieth, his heire within age, the lord which first seiseth the body in this case shall have it.

CAP. XVII.

IN itinere justic' (2) *non admittatur de cætero essonium de malo lecti* (1) *de tenemento in eodem comitatu* (3), *nisi ille, qui se facit essoniari, veraciter sit infirmus, quia si excipiatur à petente, quod tenens non est infirmus, nec in illo statu, quo minus venire potuit coram justiciariis, admittatur ejus calumnia. Et si hoc per inquisitionem convinci poterit, vertatur illud essonium in defaltam. Nec jaceat de cætero illud essonium in brevi de recto inter duos clamantes per eundem descensum* (4).

IN the circuit of the justices an essoin *de malo lecti* shall not be from henceforth allowed for lands in the same shire, unless he that caused himself to be essoined be sick indeed; for if the demandant except, that the tenant is not sick, nor in such plight but that he may come before the justices, his exception shall be admitted. And if it can be so proved by enquest, the essoin shall be turned to a default, And from henceforth such essoin shall not lie in a writ of right between two claiming by one descent.

(Fitz. Essoin, 176. 186, 187, 188, 189, 190. 192, 193, 194. 196, 197. Regist. 8.)

See Marlb. c. 12. We have before in generall spoken of the five kindes of essoines, but reserved to speak more particularly of this kinde of *essoine de malo lecti* in the exposition of this chapter, as in his proper place.

20 E. 3. essoine 27. (1) *De malo lecti.*] This essoine differeth from all other kindes of essoines, for this essoine lieth only *ad certum diem*, for he ought to appeare *ad primum diem, &c. et ad tertium diem il avera cest essoine.*

And in this case he shall have two essoiners, and the one shall cast the essoine, and the other shall sweare, that he saw the party sick, &c.

The mischiefe before this act was, that the adverse partie could not take issue, that he that offered to be essoined *de malo lecti* was in health, and not sick, and try it by a jury; but it was inquired by foure knights retourned for that purpose by the sheriffe, *si fuer' languidùs aut non*, and if they found that he was not *languidus*, then he should have fifteene dayes after to appeare, so as the party was delayed thereby fifteene dayes, and all the time before, and this was mischievous: for remedy whereof this act provideth, that the party shall take issue, that he is not *languidus*, which if it be so found 3 H. 3. essoine 186. it shall turne to a default; and if it be found that he is *languidus*, then he ought to have time to appeare a yeare and a day, and before he commeth out, he ought to have a writ *de licentia surgendi, &c.* as it appeareth by the authorities cited in the exposition of the said 12 chapter of Marlebridge.

(2) *In itinere justic'.*] Although justices in eyre are here particularly mentioned, yet this act being a beneficiall law to ouste delayes

delayes is taken by equity, and doth extend to the court of common pleas.

(2) * *De malo lecti.*] Sufficient hereof hath been spoken, onely this may be added that this essoine lieth not for an attourney, for no essoine shall be cast for an attourney but the common essoine onely.

(3) *De tenementis in eodem com'.*] This essoine *de malo lecti* doth onely lie in a writ of right right, and not in a writ of right in his nature. 15 H. 3. essoin 196.

(4) *Clamantes per eundem descensum.*] This essoine *de malo lecti* is wholly ousted in a writ of right between two claiming by the same descent. 15 H. 3. essoin 191, 192. 194. 20 E. 3. essoine 27.

As between two parceners either at the common law or by custome, &c. But if one coparcener claime the land by feoffement made by her auncester in fee, now if the other coparcener deforce her of this land in a writ of right brought against her sister, she may be essoined *de malo lecti*, and so between two brethren: so as this statute is intended where they claime the land *per eundem descensum*, and not where they derive their blood onely *per eundem descensum*; for in the case put before where they claime by severall titles, they may joyne the mise by graund assise, or by battell, which they cannot doe when they claim by one descent. Bract. l. 2. fo. 66. Britton, fo. 190. 13 E. 1. droit 51. F.N.B. 10. a.

CAP. XVIII.

CUM debitum fuerit recuperatum (1), *vel in curia regis recognitum* (2), *vel damna adjudicata, sit de cætero in electione illius* (3) *qui sequitur pro hujusmodi debito, aut damnis, sequi breve quod vicecom' fieri faciat* (4) *de terris et catallis debitoris, quod vicecom' liberet ei omnia catalla debitoris, (exceptis bobus et afris carucæ)* (5) *et medietatem terræ suæ* (6), *quousque debitum fuerit levatum* (7) *per rationabile precium et extentum* (8). *Et si ejiciatur de illo tenemento, habeat recuperare per breve novæ disseisinæ, et postea per breve de redisseisina* (9), *si necesse fuerit.*

WHEN debt is recovered or knowledged in the king's court, or damages awarded, it shall be from henceforth in the election of him that sueth for such debt or damages, to have a writ of *fieri facias* unto the sheriff for to levy the debt of the lands and goods; or that the sheriff shall deliver to him all the chattels of the debtor (saving onely his oxen and beasts of his plough) and the one half of his land, until the debt be levied upon a reasonable price or extent. And if he be put out of that tenement, he shall recover by a writ of novel disseisin, and after by a writ of redisseisin, if need be.

Fleta, li. 2. cap. 55. See the first part of the Institutes, sect. 504. verb. per Elegit. (Hob. 57. 3 Bulstr. 320. Dyer, 306. 373. 3 Rep. 12. 4 Rep. 65, 74. 5 Rep. 87, 88. 90. Fitz. Extent, 13. Fitz. Process, 51. Fitz. Execut. 35. 37. 41. 46. 66. 85, &c. Rast. 72. 327. Regist. 299. Cro. Car. 44. 2 Leon. 84. 88.)

Vide Mag. Char. ca. 8. Dier 23 El. 304. b.

At the common law where a ſubject ſued execution upon a judgement for debt or damages, he ſhould not have the body of the defendant, or his land in execution (unleſſe it were in ſpeciall caſes,) and the reaſon of the law was: that the body in caſe of debt ſhould not be detained in priſon, but be at liberty, not onely to follow his owne affaires and buſineſſe, but alſo to ſerve the king and his country when need ſhould require; nor to take away the poſſeſſion of his lands in that caſe, for that would hinder the following of his huſbandry and tillage, which is ſo beneficiall to the common wealth, whereof you may reade at large in ſir William Herberts caſe.

Lib. 3. fo. 11, 12, &c. Sir Will. Herberts caſe.

But by the common law he ſhould have execution in that caſe onely of his goods and chattels, and of his corne, and other preſent profit that grew upon his land, to which purpoſe the law gave him two ſeverall writs to be ſued within the yeare, one a *levari facias*, [395] whereby the ſheriffe was commaunded, *quod de terris et catallis ipſius A. levari fac'*, and the other called a *fieri fac'*, which alſo was onely *de bonis et catallis*.

Now the common law being underſtood, let us peruſe the words of the act.

(1) *Cum debitum fuerit recuperatum.*] That is, by judgement in an action of debt, or any action wherein damages are recovered.

(2) *Aut recognitum.*] That is, by recogniſance knowledged in any court of record that hath power to receive the ſame.

49 E. 3. 38, 39. 5 E. 3. 26. 35. 34 E. 3 Execution 129. 36 H. 6. 2, 3. 10 E. 3. 34, 35. F.N.B. 267. c. lib. 3. fol. 65. Fulwoods caſe. 21 Aſſ. 15. 15 H. 7. 5. 20 E. 2. Execution Statham. 2 R. 3. 8. F.N.B. 267. b. Regiſt. 299. 15 H. 7. 15. 21 H. 7 19. 30 E. 3. 24. 31 E. 3. Proc. 52. 47 E. 3. 26. 50 E. 3. 4. 30 E. 3. Execution. Statham. 22 Aſſ. 43. 17 E. 4 4. b. 18 E. 4. 12. 34 H. 6. 20. 19 H. 6. 4. Lib. 3. fol. 65. Fulwoods caſe.

If two do knowledge a recogniſance of C. l. *quilibet eorum in ſolido*, that is, joyntly and ſeverally, the conuſee may ſue ſeverall *ſcire fac'* againſt the conuſors upon this recogniſance.

A ſpeciall recogniſance may by expreſſe words binde the lands of the conuſor in one county onely.

(3) *Sit in electione illius.*] This election ſhall the executors or adminiſtrators of the plaintiſe, or reconuſee have, albeit they be not named; and ſo likewiſe ſhall the ſucceſſor of the conuſee have alſo: but the executors ſhall not have execution of the judgement or recogniſance in the time of the teſtator, within the yeer, without ſuing a *ſcire facias*; but otherwiſe it is of a ſtatute, &c.

When the plaintiſe or conuſee prayeth an *elegit*, the entry is *quod elegit ſibi executionem fieri de omnibus catallis, et medietate terræ*; and the writ of *elegit* is *ac cum idem H. juxta ſtatutum inde editum* (meaning this ſtatute) *elegerit ſibi liberari pro prædict'* 20. *libris omnia catalla, et medietatem terræ ipſius R.* And therefore after the ſuing out of the *elegit*, the plaintiſe, that hath a judgement in an action of debt, cannot have a *capias*, &c.

(4) *Fieri facias.*] Here under theſe words is alſo the writ of *levari facias* included,

(5) *Vel quod vicecom' liberet ei omnia catalla, exceptis bobus et afris carucæ.*] The maior and aldermen of London take a recogniſance of 250 pounds to the chamberlain of the city of London, and his ſucceſſors according to the cuſtome for orphanage money; in this caſe the chamberlain for the time being may ſue out a precept in the nature of an *elegit* to a ſerjeant at mace, and miniſter of that court to do execution upon this act: and albeit the words of this ſtatute are, *quod vicecomes liberet*; yet being a beneficiall law, by equity it is extended to every other immediate officer to every other court of record.

If

[a] If the chattels be sufficient to pay the debt, and so may appear to the sherife, whereby he may satisfie the debt, then he ought not to extend the land for the residue; and all this appeareth by the writ of *elegit* framed upon this act.

(6) *Et medietatem terræ suæ,*] [b] This is to be understood of the half of such land as the defendant had at the time of the judgement given, or of the recognisance knowledged, unlesse it be conveyed away by fraud and covin to deceive his creditors, contrary to the statutes in that case provided.

[c] A man doth knowledge a recognisance of 100 pounds to be paid at five dayes; presently after the first day he may sue an *elegit* upon this act for 20 pounds, and have the moity of the land delivered unto him and when the second day is past, he may have another *elegit* for that 20 pounds, and have the moity of the remnant delivered to him, *et sic de cæteris*; for they be in effect in nature of severall judgements in law.

* And upon these words, *medietatem terræ suæ*, the sheriffe hath extended a term for yeers, and the like.

It is to be observed, that the generall words of this act doth not take away the priviledge which the law giveth to any person; and therefore no *elegit* upon this act shall be sued against the heir of the conusor during his minority.

Upon the equall construction of these words, if the conusor be seised of Black acre, White acre, and Green acre, and after the judgement given, or recognisance knowledged, infeoffeth A. of White acre, and B. of Blackacre, and retains Green acre to himself, in this case he may have the moity of Green acre, and never intermeddle with the rest: but he cannot extend the moity of the acre in the hand of any purchaser, except he extend also the moity of all the land subject to the judgement, or recognisance; and if he omit any, the extent shall be avoided in an *audita querela*: for where it is said in books, that each purchaser shall have contribution in that case, the meaning is, that such extent of part shall be avoided, and all the land extended and equally charged; and so it is if Green acre descend to an heir, the moity thereof may be onely extended, without dealing with any of the rest: so likewise if there be two or more conusors, the lands of them all must be extended; and hereof you may read at large in sir William Herberts case, all which are just and righteous expositions.

(7) *Quousque debitum fuer' levatum.*] The *elegit* framed upon these words, saith, *tenendum ut liberum tenementum, quousque debitum prædict' inde fuer' levatum*; and yet whensoever the party pay and satisfie the debt of record, he shall enter into his land: and so it is when the tenant by *elegit* is satisfied by the ordinary extent, the tenant of the land may enter. But if it be in respect of any casuall profit, to avoid the extent he must have a *scire fac'* in respect of the incertainty.

(8) *Per rationabile precium et extentum.*] *Per rationabile precium* doth refer to goods and chattels, and *rationabile extentum* referreth to lands.

And hereby is implyed, that this apprisement and extent upon the *elegit* must be found by enquest of 12 men, and so returned of record.

That

[a] Regist. 299.

[b] 19 E. 2. Execut. 249. 2 H. 4. 14. 42 E. 3. 11. 42 Ass. 17. 3 E. 3. Execut. 107. 10 E. 2. Execut. 137. 6 E. 3. 15. 17. 7 E. 3. 7. 8 E. 3. 15. 17. 17 E. 3. 15. 30 E. 3. 26. 50. 11 H. 4. 70. 9 H. 6. 58.

[c] 16 E. 2. Execut. 138. 2 E. 2. ibid. 120. 16 E. 3. Fieri fac. 4. F.N.B. 267. b. Vide Mich. 31 E. 3. fo. 50. b. in libro meo per Fisher & Finchden.

* [396]

31 Ass. 6. 38 Ass. 4. li. 8. f. 171. Sir George Fletwoods case. 44 E. 3. 16. 7 H. 6. 2. 29 Ass. 37. 29 E. 3. 50. Sir William Herberts case, ubi supra.

29 Ass. 37. 29 E. 3. 50. Sir William Herberts case, ubi supra.

13 E. 3. Scire fac. 17. 21 E. 3. 36. 17 E. 3. 43. 46 Ass. tit. Scire fac. 47 E. 3. 11. 31 E. 3. Extent 31. Regist. 299. Fulwoods case, ubi supra.

Dier 2 Mar. 100. lib. 4. fol. 74. Palmers case.

15 H. 7. 15. 9 H. 7. 9. 22 Ass. 44. 22 E. 3. 31. 44 E. 3. 10. Temps R. 2. Pl. ult. tit. Extent. 15 E. 3. Scire fac. 115. 31 E. 3. Extent 13. 15 E. 3. ibid. 17. 22 E. 3. Recovery in value 22. 7 H. 4. 19. 22 R. 2. Execution 165. Dier 6 E. 6. 73. Regist. Judic. 13, 14. 20. * 19 E. 2. Execut. 246. 28 Ass. p. 7. F.N.B. 189. I.

That shall be said a reasonable extent, which is found by the oath of 12. men, and returned by the sherife, and filed, and there can be no re-extent granted upon surmise, that it is more then the half in value, or the like, because it extendeth onely to a chattell in lands: but before the extent be filed, the court may examine the cause, and if there be found fraud, deceit, or partiality, they may stay the filing of that writ, and grant a new.

But see 22 R. 2. 165. in dower, and in case of free-hold in Hil. 13 E. 2. fol. 74. b. the case of the hospitall of T. a *scire facias* granted for the surplusage upon a return in value, and delivered to the sherife by *habere fac' ad valorem*, for that it concerneth an inheritance, and so it was adjudged. Note the diversity, the tenant by *elegit* may for reasonable cause hold over the ordinary course of the extent, * by a reasonable construction upon this statute.

(9) *Per breve novæ disseisinæ, et per breve de redisseisina*, &c.] The words of the writ of *elegit* (as hath been said) are, *tenendum ut liberum tenementum, &c.* because this statute giveth him remedy by assise, &c. but he hath but a chattell, and no freehold; and therefore it is said, *si ejiciatur:* and the writ saith similitudinary, *ut liberū tenement'*, in respect of the assise, &c.

This branch doth give the assise to the tenant by *elegit*, and yet his executors or administrators shall have it by the equity of this act; and so shall the executors or administrators of tenant by statute merchant, and tenant by statute staple.

[397]

Tr. 15 E. 2. coram Rege. Rot. 40. John Semers case.

I have seen a record of a judgement in the raign of E. 2. that the assignee of a tenant by *elegit* should not have an assise by the purview of this statute.

Mich. 31 E. 1. coram Rege Ebor. Ranulp. de Huntingfelds case.

Tenant by statute merchant of lands, which the conusor had in the right of his wife, brought an assise upon this statute, the tenant pleaded ancient demesne, &c. and so found, &c. and yet the plaintife had judgement; and the reason of the judgement given in the record is this, *Licet manerium prædict' sit de antiquo dominico coronæ, et tenementa in eodem manerio existentia per parvum breve tantum placitabilia, et prædict' Ranulphus Huntingfeld in cognitione prædict' quam fecit præd' I. in statuto obligavit tenementa præd' in summa ejusdem cognitionis, quæ quidem obligatio naturam eorundem tenementorum non mutat, nec est ad præjudicium domini, aut exhæredationem tenentium, ex quo tenementa illa per obligationem præd' solummodo onerata sunt ad certum tempus, post quod tempus reverti debent præd' Ranulpho et uxori suæ exonerata, tenend' ut prius, &c. Consideratum est, &c.*

† 7 H. 7. 1. li. 5. fol. 105. Aldens case. * 22 Ass. 45. li. 5. ubi supra. 22 Ass. ubi supra. 8 Ass. p. 35. 9 Ass. 9. 12 Ass. 18. 2 E. 3. 42. b. 41 E 3. 2. 49 E. 3. 23. 3 H. 6. 47.

By this judgement three things are to be observed; 1. that lands in ancient demesne may be † extended by the statute *de mercatoribus, anno* 13 E. 1. 2. That ancient demesne is * no plea in assise brought by tenant by statute merchant, upon this statute. 3. That in an assise of *novel disseisin* (which is *festinum remedium*) ancient demesne shall be tryed by the recognitors of the assise.

CAP.

CAP. XIX.

CUM poſt mortem alicujus decedentis inteſtati (1), *et obligati* (2) *aliquibus in debito* (3), *bona deveniant ad ordinarium diſponend'* (4), *obligetur de cætero ordinarius* (5), *ad reſpondendum de debitis quatenus bona defuncti ſufficiunt. Eodem modo quo executores reſpondere tenerentur, ſi teſtamentum feciſſent.*

WHEREAS after the death of a perſon dying inteſtate, which is bounden to ſome other for debts the goods come to the ordinary to be diſpoſed; the ordinary from henceforth ſhall be bound to anſwer the debts as far forth as the goods of the dead will extend, in ſuch ſort as the executors of the ſame party ſhould have been bounden, if he had made a teſtament.

(Dyer, 232. 5 Rep. 83. Fitz. Brief, 822. Fitz. Execut. 77.)

(1) *Decedentis inteſtati.*] There be divers kindes of inteſtates, one that make no will at all, another that make a will and executors, and they refuſe; in this caſe he dyeth *quaſi inteſtatus*, and theſe are within the purview of this act; therefore the ordinary is the perſon whom the law appointeth to have the charge or adminiſtration of the goods and chattels of the party that dyeth inteſtate, or *quaſi inteſtatus*; and juſtly did the law in this caſe appoint the ordinary: for the law preſumed, that he that had the care of his ſoul in his life time, would after his death have care of his temporall goods and chattels, to ſee them well diſpoſed and adminiſtred. Lib. 6. fol. 67. Sir Moyle Finches caſe.

And this act was made in affirmance of the common law, as hereafter upon the expoſition of ſome parts of the act ſhall appear. 17 E. 2. Br. 822. 24 E. 3. 55. 11 E. 3. Executors 77. 18 H. 6. 23. 9 E. 4. 33. 11 H. 7. 12. F.N.B. 120. lib. 5. fol. 83. Snellings caſe. Dier 8 Eliz. 247.

(2) *Et obligati.*] This is not onely intended of an obligation or deed in writing, but howſoever he was charged in law, as for rent upon a leaſe, or upon an *aſſumpſit*, or the like.

And after it is ſaid in this chapter, *obligetur de cætero ordinar'*, where *obligetur* is not taken, that he ſhould be bound in an obligation, but that he ſhould be charged, or ſubject to an action.

(3) *In debito.*] This act is not onely intended of that which is properly a debt, but of all duties, covenants, or juſt cauſes of actions, [398]
ſuch as might be brought againſt executors.

(4) *Bona deveniant ad ordinarium diſponend'.*] Unleſſe ſome of the goods or chattels came to the hands and poſſeſſion of the ordinary, he was not to be charged by the common law; but if they came to his hands, and he would neither adminiſter and pay the debts and duties himſelf, nor commit them over to the kin and friends of the inteſtate that would, the common law did charge him, and ſo doth this act which is made in affirmance of it.

If a man dye inteſtate, and a ſtranger taketh the goods, the ordinary ſhall not have an action of treſpaſſe for taking of them (unleſſe he had taken them into his poſſeſſion.) But the executor or adminiſtrator before ſeiſure may have an action of treſpaſſe. 7 H. 4. 18.

Neither

31 E. 3. ca. 11. 19 E. 3. Administ. 20. & 24. 7 H. 4. 18. F. tit. Tresp 97. 25 E. 3. Exec. 105. 11 H. 4. 71. 18 H. 6. 22. F.N.B. 92. a. Pl. com. 278.

Neither can the ordinary have any action of debt, covenant, or any other action which belonged to the inteftate; but thofe to whom the ordinary commit adminiftration may have all thefe actions by the ftatute of 31 E. 3. but before that ftatute, there was no remedy by law given to the adminiftrators to recover thofe things in action.

[a] 41 E. 3. 2. 11 H. 4. 72. lib. 5. fo. 82, 83. Snellings cafe.

[a] But by the common law, an action of debt did lye againft the adminiftrators, but it was by the name of executors untill the faid ftatute of 31 E. 3.

[b] 12 R. 2. Adminiftrat. 21.

[b] If the ordinary take goods of the inteftate, being out of his dioceffe, he fhall not be charged as ordinary by this act, becaufe he taketh them of his own wrong, and not as ordinary, in which right he is to be charged by this act.

Lib. 5. fo. 29. the Princes cafe. 9 Eliz. Dier 255, 256. lib. fo. Sir Moyle Finches cafe.

If it be demanded what intereft the ordinary hath in the goods of the inteftate, which come to his hands; it is anfwered, that he hath fuch an intereft as the adminiftrator, to whom adminiftration is committed *durante minore ætate executoris, ad opus, commodum, et utilitatem ipfius executoris, et non aliter, feu alio modo.* So as the ordinary may adminifter for the good of the inteftate, but cannot give the goods of the inteftate, or do any thing to his prejudice.

(5) *Obligetur de cætero ordinarius.*] *Ordinarius*; this word in the law of England, in the ufuall and common fenfe fignifieth a bifhop, or he or they that have ordinary jurifdiction, and is derived *ab ordine*, to put him in minde of the duty of his place, and of that order and office that he is called unto; and this was the wifdom of antiquity, that names of men in great places fhould put them in minde (as often as they were named) of their duty: as the treafurer of England to have fpeciall care of the kings treafure; and they that had places in the kings principall courts of juftice are called juftices to put them in continuall memory to do juftice, *et fic de cæteris.*

[c] 17 E. 2. Br. 822. 5 E. 2. ibid. 16. 17 E. 3. 23. 21 E. 3. 60. 41 Aff. 29. 7 E. 4. 14. 12 E. 4. 15. 31 H. 6. 10. 15 E. 3. quare non admifit 5. Dier 18 Eliz. 350. Regift. 67. Capitulum fede vacante fuccedit epifcopo in ordinaria jurifdictione. And this is regularly true, unleffe it be by prefcription or compofition. Vide li. 3. f. 73. the dean and chapter of Norwich cafe.

[c] In this ftatute *ordinarius* is not onely taken for a bifhop, but every one that is *in loco epifcopi*; as gardeins of the fpiritualties, and fuch as have peculiar and exempt ecclefiafticall jurifdiction, and be immediate officers to the kings courts of juftice: and not onely an ordinary or gardein of the fpiritualties, or others that be *in loco ordinarii*, that of right are within this act, but alfo fuch as ufurp the place, and are in poffeffion by wrong, are to be charged by this act.

[d] Reg. 141. 11 R. 2. & 16 E. 3. Adjudg. 11 E. 3. Execut. 177. 24 E. 3. 54. 11 H. 4. 73. F N.B. 120. Pl. Com. 280.

[d] If goods of the inteftate come to the hands of the ordinary, and he dyeth; although the words be [*obligetur de cætero ordinarius*] yet his executors or adminiftrators fhall be charged in an action of debt; for when this act bindeth the ordinary, by confequent his executors or adminiftrators are bound. But if the ordinary commit adminiftration to one, and he taketh the goods into his poffeffion and dyeth no action lyeth againft his executors.

[e] 11 R. 2. Adminiftrat. 21.

[e] If the ordinary take goods into his hands of the inteftate, and after commit adminiftration, and the ordinary retaineth the goods, he fhall be charged, notwithftanding the committing of adminiftration.

CAP.

CAP. XX.

CUM justiciarii in placito mortis antecessoris consueverint admittere responsionem (1) tenentis, quod petens non est propinquior hæres (2) antecessoris, de cujus morte tenementum petitur, et hoc paratus est per assisam inquirere: concordatum est, quod in brevibus de consanguinitate, avo, et proavo, quæ sunt ejusdem naturæ, admittatur illa responsio, et inquiratur, et secundum illam inquisitionem ad judicium procedatur.

WHEREAS that justices in a plea of mortdauncestor, have used to admit the answer of the tenant, that the plaintiff is not next heir of the same ancestor, by whose death he demanded the land, and is ready to enquire the same by assise; it is agreed, that in writs of cosinage, aiel, and besaiel, which be of the same nature, his answer shall be admittted and enquired, and according to the same inquisition they shall proceed to judgement.

Fleta, li. 5. ca. 8.

(1) *Consueverint admittere responsionem.*] Hereby it appeareth that admission and allowance of the justiees ought to be holden for law, and so it is affirmed by this act.

(2) *Quod petens non est propinquior hæres.*] It is to be understood that the entry in an assise of mord' brought for (example) by P. against R. of 20 acres of land in S. is according to the words of the writ *assisa venit recognoscere si* [1] *O. pater P. cujus hæres ipse est, fuit seisitus in dominico suo ut de feodo de 20 acris terræ cum pertinentiis in S. die quo obiit. Et* [2] *si obiit infra* 50 *annos jam ultime elapsos ante teste brevis. Et* [3] *si P. propinquior hæres ejus sit.*

These three points in this assise of mordaunc' shall be inquired of by the recognitors of the assise, albeit the tenant make default, and no issue be joyned thereupon: but so it is not in the writs of aiel, besaiel, or cosinage; for they are no assises but writs of *præcipe quod reddat*, and therefore if default be made therein, judgement shall be given by default, as in other writs of *præcipe quod reddat*, without inquiry of any point of the writ: the three points of the assise are hypotheticall, the demandant affirming nothing, and the words of the other three writs here mentioned are categoricall; *præcipe A. quod juste, &c. reddat B. unum messuagium, &c. de quo W. avus prædict' B. cujus hæres ipse est, fuit seisitus in dominico suo ut de feodo die quo obiit*; now *quod petens non est propinquior hæres* is a deniall of one of the points of the writ of mordaunc'.

31 E. 1. Mord. 58.

4 E. 2. Mord. 38. 8 E. 2. ibid. 42.

And it is to be understood that when the tenant pleadeth in barre of the assise, as matter of record, or a release, or warranty, or any other barre that is out of the said three points of the assise, there the tenant beginneth his plea with *assisa non, &c.* and therefore the triall of that issue is peremptory, and the assise shall never inquire of any of the points of the writ; but when the tenant saith, that he is ready to heare the recognisance of the assise, he cannot say *assisa non*, for that should be repugnant to his owne saying; and if hee say that he is ready to heare the recognisance of the assise of one of the

2 E. 3. 9. 9 E. 3. 30. 9 Ass. 3. 10 E. 3. 4. 45. 30 E. 3. 8. 2 Ass. 10. 8 Ass. 17. 14 E. 3. Mord. 8. 29 Ass. 1. 11. 39 Ass. 13. 40 E. 3. 48. 33 E. 3. Mord. 34. 27 H. 8. 14.

the points of the writ, or traverse one of the points of the writ, yet the court *ex officio* ought to enquire of them all: and so it is if the tenant pleade in abatement of the writ, or vowch, and the demandant counterplead the vowcher, and these pleas bee tried, or adjudged for the demandant, yet the points of the writs shall bee enquired, and ought to bee found for the demandant, or else he shall not recover.

12 Ass. 48.

[400] Now the mischiefe before this statute was, that in the writs of aiel, besaiel, and cosinage, the tenant was not admitted to plead, that the demandant was not heire to him, upon whose dying seised the writ was conceived, but he must shew who was his next heire, which now by this act he need not to doe, but yet he may plead the like plea, as he might have done at the common law as he did in 6 E. 3.

6 E. 3. 55.

Mirror, c. 5. § 5. But heare what the Mirror speaking of this act saith, *Lestatut de allower un manner de exception in semblable actions ne fuit my mistier daver estre ordein sinon pur negligence des justices, car chescun affirmative est encounterable de son negative al peril del deliverant.*

12 E. 3. Mordanc' 10. 30 E. 3. 8. 33 E. 3. Mord. 34.

If the tenant saith, that he is ready to heare the recognisance of the assise, he cannot give in evidence that the demandant is a bastard, but he ought to have pleaded the same.

(3) *Antecessoris.*] This *antecessor* in a writ of mordaunc' is intended of the father, mother, brother, sister, uncle, aunt, nephew, or niece of the demandant, and of no other.

(4) *Quæ sunt ejusdem naturæ.*] The difference betweene the assise of mordaunc', and these three præcipes appeareth by that which hath been said, and yet in some respect the words of this act that they be *ejusdem naturæ* are true.

For as the writ of mordaunc' saith, *Si O. pater P. cujus hæres ipse est, fuit seisitus in dominico suo ut de feodo de 20 acris terræ cum pertinen' in S. die quo obiit.* So the words of the writ aiel be, *De quibus N. avus prædict' P. cujus hæres ipse est, fuit seisitus in dominico suo ut de feodo die quo obiit, &c.*

(5) *Et secundū illiam inquisitionem ad judicium procedatur.*] Herein is the difference between this plea in assise of mordaunc', and the other writs; for in the assise of mordaunc' the rest of the points of the writ, as hath been said, shall be enquired.

But in the writs of aiel, besaiel, and cosinage, the triall of this issue is peremptory, and thereupon the court shall proceed to judgement as here is expressed.

CAP. XXI.

CUM in statuto edito apud Glouc' (1) contineatur, quod si quis dimiserit terram alicui ad reddend' valorem quartæ partis ten' vel majoris, habeat ille qui dimisit, vel ejus hæres (postquam cessatum fuerit a solutione per biennium) actionem petendi ten' sic dimissum in dominico. Eodem modo concor-

WHEREAS in a statute made at Gloucester, cap. 4. it is contained, that if any lease his land to another to pay the value of the fourth part of the land, or more, the lessor, or his heir, after the payment hath ceased by two years, shall have an action to demand the land so leased in demean. In

concordatum est (2), *quod si quis detineat* (3) *domino suo* (4) *servitium debitum et consuetum per biennium, habeat dominus actionem petendi ten' in dominico* (5) *per tale breve.*

In like manner it is agreed, that if any withhold from his lord his due and accustomed service by two years, the lord shall have an action to demand the land in demean by such a writ.

Præcipe A. quod juste, &c. (6) *reddat B. tale ten', quod A. de eo tenuit per tale servitium, et quod ad præd' B. reverti debeat, eo quod prædictus A. in faciend' prædictum servitium * per biennium cessavit ut dicit.*

Et non solum in isto casu, sed in casu de quo fit mentio in prædicto statuto Glouc' fiant brevia de ingressu hæredi (7) *petenti super hæredem tenentem, et super eos quibus alienat' fuerit hujusmodi tenementum.*

*[401]

And not onely in this case, but also in the case whereof mention is made in the said statute of Gloucester, writs of entry shall be made for the heir of the demandant against the heir of the tenant, and against them to whom such lands shall be aliened.

Gloc', cap. 4. (6 Ed. 1. stat. 1. c. 4. Fitz. Brief, 249. 269. 6 H. 7. f. 7. Fitz. Cessavit. 1, 2, 3, 4. 7, 8. 17. 21. 22. 30. 32, 33, 34, 35. 45, 46. 50, 51. 54. 8 Rep. 118. Fitz. Cessavit, 42. 1 Inst. 154. Regist. 237.)

(1) *Cum in statuto edito apud Gloucest', &c.*] The statute of Glouc' is misrecited for [*vel ejus hæres*] are not in that statute.

1. Hereby it appeareth that the statute of Glouc' extended onely, when upon the creation of the tenure a fee farme was reserved, the deteinment whereof was more prejudice to the lord then common and usuall rents and services, and therefore that act was not extended by equity to other rents, or services.

2. That albeit the statute of Glouc' mentioneth a deed, yet if the fee farme be reserved without deed, that act extended to it, for here in the recitall of the act no deed is mentioned, so as that statute is extended to all fee farmes.

3. Here it is said *eodem modo concordatum est, quod si quis detineat domino suo servitium debitum et consuetum*; and if the statute of Glouc' had not extended to fee farmes without deed, then should not a *cessavit* lie for other services upon this act, unlesse they had been reserved by deed, by reason of these words, *eodem modo, &c.*

(2) *Eodem modo concordatum est, &c.*] By these words this act is so incorporated into the statute of Glouc'; as the letting of the land to lie fresh, the tender of the arrerages, finding of surety, &c. are to be applied to this act concerning other services.

(3) *Si quis detineat.*] These words extend as well to bodies politique or incorporate, either sole or aggregate of many, as to naturall persons; also to feme coverts and infants, unlesse the infant have the land by descent, and then although the cesser be in his time, he shall have his age, for that by intendment of law he knows not what arrerages to tender.

3 E. 3. 26.

4 E. 2. Cui in vita 22. lib. 8. fo. 44. Wittinghams case. li. 9. f. 85. Combs case.

If a villein seise and the lord enter, no *cessavit* shall lie against the lord for the cesser by the villein.

34 E. 3. bre. 924.

(4) *Domino suo.*] This is not intended onely of a lord that hath an estate in fee-simple in a seigniory, but of such also that have an estate taile, or any estate for life derived out of a fee-simple; but he in

32 E. 1. cessav. 29. 11 E. 2. cessavit. 13 E. 2. ibid. 52. 8 E. 3. receit 36. 43 E.

3. 15. 45 E. 3. 27. 33 H. 6. 53. 9 H. 7. 16. F.N.B. 209. Vet. N.B. 78.

in the reverſion ſhall not have a *ceſſavit* againſt the donee in taile or tenant for life, for he in the reverſion is not *dominus* within this ſtatute.

If the tenant ceaſe by one year, and the lord graunt over his ſeigniory, and then the tenant ceaſe another year, neither of them is *dominus* within this act. Lib. 2. fol. 93. Binghams caſe.

See the expoſition upon the ſtatute of Glouc' cap. 4. what ſervices are intended within this ſtatute, *viz.* ſervices annuall, as rent, ſuit, and the like, and not homage, or fealty, or the like, for this act ſaith *per biennium*, which implieth annuall ſervices. But this act extendeth not to rent ſervice created upon a fee farme, but a *ceſſavit* upon a fee farme muſt be conceived upon the ſtatute of Glouceſter, for which purpoſe there be ſeverall writs in the

Regiſt. 237.

Regiſter.

(5) *In dominico.*] It was the wiſdome of auncient parliaments to comprehend much matter in few words, as in this caſe, if the tenant made a leaſe for life, or a gift in taile, and a ceſſer was by

[402]

14 E. 2. bre. 815. 14 E. 3. ibid. 269. 19 E. 3. ibid. 249. 21 E. 3. 44. 30 E. 3. 22. 28 E. 3. 95. 48 E. 3. 4. 27 E. 3. 27. 39 E. 3. 15. 12 R. 2. ceſſavit 460. 33 H. 6. 53. 12 E. 4. fo. ult. 27 H. 8. 28. Kelwey 104, 105. 13 E. 3. gard 38. 1 H. 4. 3. per Burgh.

two yeares, in this caſe a *ceſſavit* ſhould be brought againſt the tenant for life or in taile, and ſuppoſe that he in reverſion did hold of him, and that the tenant for life, or in taile did ceaſe: and ſo if the tenant was diſſeiſed, and the diſſeiſor ceaſed, the writ of *ceſſavit* ſhould ſuppoſe that the diſſeiſee did hold, and that the diſſeiſor did ceaſe: and likewiſe if the tenant by whoſe hands the lord was ſeiſed of his ſervice made a feoffement in fee, the writ of *ceſſavit* ſhould ſuppoſe that the feoffee ceaſed, and that the feoffor did hold of him, *et ſic de ſimilibus:* and the reaſon of theſe and the like caſes was, for that the lord by his *ceſſavit* was to recover the land in *dominico*; and therefore theſe writs were framed and allowed accordingly: and for the ſame reaſon, if there be lord meſne and tenant, and the tenant peravaile ceaſe by two yeares; the lord ſhall have a *ceſſavit* againſt the tenant (for a *ceſſavit* doth not lie of a rent) and ſuppoſe that the meſne ceaſed.

Lib. 8. fol. 86. Buckmers caſe. 21 E. 3. 44. b. &c. Regiſt. 237. Vet. N.B. 78. 138, 139. F.N.B. 208.

(6) *Præcipe A. quod juſte,* &c.] Here is the writ of *ceſſavit* framed; now the great objection upon that which hath been ſaid, how the ceſſer can be alledged in the tenant, againſt whom the *præcipe* is brought, and the tenure alledged in another, when the writ ſo formed doth ſuppoſe him, againſt whom the *ceſſavit* is brought, to hold alſo of the demandant: the anſwer is, that the writ formed by this act is put but for example, and ſeeing that, if ſuch writs, as are above ſaid, ſhould not be maintained, no *ceſſavit* ſhould be maintenable at all in thoſe caſes, therefore they have been adjudged to be good.

Regiſt. 237.

Here is a writ in a new caſe framed by this act, and therefore the act is not to be recited, (as often we have obſerved before) but the forme preſcribed is to bee purſued; but in a *ceſſavit* upon the ſtatute of Glouc', the ſtatute is rehearſed, becauſe there is no forme of writ preſcribed by that act.

(7) *Fiant brevia de ingreſſu hæredi.*] A *ceſſavit* is properly called *breve de ingreſſu*, when it is in the *per*, or in the *per et cui*.

33 E. 3. ceſſav. 42. Pl. Com. 110. F.N.B. 209. f. lib. 8. fo. 118. D. Bonhams caſe.

Certain it is that the heire ſhall not have a *ceſſavit* for a ceſſer in the life time of the aunceſter, becauſe the heire cannot have the arrerages which the tenant in the *ceſſavit* hath power to tender, and therefore this act is to bee intended of a ceſſer in the time of the

the heire, otherwise the act should be contrary to itselfe, which in all expositions is to bee avoided.

And so it is of the aunt and neece, they shall not joyne for a cesser in the time of the mother of the neece, but for a cesser in the time of both of them the *cessavit* doth lie. 33 E. 3. ubi supra. F.N.B. ubi supra.

Se the statute of 10 E. 1. *statutum de gamletto in London, Vet. Magna Charta fol.* 122. where it is said, *implacitentur de gamletto,* which is a kinde of *cessavit,* for *gamel* or *gabble,* or *gabel* in one of the senses is taken for *census,* rent, &c. and *gamellettum* is as much to say, as to cease, or let to pay the rent, *breve de gamelletto in London est breve de cessavit in biennium, &c. pro redditu ibidem, quia tenementa fuerunt indistringibilia.* Fleta, l. 2. ca. 48. Coram Rege Pasch. 17 E. 3. Rot. 139. London.

CAP. XXII. [403]

CUM duo vel plures teneant boscum (1), *turbariam, piscariam, vel alia hujusmodi in communi* (2), *absq; hoc quod aliquis sciat suum seperale, et aliquis eorum faciat vastum* (3) *contra voluntatem alterius: moveatur actio per breve de vasto. Et habeat defendens, cum ad judicium venerit, electionem* (4) *capiendi partem suam in certo loco per vic', et per visum, et sacram', ac assignationem vicinorum ad hoc elect' et juratorum: vel quod concedat* (5) *quod nihil capiat de cætero in hujusmodi in bosco, turbaria, et aliis, nisi secund' quod participes sui capere voluerint. Et si eligat capere partem suam in certo loco, assignetur ei locus vastatus* (6) *in suam partem, secundum quod fuit antequam vastum fecit. Et est tale breve in hoc casu: scil. cum A. et B. teneant boscum pro indiviso, B. fecit vastum, &c.*

WHEREAS two or more do hold wood, turf-land, or fishing, or other such thing in common, wherein none knoweth his several, and some of them do waste against the minds of the other, an action may lie by a writ of waste; and when it is come unto judgement, the defendant shall choose either to take his part in a place certain, by the sheriff, and by the view, oath, and assignment of his neighbours sworn and tried for the same intent, or else he shall grant to take nothing from henceforth in the same wood, turf-land, and such other, but as his partners will take. And if he do choose to take his part in a place certain, the part wasted shall be assigned for his part, as it was before he committed the waste. And there is such a writ in this case, that is to say, *cum A. & B. tenent boscum pro indiviso, B. fecit vastum, &c.*

Fleta, li. 1. ca. 11. See the first part of the Institutes, 323. (21 Ed. 3. f. 29. Fitz. Waste, 25, 96. 1 Inst. 200. Regist. 76.)

(1) *Boscum,* &c.] This act extendeth not to castles, houses, or other places for the habitation of man, for one joyntenant, or tenant in common might have had for reparation of them a writ *de reparatione faciend'.* Regist. 76. 23 H. 7. Kelw. 98. F.N.B. 127. a.

(2) *Teneant, &c. in communi,* &c.] These words do include aswell joyntenants as tenants in common, for both of them hold *in communi,* and so do old books and records term them both: but though the generalty of these words do extend to coparceners, yet in good 27 H. 8 13. 21 E. 3. 29. 29 E. 3. 39.

 construction

construction they are not within the purview of this act, because they were compellable to make partition; for this act extends not to them that had remedy by the common law, as hath been said before.

This word [*teneant*] doth imply a free-hold at least.

F.N.B. 49. 59. d. 21 E. 3. 29. 3 E. 2. Waste 25. A parson of a church being tenant in common with another shall have an action of waste upon this statute; and it is holden, that an action of waste upon this act is maintainable between joyntenants, or tenants in common for lives, and yet the words of the writ be, *ad exhæredationem*.

50 E. 3. 3. If woods be given to two, and the heirs of one of them, he that hath the fee shall have an action of waste upon this statute, for no other action of waste he can have.

But if woods be letten to two, the one for life, and the other for yeers, they are not within this statute, in respect of the said word *teneant*.

(3) *Faciat vastum.*] What shall be said waste or destruction in a tenant for life, &c. shall be said waste within this act.

Habeat defendens, cum ad judic' venerit, electionem, &c.] Here the defendant hath election, either to have his part in certain, and to take the place wasted as part thereof, or that he findeth surety to take no more then belongs to his part.

[404] 31 H. 8. cap. 1. 32 H. 8. cap. 32. And the defendant hath at this day a further election, either to have an action of waste upon this act, or a writ of partition by the late statutes.

(4) *Concedat.*] That is expounded, that he finde such convenient surety, as the court shall allow of.

(5) *Assignetur eis locus vastatus.*] This is not literally to be taken, for it may be, that the place wasted is more than his portion, therefore it must be understood of so much as belong to his part.

CAP. XXIII.

HABEANT de cætero executores (1) breve de compoto, et eandem actionem, et processum (2) per illud breve, quale habuit mortuus, et haberet si vixisset.

EXECUTORS from henceforth shall have a writ of accompt, and the same action and process in the same writ as the testator might have had if he had lived.

(Fitz. Executors, 97. 4 Ed. 3. c. 7. 25 Ed. 3. stat. 5. c. 5.)

7 E. 3. 62. 19 E. 3. Account 56. Hil. 31 E. 3. fo. 36. in libro meo in Account. F.N.B. 117. b. 38 E. 3. 7. 31 E. 3. Account 57. By the common law executors should not have an action of account for an account to be made to the testator, because the account rested in privity: for remedy whereof this act was made; but *per legem mercatoriam* an action of account did lye for executors. The successor of a prior, or the like should have an action of account for an account to be made to the predecessor, because the house never dyeth.

(1) *Executors.*]

(1) *Executores.*] Administrators had no action untill the statute of 31 E. 3. No action of account was given to the executors of executors till the statute of 25 E. 3. But this act of 25 E. 3. as to the action of debt, covenant, &c. therein mentioned, is but in affirmance of the common law. 31 E. 3. cap. 11. 25 E. 3. cap. 5. Pl. Com. 286, 287. 10 E. 2. Execut. 100.

(2) *Eandē actionē et processum.*] The heir in socage dyeth before the age of 14, his executors or administrators shall have an action of account presently, and yet the heir himself should not have an action before 14, but the statute saith, *candem actionem*, and not *ad idem tempus.*

CAP. XXIV.

IN casibus in quibus conceditur breve de cancellaria de facto alicujus, de cætero non recedant querentes a cur' (2) *regis sine remedio* (1), *pro eo quod tenement' transfertur* (3) *de uno in alium. Et in registro de cancellaria* (4) *non est inventum aliquod breve in isto casu speciale, sicuti de muro, domo, mercato* (5), *conceditur breve super eum qui levavit ad nocumentum* (6). *Et si transferatur domus, murus, et his similia in aliam personam, breve non deneget': sed de cætero cum in uno casu conceditur breve, in consimili casu simili remedio indigente, sicuti prius, fiat breve* (7). *Questus est nobis A.* * *quod B. injuste, &c. levavit domum, murum, mercatum, et alia quæ sunt ad nocumentum liberi tenement' sui. Et si hujusmodi levata ad nocumentum transferantur in aliam personam, de cætero fiat breve sic: questus est nobis A. quod B. et C. levaverunt, &c. Eodem modo sicut persona* (8) *alicujus ecclesiæ* (9) *recuperare potest communiam pastur' per breve novæ disseisinæ. Eodem modo de cætero recuperet successor super disseisitorem, vel ejus hæredem per breve, quod permittat, licet hujusmodi breve prius in cancellaria non fuerit concessum. Eodem modo sicut conceditur breve utrum aliquod tenem' sit libera eleemosina alicujus ecclesiæ, vel laicum feodum, tale fiat de cætero breve utrum* (10) *sit libera eleemosina talis*

* [405]

IN cases whereas a writ is granted out of the chancery for the fact of another, the plaintiffs from henceforth shall not depart from the king's court without remedy, because the land is transferred from one to another. And in the register of the chancery there is no special writ found in this case, as of a house, a wall, a market, but the writ is granted against him that levied the nusance. And if the house, wall, or such like be aliened to another, the writ shall not be denied; but from henceforth, where in one case a writ is granted, in like case, when like remedy falleth, the writ shall be made as hath been used before: *questus est nobis A. quod D. injuste, &c. levavit domum, murum, mercatum, et alia quæ sunt ad nocumentum, &c.* And if such things levied be aliened from one to another, the writ shall be thus: *questus est nobis A. quod B. et C. levaverunt, &c.* In like manner as a parson of a church may recover common of pasture by writ of *novel disseisin*, likewise from henceforth his successor shall have a *quod permittat* against the disseisor or his heir, though a like writ were never granted out of the chancery before. And in like manner as a writ is granted to try whether land be the free alms of such a church, or the lay fee of such a man, even so from henceforth a writ shall be made to try whether it be the free

talis ecclesiæ, vel alterius ecclesiæ, in casu quo libera eleemosina unius ecclesiæ transferatur in possessionem alterius ecclesiæ. Et quotiescunque de cætero evenerit (11) *in cancellar', quod in uno casu reperitur breve, et in consimili casu* (12) *cadente sub eodem jure, et simili indigente remedio non reperitur: concordent clerici* (13) *de cancellaria in brevi faciendo, vel attermінent querentes in proximum parliamentum: et scribantur casus, in quibus concordare non possunt, et referant eos ad proximum parliamentum* (14) *: et de consensu jurisperitorum fiat breve, ne contingat de cætero quod curia domini regis deficiat* (15) *conquerentibus in justitia perquirenda.*

free alms of this church, or of another church, in case where the free alms of one church is transferred to the possession of another church. And whensoever from henceforth it shall fortune in the chancery, that in one case a writ is found, and in like case falling under like law, and requiring like remedy, is found none, the clerks of the chancery shall agree in making the writ; or the plaintiffs may adjourn it until the next parliament, and let the cases be written in which they cannot agree, and let them refer themselves until the next parliament, by consent of men learned in the law, a writ shall be made, lest it might happen after that the court should long time fail to minister justice unto complainants.

(Rast. 405. Rast. 441. 6 R. 2. c. 3. 9 Rep. 55. Rast. 538. Regist. 32. Rast. 419. Coke pla. 399. 14 Ed. 3. 17. Rast. 123. Fitz. Entry, 3. 7, 8. 10. 61. 64. 67, 68, 69. 74. 1 Inst. 54. b.)

4 Ass. 3. 4 E. 3. 36. 5 E. 3. 43. li. 5. fol. 101. Penruddocks case.

Before the making of this act, an assise of nusans did not lye against him that levyed the nusans, and against his alienee; so as by the alienation of the wrong doer, the assise of nusans failed: and he, to whom the nusans was done, was driven to his *quod permittat* (which was a writ of right in his nature, wherein was great delay) against the alienee; and the reason thereof was, for that there was no writ of assise of nusans in the Register, but that supposed that the tenant in the assise *levavit*, which is remedied by this act.

(1) *De cætero non recedant querentes a curia regis sine remedio.*] This is an ancient maxime of the common law, and the reason thereof is, *ne curia regis deficeret in justitia exhibenda*, so as in one court or other the party injured should have justice.

Bract. l. 4. fo. 231. 6 E. 2. Ass. 454. Fleta, li. 4. c. 27. 9 E. 4. 35. F.N.B. 184. g. li. 5. fol. 181. Penrud. case.

(2) *A curia*, &c.] The makers of this act knew well, that the party injured by the nusans, albeit the wrong doer made it in his own ground, yet might the party grieved (albeit he had but an estate for yeers) enter and abate, and demolish the nusans, be it house, wall, or other nusans, not onely when it was in the hands of the wrong doer, but in the hands of the alienee: but this act doth give the tenant of the free hold as speedy a remedy by law, as is the assise of *novel disseisin*, which was ever counted *festinum remedium*; and yet if the wrong doer reform the nusans before the assise, or *quod permittat* brought, the action lyeth not; howbeit, if the party had any particular losse by the nusans, he shall recover damages therefore in an action upon the case, *ne querentes recederent a curia sine remedio.*

[406]

(3) *Tenementum transfertur.*] *Transfertur* is a more generall word then *alienetur*, for *alienare* is regularly intended of the act of the

the party, but *transferre* comprehendeth also acts in law, as descents, escheats, and the like: and therefore if two coparceners levie a nusans upon their ground, and one dye, so as her part descend to her heir, the assise of nusans is maintainable against the aunt as a wrong doer, and the neece as a tenant of a moity, which moity is transferred, but not aliened to her, and so if the alienee dye seised.

(4) *In registro de cancellaria.*] This is a book of great antiquity and authority in law, whereof in another place I have spoken.

1. Part of the Institutes, sect. 101. 234. Preface to the 3. book of my Reports.

(5) *De mercato.*] Here it is to be observed, that if one hath a market, either by prescription, or by letters patents of the king, and another obtains a market to the nusans of the former market, he shall not tarry till he have avoided the letters patents of the latter market by course of law, but he may have an assise of nusans.

Note there be words in the grant of a market, *ita quod non sit ad nocumentum alterius mercati.*

And note that fairs are taken within this law, for every fair is a market, but every market is not a fair.

[a] Now in what cases a fair or market shall be said to be levied to the nusans of another, you may read in our old and latter books, this onely that hath been said is sufficient touching this point, for the understanding of this act.

(6) *Levavit ad nocumentum,* &c.] [b] A grant of a fair, &c. *Nisi sit ad nocumentum feriarum vicinarum,* where *ad nocumentum feriarum* is put but for example; for if it be *ad aliquod damnum,* either of the king, or subject in any other thing, the fair shall be revoked.

[c] *Nocumentum est triplex; 1. publicum sive generale. 2. Commune. 3. Privatum sive speciale.*

Publicum, ad nocumentum totius regni; commune, ad commune nocumentum transeuntium; privatum, to a house, a mill, &c.

[d] It is true that a private nusans may be committed three manner of wayes; *viz. Faciendo, non faciendo, permittendo, et non permittendo.*

[e] By this word *levavit,* and these words in the beginning of the chapter, *de facto alicujus,* it appeareth that this act onely extendeth to nusances that are committed by doing or disturbing; for, for not doing no assise of nusans lyeth, but an action upon the case.

[f] Though the word *levavit* is onely here, and in the writ (herein mentioned) used, yet *exaltavit, deexaltavit, obstruxit, obstupavit, arctavit, divertit, &c.* nay *prostravit,* which is the opposite to *levavit,* &c. are within this act.

(7) *Cum in uno casu conceditur breve, in cõsimili casu simili remedio indigẽte, sicuti prius, fiat breve.*] See hereafter in this chapter concerning this rule.

(8) *Eodem modo sicuti persona,* &c.] [g] A parson of a church shall have a *quod permittat* of a common in the right, and also in nature of a mordanc', &c. because the parson had an inheritance in the common in the right of his church.

But of a nusans done in the time of the predecessor against the disseisor or his heire, being an injury and wrong, no *quod permittat* did lie in that case before this statute, as it plainly appeareth by this

[a] Bract. li. 4. fo. 235. Brit. f. 159. Flet. li. 4. c. 28. 11 H. 4 5, 6. 47. 22 H. 6. 16.

[b] Pasch. 33 E. 1. Coram Rege, the Prior of Tynemouths case. Northumber.

[c] Fleta, l. 4. c. 27. Glanv. li. 9. ca. 11. li. 13 ca. 34. 19 E. 3. Barre 179.

[d] Glanv. li. 13. ca. 34, &c. Bract. li. 4. fo. 231, &c. Fleta, l. 4. c. 18 23. 26, &c. Brit. fo. 71. 2 H. 4. 11. 11 H. 4. 83. 29 E. 3. 32.

[f] Temps E. 1. Ass. 422. 7 E. 3. 56. 8 E. 3. 21. 8 Ass. 32 Ass. 2. 42 Ass. 15. 18 E. 3. 32. 15 E. 2. tit. Ass. 375. 5 H. 3. ibid. 426. 3 E. 3. ibid. 445. F.N.B. 183, 184. Regist. 452. 9. Ass. 19. 48 E. 3. 27.

[g] 13 E. 1. Juris utrum 15. 30 E. 1. Quod permittat 10. 32 E. 1. ibid. 14. & tit. Common 24. 31 E. 1. B. 874. tit. Quod permittat 8. 4 E. 3. 38. 43 E. 3. 25. 1 H. 4. 3. F.N.B. 49. c.

[407]

act it ſelfe, and the reaſon was, for that there was no writ in the Regiſter in that caſe.

Regiſt. 32, 33.

(9) *Perſona alicujus eccleſiæ.*] Theſe words doe include vicars, prebendaries, &c. and all other eccleſiaſticall perſons which could not have a *quod permittat* in the like caſe before the making of this act; for private perſons, though they had but an eſtate taile they might have had a *quod permittat*, and therefore no proviſion was made for them, but onely for parſons of a church, and the like.

Glan. l. 13. c. 23. Bract. l. 5. f. 286. Brit. fol. 234. 55. 65. Fleta, l. 5. c. 19. & 26. 11 E. 3. Juris utrum. 3. Firſt part of the Inſtit. ſect. 646. Cuſtumier de Norm. ca. 115.

(10) *Breve utrum.*] A *juris utrum* did lie at the common law for a parſon againſt a lay man, and for a lay man againſt a parſon, but no *juris utrum* did lie for one parſon againſt another before this act, becauſe it was the right of a church and no lay fee. And the words of the writ at the common law were *an ſit laicum feodum, &c.*

If an abbot hath a parſonage appropriated to him, and aliens the glebe of the parſonage, his ſucceſſor ſhall have a *juris utrum*, which he hath as parſon, and not as abbot.

20 E. 3. Juris utrum 5. 19 H. 3. ibidem 16. 8 E. 3. 60. 5 E. 3. Juris utrum 9. 19 R. 2. ibid. 17.

A parſon or chaplain of a chappel, which comes in by admiſſion and inſtitution, ſhall have a *juris utrum*, becauſe he hath no other remedy; otherwiſe it is of a gardein of an hoſpitall, a prior, and the like, becauſe they may have a writ of right.

Bract. l. 5. f. 413. Fleta, l. 2. ca. 12. Lib. 8 f. 48, 49. John Webs caſe. Firſt part Inſt. ſect. 67.

(11) *Et quotieſcunque evenerit.*] This is a moſt excellent and neceſſary rule, for before this act the juſtices did punctually hold themſelves to the writs in the Regiſter, becauſe they could not change them without act of parliament; (as elſewhere hath been ſaid) therefore by this generall law it is notably provided for expedition and adminiſtration of juſtice, that as often as it ſhould happen in the chauncery, that in one caſe there is writ (in the regiſter of the chauncery) found, and in like caſe happening under the ſame right, and needing the like remedy, a writ is not found, let the clerks of the chauncery agree in making of a writ, or adjourne the plaintiffe untill the next parliament, &c. But now let us peruſe the words.

31 E. 1. bre. 874. 38 E. 3. 13.

(12) *Conſimili caſu.*] Although there be a ſpeciall writ grounded upon this ſtatute, called by the particular name of a writ *in conſimili caſu*, yet many other writs (though they beare not the name) are grounded upon this act, as it appeareth in our books.

Firſt part of the Inſt. ſect. 67.

(13) *Concordent clerici.*] And albeit that we have treated of this in another place, yet for the underſtanding of theſe words, ſomewhat ſhall here be ſaid.

Lib. 8. f. 48, 49. John Webs caſe. Fleta, l. 2 ca. 12. 21 E. 3. fol. 38.

Theſe that here are called *clerici*, were at this time, and before called alſo *magiſtri cancellariæ*, and were aſſociated to the lord chancellor; of whom Fleta ſaith, *Cui aſſocientur clerici honeſti et circumſpecti, domino regi jurati, qui in legibus et conſuetudinibus Anglicanis notitiam habeant pleniorem, quorum officium ſit ſupplicationes, et querelas conquerentium audire et examinare, et eis ſuper qualitatibus injuriarum oſtenſarum debitum remedium exhibere per brevia regis.*

Li. 8. ubi ſupra.

And theſe writs agreed upon by theſe maſter clerks were called *magiſtralia*, for diſtinction ſake, between *brevia formata de curſu*, and theſe called *magiſtralia*, but hereof more hath been ſaid in another place.

3 E. 2. Entry 8. F.N.B. 206. f.

And one ſpeciall note is to be taken, that this generall law extends not onely to writs at the common law, but to writs alſo grounded upon acts of parliament: for example, the ſtatute of Glouceſter

Gloucester doth give a writ of entry in case of alienation by tenant in dower, to be brought in the life of tenant in * dower, which thereupon is called a writ of entry *in casu proviso:* now upon these generall words writs have been framed *in consimili casu,* that is, where tenant by the curtesie, or tenant for life doe alien, but it must be *in consimili casu* with the statute of Glocester; for where that statute speaketh of a reversion, a remainder is not *in consimili casu,* as some doe hold, that a reversion *ex assignatione,* though it be but for life, is within the act.

3 E. 2. ubi supra. 18 E. 2. Entry 74. 11 E. 2. Entry 68, ibid. 12 E. 2. 60. 7 E. 3. 17. 8 E. 3. 48. 6 E. 3. 39, 40. 16 Ass. p. 11. Regist. 237. & 235. F.N.B. 207 b. 31 E. 1. Entry 64.

(14) *Atterminent querentes usq; in proximum parliamentum.*] Matters of great difficulty were in auncient time usually adjourned into parliament to be resolved and decided there, whereof Bracton saith, *Si aliqua nova et inconsueta emerserint, quæ nunquam prius evenerunt, et obscurum, et difficile sit eorum judicium, tunc ponantur judicia in respectu usque ad magnam curiam, ut ibi per consilium curiæ terminetur:* and this agreeth with our books from time to time.

And hereof there be infinite precedents in the rols of parliament. *Vide* the statute of 14 E. 3. cap. 5. see 22 E. 3. 3. & 2 H. 7. 19.

To which end parliaments were often holden, * king Alfred or Alured did ordain by authority of parliament, that for ever twice a yeare, or oftner, if need were, in time of peace a parliament should be holden at London: *pur parlamenter sur le guidement del people de Dieu, coment gents se garderont de pecher, viveront in quiet, receiveront droit per certein usages, et saints judgements,* of whom the poet sung,

Bract. li. 1 ca. 2. Britton, fo. 143. 19 H. 3. Juris utr. 16. 1 E. 3. 7, 8. 2 E. 3. 7. 21 E. 3 31. 37. 60. 33 E. 3. Quar. Imp. 94. 37 Ass. 7. 18 Ass. p. ult. 17 E. 3. 35. 49. 39 E. 3. 21. 35. 17 E. 3. 35. 49. 40 E. 3. 34. 38. 41 Ass. p. 28. 46 E. 3. petit. 18. 13 vowcher 119. 13 H. 4. 4. 14 H. 4. 34. * Mirr. c. 2. § 3. & cap. 5. § 1.

Anglorum sic regna regens, ut non foret illi
Antea rex similis, æqualis postea nullus.

And in an ancient chronicle I reade of him, *Aluredus acerrimi ingenii princeps et doctissimus totumque novum et vetus testamentum in eulogiam Anglicæ gentis transmutavit, &c.* In historia Eliensi. lib. 2. fo. 38.

In the raigne of E. 1. parliaments were very frequent, and often holden, and for the most part one parliament in two yeares.

King Edw. 3. ordained by authority of parliament, that a parliament should be holden every year once, or more often, if need be: to what end? for maintenance and execution of lawes, and for redresse of divers mischieses, and grievances which dayly happen. 4 E. 3. ca. 14. 36 E. 3. ca. 10.

(15) *Quod curia domini regis deficiat,* &c.] For it is a rule in law, *quod curia regis non debet deficere conquerentibus in justitia exhibenda.* W. 2. ca. 51.

CAP. XXV.

QUIA non eſt aliquod breve in cancellaria, per quod querentes habent tam feſtinum remedium (1), *ſicut per breve novæ diſſeiſinæ, dominus rex voluntatem habens ut celeris fiat juſtitia, et quod dilationes* (2) *in placito communi amputentur et abbrevientur, concedit quod breve aſſiſæ novæ diſſeiſinæ locum habeat in pluribus caſibus quam prius habuit* (3). *Et concedit quod de eſtoveriis boſci* (4), *proficuo capiendo in boſco, de nucibus, et glandibus, et aliis * fructibus colligend'* (5), *de corrodio* (6), *liberatione bladi, et aliorum victualium* (7), *ac neceſſariorum* (8) *in certo loco annuatim recipiend'* (9), *tolneto, tronagio, paſſagio, pontagio, pannagio, et his ſimilibus in certis locis capiend'* (10), *cuſtodiis boſcorum, parcorum, foreſtarum, chacearum, warennarum, portarum, et aliis balivis* (11), *et officiis in feod'* (12), *jaceat de cætero aſſiſa novæ diſſeiſinæ. Et in omnibus ſupradictis caſibus modo conſueto fiat breve de libero ten'* (13). *Et ſicut prius jacuit, et locum habuit in communia paſturæ: ita de cætero locum habeat in communia turbariæ, piſcariæ, et aliis commun' his ſimilibus* (14), *quas quis habet pertinentes ad liberum tenementum, vel etiam ſine ten' per ſpeciale factum, ad minus ad terminum vitæ. In caſu etiam quando quis tenens ten' ad terminum annorum, vel in cuſtod' illud alienat in feodo* (15), *et per illam alienationem transfertur liberum ten' in feoffatum, fiat remedium per breve novæ diſſeiſinæ. Et habeantur pro diſſeiſitoribus tam ille qui feoffat, quam feoffatus: ita quod vivente altero eorum locum habeat prædictum breve. Et ſi per mortem perſonarum ceſſet remedium per prædictum breve, fiat remedium per breve de ingreſſu:*

FORASMUCH as there is no writ in the chancery whereby plaintiffs can have ſo ſpeedy remedy, as by a writ of novel diſſeiſin; our lord the king, willing that juſtice may be ſpeedily miniſtred, and that delays in pleas may be taken away or abridged, granteth that a writ of novel diſſeiſin ſhall hold place in more caſes than it hath done heretofore; and granteth, that for eſtovers of wood, profit to be taken in woods by gathering of nuts, acorns, and other fruits, for a corody, for delivery of corn and other victuals and neceſſaries to be received yearly (in a place certain) toll, tronage, paſſage, pontage, pawnage, and ſuch like, to be taken in places certain, keeping of parks, woods, foreſts, chaſes, warrens, gates, and other bailiwicks, and offices in fee, from henceforth an aſſiſe of novel diſſeiſin ſhall lie. And in all caſes afore rehearſed, according to the cuſtomed manner, the writ ſhall be *de libero tenemento*; and as before times it hath lien and holden place in common of paſture, ſo ſhall it from henceforth hold place in common of turf-land, fiſhing, and ſuch like commons, which any man hath appendant to freehold, or without freehold by ſpecial deed, at the leaſt for term of life. In caſe alſo when any holding for term of years, or in ward, alieneth the ſame in fee, and by ſuch alienation the freehold is transferred to the feoffee, the remedy ſhall be by a writ of novel diſſeiſin, and as well the feoffor as the feoffee ſhall be had for diſſeiſors, ſo that during the life of any of them the ſaid writ ſhall hold place; and if by the death of the parties remedy happen to fail by that writ, then remedy ſhall be obtained

gressu (16): et quamvis superius fiat mentio (17) de aliquibus casibus, de quibus locum non habuit prius breve novæ disseisinæ, non propter hoc credat aliquis illud breve non competere, ubi prius competebat. Et licet dubitaverint quidam, utrum in casu quo quis pascat alterius seperale (18), fieri poterit remedium per prædictum breve, teneatur pro certo, quod in casu illo per prædictum breve bonum et certum est remedium. Caveant de cætero illi qui nominati sunt disseisitores (19), quod non proponant falsas exceptiones, per quas captio assisæ differatur, dicendo quod alias transivit assisa de eodem ten' inter easdem partes, vel dicendo et mentiendo, quod breve de altiori natura pendet inter easdem partes de eodem ten', et super his et consimilibus vocent rotulos, vel recordum ad warrantum, ut per illam vocationem asportare possint vesturam, et levare redditus, et alia proficua ad magnum detrimentum querentis. Et quia prius aliam pœnam non habuit, qui hujusmodi falsas exceptiones mendaciter proposuit, nisi tantū quod post mendacium suum convictum processum fuit ad captionem assisæ: dominus rex,
[410] *cui odiosæ sunt hujusmodi falsæ exceptiones, statuit quod si quis disseisitor nominatus personaliter proponat illam exceptionem ad diem sibi datum, si defecerit de warranto quod vocavit, habeatur pro disseisitore absque recognitione assisæ, et restituat damna prius inquisita, vel post inquirenda de duplo: et nihilominus pro falsitate sua puniatur per prisonam unius anni. Et si illa exceptio proponatur per balivum, non propter hoc differatur captio assisæ, nec judicium super restitutione ten' (20), et damn': ita tamen quod si dominus illius balivi, qui absens fuerit, postmodum veniat coram justic', qui assisam ceperint, et offerat verificare per recordum, vel per rotulos, quod assisa alias transivit de eodem ten' inter easdem*

tained by a writ of entry. And albeit that above mention is made of some cases wherein a writ of novel disseisin held no place before, let no man think therefore that this writ lieth not now where it hath lien before. And though some have doubted whether a remedy be had by this writ in case where one feedeth in the several of another, let it be had for certain, that a good and a sure remedy is given in that case by the said writ. And let them which be named disseisors beware from henceforth that they alledge not false exceptions, whereby the taking of the assise may be deferred, saying, that another time an assise of the same land passed between the same parties, or saying, and falsly, that a writ of more high nature hangeth between the same parties for the same land, and upon these and like matters do vouch rolls or records to warranty, to the end that by the same vouching they may take away the vesture, and receive the rents and other profits, to the great damage of the plaintiff. And where before none other pain was limited against him that falsly had alledged such untrue exceptions, but only that after such false surmises disproved the assise should pass; our lord the king, to whom such false exceptions be odious, hath ordained, that if any being named disseisor do personally alledge the exception at the day to him given (if he fail of the warranty that he hath vouched) he shall be adjudged for a disseisor without taking of the assise, and shall restore the damages before inquired of, or to be inquired after, to the double, and shall nevertheless have a year's imprisonment for his falshood. And if that exception be alledged by a bailiff, the taking of the assise shall not be delayed therefore, nor the judgement upon the restitution of the lands and damages. Yet neverthe-less,

eaſdem partes, vel quod querens alias ſe retraxit de brevi conſimili, vel placitum pendeat per breve de altiori natura: fiat ei breve de faciendo venire ſuper hoc recordum. Et cum illud habuerit, et videant juſtic', quod recordum ita ei miſſum valeret ante judicium, quod per illud excluderetur querens ab actione ſua, ſtatim faciant juſtic' ſcire parti, quæ prius recuperavit, quod ſit ad certum diem, ad quem rehabeat defendens ſeiſinam ſuam, et damna, ſi quæ prius ſolvit per primum judicium, ſimul cum damnis quæ habuit poſt primum judicium reddit': quæ ei reſtituantur in duplo, ſicut ſupradictum eſt: et nihilominus puniatur ille qui primo recuperavit, per priſonam ſecundum diſcretionem juſtic'. Eodem modo ſi defendens, contra quem tranſivit aſſiſa, in ſua abſentia oſtendat chartas, vel quiet' clam' (21), *ſuper quarum confectione non fuerunt jurat' examinat' nec examinari poterunt, pro eo quod de eis non fiebat mentio in placitand', et probabiliter ignorare potuerunt confectionem hujuſmodi ſcriptorum: juſtic' viſis ſcriptis illis faciant ſcire parti, quæ recuperavit, quod ſit ad certum diem coram eis: et venire fac' jurat' ejuſdem aſſiſæ. Et ſi per veredictum juratorum* (22), *vel forte per irrotulamentum ſcripta illa verificaverint, puniatur ille, qui aſſiſam impetravit contra factum ſuum, per pœnam ſupradictam. Nec capiat vic' de cætero bovem à diſſeiſito, ſed à diſſeiſitore tantum* (23). *Et ſi plures ſint diſſeiſitores in uno brevi nominati, nihilominus de uno bove ſit contentus* (24)*: nec exigat bovem niſi de precio* v. s. *vel precium* (25).

leſs, that if the maſter of ſuch a bailiff that was abſent, come after before the ſame juſtices that took the aſſiſe, and offer to prove by record or rolls, that another time an aſſiſe paſſed between the ſame parties of the ſame land, or that the plaintiff at another time did withdraw his ſuit in a like writ, or that a plea hangeth by a writ of more high nature, a writ of *venire facias* ſhall be granted unto him to cauſe the ſame record to be brought; and when he hath the ſame, and the juſtices do perceive, that the record ſo ſhewed by him would have been ſo available before the judgement, that the plaintiff by force of the ſame ſhould have been barred of his action, the juſtices ſhall preſently cauſe the party to be warned that firſt recovered, that he appear at a certain day, at the which the defendant ſhall have again his ſeiſin and damages (if he before paid any by the firſt judgement given) which ſhall be reſtored him to the double, as before is ſaid; and alſo he that firſt recovered ſhall be puniſhed by impriſonment according to the diſcretion of the juſtices. In the ſame manner if the defendant, againſt whom the aſſiſe paſſed in his abſence, ſhew any deeds or releaſes, upon the making whereof the jury were not examined, nor could be examined, becauſe there was no mention made of them in pleading, and by probability might be ignorant of the making of thoſe writings; the juſtices upon the ſight of thoſe writings ſhall cauſe the party to be warned that recovered, that he appear at a certain day, and ſhall cauſe the jurors of the ſame aſſiſe to come; and if he ſhall verifie thoſe writings to be true by the verdict of the jurors, or by inrollment, he that purchaſed the aſſiſe contrary to his own deed, ſhall be puniſhed by the pain aforeſaid. And the ſheriff from henceforth ſhall not take

take an ox of the disseisee, but of the disseisor only; and if there be many disseisors named in one writ, yet shall he be contented with one ox; nor shall receive any ox but of v. s. price, or the value.

(Regist. 196, &c. 8 Rep. 45. Fitz. Ass. 138. Fitz. Avowry, 142. Rast. 58, &c. Co. pla. 60. Regist. 197. Fitz. Ass. 61. 94. 111. 134. 167. 210. 216. 330. 439. 452. Fitz. Ass. 395. Fitz. Brief, 790. Bro. Elegit. 20. Bro. disseisin, 86. 105. Rast 67. 11 H. 4. 84. Hob. 95. 11 H. 4. f. 49. 22 Ed. 3. f 4. 30 Ed. 3. f. 12. Fitz. Record. 32. Bro. Covert, 35. 1 Roll. 91. Keilw. 131, 132. Fitz. Ass. 5. 122. Fitz. Certificate, 2, 3, 4. 7, 8. 10. F.N.B. 181, &c. Rast. 110. Regist. 200. 17 E. 3. f. 28. 12 H. 4. f. 9. 7 H. 4. f. 45. Fitz. Ass. 412.)

(1) *Tam festinum remedium.*] The assise of novel disseisin is not onely *maxime festinum, sed maxime beneficiale remedium,* for many causes: [411]

1. The defendant shall not be essoigned.
2. The defendant shall not cast a protection.
3. He shall not pray in aide, but of the king.
4. He shall not vouch any stranger, nor any party to the writ, unlesse he enter into warranty maintenant.
5. The same law of receit.
6. The parol shall not demur, either for the nonage of the plaintife, or the tenant, and for divers other causes.

(2) *Ut celeris fiat justitia, et quod dilationes,* &c.] This concerneth the common-wealth, for *expedit reipublicæ, ut sit finis litium*; *Regula.* and the duty of every good judge, for *boni judicis est lites dirimere.* *Regula.*

(3) *In pluribus casibus quam prius habuit.*] It is to be observed, that at the common law there were but two forms of writs of assise of novel disseisin in the register of the chancery, that is to say, an assise *de libero tenemento,* and an assise *de communia pasturæ* for his cattell, &c. which was so necessary, as without it his free-hold could not be manured: and the assise *de libero tenemento* did lye of houses, land, rent, and other things which lay in render, whereof a *præcipe* did lye at the common law; but of all profits *aprender,* which consisted in *capiendo, colligendo, habendo, recipiendo, et exercendo,* an assise of novel disseisin did not lye at the common law; but the party was driven to his *quod permittat,* in which was great delay, and they which had but an estate for life could not maintain that writ: therefore this act doth give in all the said cases a speedy remedy by an assise in lieu of the *quod permittat,* so the said profits were to be taken or had *in certo loco*; and therefore these words, *in pluribus casibus, &c.* are verified.

4 E 2. Ass. 451. 35 Ass. p. 11. 11 H. 6. 22.

31 E. 1. Ass. 440. 4 E. 2. ib. 449. 8 E. 2. ib. 385. 16 E. 2. ib. 370.

(4) *De estoveriis bosci.*] These (as by this act appeareth) consist in *capiendo.* Lib. 5. fol. 25. lib. 8. fol. 47, 48. li. 9. fo. 112.

Of this word *estoverium,* and of the severall kindes thereof, I have spoken at large in other places.

(5) *De nucibus, glandibus, et aliis fructibus colligendis.*] These and the like consist in *colligendo,* and are to be taken in woods: *Notandum est quod sub nomine herbagii, non continetur glans, et ideo tempore glandis, et pessone excluduntur porci, et capræ, nisi ad hoc specialiter agatur, quod talem habeant communiam; glandis enim nomine* Bract. li. 4. 226.

continentur

continentur glans caſtanea, fagina, ficus et nuces, et alia quæq; quæ edi et paſci poterunt præter herbam.

Virg. Geo. 4.

Nec de concuſſa tantum pluit ilice glandis.

44 E. 3. 24, 25.

(6) *De corrodio.*] This being a reaſonable ſuſtenance for a man, conſiſteth in *habendo*, as by the writ *de corrodio habend'* appeareth.

Lib. 8. fol. 46. Jehu Webs caſe.

And albeit this act ſpeaketh *de corrodio*, yet an aſſiſe ſhall be maintained of the part of a corrodie, but therein alſo are diverſities, as you may read, lib. 8. in Jehu Webs caſe.

(7) *De liberatione bladorum, et aliorum victualium.*] Theſe conſiſt in *recipiendo*, as belonging to a corrodie.

(8) *Ac aliorum neceſſariorum.*] Theſe alſo conſiſt in *recipiendo*, as things *quæ pertinent ad victum, veſtitum, et habitationem hominis.*

[412]

(9) *In certo loco annuatim recipiendis.*] Note this clauſe, *in certo loco*, extends to eſtovers, and all the profits *aprender*, and not to the clauſe of offices. But yet the office muſt be *in certo loco*, which is ſo to be underſtord, as albeit the office be removeable, yet it muſt be *in certo loco*, when the aſſiſe is brought.

Jehu Webs caſe, ubi ſupra.

(10) *Tolneto, tronagio, paſſagio, pontagio, pannagio, et hiis ſimilibus in certis locis capiend'.*] Theſe conſiſt in *capiendo*, and of theſe you may read at large in Jehu Webs caſe, ubi ſupra.

7 E. 3. 63. 8 E. 3. 55, 56. 10 E. 3. 27. 18 E. 3. 27. 19 E. 2. Vieu. 77. 7 Aſſ. 12. 10 Aſſ. 11. 30 Aſſ. 4. 18 E. 2. Aſſ. 377. 4 E. 2. ib. 449. 8 E. 2. ib. 385. 16 E. 2. ib. 370. 7 H. 6. 8. 22 H. 6. 9. 9 E. 4. 6. 27 H. 8. a. 28 H. 8. Dier, 7. 3 Mar. Dier, 153. 31 H. 8. Br. gentes 134. * Jehu Webs caſe, ubi ſupr. F.N.B. 178. f.

(11) *Cuſtodiis boſcorum, parcorum, foreſtarum, chacearum, warrennarum, portarum, et aliis balivis.*] Of theſe and other offices, you may read at large in Jehu Webs caſe; and this act concerning theſe offices is but declaratory, for an aſſiſe did lye of them at the common law, becauſe a *præcipe* did lye of them, as in that caſe it appeareth.

(12) *Et officiis in feodo.*] This ſtatute being herein (as hath been ſaid) made in affirmance of the common law, although the ſtatute ſpeaketh onely of offices in fee *; yet ſuch as have offices in tail, or for life, ſhall have an aſſiſe, as by the authorities before cited doth appear.

† 31 E. 1. Aſſ. 440. 21 E. 3. 4. b. 27 H. 8. 12.

† And albeit the words be generall, yet this act is onely to be intended of offices of profits, and not of offices of charge, and no profit.

But this act doth extend aſwell to offices in the admirall court eccleſiaſticall court, or any other court, where either the civill or eccleſiaſticall law, or any other law then the common law, &c. of England doth rule; as to offices in temporall courts which are governed by the common law, &c. as by the authorities aboveſaid, and Jehu Webs caſe appeareth.

13 E. 3. Parl. 23. 12 Aſſ. 23. 8 Aſſ. 4. 3 E. 3. Aſſ. 175. 22 H. 6. 11. 15 E. 4. 4. 30 Aſſ. 4.

If a man be diſſeiſed of the whole office, he ſhall have an aſſiſe *de officio cum pertinen'*; and albeit the ſtatute ſpeaketh, *de officiis*, and if he be diſſeiſed of parcell of the profits, he may have an aſſiſe of that parcell: but therein alſo are diverſities, as you may read in Jehu Webs caſe.

11 Aſſ. p. 13. lib. 5. fol. 61. Je. Webs caſe.

(13) *Breve de libero tenemento.*] So as now by this act, in all the caſes aboveſaid concerning profits *aprender*, the aſſiſe of novel diſſeiſin ſhall be *de libero tenemento.*

(14) *Et ſicut prius jacuit, et locum habuit in communia paſturæ, ita de cætero in communia turbariæ, piſcariæ, et aliis communibus hiis ſimilibus.*] Bracton, who wrote before the making of this act, ſaith, *Quod locum habet aſſiſa de qualibet communia pertinen' ad liberum tenementum,*

Bract. li. 4. fol. 231. 23 H. 3. Aſſ. 438.

nementum, scil. communia pasturæ, turbariæ, &c. And in the raign of H. 3. which was before the making of this act, an assise did lye of a common of piscarie; and these opinions had great probability of reason: yet because (as hath been said) there was no writ in the Register in those cases, therefore before this act no writ did lye by the generall opinion of the judges; but now this act hath cleared the question. 12 H. 3. ib. 417. Temps R. 2. Grant 104.

(15) *In casu etiam quando quis tenet tenementum ad terminum annorum, vel in custodiam, et alienat in feodo.*] This branch is an affirmance of the common law, for the free-hold being in the lessor, or in the heir, the livery being made by the lessee for yeers, or gardein, doth work a disseisin, because by his torcious livery he disseiseth the lessor or heir, for the which they may have an assise of novel disseisin at the common law, and both the feoffor for making, and the feoffee for taking a torcious livery were both disseisors: and so it is if tenant at will, or tenant at sufferance make a lease for yeers, and the lessee enter, this is a disseisin to the lessor at the common law. 4 E. 2. Ass. 790. 19 E. 2. ib. 400. 3 E. 4. 1. 15 H. 7. 4. [413] 12 E. 4. 12.

This act speaketh first of a tenant for yeers, and yet a tenant by elegit, statute merchant, or the staple are within this law: and so it is of a tenant at will, or a tenant at sufferance, for all these have a possession, but otherwise it is of a bailife, for he hath no possession at all. See the ancient Terms, cap. Elegit. 3 E. 4. 1. 4 E. 2. Ass. 790.

2. Of gardein, which extendeth not onely to gardein in chivalry, but to gardein in socage, *et pur cause de nurture.* 8 Ass. 28. 8 E. 3. 63. 15 H. 3. Bre. 878.

3. * Of an alienation in fee, and yet an alienation in tail, or for life is within this act, because they are within the same mischief. 20 H. 3. Ass. 432.

4. † If tenant for yeers, or a gardein make a lease for life, the remainder for life, the remainder in fee, and tenant for life enter, he is a disseisor, because he taketh the first livery; and so it is of him in the remainder for life, or in fee, if he enter. * Bract. li. 4. f. 216. Brit. cap. 32. Disseisin. Fleta, li. 4. c. 17.

(16) *Fiat remedium per breve de ingressu.*] Here it is objected, that if *tam feoffator, quam feoffatus* be disseisors, by the common law, and so declared by this statute: 7 E. 3. 11. 43 Ass. 45. † 50 E. 3. 22.

1. How the lessor or heir can have a writ of entry, and suppose the entry by the lessee or gardein?

2. Whether the lessor or the heir may not have an election, either to have his assise, or his writ of entry?

To the first it is answered, that albeit it be a disseisin, having regard to the lessor or heir, for the benefit of the assise; yet between the lessee or gardein, and the feoffee, it is a feoffment, whereunto a warranty may be annexed, and a voucher had of them to recover in value (as in another place hath been said) so as the lessor or the heir may have a writ of entry in the *per* against the alienee, and principally, because it is affirmed by this act. See the first part of the Institutes, sect. 698. & 611.

To the second, this act hath prescribed a form and order concerning alienations after the act, *viz.* that living either the feoffor or feoffee, an assise should lye; and therefore living either of them, a writ of entry doth not lye: but for alienations before this act, a writ of entry might have been brought since this act. 4 E. 2. Ass. 790. 19 E. 2. ib. 400. 15 H. 3. Bre. 878.

(17) *Et quamvis superius fiat mentio,* &c.] This is but *abundans cautela,* and yet prudently added *ad majorem rei securitatem.*

(18) *Et licet dubitaverint quidam utrum in casu quo quis pascat alterius seperale,* &c.] This assise was in this case maintainable by the common law.

These

27 Aſſ. p. 30. Kelwey, 12 H. 7. 20. F.N.B. 178. h. Liure de Entries Raſt. 65.

These words are to be intended, when one claimeth common in the ſeverall land of another, and puts in his cattell to uſe the ſame; the owner of the ſoil hath two wayes to help himſelf, either to waive the poſſeſſion, and then to bring his aſſiſe as one out of poſſeſſion, as in the common caſe of a diſſeiſin, and then he ſhall have judgement to recover the land and damages; or elſe he may keep his poſſeſſion, and bring his generall writ of aſſiſe of novel diſſeiſin: and if the tenant plead to the aſſiſe, that the plaintife was tenant of the land the day of the writ purchaſed, and yet is; the plaintiſe may maintain his writ, and ſay, that the land was, and is his ſeverall, and the defendant did feed his ſeverall with his cattell, and according to this branch of this act he prayeth the aſſiſe; and in this caſe if it be found for the plaintife, he ſhall have judgement to hold the land as his ſeverall, and damages.

[414]

Note that in this caſe he is not diſſeiſed of the land, but of the ſeveralty of his land.

And this feeding is to be underſtood, when one claimeth a common appendant, appurtenant, or in groſſe, and for the uſe of the ſame doth put in his cattell; this claim, and putting in of his cattell is a diſſeiſin of the ſeveralty of the land, and ſhall have judgement, as is aforeſaid, accordingly: but if the cattell come in by way of eſcape, this is a treſpaſſe, and no diſſeiſin of the ſeveralty within this ſtatute.

Bract. li. 4. fo. 217. Fleta, li. 4. cap. 1. 27 Aſſ. p. 51. 28 Aſſ. p. 50. F.N.B. 178. i. Bract. li. 4. fo. 216.

By the common law a man that is in ſeiſin of his land may have an aſſiſe, for that he is diſſeiſed of the quiet injoying of his land; as when the lord, or any other that hath a rent, and oftentimes diſtreineth for the rent, where none is behinde, the tenant ſhall have an aſſiſe of novel diſſeiſin of the land, for that, by reaſon of the frequencie of diſtreſſes, he is diſſeiſed of the quiet injoying of his land, and cannot make his advantage thereof, and *frequentia mutat tranſgreſſionem in diſſeiſinam.*

Mirror, ca. 2. § 15. Brit. fol. 108.

And the Mirror ſaith, that diſturbance of one that is in peaceable poſſeſſion, in three caſes doth amount to a diſſeiſin: as if the lord that is in quiet poſſeſſion of his rent cometh to diſtrein, and is by the tenant diſturbed, ſo as he cannot take a diſtreſſe, this diſturbance is a diſſeiſin of the rent.

2. When the lord hath taken a diſtreſſe, and the tenant pay not his rent, but diſturb him by unjuſt ſute of a replevie.

3. When any diſtrein ſo outragiouſly (that is, ſo often) as the terre tenant cannot plough, or duly uſe his ground.

13 Aſſ. p. 1. 26 Aſſ. p. 35. 44 E. 3. 23. 7 H. 4. 16. 1 H. 4. 51, 52. Bro. covert. 68. Doct. & Stud. li. 2. fo. 113. 29 E. 3. 27. M. 18 E. 1. Coram rege Rot. 35. North. 13 R. 2. Record 32.

(19) *Caveant de cætero illi qui nominati ſunt diſſeiſitores,* &c.] A feme covert and an infant are not within this ſtatute to have corporall puniſhment by impriſonment by their plea, by vouching of a record, and failing of it.

This act doth not extend to an aſſiſe of mordanc.

See a notable record ſoon after the making of this act, upon this branch of this act, Mich. 18 E. 1. *Coram rege* Rot. 35. North.

In a formedon, or any other reall action, if the tenant plead a record, and fail thereof at the day, the demandant ſhall not have ſeiſin of the land, but onely a petit cape: for this ſtatute extendeth onely to the aſſiſe of novel diſſeiſin: and in caſe of the aſſiſe, if the tenant before this ſtatute had pleaded a record, and failed thereof, yet the aſſiſe ſhould have been taken, as appeareth by this act.

 Here

Here it is to be observed, that every man shall plead that, which is apt and pertinent to his case; and therefore a disseisor that is not tenant of the land shall not plead any thing hat concerns the tenancie of the land, as a release of all actions realls, but shall plead a release of actions personalls, or any other plea that doth excuse himself of damages. 1. Part of the Institutes, sect. 494. lib. 7. fol. 26.

(20) *Et si illa exceptio proponatur per balivum, non propter hoc differatur captio assisæ, nec judicium, super restitutione tenementi,* &c.] In an assise, as by this branch it appeareth, the bailife cannot plead any matter of record, either in barre or to the writ; for the bailife cannot plead any matter, or any plea out of the point of the assise, nor any thing that is not triable by the assise, nor any plea which he cannot conclude, *Et si trove ne soit nul tort, nul disseisin.* Hereby it appeareth what treasure may be found in the mines of these ancient statutes. 1 Ass. Pl. 1. 2 Ass. Pl. 4. 8 E. 3. 1. 8 Ass. 2. 9 E. 3. 13. 16. 9 Ass. 4. 25 Ass. 26. 8 H. 6. 9. 21 H. 6. 58. 22 H. 6. 44. 1 E. 4. 4. 8 H. 7. 11. 9 H. 7. 24. 11 H. 7. 11. F.N.B. 182. a.

And if therefore the bailife do plead any matter of record, yet the justices shall proceed, &c. and give judgement; but then the defendant named in the assise may come unto the justices, and verifie that there was such a matter of record, &c. and he shall have a certificate of assise by force of this act.

And the writ that is given in this case is after judgement, but the certificate of assise that was at the common law was after verdict; and before or after judgement when the verdict was not well examined by the justices, &c. the justices of office might examine it, whereof we need not to treat any further in this place, for that this statute doth not extend to that kinde of certificate; onely I may note two things, 1. That when the recognitors of the assise give a full generall verdict, there lyeth no certificate at the common law. 2. That if any of the recognitors of the assise that gave the verdict died, the certificate failed at the common law, for it was to supply the defect of their former verdict: see hereafter more of this matter in this chapter. [415] Bract. l. 4. fol. 289, &c. 293. Britton, fo. 239. 43 Ass. 1. 5. Regist. 200. Judic' 22. 17 E. 3. 28. 12 H. 4. 9. 2 H. 5. 5. F.N.B. 180. 183. Vet. N.B. 111, &c. Hil. 19 E. 1. coram rege Rot. 35. Suff. 8 E. 2. Ass. 412.

Note the words of the assise are *attachias eum, vel balivum suum, &c.* And the bayliffe plead in his own name; *I. de C. tanquam balivus A. de B. dicit:* and not *A. de B. per balivum suum.* 12 H. 4. 9.

(21) *Eodem modo si defendens, contra quem transivit assisa, in sua absentia ostendat chartas, vel quiet' clam',* &c.] This branch doth not onely extend to an assise of novel disseisin, but to the assise of *darrein presentment, juris utrum,* and assise of mordaunc', and some have thought to an attaint also: so as the tenant shall not onely have a certificate of an assise by the former branch upon matter of record, but also by this branch upon deeds and quiet claimes, and the reason thereof is, for that the bayliffe could not plead the same. Regist. Judic' 11, 12. 12 H. 4. 9. F.N.B. 183. e. f. & 196. c. 32 Ass. p. 1. 2 H. 5. 5. 33 H. 6. 20.

And it is to be observed, that after the bayly hath pleaded to the assise, the tenant may come before the assise taken, though it be after the assise awarded, and plead any deed, quiet-claime, or other matter of certificate, and shall not bee driven after the assise taken, &c. to sue his certificate upon this act to trouble the tenant and the recognitors of the assise, *quia frustra fit per plura, quod fieri potest per pauciora.* 11 H. 7. 11. 11 Ass. p. 3. 11 E. 3. Ass. 85. 20 Ass. 6. 50 E. 3. 20.

(22) *Venire facias jurat' ejusdem assisæ: et si per veredictum juratorum,* &c.] Upon this branch it hath been conceived, that albeit that some of the former recognitors be dead, that it shall be tried by the former and by others; for though this act doth ordain that a *venire facias* shall be awarded to the jurors of the same assise, yet the 12 H. 4. 10. 7 H. 4. 45. 31 Ass. 1. F.N.B. 183. c.

the subsequent words be, *et si per veredictum juratorum*, and saith not *praedictorum*; so as upon this act an addition may be made.

32 Ass. p. 1. 14 E. 3. receit 134. Br. certificat Dass. 13. Pasch. 31 E. 3. fol. 35. in libro meo, le Countesse de Atholes case.

In an assise the plaintiffe made title to ten marks rent by specialty of the graunt of the tenant, and the assise was taken by default, and after the tenant upon shewing of a deed of defeasance of the same rent upon certain conditions to be performed on the plaintiffes part, or otherwise the rent to cease, which he averred to be broken, which deed of defeasance did beare date in a forein county, *viz.* in London, whereupon a certificate upon this statute was prayed before the justices of assise, who adjourned the same in bank to be resolved, whether a certificate did lie upon this forein defeasaunce: where it was awarded that the certificate was maintainable, and that the deed of defeasance being denied should be tried in London, where it was found for the tenant, whereupon the certificate was remaunded to be taken in the county where the assise was brought: out of this record three things are to bee observed.

1. That a certificate doth lie upon a defeasance bearing date in a forein county (as well as upon a charter or acquitance) which was tried by jurors of that forein county, and by none of the recognitors of the assise.

2. That a certificate lieth by this act upon a recovery by default, as well as where the tenant pleadeth by bayly to the assise.

[416]

3. That the certificate must be sued and adjudged in the county where the assise was sued.

26 Ass. p. 5. 12 H. 4. 20. F.N.B. 182. c. W. 1. c. 26. 42 E. 3. 5. 4 E. 4. 10. 21 H. 7. 17. Stamf. Pl. Cor. 49. a. Itin.

(23) *Nec capiat vic' de caetero bovem à disseisito, sed à disseisitore tantum.*] This oxe which the sheriffe tooke was not any reward for doing of his office *(pro officio suo exequendo)* for that was prohibited by the statute of W. 1. cap. 26. but this was a duty due by auncient custome after the cause ended.

But where it was due onely from the disseisor, the sheriffe before this act did also incroach the like upon the disseisee, which is restrained by this act, and to be taken onely of the wrong doer, and neither of the disseisee, nor of the tenant that is no disseisor.

(24) *Et si plures sint disseisitores in uno breve nominat, nihilominus de uno bove sit contentus.*] This branch is in affirmance of the law, for seeing they are joyned in one writ, they are as to this purpose but as one disseisor, and therefore but one oxe is due unto the sheriffe.

26 Ass. p. 47.

A man that is indicted and arraigned for two felonies, shall pay but for one deliverance onely, for though the felonies be severall, yet the person that is delivered is but one.

(25) *Nec exigat bovem, nisi de precio 5. s. vel precium.*] Herein the makers of this law did adde this branch very providently, for there is nothing more incertaine then prices of things which oftentimes rise and fall, and specially of victuals, and therefore here having set down the price of the oxe, they adde, if that should not bee the just price of the oxe, which they foresaw might not continue long, then the sheriffe should have 5. s.

CAP.

CAP. XXVI.

IN brevibus de rediſſeiſina adjudicentur de cætero damna in duplo: et ſint rediſſeiſitores de cætero irreplegiabiles per commune breve. Et ſicut in ſtatuto de Merton proviſum fuit illud breve de his qui diſſeiſit' fuerint, poſtquam recuperaverint per aſſiſam novæ diſſeiſinæ, mortis anteceſſoris, aut per alias juratas ulterius de cætero habeat illud breve locum in illis qui recuperaverint per defaltam, redditionem, aut alio modo ſine recognitione aſſiſarum vel juratarum.

IN writs of rediſſeiſin from henceforth double damages ſhall be awarded, and the rediſſeiſors ſhall not be repleviable hereafter by the common writ. And like as in the ſtatute of Merton the ſame writ was provided for ſuch as were diſſeiſed after they had recovered by aſſiſe of novel diſſeiſin, of mortdaunceſtor, or other jurates; even ſo from henceforth the ſame writ ſhall further hold place for them that ſhall recover by default, reddition, or otherwiſe, without recognition of aſſiſes or jurates.

(15 H. 7. f. 8. 1 Inſt. 154. 20 H. 3. c. 3. 52 H. 3. c. 8. Raſt. 548.)

By the ſtatute of Merton both the writ of *rediſſeiſin*, and of the *poſt diſſeiſin* were given. Merton, cap. 3.

This ſtatute is an act additionall in three ſeverall points.

1. Where the ſtatute of Merton gave but ſingle damages, this act doth give double damages both in the *rediſſeiſin* and *poſt diſſeiſin*, but the jury is to give the ſingle, and the court is to double them.

2. Where notwithſtanding the ſtatute of Merton and of Marlebridge, cap. 8. he might be replevied by the common writ, yet by this act he cannot ſo be. Marlb. cap. 8.

3. Where the ſtatute of Merton extended onely to rediſſeiſins upon recoveries in aſſiſe of *novel diſſeiſin* by verdict of the recognitors, and to *poſt diſſeiſins* upon recoveries by verdict onely; this act doth extend to recoveries by default, reddition, *aut alio modo*, as upon demurrer, &c. ſo as hereby the *rediſſeiſin*, and *poſt diſſeiſin* doe lie in many more caſes then they lay before. [417]

See before in the expoſition of the ſtatute of Merton and Marlebridge.

If an aſſiſe be brought againſt A. and B. and A. is found the diſſeiſor, and B. the tenant, and the plaintiffe recovereth, and B. the tenant diſſeiſeth the plaintiffe again, the plaintiffe ſhall have no *rediſſeiſin*, but a *poſt diſſeiſin*, becauſe a *rediſſeiſin* lieth not but againſt him that was party to the former diſſeiſin.

CAP. XXVII.

POSTQUAM aliquis posuerit se in inquisitionem aliquam ad proximum diem, allocetur ei essonium: sed ad alios dies sequentes per essonium non differatur captio inquisitionis, sive prius habuit esson', sive non. Nec admittat' esson' post diem datum prece partium (1), *in casu in quo partes consentiunt venire sine essonio.*

AFTER any hath put himself to an inquest, an essoin shall be allowed him at the next day; but all the other days following, the taking of the inquest shall not be delayed by the essoin, whether he were essoined before, or no; neither shall any essoin be allowed after day given *prece partium*, in case where the parties consent to come without essoin.

(Fitz. Essoin. 15. 81. 83. 130. Dier, 224. 324. Bro. Parl. 5. Rast. 297.)

Marlb. cap. 13. The statute of Marlebridge did provide, *Quod postquam aliquis posuerit se in inquisitionem aliquam, &c. non habebit nisi unicum essonium, &c.* By which statute it was not certainly limited when he should have that one essoine, and thereof ensued a great mischiefe, for the defendant would not be essoined but at the *habeas corpus*, and then the jurors should lose their issues, and the inquest should not bee taken, to the great vexation and losse of the jurors. 9 H. 5. 12. Westm. 1. c. 41.

And therefore this statute chiefly for the ease of the jurors provideth, that the defendant should have but one essoine, and that essoine must be at the next day, and that is at the *venire facias*, and if he neglect that next time, he shall never have it after.

7 E. 2. essoin 81. 83. Dier, 15 El. 324. b. This act is to be intended onely of a plea personall, and of a common essoine, and not of an essoine *de service le roy*, for that he may cast when he will. See the exposition upon the statute of Marlebridge, cap. 13.

35 H. 6. 53. And albeit the words of this act are generall, yet it must be understood onely in cases where an essoine doth lie, which is implied by this word *allocetur*, and therefore if the defendant come in by *exigent*, or *cepi corpus*, and joyne issue *ad proximum diem*, he cannot be essoined, for that he either remaineth in ward, or goeth by mainprise, and therefore before this statute could not be essoined; and this is a branch of restraint, and not of enlargement.

(1) *Nec admittatur essonium post diem datum prece partium.*] And the reason is, for that seeing this day is given by the prayer and agreement of the parties without any essoine, this statute doth enact, that *post diem datum prece partium*, no essoine shall be admitted.

CAP.

CAP. XXVIII.

CUM per statutum Westm. 1. *statuatur quod postquam tenentes semel comparuerint in curia, non allocetur eis essonium in brevibus assisarum* (1): *eodem modo* (2) *de cætero observetur de petentibus.*

WHEREAS by the statute of Westminster the First, it was provided, that after the tenants have once appeared in the court, no essoin should be allowed them in writs of assises; in like manner it shall be from henceforth observed against the demandants.

W. 1. cap. 41. (Fitz. Essoin, 65, 66. 68, 69. 78. 149. Rast. 316.)

(1) *In brevibus assisarum.*] This act extendeth not to assises of novel disseisin no more then the said statute of W. 1. here recited doth: see before the exposition of the statute of W. 1. and the rather for that this act saith *de petentibus*, and the plaintiffe in an assise of novel disseisin is called *querens* and not *petens*, but this act extendeth to mordaunc', *juris utrum*, and attaints, and doth remedy the mischiefe of the demandants side, which was omitted in the statute of W. 1. And note that a writ of attaint is here comprehended under this word *assisa*, because it hath the quality of an assise, *viz.* to have a jury returned the first day, and so in equall mischiefe.

(2) *Eodem modo.*] This is an act of reference, that in all cases where the act of W. 1. doth take away the common essoin from the tenant after appearance, there this act doth take it from the demandant after appearance. See more of this matter in the exposition upon the said act of W. 1.

CAP. XXIX.

BREVE de transgressione (1) *ad audiendum et terminandum de cætero non concedatur coram aliquibus justiciariis, exceptis justiciariis de utroque banco* (2), *et justiciariis itinerantibus, nisi pro enormi transgressione, ubi necesse est apponere festinum remedium* (3). *Et dominus rex de gratia sua speciali* (4) *hoc duxit concedendum. Nec etiam de cætero concedatur* (5) *breve ad audiend' et terminand' appella coram justic' assign', nisi in speciali casu, et certa causa, cum*

A WRIT of trespass (*ad audiendum et terminandum*) from henceforth shall not be granted before any justices, except justices of either bench, and justices in eyre, unless it be for an heinous trespass, where it is necessary to provide speedy remedy, and our lord the king of his special grace hath thought it good to be granted. And from henceforth a writ to hear and determine appeals before justices assigned shall not be granted but in a special case, and for a cause

cum dominus rex hoc præceperit. Sed ne hujusmodi appellati, vel indictati diu detineantur in prisona, habeant breve de odio et atia (6), *sicut in Magna Charta, et aliis statutis dictum est.*

a cause certain, when the king commandeth. But lest the parties appealed or indicted be kept long in prison, they shall have a writ of *odio et atia*, like as it is declared in Magna Charta and other statutes.

Mag. Chart. c. 26. W. 1. cap. 11. Gloc'. cap. 9. (4 Inst. 182. Stat. 2 E. 3. c. 2. Regist. 123. Regist. 133. 9 H. 3. stat. 1. c. 26.)

(1) *Breve de transgressione.*] Albeit the statute mentioneth onely a writ, because commissions were in those dayes most commonly graunted by writ, as the commission to justices in eyre, justices of oier and terminer, of gaole delivery, &c. yet this act doth not onely extend to authority graunted by writ, but by commission also.

[419] Transgression here is taken in a large sense, for any outrage or misdemeanour.

Commissions of oier and terminer are of three sorts.

2 E. 3. cap. 8. One generall at the sute of the king, as to hear and determine all manner of treasons, felonies, riots, routs, trespasses, &c.

29 E. 3. 37. Another particular at the sute of the party, and that in two sorts: one naming particularly the party grieved, as *Rex dilectis et fidelibus suis A. B. & C. salutem. Ex gravi querela D. accepimus quod E. F. & G. et alii malefactores, et pacis nostræ perturbatores in ipsum D. apud N. vi et armis insultum fecerunt, &c.* And the other is more generall, and of this form, *Rex dilectis, &c. Ex clamosis querimoniis diversorum hominum de com' N. ad nostrum sæpius pervenit auditum, quod A. episcopus Winton', &c. plures et diversas oppressiones, &c.*

The third is aswell at the suit of the king, as of the party, all in one writ or commission, as hereafter in this chapter shall be touched.

The mischief before the making of this act was, that commissioners of oier and terminer, &c. were procured, and named by the parties whom the matter concerned; so as the commissioners were neither indifferent, nor of sufficient knowledge and learning.
Regist. 126, 127. F.N.B. 112. f. And the mischief was the greater, for that when a man sued out a commission of oier and terminer at the suit of the party against divers persons for taking of his goods, and for essoigning the same, to the end to waste and convert the same to their own uses; the party that sued the oier and terminer should have a writ to the sherife, rehearsing this matter, and command him to arrest the goods, and to put them in safeguard untill it be otherwise provided or
F.N.B. 112. f. adjudged by the justices of oier and terminer, &c. and if upon this sute it were found for the plaintife, the justices of oier and terminer might restore the party to his goods, or give damages to him for them, wherein it doth vary from an action of trespasse sued before justices of the one bench or the other: and where the party in particular is to be restored to his goods, or to recover damages, the sute is properly by writ, according to the words of
Regist. 123. this act (*Breve de transgressione:*) and by the statute of 34 E. 3. the
34 E. 3. cap. 1. commissioners or justices named in the writ are to be named by the court, and not by the party.

The

The ancient form of commissions of oier and terminer were of all treasons, felonies, &c. grievances, extortions, and deceits made to the king and to his people, aswell at the suit of the king, as of the party, &c. 42 Ass. p. 5.

If a commission of oier and terminer be discontinued or expired, &c. the indictments and records shall be removed into the kings bench, as to their proper center. 44 E. 3. 31. F.N.B. 243. 38 H. 8. Commiss. Br.

(2) *Exceptis justiciariis de utroque banco.*] Here is remedy for both the said mischiefs, for the justices of either benches are presumed to be men of integrity, indifferencie, skill, and knowledge.

Hereof you may read in Stamford. Plac. cor. 55, 56.

(3) *Nisi pro enormi transgressione, ubi necesse est apponere festinum remedium.*] Here it is called, *enormis transgressio.*

In the statute of 2 E. 3. cap. 2. it is called, *grand leads*, or horrible trespasses.

Fitzherbert saith, that this writ is to be granted when a great assembly, insurrection, or heinous misdemeanour, or trespas is committed in any place, then the manner and use is to make such a commission, to hear and determine such misbehaviours. F.N.B. ubi sup.

The Register termineth it, *enormis seu horribilis.* Regist. 125. a.

And if the trespas be not *enormis seu horribilis*, there lyeth a writ of *supersedeas*, or revocation, *quia non enormis, seu horribilis.* Regist. 124. b. 12 Ass. p. 21.

(4) *Dom' rex de gratia sua speciali*, &c.] This is an act of grace, for hereby the king is restrained of his power to grant commissions of oier and terminer to whom he will at his pleasure. [420] Magna Charta, c. 8. W. 1. c. 42.

The stile of the record before justices or commissioners of oier and terminer, sometimes have been, *coram rege et concilio suo apud S. &c.* and sometime, *coram concilio regis apud, &c.* whereof take one record for example, stiled thus: Nota.

Placita coram concilio regis apud Westmon' de termino Paschæ, anno regni regis E. 3. 11. Nicholas Keriels case in a commission of oier and terminer. Pasc. 11 E. 3. Coram conc. regis.

(5) *Nec etiam de cætero concedatur.*] An appeal doth lye either by writ originall, or by bill. Brit. fol. 5. 22 E. 3. Coron. 97, 98. 4 H. 6. 15. Regist. judic. 76. 3 H. 7. ca. 1. 9 H. 4. 2. 13 H. 4. 10. 17 E. 3. 13. 22 E. 4. 19. Dier, 120.

The originall writ issueth out of the chancery. By bill, as in the countie before the sherife and coroners; also before justices of gaol-delivery, if the appellee be in prison before them, and (as it appeareth by this act) before commissioners of oier and terminer, before justices of *nisi prius*, and by bill also before the justices of the kings bench.

It seemed to Fitzherbert, in abridging of the case of 44 E. 3. that justices of peace having power by the statute of 34 E. 3. (which there is called, *le novel statute*) might receive an appeal by bill, because they had power to hear and determine felonies; but that statute doth give them power to hear and determine felonies at the sute of the king, and the book at large speaketh onely of justices of gaol-delivery. 44 E. 3. 44. tit. Coron. F. 95.

(6) *Sed ne hujusmodi appellati, vel indictati diu detineantur in prisona, habeant breve de odio et atia.*] See before in Magna Charta, cap. 26. & 29. Gloc. cap. 9. this branch well explained.

CAP. XXX.

ASSIGNENTUR de cætero duo juſticiarii jurati, coram quibus, et non aliis (1) *capiantur aſſiſæ novæ diſſeiſinæ, mortis anteceſſoris, et attinctæ: et aſſocient ſibi duos, vel unum de diſcretioribus militibus com', in quem venerint: et capiant aſſiſas prædictas, et attinctas, ad plus ter per annum* (2); *viz. ſemel inter quindenam ſancti Johannis Baptiſtæ* (3), *et gulam Auguſti* (4): *et iterum inter feſtum exaltationis ſanctæ crucis, et octab. ſancti Michaelis: et tertio inter feſtum epiphaniæ, et feſtum purificationis beatæ Mariæ. Et in quolibet com', ad quamlibet captionem aſſiſæ, antequam recedant, ſtatuant diem de reditu ſuo* (5); *ita quod omnes de com' ſcire poſſint eorum adventum; et de termino in terminum adjornent aſſiſas* (6). *Si per vocationem warranti* (7), *per eſſon'* (8), *vel per defectum recognitorum, ſi ad unum diem captio earum differatur. Et ſi*
[421] *aliqua de cauſa viderint, quod utile ſit, quod aſſiſæ mortis anteceſſoris per eſſonium, vel vocationem warranti reſpectuate adjornentur in banco, liceat eis hoc facere, et tunc mittant juſticiar' de banco recordum cum brevi originali. Et cum loquela pervenerit ad captionem aſſiſæ, remittatur l quela* (9) *cum brevi originali per juſticiar' de banco, ad priores juſticiar': coram quibus capiatur aſſiſa. Sed de cætero dent juſtic' de banco in hujuſmodi aſſiſis ad minus quatuor dies per annum, coram præfat' juſtic' aſſignatis, ut parcant laboribus et expenſis. Atterminentur inquiſitiones capiendæ de tranſgreſſ' placitat' coram juſticiar' de utroque banco: niſi ita enormis ſit tranſgreſſio, quod magna indigeat examinatione. Atterminentur etiam inquiſitiones coram eis de aliis placitis*

FROM henceforth two juſtices ſworn ſhall be aſſigned, before whom, and none other, aſſiſes of novel diſſeiſin, mortdaunceſtor, and attaints ſhall be taken, and they ſhall aſſociate unto them one or two of the diſcreeteſt knights of the ſhire into which they ſhall come; and ſhall take the foreſaid aſſiſes and attaints but thrice in the year at the moſt, that is to ſay, firſt between the quinzime of Saint John Baptiſt, and the gule of Auguſt; and the ſecond time, between the feaſt of the exaltation of the holy croſs, and the utas of Saint Michael; and the third time, between the feaſt of the epiphany, and the feaſt of the purification of the bleſſed Mary. And in every ſhire at every taking of aſſiſes before their departure, they ſhall appoint the day of their return, ſo that every one of the ſhire may know of their coming, and ſhall adjourn the aſſiſes from term to term, if the taking of them be deferred at any day by vouching to warranty, by eſſoin, or by default of jurors. And if they ſee that it be profitable for any cauſe that aſſiſes of mortdaunceſtor, being reſpited by eſſoin or voucher, ought to be adjourned into the bench; it ſhall be lawfull for them to do it, and then they ſhall ſend the record with the original writ before the juſtices of the bench; and when the matter is come to the taking of the aſſiſe, the juſtices of the bench ſhall remit the matter to the former juſtices before whom the aſſiſe ſhall be taken. But from henceforth the juſtices of the bench in ſuch aſſiſes ſhall give four days at the leaſt in the year before the ſaid juſtices aſſigned, for to ſpare expence and labour. Inquiſitions of treſpaſs

placitis placitatis in utroque banco, in quibus facilis est examinatio, ut quum dedicitur ingressus, vel seisina alicujus, vel in casu quum de uno articulo sit inquirend'. Sed inquisitiones de grossis et pluribus articulis, qui magna indigeant examinatione, capiantur coram justic' de bancis, nisi ambae partes petant (10); *quod inquisitio capiatur coram aliquibus de societate, cum in partes illas venerint: quod de caetero non fiat nisi per duos justic', vel unum, cum aliquo milite de com', in quem partes consentiunt. Nec atterminentur hujusmodi inquisitiones coram aliquibus justiciariis de banco, nisi statuatur certus dies et locus in com', in praesentia partium: et dies et locus inserantur in brevi de judicio per haec verba* (11):

trespass shall be determined before the justices of both benches, except the trespass be so hainous that it shall require great examination. Inquisitions also of other pleas pleaded in either of the benches, shall be determined before them, wherein small examination is required, as when the entry or seisin of any is denied, or in case when one article is to be inquired. But inquisitions of many and great articles, the which require great examination, shall be taken before the justices of the bench, except that both parties desire that the inquisition may be taken afore some of the associates when they do come into those parts; so that from henceforth it shall not be done but by two justices, or one with some knight of the shire, upon whom the parties can agree. And such inquisitions shall not be determined by any justices of the bench, unless a day and a place certain be appointed in the shire, in presence of the parties, and the day and place shall be mentioned in a writ judicial by these words:

Praecipimus tibi quod venire facias coram justiciariis nostris apud Westmonast', in octa. sancti Michaelis, nisi talis et talis tali die et loco ad partes illas venerint, xii. &c.

Et cum hujusmodi inquisitiones captae fuerint, retornentur in bancis, et ibi fiat judicium, et irrotulentur (12). *Et si omissa forma praedicta aliquae inquisitiones capiantur, pro nullis habeantur* (13)*: excepto quod assisae ultimae praesentationis, et inquisitiones super quare impedit atterminentur in proprio com' coram uno justiciar' de banco, et uno milite, ad certos tamen diem et locum in banco statutos, sive defendens consentiat, sive non: et ibi statim reddatur judicium* (14). *Habeant de caetero omnes justiciarii de bancis in itineribus clericos irrotulantes omnia placita coram eis placitat', sicut*

And when such inquests be taken, they shall be returned into the bench, and there shall judgement be given, and there they shall be inrolled. And if any inquisitions be taken otherwise than after this form, they shall be of no effect, except that an assise of *darrein presentment*, and inquisitions of *quare impedit* shall be determined in their own shire before one justice of the bench and one knight, at a day and place certain in the bench assigned, whether the defendant consent, or not, and there the judgement shall be given immediately. All justices of the benches from

sicut antiquitus habere consueverunt (15). *Item ordinatum est, quod justiciarii * ad assisas capiend' assignati non compellant juratores dicere praecise, si sit disseisina vel non, dummodo dicere voluerint veritatem facti, et petere auxilium justic'. Sed si sponte velint* (16) *dicere, quod disseisina est, vel non, admittatur eorum veredictum sub suo periculo. Et de caetero non ponant justic' in assisis, aut juratis aliquos jurat', nisi eos qui ad hoc prius fuerunt summoniti* (17).

from henceforth shall have in their circuits clerks to inroll all pleas pleaded before them, like as they have used to have in time passed. And also it is ordained, that the justices assigned to take assises shall not compel the jurors to say precisely whether it be disseisin, or not, so that they do shew the truth of the deed, and require aid of the justices. But if they of their own head will say, that it is disseisin, their verdict shall be admitted at their own peril. And from henceforth the justices shall not put in assises or juries any other than those that were summoned to the same at the first.

(2 Bulst. 160. 12 Rep. 31. 52. Kel. 109. pl. 30. 27 Ed. 1. stat. 1. c. 4. 12 Ed. 2. stat. 2. c. 4. Regist. 186. F.N.B. 240. b. Bro. Nisi prius, 31. 13 Rep. 42. The writ of *nisi prius*. Regist. Ind. 7. F.N.B. 240. E. Rast. 437. 2 Salk. 454. 9 H. 3. stat. 1. c. 12, 13. Dyer, 135. 163. Dyer, 175. Rast. 99. 333. Plow. 92. Dyer, 173. 9 Rep. 11. 14 Ed. 3. stat. 1. c. 16.

This statute consisteth of many branches whereof we shall speak in their order: and first it is to be seen what mischiefs were before the making hereof, the principall whereof we shall touch.

1. Before the making of the statute of *Magna Charta*, assises were onely to be taken in the court of common pleas which was mischievous to the recognitors of the assise: it is provided by *Magna Charta*, that they shall be taken in the proper county once every year, and that remedy was too short, and therefore they are by this act to be taken oftner.

2. Another mischief was, that the justices of assise were not sometime but apprentices of the law, and a knight associate to them which oftentimes were favourable.

3. And if the recognitors of the assise had not given their verdict, the justices could not (before this act) have adjourned the record into the court of common pleas.

4. Also, if a forein plea had been pleaded, or forein voucher had, they could not have adjourned it into the court abovesaid.

27 E. 1. cap. 4. York 12 E. 2. ca. 3. 5. Before the making of this act, all jurors, together with the parties, came up to the kings higher courts of justice, where the cause depended, *et propter tantam, et intolerabilem populi nostri jacturam, non solum ad eorundem juratorum exonerationem, sed etiam ad celerem partibus in curia nostra placitantibus justitiam exhibendam, &c.* And this is the first act that gave the writ of *nisi prius*.

6. Also before this act some justices did rule over the recognitors, to give a precise or direct verdict without finding the speciall matter.

Now the remedies do follow.

(1) *Assignentur de caetero duo justic' jurati, coram quibus et non aliis*, &c.] Hereby it appeareth what an honourable opinion the law

law hath of the kings juſtices ſworn, that they are *omni exceptione majores.*

But this branch hath been manifoldly altered, for by the ſtatute of 27 E. 1. cap. 4. theſe inquiſitions and recognitions were to be taken *coram aliquo juſticiar' eorundem, coram quibus placitum deductum fuerit, aſſociato uno milite comitatus illius, &c.* 27 E. 1. cap. 4.

By the ſtatute of York, they are to be taken before one juſtice of the one place or the other, having aſſociate to him, *un piode home de paiis, chivalier, ou auter.* 12 E. 2. cap. 3.

But by the ſtatute of 14 E. 3. they may be taken before any juſtices of the one bench or the other, or the kings ſerjant ſworn, which is intended of any ſerjant at law, for that every ſerjant is ſworn. 14 E. 3. ca. 16.

And this act is extended to the kings attorney, being joyned with one of the juſtices or ſerjants; and albeit the king make choice of ſome ſerjants to be of his councell and fee, yet in a generall ſenſe all be called the kings ſerjants, becauſe they be all called by the kings writ. Bro. Niſi prius, 37. See the form of the *poſtea* hereafter in this chapter.

(2) *Ad plus terræ per annum.*] Hereby the former time given by Magna Charta is inlarged. [423]

These dayes are altered by later ſtatutes.

By 27 E. 1. it is provided they ſhall be taken *tempore vacationis, vide* 14 E. 3. 27 E. 1. & 14 E. 3. ubi ſupra.

(3) *Quindena ſancti Johannis Baptiſtæ.*] This return amongſt others is taken away by the ſtatute of 32 H. 8. 32 H. 8. ca. 21.

(4) *Gula Auguſti.*] Gule of Auguſt. This is alſo mentioned in the ſtatute of 27 E. 3, &c. the feaſt of S. Peter ad vincula is on this day, being the firſt day of Auguſt, as it appeareth in Pl. Com. where it is ſaid, *Al feaſt de S. Peter en la gule de Auguſt.* 27 E. 3. ſtat. 3. F.N.B. 62. i. Pl. Com. 316.

The reaſon why it is called *gula Auguſti,* you may read in Durand, in his booke *De rationali divinorum, lib.* 7. *De feſto ſancti Petri ad vincula.*

This I have added, not out of any curioſity, but that the reader might underſtand what he reads, which hath beene mine endeavour throughout all this work.

(5) *Statuant diem de reditu ſuo.*] That is, by proclamation in open court.

(6) *De termino in terminum adjornent aſſiſas.*] See the expoſition upon the ſtatute of Magna Charta. Et vide lib. 4. fol. 4. Vernons caſe, & lib. 8. fo. 57. Le countee de Rutlands caſe. Mag. Chart. ca. 12.

(7) *Per vocationem warranti.*] Forein pleas are taken within the equity of this act, and ſo are demurrers doubtfull, and other pleas and proceedings, &c. as well before as after verdict. Mag. Chart. c. 12. Br. adjorn. 29. 47 Aſſ. 1. 49 Aſſ. 23. 48 E. 3. 7. 22 Aſſ. p. 11.

In an aſſiſe, the tenant pleads a releaſe made in a forein county, whereupon the record is adjourned into the court of common pleas; that court may graunt a *niſi prius* into the forein county, for albeit in this caſe the court of common pleas hath by this act *delegatam poteſtatem* for the triall of the releaſe, yet all incidents thereunto are therewith graunted.

(8) *Per eſſonium.*] This muſt be intended of an eſſoin *ultra mare,* for the common eſſoin, or *de ſervitio regis* lieth not in this caſe.

(9) *Remittatur loquela.*] That is, the record of the aſſiſe, together with the originall writ ſhall be remaunded to be taken, &c. in the proper county before the former juſtices.

(10) *Et-*

(10) *Atterminentur etiam inquisitiones coram eis de aliis placitis, &c. in quibus est facilis examinatio, &c. Sed inquisitionem de grossis et pluribus articulis quæ magna indigeant examinatione, &c. nisi ambæ partes petant,* &c.] Upon this statute a writ in the Register is framed, *Quod inquisitiones, quæ magnæ sunt examinationis, non capiantur in patria, et de supersedendo, &c.*

Regist. 186.

42 E. 3. cap. 11.

(11) *In brevi de judicio in hæc verba.*] *Præcipimus tibi, quod venire facias coram justiciariis nostris apud Westm' in octabis sancti Michaelis, nisi talis et talis, tali die et loco ad partes illas venerint,* 12, *&c.*

[424]

The judiciall writ now in use hath [*prius*] before [*venerit,*] and therefore it taketh the name of *nisi prius.*

14 E. 3. ca. 16. 33 E. 3. attaint 77.

Although the statute of 14 E. 3. speak not of an attaint, yet is an attaint within it, for the effect of that ordinance is, that in all cases where a *nisi prius* is grauntable, it shall be graunted before justices of assise.

23 E. 3. 23. 24 E. 3. 23. 25 E. 3. 39. 14 E. 3. Nisi prius, 16. F.N.B. 241. a.

Albeit this act be generall, yet a *nisi prius* shall not be graunted where the king is party, or where the matter toucheth the right of the king, without a speciall warrant from the king, or the assent of the kings attourney.

32 H. 6. 9. F.N.B. 241. a. 11 E. 3. Visne 59.

The duke of Exeter being plaintiffe in trespasse, for the duke a *nisi prius* was prayed, and it was denied, for that the duke was of great power in that county, and if triall should be had in the country, inconvenience might thereupon follow.

(12) *Et cum hujusmodi inquisitiones captæ fuerint, retornentur in bancis, et ibi fiat judicium, et irrotulentur.*] Herewith agreeth the statute of York *ubi supra.*

By the statute of 14 E. 3. cap. 16. the chiefe justice of that place shall return the record, and shall return the verdict under his seale.

The return of the justices is, *Ad quem diem hic venerunt partes præd', et justiciarii ad assisas coram quibus, &c. miserunt hic record' in hæc verba*; and this returne is called the *postea,* because the record beginneth thus: *Postea die et loco infra contentis coram* (and nameth the justices of assise) *justiciariis ipsius domini regis ad assisas in com' N. capiend' assignat' per formam statuti venerunt tam le pl' quam le def. &c.*

Livre de entries. Rast. 101. Hil. 19 H. 7. Rot. 409. in communi banco. 2 H. 7. 10. simile. Dier, 5. Mar. 163.

If one of the justices of assise die before the returne, a *certiorari* may be awarded out of the court of common pleas to the survivor to certifie the verdict; if both the justices die, the clerk of the assise may bring it in without a *certiorari,* or a *certiorari* may be awarded to the executors, or administrators of them to certifie the record.

Statute of York. 12 E. 2. c. 4. 14 E. 3. c. 16. 17 E. 3. 23.

But this act was defective, for hereby the justices of *nisi prius* might take verdicts and inquisitions; but they could not record non-suits of the demandant or plaintiffe, or defaults of the tenant or defendant, which was remedied by the statute of York.

Regula.

(13) *Et si omissa forma prædicta aliquæ inquisitiones capiantur, pro nullis habeantur.*] For the rule of law is, *non observata forma infertur adnullatio actus*; but that rule is to be understood, *de essentiali forma,* and not *de accidentali.*

(14) *Excepto quod assisæ ultimæ præsentationis, et inquisitiones super quare impedit atterminentur in proprio com', &c. et ibi statim reddatur judicium.*] The reason of making of this branch was in respect of the daunger of laps, and therefore in favour of the patrons this clause

clause was added that the justices of *nisi prius* have power to give judgement in these two actions.

And albeit the words of this branch be, *et ibi statim reddatur judicium*, yet if the justices of *nisi prius* doe not give judgement, upon return of the *postea* judgement may be given by the court to which the return is made, for by these words the higher court is not restrained; and this branch giving to the justices of *nisi prius* power to give judgement, they have thereby power includedly, as incident, given to award execution, that is, a writ to the bishop, but that writ is not retournable; but after the record be returned into the common bench, if the former writ be not executed, that court may graunt a writ *sicut alias*, returnable into that court, all which is worthy of singular observation. 4 Mar. Dier, 135. 9 El. Dier, 260. Incident. [425]

And justices of *nisi prius* have power to inquire of incidents. 18 E. 3. 49, 50.

Also justices of *nisi prius* may amerce jurors, and demand them upon a pain, and also punish them for misdemeanors done in their presence, which are in despite of the king, and thereupon make proces, and what lieth in aide and furtherance of the businesse they may record, likewise they may record a prayer to be received. 17 E. 3. 23.

(15) *Habeant de cætero omnes justiciarii de bancis in itineribus clericos irrotulantes omnia placita coram eis placitat', sicut antiquitus habere consueverint.*] Hereby it appeareth that the justices of courts did ever appoint their clerks, some of which after by prescription grew to be officers in their courts; as here it is put for example, that the justices of the benches in their circuits had clerks that enrolled all pleas pleaded before them as auinciently they used to have, that is, as by the common law. Dier 1 Eliz. 175.

Now the cause of the making of this branch was, that the king was informed that he might erect offices for entring and inrolment of records in his courts of justice, and specially before justices of assise, which this branch declareth to belong to the justices, and that they had enjoyed the same of auncient time, that is, by the common law.

And the reason thereof is twofold. 1. For that the law doth ever appoint those, that have the greatest knowledge and skill, to performe that which is to be done. 2. The officers and clerks are but to enter, inroll, or effect that which the justices doe adjudge, award, or order, the insufficient doing whereof maketh the proceeding of the justices erroneous, then the which nothing can be more dishonourable and grievous to the justices, and prejudiciall to the party; therefore the law, as here it appeareth, did appropriate to the justices the making of their owne clerks and officers, and so to proceed judicially by their own instruments: and that this was the common law, the king cannot graunt the office of the shire or county clerk, (who is to enter all judgements and proceedings in the county court) for that the making of the shire clerk belongeth to the sheriffe by the common law, as in Mittons case it appeareth, *et sic de cæteris.* Lib. 4. fol. 32. Mittons case.

(16) *Justiciarii ad assisas capiend' assignat' non compellant juratores dicere præcise si sit disseisina, vel non, dummodo dicere voluerint veritatem facti, et petere auxilium justic'. Sed si sponte voluerint,* &c.] The first question upon this branch was, whether in case of assise, if the issue were joyned upon a collaterall matter out of the point Li. 9. f. 1. 11. 13. Dowmans case.

See the first part of the Institutes, sect. 366, 367. point of the assise, whether upon this speciall issue the jury might give a speciall verdict.

45 E. 3. 20. 42 E. 3. 1. 40 E. 3. 2. 41 E. 3. 10. 47 E. 3. 19. 16 E. 3. verdict 21. 9 H. 7. 3. Dier 28 H. 8. 32. 2 Mar. 115. 9 El. 260. 11 El. 279. 13 El. 30. 32 H. 8. 47. Pl. Com. 92. 3 E. 3. Cor. 284. 286. 43 ass. 31. 44 E. 3. 44. 26 H. 8. 5.

2. The second question was, whether it did extend to all other actions, or onely to these actions wherein the defendant or tenant might plead a generall issue.

3. Thirdly, whether in all actions the jury might give a speciall verdict upon a special issue, upon an *absque hoc*, or otherwise

In the end it hath been resolved, that in all actions reall, personall, and mixt, and upon all issues joyned generall or speciall, the jury might finde the speciall matter of fact pertinent, and tending onely to the issue joyned, and thereupon pray the discretion of the court for the law: and this the jurors might doe at the common law, not onely in cases betweene party and party, whereof this act putteth an example of the assise, but also in pleas of the crown at the kings suit, which is a proofe of the common law, for if this [426] act had made a new law, and that other like cases betweene party and party had beene taken by equity, yet the king had not beene bound thereby: and note the next precedent clause of this act, and the subsequent are both in affirmance also of the common law.

Lib. 9. fol. 13. Dowmans case.

(17) *Et de cætero non ponant justic' in assisis, aut juratis aliquos juratores, nisi eos qui ad hoc prius fuer' summoniti.*] Where this branch saith *non ponant justic' in assisis*, the meaning is that the justices shall not suffer the sheriffe to put into the pannell any men which were never summoned: for before this act if the sheriffe had made a pannell, and the jurors had not appeared, the sheriffe would have impannelled others of the same county who were never summoned, which was a wrong to them that were so newly returned, and is now prohibited by this act, whereupon any so unduly returned may have his action against the sheriffe, for this act is made for the reliefe of them that were so unduly returned.

CAP. XXXI.

CUM aliquis implacitat' (1) coram aliquibus justic' (2), proponat exceptionem (3) et petat quod justic' eam allocent, quam si allocare noluerint, si ille qui exceptionem proposuerit, scribat illam exceptionem, et petat, quod justic' sigillum suum apponant in testimonio, justiciarii apponant sigilla sua (4). Et si unus apponere noluerit, apponat alius de societate. Et si forte ad querimoniam de facto justiciariorum venire fac' dominus rex recordum coram eo, et si illa exceptio non inveniatur in rotulo, et querens ostendat exceptionem scriptam sub sigillo (5) justic' apposito, mandetur

WHEN one that is impleaded before any of the justices doth alledge an exception, praying that the justices will allow it, which if they will not allow, if he that alledged the exception do write the same exception, and require that the justices will put to their seals for a witness, the justices shall so do; and if one will not, another of the company shall. And if the king, upon complaint made of the justices, cause the record to come before him, and the same exception be not found in the roll, and the plaintiff shew the exception written,

mandetur justiciario, quod sit ad certum diem (6) *ad cognoscendum sigillum suum, vel ad dedicendum. Et si justic' sigillum suum dedicere non possit, procedatur* (7) *ad judicium secundum illam exceptionem, prout admittend' esset vel cassand'.*

ten, with the seal of a justice put to, the justice shall be commanded that he appear at a certain day, either to confess or deny his seal. And if the justice cannot deny his seal, they shall proceed to judgement according to the same exception, as it ought to be allowed or disallowed.

(9 Rep. 13. Kelyng, 15. Regist. 182.)

At the common law, before the making of this act, a man might have had a writ of error for an error in law, either *in redditione judicii, in redditione executionis,* or *in processu, &c.* and this error in law must be apparent in the record, &c. For the writ of error saith, *quia in recordo et processu, &c. error intervenit manifestus, &c.* Or for error in *fait,* by alledging matter out of the record, as death of either party, &c. before judgement: now the mischiefe before this statute was, that when the demandant or plaintiffe, or the tenant or defendant did offer to alledge any exception, (as in those dayes they did *ore tenus* at the barre) praying the justices to allow it, and the justices over-ruling it so as it was never entred of record, [427] this the party could not assign for error, because it neither appeared within the record, nor was any errour in *fait,* but in law, and so the party grieved was without remedy, for whose relief this statute was made.

(1) *Cum aliquis implacitatur.*] This act doth extend aswell to the demandant or plaintife, as to the tenant or defendant in all actions reall, personall, and mixt; and regularly it extendeth not to a stranger to the record, which is not to come in lieu of the tenant, &c. For example, if the bailife of a franchise demand conusans, and the justices over-rule the same, he cannot pray the justices to inseal a bill, because he is no party to the record: but yet one that offereth to be received, and is denyed, albeit he be none of the parties to the writ, yet because he is privie in estate, and to be *in loco tenentis,* he shall have the benefit of this act; and so it is of the vouchee, though he be no party to the writ, because he is *in loco tenentis.*

F.N.B. 21. n. & 22. a.

20 E. 3. Conusans 46.

17 E. 3. 23. a.

(2) *Coram aliquibus justiciariis.*] Albeit the letter of this branch seemeth to extend to the justices of the com' pleas only, by reason of these words, *et si forte ad querimoniam de facto justic' venire fac' dominus rex recordum coram eo,* (which is by writ of errour into the kings bench) yet that is put but for an example, and this act extendeth not onely to all other courts of record (for upon judgements given in them a writ of errour lyeth in the kings bench) but to the county court, the hundred, and court baron, for therein the judges were more likely to erre; and albeit, of judgements given in them a writ of errour lyeth not, but a writ of false judgement in the court of common pleas, yet the case being in the same, or greater mischief, the purview of this statute doth extend to those inferiour courts.

(3) *Proponat exceptionem.*] This extendeth not onely to all pleas dilatory and peremptory, &c. and (as hath been said) to prayers to be received, oier of any record or deed, and the like: but also to all challenges

11 H. 4. 52. 65. 9 Ass. p. 8. 16 E. 3. Quare non admisit 3. Regist. 182. 21 E. 4. 2. b.

21 E. 4. 12. b. F.N.B. 21. n. challenges of any jurors, and any materiall evidence given to any jury, which by the court is over-ruled.

(4) *Juſticiarii apponant ſigilla ſua.*] Here is an expreſſe commandment given to the juſtices; and yet if one refuſe, and any of the other inſeal the bill, it ſufficeth, but if they all refuſe, it is a contempt in them all; for it lyeth not in the power of the juſtices that denyed to perform the purview of this act, to take advantage

Regiſt. 182. of their own wrong, and the party grieved may have a writ grounded upon this ſtatute to the juſtices, commanding them to put their ſeals *juxta formam ſtatuti, et hoc ſub periculo quod incumbit nullatenus omittatis.*

11 H. 4. 52. 63. Regiſt. ubi ſupr. F.N.B. 22. a. And though no time be appointed by this act, when the juſtices ſhall put their ſeals, the party muſt pray the ſame before judgement; but if they deny it, then may they be commanded after judgement to put their ſeals, and then the putting of their ſeals after judgement ſhall be ſufficient.

(5) *Et querens oſtendat exceptionem ſcriptam ſub ſigillo.*] Albeit the party grieved be dead, yet his heirs or executors, &c. according to the caſe, ſhall have a writ of errour upon this bill of exception.

11 H. 4. ubi ſupr. In this caſe the plaintife can alledge no diminution, for he muſt hold himſelf to the matter in the bill ſealed; and if it be not there, it was his folly to omit it.

11 H. 4. 52. 63. (6) *Mandetur juſticiario quod ſit ad certum diem.*] Albeit ſome

[428] have holden, that the juſtices may bring in the bill under their ſeal, and acknowledge it, yet the ſurer way is to follow the order preſcribed by this act.

If the juſtice dye, yet ſhall there a *ſcire facias* go againſt his executor or adminiſtrator; for the death of the judge, which is the act of God, cannot prejudice the party, nor make the purview of this ſtatute to be of no force.

1. Part of the Inſtitutes, ſect. 102. As if a man be outlawed, and at the time of his outlawry he was beyond the ſeas in war in the kings ſervice, and brings a writ of errour to reverſe his outlawry, and obtains a certificate of the marſhall of the kings hoſt under his ſeal (as he ought to do) in this caſe notwithſtanding the marſhall dye, yet may he aſſign the ſame for errour, and upon ſhewing of the certificate have a *ſcire fac'* to the executors or adminiſtrators of the marſhall.

(7) *Et ſi juſticiarius ſigillum ſuum dedicere non poſſit, procedatur,* &c.] On the other ſide, if the judge deny his ſeal, then may the plaintife in the writ of error take iſſue thereupon, and prove it by witneſſes; for it lyeth not in the judge in this caſe to fruſtrate this excellent law made for advancement of juſtice and right.

Booke of Entries, Raſt. 275, 323. Vet. N.B. 54. For the order of proceeding herein according to this act, ſee the book of entries.

CAP.

CAP. XXXII.

CUM viri religioſi, et aliæ perſonæ eccleſiaſticæ implacitent aliquem, et implacitatus (1) *fecerit defaltam* (2), *ob quam tenement' amittere debeat: quia juſticiar' hucuſque tenuerunt, quod ſi implacitat' fecerit defaltam per colluſionem, ut cum petens occaſione ſtatuti per titulum doni, vel alterius alienationis, ſeiſinam de tenement' conſequi non poſſet, per illam defaltam conſequeretur, et ſic fieret fraus ſtatuto: ordinat' eſt per dominum regem, et conceſſum in hoc caſu, quod poſtquam defalta facta fuerit, inquiratur per patriam, utrum petens habeat jus in ſua petitione, vel non. Et ſi compertum fuerit, quod petens jus habuerit* (3), *procedatur ad judicium* (4) *pro petente, et recuperet ſeiſinam ſuam. Et ſi jus non habuerit, incurratur tenement' proximo domino feodi, ſi illud petat infra annum* (5) *a tempore inquiſitionis captæ. Et ſi infra annum non petat, ſuperiori domino incurratur, ſi petat infra dimidium annum poſt illum annum. Et ſic habeat quilibet dominus poſt proximum dominum, ſpacium dimidii anni ad petendum ſucceſſivè, quouſq; perveniatur ad regem, cui ad ultimum pro defectu aliorum dominorum tenementum incurratur. Et ad calumniandum juratores inquiſitionis, admittantur quicunque capitales domini feodorum* (6), *et ſimiliter pro rege qui calumniare* * *voluerint* (7.) *Et remaneat terra, poſtquam judicium datum fuerit in manu domini regis quouſque tenem' per petentem, vel per aliquem capitalem dominum diſrationetur, et oneretur vic' ad reſpondend' inde ad ſcaccarium.*

* [429]

WHEN religious men and other eccleſiaſtical perſons do implead any, and the party impleaded maketh default, whereby he ought to leeſe the land, foraſmuch as the juſtices have thought hitherto, that if the party impleaded make default by colluſion, that where the demandant, by occaſion of the ſtatute, could not obtain ſeiſin of the land by title of gift, or other alienation, he ſhall now by reaſon of the default, and ſo the ſtatute is defrauded; it is ordained by our lord the king, and granted, that in this caſe, after the default made, it ſhall be inquired by the country, whether the demandant had right in the thing demanded, or no. And if it be found that the demandant had right in his demand, the judgement ſhall paſs with him, and he ſhall recover ſeiſin; and if he hath no right, the land ſhall accrue to the next lord of the fee, if he demand it within a year from the time of the inqueſt taken; and if he do not demand it within the year, it ſhall accrue to the next lord above, if he do demand it within half a year after the ſame year; and ſo every lord after the next lord ſhall have the ſpace of half a year to demand it ſucceſſively, until it come to the king, to whom at length, through default of other lords, the lands ſhall accrue. And to challenge the jurors of the inqueſt, every of the chief lords of the fees ſhall be admitted, and likewiſe for the king, they that will ſhall challenge; and after the judgement given, the land ſhall remain clear in the king's hands, until it be dereigned by the demandant, or ſome other chief lord, and the ſheriff ſhall be charged to anſwer therefore at the exchequer.

Statut. de Religioſis, anno 7 E. 1. (Fitz. Coll. 1, 2. 4, 5, 6, 7. 9, 10, 11. [illegible]. 24, 25, 26, 27. 31. 40. 42. 46. 10 H. 7. f. 3. 11 Ed. 3. ſtat. 3. c. 3. 9 H. 3. ſtat. 1. c. 36.)

Notwith-

Magna Chart. cap. 36. Stat. de Religiosis, 7 E. 1. 33 H. 6. 25.

Notwithstanding the statute of *Magna Charta*, and the statute of *de religiosis*, *anno* 7 Edw. 1. yet this evasion was found out, that religious and ecclesiasticall persons did recover lands by default; which, albeit it were by consent and collusion, yet the justices did hold that these religious and ecclesiasticall persons came not to the land *per titulum doni, vel alienationis*, nor was within the generall words of the statute of 7 Edw. 1. *Aut alio quovismodo, arte, vel ingenio sibi appropriare præsumat:* for that recoveries being prosecuted in course of law were by law presumed to be just and lawfull, it was holden by the justices, that they were not within the former statute; and yet these recoveries were done *in fraudem legis*, for remedy whereof this statute was made.

2 E. 3. 10. 10 E. 3. 17. 21 E. 3. 5. 24 E. 3. 27. 38 E. 3. 12. 27. 3 E. 4. 12, 13. 1 E. 2. Collusion 11. 7 E. 3. ibid. 17. 16 E. 3. ibid. 21. 34 E. 3. ibid. 46. 20 H. 6. 38.

(1) *Et implacitatus.*] All actions brought for any lands or tenements, wherein a free-hold, inheritance, or a long term is recovered, as within this statute, as *præcipes quod reddat, quare impedit, droit de gard, ejectione firmæ, quare ejecit infra terminum, warrantia chartæ, convenuit* to levie a fine, execution *per elegit*, statute merchant, or statute staple, &c.

This act doth extend to them that are no parties to the writ, as to the vouchee, and tenant by receit and the like.

And this statute doth extend by equity when the abbot, &c. is tenant or defendant, as when a writ of right is brought against an abbot, &c. and after the mise joyned, the demandant maketh default, and is nonsute, the collusion shall be inquired, and this case wherein the abbot is tenant is within the same mischief, and therefore within the equity of this law: and so it is if a *quare impedit* be brought against a prior of the church of D. and the plaintife become nonsute, the defendant shall recover the presentment, and the collusion shall be inquired.

5 E. 2. Collus. 19. 2 E. 3. 18. 6 E. 3. 23. 25. 19 E. 3. Collusion 18.

(2) *Fecerit defaltam.*] This act doth not extend onely, according to the letter, to recoveries by default, but to all manner of recoveries by verdict, or otherwise, if they be had by collusion.

Regist. judic. 16, 17.

If it be by default, then a judiciall writ called a *quale jus* grounded upon this statute is awarded, which writ consisteth upon five parts:

1. It reciteth the recovery.

2. The doubt of the fraud, *et quia dubitatur de fraude inter eos prælocuta contra statutum.*

3. A commandement to the sherife to return a jury, *præcipimus tibi quod venire fac' coram justiciar' nostris apud Westmonast' duodecim, &c.* the charge of the jury is *ad recogn' super sacramentum suum hæc tria*; 1. *Quale jus idem abbas habuit in prædict' messuagio:* 2. *& Quis prædecessorum fuit inde seisitus ut de jure ecclesiæ suæ præd':* 3. *& Quantum illud messuagium valet per annum.*

20 E. 3. Collusion 34.

4. The fourth is another commandement to the sherife, *et interim messuagium illud in manum nostram capias, &c. et quod de exitibus ad scaccarium nobis respondeas.*

5. The sherife is commanded, *et scire facias capitalibus dominis feodi illius mediatis, et immediatis, quod tunc sint ibi audituri juratam illam, si voluerint.*

Which writ I have the more at large rehearsed, for that it giveth a great light to all the parts of this act.

[430]

And it is to be observed, that if the jury finde that his predecessor was seised of it in his demesne as of fee in the right of his church,

before the said statute *de religiosis, anno* 7 E. 1. this is a good verdict for the demandant without finding of any license; for though there were no license, the alienation was good: but if they finde that his predecessor was seised after the statute, then they ought to finde a license, or otherwise the land belongeth to the lord or king. 13 E. 3. Collusion 32. 16 E. 3. ibid 42. 34 E. 3. ibid. 40. 20 H. 6. 38.

The value of the land is inquired of, because the issues thereof are to be by this act answered to the king. 20 H. 6. 38. Stamf. Prærog. 84. b.

If there be an issue joyned in the action brought by the abbot, the jury shall not onely inquire of the issue, but of the collusion, but as concerning the collusion, it is but an inquest of office, whereof no attaint lyeth. 38 E. 3. 12. 45 E. 3. 8. 50 E. 3. 22. 14 Ass. 13. 5 E. 3. 29. 6 E. 3. 11. 20 H. 6. 38. 33 H. 6. 25. 6 R. 2. Collusion 40.

If a recovery by verdict were not within the purview of this act, such an issue of disadvantage might be joyned, and so feint evidence might be given, as this statute should be of little force.

And if the jury do not inquire of the collusion, so as the abbot, &c. recover by verdict, yet the collusion shall be inquired of by a speciall writ, and not by a *quale jus*. 33 H. 6. 25.

If an abbot bring an assise, and the tenant plead a forein release, they of the forein county cannot inquire of the collusion, but a speciall writ shall be granted.

If the tenant appear, and confesse the action, or judgement be given upon a *nihil dicit*, or a departure in despight of the court, these also are within this statute, and the collusion shall be inquired, and so if a recovery be had upon a demurrer in law, that recovery is also within the equity of this statute. 6 E. 3. 11. 17 E. 3. 5.

In some case no collusion shall be inquired at all, as if a person bring a *juris utrum*, and the jury finde that the land is the right of the church, this sufficeth without inquiring of the collusion. 29 E. 3. 35. 6 R. 2. Collusion 40. 31 H. 6. 10.

(3) *Et si compertum fuerit quod petens jus habuerit.*] This is either by jury upon triall of the issue, or by *quale jus*, if the tenant make default.

(4) *Procedatur ad judicium.*] Hereby it appeareth that the *quale jus* should be sued out after the default, and before judgement, and so it is said the use hath been; and if the collusion be found, the lord, &c. shall enter, though judgement be never given. Kelwey 134. 5 E. 3. 29.

But yet if judgement be given upon the default, yet may the *quale jus* be sued out, and so it appeareth by the Judiciall Register, and many other authorities, but execution shall cease untill the collusion be inquired. Regist. Judic. 16, 17.

In a writ of right, if judgement finall be given for the abbot, &c. the collusion shall be inquired; for albeit the judgement finall be given between them, yet the lord by this statute shall enter: and so it is of a recovery by default in a *cessavit*. 34 E. 3. Collusion 46. 13 E. 3. ibid. 28. 12 E. 3. Judgement 163. 4 E. 3. 8. Regist. Judic. 16, 17.

(5) *Et si jus non habuerit, incurratur tenementum proximo domino feodi, si illud petat infra annum,* &c.] Here be the certain times appointed when the lords mediate and immediate shall enter, whereof sufficient hath been said in the exposition of the statute *de religiosis,* 7 E. 1.

(6) *Et ad calumniandum juratores inquisitionis, admittantur quicunque capitales domini feodorum.*] Hereupon, as hath been said, the sherife shall warn the lords mediate and immediate to appear and take their challenges,

42 E. 3. 3. If any of the lords mediate or immediate be within age, in respect of these words, * *quicunque domini feodorum*, the court will advise whether any thing shall be done to his prejudice, during his minority.

(7) *Et similiter pro rege qui clamare voluerit.*] The king is alwayes (in judgement of law) present in court, and therefore any man may challenge for the king, but by the statute of 33 E. 1. they which challenge for the king must shew a cause certaine, and the truth thereof is to bee tried.

Stat. de Inquis. anno 33 E. 1.

Observe well what exposition hath beene made of this act, and how the judges extended the same by equity; for otherwise the churchmen by advice of their learned councell (whereof they had the best) would have had some evasion or other out of the letter of the law.

See the exposition before of the statute *de religiosis, anno* 7 E. 1.

CAP. XXXIII.

QUIA multi tenentes erigunt cruces (1) *in tenementis suis* (2), *aut erigi permittunt* (3), *in præjudicium dominorum suorum* (4), *ut tenentes per privilegium templariorum et hospitaliorum* (5) *tueri se possent contra capitales dominos feodorum: statutum est, quod hujusmodi ten' capitalibus dominis, aut regi incurrantur. Eodem modo* (6) *quo statuit alibi de tenementis alienatis ad manum mortuam.*

FORASMUCH as many tenants set up crosses, or cause to be set up in their lands, in prejudice of their lords, that tenants should defend themselves against the chief lords of the fee, by the privileges of templars and hospitalers; it is ordained, that such lands shall be forfeit to the chief lords, or to the king, in the same manner as is provided for lands aliened in mortmain.

Fleta, l. 2. cap. 43. Lib. 5. cap. 34. Doct. & Stud. Li. 2. ca. 34. & 46. Rot. Pat. 2 E. 3. Rot. claus. 18 E. 3.

For the better understanding of this statute, it is to be knowne that the order of the templers, otherwise knights of the temple being men professed, were by Gelasius the pope founded *anno Domini* 1117, which was *anno* 18 H. 1.

18 H. 1.

These were called *templarii*, because they were first founded in some of the edifices adjoyning and belonging to the temple, and had the charge and keeping of the lords sepulchre, and not onely entertained pilgrims that came to see the sepulchre, &c. but in their armour conducted christians that had a desire to see the city of Jerusalem, and other places in the land of Palestine, and to guard them from the Saracens and infidels.

Soone after, *viz. anno Domini* 1120, which was in *anno* 21 H. 1, the hospitallers, commonly called *milites Sancti Johannis Jerosolymitani*, being professed friers of S. John of Jerusalem, under the rule of S. Augustine, were founded, Honorius then being pope, and they were called *hospitularii*, hospitallers, because they had the care of hosting and providing hospitals for pilgrims, &c. travelling to

to Jerusalem, &c. and for their safe-conduct against Saracens and infidels. These two orders, (but especially the templers) did so overspread throughout christendome, and so exceedingly increased in possessions, revenues, and wealth, and specially in England, as you will wonder to reade in approved histories, and withall obtained so great and large priviledges, liberties, and immunities for themselves, their tenants and farmers, &c. as no other order had the like.

At the councell of Vienna holden *anno Domini* 1311, which was *anno* 4 E. 2. *Clemens quintus* then being pope, the order of the templers was by that councell dissolved throughout all Christendome, and their possessions and revenues here in England given to the hospitallers by act of parliament, *anno* 17 E. 2. [432] Councel of Vienna, anno Dom. 1311. 4 E. 2. Kelwey, 6 H. 8. fol. 169, 170. Anno 17 E. 2.

But the hospitallers continued here in England till an act of parliament made in 32 H. 8. by which act they were dissolved, so as albeit both these orders mentioned in this act are dissolved, and therefore this act may seeme to be obsolete and out of use, yet will we not omit the exposition of it for two causes; 1. for that we have hitherto omitted not one; and 2. it may serve for very good use, as hereafter shall appeare. Vet. Mag. Chart. fol. 42. second pt. 5 E. 3. 36. 35 H. 6. 46. 32 H. 8. ca. 24.

(1) *Erigunt cruces.*] The reason wherefore crosses were erected, was, for that the knights of both the said orders were *cruce signati*, and because that was the ensigne of their profession, and for that their tenants enjoyed great priviledges, to the end they might be known to be the tenants of the said orders, and thereby freed from many duties and services which other tenants were subject unto, did erect crosses upon their houses; and many tenants of other lords perceiving the state and greatnesse of the knights of both the said orders, and withall seeing the great priviledges their tenants enjoyed, did set up crosses upon their houses, as their very tenants used to doe, to the prejudice of their lords.

(2) *In tenementis suis.*] The crosse was erected upon their houses, but both the house and lands holden by one tenure were forfeited to the lord, and therefore the act saith, *in tenementis suis*.

(3) *Aut erigi permittunt.*] This word [permit] or [suffer] hath in the law two significations; first, where he that suffereth it, is party, and then it is equivalent to his owne act; as if a man suffereth a recovery against him, and the like: the other signification is when a stranger doth the act whereunto he is not party; as here if a stranger of his own head erecteth a crosse upon the tenants house, if after notice the tenant doth suffer it, this is a permission within this act; even as in waste in houses, if it be done by a stranger, the tenant must answer for it, if he repaire it not before the action brought; so if after notice the tenant doth not put down the crosse, but doth by colour thereof any thing to the prejudice of the lord, he is within this statute. 21 H. 7. 34.

(4) *In præjudicium dominorum suorum.*] Somewhat must be done to the prejudice of the lord, for if the tenant erecteth, or suffereth to be erected a crosse upon his house, this is no forfeiture of his tenancy; but if after the erection of the crosse, he claimeth and putteth in ure any of the priviledges of either of the said orders against the lord to his prejudice, then is the tenancy forfeited.

(5) *Per privilegium templariorum et hospitaliorum.*] The tenants of the knights of both these orders enjoyed great priviledges, as well Regist. f. 20, 21.

See hereafter, ca. 43. well against the king, as against the other lords; as to be free from tenths and fifteens to be paid to the king, to be discharged of purveyance, that they should not be sued for any ecclesiasticall cause before the ordinary, *sed coram conservatoribus privilegiorum suorum*; also of ancient time they claimed that a felon might take such houses having such crosses for his safety, as well as any church, and many others: now if a crosse be erected, and any of these, or other priviledges claimed and put in ure by the tenant, &c. then was his land forfeited to the lord of whom the land in truth was holden.

If after the crosse levied, the prior of S. John of Jerusalem had distrained for rent or service, and the tenant had acknowledged the
[433] tenure of him, the very lord might enter by the purview of this statute, and so if the tenant doe prove any will whereof he is made executor before the conservator of the priviledges, the lord may enter, *et sic in similibus*.

(6) *Eodem modo.*] This is an act of reference as well to the statute *de religiosis, anno* 7 E. 1. as to the 32 chapter of this parliament of Westm' the second; and therefore if the king take benefit of this act, he ought to graunt the lands over in such sort, as is prescribed by the said act of 7 E. 1.

And albeit the state of the tenancy was not hereby changed, as in the case of the mortmaine, (whereunto this act referreth) yet such were the height, power, and greatnesse of these orders, that this act doth put the matter prohibited by this act in equipage, with an alienation in mortmaine.

CAP. XXXIV.

PURVIEW est, que si home ravist feme espouse, damesclle, ou auter feme desformes, per la ou el ne soit assentus, ne avant, ne apres (1), eyt judgement de vie et de membre (2). Et ensement per la ou home ravist feme, dame espouse, damaselle, ou auter feme a force, tout soit que el soy assent apres, eyt tiel judgement come devant est dit, sil soit attaint a le suit le roy (3), et la eyt le roy sa suit. De mulieribus (5) abductis cum bonis virorum (6) suorum, habeat rex sectam de bonis sic asportatis (4.) Et si uxor sponte reliquerit virum suum, et abierit (8), et moretur cum adultero (9) suo, amittat in perpetuum actionem petendi dotem suam (7), quæ ei competere posset de ten' viri sui, si super hoc convincatur, nisi vir suus sponte, et absque cohertione ecclesiastica eam reconciliet, et secum

IT is provided, that if a man from henceforth do ravish a woman married, maid, or other, where she did not consent, neither before nor after, he shall have judgement of life and of member. And likewise where a man ravisheth a woman married, lady, damosel, or other, with force, although she consent after, he shall have such judgement as before is said, if he be attainted at the king's suit, and there the king shall have the suit. And of women carried away with the goods of their husbands, the king shall have the suit for the goods so taken away. And if a wife willingly leave her husband, and go away, and continue with her advouterer, she shall be barred for ever of action to demand her dower, that she ought to have of her husband's lands, if she be convict thereupon,

cum cohabitare permittat (10), *in quo casu restituatur ei actio. Qui monialam à domo sua abducat, licet monialis consentiat, puniatur per prisonam trium annorum, et satisfaciat domui à qua abducta fuerit, competenter* (11): *et nihilominus redimatur ad voluntatem regis* (12).

upon, except that her husband willingly, and without coertion of the church, reconcile her, and suffer her to dwell with him; in which case she shall be restored to her action. He that carrieth a nun from her house, although she consent, shall be punished by three years imprisonment, and shall make convenient satisfaction to the house from whence she was taken, and neverthelesss shall make fine at the king's will.

31 E. 1. Endictment 31. (3 Ed. 1. c. 13. 6 R. 2. c. 6. Regist. 57. 2 Roll. 247. 9 Ed. 4. f. 26. Bro. Coron. 203. Dyer, 256. Fitz. Dower, 41. 72. 94. 119. 153. Fitz. Act. sur le stat. 12. 37. 1 Inst. 32.)

(1) *Purview est, que si home ravist feme espouse, dameselle, ou auter feme desormes, per la ou el ne soit assentus, ne avant, ne apres, eyt judgement de vie et de membre.*] This clause is intended of an appeale to bee brought by the party ravished, for if she give consent either before or after, she shall have no appeale, but if shee consented neither before nor after, then shee shall have an appeale of rape, and there is no law that gives a woman an appeale of rape but this. 13 E. 3. Coron. 122.

Hereby the auncient law concerning the election given to her that is ravished is taken away. *Vide* Westm. 1. cap. 13. See the first part of the Institutes, sect. 190.

[434]

Afterwards by the statute of R. 2. a greater punishment is inflicted upon the party ravished, if she after consent to the ravisher, *viz.* that as well the ravished as the ravisher should be disabled to challenge inheritance, dower, or joynt-feoffement, &c. and that the next of blood should enter, &c. 6 R. 2. c. 6. 5 E. 4. 6. Lo. 5 E. 4. 58. 1 H. 6. 1. 9 H. 7. 25.

And moreover the husband of her that is so ravished and after gives her consent, or if she have no husband, her father, or other next of her blood shall have the appeale of rape, wherein no wager of battell shall be allowed; so as this act of R. 2. gave an appeale in case were no appeale lay before, and also to other persons, so as the woman that never consented may have her appeale upon this statute, and if she give consent afterwards, then the appeale of rape is given by the statute of 6 R. 2. Pl. Com. 45. li. 3. fol. 61. Shelleyes case. 11 H. 4. 13. 1 H. 6. 1.

If a woman be ravished by her next of kin, and consenteth to him, and hath neither husband nor father, the next of kin to him shall have the appeale, for he hath disabled himselfe by the rape, whereby he becomes a felon. 28 H. 6. Coro. 459.

(2) *Judgement de vie et de membre.*] That is to say hee shall be attainted of felony. De frangent. prisonam. 1 E. 2.

In the appeale being the suit of the party, the pardon of the king doth not discharge the party, as it doth upon the indictment at the suit of the king. 14 E. 3. cap c. 9 E. 4. 26. 22 E. 4. 23. Broke Coron. 203.

(3) *Et ensement per la ou home ravist feme, &c. a force, tout soit que el assent apres, eit tiel judgement come est avandit sil soit atteint a le sute le roy,* &c.] Hereby it appeareth that the first clause is to be intended of the suit of the party, this branch providing expresly for the suit of the king.

W. 1. c. 13. 13 E. 2. Utlag. 49. First part of the Instit. sect. 190.

See the exposition of the 13 chapter of Westm. 1. and the first part of the Institutes, sect. 190.

7 H. 3. Trespasse 244. Temps E. 1. ibid. 241.

(4) *De mulieribus abductis cum bonis virorum suorum habeat rex sectam de bonis sic asportatis.*] At the common law the husband might have had an action of trespasse, *de uxore abducta cum bonis viri.*

Regist. 97. a. F.N.B. 89. c. 42 Ass. p. 16. Dier 256.

This is also prohibited by the statute of Westm. the 1. cap. 13. and a further punishment inflicted then was at the common law, and therefore in the original writ, *de uxore abducta cum bonis viri,* it is concluded *contra formam statuti in hujusmodi casu proviso,* meaning the said statute of Westm. 1. for this act of Westm. 2. extendeth onely to the suit of the king: and if the writ be brought at the common law omitting the words, *contra formam statuti,* then it is *Si A. fecerit, &c. tunc pone, &c. quod sit, &c.* but if *contra formam statuti* be added, then the writ is, *Si A. fecerit, &c. tunc attachies B. ita quod eum habeas, &c.*

Regist. ubi sup. 14 H. 6. 2.

And albeit the words be, *habeat rex sectam,* yet may the husband also have his action, as is aforesaid.

(5) *De mulieribus.*] That is to say *uxoribus,* for of auncient time *mulier* was taken for a wife.

43 E. 3. 23. 44 Ass. 13. 7 R. 2. Trespasse 206.

If the wife be taken away, and after be divorced, or if shee die, yet the husband shall have his action, *de uxore abducta cum bonis viri;* for in this action he shall not recover his wife, but damages. And he cannot have an action for taking her away as his servant, because the law gives him an action in another forme.

47 E. 3. Action sur le stat. 37.

If the wife be *infra annos nubiles, viz.* under the age of twelve years at the time of taking away, some have holden that the husband shall not have a writ *de uxore abducta cum bonis viri.* But I hold the law is to the contrary, for she is *uxor* untill disagreement.

[435]

43 E. 3. 23.

(6) *Cum bonis virorum.*] The plaintife must in his count shew the goods in certain.

43 E. 3. ubi supr.

Albeit the words of the writ be *rapuit,* yet here it is taken for a violent taking away, and not when carnall knowledge is had, so as this action may be brought against women as well as men.

Fleta, li. 5. c. 22. Brit. ca. 109. Mirror, c. 5. § 5. 1 Part of the Institutes, sect. 36. Custumier de Norm. ca. 101.

(7) *Et si uxor sponte reliquerit virum suum, & abierit, & moretur cum adultero, amittat in perpetuum actionem petendi dotem suam, &c. nisi vir suus sponte, & sine coertione ecclesiastica eam reconciliet, & secum cohabitare permittat, &c.*] In this case of elopement, and remaining with the adulterer, &c. the wife could not be barred of her dower by the common law, no though a divorce were sued and had for the said adultery, as you may read in the first part of the Institutes, sect. 36.

43 Ed. 3. 19.

(8) *Si sponte reliquerit, & abierit, & moretur cum adultero, &c.*] Albeit the words of this branch be in the conjunctive, yet if the woman be taken away not *sponte,* but against her will, and after consent, and remain with the adulterer without being reconciled, &c. she shall lose her dower; for the cause of the bar of her dower is not the manner of the going away, but the remaining with the adulterer in avowtry without reconciliation, that is the bar of the dower: see more of these words *(reliquerit & abierit)* in this chapter.

If the wife goeth away with her husbands agreement and consent with A. B. if after A. B. commit adultery with her, and she remain with him without reconciliation, she shall be barred of her dower by this branch; whereof you shall read in an ancient parliament

parliament roll a rare and strange case, which was the first judgement that I finde given upon this branch, and the judgement was given in parliament; and the case, which I have taken out of the record it self, was this:

Sir William Paynel knight, and Margaret his wife did demand the third part of the mannour of Torpul, as the dower of the said Margaret after the death of John de Camoys her first husband, that mannour being then in the seisin of the king: the king's attorney answered, that she ought not to be endowed, *quia recessit a marito suo in vita sua, & vixit ut adultera cum prædict' Guilielmo, & non fuit viro suo reconciliata ante mortem suam, & sic per formam* * *statuti inde prius editi non debet inde dotari.* Rot. Parliam. oct. sancti Joh. Bapt. an. 30 E. 1. Rot. 2.

* Viz. this statute of W. 2. cap. 34.

The demandants replyed, and pleaded a deed of the said John Camoys under seal, in these words:

Omnibus Christi fidelibus ad quos hoc præsens scriptum pervenerit, Johannes de Camoys filius & hæres domini Radulphi de Camoys, salutem in domino. Noveritis me tradidisse & dimisisse spontanea mea voluntate domino Guiliel. Paynel militi Margaretam de Camoys filiam & hæredem Johannis de Gatesden uxorem meam. Et etiam dedisse, concessisse, & eidem domino Guilielmo relaxasse, et quietum clamasse omnia bona, et catalla quæ ipsa Margareta habet, vel de cætero habere possit, & etiam quicquid mei est de præd' Margaretæ bonis, vel catallis cum suis pertinen'. Ita quod nec ego, nec aliquis alius nomine meo in prædicta Margareta, bonis, et catallis ipsius Margaretæ cum suis pertinen' de cætero exigere seu vendicare poterimus, nec debemus imperpetuum. Volo et concedo, et per præsens scriptum confirmo, quod prædicta Margareta cum prædicto domino Guilielmo sit, & maneat, ex voluntate ipsius Guilielmi. In cujus rei testimonium sigillum meum apposui, &c. hiis testibus. Concessio mirabilis & inaudita.

And concluded their replication thus; *Virtute cujus scripti dicit, quod non vixit, ut adultera cum prædicto Guilielmo, sed ut uxor ejusdem Guilielmi.*

Whereupon the king's attorney demurred in law, and the record saith, *Et super hoc processum est ad judicium, quod non debet dotari.* [436]

By this record it appeareth, that she was barred of her dower by force of this branch, whereof the king's attorney took advantage: and in the record it is further contained, that the demandants *protulerunt quasdam alias literas episcoporum de purgatione adulterii, quæ recitantur in memorand'. Et quia super testimonio episcoporum non sunt judicia in curia regis faciend', licet literæ episcoporum in curiam regis fuer' porrectæ, nisi iidem episcopi ad mandatum regis ipsi regi rescriberent.*

This deed, for the strangenesse thereof, we have recited at large *de verbo in verbum.*

But the husband may give license to a man to carry his wife to his house, and this shall be a good bar in an action brought *de muliere abducta cum bonis viri.* 46 E. 3. Bar. 214. 1 E. 4. 1. 20 H. 7. 2. 21 H. 7. 13.

(9) *Moretur cum adultero.*] Albeit she doth not continually remain in avowtry with the adulterer, yet if she be with him and commit adultery, it is a tarrying within this statute. 3 E. 3. 2. 6 E. 3. 29.

Also if she once remain with the adulterer in avowtry, and after he keepeth her against her will; or if the avowterer turn her away, yet she shall be said *morari cum adultero* within this act.

If

If the wife doth elope from her husband's house of habitation, and commit adultery in any other the lands or mannours of her husband, this without the free reconciliation of the husband is within the purview of this statute: see hereafter in this chapter for this point.

And there be *parvæ moræ*, and *magnæ*, and both of them within this branch.

(10) *Nisi vir suus sponte, & absque cohertione ecclesiæ eam reconciliet, & secum cohabitare permittat.*] Note that cohabitation is
29 E. 3. Dower 94. not sufficient without reconciliation made by the husband *sponte*, so as cohabitation onely in the same house with the husband availeth her not; *à fortiori*, though she remain with the avowtrer in any of the lands or mannours of her husband, yet she shall be barred of her dower by this branch, without the husbands free reconcilia-
8 E. 2. Dower 153. F. N. B. 150. tion, albeit it hath been otherwise holden: and the reason that they yeelded, is because it is no elopement, whereas it appeareth before that the words of *reliquerit & abierit* are not of the substance
43 E. 3. 19. Brit. fol. 258. b. of the bar of dower, but the adultery, and the remaining with the adulterer, as is abovesaid: and albeit she and the adulterer remain within any of the lands or mannours of the husband, yet (the words being, *si uxor sponte reliquerit & abierit*) she hath left and gone from her husband in that case, which is a personall offence.
Tr. 9 E. 2. fol. 65. b. in libro meo. See the first part of the Institutes, sect. 36. for bars of dower, whereunto you may adde a case in Tr. 9 E. 2. fol. 65. *in libro meo*, that if a woman say that she is conceived with childe by her husband whiles he lived, and in truth is not, whereby the next heir is disturbed, she shall lose her dower, if she acknowledge the same before the justices.

And albeit she both cohabite, and be reconciled, yet if it be by the cohertion of the church, she shall be barred of her dower.

Regist. 71. 267. 6. E. 3. 17. F. N. B. 233. 22 E. 3. 2. Rot. Pat. part 3. lib. 9. 72. D. Husseys case. 3 E. 3. 3. 8 E. 3. 52. 29 E. 3. 24. 29 Ass. 35. 22 R. 2. Dam. 130. 12 H. 7. Kelw. 20, 21. F. N. B. 90. h. 140.

(11) *Qui monialem a domo suo abducat, licet monialis consentiat, puniatur per prisonam trium annorum, & satisfaciat domui a qua abducta fuerit competenter, & nihilominus redimatur ad voluntatem regis.*] *Monialis*, i. *Monacha, nonna, quasi non nupta, sed deo consecrata*, he that carrieth a monk out of his cloister, the abbot or prior, &c. of the house shall not have an action of trespas for the taking of him away, but his remedy is by the writ of *apostata capiendo*; but * that writ doth not lie for a nun: and therefore the common law did give an action of trespasse for taking her away, as the lord might have an action of trespasse at the common law for his ward; and this act was made to give a further punishment; for the writ in the Register doth not recite this act, but the plaintife shall not take advantage of this act, unlesse he conclude, *contra formam statuta, &c.*

*[437]

Regist. 71. 267. Now the writ *de moniale abducta* saith, *Quare vi et armis clausuras ipsius priorissæ apud L. fregit, et sororem Jocosam Ashe commonialem suam ibid' existent' cepit, et abduxit, per quod divinum servitiū in ecclesia ipsius priorissæ Sanctæ Helenæ London' multipliciter subtractum fuit, et diminutum, et alia enormia, &c.*

(12) *Et nihilominus redimatur ad voluntatem regis.*] So as albeit the abbesse or prioresse shall recover damages, and the defendant have judgment to remain in prison by three yeers, yet he shall be indicted and ransomed at the kings suit in a legall proceeding, *et sic e converso.*

CAP.

CAP. XXXV.

DE pueris masculis, sive femellis (1), *(quorum maritagium ad aliquem pertineat) raptis et abductis* (3), *si ille qui rapuit non habens jus* (2) *in maritagio, licet postmodum restituat puerum non maritatum, vel de maritagio satisfecerit, puniatur tamen pro transgressione per prisonam duorum annorum* (4). *Et si non restituerit, vel hæredem post annos nubiles maritaverit, et de maritagio satisfacere non potuerit* (5), *abjuret regnum, vel habeat perpetuam prisonam* (6). *Et super hoc habeat querens tale breve* (7):

CONCERNING children males or females (whose marriage belongeth to another) taken and carried away, if the ravisher have no right in the marriage, though after he restore the child unmarried, or else pay for the marriage, he shall nevertheless be punished for his offence by two years imprisonment; and if he do not restore, or do marry the child after the years of consent, and be not able to satisfy for the marriage, he shall abjure the realm, or have perpetual imprisonment; and thereupon the plaintiff shall have such a writ:

Si A. fecerit te securum, &c. tunc pone per vad', &c. B. quod sit coram justiciariis nostris, &c. ostens' quare talem hæred' infra ætatem existentem, cujus maritagium ad ipsum A. pertinet, apud C. inventum, tali loco rapuit et abduxit (8), *contra voluntatem ipsius A. et contra pacem, &c.*

Et si hæres sit in eodem comitatu, tunc addatur ista clausula.

And if the heir be in the same county, then this clause must be thereto added:

Et diligenter inquiras ubi ille hæres sit in baliva tua, et ipsum ubicunque inventus fuerit capias, et salvo et secure custodias, ita quod eum habeas coram præfat' justiciariis nostris ad præfatum terminum, ad reddend' cui prædictorum A. et B. reddi debeat.

Et fiat secta versus partem de qua queritur, quousque per districtionem venerit, si habeat per quod distringi poterit, vel per contumaciam (si non sit justificabilis) exigatur, et utlagetur. Si forte hujusmodi hæres ducatur, et transferatur in alium comitat' (9), *tunc vic' illius comitatus*
[438] *fiat tale breve sub hac forma:*

And suit shall be made against the party on whom complaint is made, until he come in by distress, if he have whereby he may be distrained; or else for his contumacy, in case he be not justifiable, he shall be outlawed. And if percase the heir be married, or carried into another county, then a writ shall be directed to the sheriff of the same shire in this form:

Questus est nobis A. quod B. nuper talem hæredem infra ætatem, et in custodia sua existent', tali loco in comitatu tali rapuit, et de comitatu illo ad talem locum in com' tuo abduxit, contra voluntatem ipsius A. et contra pacem, &c. Et ideo tibi præcipimus, quod prædictum hæredem, ubicunque eum in baliva

baliva tua invenire poteris, capias, et salvo et secure eum custodias, ita quod eum habeas coram justiciariis nostris, &c. tali loco et die, quem diem idem A. habet versus prædictum B. ad reddend' cui de jure reddi debeat.

Et si hæres antequam inveniri poterit, vel antequam restituatur querenti, obierit (10), *nihilominus procedat placitum inter eos, quousque terminetur, cui restitui deberet, si superstes fuisset. Nec excusabitur aut alleviabitur ille, qui injustè rapuit hujusmodi hæred' de pœna supradicta per mortem hæred', cujus extitit male fidei possessor dum vixit. Et si querens obierit ante placitum terminatum* (11), *si jus ei competebat ratione proprii feodi sui, resummoneatur loquela ad sectam hæred' querentis, et procedat placit' debito ordine. Si vero per alium titulum competat ei jus, sicut titulo donationis, venditionis, aut alio hujusmodi titulo, tunc resummoneatur loquela ad sectam executor' querentis, et procedat placit' ut prædictum est. Eodem modo si moriatur pars defendens* (12) *antequam placit' terminetur vel hæres restituatur, procedat placit' per resum' inter querentem, vel ejus hæredem, seu executores, et executores defendentis, vel ejus hæredes, si executores non sufficiant, quoad satisfactionem de valore maritagii secundum quod in aliis statutis continetur, sed non quoad pœnam prisonæ, quia quis pro alieno facto non est puniendus. Eodem modo cum pendeat placitum inter partes de custodia terræ, vel hæredis, vel utriusque per commune breve, quod incipit:* Præcipe tali, &c. quod reddat, &c. (13) *fiat resummonitio inter hæredes et executores querentis, et similiter hæredes aut executores defendentis, si mors alteram partem præveniat ante placitum terminatum. Et cum perveniatur ad magnam districtionem, detur terminus,* (14) *infra quem tres com' teneantur ad minus, in quorum quolibet comitatu fiat publica proclamatio, quod deforciator veniat ad bancum* (15) *ad diem in brevi contentum, responsurus querenti.*

And if the heir do die afore he can be found, or before he can be restored to the plaintiff, the plea shall pass between them nevertheless, until it be tried unto whom he ought to have been restored if he had been living. Neither shall the ravisher of such a one be excused or eased of the punishment aforesaid by the death of the heir, whom he did withhold by wrong during his life. And if the plaintiff die before the plea determined, if the right belong to him by reason of his proper fee, the plea shall be resummoned at the suit of the heir of the plaintiff, and the plea shall pass in due order. But if the right belongeth to him by another title, as by a title of gift, sale, or other such like, then the plea shall be resummoned at the suit of the executors of the plaintiff, and the plea shall pass as before is said. In the same manner if the defendant die before the plea be tried, or the heir be restored, the plea shall pass by resummons between the plaintiff, his heirs or executors, and the executors of the defendant or his heirs, if the executors be not sufficient to satisfy for the value of the marriage, after as it is contained in other statutes, but not as to the pain of imprisonment; for none ought to be punished for the offence of another. In the same manner when a plea hangeth between parties for the ward of land, or of an heir, or of both, by the common writ that beginneth *Præcipe tali, &c. quod reddat, &c.* Resummons shall be made between the heirs and executors of the plaintiff; and likewise the heirs and the executors of the defendant, if death prevent any of the parties before the plea determined. And when they have passed to the great distress,

renti. Ad quem diem si non venerit, (16) *et proclamatio * sic semel, secundo, et tertio testificatum fuerit, procedatur ad judicium* (17) *pro querente: salvo jure defendentis, si postmodum inde loqui voluerit* (18). *Eodem modo fiat in brevi de transgression' cum quis queritur se ejectum fuisse de hujusmodi custodiis* (19).

distress, a day shall be given, within which three county courts may be holden at the least, in every of which open proclamation shall be made, that the deforcer shall come into the bench at the day contained in the writ, to answer the plaintiff; at which day if he come not, and the proclamation be so returned once, twice, or thrice, the judgement shall pass for the plaintiff, saving the right of the defendant, if after he will claim it. In the same manner it shall be done in a writ of trespass, when any complaineth himself to be ejected from such wardships.

See the first part of the Institutes, sect. 203. (3 Inst. 171. Fitz. Gard. 18. 25. 29, 30, 31, 32. 118. 121. Fitz. Judgm. 102. 116. 123. 150. 157. 172, 204. Bro. Ravishment, 33. 1 Inst. 136. b. Hob. 93. 1 Roll. 445. 2 Roll. 354. Regist. 163. 9 Rep. 71. 74. Fitz. Brief, 823. Rast. 390. 3 Bulst. 275. 278. 281. Dyer. 289. Fitz. Brief, 776. 24 Ed. 3. f. 48. 11 H. 4. f. 54. Fitz. Executors, 52. Fitz. Gard. 110. 24 Ed. 3. f. 25. 20 H. 3. c. 6. 3 Ed. 1. c. 22. 52 H. 3. c. 7. Fitz. Proces. 33. Fitz Gard. 89. Dyer. 369. Regist. 161. &c.

This act of parliament hath made divers alterations and additions to the statute of Merton cap. 6. as hereafter in the exposition of this act shall appeare. Merton, cap. 6.

(1) *De pueris masculis sive femellis.*] The statute of Merton extended onely to heires males, and this act extendeth by express words to heires females also. Lib. 9. fol. 72. D. Husseyes case.

Also the statute of Merton concerning this matter extended to heires *infra* 14 *annos*; and this act extendeth to all that are *post annos nubiles.*

(2) *Si ille qui rapuerit jus non habens.*] The statute of Merton extended to lay men onely, this act extendeth as well to ecclesiasticall persons, regular or secular, as to lay men. D. Husseys case. ubi supra. 7 E. 3. 11.

(3) *Raptis & abductis.*] The words of the statute of Merton are *vi abductis & detentis.*

(4) *Per prisonam duorum annorum, &c.*] The statute of Merton gave imprisonment *donec emendaverit delictum, &c.* This act gives the imprisonment of two yeares, albeit the ward be delivered unmarried, or though amends be made.

The king may pardon this imprisonment for two yeares, which was added by this act. P. 34 E. 1. Coram Rege. Rot. 30.

(5) *De maritagio satisfacere non potuerit.*] The defendant shall be intended sufficient to satisfie the plaintiffe, if the plaintiffe doth not pray that the jurors should inquire of his sufficiency. 8 E. 3. 52. 22 R. 2. damages 130.

(6) *Abjuret regnum, vel habeat perpetuam prisonam.*] And in this case the election is not given to the defendant, but it is in the discretion of the court to give judgement either of abjuration, or perpetuall imprisonment. Lib. 9. fol. 73. D. Husseys case.

This punishment is also added to the statute of Merton.

Albeit the party that is by judgement abjured return again, yet

yet ſhall he not be hanged, becauſe he was not abjured for felony, but he may be puniſhed for his contempt, and remaunded.

(7) *Et ſuper hoc habeat querens tale breve, &c.*] By this branch the writ of raviſhment of gard is given, and the forme of the writ is here expreſſed.

Temps E. 1. gard 133. 3 E. 2. ibid. 6. 11 H. 3. ibid. 141. 11 E. 2. ibid. 127. 33 E. 3. ibid. 163. 1 E. 3. 19, 20. 4 E. 3. 5. 17 E. 3. 42. 26 E. 3. 65. 6 R. 2. gard. 166. 13 H. 4. 17. F. N. B. 140. e. 29. f.

The ſtatute of Merton extended to the writ of right of ward.

A gardein in ſocage cannot have a raviſhment of ward upon this act, but onely a gardein in chivalry, but the gardein in ſocage ſhall have a *raviſhment de gard.* But it was adjudged ſoone after the making of this act, that by the 24. chapter of this parliament, which giveth the writ *in conſimili caſu cadente ſub eodem jure & ſimili indigente remedio,* the gardein in ſocage ſhall maintain a writ of raviſhment of ward for the body, and a writ *de ejectione cuſtodiæ* for the land.

* For the cuſtome of the city of London concerning orphanage, ſee 32 E. 3. 8 R. 2.

32 E. 3. gard 31. 8 R. 2. gard 166. 9 E. 3. 37, 38. 22 E. 3. 19. 24 E. 3. 49. *[440]

In this writ if the iſſue be found for the plaintiffe, yet upon the context of this act the jury ſhall enquire, 1. of the value of the mariage, 2. of the age of the ward, and 3. whether he be married or no: and for the firſt and ſecond they muſt give a direct verdict; for the other they may give a conditionall verdict, as to ſay, whether he be married or no they know not, and if he be married then aſſeſſe greater damages, which enquiry is but an inqueſt of office.

9 E. 3. 37, 38. 14 E. 3 gard. 157. 19 E. 3. gard. 172, 127. 16 E. 3. ibid. 107. 17 E. 3. 57. 45 E. 3. 15. 47 E. 3 19.

Now albeit the verdict be conditionall, yet in this caſe the judgement ſhall not be conditionall, but in this caſe the plaintiffe may have judgement to recover the marriage and leſſer damages, and have execution of the body, and if the ſheriffe return that he is maried, then may the plaintiffe have a *ſcire facias* for the greater damages, and have judgement to recover them, and ſo it is in an action of detinue, &c.

11 H. 4. 80. 21 H. 6. 41. 32 H. 6. 3. 11 H. 7. 5.

(8) *Rapuit et abduxit.*] There be two ſorts of raviſhments of wards, that is to ſay, raviſhments in deeds, and raviſhments in law, and this ſtatute extends to both of them.

Firſt part of the Inſtit. ſect. 202.

Raviſhments in deed, as when one take and carry away a ward; and raviſhments in law be, as if the ward enter into religion, this is a raviſhment in law, for which the ſoveraigne ſhall anſwer, for that his admiſſion of him is a raviſhment in law.

8 E 3. 52.

If a man or a woman marry a ward to his or her daughter, or to any other, this is a raviſhment in law.

11 H. 4. 24.

A man procureth a ward to goe from his gardein, this is a raviſhment in law.

30 E. 3. 6. b. 38 E. 3. 18. 38 Aſſ.

If one raviſh a ward, or eject the lord to the uſe of a ſtranger without his privity, yet if the ſtranger agree thereunto, he is the raviſher or ejecter.

18 E. 3. 25. 41 E. 3. 15. Firſt part of the Inſtitutes, ſect. 114. many authorities there cited.

This act is intended of a gardein in chivalry, as hath been ſaid: and though the father ſhall have a writ of raviſhment of ward, *quare filium ſuum & hæredem rapuit, cujus maritagium ad ipſum pertinet*; and albeit the aunceſtor ſhall have the like action for the taking of his collaterall heire apparent, yet none of thoſe are within this ſtatute, but remain at the common law.

See the firſt part of the Inſtitutes, ſect. 114.

7. H. 4. 9.

The count in the raviſhment of ward upon this act muſt not be by *vi et armis.*

(9) *Si forte hujuſmodi hæres ducatur et transferatur in alium comitatum.*]

comitatum.] A man cannot have a writ of ravishment of ward in the county of York, and suppose the ravishment in the county of Derby, *et quod abductus fuit ab eodem comitatu usque com' Eborum.* But his originall must be in the county of Derby, and by this branch he shall have the writ here mentioned, *questus est nobis* directed to the sheriffe of York, whither the body is carried. Dier 12 El. 289. 34 E. 3. gard. 164.

If the ward be resiant in another county, then where the land is, the lord may have a writ of right of ward in that forein county where the ward is resiant. 40 E. 3. 6. 21 E. 3. 45.

(10) *Et si hæres obierit.*] Albeit the body shall be recovered in the writ of ravishment of ward given by this act, yet it is expressely provided by this branch that the death of the heir shal not abate the writ; but otherwise it is in a writ of right of ward, for in that case the death of the heire shall abate the writ; and so it is if the heire (hanging the writ) commeth to his full age, the writ of right of ward shall abate, but not the ravishment of ward, but if he be of full age at the time of the writ of ravishment brought, then the writ shall abate for the words of the writ, *cujus maritagium ad ipsum pertinet.* 46 E. 3. bre. 776. 18 E. 3. Scire fac' 10. 34 E. 1. gard 129. 30 E. 3. 14. 9 E. 4. 50.

(11) *Et si querens obierit ante placitum terminatum.*] Two joynt lords or two coparceners of a seigniory bring a writ of ward, and one of the plaintiffes die, the writ is abated, and the survivor shall not have a resummons, for this act giveth the resummons either to the heir, or to the executors, and not to any survivor, who may have a new originall; and so it is if the baron and feme be plaintiffes, and the husband dieth, the writ shall abate, and no resummons shall be sued, because one of the plaintiffes is alive, to whom the wardship surviveth, *et pars querens non obiit*; and the nature of a resummons is to continue the originall writ, for by the common law no resummons did lie but against him that was party to the originall, or which came in by voucher or receit, &c. so long as the tenant lived, and onely where the plea was put without day, without any laches or default in the party, as upon a conusans graunted and failer of right by the demise of the king, the *non venu* of the justices, or when the paroll demurred for nonage, or upon the allowance of a protection and the like; but if the process be not continued by the negligence of the plaintiffe, no resummons lieth. [441] 19 E. 3. Scire fac' 119. 38 E. 3. 36. 24 E. 3. 48. 5 H. 7. 38.

Also no resummons lieth for the defendant or tenant, because resummons is compounded of *re*, *sub*, and *moneo*: and the defendant or tenant never sued out summons, and therefore can have no resummons, neither shall a resummons be graunted but against him that was formerly summoned, and upon the resummons by this act the party cannot vary from the former plea, but onely for matter that commeth of puisne time, as a release, &c.

And where some have holden that the makers of this act were not learned in the law, because the resummons is given to the heire, where by law the heire cannot have the wardship being but a chattell, the makers of the law knew that as well as the objector, for it is said in 9 E. 3. that they were *sage gents* that were at this parliament, but seeing no resummons in this case did lie by the common law, the makers of this act gave the resummons to the heire when the wardship accrued *ratione proprii feodi*, for there the inheritance of the tenure might come in question which concerned the heir more then the wardship, *hac vice*, could concern the executors, and as if the defendant make his testament, and deviseth 11 H. 4. 54. p. Hill. 9 E. 3. 22. 18 E. 3. 4, 5. 24 E. 3. 48, 49.

the

the ward to another, yet the resummons shall be awarded by the next subsequent clause of this act against the executors, although
18 E. 3. 4. b. they have nothing in the ward, and, for their insufficiency, against the heire who cannot claime the ward being but a chattell; so *in novo casu providebant novum remedium*, and in one case charged the heire of the defendant, whom the law could not charge, and in another gave remedy to another heire upon good reason, who by law had none.

50 E. 3. 7. b. (12) *Eodem modo si moriatur pars def.* &c.] If a writ of ward he brought against two, and one of them die, no resummons shall be sued by this branch, because one of the defendants are alive, and he shall have the ward by survivor, and this branch giveth the resummons either against the executors or heire, *Et pars defendens non est mortuus.*

And the nature of a resummons (as hath been said) is to continue the originall.

24 E. 3. 48. If the plaintiffe in the writ of ward dieth, and a resummons is sued by the heire, upon the next precedent branch, if the defendant dieth the heire shall have a resummons against the executors of the defendant, for the words of this branch be, *inter querentem, vel ejus hæredem seu executores, et executores defendentis,* &c.

7 E. 3. 48. 18 E. 3. 4, 5. 24 E. 3. 49. Though this branch saith, *eodem modo*, yet for so much, as is otherwise provided for, there is no reference by these words to the former clause, for a resummons lieth not against the heire of the
[442] defendant, if the executors have assets, and it is a good plea for the heire to say that the executors have sufficient; but if the executors have assets for part, and the heire assets for part, yet no resummons is given against them both by this act.

And in a resummons against the executors upon this act of parliament *pleinment administer* is a good plea; but then the plaintiffe shall have judgement *maintenant* to recover the ward; and in a resummons against the heire for the insufficiency of the executors, it is a good plea for him, that he hath nothing by descent in fee-simple.

If the executors have not assets, so as the heire is to be charged, yet shall damages onely be recovered against him: but the punishment ordained by this act shall not be inflicted upon him, for that should be against a maxime of the common law here rehearsed, *quod quis pro alieno facto non est puniendus, et pœna ex delicto defuncti*
Bracton. *hæres teneri non debet*; and againe, *in hæredes non solent transire actiones, quæ pœnales ex maleficio sunt*: and, *toties in hæredem damus actionem de eo quod ad eum pervenit, quoties ex dolo defuncti convenitur non toties ex suo.*

And, *filius non portabit iniquitatem patris.*

(13) *Eodem modo cum pendeat placitum inter partes de custodia terræ, vel hæredis, vel utriusque, per commune breve præcipe tali, &c. quod reddat, &c.*] *Per commune breve.* Hereupon it is called, *breve de communi custodia,* that is, *breve de recto de custodia,* and to
Marl. cap. 7. that writ onely the statute of Marlebridge extended.

(14) *Et cum pervenerit ad magnam districtionem, detur terminus.*]
Marlb. cap. 7. The statute of Marlebridge gave a proclamation, *si ad magnam*
14 E. 3. Procl. 8. *districtionem non venerint, &c.* so as by that act the grand distresse must be returned before the proclamation issued, but by this act the proclamation is to issue when the grand distresse is graunted, for

for the words be, *cum pervenerit ad magnam districtionem, detur terminus, &c.* 30 E. 3. 10, 11. 49 E. 3. 19.

Also the statute of Marlebridge provided, that *bis vel ter, &c. infra medietatem anni sequentis* the proclamation should be made, so as the counties were put in certain when the proclamation should be made; now this act abridgeth the sixe months to three months, and sets the time of the proclamation in certaine. This branch extendeth onely to the writ of right of ward, as the statute of Marlebridge did, *vide* in the end of this chapter. Marlb. cap. 7.

This branch restraining the common law, extendeth not to the vowchee, but onely to the defendant in deed, and not to the defendant in law. 29 E. 3. 48. 13. Proclam. 9.

If *propter brevitatem temporis* there were but two proclamations made, the plaintiffe shall not have a writ, *cum allocatione comitat'*, because he pursued not the statute, and it was his folly that the writ contained not longer time. 2 H. 4. 1.

In a writ of ward against two, the one appeareth, and the other makes default, or if the one have nothing, and the other is distrained, no proclamation shall be awarded against the one of them, for both of them make but one defendant, and therefore either against both, or against none. 19 E. 3. Procl. 5. & 10. 17 E. 3. 70. 14 H. 4. 37.

If a distresse with a proclamation be graunted, and the defendant hath nothing but within a franchise, the sheriffe shall make the proclamations in the county, and the bayly of the liberty shall distraine him. 2 H. 4. 1.

The proclamation must be graunted in the same county where the originall is brought; and therefore if the plaintiffe surmise that the defendant hath sufficient in a forein county, he shall have a distresse at the common law, but not with proclamation by this statute. 17 E. 3. 70, 71.

(15) *Veniat ad bancum.*] This extends not to justices in eyre, nor to commissioners of oier and terminer, but the plaintife may have an action of trespasse before them at the common law. [443] 3 E. 3. Proclam. 17. 29 E. 3. 37.

(16) *Ad quem diem si non venerit,* &c.] See 17 E. 3. 19. here in the next paragraph, by which it appeareth that he must come *ad quem diem, et non ad alium.* 17 E. 3. 19.

(17) *Procedatur ad judicium.*] At the common law he could not have judgement by default without plea of the party, &c. but distresse infinite; if upon the proclamation returned the defendant be demanded, and appear, and taketh a day by *prece partium,* and at that day make default, the plaintife shall not have judgement upon this statute, because he made not default at the return of the distresse, for this act said, *ad quem diem si non venerit.* 22 E. 3. 19.

And where it is said, (*procedatur ad judicium*) yet upon this default no judgement can be yet given, but the court must award a writ to the sherife, to inquire of the value of the marriage, of the age of the ward, and whether he be marryed, &c. as is aforesaid; and upon the return of that writ, then judgement shall be given. 42 H. 3. 1. 38 E. 3. 21.

But if the defendant appear at the return of the proclamation, and confesse the action, the plaintife shall have judgement of the damages in his count.

(18) *Salvo jure defendentis, si postmodum inde loqui voluerit.*] Some have conceited upon these words [*inde loqui voluerit*] that if a man

recovereth in a writ of right of ward by default, that the defendant might have a writ of right of ward, and recover again that which
26 E. 3. Gard. 108. he formerly lost; but by reason of this word [*postmodum*] those words shall be intended, that he may have a writ of right of ward after that another tenant of the same land happen to dye his heir within age, but for the same wardship, whereof judgement is given in the writ of right of ward, the defendant is barred.

(19) *Eodem modo fiat in brevi de transgressione cum quis queritur se*
3 E. 3. 7. 30 E. 3. 10, 11. *ejectum fuisse de hujusmodi custodiis.*] The writ here intended, is an *ejectment de gard, breve de ejectione custodiæ,* which is a writ at the common law. *De attornato inde.*

Regist. 162. *Inter H. & R. de quadam transgressione eidem H. per præfatum R. illata ut dicitur.*

Regist. ubi supra. 14 E. 3. Procl. 7. By this branch, proclamation shall be made in this writ of the ejectment of gard, which shall not be made in the ravishment de gard.

CAP. XXXVI.

QUIA domini cur', et alii qui cur' tenent, et senescalli (1), *volentes gravare subditos suos* (2), *cum non habeant legalem viam eos gravandi, procurant alios movere querelas* (3) *versus eos, et dare vadium, et offerre plegios, vel impetrare brevia, et ad sectas hujusmodi querentium compellunt eos sequi comitatum, hundredum, wapentachium, et* * *cur', quousque finem fecerint cum ipsis pro voluntate sua: statutum est, quod hoc de cætero non fiat. Et si quis per hujusmodi falsas querimonias fuerit attachiatus, replegiet districtionem suam* (4) *sic captam, et poni fac' loquelam coram justiciariis, coram quibus si vicecomes, vel alius balivus, vel dominus, postquam sit districtus formaverit querimoniam suam, advocaverit justam districtionem ratione hujusmodi queremoniarum* (5) *coram eis factarum, et replicet', quod hujusmodi querimoniæ movebantur versus eos malitiosè, ad instantiam seu procurationem vic', aut aliorum balivorum, aut dominorum* (6), *admittatur illa replicatio. Et si super hoc convicti fuerint, versus dominum regem redimantur* (7), *et nihilominus*

* [444]

FORASMUCH as lords of courts, and other that keep courts, and stewards, intending to grieve their inferiors, where they have no lawful mean so to do, procure other to move matters against them, and to put in surety and other pledges, or to purchase writs, and at the suit of such plaintiffs compel them to follow the county, hundred, wapentake, and other like courts, until they have made fine with them at their will; it is ordained, that it shall not be so used hereafter. And if any be attached upon such false complaints, he shall replevy his distress so taken, and shall cause the matter to be brought afore the justices, before whom if the sheriff, bailiff, or other lord (after that the party distrained hath framed his plaint) will advow the distress lawful by reason of such complaints made unto them, and it be replied that such plaints were moved maliciously against the party by the solicitation or procurement of the sheriff, or other bailiffs, or lords, the same replication shall be admitted; and if they be convict hereupon, they shall

minus hujusmodi sic gravatis damna in triplo restituantur.	shall make fine to the king, and nevertheless restore treble damages to the parties grieved.

(22 Ed. 3. f. 15. Fitz. Avowry, 78. 13 Hen. 4. 2.)

This act was made in affirmance of the common law, and to adde a greater punishment then the common law did; for the delinquent shall be ransomed at the kings suit, and the party grieved shall recover treble damages, where he should recover but single at the common law.

If A. procure B. to sue an action in any court of record, or other inferiour court against C. he may have an action of deceit against A. at the common law, and recover his single damages. 43 E. 20. F.N.B. 98. m. Regist. Judic. 37.

(1) *Quia domini curiarum, et seneschalli,* &c.] This act extendeth to court barons, leets, and to county courts, tourns, hundreds, and not to the courts at Westminster (they being afterwards named in this act, &c.] but they remain at the common law. 41 Ed. 3. Avowry 78. 11 H. 4. 91. 13 H. 4. 2. 8 E. 4. 5.

Though *seneschalli* be here named, yet bailifes, and other officers are within this act, and the bailife, or other officer may be punished, without naming the lord. 13 H. 4. 2. 3. 41 E. 3. Avowry 78.

(2) *Volentes gravare subditos suos.*] *Subditos* is here taken for any man that is subject to their jurisdiction, and so it is to be taken in all other like places.

(3) *Procurant alios movere querelas,* &c.] These words are generall, and therefore if the lord, bailife, steward, or any other officer procure any man to sue a lawfull action, he shall be punished by this act, *Quia culpa est se immiscere rei ad se non pertinenti.* 22 E. 3. 15. 11 H. 4. 91. 13 H. 4. 2.

(4) *Repiegiet districtionem suam.*] This act extendeth onely to a replevin, and not to an action of trespasse, or any other action. 13 H. 4. 2. b.

And here a distresse is taken for an attachment.

(5) *Advocaverit justam districtionem ratione hujusmodi querimoniar',* &c.] By the letter of this branch the defendant must make an avowry, but it must be extended further then the letter; for admit that the lord, &c. will (to save himself from treble damages) make no avowry, but plead that the goods were not distrained, &c. or the like plea, whereupon issue being joyned, the plaintife after proof of the issue may give in evidence for the treble damages the purview of this act, and that the lord now defendant, procured a suit, [445] &c. contrary to this act, and that he is guilty of the distresse, or attachment, and therefore ought to yeeld treble damages; and if this be found by the jury (although it were not pleaded) the pl' shall recover treble damages; for it lyeth not in the power of the defendant by his false plea to excuse himself of treble damages given by this act: as if the disseisor alieneth to persons unknown, and in an assise brought against the disseisor he plead *Nul ten' de frank-tenement nosme in le briefe, et si trove ne soit nul tort nul disseisin,* the plaintife may give in evidence, that the said alienation was made to defraud the plaintife of his action, and that the disseisor took the profits, in which case he is to be relieved by the statutes of 1 R. 2. 4 H. 4. and 11 H. 6. Vide lib. 5. f. 60. Gooches case, a statute given in evidence, and not pleaded. 1 R. 2. cap. 9. 4 H. 4. cap. 7. 11 H. 6. cap. 4. 9 H. 6. 14. 15. lib. 1. cap. 123. Chudleys case.

See before cap. 35. in the case of ravishment of ward.

(6) *Malitiose, ad instantiam, seu procurationem vicecom', aut aliorum*
22 E. 3. 15. *balivorum, seu dominorum.*] Here it is to be observed that the procurement is the substance, and that doth imply, that it was done *malitiosè*; and therefore if the jury finde the procurement, and that it was not done maliciously, yet the court shall (for that it judicially appeareth to them) adjudge it done maliciously.

(7) *Versus dominum regem redimantur,* &c.] That is, they shall be fined to the king in that suit brought by replevin.

CAP. XXXVII.

QUIA etiam balivi, ad quos ex officio pertinet districtiones facere, gravare volentes subditos suos, ut ab eis pecuniam extorqueant, mittunt ignotos ad faciend' districtiones, ea intentione, ut subditos gravare possint, per hoc quod sic districti non habentes notitiam personarum non permittunt hujusmodi districtiones super eos fieri: statutum est, quod nulla districtio fiat (1) *nisi per balivos notos et juratos* (2). *Et si alio modo districtiones fecerint, et de hoc convicti fuerint, si gravati breve de transgress. impetraverint, restituant gravatis damna* (3) [alias in triplo] *et versus regem graviter puniantur.*

FORASMUCH also as bailiffs, to whose office it belongeth to take distresses, intending to grieve their inferiors that they may exact money of them, do send strangers to take distresses, to the intent that they might grieve their inferiors, by reason that the parties so distrained, not knowing such persons, will not suffer the distresses to be taken; it is provided, that no distress shall be taken, but by bailiffs sworn and known. And if they which do distrain do otherwise, and thereof be convict (if the parties grieved will purchase a writ of trespass) they shall restore damages to the parties grieved, and besides, shall be grievously punished towards the king.

(3 Rep. 12.)

This act is made in affirmance of the common law, and for reformation of an abuse by sherifes, who used to make bailifes to distrain, who were unknown, to the intent that the owner of the cattell might make rescous, and thereupon the sherife, &c. to extort money from him; wherefore remedy is given by this act.

Lib. 3. fol. 12. Sir William Herberts case. 25 E. 3. cap. 25. (1) *Nulla districtio fiat.*] At the time of the making of this act, this processe lay in an action of debt, (for the capias in that case is given by the statute of 25 E. 3.) so as this statute extending to an action of debt, although the latter act give a capias, yet the capias coming in lieu of the distresse is within this act.

[446]
(2) *Nisi per balivos notos, et juratos.*] By this act the bailifes must both be known and sworn: an act yet standing in force, and worthy
Fleta. to be put in execution: Fleta doth render this branch thus:

Provisum est quod nulla districtio fiat per balivos regis, nisi jurati fuerint et noti, et si quis alio modo distringeret, et de hoc convincatur ad

sectam

sectam districti, cui in hoc casu consulitur per breve de transgressione, damna reddet gravato, et versus regem graviter punietur.

Of this branch the Mirror saith thus, *Lestatute de distresses est distinguishable, car in distresses torcious sans garrant tient lieu le judgement de robbery, et per garrant chescun est receivable conus et disconus.* But the statute is in the negative, and necessary to be observed. Mirror, c. 5. § 5.

(3) *Damna.*] Some editions have *alias in triplo,* but the originall is *damna,* and not *in triplo,* and therewith agreeth Fleta.

CAP. XXXVIII.

QUIA etiam vic' hundredarii, et balivi libertatum consueverunt gravare subditos suos ponendo in assisis et juratis homines languidos, et decrepitos, perpetua vel temporali infirmitate languentes, homines etiam tempore summonition' suæ in patria non commorantes, summonendo etiam effrenatam multitudinem juratorum, ita ut à quibusdam eos in pace dimittendo pecuniam extorqueant, et sic fiunt assisæ et juratæ multotiens per pauperiores, divitibus pro suo dando domi commorantibus: statutum est, quod de cætero non summoneantur in una assis. plures quam xxiv. (1). *Senes etiam videlicet ultra 70. annos* (2), *perpetuo languidi* (3), *vel tempore summonitionis infirmi* (4), *vel in patria non commorantes* (5), *non ponantur in juratis, vel minoribus assisis* (6). *Nec etiam ponantur in assisis vel juratis, licet in proprio com' capi debeant aliqui qui minus ten' habeant, quam ad valentiam viginti solidorum per annum* (7). *Et si hujusmodi assisæ et jurat' extra comitatum capi debeant, non ponantur in eis aliqui qui minus tenement' non habeant, quam ad valentiam xl. s. per annum, illis exceptis qui testes sunt in chartis* (8), *vel aliis scriptis, quorum præsentia necessaria est, dum tamen potentes sint ad laborandum. Nec debet istud statutum extendi ad magnas assisas, in quibus oportet aliquando ponere milites in patria non residentes, propter paucitatem militum,*

FORASMUCH also as sheriffs hundreders, and bailiffs of liberties, have used to grieve those which be in subjection unto them, putting in assises and juries men diseased and decrepit, and having continual or sudden disease; and men also that dwelled not in the country at the time of the summons; and summon also an unreasonable multitude of jurors, for to extort money from some of them for letting them go in peace, and so the assises and juries pass many times by poor men, and the rich men abide at home by reason of their bribes: it is ordained, that from henceforth in one assise no more shall be summoned than four and twenty; and old men, above threescore and ten years, being continually sick, or being diseased at the time of the summons, or not dwelling in that country, shall not be put in juries of petit assises. Nor any shall be put in assises or juries, though they ought to be taken in their own shire, that may dispend less than twenty shillings yearly. And if such assises and juries be taken out of the shire, none shall pass in them but such as may dispend forty shillings yearly at the least, except such as be witnesses in deeds or other writings, whose presence is necessary, so that they be able to travel. Neither shall this statute extend to great assises, in which it behoveth many times knights to

militum, dum tamen tenement' habeant in comit'. Et si vic' vel subbalivi sui, vel balivi libertatum contra istud statutum in aliquo articulo venerint, et super hoc convincantur, restituant dampna gravatis, et nihilominus sint in misericordia domini regis. Et habeant justiciarii ad assisas capiend' assign' (9), *cum in com' venerint, potestatem audiendi querimonias singulorum conquerentium, quoad articulos in isto statuto contentos, et justiciam in forma prædicta exhibend'.*

to pass not resident in the country, for the scarcity of knights, so that they have land in the shire. And if the sheriff, or his undersheriffs, or bailiffs of liberties, offend in any point of this statute, and thereupon be convict, damages shall be awarded to the parties grieved, and they shall nevertheless be amerced to the king. And justices assigned to take assises, when they come into the shire, shall have power to hear the plaints of all complainants as to the articles contained in this statute, and to minister justice in form aforesaid.

Fleta, li. 4. cap. 5. See 21 E. 1. stat. de non ponendis. 34 E. 1. Ordinat. &c. dit super Chart. ca. 9. Marlbr. ca. 24. For Jurors. See Custumier de Norm. ca. 69. (Kelyng, 16. 28 Ed. 1. stat. 3. c. 9. 10 H. 4. f. 8. 2 Roll 163. Bro. Jurors, 24. 1 Inst. 158. Kel. 97. 8 Ed. 3. f. 30.)

The mischiefe doth plainly appeare by the preamble, and the end of these mischiefes was, that the sheriffes by such meanes did *pecuniam extorquere, &c.*

See the first part of the Institutes for the antiquity and right institution of trials by twelve men, and of the number of twelve. Sect. 234. and *Magna Charta* cap. 29.

2 H. 7. 8. Fleta ubi supra. Dier 1. Mar. 98. Fleta ubi supra.

(1) *In una assisa plures quam 24.*] This was but the abuse of the sheriffe, for though the writ, which is his warrant, is but twelve, yet regularly he must returne twenty foure, and no more, unlesse it be in speciall cases: *Supponendo, inquit Fleta, superfluam hominum multitudinem, ita quod quasdam in pace dimitterent prece vel precio*; but in a writ of right there be sixteene jurors returned onely.

F.N.B. 166. d. F.N.B. ibid. a.

(2) *Senes ultra 70. annos,* &c.] This statute is a direct prohibition in it selfe, and therefore the party grieved may have his action upon this act against the sheriffe without giving any notice either of this, or of sicknesse, or non-commorancy, and yet the use is to sue out a writ grounded upon this act to the sheriffe that he returne them not.

F.N.B. ibid. a. Regist. 177. Psalme 89. 10.

But without question notice by word were good, if notice were requisite; and this seemeth to be in affirmance of the common law, for if a coroner be *senio confractus,* it is a good cause to remove him, and the prophet David saith, *Dies nostrorum in ipsis septuaginta anni.*

(3) *Perpetuo languidi.*] As if he be *morbo paralysi percussus,* or if hee bee *leprosus,* or stricken with any other continuall sicknesse.

F.N.B. 164. Regist. 177.

It also extended to men that are blinde, deafe, of no sound memory, or so lame as they cannot well goe nor stand, and these shall take the benefit of this statute, of what age soever they bee; and this point is in affirmance of the common law, for these be good causes to remove a coroner.

(4) *Tempore summonitionis infirmi.*] This must be so intended, so infirme as he is not able to serve; and this is also in affirmance of the common law.

(5) *In patria non commorantes.*] The statute of *articuli super chartas* doth adde to this, that albeit they be commorant in the same county, yet must the jurors have two qualities, *viz.* two of the most, and one of the least, that is most neare the place, most sufficient, and least suspicious, or otherwise the demandant shall render double damages, and bee grievously amerced. Art. super Chart. cap. 9. Regist. 177. F.N.B. 165. Regist. ubi sup.

See what a coroner ought to be, *viz.* *Qui melius sciat et possit officio illi intendere.* Regist. ubi sup.

If any be returned contrary to the purview of this act, he cannot be challenged, neither can the party grieved alledge the matter for his discharge, but he must take his remedy by action against the sheriffe upon this act. [448] F.N.B. 166. d.

Now may it be a question, who is the party grieved that shall have his action, if the sheriffe returne *magis remotos, minus sufficientes, et magis suspectos?* whereunto heare what S. William Herle chiefe justice of the common pleas saith, This statute may be intended, in case where the demandant or plaintiffe is delayed of his suit by such return of the sheriffe, that he by the statute shall recover damages against him, or where the tenant or defendant after he hath lost his land, or cause by the oath of them that be so returned contrary to the forme of the statute, and after he doth convict them in an attaint, and thereby be restored, then he may have his action upon the statute to recover his damages, &c. and thereunto Hill justice agreed, which (as concerning the tenant or defendant) must of necessity be intended of this act of W. 2. for the statute of *articuli super chartas* give double damages onely to the demandant, and not to the tenant: also hereupon it followeth that the act of *articuli super chartas* is but an exposition of this act, and addeth a further penalty. 8 E. 3. 30. 7 E. 3. 26. bis.

More shall be said hereof, when we come to the said statute of *articuli super chartas.* Art. super Chart. cap. 9.

(6) *Vel in minoribus assisis.*] For as hath beene said, this act extends not to a writ of right, as hereafter in this act by expresse words it appeareth.

(7) *Qui minus tenementa habeant quam ad valenciam viginti solid' per annum,* &c.] These summes of 20 s. and 40 s. are altered by later statutes, *viz.* by 2 H. 5. and 27 Eliz. 2 H. 5. c. 3. stat. 2. 27 Eliz. ca. 10.

See the first part of the Institutes, sect. 464.

(8) *Exceptis qui testes sunt in chartis,* &c.] Here is an exception of witnesses named in the deed, who in many cases are joyned to the jury without regard had to age or yearely revenue, both because the sheriffe hath an expresse warrant to summon or distrain them by name, and for that their presence is necessary, and yet with this caution, *Dum tamen potentes sint ad laborandum.* Stat. of York, c. 2. 6 H. 3. Proc. 209. 8 H. 3. ibid. 21c. Kelw. 97. Regist. judic'. 6. b. 7. b. 56. 58. 69.

(9) *Et habeant justic' ad assisas capiend' assignat'.*] This clause is in the affirmative, and therefore the party grieved may take his remedy upon this act, either before justices of assise, or in any other court that have conusans thereof: for justices of assise could not have power in this case without expresse words, but other judges have power without any expresse words, and therefore if the meaning be to exclude other judges, then those that be named, there must be words negative, *viz.* and not in any other court, nor before any other judges.

CAP. XXXIX.

QUIA juſticiarii (ad quorum officium ſpectat unicuique coram eis placitandi juſticiam exhibere frequentius impediuntur, quo minus officium ſuum debit' modo exequi poſſint, per hoc quod vic' brevia originalia et judicialia non retornant, per hoc etiam quod ad brevia domini regis falſum retornant reſponſum : providit dominus rex et ordinavit, quod illi qui timent malitiam vic', liberent brevia ſua originalia et judicialia in pleno com', vel in retro com' (2), *ubi ſit collatio denariorum domini regis, et capiatur billettum* (1) *de vic' preſente, vel ſubvic', in quo billetto contineantur nomina petentium et tenentium in brevi nominat', et ad requiſitionem illius qui breve liberavit, apponat' billetto ſigillum vic' vel ſubvic' in teſtim', et fiat mentio de die liberationis brevis. Et ſi vicecomes vel ſubvicecomes hujuſmodi billetto ſigillum ſuum apponere noluerit, capiatur teſtimonium militum, et aliorum fide dignorum qui præſentes fuerint, qui ſigill' ſua hujuſmodi billetto apponant. Et ſi vic' brevia ſibi liberata non retornaverit, et ſuper hoc ad juſticiarios perveniat querimonia, mandetur per breve de judicio juſtic' ad aſſiſas capiendas aſſign', quod inquirent per eos qui preſentes fuerint quando breve vic' liberatum fuit, ſi ſciverint de illa deliberatione, et inquiſitio returnetur. Et ſi compertum fuerit per inquiſitionem, quod breve fuit ei liberat', adjudicentur querenti vel petenti damna, habito reſpectu ad qualitatem et quantitatem actionis, et ad periculum quod ei evenire poſſet, per dilationem quam patiebatur.* [Anno 2 E. 3. cap. 5. apud Not'.] *Et per iſtam viam fiat remedium quando vic' reſpondet, quod breve adeo tarde venit* (3), *quod præceptum regis exequi non potuit. Multociens etiam capiunt*

FORASMUCH as juſtices, to whoſe office it belongeth to miniſter juſtice to all that ſue before them, are many times diſturbed in due execution of their office, for that ſheriffs do not return writs original and judicial; and alſo for that they make falſe returns unto the king's writs; our lord the king hath provided and ordained, that ſuch as do fear the malice of ſheriffs, ſhall deliver their writs original and judicial in the open county, or in the county where the collection of the king's money is; and may take of the ſheriff or underſheriff, being preſent, a bill, wherein the names of the demandants and tenants mentioned in the writ ſhall be contained; and at the requeſt of him that delivered the writ, the ſeal of the ſheriff or underſheriff ſhall be put to the bill for a teſtimony, and mention ſhall be made of the day of the deliverance of the writ: And if the ſheriff or underſheriff will not put his ſeal to the bill, the witneſs of knights and other credible perſons being in preſence ſhall be taken, that put their ſeals to ſuch bill. And if the ſheriff will not return writs delivered unto him, and complaint thereof be made to the juſtices, a writ judicial ſhall go unto the juſtices aſſigned to take aſſiſes, that they ſhall inquire by ſuch as were preſent at the deliverance of the writ to the ſheriff, if they knew of the deliverance, and an inqueſt ſhall be returned. And if it be found by the inqueſt, that the writ was delivered to him, damages ſhall be awarded to the plaintiff or demandant; having reſpect to the quality and quantity of the action, and to the peril that might have come to him by reaſon of the delay that he ſuſtained; and by this mean

piunt placita dilationes per hoc quod vicecom' respondet, quod præcepit balivis alicujus libertatis (4), *qui nihil inde fecerint; et nominet libertates, quæ nunquam retornum brevium habuerunt. Propter quod, ordinavit dominus rex quod thesaurarius et baron' de scaccario* (5) *liberent justiciar' in rotulo omnes libertates* (6) *in quibuscunque com' qui habent retornum*
[450] *brevium. Et si vic' respondet quod retornum fecit balivo alterius libertatis, quam alicujus contentæ in prædict' rotulo, statim puniatur vicecom' tanquam exhæredator regis et coronæ suæ* (7). *Et si forte respondeat quod mandavit balivo alicujus libertatis, quæ veraciter retorn' habet* [qui inde nihil fecit (9,)] *mandetur vicecom' quod non omittat* (8) *propter aliquam libertatem prædict', quin exequatur præceptum domini regis, et quod scire faciat balivis* (10), *quibus fecit retorn' quod sint ad diem in brevi contentum ad respondendum, quare de præcepto domini regis executionem non fecerint. Et si ad diem venerint, et se acquietent, quod retornum brevis non fuit eis factum, statim condemnetur vicecom' domino illius libertatis, et similiter parti læsæ per dilationem in restitutionem damnorum. Et si ad diem non venerint balivi, vel venerint, et supradicto modo se non acquietaverint in quolibet brevi de judicio, quam diu durat placitum, præcipiatur vicecomiti quod non omittat propter libertatem, &c. Multotiens etiam vicecom' falsum dant responsum, quo ad illum articulum quod de exit'* (11), *&c. mandantes aliquando et mentientes, quod nulli sunt exitus, aliquando quod parvi sunt exitus, cum de majoribus respondere possint, aliquando non facientes mentionem de exitibus. Propter quod ordinatum est et concordatum, quod si querens petat auditum responsionis vicecom', concedatur ei. Et si offerat verificare* (12), *quod vicecom' de majoribus exitibus regi respondere potuit, fiat ei breve de judicio ad justic'*

ad

mean there shall be remedy when the sheriff returneth that the writ came too late, whereby he could not execute the king's commandment. Oftentimes also pleas be delayed by reason that the sheriff returneth that he hath commanded the bailiffs of some liberty which did nothing therein, and nameth liberties that never had the return of writs; whereupon our lord the king hath ordained, that the treasurer and barons of the exchequer shall deliver to the justices in a roll all the liberties in all shires that have return of writs. And if the sheriff answer that he hath made return to a bailiff of another liberty than is contained in the said roll, the sheriff shall be forthwith punished as a disheritor of our lord the king and his crown. And if peradventure he return that he hath delivered the writ to a bailiff of some liberty that indeed hath return, the sheriff shall be commanded, that he shall not spare for the foresaid liberty, but shall execute the king's precept; and that he do the bailiffs to wit, to whom he returned the writ, that they be ready at a day contained in the writ, to answer why they did not execute the king's precept. And if they come at the day, and acquit themselves, that no return was made to them, the sheriff shall be forthwith condemned to the lord of the same liberty, and likewise to the party grieved by the delay, for to render damages. And if the bailiffs come not in at the day, or do come, and do not acquit themselves in manner aforesaid; in every judicial writ, so long as the plea hangeth, the sheriff shall be commanded that he shall not spare for the liberty, &c. Many times also sheriffs make false returns as touching these articles, *quod de exitibus, &c.* returning sometime, and lying, that there be no issues, sometime that there are small issues, when they may return great, and sometime do make mension of no issues; wherefore it is

ad aſſiſas capiendas aſſignatos, quod inquirant in preſentia vicecomitis, ſi intereſſe voluerit, de quibus et quantis exit' vic' reſpondere potuit à die impetrationis brevis uſque ad diem in brevi contentum (13) [al' receptionis vide p. 27 *H.* 8. cap. 10. f. 3. & p. 20 *H.* 6. cap. 10. fol. 25.] *et cum inquiſitio retornata fuerit, ſi de pleno prius non reſponderit, oneretur de ſuperpluſagio* (14) *per extractas juſtic' libertates ad ſcaccarium, et nihilominus graviter amercietur pro concelamento. Et ſciat vicecom' quod redditus, blada in grangia, et omnia mobilia, præter equitaturam, indumenta, et utenſilia domus continentur ſub nomine exituum* (15).

ordained and agreed, that if the plaintiff demand hearing of the ſheriff's return, it ſhall be granted him; and and if he offer to aver that the ſheriff might have returned greater iſſues unto the king, he ſhall have a writ judicial unto the juſtices aſſigned to take aſſiſes, that they ſhall inquire in preſence of the ſheriff (if he will be there) of what and how great iſſues the ſheriff might have made return from the day of the writ purchaſed unto the day contained in the writ. And when the inqueſt is returned, if he have not afore anſwered for the whole, he ſhall be charged with the overplus by the extreats of the juſtices delivered in the exchequer, and neverthelefs ſhall be grievouſly amerced for the concealment. And let the ſheriff know, that rents, corn in the grange, and all moveables (except horſe, harneſs, and houſhold-ſtuff) be contained within the name of iſſues.

Et præcepit dom' rex, quod vic' pro hujuſmodi falſis reſponſionibus, ſemel et iterum, (*ſi ſit neceſſe*) *per*
[451] *juſtic' caſtigentur. Et ſi tertio deliquerint, alius non apponat manum quam dominus rex* (16). *Multotiens etiam falſum dant reſponſum, mandando quod non potuerunt* [exequi] *præceptum regis propter reſiſtentiam* (17) *poteſtatis alicujus magnatis, de quo caveat vic' de cætero, quia hujuſmodi reſponſio multum redundat in dedecus domini regis et coronæ ſuæ* (18).

And the king hath commanded, that ſheriffs ſhall be puniſhed by the juſtices once or twice (if need be) for ſuch falſe returns; and if they offend the third time, none ſhall have to do therewith but the king. They make alſo many times falſe anſwers, returning that they could not execute the king's precept for the reſiſtance of ſome great man; wherefore let the ſheriffs beware from henceforth, for ſuch manner of anſwers redound much to the diſhonour of the king.

Et quam cito ſubbalivi ſui teſtificentur, quod invenerunt hujuſmodi reſiſtentiam, ſtatim (*omnibus omiſſis*) *aſſumpto ſecum poſſe comit' ſui, eat in propria perſona ſua ad faciend' executionem* (19).

And as ſoon as his bailiffs do teſtifie that they found ſuch reſiſtance, forthwith all things ſet apart (taking with him the power of the ſhire) he ſhall go in proper perſon to do execution.

Et ſi inveniat ſubbalivos ſuos mendaces (20), *puniat eos per priſonam, ita quod alii per eorum pœnam caſtigentur.*

And if he find his underbailiffs falſe, he ſhall puniſh them by impriſonment, ſo that other by their example may be reformed.

Et ſi inveniat eos veraces, caſtiget reſiſtentes per priſonam, a qua non deliberentur ſine ſpeciali præcepto dom' regis (21). *Et ſi forte vic', cum venerit,*

And if he do find them true, he ſhall puniſh the reſiſters by impriſonment, from whence they ſhall not be delivered without the king's ſpecial com-

venerit, resistentiam invenerit (22), *certificet cur' de nominibus resistentium, auxiliantium, consentientium, præcipientium et fautorum, et per breve de judicio attachientur* (23) *hujusmodi per corpora ad veniendum ad cur' regis. Et si de hujusmodi resistentia convincantur, puniantur secundum quod domino regi placuerit* (24). *Nec intromittat se aliquis minister domini regis de pœna hujusmodi infligenda, quia dominus rex hoc sibi special' reservat* (25), *pro eo quod hujusmodi resistentes censentur pacis suæ et regni perturbatores.* [13 E. 1. de Mercatoribus, Articuli super Chartas, cap. 16.]

commandment. And if percase the sheriff when he cometh do find resistance, he shall certifie to the court the names of the resisters, aiders, consenters, commanders, and favourers, and by a writ judicial they shall be attached by their bodies to appear at the king's court; and if they be convict of such resistance, they shall be punished at the king's pleasure. Neither shall any officer of the king's meddle in assigning the punishment, for our lord the king hath reserved it specially to himself, because that resisters have been reputed disturbers of his peace, and of his realm.

Fleta, li. 2. ca. 61. Art. super Chart. ca. 16. (2 Ed. 3. c. 5. Regist. 86. 1 Roll, 440. 4 Rep. 65. b. 3 Ed. 1. c. 17. V.N.B. f. 43. 11 Ed. 4. f. 4. 27 H. 8. f. 3. 10 H. 7. f. 11. Fitz. Averment, 16. 26. 43. 45. 47, 48, 49. Regist. 83. 18 Ed. 1. c. 16.)

Here is a maxime of the law recited, *viz. ad officium justiciariorum spectat, unicuiq; coram eis placitanti justitiam exhibere.*

By this chapter there be five mischiefs, or rather abuses of sherifes rehearsed and provided for, which we shall handle in order, as they shall arise in this chapter.

The first mischief was, that the sherife returned not the writs to him directed, but imbezeled the same, and commonly the demandant or plaintife for default of proof was without remedy, or else without the effect of a just remedy being against a sherife, for the which a remedy is provided by this act in manner insuing.

(1) *Illi qui timent malitiam vicecom' liberent brevia sua originalia, et judicialia in pleno com', vel in retro com' ubi sit collatio denariorum domini regis, et capiatur bilettū,* &c.] This branch was taken to be short, for it was no more but *capiatur bilettum*, and no commandement to the sherife to receive the writs and to make a bill; but by the statute of 2 E. 3. the sherife and under-sherife are commanded, that they shall receive the said writs, and make a bill, and so throughout. 2 E. 3. cap. 5.

So as now it is a contempt in the sherife or under-sherife, if he make it not, and in default of them, it shall be also a contempt in the others appointed to seal it, if they refuse. [452]

In this speciall case the demandant or plaintife shall have an action against the sherife for not returning the writ, whereas regularly for not returning of a writ the sherife shall be amercied *quousque*; but for a false return, or for imbezeling of a writ, an action doth lye at the common law against the sherife. 26 Ass. 48. 38 Ass. 13. 42 Ass. 12. 8 H. 6. 1. 1 H. 6. 1. F.N.B. 93. b. 31 E. 3. Procl. 55.

And the demandant or plaintife, if he fear the malice (as this act speaketh) of the sherife, he may cause the sherife or under-sherife to be called into the court, and deliver the writ to him of record, that he may take the benefit of this statute. Regist. 85, 86. 19 H. 6. 29. Bract. lib. 5. fol. 441. b.

See the action brought upon this branch of the statute, in the book of entries Rastall. Fol. 501. 626.

(2) *Retro*

(2) *Retro comitatus.*] Is after the county court, as to pleas, be ended; it is holden further, for the collection of the kings money, that is, his green wax.

(3) *Et per iſtam viam fiat remedium quando vicecomes reſpondet quod breve adeo tarde venit,* &c.] The ſecond miſchief was, the ſherife would return a *tarde,* which by this purview is prevented; and ſo it is if the writ be delivered to the ſherife of record, as hath been ſaid.

Bract. li. 5. fo. 441. Where Bracton further in the ſame place ſaith, *Et unde infiniti ſunt caſus de genere iſto ubi vicec' per fraudem reſcribit, et prætendit non cauſam ut cauſam.*

(4) *Multotiens etiam capiunt placita dilationes per hoc, quod vicec' reſpondet quod præcepit balivis alicujus libertatis,* &c.] Here is the third miſchief, that great delays are uſed by the falſe return of ſherifes in making of mandates to fained liberties, ſuppoſing them to have return of writs, where in troth there be no ſuch liberties, for redreſſe whereof the remedy followeth.

11 E. 4. 4. a. (5) *Quod theſaurarius, et barones de ſcaccario,* &c.] Albeit it be inrolled in the chancery, that ſuch a man hath return of writs, yet is not that within the purview of this act, for that the record of the court of exchequer is onely preſcribed by this act, and therefore a *certiorari* may be awarded out of the chancery to the exchequer to the treaſurer, that he bring in the roll of the liberties in his hand to the juſtices, before whom the return is made.

(6) *Omnes libertates.*] This muſt be underſtood of a bailife of a franchiſe or ſeigniory, which have return of writs, and not to a
2 H. 4. 4. bailife created itinerant, (for example) in the county of S. and to have return of all writs, and execution of the ſame by the kings letters patents; for ſuch a grant is void, for in effect it taketh away the office of the ſherife; and therefore where ſuch a return was made upon a mandate to ſuch a new found bailife, the court was in purpoſe to have puniſhed the ſherife by this branch of this act, *tanquam exhæredatorem domini regis.*

(7) *Statim puniatur vicecomes tanquam exhæredator regis, et coronæ ſuæ.*] Becauſe he fain a liberty or franchiſe againſt the king, to the diſheriſon of the king and of his crown, foraſmuch as no man can have ſuch a liberty or franchiſe but from the crown.

This puniſhment ſhall be by ranſome and impriſonment.

[453] (8) *Quæ veraciter retornum habet, qui nihil inde fecit mandetur vicecomiti, quod non omittat.*] Here is the fourth miſchief, that where there was indeed a bailife of a liberty, who truly had return of writs, yet he upon a mandat to him would do nothing: remedy is hereby provided, that it ſhall be commanded to the ſherife, *quod non omittat, &c. quin exequatur præceptum domini regis, &c.*

Bract. li. 5. fo. 442. a. Regiſt. 82. F.N.B. 68. f. & 74. a. This branch concerning the *non omittas,* is in affirmance of the common law; and therefore Bracton who wrote before this ſtatute, treating of this matter, ſaith, *Et quo caſu cum balivi nihil inde fecerint, propter defectum eorum, præcipietur vicecomiti, quod non omitteret propter libertatem talem, quin, &c.*

4 H. 6. 25. b. 5 H. 7. 28. F.N.B. 74. a. 2 H. 6. 15. Simile. 19 H. 6. 28. 21 H. 6. 28. 8 E. 4. 5. b. Simile. (9) *Nihil inde fecit.*] This *nihil* is to be underſtood, not onely where nothing at all is done, but alſo where the bailife of the liberty maketh an inſufficient return, for that is *nihil* in law; and therefore a *non omittas, &c.* ſhall be thereupon granted; for *idem eſt nihil, et inſufficienter dicere.*

(10) *Et*

(10) *Et quod ſcire faciat balivis.*] This ſeemeth to be added by this branch to the common law.

(11) *Multotiens etiam vic' falſum dant reſponſum quoad illum articulum de exitibus.*] Now cometh the fifth miſchief, that the ſherifes would Fleta, li. 2. c. 61. return too ſmall iſſues, in which caſe by the common law the plaintife could not have an averment againſt the return of the ſherife; for the ſherife is but an officer to the court, and hath no day in 21 H. 7. 8. b. court to anſwer to the party: but this is remedied in this caſe by this branch.

(12) *Et ſi offerat verificare,* &c.] Here is the remedy given, and 27 H. 8. 3. the mean preſcribed, how the averment ſhall be proved, and 20 H. 6. 25. the plaintife muſt in his averment alledge what the value of the 22 E. 4. 10. 10 H. 7. 11. a. iſſues be.

See the book of entries for the judiciall writ to the juſtices of Raſt. 383. aſſiſe.

And where it is here ſaid, *Vicecomites falſum dant reſponſum,* this branch mentioning ſherifes extended not to bailifes of liberties, which 1 E. 3. cap. 5. Vet. N.B. fo. 53. is holpen by the ſtatute of 1 E. 3.

(13) *A die impetrationis uſque diem in brevi contentum.*] Theſe 27 H. 8. 3. iſſues, that is, the value of the land muſt be inquired, from the 20 H. 6. 25. teſte of the writ, untill the day of the return of it; and it is holden, 22 E. 4. 10. that this act extendeth not to the return of iſſues upon jurors after 10 H. 7. 11. a. b. iſſue joyned.

(14) *Et cum inquiſitio retorn' fuerit, ſi de pleno prius non reſponderit, oneretur de ſurpluſagio,* &c.] As if the ſherife return but 10 s. iſſues, 27 H. 8. 3. and it be found before the juſtices of aſſiſe, that the iſſues amounted to 50 s. the ſherife ſhall be charged with 40 s. by this branch, and ſo after that rate and proportion.

(15) *Et ſciat vicecomes, quod redditus, blada in grangia, et omnia mobilia, præter equitaturam, indumenta, et utenſilia domus continentur ſub nomine exituum.*] By this branch is explained what ſhall be Fleta li. 2. ca. 62. accounted iſſues, for the better direction of ſherifes in this caſe, that is to ſay, not onely the rent and revenue of the land, but the 27 H. 8. 3. corn in the grange, and all other moveables, as hay in the barn, 24 E. 3. 29. and other moveable or perſonall goods whatſoever, except thoſe things belonging to his riding, his apparell and utenſils of houſe: [454] and certainly this is a good and neceſſary law, if it were put in execution according to the purview of this act.

(16) *Alius non apponat manum quam dominus rex.*] That is, that the delinquent ſhall be puniſhed *coram domino rege*; that is, in the kings bench, his court of ordinary juſtice.

(17) *Multotiens etiam falſum dant reſponſum mandando, quod non potuerint exequi præceptum regis propter reſiſtentiam.*] Now we are come to the ſixth miſchief, or rather the abuſe of ſherifes, as by theſe words, *falſum dant reſponſum,* appeareth.

(18) *Caveat vicecomes de cætero quia hujuſmodi reſponſio multum redundat in dedecus domini regis, et coronæ ſuæ.*] Hereby ſuch a return Fleta, li. 2. cap. 62. is forbidden.

For this matter, ſee the expoſition upon the ſtatute of W. 1. W. 1. ca. 17.

(19) *Statim (omnibus omiſſis) aſſumpto ſecum poſſe comitatus ſui eat in propria perſona ad faciend' executionem.*] This branch is in affirmance of the common law, as appeareth in the expoſition upon the ſaid ſtatute of W. 1. where you may read of this matter at large.

(20) *Et*

(20) *Et si inveniat subbalivos suos mendaces.*] This is plain, and needeth no explanation.

(21) *Et si inveniat eos veraces, castiget resistentes per prisonam, a qua non deliberentur sine speciali præcepto dom' regis.*] This is evident in it self.

Fleta, li. 2. c. 62. (22) *Et si forte, cum venerit, resistentiam invenerit.*] Albeit by the penning of this act it may seem, that the sherife should take *posse comitatus* after complaint made, *post querimoniam factam*; yet seeing he may take *posse comitatus* by the common law, he may either take it *post, vel ante querimoniam.*

But he must take it after resistance, and not before, for *sequi debet potentia justitiam, non præcedere.*

(23) *De nominibus resistentium, auxiliantium, consentientium, præcipientium et fautorum, et per breve de judicio attachientur.*] *Fautorum*; this word is of a large extent, whereof you may read in the
16 R. 2. ca. 5. statute of 16 R. 2. and in English it properly signifieth a favourer.

(24) *Secundum quod domino regi placuerit.*] That is, according to that which shall be upon due proceeding adjudged *coram rege*, in the kings court of justice.

(25) *Nec intromittat se aliquis minister domini regis, &c. quia dominus rex hoc sibi specialiter reservat.*] That is, as hath been said, that the delinquents shall be punished *coram rege*, in his court of justice; for no man can be punished by absolute power, but *secundum*
Magna Charta, cap. 29. *legem, et consuetudinem Angliæ*, as hath been said before in the exposition of *Magna Charta*, and elsewhere hath been often said.

[455]

CAP. XL.

CUM quis alienat jus uxoris suæ, concordat' est quod de cætero secta mulieris, aut ejus hæredis (1) non differatur post obitum viri per minorem ætatem hæredis, qui warrantizare debet (2), sed expectet emptor (3) (qui ignorare non debuit quod jus alienum emit) usque ad ætatem warranti sui (4), de warrantia sua habenda (5).

WHERE any doth aliene the right of his wife, it is agreed, that from henceforth the suit of the woman, or her heir, after the death of her husband, shall not be delayed by the nonage of the heir that ought to warrantise, but let the purchaser tarry, which ought not to have been ignorant that he bought the right of another, until the age of his warrantor, to have his warranty.

(Fitz. Age, 47. 76. 126. 138. Fitz. Voucher, 180. 183. 226. 305. Rast. 139. 2 Leon, 148.)

The mischiefe before this statute was, that when the husband aliened the right of his wife, this working a discontinuance, and the wife driven to her *cui in vita*, or her heire to his *sur cui in vita*, those just actions were delayed oftentimes, when the purchaser vowched the heire of the baron being within age, untill his full age, which is remedied by this act.

18 E. 4. 16. 14 H. 7. 19. And this act restraineth the common law, and therefore it is taken *stricti juris*, as shall appeare in the exposition hereafter.

(1) *De*

(1) *De cætero secta mulieris aut ejus hæredis.*] This suit of the wife or her heire extendeth onely to a *cui in vita*, or a *sur cui in vita*, which are the proper actions upon an alienation made by the baron of the right of his wife, the former words being [*cum quis alienat jus uxoris suæ*,] for if the wife be tenant in taile, and the baron aliened in fee and died, and the wife died, the issue in taile cannot have a *sur cui in vita*, but he must have his formedon in the discender by the statute of W. 2. cap. 1. and in this action the purchaser may vowch the heire of the baron, and for his nonage the paroll shall demurre, for that action is out of this statute.

46 E. 3. age 76.

(2) * *Per minorem ætatem hæredis qui warrantizare debet.*] This by the context of this act extendeth onely to the heire of the baron who made the alienation, and therefore the heire of a stranger is out of this statute.

† The baron aliens to A. hath issue two daughters and dies, the wife brings a *cui in vita* against A. who vowcheth the daughters as heirs to the baron, whereof the one onely was within age, the paroll shall not demurre; although all the coparceners, which make but one heire, are not within age, and the words *per minorem ætatem hæredis*, yet seeing by the common law the paroll for the whole should have demurred, judgement shall be given for the demandant, and the tenant shall attend for his warranty for the whole in this case, untill the full age of the coparcener, that then is within age.

* Contr. judicat' in 14 E. 1. in Banco Rot. 81. Buck. The later authorities have over-ruled the judgement given the next yeare of the statute.
7 E. 2. age 139.
46 E. 3. ib. 76.
6 E. 3. 46.
17 E. 3. 59.
Lib. 1. fol. 15. Sir William Pelhams case.
Lib. 4. fol. 50. A. Ognels case.
Li. 6. fo. 5. Markal.

(3) *Sed expectet emptor.*] As the actions, wherein the vowcher shall be, and the heire to be vowched are set downe in certaine, so the person that is to vowch is also specified, so as if any other vowch the heire of the husband, the paroll shall demurre for his nonage, and therefore the purchaser or buyer of the husband is onely he, by reason of this word *emptor*, that is bound by this statute.

†3 E. 2. vowcher 210.
8 E. 2. judgement 240.

Therefore this *emptor* must have three properties:

1. He must be *emptor*, that is, purchaser immediately from the baron, and therefore if this *emptor* alien in fee, the alienee is *emptor*, that is a purchaser, but because he is not the immediate purchaser from the baron (albeit he may vowch the heire of the baron as assignee) yet is not hee bound by this statute.

7 E. 2. age 139.
6 E. 3. 49.
Pl. Com. 17. 47.

(2) He that is an *emptor* within this act must be the tenant in deed against whom the *cui in vita*, or *sur cui in vita* is brought, and therefore in the case before, if the second alienee vowch him that was immediate *emptor*, yet if he vowch the heire of the husband, the paroll shall demurre for his nonage, and the demandant shall not have judgement *maintenant*, because the *cui in vita*, &c. was not brought against him that was immediate *emptor*, as tenant in deed of the land, but he came in as vowchee; so it is if he that was immediate *emptor* commeth in by receit upon default of tenant for life, he is not bound by this act, *causa qua supra*.

[456]
20 E. 2. age 126.
19 E. 3. ib. 2.
9 E. 3. 4.
18 E. 4. 16.
Vide Mich. 14 E. 1. ubi sup. adjudged that this statute extendeth to the second vowchee, but the later books are to the contrary in this point also.

3. [a] He must be *ipse emptor*, and not *alter ipse*, and therefore if the immediate *emptor* dieth, albeit his heire sitteth in his auncestors seate, and is *alter idem*, yet is not the heire bound by this act, because hee is not *ipse idem*.

[a] 16 E. 3. age 47.
47 E. 3 ib. 76.
14 H. 7. 19.

[b] Now what estate an *emptor* shall have, he that purchaseth any estate of freehold, be it in fee-simple, fee-taile, or for life, he is an *emptor* or purchaser within this act, and yet the words of this act be, *qui alienat jus uxoris suæ*.

[b] 3 E. 2. vowchee 210. 8 E. 2. jugement 140. Gloc'. cap. 3.

For

For this word [*alienare*] see the statute of Glouc' and the next chapter ensuing.

Also if the baron alien, though it be for no valuable consideration, yet is he an *emptor*, that is a purchaser within this statute.

3 E. 2. vowcher 210. 8 E. 2. judgement 140. Rast. fol. 135.

(4) *Usque ad ætatem warranti sui.*] And at the full age of the vowchee the tenant shall sue a resummons.

For the order of proceeding herein see the booke of entries.

3 E. 2. ubi supra. 8 E. 2. ubi supra. 9 E. 3. 4. 6 E. 3. 46. 32 H. 8. cap. 28.

(5) *De warrantia sua habenda.*] This act doth extend as well to a warranty in law, for example, in respect of a reversion, &c. as to a warranty in deed. And albeit the stat. of 32 H. 8. doth notwithstanding the alienation of the husband, &c. give to the wife and her heires a right to enter, as by that act appeareth, so as the wife or her heires are not driven to their action, as at the time of the making of this act they were, and therefore this act may seeme to some to be of no great use, yet for divers points of notable learning, and for the discussing of like cases standing upon like reason, as you have perceived, wee held it very profitable and necessary to be explained.

CAP. XLI.

STATUIT dominus rex, quod si abbates, priores, custodes hospitalium, et aliarum domorum religiosarum (1) *fundatarum ab ipso, vel à progenitoribus suis* (2) *alienaverint* (3) *de cætero tenementa domibus ipsis ab ipso vel à progenitoribus suis collata* (4), *tenementa illa in manum domini regis capiantur* (5), *et ad voluntatem suam teneantur, et emptor amittat suum recuperare, tam de tenementis quam de pecunia, quam paiavit. Si autem domus illa à com', baron' vel ab aliis fundat' fuerit* (6), *de ten' sic alienat'* (7) *habeat ille, à quo vel à cujus antecessore ten' sic alienat' collatum fuerit, breve ad recuperand'* (9) *ten' illud in dominico, quod tale est:*

OUR lord the king hath ordained, that if abbots, priors, keepers of hospitals, and other religious houses founded by him or by his progenitors, do from henceforth aliene the lands given to their houses by him or by his progenitors; the land shall be taken into the king's hands, and holden at his will, and the purchaser shall lose his recovery as well of the lands, as of the money that he paid. And if the house were founded by an earl, baron, or other persons, for the lands so aliened, he from whom, or from whose ancestor the land so aliened was given, shall have a writ to recover the same land in demesne, which is thus:

[457] *Præcipe tali abbati, quod juste, &c. reddat B. tale ten' quod eidem domui collatum fuit in liberam eleemosynam* (8) *per præd' B. vel antecessores suos, et quod ad prædict' B. reverti debet per alienationem, quam prædict' abbas fecit de prædicto ten' contra formam collationis prædictæ, ut dic'.*

Eodem modo de ten' dat' pro cantaria sustinenda vel luminari in aliqua ecclesia vel capella, vel alia eleemosyna sustentanda

In like manner for lands given for the maintenance of a chantery, or of light in a church or chapel, or other alms

sustentanda, si ten' sic dat' alienetur (10). *Et si forte ten' sic dat'* (12) *pro cantaria, luminari, pastu pauperum, vel alia eleemosyna sustentanda vel faciend', non fuerit alienat', sed subtracta fuerit hujusmodi eleemosyna per biennium* (11), *competat actio donatori aut ejus hæredi* (13) *ad petendum tenement' sic datum in dominico, sicut statutum est in statuto Glocest'* (14) *de tenementis dimissis ad faciendum vel reddendum quartam partem valoris tenement', vel majorem.* Gloc. cap. 4.

alms to he maintained, if the land given be aliened. But if the land so given for a chantery, light, sustenance of poor people, or other alms to be maintained or done, be not aliened, but such alms is withdrawn by the space of two years, an action shall lie for the donor or his heire to demand the land so given in demean, as it is ordained in the statute of Gloucester for lands leased to do or to render the fourth part of the value of the land, or more.

(12 Rep. 72. 1 Roll, 166. Regist. 238. Fitz. Brief, 291. Fitz. Cessavit, 15. 18. 24. 44. St. 6 Ed. 1. c. 4. 11 Rep. 63.)

At the common law, as it appeareth by Glanvill, *Nec episcopus, nec abbas, quia eorum baroniæ sunt de eleemosyna domini regis, et antecessorum ejus, non possunt de dominicis suis aliquam partem dare ad remanentiam sine assensu et confirmatione domini regis.* Glanv. l. 7. ca. 1.

The meaning whereof is, that seeing those that hold of the king *per baroniam*, did hold of the king in capite, that therefore, by his opinion, they could not alien any part thereof without the kings assent; but yet if the bishop with the assent of his chapter, or the abbot with the assent of his covent, and the like, had aliened the land, the estate of the alienee could not have been avoided. Li. 5. fo. 10, 11. de jure regis ecclesiastico.

See the charter of H. 1. of the foundation of the abbey of Reading in the 26. yeare of his raigne, wherein you shall reade, *Qui autem, Deo annuente, canonica electione abbas substitutus fuerit, non cum suis secularibus consanguineis, seu quibuslibet aliis, eleemosynas monasterii male utendo disperdat, sed pauperibus, et peregrinis, et hospitibus suscipiendis curam gerat, terras censuales non ad feodum donet.*

So as no doubt the alienation was against the minde of the founder, *et contra formam donationis*, yet they having a fee-simple, the common law restrained them not from alienation, *concurrentibus his quæ in jure requiruntur.*

So as the mischiefe was, when the alienation was a barre to the successor.

(1) *Si abbates, priores, custodes hospitalium, et aliarum domorum religiosarum.*] Seeing this act beginneth with abbots, &c. and concludeth with other religious houses, bishops are not comprehended within this act, for they are superiour to abbots, &c. and these words [other religious houses] shall extend to houses inferiour to them that were mentioned before. 40 E. 3. 27. 46 E. 3. forfeiture 18. li. 2. fo. 46. Levesq; de Cant. case.

Also bishops are not properly religious, that is, regular, but secular: but yet this act doth referre to inferiour houses that are ecclesiasticall and secular, as hereafter in this chapter shall appeare. 2 Mar. Dier, 109. 33 H. 8. cap. 30. 34 & 35 H. 8. c. 15. Art. super Chart. cap. 11.

See the first part of the Institutes, sect. 133.

See Brook tit. Alienation 15. Vide h'c postea, cap. 47.

(2) *Fundatarum ab ipso, vel à progenitoribus suis.*] Albeit he that giveth the first land upon raising and creation of the house be the 33 E. 3. aide le Roy 103. F.N.B. 211. h.

the founder, though it be much lesse then the lands after given to the house in *liberam eleemosynam*, yet this act doth extend not onely to lands *ratione fundationis*, but also to lands *ratione dotationis*, so they were given *in liberam eleemosynam*. *Vide* hereafter in this chapter.

40 E. 3. 27. F.N.B. 211. Vet. N.B. 142. 46 E. 3. forfeiture 18. capit. escheat' Vet. Mag. Chart. 161.

(3) *Alienaverint*.] This act speaketh of an alienation made by abbots, &c. but it must be intended of alienations with the assent of the covent, or else the successor might recover the same by a writ of entry *sine assensu capituli*; for where acts of parliaments give remedy, it is ever intended that it shall not be illusory.

And albeit this act speaketh of the abbots that alien, it is understood when the abbots alien with consent, as is aforesaid, thereby is a right vested in the king; and albeit the abbot dieth, yet the king may have an office to finde his right, and recover the land in the time of the successor; and so may a common person have remedy in that case, as shall be said hereafter.

See the books last before mentioned.

And some have said, that this alienation is intended when the alienation is in fee, and not when the estate is made but for life, or in taile; but then should the statute bee of small effect, for then might hee make many gifts in taile, or multiply leases for many lives, without reserving the accustomed rent, and thereby utterly overthrow the house, as in former times it hath done.

Hil. 38 E. 3. Rot. 14. Coram rege Abbot de Stonleys case.

As you may reade that it was found by inquisition in the raigne of E. 3. that Thomas de Pipe, abbot of the monastery of Stonely, in the county of Warwick (of the foundation of king Henry fitz Empresse (which was H. 2.) and that he gave to the said house *in liberam eleemosynam*, the mannor of Stonely in the said county) *alienavit diversis hominibus particulariter, prout patet inferius, viz. Isabellæ de Beneshale concubinæ dicti abbatis, et Johanni filio eorundem abbatis et Isabellæ primogenito filio unum messuagium, et unam carucatam terræ, et decem mercatus redditus cum pertin' in Fynham. Habendum et tenendum ad terminum vitæ eorundem Isabellæ et Johannis absque aliquo inde reddendo annuatim:* and found also divers other leases for lives of parts of the said mannor made to divers persons, to and for the benefit of the said abbot, and of his concubine, and of her and his bastards; but it is best to use the words of the record itselfe, *Absq; aliquo inde reddendo vel præ manibus inde de eisdem percepto sed tantummodo ad opus et proficuum ipsius abbatis, et maxime pro sustentatione et inventione prædictorum Isabellæ et puerorum eorundem abbatis et Isabellæ, qui excedunt numerum monachorum suorum missas celebrantium, si forte deponeretur de statu suo, &c.*

45 E. 3. 18. F.N.B. 211.

Sometime *alienare* is taken for *alienum facere*, and therefore if land be recovered in value, &c. the founder shall have a writ of *contra formam* within this statute.

7 H. 6. 2.

If the abbot with consent of the covent doth charge the land, this is not within this act, for no land or tenement is aliened.

F.N.B. 211. Regist.

(4) *Collata*.] Lands and tenements given in free almoigne after the foundation *ratione dotationis*, are within this word [*collata*] which extendeth as well to lands *ratione dotationis*, as to lands *ratione fundationis*.

13 H. 7. 5. 8. 45 E. 3. 18. Stamf. Prer. F.N.B. 212.

(5) *In manum domini regis capiantur*.] The king in this case must have an office found for him, and a *scire fac'* against the tertenant, by the intendment and construction of this act, for all necessary incidents are to be understood, and in the *scir' fac'* the tertenant is not concluded by any trial had against the abbot.

(6) *Si*

(6) *Si autē domus illa à comite, barone, vel aliis fundata fuerit.*] Having provided remedy when the king was founder, now this act provideth when a subject is founder. 23 E. 3. contr' collat. 3.

(7) *Tenementum sic alienatum.*] These words couple all that hath beene said before to this branch.

(8) *Collatum fuerit in liberam eleemosinam.*] So as of necessity the lands and tenements within the purview of this act must be given in frankalmoigne, for so be the words of the writ framed and formed by this act. [459] Regist. 238. F.N.B. 211. a. 1. Part of the Institutes, sect. 136, 137. What Free almoigne is.

Fleta treating hereof, saith, *Alia est causa cum res detur in eleemosina, et alienetur, in quo casu provisum fuit quod breve de ingressu ad recuperandum hujusmodi tenementum alienatum in dominico. Vide* capit' Eschaetrie, Vet' Magna Charta 161. Fleta, lib. 5. ca. 24.

(9) *Habeat, &c. breve ad recuperandum.*] This branch saith, *habeat breve*: but what if the alienation be of such a tenement or hereditament, as there lieth no writ of *contra formam collationis?* As for example, if an advowson be aliened *contra formam collationis*, the founder shall present, because he can have no writ; for when a right is given, the law with it will give a remedy, so as this act is to be understood, that his remedy shall be by writ, where a writ doth lye. 29 E. 3. Contra formam collat. 8. F.N.B. 211 f. 32 E. 3. Cessavit 24. Fleta, l. 5. c. 34. For this writ.

After a recovery had by force of this writ against the abbot, there must be a *scire fac'* (as hath been said) against the tenant of the land, who is not concluded by any triall, &c. had against the abbot, &c.

Vide 32 E. 3. tit. Breve 291. for the form of this writ.

The heir shall have this writ for an alienation in the time of his ancestor, for the right of action once vested in the ancestor cannot dye. 32 E. 3. Bre. 291. 17 E. 3. Contra form. collat. i. 32 E. 3. Bre. 291. 2 H. 4. 17. F.N.B. 211. Regist. 238. Vet. N. B. 242. Lib. intrat. Rast. 126. See the last clause of this chapter.

This writ also lieth against the successor for an alienation made by the predecessor, notwithstanding these words in the writ, *prædictus abbas*; or the heir may have an action against the successor.

* This action of *contra formam collationis* consisteth onely in privity for none but onely for the founder, or donor, or his heire, and not for any stranger. * 7 R. 2. Cessavit 18. F.N.B. 211.

(10) *Eodem modo de tenemento dato pro cantaria sustinenda, vel luminari in aliqua ecclesia, seu capella, vel alia eleemosina sustinenda, si tenementum sic datum alienetur.*] *Eleemosina:* see the first part of the Institutes, sect. 133, &c. et le Custumier de Norm. cap. 32. *Tenure per omosne, et le lattin com' sur ceo.*

This is a clause of reference, *eodem modo, &c.* But this clause extendeth not to the lands or tenements parcell of the foundation of the abbey, or priory; for the former branches of this act had made sufficient provision for them. 7 H. 4. 20.

But this clause extendeth to lands or tenements given to any ecclesiasticall person, that is, either religious, as abbots, priors, &c. or secular, as parsons of churches, deans, &c. for the finding of a chauntery priest, or of a light, or any other charitable or almsdeeds, or when a chauntery is incorporated, and lands given for maintenance of the same. 10 H. 6. 5. b.

And this branch being generall, *viz. De tenemento dato pro cantaria, &c.* the same extendeth aswell to bishops, and all other secular persons, or ecclesiasticall, as religious, consisting of one sole person, or aggregate of many: and so note the diversity between this and the former branch, and the severall reasons of the same. Regist. 238. F.N.B. 209. k.

18 E. 3. 5. a. 32 E. 3. Bre. 291. cap. Eschaet. Vet. Magn. Chart. 162. See the first part of the Institutes, sect. 530.

By these words [*eodem modo*] if lands were given to an abbot, *pro cantaria sustinenda, aut pro pastu pauperum*, or other such service in certain; and the abbot aliened with consent of the covent, yet the *contra formam collationis* did lye against the abbot upon this branch, by reference to the former branch.

* [460] Regist. 238. F.N.B. 209. k. capit' Eschaet' Vet. Magna Charta, 162.

(11) *Et si forte tenementa sic data, pro cantaria, luminari, pastu* * *pauperum, vel alia eleemosina sustinenda, vel facienda, non fuerit alienata, sed subtracta fuerit hujusmodi eleemosina per biennium.*] By this branch is a cessavit given, where lands were given to finde a chaplein to sing divine service, or to finde a light in such a church, &c. or to distribute certain bread and beer every day, week, or moneth to poor people, &c.

1. part of the Institutes, sect. 137.

(12) *Tenementa sic data*, &c.] This branch extendeth not to a gift in tail, for the donor shall not have a cessavit within this statute.

7 H. 4. 20. F.N.B. 210. E. 7 E. 4. 11. per Catesby. 1. part of the Institutes, sect. 137.

It is holden, that this branch concerning the cessavit, extendeth not to lands or tenements given by the founder upon the foundation of the house; albeit, as it appeareth by the said charter of H. 1. the lands were generally given, not onely for celebration of divine service in the church, &c. but for sustentation of poor people, or other almes deeds, which are also adjudged in law divine service.

11 R. 2. View 65.

And this clause, that giveth the cessavit, referreth onely to the last branch concerning chauntries, lights, and other particular almes deeds, and not to the former branch concerning the foundations and dotations *in libera eleemosina* in generall; for this branch extendeth not at all to lands given in free almoigne, as the first and second clauses did, for in free almoigne no certain service is to be done, and therefore for them no cessavit can lye, but lyeth onely where particular divine services are mentioned.

1. part of the Institutes, sect. 136, 137.

1. part of the Institutes, sect. 137. F.N.B. 210. E.

Note here the excellent judgement of the makers of this act, for they, for alienation of lands given in free almoigne, that is, for celebration of divine services, &c. incertain, gave a *contra formam collationis*, but gave no cessavit for cesser, because no cessavit could lye for divine service incertain; but for divine service certain, both a *contra formam collationis*, and a cessavit respectively by this act doth lye, aswell as an avowry for the same at the common law.

F.N.B. 209. k. Pl. Com. 58. b. 12 H. 4. 24. 14 H. 4. 4.

(13) *Competat actio donatori, aut ejus hæredi.*] In this case the heir shall upon this branch have a *cessavit pro pastu pauperum*, for the cesser done in the life of his ancestor, but so shall not the heir of the lord in a cessavit upon the statute of Glocest': and the reason of the diversity is, for that in a cessavit brought upon this branch *de pastu pauperum*, no tender of the arrerages shall be by the tenant to the demandant, because they belong to the poor, and never belonged to the demandant or his ancestor; but the rent and service upon the statute of Gloc' belonged to the lord to whom the tender was to be made, but his heir is out of that statute, because the tender of the arrerages in the life of the ancestor belonged not to him.

(14) *Sicut statutum est in statuto Gloc'.*] Although this branch hath a reference to the statute of Gloc', yet it is to be understood, to extend to such clauses of that act, as may stand with reason of law and conveniencie, as you perceive by an example before remembred, *et sic de similibus.*

CAP.

CAP. XLII.

DE mareſcallis domini regis (1) *de feodo camerariis* (2), *cuſtodibus hoſtiorum in itinere juſtic', et ſervientibus virgam portantibus coram juſtic' apud Weſtm', qui officium illud habeant de feodo* (3), *et qui plus exigunt ratione feodi ſui quam exigere conſueverunt, ſecundum quod multi queruntur ſuper eos qui ſtatut' cur' à multo tempore viderunt et ſciunt, dominus rex inquiri fecit, quem ſtat' prædict' miniſtri de feodo habere conſueverunt temporibus retroactis, et per inquiſitionem* (4) *ſtatuit et præcepit, quod mareſcallus de feodo qui de novo exigit palefridum* (5) *de comitibus, baronibus, et aliis per partem baroniæ tenent', quando homagium fecerint, et nihilominus ad malitiam eorum alium palefridum, et de quibuſdam (de quibus palefridum habere non debuit), palefridum de novo exigunt, ordinavit quod prædictus mareſcallus de quolibet comite et barone (integram baroniam* (7) *tenente) de uno palefrido ſit contentus* (6), *vel de precio quale antiquitus percipere conſuevit* (8), *ita quod ſi ad homagium, quod fecit, palefridum vel precium in forma prædicta ceperit, ad malitiam ſuam nihil capiat;*

Et ſi fortè ad homagium nihil ceperit, ad malitiam ſuam capiat. De abbatibus et prioribus integram baroniam tenentibus, cum homagium aut fidelitatem pro baroniis ſuis fecerint, capiat palefridum vel precium, ut prædictum eſt.

Hoc idem de archiepiſcopis, et epiſcopis obſervand' eſt. De his autem qui partem baroniæ tenent, ſive ſint religioſi, ſive ſeculares, capiat ſecund' portionem partis baroniæ, quam tenent (9). *De religioſis tenent' in liberam eleemoſinam*

CONCERNING the king's marſhals of fee, chamberlains, porters in the circuit of juſtices and ſerjeants bearing vierge before juſtices at Weſtminſter, which have the ſame office in fee, and that aſk more by reaſon of their fee than they have uſed to aſk, whereupon many do complain on them, that have known and ſeen the order of the court of long time; our lord the king hath cauſed to be enquired by an inqueſt what the ſaid officers of fee have uſed to have in times paſſed, and hath ordained and commanded, that a marſhal of fee, which of new aſketh a palfray of earls, barons, and other holding by a part of a barony when they have done homage, and nevertheleſs another palfray when they are made knights, and of ſome that ought not to give any, aſk a palfray: it is in like manner ordained, that the ſaid marſhal of every earl and baron, holding by an entire barony, ſhall be contented with one palfray, or with the price of it, ſuch as he hath uſed to have of old; ſo that if he took a palfray, or the price of one, at the doing of his homage in form aforeſaid, he ſhall take nothing when he is made knight;

And if he took nothing at the doing of his homage, when he is made knight he ſhall take. Of abbots and priors holding an whole barony, when they do homage or fealty for their baronies, he ſhall take one palfray, or the price, as afore is ſaid.

And this ſhall alſo be obſerved amongſt archbiſhops and biſhops. Of ſuch as hold but a part of a barony, whether they be religious or ſecular, he ſhall take according to the portion of the part of the barony that

eleemosinam, et non per baroniam, vel partem baroniæ, nihil de cætero exigat marescallus.

that they hold. Of religious men that hold in free alms, and not by a barony, nor part of a barony, the marshal from henceforth shall demand nothing.

Et concessit dominus rex, quod per hoc statutum non præcludatur marescallus suus de feodo in plus petendo, si imposterum ostendere poterit, quod jus habeat plus petendi (10).

And our lord the king hath granted, that by this statute a marshal of fee shall not be barred hereafter to demand more, if he can shew that he hath right unto more.

Camerarii domini regis habeant de cætero de archiepiscopis (11), *episcopis, abbatibus, prioribus,* [462] *et aliis personis ecclesiasticis, comit', baron', integram baroniam tenent', rationabilem fidem cum homagium aut fidelitatem pro baroniis suis fecerint. Et si per partem baroniæ teneant, capiant rationabilem finem secundum portionem ipsos contingentem. Alii vero abbates, priores, religiosi, et seculares non tenentes per baroniam, vel partem baroniæ, non distringantur ad finem faciend'* (12), *secundum quod de tenentibus per baroniam vel partem baroniæ dictum est, sed sit camerarius de superiori indumento contentus, vel de precio indumenti: quod plus honestè dictum est pro religiosis quam secularibus, quia honestius est, quod religiosi faciant pro superiori indumento, quam exuant.*

The king's chamberlains from henceforth shall have of archbishops, bishops, abbots, priors, and other persons spiritual, of earls and barons holding an entire barony, a reasonable fine when they do their homage or fealty; and if they hold by a part of a barony, they shall take a reasonable fine according to the portion to them belonging. Other abbots, priors, and other persons spiritual and temporal, that hold no entire barony, nor part of a barony, shall not be distrained to make fine, as it is said by them that hold by a barony, or part of a barony, but the chamberlain shall be contented with his upper garment, or with the price thereof; which is done in favour of persons religious more than of lay persons; for it is more convenient that religious men should fine for their upper garment, than to be stripped.

W. 1. cap. 40.

The mischief before this statute was, that not onely the marshall, and the chamberlein of the kings house, but some inferiour officers, as the porters, or door-keepers of the justices in eyre; and likewise the bearer of rods or staves before the justices at Westminster, did extort of the subject excessive fees, more then was due to them: whereupon many that of long time had known the kings court, and other the said courts, did greatly complain; for remedy whereof this act was made; the particular mischiefs shall be specified in their due places.

The statute of W. 1. had provided against the extortion by serjeants, cryers, and marshals of justices in eyre, and of other justices; now this act provideth against the officers following.

Brit. fo. 1. b. 1. part of the Institutes, sect. cap. Grand Sergeanty. Fleta, li. 2. c. 3, 4, 5. Lib. 10. fo. 68, &c. Lib. 6. fo. 20, 21. Lib. 7. fo. 17. Fleta, li. 2. c. 6.

(1) *De mareschallis domini regis.*] This is intended of the marshall of the kings house. Of this officer Britton saith thus, *Et que le mareschal de nostre hostele teigne nostre lieu deins la vierge de nostre hostle, &c.* The steward of the kings house and this marshall have a court of justice, as elsewhere we have shewed.

(2) De

(2) *De camerariis.*] This is alſo intended of the chamberlein of the kings houſe. The l. chamberlein of the kings houſhold is a great officer of the kings houſe, ſo called becauſe his office doth principally concern the chambers, that is, matters above the ſtairs; of his office, Fleta writeth thus, *Camerarius autem, et ſubminiſtri cameræ a juriſdictione ſen', et mar' exempti ſunt, veluti omnes garderobarii, ut in quibuſdam; non enim extendit ſe juriſdictio ſen' ad modica delicta camerariorum, vel garderobariorum audienda, vel terminanda, eo quod ex conſuetudine hoſpitii ſunt exempti, dum tamen illi de quibus exigi contigerit cur' coram ſeneſch', cameris regis et reginæ, ac garderobæ aſſiduè ſint intendentes; ſed coram ipſis theſaur' et camerar' audiantur querimoniæ de hujuſmodi miniſtris et ſubditis ſuis, et terminabuntur, præſente tamen clerico regis ad placita aulæ deputato; ita quod de finibus, et amerciament' ex hujuſmodi placitis provenientibus nihil regi depereat. Debet enim camerarius decenter diſponere pro lecto regis, et ut cameræ tapetis, et banqueriis ornentur, et quod ignes ſufficienter fiant in caminis, et providere ne ullus defectus inveniatur quatenus officium ſuum contigerit.* Obſerve here, what anciently belonged to the office of the chamberlein of the kings houſhold. Fleta, ubi ſupra.

(3) *De feodo.*] Theſe words are not onely meant of them that have a fee-ſimple in their offices, but ſuch as have any fixed eſtate, either in tail or for life, and ſo are theſe words intended throughout this act; and the office of the chamberlain of the houſhold was never granted in fee: and ſome do hold, that the ſenſe of theſe words [*de feodo*] are ſuch officers as have fees due, and belonging to them. W. 1. cap. 30. See hereafter in the next chapter towards the end. [463]

(4) *Per inquiſitionem.*] Obſerve here, that before the king, the lords and commons made this law, the king did inquire by oath of a jury ſworne of the truth and certainty of the fees hereafter in this act ſet downe.

(5) *Quod mareſchallus de feodo qui de novo exigit paleſridum,* &c.] Before this act the marſhall of the kings houſe claimed and did take for his fee of every earle, baron, and of others holding by part of a barony, when they did their homage, his palfrey; and notwithſtanding, when they were made knights, did challenge and take another palfrey; wherein he did wrong in two reſpects:

1. That in that caſe hee tooke two palfreyes where hee ought to take but one.

2. That he tooke one of them, that held by part of a barony, both which are remedied by this act.

(6) *Prædictus mareſchallus de quolibet comite et barone integram baroniam tenente de uno palfrido ſit contentus, &c.*] So as by this act he ought to have but one palfrey, both at his doing of homage, and at his making of knight.

(7) *Per integram baroniam.*] What a whole barony is, and of how many knights fees it conſiſteth, hath been before ſhewed, Magna Charta, cap. 2. Mag. Chart. c. 2.

And if one had divers baronies, yet ſeeing that he was but one perſon, the marſhall ſhould have but one horſe, *de uno paleſrido ſit contentus:* and ſo it is of one that is made knight, though he hath many knights fees.

(8) *Vel de precio quale antiquitus percipere conſuevit.*] That we may ſay once for all, the auncient price of the horſe of every archbiſhop, biſhop, abbot, prior, earle, or baron holding by an entire barony is x. l. Ex pervetuſt' Manuſcript.

 Alſo

Also the auncient price of the horse of one that is made knight, or that doth homage, having no part of a barony, is v. marks.

4 H. 4. cap. 23. See the statute of 4 H. 4. cap. 23.

(9) *De hiis qui partem baroniæ tenent, sive sint religiosi, sive seculares, capiat secundum portionem partis baroniæ.*] As for example, if he hold by halfe a barony, he shall pay v. l. which is halfe the price of the horse of him, that holdeth by an entire barony, and so according to rate of the value of the horse, &c.

But the marshall shall take nothing of religious or ecclesiasticall persons that hold *in liberam eleemosynam, et non per baroniam, nec per partem baroniæ.*

(10) *Non præcludatur mareschallus de feodo in plus petendo, si in posterum ostendere poterit quod jus habet plus petendi.*] Here is a saving for the marshall of his right of demanding other fees upon better proofe made; but at the making of this act it appeared by the said inquisition, that no other fees were due to him, then are here expressed; but note there is no saving for the chamberlain.

(11) *Camerarii domini regis habeant de cætero de archiepiscopis.*] The kings chamberlaine, that is, the chamberlain of the kings boushold shall have a reasonable fine, when any ecclesiasticall or lay person, holding by an entire barony, doe his homage or

[464] fealty, and of them that hold by part of a barony a reasonable fine according to the portion which they have.

So as nothing is due to the kings chamberlain when one is made knight, as it appeareth by the context of this.

(12) *Alii vero abbates, priores religiosi et seculares non tenentes per baroniam vel partem baroniæ non distringantur ad finem faciend'.*] They which hold not by a barony, nor part of a barony shall yeeld no fine to the chamberlain, but the chamberlaine of them shall have their uppermost garment, or the price thereof; and it is more honest for the chamberlain to take the price in that case of the ecclesiasticall person, then of the secular, and the reason is there rendred, *quia honestius est, quod religiosi solvant pro superiori indumento, quam exuantur.*

CAP. XLIII.

PROHIBEATUR de cætero hospitulariis et templariis (1), *ne de cætero trahant aliquem in placitum coram conservatoribus privilegiorum suorum de aliqua re, cujus cognitio spectat ad forum regium* (2): *quod si fecerint, primo restituant damna parti gravatæ, et versus dominum regem graviter puniantur* (3). *Prohibet etiam dominus rex conservatoribus privilegiorum eorundem, ne de cætero (ad instantium hospitulariorum, templariorum, aut aliorum privilegiatorum)* (4) *concedant citationes, priusquam exprimatur*

BE it prohibited from henceforth to hospitallers and templars, that hereafter they bring no man in plea before the keepers of their privileges for any matter, the knowledge whereof belongeth to the king's court; which if they do, first, they shall yield damages to the party grieved, and be grievously punished unto the king. The king also prohibiteth to the keepers of such privileges, that from henceforth they grant no citations at the instance of hospitallers, templars, or other persons privileged, before it be

primatur ſuper qua re fieri debeat citatio (5). *Et ſi viderint hujuſmodi conſervatores, quod petatur citatio de aliqua re, cujus cognitio ſpectat ad forum regium, hujuſmodi conſervatores nec citationem faciant, nec cognoſcant. Et ſi aliter fecerint* (6) *conſervatores* (7), *reſpondeant parti læſæ de damnis, et nihilominus verſus dominum regem graviter puniantur. Et quia hujuſmodi privilegiati impetrant conſervatores, ſubpriores, præſentator', ſacriſtas, religioſos, qui nihil habent* (8) *unde læſis, aut domino regi ſatisfacere poſſint, qui audaciores ſint* (9) *ad lædend' dignitatem domini regis* (10) *quam eorum ſuperiores, quibus per eorum temporali pœna poteſt infligi: caveant de cætero prælati hujuſmodi obedientiariorum, ne permittant obedientiarios ſuos aſſumere ſibi juriſdictionem in præjudicium domini regis et coronæ ſuæ. Quod ſi fecerint, pro facto ipſorum reſpondeant ſui ſuperiores, ac ſi de proprio facto ſuo convicti eſſent* (11).

be expreſſed upon what matter the citation ought to be made. And if the keepers do ſee that a citation is required upon any matter, the knowledge whereof belongeth to the king's court, the keepers ſhall neither make nor knowledge the citation. And if the keepers do otherwiſe, they ſhall yield damages to the party grieved, and nevertheleſs ſhall be grievouſly puniſhed by the king. And foraſmuch as ſuch perſons privileged, depute keepers, ſub-priors, chantors, ſextons, which be religious men, and which have nothing to ſatisfy the parties grieved, nor the king; which be more bold to offend the king's dignity than their ſuperiors, to whom puniſhment may be aſſigned by their temporalties. Let the prelates of ſuch obedients therefore beware from henceforth, that they do not ſuffer their obedients to uſurp any juriſdiction in prejudice of the king and his crown; and if they do, their ſuperiors ſhall be charged for their fact, as much as if they had been convict upon their proper act.

(Regiſt. 39.)

(1) *Prohibeatur de cætero hoſpitulariis et templariis.*] The hoſpitallers and templars had divers great liberties and priviledges, and amongſt the reſt they held an eccleſiaſticall court before a canoniſt or ſome of the clergy whom they termed *conſervator privilegiorum ſuorum*, which judge having in deed more authority then was convenient, yet did he dayly in reſpect of the height and greatneſſe of theſe two orders, and at their inſtance and direction, incroach and hold plea of matters determinable by the common law, for *cui plus licet quam par eſt, plus vult quam licet*; and this was one great miſchiefe. [465]

Another miſchief was that this judge likewiſe at their inſtance in caſes, wherein he had juriſdiction, would make generall citations, as *pro ſalute animæ*, and the like, without expreſſing the matter, whereupon the citation was made, which alſo was againſt law, and tended to the grievous vexation of the ſubject, both which miſchiefes, or rather abuſes are remedied by this act. F.N.B. 41. a. 20 E. 3. excom. 9. 28 E. 3. 97. 20 E. 4. 20. b.

(2) *Cujus cognitio ſpectat ad forum regium.*] This branch is in affirmance of the common law.

(3) *Quod ſi fecerint, primo reſtituant damna parti gravatæ, et verſus dominum regem graviter puniantur.*] By this branch the hoſpitallers

hoſpitallers and templers are to yeeld damages to the party grieved, and to be grievouſly fined to the king, if they draw any man in plea before the conſervator of their priviledges of any thing determinable in the kings courts.

(4) *Ad inſtantiam hoſpit' templar' aut aliorũ privilegiatorũ.*] Hereby it appeareth that their juriſdiction extended reſpectively, not onely to the hoſpitallers and templers, but to perſons priviledged, or within their priviledges, and for that cauſe the judge was termed *conſervator privilegiorum.*

(5) *Probibet dominus rex conſervatoribus, &c. ne de cætero, &c. concedant citationes priuſquam exprimatur ſuper qua re ſieri debeat citatio.*] This branch is in affirmance of the common law, as before in this chapter it hath appeared; and this agreeth with Linwood, who taketh a citation *in foro eccleſiaſtico* to be, as the writ *in foro ſeculari*, for ſo it is by him defined. *Breve idem importat quod præceptum vel citatio, et in eo continetur gravamen, ſuper quo procedit actio ipſius agentis ſeu proſequentis.*

Linwood de foro compet. cap. 2.

(6) *Et ſi aliter fecerint conſervatores,* &c.] By this branch the party grieved ſhall recover his damages alſo againſt the ſaid judge, if he graunt any citation, or hold any plea of or for any matter determinable in the kings court, ſo as the party grieved ſhall have double remedy, both againſt the hoſpitallers and templers, and alſo againſt their judge, and the king to have a double fine in reſpect of the wrong done to his crown, and dignity, and the unjuſt vexation of his ſubjects.

(7) *Conſervatores.*] For this word ſee hereafter cap. 47.

Alſo if the judge did graunt a generall citation without expreſſing the cauſe, by colour whereof the party was troubled, he ſhould yeeld to the party damages, and be grievouſly fined to the king.

(8) *Et quia hujuſmodi privilegiati impetrant conſervatores, ſubpriores, præſentatores, ſacriſtas, religioſos, qui nihil habent.*] Before this act there was another miſchief or abuſe, and that was, that theſe hoſpitallers and templers, to defeat the remedy that was given to the party grieved againſt the judge in the caſes aboveſaid by the common law, did conſtitute ſubpriors, chaunters, ſextens, and other religious men, which had nothing to ſatisfie the party grieved, nor the king (whereby it appeareth that the party grieved in the caſes aboveſaid had remedy by the common law) were more bold to offend againſt the kings crown and dignity then their ſuperiors, &c. for this miſchiefe, or rather abuſe, remedy is here provided.

[466]

(9) *Qui audaciores ſint.*] The wiſdome of the common law was ever, that men of ability and ſufficient meanes to live ſhould be called to offices, and judiciall places for three cauſes:

1. Firſt, for that they would feare to offend; for men that are in place of judicature, and without meanes, are, as here it appeareth, boldeſt to offend.

2. They to maintaine their countenances are proneſt to bribe and extort.

3. That if they offend, they may be able to ſatisfie the party grieved, and the king his fine: which three cauſes doe appeare by this branch.

(10) *Ad lædendum dignitatem regis.*] Here it appeareth that incroachment of juriſdiction by eccleſiaſticall judges contrary to the kings lawes is *crimen læſæ dignitatis regis:* which appeareth by theſe

these words, and hereafter it is in this branch said, *in præjudicium domini regis et coronæ suæ.*

(11) *Quod si fecerint, pro facto ipsorum respondeant sui superiores, ac si de proprio facto suo convicti essent.*] Here is the remedy provided for the last mentioned mischiefe or abuse, *viz.* that the superiors, that is, those that appoint such judges (as are not sufficient to satisfie the party grieved his damages, and the king his fine) shall out of their temporalties satisfie the same according to the rule of *respondeat superior.*

And by the common law, if the coroner be insufficient, the whole county, who made election and choyce of him, shall *tanquam elector et superior* answer for him, and so shall the officer answer for his deputy.

Fleta, li. 6. c. 36. respondeat superior. 52 H. 3. Stat. de Scac' W. 2. c. 2. & 11. 44 E. 3. 13. 41 Ass. 10. 50 E. 3. 5. 39 H. 6. 32. 2 H 6. ca. 10. l. 11. fo. 92. The earle of Devonshires case.

Hil. 14 E. 3. ex pte remem. regis in Scac' Rot. 9. Herlizans case. 39 H. 6. 32.

CAP. XLIV.

DE custodibus hostiorum in itineribus, virgam portantibus (1) coram justic' de banco: ordinatum est, quod de qualibet assisa et jurata quam custodiunt, capiant decem denarios tantum, de chirographis nihil. De his qui recuperant demandas suas versus plures per defaltam, redditionem, vel alio modo per judicium sine assisa, vel jurat', nihil. De his qui recedunt sine die per defaltam petentis vel querentis, nihil capiant. Et si quis recuperaverit demandam suam versus plures (2) per unum breve, et per re- [467] *cognitionem assisæ vel jurat' de quatuor denariis sint contenti. Et similiter si plures in uno brevi nominati per recognitionem assisæ vel juratæ recuperaverint demandam, de quatuor denariis sint contenti. De his qui faciunt homagium in banco, de superiori panno sint contenti. De magnis assisis, attinctis, juratis, et duello percusso xii. d. tantum capiant. De his qui vocati sunt coram justic' ad sequend', vel defendend' placitum suum, nihil capiant pro egressu vel ingressu. Ad placita coronæ de qualibet duodena xii. d. tantum capiantur. De quolibet prisonario deliberato iv. d. tantum capiantur. De quolibet cujus pax proclamata*

CONCERNING porters bearing verge before justices of the bench in the circuit; it is provided, that of every assise and jury that they keep they shall take x. d. only, and for the bills nothing. Of such as recover their demands by default, confession, or otherwise by judgement without assise and jury, they shall take nothing. Of such as go without day by default of the demandant or plaintiff, they shall take nothing. And if any recover his demand against many by one writ, and by recognizance of assise or jury, they shall be content with iv. d. And likewise if many named in one writ do recover by recognizance of assise or jury, they shall be content with iv. d. Of such as do homage in the bench, they shall be content with their upper garment. Of great assises, attaints, juries, and battle waged, they shall take xii. d. only. Of such as be called before justices to sue or to defend their pleas, they shall take nothing for their comming in or forth. At the pleas of the crown, for every dozen xii. d. only shall be taken. Of every prisoner delivered iv. d. shall be taken. Of every one whose peace is proclaimed

clamata fuerit xii.d. tantum capiatur. De inventoribus occiforum, et aliis attachiat' vill', iv.d. De decennariis hominibus, al', de quatuor hominibus et propofito ac decenariis nihil capiatur. De chirographariis pro chirographo faciendo ftatutum eft, quod de quatuor folidis fint contenti (3). *De clericis fcribentibus brevia originalia et judicialia ftatutum eft, quod pro uno brevi de uno denario fint contenti. Et injungit dominus rex omnibus et fingulis jufticiariis fuis in fide et facramento quibus ei tenentur* (4), *quod fi hujufmodi miniftri contra præd' ftatutum in aliquo articulo venerint, et querimonia ad eos perveneat, pœnam eis infligant rationabilem. Et fi iterum deliquerint majorem pœnam eis infligant, qua caftigari merito debeant. Et fi tertio deliquerint, et fuper hoc convicti fuerint* (5), *fi fint miniftri de feodo* (6), *amittant feodum fuum, et fi alii fint, amittant curiam regis, nec redeant fine ipfius regis fpeciali præcepto aut gratia.*

claimed xii.d. only fhall be taken. Of the finders of men flain, and others of a town attached, iv.d. Of tythingmen nothing fhall be taken. Of cyrographers, for making a cyrografe, it is ordained, that they fhall be contented with iv.s. Of clerks writing writs original and judicial, it is ordained, that for one writ they fhall take but i.d. And the king chargeth all his juftices, upon their faith and oath that they owe him, that if fuch manner of officers offend in any article againft this ftatute, and complaint come to them thereof, they fhall execute on them reafonable punifhment; and if they offend the fecond time, they fhall award greater punifhment, that they may be duly corrected: and if they offend the third time, and be thereupon convicted, if they be officers of the fee, they fhall leefe their fee; and if they be other, they fhall void the king's court, and fhall not be received again, without the fpecial grace and licence of the king himfelf.

See W. 1. cap. 26, 27. 29. (2 H. 4. c. 8.)

(1) *De cuftodibus hoftiorum in itineribus virgam portantibus,* &c.] This noble and wife king, knowing that extortion was a grievous burthen to his fubjects, and having provided againft the fame by many laws, as before hath appeared: in this chapter he fetteth down in particular, as an addition to his former acts, what fees the porters bearing vierge before the juftices of the common pleas in their circuit, the chirographers, and clerks writing writs originall or judiciall fhould take, which were the due fees before this act; but yet it was thought neceffary that the fame fhould be fet down, and publifhed by act of parliament for three caufes.

1. That all the fubjects of the realm might take notice, and know in what cafes to give, and in what not.

2. In cafes where they ought to give, what they were to give in certainty.

3. That the officers or minifters take no more then is here prefcribed, under pretence of expedition, or other pretext whatfoever, nor to take any thing where nothing is due to them, under the pains hereby inflicted.

(2) *Et*

(2) *Et si quis recuberaverit demandam suam versus plures*, &c.] Where there were many tenants or defendants, 4. d. was before this act extorted for every tenant or defendant upon a recovery against them, where (they all being but as one tenant or defendant) there ought to be given but one 4. d. as it is declared by this act. 26 Ass. 47.

(3) *De chirographariis pro chirographo faciendo statutum est quod de 4. s. sint contenti.*] *Chirographarius* cometh of the Greek word χειρογραφεῖν, which is as much to say, as a hand writing, so called, because he writeth the chirographs, that is, the indentures of the fine, one for the buyer, another for the seller: and the fine is said to be ingrossed, when the chirographer maketh the indentures, and delivers them. F.N.B. 147. a.

By the statute of 2 Henry 4. cap. 8. it is provided, that the chirographer shall take but the said summe of 4. s. mentioned in this act for a fine levied. 2 H. 4. cap. 8.

(4) *Et injungit dominus rex omnibus, et singulis justiciariis suis in fide, et sacramento quibus ei tenentur*, &c.] By this great injunction, and commandment of so high a nature to the justices, the odiousnes of extortion appeareth, and what an high offence it is, for that most commonly it is accompanied with perjury, and that it hath a consuming quality; whereof the prophet David speaking against the enemies of Almighty GOD, saith, Let the extortioner consume that he hath, and let the stranger spoil his labour.

(5) *Et si tertio deliquerint, et super hoc convicti fuerint.*] *Convicti fuerint* is here taken for *adjudicati fuerint*. See W. 2. cap. 4.

Though this branch saith, *et super hoc convicti fuer'*, and may seem to refer to the third offence, yet cannot he be convicted of the third before he be convicted of the second, nor of the second before he be convicted of the first; and the second offence must be committed after the first conviction, and the third after the second conviction, and severall judgements thereupon given: for so it is to be understood in other acts of parliament, where there be degrees of punishment inflicted, for the first, second, and third offence, &c. there must be severall convictions, that is to say, judgements given upon legall proceeding for every severall offence, for it appeareth to be no offence untill judgement by proceeding of law be given against him.

(6) *Si sint ministri de feodo.*] This is understood of officers that have any fixed estate, although it be not in fee-simple, as in the 42. chapter is shewed; for the largest estate of any of the ministeriall offices specified in this act that ever was granted, was for term of life; and this appeareth by the diversity of punishments imposed by this act; for if they have their offices *de feodo*, that is, of a fixed estate, for the third offence *amittant feodum*, that is, *officium suum*; and if they have no fixed estate, but at pleasure, *amittant curiam regis*, that is, be forjudged the kings court.

See before, cap. 2, the sense of these words, *de feodo*.

CAP.

CAP. XLV.

QUIA de his quæ recordata ſunt (1) coram cancellario domini regis, et ejus juſtic' qui recordum habent, et in eorum rotulis irrotulatur, non debet fieri proceſſus placiti per ſummonitiones, attachiamenta (2), eſſonium (3), viſus terræ, et alias ſolemnitates curiæ (4), ſicut fieri conſuevit de contractibus et conventionibus factis extra cur': obſervandum eſt de cætero, quod ea quæ inveniuntur irrotulat' coram his, qui recordum habent, vel in finibus (5) content', ſive ſint contractus, ſive conventiones, ſive obligationes, ſive ſervitia, aut conſuetudines, recognita, ſive alia quæcunque irrotulata, quibus curia domini regis (ſine juris et conſuetudinis offenſo) authoritatem præſtare poteſt, talem de cætero habeant vigor' quod non ſit neceſſe in poſterum de his placitare (6), ſed cum venerit conquerens ad cur' domini regis, ſi recens ſit cognitio, vel finis levat', viz. infra annum, ſtatim habeat breve de executione (7) illius recognitionis factæ. Et ſi fortè à majori tempore tranſacto facta fuerit illa recognitio, vel finis levatus, præcipiatur vicecom' quod ſcire faciat parti, de qua ſit querimonia, quod ſit ad certum diem coram juſtic', oſtendens (ſi quid ſciat dicere) quare hujuſmodi irrotulat', vel in fine content' executionem habere non debeant (8). Et ſi ad diem non venerit (9), vel fortè venerit, et nihil ſciat dicere, quare executio fieri non debeat, præcipiatur vicecom', quod rem irrotulatam, vel in fine content' exequi faciat. Eodem modo mandetur ordinario in ſuo caſu (10), obſervetur nihilominus quod [W. 2. *cap.* 9.] *ſupradict' eſt de medio, qui per recognition' aut judicium obligatus eſt ad acquietandum* (11). [13 E. 1. Mercatoribus.]

BECAUSE that of ſuch things as be recorded before the chancellor and the juſtices of the king that have record, and be inrolled in their rolls, proceſs of plea ought not to be made by ſummons, attachments, eſſoin, view of land, and other ſolemnities of the court, as hath been uſed to be done of bargains and covenants made out of the court; from henceforth it is to be obſerved, that thoſe things which are found inrolled before them that have record, or contained in fines, whether they be contracts, covenants, obligations, ſervices, or cuſtoms knowledged, or other things whatſoever inrolled, wherein the king's court, without offence of the law and cuſtom, may execute their authority, from henceforth they ſhall have ſuch vigour, that hereafter it ſhall not need to plead for them. But when the plaintiff cometh to the king's court, if the recogniſance or fine levied be freſh, that is to ſay, levied within the year, he ſhall forthwith have a writ of execution of the ſame recogniſance made. And if the recogniſance were made, or the fine levied of a further time paſſed, the ſheriff ſhall be commanded, that he give knowledge to the party of whom it is complained, that he be afore the juſtices at a certain day, to ſhew if he have any thing to ſay why ſuch matters inrolled or contained in the fine ought not to have execution. And if he do not come at the day, or peradventure do come, and can ſay nothing why execution ought not to be done, the ſheriff ſhall be commanded to cauſe the thing inrolled or contained in the fine to be executed. In like manner, an ordinary ſhall be commanded in his

his case, observing neverthelesse as before is said of a mean, which by recognisance or judgement is bound to acquit.

(Fleta, 2. c. 13. p. 76. sect. 9. 1 Inst. 131. a. Bro. Debt, 10. Bro. Parl. 29. Fitz. Scire fac' 1, 2, 3. 8. 12, &c. Fitz. Execut. 18. 35. 57. 96. 100. Cro. El. 164. 13 Ed. 1. stat. 1. c. 9.)

Some diversity of opinion hath been, whether there was a *scire fac'* at the common law before this act; and the doubt grew for want of distinguishing between personall actions, and reall actions; for true it is, that in personall actions, if the plaintife after judgement given, or recognisance knowledged, sued out no processe of execution within the yeer, he could have no *scire fac'*; but the plaintife or conusee was driven to his originall, which is to be intended upon the judgement or recognisance) as in actions of debt, writs of annuity, or other personall actions, wherein debts or damages were recovered, or upon recognisances. Vide devant. ca. 18. Hil. 13 E. 2. f. 74. b. in libro meo. Adjudge. al common ley. 8 E. 3. 28, 29. 44. 21 E. 3. 55. 40 E. 3. 10. Li. 3. 3. f. 12. Sir William Herberts case, lib. 6. fol. 88. Garnons case.

But in reall actions, or upon a fine levied, though the demandant or conusee sued out no execution within the yeer after the judgement given, or fine * levyed, the demandant or conusee of the fine after the yeer might have had a *scire fac'* for the land &c. because he could not have any new originall, either upon the judgement or fine, as he might have in the other cases. Now this act giveth a *scire facias* in personall actions in lieu of a new originall. 19 H. 6. 5. 20 H. 6. 20. F.N.B. 265. g. Regist. 298, 299. 1. Part of the Institutes, sect. 505, 506 690. 18 E. 3. 33, 34. Nota dictum Wilby. 21 E. 4. 19. b.

And in reall actions, two things are remedied by this act, that is, first, the tedious processe, which was at the common law, is hereby abridged; and secondly, the great delays used therein are ousted, as views of the land, and other solemnities used in reall actions. 1 H. 5. 4.

* [470]

And the distinction abovesaid appeareth (if it be well observed) in our books, and therefore the old rule is hereby verified, *Qui bene distinguit, bene docet.* *Regula.*

And thus much being spoken for the cause of the making of this act, let us now peruse the words.

(1) *Quia de hiis quæ recordata sunt.*] Regularly upon this act, a *scire fac'* cannot be granted but upon a record; but in many cases a *scire fac'* is granted, partly upon a record, and partly upon such a suggestion, without which no proceeding could be upon the record. 2 E. 3. 7, 8. 46 E. 3. Scire fac. 134. 16 E. 3. Bre. 651. 15 E. 3. Scire fac. 115. 19 R. 2. ibid. 154. 17 E. 3. 36. 21 E. 3. 1. 4. 16. 14 H. 7. 6, 7. Hil. 13 E. 2. fo. 74. b. in libro meo le case del Mr. Hospital de T.

(2) *Non debet fieri processus placiti per summon', attachiament', esson', visus terræ. et alias solemnitates curiæ.*] Here be four things particularly named to be ousted, *viz.* processe of summons, processe of attachment, essoins, view of the land, and then generall words, other solemnities of courts.

(3) *Esson'.*] The essoin of the tenant or defendant is not onely restrained by this act, but of the priee in aid, who is a stranger to the writ, is also restrained. 2 H. 7. 10 & 11. Hill. 13 E. 2. ubi supra.

And the plaintife in the *scire fac'* shall not be essoined, although it is his own delay. 10 E. 3. 30. 12 H. 6. 8.

(4) *Et alias solemnitates curiæ.*] It hath been resolved, that a protection is within these words, and that it should not be allowed in a *scire facias*. 21 E. 4. 19.

And divers authorities are against it. 40 E. 3. 18. 47 E. 3. 3. 37 H. 6. 32 15 H. 7. 8.

Aid,

* 17 E. 3. 46. 18 E. 3. 32. 40 E. 3. 18. 37 H. 6. 32.

* Aid, age, and receit shall be granted in a *scire facias*; for *solemnitates curiæ* are properly delays in respect of the solemn judiciall proceedings of court, and these words extend not to the right of the party to have his age, or to be received, or to have aid of another.

13 E. 3. Scire fac. 118. W. 2. cap. 5.

(5) *In finibus.*] Upon a fine *sur grant et render* of an advowson, a *scire facias* shall be granted, for this is a judiciall, and no originall writ, for *de advocat' non sunt nisi tria brevia originalia.*

And though fines be here named, yet recoveries in reall actions are within the purview of this act.

36 H. 6. 32. 21 E. 4. 23. b.

(6) *Quod non sit necesse in posterum de hiis placitare.*] This branch is thus to be understood, that the tenant or defendant, though he be a stranger to the recovery, shall not plead against the recovery any thing that proveth it erroneous or voidable; but he may plead matter that proveth the recovery, void, as that it was had *coram non judice*, or the like.

* 8 E. 3. 56. 15 E 3. Age 43. 95. 10 R. 2. Fauxer de recovery 47. 3 H. 6. 34. b. 7 H. 6. 39. 10 H. 6. 5. 7 H. 7. 13. 12 H. 8. 8.

* Neither shall he in a *scire fac'* plead any thing against the title or matter of the recovery, where he may have an action, and therein falsifie the same.

† 1. Part of the Institutes, § 505.

† But the tenant or defendant may plead divers matters after the judgement given, to barre the plaintife of execution, as outlawry, or a release of actions, &c.

[471]

For receipts see Bract. l. 5. f. 377. 21 E. 3. 22. b. 21 E. 3. ubi supra.

(7) *Si recens sit cognitio, vel finis levat infra annum, statim habeat breve de executione.*] It hath been ruled that these words have relation to the teste of the recognisance, and not to the day of payment, and therefore if a recognisance be knowledged to pay a summe a year and halfe after, a *scire facias* lieth, and no *fieri facias*.

10 E. 2. exec. 137. 16 E. 2. ibid. 138. 16 E. 3. Scire fac' 4. 21 E. 3. exec' Statham.

But I take that rule to be against law, and that *recens cognitio* is as much as *recens solutio cognitionis*; for the words be *statim habeat breve de executione*, which he cannot have before the day of payment be past.

8 E. 3. 44. F. N. B. 266. c. 267. b.

If a judgement be given in a writ of annuity, the plaintiffe shall have execution within the yeare after every day of payment by *fieri fac'*, or *elegit*, though it be many yeares after the judgement; and so if a man be bound by recognisance in C. l. to pay it yearly at five severall dayes 20l. now immediately after the first day of payment he may have an *elegit*, or *fieri facias* for the 20l. and so at the second day passed, &c. and yet in both these cases there is above a yeare after the judgement given or recognisance knowledged, therefore these words *recens sit cognitio* shall relate to the day of payment of the money, which is the effect of the recognisance, and not to the teste of the recognisance, which is but the assurance for payment of the money.

And this word *recens* importeth, when the party may sue for the same, which he cannot doe before the day of payment be past, but this is to be understood, when the severall dayes of payment are contained in the recognisance it selfe, for if there be a day of payment expressed in the recognisance, and a condition or defeasance there of the same limiting other dayes of payment, there, these words *recens sit cognitio, &c.* shall relate to the day of payment expressed in the recognisance, and not to the condition or defeasance, and if there be no day of payment in the recognisance, then these words *recens cognitio, &c.* doe relate to the teste of the recognisance.

And

And albeit the plaintiffe cannot have execution within the yeare, according to the letter of this ſtatute, yet if he come within a yeare of the payment, it ſufficeth.

8 E. 3. 44.

If lands be granted and rendred by fine, and in the fine it be mentioned that W. holdeth the ſame for 26 yeares after the terme ended, he ſhall have a *ſcire facias* albeit he could have no writ of execution within the yeare; and ſo it is if a reverſion expectant upon an eſtate for life be graunted by fine, and after tenant for life liveth many yeares and dieth, the conuſee ſhall have a *ſcire facias*, and yet could he not have a writ of execution within the yeare.

If the demandant or plaintiffe taketh his proces of execution within the yeare, though it be not ſerved within the yeare, yet if he continue the ſame, he may have proces of execution at any time after the yeare.

One that is not party to the record, recogniſance, fine, or judgement, as the heire, executor, or adminiſtrator, though they be privy, and though it be within the yeare, ſhall have no writ of execution, but are to have a *ſcire facias* to enable themſelves to the ſuit; and ſo likewiſe of the tenant or defendants part, for the alteration of perſon altereth the proceſs; otherwiſe it is in caſe of a ſtatute ſtaple, or merchant, &c. becauſe the proces is given by other acts of parliament.

F.N.B. 267. d. 2 R. 3. 8. 14 H. 7. 16. b.

But if a judgement be given in the court of common pleas, and within the yeare the judgement is affirmed in a writ of error in the kings bench, the alteration of the court worketh no alteration of the proces, but he may have his writ of execution within the yeare, and not be driven to his *ſcire facias*, though it hath been otherwiſe holden, but now the common experience and later reſolutions are to the contrary.

21 Aſſ. p. 14. 14 H. 7. 15. 15 H. 7. 5. Lib. 5. fo. 88. Garnons caſe.

(8) *Et ſi forte á majori tempore tranſacto facta fuerit illa recognitio, vel finis levatus, præcipiatur vic' quod ſcire faciat parti de qua ſit querimon', &c. quare executionē habere non debeat.*] Upon theſe words, *ſcire faciat parti*, in a *ſcire fac'* upon a recogniſance out of the common pleas, the conuſee muſt name all the terre-tenants at his perill, but in other courts the writ is generall againſt all terre-tenants.

[472]

20 E. 3. Scir' fac' 121. 39 E. 3. 15. 46 E. 3. 29. b. 8 H. 6. 17.

The point of the writ is *quare executionem habere non debet*, and therefore the tenant ſhall not vowch.

21 E. 4. 19.

This ſtatute is in the affirmative, and therefore it reſtraineth not the common law, but the party may waive the benefit of the *ſcire facias* given by this act, and take his originall action of debt by the common law.

39 H. 6. 2. * 27 H. 6. 2. 35 H. 6. 24. 30 H. 6. 5.

The formes of *ſcire fac'* upon * recogniſances, &c. and likewiſe upon † fines and recoveries appeare in our books.

19 H. 6. 49. 44 E. 3. 11. 20 E. 3. Scir' fac' 121. 46 E. 3. 29. 10 H. 4. 2, 3. † 30 E. 3. 25.

And ſeeing the words of the *ſcire fac'* be, *quare executionem habere non debet*, the tenant or defendant may plead any thing in barre of execution, as hath been ſaid before.

(9) *Et ſi ad diem non venerit.*] * The party muſt either be warned, or regularly two *nihils* returned, and then by default execution ſhall be granted, and how the warning is to be made, it appeareth in our books.

17 E. 3. 74. 76, 77. Sir William Herberts caſe, ubi ſupra. * 18 E. 3. exec. 57. 33 H. 6. 42. 10 H. 6. 12. 2 H. 7. 3. l. 5 E. 4. 1. 4 H. 7. 7. Li. 5. fo. 32. Petifers caſe.

The courſe of the court of common pleas is, that upon a recovery the plaintiffe ſhall have execution upon one *nihil* returned.

(10) *Eodem*

(10) *Eodem modo mandetur ordinario in suo casu.*] This branch is to be thus intended, that if a *scire facias* be brought upon a recognisance, or upon a judgement in a writ of annuity, and the sheriffe return that the defendant is *clericus et beneficiatus nullum habens laicum feodum, &c.* the plaintiffe shall have a writ to the bishop of the same diocesse to warne the defendant, and upon warning, or two *nihils* returned, and default made, or if he appeareth, and shew no matter, wherefore execution should not be graunted, then a writ shall be awarded to the bishop to levy execution *de bonis ecclesiasticis.*

Regist. judic' fol. 22. 26.

W. 2. cap. 9.

(11) *Observatur nihilominus quod supradictū est de medio, qui per recognitionem aut judicium obligatus est ad acquietand'.*] This clause was added *in majorem rei cautelam,* that the provision before made at this parliament cap. 9. in case that in a writ of mesne, *postquam medius venerit in curiam et cognoverit, quod acquietare debet tenentem suum, vel adjudicetur ad acquietandum, si post hujusmodi cognitionem aut judicium querimonia perveniat, quod medius non acquietavit tenentem suum, tunc exeat breve de judicio, quod vic' distringat medium ad acquietandum tenentem:* whereupon fore-judger is given; now if the plaintiffe in the writ of mesne should onely take his *scire facias,* then no fore-judger should follow thereupon, therefore this clause was added, that the former generall words of this act, *sive alia quæcunque irrotulata, &c.* should not take away the benefit of the former act concerning the fore-judger in a writ of mesne, but, as hath been said, this act being in the affirmative taketh not away neither the common law, nor the benefit of the former act concerning the said fore-judger; for the plaintiffe may take advantage either of the one or other, at his election; wherein it is to be observed that an act of parliament cannot be made too plaine: but note the fore-judger is given onely against him that made the acknowledgement, or against whom judgement was given, and not against his heire, and therefore this act is an addition declarative to the former, *viz.* that a *sci' fac'* may in those cases lie against the heire.

14 E. 3. mesne 9. 46 E. 3. 31. see W. 2. c. 9. more of this matter.

[473]

CAP. XLVI.

CUM in statuto edito apud Merton, concessum fuerit, quod domini vastorum, boscorum, et pasturarum appruare se possint (1) de vastis, boscis, et pasturis illis, non obstante contradictione tenentium suorum, dummodo tenentes ipsi haberent sufficientem pasturam ad tenementa sua, cum libero ingressu et egressu ad eadem. Et pro eo quod nulla fiebat mentio inter vicinum et vicinum, multi domini vastorum, boscorum, et pasturarum hucusque impediti extiterint per contradictionem vicinorum (2) sufficientem pasturam habentium.

WHEREAS in a statute made at Merton, it was granted that lords of wastes, woods, and pastures, might approve the said wastes, woods, and pastures, notwithstanding the contradiction of their tenants, so that the tenants had sufficient pasture to their tenements with free egress and regress to the same: and forasmuch as no mention was made between neighbours and neighbours, many lords of wastes, woods, and pastures, have been hindered heretofore by the contradiction of neighbours having sufficient

bentium. Et quia forinseci tenentes non habent majus jus communicandi in bosco, vasto, aut pastur' alicujus domini, quam proprii tenentes ipsius domini: statutum est de caetero, quod statutum apud Merton provisum inter dominum et tenentes suos, locum habeat de caetero inter dominos vastorum, boscorum, et pasturarum et vicinos (3), *ita quod domini hujusmodi vastorum, boscorum, et pastur' salva sufficienti pastura hominibus suis et vicinis, appruare sibi possint de residuo. Et hoc observetur de his qui clamant pastur' tanquam pertinentem ad tenementum suum. Sed si quis clamat communiam pastur' per speciale feoffamentum, vel concessionem ad certum numerum averiorum, vel alio modo* (4), *quam de jure communi habere deberet, cum conventio legi deroget, habeat suum recuperare, quale habere deberet per formam concessionis sibi factae. Occasione molendini ventritici, bercariae* (6), *vaccariae* (7), *necessarii* (8), *augmentationis cur', aut curtilagii de caetero non gravetur quis per assisam* (5) *novae disseisinae de communia pastur'. Et cum contingat aliquando, quod aliquis jus habens appruare, fossatum aut sepem levaverit, et aliqui noctant, vel alio tali tempore quo non credant factum eorum sciri, fossatum aut sepem prostraverint* (9), *nec sciri poterit per veredictum assisae, aut juratae, qui fossatum aut sepem prostraverint, nec velint homines de villatis vicinis indictare* (10) *de hujusmodi facto culpabiles, distringantur propinquae villatae circum adjacentes, levare fossatum aut sepem, ad costum proprium, et damna restituere* (11). *Et cum* [474] *aliquis jus non habens communicandi usurpet communiam* (12) *tempore quo haeredes infra aetatem extiterint, vel uxores sub potestate virorum suorum existentes; vel pastura sit in manu tenentium in dotem, per legem Angliae, vel aliter ad terminum vitae, vel annorum, vel per feodum talliatum, et pastura illa diu fuerint usi; multi sunt*

sufficient pasture: and because foreign tenants have no more right to common in the wastes, woods, or pastures of any lord than the lord's own tenants; it is ordained, that the statute of Merton, provided between the lord and his tenants, from henceforth shall hold place between lords of wastes, woods, and pastures, and their neighbours, saving sufficient pasture to their tenants and neighbours, so that the lords of such wastes, woods, and pastures, may make approvement of the residue. And this shall be observed for such as claim pasture as appurtenant to their tenements. But if any do claim common by special feoffment or grant for a certain number of beasts, or otherwise which he ought to have of common right, whereas covenant barreth the law, he shall have such recovery as he ought to have had by form of the grant made unto him. By occasion of a windmill, sheepcote, deyry, inlarging of a court necessary, or courtelage, from henceforth no man shall be grieved by assise of novel disseisin for common of pasture. And where sometime it chanceth, that one having right to approve, doth then levy a dyke or an hedge, and some by night, or at another season, when they suppose not to be espied, do overthrow the hedge or dyke, and it cannot be known by verdict of the assise or jury, who did overthrow the hedge or dyke, and men of the towns near will not indict such as be guilty of the fact. The towns near adjoyning shall be distrained to levy the hedge or dyke at their own cost, and to yield damages. And where one, having no right to common, usurpeth common what time an heir is within age, or a woman is covert, or whilst the pasture is in the hands of tenants in dower, by the courtesy, or otherwise for term of life, or years, or in fee-tail, and have long time used the pasture, many

sunt in opinione quod hujusmodi pasturæ debent dici pertinere ad liberum ten', et quod hujusmodi possessori competere debet actio per breve nov. disseis. si ab hujusmodi pastur' deforceantur: sed de cætero tenendum est, quod habentes hujusmodi ingressum à tempore quo currit breve mortis antecessoris (13), *si antea communiam non habuerunt, non habeant recuperare per breve no. diss. si fuerint deforciati.*

many hold opinion, that such pastures ought to be said to belong to the freehold, and that the possessor ought to have action by a writ of novel disseisin, if he be deforced of such pasture; but from henceforth this must be holden, that such as have entred within the time that an assise of mortdauncestor hath lien, if they had no common before, shall have no recovery by a writ of novel disseisin, if they be deforced.

(1 Roll 365. 20 H. 3. c. 4. 11 Rep. 74. 4 Rep. 38. 13 H. 7. f. 13. Dyer, 47. 316. 339. Cro. Car. 281. 440. 580. Enforced by 3 & 4 Ed. 6. c. 3. 7 H. 4. f. 38. Skinner, 93. By 6 Geor. 1. c. 16. sect. 1. the remedy of the act is extended to the destroyers of trees, &c. by night or day, &c. 1 Lutw. 141. 156. 1 Geo. 1. stat. 2. c. 48.)

(1) *Cum in statuto edito apud Merton, concessum fuerit, quod domini vastorum, boscorum, et pasturarum appruare se possint,* &c.] Here is the statute of Merton recited, and because in that act no mention was made between neighbour and neighbour, the doubt was, whether that statute extended onely between lord and tenant, and therefore many lords of wastes, woods, and pastures have been letted to make approvement by the contradiction of neighbours, though they had sufficient pasture; for remedy whereof this statute was made.

6 H. 3. Common 26. 12 H. 3. ibid. 25.

(2) *Per contradictionem vicinorum.*] Note it is not said that the lord could not improve against a neighbour, but that the lords were letted by the contradiction of the neighbours; for by the common law the lord might improve against any that had common appendant, but not against a commoner by grant.

(3) *Statutum est de cætero, quod statutum apud Merton provisum inter dominos, et tenentes suos, locum habeat de cætero inter dominos vastorum, &c. et vicinos.*] This branch is from the making of this act an exposition of the statute of Merton, so as now the statute of Merton doth extend *inter vicinum et vicinum*; but though it be an act of exposition of a former act, yet this exposition shall take effect but *de cætero*, that is, from the making of this act of exposition. And the reason that this act had a retrospect to the statute of Merton was, *quia forinseci tenentes non habent majus jus communicandi in bosco, vasto, aut pastura alicujus domini, quam proprii tenentes ipsius domini.*

Brit. f. 144. 147. 18 Ass. Pl. 4. 18 E. 3. 43. 13 H. 7. 13. 32 H. 8. Dier 47. b. 14 Eliz. Dier 13. 16.

Vicinus is properly *qui una in eodem vico est*, but here it is taken for a neighbour, though he dwell in another town, so the towns and commons be adjoyning together; and if the lord hath common in the tenants ground, the tenant may improve within this act, for there the lord is in this case *vicinus*.

Ad assisas capt' apud Penreth in com' Cumbriæ, coram Roberto de Hereford et sociis suis, &c. die Veneris in crast' inventionis sanctæ crucis, an. regis Ed. 1. 30. Which record we have seen. In an assise brought by John of Rowbery, and Isabel his wife, against Matild of Multon, and others, of 20 acres of pasture and wood in O. the case appeareth by the verdict of the recognitors of assise, *viz.*

*Quod prædict' Matild, & similiter omnes antecess' sui domini de Gilleſland à tempore quo Waren' de Gilleſland devenit ad manus antec' suorum usi sunt hujusmodi libertate, quod nullus libere tenens infra baron' illam, se appruire posset de vasto suo, sine licentia, & voluntate præd' Matild, & antecess' suorum, nec aliquis temporibus retroactis in aliquo de vasto se appruiavit nisi satisfecerit præd' Matild, seu antecess' suis; & quæsiti si præd' Matild habeat communiam in ten' de quo, &c. dicunt quod sic ratione manerii sui de Cuquyntyngton, quod quidem maner' distat à ten' circit' per unam leucam; quæsiti si præd' Matild habeat sufficientem communiam extra ten' præd' cum libero ingressu & egressu, dicunt quod sic; dies datus est eis de audo' judo' suo apud Westm', a die Sancti Michaelis in xv. dies, &c. Postea à die Sancti Hilar' in xv. dies, anno regni domini regis nunc vicesimo venerunt præd' Walterus, & Isab' per attornatum ipsius Isab', & similiter præd' Matild per balivum suum, et petunt recordum, &c. Et quia conjunctum est per assisam istam, quod à tempore quo Waren' præd' devenit in seisina præd' Matild, ipsi antec' & similiter ipsa Matild tali libertate usi sunt, quod nullus libere tenens infra baroniam illam, se posset appruiar' de vasto suo sine licent', & voluntate præd' Matild, & antecess' suorum, nec aliquis temporibus retroactis in aliquo de vasto se appruiavit nisi prius satisfecerit præd' Matild, seu suis antecessoribus. Et ten' quod nec provisio de Merton', nec statut' domini regis nunc de appruiament' fact', seu faciend' &c. non operat' in casu proposito, cum illud de Merton' habeat locum inter dominum appruiant', et tenentem communiam clamantem. Et statutum regis nunc inter vicinum appruiantem, et vicinum communiam clamantem, et hoc de communia pertin' ad liberum ten', et casus propositus est inter dominam comm' clamantem, et tenent' appruiantem, et * hoc de communia non pertinente ad ten', imo usitata in baron' præd' per præd' Matild, & antecessores suos ratione dominii sui in eadem baronia, à tempore præd'. Consid' est quod præd' Matild, & alii inde sine die. Et quod præd' Walterus, & Isab' nihil capiant per assisam, set sint in misericordia pro falso clamor', &c.* Note this preſcription. Vide 3 E. 3. 3. 8 E. 3. 37. 46 E. 3. 13. 23. Similia. * Nota hoc.

This judgement, being given in the ſame kings time that the ſaid ſtatute of W. 2. was made, both in reſpect of the ſaid preſcription, together with the common reſerved at the time of the creation of the tenancie, as by the record it appeareth, ſtandeth well with the books of 18 E. 3. and 18 Aſſ. for there was no ſuch preſcription; and there it is holden, that if the lord had the common by reſervation at the time of the firſt feoffment, then no approvement could be made by his tenant againſt him: and note the quality of the common mentioned in the judgement.

(4) *Et hoc observetur de hiis qui clamant pasturam tanquam pertinentem ad tenementum suum. Sed si quis clamat communiam pasturæ per speciale feoffamentum, vel concessionem ad certum numerū averiorū, vel alio modo,* &c.] So here it is to be obſerved, that neither this ſtatute, nor the ſtatute of Merton doth extend to any common, but to common appendant, or appurtenant to his tenement, and not to a common in groſſe to a certain number. 12 H. 3. ubi ſupra. 3 E. 2. Common 21. See the Expoſition upon the ſtat. of Merton.

(5) *Occasione molendini ventritici, bercariæ, vaccariæ, necessarii, augmentationis curiæ, aut curtilagii de cætero non gravetur quis per assisam,* &c.] Here be five kinds of improvements expreſſed, that both between lord and tenant, and neighbour and neighbour, may be done without leaving ſufficient common to them that have it (any thing either herein, or in the ſtatute of Merton to the contrary notwithſtanding) and theſe five are put but for examples; for the lord [476] 7 H. 4. 38.

lord may erect a house for the dwelling of a beast-keeper for the safe custody of the beasts aswell of the lord, as of the commoners depasturing there in that soil; and yet it is not within the letter of this law.

(6) *Bercariæ.*] *Bercaria* signifieth a sheep-house, and is derived from from the French word *bergerie*, which also signifieth a sheep-house; and by turning *g* into *c*, the legall word is made *bercaria*, and so it is taken in this act: in Domesday it is called *berquarium*; it signifieth also a tanne-house, derived of the Saxon word *berc*. For this, see the first part of the Institutes, sect. 1. *verbo bercaria*.

Domesday, tit. Sudsex Piccam, &c.

(7) *Vaccariæ.*] *Vaccaria* is derived *à vacca*, and signifieth *stabulum vaccarum*, a cow-house, as *vaccheria* doth in Italian.

Fleta betweene *bercariæ* and *vaccariæ*, hath *dayerye*; this word I finde not in the printed books, but in ancient manuscripts, and it signifieth a dayery or milk-house; in Latine, *lactarium*.

32 Ass. 5.

(8) *Necessarii.*] Is to be applyed to *curtilagii*, both in congruity and by our books, and necessary shall not be taken according to the quantity of the free-hold he hath there, but according to his person, estate or degree, and for his necessary dwelling and abode; for if he hath no free-hold there in that town, but his house onely, yet may he make a necessary inlargement of his curtilage.

(9) *Et cum contingat aliquando, quod aliquis jus habens appruare, fossatum aut sepem levaverit, et aliqui noctanter, vel alio tali tempore quo non credant factum eorum sciri, fossatum aut sepem prostraverint*, &c.] Forasmuch as the lord, (as hath been said in the exposition upon the statute of Merton) ought to divide the parts improved, by the hedge, ditch, or other defence: now this branch provideth, that if persons unknown, either in the night or otherwise, so secretly prostrate the ditches, hedges, or other fences, as the lord cannot know against whom to bring his assise or other action; and the men of the towns next adjoyning thereunto round about do not indict the misdoers of the fact, those next towns round about shall be distrained to make the hedge or ditch at their own cost, and yeeld damages to the lord; *sed certè opus est interprete*.

(10) *Indictare.*] That is, to indict them at the kings suit, either of a ryot, force, or trespasse: but here it is demanded, what time have the next towns round about adjoyning to indict the misdoers, seeing here is no time appointed? and the answer is, that seeing no time is appointed, the law doth appoint (as in many cases it doth) a yeer and a day for the indicting of the misdoers; and by the indictment, the lord shall know against whom to bring his action.

See the first part of the Institutes, sect. 69.

(11) *Distringantur propinquæ villatæ circum adjacentes levare fossatū aut sepem, ad costū proprium, et damna restituere.*] For, *viceni vicinorum facta præsumuntur scire:* if the bordering towns do not within a yeer and a day indict the misdoers, then shall the lord or other party grieved bring his action upon this branch against the towns bordering round about the town wherein the fact was done, and judgement shall be given, that they shall at their proper costs make the ditch or hedge, &c. and yeeld damages; and after judgement given, they shall be distrained to make the hedge or ditch, &c. and

[477]

and ſo it was holden in the ſtar-chamber, Hilar. 14 Jac. in Sir William Mallories caſe. H'. 14 Jac. in Camera ſtellata.

At the parliament holden the eight day of October in 13 E. 1. at Wincheſter, remedy it given to the party robbed, upon hue and cry, (if the men of the hundred where the robbery was done, take not the offender) againſt the men of that hundred: and there is ſpeciall proviſion made, that the country ſhall have no longer ſpace then forty dayes, &c. which prevented the time limited by the law. 13 E. 1. ſtat. de Wincheſter. Lib. 7. fo. 6, 7. Milborns caſe. 27 Eliz. cap. 13. 3 E. 3. Coron. 299. Simile.

(12) *Et cum aliquis jus non habens communicandi uſurpet communiam*, &c.] This branch is in affirmance of the common law, for no man can have either common appendant or in groſſe by preſcription, but by uſage time out of minde, which is well expounded by Littleton, ſection 170. 1. Part of the Inſtitutes, § 170.

And here is to be obſerved, that uſurpations of commons in the times of infants, feme coverts, tenant in dower, tenant by the courteſie, or otherwiſe for life or yeers, or tenant in tail, ſhall not binde, though there be long poſſeſſion.

(13) *A tempore brevis mortis anteceſſoris.*] That is, *a coronatione regis* H. 3. which was in the firſt yeer of his raign, and between the coronation of H. 3. and this act, there was about 69 yeers, but yet that poſſeſſion by that time, as here it appeareth, maketh no title in law to the common, if the commencement thereof can be ſhewed ſince the time of the raign of R. 1. but the ſaid long poſſeſſion is great evidence, and a ſtrong preſumption of the right of the common, and *ſtabitur præſumptioni, donec probetur in contrarium.*

CAP. XLVII.

PROVISUM eſt, quod aquæ de Humbre, Ouſe, Trent, Doue, Arre, Derewent, Wharff. Nidd, Yore, Swale, Teſe, Tyne, Eden, et omnes aliæ aquæ in regno in quibus ſalmones capiuntur, ponantur in defenſo (1), *quo ad ſalmones capiendos, à die nativitatis beatæ Mariæ* (2), *uſque ad diem Sancti Martini* (3). *Et ſimiliter quod ſalmunculi* (4) *non capiantur, nec deſtruantur per retia, nec per alia ingenia ad ſtagna molendinorum, a medio Aprilis uſque ad nativitatem ſancti Johan. Baptiſtæ* (5). *Et in partibus ubi hujuſmodi ripariæ fuerint* (6), *aſſignentur conſervatores* (8) *iſtius ſtatuti* (7), *qui ad hoc jurati* (10) *ſæpius videant et inquirant* (9) *de hujuſmodi tranſgreſſione, et in prima tranſgr' puniantur per combuſtionem retium* (11), *et ingeniorum ſuorum. Et ſi*

IT is provided, that the waters of Humber, Owſe, Trent, Done, Arre, Derewent, Wherfe, Nid, Yore, Swale, Teſe, Tine, Eden, and all other waters (wherein ſalmons be taken) ſhall be in defence for taking ſalmons from the nativity of our lady unto St. Martin's day; and that likewiſe young ſalmons ſhall not be taken nor deſtroyed by nets, nor by other engines at milpools, from the midſt of April unto the nativity of St. John Baptiſt. And in places whereas freſh waters be, there ſhall be aſſigned overſeers of this ſtatute, which being ſworn, ſhall oftentimes ſee and inquire of the offenders; and for the firſt treſpaſs, they ſhall be puniſhed by burning of their nets and engines; and for the ſecond time, they ſhall have

si iterato deliquerint, puniantur per prisonam quarterii anni. Et si tertio deliquerint, puniantur per prisonam unius anni. Et sic multiplicata transgressione, crescat pœnæ inflictio (12).

have imprisonment for a quarter of a year; and for the third trespass, they shall be imprisoned a whole year; and as their trespass increaseth, so shall the punishment.

(13 R. 2. stat. 1. c. 19. 17 R. 2. c. 9. 22 Ed. 4. c. 2. 23 H. 8. c. 18. 25 H. 8. c. 7. 1 El. c. 17. 3 Jac. 1. c. 12. 30 Car. 2. stat. 1. c. 9. 4 & 5 W. & M. c. 23. 4 Ann. c. 21. 9 Ann. c. 26. 1 Geo. 1. stat. 2. c. 18.)

Before the making of this act, fishermen for a little lucre did very much harm, and destroy the increase of salmons by fishing for them in unseasonable times, which were between the beginning of September, and about the midst of November; and likewise for young salmons, or salmon peals, between the midst of April, and towards the end of June: against both which, provision is made by this act.

17 R. 2. cap. 9. W. 2. c. 41. li. 2. 46. the B. of Cant. case. Herein the Thames, *Thamesis nobile illud flumen* is not named, and it was holden, that the generall words extended not to inferiour rivers, and therefore the Thames is added by another act in the first place.

(1) *Ponantur in defenso.*] That is, that by this act it is prohibited that salmons, or yong salmons shall be taken between the times mentioned in this act.

(2) *A die nativitatis beatæ Mariæ.*] Which is on the eight day of September.

(3) *Usque ad diem Sancti Martini.*] Which is the eleventh day of November.

And note, that the day of Saint Martin, and the feast of Saint Martin is all one, and the feast in legall understanding beginneth and endeth with the day.

13 R. 2. ca. 19. 17 R. 2. ca. 9. (4) *Salmunculi.*] That is, yong salmons, or salmon peals, or salmon smelts; for so this act is expounded by another statute: they are also called salmon sews, or salmon issues.

(5) *Usque nativitatem Sancti Johannis Baptistæ.*] This is not taken literally for the nativity of Saint John Baptist, for that is long since past; but it is taken according to the intention of the makers, untill the day or feast of his nativity.

And such construction shall be made of covenants, or bonds to pay money, or doe any act; for example, at the annunciation of our lady, it shall be taken for the feast of the annunciation, as here the nativity, &c. is taken for the day of the nativity.

(6) *Ubi ripariæ fuerint.*] *Ripariæ* is a word derived from *ripa*, and here it signifieth the water, or river running between the banks, be it fresh or salt; and thereupon *riparius* is taken for a fisherman.

Regist. 123. 125. 64. 138. 88, &c. F.N.B. 110, 111, 112, 113. 18 E. 3. ca. 1. 4. Stat. 1. Rot. Parliam. 5 H. 4. nu. 36. 2 H. 4. Rot. Parl. nu. 22. Dier 1 El. Scrogs case. (7) *Assignentur conservatores istius statuti.*] And this assignation must be by commission under the great seal, and such a commission could not have been made without warrant by authority of parliament; for legall commissions have their due forms, aswell as originall writs, and none can be newly framed without act of parliament, how necessary soever they seem to be: as in this case it was necessary that such a commission should be granted for preservation of salmons and of their yong, and for avoiding of the destruction of the

the same, being victuall of great and precious account; and what is more necessary then increase of victuall? yet could it not be newly raised without act of parliament; but commissions of new inquiries, &c. and of new invention, have been condemned by authority of parliament, and by the common law. [479]

(8) *Conservatores.*] See this word before, cap. 43.

(9) *Qui ad hoc jurati sæpius videant, et inquirant.*] Execution of the law is the life of the law, and therefore here is provision made for the continuall, due, and speedy execution of the law.

(10) *Jurati.*] A new oath cannot be imposed upon any judge, commissioner, or any other subject without authority of parliament, as here it was; but the giving of every oath must be warranted by act of parliament, or by the common law time out of minde. Stat. de 20 E. 3. 4 H. 4. c. 18. 2 H. 5. ca. 6. 17 E. 4. ca. 2. 1 R. 3. c. 6. 5 R. 2. c. 13. 32 H. 8. ca. 46. 21 H. 8. c. 16. 1 Eliz. c. 1. 28 Eliz. ca. 4. 43 Eliz. ca. 12.

The oath of the counsellors, judges, sheriffes, under-sherifes, escheators, attorneys, maiors, and bailifes are established by act of parliament.

(11) *Et in prima transgressione punitur, per combustionem retium.*] This ought to be by indictment at the suit of the king, and the punishment cannot be inflicted upon the delinquent before upon due conviction, *secundum legem et consuetudinem Angliæ*, judgement be given. Stat. de 20 E. 3. ubi supra.

And, as hath been said in the like case, he cannot be punished for the second offence, before he be adjudged for the first, and that second offence must be committed after the judgement given for the first; nor for the third, before he be adjudged for the second, and that third must be committed after the judgement for the second; for *quod non apparet non est, et non apparet judicialiter in isto casu ante judicium.* See W. 2. ca. 44.

(12) *Multiplicata transgressione, crescat pœnæ inflictio.*] This is a maxime of the law, agreeing with those other, *Regula.*

Ex frequenti delicto augetur pœna: *Regula.*
Crescente malitia crescere debet & pœna.

CAP. XLVIII.

De visu terræ ordinatum est et statutum, quod de cætero non concedatur visus, nisi in casu quando visus est necessarius (1): *sicut si aliquis amittat tenementum per defaltam: et ille qui amisit suscitet aliud breve ad petendum idem tenement'* (3). *Et in casu quando aliquis per exceptionem dilatoriam* (2) *cassat breve post visum terræ* (4), *sicut per non tenuram, vel male nominando villam, vel hujusmodi* (5), *si suscitet aliud breve, in hoc casu et in superiori* (6) *de cætero non concedatur visus, dummodo visum habuerit in*

FOR view of land it is ordained and provided, that from henceforth view shall not be granted but in case when view of land is necessary: as if one lose land by default, and he that loseth, moveth a writ to demand the same land. And in case when one by an exception dilatory abateth a writ after the view of the land, as by non-tenure, or misnaming of the town, or such like, if he purchase another writ, in this case, and in the case before mentioned, from henceforth the view shall not be granted,

in prioribus brevibus. In brevi de dote cum petatur dos de tenemento, quod vir uxoris alienavit tenenti aut ejus antecessori (7), *cum ignorare non debeat tenens, quale ten' vir uxoris alienavit* * (8) *sibi, vel antecessori suo licet vir non obiit seisitus, nihilominus tenenti de cetero non erit visus concedendus. In brevi etiam de ingressu cassato per hoc* (9) *quod petens nominavit male ingressum, si petens suscitet aliud breve de alio ingressu, si tenens in priori brevi visum habuerit, in secundo non habebit. In omnibus etiam brevibus per quæ ten' petunt* (11) *ratione dimissionis* (14), *quam petens vel ejus antecessor fecit tenenti, et non ejus antecessori, sicut quod ei dimisit, dum fuit infra ætatem, non compos mentis* (10), *in prisona* (13), *et consimilibus* (12), *non jaceat de cætero visus, sed si dimissio facta fuerit antecessori jaceat visus sicut prius.*

granted, if he had view in the first writs. In a writ of dower, where the dower in demand is of land that the husband aliened to the tenant or his ancestors, where the tenant ought not to be ignorant what land the husband did aliene to him or his ancestor, though the husband died not seised, yet from henceforth view shall not be granted to the tenant. In a writ of entre also, that is abated because the demandant misnamed the entre, if the demandant purchase another writ of entre, if the tenant had view in the first writ, he shall not have it in the second. In all writs also where lands be demanded by reason of a lease made by the demandant, or his ancestor, unto the tenant, and not to his ancestor, as that which he leased to him, being within age, not whole of mind, being in prison, and such like, view shall not be granted hereafter; but if the demise were made to his ancestor, the view shall lie as it hath done before.

Glanv. li. 2. ca. 1. (Fitz. View. 50, 51. 57. 129. 118. Fitz. View. 1, 2. 5. 24. 41. 49. 69. 102. 118, 119. 10 H. 7. f. 8.)

8 E. 3. 55. 38 E. 3. 1. 39 E. 3. 38. & 18. 46 E. 3. 16, 17. 21 H. 6. 42. 3 E. 3. View 135. 12 E. 3. ibid. 79. 13 E. 3. ibid. 81. 24 E. 3. ibid. 95. 22 E. 3. 9. 29 E. 3. 46. 21 H. 6. 42.

(1) *De visu terræ ordinatum est et statut', quod de cetero non concedatur visus, nisi in casu quando visus est necessarius.*] There be divers books in law, wherein this maxime is cited.

(2) *Per exceptionem dilatoriam.*] The writ must be abated by exception, and therefore if the demandant be nonsuit, the tenant shall have the view again.

If the writ doth abate by conusans of the demandant, and not by the plea and exception of the defendant, the tenant shall have the view in the new writ.

If the tenant hath the view, and the demandant discontinue his suit, in a new action the tenant shall have the view.

7 E. 3. 36. 41 E. 3. 8. 30. 44 E. 3. 43. 46 E. 3. 34. 50 E. 3. 25.

(3) *Sicut si aliquis amittat tenementum per defaltam: et ille qui amisit suscitet aliud breve ad petendum idem ten'.*] This branch is not to be understood according to the letter, for if one lose by default in an assise, and the tenant bring a writ of right of the same lands against the recoveror, he shall have the view; but this branch is to be understood of a *quod ei deforceat* upon the recovery by default, which writ is grounded upon the former record, so as the tenant hath sufficient notice thereby; and therefore neither party privie nor estranger shall have view in this writ: but otherwise it is in the former case of the writ of right, for that is not grounded upon the record.

(4) *Et in caſu quando aliquis per exceptionem dilatoriam caſſat breve poſt viſum terræ.*] Here be two examples ſet down of dilatorie pleas in particular, that is to ſay, non-tenure, and miſnaming of the town where the lands do lye, both which exceptions do riſe upon the view.

A præcipe is brought againſt a feme, who abateth the writ for miſnaming of the town, the wife taketh huſband, in a new writ againſt huſband and wife they ſhall have the view; for albeit it be the act of the wife to take huſband, yet for that the huſband was not party to the firſt writ, they ſhall have the view in the ſecond.

30 E. 3. 8.

(5) *Vel hujuſmodi.*] Theſe generall words, or the like, are thus to be expounded, that the writ muſt abate for ſuch a plea dilatory, as doth riſe upon the view, as the two particular examples of non-tenure, and miſnaming of the towne doe; but when the writ abate for ſome dilatories which riſe not upon the view, then in a new writ the view ſhall be graunted; as where the writ is abated for joyntenancy, and the new writ is brought againſt them both they ſhall have the view, becauſe in the new writ another perſon is joyned; and ſo it is if any more or leſſe land be contained in the new writ: but if the firſt writ after the view abated for default of forme, or for falſe Latin, or by taking of huſband, in a new writ the tenant ſhall have the view againe, for theſe caſes are not within this word *hujuſmodi*; for they riſe not upon the view, as the two examples herein expreſſed doe.

[481]

See Circumſpecte agatis, ſimile. W. 2. c. 5. ſimile. Lib. 11. fo. 33. the Poulters caſe.

And beſides the firſt was no ſufficient writ, and an inſufficient writ and no writ is all one; ſo it is if one of the tenants after the view dieth, in a new writ the ſurviving tenant ſhall have the view againe, albeit the feme came in as a feme ſole by receit, and the huſband died, for this did not riſe upon the view, but by the act of God.

But if the firſt writ were brought in K. and the tenant plead that part of the lands extend in L. in a new writ for the lands in K. and L. though a new town be added, yet becauſe the new town was added by force of the plea of the tenant himſelfe, he was ouſted of the view.

It is not required by this act that the ſecond writ ſhould be brought freſhly by Journers accounts, though it be ſo pleaded in many books.

8 E. 3. 55. 18 E. 3. 31. 21 H. 6. 42. 6 E. 3. 15. 17 E. 3. 39, 40. 18 E. 3. 41. 38 E. 3. 1. 19 E. 3. view 111. 33 E. 3. ib. 184. 30 E. 3. 8. 21 H. 6. 42. 34 H. 6. 10. 42 E. 3. 23. 43 E. 3. 35. 29 E. 3. 17. 45. 38 E. 3. 1. 39 E. 3. 27. 6 E. 2. view 163. 5 R. 2. ibid. 63. 20 E. 2. ibid. 112. 26 H. 6. ibid. 14. 21 H. 6. 42. 21 H. 6. 55. 2 H. 6. 14. 17 E. 3. 41. b. 22 E. 3. 9.

(6) *In hoc caſu et in ſuperiori.*] This branch extendeth not to the clauſe of the recovery by default, for in the *quod ei deforceat*, the writ being grounded directly upon the former record, wherein the tenant in the *quod ei deforceat* recovered in the former writ, he hath ſufficient notice thereof, and therefore, as hath been ſaid, ſhall not have the view.

41 E. 3. 8. 30. 44 E. 3. 43. 50 E. 3. 25.

And therefore theſe words [*in hoc caſu*] are to be referred to the laſt generall words, *viz.* [*vel hujuſmodi*] and theſe words [*et in ſuperiori*] are to be referred to the two examples dilatory of non-tenure, and miſnaming of the towne.

(7) *In brevi de dote cum petatur dos de tenemento quod vir uxoris alienavit tenenti aut ejus anteceſſori,* &c.] This branch extendeth not to a writ of dower, *unde nihil habet*, for therein no view did lie at the common law, but extendeth to other writs of dower, whether for dower at the common law, or *ex aſſenſu patris, ad hoſtium eccleſiæ, &c.* or by cuſtome.

43 E. 3. 17. Temps E. 1. view 172. 20 E. 3. ib. 113.

At

22 E. 3. 9. 3 E. 3. 16. 8 E. 3. 55. 2 H. 4. 20. 5 H. 5. 4. 34 H. 6. 3. 35 H. 6. 59. Bract. l. 5. f. 377. 18 E. 3. 55.

At the common law if the huſband died ſeiſed of the land of eſtate of inheritance, whereof dower is demaunded, the heire or any claiming under him ſhould not have the view, becauſe it was preſumed that the heire was conuſant what lands his aunceſtor had at the time of his death, and herewith agreeth Bracton who wrote before this ſtatute; *Item denegatur viſus in placito dotis de terra et tenemento de quibus vir mulieris nuper obiit ſeiſitus, quia habet tenens quod tantundem valet.*

But where the huſband aliened, there at the common law view was granted, which was a delay to the demandant in dower (whoſe life did ſpend) and is taken away by this act.

30 E. 3. fo. 8.

If the baron demiſe to a feme and dieth, the feme taketh huſband, in dower againſt them they ſhall have the view; for the alienation was not made to the huſband, but to the wife, and the act ſaith *tenenti.*

2 H. 4. 1. 7 H. 4. 18. 5 E. 3. 6. 18 E. 3. 55. 30 E. 3. 3. 26 E. 3. 59. 2 E. 4. 17. 9 E. 4. 6.

(8) *Alienavit.*] If the tenant diſſeiſed the huſband of the demandant in a writ of dower, he ſhall have the view, for this is no alienation, and therefore remain at the common law.

The beſt pleading to counterplead the view in caſe of alienation is, that the tenant entred by her huſband, though the word of the act is aliened.

[482]

44 E. 3. 31. 18 E. 3. 55. 14 H. 4. 32. 3 H. 4. 18. 19 E. 2. view 76. 13 E. 3. ib. 103, 104. 14 E. 3. ibid. 93. 19 E. 3. ibid. 106.

In dower of a rent the tenant ſhall not have the view of the land, if the huſband died ſeiſed of the rent, nor the tenant of the land have view thereof, if he had the rent by the releaſe of her huſband.

Tenant in dower of two acres, the demandant to counterplead the view ſaid, that the tenant entred by her huſband, the jury found, that ſhe entred into one acre by her huſband, and into the other acre by another, the demandant recovered her dower in the one acre, and the tenant had the view for the other.

20 E. 2. view 166. 29 E. 3. 32. 2 E. 2. view 137.

(9) *In brevi etiam de ingreſſu caſſato per hoc*, &c.] A *cui in vita* is taken within this branch, and ſo is a *ſur cui in vita.*

(10) *In omnibus brevibus per quæ tenementa petuntur ratione dimiſſionis, quam petens vel anteceſſor fecerit tenenti et non ejus anteceſſori; ſicut quod ei dimiſit dum fuit infra ætatem, dum non fuit compos mentis,* &c.] This branch ſpeaketh particularly of three examples, *viz.* of the *dum fuit infra ætatem, et non compos mentis,* and *in priſona,* and generally *in conſimilibus.*

48 E. 3. 31. 46 E. 3. 34. 35 H. 6. 59.

29 E. 3. 30. view 155.

This branch extends not to theſe writs brought in the *per et cui*; for that is a degree further then this branch provideth for.

46 E. 3. 29.

(11) *Per quæ tenementa petuntur.*] Yet if any of theſe writs be brought of a rent, if the tenant demaund the view of the land, though it be of another thing, then is demanded, the tenant ſhall be ouſted of the view.

Circumſpecte agatis, ſimile. Temps E. 1. view 171. 6 E. 2. ibid. 152. 36 H. 6. view 30.

(12) *Et conſimilibus.*] By theſe words the predeceſſor of a biſhop, or the like is taken where this branch ſpeaketh *de anteceſſore* and not *de prædeceſſore.*

It is to be obſerved that the two examples here put are of a *dum fuit infra ætatem,* and *non compos mentis,* and when the heire brings either of theſe writs of the demiſe of his aunceſtor from whom he claimes the land as heire [*et conſimilibus*] ſhall be intended of writs of like nature; and therefore if a *ſur cui in vita* be brought ſuppoſing that the tenant had not entred but by one D. late huſband of E. mother to the demandant, whoſe heire he is, the tenant ſhall

shall have the view, for he claimeth not as heire to him that made the demise, and therefore it is not *actio consimilis*.

(13) *In prisona.*] At this time, *viz.* in 13 E. 1. as hereby it appeareth there lay a writ of an alienation made by dures, *dum fuit in prisona*, and the writ of *dum fuit infra ætatem*, and this writ of *dum fuit in prisona* did lie for the party himselfe that made the alienation, but so doth not the other writ of *non compos mentis*, for that lieth not for the party himselfe, but for his heire.

Bract. l. 2. fo. 16. b. Brit. f. 19. Flet. li. 2. ca. 54. l. 3. ca. 7. l. 6. ca. 6. 7. & 14. First part of the Inst. § 437, 438.

In prisona; every restraint of the liberty of a freeman is an imprisonment, although he be not within the wals of any common prison.

First part of the Inst. sect. 406.

If a man be imprisoned by order of law, the plaintiffe may take a feoffement of him or a bond for his satisfaction, and for the deliverance of the defendant, notwithstanding that imprisonment, for this is not by dures of imprisonment, because he was in prison by course of law; for it is not accounted in law dures of imprisonment, but where either the imprisonment or the dures that is offered in the prison, or at large is torcious and unlawfull, for *executio juris non habet injuriam*.

15 H. 3. dures 15. 2 E. 2. ibid. 18. 8 E. 3. 57. 8 Ass. 25. 43 E. 3. 6. 10. 6 R. 2. dures 12. 11 H. 4. 6. 4 E. 4. 17. 12 E. 4. 7.

But now albeit the writ mentioned in this act is antiquated and gone *in desuetudinem*, yet may good use be made of this part of this branch, *dum fuit in prisona*, such excellent learning may be drawn out of these auncient fountains.

It may be gathered upon this act that the feoffement made by one by dures of imprisonment is not void, but voidable; for if it were void, then no præcipe could have been maintained upon a void alienation, and this branch saith, *in omnibus brevibus in quibus tenementa petuntur ratione dimissionis, &c. dum fuit in prisona*. And so it is in the case of the infant, with whom he is paralleled in this branch, and whose cases are very like in many respects: for as in the case of an infant, if he seal and deliver a deed, he cannot plead *non est factum*, but must avoid it by plea of infancie; so it is in the case of a bond made by dures of imprisonment: and as it is in the case of the infant, that a feoffment by livery of seisin made by his own hand is voidable by entry, or action and not void; so it is in the case of a feoffment made by one by dures of imprisonment, and livery made by his own hand, as by this branch it appeareth: and as in the case of an infant, a feoffment made by letter of attorney is void, and the feoffee is a disseisor; so it is in the case of a man that maketh it in the same manner by dures of imprisonment.

[483]

Lib. 5. fo. 119. Whelpdales case. 1 H. 7. 15.

Lib. 8. fo. 42, 43, &c. Whittingams case. 14 Ass. p. 20. 39 E. 3. 28. 41 E. 3. 9. Feoffment & Faits 49. 9 H. 6. 6. 38 H. 6. 27. 2 E. 4. 21. Whittingams case, ubi supra.

And as none shall avoid the feoffment of the infant when livery is made by his own hand, but onely he himself or his heirs, which are privies in bloud inheritable, and neither privies in law, nor privies in estate: so it is in case of a feoffment made in like manner by dures of imprisonment, it is onely voidable by privies in blood inheritable, and not by privies in law or estate.

And by these resemblances and diversities this act is understood, and our books that seem *prima facie* are well reconciled: the *dures per minas, aut causa metus*, belongeth not properly to be treated of here; for this branch speaketh onely *dum fuit in prisona*; onely for affinity sake it is to be known, that a man shall avoid his deed for manuas of imprisonment, albeit he were never imprisoned: for a man shall avoid his own act for manuas in four cases, *viz.* 1. for fear of losse of life, 2. of losse of member, 3. of mayhem, and 4. of imprisonment;

39 E. 3. 28. 11 R. 2. Dures 21. 35 H. 6. 17. 38 H. 6. 21. 27. 39 H. 6. 5. 7 E. 4. 21.

imprisonment; otherwise it is for fear of battery, which may be very light, or for burning of his houses, or taking away, or destroying of his goods, or the like, for there he may have satisfaction by recovery of damages.

Bract. l. 2. fo. 16. b.

This fear, by reason of manuas, is well described by Bracton, *Metus autem est præsentis, vel futuri periculi causa, mentis trepidatio, et præsentem debemus accipere metum, non suspicionem inferendi ejus, vel cujuslibet vani et meticulosi hominis, sed talem qui cadere possit in virum constantem; talis enim debet esse metus, qui in se continet mortis periculum, et corporis cruciatum.*

13 H. 4. Dures 20. 1. Part of the Institutes, §419.

But there is a great diversity between the making of a continuall claim, or entry into lands, and the avoiding of a mans own act; for, fear of battery is a good cause to make a claim as neer the land as he dare for fear of battery (for the recontinuance of an ancient right is favoured in law) but it is no cause to avoid his own act; wherein it is observable, how fear of imprisonment (which is a manner of captivity) is more grievous and odious in law, then the fear of battery.

* See the stat. de modo levand. Fines. Li. 4. f. 127, &c. Beverlies case. Rot. Parliam. 50 E. 3. nu. 127. 6 E. 3. 39. 17 E. 3. 76. 17 Ass. 17. 13 E. 3. Audita querela 26. 20 E. 3. ibid. 27. 18 E. 3. 29. 21 E. 3. 24. 27 Ass. 53. 8 H. 6. 30. 15 E. 4. 5. 1 H. 7. 15. 16 H. 7. 5. b. 6 H. 8. Saver def. Br. 50. F.N.B. 104. k. l. 16 Eliz. Dier. 3 H. 6. 10. 7 H. 6. 38.

See more of this matter in the first part of the Institutes, *ubi supra.*

(14) *Rationе dimissionis.*] Here, as in many other places [demise] is applyed to an estate either in fee simple, fee-tail, or for term of life, and so commonly it is taken in many writs.

* But this act extendeth not to every kinde of demise or conveyance; for if the demise or conveyance be by fine or other matter of record, &c. this branch extends not to it, for regularly conveyances, or other acts of record knowledged, or made by one that is *non compos mentis*, or by dures of imprisonment, are unavoidable by him or his heirs by law: hereof see Beverleys case, lib. 4. fol. 127.

And such conveyances, or other acts of record knowledged, or made by an infant, are also unavoidable, unlesse he doth avoid them by writ of errour, or *audita querela*, during his minority; and therefore this branch is to be understood of alienations made *in paiis*, and not by matter of record.

[484]

1. Part of the Institutes, §438.

A recovery by default against an infant is erroneous, and so is a recovery by default against a man in prison, though he be lawfully imprisoned; but the infant must reverse it by writ of errour during his minority, because his infancie must be tryed by inspection, but the man in prison may reverse it when he will.

CAP. XLIX.

CHANCELLOR, treasurer, justices, ne nul de councel (1) le roy, ne clerke de la chauncery, ne del escheqer, ne de justice, ne dauter minister, ne nul del hostel le roy, ne clerk, ne lay, ne puis resceiver esglise, ne advowson de esglise, ne terre, ne tenement in fee per

THE chancellor, treasurer, justices, nor any of the king's council, no clerk of the chancery, nor of the exchequer, nor of any justice or other officer, nor any of the king's house, clerk ne lay, shall not receive any church, nor advowson of a church, land,

per done, ne per achate, ne a ferm', ne a champerty, ne en auter maner, tanque come le chose est en plee devant nous, ou devant ull' de nous ministr', ne nul lower ent soit pris. Et qui encounter cest chose face, ou per luy ou per auter, ou nul [bargeine ent] *face, soit punie a la volunt le roy* (2), *auxibien celuy qui le purchasera, come celuy qui le fra* (3). 11 E. 1. Champertie 1. Articuli super Chartas, cap. 11.

land, nor tenement in fee, by gift, nor by purchase, nor to farm, nor by champerty, nor otherwise, so long as the thing is in plea before us, or before any of our officers; nor shall take no reward thereof. And he that doth contrary to this act, either himself, or by another, or make any bargain, shall be punished at the king's pleasure, as well he that purchaseth, as he that doth sell.

(Fitz. Champerty, 1. 5, 6. 8. 12. 14, 15. Hob. 117. 3 Ed. 1. c. 25. 28 Ed. 1. c. 11. Regist. 182, 183. Rast. 119. 33 Ed. 1. stat. 2 & 3.)

(1) *Chancellor, treasurer, justices, ne nul de councel,* &c.] This is a law of addition and explanation for the statute of W. 1. cap. 25. *Purveiant que nul minister le roy, &c.* It was doubted, whether the chancellour, treasurer, justices, and those of the kings councell, being persons of such eminencie, were within these words [*nul minister le roy,*] and therefore this act by way of addition and explanation doth adde, *chancellor, treasurer, justices, et councell le roy.*

Also this act is an addition to W. 1. cap. 28. for that extendeth but to the clerks of the king, or of the justices; this act addeth, clerks of the chancery, and of the exchequer, and of any other officer; it addeth also those of the kings house, be they of the clergie or laity; and also that they shall take no reward, &c.

And it is to be observed, that neither the chancellor, treasurer, any of the justices, or any of the kings councell, nor any clerk herein mentioned, nor any of the kings house of the clergie or laity shall (hanging the plea) receive any advowson, land or tenement, by gift, purchase or fearm, either for champerty or otherwise; so as none of these persons here prohibited can acquire any advowson, land, or tenement, depending the plea, though it be *bona fide*, and not for champerty or maintenance; partly in respect of their greatnesse, and partly in respect of their places, both in the kings court, and in the courts of justice; so as the very countenance and places of these men, when they become interessed in the land *(eo ipso)* are apparent hinderances of the due and indifferent proceeding of law and justice. An excellent law and worthy to be known, and most necessary to be put in execution; so as true it is, that if any other person purchase *bona fide*, depending the suit, he is not in danger of champerty: but these persons here prohibited cannot purchase at all, neither for champerty nor otherwise, depending the plea. But these persons here prohibited must be charged upon this act, and not for champerty, unlesse they maintain.

50 Ass. p. 3. 32 E. 3. Champerty 6. where the cases were of some of these persons, otherwise they could not be law.

4 E 2. ibid. 12, &c. F.N.B. 172. E. 22 E. 3. 10. 8 E. 4. 1.

[485]

And this is a great addition to the statute of W. 1. cap. 25. which extended onely where the purchaser *(pendente placito)* did maintain.

6 E. 3. 33. F.N.B. 172. Pl. Com. 88.

And in these cases prohibited by this law, the childe cannot infeoffe the father, nor the father his childe, or the like, as they may do upon the other statutes.

And

And the prohibition here for taking of rewards is very remarkable.

(2) *Soit punie a la volunt le roy.*] These words are expounded before upon W. 1. cap. 25.

See the statute of Conspiracie, Simile. 33 E. 1. 32 H. 8. cap. 9. Simile.

And where both the said statutes conclude in effect concerning the punishment, *Et que le fra*; this act addeth, *auxibien celuy que le purchasera, come celuy que le fra*, that is, both the giver, and the taker.

W. 1. ca. 25. 28. 28 E. 1. ca. 11. 32 H. 8. ca. 9.

See the statute of W. 1. cap. 25. & 28. and the statute of 28 E. 1. cap. 11. and lastly, the statute of 32 H. 8. cap. 9. whereby all former statutes concerning maintenance, champerty, and imbracery are confirmed, and commanded to be put in due execution, and by that statute excellent provisions are made concerning the same.

31 E. 3. Champerty 5. See the statute of 11 E. 3. Vet. Magna Chart. stat. de Champerty.

(3) *Auxibien celuy que le purchasera, come celuy que le fra.*] And yet the party grieved may have his action against the purchaser onely, if he will.

We have been the more brief in exposition hereof, because we have treated of this subject before in the exposition of the statute of W. 1. cap. 25. & 28. and shall have more occasion to speak hereof when we come to the said act of 28 E. 1. cap. 11.

The cause wherefore this chapter was published in French, was, for that the said two chapters of W. 1. whereunto this act maketh additions, were likewise published in French.

See *articuli super chartas*, cap. 11.

CAP. L.

OMNIA prædicta statuta incipiant conservari (1) *ad festum Sancti Michaelis* (2) *proximo venturum, ita quod occasione aliquorum delictorum contra aliquod prædictorum statutorum citra prædictum festum perpetratorum, pœna delinquentibus, de quibus mentio fit in statutis, non infligatur. Super vero statutis in defectum legis, et ad remedia editis, ne diutius querentes cum ad curiam regis venerint recedant de remedio* (4) *desperati, habeant brevia sua in suo casu provisa* (3), *sed non placitent' usq; post festum Sancti Michaelis supradictum.*

ALL the said statutes shall take effect at the feast of St. Michael next coming, so that by occasion of any offence done on this side the said feast, contrary to any of these statutes, no punishment (mention whereof is made within these statutes) shall be executed upon the offenders. Moreover, concerning the statutes provided where the law faileth, and for remedies, lest suitors coming to the king's court should depart from thence without remedy, they shall have writs provided in their cases, but they shall not be pleaded until the feast of St. Michael aforesaid.

(1) *Omnia prædicta statuta incipiant conservari*, &c.] This was very justly added, to the intent that all men dwelling far or neer might be well informed of these laws before they were punished by them; the parliament begun *post Pasch.* and hereby day was given untill the feast of Saint Michael.

(2) *Ad*

(2) *Ad feſtum Sancti Michaelis.*] Albeit there be two feaſts of Saint Michael, Saint Michael the Archangel, and Saint Michael *de monte tumba,* commonly called, Saint Michaels in the mount in Cornwall; yet that feaſt * that is moſt notorious and of greateſt account is to be taken, and that is the feaſt of Saint Michael th'archangell celebrated on the 29 day of September, and not the feaſt celebrated the 16 day of November. 5 E. 3. 6. 20 H. 6 23. 3 H. 7. Endictment 22. 1. Part of the Inſtitutes, § 99.

Note, that both were the feaſts of Saint Michael th'archangel, but the feaſt of Saint Michael the 29 of September is the moſt notorious, both in legall proceedings, as *octabis Michaelis, &c.* and never *octabis Michaelis arch'*; and common eſtimation for payment of rents, beginning and ending of leaſes, and the like. Cambden Brit. 136, 137.

(3) *Super vero ſtatutis in defectum legis et ad remedia editis, ne diutius querentes, cum ad curiam regis venerint, recedant de remedio deſperati, habeant brevia ſua in ſuo caſu proviſa.*] *Ad remedia*; that is when any the ſtatutes made at this parliament provide remedy for the party grieved, he ſhall have an action grounded upon this act for his relief therein; and theſe words [*ad remedia*] do diſtinguiſh them from thoſe acts which give the penalty to the king alone. And hereupon they are called in ancient authors, *breve remedialia,* which are to be framed upon theſe acts by learned men, whereof Fleta ſpeaking of the maſters of the chancery, ſaith, *Ipſi autem collaterales et ſocii cancellarii eſſe; dicuntur præceptores eo quod brevia (cauſis examinatis) remedialia fieri præcipiunt.* Fleta, li. 1. c. 13. And ſometimes they are called, *brevia magiſtralia,* becauſe (being out of courſe) it is a maſters piece to frame them as they ought, Bract. li. 5. fo. 413.

(4) *Recedant de remedio.*] See before in the expoſition upon the 24 chapter of W. 2. the like clauſe.

---

[487]

STATUTUM de CIRCUMSPECTE AGATIS.

Editum Anno 13 *Edw.* 1.

REX talibus judicibus ſalutem. Circumſpecte agatis (1) *de negotiis tangentibus epiſcopum Norwicenſem* (2), *et ejus clerum, non puniend' eos ſi placitum tenuerint in curia Chriſtianitatis* (3) *de his quæ mere ſunt ſpiritualia* (4), *viz. de correctionibus quas prælati faciunt pro mortali peccato, viz. pro fornicatione, adulterio* (5) *et hujuſmodi* (6); *pro quibus aliquando infligitur pœna corporalis, aliquando pecuniaria* (7), *maxime ſi convictus fuerit de hujuſmodi liber homo. Item ſi prælatus puniat pro cimeterio non clauſo, eccleſia diſcooperta* (9), *vel non decenter*

THE king to his judges ſendeth greeting. Uſe yourſelves circumſpectly in all matters concerning the biſhop of Norwich and his clergy, not puniſhing them if they hold plea in court chriſtian of ſuch things as be meer ſpiritual, that is to wit, of penance enjoined by prelates for deadly ſin, as fornication, adultry, and ſuch like, for the which ſometimes corporal penance, and ſometime pecuniary is enjoined, ſpecially if a freeman be convict of ſuch things. Alſo if prelates do puniſh for leaving the church-yard uncloſed, or for that the

decenter ornata (8), *in quibus caſibus alia pœna non poteſt infligi quam pecuniaria. Item ſi rector petat verſus parochianos oblationes* (10) *et decimas* (11) *debitas vel conſuetas* (12), *vel ſi rector agat contra rectorem de decimis majoribus, vel minoribus, dummodo non petatur quarta pars* (13) *valoris eccleſiæ. Item ſi rector petat mortuarium* (14) *in partibus ubi mortuarium dari conſuevit. Item ſi prælatus alicujus eccleſiæ, vel advocatus petat à rectore penſionem* (15) *ſibi debitam, omnes hujuſmodi petitiones ſunt faciend' in foro eccleſiaſtico. De violentia manuum injectione in clericum* (16), *et in cauſa diffamationis conceſſum fuit alias* (17), *quod placitum inde teneatur in curia chriſtianitatis, cum non petatur pecunia, ſed agatur ad correctionem peccati, et ſimiliter pro fidei læſione* (18). *In omnibus prædictis caſibus habet judex eccleſiaſticus cognoſcere regia prohibitione non obſtante.*

the church is uncovered, or not conveniently decked, in which caſes none other penance can be enjoined but pecuniary. Item, if a parſon demand of his pariſhioners oblations or tithes due and accuſtomed, or if any parſon do ſue againſt another parſon for tithes greater or ſmaller, ſo that the fourth part of the value of the benefice be not demanded. Item, if a parſon demand mortuaries in places where a mortuary hath been uſed to be given. Item, if a prelate of a church, or of a patron, demand of a parſon a penſion due to him; all ſuch demands are to be made in a ſpiritual court. And for laying violent hands on a clerk, and in cauſe of defamation, it hath been granted already, that it ſhall be tried in a ſpiritual court, when money is not demanded, but a thing done for puniſhment of ſin, and likewiſe for breaking an oath. In all caſes afore rehearſed, the ſpiritual judge ſhall have power to take knowledge, notwithſtanding the king's prohibition.

(13 Rep. 41. 7 Rep. 44. 5 Rep. 67. 8 Ed. 4. 13. Fitz. Prohibition, 18. 20. 4 Rep. 20. Kel. 39. 22 Ed. 4. f. 20. Bro. Prohibicion, 18. 21. Bro. Act, ſur le caſe, 115. 38 H. 6. f. 29. 11 H. 4. f. 88. Regiſt. 36. 45. 50, 51. 57, &c. Raſt. pla. 483. 9 Ed. 2. ſtat. 1. c. 1.

Rot. Parl. 25 E. 3. Stat. 3. nu. 62. 19 E. 3. juriſd. 28. 27 Aſſ. p. 7. 10 H. 4. 1. 12 H. 7. 23. Pl. Com. 36. b. 2 E. 6. c. 13. verſus finem. l. 4. f. l. 47. inter Palmer & Thorp. l. 5. fol. 67. l. 7. fol. 44. Pl. Com. 36. b.

(1) *Circumſpecte agatis.*] There was alſo at this parliament holden at Weſtm' anno 13 E. 1. a writ deviſed, called *circumſpecte agatis de negotiis tangentibus epiſcopum Norwicenſem, et ejus clerum.*

Though ſome have ſaid that this was no ſtatute, but made by the prelates themſelves, yet that this is an act of parliament, it is proved not onely by our books, but alſo by an act of parliament.

(2) *De negotiis tangentibus epiſcopum Norwicenſem.*]

The biſhop of Norwich is here put but for example; but it extendeth to all the biſhops within this realme.

*[488] Glanv. l. 12. ca. 21. Bract. l. 5. fo. 463. & ſæpe alibi. Britton 226. & ſæpe alibi. Fleta lib. 6. ca. 41. Regiſt. 330. W. 2. cap. 5. 2 E. 3. 27. Smith de rep. Anglorum. l. 3. ca. 9.

*(3) *In curia chriſtianitatis.*] So called, becauſe as in the ſecular courts the kings lawes doe ſway and decide cauſes, ſo in eccleſiaſticall courts the lawes of Chriſt ſhould rule and direct, for which cauſe the judges in thoſe courts are divines, as archbiſhops, biſhops, archdeacons, &c. Linwoods words are theſe, *In curia chriſtianitatis, i. eccleſiæ, in qua ſervantur leges Chriſti, cum tamen in foro regio ſerventur leges mundi. In libro rubeo in ſcaccar' inter leges* H. 1. thus it is contained, *Sicut antiqua fuerat inſtitutione formatum ſalutari regis imperio vera nuper eſt recordatione formatum generalia comitatuum placita certis locis et vicibus, &c. interſint autem epiſcopi, comites, vicedomini, vicarii, centenarii, aldermani, præfecti, præpoſiti,*

præpoſiti, barones, vavaſores, tingrevii, et cæteri terrarum domini diligenter intendentes, ne malorum impunitas, aut gravionum pravitas, vel judicum ſubverſio ſolita miſeros laceratione confiniant. Agantur primo debita veræ chriſtianitatis jura, ſecundo regis placita, poſtremo cauſæ ſingulorum dignis ſatisfactionibus expleantur.

F. N. B. 41, &c. Linwood de foro compet. cap. Circumſpecte agatis, fol. 71. Liber rub. in cuſtod. rem. regis. cap. 48. fol. 41.

And if any deſire to look before the conqueſt concerning this matter, he may read amongſt the laws publiſhed by king Edgar, *Celeberrimus autem ex omni ſatrapia conventus bis quotannis agitor, cui quidem illius dioceſis epiſcopus et aldermanus interſunto, quorum alter jura divina, alter humana populum edoceto.*

Int' leges Regis Edgari cap. 5. Lamb. verbo Senator, Alderman, or Elderman. i. Senator, which ſignifieth the Sherive, i. Præpoſitus, ſeu cuſtos comitatus.

Thus much by reaſon of this word [*chriſtianitatis*] having been ſaid, let us return to our act.

(4) *Mere ſpiritualia.*] *Sic dicta, quia non habent mixturam temporalium:* they are here called meere ſpirituall, for that they have no mixture of the temporalties, and becauſe they are corrections *pro ſalute animæ.*

Britton ſaith, *Que ſeint eſgliſe eyt conuſance de juger de pure ſpiritualite;* hereſie, ſchiſmes, holy orders, and the like are mere ſpirituall things; note it appeareth by the conſtitution of John Stratford, archbiſhop of Canterbury in a ſynod in London *anno domini* 1380. §. *quidam etiam,* &c. that adminiſtration of the goods of a man dying inteſtate, was granted to ordinaries, *conſenſu regis et magnatum regni Angliæ tanquam pro jure et eccleſiaſtica libertate ab olim extiterit ordinatum.* And Linwood ſaith, that probate of teſtaments, *de conſuetudine Angliæ, et non de jure communi,* belong to court chriſtian: which I have added for three cauſes.

Britton fol. 11. b. Bracton l. 5. fol. 403, &c. Fleta l. 2. cap. 53. l. 6. ca. 36. &c. Linwood cap. de foro compet. fol. 7. li. 7. fo. 44. Kennes Caſe. See hereafter in this Chapter verbo Mortuary. Linwood ubi ſup.

1. That theſe things being temporall, and not meere ſpirituall, as our act ſpeaketh, belonged *not ab initio* to the court chriſtian.

2. That the eccleſiaſticall judges derive their juriſdiction therein by parliament, and the cuſtome of the realme, and not from any foreign power.

3. And laſtly, that herewith our records and books doe accord and agree.

2 R. 2. tit. Teſtam. 4. 12 H. 7. 12. b.

(5) *Pro mortali peccato, viz. fornicatione, adulterio,* &c.] There be two examples put in particular of meere ſpiritualty for correction of theſe offences.

See hereafter verbo Mortuary.

In ancient time the kings courts, and ſpecially the leets had power to enquire of, and puniſh fornication and adultery by the name of Letherwite, and it appeareth often in the book of Domeſday that the king had the fines aſſeſſed for thoſe offences which were aſſeſſed in the kings courts, and could not be inflicted *in curia chriſtianitatis.*

(6) *Et hujuſmodi.*] Theſe are to be taken for offences of like nature, as the two offences here particularly expreſſed be, as ſolicitation of any womans chaſtity, which is leſſer then theſe, and for inceſt, which is greater; and herewith agreeth Linwood, who expounding this act ſaith, *Non intelligas de omni mortali peccato, ſed de tali, cujus punitio de ſua natura ſpectat ad forum eccleſiaſticum; nam ſi de ratione cujuſlibet peccati mortalis cognoſceret eccleſia, ſic periret temporalis gladii juriſdictio.*

Linwood ubi ſup. Kennes caſe ubi ſupra.

(7) *Pro quibus aliquando infligitur pœna corporalis, aliquando pecuniaria.*] Here *pœna pecuniaria* muſt be intended by way of commutation of penance, as it is clearly expounded by the ſtatute of *Articuli Cleri*; *item ſi prælatus imponat pœnam pecuniariam alicui*

[489] Art. Cleri, cap. 2. Britton 11. b. F. N. B. 53. a.

alicui pro peccato, et repetat illam, regia probibitio locum habeat: and so doth Britton take it.

Vet. Mag. Chart. *Vide artic' contra probibit' regiam Vet' Magna Charta, pro cæmeterio non clauso.*

Register. Brit. fo. 11. lib. 5. fo. 67. Jeffreys case.] The parishioners ought to repaire the inclosure of the church-yard, because the bodies of the more common sort are buried there, and for the preservation of the burials of those, that were, or should have been whiles they lived the temples of the Holy Ghost: and *cæmeterium* is derived of the Greek verb κοιμάω, that is, *dormio*, and therefore *cæmeterium est quasi dormitorium, quia mortui dormire dicuntur usque ad resurrectionem.* And also if the church-yard be not decently inclosed, the church which is *domus Dei* cannot decently be kept, and therefore this the parishioners ought to doe *per consuetudinem notoriam et approbatam,* and the conusans thereof is allowed by this act.

Regist. 44. b.

(8) *Ecclesia discooperta, vel non decenter ornata.*] In the same manner the parishioners by this act ought to repaire the church, for that it is the place where divine service is celebrated, and the bodies of the parishioners of the best quality are buried; in respect whereof this law doth allow the ecclesiasticall court to have conusans thereof, and for the providing of decent ornaments for the celebration of divine service.

Regist. ubi supra. F. N. B. 50. n. Britton fol. 11. (9) *Ecclesia discooperta.*] This is intended not onely of the body of the church, which is parochiall, but also of any publique chappell annexed to it; but it extendeth not to the private chappell of any, though it be fixed to the church, for that must be repaired by him that hath the proper use of it; for *qui sentit commodum, sentire debet et onus*; and this the parishioners ought to doe *per consuetudinem notoriam et approbatam,* and the conusans thereof is allowed to them by this act, but the chauncell is to be repaired by the parson, &c.

Regist. 44. b.

Art' contra proh. regiam Vet Mag. Chart. Art. Cleri cap. 1, 2. 2 E. 6. cap. 13. (10) *Oblationes, decimas debitas, vel consuetas.*] *Oblationes* in the canon law are thus defined:

Oblationes dicuntur quæcunque à piis fidelibusq; Christianis offeruntur Deo et ecclesiæ, sive res solid', sive mobiles.

Cap. Cler. quæst. 13. Regist. fol. 29. & 35. F. N. B. 30. b. (11) *Decimæ.*] It appeareth by the auncient writ, *de recto de advocatione decimarum,* and by the like ancient writ of *indicavit,* whereof you may reade before in W. 2. cap. 5. *versus finem,* that the right of tithes was tried in the kings court.

† 18 E. 3 cap. 7. F. N. B. 30. g. 4 E. 3. 27. 38 E. 3. 13. 38. H. 6. 20. † And this appeareth by an act of parliament in *anno* 18 E. 3. cap. 7. and it is agreed in 4 E. 3. that before the statute (meaning W. 2. cap. 5.) every parson was ousted to demand tithes in court Christian.

Bract. li. 5. fo. 401. Brit. ubi supra. Bracton lib. 5. fol. 401. saith, *quod decimæ sunt spiritualitati annexæ:* and Britton, who was bishop of Hereford, and learned in the lawes of this realme, treating of what things the church hath conusans, omitteth tithes.

‡ Int' leges Edw. Regis, cap. 8. fol. 128. having spoken of tithes, it is said, *Hæc prædicavit beatus Augustinus et concessa sunt à rege baronibus et populo.*

Hereby it appeareth that the recitall in the statute of 1 R. 2. that pursuit for tithes of right ought, and of ancient time did pertaine to the spirituall court, must bee intended by force of former acts of ‡ parliament, (as things annexed to the spiritualty) as of W. 2. of this act made in * 13 E. 1. *articuli cleri,* cap. 1. &c. 18 E. 3. cap. 1. and is confirmed by later acts of parliament, as 27 H. 8. cap. 20. 32 H. 8. cap. 7. and 2 E. 6. cap. 13.

Now of tithes there be three kindes, prediall, perſonall, and mixt, and this act extendeth to them all, and for perſonall tithes ſee the ſtatute of 2 E. 6. cap. 13.

And true it is, that of auncient time the parſons did ſue for ſubtraction of tithes in court chriſtian, but if the right of tithes had come in queſtion, it ſhould have been tried by the common law; and therefore *in libro rubeo inter leges Henr.* 1. ſpeaking of purſute for tithes in court chriſtian, it is ſaid, *ſi rex patiatur*; but at this day it is without queſtion, as hath been ſaid, that for ſubſtraction of tithes the conuſans by force of divers acts of parliament doth belong to the eccleſiaſticall court.

(12) *Vel conſuetas.* By this act *modus decimandi*, reall compoſition, or by preſcription, or cuſtome is eſtabliſhed, for hereby are tithes divided into two parts, *in decimas debitas*, and that is *quota pars*, the tenth part, and into *decimas conſuetas*, and that is a duty perſonall due by cuſtome and uſage to the parſon, &c. in ſatisfaction of tithes; as a yearely ſumme of money, or other duty, and theſe are here called *decimæ conſuetæ*, and for this *modus decimandi* the parſon, &c. may ſue in court chriſtian, and is warranted by this act. See the act of 2 E. 6. cap. 13. 39 E. 3. juriſ. 8 E. 4. 14. 7 E. 6. 79. Doct. & Stud. 166, 167.

There is alſo a reall ſatisfaction for tithes, as if of ancient time land hath been given by the conſent of the patron and ordinary to the parſon and his ſucceſſors in ſatisfaction of tithes out of other lands, this is alſo a good diſcharge of tithes, but for this or the like reall ſatisfaction he cannot ſue in court chriſtian, but at the common law: of this reall ſatisfaction you may reade a notable record in 25 H. 3. which was before the making of this act, and the effect thereof is this: 8 E. 4. ubi ſupra. F. N. B. 41, 43. Mich. 25 H. 3. Coram Rege Rot. 5. Wilteſh.

Sampſon Foliot brought a prohibition againſt Thomas parſon of Swindon, *quare ſecutus eſt in curia chriſtianitatis de laico feodo ipſius Sampſon in Draicot, &c.* the defendant pleaded that *non eſt ſecutus placitum*, &c. *de laico feodo, ſed verum vult dicere, et dicit quod revera coram judicibus delegatis petiit ab eodem decimas feni de quodam prato in Walcot infra parochiam ſuam de Walcot, &c. et nihil petiit in parochia de Draicot, &c. Et Sampſon dicit quod anteceſſores ſui antiquitus dederunt 2. acras prati eccleſiæ de Draicot, pro decima feni, quam prædictus Thomas petit, et in eodem prato, quas eadem eccleſia adhuc habet, et ſemper hucuſque habuit, unde videtur quod illud quod prædictus Thomas petit decimas eſt in laico feodo, et quod pratum illud de quo idem Thomas petit decimas eſt in Draicot ſicut breve dicit et non in Walcot, et de hoc ponit ſe ſuper patriam*, &c. Whereupon ſeverall iſſues being joined, the jury gave this verdict, that the ſaid Thomas purſued his plea *in curia chriſtianitatis de laico feodo prædict' Sampſon, &c. pretendo ab eo decimas feni*, of the ſaid meadow of the ſaid Sampſon in Draicot, *unde anteceſſores ſui dederunt eccleſiæ de Draicot duas acras prati pro decima feni quam prædict' Thomas modo petit, et quas eadem eccleſia adhuc habet, et ſemper hucuſque habuit.* And found that the ſaid meadow, &c. did lie in Draicot, &c. and thereupon judgement is given for the plaintiffe in the prohibition, and that he ſhould recover 20. marks damages, &c. Which record, both for the antiquity thereof, and for that it agreeth with our books, being a leading caſe, I have recited the more at large. See the Regiſter fo. 34. and Glanv. li. 12. cap. 21. for this forme of writ. See the like ground of prohibition, Regiſt. fol. 38. 8 H. 6. 14. 8 E. 4. 14. F. N. B. 41. g. & 43. k. That bounds of pariſhes are to be tried by the common law. 29 E. 3. 23. 14 H. 4. 17. 5 H. 5. 18. 34 H. 6. 10, 11. 22 E. 4. 24. 12 H. 7. 22.

A man ſeiſed of 8. acres of meadow, and one of paſture, for the tithes whereof he hath been paid time out of mind v. s. iv. d. afterwards the owner builds a cornmill upon the ſame, he ſhall pay no tithes for the cornmill, becauſe the land was diſcharged *per* Mich. 26 and 27 El. in Commu. Banc. Rot 2617. Lords caſe adjudged.

45 E. 3. c. 31 H. 8. cap. 2 E. 6. ca. 13. 9 H. 5. fol. 9. 50 E. 3. 10. [491] M. 9 E. 1. Incip. 10. in com' banc. Rot. 63. Somerſet.

modum decimandi: what things be indecimable by the law, and ought not to pay tithe, vide lib. 11. fol. 48, 49. F. N. B. 53. g. &c. ſee the ſtatute of 45 E. 3. 31 H. 8. cap. and 2 E. 6. cap. 13. for diſcharge of tithes. I have read of an ancient concord *de modo decimandi,* which is worthy to be read at large, whereof we will give you the effect, *Concordia fact' inter Willum Mallet, et rectorem eccleſiæ de Aure, Heyton, Bathon' et Wellen' dioces' ex una parte, et nobilem virum Johannem de Acton militem ex altera, de modo decimandi omnia in parochia de Aure per conſenſum epiſcopi, et capituli Bathon' et Wellen', unde placitum fuit prius in cur' captum.*

See W. 2. c. 5.

(13) *Dummodo non petatur 4. pars.*] So as at this day in caſe when one perſon of the preſentation of one patron demand tithes againſt another perſon of the preſentation of another patron in court chriſtian, amounting to a fourth part, &c. the right of tithes at this day is to be tryed at the common law.

Brit. fol. 11. b. Artic. Cler. c. 1. 10 H. 4. 1.

(14) *Mortuarie.*] Or, *a corſe preſent. Mortuarium* is a gift left by a man at his death, *pro recompenſatione ſubtractionis decimarū perſonalium, et oblationū.*

2 H. 5. 10. 21 H. 8. cap. 6.

In 2 H. 5. the opinion was againſt the mortuaries, becauſe they were not contained in the ſtatute (meaning *Artic' Cleri.*)

There is no mortuary due by law, but onely by cuſtome, which is proved by the words of this act, *viz. ubi mortuarium dari conſuevit.* And this act alloweth the conuſans thereof to court chriſtian.

21 H. 8. cap. 6.

See the ſtatute of 21 H. 8. cap. 6. where mortuaries ought to be paid, for what perſons, and how much, and in what caſe none is due.

Inter communia Hil. 2 E. 2. in Scacc. poſt mort. epiſ. Bath & Wel. Tr. 36 E. 3. ib. poſt mortem epiſc. Cirenceſt. Hil. 5 E. 4. ib. Rot. 47. poſt mortem archiep. Ebor.

Some have ſaid, that the king hath a mortuary after the deceaſes of every archbiſhop and biſhop; true it is, that the king after their deceaſes hath ſix things, *viz.* (to uſe the words of the records) 1. *Optimum equum ſive palefridum ipſius epiſcopi cum cella, et freno.* 2. *Unam chlamydem ſive clocam cum capella.* 3. *Unum ciphum cum coopertorio.* 4. *Unum pelvem cum lavatorio ſive aquar'.* 5. *Unum annulum aureum.* 6. *Necnon* * *mutam canum, quæ* (ſaith the record) *ad dominum regem ratione prærogativæ ſuæ ſpectant, et pertinent.*

* *Muta* cometh of the French word, *Mente de chiens.*

Lib. Mathei Parker, publiſhed anno dom. 1573. Rot. clauſ. 7 H. 3. m. 16. Rot. Pat. 36 H. 3. m. 1. Tit. de conſuet. cap. nullus. f. 19. See before in this chapter, verbo mere ſpiritualia.

And there is a ſpeciall writ that iſſueth out of the exchequer, after the deceaſe of the biſhop, for anſwering of the ſame. And in the records this is called, *multa epiſcopi,* or *multura epiſcopi,* derived *à mulcta,* for that it was a fine, or finall ſatisfaction given to the king, that they might have power to make their laſt wills and teſtaments, and to have the probate of other mens teſtaments, and the granting of adminiſtrations: for true it is that is ſaid, *Nullā habebant epiſcopi authoritatem præter eam quam à rege acceptam referebant, jus teſtamenta probandi non habebant, adminiſtrationis poteſtatem cuiquam delegare non poterant, nec ipſi quidem teſtamenta facere de jure communi, dum id illis regnante Henrico 3. conceſſum erat, et confirmatum vivente Edw. 1. &c.*

Linwood, who wrote in the raign of H. 6. ſaith, *Beneficiatus non poteſt teſtari de communi jure, ſed de conſuetudine in Anglia.*

So as this duty, which the king hath after the death of archbiſhops and biſhops, is not any mortuary.

Regiſt. fol. 47. F.N.B. 52. b.

(15) *Si prælatus alicujus eccleſiæ, vel ejus advocatus petat à rectore penſionem.*] This act giveth conuſans of ſuit for a penſion,

when a prelate or a prior demand a penſion of a parſon of a church.

But this muſt be intended of a penſion which had his eſſence by ſome ordinance made by the ordinary upon a controverſie for tithes, or the like; by which ordinance the tithes are to be injoyned by the one, and he is to pay a penſion for the ſame to the other: for this penſion, becauſe it beginneth by an eccleſiaſticall act, and by an eccleſiaſticall judge, he may take his remedy by force of this act in the eccleſiaſticall court; but if a penſion be claimed by preſcription, there, ſeeing a writ of annuity doth lye, and that preſcriptions muſt be tryed by the common law, becauſe the common and the canon law do therein differ, they cannot ſue for ſuch a penſion in the eccleſiaſticall court, no more then if a penſion be granted by deed by a parſon with the conſent of the prior and ordinary.

3 E. 3. 17. 6 E. 3. 54, 55. 7 E. 3. 40, 41. 17 E. 3. 32. 19 E. 3. Preſcription 98. 31 E. 3. ib. 26. 31 E. 3. Juriſd. 26. 16 E. 3. Annuity 24. 40 E. 3. 3. b. Regiſt. 38. a. 11 H. 4. 68. 8 H. 6. 23. 7 E. 6. Dier, 79.

A writ of annuity muſt be brought therefore at the common law: and all this doth notably appear by a judgment in the next yeer after the making of this ſtatute, where the caſe was, that the abbot and covent of Leiceſter did by their deed under their covent ſeal, bearing date *anno* 25 H. 3. grant to the abbot of Saint Ebrulfe and his ſucceſſors a yeerly rent or annuity, for certain tithes granted by the abbot and covent of Saint Ebrulfe to the abbot of Leiceſter and his ſucceſſors; for which annuity or yeerly rent (being granted out of no lands) the abbot of Saint Ebrulfe brought a writ of annuity againſt the abbot of Leiceſter: wherein the judgement was, *Et quia cognitio placiti petendi annuū redditum directe ſecundum conſuetudinem regni ſpectat ad curiam domini regis, et in ea debet hujuſmodi placitari, et prædictus abbas de ſancto Ebr. petit quendam annual' redd' ſibi debitum per præd' contractum in præd' ſcriptis contentum inter prædeceſſorem ſuum, et prædec' præd' abbatis Leiceſt', et non aliquas decimas. Conſiderat' eſt, quod prædictus abbas de ſanct. Ebr' recuperet de cætero præd' annuum redditum verſus præd' abbatē de Leic', et ſimiliter arreragia ſua de tempore iſtius abbatis de ſanct. Ebr', quæ taxantur per juſtic' ad lx. l. et abbas de Leiceſt' in miſericordia, &c. Poſtea venit prædict' abbas de Leiceſt', et ſatisfecit præd' abbati de ſancto Ebr' de lx. l. ad tres vices, et etiam de aliis arreragiis præd' redditus uſq; ad hunc diem a tempore impetrationis brevis, de tempore præd' abbatis de ſancto Ebrulpho, &c.*

[492] Paſch. 14 E. 1. in Banc. Rot. 69. Leiceſt.

And upon this diverſity this ſtatute is well explained, and all our books reconciled.

See the ſtatute of 21 H. 8. ca. 6. where mortuaries ought to be paid, for what perſons, and how much, and in what caſes none is due.

(16) *De violenta manuum injectione in clericum.*] Note a diverſity between a ſpirituall man of the church conſecrated to the ſervice of God, and goods dedicated to divine ſervice, or meerly eccleſiaſticall: for laying of violent hands upon the perſon of any, *infra ſacros ordines*, the eccleſiaſticall court hath conuſans; but for the violent taking away, or conſuming of the ornaments of the church, or goods dedicated to divine ſervice, that court hath no conuſans, for that is not given to them; as for taking away of the bible, the book of divine ſervice, the chalice, and the like, or for the taking away of an image out of the church; but remedy muſt be taken for theſe at the common law.

7 H. 3. Prohibition 30. 5 H. 3. Prohibition 29. 31 E. 3. Bre. 58. M. 33 E. 3. Rot. 23. Coram rege caſus prioris ſancti crucis juxta turrim London. 8 R. 2. Monſtr. des faits 184.

Tr. 4 E. 3. Rot. 100. Coram rege Eſſex. Bract. li. 5. fo. 401, &c. Brit. 11. b. Regiſt. 34.

And I finde a record that William de Brinckle recovered at the common law by verdict, againſt Otho parſon of the church of Beſton, x. l. *pro ſubtractione unius bullæ papalis de ordinibus, alterius bullæ de legitimatione, et tertiæ bullæ de veniam exorantibus pro animabus anteceſſorum ſuorum.* And yet theſe were accounted in thoſe dayes ſpirituall; but by the ancient common law they have juriſdiction of no goods or chattels, but ſuch as be *de teſtamento et matrimonio.*

Artic. contra Prohib. Regiam Vet. Magna Charta. Artic. Cleri. cap. 1. 3. 11 H. 4. 81. 38 H. 6. 6. 20 E. 4. 10. b. Regiſt. 49. b. F.N.B. 41. 51. k. 52. f. 53. * Hil. 7 H. 3. Prohib. 30. Regi. 49. a. Vide ſupra verbo Mortuary. Artic. cont. Prohibit. Regiam. Vet. Mag. Chart. Regiſt. 46, 47, &c. 54. F.N.B. 51. I. K. 52. d. m. 53. a. f. 18 E. 4. 6. 22 E. 4. 20. 33 E. 3. Bre. 912. 12 H. 7. 22. Lib. 4. fol. 20. Inter Palmer & Thorp. Artic. Cleri, cap. 4.

And for laying violent hands upon one of the clergie, the end of that ſuit is onely *pro ſalute animæ,* by excommunication, or corporall penance: but if a clergie-man be arreſted by proceſſe of law, he cannot for this ſue in the eccleſiaſticall court. And if the clerk ſue in court chriſtian for damages for the battery, he is in caſe of *premunire,* for in that caſe the eccleſiaſticall judge ought to proceed *ex officio,* onely to correct the ſin.

(17) *In cauſa defamationis conceſſum fuit alias.*] Where it is ſaid here, *conceſſum fuit alias,* by it appeareth that the conuſans of defamation that concerneth meer ſpiritualty, was granted by act of parliament, implyed by this word [*conceſſum*] for otherwiſe it could not be granted.

Defamations granted to the conuſans of eccleſiaſticall judges ought to have their incidents; firſt, that it concerns matter meerly ſpirituall, as to call him heretike, ſchiſmatike, or the like: 2. That it concerns meer ſpirituall matter onely, and not mixt with any matter determinable at the common law. 3. * Although the defamation be meerly and onely ſpirituall, yet he that is defamed cannot ſue there for amends or damages, but the ſuit there ought to be for correction of the ſin, *pro ſalute animæ,* and they muſt expreſſe in particular the defamation in their libell in court chriſtian.

If a man give evidence to an inqueſt to indict one, he cannot ſue for this defamation in court chriſtian.

* [493]

Tr. 19 H. 8. Coram rege Spilm. Report.

The prior of Laund libelled in the ſpirituall court againſt Robert Lee, and John Lee, for calling the prior churls ſon, rotten churl, and cankerd churl, and a prohibition was granted, for the words concerned no ſpirituall matter, and therefore he could not ſue for them in the eccleſiaſticall court, neither could he have any action for them at the common law.

30 H. 8. Br. Action ſur le caſe 104. M. 22 H. 8. Coram rege Spilm. 23 E. 3. Stat. de Labourers. Vide ſtat. de Laboureis. 23 E. 3.

If a man call one a perjured man, he muſt take his remedy at the common law.

A ſute was in the eccleſiaſticall court for calling one falſe knave; and for the ſame cauſe a prohibition was granted, and knave *ab initio* was no word of reproach, but ſignified a man ſervant, and a knave-childe a man-childe; and this caſe was between March and Bele of Kent.

22 Aſſ. p. 7. 2 H. 4. 10. 11 H. 4. 88. 38 H. 6. 29. 20 E. 4. 10. b. Kelw. 39. Bract. lib. 5. fol. 401. & 406. b.

(18) *Pro læſione fidei.*] This is to be underſtood where the thing to be done is meer ſpirituall, and neither temporall, nor mixt with the temporalty, be it reall or perſonall, becauſe the eccleſiaſticall court cannot hold plea of the principall: and where they cannot hold plea of the principall, they cannot hold plea of the acceſſory, *Quia cujus juris (i. juriſdictionis) eſt principale, ejuſdem juris erit acceſſorium.*

And again, *Juriſdictionem non mutat fidei interpoſitio, ſacramentum præſtitum, nec ſpontanea renunciatio partium, &c. Et illud idem dicendum erit de debitis, et catallis quæ non ſunt de teſtamento, vel matrimonio.*

More

More shall be said of these matters when we come to the statute of Artic. Cleri, *anno* 9 E. 2. Vide R. book of Entries, 444. Vide Vet. Magn' Chart', part 2. fol. 70. *Prohibitio formata de stat. Articuli Cleri.*

---

[494]

STATUTUM DE QUO WARRANTO,

Editum anno 18 Edw. I.

Statutum de quo Warranto novum anno 18 *E.* 1. *qualiter brevia de quo Warranto debent terminari, et de cætero terminari.*

QUIA brevia de quo warranto et etiam judicia super placita eorundem reddend' diutinam ceperunt dilationem, eo quod justiciarii in judiciis illis reddendis de voluntate domini regis non fuerunt hucusque certiorati: idem dominus rex ad parliamentum suum post Pasch. apud Westm', anno regni sui xviii. de gratia sua speciali (1), *et propter affectionem quam habet erga prælatos, comites, et barones, et cæteros de regno suo concessit, quod omnes de regno suo quicunque fuerint, tam religiosi, quam alii, qui per bonam inquisitionem patriæ aut alio modo verificare poterunt* (2), *quod ipsi et antecessores eorum vel prædecessores usi fuerint libertatibus quibuscunq;* (3) *de quibus per brevia prædicta fuerint implacitati ante tempus regis Rich' consanguinei sui aut toto tempore suo* (4), *et hucusque continuerint: ita quod libertatibus illis non sunt abusi* (5), *quod partes adjornentur ulterius usque certum diem rationabilem coram eisdem justiciar': infra quem dominum regem adire possint cum recordo* (6) *justic' sigillo suo signat' et redire. Et dominus rex confirmabit* (7) *per literas suas patentes statum eorum. Et illi*

FORASMUCH as writs of *quo warranto*, and also judgements given upon pleas of the same, were greatly delayed, because the justices in giving judgement were not certified of the king' pleasure therein; our lord the king, at his parliament holden at Westminster, after the feast of Easter, the eighteenth year of his reign, of his special grace, and for the affection that he beareth unto his prelates, earls, and barons, and other of his realm, hath granted, that all under his allegiance, whatsoever they be, as well spiritual as other, which can verify by good enquest of the country, or otherwise, that they and their ancestors or predecessors have used any manner of liberties, whereof they were impleaded by the said writs, before the time of king Richard our cousin, or in all his time, and have continued hitherto (so that they have not misused such liberties) that the parties shall be adjourned further unto a certain day reasonable before the same justices, within the which they may go to our lord the king with the record of the justices, signed with their seal, and also

illi qui non poterunt seisinam antecessorum seu prædecessorum verificare eodem modo, quo prædictum est, deducantur et judicentur secundum legem et consuet' regni (8). *Et illi qui habent chartas regales secundum chartas illas judicentur* (9). *Præterea dominus rex de gratia sua speciali concessit, quod omnia judicia quæ reddenda sunt in placitis de quo warranto per justic' suos apud Westm' post Pasch' prædictum, et pro ipso domino rege si partes quæ amiserunt ad ipsum dominum regem revenire voluerint, tale habebunt remedium de gratia domini regis sicut superius scriptum* * *est* (10). *Concessit etiam idem dominus rex ad parcend' misis et expensis populi de regno suo: quod placita de quo warranto de cætero placitentur et terminentur in itinere justic'* (11), *et quod placita adhuc pendentia readjornentur in singulis com' suis usque adventum justiciar' in partibus illis.*

* [495]

also return; and our lord the king, by his letters patents, shall confirm their estate. And they that cannot prove the seisin of their ancestors or predecessors in such manner as is before declared, shall be ordered and judged after the law and custom of the realm; and such as have the king's charter shall be judged according to their charters. Moreover, the king of his special grace hath granted, that all judgements that are to be given in pleas of *quo warranto*, by his justices at Westminster, after the foresaid Easter, for our lord the king himself, if the parties grieved will come again before the king, he of his grace shall give them such remedy as before is mentioned. Also our said lord the king hath granted, for sparing of the costs and expences of the people of his realm, that pleas of *quo warranto* from henceforth shall be pleaded and determined in the circuit of the justices, and that all pleas now depending shall be adjourned into their own shires, until the coming of the justices into those parts.

(Fitz. Brief, 886. Kelw. 137, &c. Bro. Quo Warranto, 1, 2, 3, 4. 6. 8. 11. Bro. Prescription, 10. 14. 18. 32, 33, 34, 52. 54. 64, 65. 73. 83. 98. 107, 108. Bro. Franchise, 4. 10. 14. 22. 26. 37. Fitz. Conusance, 16. 19. 21. 26. 30, 31. 36. 39. 46. 51. 54. 57. 60, 61, 62, 63, 64. Rast. 540.)

The mischiefe before this statute, as here it is rehearsed, was that there had been [*diutina dilatio*] in writs of *quo warranto*, because the judges would not proceed to judgement (the same being finall) without being certified *de voluntate regis* by the writ *de libertatibus allocandis*, which was not onely a great delay, but a great charge to the subject: but the truth is, that this kings officers to get thanks of the king by filling of his cofers, caused very many writs of *quo warranto* for liberties to be brought; for where it is said in our chronicles, that those writs of *quo warranto* were for lands and tenements, therein they are mistaken, for it appeareth that after, that is to say, in the 31 yeare of his raigne the king did bring a *quo warranto* against the lady of S. to know by what warrant she claimed to hold the mannor of C. which belonged to his crown, as that which of ancient time was ancient demesne; and there it is affirmed and not denied, that this was the first writ that ever was seen to be brought for lands: but certaine it is, that there were an exceeding number of writs of *quo warranto* brought as well against the prelates and other of the clergy, as against the nobles and others of the

31 E. 1. bre. 886. Vide Bract. l. 5. 367. Polydor, Trivet. Abingdon. Holingf. pag. 280. a. b.

the realme for their liberties, franchises, and priviledges, for that partly by length and proces of time, and partly during the troublesome times and civill broiles and wars in the raignes of king John and H. 3. many of their charters, records of allowances, and other evidences and muniments were destroyed, wasted or made away; amongst others a *quo warranto* was brought against John Warren earle of Surrey, who appearing before the justices spake boldly and stoutly against this kinde of proceeding, as our histories doe testifie.

Certaine it is, that as well the lords spirituall and temporall, as the commons assembled in this parliament did complain hereof to the king, and besought him that he would be pleased of his grace and favour, for it was a legall course which was attempted and prosecuted in the kings name, but a matter of great rigour and extremity invented and eagerly followed by his officers, to the generall distaste and griefe of the whole realme.

The noble and wise king knowing that *summum jus* was *summa injuria*, and not intending to take advantage of the extremity of his laws in so hard a case did of his grace and favour (for so the act speaketh) *ex speciali gratia et etiam propter affectionem quam habet erga prælatos, comites, barones, et cæteros de regno suo*, provide by this act remedy for the said mischiefe.

Bracton and Fleta treating of a *quo warranto*, both of them almost *totidem verbis* sayen, *Est etiam alia actio, quæ dicitur duplex, in uno brevi, et ubi duæ concurrunt actiones, scilicet in personam, et in rem: primo in personam, quod quis sit ad respondendum quo warranto teneat aliquam libertatem seu aliam rem. In rem, cum præterea addatur in fine quam rex clamat ut jus et hæreditatem suam vel eschaetam suam, vel de antiquo dominico coronæ suæ, vel hujusmodi, vel quam talis clamat in N. contra coronam et dignitatem regis.* Bract. l. 5. fo. 367. Fleta, l. 5. cap. 9.

(1) *De gratia sua speciali.*] This, as hath been said, is an act of grace, for it bindeth the king in this particular of his prerogative, *quod nullum tempus occurrit regi*, for by this act continuance of possession of liberties from the beginning of the raigne of R. 1. till this act, which was under an hundred yeares, should be a barre to the crowne, if so it were found by inquisition, which was the time of prescription that bound the subject in case of prescription. Acts of grace. Mag. Chart. c. 8. W. 2. ca. 10. 29. 2 E. 3. fo. 28, 29. [496] First part of the Instit. sect. 190.

(2) *Qui per bonam inquisitionem patriæ, vel aliquo alio modo verificare poterint*, &c.] This is as much to say, as to prove by inquisition, or verdict of the country, who are to enquire of the fact, that is, of the possession by the time aforesaid, or to prove by matter of record (whereof juries are not to enquire) that is, by allowance before justices in eyre, &c. implied necessarily in these words [*vel aliquo alio modo*] that must be *alio modo*, then by matter in *fait* inquirable by the country; so as albeit it be said, that a possession of liberties warranted also by allowance is within this statute, that doth not exclude, but that a possession found by inquisition is within the expresse letter and meaning of this act. 2 E. 3. 28, 29. Roger Mortimers case upon this branch.

(3) *Libertatibus quibuscunque.*] This extends to all liberties, as well to those that lie in point of charter, as conusans of pleas, felons goods, and the like; as to those that may be claimed by prescription, as waife and stray, and the like. 2 E. 3. ubi supra.

The remedy is conformable to the mischiefe, for the mischiefe was, as hath been said, concerning liberties, and not concerning lands; and the *quo warranto* was framed for franchises which belong 31 E. 1. bre. 886. Bract. ubi supra. Tr. 29 E. 1 coram rege. Rot. 57. the bishop of Durhams case.

long to the crown, and ſuch as the ſubject hath, are derived from the crown, *Libertates regales ad coronam ſpectantes ex conceſſione regum à corona exierunt.*

(4) *Ante tempus conſanguinei ſui Ric. aut toto tempore ſui.*] This is king Richard the firſt, and here is called *conſanguineus*, becauſe the king derived not lineally from him, for he was elder brother to king John, who was grandfather to king Edw. 1. Note here this disjunctive [*aut*] ſo as the time of preſcription, as hath been ſaid, in the caſe of a ſubject is the time limited by this act.

(5) *Ita quod libertatibus illis non ſunt abuſi.*] This clauſe extendeth not onely to miſuſer, diſuſer, and non-uſer of liberties, but to *faux claime* of them, and the like.

(6) *Regem adire poſſint cum recordo.*] Here is an excellent pattern, that the king be informed by the judges, and by the record it ſelf, before he make any graunt or confirmation thereof; ſo carefull were they in thoſe dayes, that the king, before he paſſed any thing, might bee truly informed.

(7) *Et dominus rex ſtatum eorum affirmabit.*] In thoſe dayes, ſuch faith were given to verdicts of twelve men, as they were *vere dicta*, and *dicta veritatis*, ſo as upon one inquiſition, &c. the king by this act was to affirme the liberties according to the verdict, &c.

(8) *Deducantur et judicentur ſecundum legem communem.*] That is according to the kings prerogative of *nullum tempus occurrit regi.* Hereby it appeares that the kings prerogative is part of the law of England, and comprehended within the ſame.

(9) *Et illi qui habent chartas regales ſecundum chartas illas et earundem plenitudinem judicentur.*] Here is an excellent rule for conſtruction of the kings letters patents, not only of liberties but
[497] of lands, tenements, and other things which he may lawfully grant,
Lib. 6. fol. 5, 6. Sir John Molins caſe. that they have no ſtrict or narrow interpretation for the overthrowing of them, *ſed ſecundum earundem plenitudinem judicentur*, that is, to have a liberall and favourable conſtruction for the making of them available in law, *uſq; ad plenitudinem*, for the honor of the king.

6 E. 3. 54, 55. 7 E. 3. 40, 41. 18 E. 3. conuſans 39. 34 Aſſ. 14. 40 Aſſ. 23. 12 H. 4. 12. 14 H. 6. 12. 38 H. 6. 22. 35 H. 6. 54. 9 H. 7. 11. 10 H. 7. 13, 14. 16 H. 7. 9.

Alſo hereby is implied that they are to be conſtrued *ſecundũ earũ plenitudinem*, that is, as fully and beneficially as the law was taken at that time when they were made: and certainly theſe auncient laws were directions to the ſages of the law, for the conſtruction of the kings charters, and letters patents, as it appeareth in our books.

(10) *Præterea dominus rex de gratia ſua ſpeciali conceſſit, quod omnia judicia que reddenda ſunt in placitis de quo warranto per juſtic' apud Weſtm' poſt Paſch' prædict', et pro ipſo domino rege, ſi partes quæ amiſerunt ad ipſum dominum regem revenire voluerint, tale habebunt remedium de gratia domini regis, ſicut ſuperius eſt conceſſum.*] This was a ſpeciall grace indeed of the king, that though judgements had been given in any of his courts at Weſtminſter ſince the feaſt of Eaſter in pleas of *quo warranto* for him againſt any of his ſubjects (which judgements in law againſt the ſubjects were finall) yet, thoſe judgements notwithſtanding, the parties grieved ſhould be within the remedy of this act.

(11) *Conceſſit etiam idem dominus rex ad parcend' miſſis et expenſis populi de regno, quod placita de quo warranto de cætero et placitentur et terminentur in itineribus juſticiar'.*] The coſts, charges, and expences of the ſubjects in theſe caſes were exceſſive, and therefore,

to

to meet with this mischiefe, and that the subject might receive justice in his own country, as it were at his owne doores, it is likewise of the kings speciall grace that pleas of *quo warranto* should be heard and determined in the eyres of the justices.

Of this branch we finde a notable case in our books, and I will cite the case as I finde it of record, and as it may be gathered in our books. The archbishop of York was in possession of prisage of wines in the port of Hull, and in the raigne of E. 2. in the time of John archbishop, the same franchise was seised into the kings hands; after the decease of John archbishop, William archbishop his successor sued in parliament in the raigne of E. 3. by petition of right to be restored to the said franchise; and afterward by parliament the petitioner was restored to the possession of the said franchise, and by the same award it was adjudged that the said William archbishop the petitioner should answer the king, when and where he pleased; and the like award was made upon the petition of the said William archbishop in the parliament the morrow after the feast of S. Catherine in the fourth yeare of the same king; whereupon the king brought a writ of *quo warranto* against the said William archbishop returnable in the court of common pleas, to know by what warrant he claimed to have prisage of wines in the port of Hull; Parning that famous serjant (who after was chiefe justice, and after that lord treasurer of England, and lastly lord chauncellor of England) of councell with the archbishop, pleaded to the jurisdiction of the court, and demanded judgement, if the archbishop ought to make any answer there, for that king Edward, grandfather of E. 3. made a statute (intending this statute of 18 E. 1.) which provided, that the pleas of *quo warranto* should be pleaded before justices in eyre in the counties, and that it was ordained by a statute made in the time of king E. 3. at his parliament at Northampton (which was in 2 E. 3.) that by a writ under the great, or privy seale, no disturbance should be that common right should not be done to all, and wee intend not (saith hee) that against the said statute, which is a law common to all, that wee ought to answer in this court. The matter concerning this act of 18 E. 1. was not denied, but sir William Herle chiefe justice, that gave the rule, relying upon the award in parliament, that the archbishop should answer the king when and where hee would, and there it is said, that the award of parliament was the highest law that could bee, and thereupon serjant Parning answered over.

5 E. 3. 65. 6 E. 3. 5, &c.

[498]

Now when justices in eyre ceased, then this branch for the ease of the subject, and for saving of their costs, charges, and expences, lost his effect, for with justices of eyre this branch lived, and with them it died.

Some have supposed that Henry the second, did first institute justices in eyre, whereof one saith, *Justiciarii itinerantes constituti per H. 2. 1. Qui divisit regnum suum in sex partes, per quarum singulas tres justiciarios itinerantes constituit*; and they likewise agree, *quod hoc institutum sub Edwardo 3. evanuit.*

Rog. Hovenden poster. p'te annalium, fol. 313. Mat. Paris. Camden Brit. 129.

Wherein how men otherwise learned, but not skilfull in legall antiquities have mistaken both these points, we shall in a word or two satisfie the learned reader.

These justices itinerants, were also called *perlustrantes*; they were first instituted *ad dilationes amputandas, et ad subditorum labores, sumptusque sublevandos.*

Lucubr. Ockham.

It

Mirror, c. 2. § 15.

It appeareth by the Mirror, who had ſeene the old rolls in the raignes of ancient kings, and namely of king Alfred, and wrote of the lawes from the time of king Arthur, who ſaith, *Que auncientment ſoloient les royes en proper perſons eroer de paiis in paiis pur inquirer, oier et terminer les peches, et pur redreſſer de torts, et ceux queux ne ſont my attaine en tielz eires des perſonel treſpaſſes faitz avant remeint al judgement de Dieu. Et puis pur multiplication de peches ne purront my les royes touts faire per eux meſmes et pur ceo ilz envoieront lour commiſſaries, que ſont ore appels juſtices errants, que nount power de oier et terminer nul perſonel treſpaſſè forſque pur choſe attaine, et nient termine in le darraine eire ou puis fait* (which agreeth with our books) and further ſaith, *Eſtoiet auncient ordein que les royes per eux, ou per lour chieſe juſtices, ou per juſtices generals a touts pleas oier et terminer erraſſent de 7. ans, in 7. ans per my touts counties pur receiver les rolles de touts juſtices aſſignes, des coroners de inquiries, des eſcheators, de viſcounts, de hundreders, de bailies, et de touts ſeneſchals, &c.* And again, *Cheſcun paiis ſoloiet deſtre garnie per 40. jours per generall ſummons, &c.* All which agreeth with our books; and after he ſaith, *Abuſion eſt que juſtices et lour miniſters, que occient le gent per faux judgement, ne ſont diſtreints al fere de autres homicides, que fiſt le roy Alfred que fiſt pender 44. juſtices in un anne tant come homicides pur lour faux judgements:* and there he nameth thoſe corrupt juſtices, which is to be intended of juſtices itinerant, for there were not ſo many reſident.

Bract. l. 3. fo. 108. 115, 116. &c. Brit. fo. 127, &c. Fleta, l. 1. c. 15, &c. 2 E. 3. 27. 4 E. 3. 41. 6 E. 3. 55. 23 E. 3. 21. 6 E. 2. Aſſ. b. 496. 14 H. 7. 21. 15 H. 7. 5.

Mirror, c. 4. § Le office des juſtices in eire. ca. 5. § 1. The books aboveſaid, ubi ſupra.

And the inſtitution of juſtices itinerant, and the circuit of juſtices in the countries had his ground from holy ſcripture, for there it is ſaid, *Judicabat quoque Samuel Iſraelem cunctis diebus vitæ ſuæ, et ibat per ſingulos annos circuiens Bethel, et Galgala, et Maſphatti; et judicabat Iſraelem in ſupradictis locis, revertebaturque in Ramatha; ibi enim erat domus ejus, et ibi judicabat Iſraelem.*

1 Sam. c. 7. ver. 16.

As to the ſecond point, that juſtices in eyre ſhould ceaſe in the raigne of Edward the third, they have not onely erred *in fonte*, but *in fine* alſo, for they ceaſed not in the raigne of king Edward the third, for it is enacted by act of parliament after that kings raigne, (in reſpect of the troubles and foreine affaires) that no eyres ſhould be holden during two yeers; and after in 16 R. 2. that no eyre ſhould be holden till the next parliament; but thus much in a caſe ſo evident ſhall ſuffice. We have added thus much, not of curioſity, nor of a ſpirit of contradiction, but for two reſpects; the one, that when our hiſtorians do meddle with any legall point, or matter concerning the law, we would adviſe them, that they would before they write, conſult with thoſe that be learned, and appriſed in the laws of this realm: the other, that truth might be manifeſted, and prevail.

[499] Rot. Parliam. an. 6 R. 2. nu. 35. 16 R. 2. nu. 12.

But hereof more largely ſhall be ſpoken in the treatiſe concerning the juriſdiction of courts.

STATUT.

STATUT. DE WESTMINSTER 3.

Editum Anno 18 Edw. 1. Ad Parliamentum poſt Feſtum Hil. et Paſchæ.

In the Parliament Roll it is intituled,

Statutum Regis de Terris vendendis et emendis.

IT is called the ſtatute of Weſtm. 3. becauſe two notable parliaments had been before holden at Weſtminſter, the one called Weſtm. 1. and the other called Weſtm. 2. In reſpect whereof, and of the excellencie of it, this parliament being holden at Weſtminſter, is called Weſtm. 3.

1 part of the Inſtitutes, ſect. 140.

CAP. I.

QUIA emptores terrarum (1) *et tenementor' de feodis magnatum et aliorum dominorum in præjudicium eorundem, temporibus retroactis, multotiens in feodis ſuis ſunt ingreſſi, quibus libere tenentes eorundem magnatum et aliorum terras et ten' ſua vendiderunt, tenend' infeod' ſibi et hæredibus ſuis de feoffatoribus* [et hæredibus] *ſuis, et non de capitalibus dom' feodorum, per quod iidem capitales domini eſchaetas, maritagia, et cuſtodias terrarum et tenement' de feodis ſuis exiſtentium ſæpius amiſerunt: quod quidem eiſdem magnatibus et aliis dominis quam plurimum durum et difficile videbatur, et* [ſic] *in hoc caſu exheredatio manifeſta. Dominus rex in parliamento ſuo apud Weſtmon' poſt Paſch. anno regni ſui* 18. *videlicet in quindena Sancti Johan. Bapt. ad inſtantiam magnatum regni ſui, conceſſit, providit, et ſtatuit, quod de cætero liceat unicuique libero homini* (4), *terras ſuas, ſeu tenementa ſua, ſeu partem inde ad voluntatem ſuam* (2) *vendere* (3), *ita tamen quod feoffatus teneat terram illam, ſeu tenement' illud*

FORASMUCH as purchaſers of lands and tenements of the fees of great men and other lords, have many times heretofore entered into their fees, to the prejudice of the lords, to whom the freeholders of ſuch great men have ſold their lands and tenements to be holden in fee of their feoffors, and not of the chief lords of the fees, whereby the ſame chief lords have many times loſt their eſcheats, marriages, and wardſhips of lands and tenements belonging to their fees; which thing ſeemed very hard and extream unto thoſe lords and other great men, and moreover in this caſe manifeſt diſheritance: Our lord the king, in his parliament at Weſtminſter, after Eaſter, the eighteenth year of his reign, that is to wit, in the quinzime of Saint John Baptiſt, at the inſtance of the great men of the realm, granted, provided, and ordained, that from henceforth it ſhall be lawfull to every freeman to ſell at his own pleaſure his lands and tenements, or part of them, ſo that the feoffee ſhall hold the ſame lands

lud de capitali domino (6) *feodi illius* (5) *per eadem servitia et consuetudines* (8), *per quæ feoffator suus illa prius tenuit* (7).

lands or tenements of the chief lord of the same fee, by such service and customs as his feoffor held before.

(1 Roll, 106. Fitz. Avowry, 108. 185. 255. 12 Car. 2. c. 24.)

Lib. 3. fol. 23, 24. Walkers case. [501] Mag. Char. c. 32.

(1) *Quia emptores terrarum, &c.*] The cause of the making of this statute, appeareth by the preamble, and by that which hath been said upon the exposition of the 32. chapter of the statute of Magna Charta; where also the principall parts of this act are explained, yet some things are thereunto necessarily to be added.

31 Ass. p. 30. 2 E. 3. 33. 49 E. 3. 10.

At the common law, if A. had made a feoffment in fee to B. *reddend' inde, sive tenend' de se et hæredibus suis per* 6. *d. pro omnibus servitiis, et fac' capitalibus dominis feodi pro prædict' A. et hæredibus suis omnia servitia debita, &c.*

In this case by the first *reddend'* or *tenend'* the land had been holden of the feoffor, and all the services due shall be done to him; for to do service for a man, is to do it to him; *qui pro me aliquid facit, mihi fecisse videtur.*

3 Ass. 8. 33 E. 3. Annuity 52. 22 Ass. 53. 45 E. 3. 15. b. 4 H. 6. 20.

If the tenant had made a feoffment in fee before this statute generally, without reservation of any tenure, the feoffee should have holden of the feoffor, as he had held over; for example, if he had holden by knights service, the feoffee by creation of law had holden by knights service of the feoffor, in respect of the tenure over by him; and therefore if the lord had confirmed the estate of the feoffor, *viz.* the mesne, to hold by fealty onely (which was socage) the tenure between the tenant and the feoffor should be socage also, because the tenure created by law followeth the tenure, in respect whereof it was created.

49 E. 3. 10.

(2) *Quod de cætero liceat unicuique libero homini, terras suas, seu tenementa sua, seu partem inde ad voluntatem suam vendere.*] By the common law, the tenant might have made a feoffment in fee of the whole tenancie to be holden of the chief lord; but notwithstanding the lord might, during the life of the feoffor, take him for his tenant, and avow upon him (in respect of the former fealty, service, and privity) albeit the feoffee gave notice, and tendred him all the arrerages, which now this statute hath altred.

33 E. 3. Avowry 255. 4 H. 6. 20. 12 E. 4. 16. lib. 3. fol. 23. Walkers case.

See the exposition upon the 32. chapter of Magna Charta.

Mag. Chart. c. 32.

(3) *Vendere.*] Is here not onely taken for a sale, but for any alienation by gift, feoffment, fine, or otherwise: but sale was the most common assurance.

(4) *Libero homini.*] *i. Libere tenenti*; to every free-holder. Hereby are excluded not onely *nativi*, but also *nativè tenentes*, copy-holders, or tenants at will, according to the custome of the mannour.

(5) *Ita tamen quod feoffatus teneat terram illam, seu tenementum illud de capitali domino feodi illius.*] The generall words of this act take not away necessary incidents, as that the feoffee of all, or of part, shall give notice, and tender the arrerages before the lord shall be compelled to avow upon him: neither do these, or the former words [*de cætero liceat*] take away the fine for license of alienation, &c. of lands holden of the king *in capite*, for that belongeth to the king by the said statute of Magna Charta. See Magna Charta, cap. 32.

4 H. 6. 20. 8 E. 4. 12.

Mag. Chart. c. 32.

These

Theſe generall words have a tacite exception, *viz.* unleſſe all the lords mediate and immediate do aſſent thereunto; for, *quilibet renunciare poteſt benefic' juris pro ſe introduct'.* 27 H. 8. 26. 2 E. 2. Avowry 185.

(6) *Capitalis dominus.*] Is here taken for the next immediate lord, and ſo by degrees upward to every lord paramount, albeit the act ſpeaketh in the ſingular number: and it is to be known, that all the lands and tenements in England are holden either mediately or immediately of the king, and therefore he is *ſummus dominus ſupra omnes.*

* If the king be lord, A. meſne, C. meſne, and tenant, the tenancie commeth to the hands of the king by forfeiture or conveyance, the king granteth the lands to another in fee [*tenend' de capitali domino per ſervitia debita, et conſueta*] † this grant ſhall revive not onely the immediate tenure of C. but of A. and of the king alſo, albeit the *tenend' de capitali domino* be in the ſingular number (as here the ſtatute ſpeaketh) yet is it as much as *capitalibus dominus.* * 33 H. 6. 7. 8 E. 3. 283. 17 E. 3. 59. 46 E. 3. Petition 19. lib. 6. fol. 5, 6. Sir John Molyns caſe. Eodem libr. fol. 130, 131. Bewlies caſe. † [502]

(7) *Per eadem ſervitia et conſuetudines, per quæ feoffator ſuus illa prius tenuit.*] A. holdeth lands by knights ſervice, and giveth the ſame to B. in tail, to hold of him in ſocage; B. maketh a feoffment in fee, the feoffee ſhall not hold of the lord in ſocage, as the feoffor held, but by knights ſervice, as A. the donor held: for by the feoffment the reverſion in fee holden by knights ſervice is drawn out of the donor, and paſſeth to the feoffee; and the feoffee in this caſe cannot hold of the donor: and this caſe is not againſt the letter of the law, but within the intent and meaning thereof; for the meaning of this law was, that the feoffee ſhould hold of the lord, as the feoffor did when the feoffee held of the ſame lord; and this act was made for the advantage of the lords; and therefore in conſtruction the feoffee ſhall hold, not as the feoffor, but as the donor held. 2 E. 2. Avowry 181. 10 E. 3. 26. 18 E. 3. 7. 31 E. 3. Gard 116. 48 E. 3. 8. 1 H. 5. 5 E. 4. 8. 15 E. 4. 13. Tr. 18 Eliz. in communi banco, in Wyats caſe. Per cur' which I heard and obſerved.

If the huſband ſeiſed of land in the right of his wife make a feoffment in fee, the feoffee ſhall hold as the wife held, for the huſband had nothing but in her right.

Alſo if the tenant that holds by priority make a feoffment in fee, the feoffee ſhall not hold by priority; for this act ſaith, *per eadem ſervitia,* by the ſame ſervices, and not according to every collaterall quality.

If tenant in frank almoign alien in fee, that feoffee ſhall not hold of the lord *per eadem ſervitia,* albeit he be a man of the church; but he ſhall hold of the lord by fealty onely: for by the firſt words of this act he ſhall hold of the lord, but he cannot hold of the lord *per eadem ſervitia,* becauſe it is againſt the nature of the tenure in frank almoign, to hold of any but of the donor or his heirs; and generall words of an act ſhall not be taken to work any thing againſt the nature of the thing, or the rule of law; but he ſhall hold by fealty onely, which was as free a tenure, and as neer to the former, as can be, and therefore by conſtruction [*eadem ſervitia*] the ſame ſervices ſhall be taken as neer the ſame ſervices as may be. 1. part of the Inſtitutes, ſect. 139. Lib. 9. fol. 123. Anth. Lows caſe.

And this act extendeth to lands holden by fee fearm. 45 E. 3. 15. b.

(8) *Conſuetudines.*] Is here taken for ſervices, as in the writ *de conſuetudinibus et ſervitiis,* and not for cuſtomes. Mag. Chart. cap. 30. verb. Conſuetud.

If the meſne releaſe to the tenant, the tenant ſhall hold *per eadem ſervitia et conſuetudines,* as the meſne did; and ſo if the tenant 22 E. 3. Dower 131. 38 Aſſ. 17. 2 E. 4. 6. 7 E. 4. 12.

tenant infeoffe the mesne, the mesne shall hold *per eadem servitia*, as he did before: and so it is if the tenancie come to the mesnalty by act in law, as by escheat or descent, the mesne shall hold *per eadem servitia consuetudines*, as he held before; for albeit the tenure between the tenant and the mesne in these cases be extinct, yet the seigniory paramount, which also was issuing out of the tenancie, remaineth still.

10 Ass. p. 29. W. 2. cap. 9. Le case de Forjudger.

If there be lord mesne, mesne, and tenant, and the first mesne dyeth without heir, and the mesnalty escheat to the second mesne; or if the mesne grant the mesnalty to the mesne, the mesnalty that which is neerest to the tenancie doth drown the more remote mesnalty, and the tenant shall hold *per eadem servitia et consuetudines*, as he held before: but the second mesne shall hold of the lord paramount *per eadem servitia et consuetudines*, as he held before the extinguishment of his mesnalty for the cause aforesaid.

[503]

CAP. II.

Et si partem aliquam earundem terrarum, seu tenementorum alicui vendiderit, feoffatus illam teneat immediate de capitali domino (1), *et oneretur statim de servitiis quantum pertineat sive pertinere debet eidem capitali domino pro particula illa* (2) *secundum quantitatem terræ* (3) *seu ten' sic vendit'. Et sic in hoc casu decidat capitali domino ipsa pars servitii per manus feoffati capiend', ex quo feoffatus debet eidem capitali domino juxta quantitatem terræ seu ten' venditi, de particula illius servitii sic debiti esse intendens et respondens.*

AND if he sell any part of such lands or tenements to any, the feoffee shall immediately hold it of the chief lord, and shall be forthwith charged with the services, for so much as pertaineth, or ought to pertain to the said chief lord for the same parcel, according to the quantity of the land or tenement so sold. And so in this case the same part of the service shall remain to the lord, to be taken by the hands of the feoffee, for the which he ought to be attendant and answerable to the same chief lord, according to the quantity of the land or tenement sold for the parcel of the service so due.

(Dyer, 299. Fitz. Avowry, 101. 108. 218. Fitz. Herriot, 1. Bro. Tenures, 2. 65. 6 Rep. 1. 8 Rep. 105. 27 H. 8. f. 26. 40 Ed. 3. f. 40.)

29 H. 8. tenures Br. 64. 17 E. 3. 15.

(1) *Feoffatus ille partem illam teneat immediate de capitali domino pro particula illa.*] [*Particula illa*] is understood of a part in severalty, and not in common, and therefore it is holden that if the tenant make a feoffement in fee of the moity or third part, &c. of the tenancy, that such a feoffee is not within the purview of this statute; for a moity or a third part, &c. *pro indiviso* is not *particula*, for that word implieth a part in severalty.

17 E. 3. 15.

And this branch by reason of this word [*feoffatus*] is understood when part of the tenancy *peravaile* is aliened, and not when part of the mesnalty.

Lib. 6. f. 1. Bruerton's case. Li. 8. fo. 105, 106.

(2) *Pro particula illa.*] Is understood of services divisible and apportionable, and not of entire services, be they annuall or not annuall,

annuall, whereof you shall reade notable matter, when entire services by alienation of part shall be multiplied, and when not, and what services shall be extinct by the purchase of part by the lord, and what remaine, and what shall be apportioned, in Bruertons case in the sixt part of the reports, and in Talbots case in the eight part.

Talbots case. First part of the Institut. § 222. verbo annual. Whereunto you may adde for the case of suit-service. Mich. 18 E. 1. in Banco Rot. 232. Ro. Lutterels case. 12 E. 4. 16. 6 H. 7. 7.

Also when the lord purchaseth part, he shall hold that part *pro particula* of the lord paramount by the purview of this statute.

(3) *Secundum quantitatem terræ.*] The statute doth ordain that the feoffee of part shall hold *pro particula* of the lord, but it is necessary to be known how the same shall be apportioned: for *parum proficit scire quid fieri debet, si non cognoscas, quo modo sit facturum:* therefore admit that there be lord and tenant of twenty acres of land by fealty, and x s. rent, the lord doth purchase two acres, and taking the rent to be apportioned according to the quantity of the land doth distrain for ix s. and the tenant maketh rescous, the lord brings his assise, the tenant pleads *nul tort*, the recognitors of the assise shall extend the land according to the value, and not according to the quantity, and that the lord ought upon the true valuation of the said two acres so purchased to have but viij. s. vi. d.

Regula.

18 E. 2. avowry 218. 4 Ass. 5. 12 E. 4. 16. Pl. Com. 82.

In this case, albeit the plaintiffe did mistake the just residue upon the apportionment, yet shall he recover so much as is found by the jury to be due; for it were too hard, and a cause of multiplication of suits, and against the meaning of the makers of this act, that the lord should be driven in his assise or avowry, &c. to hit the just summe due upon the apportionment, but though he demand more, yet shall he recover but that just summe which is implied in these words, *secundum quantitatem terræ, i. secundum quantitatem valoris terræ:* but if he demand lesse in that action, he shall not recover the greater.

[504]

And so it is, if a man make a lease for yeares reserving a rent, if he graunt away part of the reversion, the rent shall be apportioned by the common law, and albeit the grauntee of part demand or claime more in his action of debt, or avowry then is due, yet shall he recover so much as the jury shall finde upon a just apportionment to be due, against a sudden opinion reported by serjant Bendloes, Hil. 6 & 7 E. 6. that the rent in that case should not be apportioned, but lost; but the law hath been often adjudged to the contrary for foure reasons:

Pasch. 39 El. Rot. 233. coram Rege inter Collins & Harding. Hil. 42. El. in Communi Banco. int' Ewer & Moile. Tr. 43. El. in Communi Banco. Rot. 243.

1. For that it is a rent service, and not a bare contract, and rent services were apportionable at the common law.

2. It is incident to the reversion, which is severable, *et accessorium sequitur naturam sui principalis.*

3. The rent, being a rent service, is severable by recovery of part, in an action of waste, or upon surrender in part.

4. Lastly, it is a generall case, and specially in case of wils, which many times are void for a third part.

And where the case hath been put of a lessee for yeares, the same law holdeth in the case of a lease for life, whereupon a rent is reserved, for the apportionment of the rent, whereby it appeareth, that there was an apportionment at the common law, *pro particula secundum quantitatem valoris, &c.* for to none of these cases our act doth extend unto.

CAP. III.

ET sciendum est quod per prædictas venditiones seu emptiones terrarum seu ten', aut partis alicujus earundem nullo modo possunt terræ seu ten' illa in parte vel in toto ad manum mortuam devenire, arte vel ingenio, contra formam statuti super hoc dudum editi (1). *Et sciendum est quod istud statut' tenet locum de terris venditis tenend' in feodo simplici* (2) *tantum. Et quod se extendit ad tempus futurum. Et incipiet locum tenere ad festum Sancti Andreæ apostoli proxim' futur' anno regni regis E. filii regis H. xviii.*

AND it is to be understood, that by the said sales or purchases of lands or tenements, or any parcels of them, such lands or tenements shall in no wise come into mortmain, either in part or in whole, neither by policy ne craft, contrary to the form of the statute made thereupon of late. And it is to wit, that this statute extendeth but only to lands holden in fee-simple; and that it extendeth to the time coming, and it shall begin to take effect at the feast of Saint Andrew the apostle next coming. Given the eighteenth year of the reign of king Edward, son to king Henry.

(9 H. 3. stat. 1. c. 32.)

(1) *Ad manum mortuam devenire, arte vel ingenio, contra formam statuti super hoc dudum edit'.*] This is understood of the statute *de* 7 E. 1. *de religiosis*, and by this branch that act is in no sort impeached by this, but standeth in full force: and note the manner of saving of former statutes in auncient times by generall words, which is the surest way.

22 Ass. 42. 3 Ass. 18. 4 H. 6. 20. 11 H. 8. 88. Kelwey. (2) *In feodo simplici.* And therefore if tenant for life graunt his estate in severall parts to severall persons, yet may the lessor distrain for the whole * rent in every part, for this act extendeth onely to tenants in fee-simple.

*[505]

1 E. 3. 3. 4 H. 6. 20. 21, 22. 20 E. 3. avowry 131. 20 E. 3. ubi supra. 38 E. 3. 7. 4 H. 6. 20. 21, &c. Lib. 2. fo. 92. Binghams case. Lib. 3. fol. 8. Heydons case.

But yet tenant for life, and tenant in taile are not wholly excluded by force of these words [*in feodo simplici*] out of this statute, for where the whole fee-simple passeth out of the feoffor, there this act extendeth to estates for life and in taile; as if an estate for life or in taile be made of land, the remainder in fee, there then tenant for life or in taile shall hold *de capitali domino* by force of this act, but otherwise it is when a reversion remaineth in the donor or lessor.

For if a man at this day make a gift in taile, *tenend' de capitalibus dominis feodi, &c.* these words are void, and he shall hold of the donor.

STATUTUM

STATUTUM DE JUDAISMO.

Ad Parliamentum tentum poſt Feſtum Sancti Hilarii, et poſt Paſch', anno 18 E. 1.

*PUR ceo que le roy ad vieu que mults des males et diſheriſons des probes homes de ſa terre ſont avenus per les uſurers que les Jewes ont fait en arere, et que mults des peches ent ount ſurs de ceo, meſque luy et ſes aunc' eyent ent grand pren de la Jewrie tout en ceo en arere, ment pur quant en le honor de Dieu et pur le common pren del people ordein le roy et eſtablie que nul Jew deſormes ne priſt rien a uſury ſur les terres rents ne ſur autres choſes, et que nul uſury ne curge * de S. Edward procheinment paſſe en avant, mes que les covenants avant faits ſoient tenus ſave que les uſurers mes ceſſent* †.

* That is from the feaſt of S. Edw. next before paſſed, which is the 18 day of March.

By the preamble hereof, two great miſchiefes did follow before the making of this ſtatute upon Jewiſh uſury; now the difficulty was how the ſame ſhould be remedied. The miſchiefes were theſe:

1. The evils and diſheriſons of the good men of the land.

2. That many of the ſins or offences of the realme had riſen and been committed by reaſon thereof, to the great diſhonor of Almighty God.

The difficulty how to apply a remedy, was, conſidering what great yearly revenue the king had by the uſury of the Jewes, and how neceſſary it was that the king ſhould bee ſupplied with treaſure; what benefit the crowne had before the making of this act appeareth by former records; as take one for many: from the 17 of December in the 50 yeare of H. 3. untill the Tueſday in ſhrovetide the ſecond yeare of Edward the firſt, which was about ſeaven yeares, the crowne had foure hundred and twenty thouſand pounds fifteene ſhillings and foure pence *de exitibus Judaiſmi*; at what time the ounce of ſilver was but xx d. and now it is more then treble ſo much, ſo as the recitall of the preamble is true, *Meſque luy et ſes aunceſtres eyent ent graund pren de la Jewrie.*

Rot. Patent anno 3 E. 1. m. 14. 17. 26. William Middleton reddit. compotum.

Many proviſions were made both by this king and others, ſome time they were baniſhed, but their cruell uſury continued; and ſoon after they returned, and for reſpect of lucre and gain, king John in the ſecond yeer of his raign granted unto them large liberties

[507] Tempore R. 1. Vet. Mag. Chart. fol. 144. Rot. Chart. 2 Johan. nu. 49. 53. 18 F.

3 I 2

† [*This appears to be little more than the preamble of the ſtatute entitled* " *Statutum de Judaiſmo,*" *which is given at length in the book quoted by lord Coke in the margin, Vet. Mag. Chart. from whence it is tranſcribed in the appendix to Ruffheads ſtatutes among thoſe of uncertaine time.*]

3. Dorf. clauf. m. 27. Dorf. Pat. 55 H. 3. m. 10.

berties and priviledges, whereby the mischiefs rehearsed in this act without measure multiplyed.

Our noble king Edw. 1. and his father H. 3. before him, sought by divers acts and ordinances to use some mean and moderation herein, but in the end it was found, that there was no mean in mischief, and as Seneca saith, *Res profecto stulta est nequitiæ modus.* And therefore king E. 1. as this act saith, in the honour of God, and for the common profit of his people, without all respect (in respect of these) of the filling of his own coffers, did ordain, that no Jew from thenceforth should make any bargain, or contract for usury, nor upon any former contract should take any usury, from the feast of Saint Edward then last past; so in effect all Jewish usury was forbidden.

Rot. 2 E. 1. m. 1. 3. 5. Rot. clauf. 3 E. 1. m. 8. 10. 13. 16. 23. Rot. Pat. 3 E. 1. m. 36. & 17. Dorf. clauf. 7 E. 1. m. 6.

Matth. Paris, pag. 833.

The king of France, *anno Domini* 1253. 37 H. 3. banished out of France all the Jews perpetually, saving merchants, and such as should get their living by the work of their hands; but soon after they returned again.

This law struck at the root of this pestilent weed, for hereby usury it self was forbidden; and thereupon the cruell Jews thirsting after wicked gain, to the number of 15060, departed out of this realm into forein parts, where they might use their Jewish trade of usury, and from that time that nation never returned again into this realm.

Holl. fol. 285. Walf. hypod. 72. Florilegus Cron. Dunstable. Banish the trade, and banish the tradesman. Divers kings had banished the Jews, and yet they returned, but no king banished their usury before.

Some are of opinion, (and so it is said in some of our histories) that it was decreed by authority of parliament, that the usurious Jews should be banished out of the realm; but the truth is, that their usury was banished by this act of parliament, and that was the cause that they banished themselves into forein countries, where they might live by their usury; and for that they were odious both to God and man, that they might passe out of the realm in safety, they made petition to the king, that a certain day might be prefixed to them to depart the realm, to the end that they might have the kings writ to his sherifes for their safe conduct, and that no injury, molestation, damage, or grievance be offered to them in the mean time: one of which writs we will transcribe:

Rot. clauf. 18 E. 1. m. 6. 18 Julii. The like writs to other counties, and intituled, *De Judæis regni Angliæ exeuntibus.* * Nota.

*Rex vic. G. Cum Judæis regni nostri universis certum tempus præfixerimus a regno illo transfretandi, nolentes quod ipsi per ministros nostros, aut alios quoscunq; aliter quam fieri consuevit, indebite pertrectentur: tibi præcipimus quod per totam balivam tuam publice proclamari, et firmiter inhiberi facias, ne quis eis infra tempus prædictum, injuriam, molestiam, damnum inferat, seu gravamen. Et cum contingat ipsos cum catallis suis, * quæ eis concessimus, versus partes London, causa transfretationis suæ, dirigere gressus suos, salvum et securum conductum eis habere facias sumptibus eorundem. Proviso quod Judæi prædicti ante recessum suum vadia christianorum quæ penes se habent, illis quorum fuerint, si ea acquietare voluerint, restituant, ut tenentur. Teste rege apud Westm. 18 die Julii, anno 18 E. 1.*

Parliam. 18 E. 1. post festum Hil. & Pasch. at which parliament the stat. of W. 3. *de quia emptores terrarum* was made.

This statute *de Judaismo* was made at the parliament *post festum Hilarii, anno* 18 E. 1. At which parliament the king had a fifteenth granted to him *pro expulsione Judæorum.* And this writ was granted in July following, the king beginning his raign, Novemb. 16. for the parliament knew, that by banishing of usury, the Jews would not remain. And thus this noble king by this means banished for ever these infidell usurious Jews; the number of which Jews thus banished, was fifteen thousand and threescore.

But

But lucre and gain, which king John had, and expected of the infidell Jews, made him *impie judaiſare*; for to the end they ſhould exerciſe the laws of their ſacrifices, (which they could not do without a prieſthood) the king by his charter granted them to have one, &c. which, for the great rarity thereof, and for that we finde it not either in our books, or hiſtories, that we remember, we will rehearſe *in hæc verba:*

Rex omnibus fidelibus ſuis, et omnibus, et Judæis, et Anglis ſalutem. Sciatis nos conceſſiſſe, et præſenti charta noſtra confirmaſſe Jacobo Judæo de Londoniis preſbytero Judæorum preſbyteratum omnium Judæorum totius Angliæ. Habendum et tenendum, quam diu vixerit, libere et quiete, et honorifice et integre, ita quod nemo ei ſuper hoc moleſtiam aliquam, aut gravamen inferre præſumat. Quare volumus et firmiter præcipimus, quod eidem Jacobo, quoad vixerit, preſbyteratum Judæorum per totam Angliam garantetis, manuteneatis, et pacifice defendatis. Et ſi quis ei ſuper eo foriſfacere præſumpſerit, id ei ſine dilatione (ſalva nobis emenda noſtra) de foriſfactura noſtra emendari faciatis tanquam dominico Judæo noſtro, quem ſpecialiter in ſervitio noſtro retinuimus. Prohibemus etiam ne de aliquo ad ſe pertinente ponatur in placitum, niſi coram nobis aut coram capitali juſticiario noſtro, ſicut charta regis Richardi fratris noſtri teſtatur. Teſte S. Bathonienſi epiſcopo, &c. Dat' per manus * *H. Cantuarienſis archiepiſcopi cancellarii noſtri apud Rothomagum* 31 *die Julii, anno regni noſtri primo.*

[508]

Rot. Chart. 1. Regis Johan. part. 1. m. 28. Chart. 171. This king had a moſt troubleſom and diſhonorable raign, God raiſing againſt him for his juſt puniſhment two potent enemies, Pope Innocent the 3. and Philip king of France. And beſides (which was the worſt) he loſt the hearts and love of his baronage and ſubjects, and at the laſt had a fearful end.

* H. id eſt, Huberti.

Walter archbiſhop of Canterbury, and chancelor of England, born in Weſtdereham in Norfolk, and brought up by Ranulph de Glanvile chief juſtice of England, founded the monaſtery of Weſtdereham, *premonſtratenſis ordinis. Vide Lib. de antiquitate Britannicæ eccleſiæ, cap.* 42. Hubertus p. 134. worthy to be read and obſerved.

At this parliament alſo of this noble king E. 1. in the 18 yeer of his raign, another kinde of Jews were ſeverely puniſhed, *viz.* the judges of the kings bench, and of the common pleas, the barons of the exchequer, and the juſtices itinerants, except two, whom for their honour we will name *(in memoria æterna erit juſtus) viz.* Sir John of Metingham chief juſtice of the common pleas, and Elias de Bekingham one of his companions, [*qui poſiti fuerunt in fornace, et prodierunt aurum:*] for they had dealt uprightly in their places, and had never ſtained their hands with ſordid bribery. But let us return to our naturall Jews.

The richeſt of theſe ſoon after this parliament, by force of the kings writ having imbarked themſelves with their treaſure in a tall ſhip of great burthen, when the ſhip was under ſail, and gotten down the Thames towards the mouth of the river beyond Quinborough, the maſter of the ſhip confederating with ſome of the mariners, invented a ſtratagem to deſtroy them, and to bring the ſame to paſſe, commanded to caſt anchor, and rode at the ſame till the ſhip at an ebbe lay on the dry ſands; the maſter and his confederates, in further execution of their wicked plot, moved and inticed thoſe rich Jews to walk with the maſter on land, for their recreation and preſervation of health, which they did: at laſt, when the maſter underſtood the tide to be coming in, he ſtole away from them, and got him back to the ſhip, whither he was, as it was before plotted, drawn up by a cord; the Jews made not ſo much haſte as he did, becauſe they knew not the danger, but when they perceived in what perill they were in (that had ſhewed

no mercie to numbers that cryed to them) cryed to him for help: his wicked and prophane anſwer to them was, that they ought rather to cry to Moſes, by whoſe conduct their fathers paſſed through the Red Sea, and that he was able to deliver them out of thoſe raging flouds which now came in upon them: and within a a ſhort ſpace ſwallowed up them all: the maſter, and ſuch other as were conſenting to this foul fact, were before the juſtices itinerants indicted, convicted of murther, and hanged.

Chron. de Dunſtable & Vet. Manuſcr. Itiner. Kanc. coram. Juſtic. Itiner. an. 18 E. 1.

And hereby it appeareth, that divine ultion did follow theſe cruell Jews, wicked and wretched men; for the debts of cruelty are ſeldom unpaid.

We will here adde a record *de Priore de Bridlington*, the information or charge is not in the record, this onely we finde:

[509]

Pl. Parlam. poſt Paſch. apud London. 21 E. 1. Rot. 4.

* Note a good expoſition upon this ſtatute.

What offence it is to deceive the king of any of his forfeitures.

* For in doing of his fealty he is ſworn.

Et quia prædictus prior cognoſcit quod prædicta pecunia præd' Judæo debebatur, viz. 300 *l. nec ei ſolvebatur ante exilium Judæorum, &* * *quicquid remanſit de eorum debitis, aut catallis in regno poſt eorum exilium domino regi fuit; conſideratum eſt quod dominus rex recuperet pecuniam præd', & dictum eſt eidem priori quod non exeat villa antequam domino regi de præd' pecunia ſatisfaciat. Et reſpondeat Johannes archiepiſcopus Eborum, quia præcepit dicto priori ſolvere valett' ſuo prædictam pecuniam in deceptionem regis, contra* * *ſacramentum & fidelitatem ſuam domino regi datam, &c. Idem in alio Rot. anno* 22 *E.* 1. *Rot.* 5.

The archbiſhop confeſſing the ſame, was adjudged to be *in miſericordia regis, ſed idem dominus rex reſervat ſibi ipſi taxationem miſericordiæ.*

This light touch we have given to this branch of this act, to the end it may be a precedent and pattern in like caſes to apply the like remedy, and will leave the reader to peruſe the reſidue of this act, which is worthy to be read, and needeth not any expoſition.

---

[510]

MODUS LEVANDI FINES,

Editum Anno 18 Edw. I.

QUANT le briefe original ſoit lie en preſence des parties devant juſtices, donques dira un countour (1) *iſſint: Sir juſtice, conge dacord'* (2)*: le juſtice dirra, que dirra?* (3) *Sir Robert, et noſmera un des parties. Donques quant ils ſerront agree de la ſumme de pecune* (4) *que eſt done al roy, donques dirra le juſtice, Cries la peace* (5). *Et*

WHEN the writ original is delivered in preſence of the parties before juſtices, a pleader ſhall ſay this, Sir juſtice, conge, de accorder; and the juſtice ſhall ſay to him, What ſaith ſir R. and ſhall name one of the parties. Then, when they be agreed of the ſum of money that muſt be given to the king, then the juſtice ſhall

*Et puis dirra le countour, Issint que la peace est tiell, a vous conge, que William et Alice sa feme, que cy sont, recognisont (7) le mannour de B. ove les appurtenances (8) contenus en le briefe (6), estre droit du R. come cell' que il ad de lour done, A. aver et tener a luy et a ses heires, de W. et Alice, et les heires A. come en demesne, rent, seigniories, courts, plees (9), purchases, gardes, mariages, reliefes, escheats, molins, avowsons de esglises, et touts auters franchises, et franke customes al avantdits manours apperteignant, rendant per a N. et ses heires, chiefes seigniours de fee, service due, et customes pur touts services. Et fait assavoir, que order de ley ne suffre mye, que final accorde soit leve en la court le roy (10) sans briefe original (11), et ceo a tout le meins devant iv. justices en bank (12), ou en eyre, et non pas aillours (13), et en presence des parties nosmes en briefe (14), queux soient de pleine age, et de bone memorie, et hors de pryson. Et si feme covert de baron soit un des parties, donques covient que el soit primerment confesse de iv. justices avantdits (15). Et si el nassent al fine, ne ceo liver' mie (16). Et la cause pur que tiel solempnitie doit estre fait en cel fine est, pur ceo que fine est ci hault barre, et de ci graund force, et de ci puissant nature en soy, que el forclos nemy solement ceux queux sont parties et privies (20) a la fine, et lour heires (19), mes touts auters gentes de mound' (21), queux sont de pleine age, hors de pryson (17), et de bone memorie, et deins les iv. meres, le jour del fine levie (22), sils ne mettront * lour claime (23) de lour action pur le pays, deins lan et le jour (18).*

*[511]

shall say, Cry the peace. And after the pleader shall say, In so much as peace is licensed thus unto you W. S. and A. his wife, that here be, do acknowledge the manor of B. with the appurtenances contained in the writ to be the right of our lord the king, which he hath of their gift, to have and to hold to him and his heirs, of the said W. and A. and the heirs of A. as in demeans, rents, seigniories, courts, pleas, purchases, wards, marriages, reliefs, escheats, mills, advowsons of churches, and all other franchises and free customs to the said manor belonging, paying yearly to R. and his heirs, as chief lords of the fee, the services and customs due for all services. And it is to be noted, that the order of the law will not suffer a final accord to be levied in the king's court without a writ original, and that must be at the least before four justices in the bench, or in eyre, and not otherwise and in presence of the parties named in the writ, which must be of full age, of good memory, and out of prison. And if a woman covert be one of the parties, then she must be first examined by four of the said justices; and if she doth not assent thereunto, the fine shall not be levied. And the cause wherefore such solemnity ought to be done in a fine, is, because a fine is so high a bar, of so great force, and of so strong nature in itself, that it concludeth not only such as be parties and privies thereto, and their heirs, but all other people of the world, being of full age, out of prison, of good memory, and within the four seas, the day of the fine levied, if they make not their claim of their action within a year and a day by the country.

(5 Rep. 39. Rast. 349. 27 Ed. 1. stat. 1. c. 1. 1 R. 3. c. 7. 4 H. 7. c. 24. 4 Rep. 125. 4 Ed. 3. f. 46. 15 Ed. 2. stat of Carlisle.)

Pl. Com. 368. a. Glanv. li. 8. ca. 1, 2, &c. Bract. lib. 5. fo. 435. lib. 3. f. 106. li. 4. fo. 256. Brit. f. 91 & 216. Fleta, l. 6. c. 52. Lib. 2. ca. 12. Lib. 5. fo. 38. Teys case. Li. 4. f. 125. Beverlies case. * Int' placita de Parliam. apud Asheridge, anno 19 E. 1. Rot. 12. The case of Margery, late the wife of Th. Weyland. 27 E 1. c. 1. acc'. First part of the Inst. sect. 441. Dier 12 El. 291. Pl. Com. 254. Stowels case. & 432. Stapletons case. Li. 6. fo. 38, 39. Teyes case.

For the antiquitie of fines, it is certaine that they were frequent before the conquest.

For what end and purpose fines, or a finall concord were first instituted, and wherefore it is called *finis*, it appeareth in the said auncient authors, *ubi supra*, which wrote before this act, * and by others, and further by an ancient record of parliament, *anno* 19 E. 1. in these words, *Nec in regno isto provideatur vel sit aliqua securitas major vel solemnior, per quam aliquis statum certiorem habere possit, vel ad statum suum verificandum aliquod solemnius testimonium producere, quam finem in curia domini regis levatum, qui quidem finis sic vocatur, eo quod finis et consummatio omnium placitorum esse debet.* See the record, for it is notable.

For the hautesse and puissant force and nature of a fine, somewhat shall be said hereafter in this chapter, in the meane time the true pleading of a fine is not, that *I. S. levavit quendam finem, sed quod quidam finis se levavit, &c.* without alledging of any season.

For the parts of a fine, see Teyes case, lib. 6.

(1) *Un countor.*] That is to say, a serjant, as before it hath been said.

(2) *Conge daccorder.*] *i. Licentia concordandi.*

For this license a fine is due to the king, which is called *finis pro licentia concordandi.* And the reason that this fine is taken, is for that the king loseth by reason of this concord the fines or amerciaments, which should have beene due to him upon the judgement or non-suit, and other advantages.

This fine *pro licentia concordandi* is an ancient flower of the crown, and is called the kings silver, and the post fine, and it is called the post fine in respect of the primer fine, or the fine in the Hamper; for in every reall action of lands or tenements of the yearly value of 5 marks, there is due in the Hamper upon the originall vi. s. viij. d. *viz.* for every v. marks of land vi. s. viij. d. and if it be under v. marks, no fine in the Hamper upon the originall is due: a writ of covenant to levy a fine (whereupon fines in these dayes are usually levied) is holden a reall writ, for which a fine in the Hamper is paid. Now the fine *pro licentia concordandi*, or the post fine is also certain, for it is as much as the primer fine, and halfe as much more. As for example *(quia exempla illustrant)* a writ of covenant is brought to levie a fine of land, of the yearly value of v. marks, there is vi. s. viij. d. due presently for the primer fine, or fine in the Hamper, but the fine *pro licentia concordandi*, or the post fine is not due till *conge d'accorder* be graunted by the court, in this case the post fine is x. s. that is as much, and halfe as much as the primer fine was, but if the land be under v. marks, so as no primer fine is due, yet shall there be a fine *per conge daccorder*, and that is also certain, *viz.* vi. s. viij. d.

And note there is no post fine due, but when there is *conge daccorder*, and in the court of common pleas there is a speciall clerk for the entring of the kings silver in a roll, which is also endorsed upon the writ of covenant.

And these fines *pro licentia concordandi* are not against *Magna Charta*, c. 29. for it is an ancient revenue of the crown.

Dier 5 El. 220. b. Lib. 5. fol. 39. Teyes case.

And the post fine is paid (as here it appeareth) for the concord, for that is the foundation and substance of the fine, for after that, and

and the kings silver entred, though the conusor dieth, the fine is good, and the land passeth, but if the kings silver be not entred, the fine may be reversed in a writ of error.

If a man bring two originall writs of covenant, the one for land in Suff. of the yearly value of vi. l. and another in Essex of xxiv. l. and albeit there be two originals, yet there is but one concord, and for that concord one entire fine is due and not severall. [512] 6 Eliz. Dier 227.

(3) *Que donera.*] The printed bookes are faulty, for they be *que dirra:* which should be *que donera,* that who is the conusee, that he may give it, and the serjant nameth him. Lib. 5. fo. 39. Teyes case.

Now the conusee doth pay the fine, *pur licence daccorder,* as here it appeareth, and if there be more then one in the fine, then he, in whom the fee reposeth by the fine, prayeth the same.

And this fine *pur conge daccorder* doe belong to the king in so high degree of his prerogative, that they passe not by his generall graunt of all fines, albeit the grant be *ex certa scientia, speciali gratia, et mero motu, &c.*

(4) *Quant ils sont agree del somme de pecunie.*] Which is easily done, for the fine upon a just computation of the primer fine, is, as is aforesaid, certaine.

(5) *Cries la peace.*] Some hath it, *Treates le peace,* that is, drawn the peace: here peace is taken for the concord, and the serjant shall say, *Le peace est tiel ove vostre conge.*

(6) *Que William et Alice sa feme, que cy sont, recognisont le mannor de B. ove les appurtenances,* &c.] Here it appeareth that they which levy the fine ought to doe it in person, and in open court expressed in these words [*que cy sont;*] and the reason thereof was, that the judges in open court might upon the view, and other good meanes discerne of their age, ideocy, *non compos mentis,* and coverture, and whether those that appeare were the same persons, all which might better be discerned in open court, and the judges informed of the truth thereof, where some people of most of the parts of the kingdome are many times present, and men will be more fearfull to offer any thing that is unjust in open court (which is the publike seat of justice) then in a private chamber, and this was in respect of the hautesse and puissant force and nature of a fine.

But this is altered by a later statute, whereby it is provided, that if any person aged or decrepit, impotent, or by casualty be so oppressed or holden, that by no meanes he is able to come before the justices in court, that in such case two or one of the justices, by assent of the residue of the bench, shall visit the party so diseased, and shall receive his conusance upon the plea, and forme of the plea, that he hath in court, whereupon the same fine ought to be levied; and if there goe but one, he shall take with him an abbot, a prior, or a knight of good fame and credence; and hereof the writ of *dedimus potestatem* had his beginning, and at the first was not graunted, but where the party was so aged, decrepit, or impotent, as he could not come to the court, and accordingly the writ of *dedimus potestatem* was framed, *ac præfatus A. adeo impotens existat quod absque maximo sui corporis periculo usq; ad Westm' ad diem in brevi prædict' content' ad recognitionem quod in hac parte requiritur faciend'* Stat. de Carlile. 15 E. 2.

faciend' laborare non sufficit; which forme albeit it continueth to this day, yet is the conusans taken of them that be in health, and
Vet. N.B. f. 103. Br. tit. fines 120. able to travell. And where that act speaketh of a justice, a *dedimus potestatem* is graunted to a serjant at law, sworn to the king, as common experience teacheth; and the chief justice of the court of common pleas may take a conusans of a fine, *virtute officii sui*,
1 H. 7. 9. a. without any writ of *dedimus potestatem*.

[513] Here is a forme of the most principall fine, *viz.* the fine *sur conusance de droit come ceo que il ad de son done*.

41 E. 3. 14. 21 E. 4. 4. It is to be known that there are two kinds of fines, *viz.* one executed, and the other executory. Executed, that is, where the present estate passeth unto, or is supposed in the conusee, for such a fine is a feoffement of record, as this fine *come ceo*, or *sur releas*, or confirmation, or *sur surrender*.

50 E. 3. 9. 28 E. 3. 95. 44 Ass. 36. 21 E. 3. fines 23. 7 H. 4. 16. 1 H. 7. 12. 22, 23, &c. 31 E. 1. grant 90. 7 E. 3. 14. 24 E. 3. 26. 39 E. 3. 1. 50 E. 3. fines 1. Glan. l. 8. ca. 3. Executory, as when no estate is vested in the conusee untill it be executed by entry or action, as fines *sur graunt et render* by the conusee, which must be made upon a fine *come ceo*, or *sur releas*, &c. or other fine which is executed, or otherwise the conusee could not make any graunt and render of that land, &c. which he had not; more shall be said hereof in the exposition upon the statute of 27 E. 1. *de finibus*.

(7) *Recognisont*, &c.] *Recognoverunt* is the auncient and usuall word in a fine for the conveyance of lands, &c. and very apt, for it is made a plea of land depending when either the demandant or tenant doth acknowledge the land to be the right of the other
Glan. l. 8. ca. 1. *per amicabilem compositionem, et finalem concordiam*, as Glanvill saith.

The agreement of the parties have altered the forme of the conusans here expressed, and doe adde, *et illud remisit et quietum clamavit*, &c. Also the fine *sur conusans de droit come ceo*, doth now comprehend a clause of warranty, which is here omitted.

13 E. 1. attaint 71. 2 E. 3. 19. 21 E. 3. 44. 32 E. 3. Scire fac' in ration. divisis. 50 E. 3. 23. 4 E. 4. 2. 18 E. 4. 22. 19 E. 4. 23. 21 E. 4. 4. (8) *Le mannor de B. ove les appurtenances.*] Of what hereditaments a fine may be levied? Regularly it may be levied of any thing whereof a *præcipe quod reddat* doth lie, as of land, rent, &c. or whereof a *præcipe quod faciat*, as the writ of customes and services, or whereof a *præcipe quod permittat*, as to have common a way, &c. or to be short, whereof a *præcipe quod teneat* doth lie, as the writ of covenant to levy a fine and the like. But of ancient times fines were levied of other things, then will be at this day allowed, and yet those ancient fines shall be holden now as available, as they were taken to be when they were levied.

17 E. 3. fo. 31. 21 E. 3. 20. 44 E. 3. 7 H. 4. 44. 8 H. 4. 23. 8 E. 4. 6. A fine cannot be levied of a mannor, or lands, that is ancient demesne, for that should be a wrong to the lord of whom the land is holden, for by the fine it should become frank fee, and not impleadable in his court, &c. and if any such fine be levied, the lord shall reverse the same in a writ of deceit, for *res inter alios acta alteri nocere non debet*.

(9) *Come in demesne, rents, seigniories, courts, pleas*, &c.] At the time of the making of this act, the forme was to enumerate in generall whereof the mannor consisted, but that forme is now also altered, and that clause wholly omitted at this day.

(10) *Le ordre del ley ne suffer my que finall concord soit levy en la court le roy sans briefe originall.*] Hereby it appeareth that this act is a declaration of the common law, and the ignorance or error of some judges was the cause of declaring of the law herein.

a First,

First, if there be no originall writ, yet the fine is not void, but voidable by law, and therefore the act saith [*Le ordre del ley ne suffer*] and that is by writ of error, and that holdeth also when there is an originall writ and the fine is levied as well of that which is contained in the writ, as of some other thing not contained: as if the writ of covenant be of the mannor of D. and the fine is of the mannor of D. and likewise of the mannor of S. it is voidable for the mannor of S. by writ of error. It holdeth also when the fine is levied immediately to a person not named in the writ of covenant; as if A. be plaintiffe in the writ of covenant against C. and C. levieth the fine to A. and B. it is voidable by writ of error, but the learning must be further expressed. 7 E. 3. 64. 24 E. 3. 28. 18 E. 4. 22. 19 E. 2. 2. Li. 3. fo. 5. Owen & Morgans case. [514]

For as concerning the thing whereof the fine is levied, it is to be knowne that in case of a fine *sur grant et render*, which containeth a double fine, there is a great diversity between the fine *sur conusans de droit come ceo, &c.* for that must be levied of the land, &c. in the originall, but the grant and render may be of another thing then is expressed in the originall: as A. bringeth a writ of covenant against B. for the mannor of D. B. cannot levie a fine to A. of a rent to be issuing out of the mannor of D. but he must levie the fine of the mannor of D. according to the writ, and his covenant therein expressed, but A. may grant and render to B. a rent out of the same mannor contained in the fine, but not out of any other land, neither can the grant and render be of any thing collaterall to the land, &c. contained in the writ, or of another nature, and neither issuing out of, nor incident to the land, &c. contained in the originall. 10 E. 3. 35. 54. 18 E. 3. 9. 19 E. 3. Abbot 13. 20 E. 3. bre. 686. 26 Ass. 37. 29 E. 3. 3. 38 E. 3. 17. 18 E. 4. 22. 19 E. 4. 2, 3. 21 E. 4. 4. b.

If two doe levy the fine, the graunt and render may bee to one of them. 24 E. 3. 35.

As concerning the persons to be named in the fine, the fine *sur conusans de droit come ceo, &c.* cannot be levied to any person that is not party to the writ of covenant, neither can the grant and render of the land, &c. be immediately *in primo gradu* to any that is no party to the writ, but mediately or in 2 *gradu, &c.* it may: for example, if a writ of covenant be brought by A. against B. of the mannor of D. B. levy a fine to A. *come ceo*, A. may grant and render the same to B. for life, or in taile, the remainder to F. in fee; for albeit the writ of covenant be *inter* A. *querent' et* B. *deforc'*, so as F. is a meere stranger to the writ, yet seeing he taketh it by way of remainder depending upon an estate warranted by the fine, it hath been allowed in our books, and hath been compared to a deed indented betweene A. and B. whereby A. doth give lands to B. to have and to hold to B. for life, or in taile, the remainder to C. (who is a stranger to the deed) in fee. 6 E. 2. fines 117. 7 E. 3. 37. 64. 10 E. 3. 32. 16 E. 3. fines 8. 18 H. 7. fines Br. 111. 30 H. 8. Bro. fines 108.

(11) *Briefe originall.*] It is not said, *briefe originall enter les parties*, but generally, and therefore a fine may be levied by a vowchee to the demandant, or by the demandant to him, and so likewise by tenant by receit to the demandant, or by the demandant to him, and yet they are not parties to the writ. 18 E. 3. 12. 8 H. 4. 5. 21 E. 4. 4. 5 H. 7. 41.

In ancient times fines were levied upon originals that were mixt, as in the assise of *darrein presentment, quare impedit*, or the like, which later times have thought to be against the height and force of a fine. For the forme of the originall writ it is to be observed, that if a fine be levied of eight severall things, as of a mannor, a rectory, a house, &c. after the naming of the mannor, the forme is, 2 E. 3. 19. 10 E. 3. 5. 18 E. 4. 22. 19 E. 4. 2, 3. 21 E. 4. 4. b. See 27 E. 1. ca. 1.

ac

ac de rectoria, necnon de messuagio; for the fourth, *ac etiam*; for the fifth, *praeterea*; for the sixth, *ac ulterius*; for the seventh, *ac etiam*; for the eighth, *ac insuper*: and if there be more, then to begin again: and I have known a chirografe of a fine discovered of forgery by not observing this order.

27 E. 1. c. 1. 4 H. 7. c. 24. 32 H. 8. c. 36. (12) *Et ceo a tout le meyns devant 4. justices en banke.*] The statute of 27 E. 1. saith, *quia fines in curia nostra levati, &c.* and by the statute of 4 H. 7. it is provided that after the engrossing of every fine to bee levied, &c. in the kings court, before his justices of the common pleas, &c. so as the number of justices here mentioned [515] are not requisite at this day: but before the making of this statute, the justices before whom the fine was levied, were named in the fine and specially upon the making of this act, to the end the number of the justices might appear; for though the number of four be not required, yet there must be above the number of one. And this 1 H. 7. 10, 11. per les justices. is the reason that a fine levied *coram Thom. Brian milite, et sociis suis justiciariis de communi banco*, were not good; because no other judge of that court was named but one, and before one a fine cannot be levied in respect of the solemnity thereof. But many writs that come out of the chancery, are *coram Thoma Brian et sociis suis.*

50 Ass. p. 9. 44 E. 3. 38. 31 H. 8. Fines Bro. 110. (13) *Et non pas ailours.*] A fine cannot be levied, to have the force of a finall concord by any that hath power *tenere placita*, but onely before the justices of the court of common pleas, or before justices in eyre (whiles they stood) *et non pas ailours*, saith this act: and therefore the king cannot grant power to hold plea for the levying of fines, against this negative statute.

(14) *Et en presence des parties nosmes en le briefe.*] The vouchee and tenant by receit are not named in the writ, and yet they may (as hath been said) levie a fine to the demandant, or the demandant to them; and these words being in the affirmative do not restrain them.

(15) *Et si feme covert de baron soit un des parties, donques covient* 24 E. 3. 62. 42 E. 3. 37. 46 Ed. 3. 15. 3 H. 6. 4. 8 H. 6. 4. *que el soit primerment confessé devant iv. justices avantdits.*] This must be understood where the husband and wife do levie a fine, for there she ought to be examined; but where the husband and wife do take by a fine, and depart with nothing, there the feme covert is not to be examined.

25 E. 3. 44. 4 E. 3. 41. 5 E. 3. 24. 6 E. 3. 22. 10 E. 3. 26. 18 E. 2. Fines 121. 4 E. 3. ibid. 43. 16 E. 3. ibid. 6. If a fine be levied of land to the husband and wife, and the husband and wife grant and render the land, there the wife shall be examined, and the examination must ever be upon the writ; and therefore a baron and feme upon a fine levied to them of land cannot grant and render a rent out of the land, because that rent is not contained in the writ.

The examination must be solely and secretly, and the effect thereof is, whether she be content of her own free good will, without any menace or threat to levie a fine of these parcels, and name them unto her, every thing distinctly contained in the writ, so as 25 E. 3. 44. she perfectly understand what she doth; and if the judge doubteth of her age, he may examine her upon her oath.

45 E. 3. tit. Examination 22. But what if the woman cannot speak any language that the judge doth understand, as Cornish, Welsh, Dutch, or the like? then there shall be a Latimer, that is, an interpreter upon his oath to interpret truly.

(16) *Et*

(16) *Et sil nassent al fine, ne ceo liera mie.*] This is so to be understood, that it ought not to be received, if she be not examined, and freely assent, as is aforesaid; but if the fine be received, and recorded, the feme covert or her heirs shall not be received to aver that she was not examined nor assented: for this should be against the record of the court, and tending to the weakning of the generall assurances of the realm.

(17) *De pleine age, et de bone memorie, et hors de pryson.*] See W. 2. cap. 48. hereof, and see Beverlies case, lib. 4. 123, 124, &c. See lib. 2. fol. 58. in Beckwiths case. Lib. 2. fo. 58. Beckwiths case.

(18) *Et la cause pur que tiel solempnitie doit estre fait en cel fine est, pur ceo que fine est ci hault barre, et de ci graund force, et de ci puissant nature en soy, que el forclos nemy solement ceux queux sont parties et privies a la fine, et lour heires, mes toutes auters gentes de mond', queux sont de pleine age, hors de pryson, et de bone memorie, et deins les iv. meres, le jour del fine levie, sils ne mettront lour claime de lour action pur le pais, deins lan et le jour.*] Here are four things to be observed: [516]

1. First, the cause that such solemnity is used in the levying of a fine, wherein three things are to be observed; 1. for that it is so high a bar, 2. of so great force, 3. of so puissant a nature.

2. The end, to make an end of troubles and controversies, and to establish concord, peace, and repose in mens possessions and inheritances; and therefore a fine is called *finalis concordia*.

3. The means to attain to the same, *viz.* to forclose two kinde of persons, *viz.* parties and privies presently, and also the strangers in the world, *in futuro*.

4. A two-fold provision full of right and equity is made for strangers; first, that they be of full age, out of prison, of good memory, and within the four seas; secondly, that they put in their claim within the yeer and the day, after the fine levied. Bract. li. 5. fo. 405, &c. Brit. f. 216. b. Fleta, li. 6. c. 53. W. 2. cap. 1. 1. Part of the Institutes, § 441

By this act, if any stranger were within age, or in prison, or *non compos mentis*, or beyond the seas at the fine levied, * he is totally and for ever excepted; so as he after his full age, or coming out of prison, or recovering his memory, or coming into the realm, or any of their heirs need not to make any claim: and hereby a woman covert was bounden, if claim were not made within the yeer and day; and the reason was, for that she had a husband that was able to put in his claim: but if the husband were within age at the time of the fine levied, though the wife were of full age, the infancie of the husband (who was to make the claim, the wife being *sub potestate viri*) should priviledge the state of the wife for ever. So as by the justice of the ancient com' law, wherof this act is a * declaration, two kinde of strangers to the fine were exempted and provided for; first such as by presumption of law had not sufficient understanding, as the infant, or *non compos mentis*; or had no notice, as the man in prison, or beyond sea, of the fine levied to make claim: and secondly, for such as had ancient rights, who are ever favoured in law, if they made their claim within the yeer and day.

* This is altered by the statute of 4 H. 7. cap. 24.

This act was made an. 18. E. 1.

* Vide Mich. 15 E. 1. in banco Rot. 107. Essex. Pasch. 10 E. 1. Rot. 72. in banco Heref. John de la Cumbes case.

(19) *Parties et privies, et lour heires.*] Parties are those that are parties to the originall. Pl. com. 357.

(20) *Privies.*] First, that is to be understood of privies in blood, not onely of the heirs by the common law, which are here named; but heirs by the custome, here comprehended under this word [*privies*] as borough English, gavelkinde, or the like, which claim, Lib. 3. fo. 23. Walkers case. Pl. com. 363. per Brown. W. 1. ca. 39. 6 E. 2. View 161. 40 Ass. Pl. 2.

19 E. 2. Count. de Vouch. 114. 12 E. 3. ibid. 326. Pl. com. Howels caſe.

claim as heirs by cuſtome; and is not intended of privies in eſtate, as joyntenants, the donor and donee, leſſor and leſſee, or the like: alſo this is to be underſtood of privies in ſucceſſion, as biſhops, abbots, and the like.

[517]

Lib. 5. fo. 123. Saffyns caſe, li. 9. fol. 105. Mary Podgers caſe. 41 E. 3. 13. li. 2. 93. Bingham, lib. 3. 84, &c. Caſe de Fines, fo. 77. Fermors caſe, li. 4. fo. 125. li. 8. 100. 72. li. 9. 87. 139. li. 10. 90. 97. lib. 11. fo. 69. 71. 78. 33 E. 3. Eſtoppel 380. 21 E. 3. 21. 8 H. 4. 9. Dier 22 El. 373. 4 E. 4. 12. Stanf. Prærog. 69. * 4 H. 7. ca. 24. 32 H. 8. ca. 36.

(21) *Mes auxy toutes auters gentes de mond'.*] In theſe words are included aſwell tenant for yeers, tenant by ſtatute merchant, and ſtaple, copy-holders, and cuſtomary-holders, as tenants of free-hold and inheritance, if they be out of poſſeſſion or ſeiſin at the time of the fine levied, for a fine levied by a ſtranger cannot barre him that is in poſſeſſion. And albeit the words of this law are very generall, yet do they not abrogate the ſtatute of W. 2. *De donis conditionalibus*, which provideth for preſervation of eſtates in tail. *Quod ſi finis ſuper hujuſmodi tenementa impoſterum levetur, finis ipſo jure ſit nullus, nec habent hæredes hujuſmodi, aut illi ad quos ſpectat reverſio, &c. neceſſe apponere clameum.* * But that branch *de donis conditionalibus* continued in force notwithſtanding this act, as to the right of the eſtate tail, untill the ſtatute of *anno* 4 H. 7. by which act, and by the ſtatute of *anno* 32 H. 8. an eſtate in tail is barred by fine with proclamations levied, and had according to thoſe acts.

[a] 6 R. 2. Eſtoppel 211.

[a] In ſome caſe the party himſelf ſhall not be concluded of his averment againſt the expreſſe fine; as if two joyntenants be in fee, and they accept a fine *ſur conuſans de droit come ceo a eux, et les heires de lun*, the eſtate is not changed, and they may plead the former feoffment to them and their heirs, and that by law they could have no other fine.

42 E. 3. 9. 41 E. 3. 14. 8 Aſſ. 33. 4 E. 3. 469. 13 Aſſ. 8. 8 H. 4. 8, 9. 12 E. 4. 15, &c. Lib. 3. fo. 88, 89. in caſe de Fines.

And in ſome caſes privies in blood, and inheritable alſo ſhall have an averment aginſt the fine, notwithſtanding this ſtatute: and therefore if tenant in tail accept a fine *ſur conuſans de droit come ceo, &c.* yet the iſſue in tail, that is privie, and heir in tail ſhall aver continuance of poſſeſſion in the father; for it ſtandeth well with the fine, which is [*come ceo que ad de ſon done*;] and ſo it is in the caſe above, if tenant in tail had granted, and rendred the land to the conuſor, the iſſue in tail might have averred continuance of poſſeſſion in the father, for the fine was executory, and nothing veſted in the conuſor untill execution: but if tenant in tail levie a fine *ſur conuſans de droit come ceo*, the iſſue in tail, though he be not barred by the fine yet he ſhall not againſt this fine aver continuance of poſſeſſion in the father, and that diverſity was holden for law after this ſtatute; neither after this ſtatute could the iſſue in tail have generally pleaded, that *partes finis nihil habuerunt*, but was ouſted thereof by this ſtatute, albeit ſome have relyed much upon theſe words in this act, *rite levatus*; now the ſtatutes of 4 H. 7. and 32 H. 8. and the expoſition thereof *ubi ſupra*, make this out of queſtion.

46 E. 3. 14. 13 E. 3. Replication 62. 17 E. 3. 53. 33 E. 3. Eſtoppell 280. 22 E. 3. 17. 33 H. 16. 18. Lib. 3. fol. 88, 89. Caſe de Fines.

4 E. 3. 46. Opinion al cont. 7 E. 3. 37. Acc. 13 E. 3. Replication 62. 11 R. 2. Eſcheat 13. 14 H. 4. 32. per Hankford. Pl. com. 357. b. Dier 3 Mar. 117. This is altered

(22) *Le jour del fine levie.*] This is to be underſtood of a compleat fine, which giveth a double notice, one by the ſolemnity of the fine in court, and another by tranſmutation of poſſeſſion in the country; as for example, one that hath a defeiſible title in land accepts a fine thereof *ſur conuſans de droit come ceo, &c.* and granteth and rendreth the ſame to the conuſor, who ſueth not execution within the yeer and day, this fine ſhall not bar him that had the ancient right, becauſe it is no compleat fine without poſſeſſion, within the meaning of this act, for that by intendment he that had right

right cannot take notice of the fine without transmutation of possession, and so out of the meaning of the law.

Note a fine *sur conusans de droit come ceo, &c.* is said to be levied when the writ of covenant is returned, and the concord and the kings silver duly entred, this maketh the land to passe, and from this shall the yeer and day be accounted, albeit the fine be ingrossed afterward.

by the statute of 4 H. 7. and five yeers given, &c. 22 H. 6. 13. Pl. com. 432.

(23) *Si ils ne mettront lour claime,* &c.] For the preserving of ancient * rights at the com' law, there were 4 manner of claims, whereof two were by matter of record, and two by act in the country; by matter of record, as by a *præcipe quod reddat*, according to the truth of the case brought within the yeer and day by him that right had, or in ancient time by an entry of a claim, entred in the record of the * foot of the fine; but first it must have been made in open court, [*appono clameum meum tali liti vel concordiæ, &c.*] And two by acts in the country, as by an actuall entry into the land, by him which right had, and whose entry was congeable, or by a continuall claim which amounted to an entry; but all these must be done by him that had a present right of action, or a present right of entry, for no other person could make any claim: and therefore if there were tenant for life, or in tail, the reversion or remainder over in [a] fee, he that had right of reversion or remainder expectant upon an estate for life, or in tail, could make no claim, because he had neither present right of action nor of entry; and therefore in that case the tenant for life, or in tail must make his claim, and that claim either by action or entry upon the foot of the fine, or by lawfull entry or continuall claim, should not onely have preserved their own right, but also the right of them in reversion or remainder; but if no claim were made by the particular tenant, the right of them in the remainder or reversion were for ever bound by the common law.

Pl. com. 358, 359, &c. in Stow. case.

*[518]

* Vide infra. Pasch. 18 E. 1. Bract. li. 5. fo. 436. nu. 7. Fleta, li. 6. c. 52. Hil. 16 E. 2. in cui in vita. Pl. com. 359. See 1. Part of the Instit. §416.

[a] Mich. 15 E. 1. in banco Rot. 107. Essex. Lucia filia Johan. de Northope. But there it is adjudged, that if tenant for life, the reversion over, and an estranger that hath nothing in the land levie a fine, without devesting or displacing of any of the estates, he in the reversion shall not be bound to make any claim, because *partes fin. nihil habuerint.*

[b] This is altred in two respects by the said act of 4 H. 7. for thereby the claim must be by action or entry, and therefore a claim entred upon the foot of the fine at this day is not available. Also they that have a right of a reversion or remainder expectant upon an estate tail, or for life, shall have five yeers after their title come unto them, as by that act appeareth.

The words of this act be, [*s'ilz ne mittont lour claime*] and yet in some case the right of one that might claim, and doth not, shall be preserved; [c] as if a disseisor be disseised, and the second disseisor levie a fine, in this case if the first disseisor enter within the yeer, this shall preserve the right of the disseisee, because the first disseisor by his entry avoided the whole estate given by the fine, and yet the disseisee might have entred himself [*et sic de similibus*;] but it must not have been an empty fine that should have barred the right of a stranger, but a fine compleat, as hath been said.

[d] This law continued untill the parliament in the four and thirtieth yeer of E. 3. and then the statute of non-claim was in that parliament made, which took away the effect and force of this law, and of the common law in this point, whereby great contention arose, and few men were sure of their possessions, which continued till the [e] parliament, *anno* 4 H. 7. and then that mischief was reformed, and the ancient common law excellently moderated by the statute of 4 H. 7. See the statute of 32 H. 8. which acts have for the common quiet and repose of all been with great wisdom and judgement

[b] 4 H. 7. c. 24. See Pasch. 18 E. 1. Rot. 1. Robert Bakuns case, a claim made upon the foot of the fine. Westmerl. And in the same roll Rob. de Hustings made the like claim for 5. s. rent. Northamp.

[c] 16 E. 2. Cont. claim 10. Pl. com. 358. b.

[d] See the 1. part of the Institutes, sect. 441.

[e] 4 H. 7. ca. 24.

32 H. 8. ca. 34. Lib. 1. fo. 96. Shellings case. Lib. 2. fo. 15, 16. Wisemans case. 93. Binghams case. Lib. 3. fo. 84, &c. Le case de Fines, & ibid. 77, &c. Fearmors case. Lib. 4. fo. 125. Beverlies case. Li. 5. fo. 124. Lib. 8. 100. 72. Li. 9. 87. 104, 105, 106. 139, 140, 141. Lib. 10. 50. 96, 97. Li. 11. 69. 71. 78. Pl. com. 360, 361. Stowels case.

judgement expounded; and that a fine with procl. and five yeers past doth bar the lord in ancient demesne of his writ of deceit, and likewise a writ of errour is also thereby barred.

And though this act of 18 E. 1. be repealed, yet may it serve in many respects to explain the statutes of 4 H. 7. and 32 H. 8. For the true understanding of the common law, and of former statutes, is the sure master expositor of the latter.

To the former reports or expositions (wherein are former authorities out of the Lord Dier & Pl. Com. cited) two things are necessary to be added; the first, wherein the statute of 4 H. 7. is altred, or strengthened by any latter act of parliament: secondly, what other case heretofore adjudged upon any branch of either of the said statutes, and not heretofore published, or any other matter, may serve for the strengthening of fines, being the common assurance of the realm, or of the estates of the subjects, concerning free-holds and inheritances.

* [519]

31 Eliz. c. 2.

* As to the first, where by the statute of 4 H. 7. it is ordained that after the ingrossing of the fine, &c. the same fine be openly and solemnely read and proclaimed in the same court the same terme, and in three termes then next following the same ingrossing in the same court, at foure severall dayes in every terme. By the statute of 31 Elizab. it is enacted, that all fines with proclamations shall bee proclaimed onely foure times, that is to say, once in the terme, wherein it is ingrossed, and once in every of the three termes holden next after the same ingrossing; and that every fine proclaimed, as is aforesaid, shall bee of as great force and effect in law to all intents, and purposes, as if the same had beene sixteene times proclaimed, according to the statutes heretofore made: a beneficiall law; for the fewer proclamations, the safer. See the statute of 1 Mar. for strengthening of fines when proclamations be not made, &c. by reason of adjournement of any terme.

1 Mar. Parl. 2. c. 7.

Dier 3 El. f. 186.

It hath beene resolved that this act extendeth where but part of the terme is adjourned, for it is a favourable law, and to be taken by equitie.

23 El. ca. 3. Vide li. 5. f. 40. Dormer's case. eodem. Lib. fo. 28. & 39. & 43, 44, 45. for amendment of fines, &c.

Another statute is made for the establishment of fines and recoveries in *anno* 23 Eliz. which is evident, and whereupon we have knowne no question made, and therefore referre the reader to the whole chapter, being a profitable and beneficiall law, and of the most part of freeholders of this realm necessary to be known.

Tr. 32 Eliz. in Communi Banc. Cottons case.

As to the second, betweene Sunie & Howes, Trin. 32 Eliz. *in communi banco*, the case was, Thomas Cotton was tenant in taile of the moity of certaine lands, and of the other moity hee was tenant for life, the remainder to William Cotton his eldest sonne in taile. William Cotton went beyond sea to Antwerpe, and after the said Thomas Cotton *anno* 19 Elizab. levied a fine of the whole with proclamations, and within the yeare William Cotton died at Antwerpe, and never came into England; William his sonne being within age entred *anno* 31 Eliz. And it was adjudged that for the moity whereof Thomas Cotton was tenant in taile, William the sonne of William was barred by this act of 4 H. 7. but for the moity of William the father, the entry of his sonne William was lawfull; for albeit that William the sonne could not take advantage of the clause that gives benefit to him that is beyond sea, and his heires to enter, or take his action within five yeares after they bee within this land, because in this case William the father after the fine levied

never

never was within the land; yet for that persons out of the realme at the time of the fine levied, amongst others having a present right, are excepted out of the body of the act (which worketh the barre) therefore where he that is beyond sea at the time of the fine levied, and never returnes, is within the exception out of the body of the act, and hee and his heires may enter or take his action at any time: but in case hee doth returne, hee and his heires must enter or take his action within five yeares after his returne: and so it is of an infant being party to the fine, and having a present right, if he dieth during his infancy, he or his heires may enter or take his action at any time: and so it is of a person that is *non compos mentis* by the act of God, if hee die whiles hee is *non compos mentis*; or a man in prison, which is by act in law, if hee die in prison; or a feme covert, which is by her owne act, if shee die whiles shee is covert, being no parties to the fine. For all these are within the reason of the case adjudged of him that is out of the realme (which going out of the realme was his owne act) and never returned.

See Pl. Com. fo. 366. a. the opinion of Brown and Saunders, lege, & perlege nil temere.

[520]

See the statute of 21 *Jacobi regis* cap. 2. for the strengthening of the estates of the subjects against the king and his successors.

---

[521]

STATUTUM DE FINIBUS LEVATIS,

Editum Anno 27 Edw. I.

QUIA fines in curia nostra levat' finem litibus debent imponere, et imponunt, et ideo fines vocantur, maxime, cum post duellum et magnam assisam in suo casu ultimum locum finalem teneant imperpetuum (1), *jamque per aliquod tempus præteritum tam tempore claræ memoriæ domini Henrici regis avi nostri quam nostro partes eorundem finium* (3) *et earum partium hæredes* (4) *contra leges et consuetudines regni nostri antiquitus usitatas super hujusmodi finibus* (2) *adnullandis et evacuandis admittebantur, proponentes quod ante finem levatum à tempore levationis ejusdem, et postea petentes seu querentes aut eorum antecessores de tenementis in finibus contentis, aut de aliqua parte eorundem semper fuerunt seisiti, et sic fines hujusmodi rite levat' per juratores patriæ falso subornatos et malitiose procuratos*

FORASMUCH as fines levied in our court ought and do make an end of all matters, and therefore are called fines principally, where after waging of battail or the great assise in their cases ever they hold the last and final place. And now by a certain time passed, as well in the time of king Henry of famous memory, our grandfather, as in our time, the parties of such fines and their heirs, contrary to the laws of our realm of ancient time used, were admitted to adnul and defeat such fine, alledging, that before the fine levied, and at the levying thereof, and since, the demandants or plaintiffs, or their ancestors, were alway seised of the lands contained in the fine, or of some parcel thereof; and so fines lawfully levied were many times unjustly defeated

curatos multotiens evacuabantur et adnullabantur minus juste: nos volentes super præmissis remedium adhibere in parliamento nostro ad Westm', statuimus, quod dictæ exceptiones seu responsiones vel inquisitiones patriæ super hujusmodi exceptionibus seu responsionibus nullo modo contra hujusmodi recognitiones et fines de cætero admittantur. Et nos vero volumus, quod statutum istud tam locum habeat ad fines prius levat' quam imposterum levand'. Et videant justic', quod notæ et fines in curia nostra imposterum levand' publice et solempniter legantur, et quod placita interim cessent omnino, et hoc fiat per duos dies in septimana secundum discretionem justic',

feated and adnulled by jurors of the country falsly and maliciously procured; we therefore, intending to provide a remedy in the premisses, in our parliament at Westminster have ordained, that such exceptions, answers, or inquisitions of the country, shall from henceforth in no wise be admitted contrary to such recognisances or fines. And further we will, that this statute shall as well extend unto fines heretofore levied, as to them that shall be levied hereafter. And let the justices see that such notes and fines, as hereafter shall be levied in our court, be read openly and solemnly, and that in the mean time all pleas shall cease; and this must be at two certain days in the week, according to the discretion of the justices.

(Rast. 349, &c. 3 Rep. 88. Fitz. Replic. 62, 63. 66. 42 Ed. 3. f. 19. 18 Ed. 1. stat. 4. of fines. 1 R. 3. c. 7. 4 H. 7. c. 24. 31 El. c. 2.)

[522] (1) *Quia fines in curia nostra levati finem litibus debent imponere, et imponunt, et ideo fines vocantur, maxime cum post duellum et magnam assisam in suo casu ultimum locum finalem teneant imperpetuum jamque per aliquod tempus præteritum.*] Herewith doe agree all our ancient authors, *viz.* Glanvill, *Nota quod talis dicitur finalis concordia eo quod finem imponit negotio, adeo ut neuter litigantium ab eo de cætero liceat decedere.*

Glanv. li. 8. c. 3.

Bract. l. 5. fo. 435. Li. 3. 106. Lib. 4. 246.

Bracton, *Item si per concordiam, et finem fact', quæ similiter peremptoria est, quia dicitur finalis concordia, et ideo finalis, quia imponit finem litibus.*

Britton, fo. 90, 91.

Britton fol. 90. & 91. *Sont ascuns choses corporels que home ne purra my bien purchaser sans aide de nostre court, sicome fees, et propretes et dount per accord del purchaser, et del donour, coviendra lever fine en nostre court parmy la quel tiel manner de purchase tiendrent effect et establete.*

See before in the exposition of the statute called *modus levandi fines,* in the parliament roll, *anno* 19 E. 1. Rot. 12. the case of Margery late wife of Thomas Weyland.

(2) *Jamque per aliquod tempus præteritum tam tempore claræ memoriæ domini Henrici regis patris nostri quam nostro partes earundem finium et earum partium hæredes (contra leges et consuetudines regni nostri antiquitus usitatus) super hujusmodi finibus,* &c.] The mischiefe, or rather the abuse before this statute, was in allowance of averments by parties and privies for adnulling of fines levied *contra leges et consuetudines regni nostri antiquitus usitatas, &c.* Whereby fines were many times unjustly avoided: and what such averments were, and wherefore they were admitted, is declared by Stoner, one of the justices of the court of common pleas, who reported that he heard

9 E. 3. f. 28.

heard Sir William Bereford knight, then chiefe justice of that court say, that in ancient times parties and privies could not avoid fines, [*proponentes*] as this act saith, *quod ante finem levatam et tempore levationis ejusdem, et postea petentes seu querentes aut eorum antecessores de tenementis in finibus contentis, aut de aliqua parte earundem semper fuer' seisiti.* But afterwards (in the raigne of H. 3. in the time of insurrections and civill warres by the graundees of this realme) it was used by the maintenance of the graundees, that parties and privies might avoid fines by such averments, which averments in the raigne of E. 1. were continued untill the making of this act; all which was affirmed by Sir William Herle chiefe justice, and further he said, that the same appeared also by this statute *de finibus*, as in truth it doth.

4 E. 3. 46.

(3) *Partes earundem finium et earum partium hæredes*, &c.] So as this act taketh away the said averment, which by the maintenance of the graundees of the realm had unjustly crept in by parties and privies; for the mischiefe before this statute was, as hath been said, that when the *conusans de droit, &c.* was made to him that had never any thing before, and the conusee graunted, and rendred the same back again at the same instant to the conusor for life, or in taile with remainder over, who alwaies was seised, and in possession of the land; privies (by colour that there was no transmutation of possession) were against law permitted to avoid fines by the averment aforesaid.

And albeit this statute extendeth to averments taken by parties and privies, and extendeth not to averments made by strangers, that are no parties nor privies to the fine, yet by the common law the hautesse and puissant force and nature of fines was such, that [523] a meer stranger could not have a generall averment against a fine; and therefore it is reported by Shard one of the justices of the court of common pleas, that it was resolved by the sages of the law, that the parties, or their heirs should have no averments against fines levied contrary to the fine to avoid it; and that a stranger should have no generall averment directly to avoid a fine, if it were not upon some speciall matter, for he that is tenant after the fine levied, is intended tenant under the state of some of the parties to the fine, to whom by the common law a generall averment is not given more then to the party or privie: and the speciall matter which giveth him the averment is, that after that he pleads that the parties to the fine had nothing in the land at the time of the fine levied, he doth formerly adde, that either he himself, or some other whose estate he hath, was seised at the time of the fine levied, &c. But yet that matter is not traversable, but a mean to traverse and avoid the fine, and therefore the tenant that pleads that plea doth conclude, *et de hoc ponit se super patriam*, without a further replication; for Littleton himself that famous lawyer reporteth, that it was adjudged in the time of Sir John June, chief justice of the court of common pleas (who was constituted chief justice of that court, Februar. 9. *anno* 14 H. 6. and continued untill the 20 of Jan. *anno* 17. of the same king, and then was made chief justice of the kings bench) that when the tenant pleads in bar against a fine, *quod partes finis nihil habuerunt in ten' tempore levationis finis, nec aliquis eorum aliquid habuit, sed quidam T. B. adtunc fuit seisitus, &c. cujus statum, &c. Et de hoc ponit se super patriam, et prædictus querens similiter.* And if it be found, that the parties to the fine had nothing, &c. the fine shall

17 E. 3. 54. Wakes case. 13 E. 3. Replication 62. 32 E. 3. Vouch. 96. 13. ibid. 119. Garranty 37. 41 E. 3. 14. 14 H. 4. 33. b.

40 E. 3. 30. b. Dier 12 Eliz. 290, 291. 33 H. 6. 21. 22 H. 6. 57. 17 E. 3. 53. 32 E. 3. Replication 63. 42 E. 3. 21. 19 R. 2. Replication 53. 14 H. 4. 53. 12 E. 4. 13. 3 H. 7. 9. Dier 12 Eliz. 291. 33 H. 6. 21, &c. ubi supra. 40 E. 3. 30. b. 41 E. 3. fo. 14. Dier 12 Eliz. 250, 291.

ſhall be avoided, though the ſpeciall matter of the ſeiſin of himſelf, or of a ſtranger at the time of the fine levied be not found. And ſo it is in the caſe of the like plea to avoid a recovery, or in caſe of a counterplea of a voucher, and the like: all which you may read in that report; and this kind of pleading remains at the com: law ſince the ſtatute of 4 H. 7,

Dier ubi ſupra. Pl. com. 354. 432.

13 E. 3. Replic. 62. 17 E. 3. 53.

(4) *Et earum partium hæredes.*] This is not intended of an heir in blood onely, but of the heir of the land; for *hæres dicitur ab hæreditate:* and therefore if the heir apparant be ſeiſed of land, and the anceſtor levie a fine of the ſame land, and dyeth, this ſhall not bar the heir, for he claims not the land, whereof the fine is levied, as heir unto him.

Rot. Parl'am. an. 14 E. 3. nu. 31. The caſe of ſir John Stanton, and Anne his wife in a Formd. 13 E. 3. Vouch. 119.

See in the parliament roll of *anno* 14 E. 3. a notable caſe of an averment taken by a ſtranger againſt a fine, and afterwards adjudged, which caſe is abridged by Fitzherbert, 13 E. 3. tit. Voucher 119. but more effectually in the parliament roll.

22 E. 3. 4. 24 E. 3. 36. 78, 79. 29 E. 3. 18. 18 Aſſ. 6. 21 Aſſ. 28. 25 Aſſ. p. 3. 43 Aſſ. 6. 23 Aſſ. 13. 15 E. 3. Maint. de Bre. 55. 3 E. 3. ibid. 13. 14. Itiner. North. 17 E. 2. ibid. 1. 1 E. 3. 5. 2 E. 3. 30. 24 E. 3. 79. 4 E. 3. 30. 8 E. 3. 33. 24 E. 3. 79.

But ſeeing the learning concerning averments of parties and privies, and of ſtrangers hath been delivered as is aforeſaid; it is objected, that when joyntenancie is pleaded by fine in abatement of the writ, that a ſtranger for maintenance of his writ could not take any generall averment againſt the fine. And this being agreed unto them, as is aboveſaid, then they proceeded, that in the caſe of a fine the demandant could have no replication thereunto, as to ſay that the other joyntenant not named in the writ by his deed releaſed before the writ brought, or that they both infeoffed A. which reinfeoffed the tenant; and this was ſaid to be in reſpect of the height, and puiſſant force and nature of the fine: but to this it was anſwered, that the ſame held at the common law in caſe of joyntenancie by deed, and therefore that could not be the cauſe thereof. Then another reaſon was ſought for, and that was, that the land was the free-hold of another, and therefore it ſhould not be put in tenancie (that is, in plea of law in danger to be loſt) without the party himſelf: but if the fine or deed were made by the demandant himſelf to the tenant and another, then he might confeſſe and avoid the fine; as to ſay, that ſince that time the joyntenant infeoffed him, or the like, becauſe the demandant was party. But again it was affirmed, that that reaſon could not hold in reſpect of the ſtrangers free-hold, for that might hold alſo where joyntenancie is pleaded without fine or deed, but there it is evident that the demandant ſhall maintain his writ, and try a third perſons free-hold, nay the judges themſelves were ſometimes ſo fearſull to weaken the ſtrength and force of fines, and ſometime ſo bedazeled with the bright ſolemnity of the fine, as Sir John Stoner chief juſtice of the court of common pleas did ſay, that an averment ought to be had againſt a fine, both by conſcience and the law of God; and yet leſt the fine ſhould be avoided, he would be adviſed. This doubtfulneſſe grew, for that the true diverſity was not obſerved between averments, where they were made by parties and privies, and where by ſtrangers, nor the true pleading thereof reſolved upon.

[524]

12 E. 2. Aſſ. 116.

13 E. 3. Garranty 17.

3 E. 3. 25. b. 24 E. 3. 78. 14 H. 6. 8. 25. Dier 13 Eliz. 290, 291.

Now, that truth (the mother of juſtice) might not be ſuppreſſed, it hath been reſolved that againſt a joyntenancie pleaded by fine, the demandant may confeſſe and avoid the fine, as to ſay, that the joyntenant not named releaſed before the writ brought, or that they both infeoffed one, who reinfeoffed the tenant, or the like; for theſe

or the like pleas confeſſing and avoiding the fine, do in no ſort weaken the ſtrength or force of the ſame.

But againſt joyntenancie by fine the demandant cannot take a generall averment, that the tenant is ſole ſeiſed, for that ſhould ſeem to weaken the force of the fine: and the ſtatute of *conjunctim feoffatis, anno* 34 E. 1. extends not to joyntenancie by fine, but to joyntenancie by deed onely, to take the generall averment againſt the deed, that the tenant is ſole ſeiſed: and thus are all the books (whereof there be many) that ſeemed *prima facie* to diſagree, well reconciled. And this ſtatute *de conjunctim feoffatis,* extends not onely to aſſiſes, but to writs of dower, and other reall writs of *præcipe quod reddat,* * but not to writs of gard, or the like.

Stat. de Conjunctim feoffatis, 34 E. 1. c. 1. 17 E. 2. Maint. de Bre 1. Regiſt. 12. 1 E. 3. 5. 2 E. 3. 20. 4 E. 3. 30. 8 E. 3. 33. 15 E. 3. Maint. de Bre. 55. 3 E. 3. ibi. 13, 14. 18 Aſſ. 6. 21 Aſſ. 28. 22 E. 3. 45, 46. 22 Aſſ. 54. 23 Aſſ. 13. 24 E. 3. 76, 79, 29 E. 3. 18.

† Green chief juſtice, *anno* 24 E. 3. granted, that this act of 34 E. 1. was made more in damage of the people, then in amendment of the common law.

43 Aſſ. p. 6. 32 Aſſ. p. 4.
† 9 H. 6. 1. 34 H. 6. 16.

* 37 Aſſ. p. 3. 41 E. 3. 15. 49 E. 3. 17. 7 R. 2. Maint. de Bre. 8.

---

[525]

Confirmationes Chartarum de Libertatibus Angliæ et Foreſtæ.

Anno viceſimo quinto Edwardi primi.

CAP. I.

EDWARD per la grace de Dieu roy Dangleterre, ſeigniour Dirlande, et duke Daquitaine, a touts ceux que ceſtes letters preſents (1) *oiront, ou verront, ſalutem. Saches nous al honor de Dieu, et de ſaint eſgliſe, et au profit de noſtre realme* (2), *avoir grant pur nous, et pur nous heires, que la chartre des franchiſes, et la chartre de la foreſt, les queux fuerent faitz per commen de tout royalme* (3) *en le temps le roy Henry pier, ſoient tenus en touts lour points, ſans nul blemiſment, et volons que meſmes cels chartres deſous noſtre ſeale ſoient envoyes a nous juſtices auxi bien de la foreſt, come as autres: et a touts les viſcontes des counties, et a touts nous autres miniſtres, et a touts nous cities parmy le realme enſemblement*

EDWARD, by the grace of God, king of England, lord of Ireland, and duke of Guian, to all thoſe that theſe preſent letters ſhall hear or ſee, greeting. Know ye that we, to the honour of God and of holy church, and to the profit of our realm, have granted for us and our heirs, that the charter of liberties, and the charter of the foreſt, which were made by common aſſent of all the realm, in the time of king Henry, our father, ſhall be kept in every point without breach. And we will that the ſame charters ſhall be ſent under our ſeal, as well to our juſtices of the foreſt, as to others, and to all ſheriffs of ſhires, and to all our other officers, and to all our cities throughout the realm, together

ment ove nous briefes (4), *en les queux ſerra contenus que ils facent les avantdits chartres publier, et que ils facent dire al people, que nous les avons grants en touts points, et a nous juſtices, viſcontes, maires, et autres miniſtres, que les loies de la terre de ſous nous ount a guier meſmes les chartres* (5) *en touts lour points empledes devant eux en jugement, facent allower : ceſtaſcavoir le grande chartre come ley common, et la charter de la foreſt, en amendement de noſtre realme* (6).

together with our writs, in the which it ſhall be contained, that they cauſe the foreſaid charters to be publiſhed, and to declare to the people that we have confirmed them in all points; and that our juſtices, ſheriffs, mayors, and other miniſters, which under us have the laws of our land to guide, ſhall allow the ſaid charters pleaded before them in judgement in all their points, that is to wit, the great charter as the common law, and the charter of the foreſt, for the wealth of our realm.

(28 Ed. 1. ſtat. 3. c. 1.)

For the ſtile of the kings, and for the king that ſpake firſt in the plurall number [*nous*] as our king here doth, ſee *Magna Charta*, cap. 1. and the firſt part of the Inſtitutes, ſect. 1.

(1) *Per ſes letters patents.*] Acts of parliaments are many times in form of charters, or letters patents, *vide Magna Charta*, cap. 1. & *liber* 8. fol. 1, &c. *in caſu principis*

The title of theſe ſtatutes is, *Confirmationes chartarum de libertatibus Angliæ et foreſtæ*; and true it is, that hereby the ſaid charters are expreſly confirmed: but they are alſo excellently interpreted

[526] (which is a confirmation in law) for here is nothing enacted, but it is included within *Magna Charta*.

(2) *Al honour de Dieu, et de ſaint eſgliſe, et au profit de noſtre realme.*] This is, or ſhould be the true end of all parliaments.

See *Magna Charta* in the ſtile thereof, and all ſucceeding parliaments have in effect followed this precedent.

(3) *Per commen de tout realme.*] That is, by the common aſſent of the realm by authority of parliament; and many times *per communitatem Angliæ*: it ſignifieth alſo an act of parliament; for it cannot be *per communitatem Angliæ*, but by parliament, as hereafter ſhall be ſhewed.

(4) *Soient envoyes a nous juſtices, &c. et a touts nous cities, &c. enſemblement ove nous briefs.*] Before printing, and till the raign of H. 7. ſtatutes were ingroſſed in parchment, and by the kings writ proclaimed by the ſherife of every county: this was the ancient law of England, that the kings commandments iſſued, and were publiſhed in form of writs (as here it was:) an excellent courſe, and worthy to be reſtored.

(5) *Que les loyes de la terre de ſous nous ount a guier meſmes les chartres*, &c.] This is a clauſe worthy to be written in letters of gold, *viz.* that our juſtices, ſherifes, maiors, and other miniſters, which under us have the laws of our land to guide them, ſhall allow the ſaid charters in all their points, which in any plea ſhall come before them in judgement: and here it is to be obſerved, that the laws are the judges guides, or leaders, according to that old rule, *Lex eſt exercitus judicum tutiſſimus ductor*, or *lex eſt optimus judicis zenagogus*, and *lex eſt tutiſſima caſſis*.

There is an old legall word, called [*guidagium*] which ſignifieth an office of guiding of travellors through dangerous and unknown wayes;

wayes; here it appeareth, that the laws of the realm hath this office to guide the judges in all causes that come before them in the wayes of right justice, who never yet misguided any man, that certainly knew them, and truly followed them.

(6) *Le grand chartre come ley common, et la chartre de la forest, en amendement de nostre realme.*] The sense hereof is, that the great charter, and the charter of the forest are to be holden for the common law, that is, the law common to all; and that both the charters are in amendment of the realm; that is, to amend great mischiefs and inconveniences which oppressed the whole realm before the making of them.

CAP. II.

ET volons, que si nul judgement soit done desormes encountre les points des chartres avantdits per justic', ou per autres de nous ministres, que encountre les points des chartres tenont plee devant eux, soit defaite, et pur nient tenus.

AND we will, that if any judgement be given from henceforth contrary to the points of the charters aforesaid by the justices, or by any other our ministers that hold plea before them against the points of the charters, it shall be undone, and holden for nought.

(42 Ed. 3. c. 1.)

Whatsoever judgement is given against the statute of *Magna Charta*, or of *Charta de foresta* is made void by this act, and may be reversed by writ of error, because the judgement is given against the law, for this act saith, *soit defait, et pur nient tenus.* [527]

CAP. III.

ET volons que mesmes cestes charters desous nostre seale soient envoys as esglises cathedrals par my nostre royalme, et la demoergent, et soient deux foits per an lieus devant le people.

AND we will, that the same charters shall be sent, under our seal, to cathedral churches throughout our realm, there to remain, and shall be read before the people two times by the year.

Here it is to be observed what care was taken for the preservation of these charters, and of this act of parliament, for it is good chance to obtaine, but great wisdome to keep.

CAP. IV.

ET que archeveſques et eveſques denuncent les ſentences dexcommengement countre touts iceux, que countre les avantdits chartres vendrount en dict ou en fait, ou en eide, ou en counſeil, ou en nul point enfraindrant, ou countre vendront. Et que cels ſentences ſoient denuncies et publies deux foits per an per les prelates avantdits. Et ſi meſmes les prelates en nul de eux ſoient negligentes en la denunciation ſuiſdit faire, per les archeveſques de Canterbrie, et Deverwike, que pur temps ſerront, ſicome covient, ſoient repris et deſtreintx a meſme cel denunciation faire en la forme avantdit.

AND that all archbiſhops and biſhops ſhall pronounce the ſentence of excommunication againſt all thoſe that by word, deed, or counſel do contrary to the foreſaid charters, or that in any point break or undo them. And that the ſaid curſes be twice a year denounced and publiſhed by the prelates aforeſaid. And if the ſame prelates, or any of them, be remiſs in the denunciation of the ſaid ſentences, the archbiſhops of Canterbury and York for the time being ſhall compel and diſtrein them to the execution of their duties in form aforeſaid.

Stat. de Tallagio, &c. cap. 5.

This excommunication the prelates could not pronounce without warrant by authority of parliament, becauſe it concerned temporall cauſes.

CAP. V.

*ET pur ceo que aſcuns gents de noſtre realme ſoy doubtent, que les eides (1) et les miſes (2), queux il nous ount fait avant ſes heurs pur nous guerres (3) et auter boſoignes de lour graunt et lour bon voluntie, en quel maner que faits ſoient, puiſſont turner en ſervage a eux et a lour heires, pour * ceo que ils ſerront autre foits troves en rolle, et auxint priſes que ount eſte faits parmy le royalme per nous miniſters en noſtre noſme. Nous avons grantes pur nous et pur nous heires, que mes tielx eides, miſes ne priſes, ne trerons a cuſtome pur nul choſe que ſoit fait, ou que per rolle, ou en autre maner poet eſtre trove.*

* [528]

AND for ſo much as divers people of our realm are in fear, that the aids and taſks which they have given to us beforetime towards our wars and other buſineſs, of their own grant and good will (howſoever they were made) might turn to a bondage to them and their heirs, becauſe they might be at another time found in the rolls, and likewiſe for the priſes taken throughout the realm by our miniſters: we have granted for us and our heirs, that we ſhall not draw ſuch aids, taſks, nor priſes into a cuſtom, for any thing that hath been done heretofore, be it by roll or any other precedent that may be founden.

(1) *Eydes*

(1) *Eydes et mises.*] *Auxilia* at this time was a generall word, not onely including aides due by law, and tenure, as *aide pur faire fits chivalier, pur file marier, &c.* but aides also graunted by the free will of the subjects in parliaments, which afterwards were called subsidies; and here this word *eides* is taken for an aide graunted by authority of parliament. See hereafter for this word, Stat. de Tallag. non conced. 34 E. 1.

(2) *Mises.*] Are properly taken for expences or charges, but here in this act they are taken for tasks, taxes, tallages, or takings. See the statute of 34 E. 1. ubi sup.

(3) *Pur nous guerres,* &c.] The king had obtained by free consent, and good will in parliaments precedent aids, subsidies or tasks for the maintenance of his warres in forein parts, which howsoever they were graunted in full parliament, yet (as here it appeareth) many men doubted, might turne in servage of the subjects of the realme, for that it was holden that they ought not to contribute to the maintenance of the kings warres out of the realme; and thereupon Bohun earle of Hereford, and Essex high constable of England, and Bigot earle of Norffolk, and Suffolk, and marshall of England, for that it concerned matter of armes and warre, exhibited a petition to the king in French, in *anno* 25 E. 1. before the making of this act, which I have seen auncienly recorded, on the behalfe of the commons of England, concerning the said matter, and thereupon the king at this parliament yeelded to this act, that such eides, tasks, or takings should not be drawn to custome for any thing that had beene done in that behalfe. Vide Calvins case. lib. 7. fol. 7, 8, &c.

But yet this matter was never in quiet untill it was more particularly explained by divers acts of parliament, which we have drawn into one body of a law divided into severall branches.

1. No man shall be charged to arme himselfe, or to finde men of armes, or any hoblers or archers (other then those that hold by such services, or devoires of the king, or of other lords) if it be not by common consent, and graunt in parliament. 1 E. 3. c. 5. & c. 7. 25 E. 3. cap. 8. 1 E. 3. cap. 5. 4 H. 4. cap. 13. 18 E. 3. cap. 7. 4 H. 4. cap. 13.

2. No man shall be compelled to goe to the kings warre out of his shire, but where necessity of sudden comming of strange enemies into the realme.

3. No man shall be charged to give any wages either to the preparers or conveyors of souldiers, or to the souldiers to goe into Scotland, Gascoin, or elsewhere; but that men of armes, hoblers, and archers, chosen to goe into the kings service out of England, shall be at the kings wages from the day they depart out of the counties where they were chosen, till they return. Lib. 7. cap. 7, 8. Calvins case. Rot. Parl. 1 H. 5. nu. 17. 7 H. 5. nu. 9, &c. See 25 E. 3. cap. 7. Rot. parl. 4 H. 4. nu. 48. 20 R. 2. nu. 48. 4 H. 4. cap. 13. 11 H. 7. c. 7. 19 H. 7. c. 1. vid. Rot. clausus 44 E. 3. Sir Rich. Pembrughs case. Vide Mag. Chart. c. 20. verb. Exile. Confirm. chart. 25 E. 1.

Which acts of parliament are but declarations of the ancient law of England.

And according to this ancient law, the commons after the said declaratory acts of parliament did, when this point concerning maintenance of warres out of England came in question, make their continuall claim of their auncient freedom and birth right, as in 1 H. 5. and in 7 H. 5. &c. the commons made protestation that they were not bound to the maintenance of warre in Scotland, Ireland, Calice, France, Normandie, or other forein parts, and caused their protestations to be entred into the parliament roll where they yet remain; which in effect agreeth with that, which upon like occasion was made in this parliament of 25 E. 1.

But here may be observed, that when any ancient law or custome of parliament is broken, and the crown possessed of a precedent, [529]
how

how difficult a thing it is to reſtore the ſubject again to his former freedome and ſafety.

Now how of ancient time ſoldiers were levied, muſtered and entred of record, &c. (an excellent military policy) which will conduce much to the finding of the true ſenſe of this, and other ſtatutes, concerning this matter, ſee the third part of the Inſtitutes, cap. Felony in ſoldiers that depart, &c. in the expoſition of the ſtatute of 18 H. 6. cap. 19. See the ſtatutes of 11 H. 7. cap. 7. and 19 H. 7. cap. 1.

CAP. VI.

ET auxint avons graunt pur nous, et pur nous heires, as archeveſques, eveſques, abbes, priors, et as autres gents de ſ. egliſe, as countes, barons, et a tout la comminalty de la terre, que mes per nul beſoigne tiels manners des aides, miſes, ne priſes, ne prendrons forſque de common aſſent de tout le royalme, et pur le common profit de ceo: ſaves le auncient aides, et priſes dues et accuſtomes (1).

MOREOVER we have granted for us and our heirs, as well to archbiſhops, biſhops, abbots, priors, and other folk of holy church, as alſo to earls, barons, and to all the communalty of the land, that for no buſineſs from henceforth we ſhall take ſuch manner of aids, taſks, nor priſes, but by the common aſſent of the realm, and for the common profit thereof, ſaving the ancient aids and priſes due and accuſtomed.

(34 Ed. 1. ſtat. 4. c. 1.)

The cauſe of the making of this branch, and of ſuch ſpeciall mentioning of the clergy was, that the king did againſt the auncient lawes and cuſtomes of the realme collect money by commiſſion without aſſent of parliament, not onely of earls, barons, and comminalty, but of the clergy, who in thoſe dayes claimed a priviledge, and immunity from ſecular aides and ſubſidies, (by pretext of a late conſtitution made by Pope Boniface:) the clergy ſtood ſo ſtoutly in defence of their privilege, that ſir Robert de Brabazon the kings chiefe juſtice pronounced openly in the kings bench, *(in terrorem)* that from thenceforth no juſtice ſhould be done for them at their ſuit, but juſtice ſhould bee done againſt them in the king's courts at any other mans ſuit. But at this parliament this branch gave ſatisfaction to all, for hereby it is enacted that every aide and taſk and other taking muſt have two ſpecial properties, the one in the creation, viz. that it bee given by the common conſent of the whole realme in parliament; the other in the execution, viz. that it be given and imployed for the common benefit of the whole realme, and not for private or other reſpects; which words [*et pur le common profit de ceo*] in the impreſſion of Tottell are injuriouſly omitted.

Vid. Stat. de 34 E. 1. De Tallagio non concedendo.

(1) *Saves les auncient aides et priſes dues et accuſtomes.*] The auncient aides are here intended, *aide pur file marier, pur faire fits chivalier*, and reliefes by reaſon of tenures, and the auncient takings or ſeiſures are here intended, ſuch as were due to the crown, *jure prærogativæ*,

prærogativæ, as waifes, strayes, the goods of felons, and out-laws, deodands, and the like, [*ratione tenuræ*] as heriots, and such other as did lie in seisure or taking by reason of any tenure or custome.

CAP. VII. [530]

ET pur ceo que touts le pluis de la comminaltie du realme seisent durement greve de la maletot des leyns, cestascavoir, de chescun sacke de leyn quarant soulz (1), *et nous ont pries, que nous les voudrons relesser: nous a lour prier les avons pleinment relesses. Et nous avons graunt pur nous et pur nous heires, que mes celes ne prendrons sans lour common assent, et lour bon volunte* (2). *Sauve a nous et a nous heires la custome des leyns* (4), *pealx, et quires avant grauntes per la comminaltie avantdit* (3). *En tesmoignances des queux choses nous avons fait faire cestes nous letters overts. Tesmoigne Edwarde nostre fits a Londres le x. jour Doctobre, lan de nostre reigne xxv.*

AND for so much as the more part of the communalty of the realm find themselves sore grieved with the maletent of woolls, that is to wit, a toll of forty shillings for every sack of wooll, and have made petition to us to release the same; we at their requests have clearly released it, and have granted for us and our heirs, that we shall not take such things without their common assent and good will, saving to us and our heirs the custom of woolls, skins, and leather, granted before by the communalty aforesaid. In witness of which things we have caused these our letters to be made patents. Witness Edward our son at London the tenth day of October, the five and twentieth year of our reign.

(2 Inst. 76.)

(1) *Et pur ceo que tout le pluis de la comminaltie du realme seisent durement greve de la maletot des leynes. s. de chescun sacke de leyn 40. s. &c.*] The grievance was that the king had lately, without common assent of parliament, set a charge of forty shillings upon every sack of wool, here called by the name of maletct, that is, the ill toll or charge, for the word [imposition] was not yet heard of in any record. See before the statute of Magna Charta cap. 30.

See more of this matter in the exposition upon the 30. chaper of Magna Charta.

This is an excellent precedent, that when grievances are found out, and proved, that they bee put downe and overthrowne by authority of parliament.

(2) *Et nous avons graunt pur nous et pur nous heires, que mes celes ne prendrons sans lour common assent et lour bone volunt.*] This is worthy of observation, whereof you may reade in the exposition of the 30 chapter of Magna Charta.

(3) *Avant graunts per le comminaltie avantdit.*] By the comminalty aforesaid, that is, by act of parliament for the comminalty of England cannot graunt but by parliament.

And some say that the comminalty are here named for three respects: 1. For that they are the greater part. 2. For all aids Rot. Pat. 3 E. 1. m. & 9.

and

Mich. 26 E. I. int' retorn' brev. in Scacc'. per communitatem Angliæ, &c. vid. Magna Chart. cap. 30. * Art. super Chart. cap. I.

and subsidies begun with them. 3. For that the farre greater benefit to the king comes from them. For in subsidies the cominalty filleth the kings coffers; but some have said that * commune and comminalty doe signify as much as the people, that is, all the subjects of the realme, and so it was taken in divers parliaments in this kings raigne, and in this also, so as commune should signify the people, and commons a part of them.

[531]

(4) *Les customes de leynes.*] The customes here intended to be granted by parliament, were 6. s. 8. d. for the transportation of a sack of wool, and 6. s. 8. d. for every 300 pelts transported, and 13. s. 4. d. for the transportation of a last of leather.

Rot. Pat. 3 E. I. m. I. & 9. Rot. Finium. 3 E. I. Acc. Mich. 26 E. I. in Scacc. inter retorn. brevium ex rem. Thesaur. See in the Exposition upon the statute of Magna Chart. ca. 30.

These customes were granted to king Edw. I. as it appeareth in Rot. patent. 3 E. I. *Cum prælati, magnates, et tota communitas regni nostri nobis concess' quandam novam consuetudinem de lanis, pellibus, et coriis tam in Anglia, quam in Hibernia, et Wallia regnum nostrum exeuntibus imperpetuum nobis, et hæredibus nostris, percipiend' in forma subscripta, viz. de quolibet sacco lanæ dimidiam marcam, de singulis trescentis pellibus lanutis quæ faciunt unum saccum dimidiam marcam, et de qualibet lasta coriorium unam marcam, illorum scilicet coriorium, pellium, et lanarum, quæ portus Angliæ, Hiberniæ, et Walliæ regnum nostrum exibunt*, &c.

---

[532]

STAT. DE TALLAGIO NON CONCEDENDO,

Edit. Anno 34 Edw. I.

CAP. I.

NULLUM tallagium (1), vel auxilium (2) per nos, vel hæredes nostros in regno nostro ponatur, seu levetur sine voluntate, et assensu archiepiscoporum, episcoporum, comitum, baronum, militum, burgensium, et aliorum liberorum com' de regno nostro (3).

NO tallage or aid shall be taken or levied by us or our heirs in our realm, without the good will and assent of archbishops, bishops, earls, barons, knights, burgesses, and other freemen of the land.

(25 Ed. I. stat. I. c. 6.)

Albeit that this act is not next in course of time, yet being next in matter, we have thought good to handle this act before others.

There were two causes of the making of this act; the first was, that where king E. I. having conceived just displeasure against the French king, for the injury done unto him, in with-holding Aquitaine, and other his inheritance in France; and where the French king had grievously, and with strong hand vexed and over-

over-layed Guy earl of Flanders, and had won much of his lands from him: king Edw. the first intending to aid and assist the said earl, and to rescue him out of the hands of the French king, who was ready to devour him and his earldom, did require specially of Humfrey le Bohun earl of Hereford and Essex, and constable of England, and of Roger Bigot earl of Norffolk and Suffolk, marshall of England, and of all the Earls, barons, knights, and esquires, and of all free-holders of 20. l. land within his kingdom, whether they held of the king in *capite*, or of other whatsoever, to contribute to his wars in Flanders in rescue of the said earl, or finde able men to go with him on that journey: which the constable and marshall, and many of the nobility, and of the knights and esquires, and specially John Ferrers taking part with them, and all the free-holders abovesaid vehemently denyed, unlesse it were so ordained and determined by common consent of parliament, as had been before enacted in the parliament of anno 25 E. 1. by the act of *confirmationes chartarum*, as before it appeareth.

The second cause was, that the king the yeer before had taken a tallage of all cities, boroughs and towns, without assent of parliament; whereupon grew great murmuring and discontentment among the commons. For pacifying of which discord between the king and his nobles, and for the quieting of the commons, and for a perpetuall and a constant law for ever after both in this and other like cases, this act was made in the four and thirtieth yeer of his reign.

(1) *Nullum tallagium.*] *Tallagium*, or *tailagium* cometh of the French word *tailer*, to share or cut out a part, and metaphorically is taken when the king or any other hath a share or part of the value of a mans goods or chattels, or a share or part of the annuall revenue of his lands, or puts any charge or burthen upon another; so as *tallagium* is a generall word, and doth include † all subsidies, taxes, tenths, fifteens, impositions, or other burthens or charge put or set upon any man, and so is expounded in our books, here it is restrained to tallages, set or levied by the king or his heirs.

* *Robertus de Haye impl' Richardum le Waleyes cum al' pro captione averiorum in duobus locis, apud Lindefield vocat' Northflet & Southuse, ipsi dicunt quod Willielmus filius Walteri le Haye tenet de eo quædam ten' apud Lindefand per servitium xi. s. & per tallagium ei faciend' ad voluntatem ipsius Richardi, & quia ipsum Willielmum talliavit, anno regis nono, una vice ad ii. s. & alia vice anno decimo, ad xviii. d. quod tallagium ei aretro fuit pro prædictis ii. s. per annum, ipsum Willielmum districxit super feodum suum pro præd' arreragiis: Robertus dic' quod præd' Willielmus tenuit de eo prædict' ten' per certum servitium, & non per tallagium ad voluntatem suam, & dic' quod de illo servitio nihil ei aretro fuit &c. Richardus dicit quod advocat prædictam districtionem super prædict' Willielmum, & non super ipsum Robertum; et petit judicium si idem Robertus, qui non est tenens suus, nec districtio super ipsum advocatur, possit servitium suum dedicere: ideo considerat' est quod prædictus Richardus inde sine die. Et prædictus Robertus nihil cap' per breve suum, set sit in misericordia pro falso clam' suo; et prædictus Richardus habeat returnum averiorum, &c.*

(2) *Auxilium.*] And this word was used in the statute of 25 E. 1. whereof somewhat hath been said in the exposition thereof.

You

† [533] For this word Tallage, vide 15 E. 3. Avowry 106. F. N. B. 14. 16. 38 H. 6. 10. 32 E. 3. Monstr. 16. 3 E. 3. Quo War. Bre. 2. Clauf. 19 H. 3. m. 16. ibid. m. 13. Clauf. 11 H. 3. m. 17. Regist. 142, 143. F. N. B. 150. 13 E. 1. Vill. 38. Rot. Alma. 12 E. 3. part 1. m. 22. Rot. Parliam. 6 E. 3. nu. 4. 1 E. 2. Stat. de Militibus, Rot. Parliam. 13 H. 4. nu. 14. 19 H. 6. 32. 38 H. 6. 10. Rot. Pat. 1 H. 7. part 3. m. 16. Vide in Waste Tallage de Villens, &c. Modus tenend. Parli. Vet. Manuscript.

* Mich. 11 E. 1. in banco Rot. 49. Sussex.

You may read further in that ancient record intituled *De modo tenendi parliamentum tempore regis Edw. filii Etheldredi*; *debent auxilia peti in pleno parliamento.* So, as hath been ſaid before in the expoſition upon the 30. chapter of Magna Charta, and of 25 E. 1. Theſe acts are but declarations of the ancient common laws of this realm.

* Vide fol. 41. Math Par. 247. Walſ. 40. Forteſcue, ca. 9. fol. 13. & cap. 12. 18. 34. & 35.

(3) *Nullum tallagium, vel * auxilium per nos, vel hæredes noſtros in regno noſtro ponatur, ſeu levetur ſine voluntate, et aſſenſu archiepiſcoporum, epiſcoporum, comitum, baronum, militum, burgenſium, et aliorum liberorum com' de regno noſtro.*] Theſe words are plain without any ſcruple, abſolute without any ſaving. *Abſoluta ſententia expoſitore non indiget.*

And this is as much as to ſay, that no ſubſidy, taſk, tenth, fifteenth, impoſition, or other aid or charge whatſoever, ſhall by the king or his heirs be put or levied without the common councell of the realm, that is, by the will and aſſent of the archbiſhops, biſhops, earls, barons, knights, burgeſſes, and others of the counties, that is to ſay, by grant and common aſſent in parliament.

Within this act are all new offices erected with new fees, or old offices with new fees, for that is a tallage put upon the ſubject, which cannot be done without common aſſent by act of parliament. And this doth notably appear by a petition in parliament in *anno* 13 H. 4. where the commons complain, that an office was erected for meaſurage of clothes and canvas, with a new fee for the ſame by colour of the kings letters patents, and pray that theſe letters patents might be revoked, for that the king could erect no offices with new fees to be taken of the people, who may not ſo be charged but by parliament.

Rot. Parliam. 13 H. 4. nu. 43.

The royall anſwer of the king in parliament was, that the ſtatutes therefore provided ſhall be obſerved, which ſtatutes were the ſaid act of 25 E. 1. and this of 34 E. 1. &c. and accordingly judgement was alſo given in the kings bench, ſo as this point was both reſolved in parliament, and adjudged by law according to theſe ſtatutes; and hereby it appeareth that theſe were acts of parliament.

[534]

13 H. 4. fol. 16, 17.

Rot. Parl. 22 E. 3. nu. 31. Rot. Parl. 25 E. 3.

King Edw. 3. had granted to Robert Poley a new office of meaſuring of worſteads, with a new fee; and it was at the petition of the commons reſolved in parliament to be void, and afterward revoked as void by authority of parliament; and the like law is in all like caſes.

Note that the words of this branch are generall, *Nullum tallagium, &c. ponatur, ſeu levetur ſine voluntate, &c.* and ſaith, *Per nos, et hæred' noſtros*, but not *Pro nobis, aut ad opus noſtrum.* But generally ſo as all tallages, burthens, or charges put upon the ſubject by the king, either to or for the king, or to or for any ſubject by the kings letters patents, or other commandement or order, is prohibited by this act unleſſe it be by common conſent of parliament; and note that the words are in the disjunctive, [*Ponatur ſeu levetur*] ſo as if it be ſet by the king, although it be not levied by him, but by a ſubject, as it was in the caſes aboveſaid, it is within the purview of this ſtatute.

CAP.

CAP. II.

NULLUS miniſter noſter, vel hæredum noſtrorum capiat blada, correa, aut aliqua alia bona cujuſcunque, ſine voluntate et aſſenſu illius, cujus fuerint bona.

NO officer of ours, or of our heirs, ſhall take corn, leather, cattle, or any other goods, of any manner of perſon, without the good will and aſſent of the party to whom the goods belonged.

(12 Rep. 19.)

Of this branch we ſhall have juſt occaſion to ſpeak when we come to the ſtatute of 28 E. 1. cap. 2. and therefore do purpoſely omit to ſpeak of it here.

CAP. III.

NIHIL capiatur de cætero nomine, vel occaſione maletot de ſacco lanæ.

NOTHING from henceforth ſhall be taken of ſacks of wooll by colour or occaſion of male-tent.

See for Maletot 25 E. 3. cap. 6. and Magna Charta, cap. 30. and albeit it was ouſted before, yet *nunquam nimis dicitur, quod nunquam ſatis dicitur*; by this act it is both prohibited by the generall purview, and alſo by this particular branch.

CAP. IV.

VOLUMUS et concedimus pro nobis et hæredibus noſtris, quod omnes clerici et laici de regno noſtro habeant omnes leges, libertates, et liberas conſuetudines ſuas ita libere et integre, ſicut eas aliquo tempore melius et plenius habere conſueverunt. Et ſi contra illas quocunque ar-
[535] *ticulo in præſenti charta contento ſtatuta fuerint edita per nos et anteceſſores noſtros, vel conſuetudines introductæ: volumus et concedimus, quod hujuſmodi conſuetudines et ſtatuta vacua et nulla ſint in perpetuum.*

WE will and grant for us and our heirs, that all clerks and laymen of our land ſhall have their laws, liberties, and free cuſtoms, as largely and wholly as they have uſed to have the ſame at any time when they had them beſt; and if any ſtatutes have been made by us or our anceſtors, or any cuſtoms brought in contrary to them, or any manner of article contained in this preſent charter, we will and grant, that ſuch manner of ſtatutes and cuſtoms ſhall be void and fruſtrate for evermore.

This containeth a restitution generall to the subjects of all their lawes, liberties, and free customes, as freely and wholly, as at any time before in the better and fuller manner they used to have the same, and this doth not onely extend to *Magna Charta*, and *Charta de Foresta*, but to all other laws, liberties, or freedomes, and free customes whatsoever.

42 E. 3. ca. 1. simile. But what if any act of parliament have been made contrary to any article in this act contained; this later clause, viz. *Et si contra illas*, &c. containeth a repeale of all statutes made by king E. 1. or any of his auncestors against any article in this act contained, that is to say, concerning the first chapter, *Nullum tallagium*, &c. or the second, *Nullus minister noster*; or the third, *Nihil capiatur*; or this fourth, which is most generall, *Volumus et concedimus*, &c.

Hereby it may be observed how prudent antiquity could containe much matter in few words.

CAP. V.

REMISIMUS etiam Humfredo le Bohun, comiti Hereford' et Essex, constabular' Angliæ, et Roger' Bigot comiti Norff. et Suff. marescallo Angliæ, et aliis comitibus, baronibus, militibus, armigeris, et I. de Ferreres, ac omnibus aliis de eorum societate, confœderatione, et concordia existentibus: necnon et omnibus viginti libratas terræ tenentibus in regno nostro, sive de nobis teneant in capite, sive de alio quocunque ad transfretand' nobiscum in Fland' certo die vocatis, rancorem (1) *et malam voluntatem* (2) *erga nos habitam, ac etiam transgressiones si quas nobis fecerint* (3), *usque ad præsentis chartæ confectionem. Et ad majorem hujusmodi rei securitatem volumus et concedimus, quod omnes archiepiscopi* (4), *et episcopi in perpetuum habeant in suis cathedralibus ecclesiis, habitanti præsenti charta lecta excommunicare, et publice in singulis parochialibus ecclesiis suarum dioc' excommunicatos denunciare bis in anno omnes illos, qui contra tenorem præsentis chartæ vim et effectum quoquo modo vel articulo scienter fecerint, aut fieri procuraverint. In cujus rei testimonium præsenti chartæ sigillum nostrum est appensum una cum sigillis archiepis-*

MOREOVER, we have pardoned Humfrey Bohun earl of Hereford and Essex, constable of England, Roger earl of Norfolk and Suffolk, marshal of England, and other earls, barons, knights, esquires, and namely John de Ferrariis, with all other being of their fellowship, confederacy, and bond, and also to all other that hold xx pound land in our realm, whether they hold of us in chief, or of other, that were appointed at a day certain to pass over with us into Flanders, the rancour and evil-will born against us, and all other offences that they have done against us, unto the making of this present charter. And for the more assurance of this thing, we will and grant, that all archbishops and bishops for ever shall read this present charter in their cathedral churches twice in the year, and upon the reading thereof in every of their parish churches, shall openly denounce accursed all those that willingly do procure to be done any thing contrary to the tenor, force, and effect of this present charter in any point and article. In witness of which thing we have set our seal to this present charter, together with the seals

archiepiscoporum, episcoporum, &c. (5) *qui sponte juraverunt, quod tenorem præsentis chartæ, quantum in eis est, in omnibus causis et singulis articulis servabunt, et ad observationem fidele auxilium præstabunt, &c.* (6)	seals of the archbishops, bishops, &c. which voluntarily have sworn that, as much as in them is, they shall observe the tenor of this present charter in all causes and articles, and shall extend their faithful aid to the keeping thereof, &c.

If you compare our English histories with this act of parliament, the old saying shall bee verified, that records of parliament are the truest histories. [536]

Although the king had conceived a deep displeasure against the constable, marshall, and others of the nobility, gentry, and commons of the realme, for denying of that which he so much desired, yet for that they stood in defence of their laws, liberties, and free customes, the king, who (as sir William Herle chief justice of the common pleas, who lived in his time, and served him, said) was the wisest king that ever was, did not onely restore the same to them as is aforesaid, but granted a special pardon to those of whom he had conceived so great displeasure; such a one as you shall not reade of the like, for hereby he pardoned three things: 5 E. 3. fol. 14.

(1) 1. *Rancorem.*] Rancor is taken here metaphorically for a festring of indignation, or displeasure in the minde of the king, which the king releaseth and dischargeth them of the same, and incidently restoreth them to his favour.

(2) 2. *Malum voluntatem.*] Ill will or unkindnesse: of this so much may be said as hath been said of rancor.

(3) 3. *Et etiam transgressiones, si quas fecerint.*] Here these words [*si quas fecerint*] are added, lest by acceptance of a pardon of transgressions they should impliedly confesse that they had transgressed: so carefull were the lords and commons in former times to preserve the ancient laws, liberties, and free customs of their country.

(4) *Et quod omnes archiepiscopi, &c.*] Here power is given to archbishops and bishops twice in the yeare, upon the reading of this act, to excommunicate all the violaters thereof, &c. 25 E. 1. Confirm. Chartar, cap. 4.

(5) *In cujus rei testimonium præsenti chartæ sigillum nostrum est appensum una cum sigillis archiepiscoporum, episcoporum, comitum, baronum,* &c.] *Nota* the solemnity of this act, in that all the archbishops, bishops, earles, barons, &c. did put their seale thereunto: a rare example, which was done for the obliging of them the more firmly to the observation of this act, which concerned the laws, liberties, and free customes of their country. Rot. Parl. 7 H 4. nu. 60. simile. 28 E. 1. bre. procerum, & comitat. 70. cap. sigillat. Walf. pag. 48.

(6) *Qui sponte juraverunt, quod tenorem præsentis chartæ, quantum in eis est, in omnibus causis et singulis articulis servabunt, et ad observand' fidele auxilium præstabunt,* &c.] And for their greater obligation for the due observation of this act, they tooke a voluntary corporall oath.

Here note, that either houses of parliament being courts may take voluntary oathes, as here it appeareth.

ARTICULI SUPER CHARTAS,

Edit. Anno 28 *Edw.* 1.

PUR ceo que les points de la graund chartre, des fraunchiſ. et de la foreſt, les queux le roy Henry pier noſtre ſeigniour le roy qui ore eſt, granta a ſon people (1) *pour le preue de ſon roialme, ne ont pas eſte tenus, ne gardes avant ces heures, pour ceo que avant ces heures peine ne fuit eſtablie* (2) *vers les treſpaſſants countre les points des chartres avantdits: noſtre ſeigniour le roy les adde novel graunt, renovele et confirme. Et a la requeſtes des prelates, counts, et barons* (3) *a ſon parliament a Weſt', en quareſme lan de ſon reign xxviii. ad certains points affirme, et peine ordeigne, et eſtablie, encounter touts yceux, que encountre les points des avantdits chartres, ou nul point de eux, en nul manner viendront, on miſprendrent, en la forme que lenſuit.*

FORASMUCH as the articles of the great charter of liberties, and of the charter of the foreſt, the which king Henry, father of the king that now is, granted to his people for the weal of his realm, have not been heretofore obſerved ne kept, becauſe there was no puniſhment executed upon them which offended againſt the points of the charters before mentioned; our lord the king hath again granted, renewed, and confirmed them at the requeſt of his prelates, earls, and barons, aſſembled in his parliament holden at Weſtminſter, the eight and twentieth year of his reign, and hath ordained, enacted, and eſtabliſhed certain articles againſt all them that offend contrary to the points of the ſaid charters, or any part of them, or that in any wiſe tranſgreſs them, in the form that enſueth.

One cauſe of the making of this act was, that albeit the king had confirmed the ſaid charters at his parliament holden in 25 E. 1. and ſtiled the act by the name of *Confirmationes chartarum de libertatibus Angliæ et Foreſtæ*, yet becauſe there was a ſaving in that act [*Saves les auncient aides et priſes dues et accuſtomes*] although they were to be underſtood of aids by reaſon of tenure, &c. as in the expoſition thereof it appeareth, yet it was a colour for the kings officers and miniſters to make an evaſion when the parliament was: and thereupon the lords of parliament did importune the king to confirme the ſaid charters; which the king promiſed to doe: but when it came to be ſet downe in forme of an act, the king would have added a ſaving of the right of his crown, which the lords did mainly inveigh againſt, and preſſed the king with his promiſe to confirm them as abſolutely as his noble father king H. 3. had graunted them; which in the end he yeelded unto, as by this act it appeareth.

And another cauſe of the making of this act, as by the preamble is ſuggeſted, was, that there was no certaine puniſhment in many points eſtabliſhed by the ſaid charters againſt the violaters of the ſame, which alſo by this act are remedied.

(1) *Grant*

(1) *Grant a son people.*] This word *populus* here doth include all the king's subjects, both the prelates, and other of the clergy, and the nobles and commons of this realme, for all bee the kings people, [*son people.*]

(2) *Peine ne fuit establie.*] Some reade it [*peine ne fuit execute*] that is true in effect, but the originall is *peine ne fuit establie*, that is, no paine was set down in certain.

(3) *A le request les prelates, countes, et barons.*] These articles [538] were preferred by the lords of parliament, because they had a promise of the king to passe the said articles; there were at this parliament 93. earles and barons of the realme, besides the lords of the clergy, which then were many.

The title is here *Articuli super chartas*, sometime they styled it by the name of *Novi articuli super chartas*, sometimes, *Explanations sur les chartres*; and justly they are called *Articuli super chartas*, meaning *Magna Charta*, and *Charta de Foresta*, for that they contain the substance of all that is contained in these articles.

Rot. Parl. 5 H.4. nu. 61. 2 E. 3. 27. Piers de Salt. marsh. Case. Vide li. 10. fo. 74. Le Case de Marshalsea.

CAP. I.

CESTASCAVOIR, que de cy en avant la grand chartre des franchises Dengleterre, grante a tout la commune Dengleterre (1), *et la chartre de la forest in mesme le maner grante, soient tenus, gardes, et maintenus en chescun article, et chescun point, auxy pleinment come le roy les ad graunte, renovele, et per sa chartre confirme* (2). *Et que celles chartres soient bailles a chescun viscont* (3) *Dengleterre desoubes le seale le roy, a lier quatre foits per an devant le people en pleine countie: cestascavoir, au prochein countie apres la saint Michael, au prochein countie apres le Noel, au prochein countie apres la Pasche, et au prochein countie apres la saint Johan' Baptist. Et a ceux deux chartres en chescun point, et en chescun article dicele, firmement tener, et garder, ou remedie ne fuit avant per la common ley, soient esleus en chescun countie per la commune de mesme la countie trois prodes homes chivalers, ou auters loialx, sages, et avises, que soient jures et assignes per les letters le roy overtes de son graund seale, de oier et terminer, sans auter briefe*

THAT is to say, that from henceforth the great charter of the liberties of England, granted to all the commonalty of the realm, and the charter of the forest, in like manner granted, shall be observed, kept, and maintained in every point, in as ample wise as the king hath granted, renewed, and confirmed them by his charter. And that the charters be delivered to every sheriff of England under the king's seal, to be read four times in the year before the people in the full county, that is to wit, the next county-day after the feast of Saint Michael, and the next county-day after Christmas, and at the next county after Easter, and at the next county after the feast of Saint John. And for these two charters to be firmly observed in every point and article (where before no remedy was at the common law) there shall be chosen in every shire-court, by the commonalty of the same shire, three substantial men, knights, or other lawful, wise, and well-disposed persons, which shall be justices sworn and

briefe que lour common graunt, les pleints que se ferront de touts yceux, que contreviendront (5) ou mesprendront en nul des dits points des avantdits chartres en counties ou ils sont assignes, auxibien dedeins franchises, come dehors, et auxibien des ministers le roy hors de lour places, come des auters, et les pleints oier de jour en jour sans delay: et les terminent sans allower les delayes, que sont allowes per la common ley (6), et que mesme ceux chivalers eyent poyer de punier touts ceux que ser- [539] *ront attaints de trespas fait, encountre nul point des chartres avantdits, ou remedy ne fuit avant per la common ley (4), auxy come avant est dit, per imprisonment, ou per ransome, ou per amerciament, solonque ceo que le trespas le demaund. Et pur ceo nentende pas le roy, ne nul des soyens que a cest ordeignement fuerent, que les chivalers avantdits, teignent nul plee per le power que done lour soit, en cas ou avant ces heures fuit remedie purview solonque la common ley per briefe: ne que prejudice soit fait a la common ley, ne a les chartres avantdits, en nul de lour points. Et voit le roy, que si touts trois ne soient presentes, ou ne perront a touts les soits attendre, a faire lour office en la forme avantdit, que deux des trois le facent. Et ordeigne est, que les viscounts, et les bailifes le roy, soient attendants a les commandements des avantdits justices, en quant que appent a lour office. Et oustre ces choses granis sur les points des chartres avantdits, le roy de sa grace especiall, en allegeance des grevances, que son people ad eu per les guerres que ont este, et en amendement de lour estate, et pur tant que ils soient plus prestes a son service, et plus voluntiers aidants, quant il en avera a faire (7), ad grant ascuns articles, les queux il entend' que tiendront auxibien lieu a son people, & auxi grand profit ferront, ou plus que les points avant grantes.*

and assigned by the king's letters patents under the great seal, to hear and determine (without any other writ, but only their commission) such plaints as shall be made upon all those that commit or offend against any point contained in the foresaid charters, in the shires where they be assigned, as well within franchises as without, and as well for the king's officers out of their places, as for other, and to hear the plaints from day to day without any delay, and to determine them, without allowing the delays which be allowed by the common law. And the same knights shall have power to punish all such as shall be attainted of any trespass done contrary to any point of the foresaid charters (where no remedy was before by the common law) as before is said, by imprisonment, or by ransom, or by amerciament, according to the trespass. Nevertheless the king, nor none of those that made this ordinance, intend, that by virtue hereof any of the foresaid knights shall hold any plea by the power which shall be given them in such case, where there hath been remedy provided in times passed, after the course of the common law by writ, nor also that any prejudice should be done to the common law, nor to the charters aforesaid in any point. And the king willeth, that if all three be not present, or cannot at all times attend to do their office in form aforesaid, that two of them shall do it. And it is ordained, that the king's sheriffs and bailiffs shall be attendant to do the commandements of the foresaid justices, as far forth as appertaineth unto their offices. And besides these things granted upon the articles of the charters aforesaid, the king of his special grace, for redress of the grievances that his people hath sustained by reason of his wars, and for the amendment of their estate, and to

to the intent that they may be the more ready to do him ſervice, and the more willing to aſſiſt and aid him in time of need, hath granted certain articles, the which he ſuppoſeth ſhall not only be obſerved of his liege people, but alſo ſhall be as much profitable, or more, than the articles heretofore granted.

(1) *A le commune d'Angleterre.*] Here *commune* is taken for people, ſo as [*tout le commune*] is taken here for all the people; and this is proved by the ſenſe of the words, for *Magna Charta* was not granted to the commons of the realm, but generally to all the ſubjects of the realm, *viz.* to thoſe of the clergie, and to thoſe of the nobility, and to the commons alſo: and that [*commune*] in this place ſignifieth people, it is proved by the preamble, for there the great charter, and the charter of the foreſt, are rehearſed to be granted by king H. 3. to his people; and here they are ſaid to be granted [*a le commune:*] and ſee before 25 E. 1. Confirmat. Chart. cap. 1. & cap. 6. for this word *commune* and *comminaltie:* ſo as [*a le commune*] here ſignifieth not to the commons of the realm, but to the people of the whole realm; and herewith agreeth our books, that for a common nuſance, which concerns *le commune, ou le comminaltie, le ſuite ſerr' done au roy,* where [*commune*] and [*comminaltie*] include all the kings ſubjects. a E. 3. 26, &c.

(2) *Auxi pleinement come le roy, les ad grante, renovele, et per ſon chartre confirme.*] Here it is to be underſtood, that this king Edw. 1. the 28 day of March, in this 28 yeer of his raign had abſolutely confirmed, ſo as now by force of this act of parliament in *an.* 34 E. 1. it hath onely the force of a charter, but this is eſtabliſhed by this act of parliament. [540]

(3) *Et que les chartres ſont bailles a cheſcun viſc', &c.*] And that theſe charters ſhould be read four times in the yeer in full county; here is order taken for the publiſhing of theſe charters.

See the ſtatute de Confirmat. Chart. cap. 1. 3, 4.

(4) *Ou remedie ne fuit avant per le common ley.*] That is, where no action was given by the kings writ to be purſued at the common law.

(5) *Apres le ſaint Michael, &c. Soient eſleus en cheſcun countie, per la commune de meſme le countie, trois prodes chivaliers, ou auters loyals, ſages, et aviſes, que ſoient jurees et aſſignes per les letters le roy overtes de ſon grand ſeale, de oier et terminer ſans auter briefe que lour commen grant, les pleints que ſe ferront de touts ceux, que contrevien-dront,* &c.] Here, for the better execution of thoſe glorious two lights, *Magna Charta,* and *Charta de Foreſta,* a new court and new juſtices were appointed, with limitation that they ſhould meddle onely with thoſe points againſt thoſe charters, for the which before this act there was no remedy by the common law.

Here by the way it is to be obſerved, that three new things which have fair pretences are moſt commonly hurtfull to the common-wealth, *viz.* 1. New courts (as here was one) for commonly they tend to the grievous vexation and oppreſſion of the ſubject,

ſubject, and not to that glorious end that at the firſt was pretended; for erect new courts, and conſtitute great men to be judges, and make what limitations you will, they will never want authority and juriſdiction. 2. New offices either in courts of juſtice, or out of them, which cannot be done as here it was, but by parliament; but they under pretence of the common good are exerciſed to the intolerable grievance of the ſubject. 3. New corporations trading into forein parts, and at home, which under the fair pretence of order and government, in concluſion tend to the hinderance of trade and traffique, and in the end produce monopolies. But now to the text.

(6) *Et auxibien des miniſters le roy hors de lour places, come des auters: et les pleintes oier de jour en jour ſans delaie: et les terminent ſans allower les delaies, que ſont allowes per la commen ley.*] Here was the firſt ground for the raiſing of the juſtices of *trebaſton*, or *trailbaſton*, ſo called (in reſpect of their precipitate proceeding from day to day, without ſuch convenient leiſure and time as common law allowed) for that their proceedings were as ſpeedy and ready as one might draw a ſtaff.

Rot. Pat. 33 E. 1. in Dorſæ. m. 1. 2 E. 3. fol. 27. 27 Aſſ. 57. Stat. de Ragman. Vet. Chart. part 2. fol. 28. Matth. Paris. 450. Holl. 312, 313. Stare 33 E. 1. Vet. N. B. 52.

Their authority was increaſed in *anno* 33 E. 1. and if you deſire to read their commiſſion, you may read the ſame in Rot. Pat. *anno* 33 E. 1.

They in the end had ſuch authority as juſtices in eyre; but albeit they had their authority by act of parliament, yet if they erred in judgement, a writ of errour did lye by the generall rule of the common law to reverſe their judgement in the kings bench; which being once reſolved and known, and their juriſdiction fettered with ſo many limitations, their authority by little and little vaniſhed.

[541]

(7) *Le roy de ſa grace eſpecial, &c. et pur tant que ils ſoient plus preſtes a ſon ſervice, et plus voluntiers aidants, quant il en avera a faire.*] Here is to be obſerved, that the ſubject ought to retribute to the king for a bill of grace two things, firſt: to be the more ready to do him ſervice; and ſecondly, to aid him in time of need.

CAP. II.

EN primes pur ceo que un grande grievance (1) *eſt en ceſt realme, et dammage ſans nombre, de ceo que le roy et ſes miniſters de ſa meignee, auxibien les aliens come les deniſens, fent lour priſes* (2) *per la ou ils paſſent parmy le realme, et pernent les biens des gents, des cleres, et des layes, ſans rien paier, ou bien meins que la value* (3). *Ordeine eſt, que de cy en avant, nul ne preign' priſes parmy realme, forſque les parnours le roy, et ſes*

SECONDARILY, foraſmuch as there is a great grievance in this realm, and damage without meaſure, for that the king and the miniſters of his houſe, as well of aliens as denizens, do make great priſes where they paſs through the realm, and take the goods as well of clerks as of lay-people, without paying therefore any thing, or elſe much leſs than the value: it is ordained, that from henceforth none do take any ſuch priſes

ſes purveyours pour loſtell' le roy (4). *Et pur les parnours le roy, et purveyours pour ſon hoſtell', ne preignent riens, forſque pur meſme loſtell'* (5): *et des priſes que ilz ferront par my le pais, de manger ou de boire, et des auters menus neceſſaries pur loſtell', que ils facent la paie ou gree a ceux, des queux les choſes ſerront priſes* (6). *Et que touts ceux parnours le roy, purveyours, ou achatours, eient de cy en avant lour garrante oveſque eux du grand ſeale, ou du petite ſeale le roy, conteinant lour poiar, et les choſes dont ils ferront priſes* (7), *au purveyance: le quel garrant ils monſtrent a ceux des queux ils ferront la priſe, avant ceo que ils impreignent rien* (8). *Et que ceux parnours, purveyours, ou achatours le roy, ne preignent plus que beſoigne, et meſter ne ſoit* (9), *pour le roy et ſon hoſtell', et de ſes enfants. Et que riens ne preignent pur ceux que ſont as gages, ne pur nul auter. Et que ils reſpoignent en loſtell', ou en la gardrobe pleinment de toutes lour priſes, ſans faire lour largeſſes aillours, ou liveries des choſes, que pur le roy ſerront priſes* (10). *Et ſi nul parnour del hoſtell' le roy, per garrantie que il eit, face priſes, ou liveres en auter maner, que deſus neſt dit, per plaint fait al ſeneſchall', et au treaſorer del hoſtell' le roy, ſoit la verite inquiſe. Et ſi de ceo*

[542] *ſoit atteint, ſoit gre maintenant fait al pleintif, et ſoit ouſte de ſervice le roy pur touts jours, et demoerge en priſon a la volunte le roy. Et ſi null' face priſes ſans garrante, et les emporte encountre la volunte* (12) *de celuy a que les biens ſont, ſoit maintenant arreſte per la ville, ou le priſe ſerra fait, et ameſne a la prochein gaole. Et ſi de ceo ſoit atteint, ſoit la fait de luy, come de laron* (11), *ſi la quantite des biens le demand'. Et quant as priſes faire en faires, et en bons villes, et en portes pur*

priſes within the realm, but only the king's takers, and the purveyors for his houſe; and that the king's takers and purveyors of his houſe ſhall take nothing, but only for his houſe. And touching ſuch things as they ſhall take in the country, of meat and drink, and ſuch other mean things neceſſary for the houſe, they ſhall pay or make agreement with them of whom the things ſhall be taken. And that all the king's takers, purveyors, or catours, from henceforth ſhall have their warrant with them, under the king's great or petty ſeal, declaring their authority, and the things whereof they have power to make priſe or purveyance; the which warrant they ſhall ſhew unto them whoſe goods they take, before they take any thing. And that thoſe takers, purveyors, or catours for the king, ſhall take no more than is needful or meet to be uſed for the king, his houſhold, and his children. And that they ſhall not take any thing for them that be in wages, nor for any other. And that they ſhall make full anſwer in the king's houſe, or in the wardrobe, for all things taken by them, without making their largeſſes any other where, or liveries, of ſuch things as they have taken for the king. And if any taker for the king's houſe, by reaſon of his warrant, make any priſe or livery, otherwiſe than before is mentioned, upon complaint made to the ſteward, and to the treaſurer of the king's houſe, the truth ſhall be enquired. And if he be attainted thereof, he ſhall forthwith make agreement with the party, and ſhall be put out of the king's ſervice for ever, and ſhall remain in priſon at the king's pleaſure. And if any make priſe without warrant, and carry it away againſt the will of the owner, he ſhall immediately be arreſted by the town where the priſe was

pur la grande garderobe le roy, eient les pernours lour commen garrant per le grand seale (13). *Et des choses que ils prendront, eient la tesmoign' du seale du gardein de la garderobe. Et des choses issint per eux prises, de nombre, de quantite, et de value soit fait dividende entre les pernours, et les gardeins des faires, maires, ou chief baylies des villes, et portes, per la vieu des merchants, des queux les biens serront issint prises. Et riens ne luy soit suffert de plus prendre, que il ne mette en dividende. Et cell' dividende soit port en garderobe soubs le seale le gardein, maire, ou chiefe bailife avantdits: et la demoerge tanque sur laccompte du garderobe le roy. Et sil soit trove que nul eit autrement prise que faire ne deveroit, soit puny sur laccompte per le gardein de la garderobe le roy, solonq; sa deserte. Et si nul face tielx prises sans garrante, et sur ceo soit atteint, soit fait de luy come de ceux que font prises pur lostell' le roy sans garrante, come desus est dit* (14). *Et nentende mye le roy, ne son counsail, que per cest estatute rien decresse au roy de son droit des auncient prises dues et accustomes, come des vins, et auters biens: mesque en toutes pointes pleynment luy soit save* (15).

was made, and shall be committed to the next gaol; and if he be attainted thereupon, it shall be done unto him as unto a felon, if the quantity of the goods do so require. And concerning prises made in fairs, and good towns, and in ports, for the king's great wardrobe, the takers shall have their common warrant under the great seal. And for the things that they shall take, it shall be testified under the seal of the keeper of the wardrobe; and of those things that they have taken, the number of the things, the quantity, and the value, shall be specified in a divident made between the takers and the keepers of fairs, mayors, or chief bailiffs of towns and ports, by the view of merchants, whose goods shall be so taken; and they shall not be suffered to take any more than is contained in their divident; and the said divident shall be taken into the wardrobe under the seal of the warden, mayor, or chief bailiff aforesaid, and there shall remain until the accompt of the keeper of the king's wardrobe; and if it be found, that any hath taken otherwise than he ought to do upon his accompt, he shall be punished by the keeper of the kings wardrobe after his desert; and if any make such prises without warrant, and be attainted thereupon, he shall incur the same pain as they which take prises for the king's house without warrant, as before is said. Nevertheless the king and his council do not intend, by reason of this estatute, to diminish the king's right, for the ancient prises due and accustomed, as of wines and other goods, but that his right shall be saved unto him whole in all points.

This chapter is confirmed by 18 E. 1. cap. 2. (4 Ed. 3. c. 4. 5 Ed. 3. c. 2. 10 Ed. 3. stat. 2. c. 1. 25 Ed. 3. c. 1. 36 Ed. 3. c. 2. 12 Car. 2. c. 24.)

Seeing

Seeing by many acts of parliaments the kings purveyance is limited in certain, so as the law there is certain, and without question; it shall not be impertinent nor unnecessary to learne from antiquity, how, and in what sort the kings houshold was in those dayes provided of victuals: certain it is, that aswell before as after the conquest, the king upon his ancient demesnes of the crown of England, had houses of husbandry, and stocks for the furnishing of necessary provisions for his houshold; and the tenants of those mannours did by their tenures, manure, till, &c. and reap the corn upon the kings demesnes ‡, mowed his meadowes, &c. repaired the fences, and performed all necessary things belonging to husbandry upon the kings demeanes: in respect of which services, and to the end they might apply the same the better, they had many liberties and priviledges, as that they should not be sued out of the court of that mannor, nor impannelled of any jury or inquest, nor appeare at any other court, but onely at the court of the said mannor, nor be contributory to the expences of the knights of the shire which serve at parliament, nor pay any toll, &c. which liberties and immunities continue to this day, albeit the originall cause thereof is ceased: now all the mannors that were in the hands of Edward the Confessor before the conquest, or in the hands of William the Conqueror, and so appeare in the booke called Domesday, are accounted the auncient demeanes of the crowne of England, and had beene the demeanes of the crown long before.

* Inter leges Canut. regis ca. 67. Omnibus hanc porro impartimus allevationē ut quo prius opprimebat' onere populum liberemus: inprimis præfectis meis omnibus mand', ut ex prædiis meis propriis quæ mihi fuerint ad victum necessaria suppeditent, neque alius quisquam victui nostro alimenta præstare invitus cogatur. Itaq; si eorum aliquis hoc nomine mulctam petierit, is proprii capitis æstimationem regi dependito.

In libro rubeo scacc. cap. A quibus et ad quid fuit argent' examinatio; you shall reade that which is very observable. *In primitivo regni statu post conquisitionem, regibus de fundis suis non auri et argenti pondera, sed sola victualia solvebantur, ex quibus in usus quotidianos domus regiæ necessaria ministrabantur, &c.* And see the reason wherefore these provisions of victualls were changed.

Lucubrat.

‡ [543]

And this is evident by many records, but by little and little this course of good husbandry vanished.

When the kings own provisions for the most part failed, then to supply necessary provisions, there was a continuall market kept at the court gate, where the king was better served with viands for his houshold, then by purveyors, the subject better used, and the king at farre lesse charge in respect of the multitude of purveyors, and the officer of this market was called *clericus mercati hospitii regis*, the clerk of the market of the kings house, so as he retaineth his name still according to the first institution, although the good end thereof ceaseth; when this market was discontinued, then purveyors started up, and the number of them dayly increased, who by the lawes and statutes of this realme ought to observe five things: 1. To take onely for the kings houshold. 2. With the consent of the owner. 3. For the price as was sold in the market. 4. To take no more then was necessary for the kings houshold. 5. Where it might best be spared, and where more plenty was.

Rot. claus. 13 H. 3. m. 10. in dors. Rot. finium 3 E. 1. 35. Kelwey, 114. Brit. 75, 76. Fleta, lib. 2. cap. 8. & 11.

Rot. Parl. 50 E. 3. nu. 87. & 152. 12 R. 2. cap. 4. Lib. intr' Co. 445. 32 H. 8. ca. 20. The number of purveyors enacted to be abridged. 34 E. 3. ca. 3. 36 E. 3. ca. 2. That they be sufficient men.

All which was inquirable before the justices in eyre, before our statute made in 28 E. 1. and at the first they were called *emptores*, buyers; and it was a speciall article inquired by the justices in eyre, *de prisis fact' per vicecomites, vel constabular', vel alios balivos contra voluntatem eorum quorum catalla fuerint*; and this was before the making of our statute of 28 E. 1.

Bract. l. 3. fo. 117. cap. Itin' sæpe. Brit. fol. 33. 36. Fleta, l. 1. ca. 20. Lib. 2. cap. 16. Fortescue, c. 36. fol. 43 See the statutes hereafter mentioned.

And

Stat. de Tallagio. 34 E. 1. 4 E. 3. c. 3. 18 E. 3. c. 7. Int' brevia 6 H. 3. Balivus de Hoyl and Lenne, & Gernem. 7 H. 3. tit. Waſte 141. Pl. Com. in caſe de Mynes.

And for a concluſion hereof it is declared by authority of parliament, in theſe words, *Nullus miniſter noſter, vel hæredum noſtrorum, capiat blada, corea, vel aliqua alia bona cujuſcunque ſine voluntate et conſenſu illius cujus fuerint bona:* and this is confirmed and eſtabliſhed by the ſtatute of 18 E. 3.

So as no queſtion can bee hereof made, and if you reade of any taking or purveyance in auncient time it muſt bee taken with theſe limitations; and the reaſon why theſe words, *ſine voluntate et conſenſu, &c.* without the will and agreement, were expreſſed, was for that purveyors would take the goods of ſuch men as had no will to ſell them, but to uſe or ſpend them for their own neceſſary uſe.

(1) *En primes pur ceo que un graund grevance, &c.*] The miſchiefe before this ſtatute was, that the inſolency of the purveyors [544] bearing themſelves ſo proudly under the great officers of the kings houſhold, grew to that height that they would take what and how much as it pleaſed them, and many times where it might be leaſt forborne or ſpared, and for others then for the kings houſhold, and ſometimes would pay nothing, and many times leſſe then the true value, and many perſons would make purveyance without any warrant at all; of theſe great grievances and loſſes without number, infinite damages, the ſubjects complained of at this parliament, and for reſtraining of the abuſes of the purveyors and reliefe of the ſubjects, this act of parliament was made.

Paſch. 30 E. 1. coram rege Kanc'. The Cinque ports caſe. * Rot. Cha. 17 July, anno 6 E. 1. Baronibus 5. Port. conceſſus.

(2) *Font lour priſes*] Of the French word *priſe,* comes the word *priſa,* uſed in law for the things taken by purveyors: *recta priſa,* right taking or purveyance is there expounded, *viz. De uno dol' ante malum et alio poſt malum* * and ſo explained in the charter of E. 1. This is called *recta priſa,* right taking or purveyance, becauſe it diſtinguiſhed it from the taking or purveyance againſt right. *Vide ſpeculum regis M.S.* written by Iſlep archbiſhop of Cant. to king E. 3.

In ligul. de præcept. de Term. Hil. anno 16 E. 2. Nota pro juſtic. de banco regis & eorum honore & ſuprema juriſdictione. * Purveyance. 28 E. 1. Art. ſuper Chart. ca. 2. 28 E. 1. Art. ſuper Chart. c. 20. Anno 33 E. 1. de conſpirat.

*Edwardus Dei gratia rex Angliæ, dominus Hiberniæ, & dux Aquitan' dilectis & fidelibus ſuis Henric' le Scrop' & ſociis ſuis juſtic' noſtris ad placita coram nobis tenend' aſſignat', ſalutem. Miramur quod cum vos præfat' locum noſtrum in placitis hujuſmodi teneatis, & noſtram præſentiam per loca per quæ regno noſtro tranſieritis in præmiſſis ſupplere debeatis, * de priſis bladorum, victualium, et aliorum bonorum ſubditorum noſtrorum, contra voluntatem eorundem, conſpiratoribus, tranſgreſſoribus, informatoribus falſarum querelarum, conventiculis & confederationibus illicitis factis non inquiritis, nec ulterius facitis quod deceret: volentes igitur hujuſmodi mala puniri prout decet, vobis mandamus firmiter injungentes quod de hujuſmodi priſis, conſpirationibus, tranſgreſſionibus, informationibus falſarum querelarum, conventiculis, & confederationibus exnunc per ſingula loca per quæ tranſieritis, tam infra libertates quam extra, cum omn' diligentia & modis quibus poteritis inquiratis, & omnes illos quos legitime convinci contingit, puniatis juxta formam ſtatutorum, & articulorum inde editorum, & ſecundum legem, & conſuetudinem regni noſtri in hac parte talit' vos habentes, quod querela ad nos inde non perveniat iterata. T. me ipſo apud Newarke, xxx. die Januarii, anno regni noſtri 16. per ipſum regem.*

4 E. 3. c. 3. 25 E. 3. ca. 1. 36 E. 3. ca. 2.

(3) *Ou bien meynes que la value.*] Hereby it appeareth that the very value ought to be paid for the things purveyed according to that which appeared in our auncient authors.

(4) *Forſque*

(4) *Forſque le pernours le roy, et les purveyors pur le hoſtle le roy.*] Herewith agreeth many later ſtatutes, and explained to be the houſhold of the king and queene, at this parliament, cap. 5. that the chauncellor and juſtices of the kings bench ſhould follow the court, and by pretext thereof purveyance was made for them as part of the houſhold, which laſted untill 4 E. 3. cap. 3. at what time (the chauncellor and judges diſcontinuing to follow the court) it is provided againſt them, and all other that be not of the kings houſhold.

4 E. 3. c. 3. 25 E. 3. ca. 1. 36 E. 3. c. 2. Rot. Pat. 10 E. 2. pt. 2. m. 20. li. 10. fol. 73. In caſe de Marſhalſca.

(5) *Ne pernont riens forſque pur meſme le houſholde*, &c.] All this is in affirmance of the auncient common above mentioned, and ratified by the later acts of parliament laſt above remembered.

(6) *Et des priſes que ilz ferront per my le pays de manger ou de boyer, et des auters menus neceſſaries pur le hoſtele, que ilz facent le paie ou gree a ceux des queux le choſes ſerront priſes.*] This is to be underſtood, when the king is paſſing in the country, as in his progreſſe, or in any journey, as it appeareth by the preamble; there the purveior may take meat and drink, which this act here in reſpect of the kings paſſage calls ſmall things, but he muſt pay the very value therefore, and make preſent payment, or agree with the party. [545]

This is made certaine by a latter ſtatute, that in all caſes where the thing to be taken is under 40 ſhillings, there preſent payment to be made, or elſe the owner may retaine and reſiſt, and for the tryall of the true value, the thing to be taken is to be praiſed or priced according to the very value by the lord or his baily, or the conſtable, and foure good men of the town where ſuch taking ſhall be, there to be ſworne, in covenable and eaſie manner without threats or dures and by indenture the quantity of the thing taken, the price, and of what perſons; but if it be not in the kings paſſage, but for his ſtanding houſe, then the king cannot take any beere or ale, becauſe it is a manufacture, no more then he can take for his ſtanding houſe any other victuall made by art and labour of mans hand, as bread, or the like; but mault, having the ſubſtance of the barley remaining, and having nothing added to it, is no ſuch manufacture, as it appeareth by a later act of parliament. But then the king by his officers muſt convert it into beere; for he cannot ſell, or otherwiſe imploy the ſame, which hath been the cauſe that never any mault was taken, and it muſt be taken at the very value in the market.

4 E. 3. cap. 3. 5 E. 3. cap. 2. 36 E. 3. c. 2. &c.

36 E. 3. cap. 2.

(7) *Eyent de cy en avant lour garrante, ove eux du grand ſeale, ou de petit ſeale le roy, conteynant lour power, et les choſes dont ils ferront priſes.*] By latter ſtatutes the commiſſion muſt be under the great ſeal onely, and every halfe yeare to be renewed.

36 E. 3. cap. 2. 2 & 3 Ph. & Mar. cap. 6.

(8) *Le quel garrant ils monſtrent a eux des queux ils ferront le priſe avant ceo que ils impreignent rien.*] This is evident, and confirmed by later ſtatutes.

(9) *Ne preigne plus que beſoigne et meſter ne ſoit*, &c.] The ſtatute of 36 E. 3. confirmeth this, and doth adde, that the takings muſt be in ſuch places where greateſt plenty is, and in a covenable time.

I have reade a booke called *Speculum Regis*, written in Latin by Simon Iſlip archbiſhop of Canterbury to king Edward the third, wherein he ſharply inveigheth againſt the intolerable abuſes of purveiors and purveyance in many particulars, and earneſtly adviſeth, Speculum Regis.

viseth, and instantly presseth the king to provide remedy for those insufferable oppressions and wrongs offered to his subjects, which the king keeping with him, and often perusing, it wrought such effect, that the king at divers of his parliaments, but specially at his parliament holden in the 36 yeare of his reign, of his own will, without motion of the great men or commons, as the record of parliament speaketh, caused to be made many excellent lawes against the oppressions, malice, and falshood of purveyors.

(10) *Et que ils respoinent in lostel ou en la garde robe pleinment de touts lour prises sans faire lour largesses ailours, ou liveries des choses, que pur le roy serra prises.*] This account is to be made by this act for victuals, &c. to the houshold, that is, to the officers of the green cloth; and for such things as belong to the wardrobe to the master of the wardrobe.

[546] (11) *Et si nul face prises sans garrant, et les emport encounter le volunt de celuy, &c. Et si de ceo soit attaint, soit fait de luy, come de laron.*] By this branch, if any purveyor take any thing without warrant, &c. it is felony. And here it is to be observed, that these words, *come de laron,* shall be understood of a theefe that stealeth above the value of 12 pence; for he that committeth petit larceny is not *un laron* within this act.

Vid. the forme of an inditement in Lambards Justice of Peace in fine libri.

(12) *Encounter le volunt.*] That is, when he takes it as the kings purveyor, pretending to have a warrant where he hath none, this is in law as against his will, for with his will he would not have suffered him to take it, if he had knowne he had no warrant; but if the owner knew that he had no warrant, and yet willingly sold it him, then cannot it be said, that he carried it away against his will.

5 E. 3. cap. 2. 25 E. 3. cap. 1. Hol. Cronic' fol. 39. 369. 36 E. 3. ca. 2. 4. 7 R. 2. cap. 4. 32 E. 3. tit. Barre 259. Stamf. Pl. cor. 37. a. Li. 8. fo. 146. b. le 6 Carpent. case. Hill. 23 E. 3. coram rege apud Ebor' inditements de purveyors. Lib. 2. ca. 6, 7.

If the purveyors take any thing without praisment made by the constables, or other discreet men thereto sworne, or otherwise against that statute, it is felony, and divers purveyors in 20 E. 3. were attainted and hanged for offending against these lawes.

If any purveyor make any takings or buyings, or take any carriage in any other manner then is conteined in his commission, it is felony; or if the purveyor take more then he deliver, and have not paid for that which is taken, it is felony.

And at the sessions at Newgate holden in January, *anno* 32 Eliz. Nichols one of the queenes purveyors was attainted and hanged for offending of this law.

(13) *Et quant as prises faits en faires, et en bones villes, et en ports per le grand gardrobe le roy, eyent les pernours lour common garrant per le grand seale.*] For the wardrobe see Fleta.

And the letter of the law is plaine.

(14) *Et si nul face tiels prises sans garrant, et sur ceo soit attaint, soit fait de luy come de ceux que sont prises pur le hostel le roy sans garrant, come de suis est dit.*] That is to say, let it be done of him as a theefe.

(15) *Et nentend mye le roy ne son counsaile, que per cest statute rien decresse al roy de son droit des auncient prises dues, et accustomes, come des vines, et auters biens: mesque en touts points pleinment luy sont save.*] *Vide* 25 E. 1. *confirm' chartarum,* the like saving explained, and whereof this ancient prices is to be intended.

Confirm. Chart. cap. 6.

And hereby it may appeare how necessary it was, first to know what belonged to the king of common right, and at the common law.

But

But to prevent all ſcruples by colour of this ſaving, the ſaid act of parliament *de tallag' non conced' anno* 34 E. 1. was made after this act of 28 E. 1. which is a generall negative law, without any ſaving.

34 E. 1. de tall' non conced. c. 2.

And therefore what ſubſequent acts of parliament have given to the king, the ſame ought to be obſerved and kept in ſuch manner and order as thereby is preſcribed.

CAP. III.

DES eſtates des ſeneſchals, et des marſhals (2), *et des plees que eux devoient tener, et coment* (1)*: ordeine eſt, que deſormes ne teigne plee de franktenement* (3), *ne de dette, ne de covenant, ne de contract des gents de people, forſque tantſolement de treſpaſſes del hoſtell, et dauters treſpaſſes fait dedeins la vierge, et des contracts et covenants, que aſcun del hoſtel le roy avera fait a auter de meſme le hoſtel, et en meſme le hoſtel, et nemy ailours* (4). *Et nul plee de treſpaſſe ne pledront, auter que ne ſoit attache* (5) *per eux, avant ceo que le roy iſſera* (6) *hors de la vierge, ou la treſpaſſe ſerra fait. Et les pleder' haſtivement de jour en jour, iſſint que ils ſoient pledes et termines avant ceo que le roy iſſera hors des boundes de cel vierge* (7), *ou le treſpaſſe fuit fait. Et ſi par cas dedeins les bounds de cel vierge ne poient eſtre termines, ceſſent tiels plees devant le ſeneſchalle, et ſoient les plees a la common ley. Ne deſormes ne preigne ne ſeneſchalle conuſances des dets, ne dauter choſe, forſque des gents del hoſtel avantdit, ne nul auter plee en tiend per obligac'* (8) *fait a le diſtreſſe le ſeneſchalle, ou le mareſchalle. Et ſi les ſeneſchals, ou le mareſchals rien facent encounter ceſt ordinance, ſoit lour fait tenus pur nul. Et pur ceo que avant ces heures mults des felonies faits dedeins la vierge ount eſtre depunies* (9), *pur ceo que les coroners de pays ne ſe ont pas entermis denquirer des tiels maners des felonies dedeins la vierge*

CONCERNING the authority of ſtewards and marſhals, and of ſuch pleas as they may hold, and in what manner, it is ordained, that from henceforth they ſhall not hold plea of freehold, neither of debt, nor of covenant, nor of any contract made between the king's people, but only of treſpaſs done within the houſe, and of other treſpaſſes done within the verge, and of contracts and covenants that one of the king's houſe ſhall have made with another of the ſame houſe, and in the ſame houſe, and none other where. And they ſhall plead no plea of treſpaſs, other than that which ſhall be attached by them before the king depart from the verge where the treſpaſs ſhall be committed; and ſhall plead them ſpeedily from day to day, ſo that they may be pleaded and determined before that the king depart out of the limits of the ſame verge where the treſpaſs was done. And if it ſo be that they cannot be determined within the limits of the ſame verge, then ſhall the ſame pleas ceaſe before the ſteward, and the plaintiffs ſhall have recourſe to the common law. And from henceforth the ſteward ſhall not take cogniſance of debts nor of other things, but of people of the ſame houſe, nor ſhall hold none other plea by obligation made at the diſtreſs of the ſteward and of the marſhals. And if the ſteward or marſhals do any thing contrary to this ordinance, it ſhall be holden as void.

vierge (10), *mes le coroner del hostel le roy, que est passant, de quoy issue nad my este fait en du manner, ne les felons mis en exigent* (11), *ne utlages, ne rien de ceo present en eyre, que ad ēe a graund damage du roy, et a meins bone garde de la peace: ordeine est, que desormes en case de mort de home, ou office de coroner appent as viewes, et enquests de ceo faire, soit maund al coroner del pays, que ensemblement ove le coroner del hostel le roy face loffice que appent, et le metter enrolle. Et ceo que ne purra mie devant le seneschal estre termine, pur ceo que les felons ne purront estre attaches, ou pur auter encheson, demurge a la common ley, issint que les exigents, utlagaries, et presentments en eyre soient de ceo faits per le coroner du pays, auxy come des auters felonies faits hors de la vierge. Mes pur ceo ne soit lesse* *, *que les attachments ne soyent faits freshment sur les felonies faits.*

*[548]

void. And forasmuch as heretofore many felonies committed within the verge have been unpunished, because the coroners of the country have not been authorized to enquire of such manner of felonies done within the verge, but the coroner of the king's house, which never continueth in one place, by reason whereof there can be no trial made in due manner, nor the felons put in exigent, nor outlawed, nor any thing presented in the circuit, the which hath been to the great damage of the king, and nothing to the good preservation of his peace; it is ordained, that from henceforth in cases of the death of men, whereof the coroner's office is to make view and enquest, it shall be commanded to the coroner of the country, that he, with the coroner of the king's house, shall do as belongeth to his office, and inroll it. And that thing that cannot be determined before the steward, where the felons cannot be attached, or for other like cause, shall be remitted to the common law, so that exigents, outlawries, and presentments, shall be made thereupon in eyre by the coroner of the country, as well as of other felonies done out of the verge; nevertheless they shall not omit, by reason hereof, to make attachments freshly upon the felonies done.

(10 Ed. 3. stat. 2. c. 2. 13 R. 2. stat. 1. c. 2. 15 H. 6. c. 1. 1 Bulstr. 208. 2 Inst. 547. 4 H. 6. f. 8. 10 H. 6. f. 13. Bro. Action sur le stat. 38. 44. 6 Rep. 12. 20. 10 Rep. 71. 4 Rep. 46. 33 H. 8. c. 12. 2 Leon, 160. 18 Ed. 3. stat. 2. c. 7.)

(1) *Des estates, des seneschals, et des marshals, et des plees, que eux devoient tener et coment.*] Here in this short and effectuall preamble three things are to be observed:

1. *Des estates,* that is the extent of the jurisdiction or state of the steward and marshall, whereupon they may justly and safely stand.

2. What pleas they ought to hold, where this word *(devoient)* is observable; for this act doth restore and confine this court of the marshalsea to his right and just jurisdiction, and to hold those pleas which the steward and marshall ought, that is, of right ought to hold.

3. How

3. How and in what order and manner thoſe pleas ought to be holden, expreſſed in this word *coment*.

Hereby it appeareth, that this act is in affirmance of the common law, and purpoſely made for relieving the ſubject againſt the uſurpations and incroachments of the ſteward and marſhall.

(2) *Des seneſchals et marſhals*, &c.] Theſe words are generall, but they are to be underſtood of the ſteward of the court of the marſhalſea of the houſhold, who is ever a profeſſor of the common law, and not of the ſteward of the kings houſhold; and the marſhall is here to be underſtood the marſhall of the houſhold, and the marſhalſea is to be underſtood of the houſhold, and not of the kings marſhalſea; for that belongeth to the kings bench.

Lib. 10. fol. 68. in caſe of the Marſhalſea.

(3) *Ordeine eſt, que ne teigne plee de franktenement.*] This is negative, abſolute, and in affirmance of the common law.

(4) *Ne de dette, ne de covenant, ne de contract des gents de people, forſq; tant ſolement des treſpaſſes del hoſtel, et dauters treſpaſſes faits deins la vierge, et des contracts et covenants, que aſcun del hoſtel le roy avera fait al auter de meſme le hoſtel, et nemy ailours.*] Here by this act it is declared, that the ſaid ſteward and marſhall cannot hold plea but of three actions, *viz.* of debt, covenant, and treſpaſſes: in debt and covenant both the parties muſt be of the kings houſhold; in treſpaſſes it ſufficeth that one of the parties be of the kings houſhold.

And though this act ſpeaketh generally of treſpaſſes, yet is it onely intendable of treſpaſſes *vi et armis*, as of battery, or taking away of goods, and not of treſpaſſes *quare clauſum fregit*, nor of treſpaſſes and ejectment, nor of treſpaſſes *ſur le caſe*, nor of detinue, nor of any other perſonall action, nor of any reall or mixt action, notwithſtanding the generall words of the ſtatute of 33 H. 8. as you may reade at large in the caſe of the * marſhalſea; for particular juriſdictions derogating from the juriſdiction of the generall courts of the common law are ever taken ſtrictly.

38 E. 3. 17. Regiſt. 185. & 111. 6 R. 2. action ſur le ſtatute pl. ult. 3 H. 6. eſtopp. 18. action ſur leſtat. 13. 7 H. 6. 30. 10 H. 6. 13. 14 H. 6. 6. Lib. 5 E. 4. 129. 19 E. 4. 8. b. 20 E. 4. 16. 22 E. 4. 11. 16. 31. F.N.B. 241, 242. Hil. 5. Jac. coram rege rot. 876. 33 H. 8. ca. 12. * Lib. 10. fo. 60. en caſe de Marſhalſea.

(5) *Et nul plee de treſpaſſes pledront, auter que ne ſoit attache.*] This is explained in the caſe of the marſhalſea, *ubi ſupra.*

(6) *Avant que le roy iſſera.*] Albeit the king himſelfe do goe out of the bounds of the vierge for his recreation, as to hunt, with no purpoſe to reſt, tarry, abide, or make his repoſe there, and his councell and houſhold continue where they were, this is no removing within this ſtatute: but when the king goeth in progreſſe, there his houſhold goeth with him, there the king removeth within this act.

32 H. 8. cap. 20. F.N.B. 241.

(7) *Hors des bounds de ceſt vierge.*] The bounds of the vierge. See Fleta * and the Mirror, that the bounds of the vierge was 12 miles round about the kings houſe, ſo as it ſeemeth, that 13 R. 2. was but in affirmance of the common law. *Vide* 33 H. 8. the bounds of the kings houſe, or palace.

The caſe of the Marſhalſea, ubi ſupra.

* [549]

13 R. 2. cap. 3. 33 H. 8. cap. 12.

(8) *Ne nul auter plee teigne per obligation.*] This is alſo notably explained in the ſaid caſe of the marſhalſea, *ubi ſupra.*

(9) *Et pur ceo que avant ceux heures mults des felonies faits deins la vierge, ount eſtre diſpunies.*] Here are to be obſerved, that as the actions aboveſaid determinable before the ſteward and marſhall, are confined to the vierge; ſo felonies alſo determinable before the ſteward and marſhall, are alſo confined to the vierge: and as they are limited of all the cauſes of actions riſing within the vierge onely to three, and they not generally extending to all, but ſpecially

2 H. 4. cap. 23. 9 R. 2. cap. 5. 18 E. 3. cap. 7.

cially confined to certaine particular perſons; ſo of felonies done within the vierge, the juriſdiction of the ſteward and marſhall extend not to all, but to certaine, and thoſe againe limited to certaine perſons: for of ancient time they had generall authority, as juſtices in eyre, and as vicegerents of the chiefe juſtice of England within the vierge, at what time they held plea of all felonies within the vierge, which power is now vaniſhed; but as ſteward and marſhall of the court of marſhalſea of the kings houſhold, the title of their court in criminall cauſes was, *placita coronæ aulæ hoſpitii domini regis coram ſeneſchallo et mariſchallo*, and alwayes confined to felonies done within the circuit of the kings houſhold, the bounds whereof are made certaine by the ſaid act of 33 H. 8. And by that act it is provided, that all treaſons, miſpriſions of treaſons, murthers, manſlaughters, bloudſheds, and other malicious ſtrikings, by reaſon whereof bloud is or ſhall be ſhed, which ſhall be done in any of the kings palaces or houſes, &c. ſhall be enquired, tried, heard, and determined before the lord ſteward for the time being of the kings houſhold, or in his abſence before the treaſurer, and controller, and ſteward of the marſhalſea, or any two of them, whereof the ſteward to be one: ſo as theſe great officers and councellors of ſtate, the lord ſteward, treaſurer, and controller have no juriſdiction in theſe criminall cauſes, but onely within the circuit of the kings palace or houſe: and it is to be obſerved, that this court of the marſhalſea of the kings houſe was, as bookes ſpeak, of ancient time inſtituted for thoſe of the kings houſe, but they have incroached beyond their true juriſdiction: and Standford ſaith, that the ſteward and marſhall before the ſaid act of 33 H. 8. might have heard and determined all felonies, &c. perpetrate within the kings palace or houſe.

Vid. le caſe de Marſhalſea, ubi ſupra.

Stanf. pl. cor. fol. 57.

L. 5 E. 4. 13. of this incroachment complaint hath been made in parliament. 8 H. 4. nu. 42. Stanf. ubi ſupra.

A robbery was committed in a towne within the vierge, and this appearing to the court, yet the ſame was enquired of, heard, and determined in the kings bench, and ſo it may be before juſtices of oire and terminer, and juſtices of peace, becauſe their juriſdiction is generall through the whole county; but of an offence within the kings palace it ſhall be heard and determined according to the ſaid act of 33 H. 8. upon which act this is obſervable, that if a man ſtrike in the kings palace, where his royall perſon is reſiant, unleſſe bloud be ſhed he loſeth not his hand; but in Weſtminſter hall, when the kings courts ſit, or before the juſtices of aſſiſe ſitting in their place, if any man ſtrike another, though he draw no bloud, yet ſhall he loſe his right hand, ſo great honour and reverence doe lawes give to the kings courts: for in judgement of law the king himſelfe is alwayes preſent to miniſter juſtice by his judges in thoſe courts of juſtice, according to his kingly office to all his ſubjects, *ſecundum legem et conſuetudinem Angliæ*.

Paſch' 12 E. 2. rot. 280. coram rege, the caſe of William Swetton, lib. 4. fo. 47. Kath. Wroths caſe.

41 E. 3. coron. 280. 22 E. 3. 13. 19 E. 3. judgemt. Dyer, 3 El, 188.

(10) *Les coroners de pays ne ſoient pas intermis denquirer des felonies deins la vierge.*] This is underſtood of felonies of the death of man; for the enquiry of that felony belongs to the office of the coroner of the vierge, and ſo it is hereafter in this act explained, *Office del coroner appent a views et enqueſts de ceo faire.*

[550]

Hereby it appeareth, that by the common law the coroner of the county could not intermeddle within the vierge, but the coroner of the vierge, and that if he took an inditement of the death of man, it was not allowable in law; and ſo it is if the coroner of the kings houſe take an inditement of the death of man out of the vierge, it

Brit. fol. 1. Lib. 4. fol. 46, 47. ubi ſupra.

it is void, and *coram non judice.* And if an inditement of the death of a man being ſlaine out of the vierge, be taken before the coroner of the kings houſe, and the coroner of the county, and ſo entred of record, it is inſufficient, becauſe the coroner of the kings houſe joyned with him, who had no authority.

(11) *Ne les felonies miſe in exigent,* &c.] And yet the felony was not diſpuniſhable; for at this time it might after the remove of the king be inquired of in the kings bench, if the bench ſate in that county, or before juſtices of oire and terminer, &c. or if the coroner of the vierge had taken an inditement, though the king went out of the vierge, yet the inditement ought to be removed into the kings bench; for that is the center whereunto all records of that nature doe fall, and there the offence might be heard and determined.

But this act was made for more ſpeedy proceeding, for being removed into the kings bench, there ought to be 15 dayes, &c. Lib. 9. fol. 118, 119. Seignior Zanchers caſe.

And if a murder had been committed within the vierge, and the king had removed before any inditement taken by the coroner of the vierge, the coroner of the county might have inquired of the ſame at the common law, *ne maleficia remanerent impunita.*

See the ſtatute of Magna Charta, *Nullus vicecomes, conſtabular', coronator, vel alii balivi noſtri teneant placita coronæ noſtræ.* See the expoſition of that ſtatute concerning this branch for awarding of exigents, &c. Magna Charta, cap. 17.

Albeit the treaty of theſe matters concerning the marſhalſea doe properly belong to the juriſdiction of courts, yet it is pertinent to this place to ſay ſo much as ſerved for the expoſition of this chapter.

See the ſaid caſe of the marſhalſea thorowout, which indeed doth open the windowes of the greateſt part of this act.

CAP. IV.

OUSTER ceo nul common plee ne ſoit deſormes tenus a leſchequer, encounter la forme de la graund charter.

MOREOVER no common pleas ſhall be from henceforth holden in the exchequer, contrary to the form of the great charter.

(Dyer, 250. 9 H. 3. c. 11. Regiſt. 187.)

Here is intended the 11. chapter of Magna Charta, whereof this chapter (according to the title of *Articuli ſuper chartas)* is an expoſition; for where that chapter is, *communia placita non ſequantur curiam noſtram, ſed teneantur in loco certo,* this chapter expoundeth the ſame, that from henceforth no common plea ſhall be holden in the exchequer againſt the forme of the great charter: for *curia noſtra* in *Magna Charta* are taken collective, and include as well the exchequer as the kings bench.

2. This act maketh it without queſtion; for admit that the court of the kings bench had been named in that chapter of *Magna Charta,* and this act prohibiteth that no common plea ſhould be holden in the exchequer againſt the forme of *Magna Charta,* that

is, againſt the forme that *Magna Charta* provideth for the kings bench: and this is alſo confirmed by a ſtatute made in the reigne of E. 1. and tranſcribed to the exchequer under the great ſeale, *in*
[55¹] *anno* 10 E. 1. called the ſtatute of Roteland, in theſe words: *Sed quia quædam placita, &c.*

Now that this was a ſtatute, the title or ſtile of the act is, *Statutum novum de ſcaccario, aliter dictum, ſtatutum de Roteland. In libro rubeo* it is called *ſtatutum de Roteland,* and there is a writ in the Regiſter under the title of *brevia de ſtatut', rex theſaurario, et baronibus ſalutem: cum ſecundum legem et conſuetudinem regni noſtri communia placita coram vobis ad ſcaccarium prædictum placitari non debent, niſi placita illa nos vel aliquem miniſtrorum noſtrorum ejuſdem ſcaccarii ſpecialiter tangunt, &c.* which writ reciteth the words of the ſtatute of Rutland, and in the margent of the writ is quoted *ſtatutum de Roteland,* ſo as without queſtion this act was made by authority of parliament, ſo as without queſtion whatſoever pleas were holden in the exchequer, in the raigne of H. 2. when Glanvile wrote, yet now by two acts of parliament their juriſdiction is limited and ſettled: and therefore reject a late opinion contrary to ſuch authority, and never read nor heard of before.

Regiſt. fol. 187. 8 Eliz. Dyer, fol. 250.

Pl. com. 208, 209.

Per Saunders.

The exchequer is an ancient court of record for the kings affaires, touching his rights and revenues of his crowne, and for debts and duties, and other things due to the king in the right of his crowne. Britton treating of the juriſdiction of the exchequer, ſaith, *A oier et determiner touts les cauſes que touchent nous detts, et auxi a nous fees, et les incidents choſes, &c.*

[a] Yet in three caſes the court of exchequer hath juriſdiction of common pleas between common perſons in perſonall actions onely.

1. Where an officer or miniſter is one of the parties in any perſonall action, becauſe that his abſence in other courts may hinder the affaires of the king in his court of exchequer.

2. Any man that is a priſoner of this court, or an accountant that is entred into his account, or any other that ought to have the like priviledge of this court of exchequer, ſhall not bee ſued in any perſonall action but in this court; and the reaſon is, becauſe neither of theſe acts of parliament take away the priviledge of any court: for then, if the party priviledged were ſued in any other court, he ſhould not in reſpect of his priviledge of the exchequer anſwer there; and therefore leſt the party ſhould be without remedy, he may commence his action perſonall againſt him in the exchequer, for ſtatutes muſt be ſo expounded, as there be no failer of juſtice.

Mirr. c. 4. de juriſdict. Flet. li. 2. cap. 25, 26. 38 aſſ. p. 20. 40 aſſ. p. 35. 14 E. 3. ſcire fac' 122. 2 E. 3. 24, 25. Pl. com. 208, 320. Brit. fol. 2. 29. 38. [a] Regiſt. 187. b. Stat. de Roteland, ubi ſupra. 2 E. 3. 25. lib. rubeus 36. 9 E. 4. 33. See the expoſition of Magna Charta, cap. 11.

3. He that is a farmer, or indebted to the king, for the kings more ſpeedy ſatisfaction of his debt or duty, ſhall ſue his debtor by a *quo minus* in the exchequer, and this appeareth by Britton, who treating of the juriſdiction of the exchequer, ſaith, *Et que il eyt power a conuſter de dett, que lun doit a nous detters per ou nous puiſſons pluis toſt approcher a noſtre.*

Now concerning the old court and the new court of exchequer, mentioned in 2 E. 3. and other matter concerning this court of exchequer, for that the ſame doe properly belong to the treaty concerning the juriſdiction of courts, we ſhall no further ſpeake of it here, for that ſufficient hath been ſaid already for the underſtanding of this chapter.

2 E. 3. 25. 20 E. 3. ley 52. 44 E. 3. 44. 2 H. 4. 7. 11. 8 H. 5. 6. 8 H. 6. 34. 32 H. 8. 24. 7 E. 4. 30. 11 H. 7. 29. 27 H. 8. 23. Brit. fol. 2. Flet. ubi ſupra, Dier, 2 El. 174. 3 El. 201. 16 El. 328. Pl. com. 208. a. b.

CAP.

CAP. V.

ET dauter part le roy voit que le chauncellor et les juſtices de ſon bank (1) *luy ſuivent, iſſint que il eyt touts jours pres de luy aſcun ſages de la ley, que ſachent les beſoignes* (2), *que veignent a la court duement deliverer a touts les foits que meſtier ſerra.*

AND on the other party, the king will, that the chancellor and the juſtices of his bench ſhall follow him, ſo that he may have at all times near unto him ſome ſages of the law, which be able duly to order all ſuch matters as ſhall come unto the court at all times, when need ſhall require.

The true cauſes wherefore the chancellour followed the kings court were firſt, that the great ſeale is *clavis regni*, and in the cuſtody of the chancellour, and meet it was, that the king ſhould have the key of his kingdome about him. [552]

2. That *curia cancellariæ*, was *officina juſticiæ*; for in thoſe dayes not only originall writs *in regiſt' cancellariæ*, but all commandements upon any occaſion for the ſafety of the realme, or the good government thereof were by writs, and paſſed under the great ſeale: and therefore neceſſary in thoſe dayes, that the chancellour, having the cuſtody of the great ſeale, ſhould be about the king at all times; and this is the cauſe that the court of chancery cannot be adjourned.

3. The ſtile of the court of chancery is *coram domino rege in cancellaria*. But where ſome hath ſuppoſed, that at the making of this ſtatute the chancellour held a court of equity, and that the judges in this act named attended on the king to decide matter of law, and the chancellour attended on him to decide matter of equity, it is mainly oppoſed, that at this time the chancellour had no court of equity, but onely a court of record of ordinary juriſdiction, according to the courſe of the common law. Maſter Lambert that was a maſter of the chancery, and had the keeping of the records of the Tower, and had abridged many of the principall of them (which I have ſeen) and was well learned, and beſides a great ſearcher of antiquities, in his treatiſe of the juriſdiction of courts ſaith, that he could not find that the chancellour held any court of equity, nor that any cauſes were drawne before the chancellour for help in equitie before the time of Hen. 4. in whoſe dayes, by reaſon of the inteſtine troubles, feoffments to uſes did firſt begin, as ſome think, or elſe did firſt grow common and familiar, as all men muſt agree: ſo he. And he that adviſedly reads our ancient authors, which ſpeak of the court of chancery, they all ſpeak of the ordinary juriſdiction of the chancellour, but none of them of any court of equity.

Alſo the booke called the Diverſitie of Courts, written in the reigne of Ed. 3. treateth of the juriſdiction of the chancellour according to his ordinary power, but nothing of that which he holdeth in cauſes of equitie. Neither ſhall you find in any booke caſe, or reports of the law, any mention made of any court of equity before or in the reigne of H. 5. and yet all of them ſpeake of the ordinary power

Glanvile, Bract. Brit. fol. 12. Flet. lib. 2. cap. 12, 13. Mirr. cap. 2. § 13. & cap. 4. de ordinance, de judgement & juriſdiction.

2 E. 3. 20. 10 E. 3. 59, 60. 13 E. 3. prohibit. 1. 24 E. 3. 65.

26 E. 3. 61. 42 aſſ. 5. 43 aſſ. 35. * 31 H. 6. ſub pœna, 19. & 23. 35 H. 6. ibid. 22. 37 H. 6. 35. 5 E. 4. 7. 7 E. 4. 24, 29. 16 E. 4. 4. 22 E. 4. 6. 7 H. 7. 2. 14 H. 8. 7, 9. 24. b.

power or juriſdiction of the chancellour. But in the reigne of H. 6. and E. 4. caſes have been reported where the chancellour hath heard ſome few cauſes in equity by Engliſh bill, and moſt of them concerning uſes of lands. It is true, that the chancellour ſaid in 2 E. 3. in the court of chancery at Weſtminſter, in Theoband de Verons caſe, in a caſe that concerned livery, which belonged to his ordinary power, that the court of chancery is a court of equity, where we grant a writ to every man that comes to demand his heritage, according to that which is found by office, &c. So he. And in that extent of equity, all the courts at Weſtminſter are courts of equity, *viz.* to adminiſter juſtice according to the common law; and thereupon it is ſaid in 10 E. 3. that the chancery and the kings bench is one place or court; but here it is to be noted, that at this time, and before, the court of chancery was a ſettled court in a certaine place, to the great benefit and eaſe of the ſubject.

Sir Robert Parning, that was lord chancellour in 14 E. 3. and had been chiefe juſtice of the common pleas, would in the terme time come and ſit in the court of common pleas to heare matters in law debated and reſolved, when he was lord chancellour, and ſpeak to them himſelfe, as it appeareth, Hillar. 17 E. 3. fol. 14. b. & Trin. 17 E. 3. 37. b. and in both theſe termes Sir John de Stonore knight was chiefe juſtice of the court of common pleas.

Vide Rot. parliament, 45 E. 3. nu. 8.

And Sir Robert de Thorpe knight, being chiefe juſtice of the common pleas, was made chancellour 26 *Martii*, 45 E. 3. and yet in Michaelmas terme following he ſate in the court of common pleas, and ſpake to matters in law, Mich. 45 E. 3. fol. 12. b. Trin. 45. E. 3. 19, 22, 23, b. 24, 25, 26, 27, 28. William de Finchden then being chiefe juſtice of the court of common pleas.

So Sir Knivet knight, being chiefe juſtice of the kings bench, was made chancellour of England, 5 *Julii*, 46 E. 3. and in

[553]

47 E. 3. fol. 13. b. Finchden chiefe juſtice of the common pleas in a matter of law depending in that court ſaid, that he would conferre with the chancellour and the juſtices of the kings bench, and in the end judgement was given by the advice of the chancellour (*viz.* Knivet) and all the judges of the realme. In 49 E. 3. 4. b. Knivet chancellour argueth a matter in law, and giveth judgement.

Alſo peruſe all the acts of parliament printed and not printed, and you ſhall find none that giveth him power to hold any court of equity, where ſome have thought, that the ſtatute of 36 E. 3. cap. 9. doth give the chancellour power to draw men before him for reliefe in equity, but that ſtatute without queſtion referreth to his ordinary power; for thereby it is provided, that if any man, that finds himſelfe grieved contrary to the articles above written, or others contained in divers ſtatutes, will come into the chancery, or any for him, and thereof make his complaint, he ſhall preſently there have remedy by force of the ſaid articles and ſtatutes, without purſuing elſewhere to have remedy; that is, the party grieved ſhall have an originall writ in the chancery grounded upon theſe ſtatutes for his reliefe, although no certaine remedy be expreſſed in the ſtatutes without purſuit in parliament, which act is but a declaration of the common law, as oftentimes hath been obſerved before, and giveth no ſhadow to the chancellour of any abſolute power.

If you look into the parliament rolls: the firſt decree in chancery that I find made by the chancellour was in 17 R. 2. John de Wyndeſor complaineth in parliament againſt Sir Ri. le Scrope, and requireth to be reſtored to the mannors of Rampton, Cotenham, and Weſtwike in Cambridgeſhire, the which were adjudged and ordered to him by the kings award, then being in the poſſeſſion of Sir John Liſley, and now withholden by Sir Richard le Scrope, who by champerty bought the ſame: briefly, the caſe, as in the parliament roll it appeareth, was this: upon the petition of John de Windeſor againſt Sir John Liſley for the ſaid mannors, they compromitted the matter to the kings order and award; the king committed the ſame to the councell, they hearing the ſame, doe order and adjudge the matter in controverſie for Sir John de Wyndeſor under the privie ſeale, and ſent a warrant to Arundell archbiſhop of Canterbury, then chancellour of England, to confirme the kings award made by advice of his councell, who forthwith without more adoe confirmed it by his decree, and granted an injunction under the great ſeal againſt Sir John Liſley. After Sir John Liſley by petition to the king requireth that his title to the ſaid mannors might be tried and determined as it ought by the common law, notwithſtanding any former matter; the king by privie ſeale giveth warrant to the chancellour to make a ſuperſedeas, which the chancellour without any ſticking at it did by privie ſeale: after which Sir Richard le Scrope purchaſed the ſaid mannors: upon the deliberate hearing of the whole matter by the lords of parliament, it was reſolved, that the purchaſe of the ſaid mannors was no champerty, and it was adjudged, that Sir John de Wyndeſor ſhould take nothing by his ſute, but ſtand to the common law, and that Sir Richard le Scrope ſhould goe without day. Rot. parliament. 17 R. 2. nu. 10.

It is thought, that this court of equity began under Henry Beauford, ſonne of John of Gaunt, that great biſhop of Wincheſter, afterwards cardinall in the reigne of Hen. 5. and in the beginning of H. 6. and increaſed while John Kemp, biſhop of York and cardinall was lord chancellour in the 28 yeare of H. 6. But it increaſed moſt of all, when Cardinall Wolſey was lord chancellour of England, *anno* 8 H. 8. and continued untill the 21 year of the ſame king: of whom the old ſaying was verified, that great men in judiciall places will never want authority. But the juriſdiction of this court belongeth to another treatiſe; and therefore thus much, which was pertinent to the underſtanding of this branch of this act, upon this juſt occaſion ſhall ſuffice: only thus much for the honour and antiquity of that court, you reade, that in the time of king Alfred (who began to reigne *anno Domini*, 872. and reigned 29 yeares and ſix moneths) he gave a pardon to Wolſton, and that it was inrolled in the court of chancery, which record Wolſton vouched. Mirror, c. 5. § 1. [554]

(1) *Et les juſtices de ſon bank.*] The cauſes of their attendance on the king are afterwards in this chapter ſet downe; therefore we purpoſely omit to ſpeak of this high and honourable court, but referre the ſame to the treatiſe of the juriſdiction of courts, onely this may be obſerved, that albeit this court and the chancery became to have certaine and ſetled places about one time, yet the returne of writs *coram rege* are ſtill *coram nobis ubicunque fuerimus in Anglia.* Flet. lib. 2. cap. 2.

(2) *Issint que il eyt touts jours pres de luy ascun sages de la ley, que sachent les besoignes,* &c.] This clause referreth to the judges of the kings bench, who are termed *sages de la ley*, and which could decide the businesse which came to the court, and duly deliver justice to all when need should be. This proveth also, that at this time the chancellour held no court of equity; for the sages of the law (the judges of the kings bench) were duly to deliver justice to all: and hereunto may be applyed the said booke in 10 E. 3. that the court of chancery and of the kings bench was but one place (that is) to be guided by one and the same law.

See more before in this chapter concerning the chancery. 10 E. 3. 59, 60.

At the making of this act John Langton bishop of Chichester was lord chancellour of England: and at this time Sir Roger Brabazon knight, a man excellently learned in the lawes of the realme, was chiefe justice of the kings bench, and three other learned judges, here called *sages de la ley*, were his companions: these in Fleta and ancient records are called, *locum tenentes regis*.

Flet. ubi supra. 17 E. 1. coram rege.

CAP. VI.

DESOUTH le petit seale (1), *ne issera desormes nul briefe que touche le common ley.*

THERE shall no writ from henceforth, that toucheth the common law, go forth under any of the petty seals.

The print that saith [*de touts les privie seales*] is not according to the record.

For the better understanding of this act, it is to be understood, that at the making of this statute, the king had three seales: first, *magnum sigillum*, the great seale; 2. *parvum sigillum*, the little or petit seale; 3. *signettum*, the signet.

The great seale is in the custody of the lord chancellour or lord keeper of the great seale; and there is a speciall officer in the court of chancery, called *sigillator*, who hath the sealing of writs, and other things that passe the great seale. *Parvum sigillum*, the little or petit seale, after this time called the privie seale: this seale is in the custody of the clerke of the privie seale, sometime called keeper of the privie seale, after called lord privie seale, of whom Fleta saith thus, *Custodi sigilli privati associentur clerici honesti, et circumspecti domino regi jurati, qui in legibus et consuetudinibus Anglicanis noticiam habeant pleniorem, quorum officium sit supplicationes et querelas conquerentium audire et examinare, et eis super qualitatibus injuriarum ostensarum debitum remedium exhibere per brevia regis.* By this ancient writer three things are to be observed:

2 E. 3. cap. 8. rot. parliam. 50 E. 3. nu. 10. 11 R. 2. cap. 11. 12 R. 2. cap. 2. cap. 11. Flet. lib. 2. ca. 13.

1. That the clerkes, associates to the keeper of the privie seale, are those that we now call the masters of requests, *magistri à libellis supplicum*, whose office is here lively purtrayed out, *viz. quorum officium sit supplicationes et querelas conquerentium audire et examinare*.

2. Of

2. Of what quality ought theſe maſters of the requeſts to be? They muſt have three qualities: 1. they muſt be *honeſti et circumſpecti: 2. domino regi jurati: 3. qui in legibus et conſuetudinibus Anglicanis notitiam habeant pleniorem.*

3. To what end did they heare and examine the matters contained in theſe petitions? *Ut eis (id eſt) conquerentibus ſuper qualitatibus injuriarum oſtenſarum debitum remedium exhibere per breve regis.* So as their office was, that being learned in the law, they ſhould direct ſuch as petitioned to the king, to take their remedy by the kings writ, that is, by originall writ in the chancery. And hereby it appeareth, that this act is but in affirmance of the common law; for no writ before this act could have been ſealed by the privie ſeale.

Sigillum regis generally ſpoken is the great ſeale; and ſo is Bracton to be underſtood, where he ſaith, *ſi aliquis accuſatus fuerit vel convictus, quod ſigillum domini regis falſaverit, conſignando inde chartas, vel brevia, &c. pro voluntate regis judicium ſuſtinebit.* Bract. lib. 3. fol. 119. Brit. fo. 10. b. acc'.

And the Mirror yet more plainly, *Inter les exceptions al power del judge; ſi le commiſſion (i. le briefe) ne ſoit ſeale del ſeale le roy de ſa chancery, car al privie ſeale le roy, &c. ne auter forſque ſolement al ſeale, que eſt aſſigne dẽe conue de la cominaltie del people, et noſmement en juriſdictions et breves originals, neſtoit a nul obeyer, &c.* And in another place he ſaith, *Et iſſint ordeineront nous auncients un ſeale, et un chancellour pur le garder, et pur doner briefes remediels a touts ſauns danger, &c. per cel ſeale ſolement eſt juriſdiction aſſignable a touts pleintifes ſans difficultie, &c.* Mirr. cap. 3. cap. Except al poier de le judge. cap. 4. Ordinance de judgement.

There are foure clerkes of the privie ſeale, who give their attendance on the lord privie ſeale: the principall office and charge of the lord privie ſeale and of his clerkes is about ſuch things as paſſe by bill ſigned, and are to goe to the great ſeale: of this you may reade in the ſtatute of 27 H. 8. cap. 11. & lib. 8. fol. 18. *in caſu principis.*

(1) *Deſouth le petit ſeale.*] This act ſaith not, that all writs which concerne the common law ſhall paſſe under the great ſeale; but no writ ſhall paſſe under the privie ſeale which touch the common law: for it is to be knowne, that the courts of the kings bench and the common pleas had at the making of this ſtatute ſeverall ſeales, whereby they ſealed judiciall writs: as the ſeale belonging to the court of kings bench is in the cuſtody of the chief juſtice; and ſo likewiſe the ſeale belonging to the court of common pleas is in the cuſtody of the chiefe juſtice of that court; and the ſeale belonging to the court of exchequer is in the cuſtody of the chancellour of that court. *Ad cancellarium ſcaccarii pertinet cuſtodia ſigilli regis. Officium cancellarii eſt ſigillum regis cuſtodire, ſimul cum controrotulis ſuis pro proficuo regni.* And theſe ſeales are incidents inſeparable to the ſaid courts for the ſealing of all judiciall writs, &c. which, for adminiſtration of juſtice diſtributive to all men, are reſpectively under the ſaid ſeales, and without which the courts cannot adminiſter juſtice: and therefore the profits coming of theſe ſeales have been letten and demiſed of ancient and later times, but the ſeales themſelves were never demiſed, or letten, nor could be, nor any other keeper appointed to be keeper of them, then hath been time out of mind. Lib. 2. fol. 17. Lanes caſe. Ockam. cap. de officio cancellarii. Flet. li. 2. c. 25. Rot. pat. an. 24. E. 3. part. 2. m. 12. ibid. 30 E. 3. part 3. m. 12.

No eſſoine *de ſervitio regis* can be warranted by the king under his privie ſeale, nor protection granted under the privie ſeale, but both 34 H. 6. 1. 35 H. 6. 2. Lib. 11. fo. 92. in le countee de Devons caſe.

both of them under the great ſeale, becauſe they tend to the great delay of juſtice, if they be not duly obtained: and therefore the law doth require the great ſeale in theſe caſes. But a warrant of the king under the privie ſeale to iſſue out mony out of his coffers is ſufficient; becauſe it concerneth but a chattell in poſſeſſion. And in matters of ſmall moment, and which can work no delay to the ſubject, the privie ſeale is ſufficient; as to grant a *ſuperſedeas* of a proceſſe in the kings owne caſe, or to grant a *niſi prius* where the king is party, or to allow a plea againſt the king, to cancell a recognizance made to the king, to diſcharge a debt, or the like.

4 E. 4. 16. 32. 40. 46 E. 3. petit. 19. 48 E. 3. 30 F.N.B. 85. Pl. com. fol. 20. Dyer, 5 Mar. 161. b. 7 El. 232. b.

[556]

At the making of this ſtatute the king had another ſeale, and that is called *ſignettum*, his ſignet. This ſeale is ever in the cuſtody of the principall ſecretary. And there be foure clerkes of the ſignet, called *clerici ſignetti* attending on him. The reaſon wherefore it is in the ſecretaries cuſtodie, is, for that the kings private letters are ſigned therewith. Alſo the duty of the clerk of the ſignet is to write out ſuch grants or letters patents as paſſe by bill ſigned (that is, a bill ſuperſcribed with the ſignature, or ſigne manuall, or royall hand of the king) to the privie ſeale, which bill being tranſcribed and ſealed with the ſignet is a warrant to the privie ſeale, and the privie ſeale is a warrant to the great ſeale. Such was the wiſdome of prudent antiquity, that whatſoever ſhould paſſe the great ſeale ſhould come through ſo many hands, to the end that nothing ſhould paſſe that great ſeale, that is ſo highly eſteemed and accounted of in law, that was againſt law, or inconvenient; or that any thing ſhould paſſe from the king any wayes, which he intended not, by undue or ſurreptitious meanes.

F.N.B. fol. 85. e.

And of the ſignet the law in ſome caſes taketh notice; for a *ne exeat regnum* may be by the kings writ under the great ſeale, or by commmandement under the privie ſeale, or under the ſignet; for in this caſe the ſubject ought to take notice as well of the privie ſeale and ſignet, as of the great ſeale: for this is but a ſignification of the kings commandement, and nothing paſſeth from him. But a warrant under the privie ſignet to iſſue any treaſure is not ſufficient, but there it ought to be either under the great or privie ſeale. The miſchiefe before this act was not concerning writs under the ſignet; for that was not attempted, but under the petit or privie ſeale, which this act ouſteth as a thing done againſt *Magna Charta*, cap. 29. where it is ſaid, *nec ſuper eum ibimus, nec ſuper eum mittemus, niſi per legale judicium parium ſuorum, vel per legem terræ*. And to grant writs under the privie or petit ſeale was *contra legem terræ*.

Hill. 1 E. 4. rot. 14. indorſ. in Scaccario, Petilians caſe. Lib. 11. fo. 92. in le countee de Devons caſe. Vid. 42 E. 3. ca. 3.

CAP.

CAP. VII.

LE constable du chastle de Dover (1) ne plede desormes a la port de chastle nul plee forreine du countie, que ne touche la gard du chastle. Et le dit constable ne distreiner (2) les gents du cinque ports, a pleader ailours ne en auter manner que ils devoient, solonque la forme des charters que ils ount des royes, de lour franchises auncients affirmes per le grand charter.

THE constable of the castle of Dover shall not from henceforth hold any plea of a foreign county within the castle gate, except it touch the keeping of the castle. Nor shall the said constable distrain the inhabitants of the cinque ports to plead any otherwhere, nor otherwise, than they ought after the form of their charter obtained of the king for their old franchises confirmed by the great charter.

(Regist. 185.)

(1) *Constable du chastle de Dover.*] It is to be knowne, that he that is the constable, or liestenant, or keeper of the castle of Dover, is also the warden of the cinque ports. And the kings writs directed to him, are directed, *Rex, &c. B. constabulario castri sui de Dover, et custodi quinque portuum suorum.* But he is commonly called lord warden of the cinque ports. The cinque ports be, Hastings, Dover, Hithe, Rumney, and Sandwich, whereunto Winchelsey and Rye (as most of note) and other townes be adjoyned. F.N.B. 240. b. Regist. fol. 132. F.N.B. 240.

The constable of Dover and lord warden hath two jurisdictions, *viz.* 1. the authority of an admirall; and the speciall charge is committed to one that is not onely of great prowesse, wisdome, and experience in military knowledge, and specially in sea-service; but also of approved trust and loyalty, because, in regard of their situation, they require the vigilant care of their particular admirall, and his residence thereupon, in respect of the danger of the invasion of enemies by reason of the narrownesse of the sea there, and that this realme was never conquered by any enemy, but landing at one of these five ports; as by the Roman at by the Saxon at and by the Norman at Hastings. But with this jurisdiction our statute dealeth not withall, [557]

2. This constable of the castle of Dover mentioned in our act hath a jurisdiction to hold plea by bill concerning the guard of the castle, &c. according to the course of the common law, and of this jurisdiction doth our statute speak. Bract. lib. 5. fol. 411. b. Flet. lib. 6. cap. 36.

And it is to be knowne, that of such things, whereof the constable of Dover and lord warden hath jurisdiction, he is the immediate officer to the court, and, as it hath been said, writs shall be directed to him, as in all reall actions &c. for land within the cinque ports. And true it is, that they of the cinque ports have great liberties and priviledges, in respect of their necessary attendance in the ports for the defence and safety of the realme: but yet the cinque ports are not exempted out of the county, for divers causes: 49 E. 3. 24. 12 E. 4. 17, 18. 1 E. 3. 1. b. 30 H. 6. 5. 1 E. 4. 10. 21 E. 3. 49. F.N.B. 132. 33 E. 3. Jurisd. 60. 11 R. 2. brev. 636.

1. The

1. The conſtable of Dover hath no generall juriſdiction within the cinque ports, but it is limited; for example, if a man be murdered in any of the cinque ports, the wife ſhall have an appeale againſt the murderer directed to the ſherife of the county, and he ſhall execute the writ within the cinque ports, for the conſtable hath no juriſdiction to hold plea thereof, as it was reſolved, Trin. 42 Eliz. in an appeale brought by Dorothy Waes againſt Baynes, for the murder of her huſband at Feverſham in the county of Kent. And ſo it is, if he be *in cuſtodia mareſcalli*, the appeale may be brought by bill againſt him for murder in any of the cinque ports. Alſo if the conſtable of Dover hold plea of a forraine plea, contrary to the purport of this ſtatute, an action upon the ſtatute doth lye againſt him, and the writ may be directed to the ſherife of the county, and he may ſerve it within the cinque ports.

Trin. 42 Eliz. coram rege in appeale.
19 H. 6. 1, 2.

Vide a notable Record, Paſch' 30 E. 1. coram rege, Kanc'.

2. If a ſtranger doth treſpaſſe, &c. in the cinque ports, &c. the ſuit ſhall be by writ, leſt the treſpaſſe ſhould be diſpuniſhable.

50 E. 3. 5.

3. If a *præcipe* be brought againſt one for land within the cinque ports, and he appeare and plead to it, and judgement be given againſt him in the court of common pleas, this judgement ſhall bind him for ever; for the land is not exempted out of the county, and the tenant may wave the benefit of his priviledge.

4. The priviledge extendeth not but to certaine particular townes, whereof the kings courts cannot judicially take notice.

But otherwiſe it is of a judgment given in the common pleas in a *præcipe* of lands that lye in any of the county palatines of Cheſter, Lancaſter, and Durham; for they are exempted from the juriſdiction of the kings courts, and within them are *jura regalia*, and plenary juriſdiction, and ſo knowne to the kings courts: for they take notice of all the counties of England, becauſe they be immediate to them for direction of writs: and therefore although the tenant doth admit the juriſdiction of the court in thoſe caſes, the judgement againſt him for many of ſuch lands is void. And thus are the doubts in ſome books in this and other like caſes fully reſolved.

9 H. 7. 12.
33 H. 6. 33.
39 H. 6. 21.
12 E. 4. 16.
45 E. 3. juriſ.
53. 40 E. 3. 24.
49 E. 3. 24.
50 E. 3. 5.
14 H. 4. 20.
Bract. lib. 5. fol. 411. Flet. lib. 6. cap. 36. Dyer, 23 El. 376.
30 H. 6. 6.
49 E. 3. 24.
33 E. 3. juriſd. 60. diverſity des courts. cap. 5. Ports.
Brook, Cinque ports 25.
30 H. 6. 6.
Pl. com. 37. b.

It is further to be underſtood, that the maior and jurats of the ſeverall cinque ports have power to hold pleas, &c. and upon their judgement no writ of error out of the chancery doth lye returnable in the kings bench, nor writ of falſe judgement returnable into the court of common pleas: but by the franchiſe and cuſtome of the cinque ports ſuch an erroneous judgement ſhall be by bill, in the nature of a writ of errour, examined *coram domino cuſtode ſeu gardiano quinque portuum, apud curiam ſuam de Shipwey*. And if the judgement be erroneous, it ſhall be reverſed by the warden of the cinque ports, and the maior and jurats ſhall be fined, and the maior removed from his place, and yet the court is a court of record.

And this kind of juriſdiction could not begin by letters patents, but by parliament. And I find in the book of Domeſday of the liberties and franchiſes granted to the cinque ports, as granted in the reigne of king Edward the Confeſſour.

[558]
See the termes of the law, verb. cinque ports.

And this manner of reverſing of a judgement, and the judgement thereupon, is the onely phenix of the law for three reſpects:

Firſt, that a judgement in a court of record ſhall be reverſed or affirmed without the kings writ purchaſed out of the chancery.

Secondly,

Secondly, that they being judges of record ſhall be fined, where in a writ of falſe judgement the ſuiters ſhall be but amerced.

And thirdly, that the maior that gave the judgement ſhall be removed from his place. But our act extends only to courts holden before the conſtable in our act mentioned, and not to the court holden before the maior and jurats. Rot. cart. 1 Johan. part. 2. m. 12. 2. Johan. m. 51. Rot. clauſ. 8 H. 3. & 10 H. 3. in dorſ. m. 18. Paſch. 9 E. 1. *coram rege* Kanc' Rot. 35. Rot. Parliam. 18 E. 1. fol. 6. Hill. 21 E. 1. rot. 4. Paſch. 21 E. 1. fol. 4. Rot. Vaſc. an. 22 E. 1. nu. 2, 3, 7. 13. Rot. clauſ. 23 E. 1. Rot. pat. 34 E. 1. m. 25. Rot. parliam. 13 E. 3. nu. 11. Pat. 33 E. 3. m. 6. Rot. brevium, 1 E. 3. part. 1. Rot. clauſ. 10 R. 2. bis. Rot. clauſ. 8 H. 6. m. 15.

He that deſires to reade more of the liberties and priviledges of the cinque ports, he may reade the records (amongſt many others) next before cited.

(2) *Et le dit conſtable ne diſtreinera*, &c.] This branch is evident; and therefore without further expoſition, with one record of parliament I will conclude this chapter.

The commons of the county of Kent complained againſt the officers of the caſtle of Dover, for arreſting them by their catchpoles to anſwer before them, whereunto they were not bound. The anſwer hereunto was, that the officers ſhould have no juriſdiction out of the fee of the honour and caſtle of Dover, nor ſhould make no proceſſe by *capias* out of the liberties of the cinque ports. Rot. parliament. nu. 135.

CAP. VIII.

LE roy ad grant a ſon people, que ils eyent election de lour viſcount en cheſcun countie, ou viſcount neſt my de fee, ſils voilont.

THE king hath granted unto his people, that they ſhall have election of their ſheriff in every ſhire (where the ſhrivalty is not of fee) if they liſt.

(9 Ed. 2. ſtat. 2. 14 Ed. 3. ſtat. 1. c. 7.)

Of ancient time before the making of this act ſuch officers or miniſters as were inſtituted either for preſervation of the peace of the county, or for execution of juſtice, becauſe it concerned all the ſubjects of that county, and they had a great intereſt in juſt and due exerciſes of their ſeveral places, were by force of the kings writ in every ſeverall county choſen in full or open county by the freeholders of that county: as before the inſtitution of juſtices of peace there were *conſervatores pacis* in every county, whoſe office (according to their names) was to conſerve the kings peace, and to protect the obedient and innocent ſubjects from force and violence. Theſe conſervators by the ancient common law were by force of the kings writ choſen in full and open county *de probioribus et potentioribus comitatus*, &c. by the freeholders of the county; after which election ſo made and returned, then in that caſe the king directed Vid. inter leges Sancti Edwardi, Lamb. fol. 136. Hovenden annal. cap. 35. F.N.B. 163. k. Rot. pat. an. 5 E. 1.

directed a writ to the party so elected. *Edwardus Dei gratia rex Angliæ, dominus Hiberniæ, et dux Aquitaniæ, dilecto et fideli Johanni de Bretun salutem. Cum vicecomes noster Norff. et Cōītas ejusdem comitatus elegerunt vos in custodem pacis nostræ ibidem, vobis mandamus quod ad hoc diligenter intendatis, prout idem vicecomes vobis scribi faciet ex parte nostra, donec aliud inde præceperimus. In cujus rei, &c. datum, &c. apud Cestr'. 2. die Sept. anno regni nostri* 5. And so it was then, and yet is of coroners to be chosen in full and open county by the freeholders of the county by force of the kings writ: and though the words of this writ be *de assensu comitatus*, and of the other, *per communitatem ejusdem comitatus*, and by this act, by the people, yet ought the election to be by the freeholders of the county: and so it was then, and yet is of the knights of the shires for the parliament, and of the verderors of a forest.

This Bretun was lord of the mannor of Wichingham in Norff.

[559]

Regist. 177. F.N.B. 163. k. 4 E. 4. 44. F.N.B. 164. c. Regist.

9 E. 2. Linc. de Vicecom. 14 E. 3. cap. 7. 23 H. 6. ca. 8. 12 R. 2. ca. 3. Fortescue, ca. 24. & 26. W. 1. cap. 5.

And likewise it was of ancient time of the sherife of the county, and restored by this act to the freeholders of the county; but this is altered by divers acts of parliament, *viz.* the act of 9 E. 2. *Lincoln de vicecomitibus*, 14 E. 3. 12 R. 2. and 23 H. 6. The knights and burgesses of parliament were then, and yet are eligible as daily experience teacheth. Now because that these and others were eligible, the statute of W. 1. provideth, that elections should be freely and duly made without any disturbance, as by that act appeareth. See hereafter cap. 13.

But I could not let passe a resolution of all the judges of England in 34 H. 6. which grew upon this occasion upon a reference by the kings privie councell to Sir John Fortescue, and Sir John Prisot chiefe justices, and to the rest of the justices concerning a sherife constituted by the king himselfe, it is thus in the councell booke recorded, 3 *Martii anno* 34 Hen. 6. as followeth in these words:

Sherife.

Upon a demaund that my lord chancelor made to the chiefe juges, and to the remnant of the juges, howe that the kings lawes, neyther justice might not be executed in Lincolnshire, bycause ther was no sherriefe there, and that the kinge by his letters patents under his great seale had deputed certaine men for to have be sherriefes there? what them seemed should be doon in this behalfe. So that the kings lawes and justice might ben executed in that shire, as it is executed in other shires of England.

The ij chiefe justices the same day came unto my lords of the kings counsiel in the sterred chamber, and upon the abouesaid demaund sayde, that them semed, and so it semed unto the remnant of the juges, that the king did an errour, when that he made another person sherriefe of Lincolnshire then was chosen and presented unto his highnes after theffect of the statut in such behalfe made.

And though that he that so was made sherrief wolde not take it vpon him, ought not to be so punished, and to make also great a fine for his disobeissance, as that yif he had be one of the iij. persons that were chosen to be sherriefs after the teneur of the statute.

And furthermore them semed, that the king should have recours to the three persons that were chosen after the teneur of the statut, and make one of hem sherrief by letters patents beringe date ether at the day of thelection of hem, or els at Michelmas.

And

And though that ſithence the ſaid election any of hem have gete him an exemption, that he ſhould not be made ſherriefe, yet them ſemeth that he ſhould be charged to take the ſaid office vpon him.

And furthermore them ſemeth, that yif none of the ſaid iij. perſons choſen be made, that then ſome other thrifty man dwelling in a foreine ſhire be entreted to occupie the ſaid office for this yeare. And the next yeare, that in eſchuing of ſuch inconveniences, that the order of theſtatut in ſuch behalfe made be obſerved and kept.

To the king our ſoueréigne lord, and to the lords ſpirituell and temporell of his moſt noble counſail.

Beſechith mekely your humble liegeman John Tempeſt knight, to graunt your letters under your privie ſeale to be made in forme following, and he ſhall pray to God for your moſt noble eſtate.

Henry, &c. To the treſorer and barons of our eſchequer. Foraſmuch as our truſty and welbeloued John Tempeſt knight, by us ordeyned and deputed to be ſheriefe of Lincolnſhire for this yere, hath for certaine cauſes for him alledged vtterly refuſed to [560] take vpon him the charge of the ſaid office, without that it like vs ſo to puruei for him, that he take no loſſe in the ſaid office, like as we haue doon nowe in late yeeres for othir that haue ben ſheriefs of the ſaid ſhire. We conſidering the hurts and manifold inconveniences that ſhould enſue not only to us, but alſo to our ſubgites, namely, in letting of their ſuites at commune law, if the ſaid ſhire ſhould long ſtand deſtitute of a ſheriefe; wol and by thadvice of our counſail haue graunted to the ſaid John, that he ſhall occupie the ſaid office by approwment, and ſo accompte for this yere. And therefore we charge you, that in his accompt that he ſhalbe to yeilde unto us bycauſe of his ſaid office, ye charge him not with the hoole extent of the ſaid ſhire, that is to ſay, of thees twoo fermes called *de reman' firmæ com' poſt terras dat'* and *firma com' numero.* And alſo of thees particular prouffites, called *de firmis ballivorum, auxilium vic' francipleg' certi fines,* iſſues, prouffites, nor none othir things by him to be reiſed by vertue of the ſommons of the pipe, or of the grenewex in the ſaid ſhire, ſaue onely of ſuch parcelles as he with his true diligence ſhall arrere and gader. And that of all the remenant that ſhall come and grow vnto us of the ſaid ſhire, ye vtterly and clerely diſcharge and acquite the ſaid John Tempeſt knight ſheriefe aforeſaid by his othe, or by th'othe of his deputy ſufficiant accompting for him, withouten any iſſue, tryall, or auerrement betwix vs, and him to be had therein. Yeuen, &c.

T. Cant'.		R. Saliſbury.
W. Ebor.	R. York.	R. Sancti Johannis.
T. London.		Stourton,
J. Lincoln.		W. Faucomberge.

XIX. die Novembris, an. 34. *apud Weſtm' in camera ſtellata rex de aviſamento conſilii voluit, et mandavit, quod cuſtos privati ſigilli ſui literas ſub eodem ſigillo fieri faceret ſecundum tenorem infraſcriptum dominis ſe ſubſcribentibus, ut patet attent' ut Henricus Ratford* Indorſiament.

qui fuit vicecomes anno præterito ejuſdem com', et nonnulli alii vicecomites retroactis temporibus eodem modo habuerunt, et occupaverunt.

T. Kent.

Which aboveſaid unanimous opinion, being the adviſed reſolution of two ſuch famous chiefe juſtices, and of all the judges of England, and finding it in the councell book, I thought fit to be publiſhed in ſuch words, as it is there ſet downe, as a ſure and juſt expoſition of the ſtatutes concerning the making of ſherifes.

CAP. IX.

LE roy voet et commaund, que nul viſcount, ne bailife, ne mitte en enqueſts, ne in juries plus des gents, ne auters ne en auter manner que il neſt ordeine per eſtatute (1), *et que ils mittent en tiels enqueſts* (2) *et juries le plus procheines* (3), *le plus ſuffiſants, et meynes ſuſpicious. Et que auterment le ferra, et de ceo ſoit attaint, rend' al plaintife ſes damages au double* (4), *et ſoit en la greve mercie le roy.*

THE king willeth and commandeth, that no ſheriff nor bailiff ſhall impanel in inqueſts nor in juries over many perſons, nor otherwiſe than it is ordained by ſtatute; and that they ſhall put in thoſe inqueſts and juries ſuch as be next neighbours, moſt ſufficient, and leaſt ſuſpicious. And he that otherwiſe doth, and is attainted thereupon, ſhall pay unto the plaintiff his damages double, and ſhall be grievouſly amerced unto the king.

(1 Inſt. 158. a. 34 Ed. 3. c. 4. 42 Ed. 3. c. 11. Regiſt. 178, 179, 180. 13 Ed. 1. ſtat. 1. c. 38.)

1. part Inſtitut. ſect. 234.

Of the antiquity and right inſtitution of the tryall by 12, and of the number of 12, &c. See the firſt part of the Inſtitutes.

[561]

(1) *Ordeine per leſtatute.*] That is, by the ſtatute of W. 2, cap. 38. See the ſtatute of 21 E. 1. *Vet. Magna Charta* 87. and ſee before in the expoſition of the ſtatute of W. 2. cap. 38.

(2) *Enqueſts.*] This act doth extend to all enqueſts *ex officio*, or for tryall of an iſſue between the king and the ſubject, or between party and party, alſo to all ſuits or proceedings, either criminall or civill, reall, perſonall, or mixt, publike or private, grand or petit, aſſiſes or enqueſts.

Vid. 7 E. 3. 26. bis. 8 E. 3. 30. Regiſt. 178, 179. 180. Forteſcue, cap. 27. F.N.B. 165. a. and 166. d. lib. 8. fol. 118. Bonhams caſe. See the firſt part of the Inſtitutes, ſect. 234. W. 2. cap. 38. Magna Charta, cap. 29. Regiſt. 186. & 187.

(3) *Le pluis procheine*, &c.] If the purview of this act were well executed, then were the right inſtitution of tryall by juries obſerved; for then every juror muſt have two moſts, and one leaſt, *viz.* moſt neere, moſt ſufficient, and leaſt ſuſpicious. See the Regiſter, and F. N. B. how the party grieved may have remedy upon this ſtatute, and that in writs of aſſiſe, attaints, and other actions, where there be juries at the firſt day, or when a *venire fac'* is awarded to the ſherife to returne a jury, the demandant or plaintife, the tenant or defendant may have a writ to the ſherife to returne jurors according to this act, and if he doth not accordingly, an attachment lyeth againſt him. And where the party plead to iſſue,

iſſue, and ſuffer the jury to be ſworne, or challengeth them, and tried indifferent, and paſſe againſt him; it is ſaid, that he hath no remedy, but firſt to reverſe the judgement by writ of attaint, and then to take his remedy upon this ſtatute. But ſee the ſtatutes of 20 E. 3. cap. 6. and 34 E. 3. cap. 4. 42 E. 3. cap. 11. & 4 E. 3. cap. 11. & 5 E. 3. cap. 10.

(4) *Ses damages au double.*] That is double the value of the land, debt, damages, or other thing that he loſt, or was barred of by reaſon of that verdict.

CAP. X.

EN droit des conſpirators (1), *faux enformers* (2), *et malveyes procurers* (3) *des douſeins* (4), *enqueſts, aſſiſes, et juries, le roy ad ordeine remedie as plaintiffes per briefes de chancelarie. Et jademeins voet le roy, que les juſtices de lune bank et de lauter, et juſtices daſſiſes prend' aſſignes, quant ils veignent en pais a faire lour office, de ceo facent lour enqueſts a cheſcun pleint ſans briefe, et ſans delay facent droit as pleintifes.*

IN right of conſpirators, falſe informers, and evil procurers of dozens, aſſiſes, inqueſts, and juries, the king hath provided remedy for the plaintiffs by a writ out of the chancery. And notwithſtanding, he willeth that his juſtices of the one bench and of the other, and juſtices aſſigned to take aſſiſes, when they come into the country to do their office, ſhall, upon every plaint made unto them, award inqueſts thereupon without writ, and ſhall do right unto the plaintiffs without delay.

(Kel. 81. Regiſt. 188. Raſt. 123, &c.)

(1) *Conſpiratours.*] Theſe are deſcribed by the ſtatute of 33 E. 1. Definitio de conſpirat. 33 E. 1. Vet. Mag. Chart. 90. b.

(2) *Faux enformers.*] Theſe are to be underſtood of imbracers, and under-hand inſtructers, and leaders of jurors returned, and albeit the matter which he enformeth be true, yet is he a falſe informer, becauſe he doth it in an undue and unjuſt manner.

(3) *Malveis procurors.*] That is underſtood of ſuch as uſe to packe juries by nomination, or other practice, or procurement.

(4) *Douſeins, duodenæ in letis,* &c.] Note here this law beginneth with the inferiour, as douſeins in leets, and therefore the makers of the act doe particularize the reſt, *viz.* inquiſitions, aſſiſes, and juries. F.N.B. 116. a.

[562]

(5) *Le roy ad ordeine remedie per briefe de chancelarie.*] The ordinance here mentioned, whereby a writ is given againſt conſpirators (which writ was framed *per Gilbertum de Rowberie clericum de concilio domini regis,* and allowed by authority of parliament) was enacted at the parliament holden an. 21 E. 1. Rot. 2. which ordinance you may reade in *Vet. Magna Charta.* But there it is ſet downe to be made in 33 E. 1. where in truth it was made in 21 E. 1. which errour there, and the miſtaking of Richard Tottell the printer, in quoting 33 E. 1. to this branch (as if the makers of this act had been indued with a propheticall ſpirit) would in the next impreſſion be amended. This Gilbert de Rowberie was one of the kings juſtices of his bench, as hereafter ſhall appeare. Vet. Mag. Chart. 111.

This

Regist. F.N.B. 114, 115. &c. Stamf. pl. cor. 172. &c.

This ordinance was but in affirmance of the common law; for the writ of conspiracy was maintainable both in cases criminall concerning life, and civill, as it appeareth in the Register and F.N.B. and plentifully in our bookes: and in cases concerning life, if the conspirators be indited and convicted at the kings suit, judgement villanous shall be given against him, but not at the suit of the party, which judgement is by the common law; for it is given by no statute.

27 ass. p. 59. 24 E. 3. 34.

43 E. 3. consp. 11. 4 H. 5 judgem. 220. Stamf. pl. cor. 175. 198. lib. 9. fol. 56. Poulters case. 5 E. 3. cap. 10. 34 E. 3. cap. 8. 38 E. 3. cap. 12. 41 E. 3. 15.

(6) *Et jademaines voit le roy que les justices de lun bank et lauter,* &c.] See the statutes of 5 E. 3. 34 E. 3. 38 E. 3. &c. by the which this statute is inlarged as to the justices. And a notable case in 41 E. 3. in expounding of these statutes, and upon like reason this act concerning the proceeding by bill, according to the words of this branch, *sans briefe, et sans delay.*

Coram rege apud Linc. Hil. 29 E. 1. rot. 19. Secundum ordinationem regis, i. 21 E. 1. ubi supra.

In the next yeare after the making of this act, which was in the 29 yeare of E. 1. William de Welbye brought an action by originall writ of conspiracy, returnable in the kings bench against William of Hemswell, parson of the church of Newton, and John of Malden, parson of the church of Askerbye, *secundum ordinationem regis*; for that they *per conspirationem et confederationem inter eos malitiose fact' apud Groham, &c. anno regni domini regis nunc 29, procuraverunt et fecerunt præfatum Willum de Welbye citari coram Nicholao de Whitechurch archidiacono episc' Lincoln' ad respondendum præfat' Will' &c.* for a trespasse, whereof he had been acquitted in the kings court. Hemswel pleaded not guilty. Malden the other parson pleaded that he was *communis advocatus, et pro suo dando, &c.* and justified as an attorney, and denied that he conspired, &c.

Gilbert de Rowbery. F.N.B. fol. 116. k. 3 E. 3. 19. 8 E. 3. 18. 11 H. 4. 2. 22 R. 2. bre' 88. 18 E. 4. 1. 24 E. 3. 34. Vid. 22 E. 3. 1.

Whereupon issues being joyned, it was found before Gilbert de Rowberie, that Malden the parson of Askerbye was *communis advocatus,* and was not guilty of the conspiracy, &c. and the other was found guilty, and judgement was given against him; for in this and the like a conspiracy will lye against one: otherwise it is in case of felony. By this record it appeareth, that a writ of conspiracy doth lye upon the said act of 21 E. 1. (for the conspiracy was alledged before our statute) for a conspiracy between two for the one of them to sue the plaintife in the spirituall court: and note the record saith, *contra ordinationem domini regis.* And note, it did lye for conspiracy in a suit in the ecclesiastical court.

CAP. XI.

DE rechiefe pur ceo que le roy avoit avant ordeine per lestatute, que nul de ses ministers ne prist nul plee a champertie; et per cel estatute auters ministers nestaient pas avant ces heures a ceo lies: voit le roy, que nul minister, ne nul auter, pur part avoier des choses que sont en plee' (1), *enpreigne les besoignes que sont en plee. Ne nul sur*

AND further, because the king hath heretofore ordained by statute, that none of his ministers shall take no plea for maintenance, by which statute other officers were not bounden before this time; the king will, that no officer nor any other (for to have part of the thing in plea) shall not take upon him the business that

sur tiel covenant (4) *son droit ne lesse a auter. Et si ul le face, et de ceo soit attaint, soit forfait, et encurr' devers le roy des biens, et des terres le parnour, a la value de tant* (2) *come sa part de son purchase per tiel emprise amounter'. Et a ceo attend', soit rescue celuy que suer voudr' pur le roy devant les justices, devant queux* (3) *le plee avera este, et per eux soit lagard' fait. Mes en ceo case nest mye a entender, que home ne poit aver counsaile des countours, et des sages gents* (5) *pur son donant, ne de ses procheine amies* (6).

that is in suit; nor none upon any such covenant shall give up his right to another; and if any do, and he be attainted thereof, the taker shall forfeit unto the king so much of his lands and goods as doth amount to the value of the part that he hath purchased for such maintenance. And for this atteindre, whosoever will, shall be received to sue for the king before the justices, before whom the plea hangeth, and the judgement shall be given by them. But it may not be understood hereby, that any person shall be prohibit to have counsel of pleaders, or of learned men in the law for his fee, or of his parents and next friends.

(3 Ed. 1. c. 25. 13 Ed. 1. stat. 1. c. 49. 13 H. 4. f. 17. Fitz. Champerty. 3, 4. 6. 12. 14, 15. 2 Inst. 118. 1 Ed. 3. stat. 2. c. 14. 1 R. 2. c. 4. 32 H. 8. c. 9. 21 Ed. 3. f. 52. Bro. Champerty, 11. Rast. 119. 427, &c.

The cause of the making of this statute was, that where the statutes of W. 1. 11 E. 1. and W. 2. of champerty were particular, and extended only to the kings ministers, the chancellour, the treasurer, justices, the kings councellers, clerkes of the chancery, of the exchequer, and of justices, and to those of the kings houshold, clerke or lay. Now this act is generall, and doth extend to all persons; for the words are generall, *nul minister, ne nul auter.* W. 1. cap. 25. W. 2. cap. 29. Stat. de Champertie, an. 11 E. 1. Vet. Mag. Chart. fo. 80. b.

(1) *Pur part aver des choses que sont in plea.*] If A. bargaine with B. owner of the mannor of D. B. is impleaded, B. enfeoffed A. hanging the suit according to the bargaine, though this be within the letter of the law, yet is it not within the meaning. On the other side, it is adjudged champerty, if he maintaine any party hanging the plea to have part, though he purchase not, nor take any state. And this act extendeth to all actions, as well personall, reall, and mixt. If the tenant hanging the plea grant a rent out of the land, this is champerty, and yet it is no part of the thing in demand, but it is within the same mischiefe. In an assise brought against the disseisor, and the tenant maintaine the plea upon covenant or promise after recovery to have part; although the disseisor hath nothing in the land, yet shall he have an action of champerty, because he may be charged with damages, and the tenant shall have his action also. 19 R. 2. champert. 15. Pl. com. 465. 30. ass. p. 15. 8 E. 4. 13. 47 E. 3. 9. F.N.B. 172. k. 47 E. 3. 9. F.N.B. 172.

If the husband and wife be impleaded, and one doth maintaine for champertie, the husband onely may have the action, or the husband and wife may joyne. 47 E. 3. 9.

And this action may be brought hanging the principall plea before judgement; and if the demandant be non-suit, yet may he have an action of champerty. 47 E. 3. 9. 33 E. 3 mainten. 26.

If two be impleaded in a reall action, and one doth maintaine the demandant to have part, the tenants bring a writ of champerty, the non-suit of one is not the non-suit of the other, because the 47 E. 3. 6. Lib. 6. fol. 25.

action of champerty being but accessary, doth follow the nature of the principall action.

If the tenant make a feoffment in fee hanging the writ, if one doth maintaine the demandant to have part, the feoffor shall have the action of champerty; for he remaines tenant to the demandant.

8 E. 4. 13. (2) *A la value de tant, &c.*] That is to say, the value of the land.

See the statute of 32 H. 8. cap. 9.

(3) *Devant les justices devant queux.*] See the statute of 4 E. 3. cap. 11.

Regist. 183. 22 H. 6. 7. Note, the party grieved may upon this statute either have a writ directed to the sherife, or a writ directed to the justices before whom the principall action dependeth.

F.N.B. 172. I. (4) *Ne nul sur tiel covenant.*] Here it is taken for a promise or contract by parol, as well as by deed.

1 E. 3. c. 14. 1 R. 2. c. 4. 32 H. 8. c. 9. See the statutes of 1 E. 3. 1 R. 2. and 32 H. 8.

(5) *Mes en ceo case nest my a entender, que home ne poet aver councell de ses countours, ne des sages gents.*] *Councell, consilium,* is taken for [564] advice and direction in law, and that is to be had of three persons, *viz.* 1. of serjeants at law, *servientes ad legem,* expressed here under the name of *countors:* 2. of apprentices of law, *apprenticii legis,* in pleading called *homines consiliarii, et in lege periti,* expressed here under this word *sages.* And these have *officium ingenii:* 3. Attornies of law, that have *officium laboris,* in following the advice of the learned, and dispatching of matters of course and experience, and they are under these words, *sages gents. Consilium* is also taken for assistance, maintenance, and comfort in their suits. And so it is taken here.

(6) *De ses prochein amyes.*] That is, of their next of bloud, who are or ought to be their surest assistants, aiders, and comforters; for *naturæ vis maxima,* and as some say, *natura bis maxima.*

And according to this diversity of signification, if the serjeant at law, apprentice, or attorney doe take a feoffment hanging the plea, or the like to maintaine the tenant, though it be *pro suo dando,* in lieu of his fee, yet is this champerty within the purview of this statute; for their counsell, that is, their advice and direction in their profession of law is excepted: but to take any estate in the land, hanging the writ, for maintenance, is to become a party, and in no sort allowed to them by this act.

6 E. 3. fo. 33. 20 H. 6. 12. Pl com. 305. F.N.B. 172. h. Li. 7. fo. 13, 14. Calvins case. 21 H. 6. 16. b. 29 H. 6. maintenance 12. 19 E. 4. 3. b. 34 H. 6. 26. 39 H. 6. 5. 6 E. 4. 5. 9 E. 4. 32. 14 H. 7. 2, &c.

But if a father be impleaded, he may infeoffe his son for his assistance, maintenance, and comfort; for that is natures profession for the son *assistere, manutenere, et consolari, et e converso, et sic de similibus: et sic alia est professio legis, et alia naturæ.*

So it is, that the son may of his owne mony, and in his owne name give fees to his fathers councell, or attorney, without any expectation of repayment, and so may the father to his sons councell; for he is *procheine amye,* but so cannot the serjeant nor apprentice, for that their counsell, advice, and direction in law is only saved to them. But the attorney may in his masters name lay out his owne mony to his councell, to be repaid to him by his master againe.

In like manner, and by the like reason, if the father be demandant in a *præcipe,* he may promise and contract with the son to assure him

him the land after the recovery, and is not any champerty within this act, and so of any other ancester and his heire apparant: but so it is not of the serjeant, apprentice, or attorney; for they cannot contract to have any part of the thing in demand after the recovery, *et sic de similibus.* And therefore Penros case maketh not against this, nor any thing that hath been said: for there the case (as Hanckford imperfectly citeth it) was, that in a writ of champerty brought against Penros, for that he had parcell of the land recovered against him at another mans suit, Penros said that he was of councell with the party which recovered, and had that land for his wages: but let us take the ford as we find it (though Fitzherb. in abridging this case, not knowing what to make of it, omitted it) the taking of the state for his wages after the recovery could be no champerty, unlesse there had been a covenant or promise hanging the plea on the demandants part, to make the same after the recovery, which was not alledged but only the taking of the state: neither doth it appeare what became of Penros plea: and we are of opinion, that it shall remaine for ever a blemish to his reputation, as often as it is cited; for, *quamvis aliquid ex se non sit malum, tamen si sit mali exempli, non est faciendum.*

13 H. 4. 19.

F. tit. Mainten. 23.

(6) *De ses prochein amyes,* &c.] Of *prochein amyes* you have heard before, this is to be added, that there be not onely *prochein amyes* in bloud, but in estate also: and therefore as the next of bloud is *prochein amy,* in respect of the expectancie of a discent (and yet it may be it shall never descend to him: for *solus deus facit hæredes, non homo*) so they that have reversions, or remainders expectant upon estates in taile, life or lives, are *prochein amyes* in estate, and are excepted out of this law, and yet it may be the land shall never come in possession to them: and therefore if a *præcipe* be brought against a tenant for life, and he surrender to him in the reversion or remainder, hanging the writ, for maintenance, this is no champerty within this act, no more then it is when the tenant infeoffeth his heire apparent: and so it is if tenant in taile, hanging the writ, conveyeth the land to him in reversion or remainder, this is no champerty for the cause aforesaid within this act.

17 E. 3. champerty 14. per les Justices. 19 E. 4. 3. b. F.N.B.

[565]

For the word *prochein amy, proximus amicus,* or *amicus propinquus,* see Littl. W. 1. and W. 2. &c.

Littl. sect. 123. W. 1. ca. 48. W. 2. ca. 15.

CAP. XII.

De rechiefe voet le roy que distresses, que sont a faire pur sa dett, ne soyent faits per bestes des charues, tanque come home poet auter trover, solonque ceo que est ordeine ailours per estatute (1), *ove la paine, &c. Et ne voet que trope greve distresse soit prise pur sa dett, ne trope loigne mesne* (2). *Et si le dettour poet trover suffisant, et covenable suretie* (3), *jesq; a un jour deins*

FROM henceforth the king will, that such distresses as are to be taken for his debts shall not be made upon beasts of the plough, so long as a man may find any other, upon the same pain that is elsewhere ordained by statute, &c. And he will not that overgreat distresses shall be taken for his debts, nor driven too far; and if the debtor can find able and convenient surety

deins le jour al viscount, dedeins le quel home puisse purchaser remedie a faire gree de la demaund, soit la distres relesse endementiers, et que auterment le fra soit grevement punie.

surety until a day before the day limited to the sheriff, within which a man may purchase remedy to agree for the demand, the distress shall be released in the mean time; and he that otherwise doth, shall be grievously punished.

(4 H. 7. f. 8. 51 H. 3. stat. 4. 52 H. 3. c. 4. Regist. 97. 185. Rast. pla. 226.)

51 H. 3. Vet. N. B. fo. 89. b. Regist. 97. b. Rast. pl. 118. 393. 450. (1) *Per statute.*] This is intended of the statute intituled, *statutum de districtionibus scaccarii, editi an.* 51 H. 3. which by mistaking is in the abridgement of statutes, tit. Distresses 10. supposed to be in *anno* 21 E. 1. which should be made 51 Hen. 3. the words of that act (amongst other things) are, *Que nul home de religion, ne auter soit distrein per les bestes, queux gaingnont sa terre, ne per les barbites pur la det le roy, ne pur le dett dauter home, ne pur auter encheson per les baillies le roy, ne per auters homes tanque come un trove auter distres,* F.N.B. 174. Regist. 97. 185. Marlbridge, c. 15. *ou auters chateux suffisantes, dont ils poient lever le det, ou que suffist la demande, &c.* But hereof sufficient hath been said in the exposition of the statute of Marlebridge.

(2) *Et ne voet que trope greve distres soit prise, ne trope loigne* F.N.B. 174. Regist. 97. *mesne.*] This is also provided for by the said act of 51 H. 3, and sufficient also hath hereof been said in the exposition of the said statute of Marlebridge, cap. 15. and these acts were made to take away the abuse of the sherifes, bailifes, and other ministers.

Act of grace. Vid. Mag. Chart. cap. 8, &c. Reg. 185, 186. F.N.B. 174. b. 36 E, 3. ca. 9. (3) *Et si le dettor poet trover suffisant et covenable suertie, &c.*] This is an act of grace, and upon this act there lyeth a writ directed to the sherife, commanding him to receive surety according to this act, which if he refuse, an attachment lyeth against him, or the party offering suretie according to this act, if it be refused, may have an action against the sherife, &c.

[566]

CAP. XIII.

ET pur ceo que le roy ad grant (1) *le election des viscounts a ceux des counties, voit le roy que ils eslient tiels viscounts, que ne les charge my: et ne mittent nul minister en bailie pur lower, ne pur don'. Et que tiels ne se herbergent trope sovent en un lieu, ne sur les povers, ne sur les religious.*

AND forasmuch as the king hath granted the election of sheriffs to the commons of the shire; the king will, that they shall chuse such sheriffs that shall not charge them, and that they shall not put any officer in authority for rewards or bribes; and such as shall not lodge too oft in one place, nor with poor persons, or men of religion.

(1) *Ad grant.*] This grant was made before at this parliament, cap. 8.

By this act five things are to be observed by the sherife: first, that he be not chargeable to the county: 2. that he shall put no minister

minister in office under him for hire, gift, or bribe: 3. that they shall not too often lodge or harbour in one place: 4. that they shall not lodge or harbour at all with those that are poore: 5. nor with religious men.

And albeit the manner of making of sherifes be altered, as before in the exposition of the eighth chapter doth appeare, yet the said articles are to be observed by him: for they follow the office of the sherife without respect of the maner of his making: and therefore if any sherife take any hire, gift, or bribe of any undersherife, baylife, keeper of the gaole, or other minister for his office or place, he may be indited, and fined, and imprisoned.

See other statutes against sale of offices, &c. 12 R 2. 11 H. 4. 5. E. 6. And in like manner touching the rest of the articles prohibited by this chapter, see the next chapter. 12 R. 2. cap. 2. 11 H. 4. Rot. parl. nu. 28. 5 E. 6. ca. 16.

CAP. XIV.

De rechiefe voit le roy, que les bailifes et les hund' du roy, ne les auters grand seigniors de la terre ne soient lesses a trope grand summe a ferme, per quoy le people soit greve, ne charge per contribution faire a tiels fermes.

From henceforth the king will, that the bailiwicks and hundreds of the king, nor of other great lords of the land, be not let to ferm at over great sums, whereby the people are over-charged by making contribution to such ferms.

This act was made for avoiding of extortion and oppression; for they that buy deare, must sell deare. For addition to this law it was enacted, that sherifes should not let their hundreds and wapentakes but for the old rent, and not above. 4 E. 3. ca. 15.

After by another act neither sherife, nor bailifes, or hundredors in fee should let any hundreds, &c. but for the ancient ferme, without any thing increasing. 14 E. 3. ca. 9.

And by another statute it was provided, that he should not let his bailiwicke at all to any man, and that it should be parcell of his oath. Upon which act some doubt was conceived, whether if he let not his whole bailiwicke, it was within that law; and besides, there was no penalty inflicted by that act; therefore by another law it is enacted, that no sherife shall let to ferme in any manner his county, nor any of his bailiwickes, hundreds, or wapentakes, upon paine of forfeiture of xl. li. 4 H. 4. ca. 5. 23 H. 6. ca. 10. 20 H. 7. 12. &c. 21 H. 7. 36. Pl. com. 87. & 124. Vid. Mag. Chart. cap. 8, &c.

And this act, as to the king, is a bill of grace.

CAP. XV. [567]

En summons (1) et attachments (2) en plea de terre (3), desormes conteigne la summons ou lattachment le terme de xv. jours a tout la meyns (4), solonque

In summons and attachments in plea of land, the summons and attachments from henceforth shall contain the term of fifteen days full at the least

solonque la common ley, sil ne soit en attachment des assises prender en presence le roy (5), ou devant les justices del common bank, ou des plees devant justices en eire, durant le eire.

least according to the common law, if it be not in attachment of assises taken in the king's presence, or of pleas before justices in eyre during the eyre.

See Marlbridge, cap. 12. & 26. (Fitz. Jour. 16, 17. 36. Bro. Attach. 3, 4. 6, 7, 8, 9, 10. 13. 15, 16, 17.)

F.N.B. 177. d. e. 11 ass. p. 30. 22 ass. p. 79. 30 ass. 26. & 44.

The printed bookes leave out *(ou devant les justices del common bank)* which ought to be added.

* 12 E. 4. 11. Glan. li. 1. ca. 7. Bract. li. 4. fo. 255. & 182. Brit. fol. 279. b. Flet. li. 6. ca. 6.

This statute was made in affirmance of the common law, as by the expresse words of the statute it appeareth, contrary to a sudden and misconceived opinion in our * bookes: for Glanvile saith, *Summonebitur per intervallum quindecim dierum ad minus:* and therewith agreeth Bracton and Britton, *Et si ascun soit resonablement summon, il doit aver space de xv. jours au meynes, de soy garner de son respons.* And Fleta saith, *Nec etiam sufficit quod summonitio fiat ad statim respondendum, sed decet quod quilibet habet tempus xv. dierum ante diem litis, et si summonitio minus spacium, pro illegitima debet reputari, nisi in causis specialibus; ut sunt causæ mercatorum, et crucesignatorum, et hujusmodi quæ instantiam desiderant et celeritatem, &c.* And all these authors wrote before the making of our act: and the author of the Mirror that wrote of the ancient lawes of this realme, speaking of the time of summons, saith, *Et reasonable respit al meyns de xv. jours de purveire respons, et de parer en judgement.* And the cause wherefore the common law set downe the certaine time of 15 dayes was, for that a dayes journey is accounted in law 20 miles, *rationabilis dieta constat ex viginti miliaribus:* for *dieta* both in the common and civill law signifieth a dayes journey, *continet legalis dieta viginti miliaria.* And therefore 15 dayes was accounted by the common law a reasonable time of summons or attachment, within which time wheresoever the court of justice sate in England, the party summoned or attached, wheresoever he dwelt in England, afore the kings writ did come, might *per prædictas dietas computatas,* by the said account of dayes journies appeare in court, &c.

Mirr. c. 2. § 19.

Bract. lib. 4. fo. 235. b. 19 H. 7. ca. 1. the like account is made. Lib. intr. tit. Journies accounts, f. 382. li. 6. f. 10. & 11. Spencers case. 18 E. 3. 42. 32 E. 3. Journies acc' 16. Custumere, c. 61. fol. 76, 77. 12 E. 4. 11.

(1) *En sommons.*] In a writ of pone, to remove a replevin at the suit of the defendant, the writ saith, *et dic præfato querenti, quod sit coram justiciariis nostris apud Westm' tali die,* there ought to be a warning by 15 dayes, for that this *(dic querenti)* is in nature of a summons, and so the writ of *venire fac'* for returning of a jury is in nature of a summons: but this statute extends not to a writ of errour, nor to dayes of prefixion, as upon a forreine voucher in London, and the like.

1 E. 5. 2. b. Bract. lib. 4. fol. 255.

This act speaketh of a summons, and so it is in a resummons.

(2) *Et attachments.*] And so it is in a re-attachment.

1 E. 5. 2. b. Dyer 8 El. 252. 9 E. 4. 18.

(3) *En plea de terre.*] Upon an originall writ in any reall action the tenant must be summoned by 15 dayes, as is aforesaid; but if the originall writ be returned *tarde,* the *sumoneas sicut alias* must have nine returnes between the *teste* and the returne: for albeit the *summoneas sicut alias* be in lieu of the summons in the originall, yet being a judiciall processe in a reall action, there must be nine returnes, &c. and the summons thereupon ought to be made by 15 dayes, or more, before the returne.

[568] 24 E. 3. 35. 46. 22 E. 3. 7. 31 H. 6. 13. 27 H. 6. 2.

(4) *Le terme de 15 jours a tout le meynes.*] These 15 dayes or more must be before the day of the returne of the writ, and the day of the returne must be accounted none of them.

(5) *Si*

(5) *Si ne ſoit en aſſiſes prender en preſence del roy*, &c.] *En preſence del roy*, that is, in the kings bench, for there all pleas be *coram rege*. It was accorded in 7 E. 2. by Sir Guilliam Inge chiefe juſtice of the kings bench, and the juſtices, that in writs of attaints upon an aſſiſe of *novel diſſeiſin* taken in the kings bench, there ſhall be a certaine day given as in the aſſiſe; for example, the Monday, or the morrow, or in the *utas* or *quinden'* of Eaſter: but it behoveth that the tenant hath garniſhment by 15 dayes in the attaint, for this ſtatute of *articuli ſuper chartas* doth not give any leſſe terme, but only in an aſſiſe of *novel diſſeiſin* in the kings bench, common pleas, or in eire. Regiſt. 204. a. 7 E. 2. per les Juſtices. F.N.B. 109. a.

This branch, as to the kings bench, ſeemeth to be in affirmance of the common law; for in criminall cauſes, which concerne the life of man, if a man be indited of treaſon or felony in the county where the kings bench doth ſit, the *venire fac'* for the returning of the jury need not have 15 dayes between the *teſte* and the returne, nay the entry may be *ideo immediate venit inde jurata, &c.* But if the inditement be taken in any other county, and removed into the kings bench, there ought to be 15 dayes between the *teſte* of the *venire fac'* and the returne. Li. 9. f. 118. b. Seignior Zanchars caſe.

* Commiſſioners of oire and terminer may in caſe of treaſon, felony, miſpriſion, treſpaſſe, &c. trie the priſoner the ſame day they award the *venire fac'*, as by divers preſidents ancient and late doe appeare; but the commiſſioners muſt make a precept in parchment under their ſeales for the returning of a jury immediately the ſame day, if they will, or any day after, and likewiſe juſtices of gaole delivery, or juſtices of peace may trie the priſoner the ſame day, or any day after, but need not make any particular precept: for the juſtices of gaole delivery, and juſtices of the peace make a generall precept in parchment under their ſeales for the ſommons of the ſeſſions, and for returne of juries, &c. and therefore any particular precept is not requiſite. * Hil. 2. H. 4. rot. 4. Thomas Marks eveſq' de Carlile, treaſon. Lunæ poſt feſtum Mich. an. 1. H. 8. Sir Richard Empſon, treaſon. 10 Decem. 3 E. 6. Thomas Bonham, before Portman chiefe juſtice, and other juſtices, treaſon. 2 Decem. 3 E. 6. before Lyſter, Mountague Cholmeley, &c. Robert Bell, treaſon. 4 Auguſt 10 El. John Felton, &c. London, treaſon. Hill. 36. El. Doct. Lopes in London, &c. treaſon. Paſch' 9 H. 8. Kelwey. Holl. Chronic. 8 H. 8. fol. 843. 22 E. 4. tit. coron. 44.

There was a generall ſommons made 40 dayes before the ſitting of the juſtices in eire.

* We have the rather ſpoken ſomewhat hereof, becauſe there is a report of the reſolution of the judges, that commiſſioners of oire and terminer, or juſtices of peace cannot trie a priſoner that pleads not guilty the ſame day that he pleads, &c. But herein at this day not onely *juriſperiti*, but *uſuperiti* alſo doe agree. * 4 H. 5. tit. enqueſt 55.

CAP. XVI.

SOIT fait de ceux que ſont faux retornes des briefes al maundement le roy, per quoy droiture eſt delay, auxy come ordeine eſt en le ſecond eſtatute de Weſtminſter ove la peine.

THAT ſhall be done with them that make falſe returns (whereby right is deferred) as it is ordained in the ſecond ſtatute of Weſtminſter, with like pain.

(13 Ed. 1. ſtat. 1. c. 39.)

This is an act of confirmation, whereby the ſtatute of W. 2. cap. 39. touching falſe returnes, is confirmed.

CAP. XVII.

ET pur ceo que mults misfeaſors ſont en la terre pluis que ne ſolent, et robberies, arſions, e homicides faits ſans number, et la peace meynes bien garde, pur ceo que leſtatute, que le roy fiſt faire nadgaires paſſes a Wincheſter, nad pas eſte tenus: voit le roy que cel eſtatute ſoit de novel envoy en cheſcun countie, et ſoit lie et publie 4 foits per an (1), *auxybien come les deux graund charters* (2), *et firmement gardes en cheſcun point, ſur les paines que la cyens ſont aſſeſſes. Et a cel eſtatute garder et mainteiner, ſoient charges les trois chivaliers* (3), *que ſont aſſignes per mye les counties pur redreſſer les choſes faits encounter les grand charters, et de ceo eyent garrantie.*

AND foraſmuch as there be more malefactors in the realm, than had wont to be, and that robberies, burnings, and man-ſlaughters are committed out of meaſure, and the peace little obſerved, by reaſon that the ſtatute which the king not long paſt cauſed to be made at Wincheſter is not obſerved; the king will, that the ſame ſtatute be ſent again into every county, to be read and publiſhed four times in the year, and kept in every point as ſtraitly as the two great charters, upon the pains therein limited. And for the obſerving and maintenance of this ſtatute, the three knights that be aſſigned in the ſhires for to redreſs things done againſt the ſaid great charters, ſhall be charged, and ſhall have their warrant therefore.

(13 Ed. 1. ſtat. 2. c. 1.)

Vid. Flet. lib. 1. cap. 24. this ſtatute of Wincheſter recited.

The effect of the ſtatute of Wincheſter made at a parliament holden in 13 E. 1. is this, that from thenceforth every country ſhould be ſo well kept, that immediately upon ſuch robberies and felonies committed, freſh ſuit ſhould be made, &c.

Vid. li. 7. f. 6, 7. caſes ſur ceſt, ſtatute. 3 E. 3. coron. 293.

The letter of this ſtatute is generall; and firſt, concerning the place: if a man be robbed in his houſe, it is not within the meaning of this ſtatute. Secondly, the time: if a man travell in the night, and be robbed, he ſhall not take the benefit of this act, as you may reade at large, lib. 7. *ubi ſupra.*

28 E. 3. ca. 11. 27 Eliz. ca. 13.

See the ſtatutes of 28 E. 3. and 27 Eliz. which have in ſome points altered, in ſome explained, and added divers articles to this ſtatute of Wincheſter.

Dyer 23. El. 370. Brit. f. 20. 32. b. & 263. 160. Elegit.

Britton maketh mention of the ſtatute of Wincheſter in theſe words, *ſolonque noſtre ordinance de nous ſtatutes de Wincheſter*, and of the ſtatute of W. 2. *an.* 13 E. 1. So as he wrote not his book in 5 E. 1. as Priſot ſuppoſed: neither died he in 3 E. 1. *anno Dom.* 1272. as Bale, fol. 111. hath miſtaken; but certainly he wrote his booke after 13 E. 1.

And it appeareth by Fleta, *ubi ſupra*, that the time given to the country by the ſtatute of Wincheſter is not within 40 dayes, as the booke of ſtatutes lately printed miſtakes it, but *infra dimid' anni*, and ſo is the printed booke of ſtatutes by Berthelet; and therefore it would be reformed accordingly. True it is, that the ſtatute of

28 E.

28 E. 3. doth expreſly ſet downe 40 dayes; but yet the words of the ſtatute of Wincheſter muſt remaine as they were. 28 E. 3. ca. 11.

For actions brought upon the ſtatute of Wincheſter, ſee Hil. 4 H. 8. rot. 525. Paſch. 4 H. 8. rot. 310. Mich. 6 H. 8. rot. 1. Paſch. 12 & 13 Hen. 8. rot. 4 Eliz. rot. 508. &c. which were before the ſtatute of 27 Eliz, Lib. intr' Raſt. 580. Lib. 7. fo. 6. ubi ſupra.

See Trin. 28 Eliz. rot. 75. Aſhpoles caſe, and Trin. 29 El. rot. 1027. Milborns caſe. Lib. intr' Co. fol. 348.

Which precedents I have addded, becauſe they ſerve both for expoſition of the ſaid ſtatutes, and for direction to the party grieved to attaine to the benefit of the ſame. Lib. 7. fol. 6. ubi ſupra.

If any deſire to ſee ſome precedent neerer the making of the ſtatute of Wincheſter, let them ſee the record of that notable caſe of Ellice Caller in 2 E. 3. and they ſhall perceive, that actions grounded upon this ſtatute were not ſubject to ſuch captious and curious exceptions, as now they be. There the caſe was, that Ellice Caller was robbed in the hundred of H. in the confines of two counties, &c. and brought his action upon this ſtatute, and had judgement, and ſued execution to the ſherife of Stafford, who returned, that he had levied x. marks of the men of the biſhop of Coventry and Litchfield of the hundred of H. the biſhop came and ſaid, that the hundred of H. was of the right of his church of Saint Cadde of Litchfield, and ſhewed forth to the court the charter of king Richard the firſt, by the which he granted to E. then biſhop of Coventry and Lichfield, and to his men, that they ſhould be quit of murder and larceny, that is, to be quit and diſcharged of every thing that lyeth in charge of his men, by reaſon of murder or felony; as of amerciaments and of preſentments of murder and felony. But the authority of the booke is, that the biſhops men ought not to be diſcharged, and Shard that giveth the rule, giveth alſo two reaſons thereof. Hill. 2 E. 3. fo. 6. & 7. [570]

Firſt, that the charter of Rich. 1. could not diſcharge this action, for that at the time of that charter an action againſt the inhabitants, by reaſon of robbery, &c. was not granted, but it was granted long after, that is to ſay, *in anno* 13 E. 1. and we doe not entend, that by reaſon of the charter, being more ancient then the ſtatute of Wincheſter, you may barre or diſcharge the execution.

Secondly, albeit the king by his charter may grant, that a man may be acquited againſt him and his ſucceſſors, yet thereby the action or right of the party cannot be taken away.

The burgeſſes of the towne of Tewkſbury in the county of Gloceſter brought an action of debt upon the ſtatute of 8 H. 6. which hath reference to this ſtatute of Wincheſter, if ſatisfaction be not made for the robbery therein mentioned within 15 dayes after proclamation, and the action is given againſt the comminalties of the foreſt of Deane, which are adjacent to the river of Severn, and of the hundreds of Bledſtow and Weſtbury, and the writ was, *Præcipe communitati foreſtæ de Deane, et hundredis de B. & W.* and exception was taken to the writ, for that the writ ought to have been, *Præcipe communitati foreſtæ de Deane, et hundredorum de B. et W.* according to the words of the ſtatute of 8 H. 6. as one entire comminalty; and yet the writ was awarded good, for that it was the ſame in effect, though it had been the better, if it had accorded with the words of the ſtatute. 11 H. 6. fo. 47. a. 8 H. 6. ca. 27.

It is ſaid, that one that took upon him the profeſſion of the law, made a motion, that all the ſuperfluous caſes of the law reported in our bookes might be rejected, and left out of the next impreſſion,

and

and principally thoſe that Fitzherhert had not vouchſafed to abridge. But indeed the motion was ſuperfluous and ſmoakie, and therefore vaniſhed; for there is no caſe reported in our bookes, but is worthy of obſervation; for thereof great uſe may be made at one time or other, if it be well underſtood and remembred, and we ſhould have been right ſorry, if theſe two excellent caſes, amongſt many others, had been rejected.

(1) *Et ſoit lye et publie 4 foits per ann'.*] This is evident.

(2) *Auxybien come les deux grand charters.*] Here it is to be obſerved, that *Magna Charta*, and *Charta de foreſta* are called, *les deux grand charters.*

By the firſt chapter of the acts of this parliament it is provided, that theſe two charters ſhal be read foure times every yeare before the people in full countie, that is to ſay, in the next county after the feaſt of Saint Michael, and after the feaſt of the nativity of our Saviour, after Eaſter, and after the nativity of Saint John Baptiſt, and ſo oft, and at thoſe times, ought the ſtatute of Wincheſter to be read and publiſhed.

(3) *Soit charge les trois chivaliers.*] Theſe three knights are authoriſed before cap. 1.

[571]

CAP. XVIII.

EN droit des waſtes et deſtructions faits en gards per eſcheators et ſubeſcheators (1) *de meaſons, bois, parkes, viuers* (2); *et de touts auters choſes, que eſchient en les maynes le roy* (3): *voit le roy, que celuy que aver' le dam' reſcere, eit briefe de waſt* (4) *en la chancery vers leſcheator de ſon fait, ou ſubeſcheator de ſon fait, ſil eyt de quoy reſponder, et ſil nad de quoy, ci reſpond' ſon ſoveraigne* (5) *per autiel peine, quant as damages, come' darreine ordeine eſt per eſtatute* (6) *ſur ceux que ſont waſt en gardes.*

FOR redreſs of waſtes, and deſtructions done by eſcheators or ſubeſcheators in the lands of wards, as of houſes, woods, parks, warrens, and of all other things that fall into the king's hands; the king will, that he which hath ſuſtained damage, ſhall have a writ of waſte out of the chancery againſt the eſcheator for his act, or the ſubeſcheator for his act (if he have whereof to anſwer) and if he have not, his maſter ſhall anſwer by like pain concerning the damages, as is ordained by the ſtatute for them that do waſte in wardſhips.

(6 Ed. 1. ſtat. 1. c. 5. 14 Ed. 3. ſtat. 1. c. 13. 36 Ed. 3. c. 13. Regiſt. 72. Raſt. 693. 12 Car. 2. c. 24.)

36 E. 3. ca. 13. & Magna Chart. cap. 5.

Where ſome have thought that the eſcheator and undereſcheator are not within the ſtatute of Magna Charta; and therefore in this point the title of *confirmatio chartarum* is not apt as to this chapter, let them reade the ſtatute of 36 E. 3. and they will be ſatisfied.

* Regiſt. 301. cap. Eſcheatrie. Mirr. ca. 1. § 5. Statut. de Scacc. 51 H. 3.

(1) *Per eſcheators et ſubeſcheators.*] Of their * names, and whence they are derived, of their antiquity and office, of their number in ancient time, and what alteration hath been by acts of parliament

liament of later times, you may reade in the firſt part of the Inſtitutes.

(2) *Parkes, viuers.*] Here vivers, *vivaria*, are taken for fiſhponds and warrens, as heretofore we have obſerved.

(3) *Et de touts auters choſes, que eſchient en le maynes le roy.*] [a] That is, of all other things which caſually fall, or eſcheat, or come into the kings hands.

(4) *Eyt briefe de waſte.*] [b] For the action of waſt againſt the eſcheator, ſee the Regiſter, F.N.B. &c.

(5) *Reſpond' ſon ſoveraigne.*] *Reſpondeat ſuperior*, that is, the eſcheator ſhall anſwer for the deputy eſcheator, or under-eſcheator.

(6) *Per eſtatute.*] That is, by the ſtatute of Glouceſter, *anno* 6 E. 1. cap. 5. and W. 2. *anno* 13 E. 1. cap. 21.

And it is to be obſerved (that we may note it once for all that in this and other ancient acts of parliament that have relation or reference to any former, there is not any mention made of the yeare or chapter of the former ſtatute, but the generall reference was then thought the ſureſt, and the more parliamentary way.

Brit. fol. 33, 34. Flet. lib. 1. ca. 6. Rot. Parl. 18 E. 1. fol. 7. & 21 E. 1. rot. 1. 28 E. 1. cap. 18. 29 E. 1. de eſcheat. 14 E. 3. cap. 8. 1 H. 8. c. 8. F.N.B. 100. Stamf. pr. 81. 1. part of the Inſtitutes, ſect. 4.

[a] See the firſt part of the Inſtitutes, ubi ſupra.

[b] Regiſt. 72. F.N.B. 59. b. Vet. N. B. fo. 36. Stamf. prer. 81. 14 E. 3. ca. 13. 36 E. 3. ca. 13.

CAP. XIX.

[572]

DE rechieſe la ou leſcheator, ou le viſcount ſeiſient en la mayne le roy (1) auters terres, la ou il nad reaſon de ſeiſier: et puis quant trove eſt la non reaſon, les iſſues du meſne temps ont eſtre ceo en arere retenus, et nemy rendus, quant le roy ad la mayne ouſte: voit le roy que deſormes, la ou terres ſont iſſint ſeiſies, et puis la mayne ouſte pur ceo que il nad reaſon de ſeſier, ne ceo tener, ſoient les iſſues pleinment rendus a celuy a que la terre demurt, et avera le damage reſceive.

FROM henceforth, where the eſcheator or the ſheriff ſhall ſeiſe other mens lands into the king's hands (where there is no cauſe of ſeiſer) and after, when it is found no cauſe, the profits taken in the mean time have been ſtill retained, and not reſtored, when the king hath removed his hand; the king will, that if hereafter any lands be ſo ſeiſed, and after it be removed out of his hands by reaſon that he hath no cauſe to ſeiſe nor to hold it, the iſſues ſhall be fully reſtored to him to whom the land ought to remain, and which hath ſuſtained the damage.

Vide W. 1. cap. 24. (Regiſt. 314. Raſt. 604.)

See the ſtatute of 29 E. 1. *de eſchaetoribus*, commonly called the ſtatute of Lincoln, made the yeare after this law; and upon theſe two ſtatutes ten points are to be obſerved;

1. That by the common law, although the ſeiſure was not lawfull, yet for the meſne profits upon the livery, or *ouſter le mayne*, the party grieved was not reſtored to the meſne profits, which miſchiefe is remedied by theſe two ſtatutes.

2. Iſſues are intended rents and things leviable by the eſcheator, which may be reſtored, though the eſcheator hath accounted for them,

24 E. 3. 28, 29. 59. 5 E. 3 6.

them, and not paid; but the mony, being once in the kings coffers, shall not be restored.

3. That though both these statutes speake onely of an *ouster le mayne*, yet being both beneficiall lawes for restitution to be made to the party grieved, by equity they extend to liveries.

4. Where the words seem to extend onely to seisures before office, and after by the office that is found the king is not intitled, yet by construction the same extend onely to seisures after office found. See hereafter *verbo Seisent*.

24 E. 3. 33. 9 E. 4. 52. Kelway, 1 H. 8. 156.

5. These statutes extend by equity to *ouster le mayne*, and *amoveas manus* upon petitions, and *monstrans de droits*, not only in cases concerning wardship, but freehold and inheritance.

6. These statutes extend also by like equity to *ouster le maynes* upon traverses, although traverses were not in use at the time of the making of these statutes.

28 H. 6. fo. 9. b. 5 H. 5. 2. 30 ass. 28. F.N.B. 260. 4 H. 7. 5. Dyer, 8 El. 248, 249. 21 E. 3. 1. 21 ass. 15. 12 R. 2. livery 28. 40 ass. * 21 E. 3. 1. 21 ass. 15. 40 ass. 36. 9 E. 4. 51, 52. * 18 E. 3. liver. 3. 24 E. 3. 65. Darcies case. 44 E. 3. 12. Stamf. pr. fol. 11. & 80, 81. Brok. reseis. 13. 24 E. 3. 33.

7. By the said statute of 29 E. 1. if any former office or record be found after livery, or *ouster le mayne*, that maintaineth the title, by reason whereof the king is seised, the king upon that record shall not reseise *maintenant*, but thereupon sue out a *scire facias*, &c.

8. But if an * office be found, which doth entitle the king to the land by a title growne to him since the livery, or *ouster le mayne*, neither of these statutes restraine the king, but that he may reseise without a *scire facias*.

9. * There is a diversity, when the party hath a livery or *ouster le mayne* upon an insufficient office, or by erroneous processe, there though the party hath right, yet the king shall reseise without *scire fac'*: for a livery mis-sued is as it had been never sued, and the statute of 29 E. 1. is to be understood of a livery or *ouster le mayne*, duely and lawfully sued for that which is insufficient is nothing in law: but when the party sueth out his livery or *ouster le mayne* duely and according to law, where in truth he hath no right, but the king, if he had been apprised of his title appearing of record, no livery or *ouster le mayne* ought to have been granted, yet there upon that record the king cannot reseise without a *scire facias*.

[573]

10. Some have holden, that at the common law he that was in possession of the land, &c. by judgement, as in case of an *ouster le mayne*, livery, or *amoveas manum*, that no reseisure could be made for the king without a *scire facias*, and therein to avoid the former record by matter of as high nature: for the generall rules of law be, *Nihil tam conveniens est naturali æquitati, unumquodque dissolvi eo ligamine, quo ligatum est: et judicia sunt tanquam juris dicta, et pro veritate accipiuntur.*

5 E. 6. tit. Office. Br. 55. Lib. 8 fol. 169. Paris Stoughton case.

(1) *Seisient en la mayne le roy.*] This seisure is intended after office: for before office lands or tenements cannot be seised into the kings hands, and so is the common experience at this day.

See the statute of W. 1. cap. 24.

That we passe over nothing that the statute of 29 E. 1. giveth us occasion to remember which is worthy of observation: it is there said, that the statute was commanded to be observed *de concilio venerabilis patris Walteri de Langton, Coventr' et Lichfield episc', tunc ejusdem regis thesaurarii, et Johannis de Langton cancellarii*, who then had the dealing with wards, &c. we will speak somewhat of both these great officers.

This Walter de Langton, a gentleman of an ancient and faire deſcended family, was made lord treaſurer of England in the 23 yeare of king Edward the firſt; he was a grave and a wiſe man, and was much favoured by the king, and in great authority under him, the rather, for that he with great diſcretion and moderation did wiſely diſſwade prince Edward (who after was king by the name of Edward the ſecond) from ſuch diſhonourable and diſſolute courſes as he took, and was the principall motive that Pierce Gaveſton, the wicked corrupter of the princes youth, was baniſhed the realme. The prince in requitall hereof, on a time amongſt other injuries, gave the treaſurer foule and diſgracefull words, whereof the noble king underſtanding, deemed the offence done unto himſelfe; for ſo I find it of record in the ſame kings time, which record ſpeaketh in theſe termes: *Et hoc expreſſè nuper apparuit, cum idem rex filium ſuum primogenitum, et chariſſimum principem Walliæ, pro eo quod quædam verba groſſa et acerba cuidam miniſtro ſuo dixerat, ab hoſpitio ſuo fere per dimid' an' amovit, nec ipſum filium ſuum in conſpectu ſuo venire permiſit, quouſque dicto miniſtro de præd' tranſgreſſione ſatisfecerat: quia, ſicut honor et reverentia qui miniſtris domini regis ratione officii fiunt, ipſo regi attribuuntur: ſic dedecus et contemptus miniſtris ipſius domini regis fact' eidem domino regi inferuntur.* But we are ſorry to remember, that the favour of a king, and the height of proſperity, which rightly uſed are the bleſſings of God, ſhould make him preſume to defile his hands with corrupt and ſordid bribery, and to beguile himſelfe to thinke that no man ſhould dare to bring him in queſtion. True it is, that he was judicially convicted in the firſt yeare of king Edward the ſecond, but it was before foure of the principall judges of the realme and in effect upon his owne confeſſion. Coram rege Mich. 33 E. 1. Rot. 75.

All theſe briberies you may reade in a bundle of the records remaining in the treaſury, intitled *Placita apud Winſor coram Roberto de Brabazon, Will' de Bereford, Rogero de Heigham, et Will' Inge juſticiariis, &c. aſſignatis in cro' Sancti Andræ apoſtoli, anno regni regis E. filii regis E. primo, rot. 3. 8. 14. &c. Servile eſt expilationis crimen, ſola innocentia libera.* Hiſtories may ſafely be beleeved, when there is a record to warrant them.

John Langton named alſo in the act of 29 E. 1. was then biſhop of Chicheſter, and lord chancellour of England, he was of a great ſpirit, and feared not the face of great men in that dangerous time to doe that which he ought: for whereas Thomas the noble earle of Lancaſter had lawfully married Alice onely daughter and heire of Henry Lacie earle of Lincoln, ſon and heire of William de Longa Spatha earle of Saliſbury; and John earle Warren and of Surrey had to wife the kings niece, that is, Joan daughter of Henry earle of Barre, and of Elinor his wife daughter of king Edward the firſt, yet the ſaide earle Warren by great force and ſtrong hand *(ut dicebatur aſſenſu regio)* cauſed the ſaid Alice counteſſe of Lancaſter to be fetched from the earle of Lancaſters houſe in Canford in Dorſetſhire, and in great pomp and bravery (in deſpight of the earle of Lancaſter) to be brought to him to his caſtle of Ryegate in Surrey, where they lived in open advoutry. This worthy biſhop looking neither above him nor about him, but according to his office and duty called the ſaid earle Warren in queſtion for the ſaid ſhamefull and open adultery, and by eccleſiaſticall cenſures excommunicated him for the ſame, as he well deſerved: [574] Vid. Paſch' 8 E. 2. rot. 111. Coram rege.

An. Dom. 1317. & 10 E. 2. deserved: in revenge whereof the earle, adding a new offence to the old, came with many of his followers weaponed for the purpose towards the bishop, to lay violent hands on him: but the bishop himselfe being a man of great courage, and being well attended with gentlemen and other his houshold servants, understanding thereof, they addressed themselves, and having put themselves in good order, issued out, and encountred with the earle and his men, and not onely manfully defended themselves against that barbarous attempt, but valiantly overcame the earle and his followers, and took them into their possession, and laid the earle and his gallants fast in prison by the bishops commandement.

Armaque in armatos sumere jura sinunt.

But, fearing that one of Virgils verses should be applied to us,

Virg. 5. Æneid. *Sed jam age, carpe viam, susceptum perfice munus,*

We will returne to our statute.

CAP. XX.

ORDEIGNE est que nul orfeure d'Angleterre ne ailors de la seigniorie le roy, ne ouere, ne face de ci en avant nul manner de vessel, ne joialx, ne auter chose dore ne dargent, que ne soit de bone et veray allay, cestassavoir, ore de certaine touche (1), *et argent del allay del esterling* (2), *ou de melior allay, solonque le volunt de celuy, a que les ouerers sont. Et que nul ouer pejor argent que money* (3). *Et que nul maner de vessel dargent ne depart hors des maines des ouerours, tanquel el soit assay per les gardeins de la mister'* (4) *et auxy que el soit sign' dun teste dun leopard* (5). *Et que nul ne ouere pejor ore que de touche de Paris* (6). *Et que les gardeins du misterie allent de shope en shope enter les orfeours, assaiants que lore soit tiel come la touche avantdit. Et sils trovont ul pejor que la touche, que lour soit forfeit al roy. Et que nul ne face auneux, croix, ne firmaux* (7). *Et nul ne mett' pire en ore, si il ne soit naturel* (8). *Et que taillours des aimans et des seales, rendant a chescun son poyz dargent et dore auxy avant come ils le purront scaver sur lour soialtie. Et les joyaux dore, que*

IT is ordained, that no goldsmith of England, nor none otherwhere within the king's dominion, shall from henceforth make, or cause to be made, any manner of vessel, jewel, or any other thing of gold or silver, except it be of good and true allay, that is to say, gold of a certain touch, and silver of the sterling allay, or of better, at the pleasure of him to whom the work belongeth; and that none work worse silver than money. And that no manner of vessel of silver depart out of the hands of the workers, until it be essayed by the wardens of the craft; and further, that it be marked with the leopard's head; and that they work no worse gold than of the touch of Paris. And that the wardens of the craft shall go from shop to shop among the goldsmiths, to essay if their gold be of the same touch that is spoken of before; and if they finde any other than of the touch aforesaid, the gold shall be forfeit to the king. And that none shall make rings, crosses, nor locks, and that none shall set any stone in gold, except it be natural. And that gravers

*que ils ont entermaines de veil ouere, que ils ſeu deliveront a plus toſt que ils purront. Et ſils * achatent deſor en avaunt de meſme cell' oueraige, que ils lachatent pur defere, et nemy pur revender. Et touts les bones villes Dengleterre, la ou il y ad orfeures, que ils facent per meſme leſtatute, come ceux de Londres ſont. Et que un veigne de cheſcun ville pur touts, a Londres, de quer' lour certaine touche. Et ſi ull' orfeure ſoit attaint que autrement le face que deſuis neſt ordeine, ſoit punie per priſon, et per ranſome a la volunt le roy. Et en touts les choſes deſuis dits, et cheſcun de els voit le roy, et tenend' il et ſon councel, et touts ceux que a ceſt ordeinment fuerent, que le droit et la ſeigniorie de la corone ſaves luy ſoient per touts, &c.* (9)

gravers or cutters of ſtones and of ſeals ſhall give to each their weight of ſilver and gold (as near as they can) upon their fidelity; and the jewels of baſe gold which they have in their hands, they ſhall utter as faſt as they can; and from henceforth, if they buy any of the ſame work, they ſhall buy it to work upon, and not to ſell again; and that all the good towns of England, where any goldſmiths be dwelling, ſhall be ordered according to this eſtatute as they of London be; and that one ſhall come from every good town for all the reſidue that be dwelling in the ſame, unto London, for to be aſcertained of their touch. And if any goldſmith be attainted hereafter, becauſe that he hath done otherwiſe than before is ordained, he ſhall be puniſhed by impriſonment, and by ranſom at the king's pleaſure. And notwithſtanding all theſe things before-mentioned, or any point of them, both the king and his council, and all they that were preſent at the making of this ordinance, will and intend that the right and prerogative of his crown ſhall be ſaved to him in all things.

(Altered by 8 & 9 W. 3. c. 8. ſ. 9. and 6 G. 1. c. 11. ſ. 41. 21 Jac. 1. c. 28. 37 E. 3. c. 7. 2 H. 6. c. 14. 17 E. 4. c. 1. 4 H. 7. c. 2. 18 El. c. 15.)

(1) *Ore de certeine touche.*] The pound of gold and ſilver containeth 12 ounces: 12 graines of fine gold make a caret, 24 carets of fine gold make an ounce, 12 ounces make a pound of fine gold of the touch of Paris; but by the ſtatute of 18 Eliz. 22 carets fine make an ounce.

See hereafter in this chapter.

18 Eliz. cap. 15.

(2) *Et argent del allay de eſterling.*] In our law it is called *ſterlingum.* For the name of eſterling or ſterling money there be divers opinions.

37 E. 3. cap. 7.

Our hiſtorians thinke it is ſo called, *ab effigie ſturni, aviculæ, quæ in altera parte nummi impreſſa fuit, nam ſturnus anglicè* ſterling *dicitur, &c. vel quod numulus in altera parte haberet notam ſtellæ, quam Angli* ſter *vocant.*

Polid. Virg. fol. 304, &c.

And with the conceit of the ſterling agreeth * Linwood the civilian in his gloſſe upon the provinciall conſtitutions.

* Tit. de teſtamentis cap. Item quia verbo centum ſolid.

The Scots thinke it ſhould take his name of a towne in Scotland, called Striveling, *alias* Sterling.

Maſter Skene.

But

The name. Hovend. parte poster. annalium. fol. 377. b. 20 E. 1. Vet. Mag. Chart. 167. The time. Dier, 7 El. fol. 82. The value.

But the esterling or sterling peny tooke the name of the workmen, being Esterlings, that both coined it, and gave it the allay as the florence of gold is called of the Florentines, and the portagues of the Portugals, &c.

And the esterling penny was first coined by the Esterlings in the reigne of Henry the second; and now money of that allay is counted the lawfull money of England.

20 pence of silver made an ounce, and twelve ounces made a pound of fine silver, and eleven ounces of fine silver, and one ounce of allay maketh a pound weight of sterling silver intended by this act.

By the statute of 18 Eliz. plate of silver ought to be of the fines of xi. ounces two peny weight.

9 H. 5. stat. 2. cap. 4. & 6. 3 H. 7. 10. a. b. 3 H. 7. ubi supr.

Allay is the mixture of a baser metall then silver or gold, called in our bookes false metall.

And if more allay be put into the money then is limited to them by the indenture between the king and them, or make it of lesse weight, it is treason, and herewith agreeth Britton, treating of treason, where he saith, *Auxy le fesors de nostre money counterfeit, ou plus de allay mys en nostre money que mister ne serra solonque le forme et usage de nostre realme,* and hereunto accordeth Fleta.

Brit. fol. 10. b. Flet. li. 1. c. 22.

What kind of coine. Regist. 135. F.N.B. 82. Stat. de 31 E. 1. de ord. mensur. lib. intrat.

The ancient currant silver was the penny: for so I find in the Register in an action of account against a receiver, the plaintife supposed the defendant to be *receptor denariorum:* and when a man wageth his law in an action of debt, the entry is, *quod non debet præfato quærenti* 4. *libras nec aliquem denarium inde.* And at the making of this statute in 28 E. 1. the peny was the currant money of England: it is called in Latine *denarius,* and very aptly to be derived *à numero denario,* as it is taken by us; *quilibet enim denarius argenti valebat* 10. *denarios æris: denarii dicti, quia denosære valebant*; *quilibet denarius puri auri valebat* 10. *denarios puri argenti.*

Denarius unde.

[576]

Penny in English cometh of the Saxon word pennyȝ.

Rot. clauf. an. 13 H. 3.

In 13 H. 3. there was found by a plowman in tilling the earth money in vessels so ancient, as it was not knowne; the record saith, *De veteri moneta ignota in doliis arando reperta, &c.*

Rot. clauf. an. 3 H. 8.

The richest king of England of treasure, that I have read of, was king Henry the seventh, who left at his death in ready mony fifty and three hundred thousand pounds, most of it in foraine coine.

37 E. 3. cap. 7. 2 H. 5. ca. 4. Sta. 2. 2 H. 6. cap. 14.

(3) *Et que nul oure, pejor argent que monie.*] The sense hereof is, that none shall gild worse silver then of the fines of sterling; for such ought the mony to be, and all silver vessell ought to be of the allay of good sterling: for the plate of England is both for the honour, and riches of the realme.

(4) *Tanque il soit assaie per les gardens del misterie.*] This is evident of itselfe.

(5) *Auxy que soit signe dun teste de leopard.*] This is observed to this day: the statute of 37 E. 3. added, that every goldsmith should have his private marke, &c. to the end it may be knowne who made it; besides the surveyors must set their marke; and then an alphabeticall letter must be also set unto it, so as it must have foure markes.

37 E. 3. cap. 7.

For these matters see the statutes of 2 H. 6. ca. 14. 17 E. 4. ca. 1. 4 H. 7. ca. 2. 18 Eliz. cap. 14.

(6) Et

(6) *Et que nul ne oure pejor ore que de touche de Paris.*] Of this ſufficient hath been ſaid before.

(7) *Et que nul ne fac' auneux, croix, ne firmeaux.*] This branch is repealed by 21 *Jacobi regis, cap.* 28. *verſus finem.*

(8) *Et nul mett' pier en ore, ſi il ne ſoit naturel.*] Counterfeit ſtones ſhould not be ſet in gold, to the end that the ſubject ſhould not be deceived thereby.

(9) *Que le droit et le ſeigniorie de la corone ſaves luy ſoient per touts.*] Here is offred juſt occaſion to ſpeake what prerogative the king hath in ſilver and gold, and firſt and principally in making of money currant within the realme.

It is ſaid by thoſe that were of councell with the king in the caſe of the mines, that it doth pertaine to the king onely to put a value to the coine, and to make the price of the quantity, and to put a print to it; which being done, the coine is currant for ſo much as the king hath limited. Before we ſpeak to this, let us ſee what our ancient authors and acts of parliament have holden and enacted concerning the monies of England *in genere*, and then ſhall we the better conceive of this opinion.

Plo. com. 316.

The Mirror treating, *Des articles per veiels roys ordeins*, ſaith thus, *Ordein fuit que nul roy de ceſt realme ne poet changer ſa money, ne impairer, ne amender, ne auter money faire, que de ore ou dargent ſans laſſent de touts ſes counties*, that is, without aſſent of parliament.

Mirror, cap. 1. § 3.

For the better underſtanding hereof, and of that which ſhall be ſaid hereafter, it is to be underſtood, *quod metallorum ſunt ſeptem ſpecies, viz. aurum, argentum, æs, ſive cuprum (ſic dictum, quia primo inventum fuit in Cypro) ſtannum, ferrum, plumbum, et aurichalchum.* Now as to the making of coine theſe metals by the law of England are ſubdivided *in metallum legale, ſive verum, et metallum illegitimum ſive falſum.* And this ſubdiviſion appeareth both by act of parliament, and by our bookes.

Eucilides, lib. 1. cap. 1. Geo. agricol. lib. 10. cap. 1.

[577]

Quicunque in emptionibus et venditionibus obulum ſeu quadrantem legalis metalli, et debitam habentem formam recuſare præſumpſerit, tanquam regiæ majeſtatis contemptor capiatur, et in carcerem detrudatur. By this act it appeareth, that no ſubject can be enforced to take in buying or ſelling, or other payment, any money made, but onely of lawfull metall, that is, of ſilver or gold, as the Mirror hath told you, and by this it is proved, that having reſpect to money, there is an unlawfull metall, and theſe be the other five.

Statutum de dimiſſione denariorum, an. 20 E. 1. Vet. Mag. Chart. fol. 167.

The mony of England is the treaſure of England, and nothing is ſaid to be treaſure trove but gold and ſilver. See the third part of the Inſtitutes, cap. *Treaſure trove.* And this is the reaſon that the law doth give to the king mines of gold and ſilver, thereof to make money, and not any other metall which a ſubject may have, becauſe thereof money cannot be made. And hereof there is great reaſon, for the value of money being the meaſure of all contracts, &c. is in effect the value of every man. And herewith agreeth the booke in 3 H. 7. *Quod ille qui facit monetam contra ordinationem, &c. allaiatam, viz. alcamino, vel alio falſo metallo, proditio eſt*, where all the ſaid five baſe metals (as to be put in coine) are deemed falſe metals. Bracton calleth money made of them *monetam reprobam, et monetam falſam.*

Pl. com. 316. the point adjudged. In nummis tria requiruntur, metallum legale, pondus, & forma. 3 H. 7 ubi ſupra. 9 E. 3 cap. 2. Glanv. lib. 14. cap. 7. Bract. lib. 3. fol. 118. Flet. lib 1. c. 22.

To omit many things that might be ſaid to the ſame intent, and to confirme this point with an act of parliament made in the 25 yeare

25 E. 3. cap. 13. 9 H. 5. stat. 2. ca. 6. See the third part of the Institutes, cap. Felony, by bringing in of certaine coine, &c.

yeare of the reigne of that wise and victorious king Edward the third, in these words: " *Item,* it is accorded, that the mony of " gold and silver which now is currant, shall not be impaired in " weight, or allay, but as soon as a good way may be found, that " the same be put in the ancient state, as in the sterling."

By this act three things are to be observed: 1. That the money of England must either be of gold or silver: 2. That the currant money of England cannot be impaired either in weight or in allay: 3. That the allay of the sterling was the ancient currant mony of England. And herewith agreeth the statute of 9 H. 5.

Rot. Parl. 17 E. 3. nu. 15.

By an act made, not in print, it is enacted, that silver shall be coined according to the old esterling in poize, and allay, to be currant amongst the subjects, and not to be carried over, on paine of death. And if the Flemings shall coine their silver accordingly, that the same be currant amongst merchants. And that the sterling mony was the ancient currant money of England. That in the

Rot. fin. an. 28 E. 1. Holl. pag. 309. a. Walf. an. 28 E. 1.

raign of E. 1. there were divers white monies called pollards, crocards, staldings, eagles, leonines, and steepings artificially made of silver, copper, and sulphur, and yet currant within the realme; and for that two pieces of those monies were but of the value of one sterling, king E. 1. by his proclamation utterly forbad the

See Matth. Paris. 31 H. 2.

same. And yet to look somewhat higher, Matth. Paris 33 H. 3. pag. *Denarius Angliæ qui nominatur sterlingus rotundus sine tonsura ponderabit 12 grana frumenti in medio spicæ, et 20 denarii faciunt unciam, et 12 unciæ faciunt libram, &c.*

Inter leges H. 1. cap. 11. de jure regis.

And yet to ascend to former times, *Hæc sunt jura quæ rex Angliæ solus et super omnes habet in terra sua, &c. viz. murdrum, falsaria monetæ suæ, incendium, hamsockna, forstall', firdinga, flemen firmæ, præmeditat' assultus, roberia, &c.*

But I will desire the studious reader to cast his eyes upon the lawes before the conquest.

Inter leges Ethelstani regis, cap. 14. & Edgari, cap. 8. & Canuti regis, cap. 8.

Si quis nummum corripuerit, ei manus scelere violata præciditor, eamque prece vel pretio redimi nefas esto, &c.

In dimensione et pondere nihil esto iniquum, ab iniquitate deinceps quisque temperat, &c.

7 E. 2. cap. 12.

And melting of the good monies of the realme, and altering the same into base coine was deemed in parliament amongst the rest of the calamities that then fell upon this realme. And that the law

[578]

is this, it is best for the king; for by the impairing of the coine of England either in weight or in allay, the king hath the greatest losse both in his owne revenues, forfeitures, and subsidies, and also in the disvaluation of his subjects: for the king can never be rich, or his kingdomes safe, when his subjects be poore, and the finenesse and goodnesse of his coine is *inter magnalia et regalia coronæ.*

25 E. 3. cap. 20.

At the aforesaid parliament of 25 Ed. 3. another excellent law was made in these words: " *Item,* it is accorded and assented, that " the moniers, and other wardens and ministers of the money shall " receive plate of gold and silver by the weight, and not by num- " ber, and in the same manner shall deliver the mony, when it " shall be made, by weight, and not by number, without delay.

Queen Elizabeth (*Angliæ amor*) finding in the beginning of her raigne some copper money, and all too much, and against law allayed, amongst many others, reformed the same, as upon her tombe in Westminster it appeareth, *Religio reformata, pax fundata, moneta ad*

ad ſuum valorem reducta, claſſis inſtructiſſima apparata, gloria navalis reſtituta, rebellio extincta, Anglia totos 40 annos prudentiſſimè adminiſtrata, ditata, et munita, Scotia à Gallis liberata, Gallia ſublevata, Belgia ſuſtentata, Hiſpania coercita, Hibernia pacata, orbiſque terrarum ſemel atque iterum circumvagatus.

Now for the kings prerogative in the mines or veines of gold and ſilver (for he hath no prerogative in any other metall) you may reade at large in the caſe of the mines. If you deſire to reade other authorities not cited there *de aurifodinis, argenti fodinis, et aliis mineris,* you may reade Bracton, Fleta, the Regiſter, and other ancient authors, records, and book-caſes. And to this you may adde a record which we lately found out.

Pl. com. in the caſe of the mines, fol. 314, &c. Bract. lib. 2. fol. 122. b. Flet. lib. 4. cap. 19. Glanvil. lib. 14. cap. 2. Mich. 33 E. 1. rot. 126. coram rege, Derby. Rot. Parl. 3 R. 2. nu. 43. Regiſt. 165. 21 E. 3. fol. 60. 27 aſſ. 19. 43 E. 3. 35, &c.

* *Patrius del Gile & xxvi. alii minetarii apud Aldeneſton implacitantur per Henr' de Whiteby, & Joannam uxorem ejus pro eo quod ſucciderunt arbores ſuas apud Aldeneſton vi & armis, & eas aſportaverunt ad valentiam lx. li. &c. Ipſi dicunt quod tenent mineram de Aldeneſton ad firmam de dom' rege, & dicunt quod talis eſt libertas mineræ prædictæ, quòd minetarii ejuſdem mineræ poſſunt capere boſcum, cujuſcunque fuerit, propinquiorem & utiliorem venæ argenteæ prædictæ mineræ, quam invenire contigerit. Et quod iidem minetarii poſſint capere pro voluntate ſua boſcum illum ad mineram illam ardendam & fundendam. Et licitum eſt eis capere boſcum illum ad ædificandum, & ardendum, & claudendum. Et quod licitum eſt eis boſcum illum dare miniſtris mineræ prædictæ pro ſtipendiis ſuis. Et etiam licitum eſt divitibus ejuſdem mineræ dare pauperibus de boſco illo ad ſuſtentationem ſuam quantum voluerint. Et dicunt, quòd, quia prædictus boſcus fuit propinquior & utilior cuidam venæ quam ipſi invenerunt, ipſi ſucciderunt boſcum prædictum ad comburendam, & fundendam mineram prædictam, & ad ædificandum, claudendum, & ad dandum pauperibus & miniſtris ejuſdem mineræ pro ſtipendiis ſuis, ſicut prædictum eſt. Dicunt etiam, quod non eſt licitum aliquibus dominis boſcorum poſtquam opī minetarii inceperint ſuccidere in boſcis illis ad mineram prædictam, ſicut prædictum eſt, aliquid de boſcis illis vendere, nec dare, niſi tantum inde capere rationabilia eſtoveria ſua. Et dicunt quòd ipſi & anteceſ. ſui, nomine domini regis in boſcis vicinis quorumcunque fuerint ad mineram tali libertate uſi ſunt à tempore quo non extat memoria, unde bene advocant quod ipſi ſucciderunt prædictum boſcum ratione ejuſdem libertatis, & non contra pacem, &c. Et Henr' & Joan' bene cognoſcunt quod licitum eſt minetariis prædictis capere de propinquioribus & utilioribus boſcis ad mineram regis ardendam & fundendam, ſet dicunt, quod, ultra neceſſaria ſufficientia ad mineram illam ardendam & fundendam, vi & armis boſcum ſuum ad valentiam xl. li. ſucciderunt, vendiderunt, et aſportaverunt, de quo nihil proficui ad mineram regis devenit, nec ad ejuſdem mineræ promotionem. Et quod ita ſit, petunt quod inquiratur; unde ſi boſcus ille et alii de partibus illis deſtruantur, & ad aliqua alia inde facienda, quam ad mineram prædictam comburend' & fundend', hoc erit ad dampnum domini regis; pet' judic' ſi minetarii prædicti ad præmiſſa quæ allegant, cum in manifeſtum dampnum domini regis redundant, admitti debeant, &c. cum deſtructis boſcis illis ceſſabit mineræ illius proficuum, &c. dies dat' eſt in tres Paſch', &c.*

* Mich. 18 E. 1. in banco rot. 139. Cumberl. Minera argent. de Aldeneſton. Libertates mineræ.

[579]

Modo reddit Oxenford lx. li. ad numerum de 20 in ora, (i.) ad numerum de xx. d. in uncia, ſic interpretatur in lib. abbatiæ de Burton in [a] *com' Staff.*

Domeſday Oxenford &c. ora Oxenford. & ibi ſæpe.

Mich. 37 H. 3. [illegible]

[a] Duæ horæ quæ valent 32. d.

* Moneta unde. Isidor. lib. 16. Ethic. cap. 17. * *Moneta appellata est, quia nos monet ne qua fraus in metallo vel pondere fiat:* [b] *Pecunia à pecudibus est appellata, sicut à juvando jumenta dicta sunt, quia in pecudibus universa antiquorum substantia constabat: antiquissimi non dum auro et argento invento,* [c] *ære utebantur, nam prius ærea pecunia in usu fuit, postea* [d] *argentea, deinde* [e] *aurea subsequuta. Sed ab ea quæ incepit nomen retinuit, unde ærarium dicitur, quòd prius æs fuit in usu. Hæc Isidorus.*

[b] Pecunia unde.
[c] Unde æs, vide Cæsars Commen.
[d] Argentea pecunia quando.
[e] Aurea quando.
[f] Nummus unde.

[f] Νόμισμα ἀπὸ τοῦ νόμου, *hoc est, â lege* ο *in* υ *commutato, quia cum antea permutatione mercium homines uti solerent lege, lege usus nummi introductus est.* Some deriveth it, *à Numa Romanorum rege, quia ipse primus imaginibus notavit, et titulo nominis sui præscripsit.* Others imagine, *quòd dicitur nummus, eò quòd nominibus effigieque signatur.*

Ferlingus unde, Stat. de 51 H. 3. Assisa panis, &c. *Panis Wastelli de Ferlingo, (i.) quadrantis, derivatur à verbo Saxonico* feorðling, *per contractionem ferling.*

Where you reade *de auri fodinis* and *argenti fodinis*, it is affirmed by merchants that have travelled for gold, that there are silver mines, that is, there is oare or soile of silver digged out of the earth, and out of that by art is silver tried, but there is no oare or soile of gold, but it is gold originally in smaller pieces as it were dust, which being washed downe to the shoare, it is found by the yellownesse of the water. And this is confirmed by Job; for he saith, *Habet argentum venarum suarum principia, et auro locus est in quo conflatur:* surely, there is a veine for the silver, and a place for gold where they finde it. And soon after, *locus sapphiri lapides ejus, et glebæ illius aurum:* the stones of it are a place of saphires, and the dust of it is gold. And yet for distinction sake it is called *aurifodina.*

Jobi, ca. 28. ver. 1. & ver. 6.

Diodorus Siculus, lib. 5. ca. 8. fol. 142. b. Polibius, lib. 3. For *stannum*, tinne, England hath of ancient time furnished other countries, both farre and neare, as you may reade in Diodorus Siculus, who lived in Augustus time. But Polibius, who wrote about two hundred yeares before him, affirmed this island to be abundantly stored with tinne; and we have taken the greater liberty herein (to delight, if we could, the reader) for that herewith we conclude this last chapter of this excellent parliament.

---

[580]

STATUTUM DE ASPORTATIS RELIGIOSORUM,

Editum Anno 35 Edw. I. *apud Carliolen.*

NUPER ad notitiam domini regis ex gravi querela magnatum, procerum, et aliorum nobilium regni (1) sui pervenit; quod cum monasteria, prioratus, et domus religiosæ (2) ad laudem et honorem Dei, et ad exultationem sanctæ ecclesiæ per regem et progenitores

OF late it came to the knowledge of our lord the king, by the grievous complaint of the honourable persons, lords, and other noblemen of his realm, that whereas monasteries, priories, and other religious houses were founded to the honour and glory of

progenitores suos, et per dictos magnates, nobiles, et eorum antecessores fundata fuissent, et terræ et tenementa quæ plurima essent data per ipsos dictis monasteriis, prioratibus, et domibus, ac viris religiosis in eisdem Deo servientibus, ut in hujusmodi monasteriis, prioratibus, et domibus religiosis, tam clerici quam laici admitterentur, secundum suarum sufficientiam facultatum; et infirmi ac debiles sustentarentur, hospitalitates, eleemosynarum largitiones, et alia pietatis opera exercerentur; et pro animabus fundatorum prædictorum, et hæredum suorum fierent in eisdem: abbates, priores, et custodes eorumdem domorum, et quidam eorum superiores alienigenæ (3), *utpote abbates, et priores Clunacen', et Præmontraten', et sanctorum Augustini et Benedicti ordinum, et cæteri qui plures alterius religionis et ordinis noviter per singula monasteria, et domos eis subjecta in Anglia, Hibernia, Scotia, et Wallia* (4) *diversa tallagia, census, et impositiones insolitas graves, et importabiles* (5), *domino regi et magnatibus suis inconsultis, fieri statuerunt, et pro suo libito ordinaverunt, contra leges et consuetudines dicti regni* (6). *Ex quo fit, ut numerus religiosorum et aliorum servitorum in hujusmodi domibus et locis religiosis per tallagia hujusmodi, census, et impositiones oppressis, minuitur cultus divinus* (7), *et eleemosynæ pauperibus, infirmis, et debilibus subtrahuntur, et salutes vivorum, et animæ mortuorum miserabiliter defraudantur: hospitalitates, eleemosynarum largitiones, ac cætera cessant opera pietatis, sicque quod olim in usus pios, et ad divini cultus augmentum charitativè fuerat erogatum, jam in censum reprobum est conversum* (8). *Unde prætereа, quæ*
[581] *prætermittentur, scandalum non modicum crescit in populo, et damna innumera, et exhæredationem fundatorum prædictorum, et hæredum suorum, procul dubio pervenisse*

of God, and the advancement of the holy church, by the king and his progenitors, and by the said noblemen and their ancestors, and a very great portion of lands and tenements have been given by them to the said monasteries, priories, and houses, and the religious men serving God in them, to the intent that clerks and laymen might be admitted in such monasteries, priories, and religious houses, according to their sufficient ability, and that sick and feeble men might be maintained, hospitality, almsgiving, and other charitable deeds might be done, and that in them prayers might be said for the souls of the said founders and their heirs; the abbots, priors, and governours of the said houses, and certain aliens their superiours, as the abbots and priors of Cestercienses, and Premonstratenses, and of the order of St. Augustine, and St. Benedict, and many more of other religion and order, have at their own pleasures set divers unwonted, heavy and importable tallages, payments, and impositions upon every of the said monasteries and houses in subjection unto them in England, Ireland, Scotland, and Wales, without the privity of our lord the king and his nobility, contrary to the laws and customs of the said realm; and thereby the number of religious persons, and other servants in the said houses and religious places being oppressed by such tallages, payments, and impositions, the service of God is diminished, alms being not given to the poor, the sick, and feeble, the healths of the living and the souls of the dead be miserably defrauded, hospitality, almsgiving, and other godly deeds do cease; and so that which in times past was charitably given to godly uses, and to the increase of the service of God, is now converted to an evil end; by permission whereof there groweth great scandal

venisse noscuntur: et adhuc verisimiliter præsumuntur pervenire, nisi tantis et tam gravibus detrimentis celeri et salubri remedio obvietur. Considerans igitur præfatus dominus rex sibi et populo suo valde fore damnosum, si tam grandes jacturas et insolentias sustineret diutius sub dissimulatione transire.

scandal to the people, and infinite losses and disheritances are like to ensue to the founders of the said houses and their heirs, unless speedy and sufficient remedy be provided to redress so many and grievous detriments. Wherefore our foresaid lord the king, considering that it would be very prejudicial to him and his people if he should any longer suffer so great losses and injuries to be winked at,

Volensque idcirco monasteria, prioratus, et alias domos religiosas, et loca in regno et terris dominio suo subjectis constituta secundùm voluntatem et pia vota fundatorum ipsorum manutenere et defendere, et contra hujusmodi oppressiones de congruo remedio providere de cætero, ut tenetur de consilio comitum, baronum, magnatum, procerum, et aliorum nobilium, et regni sui comitatum in parliamento suo (9) *apud Westmonast' die dominica proxim' post festum Sancti Matthiæ apostoli anno regni sui* 33. *habito ordinavit et statuit, ne quis abbas, prior, magister, custos, seu quivis alius religiosus, cujuscunque conditionis, aut status seu religionis exstat sub potestate et jurisdictione sua constitutus, censum aliquem per superiores* (10) *suos abbates, priores, magistros, custodes religiosarum domorum, vel locorum impositum, vel inter se ipsos aliqualiter ordinatum extra regnum et dominium suum sub nomine redditus, tallagii, apporti seu impositionis cujuscunque, vel alias nomine excambii, venditionis mutui, vel alterius contractus quocunque nomine censeatur, per se vel mercatores, aut alios clam vel palam, arte vel ingenio defer' vel transmittat, seu deferri faciat quoquo modo, nec etiam ad partes exteras se divertat causa visitationis, aut alio colore quæsito, ut sic bona monasteriorum et domorum suarum extra regnum et dominium prædictum abducat. Et si quis contra præsens statutum venire præsumpserit, considerata qualitate delicti, et regiæ prohibitionis pensato*

And therefore being willing to maintain and defend the monasteries, priories, and other religious houses erected in his kingdom, and in all lands subject to his dominion, and from henceforth to provide sufficient remedy to reform such oppressions, as he is bound by the counsel of his earls, barons, great men, and other nobles of his kingdom in his parliament holden at Westminster, in the five and thirtieth year of his reign, hath ordained and enacted, that no abbot, prior, master, warden, or other religious person, of whatsoever condition, state, or religion he be, being under the king's power or jurisdiction, shall by himself, or by merchants or others, secretly or openly, by any device or means, carry or send, or by any means cause to be sent, any tax imposed by the abbots, priors, masters or wardens of religious houses their superiors, or assessed amongst themselves, out of his kingdom and his dominion, under the name of a rent, tallage, or any kind of imposition, or otherwise by the way of exchange, mutual sale, or other contract howsoever it may be termed; neither shall depart into any other country for visitation, or upon any other colour, by that means to carry the goods of their monasteries and houses out of the kingdom and dominion aforesaid. And if any will presume to offend this present statute, he shall be grievously punished according to the quality of his offence, and

pensato contemptu, graviter puniatur (11).

Praeterea inhibet praefatus dominus rex omnibus et singulis abbatibus, prioribus, magistris, et custodibus religiosarum domorum et locorum, alienigenis quorum potestati, subjectioni, et obedientiae domus eorumden ordinum in regno et dominio suo existentes, subdunt', ne de caetero tallagia (12), *census, impositiones, apporta, seu alia quaecunque onera aliquibus*
[582] *monasteriis, prioratibus, seu aliis domibus religiosis eis (ut praedicitur) sic subjectis imponant, seu faciant aliqualiter assidere, et hoc sub foris factura omnium, quae in potestate sua obtinent, et foris facere poterunt in futurum* (13).

Et insuper ordinavit dominus rex et statuit, quod abbates Cisterc', et Praem' ordinum (14) *aliorum religiosorum, quorum sigillum in custod' abbatis, et non conventus, prius residere tantummodo consuevit, de caetero habeant sigillum commune, et illud in custod' prioris monasterii seu domus et quatuor de dignioribus, et discretioribus ejusdem loci conventus, sub privato sigillo abbatis ipsius loci custod' deponend'. Ita quod abbas, seu prior domus cui praeest, per se contra aliquem seu oblig' nullatenus possit firmar', sicut hactenus fieri consuevit. Et si forsan aliqua scripta oblig' donationum, emptionum, venditionum, alienationum, seu aliorum quorumcunque contract' alio sigillo, quam tali sigillo communi, sicut praemittitur custodito, inveniantur à modo sigillata, pro nullis penitus habeantur, omnique careant firmitate. Caeterum intentionis domini regis non existit* (15) *abbates, priores, et alios religiosos alienigenas per ordinationes et statuta expressa superius ab officio visitationis in regno et in dominio suo exercendo excludere, quin per se ipsos vel alios, monasteria et alia loca eis in regno et in dominio suis praedictis subjecta, juxta officii sui debitum in his duntaxat*

and according to his contempt of the king's prohibition.

Moreover, our foresaid lord the king doth inhibit all and singular abbots, priors, masters and governors of religious houses and places, being aliens, to whose authority, subjection, and obedience the houses of the same orders in his kingdom and dominion be subject, that they do not at any time hereafter impose, or by any means assess any tallages, payments, charges, or other burdens whatsoever, upon the monasteries, priories, or other religious houses in subjection unto them (as is aforesaid) and that upon pain of all that they have or may forfeit.

And further, our lord the king hath ordained and established, that the abbots of the orders of Cestercienses and Premonstracenses, and other religious orders, whose seal hath heretofore been used to remain only in the custody of the abbot, and not of the covent, shall hereafter have a common seal, and that shall remain in the custody of the prior of the monastery or house, and four of the most worthy and discreet men of the covent of the same house, to be laid up in safe keeping under the private seal of the abbot of the same house; so that the abbot or prior, which doth govern the house, shall be able of himself to establish nothing, though heretofore it hath been otherwise used. And if it fortune hereafter, that writings of obligations, donations, purchases, sales, alienations, or of any other contracts, be sealed with any other seal than such a common seal, kept as is aforesaid, they shall be adjudged void and of no force in law. But it is not the meaning of our lord the king to exclude the abbots, priors, and other religious aliens, by the ordinances and statutes aforesaid, from executing their office of visitation in his

duntaxat quæ ad observantiam regularem, et ordinis sui disciplinam pertinent, libere valeant visitare. Proviso quod illi qui officium hujusmodi visitationis exercuerint, nihil de bonis aut rebus hujusmodi monasteriorum, prioratuum, et domorum extra præfatum regnum et dominium, præter rationabiles et moderatas eorum expensas, deferant, vel deferri procurant.

his kingdom and dominion; but they may visit at their pleasures, by themselves or others, the monasteries and other places in his kingdom and dominion in subjection unto them, according to the duty of their office, in those things only that belong to regular observation, and the discipline of their order. Provided, that they which shall execute this office of visitation, shall carry, or cause to be carried out of his kingdom and dominion, none of the goods or things of such monasteries, priories, and houses, saving only their reasonable and competent charges.

Et licet ordinationum et statutorum præscriptorum pronunciatio et publicatio à parliamento proximo præterito (16) *usq; ad præsens parliamentum apud Carliolum in octabis Sancti Hilarii, anno regni ejusdem regis Edwardi* 35. *certis ex causis, et ut cum majore deliberatione et maturitate procederent* (17), *remanserit in suspenso, dominus rex post deliberationem plenariam et tractatum cum comitibus, baronibus, proceribus, et aliis nobilibus et comitibus regni sui habitum in præmissis, de consensu eorum unanimi et concordi ordinavit et statuit, ut ordinationes et statuta prædicta* [583] *sub forma modis et conditionibus supra contentis à primo die Maii prox' futur' in antea inviolabiliter observentur perpetuis temporibus valitura: quodque transgressores ipsorum pœnis extunc subjaceant annotatis.*

And though the publication and open notice of the ordinances and statutes aforesaid was stayed in suspence for certain causes sithence the last parliament, until this present parliament holden at Carlisle in the octaves of Saint Hilary, in the five and thirtieth year of the reign of the same king Edward, to the intent they might proceed with greater deliberation and advice; our lord the king, after full conference and debate had with his earls, barons, nobles, and other great men of his kingdom, touching the premisses, by their whole consent and agreement hath ordained and enacted, that the ordinances and statutes aforesaid, under the manner, form, and conditions aforesaid, from the first day of May next ensuing, shall be inviolably observed for ever, and the offenders of them shall be punished as is aforesaid.

(25 Ed. 3. stat. 6. Hob. 148. 3 Bulstr. 45. 5 Ed. 3. c. 3. 4 Ed. 3. c. 6. 8 Rep. 118.)

The reason wherefore this parliament was holden at Carlisle, appeareth by the writ of parliament directed to the lords, *viz. Quia super ordinationem et stabilimentum terræ nostræ Scotiæ, necnon et aliis negotiis nos, et statum regni nostri specialiter tangentibus, apud Carliolum in octab' sancti Hillarii proxim' futur' parliamentum tenere, &c.*

There were two mischiefes before the making of this act, but both of them tended to one end, *viz.* the grievous oppression of churches

churches and monasteries; the one from the pope, the other mentioned in the preamble.

For the first, *In hoc parliamento per majores graves depositæ fuerunt querimoniæ de oppressionibus ecclesiarum, et monasteriorum multiplicibus, et extortionibus pecuniarum per clericum domini papæ, magistrum Wil' testa noviter in regno inductum: præceptum est eidem clerico de assensu comitum et baronum, ne de cætero talia exequatur*; for the king and the lords adjudged it unjust, that the pope should take any profit of the houses of their foundation: and therefore this act dealeth not herewith, but the lords prohibited his collector, and left the party grieved to his remedy by prohibition, or other remedy by law, as had been before, and after was used, as by the records and authorities quoted in the margent (amongst many others) which are worthy your reading, more at large appeareth: and so much for that first mischiefe. The other mischiefe appeareth at large in the preamble, wherein the pope, having so great power over the abbots and priors aliens, had a hand for his owne benefit.

Rot. claus. 17 H. 3. m. 37. Rot. Franc' 16 H. 3. Rex, &c. Justic' suis de banco. 29 H. 3. tit. 3. à tergo. 39 E. 3. tit. 22. à tergo. 48 E. 3. tit. 33. Bract. lib. 4. fol. 250. b. Rot. Parl. 50 E. 3. nu. 64, &c. to the 117. 51 E. 3. nu. 78. Rot. Parl. 13 R. 2. nu. 43. 2 H. 2. fol. 10, &c. 4 H. 4. rot. claus. m. 11. * Rot. Parl. 17 E. 3. nu. 59.

* The commons complaine against provisions coming from Rome, whereby strangers were enabled within this realme to enjoy ecclesiasticall dignities, &c. by meanes whereof daily almes was decayed, the treasure of the realm transported, the secrets of the realme discovered, and the clerkes within the realm impoverished; and that the pope had in most covert wise granted to two new cardinals sundry ecclesiasticall livings within the realm, and namely, to cardinall Paragots above 10,000 marks yearly taxe: they therefore require of the king and lords some remedy, for that they neither could, nor would any longer beare those strange oppressions, or else to help them to expell out of this realm the popes power by force. The answer of the king was, that he understood well these mischiefes, and willeth, that between the lords and commons some remedy might be found, whereunto he might assent: hereupon the lords and commons sent for this act of 35 E. 1. upon the like complaint, thereby forbidding, that any thing should be attempted, or brought into the realme, which should tend to the blemishment of the kings prerogative, or in prejudice of his lords or commons, and so at that time, upon consideration had of this act of 35 E. 1. and for further remedy, an act of provision was made.

Also the statute of 25 E. 3. made against provisions, reservations, &c. reciteth this statute of 35 E. 1. and grounded that act upon the same. So as this act (as you may perceive) hath been of very great and high account. And now let us peruse the words thereof.

25 E. 3. stat. unic. * 25 E. 3. de provisor' per l'assent des counts, barons, & auters nobles. 9 E. 3. cap. 2. 27 E. 3. stat. stap. per les prelates, counts, barons, & auters grandees des counties, &c. Vid. 9 E. 2. stat. of shrieves. 7 E. 1. de Religiosis. W. 2. in the preamble.

(1) *Ex gravi querela magnatum, procerum, et aliorum nobilium regni.*] It is recited by the said act of 25 E. 3. that this act of 35 E. 1. was made at the petition of the comminalty of the realme, and here it is said, *ex gravi querela magnatum, &c.* and yet both stand well together; for knights of the shire, and other gentlemen of the house of commons are included under these words, *aliorum* * *nobilium*: for *nobilitas est duplex, superior et inferior*; *superior* belongeth to the lords of parliament, and *inferior* to knights and gentlemen of name and bloud, who are in this act termed *nobiles*.

(2) † *Quod cum monasteria, prioratus, et domus religiosæ, &c.*] Here is rehearsed the end of the erection of religious houses, *viz. ad laudem et honorem Dei, et exaltationem sanctæ ecclesiæ per regem, et progenitores*

† [584]

genitores suos, et per dictos magnates, et nobiles, et eorum antecessores fundata fuissent, &c.

4 R. 2. nu. 13.

(3) *Quidam eorum superiores alienigenæ.*] It appeareth in a parliament roll, that the clergy, (whereof priors aliens were part) had a third part of the possessions of the realme. These abbots, priors, and prioresses aliens were justly complained of, as by this act appeareth, and many times upon like complaints faire promises were made for reformation, but no amendment could be had, till they were taken away, and their possessions given to the king by act of parliament. See the parliament rolls of 4 H. 4. and 1 H. 5.

Rot. Parl. 1 R. 2. nu. & 13 R. 2. nu. 19. rot. parl. an. 4 H. 4. nu. 23. & 48. 1 H. 5. cap. 7. & Rot. Parl. 1 H. 5. nu. 38. 22 E. 4. 44. 38 H. 6. 34. 21 H. 7. fol. 1. &c. 13 E. 3. 264. 14 E. 3. 21. 20 E. 3. annuity 24. 40 E. 3. 10. 27 ass. 48. 14 H. 4. 37. 22 E. 4. 44. 21 H. 7. 7. 7 R. 2. cap. 12. 13 R. 2. cap. 1 H. 5. ca. 7.

Note, these priors, and prioresses aliens were Normans, and French men, and in time of warre with France, the king by the common law might and did seise the possessions of the priors aliens within this realm into his hands, without any office, &c. See the statutes of 7 R. 2. 13 R. 2. 1 H. 5. against Frenchmen and aliens, to receive or have any benefice in England.

(4) *In Anglia, Hibernia, Scotia, et Wallia.*] For Scotland, &c. see divers records and authorities in law, Rot. Parl. Pasch. 21 E. 1. rot. 1. & rot. 2. *magnum placitum inter regem de Norwey, et regem Scotiæ.* Rot. Vasc. 22 E. 1. m. 23. Trin' 25 E. 1. coram rege, rot. 6. Norff. Robertus de Tony, &c. Mich. 33 E. 1. coram rege, rot. 127. Scotia. 28 E. 1. the letters of all the nobility of England in the name of themselves, and of the whole comminalty in parliament assembled to the pope, a duplicat whereof under the seales remaine in the exchequer, which we have seen, and a copy whereof we have. In the same yeare reade also the kings letters to the pope, which Walsingham rehearseth, pag. 49. and the lords letters, pag. 54. Reade also Walsing. pag. 17. &c. where many more authors be cited, and pag. 31, 32. 121. 138. & Matth. Westm' pag. 420. 428. 443. 452, &c. Holl. fol. 116, 117. Policron. lib. 7. cap. 39. Stow, 303. Fox, 269. 341. Rot. Parl. 14 E. 3. nu. 13. Stat. 2. & 42 E. 3. nu. 7. See in the parliament rolls, in every parliament *petitiones Scotiæ.* Rot. pat. 10 E. 3. 2. part comes Arundel, &c. Brit. fol. 25. a. b. 6 E. 3. 18. 1 E. 3. 17. per Cant' 8 R. 2. cont'. claim 13. 7 H. 4. corody 7. 13 H. 4. 4. & 5. 8 H. 5. 4. 7 E. 4. 27. Fortescue, fol. 17. Pl. com. 126. Dier, 13 El. in manuscript.

(5) *Diversa tallagia, census, et impositiones insolitas, graves et importabiles, &c.*] See the exposition upon the statute of Magna Charta, cap. 30. when the king began to use the word of imposition; but here is the first statute that we remember, wherein this word imposition was used; and observe well from whom it came; and therefore here these impositions be called *insolitæ*, and this word *noviter, &c.* expresseth so much; and because they were unaccustomed and newly imposed, they were *graves* and *importabiles*, and against the lawes and customes of the realme.

12 H. 7. cap. 6. accord.

(6) *Contra leges et consuetudines dicti regni.*] Here it appeareth, that tallages, assessements, or impositions, set by any superiour, foreiner, or other, ecclesiasticall or temporall, upon his inferiour, or any other, though they have never so faire pretexts, as to recover the holy land, &c. are against the law and custome of the kingdome of England.

Rot. parl. 17 E. 3. ubi supra. nu. 59.

And here it is to be observed, how this act hath since the 17 yeare of E. 3. been dealt withall; for at that yeare a branch of this statute was recited, that forbad that any thing should be attempted or brought

brought into the realme, which should tend to the blemishment of the kings prerogative, or in prejudice of his lords and commons, which now is wholly omitted,

> *Accipe nunc horum insidias, et crimine ab uno*
> *Disce omnes*———

(7) *Minuitur cultus divinus*, &c.] That acts of parliament have been made at the petition sometime of the nobles, many times of the commons, and of the lords and commons in causes ecclesiasticall for the honour of God, for advancement of divine worship, for the instruction of Gods people, and maintenance of workes of piety, and the like, appeareth in this act, and in many other acts of parliament: for *reges qui serviunt Christo, faciunt leges pro Christo*. To omit the ancient statutes made in parliament before the conquest of master Lamberts edition, we will recite some few which shall suffice in a matter so frequent and evident, W. 2. 13 E. 1. cap. 43. 21 E. 3. fol. 60. the bishop of Norwich his case, 25 E. 3. cap. 22. 25 E. 3. *stat. de provisoribus*, 27 E. 3. cap. 1. 36 E. 3. cap. 8. 38 E. 3. stat. 2. cap. 1. & cap. 4. 45 E. 3. cap. 3. Rot. parl. 51 E. 3. nu. 13. 3 R. 2. ca. 3. 7 R. 2. cap. 12. 12 R. 2. ca. 15. 13 R. 2. stat. 2. cap. 2. & 3. 16 R. 2. cap. 5. 2 H. 4. cap. 3. & 4. 4 H. 4. cap. 12. & 13. 6 H. 4. cap. 1. 7 H. 4. cap. 6. & 8. 9 H. 4. cap. 8. 1 H. 5. cap. 5. 3 H. 5. cap. 4. 2 H. 5. cap. 3. 2 H. 5. stat. 2. ca. 2. 4 H. 5. ca. 6. 3 H. 7. cap. 6. 11 H. 7. cap. 8. and generally, all statutes that take away priviledge and benefit of clergy and sanctuary. [585]

(8) *Sic quod olim in usus pios, et ad divini cultus augmentum charitativè fuerat erogatum, nunc in censum reprobum est conversum.*] If it be observed of whom they are spoken, these words are sharp and bitter: for, as a reprobate is *abjectus et creatus diabolo*, so a reprobate sense is an abject and damned sense, and the like is frequent in parliaments, when any thing is attempted or done against the honour of God, the prerogative and dignity of the king, the lawes of the realme or the common-wealth.

Lib. 11. f. 73. b. Magd. Coll. case.

* The pope, for divers usurpations, is called the common enemy to the king and the realme.

[a] By brocage and unlawfull meanes the pope receiveth so much of ecclesiasticall dignities in this realme, as is more then the kings warres, who then was, and of long time had been in an open and chargeable warre with France.

[b] Note, in the roll of parliament of the statute of provisors, there are more sharp and biting words against the pope, then in the print, a mysterie often in use, but not to be knowne of all men.

[c] That the brocars of the sinfull city of Rome for money promote many caitifes, being altogether unlearned, and unworthy, to a thousand markes livings yearly, where the learned and worthy can hardly obtaine twenty markes, whereby learning decayeth.

Rot. Parl. * 18 E. 3. stat. 1. nu. 38. Vid. 17 E. 3. nu. 59. [a] 25 E. 3. nu. 13. [b] 38 E. 3. ca. 1, 2, 3, 4. [c] Rot. parl. 50 E. 3. nu. 96. Rot. parl. 18 E. 3. nu. 32. stat. 2. Rot. parl. 51 E. 3. nu. 13. 3 R. 2. c. 3. & Rot. parl. nu. 37. 6 H. 4. c. 1. of the horrible mischiefes and damnable customes introduct of new into the court of Rome, &c. 3 H. 5. nu. 11.

(9) *De concilio comitum, baronum, magnatum, procerum, et aliorum nobilium, et regni sui comitatuum in parliamento suo*, &c.] Here the prelates are omitted, and this statute was made by the king, the nobles, and the comminalty; and it is objected, that therefore this is no act of parliament, and for authority of the roll of parliament in 21 R. 2. is cited, where it is said, that divers judgements were heretofore undone, for that the clergy were not present. To this some have

have anſwered, that a parliament may be holden by the king, the nobles, and commons; and never call the prelates to it: but we hold the contrary to both theſe, and ſhall make it manifeſt by records of parliament, wherein for the better underſtanding hereof, we will obſerve this order: firſt, that the biſhops ought to be called to parliament: ſecondly, where acts of parliament are good without them: and laſtly, that this act of 35 E. 1. is an act of parliament.

To the firſt, every biſhop hath a barony, in reſpect whereof, *ſecundum legem et conſuetudinem parliamenti*, he ought to be ſummoned to the parliament as well as any of the nobles of the realme: and likewiſe 26 abbots, and two priors had baronies, and thereby were [586] alſo lords of parliament; and when the monaſteries were diſſolved, the lords houſe loſt ſo many members that had voices in parliament. But ſeeing it was done by authority of parliament, it was no impeachment to the proceedings in parliament.

To the ſecond, if they voluntarily abſent themſelves, then may the king, the nobles and commons make an act of parliament without them, as where any offender is to be attainted of high treaſon, or felony, and the biſhops abſent themſelves, and the act proceed, the act is good and perfect.

Likewiſe if they be preſent, and refuſe to give any voices, and the act proceed, the act of parliament is good without them.

Alſo where the voices in parliament ought to be abſolute, either in the affirmative or negative, and they give their voices with limitation or condition, and the act proceeds, the act is good; for their conditionall voices are no voices.

Of every of theſe we will produce examples out of the records and rolls of parliament.

Dorſ clauſ. an. 15 E. 2. m. 25.

See Vet. Magn. Chart. 2. part fol. 56.

At a parliament holden *à die nativitatis Sancti Johannis Baptiſtæ, in 3 ſeptimanas anno* 15 E. 2. the prelates, countes, barons, and commons of the realme charge Sir Hugh Spencer the father earle of Wincheſter, and Hugh his ſonne earle of Gloceſter with many high and hainous offences, as the act called *exilium Hugonis Leſpencer patris et filii*; the earles and barons, peeres of the realme, in the preſence of the king pronounce judgement againſt them, as by the act appeareth: and after at a parliament holden at York, *à die Paſch' in 3 ſeptimanas*, the ſaid judgement and attainder againſt them (by the kings exorbitant favour towards them, whoſe favourites they were) was adnulled; and one of the cauſes was, for that the ſaid judgement was given without the prelates, whereas the ſame being an act of parliament, and entered into the parliament roll, as other acts at that parliament were, and the conſent of the biſhops doth manifeſtly appeare, for that they were parties to the charge, and after it was adjudged by authority of parliament, that the ſaid judgement againſt them was good, and confirmed the ſame; ſo as they that beheld but on the outſide of the adnullation, and looked not into all parts of the former act, and knew not the act of 1 E. 3. might ſay, as the commons ſaid, as is aforeſaid, in 21 R. 2.

Dorſ. clauſ. 15 E. 2. m. 13. in ſchedula.

1 E. 3. ca. 1.

5 R. 2. ſtat. 2. c 3. ſee the ſtatute at large.

At the parliament holden in the third yeare of king Richard the ſecond, a bill was exhibited againſt the clergy with many bitter words, for the ill diſpoſing of the dignities, offices, parſonages, canonries, prebends, and other benefices, whereof they were patrons, and were in their gift, whereof many inconveniences followed; the biſhops and other prelates taking great offence at this bill, ab-

ſented

sented themselves, whereupon the king, upon the complaint of his commons, by the advice and common assent of all the lords temporall, passed the bill.

In the same parliament great complaint was made of the extortions committed by the bishops and their officers; and thereupon a bill was framed, that justices of peace might enquire thereof, and a forme of a commission desired to be enacted; the prelates and clergy made their protestation expresly against the said bill to heare extortions, &c. tending to the blemishing of the liberty of the church, &c. whereunto it was replyed for the king, that neither for their said protestation, nor other words in their behalfe, the king would not stay to grant to his justices in that case, and all other cases, as was used to be done in times past, and was bound to doe by vertue of his oath done at his coronation, whereupon the act and forme of a commission passed as was desired. Rot. parl. 3. R. 2. nu. 38. & 40. See 7 R. 2. c. 12.

At the parliament holden in the 11 yeare of Richard the second, in the beginning of the parliament holden in that yeare, the archbishop of Canterbury made openly in the parliament a solemne protestation for himselfe, and the whole clergy of his province, which he desired might be entred, and so it was: the effect whereof was, that albeit they might lawfully be present in all parliaments, yet for that in this parliament matters of treason were to be entreated of, whereat by the canonicall law they ought not to be present; they therefore absented themselves, saving their liberties therein otherwise: the like protestation did the bishop of Duresme and Carlisle make. At which parliaments divers statutes were made, nothing concerning life or member, as the 7 chapter concerning merchants, the 8 chapter touching annuities, the 9 chapter against new impositions, the 11 concerning keeping of assises, &c. all which were good and perfect statutes, and yet the prelates assented not to them. Rot. parl. 11 R. 2. nu. 9, 10. [587]

At the parliament holden in the 13 yeare of Richard the second, when the two bill were read, the one intitled a confirmation of the statute of provisors, and the forfeiture of him that accepteth a benefice against that statute; the other intitled the penalty of him that bringeth in a sommons or sentence of excommunication of the pope against any person upon the statute of provisors, and of a prelate executing it, both which bills tended to restraine the popes authority, which he claimed in disposing of ecclesiasticall promotions within this realme. The archbishops of Canterbury and Yorke for the whole clergy of their provinces made their solemn protestations in open parliament, that they in no wise meant or would assent to any statute or law in restraint of the popes authority, but utterly withstood the same, the which their protestations at their requests were inrolled, and yet both bills passed by the king, lords, and commons, which are in print. 13 R. 2. ca. 2. 13 R. 2. ca. 3. Vid. 1 H. 5. c. 7. Rot. Parl. 13 R. 2. nu. 24.

See the statute of 16 R. 2. and many others. 16 R. 2. ca. 5.

It is enacted by the king, lords temporall, and commons, that no man should contract or marry himselfe to any queen of England, without the speciall licence and assent of the king, on paine to lose all his goods and lands. Rot. Parliament. 6 H. 6. nu. 27.

The bishops and clergy being present, assented to this bill, as farre forth as the same swerved not from the law of God, and of the church, and so as the same imported no deadly sinne, this was holden no assent; and therefore it was enacted by the king,

king, lords temporall, and commons, and ſo ſpecially entred, omitting the prelates.

And thus much as concerning the ſecond article ſhall ſuffice.

Rot. Patent. 7 E. 2. 1. part m. 6. 4 E. 3. c. 6. 5 E. 3. ca. 3. 25 E. 3. ſtat. unic. and by the record of parliament in 17 E. 3. ubi ſupra. 20 E. 3. Abb. 14. 27 H. 6. annuitie 41.

As to the third point, when an act is ſpecially entred, that it was enacted by the king, the lords temporall, and commons, it muſt be intended, that the biſhops abſented themſelves, or if they were preſent, proteſted againſt it, or gave ſuch voices as were *contra legem et conſuetudinem parliamenti*. And for this act of 35 E. 1. in letters patents made within 8 yeares after this ſtatute, it is affirmed to be an act of parliament; by foure acts of parliament in the 4 and 5 and 25 yeare of E. 3. the ſame is holden for an act of parliament, and ſo it is in 13 R. 2. cap. 2. ſtat. 2.

(10) *Cenſum aliquem per ſuperiores*, &c.] This branch is plaine, and needeth no expoſition.

(11) *Conſiderata qualitate delicti, et regiæ prohibitionis penſato contemptu, graviter puniatur.*] That is, by fine and impriſonment, according to the quality of the offence.

(12) *Ne de cætero tallagia*, &c.] Hereby are all ſuch tallages forbidden.

Vid. ſtat. de moneta mag. ca. 3. Vet. Mag. Chart. fo. 38. 20 E. 3. cap. 1.

(13) *Et hoc ſub forisfactura omnium, quæ in poteſtate ſua obtinent, et forisfacere poterunt in futuro.*] This is the like forfeiture as is given by other ſtatutes in caſe of *præmunire*, *viz.* the forfeiture of his lands, which he may forfeit, and of his goods, and to be impriſoned at the will of the king.

[588]

27 H. 6. annuitie 41. Lib. 8. fo. 118. Doct. Bonhams caſe.

(14) *Quod abbates Ciſterc' et Præmonſtr' ordinum*, &c.] This branch (as it hath been reſolved) is impoſſible, and inconvenient to be obſerved: impoſſible, becauſe it is hereby enacted that the common ſeale, &c. ſhould be in the cuſtody of the prior, and of foure of the worthieſt and diſcreeteſt of the covent, ſealed up with the private ſeale of the abbot, &c. and if any writing, &c. ſhould be ſealed with any other ſeale then with the ſaid common ſeale ſo (as is aforeſaid) kept in cuſtody, it ſhould be void, &c. for if it be kept in cuſtody under the ſeale of the abbot, then no writing can be ſealed by the abbot, and if the abbot taketh it out, and ſeale, &c. then is it not kept in cuſtody under his private ſeale; and therefore it was reſolved by the whole court of the common pleas, that this branch, being impoſſible to be obſerved, is void; the court alſo reſolved, that it was inconvenient: for they ſaid, that if the ſtatute ſhould be obſerved, every deed that paſſed under the common ſeale might be undone by a ſimple ſurmiſe, &c.

Bract. li. 1. ca.

Bracton ſaith, that *lex eſt ſanctio juſta, jubens honeſta, et prohibens contraria*; ſo as every law muſt have three qualities: 1. it muſt be *juſta*: 2. *jubens honeſta*: 3. *prohibens contraria*. And if it be *juſta*, it muſt have five properties: 1. it muſt be *poſſibilis*, 2. *neceſſaria*, 3. *conveniens*, 4. *manifeſta*, 5. *nullo privato commodo, ſed communi utilitati edita*. And this is grounded upon holy writ, *Legum conditores juſta decernunt. Væ qui condunt leges iniquas, et ſcribentes injuſtitiam ſcripſerunt.*

Prov. ca. 8. ver. 15. Eſa. c. 10. ver. 1.

(15) *Cæterum intentio domini regis non exiſtit*, &c.] By this branch the power of viſitation is reſerved with three reſtrictions or limitations: 1. *juxta officii ſui debitum*, 2. *in his duntaxat, quæ ad obſervantiam regularem, et ordinis ſui diſciplinam pertinent*: 3. *proviſo quod, &c. nihil, &c. extra præfatum regnum, &c. deferant.*

(16) *Et licet ordinationum et ſtatutorum, &c. à parliamento proxim' præterito.*] That is, at a parliament holden at Weſtminſter, *die*

die dominica prox' poft feftum Sancti Mathæi apoftoli, in the 33 yeare of E. 1.

(17) *Cum majore deliberatione et maturitate procederent.*] According to the ancient rule, *deliberandum eft diu, quod ftatuendum eft femel.*

STATUTUM DE FRANGENTIBUS PRISONAM.

Editum anno 1 Edw. II.

[589]

DE prifonariis prifonam frangentibus, dominus rex vult et præcipit, quod nullus de cætero, qui prifonam fregerit (1), *fubeat judicium vitæ vel membrorum* (2) *pro fractione prifonæ tantum, nifi caufa* (3), *pro qua captus et imprifonatus fuerit, tale judicium requirat, fi de illa fecundum legem et confuetudinem terræ fuiffet convictus, licet temporibus præteritis aliter fieri confuevit.*

CONCERNING prifoners which break prifon, our lord the king willeth and commandeth, that none from henceforth that breaketh prifon fhall have judgement of life or member for breaking of prifon only, except the caufe for which he was taken and imprifoned did require fuch judgement, if he had been convict thereupon according to the law and cuftom of the realm, albeit in times paft it hath been ufed otherwife.

(3 Inft. 69, 70. Kel. 87. Fitz. Coron. 134.)

At a parliament holden at Weftminfter *in cro' affumptionis beatæ Mariæ, anno regni* E. 1. 23. the like act of parliament was made with the like title as this is, *totidem verbis*; and therefore it may be, that it was recited and affirmed at the parliament holden in 1 Ed. 2. which onely is mentioned in our printed bookes.

Inter placita & mem. coram domino rege, anno 23 E. 1.

It appeareth by our ancient authors of the law, that if a prifoner, whatfoever the caufe was for which he was committed, had broken the kings prifon, and efcaped out, it was felony; becaufe, *intereft reip. ut carceres fint in tuto:* but yet it muft have been an actuall breaking of the prifon; for if the doore had been open, and he had gone out, or if others without his privity had broken open the prifon doore, &c. and he goeth out, and efcapeth, or if the gaoler himfelfe had let him out; in thefe cafes it had been no felony, becaufe the prifoners did not actually breake the prifon. And fo it is of a felon that is under cuftody of the kings officer (which is an imprifonment in law) and divers men doe refcue or take him by force out of the cuftody of the kings officer, this is felony in them all by the common law. And fo doth Huffey chiefe juftice report the cafe, that in the raigne of Ed. 4. when he was attorney, it was refolved by Billing chiefe juftice, Choke, and the judges, that the refcous of a felon, to take him out of cuftody and prifon, was alwaies felony

Bract. li. 2. fol. Brit. fol. 17. Flet. li. 1. c. 26. Stanf. pl. cor. 30. b.

1 H. 7. fo. 6. a.

by the common law, but of the prisoner himselfe it was not, &c. which must of necessity be intended, when other men did rescue him, or brake open the prison without his privity, and these words in the report *(tanque lestatute fuit fait de frangentibus prisonam)* ought to be omitted.

Mirr. ca. 5. § 1.

Forasmuch as every man desireth to be at naturall liberty, the Mirror complaines of the common law in this point, and saith, *abusion est a tener escape de prisoner, ou de bruserie del gaole pur peche mortell, car cel usage nest garrant per nul ley, ne in nul part est use forsque in cest realme, et en France, cins est leu garrantie de ceo faire per la ley de nature. Hoc ille.*

[a] 1. ass. p. 6. 1 E. 3. 17. 3 E. 3. coro. 312. 22 E. 3. ib. 251. [b] 11 E. 2. det. 172. 13 E. 3. barr. 153. 27 ass. 27. 8 H. 4. 18. 20 E. 4. 5. Brit. 72. 5 H. 4. cap. 10. * 22 E. 3. coron. 250. 8 E. 2. ibid. 419. 23 H. 8. ca. 11. 1 E. 6. c. 12.

(1) *Nullus de cætero qui prisonam fregerit.*] *Nota,* [a] he that is in the stockes, or under lawfull arrest, is said to be in prison, although he be not *infra parietes carceris:* and therefore this branch extendeth as well to a prison in law, as to a prison in deed. [b] Albeit divers lords of liberties have custody of the prisons, and some in fee, yet the prison it selfe is the kings *pro bono publico:* and therefore it is to be repaired at the common charge: for no subject can have the prison it selfe, but the king only: and therefore Britton, *ubi supra,* speaking of the kings prison, doth include all prisons. * For that which was called the bishops † prison, see the statutes of 23 H. 8. and 1 E. 6. This *(fregerit)* is intended an actuall breaking of prison as hath been said.

† [590]

1. ass. p. 6. 3 E. 3. coron. 333. Fitz. Justice of Peace, fol. 23.

If the sherife have a *capias* upon an inditement of felony against A. and coming to arrest him, is so disturbed, that he cannot arrest him, this is no felony; for A. was never in prison: and therefore prison in that case could not be broken.

15 H. 7. 1, 2. Pl. com. fo. 13.

In some cases it is lawfull for the prisoner to break prison both at the common law, and notwithstanding this statute: as if the prison be set on fire, either by lightning or otherwise, unlesse it be by the privity of the prisoner, he may break prison for safeguard of his life. *Et sic in similibus.* For, *quodcunque aliquis ob tutelam corporis sui fecerit, jure id fecisse videtur.* But it must be, *inevitabilis necessitas.*

1 H. 6. 5. 9 E. 4. 26. See W. 2. ca. 34. Rot. parl. an. 2 H. 6. nu. 60. Vid. 14. El. ca. 2.

(2) *Subeat judicium vitæ vel membrorum.*] These words at the making of this act extended as well to treason as to felony. In 2 H. 6. it was enacted to continue till the next parliament, that if any be indited, appealed, or taken for suspicion of high treason, and breake the same prison, it should be high treason. And the reason of that act was, because that by the statute of 25 Ed. 3. *de proditionibus,* no other offence then is therein mentioned can be adjudged high treason, untill it be declared by act of parliament; and therefore that act of parliament being in the negative, if a man be indited or appealed for high treason, and breake the prison, this breaking of prison is not high treason, till it be so declared by parliament because such offence is not mentioned in the act of 25 E. 3. and therefore according to the act of 25 E. 3. it is so declared by the act of 2 H. 6. And yet the resolution of the judges in 1 H. 6. is good law: for there the case is, that a man outlawed of felony was in prison in the kings bench, in which prison he knew that certaine persons were there committed for high treason, and brake prison, and carried and led out the prisoners that were there in gaole for treason; and seeing there be no accessaries in high treason, this was an abetting and aiding of them for their escape, he knowing them to be imprisoned for high treason; and thereof he was indited, and arraigned,

Rot. parl. 2 H. 6. nu. 18. Sir John Mortimers case declared in parliament to be treason. 2 H. 6. ca. ult. in print. Stanf. pl. coron. 32. f.

arraigned, and pleaded not guilty, and was found guilty. And it was adjudged by all the justices, that hee was a traitor, and was drawne and hanged, which are the words of the booke. And the principall end of this case was to prove, that a man attainted of felony might be indited, arraigned, tried, and adjudged for high treason, for the benefit of the king, and the odiousnesse of the offence, and the scope and end of the case is ever to be observed; for in that case it must be also intended, that the treason was committed before the felony. And it is to be remembred, that the statute of 1. Mar. doth not onely repeale all treasons, but all declarations of treason made by any act of parliament, since the said act of 25 E. 3. A man imprisoned for petit larceny, or for killing of a man, *se defendendo*, or by misfortune, and breake prison, it is no felony, because he shall not for the first offence *subire judicium vitæ vel membri. Et sic de similibus.*

Vid. Stanf. pl. coron. 107. b.

1. Mar. the first statute.

(3) *Nisi causa,* &c.] This act speaking of a cause, is to be intended of a lawfull cause; and therefore false imprisonment is not within this act,

Imprisonment is a restraint of a mans liberty under the custody of another, by lawfull warrant in deed or in law. Lawfull warrant is, when the offence appeareth by matter of record, or when it doth not appeare by matter of record. By matter of record, as when the party is taken upon an inditement at the suit of the king, or upon an appeale at the suit of the party. When it doth not appeare by matter of record, as when a felony is done, and the offender by a lawfull *mittimus* is committed to the gaole for the same. But between these two cases there is a great diversity: for in the first case, whether any felony were committed, or no, if the offender be taken by force of a *capias*, the warrant is lawfull; and if hee break prison it is felony, albeit no felony were committed. But in the other case, if no felony be done at all, and yet he is committed to prison for a supposed felony, and breake prison, this is no felony, for there is no cause; and the words of this act are, *nisi causa, pro qua captus fuerit, tale judicium requirit.* So as the cause must be just, and not feigned; for things feigned require no judgement.

See Mag. Chart. cap. 29.

[591]

If A. give B. a mortall wound, for which A. is committed to prison, and breaketh prison, B. dyeth of the wound within the yeare, this death hath relation to the stroke; but because relations are but fictions in law, and fictions are not here intended, this escape is no felony, 11 H. 4. 11. Plowd. com. 401. Coles case.

Seeing the weight of this businesse touching this point, to make the escape either in the party, or in the gaoler felony, dependeth upon the lawfulnesse of the *mittimus*, it shall be necessary to say somewhat hereof: first, it must be in writing in the name, and under the seale of him that makes the same, expressing his office, place, and authority, by force whereof he maketh the *mittimus* and is to be directed to the gaoler, or keeper of the gaole or prison. 2. It must containe the cause (as it expresly appeareth by this act, *nisi causa pro qua captus, &c.*) but not so certainly, as an inditement ought, and yet with such convenient certainty, as it may appeare judicially, that the offence *tale judicium requirit* as *pro alta proditione, viz. in personam domini regis,* or *pro contrafactura magni sigilli domini regis, &c.* or *pro contrafractura monetæ domini regis,* or *pro parva proditione, viz. pro morte (talis) magistri sui,* or *pro felonia, viz. pro morte talis, &c.*

25 E. 3. 42. b. coron. 134. 32 E. 3. coron. 248. 9 E. 4. 52.

&c. or *pro burglaria*, or *robberia*, &c. or *pro felonia*, *viz.* for stealing of a horse, &c. or the like, so as it may in such a generality appeare judicially, that the offence *tale judicium requirit*. And this is proved both by reason and authority. By reason, first, for that it is in case of felony, *quæ inducit ultimum supplicium*; and therefore ought to have convenient certainty, as is aforesaid. 2. Also it must have convenient certainty, for that a voluntary escape is felony in the gaoler. 3. If the *mittimus* should be good generally *pro felonia*, then as the old rule is, *ignorantia judicis foret calamitas innocentis*; for the truth of the case may be, that he did steale charters of land, or wood growing, or the like, which in law are no felonies; and therefore in reason in a case of so high nature concerning the life of man, the convenient certainty ought to be shewed.

By authority. The constant forme of the inditement in that case for escape either by the party, or voluntarily suffered by the gaoler is, that he was arrested *pro suspicione cujusdam feloniæ*, *viz. pro morte cujusdam M.N. felonice interfecti*, or the like; for the inditement must rehearse the effect of the *mittimus*, which directly proveth, that the cause in such a generall certainty ought to be shewed. *Vid.* 25 E. 3. fol. 42.

Also if a man be indited of treason, or indited or appealed for felony, the capias thereupon, whereby the party is to be arrested, comprehendeth the cause. *A fortiori* the *mittimus*, whereby the party is to be arrested, having no such ground of record as the capias hath, must, pursuing the effect of the *capias*, comprehend the cause in convenient certainty. 25 E. 3. fol. 42. pl. 32. there ought to be a certaine cause: and in the same leafe, pl. 35. in case of breaking of prison, the cause of the imprisonment ought to be shewed.

25 E. 3. fo. 42.

9 E. 4. 26. 41 ass. 5. 22 E. 3. coron. 242, 243. 248. 43 E. 3. ib. 424. 3 E. 3. ibid. 312. 328. 333. 345, 346. 2 E. 3. f. 1. 26 ass. 51. 22 E. 3. 13. 27 ass. 42. 27 ass. p. 116. 15 E. 2. coro. 38. 9 H. 4. 1. 10 H. 4. 7. 11 H. 4. 11. 8 E. 2. coro. 422. 430, 431 27 H. 6. 7. 39 H. 6. 33. 1 R. 3. ca. 3. 2 H. 5. ca. 7. 21 H. 7. 17.

If a man be indited, *quod felonice fregit prisonam*, &c. generally, it is not good; for the inditement ought to rehearse the specialty of the matter according to the statute, that he being imprisoned for felony, &c. *fregit prisonam*. We have quoted many other books, which though they be not so certainly reported, as might have been wished, yet the judicious reader will gather fruit of them. But see before the exposition of *Magna Charta*, cap. 29. *verbo*, *Aut per legem terræ*, and observe well the words of the writ of *habeas corpus*, for a direct proofe that the cause ought to be shewed.

Lastly, see hereafter in the exposition of the statute of *articuli cleri*, the resolution of all the judges of England, the answer to the 21 and 22 objections, which we will in no sort abridge for the excellency thereof, but referre you to the fountaines themselves.

Hereupon it appeareth, that the common warrant or *mittimus* to answer to such things as shall be objected against him, is utterly against law.

[592]

Now as the *mittimus* must containe the cause, so the conclusion must be according to law, *viz.* the prisoner safely to keep, untill he be delivered by due order of law, and not untill he that made it shall give other order, or the like.

4 E. 3. 17. 1 H. 7. 6.

And if the warrant be not lawfull, if the gaoler suffer such a prisoner to escape voluntarily, it is no felony in him. But admit the warrant be lawfull, and in particular for felony, and the gaoler suffer him willingly to escape, untill the prisoner be attainted, the gaoler shall not answer to the escape, though the prisoner be indited; for the

8

the felony of the prisoner shall not be tryed between the king and the gaoler, because the prisoner is a stranger thereunto. But if the warrant be lawfull, and there is a felony done, and one is lawfully committed for the same, if he breake prison he may be indited for that escape before he be attainted of the offence, because he is party. And albeit the gaoler be *de facto, et non de jure,* yet shall he be charged for the escape. 39 H. 6. 33.

And certainly this law of *nisi causa, &c.* agreeth with that judiciall saying of Felix in the holy history, *sine ratione mihi videtur mittere vinctum, et causas ejus non significare.* And whatsoever Felix was, yet according to that old rule, *Veritas à quocunque dicitur à Deo est.* Act. Apost. c. 25. ver. 27.

(4) *Tale judicium requirit.*] If a man be committed by lawfull warrant for suspicion of felony done, if he breake prison, he may be indited for that escape, albeit the commitment be for suspicion of felony, and yet no judgement can be given against him for suspicion, but for the felony it selfe, whereof he is suspected; and so be many presidents. 43 E. 3. cor. 454. 44 ass. 12. Rot. Parl. 2 H. 6. nu. 18. Sir John Mortimers case. 1 H. 6. 5. 1 Mar. Dyer 99.

And albeit the words be in the present time, yet if a felony be made after by parliament, it is within the provision of this statute.

For other matters concerning escapes, you may reade the learned treatise of justice Stanford, pl. coron. fol. 30, 31. &c. which need not here to be inserted.

STATUTUM DE MILITIBUS, [593]

Editum Anno primo Edw. II.

THIS writ king Edward the second granted in the time of the parliament, and caused it to be entred of record; and therefore is here stiled by the name of a statute or ordinance, and the very frame of the writ doth prove it to be no act of parliament: but let us take the ford as we find it, and peruse the words thereof.

Cap. 1. *DOMINUS rex concessit, quod omnes illi qui milites esse debent, et non sunt (1), et districti fuerint ad arma militaria suscipienda infra festum natalis Domini, habeant responsum ad prædicta arma militaria suscipienda usque in octab' sancti Hilarii sine actione: et extunc distringantur, nisi interveniant.*

2. *Item*

OUR soveraigne lord the king hath graunted that all such as ought to be knightes, and bee not, and have beene distrained to take upon them the order of a knight within the feast of the nativitie of our Lord, shall have respite to take the foresaid armes of a knight, untill the utas of Saint Hillarie without occasion, and after that

that they ſhall bee diſtrained except they make ſome other meane.

2. *Item conceſſit quod ſi aliquis queſtus fuerit in cancellaria, quod diſtrictus fuerit, &c. et non habeat xx. li. terræ in feodo, vel ad terminum vitæ ſuæ, et hoc velit verificare per patriam, tunc diſcretis et legalibus militibus de comit' ad prædictam inquiſitionem capiendam ſcribatur. Et ſi per illam inquiſitionem ita fuiſſe conſtiterit, fiat ei remedium, et ceſſet diſtrictio.*

Alſo hee hath graunted that if any will complaine in the chauncerie, becauſe hee was diſtrained, &c. and hath not xx.li. yeerely in fee, or for terme of life, and will prove that by the countrey, then it ſhall bee written unto the more diſcreette and ſage knightes of the ſhire, to take the ſayd inquiſition, and if it fortune to bee tryed ſo by the ſame inqueſt, hee ſhall have remedie and the diſtreſſe ſhall ceaſe.

3. *Item ſi aliquis implacitatus fuerit de tota terra ſua, vel etiam de parte ejuſdem, ita quod reſiduum non ſufficiat ad valentiam xx. li. et hoc poſſit verificare, tunc ceſſet diſtrictio, donec placitum illud terminetur.*

Alſo if any bee impleaded for all his land or for part of the ſame, ſo that the reſidue bee not ſufficient to the value of xx. li. and can prove the ſame, then the diſtreſſe ſhall ceaſe untill the ſame plea be determined.

4. *Item ſi quis eorum teneatur in certis debitis atterminatis ad ſcaccarium, ad certam ſummam inde percipiendam per annum, et reſiduum terrarum ſuarum ultra prædictam ſummam valorem xx. li. annuarum non attingat, ceſſet diſtrictio donec prædictum debitum fuerit ſolutum.*

Alſo if any of them bee bounden in certaine debtes awarded in the eſchequer for a certaine ſumme to be received yeerely out of his lands, ſo that the reſidue thereof doth not amount to the yeerely value of xx. li. beſides the ſame ſumme: the diſtreſſe ſhall ſeaſe untill the foreſaid debte be cleerely paide.

5. *Et nullus diſtringatur ad arma militaria ſuſcipienda antequam venerit ad ætatem 21 annorum.*

And none ſhall be diſtrained to take upon him the order of a knight before that he come unto the age of xxi. yerres.

6. *Item nullus ratione terræ ſuæ, quam tenet in maneriis, quæ nunc ſunt de antiquo dominico coron', et tanquam ſokemannus, et quæ terra dabit tallagium, quando dominica regis tallientur, diſtringatur ad arma militaria ſuſcipienda.*

Alſo none by reaſon of any land that he holdeth in manors which be now in auncient demeane of the crowne as a ſockeman, and which lands muſt alſo give tallage when the kings demeanes are tayled, ſhall be diſtrained to take upon him the order of a knight.

7. *Item de illis qui terras ſuas tenent in ſocagio de aliis maneriis quam de maneriis coronæ, et nullum faciunt ſervitium*

[594]

Alſo of them that hold their lands in ſocage of other manors then of the manors of the king, doing no forreine ſervice, the rolles of the chauncerie ſhall

vitium forinsecum, scrutentur rotuli de cancellaria de tempore prædecessorum domini regis, et fiat secundum quod fieri consuevit.

shall be searched for the time of the kings predecessors. And it shall bee done as it hath used to be done.

8. *Eodem modo fiat de clericis infra sacros existentibus laicum feodum tenentibus, qui milites esse deberent, si laici fuissent.*

In like mannor shall be done of clerkes being within orders, holding lay fee which should be knights if they were laye.

9. *Item nullus distringatur pro burgagiis suis, licet valorem xx. li. attingant, aut plus.*

Also none shall be distrained for his burgage lands, although they doe amount to the value of xx li. yeerely or more.

10. *Item qui milites esse debent et non sunt, qui per modicum tempus terras suas tenuerunt, et similiter qui nimiam senectutem, vel defectum membrorum habent, seu morbum incurabilem, vel onus liberorum, vel placitorum allegant, vel alias causas necessarias prætendunt: adeant ad Robertum Typtost, et Anto' de Berk, et coram eis fines faciant: quibus est injunctum, quod secundum discretionem eorum, rationabiles fines admittant de viris prædictis.*

Also they that ought to be knights and be not, which have holden their lands in their hands but a small time, and likewise such as should be knights that do pretend great age, or default of their members, or any other incurable disease, or charge of their children, or of suites, or do alledge such necessary excuses, they shall resort unto Robert Typtoffe and Anthonie de Berke, and shall make fine before them, to whom it is enjoyned that according to their discretions they shall admitte the reasonable fines of all such persons. [*Rastell's Translation.*]

(1) *Dominus rex concessit, quod omnes illi qui milites esse debent, et non sunt.*] That is, the king doth grant, that all they which ought to be knights, and be not, &c. In these words consist the locke and the key of this writ, *viz.* who by the common lawes of this realme ought (that is, *de jure*) to be compelled to be a knight. For the understanding whereof, and of all the parts of this writ, seven things fall into consideration. (There being foure kinds of knights, *viz.* knights of the garter, knights banaret, knights of the bath, and knights bachelor of the spurre, 3 E. 4. cap. 5.)

First, of what degree knighthood is. This writ being understood of a knight bachelor.

It is resolved in our bookes without any contradiction, that the name of this knight is a name of dignity, and of the inferiour degree of nobility; and therefore is parcell of his name. And in writs and inditements he ought to be named knight by the common law; but so it is not of the state of an esquire or gentleman. * Britton stileth a knight honourable, and in the record of 9 E. 1. Sir John Acton knight hath the addition of *nobilis*; and certaine it is, that, seeing it is a name of dignity, it followeth, that he ought to have sufficient revenue to maintaine that dignity. See W. 1. cap.

11 E. 3. brev. 259. 26 E. 3. brev. 250. 42 E. 3. 9. 22 R. 2. brev. 925. 4 H. 4. 2. 7 H. 4. 7. 11 H. 4. 19. 14 H. 4. 21. 7 H. 6. 15. 14 H. 6. 15. 22 H. 6. 32 H 6. 29. 35 H. 6 55. 5 E. 4. 19. 15 E. 4. 14. 18 E. 4. 20. 21 E. 4. 71.

* Brit. cap. 25. fo. 49. b. Mich. 9 E. 1. in banco rot. 63. Somerset.

10. *verbo chivalers*, that in ancient times coroners ought to have been knights, and the reason was, for that being knights, the law did intend, that they had sufficient to answer both the king and the subject, if cause should require. But hereof more shall bee said hereafter.

In the meane time this is to be observed, that the greater dignity doth never drowne the lesser dignity, but both stand together in one person: and therefore if a knight be created a baron, yet he remaineth a knight still; and if the baron be created an earle, yet the dignity of a baron remaineth, *et sic de cæteris*. But if an esquire (which is no name of dignity be made a knight, the degree of the esquire is changed, and gone, and cannot so be named in any judiciall proceeding.

7 E. 4. 7. adjudge. 32 H. 6. 29.

2. Secondly, of what quality he that is to be a knight ought to be, *debet*, &c. We have not found that a baron, being a lord of parliament, or higher degree, hath been distrained *ad arma militis suscipienda*. But he that is distrained, &c. ought to be a gentleman of name and bloud, *claro loco natus*, or else *non debet*, he ought not to be compelled by this writ to take the dignitie of knighthood upon him.

[595]

Vid. 7 E. 3. ea. 19. Un gentlehome de estat. Pat. 38 E. 3. part. 1. m. 10. Rex licentiamdedit Johanni Beverly armigero suo, &c. Rot. claus. 19 R. 2. in dors. proclam. Nequis miles, armiger, &c. 11 H. rot. claus. m. 2. Omnes qui tenent per servitium militare in capit milites fiant.

* See here cap. 6 & 7 Glanv. lib. 7. cap. 9. Burgensis.

Of ancient time those that held by knights service were regularly gentile, and those which held by socage, or in burgage, were yeomen or burgesses: and this appeareth by the ancient rule of law, * *Lex Angliæ nullum scutagium aut servitium militare de sockmannis aut burgensibus expetit*. It appeareth also by many ancient records, and particularly by this writ, that *sockmannus, &c. et qui terras tenent in socagio, &c. et nullum faciunt forinsecum servitium*, that is, those which hold in socage, of what value soever, and doe no knights service, ought not to be knights, *non debent, &c.* And our writ saith, *Nullus distringatur pro burgagiis suis, &c.* no man ought to be distrained to be a knight for the land which he holds in burgage, &c. of what value soever. But though it were of ancient time a badge of gentry to hold by knights service, yet now *tempora mutantur*, and many a yeoman, burgesse, or tradesman purchase lands holden by knights service, and yet *(non debet)* ought not for want of gentry be a knight. At this day the surest rule is, *Nobiles sunt qui arma gentilicia antecessorum suorum proferre possunt*; therefore they are called *scutiferi, armigeri, &c.* When a knight is degraded, one of his punishments, is, *quod clypeus suus gentilicius reversus erit*, and here his armes be reversed that beareth none.

Mich. 9 E. 2. fol. 61. in libro meo. Dower de socage terre, & nemy de terre tenus per service de chivaler, Lit. de la pluis beale. [a] 31 H. 8. cap. 3. 9 H. 3. prescript. 63. 26 H. 8. 4. b. Bract. fol. 77. Glanvil. fol. 46. In Bundello. eschaet. an 1 E. 3. acc'.

Lands and tenements anciently holden by knights service, belonging to the nobility and gentry of the realme, are not of the custome of gavelkind, which belonged to the yeomanry, and were holden in socage for the service of the plow: and this appeareth by the judgement of the whole parliament in [a] 31 H. 8. cap. 3. and by the booke of 9 H. 3. tit. Prescription 63. and 26 H. 8. fol. 4. and the reason thereof was, because the lands and tenements holden by knights service should not be carried by descent into many hands of issues males, whereby the service for defence of the realme in a few descents should be lost or diminished, and the owners (the lands being divided into so many hands) should not be able to maintaine the countenance of their order and degree. *Inter statuta seu institutiones H. 1. cap. 11. Militibus qui per loricas terras suas deserviunt, terras dominicarum carucarum suarum quietas ab omnibus gildis, et ab omni opere ipso dono meo concedo; ut sicut benignitas mea propensior est in eis,* *ita*

ita mihi fideles ſint: et ſicut tam magno gravamine alleviati ſunt, ita equis et armis ſe bene inſtruant, ut apti et parati ſint ad ſervitium meum, et ad defenſionem regni mei. And where it is enacted by the ſtatute of *prerogat' regis, cap.* 16. *quod fœminæ non participabunt cum maſculis,* it is to be underſtood of ſuch as be in equall degree; as the ſiſter ſhall not inherit with the brother, becauſe they be in equall degree; but the daughter of the ſonne ſhall have a part with her uncle, for they be not in equall degree.

Prerogat. regis, cap. 16. Vid. Paſch. 4 E. 1. in com' banco rot. 22. Kanc' for the cuſtome of gavelkind, Hill. 10 E. 1. in banco Kanc' per de Benbrokes caſe, & m. 18 E. 1. in banco rot. 68. Suff. Laurence le Fryes caſe.

A knight is by creation, and not by deſcent, a gentleman is by deſcent, and yet I read of the creation of a [b] gentleman; and thus it was: a knight of France came into England, and challenged John Kingſton (a good and a ſtrong man at armes, but no gentleman) as the record ſaith, *ad certa armorum puncta, &c. perficienda. Rex, ut prædictus Johannes honorabilius in præmiſſis accipiatur, ipſum Johannem ad ordinem generoſorum adoptavit, et armigerum conſtituit, et certa honoris inſignia ei conceſſit, &c.* Note, the king made him no knight, as his adverſary was, becauſe he was no gentleman.

[b] Rot. patent. an. 13 R. 2. part. 1. 7 H. 4. fol. 7. 1 H. 5. cap. 1.

But for any thing that I have reade and doe remember in the raigne of H. 4. or ever before, gentlemen of name and bloud had very rarely the addition of *generoſus* or *armiger,* as of a ſtate or degree, but were diſtinguiſhed from yeomen, who ſerve by the plow, by their ſervice, *viz.* knights ſervice, *forinſecum ſervitium,* but in the raigne of H. 5. and ever ſince, they have had the addition of gentlemen or eſquires, and the reaſon thereof is this: it is enacted by the ſtatute of 1 H. 5. that in every writ originall of actions perſonals, appeales, and inditements, in which proceſſe of outlary doe lye, that to the name of the defendants addition be made of the eſtate or degree, or myſterie: and hereupon in thoſe writs addition was made as the caſe required, of *generoſus* or *armiger*; for if a gentleman were named in ſuch a writ huſbandman, or yeoman, he may abate the writ, by pleading that he is a gentleman. And after this the like additions were made in commiſſions, and after that in grants and conveyances, &c.

1 H. 5. cap. 5. [596]

14 H. 6. 15. 22 H. 6. 3. 28 H. 6. 8. 38 H. 6. 10. 23 H. 6. cap. 15.

And great diſcord and diſcontentment would ariſe within the realme, if yeomen and tradeſmen ſhould be called to the dignity of knighthood, to take the place and precedency of the ancient and noble gentry of the realme. And the eldeſt ſonne of a knight is an eſquire, as his father ought to be, before he was called to the dignity of knighthood.

Thirdly, of what livelihood or revenue a knight ought to be, *debet, &c.* And it is certaine, that he ought to have a knights fee: *i. feodum unius militis.* Herein three things are to obſerved: firſt, whether the law doth determine of what yearly value a knights fee (*viz.* the lands and revenue of a knight) ought to be. Secondly, if the law define not the certainty of the value, what is eſteemed in law a knights fee, Thirdly, what eſtate he ought to have in it. 3.

To the firſt, the law doth reſpect rather the value, then the content, *viz.* to be of ſufficient value to maintaine the degree of a knight, but doth not determine of any certaine yearly value: for nothing is more incertaine than the values of lands in ſucceſſion. And therefore in a writ in the raigne of H. 3. no value was expreſſed, but a writ iſſued out of the chancery generally to diſtraine *omnes qui tenent per ſervitium militare.*

Lib. 9. fol. 124. Lowes caſe. 1. part Inſtitutes, ſect. 112. Sir Tho. Smith, lib. 1. cap. 18. 11 H. 3. ubi ſup.

At the making of *Magna Charta* a knights fee was accounted the value of 20 li. and the fourth part thereof was a knights reliefe.

9 H. 3. Magn. Chart. cap. 2.

 In

Glanv. lib. 9. ca. 4. lib. 7. fol. 33. b. Rot. parl. 20 E. 1. rot. 4.
* Trin. 1 E. 2. coram rege, rot. 4. Linc'.
[a] Rot. clauf. 19 E. 2. m. 16. in dorf.
[b] Brev. regis, part 1. & 2. 2 R. 2.
[c] Rot. parl.
* Hill. 40 H. 3. pag. 254. a. 30. ibid. a. 60.

In *anno* 20 E. 1. the value of the knights fee in the writ was 40 li. by our writ in 1 E. 2. 20. li. * Trin. 1 E. 2. 48. *carucat' terræ faciunt unum feodum militis*. This was in the fame year that this writ was granted. [a] 19 E. 2. *feodum unius militis annui valoris* 40 li. [b] 2 R. 2. 10. li. *per annum*. 7 H. 6. fol. 15. 10 li. *per annum*. [c] 18 Hen. 6. nu. 43. 40 li *per an. &c.* So as (as hath been faid) nothing is more incertaine then the values of lands; but he muft have *feodum unius militis*. And in feverall ages a knights fee, as before it appeareth, was valued at feverall values. * The king caufed a proclamation to be fet forth, that all fuch as might difpend 15 li. in lands, fhould receive the order of knighthood, and thofe that would not, or could not, fhould pay theirfines.

There was 5 markes fet on every fhriefes head, becaufe they had not diftrained every perfon that might difpend 15 li. lands, to receive the order of knighthood, as was to the fame fhriefes commanded.

[d] Vid Camden. Brit. pag. 126. Note, a baron & others of higher degrees are prefumed to have greater livings, as appeareth by their reliefe, Mag. Chart. cap. 2. li. 2. fol. 124. ubi fupr. Glanv. lib. 2. ca. 3. acc'. Pafch' 3 E. 1. coram Rogero de Seton & fociis fuis, rot. 10. Ralph Normanvils cafe. 19 E. 2. ubi fupr.
[e] See here, cap. 3.

[d] As to the fecond it appeareth before, that he ought to have a knights fee: then the onely queftion is, what quantity of land a knights fee is. And without doubt this fhall not be accounted by the acres; for fome acre is of far greater value then another: and therefore that fhould be as uncertaine as the values be; but this is refolved by prudent fages of the law of ancient time, who have reduced a knights fee to a certaine number of carues, or plow lands, which though they be incertaine (for if the land be fertile and heavie, there goeth to a plow land the leffe; and if it be lighter, a greater quantity) yet it is as neere to certainty as can be, and this computation time cannot alter: and therefore a knights fee containeth [e] 12 plow lands. And by this writ it appeareth, that a knights fee is here valued at 20 li. *per an.* And if he be impleaded for it, or any part thereof, &c. that he fhall not be compelled to be a knight, untill the action be determined. And fo likewife, if he be indebted to the king, and his debt ftalled, he fhall not be compelled to be a knight, untill his debt be paid: and the reafon hereof is, that povertie fhould not be apparelled with honour and dignity.

[597]

As to the third, he ought to have an eftate in fee-fimple or fee-taile, as it appeareth in 20 E. 1. *ubi fupra, in feodo et hæreditate.* Or as tenant by the curtefie (which in this writ is intended by the name of tenant for life) whofe heire by poffibility may inherit.

4. The end.

Fourthly, to what end he ought to be called to this dignity of knighthood. And our writ doth truly anfwer, *ad arma militaria fufcipienda*, to take upon him the military armes, or the armes of a knight for the honour, and fervice, and defence of the realme; this is *pro bono publico.*

The writs of parliament are to returne two knights for every county *gladiis cinctos*, not that they fhould come to the parliament girt with fwords, but that they fhould be able to do knights fervice, *et arma militaria exercere*, the fword being named, for that it is the warden of all weapons: and therefore this end ought not to be pretended, and a private intended. *Dicuntur arma, quia armos tegunt, et ab humeris dependent, et continent fcutum, gladium, tela, et ea quibus præliantur.* No infufficient men are to be called *ad arma militaria fufcipienda, ne dignitas hujus ordinis vilefceret.*

Fifthly,

Fifthly, of what age he ought to be, &c. when he is called, *debet,* 5.
&c. By this writ it appeareth, that he ought to be above 21, and this agreeth with Littleton, and other authorities and records; but this is so to be understood, that he cannot be compelled to be a knight before 21, but if he be made a knight before that age, it is good enough.

* And above the age of 60 (which in this writ is called *nimia senectus*) no man ought to bee compelled *ad arma militaria suscipienda,* or to serve as a souldier. If the plaintife in an appeale of death, &c. be of the age of 60, or maimed, or of any great infirmity, so as hee is not able to fight, hee shall not bee compelled to wage battell. And by this writ it appeareth, that if hee hath *defectum membrorum, seu morbum incurabilem, vel alias causas rationabiles,* that hee shall not be compelled *ad arma militaria suscipienda,* because he is not able to performe the service and duty of knighthood.

* See here, ca. 10. Rot. claus. an. 7 E. 3. part. 1. mem. 25. & m. 22, 23. Rot. parl. 5 H. 4. nu. 24, 25. 33 H. 8. cap. 22 E. 4. 19. 15 E. 2. coron. 185. Brit. fol. 40. Fitz. N.B. 163. n. simile.

See here, cap. 10.

Sixthly, by what meanes hee ought to bee called, *debet, &c.* hee 6.
ought to bee called by writ. It hereby appeareth, that this writ issueth out of the chancery to the shriefe, commanding him, *quod proclamari faciat, quod omnes illi qui habent* * *terræ, arma militaria suscipiant citra (tale festum) et quod summoneri fac eos', &c.* and this writ is returnable into the chancery at a certaine returne. At which day of the returne it is necessary for them that are summoned to appeare; for if they make default, it is finable (which, it may be, is the marke that is aimed at) but if they appeare, and take the dignity upon them, or refuse for the causes aforesaid, or any of them, they ought not be fined.

7 H. 6. 15. See here, cap. 2.

* The yearly value of the land.

This writ and the returne thereof is by writ of *mittimus* transmitted into the court of exchequer, who cannot make a commission to others concerning this matter, but ought to proceed legally themselves, because they have but *delegatam potestatem, quæ non potest delegari,* and they are learned and sworne judges, and able to allow the parties their just exceptions.

For writs of summons or *distringas* for the dignity of bachelor knighthood, see Rot. claus. 29 H. 3. m. 9. 44 H. 3. *parte prima. ibid.* 6 E. 1. *dors.* 8. *ibid.* 6 E. 2. *dors.* 29. &c.

Seventhly, if he ought to be a knight, and refuse, or make 7.
default, how often he may be fined.

He can by the law be fined but once, no more then an apprentice at law, that is called by writ *ad statum et gradum servientis ad legem,* if hee refuse, and be fined, he cannot be fined againe; for so he might be fined infinitely, *et infinitum in jure reprobatur.*

Rot. Parl. 18 H. 6. nu. 43. 14 H. 6. 2, 3. Fitz. N.B. 231. b. Le Roy navera que un pension.

The commons petitioned (to have a declaratory law) that no person once making fine for not being knight, be never after called thereunto againe. But this was but to avoid charge and vexation. *Vid.* Dyer, 35 H. 8. 55. Brook briefe 150, *fine pur contempts* 19.

We doe not remember that we have read any thing touching [598]
this matter in Bracton, Britton, Fleta, Mirror, the Register, or F.N.B.

No clerke within holy orders, be hee regular or secular, though hee hath a knights fee, can be made a knight, as by this writ it appeareth.

See here, cap. 7.

See Matth. Paris, *an.* 29 H. 3. pag. 882. *Rex die natali Johannem de Gatesden clericum, et multis ditatum beneficiis, sed omnibus ante expectatum resignatis, quia sic oportuit, baltheo cinxit militari.* This last

See here, cap. 10.

last clause, *item qui milites esse debent, et non sunt*, and yet have just cause of excuse (as for instance, that they are impleaded for their land, which before by this writ is allowed for a good excuse, &c. or have any other of the just causes of excuse here expressed, and yet will not stand to a legall and chargeable pleading and proceeding) they may, if they will, redeem their vexation and charge, and submit themselves to a reasonable fine: and therefore by this writ Robert Tiptost, and Anthony de Berke are appointed to assesse reasonable fines; but this must be understood by consent, for this was no legall proceeding. I find in the parliament roll *de anno* 18 E. 1. rot. 6. that Robert Tiptost was *justiciarius domini regis*. And so, it is like, Anthony Berk was; but certainly what he was, we have not yet found.

For knights of the bath.

Writs to divers *ad ordinem militiæ de balneo suscipiendum juxta antiquam consuetudinem in creatione usitatam, Rot. claus. in dorso*, 10 *H*. 7. 20. *Septembris*.

For knights banerets.

See Rot. Vasch' 13 E. 3. m. 13. William de la Pole created. Rot. *eodem* m. 1. Rich. de Cobham created. Rot. Pat. 15 E. 3. part 2. m. 22. John Coupland created. See Matth. Paris, pag. 1354, 1355. &c. Camden Brit. 124.

---

[599]

ARTICULI CLERI,

Edit' Anno nono Edw. II.

LONG before the making of this statute, that is, *anno* 42 H. 3. *anno Domini* 1258, Boniface younger sonne of Thomas earle of Savoy, archbishop of Canterbury, uncle of Elianor queen of England, who was daughter of Reymond earle of Province by Beatrix daughter of Thomas earle of Savoy, and sister to the said Boniface, made divers and many canons and constitutions provinciall directly against the lawes of the realme, which canons begun thus: *Universis Christi fidelibus ad quos præsens pagina pervenerit, Bonifacius miseratione divina Cantuariensis archiepiscopus, totius Angliæ primas, et sui suffraganei in verbo salutari salutem*, And ending thus: *Actum apud Westm', sexto iduum Junii anno Domini* 1258. *In quorum omnium robur et testimonium, &c.* which being exceeding long, we could not here insert. But the effect of them is, so to usurp and incroach upon many matters, which apparently belonged to the common law, as, amongst many others, the tryall of limits and bounds of parishes, and right of patronage, against tryall of right of tithes (by *indicavit*) against writs to the bishop upon a recovery in a *quare impedit*, &c. in the kings courts. That none of their possessions or liberties, which any of the clergy had in the right of their church, should be tryed before any secular judge; (so as they would not have conusance of things spirituall, but of temporall also) and concerning distresses and attachments within their fees, and

and in effect, that no *quo warranto* ſhould be brought againſt them, when they had been long in poſſeſſion, with an invective againſt the perverſe interpretation by the judges of the realme (ſo they termed it) of charters, &c. granted to them, and in ſubſtance againſt the ancient and juſt writs of prohibition in caſes, where by the lawes of the realme they are maintainable: and commandement given to admoniſh the king, and interdict his lands and revenues, and thundred out excommunications againſt the judges and others if they violated, or obeyed not the ſaid canons and conſtitutions. And this was the principall ground of the controverſies between the judges of the realme and the biſhops: for this cauſed eccleſiaſticall judges to uſurp and incroach upon the common law. But notwithſtanding the greatneſſe of the archbiſhop Boniface, and that divers of the judges of the realm were of the clergy, and all the great officers of the realm, as chancellor, treaſurer, privie ſeale, &c. were prelates; yet the judges proceeded according to the lawes of the realm, and ſtill kept, though with great difficulty, the eccleſiaſticall courts within their juſt and proper limits. The courts by pretext of theſe canons being at variance, at length at a parliament holden in the 51 yeare of Henry the third, Boniface, and the reſt of the clergy complained (which was *ultimum refugium*, and yet the right way) and exhibited many articles as grievances, called *Articuli Cleri*. The articles exhibited by the clergie either by accident or induſtry are not to be found; ſome of the anſwers are extant, *viz. ad* 16 *articulum de uſuris reſpondetur, quod licet epiſcopus, &c. ad* 17 *articulum de defamatione, &c. reſpondetur, ſi aliquis defamatus, &c. ſi autem certæ perſonæ nominatæ fuerint, per quas rei veritas melius ſcire poterit, nominantur, ad proband' matrimonium vel teſtamentum: et ſimiliter in accuſationibus tales perſonæ impediendæ non ſunt, quia teſtimonium perhibent veritati, ſed propter hoc non eſt congregatio laicorum faciend', quia per congregationem hujuſmodi ſervitia dominus poſſit deperire.* Ex fragmento Rot. parl. anno 51 H. 3.

Ad 18 *artic' dominus poſuit remedium.*

Ad 19 *artic' reſpondetur, quod archiepiſcopus de epiſcopatu vacante non ſe intromittat quantum ad temporalia, ſed tantum ſe de ſpiritualibus intromittat, &c.* [600]

Ad 20 *artic' reſpondetur, quod de clericis occiſis, et de hiis qui forſan occidi contigerit, in futurum fiat juſtitia, ſecundum legem et conſuetudinem terræ, &c.*

Ad 21 *artic' reſpondetur, quod excommunicatus per ordinarium, aut alium judicem competentem, et denunciatus taliter, debebit ab aliis evitari, niſi forſan excommunicatus conqueratur ſe eſſe injuſte excommunicatum pro aliqua re temporali, de qua non debeat coram ordinario reſpondere, ad cujus probationem debet admitti, ſed in cæteris quæ proponit, ut actor, eſt interim evitandus.*

Ad 22 *artic' mandabitur juſticiariis, quod non fiant aliquæ priſæ per totam terram de bonis aliquorum, niſi debitæ priſæ et conſuetæ.*

Ad 23 *artic' reſpondetur, quod cum aliqui teneant aliquod de rege in capite unde cuſtodia debeatur, cuſtodiæ omnium terrarum de quibuſcunque tenentes illi tenementa illa teneant cum acciderint (ſi inde cuſtodia habere debeatur) hactenus ex conſuetudine approbata ſpectarunt ad regem, ſed epiſcopi ſi expedire videant, inhibeant tenentibus ſuis, ne aliqua tenementa ſibi perquirant de feodis regis.*

Theſe

These answers are yet extant of record, and are worthy to be read at large as they yet remaine; whereunto we referre the reader. This is to be observed, that none of Boniface's canons against the lawes of the realme, and the crowne and dignity of the king, and the birth-right of the subject, are here confirmed.

Prohibitio formata de statut' Artic'Cleri. Vet. Magn. Chart.

What the residue of the articles and the answers were, may be collected by that act of parliament entitled *prohibitio formata de statuto articuli cleri*, which was made in the time of Edward the first, about the beginning of his raign, which beginneth thus: *Edwardus, &c. prælatis, &c.* wherein divers points are to be observed against the canons of Boniface: 1. *Quod cognitiones placitorum super feodalibus et libertatibus feodalium, districtionibus, officiis ministrorum, executionibus contra pacem nostram factis, felonum negotiationibus, consuetudinibus secularibus, attachiamentis, vi laica malefactoribus rectatis, robberiis, arrestationibus, maneriis, advocationibus ecclesiarum, sufficientibus assisis juratis, recognitionibus laicum feodum contingentibus, et rebus aliis, et causis pecuniarum, et de aliis catallis et debitis quæ non sunt de testament' vel matrimon' ad coronam et dignitatem regiam pertineant, et de regno de consuetud' ejusdem regni approbata, et hactenus observata.*

2. *Et proceres, et magnates, aut alii de eodem regno temporibus nostrorum prædecessorum regum Angliæ, seu nostra authoritate alicujus non consueverunt contra consuetudinem illam super hujusmodi rebus in causa trahi vel compelli ad comparendum coram quocunque judice ecclesiastico.*

Vid. Brit. fo. 35. b. Registr. 36. b. 29 E. 3. 29. F.N.B. 41. a. Vid. Vet. Magn. Chart. fol. 91. Bertelets impression.

3. *Et quod vicecomes non permittant, quod aliqui laici in baliva sua conveniunt ad aliquas recognitiones per sacramenta sua faciend', nisi in causis matrimonialibus et testamentariis.* Of the substance of this prohibition, Britton speaketh in these words, *et queux ount suffert pleader en court christian auters pleas, que de testament ou matrimonie, et de pure spiritueltie sans deniers prender de lay home. Ou suffert lay home iorrer devant lordinary.*

After this the clergy, at a parliament holden in the raigne of the same king E. 1. preferred articles intitled *articuli contra prohibitionem regis*, fearing lest by reason of some generall words therein they might be prohibited in causes, which of right belonged to the ecclesiastical jurisdiction, in these words, *sub hac forma impetrant laici prohibitionem in genere super decimis, oblationibus, obventionibus, mortuariis, redemptionibus penitentiarum, violenta manuum injectione in clericum vel cōmissarium, et in causa defamationis, in quibus casibus agitur ad pœnam canonicam imponendam.* And a just and legall answer was made thereunto, as thereby appeareth. But it is to be observed, that they claimed nothing which was against the true meaning of the said act, called *prohibitio formata de statuto artic' cleri*, nor any of Boniface's canons to bee confirmed: and so these matters rested, untill the parliament holden at Lincoln in the ninth yeare of Edw. 2. where Walter Reynolds bishop of Canterbury (whom the king favoured, saith one, singularly for the opinion he had of his fidelity and great wisdome, and *Walterus archiepiscopus Cantuariensis regi gratiosissimus fuit, hæc regis æquissima responsa ad prælatorum petita obtinuit*) in the name of himselfe and of the clergy, preferred these 16 articles, and by authority of parliament had the answers here following *seriatim* to every one of them. And now it may seem high time that we should descend to the perusall of the preamble, and the articles and answers. But before we come to it, it shall conduce

[601]

Mat. Parker, fol. 229.

duce much to the right underſtanding of divers parts of this act of parliament, to report unto you what articles Richard Bancroft archbiſhop of Canterbury exhibited in the name of the whole clergy in Michaelmas terme *anno* 3 *Jacob. regis* to the lords of the privie councell againſt the judges of the realm, intitled, Certain articles of abuſes, which are deſired to be reformed, in granting of prohibitions, and the anſwers thereunto, upon mature deliberation and conſideration, in Eaſter terme following, by all the judges of England, and the barons of the exchequer, with one unanimous conſent under their hands (reſolutions of higheſt authorities in law) which were delivered to the lords of the councell. And we, for diſtinction ſake (becauſe we ſhall have occaſion often to cite them) call them *Articuli Cleri* 3 *Jacobi*.

His Majeſty hath power to reforme abuſes in prohibitions. 1.

The clergy well hoped, that they had taken a good courſe in ſeeking ſome redreſſe at his majeſties hands concerning ſundry abuſes offered to his eccleſiaſticall juriſdiction, by the over frequent and undue granting of prohibitions; for both they and we ſuppoſed (all juriſdiction, both eccleſiaſticall and temporall being annexed to the imperiall crowne of this realme) that his highneſſe had been held to have had ſufficient authority in himſelfe, with the aſſiſtance of his councell, to judge what is amiſſe in either of his ſaid juriſdictions, and to have reformed the ſame accordingly; otherwiſe a wrong courſe is taken by us, if nothing may bee reformed that is now complained of, but what the temporall judges ſhall of themſelves willingly yeeld unto. This is therefore the firſt point, which upon occaſion lately offered before your lordſhips by ſome of the judges, we deſire may be cleared, becauſe we are ſtrongly perſwaded as touching the validity of his majeſties ſaid authority, and doe hope we ſhall be able to juſtifie the ſame, notwithſtanding any thing that the judges, or any other can alledge to the contrary. Objection.

No man maketh any queſtion, but that both the juriſdictions are lawfully and juſtly in his majeſty, and that if any abuſes be, they ought to bee reformed: but what the law doth warrant in caſes of prohibitions to keep every juriſdiction in his true limits, is not to be ſaid an abuſe, nor can be altered but by parliament. Anſwer of the judges.

The formes of prohibitions prejudiciall to his majeſties authority in cauſes eccleſiaſticall.

Concerning the forme of prohibitions, foraſmuch as both the eccleſiaſticall and temporall juriſdictions be now united in his majeſtie, which were heretofore *de facto*, though not *de jure* derived from ſeverall heads, we deſire to be ſatisfied by the judges, whether, as the caſe now ſtandeth, the former manner of prohibitions heretofore uſed importing an eccleſiaſticall court to be *aliud forum à foro regio*, and the eccleſiaſticall law not to be *legem terræ*, and the proceedings in thoſe courts to bee *contra coronam et dignitatem regiam*, may now without offence and derogation to the kings eccleſiaſticall prerogative be continued, as though either the ſaid juriſdictions remained now ſo diſtinguiſhed and ſevered as they were before, or that the lawes eccleſiaſticall, which wee put in execution, were not Objection. [602]

not the kings and the realmes ecclesiasticall lawes, as well as the temporall lawes.

Answer. It is true, that both the jurisdictions were ever *de jure* in the crowne, though the one sometimes usurped by the see of Rome; but neither in the one time, nor in the other hath ever the forme of prohibitions been altered, nor can bee but by parliament. And it is *contra coronam et dignitatem regiam* for any to usurp to deale in that, which they have not lawfull warrant from the crowne to deale in, or to take from the temporall jurisdiction that which belonged to it. The prohibitions doe not import, that the ecclesiasticall courts are *aliud* then the kings, or not the kings courts, but doe import, that the cause is drawne into *aliud examen* then it ought to be: and therefore it is alwaies said in the prohibitions (be the court temporall or ecclesiasticall, to which it is awarded) if they deale in any case which they have not power to hold plea of, that the cause is drawn *ad aliud examen* then it ought to be; and therefore *contra coronam et dignitatem regiam*.

3. A fit time to be assigned for the defendant, if he will seek a prohibition.

Objection. As touching the time when prohibitions are granted, it seemeth strange to us, that they are not onely granted at the suit of the defendant in the ecclesiasticall court after his answer (whereby hee affirmeth the jurisdiction of the said court, and submitteth himselfe unto the same;) but also after all allegations and proofes made on both sides, when the cause is fully instructed and furnished for sentence: yea, after sentence, yea after two or three sentences given, and after execution of the said sentence or sentences, and when the party for his long continued disobedience is laid in prison upon the writ of *excommunicato capiendo*, which courses, forasmuch as they are against the rules of the common law in like cases (as we take it) and doe tend so greatly to the delay of justice, vexation, and charge of the subject, and the disgrace and discredit of his majesties jurisdiction ecclesiasticall, the judges (as we suppose) notwithstanding their great learning in the lawes, will be hardly able in defence of them to satisfie your lordships.

Answer. Prohibitions by law are to be granted at any time to restraine a court to intermeddle with, or execute any thing, which by law they ought not to hold plea of, and they are much mistaken that maintaine the contrary. And it is the folly of such as will proceed in the ecclesiasticall court for that, whereof that court hath not jurisdiction; or in that, whereof the kings temporall courts should have the jurisdiction. And so themselves (by their extraordinary dealing) are the cause of such extraordinary charges, and not the law: for their proceedings in such case are *coram non judice*. And the kings courts that may award prohibitions, being informed either by the parties themselves, or by any stranger, that any court temporall or ecclesiasticall doth hold plea of that (whereof they have not jurisdiction) may lawfully prohibit the same, as well after judgement and execution, as before.

4. Prohibitions unduly awarded heretofore in all causes almost of ecclesiasticall cognizance.

Objection. Whereas it will be confessed, that causes concerning testaments, matrimony, benefices, churches, and divine service, with many offences

offences againſt the 1, 2, 3, 4, 5, 7, 9. and 10. commandements, are by the lawes of this realm of eccleſiaſticall cognizance, yet there are few of them, wherein ſundry prohibitions have not been granted, and that more ordinarily of latter times, then ever heretofore, not becauſe we that are eccleſiaſticall judges doe give greater cauſe of ſuch granting of them, then before have been given, [603] but for that the humour of the time is growne to be too eager againſt all eccleſiaſticall juriſdiction. For whereas (for examples ſake) during the raigne of the late queen of worthy memory, there have been 488 prohibitions, and ſince his majeſties time 82 ſent into the court of the arches; we humbly deſire your lordſhips, that the judges may be urged to bring forth one prohibition of ten, nay the twentieth prohibition of all the ſaid 488, and but 2 of the ſaid 82, which upon due conſiderations with the libels in the eccleſiaſticall court, they ſhall be able to juſtifie to have been rightly awarded: we ſuppoſe they cannot; our predeceſſors, and we our ſelves have ever been ſo carefull not to exceed the compaſſe and limits of the eccleſiaſticall juriſdiction: which if they ſhall refuſe to attempt, or ſhall not be able to performe, then we referre our ſelves to your lordſhips wiſdomes, whether we have not juſt cauſe to complaine, and crave reſtraint of this over laviſh granting of prohibitions in every cauſe without reſpect. That which we have ſaid of the prohibitions in the court of the arches, we verily perſwade our ſelves may be truly affirmed of all the eccleſiaſticall courts in England, which doth ſo much the more aggravate this abuſe.

Anſwer. It had been fit they ſhould have ſet downe ſome particular caſes, in which they find the eccleſiaſticall courts injured by the temporall (as their lordſhips did order) unto which we would have given a particular anſwer; but upon theſe generalities nothing but clamour can be concluded. And where they ſpeake of multitudes of prohibitions; for all granted to, or in reſpect of any eccleſiaſticall court, we have heretofore cauſed diligent ſearch to be made in the kings bench and common pleas, from the beginning of his majeſties raigne, unto the end of Hilary term, in the third yeare of his raigne; in which time we find, that there were granted unto all the eccleſiaſticall courts in England out of the kings bench but 251. whereof 149. were *de modo decimandi*, upon unity of poſſeſſion, for trees of 20 yeares growth and upwards, and for barren and heath ground, and all out of the common pleas, but 62. whereof 31. were ſuch as before, and the reſt grounded upon the bounds of pariſhes, or ſuch other cauſes as they ought to be granted for; but for that which was done in the late queenes time, it would be too long a ſearch for us to make, to deliver any certainty thereof. And for his majeſties time, they requiring to have but two to be lawfully warranted upon the libell in the eccleſiaſticall court, we have ſix to ſhew to be lawfully warranted upon the libell there, and ſo are all the reſt of like kind, by which it will appeare, that this ſuggeſtion is not onely untrue, but alſo, that the extraordinary charges growing unto poore men, are of neceſſity by meanes of the undue practices of eccleſiaſticall courts.

The multiplying of prohibitions in one and the ſame cauſe, the libell being not altered. 5.

Objection. Although it hath been anciently ordained by a ſtatute, that when a conſultation is once duly granted upon a prohibition made

to

to the judge of holy church, the ſame judge may proceed in the cauſe, by vertue of that conſultation, notwithſtanding any other prohibition to him delivered, provided that the matter in the libell of the ſame cauſe be not engroſſed, enlarged, or otherwiſe changed; yet notwithſtanding prohibitions and conſultations in one and the ſame cauſe, the libell being no waies altered according to the ſaid ſtatute, are lately ſo multiplyed, as that in ſome one cauſe, as aforeſaid, two, in ſome three, in ſome other ſix prohibitions, and ſo many conſultations have been awarded, yea divers are ſo granted out of one court: as for example, when after long ſuit a conſultation is obtained, it is thought a ſufficient cauſe to ſend out another prohibition in revocation of the ſaid conſultation, upon ſuggeſtion therein contained, that the ſaid conſultation *minus commode emanavit.* By which pretty device the judges of thoſe courts which grant prohibitions, may, notwithſtanding the ſaid ſtatute, upon one
[604] libell not altered, grant as many prohibitions as they liſt, commanding the eccleſiaſticall judges in his majeſties name, not to proceed in any cauſe that is ſo divers times by them prohibited, whereby the poore plaintifes doe not know when their conſultations (procured with great charge) will hold, and ſo finding ſuch and ſo many difficulties, are driven to goe home in great griefe, and to leave the cauſes in Weſtminſter hall, the eccleſiaſticall judges not daring to hold any plea of them. Now may it pleaſe your lordſhips, the premiſſes being true, we humbly deſire to heare what the judges are able to produce for the juſtifying of theſe their proceedings.

Anſwer. It were fit they ſhould ſet downe particular cauſes, whereupon this grievance is grounded, and then we doubt not but to anſwer it ſufficiently, without uſing any pretty device, ſuch as is ſet downe in this article.

6. The multiplying of prohibitions in divers cauſes, but of the ſame nature, after conſultations formerly awarded.

Objection. We ſuppoſe, that as well his majeſties eccleſiaſticall juriſdiction, as alſo very many of his poore, but dutifull ſubjects, are greatly prejudiced by the granting of divers ſeverall prohibitions, and conſultations in cauſes of one and the ſame nature and condition, and upon the ſelfe ſame ſuggeſtions: for example, in caſe of beating a clerke, the prohibition being granted upon this ſuggeſtion, that all pleas *de vi et armis* belong to the crowne, &c. notwithſtanding a conſultation doth thereupon enſue, yet the very next day after, if the like ſuggeſtion be made upon the beating of another clerke, even in the ſame court another prohibition is awarded. As alſo, where 570 prohibitions have been granted ſince the late queenes time into the court of arches (as before is mentioned) and but 113 conſultations afterwards upon ſo many of them obtained: yet it is evident by the ſaid conſultations, that (in effect) all the reſt of the ſaid prohibitions ought not to have been awarded, as being grounded upon the ſame ſuggeſtions, whereupon conſultations have been formerly granted: and ſo it followeth, that the cauſes why conſultations were awarded upon the reſt of the ſaid prohibitions, were for that either the plaintifes in the court eccleſiaſticall were driven for ſaving of further charge, to compound, to their loſſe, with their adverſaries, or were not able to ſue for them; or being able, yet through

through ſtrength of oppoſition againſt them, were conſtrained to deſiſt; which is an argument to us, that the temporall judges doe wittingly and willingly grant prohibitions, whereupon they know, before hand, that conſultations are due: and if we miſtake any thing in the premiſſes, we deſire your lordſhips, that the judges, for the juſtification of their courſes, may better enforme us.

Anſwer. It ſhall be good, the eccleſiaſtical judges doe better enforme themſelves, and that they put ſome one or two particular caſes to prove their ſuggeſtions, and thereupon they will find their owne errour; for the caſe may be ſo, that two ſeverall miniſters ſuing in the eccleſiaſticall court for beating of them in one and the ſelfe ſame forme, that the one may and ought to have a conſultation, and the other not. And ſo it is in caſes of prohibitions, *de modo decimandi*; and hereof groweth the overſight in making this objection. And we aſſure our ſelves, that they ſhall not find 570 prohibitions granted into the arches ſince her late majeſties death; for we find (if our clerkes affirme truly upon their ſearch) that out of the kings bench have been granted to all the eccleſiaſticall courts in England but 251 prohibitions (as before is mentioned) from the beginning of his majeſties raigne, unto the end of Hilary terme laſt; and out of the common pleas not 63. And therefore it cannot be true, that ſo many have paſſed to the arches in that time, as is ſet downe in the article; and this article in that point doth exceed that which is ſet downe in the fourth article by almoſt 500, and therefore whoſoever ſet this downe, was much forgetfull of that which was before ſet downe in the fourth article, and might well have forborne to lay ſo great a ſcandall upon the judges, as [605] to affirme it to be a witting and willing errour in them, as is ſet downe in this article.

7. New formes of conſultations, not expreſſing the cauſe of the granting of them.

Objection. Whereas upon the granting of conſultations, the judges in times paſt did therein expreſſe and acknowledge the cauſes ſo remitted to be of eccleſiaſticall cognizance, which were preſidents and judgements for the better aſſurance of eccleſiaſticall judges, that they might afterward hold plea in ſuch caſes, and the like; and were alſo ſome barre as well to the temporall judges themſelves, as alſo to many troubleſome and contentious perſons from either granting or ſeeking prohibitions in ſuch caſes, when ſo it did appeare unto them upon record, that conſultations had been formerly granted in them; they the ſaid temporall judges have now altered that courſe, and doe onely tell us, that they grant their conſultations *certis de cauſis ipſos apud Weſtm' moventibus*, not expreſſing the ſame particularly, according to their ancient preſidents. By meanes whereof the temporall judges leave themſelves at liberty without prejudice, though they deny a conſultation; at another time upon the ſame matter contentious perſons are animated, finding no cauſe expreſſed, why they may not at another time ſeeke for a prohibition in the ſame cauſe; and the eccleſiaſticall judges are left at large to thinke what they liſt, being no way inſtructed of the nature of the cauſe which procured the conſultation: the reaſon of which alteration in ſuch conſultations, we humbly intreat your

lordships, that the judges, for our better instruction, may be required to expresse.

Answer. If we find the declaration upon the surmise, upon which the prohibition is granted, not to warrant the surmise, then we forthwith grant a consultation in that forme which is mentioned, and that matter being mentioned in the consultation would be very long and cumbersome, and give the ecclesiasticall court little information, to direct them in any thing thereafter; and therefore in such cases, for brevity sake, it is usuall: but when the matter is to receive end by demurrer in law, or tryall, the consultation is in another forme. And it is their ignorance in the arches, that will not understand this, and we may not supply their defects with changing our formes of proceedings, wherein if they would take the advice of any learned in the lawes, they might soon receive satisfaction.

8. That consultations may be obtained with lesse charge and difficulty.

Objection. The great expences and manifold difficulties in obtaining of consultations are become very burthensome to those that seeke for them; for now a dayes, through the malice of the plaintifes in the temporall courts, and the covetous humours of the clerkes, prohibitions are so extended and enlarged, without any necessity of the matter (some one prohibition containing more words and lines then forty prohibitions in ancient times) as by meanes thereof the party in the ecclesiasticall court, against whom the prohibition is granted, becomes either unwilling, or unable to sue for a consultation, it being now usuall and ordinary, that in the consultations must be recited *in eadem verba* the whole tenour of the prohibition, be it never so long; for the which (to omit divers other fees, which are very great) he must pay for a draught of it in paper viii. d. the sheet, and for the entry of it xii. d. the sheet. Furthermore, the prohibition is quicke and speedy: for it is ordinarily granted out of court by any one of the judges in his chamber, whereas the consultation is very slowly and hardly obtained, not without (oftentimes) costly motions in open court, pleadings, demurrers, and sundry judiciall hearings of both parties, and long attendance for the space of two or three, nay, sometimes of eight [606] or nine years before it be obtained. The inconvenience of which proceedings is so intolerable, as we trust, such as are to grant consultations will by your lordships meanes not onely doe it expeditely, and moderate the said fees; but also reforme the length of the said consultations, according to the formes of consultations in the Register.

Answer. It were fit the particular cause were set downe, whereupon the generall grievance, that is mentioned in this article, is grounded; and that done, it may have a full answer: for a prohibition is grounded upon the libell, and the consultation must agree therewith also; and therefore we doubt not, but the ground of this grievance, when it is well looked into, will grow from themselves in interlacing of much nugatory and unnecessary matter in their libells: and for the fees taken; wee assure our selves, none are taken, but such as are anciently due and accustomed; and it will appeare, that we have abridged the fees, and length of pleadings, and

and use no delayes, but such as are of necessity, and we wish they would doe the like, and upon examination it will appeare of which side it growes, that the fees or delayes are so intolerable. And where in ancient time such as sued for tithes, would not sue but for things questionable, and never sought at their parishioners hands their tithes in other kinds then anciently they had been used to have been paid; now many turbulent ministers do infinitely vexe their parishioners for such kinds of tithes as they never had, whereby many parishes have been much impoverished: and for example, we shall shew one record, wherein the minister did demand seventeen severall kinds of tithes, whereupon the partie suing a prohibition had eight or nine of them adjudged against the minister upon demurrer in law, and other passed against him by tryall, and this must of necessity grow to a matter of great charge; but where is the fault, but in the minister that gave occasion? and we will shew one other record, wherein the party confessed to some of us, that hee was to sue his parishioner but for a calfe and a goose; and that his proctor neverthelesse put in the libell or demand of tithes, of seven or eight things more then he had cause to sue for: this enlarged the prohibition, and gave occasion of more expence then needed; and where is the fault of this, but in the ecclesiasticall courts? and as in these, so can wee approve in many others; and therefore wee must retort the cause and ground of this grievance upon themselves, as more particularly may appeare by the severall presidents to be shewed in this behalfe.

Prohibitions not to be granted upon frivolous suggestions. 9.

Objection. It it a prejudice and derision to both his majesties ecclesiasticall and temporall jurisdictions, that many prohibitions are granted upon trifling and frivolous suggestions, altogether unworthy to proceed from the one, or to give any hinderance or interruption to the other: as upon a suit of tithes brought by a minister against his parishioner, a prohibition flyeth out upon suggestion, that in regard of a speciall receipt, called a cup of buttered beare made by the great skill of the said parishioner to cure a grievous disease called a cold, which sorely troubled the said minister, all his tithes were discharged. And likewise a woman being convented for adultery committed with one that suspiciously resorted to her house in the night time, the suggestion of a prohibition in this case was, that *omnia placita de nocturnis ambulationibus* belong to the king, &c. Also where a legatary sued for his legacy given in a will, the prohibition was, *Quia omnia placita de donis et concessionibus spectant ad forum regium, et non ad forum ecclesiasticum, dummodo non sint de testamento et matrimonio*; as if a legacy were not *donatio de* or *in testamento*, with many other of like sort. The reformation of all which frivolous proceedings, so chargable notwithstanding to many poore men, and the great hinderance of justice, we humbly referre to your lordships consideration.

Answer. We grant none upon frivolous suggestions, but for the case put, it is ridiculous in the minister to make such a contract (if any such [607] were) but that maketh not the contract void, but discovereth the unworthinesse of the party that made the same, and yet no fault in granting the prohibition; but when it shall appeare unto us, that such a matter is suggested by fraud of any clerke or counceller at

at law, we will not remit ſuch offences, but will exclude ſuch attorney from the court, and ſuch councellers from their practice at the barre. And if they will ſuggeſt adultery to one, againſt whom they prove but night-walking, and doe adjudge him for it, we are in ſuch a caſe to prohibite their proceedings: for that is a matter meerly pertinent to the temporall court; ſo, if it appeare hee hath entred the houſe as a thiefe, or a burglarer, and ſo in many other caſes alſo. And if any ſurmiſe a legacy from the dead, where it was but a promiſe of payment in his life time, in that caſe ſuch a ſuit is to be prohibited: but if in theſe caſes the parties were named, then we might ſee the record, and thereupon be directed to ſhew upon what conſideration theſe prohibitions were granted, otherwiſe wee ſhall thinke that theſe are caſes newly invented.

10. No prohibition to be granted at his ſuit, who is plaintife in the Spirituall Court.

Objection. We ſuppoſe it to be no warrantable nor reaſonable courſe, that prohibitions are granted at the ſuit of the plaintife in the eccleſiaſticall court, who having made choice thereof, and brought his adverſary there into tryall, doth by all intendment of law and reaſon, and by the uſage of all other judiciall places conclude himſelfe in that behalfe; and although he cannot be preſumed to hope for helpe in any other court by way of prohibition, yet it is very uſuall for every ſuch perſon ſo proceeding onely of meere malice for vexation of the party, and to the great delay and hinderance of juſtice, to find favour for the obtaining of prohibitions, ſometimes after two or three ſentences, thereby taking advantage (as he muſt plead) of his owne wrong, and receiving aide from that court, which, by his owne confeſſion, he before did contemne; touching the equity whereof, we will expect the anſwer of the judges.

Anſwer. None may purſue in the eccleſiaſticall court for that which the kings courts ought to hold plea of, but upon information thereof given to the kings courts, either by the plaintife, or by any meere ſtranger, they are to be prohibited, becauſe they deale in that which appertaineth not to their juriſdiction, where if they would be carefull not to hold plea of that which appertaineth not to them, this needed not: and if they will proceed in the kings courts againſt ſuch as purſue in the eccleſiaſticall courts for matter temporall, that is to be inflicted upon them, which the quality of their offence requireth; and how many ſentences howſoever are given, yet prohibitions thereupon are not of favour, but of juſtice to be granted.

11. No prohibition to be granted, but upon due conſideration of the libell.

Objection. It is (we are perſwaded) a great abuſe, and one of the chiefe grounds of the moſt of the former abuſes, and many other, that prohibitions are granted without ſight of the libell in the eccleſiaſticall court; yea, ſometimes before the libell be there exhibited, whereas by the lawes and ſtatutes of this realme (as we thinke) the libell (being a briefe declaration of the matter in debate betweene the plaintife and defendant) is appointed as the only rule and direction for

for the due granting of a prohibition, the reason whereof is evident, *viz.* upon diligent consideration of the libell it will easily appeare, whether the cause belong to the temporall or ecclesiasticall cognizance, as on the other side without sight of the libell, the prohibition must needs range and roave with strange and forraigne suggestions at the will and pleasure of the devisor, nothing pertinent to the matter in demand: whereupon it cometh to passe, that [608] when the judge ecclesiasticall is handling a matter of simony, a prohibition is grounded upon a suggestion, that the court tryeth *placita de advocationibus ecclesiarum, et de jure patronatus.* And when the libell containeth nothing but the demand of tithe wooll, and lamb, the prohibition surmiseth a custome of paying of tithe pigeons. So that if it may be made a matter of conscience to grant prohibitions only, where they doe rightly lye, or to preserve the jurisdiction ecclesiasticall united to his majesties crowne, it cannot (we hope) but seem necessary to your lordships, that due consideration be first had of the libell in the ecclesiasticall court, before any prohibition be granted.

Who hath an advowsion granted to him for money, being sued for simony, shall have a prohibition; and it is manifest, that though in the libell there appeare no matter to grant a prohibition, yet upon a collaterall surmise the prohibition is to be granted: as where one is sued in a spirituall court for tithes of *silva cædua*, the party may suggest, that they were grosse or great trees, and have a prohibition, yet no such matter appeareth in the libell. So if one bee sued there for violent hands laid on a minister by an officer, as a constable, hee being sued there may suggest, that the plaintife made an affray upon another, and he to preserve the peace laid hands on him, and so have a prohibition. And so in very many other like cases, and yet upon the libell no matter appeareth why a prohibition should be granted: and they will never shew, that a custome to pay pigeons was allowed to discharge the payment of wooll, lamb, or such like. Answer.

No prohibition to be granted under pretence, that one witnesse cannot be received in the ecclesiasticall court, to ground a judgement upon. 12.

There is a new devised suggestion in the temporall courts commonly received and allowed, whereby they may at their will and pleasure draw any cause whatsoever from the ecclesiasticall court: for example, many prohibitions have lately come forth upon this suggestion, that the lawes ecclesiasticall doe require two witnesses, where the common law accepteth of one; and therefore it is *contra legem terræ*, for the ecclesiasticall judge to insist upon two witnesses to prove his cause: upon which suggestion, although many consultations have been granted (the same being no way as yet able to warrant and maintaine a prohibition) yet because we are not sure, but that either by reason of the use of it, or of some future construction, it may have given to it more strength then is convenient, the same tending to the utter overthrow of all ecclesiasticall jurisdiction, we most humbly desire, that by your lordships good meanes, the same may be ordered to be no more used. Objection.

If the question be upon payment, or setting out of tithes, or upon the proofe of a legacy, or marriage, or such like incidence, Answer.

we are to leave it to the tryall of their law, though the party have but one witnesse; but where the matter is not determinable in the ecclesiasticall court, there lyeth a prohibition either upon, or without such a surmise.

13. No good suggestion for a prohibition, that the cause is neither testamentary, nor matrimoniall.

Objection. As the former device last mentioned endevoureth to strike away at one blow the whole ecclesiasticall jurisdiction; so there is another as usuall, or rather more frequent then the former, which is content to spare us two kind of causes to deale in, *viz.* testamentary, and matrimoniall: and this device insulteth mightily in many prohibitions, commanding the ecclesiasticall judge, that be the cause never so apparently of ecclesiasticall cognisance, yet hee shall surcease; for that is neither a cause testamentary, nor matrimoniall: [609] which suggestion, as it grew at the first upon mistaking, and omitting the words, *de bonis et catallis, &c.* as may appeare by divers ancient prohibitions in the Register; so it will not be denied, but that, besides those two, divers and sundry other causes are notoriously knowne to be of ecclesiasticall cognizance, and that consultations are as usually awarded (if suit in that behalfe be prosecuted) notwithstanding the said suggestion, as their prohibitions are easily granted; which, as an injury, marching with the rest to wound poore men, protract suits, and prejudice the courts ecclesiasticall, we desire that the judges will be pleased to redresse.

Answer. If they observe well the answer to the former objections, they may be thereby satisfied, that we prohibit not so generally as they pretend, nor doe in any wise deale further then we ought to doe, to the prejudice of that which appertaineth to that jurisdiction; but when they will deale with matters of temporall contracts, coloured with pretended ecclesiasticall matter, wee ought to prohibit them with that forme of prohibitions, mentioning, that it concerneth not matter of marriage, nor testamentary: and they shall not find that we have granted any, but by form warranted, both by the Register, and by law: And when suggestions, carrying matter sufficient, appeare to us judicially to be untrue and insufficient, we are as ready to grant consultations as prohibitions: and we may not alter the forme of our prohibitions upon the conceits of ecclesiasticall judges, and prohibitions granted in the forme set downe in the article, are of that forme which by law they ought to be, and cannot be altered but by parliament.

14. No prohibition upon surmise onely to be granted, either out of the kings bench, or common pleas, but out of the chancery onely.

Objection. Amongst the causes whereby the ecclesiasticall jurisdiction is oppressed with multitude of prohibitions upon surmises onely, this hath a chiefe place, in that through incroachment (as wee suppose) there are so many severall courts, and judges in them, that take upon them to grant the same, as in the kings bench five, and in the common pleas as many, the one court oftentimes crossing the proceedings of the other, whereas wee are perswaded, that all such kinds of prohibitions, being originall writs, ought onely to issue out

out of the chancery, and neither out of the kings bench, nor common pleas. And that this hath been the ancient practice in that behalfe, appeareth by some statutes of the realme, and sundry judgements at the common law; the renewing of which practice carrieth with it an apparant shew of great benefit and conveniency, both to the church, and to the subject: for if prohibitions were to issue onely out of one court, and from one man of such integrity, judgement, sincerity, and wisedom, as we are to imagine the lord chancellour of England to be endued with, it is not likely, that he would ever be induced to prejudice and pester the ecclesiasticall courts with so many needlesse prohibitions: or, after a consultation, to send out in one cause, and upon one and the same libell not altered, prohibition upon prohibition, his owne act remaining upon record before him to the contrary. The further consideration whereof, when, upon the judges answer thereunto, it shall be more thoroughly debated, wee must referre to your lordships honourable direction and wisdome.

Answer

A strange presumption in the ecclesiasticall judges, to require that the kings courts should not doe that which by law they ought to doe, and alwayes have done, and which by oath they are bound to doe! and if this shall be holden inconvenient, and they can in discharge of us obtaine some act of parliament to take it from all other courts then the chancery, they shall doe unto us a great ease: but the law of the realme cannot be changed, but by parliament; and what reliefe or ease such an act may worke to the subject, wise men will soone finde out and discerne: but by these articles [610] thus dispersed abroad, there is a generall unbeseeming aspersion of that upon the judges, which ought to have been forborn.

No prohibition to be awarded under a false pretence, that the ecclesiasticall judges would hold no plea for customes for tithes. 15.

Objection.

Amongst many devices, whereby the cognizance of causes of tithes is drawn from ecclesiasticall judges, this is one of the chiefest, *viz.* concerning the tryall of customes in payment of tithes, that it must be made in a temporall court; for upon a quirke and false suggestion in Edward the fourth his time, made by some sergeants, a conceit hath risen (which hath lately taken greater strength then before) that ecclesiasticall judges will allow no plea of custome or prescription, either in *non decimando*, or *in modo decimandi*; and thereupon, when contentious persons are sued in the ecclesiasticall court for tithes, and doe perceive, that upon good proofe judgement will be given against them, even in their owne pleas, sometimes for customes, doe presently (knowing their own strength with jurors in the country) flie unto Westminster hall, and there suggesting that they pleaded custome for themselves in the ecclesiasticall courts, but could not be heard, doe procure thence very readily a prohibition; and albeit the said suggestion be notoriously false, yet the party prohibited may not bee permitted to traverse the same in the temporall court (directly contrary to a statute made in that behalfe): neither may the judge prohibited proceed without danger of an attachment, though himselfe doe certainly know, either that no such custome was ever alledged before him, or being alledged, that he did receive the same, and all manner of proofes

 offered

offered thereupon: which course seemeth the more strange unto us, because the ground thereof laid in Edward the fourth his time, as aforesaid, was altogether untrue, and cannot with any sound reason be maintained: divers statutes and judgements at the common law doe allow the ecclesiasticall courts to hold plea of such customes; all our bookes and generall learning doe therewith concurre, and the ecclesiasticall courts, both then and ever since, even untill this day, have, and still doe admit the same, as both by our ancient and recent records it doth and may to any most manifestly appeare. And besides, there are some consultations to bee shewed in this very point, wherein the said surmise and suggestion, that the ecclesiasticall judges will heare no plea of customes, is affirmed to be insufficient in law to maintaine any such prohibition: and therefore we hope, that if we shall be able, notwithstanding any thing the judges shall answer thereunto, to justifie the premisses, your Lordships will be a meanes, that the abuses herein complained of, having so false a ground, may be amended.

Answer. The temporall courts have alwayes granted prohibitions as well in cases *de modo decimandi*, as in cases upon reall compositions, either in discharge of tithes, or the manner of tithing: for that *modus decimandi* had his originall ground upon some composition in that kinde made, and all prescriptions and compositions in these cases are to be tryed at the common law, and the ecclesiasticall courts ought to be prohibited, if in these cases they had plea of tithes in kind: but if they will sue in the ecclesiasticall court *de modo decimandi*, or according to composition, then we prohibit them not: and the cause why the ecclesiasticall judges find fault herewith, is, because many ministers have growne of late more troublesome to their parishioners, then in times past; and thereby worke unto these courts more commodity, whereas in former ages they were well contented to accept that which was used to be paid, and not to contend against any prescription or composition; but now they grow so troublesome to their neighbours, as, were it not for the prohibition (as may appeare by the presidents before remembred) they would soone overthrow all prescriptions and compositions that are for tithes, which doth and would breed such a
[611] generall garboile amongst the people, as were to be pitied, and not to be permitted. And where they say, there bee many statutes that take away these proceedings from the temporall courts, they are much deceived; and if they looke well unto it, they shall find even the same statutes (they pretend) to give way unto it. And it is strange they will affirme so great an untruth, as to say, they are not permitted to traverse the suggestion in the temporall court; for both the law and daily practice doth allow it.

16. The customes for tithes are onely to be tried in the ecclesiasticall courts, and ought not to be drawne thence by prohibitions.

Objection. Although some indiscreet ecclesiasticall judges, either in the time of king Edward the fourth, or Edward the sixth, might, against law, have refused in some one cause to admit a plea of custome of tithes, to the prejudice of some person whom he favoured, and might thereby peradventure have given occasion of some one prohibition (but whether they did so or no, the suggestion of a lawyer for his fee is no good proofe) yet forasmuch as by three statutes made

made ſince that time, wherein it is ordained, *viz.* both that tithes ſhould be truly paid, according to the cuſtome, and the tryall of ſuch payments, according to cuſtome upon any default or oppoſition, ſhould be tryed in the kings eccleſiaſticall courts, and by the kings eccleſiaſticall lawes, and not otherwiſe, or before any other judges then eccleſiaſticall, we moſt humbly deſire your lordſhips, that if according to the ſaid lawes we be moſt ready to heare any plea of cuſtomes your lordſhips would be pleaſed, that the judges may not be permitted hereafter to grant any prohibitions upon ſuch falſe ſurmiſes; or if they ſhall anſwer, that wee miſtake the ſaid ſtatutes, that then the ſaid three ſtatutes may bee throughly debated before your lordſhips, leſt under pretence of a right, which they challenge, to expound theſe kind of ſtatutes, the truth may be over-borne, and poore miniſters ſtill left unto country tryalls, there to juſtifie the right of their tithes before unconſcionable jurors in theſe caſes.

The anſwer to the former article may ſerve for this; and where the objection ſeemeth to impeach the tryall at the common law by jurors, we hold, and ſhall be able to approve it to be a farre better courſe for matter of fact upon the teſtimonie of witneſſes, ſworne *viva voce*, then upon the conſcience of any one particular man, being guided by paper proofes; and we never heard it excepted unto heretofore, that any ſtatute ſhould be expounded by any other then the judges of the land; neither was there ever any ſo much over-ſeen, as to oppoſe himſelfe againſt the practice of all ages to make that queſtion, or to lay any ſuch unjuſt imputation upon the judges of the realme. Anſwer.

No prohibition to be granted, becauſe the treble value of tithes is ſued for in the eccleſiaſticall court. 17.

Whereas it appeareth plainly by the tenour of the ſtatute of Edw. 6. cap. 13. that judges eccleſiaſticall, and none other, are to heare and determine all ſuits of tithes, and other duties for the ſame, which are given by the ſaid act; and that nothing elſe is added to former lawes by that ſtatute, but onely certaine penalties, for example, one of treble value: foraſmuch as the ſaid penalty, being onely deviſed as a meanes to worke the better payment of tithes, and for that there are no words uſed in the ſaid ſtatute to give juriſdiction to any temporall court, we hold it moſt apparant, that the ſaid penalty of treble value, being a duty given in the ſaid ſtatute for non-payment of tithes, cannot bee demanded in the temporall court, but onely before the eccleſiaſticall judges, according to the expreſſe words of the ſaid ſtatute: and the rather, wee are ſo perſwaded, becauſe it is moſt agreeable to all lawes and reaſon, that where the principall cauſe is to bee decided, there all things incident and acceſſary are to bee determined. Beſides, it was the practice of all eccleſiaſticall courts in this realme, immediately after the making of the ſaid ſtatute, and hath continued ſo ever ſince to award treble damages (when there hath been cauſe) without any oppoſition, untill about ten yeares paſt, when, or about which time, notwithſtanding the premiſſes, the temporall judges began to hold plea of treble value, and doe now accompt it ſo proper and peculiar to their juriſdictions, as by colour thereof they admit ſuits originally for the ſaid penalty, and doe make thereby Objection [612]

(very

(very absurdly) the penalty of treble value to bee principall, which is indeed but the accessary; and the cognizance of tithes to bee but the accessary, which in all due construction is most evident to be the principall, thereby wholly perverting the true meaning and drift of that statute, whereupon if in the spirituall court the treble value be now demanded by the libell as a duty, according to that statute, or that sentence be awarded directly and sincerely upon the said libell, presently, as contentious persons are disposed, a prohibition is granted, and some sharp words are further used, as if the ecclesiasticall judges were in some further danger for holding of these kind of pleas: and therefore we most humbly desire, that if the judges shall insist in their answers upon such their straining of the said statute, your lordships will be pleased to heare the same further debated by us with them.

Answer. If they observe well the statute, they shall find, that the ecclesiasticall court is by that statute to hold plea of no more, then that which is specially thereby limited for them to hold plea of; and the temporall court not restrained thereby, to hold plea of that which is not limited unto the ecclesiasticall court by that act, and of that they had jurisdiction of before: and the forfeiture of double value is expresly limited to be recovered before the ecclesiasticall judges; but where a forfeiture is given by an act generally not limiting where to be recovered, it is to be recovered in the kings temporall courts, and the cause why it is so divided, seemeth to be for that, where by that act, temporall men were to sue for their tithes in the ecclesiasticall court, where it was then presumed they were to have no great favour: therefore the party grieved might (if he would) pursue for the forfeiture of the treble value in the temporall court, where hee was to recover no tithes; but if he would sue where he might also recover the tithes, then hee would pursue for the double value: for that is specially appointed to be recovered in the ecclesiasticall court, but not the treble value. And although they alledge, that they sometimes used to maintaine suit for the treble value, yet as soon as that was complained of to the kings courts, they gave remedy unto it as appertained.

18. No prohibition to be awarded, where the person is stopped from carrying away of his tithes by him that setteth them forth.

Objection. As the said statute of Edward the sixth last mentioned assigneth a penalty of treble value, if a man upon pretence of custome, which cannot be justified, shall take away his corne before he hath set out his tithes; so also in the said statute it is provided, that if any man having set out his tithes, shall not afterwards suffer the parson to carry them away, &c. he shal pay the double value thereof so carried away, the same to be recovered in the ecclesiasticall court. Howbeit the clearnesse of the statute in this point, notwithstanding meanes are found to draw this cause also from the ecclesiasticall court; for such as of hatred towards their ministers are disposed to vexe them with suits at the common law (where they finde more favour to maintaine their wrangling, then they can hope for in the ecclesiasticall court) will not faile to set out their tithes before witnesses, but not with any meaning or intent that the parson shall ever carry them away; for presently thereupon they will cause their owne servants to load them away to their owne

owne barnes, and leave the parson as he can to seek his remedy; which if he do attempt in the ecclesiasticall court, out cometh a prohibition, suggesting, that upon severance and setting forth of the tenth part from the nine, the same tenths were presently by law in the parsons possession, and being thereupon become a lay chattell, must be recovered by an action of trespasse at the common law, whereas the whole pretence is grounded upon a meere perverting of the statute, which doth both ordain, that all tithes shall be set forth truly and justly without fraud and guile; and that also the parson shall not be stopped or hindered from carrying them away, neither of which conditions are observed when the farmer doth set them forth, meaning to carry them away himselfe (for that is the fraudulent setting of them out;) and also, when accordingly hee taketh them away to his own use; for thereby hee stoppeth the parson to carry them away: and consequently, the penalty of this offence is to bee recovered in the said ecclesiasticall courts, according to the words of the said statute, and not in any court temporall: wherefore we most humbly desire your lordships, that either the judges may make it apparant to your lordships, that we mislike this statute in this point, or that our ecclesiasticall courts may ever hereafter be freed from such kinds of prohibitions. [613]

Answer. For the matter of this article it is answered before, and where the truth of the case is, that he that ought to pay prediall tithes, doth not divide out his tithes, or doth in any wise interrupt the parson or his deputy, to see the dividing or setting of them out: that appearing unto us judicially, we maintain no prohibition upon any suit there for the double value, but if after the tithes severed, the parson will sell the tithes to the party that divided them, upon the surmise thereof, we doe, and ought to grant a prohibition; but if that surmise doe prove untrue, we do as readily grant a consultation, and the party seeking the same, is, according to the statute, to have his double costs and damages.

No prohibition to be granted upon any incident plea in an ecclesiasticall cause. 19.

Objection. We conceive it to be great injury to his majesties ecclesiasticall jurisdiction, that prohibitions are awarded to his ecclesiasticall courts upon every by, and every incident plea or matter alledged there in barre, or by way of exception, the principall cause being undoubtedly of ecclesiasticall cognizance: for example, in suit for tithes in kind, if the limits of the parish, agreements, compositions, and arbitraments, as also whether the minister that sueth as parson, be indeed parson or vicar, doe come in debate by way of barre, although the same particulars were of temporall cognizance (as some of them wee may boldly say are not) yet they were in this case examinable in the ecclesiasticall court, because they are matters incident, which come not in that case finally to be sentenced and determined, but are used as a meane and furtherance for the decision of the maine matter in question. And so the case standeth in other such incident pleas by way of barre; for otherwise either party in every cause might at his pleasure, by pleading some matter temporall by way of exception, make any cause ecclesiasticall whatsoever subject to a prohibition, which is contrary to the reason of the common law, and sundry judgements thereupon given,

given, as wee hope the judges themſelves will acknowledge, and thereupon yeeld to have ſuch prohibitions hereafter reſtrained.

Anſwer. Matters incident that fall out to be meere temporall, are to be dealt withall in the temporall, and not in the eccleſiaſtical court, as is before particularly ſet downe in the eleventh article.

20. That no temporall judges, under colour of authority to interpret ſtatutes, ought, in favour of their prohibitions, to make cauſes eccleſiaſticall to be of temporall cognizance.

Objection. Although of late dayes it hath been ſtrongly held by ſome, that the interpretation of all ſtatutes whatſoever doe belong to the judges temporall, yet we ſuppoſe, by certain evil effects, that this [614] opinion is to bee bounded within certaine limits; for the ſtrong conceit of it hath already brought forth this fruit, that even thoſe very ſtatutes which doe concerne matters meerly eccleſiaſticall, and were made of purpoſe with great caution, to preſerve, enlarge, and ſtrengthen the juriſdiction eccleſiaſticall, have been by colour thereof turned to the reſtraining, weakening, and utter overthrow of the ſame, contrary to the true intent and meaning of the ſaid ſtatutes: as for example (beſides the ſtrange interpretation of the ſtatutes before mentioned, for the payment of tithes) when parties have been ſued in the eccleſiaſtical courts, in caſe of an inceſtuous marriage, a prohibition hath been awarded, ſuggeſting, under pretence of a ſtatute in the time of king Hen. 8. that it appertaineth to the temporall courts, and not to the eccleſiaſticall, to determine what marriages are lawfull, and what are inceſtuous by the word of God. As alſo a miniſter, being upon point of deprivation for his inſufficiency in the eccleſiaſticall court, a prohibition was granted, upon ſuggeſtion that all pleas of the fitneſſe, learning, and ſufficiency of miniſters belong only to the kings temporall courts, relying, as wee ſuppoſe, upon the ſtatute of 13 Eliz. by which kind of interpretation of ſtatutes, if the naming, diſpoſing, or ordering of cauſes eccleſiaſticall in a ſtatute ſhall make the ſame to be of temporal cognizance, and ſo aboliſh the juriſdiction of the eccleſiaſticall court, without any further circumſtances, or expreſſe words to warrant the ſame, it followeth, that foraſmuch as the common book and articles of religion are eſtabliſhed and confirmed by ſeverall acts of parliament, the temporall judges may challenge to themſelves an authority to end and determine of all cauſes of faith and religion, and to ſend out their prohibitions, if any eccleſiaſticall judge ſhall deale or proceed in any of them: which conceit, how abſurd it is, needeth no proofe, and teacheth us, that when matters meerly eccleſiaſticall are comprized in any ſtatute, it doth not therefore follow, that the interpretation of the ſaid matters doth belong to the temporall judges, who by their profeſſion, and as they are judges, are not acquainted with that kind of learning: hereunto, when we ſhall receive the anſwer of the judges, we ſhall be ready to juſtifie every part of this article.

Anſwer. If any ſuch have ſlipt, as is ſet downe in this article, without other circumſtances to maintaine it, we make no doubt, but when that appeared to the kings temporall court, it hath been preſently remitted; and yet there be caſes, that we may deale both with marriages and matters of deprivation, as where they will call the marriage in queſtion after the death of any of the parties, the marriage

marriage may not then be called in queſtion, becauſe it is to baſtard and diſinherit the iſſues, who cannot ſo well defend the marriage, as the parties both living themſelves might have done; and ſo is it, if they will deprive a miniſter not for matter appertaining to the eccleſiaſticall cognizance, but for that which doth meerly belong to the cognizance of the kings temporall courts. And for the judges expounding of ſtatutes that concerne the eccleſiaſticall government or proceedings, it belongeth unto the temporall judges; and wee thinke they have been expounded as much to their advantage, as either the letter or intention of lawes would or could allow of. And when they have been expounded to their liking, then they could approve of it; but if the expoſition be not for their purpoſe, then will they ſay, as now they doe, that it appertaineth not unto us to determine of them.

That perſons impriſoned upon the writ of *de excommunicato capiendo* are unduly delivered, and prohibitions unduly awarded for their greater ſecurity. 21.

Objection. Foraſmuch as impriſonment upon the writ of *excommunicato capiendo* is the chiefeſt temporall ſtrength of eccleſiaſticall juriſdiction, and that by the lawes of the realm none ſo committed for their contempt in matters of eccleſiaſticall cognizance, ought to be delivered untill the eccleſiaſticall courts were ſatisfied, or caution given in that behalfe, we would gladly be reſolved by what authority the temporall judges do cauſe the ſherifes to bring the ſaid [615] parties into their courts, and by their owne diſcretions ſet them at liberty, without notice thereof firſt given to the eccleſiaſticall judges, or any ſatisfaction made either to the parties at whoſe ſuit he was impriſoned, or the eccleſiaſticall court, where certaine lawfull fees are due: and after all this, why doe they likewiſe ſend out their prohibitions to the ſaid court, commanding, that all cenſures againſt the ſaid parties ſhall be remitted, and that they be no more proceeded with for the ſame cauſes in thoſe courts. Of this our deſire, we hope your lordſhips do ſee ſufficient cauſe, and will therefore procure us from the judges ſome reaſonable anſwer.

Anſwer. We affirme, if the party excommunicate be impriſoned, wee ought upon complaint to ſend the kings writ for the body and the cauſe, and if in the returne no cauſe, or no ſufficient cauſe appeare, then we doe (as we ought) ſet him at liberty; otherwiſe, if upon removing the body, the matter appeare to be of eccleſiaſticall cognizance, then we remit him againe; and this we ought to doe in both caſes; for the temporall courts muſt alwaies have an eye, that the eccleſiaſticall juriſdiction uſurp not upon the temporall.

The kings authority in eccleſiaſticall cauſes is greatly impugned by prohibitions. 22.

Objection. We are not a little perplexed touching the authority of his majeſtie in cauſes eccleſiaſticall, in that we find the ſame to be ſo impeached by prohibitions, that it is in effect thereby almoſt extinguiſhed; for it ſeemeth, that the innovating humour is growne ſo rank, and that ſome of the temporall judges are come to be of opinion, that the commiſſioners appointed by his majeſty for his cauſes

causes ecclesiasticall (having committed unto them the execution of all ecclesiasticall jurisdiction annexed to his majesties imperiall crowne, by virtue of an act of parliament made in that behalfe, and according to the tenour and effect of his majesties letters patents, wherein they are authorised to imprison, and impose fines, as they shall see cause) cannot otherwise proceed, the said act and letters patents notwithstanding, then by ecclesiasticall censures onely: and thereupon of latter dayes, whereas certaine lewd persons (two for example sake) one for notorious adultery and other intolerable contempts, and another for abusing of a bishop of this kingdome with threatning speeches, and sundry railing termes (no way to be endured) were thereupon fined and imprisoned by the said commissioners, till they should enter into bonds to performe further orders of the said court; the one was delivered by an *habeas corpus* out of the kings bench, and the other by a like writ out of the common pleas: and sundry other prohibitions have been likewise awarded to his majesties said commissioners upon these suggestions, *viz.* that they had no authority either to fine or imprison any man; which innovating conceit being added to this that followeth, That the writ of *de excommunicato capiendo* cannot lawfully be awarded upon any certificate or *significavit* made by the said commissioners, wee find his majesties said supreme authority in causes ecclesiasticall (so largely amplified in sundry statutes) to be altogether destitute in effect of any meanes to uphold it, if the said proceedings by temporall judges shall be by them maintained and justified; and therefore wee most humbly desire your lordships, that they may declare themselves herein, and be restrained hereafter (if there be cause found) from using the kings name in their prohibitions, to so great prejudice of his majesties said authority, as in debating the same before your lordships will hereafter more fully appeare.

Answer. We doe not, neither will we in any wise impugne the ecclesiasticall authority in any thing that appertaineth unto it; but if any by the ecclesiasticall authority commit any man to prison, upon complaint unto us that he is imprisoned without just cause, we are to send to have the body, and to be certified of the cause; and if [616] they will not certifie unto us the particular cause, but generally, without expressing any particular cause, whereby it may appeare unto us to be a matter of the ecclesiasticall cognizance, and his imprisonment be just, then we doe and ought to deliver him: and this is their fault, and not ours. And although some of us have dealt with them to make some such particular certificate to us, whereby wee may bee able to judge upon it, as by law they ought to doe, yet they will by no meanes doe it; and therefore their errour is the cause of this, and no fault in us: for if we see not a just cause of the parties imprisonment by them, then we ought, and are bound by oath to deliver him.

23. No prohibition to be granted, under pretence to reforme the manner of proceedings by the ecclesiasticall lawes, in causes confessed to be of ecclesiasticall cognizance.

Objection. Notwithstanding that the ecclesiasticall jurisdiction hath been much impeached heretofore through the multitude of prohibitions, yet the suggestions in them had some colour of justice, as pretending,

pretending, that the judges ecclesiasticall dealt with temporall causes: but now, as it seemeth, they are subject to the same controlments, whether the cause they deale in be either ecclesiasticall or temporall, in that prohibitions of late are wrestled out of their owne proper course, in the nature of a writ of errour, or of an appeale: for, whereas the true and onely use of a prohibition is to restraine the judges ecclesiasticall from dealing in a matter of temporall cognizance, now prohibitions are awarded upon these surmises, *viz.* that the libell, the articles, the sentence, and the ecclesiasticall court, according to the ecclesiasticall lawes, are grievous and insufficient, though the matter there dealt withall be meerly ecclesiasticall: and by colour of such prohibitions, the temporall judges to alter and change the decrees and sentences of the judges ecclesiasticall, and to moderate the expences taxed in the ecclesiasticall courts, and to award consultations upon conditions: as for example, that the plaintife in the ecclesiasticall court shall except of the one halfe of the costs awarded, and that the register shall lose his fees; and that the said plaintife shall be contented with the payment of his legacy, which was the principall sued for, and adjudged due unto him at such day, as they the said temporall judges shall appoint, or else the prohibition must stand. And also where his majesties commissioners, for causes ecclesiasticall, have not been accustomed to give a copy of the articles to any party, before he hath answered them; and that the statute of Hen. 5. touching the delivering of the libell, was not onely publikely adjudged in the kings bench, not to extend to the deliverance of articles, where the party is proceeded with *ex officio*, but likewise imparted to his majestie, and afterwards divulged in the starre-chamber, as a full resolution of the judges, yet within 4 or 5 moneths after, a prohibition was awarded to the said commissioners out of the kings bench, upon suggestion, that the party ought to have a copy of the articles, being called in question *ex officio*, before he should answer them; and notwithstanding that a motion was made in full court shortly after for a consultation, yet an order was entred, that the prohibition should stand untill the said partie had a copy of the said articles given him; which novell and extraordinary courses doe seem very strange unto us, and are contrary not onely to the whole course of his majesties lawes ecclesiasticall, but also to the very maximes and judgement of the common law, and sundry statutes of this realme, as wee shall be ready to justifie before your lordships, if the judges shall endeavour to maintaine these their proceedings.

Answer. To this we say, that though where parties are proceeded withall *ex officio*, there needeth no libell, yet ought they to have the cause made knowne unto them for which they are called *ex officio*, before they be examined, to the end it may appeare unto them before their examination, whether the cause be of ecclesiasticall cognizance, otherwise they ought not to examine them upon oath. And touching the rest of this article, they doe utterly mistake it.

[617]

24. That temporall judges are sworne to defend the ecclesiasticall jurisdiction.

Objection. We may not omit to signifie unto your lordships, that (as wee take it) the temporall judges are not onely bound by their ancient oath,

oath, that they ſhall doe nothing to the dis-heriſon of the crown, but alſo by a latter oath unto the kings ſupremacy, wherein they doe ſweare, that, to their power, they will aſſiſt and defend all juriſdictions, priviledges, preheminences, and authorities united and annexed to the imperiall crowne of this realme; in which words the eccleſiaſticall juriſdiction is ſpecially aimed at: ſo that whereas they doe oftentimes inſiſt upon for their oath, for doing of juſtice in temporall cauſes, and do ſeldome make mention of the ſecond oath taken by them for the defence of the eccleſiaſticall juriſdiction, with the rights and immunities belonging to the church; we think, that they ought to weigh their ſaid oaths better together, and not ſo farre to extend the one, as that it ſhould in any ſort prejudice the other: the due conſideration whereof (which we moſt inſtantly deſire) would put them in mind (any ſuggeſtion to the contrary notwithſtanding) to be as carefull not to doe any thing that may prejudice the lawfull proceedings of the eccleſiaſticall judges in eccleſiaſticall cauſes, as they are circumſpect not to ſuffer any impeachment, or blemiſh of their owne juriſdictions and proceedings in cauſes temporall.

Anſwer. We are aſſured, that none can juſtly charge any of us with violating our oaths, and it is a ſtrange part to taxe judges in this manner, and to lay ſo great an imputation upon us; and what ſcandall it will be to the juſtice of the realme to have ſo great levity, and ſo foule an imputation laid upon the judges, as is done in this, is too manifeſt. And we are aſſured it cannot be ſhewed, that the like hath been done in any former age; and for leſſe ſcandals then this of the juſtice of the realme, divers have been ſeverely puniſhed.

25. That excommunication is as lawfull, as prohibition, for the mutuall preſervation of both his majeſties ſupreme juriſdiction.

Objection. To conclude, whereas for the better preſerving of his majeſties two ſupreme juriſdictions before mentioned, *viz.* the eccleſiaſticall and the temporall, that the one might not uſurp upon the other, two meanes heretofore have of ancient time been ordained, that is to ſay, the cenſure of excommunication, and the writ of prohibition; the one to reſtraine the incroachment of the temporall juriſdiction upon the eccleſiaſticall, the other of the eccleſiaſticall upon the temporall, we moſt humbly deſire your lordſhips, that by your meanes the judges may be induced to reſolve us, why excommunications may not as freely be put in ure for the preſervation of the juriſdiction eccleſiaſticall, as prohibitions are, under pretence to defend the temporall, eſpecially againſt ſuch contentious perſons, as doe wittingly and willingly, upon falſe and frivolous ſuggeſtions, to the delay of juſtice, vexation of the ſubjects, and great ſcandall of eccleſiaſticall juriſdictions, daily procure, without feare either of God or men, ſuch undue prohibitions, as we have heretofore mentioned.

Anſwer. The excommunication cannot be gain-ſaid, neither may the prohibition be denied upon the ſurmiſe made, that the matter purſued in the eccleſiaſticall court is of temporall cognizance, but as ſoon as that ſhall appeare unto us judicially to be falſe, we grant the conſultation.

For

For the better satisfaction of his majesty, and your lordships, touching the objections delivered against prohibitions, we have thought good to set downe (as may be perceived by that which hath been said) the ordinary proceeding in his majesties courts therein; whereby it may appeare both what the judges doe, and ought to doe in those causes; and the ecclesiasticall judges may doe well to consider, what issue the course they herein hold can have in the end: and they shall find it can be no other, but to cast a scandall upon the justice of the realme; for the judges doing but what they ought, and by their oaths are bound to doe, it is not to be called in question: and if it fall out, that they erre in judgement, it cannot otherwise be reformed, but judicially in a superiour court, or by parliament. [618]

Subscribed by all the judges of England, and the barons of the exchequer, Pasch. 4 *Jacobi*, and delivered to the lord chancellour of England.

Which answers and resolutions, although they were not enacted by authority of parliament, as our statute of *Articuli Cleri* in 9 E. 2. was; yet, being resolved unanimously by all the judges of England, and barons of the exchequer, are for matters in law of highest authority next unto the court of parliament.

Magna est veritas, et prevalet.

But now we will peruse the preamble, and after every chapter in order, and proceed to the exposition of the same; which office the clergy claimed, *viz.* to interpret all statute lawes concerning the clergy; but it was resolved by all the judges of England, that the interpretation of all statutes concerning the clergy, being parcell of the lawes of the realme, doe belong to the judges of the common law. Artic' Cleri. 3 Jac. ad artic. 20.

EDWARDUS Dei gratia rex Angliæ, &c. omnibus ad quos præsentes literæ pervenerint, salutem. Sciatis quod cum dudum, temporibus progenitorum nostrorum quondam regum Angliæ, in diversis parliamentis suis (1); *et similiter postquam regni nostri gubernacula suscepimus, in parliamentis nostris* (2), *per prælatos, et clerum* (4) *regni nostri plures articuli continentes gravamina aliqua ecclesiæ Anglicanæ, et ipsis prælatis et clero illata (ut in eisdem asserebatur) porrecti fuissent, et cum instantia supplicatum, ut inde apponeretur remedium oppartunum: ac nuper in parliamento nostro apud Lincoln', anno regni nostri ix.* (3) *articulos subscriptos, et quasdam responsiones ad aliquos eorum prius factas, coram concilio nostro recitari, ac quasdam responsiones corrigi, et cæteris*

THE king to all to whom, &c. sendeth greeting. Understand ye, That whereas of late times of our progenitors sometimes kings of England, in divers their parliaments, and likewise after that we had undertaken the governance of the realm, in our parliaments many articles containing divers grievances (committed against the church of England, the prelates and clergy) were propounded by the prelates and clerks of our realm; and further, great instance was made that convenient remedy might be provided therein: and of late in our parliament holden at Lincoln, the ninth year of our reign, we caused the articles underwritten, with certain answers made to some of them heretofore, to be rehearsed before our council, and made certain answers to

teris articulis subscriptis per nos, et dictum concilium nostrum fecerimus responderi: quorum quidem articulorum et responsionum tenores subsequuntur in hunc modum.

to be corrected; and to the residue of the articles underwritten, answers were made by us and our council; of which said articles, with the answers of the same, the tenors here ensue.

(1) *Cum dudum temporibus progenitorum nostrorum, &c. in diversis parliamentis.*] That is, in the said parliament holden *anno* 51 H. 3. *Articuli Cleri*, and of the said acts in the raigne of E. 1. called *prohibitio formata super Artic' Cleri*, and *Articuli contra prohibitionem regiam*, which have been cited before.

Rot. parl. 5 E. 2. m. 3. & 8 E. 2.

(2) *In parliamentis nostris.*] *Viz.* 5 E. 2. & 8 E. 2.

(3) *Ac nuper in parliamento nostro apud Lincoln' anno regni nostri nono.*] There were two parliaments holden in this ninth yeare, *viz.* the one at Lincolne, 15 Hill. mentioned in this preamble; and the other, 15 Pasch' *anno nono* at Westminster: and as one saith, *Merito in parliamento conquesti sunt, quia lex Angliæ sine parliamento mutari non potest.*

[619]

Vid. artic' Cler' anno 3 Jacobi regis ad artic' 1. & 13.

And note well what is said there, *viz.* what the law doth warrant in cases of prohibition, to keep every jurisdiction in his true limits, cannot be altered but by parliament.

Vid. ubi supra ad artic' 3. Vid. ad artic' 10. 21.

(4) *Per prælatos et clerum*, &c.] In these parliaments complaint was made by the clergy onely; but the kings courts, that may award prohibitions, being informed by the parties themselves, or by any stranger, that any court temporall or ecclesiasticall doe hold plea of that whereof they have not jurisdiction, may lawfully prohibit the same, as well after judgement and execution, as before; and so resolved by all the judges of England, and barons of the exchequer, agreeable to make authorities in law.

CAP. I.

INPRIMIS laici impetrant prohibitiones in genere super decimis, obventionibus, oblationibus, mortuariis, redemptionibus penitentiarum, violenta manuum injectione in clericum vel conversum, et in causa diffamationis: in quibus casibus agitur ad pœnam canonicam imponendum: rex ad istum articulum respondit, quod in decimis, oblationibus, obventionibus, mortuariis, quando sub istis nominibus proponuntur, prohibitioni regiæ non est locus; etiamsi, propter detentionem istorum diuturnam, ad æstimationem eorundem pecuniariam veniatur. Sed si clericus, vel religiosus decimas suas in horreo suo con-

FIRST, whereas lay-men do purchase prohibitions generally upon tythes, obventions, oblations, mortuaries, redemption of penance, violent laying hands on clerks or converts, and in cases of defamation, in which cases spiritual penance ought to be enjoined; the king doth answer to this article, that in tythes, oblations, obventions, mortuaries (when they are propounded under these names) the king's prohibition shall hold no place, although for the long withholding of the same the money may be esteemed at a sum certaine. But if a clerk or a religious man

congregatas, vel alibi existentes vendiderit alicui pro pecunia: si petatur pecunia coram judice ecclesiastico, locum habet regia prohibitio, quia per venditionem res spirituales fiunt temporales, et transeunt decimæ in catalla.

man do sell his tythes being gathered in his barn, or otherwise, to any man for money, if the money be demanded before a spiritual judge, the king's prohibition shall lie; for by the sale the spiritual goods are made temporal, and the tythes turned into chattles.

(8 Ed. 4. 13. Cro. El. 753. 12 Rep. 29. 13 Rep. 41. Rast. 484, &c.)

Of these sufficient hath been said in the exposition upon the statute of *Circumspecte agatis:* whereunto we referre the reader; only this wee may adde (which wee have reserved to this place) the resolution of all the judges of England to the 5. 8. 15, 16. 18. articles in *Artic' Cleri, 3 Jacobi regis,* in many cases concerning tithes, &c.

CAP. II.

ITEM si sit contentio de jure decimarum, originem habens de jure patronatus, et earundem decimarum quantitas ascendat ad quartam partem bonorum ecclesiæ, locum habeat regia prohibitio, si hæc causa coram judice ecclesiastico ventilet'. Item, si prælatus imponat pœnam pecuniariam alicui pro peccato (1), *et repetat illam, regia prohibitio locum habet.* [620] *Veruntamen, si prælati imponant pænitentias corporales, et sic puniti velint hujusmodi pœnitentias per pecuniam redimere sponte, non habet locum regia prohibitio, si coram prælatis pecunia ab eis exigatur.*

ALSO if debate do arise upon the right of tythes, having his original from the right of the patronage, and the quantity of the same tythes do come unto the fourth part of the goods of the church, the king's prohibition shall hold place, if the cause come before a judge spiritual. Also if a prelate enjoin a penance pecuniary to a man for his offence, and it be demanded, the king's prohibition shall hold place. But if prelates enjoine a penance corporal, and they which be so punished will redeem upon their own accord such penances by money, if money be demanded before a judge spiritual, the king's prohibition shall hold no place.

(Co. 465. Regist. 35.)

This is intended of the kings writ of *indicavit,* whereof, and of the tryall of the right of tithes at the common law, we have spoken sufficiently for the understanding of this branch of this act, in the exposition of the statute of W. 2. cap. 5. *versus finem,* and the statute of *circumspecte agatis, &c.*

Vid. Registr. 48, &c.

(1) *Item, si prælatus imponat pœnam pecuniariam alicui pro peccato, &c.*] For the understanding hereof, wee referre the reader to the exposition upon the statute of *Circumspecte agatis,* where sufficient hath been said of this matter.

CAP. III.

INSUPER, si aliquis violentas manus injecerit in clericum, pro violentia facta debet emendari coram rege: pro excommunicatione vero, coram prælato, ubi imponatur pœnitentia corporalis; quod si reus velit sponte per pecuniam redimere, dand' prælato vel læso, potest repeti coram prælato: nec in talibus regia probibitio locum babet.

MOREOVER, if any lay violent hands on a clerk, the amends for the peace broken shall be before the king, and for the excommunication before a prelate, that penance corporal may be enjoined; which if the offender will redeem of his own good will, by giving money to the prelate, or to the party grieved, it shall be required before the prelate, and the king's prohibition shall not lie.

(Regist. 51, 52. 57.)

For this matter, we referre the reader to the statute of *Circumspecte agatis:* to that we adde the resolution of all the judges of England touching this matter, *ad Artic'* 6. & 11. *in Articulis Cleri,* 3 *Jacob.* which you may reade before, since we began with this statute.

And here it is to be noted, that where the article of the clergy, cap. 1. *de violenta manuum injectione in clericum vel conversum,* answer is made to the clerke, but no answer is made at all to the convert.

CAP. IV.

IN diffamationibus etiam corrigant prælati supradicto modo, regia prohibitione non obstante, primo injungendo pœnam corporalem: quam si reus velit redimere libere, percipiat prælatus pecuniam, licet regia prohibitio porrigatur.

IN defamations also prelates shall correct in manner abovesaid, the king's prohibition notwithstanding; first injoyning a penance corporal, which if the offender will redeem, the prelate may freely receive the money, though the king's prohibition be shewed.

(4 Rep. 20. Regist. 49. Rast. 487, &c.)

Hereof also sufficient hath been said in the exposition upon the statute of *Circumspecte agatis.*

CAP.

CAP. V.

ITEM, ſi aliquis in fundo ſuo molendinum erexit de novo, et poſtea à rectore loci exigatur decima de eodem, exhibetur regia prohibitio ſub hac forma:

ALSO if any do erect in his ground a mill of new, and after the parſon of the ſame place demandeth tithe for the ſame, the king's prohibition doth iſſue in this form:

Quia de tali molendino hactenus decimæ non fuerunt ſolutæ, prohibemus, &c. et ſententiam excommunicationis, ſi quam hac occaſione promulgaveritis, revocetis omnino.

Reſponſio: In tali caſu nunquam exivit regia prohibitio de principis voluntate (1), *qui et decernit talem perpetuo non exire.*

The anſwer. In ſuch caſe the king's prohibition was never granted by the king's aſſent, nor never ſhall, which hath decreed that it ſhall not hereafter lie in ſuch caſes.

See hereafter the expoſition of the ſtatute of 2 E. 6. cap. 17. verb. by the lawes of the realme. Vid. inter leges Edwardi regis, cap. 8. fo. 128. (1 Roll, 405. 2 Roll, 84.)

The forme of this prohibition is juſtly condemned, for that the ſubſtance of it was a *non decimando*, becauſe the mill was newly erected; but yet hereby, and by our bookes it appeareth, that ſome tithe or other is due for a mill, be it new, or old.

See 2 E. 6. c. 13. every perſon ſhall juſtly, &c. ſet out, yeeld, and pay all prediall tithes in their proper kind, as they riſe, and happen, &c. which (ſay they) cannot be applyed to the taking of the toll-diſh. Regiſtr. 48. b. F.N.B. 51. h.

But this is (as ſome doe hold) a perſonall [a] tithe, coming from the gaine of the miller, by his induſtry and labour: as of a fiſherman of the tithe of his gain by fiſhing, called *decimæ de piſcationibus*, or the like.

The words are generall, *molendinum erexit*, and doe extend to all kind of mills, as private mills, and to publike, as to fulling mills, paper mills, &c. whereof there is no tithe to bee paid, but perſonall, if any bee; which is a good proofe (ſay they) that ſo it ought to be of corne mills; and if the parſon ſhould have the tenth toll-diſh, then ſhould he have not onely tithe corne, but alſo tithe of the ſame corne ground at the mill, and ſo a double tithe, which he ſhall not have of a fulling mill, paper mill, &c. No tithe ſhall be demanded of the rawyn, or after-paſture, or of ſtubble, becauſe the parſon ſhall not have a double tithe of one and the ſame thing in one yeare. If the parſon hath tithe of fruit that groweth on fruit-trees, and in the ſame yeare the owner fell downe the fruit-trees, and make billets or fagots of them, he ſhall have no tithe of them, as it was holden Hill. 8 Jacob. Rot. 1109. *in communi banco, inter* Baxter & Hopes.

[a] Rot. clauſ. 7 E. 2. Decimæ de molendino Ewell. Mich. 8 & 9 H. 3. coram rege, rot. 6. See Linwood, tit. de Decimis, fol. 141, 142. Mich. 9 & 10 H. 3. coram rege, rot. 15 Jo. Fitzroberts caſe.

[b] Every perſon exerciſing merchandizes, bargaining and ſelling, clothing, handicraft, or other art or faculty, being ſuch kind of perſons, and in ſuch places, as heretofore, within 40 yeares, before the ſtatute of 2 E. 6. have accuſtomably uſed to pay ſuch perſonall tithes, or of right ought to pay, other then ſuch as be common day-labourers, ſhall yearly, before the feaſt of Eaſter, pay for his perſonall

[b] 2 E. 6. cap. 13.

ſonall tithes the tenth part of his cleare gaines, his charges and expences, according to his eſtate, condition, or degree, to be therein abated, allowed, or deducted, &c. And the ordinary hath power to call the parties before him, and to examine them by all lawfull and reaſonable meanes, other then upon oath, concerning the true payment of perſonall tithes.

Nota, in this deſcription of perſonall tithes, the words be, clothing, handicraft, or other art and faculty; within which generall words, the millers of fulling mills, rape mills, corne mills, and other mills be included; for a miller is of an art and faculty.

* Mich. 25 & 26 El. rot. 2617. in communi banco. Mich. 29 & 30 Eliz. rot. 254. Nicholas Muſſels caſe, ibid. Vid. lib. 11. fol. 48, 49. & 81.

Exigatur decima.] Some do hold, that the parſon ſhall have the tenth toll-diſh, as a prediall tithe.

* He that deſireth to reade more concerning this matter, let him ſearch for two records of prohibitions in the court of common pleas, in the raigne of the late queen Elizabeth.

[622] Note, that in many caſes the common law and the canon law differ concerning the payment of tithes; the common law adjudging many things not tithable, which by the canon law ought to pay tithes: and this caſe of tithes of mills was never (that I know) judicially determined.

See the expoſition of the ſtatute of *Circumſpecte agatis, verbo Conſuet'*.

(1) *De principis (i. regis) voluntate.*] *i. Curiæ regis, in qua rex ſive princeps repræſentatur.*

CAP. VI.

ITEM, ſi aliqua cauſa, vel negotium, cujus cognitio ſpectat ad forum eccleſiaſticum, et coram eccleſiaſtico judice fuerit ſententialiter terminatum, et tranſierit in rem judicatam (1), *nec per appellationem fuerit ſuſpenſum, et poſtmodum coram judice ſeculari, ſuper eadem re inter eaſdem perſonas quæſtio moveatur, et probetur per teſtes vel inſtrumenta, talis exceptio in foro ſeculari non admittatur. Reſponſio: Quando eadem cauſa diverſis rationibus* (2) *coram judicibus eccleſiaſticis et ſecularibus ventilatur, ut ſupra patet de injectione violentarum manuum in clericum, dicunt quod (non obſtante eccleſiaſtico judicio) curia regis ipſum tractat negotium, ut ſibi expedire videtur.*

ALSO if any cauſe or matter, the knowledge whereof belongeth to a court ſpiritual, and ſhall be definitively determined before a ſpiritual judge, and doth paſs into a judgement, and ſhall not be ſuſpended by an appeal; and after, if upon the ſame thing a queſtion is moved before a temporal judge between the ſame parties, and it be proved by witneſs or inſtruments, ſuch an exception is not to be admitted in a temporal court. The anſwer. When any one caſe is debated before judges ſpiritual or temporal (as above appeareth upon the caſe of laying violent hands on a clerk) it is thought, that notwithſtanding the ſpiritual judgement, the king's court ſhall diſcuſs the ſame matter as the party ſhall think expedient for himſelf.

(4 Rep. 16. 20.)

(1) *Fuerit*

(1) *Fuerit ſententialiter terminatum, et tranſierit in rem judicatam,* &c.] The like article was preferred 3 Jac. and anſwered and reſolved by all the judges of England, which you may reade there, and need not here to be rehearſed. Art. Cleri, 3. Jac. ad artic' 21.

(2) *Diverſis rationibus.*] For the ſpirituall judges proceedings are for the correction of the ſpirituall inner man, and, *pro ſalute animæ*, to injoyne him penance; and the judges of the common law proceed to give damages and recompence for the wrong and injury done: as if one lay violent hands of a clerke, the ſpirituall judge, *pro ſalute animæ*, ſhall injoyne him penance, and the clerke may have his action of battery, and recover damages for the injury done to him; and ſo in the caſe of uſury, and the like: ſo as this act ſaith well, that *eadem cauſa diverſis rationibus coram judicibus eccleſiaſticis et ſecularibus ventilatur*; and therefore this article of the clergy was deſervedly rejected.

CAP. VII.

*ITEM, litera regia ordinariis dirigitur, qui aliquos ſuos ſubditos excommunicationis vinculo innodarunt, quod eos abſolvant infra certum diem; alioquin quod compareant reſponſur' quare eos excommunicaverunt. Reſponſio: rex * decernit, quod talis litera nunquam in poſterum exire permittatur, niſi in caſu quo poſſit inveniri, lædi per excommunicationem regiam libertatem.*

*[623]

ALSO the king's letter directed unto ordinaries, that have wrapped thoſe that be in ſubjection unto them in the ſentence of excommunication, that they ſhould aſſoil them by a certain day, or elſe that they do appear, and ſhew wherefore they have excommunicated them. The anſwer. The king decreeth, that hereafter no ſuch letters ſhall be ſuffered to go forth, but in caſe where it is found that the king's liberty is prejudiced by the excommunication.

(5 El. c. 23. Regiſt. 65.)

Here was a miſtaking in the article of the clergy; for never was any writ of the king here called *litera regis*, granted in caſe of excommunication, but in certaine caſes, as, when a man is juſtly excommunicated, and taken by force of the kings writ *de excommunicato cap.* if the biſhop, upon the kings writ *de cautione admittenda, &c.* doe not deliver him, then ſhall a writ out of the chancery goe to the ſheriſe, upon the refuſall of the biſhop to deliver him; or if the excommunication be unjuſt, that is, if the party be excommunicated for a matter which belongs not to eccleſiaſticall conuſance, and taken by force of the kings writ, then the party grieved ſhall have a writ out of the chancery to the ſheriſe, to deliver him out of priſon. And this appeareth by our ancient books written before this act, and by ancient records and book-caſes in all ſucceſſion of ages ever ſince; and in both the caſes aboveſaid, *regia libertas læſa fuit*, and thereupon the ſubject had reliefe by the kings writ; and therefore the anſwer to this article was very pertinent, *Niſi in caſu quo poſſit inveniri, lædi per excommunicationem regiam libertatem.* And the

Regiſt. 65, 66, 67, 70. Bract. lib. 5. fol. 408, 409, 427, 443. Flet. lib. 6. c. 43. 5 E. 3. 8. 8 E. 3. 9. 14 H. 4. 14, 15. 3 H. 4. 4.

Doctor & Stud. lib. 2. cap. 32. Vet. N.B. 33, 35. F.N.B. 62. &c. Dorf. clauf. 21 R. 2. m. 10. Hill. 22 E. 1. apud Sandw. coram rege, rot. 2. William de Valences cafe.

the contempt of the bifhop in thofe cafes is the greater, for that *breve regis de excommunicato cap. de gratia regis procedit.* And fo it is if a man be excommunicated, and offer to obey and performe the fentence, and the bifhop refufeth to accept it, and to affoile him, he fhall have a writ to the bifhop, requiring him, upon performance of the fentence, to affoile him, &c. and the reafon thereof is, for that by the excommunication, the party is difabled to fue any action, or to have any remedy for any wrong done unto him, fo long as he fhall remaine excommunicate. And alfo the party grieved may have his action upon his cafe againft the bifhop, in like manner as he may when the bifhop doth excommunicate him for a matter which belongeth not to ecclefiafticall conufance. Alfo the bifhop in thofe cafes may be indited at the fuit of the king, as by many notable records may appeare: Mich. 7 E. 1. *coram rege*, Rot. 33. Robertus Sprot, Hill. 7 E, 1. *coram rege*, Rot. 8. Magifter R. de Petchford, Pafch' 32 E. 1. *coram rege*, Rot. 33. Walterus de Wilton, Hill. 35 E. 1. *coram rege*, Rot. 52. Gloc' Prior de Glocefters cafe, Mich. 19 E. 2. *coram rege*, Rot, 53. Linc' Philip Whites cafe, Trin. 20 E. 3. *coram rege*, Rot. 46, 289. Frefiles cafe.

28 E. 3. 97. 14 H. 4. 14. 3 H. 4. 4. 22 E. 4. 20. b. 9 H. 7. 22. Fitz. N.B. 6. f.

And it is to be obferved, that at the common law a certificate of the bifhop, whereupon a *fignificavit*, that is, a writ *de excommunicato capiendo* was to be granted, ought to expreffe the caufe, and the fute againft him fpecially in the certificate.

5 El. cap. 23.

See more the ftatute of 5 El. cap. 23. concerning the awarding and returning the writ *de excommunicato capiendo.*

See the firft part of the Inftitutes, fect. 201. concerning this matter.

CAP. VIII.

ITEM, barones de fcaccario domini regis, vendicantes fibi ex privilegio (1), *quod non debent extra illum locum conquerenti cuicunque refpondere, extendunt illud privilegium ad clericos commorantes ibidem, vocatos ad ordines, feu ad refidentiam; et diocefanis inhibeant, ne aliquo modo aliquave ex caufa, dum fint in fcaccario, et in fervitio domini regis, trabant ad judicium quovifmodo. Refponfio: Placet domino regi, ut clerici fuis obfequiis intendentes, fi delinquant* (2) *per ordinarios (ut cæteri) corrigantur: fed tempore quo occupantur circa fcaccarium, ad refidentiam* (3) *in fuis faciendam ecclefiis non teneantur. Hic additur de novo, per concilium domini regis* (4). *Rex et antecefsores fui, à tempore*

[624]

ALSO barons of the king's exchequer claiming by their privilege, that they ought to make anfwer to no complainant out of the fame place, extend the fame privilege unto clerks abiding there, called to orders or unto refidence, and inhibit ordinaries that by no means, or for any caufe, fo long as they be in the exchequer, or in the king's fervice, they fhall not call them to judgement. The anfwer. It pleafeth our lord the king, that fuch clerks as attend in his fervice, if they offend, fhall be correct by their ordinaries, like as other; but fo long as they are occupied about the exchequer, they fhall not be bound to keep refidence in their churches. This is added of new by the king's council. The

tempore cujus contrarii memoria non existit, usi sunt, quod clerici suis immorantes obsequiis, dum obsequiis illis intenderint, ad residentiam in suis beneficiis faciendam minime compellantur; nec debet dici tendere in præjudicium ecclesiasticæ libertatis, quod pro rege et republica necessarium invenitur (5).

The king and his anceftors fince time out of mind have ufed, that clerks, which are employed in his fervice, during fuch time as they are in fervice, fhall not be compelled to keep refidence at their benefices. And fuch things as be thought neceffary for the king and the commonwealth, ought not to be faid to be prejudicial to the liberty of the church.

(Regift. 58.)

(1) *De privilegio*, &c.] The court of the exchequer may grant a prohibition to the ordinary, for any that ought to have the priviledge of the exchequer, where the court may give the party remedy, or where a fute dependeth in the court of exchequer for the fame caufe, or where the kings fervice, which is the caufe of the priviledge, is hindered by the fuit before the ordinary: as for non-refidence, &c. during that time that he gave his neceffary attendance in the exchequer for the kings fervice.

(2) *Si delinquant.*] This extendeth onely *ad delicta, i. crimina,* whereof the ecclefiafticall court hath conufance, as herefie, adultery, and the like, which the ordinary may correct; and not unto civill actions.

(3) *Ad refidentiam.*] There is an ancient writ, called *de non refidentia clerici regis*, the words of which writ be, *Cum clerici nostri ad faciend' in beneficiis suis residentiam personalem, dum in nostris immorantur obsequiis compelli, aut alias super hoc molestari, seu inquietari non debeant: nosque ac progenitores nostri quondam reges Angliæ, hujusmodi libertate et privilegio pro clericis nostris à tempore quo non extat memoria semper hactenus usi sumus: vobis mandamus, quod dilectum clericum nostrum A. parsonam ecclesiæ de B. vestræ diœces. qui in cancellaria nostra, nostris jugiter intendit obsequiis, ad personalem residentiam in beneficio suo prædict' faciendam, dum in eisdem obsequiis nostris immoretur, nullatenus compellatis. Et sequestrum si quod in fructibus, aut aliis bonis ecclesiæ suæ prædictæ ea occasione per vos, aut vestros fuerit appositum, sine dilatione relaxari faciatis. Teste, &c.* Regift. 58. b. F N.B. 44. g.

(4) *Per concilium domini regis.*] Here *concilium domini regis* is taken for *commune concilium regni*, as it is termed in originall writs, and in other legall records, and fo it is taken in other acts of parliament, and in the preamble of this act alfo, where it is faid, *Ac nuper in parliamento nostro apud Lincoln', &c. coram concilio nostro, &c.*

This branch is generall (and not limited, as the former is, to the priviledge of the exchequer) but extendeth to any other fervice of the king for the common-wealth: as if hee be imployed as an embaffadour into any forraine nation, or the like fervice of the king, which is *pro republica*, for the common-wealth, as hereafter it is faid, which ever muft be preferred before the private.

(5) *Nec debet dici tendere in præjudicium ecclesiasticæ libertatis, quod pro rege et republica necessarium invenitur.*] The clergy in this parliament inveighing vehemently againft this anfwer, and that it [625]
tended

tended to the breach of the ecclesiasticall liberty, which was granted to them by *Magna Charta*, and often confirmed by other acts of parliament, *quod ecclesia Anglicana libera sit, &c.* To which it was answered, that the words subsequent explained those words, *et habeat omnia jura sua et libertates suas illæsas*; so as the clergy cannot claime any right, but *jus suum*, nor any liberty, but *libertates suas:* and the point here in question, *viz.* to proceed against a clerke for non residence, whiles hee was in the kings service for the commonwealth, was neither *jus suum*, nor *libertas sua*, but *libertas regis:*
Registr. 58. b. and therefore the parliament thought it fit to declare, that the king and his ancestors had used this liberty or prerogative time out of mind. And where it was said, that this tended *in præjudicium ecclesiasticæ libertatis*, the parliament thereunto answered (which is worthy to be written in letters of gold) *nec debet dici in præjudicium ecclesiasticæ libertatis, quod pro rege et republica necessarium invenitur.*

Regularly personall residence is required of ecclesiasticall persons upon their cures; and to that end, by the common law, if hee that hath a benefice with cure, be chosen to an office as to an office of bailiffe, or bedle, or the like secular office, he may have the kings writ, *quod non eligatur in officium, &c. quia non est consonum, quod is, qui pro salubri statu animarum eleemosynis, et aliis piis operibus, infra, &c. manutenendis et sustentandis continue deservit, extra &c. in secularibus negotiis compellatur, vobis præcipimus, quod districtioni et compulsioni, si quas &c. eidem &c. ad officium balivi, bedelli, &c. in manerio, &c. assumend' feceritis, omnino supersedeatis, et eas sine dilatione relaxetis, et denarios, si quos per amerciamenta, vel alio modo ex causa præd' ab eo levaveritis, eidem &c. restitui faciatis immediate, sub periculo quod incumbit. Teste, &c.*

And this writ of ancient time was granted at the petition of the
2 Tim. 2. ver. 4. clergy, and grounded upon holy writ, *Nemo militans Deo implicat se*
34 H. 6. 40. a. *negotiis secularibus, ut ei placeat cui se probavit.* And the opinion of Sir John Prisot, chiefe justice of the common pleas, is notable; to those lawes which holy church hath out of the scripture, we ought to yield credit; for that (saith he) is the common law, upon which all lawes are founded: and the intendment of the common
30 H. 6. fo. 8. a. law is, that a parson, &c. is resident upon his cure; for in an action of debt brought against J. S. *rectorem de* D. the defendant pleaded, that he was demurrant, and conversant at B. in another county: and the rule of the booke is, that seeing the defendant denied not that he was rector of the church of D. he shall be deemed by law to be demurrant and conversant there for the cure of soules; and therefore the plea was over-ruled.

We could not over-passe an ancient and an excellent record concerning non-residence, in the 48 yeare of king Henry the third, for it is worthy of rehearsall for many purposes: at that time one Peter Egneblanke a stranger, borne in Savoy, was bishop of Hereford: this bishop then was, and long before had been a non resident, an unfaithfull steward, and altogether carelesse of his pastorall charge: the king travelling (for the defence and safety of the Marches) came to the citie of Hereford, where finding the bishop absent, the people neither informed nor reformed *per verbum salutis, et virgam correctionis*, divine service neglected, and all things out of order, as by the writ following appeareth, which

which we hold worthy to be rehearsed *de verbo in verbum*, as it is of record.

Rex episcopo Hereford' salutem, Pastores gregibus praeponuntur, ut, diei noctisque vigilias exercendo, oves famelicas in fertilitatis pascua introducant: errantes vero per verbum salutis, & virgam correctionis in unius ovilis conservare studeant indissolubilem unitatem: sed sunt nonnulli qui hanc doctrinam damnabiliter contempnentes, & sua ab aliis pecora distinguere nescientes, lac & lanam tollunt, qualiter dominicus grex alatur non curantes, temporalia rapiunt, & quis in parochia fame pereat, aut periclitetur in moribus, non attendunt; qui non pastores, sed mercenarii potius dici promerentur: hoc siquidem, dum hiis diebus ad disponendum de regni nostri praesidiis in partes Marchiae nos transferremus, in ecclesia vestra Hereff. (dolenter referimus) nos invenisse quam adeo invenimus pastoris solatio destitutam, ut ne dum episcopum, sed nec officialem haberet, vicarium, aut decanum, qui quicquam spiritualitatis exercere possit in eadem. Sed ecclesia ipsa, quae olim deliciis affluere consuevit, & canonicis qui ibidem nocturnis et diurnis officiis vacare, & opera charitatis exercere deberent, eam deserentibus & longe degentibus in remotis, stola jocunditatis exuta cecidit in terram, viduitatis suae detrimenta deplorans, nec est qui consoletur eam ex omnibus caris ejus: sane, dum haec vidimus & consideramus diligenter, pietatis aculeus viscera nostra commovit, & compassionis gladius intima cordis nostri acrius vulneravit, ut tantam ecclesiae matris nostrae injuriam ulterius dissimulare non possimus, nec pertransire incorrectam. Quapropter vobis mandamus firmiter injungentes, quatenus ad ecclesiam vestram praedictam, occasionibus quibuscunque postpositis, cum ea qua poteritis celeritate vos transferre curetis, commissum vobis in eadem cura pastorali officium personaliter executur' &c. Alioqui scire vos volumus pro constanti, quod si istuc facere non curaveritis, bona temporalia, & omnia quae ad baronium ipsius ecclesiae pertinent, quae donatione constat eidem fuisse collata, & quae hactenus colligi, & salvo custodiri praecepimus in commodum & utilitatem ipsius ecclesiae convertenda, cessante jam causa in manu nostra totaliter capiemus, nec ulterius sustinebimus, quod temporalia metat, qui spiritualia ad quae ex officii sui debito tenetur, irreverenter subtrahere non formidat, aut quod emolumenta percipiat, qui incumbentia ejusdem onera subire recusat. Test' R. apud Hereff. primo die Junii anno regni sui xlviii. [626]

By this writ the king telleth the bishop what his pastorall office and duty was, rehearseth the damnable and damned events of non-residency, commandeth him to be personally resident, and representeth to him the danger, if he doth it not. And this writ, commanding residence, ought to have been put into the Register of writs, rather then the writ *de non residentia clerici regis: hoc non omittendum, illud faciendum.*

The Englishman hath ever been desirous to be taught and directed in the way of his salvation; and therefore hath often complained in * parliament against non residents, unlearned pastors, and pluralities, which you may reade in the fountaines themselves.

* Rot. parl. 35 E. 1. lestatute de Carlile. 18 E. 3. nu. 32. Rot. parl. 3 R. 2. nu. 38. 3 R. 2. stat. 2. cap. 2. 7 R. 2. nu. 35. 17 R. 2. nu. 43. 1 H. 4. nu. 50. 2 H. 4. nu. 26. 6 H. 4. nu. 48. 7 H. 4. nu. 114. 11 H. 4. nu. 70. 3 H. 6. nu. 38. 4 H. 6. nu. 31. &c.

After that Thomas Wolsey in the seventh year of Henry the eight was made cardinall, and grew into the height of his authority and favour with the king, he hated both parliaments, and the common lawes (the principall meanes to keep greatnesse in order, and due subjection) as it is contained in his inditement, which he confessed of record, that hee intended (that I may use the very words of

Mich. 21 H. 8. coram Rege. of the record) *Antiquissimas Angliæ leges penitus subvertere, et enervare, universumq; hoc regnum Angliæ, et ejusdem regni populum legibus imperialibus vulgo dictis legibus civilibus, et earundem legum canonibus imperpetuum subjugare et subducere, &c.* And for execution of his intended plot, he was the meane that but one parliament was holden in fourteen yeares, *viz.* from the seventh yeare, till the one and twentieth yeare of Henry the eight, and that one was principally [627] holden for the attainder by parliament of Edward the good duke of Buckingham, whom he hated, and the confiscation of all that he had. Now the cardinall, being a great protector of non-residents, was no sooner attainted by that law (which he sought to alter) but 21 H. 8. cap. 13. Vid. 33 H. 8. cap. 28. at the parliament holden in 21 H. 8. a law was made against non-residence, which was excellent for that time, but now had need of some alterations and additions.

CAP. IX.

ITEM, ministri domini regis, ut vicecomites, et alii, ingrediuntur feoda ecclesiæ (1) ad faciendum districtiones, et aliquando capiunt animalia rectorum (2) in via regia, quando non habent nisi terram pertinentem ad ecclesiam. Responsio: Placet domino regi quod de cætero districtiones fiant hujusmodi, nec in via regia, nec in feodis, quibus olim (4) ecclesiæ sunt datatæ (3), vult tamen districtiones fieri in possessionibus de novo à personis ecclesiasticis acquisitis.

ALSO the king's officers, as sheriffs and other, do enter into the fees of the church to take distresses, and sometime they take the parson's beasts in the king's highway, where they have nothing but the land belonging to the church. The answer. The king's pleasure is, that from henceforth such distresses shall neither be taken in the king's highway, nor in the fees wherewith churches in times past have been indowed; neverthelefs he willeth distresses to be taken in possessions of the church newly purchased by ecclesiastical persons.

(52 H. 3. c. 15. Regist. 98. 183.)

(1) *Ingrediuntur feoda ecclesiæ.*] See the exposition upon the Marlbridge, ca. 15. statute of Marlebridge: this is to be added, that the statute of Marlebridge was construed to extend onely to lay men, and this statute to men of the church: and this appeareth by the Register; for if a lay man bring an action upon the statute for distraining in Reg. 187, 188. F.N.B. 173. e.f. the kings high-way, he reciteth the statute of Marlebridge: and if a parson bring an action for distraining in the high-way, he groundeth it upon this statute.

(2) *Rectorum.*] Here parsons be named but for example; for this law extended to abbots, priors, and the like; for afterwards the words be *personæ ecclesiasticæ:* but this law bindeth not the king, when he is party, for any debt, or duty due unto him, because the distresse or other processe for the king is not expresly named in the act, but *districtiones* generally: and this appeareth by a book-27 Ass. p. 66. case: a prior brought a bill of trespasse against J. for entering into his

his ſanctuary, that is, within the circuit of the ſcite of his priorie, and tooke away his beaſts: J. ſaid that he was ſheriffe, and that the prior loſt iſſues in the court of common pleas, and a writ iſſued to him to levie the iſſues, and that hee entred into the ſanctuary, &c. becauſe he could not find a diſtreſſe without; whereupon the plaintife demurred, and judgement was given againſt the plaintife, which proveth, that the ſheriffe in that caſe could not have returned upon the proceſſe to him directed, *Clericus beneficiatus nullum habens laicum feodum.*

(3) *Nec in feodis quibus olim eccleſiæ ſunt dotatæ.*] Here *dotatæ* is taken in a large ſenſe; for here the fees that they have *ratione fundationis*, or *ratione dotationis* are included; and here is alſo to be noted, that the poſſeſſions of the church are the indowment of the church, and they accounted as tenants in dower, as in another place hath been obſerved.

(4) *Olim.*] This word is well expounded afterwards in this act, to be thoſe that are not *de novo acquiſita.*

Concerning taſkes, tenths, and fifteenes granted by parliament to the king, the poſſeſſions of eccleſiaſticall perſons, which they acquired ſince 20 E. 1. either by purchaſe or act in law, as by others, &c. were chargeable thereunto: but thoſe which they had at that time were not charged therewith; and the reaſon thereof was this, the pope (after the example of the high prieſt amongſt the Jewes, who had of the Levites *decimam partem decimæ)* claimed by pretext thereof a yearly tenth part of the value of all eccleſiaſticall livings: this portion or tribute was by ordinance yeelded to the pope in 20 E. 1. and a valuation then made of the eccleſiaſticall livings within this realme, to the end the pope might know, and be anſwered of that yearly revenue, ſo as the eccleſiaſticall livings chargeable with that tenth (which was called ſpirituall) to the pope, were not chargeable with the temporall tenths or fifteenes granted to the king in parliament, leſt they ſhould be doubly charged, but their poſſeſſions acquired after that taxation were liable to the temporall tenths or fifteenes, becauſe they were not charged to the other; and ſo it was declared by act of parliament in 18 E. 3. which never was printed; ſo as the tenths of eccleſiaſticall livings were not yeelded to the pope *de jure*, after the example of the high prieſt amongſt the Jewes; for then hee ſhould have had the tenths of all eccleſiaſticall livings whenſoever they were acquired; but he contented himſelfe with what he had got, and never claimed more: and that he might the better keep and enjoy that which he had got, the popes did often after grant the ſame for certaine termes to divers of the kings of England, as by our hiſtories appeare. And albeit theſe yearly tenths are perpetually annexed to the crown of England by act of parliament yet hereby the ſtudent ſhall better underſtand the bookes of law that treat hereof.

17 E. 3. 44. b. 27 E. 3. 28. b. 11 H. 4. 35.

[628]

Numeri, ca. 18. ver. 26.

Rot. parl. 18 E. 3. nu. 44. never printed.

26 H. 8. ca. 3. 1 Eliz. ca. 1.

CAP.

CAP. X.

ITEM, quandocunque aliqui confugientes ad ecclesiam abjurant terram (1), *secundum regni consuetudinem, et prosequuntur laici eos, vel inimici eorum, et à publica strata abstrahuntur, et suspenduntur, vel statim decapitantur* (2), *et dum sint in ecclesia custodiuntur per armatos infra cœmeterium, quandoque infra ecclesiam ita arcte, quod non possunt exire locum sacrum causa superflui ponderis deponendi, nec permittitur eis necessaria ad victus ministrari. Responsio: Qui terram abjuraverint, dum sint in strata publica, sint in pace domini regis, nec debent ab aliquo molestari: et dum sint in ecclesia, custodes eorum non debent morari infra cœmeterium, nisi necessitas, vel evasionis periculum hoc requirat: nec arctentur confugere, dum sint in ecclesia, quin possint habere vitæ necessaria* (3): *et exire libere pro obsceno pondere deponendo. Placet etiam domino regi, ut latrones vel appellatores* (5), *quandocunque voluerint, possint sacerdotibus sua facinora confiteri: sed caveant confessores, ne erronice hujusmodi appellatores informent* (4).

ALSO where some flying unto the church, abjure the realm, according to the custom of the realm, and lay-men or their enemies do pursue them, and pluck them from the king's highway, and they are hanged or headed; and whilst they be in the church, are kept in the church-yard with armed men, and sometime in the church, so straitly, that they cannot depart from the hallowed ground to empty their belly, and cannot be suffered to have necessaries brought unto them for their living. The answer. They that abjure the realm, so long as they be in the common way, shall be in the king's peace, nor ought to be disturbed of any man; and when they be in the church, their keepers ought not to abide in the church-yard, except necessity or peril of escape do require so. And so long as they be in the church, they shall not be compelled to flee away, but they shall have necessaries for their living, and may go forth to empty their belly. And the king's pleasure is, that thieves or appellors (whensoever they will) may confess their offences unto priests; but let the confessors beware that they do not erroneously inform such appellors.

(1 Jac. 1. c. 25. 21 Jac. 1. c. 28.)

[629]
Bract. lib. 2. fo. 135. &c. Brit. fol. 24. &c. Flet. li. 1. c. 29. Stamf. pl. coro. fo. 116. f. &c. 21 Jacobi Regis, cap.

(1) *Abjurant regnum.*] Concerning abjuration you may plentifully read in our ancient authors, and other bookes of the lawes, and specially in Stamford pl. coron. fol. 116. &c. wherein we are the more briefe, because it is enacted by the statute of 21 Jac. regis, that no sanctuary, or priviledge of sanctuary, after that statute be admitted or allowed in any case; and if the offender be barred of the priviledge of sanctuary to be allowed to him, then can hee not flee to any church, as to a sanctuary, for the tuition of his life, and consequently abjuration is taken away.

(2) *Decapitantur.*] This was mistaken in the petition: for no man can be beheaded but for treason; and no man could abjure

 for

for treason, because the coroner had no power to take any confession for treason, albeit the coroner had a speciall commission from the king to doe it.

See 1 Jacobi regis, cap. 25.

(3) *Quin possint habere vitæ necessaria.*] This is thus to be understood, that he shall have *necessaria vitæ* so long as he behaves himselfe according to the law, and the priviledge of the place; but if hee had continued 40 dayes, and would not abjure, then *vitæ necessaria* shall be denied unto him, and they should be punished that ministred the same unto him.

Bract. li. 2. fo. 135. &c. Brit. fol. 24, 25. Flet. li. 1. c. 29. 3 E. 3. coron. 313. Stamf. ubi supra.

(4) *Placet etiam domino regi, ut latrones, vel appellatores, quandocunque voluerint, possint sacerdotibus sua facinora confiteri, sed caveant confessores, ne erronice hujusmodi appellatores informent.*

(5) *Latrones vel appellatores.*] This branch extendeth onely to theeves and approvers indited of felony, but extended not to high treasons: for if high treason be discovered to the confessor, he ought to discover it, for the danger that thereupon dependeth to the king and the whole realme; therefore this branch declareth the common law, that the priviledge of confession extendeth onely to felonies: and albeit, if a man indited of felony becometh an approver, he is sworne to discover all felonies and treasons, yet is hee not in degree of an approver in law, but onely of the offence whereof he is indited; and for the rest, it is for the benefit of the king, to move him to mercy: so as this branch beginneth with theeves, extendeth onely to approvers of theevery or felony, and not to appeales of treason; for by the common law, a man indited of high treason could not have the benefit of clergy (as it was holden in the kings time, when this act was made) nor any clergy-man priviledge of confession to conceale high treason: and so was it resolved in * 7 Hen. 5. whereupon frier John Randolph the queene dowagers confessor, accused her of treason, for compassing of the death of the king: and so was it resolved in the case of Henry Garnet, superiour of the jesuites in England, who would have shadowed his treason under the priviledge of confession, although in deed he was not onely consenting, but abetting the principall conspirators of the powder-treason, as by the record of his attainder appeareth; and albeit this act extendeth to felonies onely, as hath been said, yet the caveat given to the confessors is observable, *ne erronice informent.*

12 E. 4. 10. b. 19 E. 2. cor. 387. 6 H. 6. coro. 231. 19 H. 6. 47. See W. 2. ca. 41. § Si Abbates, &c. li. 2. fo. 46. Levesque de Cant' case, &c. 20 E. 2. coro. pl. 283. 19 H. 6. 47.

* Rot. Parl. anno 7 H. 5. nu. 13. Hill. 3 Jac.

CAP. XI.

[630] *ITEM petitur, quod dominus rex, et regni magnates non onerent domos religiosas, vel ecclesiasticas personas pro corodiis, pensionibus (1), vel perhendinationibus (2) faciendis in domibus religiosis, et aliis locis ecclesiasticis, carectis et equis sibi mittendis, cum per hoc prædictæ domus depauperentur cultusque*

ALSO it is desired that our lord the king, and the great men of the realm do not charge religious houses, or spiritual persons, for corodies, pensions, or sojourning in religious houses, and other places of the church, or with taking up horse or carts, whereby such houses are impoverished, and God's service diminished.

tusque divinus in hac parte diminuatur, et propter hujusmodi onera compelluntur sæpissime presbyteri, et alii ministri ecclesiastici divinis officiis deputati à locis recedere supradict'. Responsio: Placet domino regi, quod super contentis in petitione, de cætero indebite non onerentur. Et si per magnates, aut alios contra fiat, habeant inde remedium juxta formam statutorum (3) tempore dom' E. regis patris domini regis nunc editorum: et fiat consimile remedium de corodiis, et pensionibus (4) per coertionem exactis, de quibus non fit mentio in statutis.

nished, and, by reason of such charges, priests, and other ministers of the church deputed unto divine service, are oftentimes compelled to depart from the places aforesaid. The answer. The king's pleasure is, that upon the contents in their petition, from henceforth they shall not be unduly charged. And if the contrary be done by great men or other, they shall have remedy after the form of the statutes made in the time of king Edward, father to the king that now is. And like remedy shall be done for corodies and pensions exacted by compulsion, whereof no mention is made in the statutes.

(3 Ed. 1. c. 1.)

(1) *Pro corodiis, et pensionibus.*] See hereafter in the end of this chapter, to whom, and in what cases corodies and pensions be due.

(2) *Perhendinationibus.*] See hereof W. 1. cap. 1.

Rast. pl. fo. 373. (3) *Juxta formam statutorum.*] That is to say, of W. 1. *anno* 3 E. 1. cap. 1.

Regist. fol. F.N.B. 230. b. 14 H. 6. 11. 2 E. 2. cui in vita 18. 6 E. 2. ibid. 25. Bract. li. 3. fo. 221. 14 E. 3. corody 5. 15 E. 3. ibid. 4. 11 ass. 22. 24 E. 3. f. 33. 38 ass. 22. 44 E. 3. 24. 50 ass. 6. 10 H. 4. 33. 14 H. 6. 11. 39 H. 6. 28. 1 E. 4. 10. 8 H. 7. 12. F.N.B. 231. Vid. rot. claus. in dors. 8 H. 4. m. 13. & 9 H. 4. m. 33, 34. penc' coram rege, Mich. 32. E. 1. Northampton.

(4) *Consimile remedium de corodiis et pensionibus.*] Albeit *corodium* is derived *à con et rodere, i. simul comedere*; yet to a corody belong not onely *victus*, but *vestitus, et alia vitæ necessaria*, which is called *sustentatio congrua*, as much as a monke of the same house hath; and a pension is a yearly annuity to be granted to one of the kings chapleines. The king shall have a corody for his vadelet, and a pension for his chaplein, out of all the religious and ecclesiasticall houses of his foundation (unlesse the tenure be in frankalmoigne) but by reason of dotation, if he be not founder, he shall have none, unlesse it be by speciall grant. A common person shall have no corody, nor pension, &c. though he be founder, unlesse it be by speciall grant. The abbot, &c. shall not be charged with a new pension, though the chaplein dye, during the life of the king; but if the abbot, &c. dye, his successor shall be charged, *ratione creationis* with a pension. If the vadelet dye, another shall have the corody during the kings life; but if the abbot, &c. dye, no new corody during the life of the former vadelet.

CAP.

CAP. XII.

ITEM, si aliqui de tenura domini regis vocantur coram ordinariis, extra parochiam in qua degunt, si propter suam contumaciam manifestam excommunicentur, ac post quadraginta dies pro eorum captione scribatur, prætendunt se privilegiatos, quod extra villam seu parochiam suam non debent vocari, et sic denegatur breve regium pro captione eorundem. * *Responsio: Nunquam fuit negatum, nec negabitur in futurum.*

*[631]

ALSO if any of the king's tenure be called before their ordinaries out of the parish where they continue, if they be excommunicate for their manifest contumacy, and after forty days a writ goeth out to take them, they pretend their privilege, that they ought not to be cited out of the town and parish where their dwelling is; and so the king's writ that went out for to take them is denied. The answer. It was never yet denied, nor shall be hereafter.

The writ *de excommunicato capiendo,* commonly called a *significavit,* was never denied; for this cause, that hee that held of the king had such a priviledge, that they should not be called out of the towne or parish where they lived; and therefore the answer (which must ever be conforme to the petition) ought of necessitie to be taken, that for that cause the kings writ was never, nor should be denied.

But for the better understanding hereof, at the parliament holden at Clarendon, in the eleventh yeare of Henry the second, *Facta est recognitio, seu recordatio cujusdam partis consuetudinum antecessorum regis, viz. Henrici (primi) avi sui, quæ observari debebant in regno, et ab omnibus teneri propter dissensiones et discordias sæpe emergentes inter clerum et justiciarios Domini regis, et magnatum regni.* Amongst the rest, this was agnized and declared in these words: *Nullus qui de rege tenet in capite, nec aliquis dominicorum ministrorum ejus excommunicetur, nec alicujus eorum terræ sub interdicto ponantur, nisi prius dominus rex, si in regno fuerit, conveniatur, vel justiciarius ejus, si fuer' extra regnum, ut rectum de eo faciat, ut quod pertinebat ad regis curiam, ibi terminetur, et de eo quod spectat ad curiam ecclesiasticam ad eandem mittatur, et ibidem terminetur.* And the reason of this law was, for that the tenures by grand serjeantie, and knights service *in capite* were for the honour and defence of the realme; and concerning those that served the king in his houshold, their continuall service and attendance upon the royall person of the king was necessary.

8 Kal. Febr. anno 11 H. 2. apud Clarendon, commonly called Assisa de Clarendon, Bract. li. 3. fol. 136. See cap. 15.

Of this law the clergy here complained not, and other then this concerning tenure, &c. in the petition mentioned, we remember not any; so as we may conclude this point, that this writ *de excommunicato capiendo* (as hath been said) *procedit de gratia regis.*

Vid. ca. 7. before. Rot. clauf. in dorf. 17 R. 2. m. 10.

CAP. XIII.

ITEM petitur quod personæ ecclesiasticæ, quas dominus rex ad beneficia præsentet ecclesiastica, si episcopus eas non admittat, ut puta propter defectum scientiæ, vel aliam causam rationabilem, non subeant examinationem laicarum personarum in casibus antedictis, prout his temporibus attentatur de facto, contra canonicas sanctiones: sed adeant judicem ecclesiasticum, ad quem de jure pertinet pro remedio, prout justum fuerit, consequendo. Responsio: De idonietate personæ (1) *præsentatæ ad beneficium ecclesiasticum pertinet examinatio ad judicem ecclesiasticum: et ita est hactenus usitatum* (2), *et fiat in futurum.*

ALSO it is desired that spiritual persons, whom our lord the king doth present unto benefices of the church (if the bishop will not admit them either for lack of learning, or for other cause reasonable) may not be under the examination of lay persons in the cases aforesaid, as it is now attempted, contrary to the decrees canonical, but that they may sue unto a spiritual judge for remedy, as right shall require. The answer. Of the ability of a parson presented unto a benefice of the church the examination belongeth to a spiritual judge; and so it hath been used heretofore, and shall be hereafter.

(4 Mod. 135. Regist. 53.)

[632]

Regist. 53. b. 38 E. 3. 2. 29 E. 3. 44. 5 R. 2. tryall 54. 11 H. 4. 34 H. 6. 40. per Prisot, 5 H. 7. 19. 11 H. 7. 7. 37. 15 H. 7. 7. 9 El. Dyer, 154. 13 El. Dyer, 332. li. 5. fol. 57. Specots case.

(1) *De idonietate personæ.*] It is required by law, that the person presented be *idonea persona*; for so be the words of the kings writ, *præsentare idoneam personam.* And this *idonietas* consisteth in divers exceptions against persons presented: first, concerning the person, as bastardy, villenage, outlawry, excommunication, a layman, under age, and the like: secondly, concerning his conversation, as if he be *criminosus, &c.* Thirdly, concerning his inability to discharge his pastorall duty, as if hee be unlearned, and not able to feed his flocke with spirituall food, &c. And the examination of the ability and sufficiency of the person presented belongs to the bishop, who is the ecclesiasticall judge; and in this examination he is a judge, and not a minister, and may and ought to refuse the person presented, if he be not *idonea persona.* And if the cause of refusall be for default of learning, or that he is an heretick, schismatick, or the like, belonging to the knowledge of ecclesiasticall law, there he must give notice thereof to the patron; but if the cause be temporall, as a felon, or homicide, or other temporall crime; or if the disability grow by any act of parliament, or other temporall law, there no notice ought to be given, unlesse notice be prescribed to be given thereby. But in a *quare impedit* brought against the bishop, for refusall of the clerke, he must shew the cause of his refusall specially and directly (for whether the cause thereof be spirituall or temporall, the examination of the bishop concludes not the plaintife) to the intent the court, being judges of the principall cause, may consult with learned men in that profession, and resolve whether the cause be just or no; or the party may deny the same, and then the court shall write to the metropolitane to certifie the same; or if the cause bee

bee temporall, and sufficient in law (which the court must decide) the same may be traversed, and an issue thereupon joyned, and tried by the country. And yet in some cases, notwithstanding this statute, *idonietas personæ* shall be tried by the country, or else there should be a failer of justice (which the law will never suffer) as if the inability or insufficiency be alledged in a man that is dead, this case is out of this statute: for the bishop cannot examine him, and the words of this act be, *de idonietate personæ præsentatæ ad beneficium eccles. pertinet examinatio, &c.* And consequently, though the matter be spirituall, yet shall it be tried by a jury, and the court, being assisted by learned men in that profession, may instruct the jury as well of the ecclesiasticall law in that case, as they usually doe of the common law. 39 E. 3. 2. 40 E. 3. 25.

(2) *Et ita est hactenus usitatum.*] So as this act is a declaration of the common law and custome of the realme.

CAP. XIV.

ITEM, si vacet aliqua dignitas, ubi electio est facienda, petitur quod electores libere possint eligere, absque incussione timoris à quacunque potestate seculari: et quod cessent preces, et oppressiones in hac parte. Responsio: Fiant libere, juxta formam statutorum et ordinationum.

ALSO if any dignity be vacant, where election is to be made, it is moved that the electors may freely make their election without fear of any power temporal, and that all prayers and oppressions shall in this behalf cease. The answer. They shall be made free according to the form of statutes and ordinances.

(3 E. 1. c. 5.)

The clergy either remembred not the statute of W. 1. or if they did, they doubted whether it extended to ecclesiasticall elections, although without question it did, and so it is declared by this act, and it is an excellent law, and worthy to be put in execution. W. 1. cap. 5.

See more hereof before in the exposition upon the statute of W. 1.

CAP. XV. [633]

ITEM, licet clericus coram seculari judice judicari non debeat, nec aliquid contra ipsum fieri, per quod ad periculum mortis, vel ad mutilationem membrorum valeat perveniri: seculares tamen judices clericos ad ecclesiam confugientes, et reatus suos forte confitentes

MOREOVER, though a clerk ought not to be judged before a temporal judge, nor any thing may be done against him that concerneth life or member; nevertheless temporal judges cause that clerks fleeing unto the church, and paradventure confessing

confitentes faciunt abjurare regnum, et eorum abjurationes admittunt ex illa causa, quanquam eorum judices super hiis non existant: sicque datur laicis indirecte potestas hujusmodi clericos cruciandi, si ipsos post hujusmodi abjurationem in regno contigerit inveniri: super quo petunt prælati, et cler' tale remedium adhiberi, ut immunitas ecclesiæ, et personarum ecclesiasticarum conservetur illæsa. Responsio: Clericus ad ecclesiam confugiens (1) *pro felonia, pro immunitate ecclesiastica obtinenda, si asserit se esse clericum, regnum non compellatur abjurare, sed legi regni se reddens gaudebit ecclesiastica libertate, juxta laudabilem consuetudinem regni* (2) *hactenus usitatam.*

confessing their offences, do abjure the realm, and for the same cause admit their abjurations, although hereupon they cannot be their judges, and so power is wrongfully given to lay persons to put to death such clerks, if such persons chance to be found within the realm after their abjuration; the prelates and clergy desire such remedy to be provided herein, that the immunity or privilege of the church and spiritual persons may be saved and unbroken. The answer. A clerk fleeing to the church for felony, to obtain the privilege of the church, if he affirm himself to be a clerk, he shall not be compelled to abjure the realm; but yielding himself to the law of the realm, shall enjoy the privilege of the church, according to the laudable custom of the realm heretofore used.

Custumier de Norm. c. 83. (28 H. 8. c. 1. 1 Jac. 1. c. 25. 21 Jac. 1. c. 28.)

Here the claim of the clergy is generall, that *clericus coram seculari judice judicari non debeat, nec aliquid contra ipsum fieri, per quod ad periculum mortis, vel mutilationem membrorum valeat perveniri:* let us see what priviledge the clergy had allowed unto them in criminall cases: first, let us observe what our ancient authors have holden in that case: secondly, what records of parliament, and other records have delivered to us: thirdly, what acts of parliament have established in these cases: fourthly, what have the judgements and resolutions been of judges in our bookes and eports. And lastly, from what root this priviledge of clergy sprang, to exempt them from the common justice of the realme.

Custumier ubi supra.

Bracton saith, *Cum clericus cujuscunque ordinis vel dignitatis captus fuerit pro morte hominis, vel alio crimine, et imprisonatus, et de eo petatur curia christianitatis ab ordinario loci, &c. imprisonatus statim ei deliberetur, &c. donec à crimine sibi imposito se purgaverit competenter, vel in purgatione defecerit, propter quod debet degradari, &c. cum autem clericus sic de crimine convictus degradetur, non sequitur alia pœna pro uno delicto, vel pluribus, ante degradationem perpetratis.* Here three things are to be noted: first, that he beginneth with the greatest felony, that is, the death of man: secondly, that albeit he were found guilty, and could not purge himselfe before the ordinary, yet all that the ordinary could doe was to degrade him. Thirdly, that he could have no other punishment for that felony, or any other formerly done, but degradation.

See the statute of 23 H. 8. cap. 11. & ca. 1. 1 E. 6. cap. 10, &c. Bract. lib. 3. fol. 123. b.

Britton also speaketh only of felony: *Et si le clerk encoupe de felonie alledge clergie, et soit tiel trove, et per ordinarie demand, si soit enquise coment il est mescru, et sil soit nient mescru, &c. soit arge tout quits,*

Brit. fol. 11. Stamf. pl. cor. 123. c. 8 E. 2. coron. 417. 17 E. 2. ib. 386. 3 H. 7. 12.

quits, et s'il soit mescrue, si soient ses chateux taxes, et ses terres prises in nre. maine, et son cors deliv' al ordinarie.

According to Britton, when one of the clergy was indited of felony, &c. and the ordinary demanded him, yet to the end (saith the * record) *ut sciatur qualis deliberaretur ordinario*, an enquest was charged by the court to enquire, whether he were guilty, or no. And though hee was found guilty by this enquest of office, yet was he delivered to the ordinary, and his chattels seised, and his lands taken into the kings hands, as Britton saith. [634]

* Mirr. cap. 3. del exception de clergie accord.

Fleta saith, *Si criminaliter agatur versus clericum, quamvis clericus respondere voluerit in foro seculari, judex tamen ecclesiasticus cognitionem habere non poterit, nec regiam auferre jurisdictionem: In causa enim sanguinis non poterit ecclesiasticus judex cognoscere, neque judicare, nisi irregularitatem committat. Et quamvis neminem valeat morti condemnare, degradare tamen poterit criminum convictos, vel perpetua carceris inclusione custodire.* Flet. lib. 6. ca. 36.

The Mirror hath generall words, *Lesglise et cy enfranchise que nul lay judge ne poet aver conusans de clarke, tout le voiloit le clarke conustre pur son judge, &c.* Mirr. ubi supra.

Two of these ancient authors have spoken of felony, and so are the other two to be intended; for the priviledge of the church did not extend to high treason, *crimen læsæ majestatis*, as by divers judiciall records and authorities in law shall appeare.

Walter de Berton clerke counterfeited the great seale, which was high treason, *crimen læsæ majestatis*, whereof he was indited and convicted: for so the record saith, *Qui convictus fuit pro falsificatione sigilli domini regis, quod tradatur episcopo Sarum, qui eum petiit ut clericum suum, sub pœna et forma qua decet, quia videtur concilio, quod in tali casu non est admittenda purgatio.* Rot. Parl. anno 21 E. 1. rot. 9.

This delivery to the ordinary was by ordinance of parliament *de gratia, et non de jure:* for it was resolved, that hee could not make his purgation; and therefore hee was delivered to him *sub pœna, &c.* In the reigne of Ed. 3. it was taken for a generall rule, *quod privilegium clericale non competit seditioso equitant' cum armis, platis et cotearmuris, secundum leges Angliæ.* Trin. 21 E. 3. coram rege, rot. 173. Hertford.

In 17 E. 2. in the time of the parliament, Adam de Orleton, bishop of Hereford, was indited of high treason, for being party and privie, aiding and abetting of Roger Mortimer earle of March with horse and armes in his open rebellion; and because he could not have any priviledge of clergy by the common law, the archbishop of Canterbury, Yorke, and Dublin, and their suffragan bishops, came to the barre (in that disordered time) and with force tooke him from the barre: all which was done by pretext and colour of the canons of the church, which you may reade in Linwood. 17 E. 2. rot. Rom. m. 6. Henricus Blanford. Linwood tit. de foro compet' cap. Contingit.

But, omitting many other things that might be here rehearsed, let us see what acts of parliament have ordained in this case; for the clergy never thought themselves sure of this priviledge, till it was confirmed to them by authority of parliament. By the statute of W. 1. it is provided, *Que quant clerke est prise pur ret de felonie, et soit demand per lordinarie, a luy soit liver solonque le priviledge de saint esglise, in tiel perill come ils appent, solonque le custome avant ces heures use, &c.* where note, this act extendeth but to felony. W. 1. cap. 2. See Marlbridge, cap. 27. See hereafter, cap. 5.

See the exposition of the statute of W. 1. in this point, and the charge as is given to ordinaries, that none be delivered without due

4 H. 4. cap. 3. 23 H. 8. cap. 1. due purgation; but it is worthy our paines to reade the statutes of 4 H. 4. and 23 H. 8.

Pl. coram domino rege apud Sandwicum in cro' Hilarii, an. 22 E. 1. rot. 15. Kanc'. After this statute, and in this kings time, Guinandus de Briland, parson of Snodiland in the county of Kent (in which towne Solomon de Rolfe, one of the kings justices in eire, and one that punished the extortions and other crimes of the clergy, dwelt) came to dine with Solomon de Rolfe, and brought poyson with him of his malice prepensed, to murder by poyson the said Solomon; and the record of his inditement saith, *Cum eo comedit, et posuit venenum in cibo et in potu ipsius Solomonis, et ipsum impoisonavit, per quod, post quindecim dies sequentes inde obiit:* and albeit of all felonies, murder is the worst, and of all murders, murder by poyson is the most unavoidable and detestable, and Guinand being indited and arraigned upon the said inditement, *et quæsitus qualiter se vellet acquietare,* [635] *dicit, quod clericus est, et non potest hic inde respondere, et super hoc venit frater Thomas episcopus Roffensis, et petit ipsum tanquam clericum, &c. Et ut sciatur qualis deliberare debet, inquiratur rei veritas per patriam; et jurat' &c. dicunt super sacramentum suum, quod prædict' Guinandus dedit prædict' Solomoni venenum unde impoisonatus fuit, et inde obiit, ut prædictum est.* But in the end he was delivered to the ordinary, as by the record it appeareth, and thereby, for any thing that wee find in that or any other record, he escaped the sentence of death, which was due for his offence by the law of God, and by the common law of the realme grounded upon the same, Genes. cap. 9. ver. 6. *Quicunque effuderit humanum sanguinem, fundetur sanguis illius, ad imaginem quippe Dei factus est homo.* Numer. cap. 35. ver. 29, 30, 31. 33. And againe, in the book of Numbers, *Hæc sempiterna erunt et legitima in cunctis, homicida sub testibus punietur, &c. non accipies pretium ab eo, qui reus est sanguinis, statim et ipse morietur, ne polluatis terram habitationis vestræ quæ insontium cruore maculatur, nec aliter expiari potest, nisi per ejus sanguinem, qui alterius sanguinem fuderit.*

8 E. 2. coron. 419. 22 E. 3. ib. 248. In 8 E. 2. a clerke convict for felony, and delivered to the ordinary, murdered his keeper, and fled, *et non obstante clerimonia sua,* hee was hanged. And the like was done in 22 E. 3.

The abuse of delivery of clerkes to the ordinary grew so intolerable, as in the end it was taken away; as hereafter shall be shewed.

See the statute of 18 E. 3. cap. 2. concerning this matter.

Rot. Parl. 25 E. 3. nu. 68, &c. At the parliament holden *in anno* 25 E. 3. the clergy did complaine, that one Hanketun Honby a knight, and one of the clergy, had judgement given against him for high treason to be hanged, drawne, and quartered: also for a judgement given against a priest at Nottingham, for killing of his master, sir Thomas Cibethorp, a clerke of the chancery, one of the kings justices.

25 E. 3. ca. 4. & 5. 4 H. 4. cap. 3. And lastly, for hanging of divers monkes of Combe for felony. Thereupon at this parliament an act of parliament was made, wherein it is recited, that the prelates had grievously complained, praying thereof remedy, for that secular clerkes, as well chapleines, as other monkes, and other people of religion had been drawne, and hanged by award of the secular justices, in prejudice of the franchises of holy church, &c. It is accorded and granted by the king, that all manner of clerkes, as well secular as religious, which should be convict before secular justices for any treasons or felonies touching other persons, then the king himselfe or his royall majestie, should freely have and enjoy the priviledge of holy church, &c.

&c. Hereby two things are to be observed: first, that hee shall not be delivered to the ordinary before hee be convicted: secondly, that the priviledge of the church extended not to high treason touching the king, *crimen læsæ majestatis*, but to petit treasons and felonies touching other persons.

About six yeares after this act, the abbot of Missenden in the county of Buckingham, was adjudged to be drawne and hanged for high treason, *viz.* for *contrafactione, et resectione legalis monetæ*. Coram rege Mich. 31 E. 3. rot. 55. Buck.

At the parliament holden in the first yeare of H. 4. on the first Thursday after the bishop of Canterbury had willed the lords, that in no wise they should disclose any thing that should be there spoken, the earle of Northumberland demanded of the lords what were best to be done for the life of king Richard the second; thus farre are the words of the roll of the parliament: at this time spake that worthy prelate John Merkes bishop of Carlisle, and said, that they ought not to proceed to any judgement against king Richard for foure causes: first, that the lords had no power to give judgement upon him that was their superiour, and the lords annointed: secondly, that they obeyed him for their soveraigne lord and king 22 yeares or more: thirdly, if they had power to give judgement against him, they ought in justice to call him to his answer; for that (said he) is granted to the cruellest murderer, or arrantest thiefe in ordinary courts of justice: fourthly, that the duke of Lancaster had done more trespasse to king Richard and his realme, then king Richard had done to him or them, &c. and desired, that if they would proceed against him, that the names of them that so would proceed might be entred into the parliament roll. [636] It is true, that the parliament roll omitteth this speech of the bishop, but it appeareth by the parliament roll, that the lords proceeded against king Richard, and adjudged him to perpetuall prison, whose life they would by all meanes to be saved, as the roll reporteth. The names of the bishops, and lords, and knights that assented, are set downe, as the roll of the parliament reports; so as it seemeth, that the stout and resolute speech of the worthy bishop wrought some effect: for this speech he was arrested by the earle marshall, and being for a small time committed to the custody of the abbot of Saint Albons was soon delivered; against him never any judiciall proceeding was had for this speech in parliament: but this bishop, transported with excesse of zeale, and affectionate desire of the enlargement and restitution of king Richard, was party and privie to the conspiracie of Thomas Holland earle of Kent, John Holland earle of Huntingdon, John Montacute earle of Salisbury, Edward earle of Rutland, Thomas lord Spencer, and others, to kill the king, under colour of jousting and pastimes in the Christmasse time, at the castle of Windesor, where the king lay in the first yeare of his reigne: for this he was indited of high treason, arraigned, tryed, and had judgement as in case of high treason. But *cor regis in manu domini*, the king pardoned him, and set him at liberty. Many more presidents might to this end be produced, but we will conclude this point with a resolution of all the judges in 24 H. 8. A priest was attainted by verdict at the gaole-delivery at Newgate, for clipping of the kings coine, *viz.* George Nobles, and by advice of all the judges judgement was given against him to be drawne and hanged, as another lay person, because

Rot. Parl. 1 H. 4. nu. 73.

Vid. Rot. Parl. an. 2 H. 4. nu. 30. See the record of his attainder, Hill. 2 H. 4. coram rege, rot. 6.

Trin. 24 H. 8. Justice Spilmans report.

because it was high treason, and without degradation he was executed at Tiborne.

Now for murder, burglary, robbery, sodomy, rape, burning of houses, and many other felonies, the benefit and priviledge of clergy is taken away by divers acts of parliament, whereunto the bishops were party, whereof you may reade, lib. 11. Alexander Poulters case, and where the benefit and priviledge of clergy remaineth, the party that takes the benefit of it shall not be delivered to the ordinary, nor make any purgation (which had been much abused) but forthwith be enlarged and delivered out of prison by the justices, by whom such clergy is allowed, as by another act of parliament, whereunto the bishops were party appeareth.

Lib. 11. fol. 29. Alexander Poulters case. 23 H. 8. ca. 1. 25 H. 8. c. 3. 28 H. 8. c. 1. 32 H. 8. cap. 3. 1 E. 6. cap. 12. 5 E. 6. cap. 9. 8 El. cap. 4. 39 El. ca. 9. & 15. 18 El. ca. 7.

* Amongst the ancient customes and liberties of England recognized and declared in the parliament before mentioned, holden in the eleventh yeare of Henry the second, this was one, *Cleri accusati de quacunque re, summoniti à justiciario regis, veniant in curiam ipsi responsuri ibidem de hoc, unde videbitur curiæ regis quod ibi sit respondendum, et in curia ecclesiastica, unde videbitur quod ibi sit respondendum, ita quod regis justiciarius mittet in curiam sanctæ ecclesiæ, ad videndum quomodo res ibi tractabitur, et si clericus convictus, vel confessus fuerit, non debet eum de cætero ecclesia tueri.* So as in effect the ancient law and custome of England in that case is restored.

* 11 H. 2. apud Clarendon, ubi sup. cap. 12.

Pollchro. lib. 4. cap. 24. Gaius Pope.

Lastly, out of what root this priviledge sprang? It took his root from a constitution of the pope, that no man should accuse the priests of holy church before a secular judge, which being contrary to the crowne and dignity of the king, and the common law bound not here, till it was confirmed by parliament, and the rather, for that the church had no power to punish the offence; but where their claime was generall, the parliament of Edw. 1. and custome of the realme restrained it onely to felony, so as they were to answer to high treason, and all offences under felony.

Vid. Stamf. pl. cor. 122, 123, &c.

(1) *Clericus ad ecclesiam confugiens,* &c.] By this law, if any that was *infra sacros ordines* committed felony, and for his tuition fled to a church, if he claimed the priviledge of his clergy, he should not be compelled to abjure, but submitting himselfe to the law of the kingdome, he should enjoy the priviledge of his clergy. See more of this matter in the next § *secundum laudab'.*

[637]

Vid. W. 1. ca. 2. solonque le custome avant ces heures use.

(2) *Secundum laudabilem consuetudinem regni.*] So as this priviledge of the clergy took not his vigour or strength by force of any forraine councell or canon, but by authority of parliament, and by the laudable law and custome of the kingdome, a point worthy of observation, the answer being so cautelously penned in those dayes, lest any thing in the petition should countenance any forraigne jurisdiction: but so farre as *lex et consuetudo regni* have allowed of the priviledge of the clergy, so farre, and no further it is to be allowed; and yet with this limitation, so as the clerke would submit himselfe (as hath been said) to take it by the law of the kingdome expressed in these words, *sed legi regni se reddens, &c.*

4 H. 7. cap. 13.

He that is within orders hath a priviledge, that albeit hee have had the priviledge of his clergy for a felony, he may have his clergy afterwards againe, and so cannot a lay-man; and he that is within orders, and hath his clergy allowed, shall not be branded in the hand. But these priviledges are given by act of parliament.

CAP.

CAP. XVI.

ITEM, quanquam confessio coram illo qui non est judex confitentis, locum non teneat, nec sufficiat ad faciend' processum, vel sententiam proferendam: quidam tamen seculares judices clericos, qui de foro suo in hac parte non existunt, reatus proprios, et enormes, ut puta furta, roberias, homicidia, coram eis confitentes, admittunt accusationem illorum, quam ipsi communiter vocant appellum, ipsos sic confitentes, et accusantes, seu appellum facientes, non liberant prælatis eorum post præmissa, quanquam super his fuerint sufficienter requisit', licet coram eis etiam per confessionem propriam judicari vel condemnari nequeant, absque violatione ecclesiasticæ libertatis. Responsio: Appellatori (1) *in forma debita, tanquam clerico, per ordinarium petita libertatis ecclesiasticæ beneficio, non negabitur. Nos desiderantes statui ecclesiæ Anglicanæ, et tranquillitati, et quieti prælatorum, et cleri prædictorum (quatenus de jure poterimus) providere, ad honorem Dei, et emendationem status dictæ ecclesiæ, et prælatorum, et cleri prædictorum, omnes et singulas responsiones prædictas, ac omnia et singula in eisdem responsionibus content' ratificantes et approbantes, ea pro nobis et hæredibus nostris concedimus, et præcipimus in perpetuum inviolabiliter observari: volentes, et concedentes pro nobis et hæredibus nostris, quod prædicti prælati, et clerus, et eorum successores in perpetuum in præmissis jurisdictionem ecclesiasticam exerceant, juxta tenorem responsionum prædictarum, absque occasione, inquietatione, vel* [638] *impedimento nostri, vel nostrorum hæredum, seu ministrorum quoruncunque. In cujus, &c. Test. &c.*

ALSO notwithstanding that a confession made before him that is not lawful judge thereof, is not sufficient whereon process may be awarded, or sentence given; yet some temporal judges (though they have been instantly desired thereto) do not deliver to their ordinaries, according to the premisses, such clerks as confess before them their heinous offences, as theft, robbery, and murther, but admit their accusation, which commonly they call an appeal, albeit to this respect they be not of their court, nor can be judged or condemned before them upon their own confession, without breaking of the churches privilege. The answer. The privilege of the church, being demanded in due form by the ordinary, shall not be denied unto the appealour, as to a clerk. We desiring to provide for the state of holy church of England, and for the tranquillity and quiet of the prelates and clergy aforesaid, as far forth as we may lawfully do, to the honour of God, and emendation of the church, prelates, and clergy of the same; ratifying, confirming, and approving all and every of the articles aforesaid, with all and every of the answers made and contained in the same, do grant and command them to be kept firmly, and observed for ever; willing and granting for us and our heirs, that the foresaid prelates and clergy, and their successors, shall use, execute, and practise for ever the jurisdiction of the church in the premisses, after the tenour of the answers aforesaid, without quarrel, inquieting, or vexation of us or of our heirs, or any of our officers whatsoever they be.

T. R.

T. R. at York, the xxiv. day of November, in the tenth year of the reign of king Edward, the son of king Edward.

Wee have been the longer in exposition of the former chapter, because wee should be the shorter in this which somewhat concerneth the same matter.

(1) *Appellatori, i. Probatori.*] Albeit the clergy here pretended, that the confession of a clerke (when he was indited of felony, and confessed the felony, and became an approver) was *coram non judice*; yet the continuall opinion and resolution of the judges were against this: for they resolved, that such a clerke as confessed the felony before a secular judge, could not make his purgation, and consequently, the confession did bind him: and therefore Shard in 25 E. 3. spake in the person of a prelate. And when the clerke was delivered to the ordinarie, without any purgation to be made, he ought to have degraded him; but commonly, if the offender were a monke, he delivered him to his abbot to remaine in the abbey perpetually: and if he were secular, he remained in the bishops prison, &c. in a very favourable manner; which abuses grew so odious and insufferable in encouragement of malefactors in their wickednesse, as they were justly taken away, as is aforesaid.

10 E. 3. cor. 247. 27 H. 6. fol. 7. 13 E. 4. 3. 3 H. 7. 2. 25 E. 3. coron. 128. Vid. 12 R. 2. coron. 109. & 247. 8 E. 2. coron. 417.

An appeale of robbery was brought against J. de B. monke of L. who pleaded not guilty, and put himselfe upon the tryall of the country, who found him not guilty, whereupon the abbot of L. and the said Monke, brought a writ of conspiracie against divers, which procured and abetted the said appeale, and recovered a 1000 markes in damages, which could not have been recovered, unlesse the monke had been *legitimo modo acquietatus*, before a competent judge: and hereby it appeareth, that a clerke might wave the priviledge of his clergy, if he would, and be tryed by the course of the common law. And note, when hee knew himselfe free and innocent, then hee would be tryed by the common law; but when he found himselfe fowle and guilty, then would he shelter himselfe under the priviledge of his clergy: and though they committed temporall crimes, yet would they not be tryed by the temporall lawes, which was the more against reason, because no other law within this realme could punish them for the same, but the temporall lawes onely.

24 E. 3. 73. a. 22 E. 3. cor. 276. lib. 11. fol. 77. Magd. Colledge case.

The Expoſition of 18 Edw. 3. Cap. 7. of Tithes.

* *ITEM que per la ou briefes de ſcire fac' eient eſtre grantes* (1) *a garner prelates religious et auters clerkes* (2), *a reſpondre des diſmes a noſtre chancerie, et a monſtrer ſils eient riens pur enſachent riens dire pur quoi tiels diſmes a les demandants ne deinent eſtre reſtitus, et a reſponder auxibien aux nous, come a partie de tieux diſmes.* † *Que tieux briefes deſere en avant ne ſoient grantes, et que les proceſſes pendants ſur tieux briefes ſoient anientes et repeales, et que les parties diſmiſes devant ſecular juges de tiels manners de pleas : ſaves a nous noſtre droit* (3), *tiel come nous et nous anceſtres avouns eit, et ſoloions avoir de reaſon. En teſtimoinance de quele choſe, a le requeſt des dites prelates a ceſtes preſentes lettres avons fait metre noz ſeale. Done a Londres le* 8 *jour de July lan de noſtre reigne Engleterre diſoitiſme, et de France quints.*

ITEM, whereas writs of ſcire facias have been granted to warn prelates, religious and other clerks, to anſwer diſmes in our chancery, and to ſhew if they have any thing, or can any thing ſay, wherefore ſuch diſmes ought not to be reſtored to the ſaid demandants, and of anſwer as well to us, as to the party of ſuch diſmes ; that ſuch writs from henceforth be not granted, and that the proceſs hanging upon ſuch writs be adnulled and repealed, and that the parties be diſmiſſed from the ſecular judges of ſuch manner of pleas ; ſaving to us our right, ſuch as we and our anceſtors have had, and were wont to have of reaſon. In witneſs whereof, at the requeſt of the ſaid prelates, to theſe preſent letters we have ſet our ſeal. Dated at London the eighth day of July, the year of our reign of England the eighteenth, and of France the fifth.

* Le preamble. † Le act.

Before we enter into the expoſition of this act, we will cleare it of an objection againſt the life of it, *viz.* That it ſhould be no act of parliament, but an ordinance made by the king onely at the requeſt of the prelates: and that the king to theſe letters had put his ſeale, and the *teſte* and date as done by the king only; all which, ſay they, appeare in the parliament roll, and that the clauſe of *En teſtimoinance de quel choſe, &c.* is left out of the print.

But hereunto we anſwer, that by the ſaid clauſe *En teſtimoinance de quel &c.* is to be underſtood, that this act was ſo plauſible to the prelates, that they requeſted the king, that it might be exemplified under the great ſeale for the better preſervation thereof, which the king granted. This parliament began the Munday after the *Octab. Trinitatis,* which was 16 *Junii*; and this exemplification was 8 *Julii* after this act was paſſed, there being but ſeven acts paſſed at this parliament. And *en teſtimoinance de quel,* and the whole clauſe following, are words of an exemplification. Vide Rot. Parl. 18 E. 3. nu. 31.

Now that this ordinance before the clauſe of the exemplification is an act of parliament, firſt, is proved by divers reaſons, *viz.* The title of the parliament is, *Incipit ſtatutum regis Edwardi anno regni*

ſui

sui decimo octavo. Secondly, it is entred in the parliament roll. Thirdly, it was by force of the kings writ (as the usage then was) proclaimed as an act of parliament, which writ in French we thinke good to transcribe in these words: *Edward per le grace de Dieu roy Dangleterre et de France, et seignieur Dirland a nostre viscount de Nottingham, salus. Saches que a nostre parliament tenus a Westm' le Lundye procheine apres les octaves de la Trinity procheine passes entre autres choses monstres, assentus, et accordes en dit parliament, si furent monstres, assentus et accordes les choses sous escrites.* And after a rehearsall of all the statutes, whereof this seventh chapter is one, the conclusion is, *Et pur ceo vous mandous, que touts les statutes faces crier et publier, et fermement tener per mye vostre baillie solonque la forme et tenur dicelle. Et ceo ne lesses en ascun mannere, &c.*

[640] And F.N.B. 30 E. taketh it for a statute, and so it hath ever been by the generall consent from time to time of learned men. And if it should not be a statute, it would worke great trouble and disquiet in the realme. Now that wee have cleared this objection, let us peruse the words of the act.

(1) *Ou briefes de scire facias eient estre grantes,* &c.] This rehearsall in this statute is true; for wee have found, that upon divers matters of record, that is to say, enrolled, returned, or removed into the chancery: first, upon tithes granted by the kings letters patents, which are inrolled in the chancery, writs of *scire fac'* were brought in that court: as taking one example for many: in 17 E. 3. a *scire fac'* was brought by the king, and the dean and canons of the kings free chappell of Saint Martins London, upon letters patents of Mawd, *quondam reginæ Angliæ* of tithes, &c. against the abbot of Saint Johns of Colchester, who took the same after severance, whereunto the abbot pleaded, &c. worthy to be seen.

In bundello brevium, an. 17 E. 3. part. 1. & 3. in turri London, vic. Essex.

(2) *A garner prelates religious et auters clerks,* &c.] Note, this *scire fac'* was not brought against the possessors of the land for substraction of tithes, but against the prelates, or other clerkes, which took the tithes after they were severed. See 6 E. 1. *in bundello petitionum in turri London,* where the petition was for substraction of tithes, to be put in possession: the answer was in parliament *anno* 6 E. 1. *Rex non intromittit se de hiis quæ taliter spectant ad forum ecclesiasticum, prosequatur jus suum versus clericum coram ordinario.* Herewith agreeth Bracton, lib. 5. fol. 403. & 407.

Commissions out of the chancery were directed to certaine persons, giving them authority to enquire, whether such a spirituall person ought to have tithes of such lands, whereupon inquisitions were taken and returned; and if it were found for the spirituall person, upon this record he might have a * *scire fac'* against any prelate religious, or other clerke that took them after severance.

* See 22 Ass. p'. 75.

[a] Rot. claus. 7. E. 2.

[a] *Compertum est per inquisitionem rectorum, et vicariorum vicinorum de Ewel, quod vicarius ecclesiæ ibidem percipere debet minutas decimas omnium animalium ibidem, et molend' aquatic' ibidem.* But no *scire fac'* was sued hereupon, for that the vicar was to sue for substraction of these tithes against the owner of the land in the spirituall court.

[b] In fin. Term. Trin' 10 regis Johannis.

[b] Also upon a fine executory of tithes before this act, the tenour whereof was removed into chancery, a *scire fac'* did lye therefore against the spirituall person that perned the same after they were severed.

(3) *Savant*

(3) *Savant a nous nostre droit*, &c.] By force of this [c] saving not onely the king himselfe, but the provost of C. being the kings patentee of tithes of the new assarts in the forest of Rockingham in the county of North-hampton, brought a *scire fac'* in the chancery after this statute, against certaine persons of holy [d] church, who had taken the tithes granted to him, to have execution of the said tithes, according to the kings letters patents. The [e] defendants pleaded to the jurisdiction of the court, that the conusance of this cause for tithes appertained to court christian, and not to the chancery, whereunto it was answered by the court, that that was to be understood, where the suit was taken against them that ought to pay the tithes (that is to say) for substraction of tithes, and not when it was brought against them, that were wrongfull takers of the tithes. And all this is well warranted by the book, whereupon the defendants pleaded to issue, and the record delivered over to be tried in the kings bench. See Hill. 32 E. 1. *coram rege* Wigorn' the Prior of Worcesters case resolved by the chancellor, treasurer, and all the judges and barons, that appropriation of tithes is no mortmaine, [f] *Quia decimæ sunt meræ spirituales, quarum cognitio ad curiam christianitatis pertinet, et non ad curiam istam.*

And yet the inference that Fitzherbert maketh, that before this statute of 18 E. 3. the right of tithes was tryed in the kings court was true: for upon a *scire facias* by a spirituall person against a spirituall person, and for tithes * which were spirituall, the right of tithes was tried in the *scire fac'* before this statute, albeit the tithes were severed, which is now taken away in case of the *scire fac'* by this statute.

And at this day, albeit in case of tithes, the parties by pleading admit the jurisdiction of the court, yet if it be between spirituall persons, and the right of tithes come to be tried, albeit it be after the tithes severed, the court *ex officio* shall ouste the court of jurisdiction, which we hold, where the right of patronage was not drawne in question, was wrought by the construction and consequent of the said statute of 18 E. 3. for before that statute right of tithes, after severance was tried in a *scire fac'* by the common law in certaine cases. But when the right of tithes trench to the dissolution or diminution of the advowson, &c. in certaine cases, the right of tithes at this day (as hath beene said) shall be tried *in brevi de recto advocat' decimarum*, and in the *indicavit:* but neither of these writs give any jurisdiction to the kings court, to hold plea for subtraction of tithes, but that is sent to the ecclesiasticall court to determine.

[c] 22 Ass. pl. 75. 38 Ass. pl. 20. Bro. tit. Dismes 10 Pla. Parlam. Hill. & Pasch. 18 E. 1. the Bish. of Carlisles case, to whose predecessors Hen. rex vetus concessit omnes decimas in Foresta de Englewe. 14 H. 4. 17.

[d] Note, this act of 18 E. 3. is not mentioned in this book of 22 Ass. because the case was taken to be within the saving.

[e] Note, albeit this book was after the stat. yet doth it open the true sense & reason of the common law before this statute of 18 E. 3.

[f] Pasch. 20 E. 1. in banco regis, rot. 135. Buck. F.N.B. 30 E.

*[641]

28 E. 3. f. 6. 8. a. b. 22 E. 4. 23. 24. 20 H. 6. 17. 31 H. 6. 11. 35 H. 6. 39. 47. 38 H. 6. 12. 6 E. 4. 3.

Trin. 5 E. 1. in Banco. 29 Norff. Pasch. 12 E. 1. Rot. 28. Norff. Abb. de Selbies case. Pasch. 19 E. 1. in Banco Rot. 45. Pasch. 7 E. 1. in Banco Rot. 78. Gloc'. Eliz. Penbreges case. Mich. 9 E. 1. in Banco Rot. 88. Salop. Bract. l. 5. 402. Placita de advocat. Eccl. spectant ad Coronam. Fleta, l. 6. ca. 36. Glanv. l. 4. ca. 13. acc'. 18 E. 2. bre. 825. 4 E. 3. 27. Rot. pat. 27 E. 3. 1. ps. nu. 18. F.N.B. 44. k. 45. b. c. d. 50. q. r. 51. c. 1. 30. e. g. 37. e. Vid. bre. de Indicav. Vid. Regist. 29. b. de rect. advocat. decim. Regist. 36. b. prohibition. de decimis reparatis. W. 2. ca. 5. 4 E. 3. 27. per Parning. 7 E. 3. 42. 8 E. 3. 49. 38 E. 3. 13. 16 E. 3. Quare Impedit. 147. 31 H. 6. 13. 38 H. 6. 20. 12 E. 4. 13. 2 H. 7. 12. Doct. & Stud. lib. 2. cap. 25. fol. 108.

Nullus pro decimis quæ sunt spirituales de aliqua reparatione pontis seu aliquibus oneribus temporalibus onerari debet. But at this day if tithes be in the hands of temporall men, they are by reason of them contributory to temporall charges.

Hil. 35 E. 3. coram Reg. Rot. 72. Mid. Vid. 32 H. 8. ca. 7. Dier 7 E. 6 83 l. 11. fo. 25. b. in Henry Harpers case.

10 H. 7. f. 18. a. per Brian. 44 E. 3. 5. Doct. & Stud. lib. 2. cap. 55. 7 E. 6. Dier fo. 84. & F.N.B. 54. b. Lib. 2. fo. 44. in Levesque de Winchesters case. But Parning in 7 E. 3. fo. 5. pl. 8. who not long after was lord treasurer, and after lord chauncellor, vowcheth it truly, for hee saith that of auncient time before a new constitution made by the pope, the patron of one church might grant his tithes to another parish, that is, by the constitutions made by pope Innocent 3. anno dom. 1200. in his decretall epistle, which you shall finde in his 6. Epistle. Decret. lib. 1. p. 452. edit. Colon. See the statutes of 18 E. 3. cap. 7. 1 R. 2. cap. 14. 5 H. 4. ca. 1. 27 H. 8. c. 20. 32 H. 8. c. 7. 2 E. 6. c. 13. Regist. 179, 180. † Anno 2 Regis Johannis. In bundello petitionum parliam. anno 6 E. 1. in Turri.

Where it is said in some of our books, that of auncient time before the councell of Lateran, any man might have given his tithes to what spirituall person he would, and that at that councell it was provided that tithes in one parish should be given to the rector or parson of the same parish, that hee that gave the spirituall food, should reap temporall, &c. The truth is, that I have perused the councels holden at Lateran, and specially that holden under pope Alexander the third, *anno Domini* 1179, *anno* 25 H. 2. and cannot finde any such decree: but pope Innocent the third, in a decretall epistle, in or about the yeare of our lord † 1200. and the first yeare of king John dated at Lateran, directed to the archbishop of Canterbury, *ut ecclesiis parochialibus juste decimæ persolvantur*, hath these words, *Pervenit ad audientiam nostram, quod multi in diocesi tua decimas suas integras vel duas partes ipsarum non illis ecclesiis in quarum parochiis habitant, vel ubi prædia habent, et à quibus ecclesiastica percipiunt sacramenta, persolvunt, sed eas aliis pro sua distribuunt voluntate. Cum igitur inconveniens esse videatur, et à ratione dissimile, ut ecclesiæ, quæ spiritualia seminant, metere non debeant à suis parochianis temporalia, et habere; fraternitati tuæ authoritate præsentium indulgemus, ut liceat tibi super hoc, non obstante contradictione vel appellatione cujuslibet, seu consuetudine hactenus observata, quod canonicum fuerit ordinare et facere quod statueris per censuram ecclesiasticam firmiter observari, nulli ergo, &c. confirmationis, &c.* Dat. Lateran. *nonas Julii.* And (that I may speake once for all) this epistle decretall bound not the subjects of this realme, but the same being just and reasonable they allowed the same, and so became *lex terræ*.

See Linwood *cap. de locato et conducto, fo.* 117. *verbo portiones*, where he saith, *Quod ante consilium Lateranense, anno Domini* 1179. *bene potuerunt laici decimas in feudum retinere, et eas alteri ecclesiæ dare, non tamen post dicti consilii, &c.* And thus began portions of

[642]

tithes, that the parson of one parish hath in another. *Vide concilium Lateran', anno Domini* 1215. 17 *Joh. regis.*

Albeit the parochiall right of tithes is now established by divers acts of parliament as before it appeareth (a matter tending to the exceeding benefit and quiet of the clergy) yet he that is desirous to know what the auncient lawes of England were concerning the

Having spoken of tithes, it is said. * *Hæc prædicavit beatus Augustinus, & concessa sunt à rege baronibus, & populo, &c.* Lamb. 128. Vide inter leges Edwardi regis, * ca. 8. ubi supra. de bosco.

paiment of tithes before the conquest, let him reade *Fædus Edvardi et Guthruni regum, cap.* 6. *et inter leges Ethelstani cap.* 1. *Inter leges Edmundi regis, cap.* 2. *Leges Edgari regis, cap.* 2. & 3. *Leges Canuti regis, cap.* 8, 10, 11, 12. *et leges Edwardi regis,* * *cap.* 8, 10. *Quas Willielmus Conquestor recitavit, et confirmavit.* All which lawes M. Lambard hath well translated out of the Saxon into the Latine tongue, which was faithfully, but not so accurately, done before him, which wee have.

There hath been great controversie heretofore concerning the tithes of wood, as appeareth by divers petitions in parliament, which petitions together with the answers we will recite, and incidently will shew, how that controversie is quieted, and ended.

That no man be impleaded for tithes of wood, or underwood, but in places accustomed. The answer was, as heretofore the same shall be. *Item pria le commen, que come * constitution soit fait per les prelats a prender dismes de chescun maner de boyes, quel chose ne fuit unques usee, et que niefs, et femes poent faire testaments, que est contre reason, que plese per luy, et per son bon counseil ordeiner remedie, et que son people demoerge en mesme lestate quilz soloient estre en temps de touts ses progenitors, et que prohibitions soient grantes a touts ceux que sont impledes de dismes de bois sans avoir consultation.* Whereunto the answer of the king was, the king willeth that law and reason be done.

Rot. Parl. anno 17 E. 3. nu. 52. Rot. Par. 18 E. 3. Artic. 9. * This constitution was made in ann. 17 E. 3. an. dom 1343. Vide Linwood. Note the asseveration of the whole body of the realm in this petition, concerning the paiment of tithewood. Rot. Par. 21 E. 3. Artic. 48. Note also these asseverations.

Item monstre la commune come nadgaires lercheuesque de Canterbury, et les auters prelates ordeinerent une constitution a doner dismes de subbois vendus tantsolement la ou avant ses heures nulles dismes furent dones, ore des gents de Seint Esglise per force de la constitution pernent et demandent les dismes auxibien de gros bois, come de subbois vendus et neient vendus, econtre ce qui is ont uses puis temps de memorie a la grand damage de la commune de quoi ilz priont remedie, de lun point et del autre.

Whereunto the answer is, the archbishop of Canterbury, and the other bishops have answered, that such tithe is not demaunded by reason of the said constitution, but of underwood. But the subject being still molested for woods not tithable complained again in *anno* 25 E. 3. all which were preparatives to a good law made in *anno* 45 E. 3. cap. 3. *De grosse boyes dage de vint ans, ou de greinder age nul dismes serra demands in nosme de cest parol sylva cædua, est ordeine et establie que prohibition en ceō case, soit grant, et sur ceo attachment come ad estre use avant ceux heures.*

Rot. Parl. 25 E. 3. nu. 37. Rot. Parl. 45 E. 3. nu. and in the print cap. 3.

It appeareth before that all the bishops claimed onely tithes *de subbois*, of underwood, under the name of *silva cædua*, so as of hautboyes, of great wood no tithes were claimed; but herein rested two doubts; 1. what should be said high or great wood. 2. Of what age the same should be, because it is parcell of the inheritance.

As to the first, this act, which is declaratory of the common law, as it appeareth by the book in 50 E. 3. fol. 10. b. 9 H. 6. fol. 56. Pl. Com. fol. 471. and this act it selfe proveth it, for it concludeth, *Come ad estre use devant ceux heures*; and this is confirmed by divers judgements hereafter cited.

And it is to be understood that this act useth these words *grosse boyes*, and not *haut boyes*, or *graund boyes*, which word is also used in the books of 50 E. 3. and 9 H. 6. And in this act this word [*grosse*] signifieth specially such wood as hath been, or is either by the common law or custome of the country timber, for this act extends not to other woods, that have not beene, or will not serve for timber, though they be of the greatnesse or bignesse of timber. And it is to be observed, that the prohibition in 50 E. 3. for suing for tithes in court christian of grosse boys, was grounded upon the common law, without mentioning of this act.

Li. Intrat. R. fo. Regist. fo. 44. See the old book of Entries, fo. 34. b. & 34. a. premunire, printed anno dom. 1546. 50 E. 3. 10. 9 H. 6. 56. Pl. Com. 47. Lib. 11. fol. 48. b. Lifords case.

[643]

Here it is to be demanded, to what kinde of wood grosse boys do extend? And the answer is, that oake, ash, and elm, are included within these words; and so is beech, horsbeche, and hornbeam, because they serve for building, or reparation of houses, mills, cottages, &c. against the opinion in Plowd. Comment. fol. 470. in Molyns

See the first part of the Inst. f. 3. wast in beech. So it was adjudged coram rege Pasch. 2 Jac. Regis rot. 292. between

Henry Hall, and Dorothy Fettiplace. Kanc. Molyns case, holden without argument, which opinion the whole court upon deliberate advice held to be no law.

[a] Pl. Com. f. 470. Molyns case, Tr. 26 El. coram rege.

[b] Hil. 2 Jac. in Com. Kanc. Rot. 229. int. Brooke et Rogers.

[c] Lib. 11. f. 49. Lifords case. Doct. & Stud. fo. 174, 175.

[d] Regist. fo. 49. lib. 11. fo. 49.

[a] It was resolved by the whole court, that asp is also comprehended within grosse boys, because it may serve for building, or reparation, *ut supra*. But otherwise it is of birch (as it was said) it was adjudged in the case of Lennard *custos brevium*, because that kinde of wood serveth not for building.

[b] If a timber tree be *arida, sicca, et non portans folia nec fructus in æstate, nec existens maeremium*, and the owner cut it down, and convert it to fuell, &c. no tithe shall be paid thereof for the inheritance which was once in it.

[c] So for the bark of oakes, being timber trees, no tithes shall be paid, because it is parcell of the tree, and renueth not *de anno in annum*. [d] But for acorns tithe shall be paid, because they renue yeerly.

As to the second doubt, of what age those grosse or timber trees, whereof no tithes should be had, should be; the statute resolveth this doubt in these words, *Grosse boys del age de 20. ans, ou greinder.* Which point was also declaratory of the common law, as by the conclusion of this act, and the authorities aforesaid appeareth: for this *grosse boys* thus described, it appeareth by the act, that parsons and vicars sued for tithes of them, *en nosme de cest parol, sylva cædua.*

50 E. 3. 10. b. 44 E. 3. 32. a. merisme.

Del age de 20 ans.] This is the age, as to bar all suits in court christian for tithes. And these words are to be understood of grosse trees, which may serve for timber, and grow out of the own stubs: for if a man usually top or lop timber trees, tithes shall not be paid, though they be under the age of 20 yeers. For as the law priviledgeth the body of the tree, being parcell of the inheritance, so it doth priviledge the branches also.

Pl. Com. 470. b. Doct. & Stud. fo. 175. Br. dismes 14. li. 11. fo. 49. Lifords case.

So if a man cut down timber trees, tithe shall not be paid for the germyns or branches which grow out of the roots, of what age soever; for that the root is parcell of the inheritance.

Pl. Com. 470. So resolved Pasch. 29 El. coram rege. Lib. 11. fo. 49. Lifords case.

The bishops, and others of the clergie taking upon them to interpret this statute, which belonged not unto them, gave out and published that this ordinance did not restrain their ancient jurisdiction, and that this ordinance was never affirmed for a statute: and thereupon the subject was still vexed in court christian, both contrary to the common law, and the said statute: and thereupon a bill was exhibited in the next parliament following, holden in the 47 yeer of E. 3. reciting the statute of 45 E. 3. and then shewing that the persons of holy church intending that this ordinance did not restrain their ancient incroachments; and surmising, that this was not affirmed for a statute, held plea in court christian to the contrary of the ordinance aforesaid, to the great damage of the people. Wherefore may it please our soveraign lord the king to affirm the said ordinance for a statute to indure for all times to come; and that a speciall prohibition upon the same statute thereupon be made in the chancery, prohibiting that they should not hold plea in court christian of tithes of wood of the age aforesaid. Whereunto the answer was, that such prohibition be granted, as hath been used of ancient time. Which answer being compared with the conclusion of the act of 45 E. 3. hath given such an end to both these points, as no question hath been made thereof at any time since. And to say the truth, that the surmise that this act of

45 E.

45 E. 3. was but an ordinance, and no ſtatute, was but a meer cavill, without any colour of probability: for 1. it is entred in the parliament roll amongſt the other ſtatutes made at that parliament. 2. It is under the title in that roll of ſtatut. E. 3. *de anno regni ſui* 45. 3. It was proclaimed by the ſherifes (as the uſage in thoſe dayes was) amongſt the reſt of the ſtatutes of that parliament. 4. It hath the phraſe of an act of parliament [*Ordeine eſt et eſtablie*] agreeing therein in effect with the other acts in that parliament. 5. It hath the conſent of the lords and commons (who joyn in the petition in the preamble) and of the king. 6. Infinite prohibitions upon this ſtatute, as taking ſome few precedents, whereof we have the number roll, of ſuch as be not in print.

Coram rege Tr. 27 E. 1. Rot. 28. *Linc. Magiſter Willielmus perſona eccleſiæ de Epworth attachiatus fuit ad reſpondend' Stephano de Rodnes de Gener' laco, et Willielmo Stel de Cottingham de placito quare ſecutus fuit placitum in curia Chriſtianitatis, de catallis et debitis quæ non ſunt de teſtamento, vel matrimonio contra prohibitionem regis, &c. Et unde queruntur, quod cum prædictus magiſter Willielmus ſecutus fuit placitum verſus eos in curia Chriſtianitatis coram offic' epiſcopi Lincol' de catallis et debitis laicis, viz. de quercubus et aliis arboribus per ipſos empt' de quodam Rogero Mubey. Et idem Stephanus et Willielmus ſuper hoc protuliſſent prohibitionem domini regis coram prædict' officiariis in eccleſia omnium Sanctorum de Northt' die Martis prox' poſt feſtum Sancti Nicholai, anno regni regis nunc 25. et ei inhibuiſſent ne placitum illud contra prohibitionem prædictam ulterius ſequeretur in præſentia Rogeri de Waldebye, Gened' de Cave, Willielmi de Clere, et Thomæ de Redneſſe tunc ibidem præſentium, idem tamen magiſter Willielmus non obſtante prohibitione prædicta placitum præd' ulterius ſecutus fuit quouſque ipſi per ſectam ſuam prædictam excommunicati fuerunt; unde dicunt quod deteriorati ſunt et dampnum habent ad valentiam C. l. et in contempt' domini regis mille libr', &c.*

Regiſt. 34. the ſame prohibition, & 50 E. 3. 10.

De quercubus & arboribus. Vide Paſch. 15 E. 1. in banco Rot. 52. Linc. mille quercus, &c.

Et prædictus magiſter Willielmus venit et defendit, &c. et dicit quod nullum placitum de bonis et catallis laicis ſecutus fuit in curia chriſtianitatis contra prohibitionem domini regis ſicut ei imponunt, et vadiavit eis inde legem ſe 12. manu, &c. And had a day to make his law, at which he came; and *incepit* (ſaith the record) *jurare, et poſt quartum juratum defecit de lege, ideo conſideratum eſt, quod prædict' Stephanus et Willielmus recuperarent damna ſua prædicta centum librarum, et fecit finem cum rege ad* 40 *l.*

It is to be noted, that the parſon ſtood not upon his right to have tithes of oake and other trees; but the colour he had to wage his law, was in reſpect of theſe words, *De bonis et catallis laicis*, and tithes are not lay-chattels: but he durſt not in that caſe ſtand to it to make his law, but upon failing therein, judgement was given againſt him of the damages, as the plaintifes had counted.

The law at this day, and long after was holden, that in this caſe he might wage his law. 18 E. 3. 4. 24 E. 3. 39. ſo adjudged, 32 E. 3. tit. Ley. 62. But in 44 E. 3. fo. 32. it is otherwiſe ruled, becauſe it is not in a writ of contempt; and ſo hath the law been taken ever ſince.

See lib. Intrat. Raſt. fol. 448. b. nu. 2. 449. a *prohibition ſur leſtatute de* 45 E. 3. *circa* 14 H. 7. The old book of Entries, fol. 34. b.

Hil. 33 H. 8. Rot. 78. Inter Stelling et Spooner.
Ibidem Rot. 103. Inter Peiers et Dixon.
Mich. 34 H. 8. Rot. 116. Inter Felton et Glover.
Paſch. 36 H. 8. Rot. 116. Inter Smy et Ap. Richard.
Mich. 36 H. 8. Rot. 1. conſimilis prohibitio.
Hil. 36 H. 8. Rot. 1. conſimilis prohibitio.
Paſch. 38 H. 8. Rot. 1. conſimilis prohibitio.

Prohibitions coram rege tempore H. 8.

Mich. 38 H. 8. Rot. 1. consimilis prohibitio.

Coram rege tempore E. 6.

Trin. 1 E. 6. Rot. 94. consimilis prohibitio. Inter Herne & Croft.

Mich. 2 E. 6. Rot. 97. Inter Heford & Howe.

Mich. 3 E. 6. Rot. 1. consimilis prohibitio.

Pasch. 4 E. 6. Rot. 1. consimilis prohibitio.

Hil. 5 E. 6. Rot. 2. consimilis prohibitio.

Trin. 6 E. 6. Rot. 1. consimilis prohibitio.

[645]

Coram rege tempore Mariæ.

Mich. 1 Ph. et Mar. Rot. 159. Inter Gray et Philpot, consimilis prohibitio.

Pasch. 1 Mar. rot. 1. consimilis prohibitio.

Hil. 1 et 2 Ph. et Mar. Rot. 1. consimilis prohibitio.

Pasch. 1 et 2 Ph. et Mar. Rot. 3. consimilis prohibitio.

Trin. 1 et 2 Ph. et Mar. Rot. 10. consimilis prohibitio.

Mich. 2 et 3 Ph. et Mar. Rot. 4. consimilis prohibitio.

2 et 3 Ph. et. Mar. Rot. 1. consimilis prohibitio.

3 et 4 Ph. et Mar. Rot. 2. consimilis prohibitio.

Hil. 4 et 5 Ph. et Mar. Rot. 1. consimilis prohibitio.

Mich. 4 et 5 Ph. et Mar. Rot. 1. consimilis prohibitio.

We could cite a world of other examples of this kinde, out of the kings bench, chancery, and common place, but in a case whereof never any learned man made any doubt, these shall suffice.

But this is against the provinciall constitution of Simon Mepham, *anno Domini* 1332. *anno* 6 E. 3. and the exposition of Linwood thereupon.

Regist. 44. a. b. See the old book of Entries, fol. 34. a. the like prohibition. The latter book of Entries, R. 449. a. b. Old book of Entries, 34. a. 31 H. 8. tit. prohib. Brook 17. Regist. 49. a.

There is a consultation *de sylva cædua*, where the prohibition was, *De catallis et decimis quæ non sunt de testamento et matrimonio*; and yet in the consultation there is a restraint (according to the common law, and the said act of 45 E. 3.) *Dummodo tamen de grossis arboribus in hac parte non agatur, &c.*

If any sue in court christian for tithes *de grossis arboribus ultra ætatem 20 annorum*, he incurs the danger of a *præmunire*, if so it be contained in the libell.

In the Register it is said by Herlaston, *Concordatum fuit coram concilio regis in parliamento apud Sarum, quod consultationes fieri debent de sylva cædua, eo non obstante, quod non renovatur per annum; et super hoc facta fuit quædam consultatio pro abbate de Notley, de sylva cædua.*

Great question hath been made, when this parliament at Salisbury was holden, but we shall make it evident, that it was holden the Friday next after the feast of Saint Mark the Evangelist, in the seventh yeer of R. 2. which appeareth by William de Herlaston here named, who was a clerk of the chancery, and as here it appeareth, inserted this into the Register.

Regist. f. 80. b.

This Herlaston lived at the time of the holding of this parliament at Salisbury; for afterward in the same Register, fol. 80. b. it is said, *Nota que nul home serra prise, ne imprison, pur vert ne pur venison, si il ne soit trove ove le mayneur, ou si il ne soit indite, &c. Et vide inde statute R. 2. de anno 7. cap. 4. Quando quis taliter fuerit indictatus, et virtute indictamenti illius est convictus, ita quod non ponet se super patriam, et sic fiet de illis, qui indictati sunt de receptamento, ac si essent principales transgressores per Herlaston.*

7 R. 2. cap. 4.

And in the Register, fol. 261. a. you shall finde this note, *Hoc breve concessum fuit pro hominibus de Odiham, et concessum fuit pro omnibus aliis antiquis dominicis per cancellarium Lescrope, et W. de Herlaston.*

laſton. Now this Leſcrope lord of Bolton was chancellor in *annis* 2 & 5 R. 2. as we finde of record.

Thus have we diſcovered the clerk that inſerted into the Regiſter the ſaid *concordatum* in the parliament at Saliſbury: but looking diligently into that parliament roll, no ſuch *concordatum* as Herlaſton inſerted into the Regiſter can be found, and therefore you muſt take it upon the truſt and credit of this clerk. But admitting that any ſuch *concordatum* had been, as in the Regiſter it is ſet down, it may well ſtand with law: for in the Regiſter, fol. 44. there is a conſultation (as before hath been ſaid) *de ſylva cædua*, and is conſonant to law, having ſuch a reſtraint in the ſame writ, as is aforeſaid.

A country may preſcribe to be quit of tithes of wood, or any other tithe, ſo there be ſufficient maintenance and ſuſtentation of the incumbent beſides; but a town cannot ſo preſcribe. Doct. & Stud. 147. b. Br. Diſmes 14.

Rex tali judici ſalutem. Monſtravit nobis venerabilis pater H. Lincoln' epiſcopus (1), *quod cum I. præcentor eccleſiæ beatæ Mariæ Lincoln' teneat de dono ſuo omnes decimas dominicarum terrarum ſuarum vel dominici ſui de N. quas idem epiſcopus et prædeceſſores ſui epiſcopi loci prædicti libere conferre conſueverunt: Prior beatæ Catherinæ extra Lincoln. clamans decimas illas pertinere ad eccleſiam ſuam de B. trahit eum inde in placitum, &c.* (2). *Et quia placitum prædictum tangit coronam et dignitatem noſtram, præſertim cum collatio earundem decimarum ad nos poſſit devolvi ratione cuſtodiæ vel eſcaetæ, quia etiam conſimiles decimas conferimus in quibuſdam dominicis, et ſimiliter quamplures magnates regni noſtri in dominicis ſuis: vobis prohibemus ne placitum illud teneatis in curia chriſtianitatis, nec aliquid quod in derogationem regiæ dignitatis noſtræ cedere valeat in hac parte attentetis, ſeu per alios attentari faciatis, quoviſmodo. T. &c.* Regiſt. 36. b. [646]

Opus eſt interprete, therefore we will peruſe the words of this writ in ſuch order as they doe lye in the ſame.

(1) *Venerabilis pater H. Lincoln. epiſcopus.*] Is intended as I take it of Hugh biſhop of Lincoln, who deceaſed ſoone after: and hereby it appeareth, that this writ was in uſe before the ſaid conſtitution of pope Innocent the third, as alſo is proved by latter words of this writ, which we ſhall obſerve when we come to it. This was S. Hugh, biſhop of Lincolne, as wee conceive it.

(2) *Quod cum præcentor eccleſiæ beatæ Mariæ Lincoln. de dono ſuo teneat omnes decimas dominici de N. &c. Prior beatæ Katherinæ extra Lincoln. clamans decimas illas ad eccleſiam ſuam de B. trahit eum inde in placitum*, &c.] Here it may be demanded that ſeeing the ſuit is between ſpirituall perſons, and for tithes which are ſpirituall things, wherefore they ſhould bee prohibited. Hereof three reaſons are rendred in this writ. Firſt, *quia placitum prædictum tangit coronam et dignitatem noſtram.* For all advowſons are lay fee, and pleas of them doe belong to the kings law, and ſeeing the whole benefit of the patron of this advowſon conſiſteth in conferring of theſe tithes to any of his chaplains, &c. And if the tithes be recovered, the advowſon vaniſheth as a thing without fruit or benefit, and therefore the eccleſiaſticall court cannot hold plea of them.

Bre. de Indicavit. Bre. de recto advoc. decimarum. Regist. 29. b. Artic. cleri c. 2. 12 E. 4. 13. b. 4 E. 3. 2. Glan. li. 4. c. 13. Bract. lib. 5. fo. 402. 403. Fleta, li. 6. c. 36. Fitz. N.B. 30. g. Vet. N.B. 24. a. Vide Mich. 2 E. 1. in communi banco, Rot. 52. Leic. the Prior of S. Mary de pratis case. indicavit bre. de indicavit super 4. partem.

Quia tangit, &c. See the writ of *indicavit, et breve de recto de advocatione decimarum,* before in this second part of the Institutes W. 2. cap. 2. *versus finem, & Articuli cleri* cap. 2. And if the suit in the ecclesiasticall court were for substraction of tithes, after the right of the advowson be tryed for the patron of the person that sueth, he shall proceed in the ecclesiasticall court.

2. The second reason yeelded in this writ is, *Præsertim cum collatio earundem decimarum ad nos possit devolvi ratione custodiæ, &c.* And if the tithes should be recovered, as hath been said, the advowson should vanish, &c.

3. *Quia etiam consimiles decimas conferimus in quibusdam dominicis, et similiter quamplures magnates nostri in dominicis suis, &c.*

By this it is probable, that the king speaking in this writ for himselfe and the grandees of the realme in the present time, that this writ was in use before the constitution that confined tithes to parishes, and hereby it is proved that at this time the king, and the nobles of the realme might give their tithes to what spirituall person they would. Lastly albeit the king and the nobles be for honour sake named in the writ, yet the liberty of granting of tithes extended at this time to all the kings subjects.

The marginall note in the Register is *de decimis separatis,* so called because they had been granted to some spirituall person, and not annexed to any parish church.

Extravagant tit. de Decimis, ca. 13. quoniam.

For the better understanding of the opinion of Sir William Herle in the said book of 7 E. 3. which is, *Ore ne poet home ses dismes que sont hors de parish; grant a que il voudra, car levesque del lieu les averd.*

[647]

Mich. 5 E. 3. cor. Rege. Rot. 168. Cumbr. 22 Ass. p. 75. 38 Ass. p. 2. 14 H. 4. fo. 17. Br. dismes 10. Acc' Rot. Parl. 18 E. 1. fo. 8. Lib. 5. fo. 15. in Caudries case. Li. 2. fo. 44. in Levesque de Winchesters case.

Hee grounded his opinion in this case upon the canon law, which is, that the bishop is to have all tithes growing in lands not assigned to any parish within his diocesse. Yet this canon being against the law of the land, never had allowance within this realme, for in such part of forests as are out of any parishes, the king shall have them. See a notable record, term' Mich. *an.* 5 E. 3. *coram rege* Rot. 168. *Cumbria*; adjudged for the king against the canon, and the opinion of Herle. And this had been formerly resolved in parliament, *inter placita coram ipso domino rege et ejus concilio ad parliament' sua post festum Sancti hilarii, et etiam post festum Pasch', anno* 18 *E.* 1. *fo.* 8. *int' episcopum Carlisle, et priorem ejusdem de decimis assartorum vocat' Linthwait et Kirkethwait in foresta de Englewood.* The words of which record are, *Quod decimæ prædictæ pertinent ad regem, et non ad alium, quia sunt infra bundas forestæ de Englewood, et quod rex in foresta sua prædicta potest villas ædificare, ecclesias construere, terras assertare, et ecclesias illas cum decimis terrarum illarum pro voluntate sua cuicunque voluerit conferre, &c.*

Rot. Parl. anno 8 E. 2. nu. 17. in dorf.

And E. 1. granted tithes comming of land within the forest of Deane, as were not within any parish, to the bishop of Landaffe, and his successors.

An

An Expoſition upon the Statute entituled, An Act for the true Paiment of Tithes.

Anno 2 *E.* VI. *cap.* 13.

THE noiſe of the diſſolution of monaſteries in the parliament holden in the 27 yeare of H. 8. (lay-men taking ſmall occaſions to withdraw their tithes) was the occaſion of the making of the ſtatute of 27 H. 8. c. 20. The principall cauſe of the making of the ſtatute of 32 H. 8. cap. 7. was to inable lay-men, that had eſtates or intereſts in parſonages, or vicarages impropriate, or otherwiſe in tithes, to ſue for ſubtraction of tithes in the eccleſiaſticall courts, and to provide that no parſon ſhould be ſued, or compelled to pay any manner of tithes for any mannors, lands, tenements, or hereditaments, which by the laws or ſtatutes of this realme were diſcharged, or not chargeable for payment of any ſuch tithes. 27 H. 8. ca. 20. acc'. Vid. 31 H. 8, ca. 20. verſ. finem.

This act of 2 E. 6. is an act of addition, as by the words thereof hereafter following appeare.

Where in the parliament holden at Weſtminſter the fourth day of February, anno 27 H. 8. there was one act made concerning paiment of tithes prediall, and perſonall: and alſo in another parliament holden at Weſtminſter, 24 July, 32 H. 8. another act was made concerning true paiment of tithes, and offerings: in which ſeverall acts, many and divers things be omitted and left out, which were convenient and very neceſſary to be added to the ſame. In conſideration whereof, and to the intent the ſaid tithes may be hereafter truly paid, according to the minde of the makers of the ſaid act: bee it ordained and enacted, &c. that not onely the ſaid acts made in the ſaid 27 and 32 yeare of H. 8. concerning true paiment of tithes, and every article, and branch therein contained, ſhall abide and ſtand in their full ſtrength and vertue: but alſo be it further enacted by the authority of this preſent parliament, that every of the kings ſubjects ſhall from henceforth truly and juſtly, without fraud or guile, divide (2), ſet out, yeeld, and pay all manner of their predial tithes (1), in their proper kinde, as they ariſe and happen, in ſuch manner and forme, as hath been of right yielded and payd within 40 yeares (3) next before the making of this act, or of right or cuſtome ought to have been paid (4). And that no perſon ſhall from henceforth (5) take or carry away any ſuch or like tithes, which have been yeelded or payd within the ſaid 40 yeares or of right ought to have been payd in the place or places tithable of the ſame, before he hath juſtly divided or ſet forth for the tithe thereof, the tenth

27 H. 8. ca. 20. — 32 H. 8. cap. 7. — [649]

part of the ſame, or otherwiſe agreed for the ſame tithes with the parſon, vicar, or other owner, proprietory or farmer of the ſame tithes, under the paine of forfeiture of treble value of the tithes ſo taken or carried away.

(1) *Prediall tithes.*] This branch extends only to prediall tithes.

Paſch. 1 Ja. Rot. 1119. *in communi banco. Int. Booth et Southraie* in debt upon this ſtatute by the parſon of the church *pro non extrapoſitione decimarum pro caſeo, vitulis, agnis, cerafis, volemis et pyris* to have the treble value, &c. The defendant pleaded *nihil debet per patriam,*and it was found againſt him. And it was moved in arreſt of judgement that the ſaid tithes of cheeſe, of calſes, and lambes were no prediall tithes, and therefore not within this branch of the ſtatute; and this act is penall, and ſhall not be taken by equity, *quod fuit conceſſum per totam curiam.* And it was reſolved, *quod decimarum tres ſunt ſpecies, quædam perſonales, quæ debentur ex opere perſonali, ut artificio, ſcientia, militia, negotiatione, &c. Quædam prædiales, quæ proveniunt ex prædiis, i. e. ex fructibus prædiorum, ut blada, vinum, fenum, linum, canabium, &c. ſeu ex fructibus arborũ, ut poma, pyra, pruna, volema, ceraſa, et fructus hortorum, &c. Quædam mixtæ, ut de caſeo, lacte, &c. aut ex fœtibus animaliũ, quæ ſunt in paſcuis, et gregatim paſcuntur, ut in agnis, vitulis, hædis, capreolis, pullis, &c. Ex prædialibus ſunt quædam majores, quædam minutæ. Majores, ut frumentum, ſigilo, zizania, &c. fenum, &c. minores ſive minutæ, quidam dicunt, ſunt quæ proveniunt ex menta, aneto, oleribus, et ſimilibus juxta illud dictum Domini, Luk.* 11. *verſ.* 42. *Væ, qui decimatis mentam et rutum et omne olus, et præteritis judicium et charitatem Dei; hæc autem oportuit facere, illa non omittere. Alii dicunt quod in Anglia conſiſtunt decimæ minutæ in lino quæ ſunt prædiales, et lana, lacte, caſeis, et in decimis animalium, agnis, pullis, et ovibus, decimæ etiam mellis et ceræ numerantur inter minutas, quæ ſunt mixtæ. Vide Linwood cap. de decimis cap. Quoniam, fol.* 140. *verb. talibus decimis.*

Deut. 4. verſ. 29. Here is ſhewed the true uſe whereto tithes ſhould be imployed.

And the Levite (to whom tithes were aſſigned) ſhall come, and the ſtranger, the fatherleſſe, and the widow which are within thy gates ſhall eat and be filled.

The firſt addition. Simile in the ſame tearme in the caſe of Webb parſon of Fretteuden in Kent.

(2) *Henceforth truly and juſtly without fraud or guile divide,* &c.] Trin. 44 Eliz. *coram rege.* In a prohibition between Walter Heale and John Sprat, the caſe was, Walter Heale ſet out his prediall tithes, and divided them juſtly from the 9 parts, and ſoone after carried the ſame away. Sprat ſued for ſubſtraction of the ſame in the eccleſiaſticall court, Heale pleaded that hee had ſet them out *ut ſupra,* whereunto Sprat ſaid, that preſently after his ſetting out, &c. he carryed them away *in fraudem legis.* Adjudged that this was fraud and guile within this act, albeit he did juſtly devide the ſame within the letter of this law. It was further reſolved, that if the owner of the corne before ſeverance grant the ſame to another of intent that the grantee ſhould take away the ſame to the end to defraud the parſon, &c. of his tithe, this is fraud and guile within this ſtatute.

Lib. Int. Coke 384.

(3) *Within forty yeares.*] This time of 40 yeares is here ſet downe becauſe it is the uſuall time for the proofe *de modo decimandi.*

[650]

(4) *Or of right or cuſtome ought to have been yeelded,* &c.] The ſenſe of theſe words [as hath been of right yeelded] is of tithes

tithes to be yeelded *in ſpecie* within 40 yeares, and the ſenſe of the words [or of right or cuſtome] is, or by rightfull cuſtome *de modo decimandi* ought to have been paid.

(5) *And that no perſon from henceforth*, &c.] Albeit this branch doth not give the forfeiture to any perſon in certaine, and therefore it was pretended that the forfeiture ſhould be given to the king. And thereupon, upon this branch, the attourny generall, Hil. 29 Eliz. did exhibit an information in the exchequer againſt Wood of Cambridgeſhire for this treble forfeiture for carrying away his tithes before they were juſtly divided. The defendant pleaded not guilty, and by a jury at the barre he was found guilty, and in arreſt of judgement it was moved that in this caſe the forfeiture was not given to the king, for that the words of the act be, under the paine of the forfeiture of the treble value of the tithes ſo taken away. And whenſoever a forfeiture is given againſt him that doth diſpoſſeſſe, &c. the owner of his property, as here he doth of his tithes, there the forfeiture is given to the party grieved or diſpoſſeſſed, and the rather for that this is an additionall law, as hath been ſaid, and made for the benefit of the propriator of the tithes. And ſo it was adjudged by Sir Roger Manhood and the whole court of the exchequer Paſch. 29 Eliz. And this was the firſt leading caſe, that was adjudged upon this point, and ever ſince it hath been received for law, and the party intereſted in the tithes doth in an action of debt recover the treble value. And ſo it was alſo adjudged Hil. 40 Eliz. Rot. 699. where Rob. Bedell and Sarah his wife in the right of his wife joyned in an action of debt for the treble forfeiture. A record well examined and adjudged, and worthy to be a precedent. In which caſe it was reſolved that the generall allegation in the count, that the defendant *anno* 38 Eliz. *grano ſeminavit* 20 *acras terræ*, *&c.* *et quod decimæ inde attingunt ad valorem* 150*l.* without ſhewing what kind of graine, was good.

The ſecond addition.

And be it alſo enacted by the authority aforeſaid, that at all times whenſoever, and as often (6) as the ſaid prediall tithes ſhall bee due at the tithing time of the ſame, it to be lawfull to every party to whom any of the ſaid tithes ought to be paid, or his deputy or ſervant to view and ſee their ſaid tithes to be juſtly and truly ſet forth and ſevered from the nine parts, and the ſame quietly to take and carry away. And if any perſon carry away his corne, or hay, or his other prediall tithes before the tithe thereof be ſet forth, or willingly withdraw his tithes of the ſame, &c. that then upon due proofe thereof made before the ſpirituall judge, or any other judge, to whom heretofore he might have made complaint, the party ſo carrying away, withdrawing, letting, or ſtopping ſhall pay the double value (7) of the tenth, or tithe ſo taken, loſt, withdrawn, or carryed away, over and beſides the coſts, charges, and expences (8) of the ſuit in the ſame, the ſame to be recovered before the eccleſiaſticall judge, according to the kings eccleſiaſticall lawes.

The third addition.

Mich. 9 E. 2. fol. 61. in libro meo. Labbe de Ofneis case. 19 R. 2. action sur le case, 52. 17 H. 6. Jurisdiction, 58. So resolved by all the judges of England, Pasch. 4 Jac. Vide Artic. cleri 4 Jac. Artic. 16. *[651]

(6) *That at all times whensoever, and as often*, &c.] The first part of this branch is declaratory of the common law, because for the stopping of his way, &c. an action of the case did lye at the common law.

(7) *Shall pay the double value*, &c.] The reason why the double value, &c. is by this branch to be recovered in the ecclesiasticall court, where by the former branch, the parson, &c. at the common law shall recover the treble, is, * for that in the ecclesiasticall court hee shall recover the tithes themselves, and therefore the value recovered in the ecclesiasticall court is equivalent with the treble forfeiture at the common law.

(8) *Besides the costs, charges, and expences*, &c.] So as the suit in the ecclesiasticall court is more advantagious then the suit for the treble forfeiture at the common law: for at the common law he shall recover no costs, but he shall recover in the ecclesiasticall court costs and expences. But then it is demanded, whether in an action of debt for the treble value at the common law, if the plaintiffe be nonsuite, or if the verdict passe for the defendant, the defendant shall recover his costs by the statute of 23 H. 6. c. 15. And the answer is, that in that case he shall recover no costs, and so it was adjudged. Trin. 43 Eliz. *in communi banco, inter* Dounton plaintiffe in debt upon this statute, and S. Moile Finch defendant, that this action of debt is no action of debt within the statute of 23 H. 8. because it is neither upon a specialty or by contract; neither is this action upon this statute any action for wrong personall immediately done to the plaintiffe, for it is a *non-fesance, viz.* a not-setting out of the tithes, Trin. 42 Eliz. *in communi banco* adjudged in an action of debt for the treble value upon this statute, not guilty, or *nihil debet* are good uses, and so upon the statute of 5 Eliz. upon perjury.

The fourth addition.

And be it further enacted, &c. that all and every person which hath or shall have any beasts or other cattel tithable (9), going, feeding, or depasturing in any wast or common ground, whereof the parish is not certainly knowne, shall pay their tithes for the increase of the said cattel so going in the said wast or common to the parson, vicar, proprietory, portionary, owner or other their farmours or deputies, of the said parish, hamlet, towne, or other place, where the owner of the said cattell inhabiteth, or dwelleth.

Rot. parl. 18 E. 1. fol. 8. Int. Episcopum Carliel. & decan. 22 ass. p. 75.

(9) *All and every person which hath or shall have any beasts or other cattel tithable*, &c.] Where the king ought to have the tithes within the wasts or commons in his forests, which are not within any parish, this branch giveth the tithes of the increase of cattle to the parson of the parish where the owner dwelleth.

The fifth addition.

Provided, &c. that no person shall be sued, or otherwise compelled to yield, give, or pay, any manner of tithes for any mannours, lands, tenements, or hereditaments, which by the lawes (10), and statutes (11) of this realme or by any priviledge or prescription (12) are not chargeable with the payment of any such tithes (13), or that be discharged by any composition reall (14).

(10) *By the lawes of the realme*, &c.] (and so speaks the statute of 32 H. 8. cap. 7.) That is, by the common lawes and customes of the realm, *terræ sunt indecimabiles*: hereof you may read divers examples lib. 8. fol. 48, 49, 81.

Note, that tithes shall not be payd of any thing that is of the substance of the earth and are not annuall, as of quarries of stone, turfe, flagges, tynne, lead, brick, tyle, lyme, marle, coales, chalke, pots of earth, and the like, nor of beasts that be *feræ natura*, as deere, &c. nor of agistment of such beasts, as the parson hath tithe of, nor of cattle that manure the ground; but of barren beasts he shall have tithe for agistment, or herbage of them, unlesse they be nourished for the pale or plough, and so imployed. Mich 41 & 42 Eliz. *coram rege* in prohibition *int*. Greene & Hull. & Mich. 37 & 38 Eliz. *inter* Grisman & Lewes *in communi banco*. Nor of rakings left without covin, nor of after pasture. No tythes shall bee payd for *sylva cædua* imployed to hedging or for fewell, for maintenance of the plough or pale. Nor for the herbage of meres, bawkes, nor fearne, locks of wooll, or stubble, &c. but are freed thereof by the common law and custome of the realme. *Vide* Hil. 8 Jac. *coram rege* Tho. Baxters case. And in that case it was resolved and adjudged, that a parson shall not have two tithes of one land in one yeare, as of corne, and of the stubble or herbage, of hay, and of the after-pasture, *et sic in similibus*. But if the soyle of an orchard be sowne with any kinde of graine, the parson shall have tithe of the fruit trees and of the graine, for they be of severall and distinct kindes. But if he pay tithe for the fruit of the trees, and after cut downe the trees, and sell them in billet, or faggot, he shall pay no tithe, for they bee not of severall kindes.

So resolved; Mich. 21 & 22 Eliz. coram rege per Wray chiefe justice & totam curiam. F.N.B. 53. g. Regist. 54. b. Rot. parl. 51 E. 3. nu. 57. 7 H. 12 H. 8. 4. b. 4. nu. 105.

[652]

If a man pay tithe for his corne, and after grindeth the same corne at a mill within the same parish, no tithe meale shall be payd therefore. *Vide Artic' Cleri*. cap. 2.

Decimam partem separabis de cunctis fructibus quæ nascuntur in terra per annos singulos, &c. Decimam frumenti tui, et vini, &c. Thou shalt tithe all the increase of thy seed that the field bringeth forth yeare by yeare, as of corne, wine, &c. Deut. 14. vers. 22, 23.

Register 54. b. F.N.B. 53. E. Brooke Dismes. 16.

All canons and constitutions made against the lawes &c. of the realme are made void. 25 H. 8. cap. 19.

(11) *By the statutes*, &c.] *Viz*. 27 H. 8. cap. 20. 31 H. 8. cap. 13. 32 H. 8. cap. 7.

(12) *By prescription*.] The orders of *Cistercienses, Templarii, et Hospitularii decimas prædiorum suorum, quæ propriis manibus aut sumptibus excolunt, non tenentur solvere, &c.* *Vide* Dier, 10 Eliz. fol. 277, 278. & 2 H. 4, 5. cap. 14.

This priviledge to these three orders of religion was granted to them by the councell of Lateran, *anno Domini* 1215. & *anno* 17. *Johannis regis*, and was allowed by the generall consent of the realme, but this priviledge extendeth only to the lands which they had before that generall councell.

Pope Innocent the third by his bul discharged those of the order of Premonstratenses of the payment of tithes of such lands as were of their owne manurance, or other improvement. Note, about the yeare of our lord 1150. most of all religious orders were exempt from payment of tithes out of their possessions kept in their owne hands. Which pope Adrian the fourth about that time restrained

Innocent the 3. in epist. decretali. lib. 1. pag. 262. Vid. 38 E. 3. 6. a.

to

to *Cistercienses, Templarii, et Hospitularii,* and that all other orders should pay tithes, &c.

2 H. 4. cap. 4.

By the statute of 2 H. 4. not only the Cisterciensés, but all other religious and seculars which put any bulls in execution for discharge of tithes of their lands in the hands of their farmours should be in danger of a premunire.

28 H. 8. cap. 16. Vid. 25 H. 8. cap. 21. Vid. 11 H. 4. 76. 12 H. 8. 5, 6.

By the statute of 28 H. 8. it is enacted that all bulls, briefes, faculties, dispensations, of what names, natures, or qualities whatsoever they be of, heretofore had or obtained of the bishop of Rome, or of any of his predecessours, or by authority of the sea of Rome, by or to any subjects, resiants, or bodies politique or corporate of or in this realme, or of or in other the kings dominions, should from thenceforth be clearely voyde, and of no value, force, strength, nor vertue, and should never after that act be used, admitted, allowed, pleaded, or alledged in any places or courts of this realme or any other the kings dominions, upon paine contained in the statute of premunire, &c. This is a generall law, and plenarily and strictly penned against all bulls, &c. True it is, that there are some exceptions or qualifications in the act, which you may read there; but there is no exception or qualification therein for any dispensation or discharge of not payment of tithes by any bull of the pope. And we are of opinion, that the pope by his bull could not discharge any subject of this realme of payment of tithes, for it should be against the liberty of the subject, when he had liberty to grant his tithes to what spirituall person he would, and against the right of the persons, &c. of parishes, after parochiall rights were established.

Præmunire.

[653]

Vid. Dier 10 Eliz. 277, 278. Vid. 25 H. 8. cap. 19. Vid. 18. Eliz. Dier, fol. 347. Westons case. Extr. tit. de Eccl. ædific. cap. 4. De his Lindwood fol. 39. verb. reparat. Extr. tit. de offic. judicis ordinar. cap. 4. cum vos. Lindwood fol. 121. verb. legitima. Rot. Clau. 30 H. 3. m. 4. in turri Lond. Pat. 13 E. 1. m. 11. ib. de monitura episcopi Hil. 2 E. 2. in mem. Scaccarii. Tr. 36 E. 3. ib. proces vers. episcopum, Cestr. Hil. 5 E. 4. int. communia Rot. 47. Larcheveque de Yorkes case.

This act of 28 H. 8. extendeth not to general councells, but leave them as they were before, but all canons (as elsewhere hath been said) which are against the prerogative of the king, the common law or custome of the realme, are of no force. Let not therefore only serjants, apprentices, and attournyes, but the parties themselves be well advised how they plead or alledge any bull, briefe, faculty, or dispensation from Rome, &c. which is not warranted by this act, the punishment being so penall as a premunire, if they plead or alledge any bull, &c. against that act.

And in some cases, this maketh for the clergy. By the canon law parish churches are to be repaired by the parsons of the parish, but the custome of this realme being that the parish churches are to be repaired by the parishioners or inhabitants of the parishes, this canon bound not the clergy.

Also by another canon, neither arch-bishop nor any other of the clergy could by their testament bequeath any thing wherein he had property in the right of his church; but this being contrary to the custome of the realme originally obtained by the bishops of this realme for themselves and their whole clergy, for which at this day a recompence is given to the king, as elsewhere we have shewed.

[a] Regist. 38. F.N.B. 41. g. 8 E. 4. 24. 18 H. 6. 14. [b] Doct. & Stud. 174.

(12) [a] *Prescription.*] As *modus decimandi*, lands given in satisfaction, &c. [b] And a country may prescribe to be quit of tithes, or in *non decimando*. But for the better understanding both of this statute, and of our books, it is good to be knowne what the time of prescription for tithes is by the canon law, and by what authority. And the time for prescription in that case is forty yeares, by which time of prescription a spirituall person may gaine by the canon

canon law a right of tithes in another parish, &c. [c] And this prescription hath this ground and warrant by a decretall epistle of pope Alexander the third, *anno Domini* 1180. But this canon being against the common law which alloweth no prescription unlesse it be time out of mind of man, never had allowance in England. [d] Of prescription according to the common law, you may read in the first part of the Institutes sect. 170. at large. And the epistle decretall of pope Alexander we have thought good to recite *in hæc verba, Alexander Mauricio episcopo: Ad aures nostras te significante pervenit, duas ecclesias sæpius sub examine tuo litigare super decimis, quas una ecclesiarum in alterius parochia* 40 *annis possedit, ac per hoc petit ejus actionem extentam, altera vero volens eas jure parochiali evincere præscriptionem non debere sibi obesse proponit; ideo quid juris sit in hoc casu tua nos duxit fraternitas consulendos. Tuæ itaque fraternitati literis præsentibus innotescat, quod jure * divino et humano melior est conditio possidentis, quoniam * quadragenalis præscriptio omnem prorsus actionem secludit.*

[c] 20 H. 6. fol. 17. ac. prescription per le ley de St. Eglise est 40. ans, et en nostre ley nest vailent. prescrip. per C. ans. 2 E. 4. 15, 6 E. 4. 3.
[d] 1. part. Institut. sect. 170.

* Jure Canonico.
* This is le ley de St. Esglise mentioned in 20 H. 6.

[e] Mich. 43 & 44 Eliz. In a prohibition between Nowell and Hicks vicar of Edmonton in Midd. the plaintiffe in the prohibition alledged a custome within the said parish of Edmonton time out of mind of man to pay for every lambe a penny, &c. And issue was taken upon the custome, and the jury found, &c. before twenty yeares last past time out of mind, that there was within the said parish such a custome, and *modus decimandi*; but for twenty yeares last past by reason of suits and troubles, the inhabitants of the said parish had payd tithe lambs in kinde. And in this case these two points were adjudged. First, when a custome doth create an inheritance, this cannot be waved or adnulled by payment or other matter *in paiis*. 2. Albeit that the *modus decimandi* had not been yeelded or payd by twenty yeares, yet the prescription may be generall, for that the custome once established doth continue. As if a man hath a common of pasture, &c. and taketh a lease of the land, &c. for many yeares, yet after the yeares ended he may prescribe generally; for the inheritance of the common continued: and if the law should be otherwise, it were dangerous for the parties that doe prescribe for one yeare, and tenne or twenty yeares, &c. is all one in judgement of law. And so herewith doe agree the books in 15 E. 3. tit. judgement 133. in a writ of mesne. 14 E. 3. *ibidem* 155.

[e] Mich. 43 & 44 Eliz. coram rege.

[654]

Edmundus de mortuo mari attachiatus fuit ad respondendum Johanni de Segrave et Christianæ uxori ejus, quare impedit eos habere liberam chaceam in bosco suo de Kinkeswood pertinen' ad manerium suum de Stotesden quod tenent de rege in capite, et quod habent ex feoffamento Hugonis le Plessye quondam domini dicti manerii. Edmundus dicit quod Rogerus pater suus obiit seisitus inde tenend' in suo seperali, et quod prædictus Hugo tempore quo feoffavit prædictos Johannem et Christianam de dicto manerio, non fuit seisitus de dicta chacea. Et de hoc ponit se super patriam, et præd' Johannes et Christiana similiter. Jur' dicunt quod Johannes de Plessy pater prædicti Hugonis de Plessy fuit seisitus de prædicta chacea dum fuit dominus dicti manerii, et dicunt quod dictus Hugo voluit ibidem fugasse, postquam prædictum manerium pervenit ad manum suam, set Rogerus de mortuo mari ipsum impedivit et non permisit. Et dicunt quod Hamo le Strange, et Hugo de Turbervile parentes uxoris ipsius Hugonis ex rogatu ipsius Hugonis venerunt ad manerium de Stotesden, et prædictam chaceam simul

Mich. 13 E. 1. in banco Rot. 119. Salop. Free chase appendant al mannor. Issue, non fuit seisitus. Verdict.

simul cum prædicto Hugone intraverunt nomine ipsius Hugonis cum equis et armis, et in ea cum equis et armis per tres dies fugaverunt absque impedimento prædicti Rogeri de mortuo mari aut hominum suorum. Et quesit' jur' &c. dicunt quod illud fecerunt tempore pacis, et absque impedimento prædicti Rogeri aut hominum suorum eo quod dictus Rogerus nescivit quod ibi fugaverunt, et quod ab eo tempore dictus Hugo nunquam fugavit ibi; quia quotiescunq; fugare ibidem voluit, dictus Rogerus ipsum impedivit. Postea term' Trin' anno 20 *venerunt partes, et petierunt judicium suum per attornatos suos. Judicium redditum, quod quia Johannes de Plessy fuit de chacea seisitus tanquam pertinen', &c. Et postea dictus Hugo per tres dies continue tempore pacis seisinam suam obtinuit absque impedimento Rogeri de mortuo mari, aut alicujus paren' suorum, per quod videtur cur' quod seisina illa est sufficiens, bona, et pacifica in hoc casu; consideratum est, quod Edmundus injuste impedivit dictos Johannem et Christianam de prædicta chacea, et ipsi re' chaceam illam et dampn'* 100*s.*

Multiplex interruptio non tollit præscriptionem semel obtentam. Note an interruption to chace is no disseisin thereof, but at the will of the owner. Judgement. Seisina bona debet esse pacifica. Mich. 2 E. 2. coram rege. Warw. in monstraverunt.

The mannour of Brimsgreen and Norton was ancient demesne, and in the kings hands, and William of Brimingham and his ancestours time out of minde and before the conquest had taken toll aswell of the tenants of the said mannour as of others, whereupon judgment was given, as it appeareth in the record in these words: *Et quia manifeste constat, &c. quod manerium de Brymmesgreen et Norton est de antiquo dominico coronæ Angliæ, et à tempore quo non extat memoria, extitit in seisina progenitorum reg' quondam regum Angliæ, et adhuc in seisina domini regis nunc existit. Et homines de eodem manerio sicut et cæteri homines de antiquis dominicis coronæ domini reg' quieti esse debeant à præstatione theolonii per totum regnum Angliæ, ut prædictum est, &c. Et super hoc viso et lecto recordo placiti prædicti manifestè patet quòd predict' Willielmus de Brimingham recognovit quòd ipse et antecessores sui habuerunt mercatum in prædicta villa de Brimingham, et theolonium de omnibus mercandisis in eadem villa, de quibus theolonium præstari deberet, perceperunt et habuerunt, et etiam de hominibus de Bremesgreen et Norton, quam de aliis ibidem vendentibus et ementibus ante Conquestum, et sine temporis interruptione, et quòd ipse statum eorundem antecessorum continuavit distringendo et percipiendo ab eisdem hominibus theolonium, tam pro minutis, ut pro victualibus et aliis necessariis suis, quam de aliis quibuscunque mercandisis sicut de aliis mercatoriis. Consideratum est quòd prædicti Richardus, Robertus, Johannes, et omnes alii de manerio prædicto, quieti sint imperpetuum à præstatione theolonii in villa prædicta præstandi secundum legem et consuetudinem in regno usitat', et quod recuperent damna, quæ taxantur per discretionem justiciarior' ad vigint marc'. Et prædictus Willielmus pro injusta continuatione, usurpatione antecessorum suorum in misericordia. Et inhibitum est eidem Willielmo ne homines de manerio prædicto de cætero distring' ad theolonium in dicta villa de Brimingham præstand' contra legem et consuetudinem prædictas, &c.*

Nota, ante Conquestum. Note a possession beyond time of memory shall not stand, but give place to law. Consuetudo licet sit magnæ authoritatis, nunquam tamen præjudicat veritati.

[655]

Abbas de Sancto Edmundo implacitat Rogerum de Bigod com' Norff' maresc. Angl', et duos alios pro captione duorum leporariorum suorum in villa de magna Thorpe. Comes dicit, quod dicta villa est infra præcinctum demid' hundredi sui de Ersham quod tenet ingarennatum prout Rogerus avunculus suus, cujus hæres ipse est, illud tenuit, et quia invenit prædictum abbatem ibidem fugantem, ipse cepit, &c. Abbas dicit quòd ratione terrarum suarum ibidem ad ipsum pertinet fugare, prout omnes prædecessores sui ibidem fecerunt, &c. Ideo ven' jur' qui per speciale veredictum dicunt, quòd abbas et prædecessores sui solebant ante bellum de Lewes

Trin. 18 E. 1. banco rot. 50. Norff. Nota pro leporariis. Ingarennatum pertinet fugare. Verdict speciall. Bellum de Lewes 48 H. 3. anno Domini, 1264.

Lewes ibidem semper fugare. &c. *Et dicunt quod tam Rogerus comes, quam Rogerus nunc ipsum abbatem et homines suos sæpe impedivit ibidem fugare, et leporarios suos surripuerunt.*

(13) *Not chargeable by payment of tithes,* &c.] As by unity of possession. lib. 2. fol. 46, 47, 48, 49. lib. 11. fol. 10, 11, 14, 16.

(14) *Discharged by any composition reall,* &c.] Either before time of memory, or within time of memory, that is by parson, patron, and ordinary. *Vide* 8 H. 6. 22, 23. 9 H. 6. 17. 41 E. 3. 27. 17 E. 3. 11. 38 E. 3. 6. 8. 12 H. 4. 13. 19 H. 6. 75. 32 H. 6. 4. 34 H. 6. 36. 31 H. 6. 28. 35 H. 6. 5. a. 37 H. 6. 25. 1 E. 4. 6. 8 E. 4. 14. 18. 14 H. 7. 3. 26 H. 8. 7. 27 H. 8. 20, 21.

*Concordia facta inter Willielmum Mallet et rectorem ecclesiæ de Aure beiton Bathon, et Wellen' diocesʹ ex una parte, et * nobilem virum Johannem de Acton mil' ex altera parte, de * modo decimandi omnia infra parochiam de Aure per consensum episcopi et capitul' Bathon' unde placitat' fuit prius in curia Cantuar'. Nota.* Mich. 9 E. 1. in banco rot. 63. Somerset. * Miles est nobilis. * Modus decimandi per realem compositionem.

Provided, &c. that all such barren (15), heath (16), or wast (17) ground, other then such, as be discharged for the payment of tithes by act of parliament, which before this time have lyen barren and payd no tithes by reason of the same barrennesse, and now be or hereafter shall be improved and converted into arable ground or meadow, shall from henceforth, after the end and tearme of seven yeares, next after such improvement fully ended and determined, pay tithe (18) for the corne and hay growing upon the same, any thing in this act to the contrary in any wise notwithstanding. The fifth addition, with a proviso.

(15) *Barren.*] *Terra sterilis ex vi termini est terra infæcunda, nullum ferens fructum.* Virgil. *Infelix lolium, et steriles dominantur avenæ.*

But it is not only so strictly taken in this act, but hath also a more restrained sense. For albeit it doth yeeld some fruit, yet if it be barren land, *quoad agriculturam,* as to tillage, which this branch meant to advance, it is within this act, for albeit barren ground (as to tillage) doth pay tithe wooll and lambe, yet is it within this act, and this appeares by the next proviso in this act for the payment of such tithe as during the seven yeares before the improvement was payd. But yet if the ground be not apt for tillage, yet if it be not *suapte natura* barren, it is not within this act. As if a wood be stubbed and grubbed, and made fit for the plough, and imployed thereunto, yet shall it pay tithes presently, for wood-ground is *terra fertilis, et fæcunda.* Dier, 2 Eliz. fol. 170, 171. lib. Int. Coke 462, 463. [656] 6 E. 6. ex libro Bendloes.

Devenere locos lætos, et amæna vireta
Fortunatorum nemorum, sedesq; beatas. Virgi Æneid.

And so was it resolved Hil. 9 Jac. reg. upon the motion of Serjant Houghton by the whole court of common pleas.

In a prohibition between Sharington and Fleetwood for tithes in Orwell in the county of Lancaster, it was resolved, that if marish meadow, or other land for not cleansing of the trenches or sewers, or by suddaine accident or inundation of waters be surrounded; or by ill husbandry or unprofitable negligence any land become overrunne Hil. 38 Eliz. coram rege.

runne with bushes, furres, whinnes, and bryers, yet are not they or any of them said to bee barren land within this statute, because of their owne nature they are fruitfull, and the parson, &c. shall not by this act be barred of his tithes by the ill husbandry or negligence of the owner or possessour.

(16) *Heath.*] In French it is called *bruyere*; in legall Latin *bruera*, Regist. 2. In domesday it is called *bruaria*; *Latinè erix, erica* an unprofitable kinde of ground, but wholly barren, for thereon sheep and beasts will bruise, and some poore people the flags and turfes thereof doe apply to fewell; and this heath cannot without great skill, charge and industry bee converted to tillage.

Lib. Intr. Coke ubi supra.

It sendeth forth a flower in autumne (when all others cease) which bees doe exceedingly covet, as it is said, this is within this act. Some say, *est quoddam genus myricæ*, a kinde of wilde tameriske, and in Lincolnshire a litle religious house was called Temple bruer, because it was seated in the heath.

Lib. Intr. Coke ubi supra.

(17) *Wast.*] It is called *vastus fundus*, wast ground, because it lyeth as wast with little or no profit to the lord of the mannour, and is so called to distinguish it from the residue of the demesnes in the lords hands, and cannot without great charge and industry be improved or converted to tillage being *suapte natura* unprofitable, and being converted to tillage it shall pay no tithes by the space of seven yeares.

(18) *Shall after the end and terme of seven yeares next after such improvement pay tithe.*

Dier, 2 Eliz. 170. b.

Note, here are no expresse words of discharge of the tithes during the seven yeares, but by reasonable construction it doth implyedly amount to a discharge during the seven yeares, and the seven yeares are to be accounted next after the improvement.

The sixth addition with the proviso.

And be it enacted, &c. that every person exercising merchandizes, bargaining, and selling, clothing, handicraft, or other art or faculty, being such kinde of persons as heretofore within these forty yeares have accustomably used to pay such personall tithes, or of right ought to pay (other then such as bee common day-labourers) shall yearly, &c. pay for his personall tithes, the tenth part of his cleare gaines (19), his charges, &c. deducted; and where handicrafts men have used to pay their tithes within [657] this forty yeares, the same custome of payment of tithes (20) to be observed. And if any person refuse to pay his personall tithes, &c. it shall be lawfull to the ordinary of the same diocesse, &c. to call the same party before him, and by his discretion to examine him by all lawfull and reasonable meanes other then by the parties owne corporall oath (21), concerning the true payment of the said personall tithes.

(19) *Pay for his personall tithes the full tenth part of his cleare gaines*, &c.] Of personall tithes we have spoken before. Vid. 37 H. 8. cap. 12. Vid. Linwood, tit. de Decimis, fol. 141, 142.

(20) *Custome of payment of tithes.*] Nota, there may be *modus decimandi* for personall tithes.

(21) *By all lawfull and reasonable meanes, other than by the parties owne corporall oath.*] Here is just occasion offered to speake *de*

juramento

Juramento calumniæ, wherein we will endeavour to find out three things: first, the beginning of the bringing in of this oath: secondly, how the law hath stood therein in former ages: and thirdly, what the right is at this day.

By a constitution *domini Othonis diaconi cardinalis Sancti Nich. apostolicæ sedis legati*, at a provinciall councell, holden *octab' Sancti Martini in ecclesia Sancti Pauli London, an. Dom.* 1236. *anno* 21 H. 3. it was ordained in these words: *Jus-jurandum calumniæ in causis ecclesiasticis et civilibus de veritate dicenda in spiritualibus, quout veritas facilius aperiatur, et causæ celerius terminentur, statuimus præstari de cætero in regno Angliæ, secundum canonicas et legitimas sanctiones obtenta, consuetudine in contrarium non obstante.* By this it appeareth, that by the custome of the realme of England, *juramentum calumniæ* was not to be ministred: but to confesse the truth, the custome was not so generall, as in this canon is alledged; for lay-men were free by the custome of the realme for taking of that oath, unlesse it were *in causis matrimonialibus et testamentariis*: and in those two cases the ecclesiasticall judge might examine the parties upon their oath, because contracts of matrimony were often made in private, and legitimation of children depended thereupon. And in causes testamentary many things consist in secrecie, and the truth therein is to be drawn out by oath, *et interest reipublicæ testamenta hominum rata haberi.* And this appeareth by a * prohibition by authority of parliament directed to the sherifes, &c. *Quod non permittant quod aliqui laici in baliva sua in aliquibus locis conveniant ad aliquas recognitiones p. sacramenta sua facere, nisi in causis matrimonialibus et testamentariis.* But this custome extended not to them of the clergy, but to lay-people only, for that they of the clergy being presumed to be learned men, were better able to take *juramentum calumniæ:* for concerning the testimony of witnesses in the ecclesiasticall court, that act, or the custome of the realme extends not unto. 1.

* Prohib. format' super Artic' Cleri, tit. Prohib. Rastall 4. vet. Magn. Chart. 2. part. fol. 70. a. Vid. ass. de Clarendon, 10 H. 2. Brit. fol. 35. b. acc' Hill. 7 E. 3. rot. 285. in communi banc. Hill. 7 H. 6. rot. 135. ibid. Trin. 3 H. 6. rot. 41. ibid. 19 E. 4. 10. per Brian, that it is a statute. 20 E. 4. 3. b. [a] Regist. fol. 36. b. F.N.B. 53. d. A prohibition, and thereupon an attachment, contra consuetudinem regni, but there is a consultation for witnesses. Fitzh. justice of peace 72. Lamb. justice of peace, 338.

But if in a penall law the jurisdiction of the ordinary be saved, as by 1 Eliz. [b] for hearing of masses, or by 13 Eliz. [c] for usury, or the like, neither clerke nor lay-man shall be compelled to take *juramentum calumniæ*, because it may be an evidence against him at the common law upon the penall statute.

[b] Dyer manuscript. propria manu, Trin. 9 Eliz. in communi banco, Leighs case, Habeas corpus. [c] 18 Eliz. Dyer 175. in margine, Hindes case, Habeas corpus.

But it is objected, that this oath hath long continued in the ecclesiasticall court. To this it is answered: First, that it had the warrant of an act of parliament (as it was holden) in 2 Hen. 4. cap. 15. whereby it was enacted, *Quod diocesanus per se, vel commissarios suos contra hujusmodi personas, &c. ad omnem juris effectum publice, et judicialiter procedat et negotium hujusmodi terminet juxta canonicas sanctiones.* By this statute, and the said provinciall constitution, and other the canons of the church, the diocesans, &c. ministred the said oath, even in the case of heresie, &c. This statute of 2 H. 4. was repealed by the act of 25 H. 8. (which act is partly declaratory of the ancient law of the realme) in these words: "It standeth not "with the right order of justice, nor good equity, that any person "should 2.

[658]

25 H. 8. cap. 14. & 1 E. 6. cap. 12.

This statute of 2 H. 4. was revived in an. 1 & 2 Phil. & Mar.

ca. 6. and repealed again an. 1 Eliz. 1. & so remaineth.

" ſhould be convict, and put to loſſe of life, good name, or goods, " unleſſe it were by due accuſation and witneſſe, or by preſentment, verdict, confeſſion, or proceſſe of outlawry, &c. And " that it is not reaſonable, that any ordinary, upon any ſuſpicion " conceived of his owne fantaſie, without due accuſation or preſentment ſhould put any ſubject of this realm in any infamy and " ſlander of hereſie, to the perill of life, or loſſe of name, or " goods." And in a former clauſe of the ſaid act it is ſaid: " That the moſt expert and beſt learned man of this your realm, " diligently lying in wait upon himſelfe, can eſchew and avoid " the penalties and dangers, &c. if he ſhould be examined upon " ſuch captious interrogatories, as is, and hath been accuſtomed to " be miniſtred by the ordinaries of this realme, in caſes where they " will ſuſpect any man of hereſie, &c.

Secondly, the words of the ſaid act of parliament are *contra voluntatem eorum*, and of the Regiſter, *ipſis invitis*; ſo as ſuch as willingly have taken it, ſerveth for no poſſeſſion againſt the law.

3. But now laſtly it is to be ſeen, how the right ſtandeth touching this oath at this day. It is confeſſed, as before it appeareth, as well by the ſaid provincial conſtitution of Otho, as by the Regiſter, that the ſaid conſtitution was *contra conſuetudinem regni*, whereupon it followeth, that no cuſtome of the realme can be taken away by a canon of the church, but only by act of parliament, and ſpecially in caſe of an oath, which is ſo ſacred a thing, and which generally concerneth all the nobility, gentry, and comminalty of the realme of both ſexes. And by the ſtatute of * 25 Hen. 8. cap. 19. no canon againſt the kings prerogative, the law, ſtatutes, or cuſtome of the realme, is of force, which is but declaratory of the common law.

Vid. the third part of the Inſtitutes, cap. Perjury.
* 25 H. 8. ca. 19. Rot. pat. an. 15 E. 2. part 1. m. 8. 19 E. 3. quare non admiſit 7. 10 H. 7. fo. 6. per Brian.
See the fourth part of the Inſtitutes, cap. The Court of Convocation.
d Doct. Coſin in his book intitled, An Apology, &c. cap. 13.

[d] Wee have read over what Doctor Coſin hath in his book ſpoken for the maintenance of this oath, and certainly, he toucheth not the ſtate of the queſtion, as will appeare to the learned reader.

To conclude: This branch of 2 Ed. 6. giveth no life to any forceleſſe canon, which is againſt any law or cuſtome of the realme, but, according to the law and cuſtome of this kingdome prohibiteth the ordinary in caſe of perſonall tithes to examine the party upon his corporall oath; for the parliament did take that to be no lawfull and reaſonable meanes (whereof it ſpeaketh); for a parliament would never have prohibited any thing that was lawfull and reaſonable; and yet the cleare gains of merchants, clothiers, or handicraft men do lye in great ſecrecie, and hardly to be proved by witneſſes. And before, in the clauſe concerning the ſecond addition, for recovery of predial tithes, it is ſaid; upon due proofe thereof, made before the ſpirituall judge, &c. for that they are open, viſible, and eaſie to be proved by witneſſes: and at this time the ſtatute of 2 H. 4. ſtood repealed.

L. 18. F. de pœna. Cogitationis pœnam nemo meretur.

No perſon eccleſiaſticall or temporall ought in any eccleſiaſticall court to be examined upon the cogitation of his heart, or what hee thinketh, &c. as it was holden by the judges in the parliament holden 4 Jac. and as it was after holden in the court of common pleas, Mich. 6 Jac. in Doctor Wolſtons caſe in a prohibition.

Provided

Provided, &c. that all and every person and persons, which by the lawes or customes of this realme ought to make or pay their offerings, shall yearly from henceforth well and truly content and pay his or their offerings (22) to the parson, &c. of the parish or parishes, where it shall fortune or happen him or them to dwell or abide, &c. The 7. addition.

(22) *Offerings.*] Offerings or oblations, *oblationes*, these are of two sorts, viz. free or voluntary, and consuet; or by custome, as here it appeareth. Offerings and obventions are in London the profits of the church, and not in corn, or other manner. [659]

A writ of right of advowson brought of the fourth part of the tithes and offerings of the church of Saint Dunstan in the West in Fleetstreet London, and adjudged to be good. 30 E. 3. 1. in account. 38 E. 3. 13. per Finch. acc'.

See lib. 11. fol. 16. Doctor Grants case. Vid. there for obventions, 38 E. 3. 13. and 16 E. 3. ubi sup. and see here the 10 addition. Vid. the next addition. 16 E. 3. quare Imped. 147.

Provided, &c. That this act, or any thing therein contained, shall not extend to any parish, which stands upon and towards the sea coasts, the commodities, and occupying whereof consisteth chiefly in fishing, and have by reason thereof used to satisfie their tithes by fish, but that all and every such parish and parishes shall hereafter pay their tithes, according to the laudable customes, as they have heretofore of ancient time within these 40 yeares used and accustomed, and shall pay these offerings, as is aforesaid. The 8. addition.

Provided that this act, &c. shall not extend in any wise to the inhabitants of the citie of London and Canterbury, and the suburbs of the same, ne to any other towne or place, that hath used to pay their tithes by their houses, otherwise then they ought or should have done before the making of this act, any thing in this act to the contrary in any wise notwithstanding. The 9. addition.

Mich. 5. Jac. *in communi banco*, between John Skidmore and Robert Eire plaintifes in a prohibition against John Bell parson of Saint Michael Queenhithe in London: the case upon the said statute of 37 H. 8. and the decree thereupon was this: the said parson libelled before the chancellor of London for the tithes of an house, called the Bores Head in Breadstreet in the said parish, by force of the said act and decree, the ancient farme rent whereof was five pounds, at the time of the said decree, and after, and that of late a new lease was made of the said house, rendring the rent of five pounds *per annum*, and over that a great in-come or fine, which was covenanted and agreed to be paid yearly at the same day; that the rent was paid as a summe in grosse, and that so much rent might have been reserved for the said house, as the rent reserved, and the summe in grosse amounted unto; which reservation and covenant, &c. were made to defraud the said parson of the tithes of the true rent of the said house, which to him did appertaine by the purport and true intention of the said decree. And in this case foure points were resolved by the whole court.

First, if so much rent be reserved as was accustomed to be paid at the making of the said decree in 37 H. 8. (whatsoever fine or in-come be paid) that the parson can averre no covin; for the words of the decree be; Where any lease is or shall be made of any dwelling house, &c. by fraud or covin in reserving lesse rent then hath been accustomed, or is paid, &c. So as if the accustomed rent be reserved, no fraud can be alledged; for the fraud by the decree is, when lesser rent then was then accustomed to be paid, is reserved; or if no rent at all be reserved, &c. for then tithe shall be paid according to the rent, that then was last before reserved to be paid. The words of the decree are: Or that any lease shall be made without any rent reserved upon the same by reason of any fine or income, then the fermor shall pay for his tithes after the rate aforesaid, according to the quantity of such rent, as the house was lastly letten for, without fraud or covin, before the making of such lease. So as the decree consisteth upon foure points, viz. First, where the accustomed rent, &c. was re-
[660] served. Secondly, where the rent was increased, there the tithes should be paid according to the whole rent. Thirdly, where lesser rent was reserved. Fourthly, where no rent was reserved, but had been formerly reserved. And this act and decree were very beneficiall for the clergy of London, in respect of that which they had before: and the defendant in his libell confesseth, that the accustomed rent, &c. was reserved: and therefore no cause of suit.

Secondly, it was resolved, that such houses as were never letten to farme, but inhabited by the owner, this is *casus omissus*, and shall pay no tithes by force of the decree.

Thirdly, it was resolved, that where the decree saith, Where no rent is reserved by reason of any fine or in-come paid before-hand, albeit no fine or in-come be paid in that case, yet if no rent be reserved, the parson shall have his tithes according to the decree, for that is put but for an example or cause, why no rent is reserved, and whether any fine or in-come were paid, or no, is not materiall, as to the parson.

Fourthly, it was resolved, that the parson could not sue for the said tithes in the ecclesiasticall court, for that the act and decree that raised and gave these kind of tithes, did limit and appoint how, and before whom the same should bee sued for, viz. That if a controversie were moved in the city for not payment of those tithes, or concerning the true rent or tithes, that then upon complaint made by the party grieved to the lord maior of London, hee by advice of his assistants should make a finall end, with costs to be awarded by his discretion. And if the maior doth not make an end of it within two moneths, or if any of the parties find themselves grieved, that then the lord chancellor within three moneths shall make an end thereof with costs, according to the true intention of the said decree: therefore as the decree gave a new and speciall kind of tithings; so it did appoint new and speciall judges to heare and determine the same. And in the end it was awarded, that the prohibition should stand. Vid. for tithes in London, 27 H. 8. cap. 20. and 32 H. 8. cap. 7.

Sec lib. 5. fo. 73. the case of Orphanage, in London.

The 10. addition.

And be it further enacted, &c. that if any person do substract or withdraw any manner of tithes, obventions (23), profits, commodities,

commodities, or other duties before mentioned, or any part of them, contrary to the true meaning of this act, or of any other act heretofore made, that then the party so substracting or withdrawing the same, may or shall be convented and sued in the kings ecclesiasticall court by the party from whom the same shall be substracted or withdrawne, to the intent the kings judge ecclesiasticall shall and may then and there heare and determine the same, according to the kings ecclesiastical lawes. And that it shall not be lawfull unto the parson, vicar, proprietorie, owner, or other their fermors or deputies, contrary to this act to convent or sue such with-holder of tithes, obventions, or other duties aforesaid, before any other judge then ecclesiasticall. And if any archbishop, bishop, chancellor, or other judge ecclesiasticall give any sentence in the aforesaid causes of tithes, &c. and (no appeale ne prohibition hanging) and the party condemned do not obey the said sentence; that then it shall be lawfull for every such judge ecclesiasticall to excommunicate the said party so, as aforesaid, condemned and disobeying: In the which sentence of excommunication, if the said party excommunicate, wilfully stand and endure still excommunicate by the space of 40 daies next after, upon denunciation, and publication thereof in the parish church, or the place or parish, where the party so excommunicate is dwelling, or most abiding, the said judge ecclesiasticall may then at his pleasure signifie unto the king into his court of chancery of the state and condition of the said party so excommunicate, and thereupon to require processe *de excommunicato capiendo* (24), to be awarded against every such person as hath been so excommunicate. [661]

(23) *Obventions.*] Obventions aforesaid are offerings.

That the jurisdiction of tithes belong to the ecclesiasticall court, it appeareth by the acts of parliament, viz. of *Circumspecte agatis, an.* 13 E. 1. *Artic' Cleri anno* 9 E. 2. 18 E. 3. cap. 7. 1 R. 2. cap. 13. 27 H. 8. cap. 20. 32 H. 8. cap. 7. and this act.

Of ancient they were determined in the sherifes turne, as it appeareth in *lib. rubeo inter leges* H. 1. cap. 8. After by *scire fac'* at the common law before the statute of 18 E. 3. Vid. Rot. claus. 21 H. 3. m. 3. & Rot. Eschaet' 8 E. 1. nu 67. Regist. fol. 165. a writ of covenant to levie a fine *de decimis garbarum*, &c. 38 H. 6. 20. F. N. B. 30. e. f. 4 E. 3. 27. 29. 7 E. 3. fol. 5. per Parning. 8 E. 3. 49. Bracton, lib. 5. fol. 401. Britton, cap. 4. fol. 11. omitted tithes, &c. Fleta, lib. 6. cap. 36. 28 E. 3. 97. Vid. Mich. 7 E. 1. coram Reg. rot. 21.

At this day a writ of right of advowson lyeth *de advocatione decimarum ecclesiæ*, &c. for the tithe is the profit of the church; and if the tithes be taken away, the advowson is of none effect, and the esples in a writ of right of advowson (which is the fruit of the advowson) are alledged in the parson, in taking of the great and small tithes by the presentment of the patron. See 16 Ed. 3. tit. *Quare Imped.* 147. 30 E. 3. fol. 1. 38 E. 3. 13. 45 E. 3. 12. Brit. cap. 4. and the writ of *indicavit*, whereof you may 4 E. 3. 27. per Shard & per Stoner, &c. 26 H. 8. 3. F.N.B. 30. c. F.N B. 30. c. Vet. N.B. 31. 4 E. 3. 27. 8 E. 3. 49. 31 H. 6. 16. 12 E. 4. 13.

13 H. 7. 16. 31 H. 8. prohib. 17. may reade at large before in the expofition of the ftatute of W. 2. cap. 5.

This 10. addition for the eftablifhment of ecclefiafticall jurifdiction for tithes was made, but by the generality thereof (which obferve well) it fhould have been doubted, whether the writ of right of advowfon of tithes, and of *indicavit* had been taken away; but to cleare the doubt, there is hereafter a fpecial provifion therefore, as hereafter fhall be fhewed. See the 12. addition.

(24) *Proceffe de excommunicato capiendo.*] See the ftatute of 5 Eliz. cap. 23. for divers notable things concerning this matter; but none of the penalties of that ftatute doe extend to the proceeding upon caufe of tithes, but onely upon nine caufes belonging to ecclefiafticall jurifdiction particularly expreffed in that act.

The 11. addition. Be it further enacted, &c. that if any party at any time hereafter, for any matter or caufe before rehearfed (25), limited, or appointed by this act to be fued or determined in the kings ecclefiafticall court, or before the ecclefiafticall judge, doe fue for any prohibition in any of the kings courts, where prohibitions before this time have been ufed to be granted: that then in every fuch cafe the fame party, before any prohibition fhall be granted to him or them, fhall bring and deliver to the hands of fome of the juftices or judges of the fame court where fuch party demanded prohibition, the very true copy of the libell depending in the ecclefiafticall court concerning the matter, wherefore the partie demandeth prohibition, fubfcribed or marked with the hand of the fame party; and under the copy of the faid libell fhall be written the fuggeftion, wherefore the party fo demandeth the faid prohibition. And in cafe the faid fuggeftion by two honeft and fufficient witneffes at the leaft, be not proved true in the court (26) where the faid prohibition fhall be fo granted within 6 moneths next following after the faid prohibition fhall be fo granted and awarded, that [662] then the party that is letted or hindered of his or their fuit in the ecclefiafticall court by fuch prohibition, fhall upon his or their requeft and fuit, without delay, have a confultation granted in the fame cafe in the court, where the faid prohibition was granted, and fhall alfo recover double cofts and damages againft the party that fo purfued the faid prohibition, the faid cofts and damages to be affigned or affeffed by the court, where the faid confultation fhall be fo granted; for which cofts and damages the party to whom they fhall be awarded may have an action of debt by bill, plaint, or information in any of the kings courts of record, wherein the defendant fhall not wage his or their law, nor have any effoine or protection allowed or admitted.

(25) *Rehearfed.*] This word is very materiall, for this additional act of 2 E. 6. extendeth onely to prediall and perfonall tithes; but in as much as this act doth rehearfe the ftatutes of 27 H. 8. cap. 20. and 32 H. 8. cap. 7. both which ftatutes extend unto

unto all kind of tithes, viz prediall, perſonall, and mixt, and to offerings alſo; therefore this branch extendeth to them all. And it is to be obſerved, that this branch reſpecteth the cauſe of ſuit, viz. for tithes or offerings, and not the cauſe of the prohibition. Vid. Dyer, 2 Eliz. fol. 170.

(26) *And in caſe the ſaid ſuggeſtion, &c. be not proved true in the court,* &c.] This clauſe was made in favour of the clergy for proofe by witneſſes, which they had not at the common law.

If the ſuggeſtion be in the negative, as if the proprietary of a parſonage impropriate ſue for tithes, and the cauſe of the ſuggeſtion be, that the parſonage is not impropriate; or if the parſon of Dale ſue for tithes of lands in that pariſh, and the party ſue a prohibition, for that the land lieth not in that pariſh, or that the parſon that ſueth for tithes was not inducted, &c. or any the like cauſe in the negative of any matter of fact, hee ſhall not produce any witneſſe by force of this branch, becauſe a negative cannot be proved: and therefore a prohibition upon cauſes in the negative remains at the common law.

If a man plead a deed in barre, wherein witneſſes be, and iſſue is joyned, *non eſt factum*, and proceſſe is awarded againſt the witneſſes, who are joyned to the jury, and it is found *non eſt factum*, notwithſtanding this joynder, the party grieved ſhall have an attaint: for it is a maxime in law, That witneſſes cannot teſtifie in the negative, but in the affirmative: otherwiſe it is, if they found it to be the deed of the party in the affirmative, there no attaint doth lye. Vid. 11. aſſ. p. 19. 22 aſſ. p. 15. 23. aſſ. p. 11. 40 aſſ. p. 23. 12 H. 6. 6. F.N.B. 106. h. So it is, if the ſuggeſtion be grounded upon any matter in law, for that the ſuit for tithes in that kind are not due by law. As if the libell be in the eccleſiaſticall court, for the tithe of tiles, turfes, or the like, there need no witneſſes to be produced; for that matters in law are to be decided by the judges, and not to be proved by witneſſes: and *quod conſtat curiæ, opere teſtium non indiget*, and the cauſe of this prohibition, or the like, appeareth in the libell it ſelfe. See before *Artic' Cleri 3. regis Jacobi, Artic'* 18.

Provided alwaies, and be it enacted by the authority aforeſaid, that this act, or any thing therein contained, ſhall not extend to give any miniſter or judge eccleſiaſticall any juriſdiction to hold plea of any matter, cauſe, or thing, being contrary or repugnant to, or againſt the effect, intent, or meaning of the ſtatute of Weſt. 2. (27) the fifth chapter, the ſtatutes of *Articuli Cleri* (28), *Circumſpecte agatis* (29), *Sylva cædua* (30), the treatiſe *de regia prohibitione* (31), ne againſt the ſtatute of *anno primo Edwardi tertii* the tenth chapter (32), or any of them, ne yet hold plea in any matter, whereof the kings court of right ought to have juriſdiction (33): any thing therein contained to the contrary in any wiſe notwithſtanding.

A proviſo touching the 11 addition.

[663]

(27) *Statute of W. 2. cap. 5.*] Hereby, if need were, the writ of indicavit, and the writ of right of the fourth part of tithes, and all dependances thereupon are ſaved. See before in the expoſition of this act of W. 2. cap. 5. anno 13 E. 1.

(28) *Articuli cleri,*] These articles were established by act of parliament anno 9 E. 2. See before in the exposition upon these articles. By this act also cap. 2. the writs of indicavit, and of right of advowson of tithes are saved.

10 H. 4. 1. b. (29) *Circumspecte agatis.*] This act is (as here it appeareth) a statute, and enacted anno 13 E. 1. See before the exposition hereof.

(30) *Silva cædua.*] Here is intended the statute of 45 E. 3. cap. 3. concerning tithes *de silva cædua,* and not of great wood above 20 yeares growth.

Hill. 7 H. 4. pl. 2. (31) *The treatise de regia prohibitione.*] Herein some difference is in our bookes; for in Hill. 7 H. 4. it is said, that the statute *de regia prohibitione* doth rehearse how *per venditiones spirituales fiunt temporales* which clause is in *Artic' Cleri,* cap. 1. *in fine.* Also in 31 H. 6. 13, 14. 31 H. 6. it is said, that the statute *de regia prohibitione,* and recite the effect of the second chapter of *Artic. Cleri.* So as by these bookes the statute *de regia prohibitione* is the statute of *Artic' Cleri*: but it cannot be so conceived in this act, because herein they are distinguished as two severall statutes, and so in truth in the intendment of this act they are: and the treatise *de regia prohibitione* intended by this act is that treatise *de regia prohibitione,* intitled *Prohibitio formata super artic'.* Vide Vet. Mag. Chart. part 2. fol. 7. Rastall abridg. stat. tit. prohib. pl. 6.

21 E. 3. 29. a. Concerning lay fee, &c. this is affirmed to be a statute. (32) *Statute of* 1 *E.* 3. *cap.* 10.] This is misprinted; for the act is 1 E. 3. stat. 2. cap. 11. that if any suit be in the spirituall court against inditers, a prohibition doth lye. This act is in affirmance of the common law. Vide Regist. fol. 39. lib. intr. R. 447. b. tit. Defamation.

(33) *Ne yet hold plea in any matter where the kings court of right ought to have jurisdiction.*] So provident the makers of this statute were to keep both jurisdictions within their proper bounds, a great meanes to make both church and common-wealth flourish. And this is a large and a generall saving of the jurisdiction of the kings courts of the common law.

The 13. and last addition. Provided neverthelesse, where heretofore such a custome hath been in many parts of Wales, that of such cattell and other goods as have been given with marriage of any person, there tithes have been exacted and levied by the parsons and curats in those parts; which custome being dissonant from any part of this realme, as it seemeth, when the country of Wales was through civill dissention unculted for want of other sufficient profits, that might otherwise grow to the curats and ministers there, to have been for that time tolerable (34), so now the countrie being now well manured and husbanded, and the tithe is duly paid there of corne, hay, wooll, and cheese, and of other increase of all manner of cattell, as it is commonly in all other parts of this realme, the same custome seemes to be grievous and unreasonable, specially where the benefices are else sufficient for the finding of the said ministers and curats: that it be therefore enacted by the authority aforesaid, [664] that from and after the first day of May next coming no such tithes of marriage goods be exacted or required of any person within the said dominion of Wales, or marches of the same: any

any thing in this act contained, or any other act, custome, prescription had or made to the contrary hereof notwithstanding.

(34) *To have been for that time tolerable.*] Here is first to be noted, that a custome once reasonable and tolerable, if after it become grievous, and not answerable to the reason, whereupon it was grounded, yet is to be (as here it appeareth) taken away by act of parliament; for an inheritance once fixed cannot be taken away, but by parliament. Secondly, here is to be noted, that by custome a parson, &c. may have tithes of such things, as are not tithable of common right.

An Exposition upon the Statute of 1 H. 5. Cap. 5. of Additions.

ORDEINES est et establies, que en chescun briefe originall (1) *des actions personels, appeales, et indictments, et en queux exigends serr' agard'* (2), *que aux nosmes des defendants en tiels briefes originals, appeales, et indictments soient faits addition de lour estate, ou degree* (3), *ou de mestier* (4), *et les villes* (5) *ou hamlets* (6), *lieux* (7), *et les counties* (8) *de queux ils fueront ou sont, ou en queux ils sont ou fueront conversantes. Et si per proces sur les dits briefes originals, appeales, ou indictments, en queux les dits additions soient enterlesses ascuns utlagaries soient pronouncies, que ils soient voides* (9), *irrites, et tenus pur nul. Et que avant les utlagaries pronouncies les dits briefes et endictments soient abatus per exception du partie* (10), *per la ou en icell' les dits additions soient enterlesses. Purview touts foits, que mesq; les dits briefes dactions personels ne soient accordants as recordes, et faits* (11) *per le surplusage de additions suisdits, que pur cel cause ils ne soient abatus. Et que les clerkes del chancellarie* (12), *south que nosmes tiels briefes isseront escriptes ne*

ITEM it is ordained and established, that in every original writ of actions personals, appeals, and indictments, and in which the exigent shall be awarded, in the names of the defendants in such writs original, appeals and indictments, additions shall be made of their estate or degree, or mystery, and of the towns, or hamlets, or places, and counties, of the which they were, or be, or in which they be or were conversant; and if by process upon the said original writs, appeals, or indictments, in the which the said additions be omitted, any utlagaries be pronounced, that they be void, frustrate, and holden for none; and that before the utlagaries pronounced, the said writs and indictments shall be abated by the exception of the party, where in the same the said additions be omitted. Provided always, that though the said writs of additions personals be not according to the records and deeds, by the surplusage of the additions aforesaid, that for that cause they be not abated; and that the clerks of the chancery, under whose names

ne enterlessent, ne facent omission des dits additions, come desuis est dit, sur peine destre punis, et faire fine al roy per discretion de le chancellor (13). *Et commencera cest ordinance a tener lieu al suit de partie, de la feast de Saint Michael prochein ensuant* (14).

names such writs shall go forth written, shall not leave out, or make omission of the said additions as is aforesaid, upon pain to be punished, and to make a fine to the king, by the discretion of the chancellor. And this ordinance shall begin to hold place at the suit of the party, from the feast of St. Michael next ensuing forward.

(4 Ed. 4. f. 10. 6 Rep. 67. Cro. El. 198. Cro. Jac. 610. Dyer, 46. Bro. Addit. 4, 5. 7, 8, 9, 10. 12. 14, 15. 19. Fitz. Brief, 30. 36. 40. 47. 49. 51. 61. 67. 72. 75. 109. 122. 124, 125. 129. 151. 163. 169. 201. 236. 940. 2 Leon. 183. 200. 3 H. 6. 30. b. pl. 17. 2 Roll, 225. 3 Mod. 139. 1 Shower, 16. Hob. 129. Mod. Cases in Law, 52. 8 H. 6. c. 12. 5 El. c. 23.)

We shall, in expounding the words of this act, shew what was the common law before the making hereof.

3 H. 6. 30. 14 H. 6. 21. 35 H. 6. 30. 10 E. 4. 16. a. 18 E. 4. 9. * 10 E. 4. 16. 10 H. 7. 21. 13 H. 7. 21.

(1) *En briefe originall.*] Though it be in writ originall, yet if the plea be not holden upon the originall, this act extendeth not to it; as in a *recordare* to remove a plaint of replevin into the common place, because the plea is holden upon the plaint, this act extends not to it. * So in a returne of rescous, though there lyeth processe of outlawry, yet this statute extends not to it, because this act speaketh only of writs originall.

9 ass. pl. 1. 9 E. 3. ass. 449. 7 H. 4. 39.

(2) *Des personels actions, &c. en queux exigends serr' agard'.*] In an assise of *novel disseisin*, if the disseisin be found with force and armes, a *capias pro fine* and exigent doe lye for the king; yet the defendant shall have no addition within this statute, for that the originall writ is in the realty, and this act extendeth onely to personall actions.

* 17 E. 3. 44. b. 11 H. 6. 11. in maintenance. 27 H. 6. 3. 10 E. 4. 16. 10 E. 4. 12. 35 H. 6. 12.

Aux nosmes des defendants.] * Regularly by the common law every naturall man, having no name of dignity, ought to be named in all originalls, and other suits by his christian name and sirname, and that before this act * sufficed; but if he had a name of inferiour dignity (as knight, or banneret) he ought to be named by his christian name and sirname, and by the addition of his name of dignity by the common law, which is implyed in these words: *aux nosmes des defendants.*

* [666]

27 H. 6. 9. 10 H. 6. 1. 7 E. 4. bre. 163. 18 E. 4. 21. 8 E. 3. 247. 24 E. 3. 31. 39 E. 3. 17. 35 H. 6. 12. 32 E. 3. bre. 291. 32 H. 6. 28, 29.

If there be a corporation of one sole person that hath a fee-simple, and may have a writ of right, he may be named in originals, &c. by the common law by his christian name, without any sirname; for the name of his corporation is in lieu of his sirname (some say both christian name and sirname) as John abbot of D. &c. John bishop of N. but otherwise it is of a parson: for hee must be named by his christian name and sirname.

* 12 E. 4. 10. 18 E. 4. 9. 21 E. 4. 158.

* If it be a corporation aggregate of many able persons; as maior and comminalty, dean and chapter, master of an hospital and confreres, &c. the maior, deane, or master need not be named by his christian name, because that such a corporation standeth in lieu both of the christian name and sirname.

2 H. 6. 29. 7 E. 3. 26. 25 E. 3. 39, 40. 7 E. 4. brev. 163.

If a man be created by letters patents duke, marquesse, earle, viscount, or baron, the dignity is so incorporated to him, according to the state given unto him by those letters patents, as the duke, &c. by

by the common law might be named by his christian name, and by the name of his dignity, which standeth in lieu of his sirname: as *Præcipe Johanni duci Lancastriæ*. And the reason thereof is, for that the king by those letters patents creates him to the state, honour, and degree of duke, *et imponit ei stilum et titulum ducis Lanc' &c. habend' &c. et sic in similibus*. And albeit a creation by writ hath not the same words, yet it hath the same effect.

5 E. 3. 28. 99. 22 ass. 24. Nota, nobility in a manner incorporated.

And it is to be observed, that *surnosme* is derived of *sur (id est) super*, and *nosme* (that is) *nomen, quasi super nomen*, because it is superadded to the christian name, which legally is *prænomen*, in Latine *cognomen, quia conjunctum nomen*.

(3) *Soient faits addition de lour estate, ou degree, ou de mestier.*] Estate, *status à stando*, the condition wherein any subject standeth. Degree, *gradus à gradiendo*, the degree wherein any subject standeth. So as in legall understanding these two words are of * one signification, and doe extend to persons of nobility, of dignity, and under the degree of nobility and dignity; as yeoman, &c. and doe extend as well to the clergy as to the temporalty, and to graduates and degrees in universities in any kind of profession.

* 37 E. 3. ca. 8. 22 E. 4. cap. 1. 8 E. 4. cap. 2. 13 R. 2. stat. 2. cap. 1.

State of a lord, 3 E. 4. cap. 5. *sæpe*. 22 E. 4. cap. 1.

Under the estate of a knight, & cap. 14. of the estate of carriers, plowmen, &c. and the estate of a groome attending to husbandry, cap. 13. degree and estate of clerkes, 37 E. 3. ca. 10.

Degrees applied to all, as well women as men. 3 E. 4. cap. 5.

No yeoman, nor lower estate then an esquire. 16 R. 2. cap. 4.

Under the degree of a knight or lords son, 20 R. 2. cap. 2.

Under the degree of a barons son, or knight, 24 H. 8. cap. 13. 8 Eliz. cap. 11.

So as in legall understanding, *status* and *gradus sunt synonyma*. And so in the ancient writ of the call of a serjeant, * *ad statum et gradum servientis ad legem*.

* Fortesc. ca. 50. 14 H. 6. 15. Br. tit. Addition 44.

The estates and degrees against whom originall writs may be brought, are the queen, consort of the king, the prince of Wales, dukes, * marquesses, earles, viscounts, and barons. These are of the greater nobility.

* Marchiones. 26 H. 6. bre. 100.

Knights of Saint George, knights bannerets, knights of the bathe, knights of the chamber, [b] *milites cameræ*, knights batchelors, baronets, esquires, gentlemen. These are of the lesser nobility.

[b] Rot. pat. 29 E. 3. part. 1. m. 29.

Cives, burgenses, and yeomen, which are of the lowest estates or degrees.

Armigeri, scutiferi, unde scutagium, generosi.

There is another division made in our * books of lesser nobility, *viz.* some be names of dignities, as all the knights abovesaid, and baronets; and some of worship, as esquires and gentlemen.

* 14 H. 6. 14. Camb. Brit. p. 24.

Baronets were first raised and created by king James, of an estate to them and the heires males of their bodies: and where in some * statutes and records baronets are named, it is *vitium impressoris, seu scriptoris*, and should be bannerets, who were not of inheritance, for that they were knights, which dignity was not descendable, nor yet is. Bannerets rightly named. Rot. Parl. 46 E. 3. nu. 10. 50 E. 3. nu. 40. 1 H. 4. nu. 53, &c. In letters patents, Rot. Pat. *anno* 13 E. 3. m. 13. Will. de la Pool *statum et honorem baneretti*, part 2. 15 E. 3. m. 22, 23. & Rot. Pat. *anno* 7 R. 2. 8. octab' Thomas Camois banerettus, &c. 22 E. 3. fol. 18. a banner, *quia nomen habet à vexillo*, of the banner, &c. Corruptly baronet,

[667]

* Rot. Parl. 2 R. 2. nu. 13, 14. 13 R. 2. stat. 2. cap. 1. 14 R. 2. cap. 11. 16 R. 2. cap. 6.

Vid. Camb. ubi sup.

ronet, in 35 H. 6. 46. for baron. But let us proceed to ſome more profitable matter.

There have been within this realme ſince the conqueſt divers names of dignities, which are growne to dis-uſe, and in a manner

Lib. rubr. 8. Bract. lib. 1. cap. 8.

loſt: as, *vicedomini, vidams. Vavaſores, viri* (as Bracton ſaith) *magnæ dignitatis. Vavaſor enim nihil melius dici poterit, quam vas ſortitum ad valetudinem: unde vavaſoria* in divers ancient records. Cambden Brit. 123. *vavaſores ſive valvaſores proxime poſt barones locum olim tenuerunt.* See Chaucer our Engliſh poet in the Franklyns prologue.

Some doe hold, that it had been more fit to have revived ſome of the ancient dignities, then to have created any of a new invention.

We have ſpoken of all the names of dignity, let us now ſpeake of the names of worſhip.

Eſquier, armiger, ſcutifer, &c.] In legall underſtanding he is derived *ab armis, quæ in clypeis gentiliciis honoris inſignia geſtant.* In Spaniſh *eſcudero, ab eſcudo, id eſt, ſcuto.*

37 E. 3. cap. 10. 1 R. 2. ca. 7. 16 R. 2. ca. 4. 20 R. 2. ca. 2. 7 H. 4. 7. 28 H. 6. 8. 32 H. 6. 28, 29. * 3 E. 4. cap. 5. Rot. Parl. anno 1 E. 4.

In this ſenſe, as a name of eſtate and degree, it was uſed in divers acts of parliament before the making of this act, and * after this act alſo. Et Rot. Parl. an. 1 E. 4. John lord Audeley, an ancient and a noble baron, was named *Johannes Audeley armiger,* for that all the reſt of the barons that appeared at that parliament were knights: and all dukes, marqueſſes, earles, viſcounts, and barons of other nations, or which are not lords of the parliaments of England, are named *armigeri,* if they be no knights; and if knights, then are they named *milites.*

The ſonnes of all the peeres and lords of parliament in the life of their fathers, are in law eſquires, and ſo to be named. By this ſtatute the eldeſt ſon of a knight is an eſquire.

See before ſtat. de Militibus, anno [illegible] E. 2.

Gentleman, generoſus, Gentill home.] This is alſo a good addition. And every gentleman muſt be *arma gerens,* and the beſt tryall of a gentleman in bloud (which is the loweſt degree of nobility) is by bearing of armes. For as in ancient time the ſtatues or images of their anceſters were prooſes of their nobility, which was a ſolemne and honourable, but yet a cumberſome tryall, whereof, and how in time they decayed, the poet ſpeaketh,

Juvenal. ſat. 8.

Stemmata quid faciunt? quid prodeſt pontice longo
Sanguine cenſeri, pictoſque oſtendere vultus
Majorum, et ſtantes in curribus Æmylianos,
Et curios jam dimidios, naſumque minorem
Corvini, et Galbam auriculis naſoque carentem? &c.
Tota licet veteres exornent undique ceræ
Atria: nobilitas ſola eſt atque unica virtus.

Cicero. *Flavia gens obſcura quidem, et ſine imaginibus.*
Cicero. *Nobiles ſunt qui imagines generis ſui proferre poſſunt.*

So of later times coat-armes came in lieu of thoſe ſtatues or images, and are the moſt certaine prooſes and evidence of nobility and gentry. So as in theſe daies the rule is, *nobiles ſunt qui inſignia gentilicia generis ſui proferre poſſunt.*

[668] There is ſmall difference between an eſquire and a gentleman; for every eſquire is a gentleman, and every gentleman is *arma gerens.*

And

And *generosus* and *generosa* are good additions: and if a gentlewoman be named spinster in any originall writ, &c. appeale, or inditement, she may abate and quash the same; for she hath as good right to that addition, as baronesse, viscountesse, marchionesse or dutchesse have to theirs.

[a] A man may have an addition of gentleman within this statute, if hee be a gentleman by office (though he be not by birth) as many of the kings houshold, and of other lords, be; and * clerkes, being officers in the kings courts of record: and if they be out of their office, they are but yeomen; and yet as long as they continue in their office, they ought to be named gentlemen, as their due addition.

A gentleman by [b] reputation, that is, neither gentle by birth, nor by office, nor by creation, but commonly called gentleman, and knowne by that name, is a sufficient addition within this act. And so was it adjudged in [c] Caters case, Hill. 25 Eliz. *in communi banco*, but if he be named yeoman, hee cannot abate the writ.

A French knight challenged [d] John Kingston yeoman, the kings subject, at certaine points and deeds of armes, &c. *unde rex* (saith the record) *ut dictus Johannes honorabilius in præmissis accipiatur, ipsum Johannem in ordinem * generosorum adoptavit, et armigerum constituit, et cætera honoris insignia concessit.* And such a gentleman or esquire so created, is an addition within this statute.

[e] Since the making of this statute, esquire and gentleman were more frequently by force of this act used, as additions in originalls, &c. and afterwards were commonly used in deeds and other specialties. * He that hath taken any degree in either university, may be named by that degree without question, being within the direct letter and meaning of this act; and if he hath taken any degree in divinity, he may have the addition of clerke.

[f] *Yeoman or yeman.*] This is a Saxon word ȝeuen gemen, the G being turned in common speech (as is usuall in like cases) into a Y. In [g] legall understanding a yeoman is a free-holder, that may dispend 40 shillings, anciently 5 nobles *per annum:* and he is called *probus et legalis homo.*

And as of ancient time the [h] gentleman held *per servitium scuti*, by knights service, so the yeoman held *per servitium socæ*, by socage. Of this degree see Fortescue, cap. 25. & 29.

[i] This degree is a good addition within this statute, and is applyed onely to the man, and not to the woman.

We have omitted * citizens and burgesses (albeit they are such as are called to parliament) yet because they are no sufficient additions (being too generall) within this act, we have omitted them.

(4) [k] *Mistier.*] *i. ars, seu artificium, Latinè dicitur, mysterium, Anglicè* mysterie. *Mistier derivatur à maistre, Latinè magisterium,* because no man ought to exercise it, but he that is a master of it. *Mistier* is a large word, and includeth all lawfull arts, trades, and occupations, as taylor, merchant, mercer, husbandman, labourer, and the like. But [l] servant, groome, or fermor are no additions within this act, because they are not of any mysterie. And [m] chamberer, butler, pantler, or the like, are additions of offices, and not of any mysterie or occupation.

Neither doth this act extend to unlawfull practices, as extortioner, maintainer, abetter, hereticke, &c.

Trade

21 E. 4. 15. Lib. int. Rast. 108. 10 E. 4. 16. 28 H. 6. 3, 4. 7 E. 6. Dyer, fo. 88. lib. int. fol. 107. nu. 9. de gradu hominis generosi, et non de gradu hominis vocat' a yeoman.
[a] 28 H. 6. fo. 4. a. 5 E. 4. 33. acc' 14 H. 6. 15.
* 20 H. 6. 30. b.
[b] Reputatio est vulgaris opinio, ubi non est veritas.
[c] Lib. 6. fol. 67. Hill. 25 Eliz. in communi banco, Caters case. Lib. int. R. fol. 107. nu. 8. Vid. lib. int. fol. 107. nu. 7. a fellow of Clements Inne, &c.
[d] Rot. pat. 13 R. 2. part 1.
* Nota, the creation of a gentleman.
[e] 21 H. 6. bre. 89. 28 H. 6. 8. 7 H. 4. 7. 16 H. 6. 28.
* 35 H. 6. 55. b.
[f] Lib. 6. fol. 67.
[g] See the first part of the Institutes, sect. 464. 2 H. 5. cap. 3. See the first part of the Institutes, sect. 95.
[h] Fortesc. ca. 25. & cap. 29.
[i] 10 E. 4. 16. 1 H. 4. cap. 7. 2 H. 4. cap. 21.
* 27 H. 6. 4. 4 E. 4. 10. 5 E. 4. 142. 1 H. 5. 3. 35 H. 6. 12.
[k] 22 E. 4. 1. 2 R. 3. 2. 9 H. 6. 65. 35 H. 6. 55. 4 H. 6. 26. 5 E. 4. 33. 3 H. 6. 31. 11 H. 6. 11.
[l] 7 E. 4. 10. 9 E. 4. 50. 28 H. 6. 4.
[m] 5 E. 4. 32.

Trade *dicitur à tradendo, quia tradit nobis necessaria:* the Saxon word is Cꞃæꝼꞇ, Cræft, *hodie* craft, *id est*, trade.

14 H. 6. 15. 5 E. 4. 33. [669] If a man have divers arts, trades, or occupations, he may be named by any of them: but if a gentleman by birth be a mercer (as many younger sonnes of gentlemen be bound prentices to arts and trades in London, and elsewhere) if he in an originall, &c. be named mercer, or of any other trade, whereof hee is in truth, he may abate the writ, &c. for he ought to be named by the degree of a gentleman, because it is worthier then the addition of any mysterie.

27 H. 6. 4. 4 E. 4. 10. 5 E. 4. 142. 35 H. 6. 12. And so it is, if one man be a duke, a marquesse, earle, viscount, and baron, all these dignities stand distinctly in him, and the greater drowneth not the lesser, yet shall hee be named in originall writs, &c. by the worthier dignity, *viz.* by the name of a duke onely within this act.

Having diligently observed the order of this act, we find, that in some cases the order thereof is observed, and in others not. In appeales and inditements of treason or felony, &c. against the greater nobility, as dukes, marquesses, the order of the statute is pursued, *viz.* For, 1. the estate and degree (for example) of a duke, &c. is named, and after the towne and county. *Edwardus dux Buckingham nuper de N. in com' Glouc'.* And so it is when one is named of a citie, which is a countie of it selfe, the like order is observed: as *J. S. pannarius de London in com' civitatis London.*

But in case of the lesser nobility, and all other under them, the towne and county are named before the addition: as, *Th. C. nuper de D. in com' M. miles. Jo. C. nuper de D. in com' M. armiger. N. C. nuper de D. in com' M. merchant, &c.*

7 H. 6. 39. 22 H. 6. 29. 21 E. 4. 51. (5) *Et les villes, ou hamlets, ou lieus, et les counties.*] *Villes.* For these see the first part of the Institutes, sect. 171. And if there be *D. major*, and *D. minor*, and not *D. tantum*, he cannot be named of *D.* for there is no such towne.

(6) *Hamlets.*] See the first part of the Institutes, *ubi sup.* And it is at the election of the party to name him of the hamlet or towne.

(7) *Lieus.*] These be understood of places knowne out of any towne or hamlet, 14 H. 6. 24. 35 H. 6. 30. 21 E. 4. 89. 4 E. 3. 129. 19 E. 3. bre. 467. 7 H. 6. 24. 37. 20 H. 6. 30. 7 H. 4. 27. 17 E. 3. 56. 43 E. 3. 5.

Bract. lib. 3. fol. 124. b. 19 H. 6. 1. By the ancient common law of England, *secundum antiquam consuetudinem dici poterit de familia alicujus, qui hospitatus fuerit cum alio per tres noctes, et vocatur Hoghenehyne.*

(8) *Counties.*] See the first part of the Institutes, sect. 61. & 248.

See the first part of the Institutes, sect. 171. 7 H. 6. 1. 27 H. 6. 4. 4 E. 4. 10. 5 E. 4. 142. 21 E. 4. 15. * 22 H. 6. 47. 35 H. 6. 30. 4 E. 4. 41. 5 E. 4. 20. 21 E. 4. 2. 1 E. 3. 8. lib. 4. fol. 14. Arundell.

But seeing that ancient boroughes were first townes, and cities were formerly boroughes, if a citie be a countie of it selfe, wherein are divers parishes, yet the addition *de London*, or *nuper de London*, is sufficient within this statute.

* The addition of a parish, if there be two or more townes within it, is not good, but if there be one towne, the addition of parish is good within this statute: and it shall not be intended (if it be not pleaded) that there be more towns then one in the parish; for *non præsumitur pluralitas.*

This statute extends not to some cases, though the defendant be

not

not named of any towne, hamlet, or place. ° As in an action of debt, the writ is, *præcipe R. G. rectori ecclesiæ de T.* without alledging in what town, hamlet, or place he is dwelling. So if the *præcipe* in an action of debt be, *Prec' Tho' Chase cancellario universitatis Oxon'*, without saying *de Oxonia.* So in a writ brought against the husband and his wife, or the abbot and his commoigne, the plaintife need not shew in what towne, &c. the wife or commoigne dwell; for the law shall intend (which ever intendeth the best) that the parson is resident upon his rectory, the chancellor upon his office, the wife with her husband, and the monke with his soveraigne.

° 7 H. 6. 1. 10 H. 6. 8. 8 H. 6. 38. 3 H. 6. 31.

p The addition as well of the estate, degree, or mysterie, as the towne, hamlet, or place, ought by force of this act to be alledged *in primo nomine*; for the proper use of an *alias dict'* is, to agree with the record, or specialty whereupon the writ is grounded, and is not traversable.

p Alias dict' 30 H. 6. 5. & 6. 32 H. 6. 33. 36 H. 6. 28. 4 E. 4. 10. 21 E. 4. 15. 18. 33 H. 8. Dyer, 50. b. 1 E. 4. 1. 5 E. 4. 141. 26 H. 6. bre. 100. 28 H. 6. 9.

[670]

The addition of the estate, degree, or mystery ought to be by force of this act, as the defendant was of at the day of the writ purchased, and not with a *nuper*, as *nuper armiger, nuper monachus, aut nuper comes de D. &c.* but a *nuper* may be of the towne, &c. because men doe often remove their habitation. And this distinction appeareth by the act it selfe, by reason of these words in the act, relating to the townes, hamlets, &c. *Ou ils fuer', ou sont.*

9 E. 4. 2. 21 H. 6. 3. b. 2 H. 6. 4. 32 H. 6. 20. 29. 5 E. 3. 28.

The end of the purview of this act was, that the person of the defendant in originalls, &c. where processe of outlawry did lye, should be so described by certaine additions, as one man might not be troubled for another. See other statutes made to the same end. 8 H. 6. cap. 10. * 6 H. 8. cap. 4. 5 E. 6. cap. 26. 31 El. cap. 3. & 9.

* Dyer, 4 Eliz. 213, 214.

(9) *Ascũs utlagaries sont pronounce, que ils soient voides, &c.*] This being a judgement in law is interpreted to be made void by a writ of error, or by the plea of the party coming in upon a *cap. utlegat'*, according to the course of the common law: for though the words of the statute be *voides*, yet it is but voidable by a writ of error, or plea; which is worthy of observation. 19 H. 6. fol. 1. 8 H. 6. cap. 10. pl. com. 137. b. 7 H. 6. 27. 39. 10 H. 6. 8. 11 H. 6. 19. 67. 19 H. 6. 58, &c. 20 H. 6. 20. 21 H. 6. 23. 55. 37 H. 6. 1. 38 H. 6. 1. 22 H. 6. 18. & 23. 36. 30 H. 6. 1. 21 E. 4. 94. 73. 1 E. 4. 2. 2 E. 4. 10. 4 E. 4. 10. 41, 42. 22 E. 4. 37. 10 E. 4. 13. 5 H. 7. 16. 11 H. 7. 5. 21 H. 7. 13. 3 El. 192. b. 4 El. Dyer, 213, 214.

(10) *Per exception du partie.*] But if the defendant, albeit hee hath not such addition as this act requireth, yet if he appeareth upon processe, and plead, taking no advantage thereof by exception, he hath lost the benefit of this act.

7 H. 6. 37. 35 H. 6. 12. 5 E. 4. Vid. Br. tit. error 69.

(11) *Ne soyent accordant al records et faits, &c.*] *Abundans cautela non nocet*; but if the addition prescribed by this act had varied from the record or deed, yet being injoyned by act of parliament to be contained in the writ, &c. such variance should not have abated the writ, albeit this clause had been omitted; but yet an act of parliament cannot be made too plaine.

3 H. 6. 24. 35. 28 H. 6. 9. 21 E. 4. 95.

(12) *Et que les clerkes del chancerie.*] *i. e. les coursetours. Clerici de cursu*, that make out originall writs. Of these there be in the chancery twenty in number. To every of these are appointed certaine counties, and are a corporation of themselves.

Fleta, lib. 2. ca. 12. 14 & 15 H. 8. cap. 8.

(12) *Destre*

(13) *Destre punies, et faire fine per le discretion del chancellor.*] This extendeth to the lord keeper of the great seale, as often elsewhere hath been observed.

(14) *Et commencera cest ordinance a tener lieu al suit de partie de la feast de S. Michael prochein ensuant.*] This parliament began 15 Pasch' 1 H. 5. And this statute was made, when acts of parliament were not printed, but were by the sherifes proclaimed in every county (as elsewhere hath been shewed:) and therefore to the end the subject might take notice thereof, day was given by this act untill the feast of Saint Michael the archangel following; but at the kings suit this act began presently, for that the kings learned councell were attendants in parliament, and had sufficient notice of this act.

---

[671] An Exposition upon the Statute of 27 H. 8. ca. 16. intitled, An Act concerning Inrolments of Bargaines, and Contracts of Lands and Tenements.

BE it enacted by the authority of this present parliament, that from the last day of July, which shall be in the yeare of our Lord God 1536. no mannors, lands, tenements, or other hereditaments shall passe, alter, or change from one to another, whereby any state of inheritance or freehold shall be made (1), or take effect in any person or persons, or any use thereof to be made, by reason onely of any bargaine (2) and sale thereof (3); except the same bargaine and sale be made by writing (4) indented (5), sealed and inrolled (6) in one of the kings courts of record at Westminster (7), or else within the same countie or counties where the same manors, lands, or tenements so bargained and sold, lye or be, before the *custos rotulorum* (9), and two justices of the peace (8), and the clerke of the peace of the same countie or counties, or two of them at the least, whereof the clerke of the peace to be one: and the same inrolment to be had and made within six moneths next after the date of the same writings indented (10), the same *custos rotulorum*, or justices of the peace, and clerke, taking for the inrolment of every such writing indented before them, where the land comprised in the same writing exceed not the yearly value of 40 shillings, 2s. (11) that is to say, 12d. to the justices, and 12d. to the clerke, and for the inrolment of every such writing indented before them, wherein the land comprised exceed the summe of 40 shillings yearly value, 5s. that is to say, 2s. 6d. to the said justices, and 2s. 6d. to the said clerke for the inrolling of the same. And that the clerke of the peace for

for the time being, within every ſuch county, ſhall ſufficiently inroll and ingroſſe in parchment (12) the ſame deeds or writings indented, as is aforeſaid, and the rolls thereof, at the end of every yeare ſhall deliver unto the *cuſtos rotulorum* (13) of the ſame county for the time being, there to remaine in the cuſtody of the ſaid *cuſtos rotulorum* for the time being, amongſt other records of every of the ſame counties, where any ſuch inrolments ſhall be ſo made, to the intent that every party that hath to doe therewith may reſort and ſee the effect and tenour of every ſuch writing ſo inrolled.

(1) *Of inheritance, or freehold ſhall be made, &c.*] After the ſtatute of 27 H. 8. cap. 10. of transferring uſes into poſſeſſion. If a man by his deed had bargained, and ſold for valuable conſideration, any lands, &c. of any eſtate of inheritance, free-hold, or for yeares, the ſame had been executed by the ſaid act of 27 H. 8. cap. 10. Now this act of inrolments reſtraines onely eſtates of inheritance and free-hold; and therefore bargaines and ſales for yeares, for what number ſoever, are not reſtrained by this act, though it be not by deed indented nor inrolled. Lib. 2. fol. 36. Sir Rowl. Heywards caſe.

(2) *By reaſon only of any bargaine, &c.*] If a man for valuable conſideration by deed indented doe bargaine and ſell lands to another and his heires, and before the deed be inrolled he levieth a fine, or maketh a feoffment to the bargainee and his heires of the ſame lands, and after, and within the ſix moneths the deed is inrolled, the bargainee ſhall be in by the fine or feoffment, and not by the bargaine and ſale, both by reaſon of this word only, &c. and that the eſtate by the common law veſted ſhall be preferred. Lib. 8. 94. Foxes caſe. [672] Trin. 33 Eliz. in communi banco, int' Ric. Libbear. plaintife en waſte, & Eliz. Hynd defendant, lib. 5. fol. 71. Hynds caſe.

(3) *Of any bargaine and ſale thereof.*] Firſt, what is a bargain and ſale? &c. A bargaine and ſale is a reall contract * upon valuable conſideration for paſſing of mannors, lands, tenements, or hereditaments by deed indented and inrolled within ſix moneths after the date of it, without livery of ſeiſin, or attornement of tenants. * Pl. com. 307. a. 30 H. 8. tit. attornement, Br. 29.

If the bargainor be in poſſeſſion, this is a facile and ready aſſurance, but the feoffment reduceth and reſtoreth the poſſeſſion to the feoffor, and paſſeth the land to the feoffee, though the feoffor had been diſſeiſed, &c. and the inrolment is not pleadable as the feoffment is. 19 H. 6. 6.

Secondly, whether theſe words of [bargain and ſale] only, or equipollent words may be uſed, &c. to take effect by force of this ſtatute? Though it be good to uſe thoſe words mentioned in this act, yet are they not of neceſſity to be uſed; for whatſoever word upon valuable conſideration would have raiſed an uſe of any lands, tenements, or hereditaments at the common law, the ſame doe amount to a bargaine and ſale within this ſtatute: as if a man by deed indented and inrolled according to this act doth covenant for valuable conſideration to ſtand ſeiſed of lands to the uſe of another, &c. this is in nature of a bargaine and ſale within this act. Lib. 8. fol. 93, 94. Foxes caſe. Lib. 7. fol. 40. Bedles caſe. Lib. 8. fol. 93, 94. Foxes caſe. Lib. int. Co. 116. a. b.

A. ſeiſed of certaine lands in fee, demiſed the ſame to C. for life, the remainder for life reſerving a rent at the feaſt of Saint Michael, and of the annuntiation; A. by indenture, in conſideration of 50 pounds, doth demiſe, grant, ſet, and to farme let the ſame lands to B. for 99 yeares, reſerving a rent at the ſame feaſts preſently, and C. the leſſee for life did not attorne; and it was adjudged, that the ſaid Lib. 8 fol. 93, 94. Foxes caſe. Vid. li. 2. fo. 35. Sir Rowland Heywards caſe.

ſaid demiſe and grant upon the conſideration of 50 pounds amounted to a bargaine and ſale for the ſaid terme. So if a man for valuable conſideration doth by deed indented and inrolled alien or grant the land to a man and his heires, &c. this is a bargaine within this ſtatute, *et ſic de ſimilibus*. But inaſmuch as the intention of the parties is the principall foundation of the creation of uſes, if by any clauſe in the deed it appeareth, that the intention of the parties was to paſſe it in poſſeſſion by the common law, there no uſe ſhall be raiſed: and therefore if any letter of attorney be in the deed, or a covenant to make livery, or the like, there nothing ſhall paſſe by way of uſe, but according to the intention of
4 Mar. Dyer, fol. 146. Villiers caſe. the parties poſſeſſion by the common law. And albeit no valuable conſideration be expreſſed in the indenture, yet if any were given, the ſame may be averred, and the land doth ſufficiently paſſe.

Lib. 11. fol. 25. a. Harpers caſe. Lib. 1. fol. 176. Mildmayes caſe. A. by deed indented and inrolled in conſideration of 100 pounds paid by B. bargaineth and ſelleth the land to B. C. and D. parties to the indentures: in this caſe the land paſſeth to them all; for although the valuable conſideration be expreſſed to be paid by one, yet it muſt be intended, that it was paid for them all, to the end, that the land may paſſe to them all, according to the meaning of all the parties, and a conſideration given by one of the parties, is ſufficient to convey the land to them all.

(4) *Except the ſame bargaine and ſale be made by writing.*] Firſt, it muſt be by writing, and not by print or ſtamp.

* Lib. 5. fol. 20. b. Stiles caſe. Secondly, it muſt be * written in parchment or paper, and not upon wood, ſtone, lead, or other materiall.

See Stiles caſe, ubi ſupra. (5) *Indented.*] If the deed begin, *Hæc indentura*, or, This indenture, yet if the deed be not indented, it is no indenture; but if the deed be indented, though the deed doth begin, This deed made, without mentioning the word of indenture, yet is it a writing indented within this ſtatute.

[673] Trin' 29 Eliz. in the kings bench. In an action of debt between Scudamore and others plaintifes, and Vandenſtene defendant, upon an indenture of charter party the caſe was this: the indenture of charter party was made between Scudamore and others owners of the good ſhip, called B. whereof Robert Pitman was maſter, on the one partie, and Vandenſtene on the other party. In which indenture the plaintiſe did covenant with the ſaid Vandenſtene and Robert Pitman, and alſo Vandenſtene covenanted with the plaintiſe and Robert Pitman, and bound themſelves to the plaintiſe and Robert Pitman for performance of covenants in 600 pounds. And the concluſion of the ſaid indenture was, "In witneſſe whereof the parties aboveſaid to theſe preſent "indentures have put to their ſeals." And the ſaid Robert Pitman to the ſaid indenture put his hand and ſeal, and delivered the ſame. The defendant in barre of the ſaid action pleaded the releaſe of Pitman, &c. whereupon the plaintiſe demurred. And it was adjudged, that the releaſe of Pitman did not barre the plaintiſe, becauſe hee was no party to the indenture. And the diverſity was taken and agreed betweene an indenture reciprocall betweene parties on the one ſide, and parties on the other ſide, as this was; for there no bond, covenant, or grant can be made to or with any
See the firſt part of the Inſtitutes, ſect. 66. fol. 52. Vid. 4 E. 2. tit. Obligation 16. that is not party to the deed. But where the deed indented is not reciprocall, but is without a between, &c. as, *omnibus Chriſti fidelibus*, &c. there a bond, covenant, or grant may be made to divers ſeverall perſons.

(6) And

(6) *And inrolled.*] Albeit the indenture (as hath been said) may be either of parchment or paper, yet the inrolment must be in parchment onely; and so it is expressed in the clause of inrolment by the clerke of the peace, *viz.* That hee shall sufficiently inroll and ingrosse * in parchment the same. And so much is implied, when the inrolment is in any of the kings courts of record at Westminster; and so was it adjudged, as M. Plowden cited it before the lords in parliament, *anno* 23 Eliz. in the great case between Herbert and Vernon, which I heard, and observed.

39 E. 3. 39. 40 E. 3. 5.

* Nota.

A deed knowledged by the husband and wife shall by the common law be inrolled onely for the husband, and not for the wife, by reason of the coverture, and though it be inrolled for both, it bindeth her not. Otherwise it is by custome, and none hath power to examine a feme covert without writ. 29 H. 8. tit. Faits inroll' Br. 14. 7 E. 4. 5. *Vid.* 34 H. 8. ca. 22. 18 E. 3. 29. 45 ass. 8. 14 E. 3. execution 73. 19 R. 2. estoppel 281. 21 E. 3. 43. 24 E. 3. 64. 21 Eliz. Dyer, fol. 363. Kelwey 12 H. 7. fol. 4. &c. 12 H. 4. 12. 29 H. 8. faits inroll Br. 15. lib. 10. Mary Portingtons case, fol. 42.

If an infant acknowledgeth a recognizance, statute merchant, statute staple, or obligation in the nature of a statute staple, or inroll an obligation, in all these cases he must avoid it in an *audita querela*, during his minority; for it must be tryed by inspection, and these concerne but personall duties. But if an infant bargaine and sell lands which are in the realty by deed indented and inrolled, he may avoid it when he will; for the deed was of no effect to raise an use: and this statute is to be intended of lawfull and effectuall bargaines and sales, and such as would have raised uses at the common law, and doth onely restraine the execution of them that be of effect, except the deed be inrolled. And this standeth with the reason of the common law, that none but effectuall deeds ought to be inrolled; and therefore a deed of feoffment ought not to be inrolled before livery. But in case of a fine the infant must reverse it during his minoritie: for the conusance is taken by force of the kings writ before a judge, and is voidable by the common law.

Vid. Regist. fol. 150. F.N.B. 104. k. Dyer, 7 El. 132. b. Harrisons case. 7 E. 4. 5. 13 E. 3. audit. querela 26. 17 E. 3. 76. 10 E. 3. enfant 61. 28 E. 3. audita quer. 27. 8 H. 6. 30. 15 E. 4. 51. 1 H. 7. 15. 11 H. 7. 5. 48 E. 3. 33. 16 H. 7. 5. 44 E. 3. 7. b.

That upon a bargaine and sale by deed indented and inrolled, a rent may be reserved, for the use and possession passeth *tanquam uno flatu.* See lib. 2. fol. 54. in Sir Hugh Cholmleys case.

(7) *In any of the kings courts of record at Westminster.*] That is, in the kings bench, the chancery, the common pleas, and the exchequer. And though the words be, at Westminster, for that at the time of the making of this act, these courts were there; yet if these be adjourned into another place, the inrolment may be in any of these courts; for the inrolment is confined to the courts, wheresoever they be holden.

[674]

(8) Or else in the same county, &c. before the custos rotulorum, and two justices of peace, and the clerke of the peace, &c.

(9) *Custos rot.*] This officer is a justice of peace, and is of the gift of the lord chancellor, or lord keeper, and he may exercise his office by deputy. He hath the keeping of all bargaines and sales by deed indented and inrolled, and of all the records and rolls of the sessions of peace, * and of the commission of peace it selfe, and thereof he taketh the name of his office to put him in mind of his duty. He hath the gift of the clerkship of the peace, to exercise by

37 H. 8. cap. 1. 3 E. 6. cap. 1.

* 9 E. 4. 2. 10 H. 7. 7.

by himselfe or his deputy, but he continueth no longer in his place, then the custos rotulorum doth.

Dyer, 5 El. 218. Pasch' 4 El. rot. 812. adjudge sur demurrer, Pophams case. Lib. int' Coke fol. 596. Lib. 5. fo. 1. b. Claytons case.

(10) *The same inrolment to be had within six moneths next after the date of the same writing indented.*] The six moneths shall be accounted after the computation of 28 dayes to the moneth. After the date, and after the day of the date upon this act is all one; so as the date it selfe is taken exclusive. And yet in the report of justice Dalison it is said, that it was holden *anno* 4 Eliz. that if it be inrolled the same day it beares date, it is sufficient; but the safer way is to inroll it after the day of the date. And yet where it hath a date, and is delivered after, it shall take effect to passe from the bargainor from the delivery; for then it became his deed, and not from the date: but the deed must be inrolled within six moneths after the date.

Every deed shall be intended to be delivered on the same day that it beares date, unlesse the contrary be proved. And it is the best course (according to the intendment of law) to deliver it the same day that it beares date. But if the deed indented hath no date, then the day of the delivery is the day of the date of that deed, and may be inrolled within six moneths after the delivery. And when the deed is inrolled within the six moneths, then it passeth from the delivery of the deed. And albeit after the delivery and acknowledgement, either the bargainor or the bargainee dye before inrolment, yet the land passeth by this act; for the words thereof be: No mannors, lands, tenements, or hereditaments shall passe of any estate of inheritance or freehold, * except the deed be inrolled. So as by the common law and the statute of 27 Hen. 8. of uses, it should have passed. And by the words of this statute, when the deed is inrolled, it passeth *ab initio*.

Lib. 5. fol. 1. b. Claytons case, ubi sup. adjudge Trin' 21 Eliz. in communi banco 6 E. 6. faits inrol Br. 9. per les justices.

* Nota, except is more then unlesse.

Trin' 42 Eliz. rot. 1037. in communi banco in repl.

Between Andrew Mallery plaintife, and Jennings and others defendants, the case was this: one Sewster was seised of certaine lands in fee, and knowledged a recognizance to Turner, whose executrix brought a *scire fac'* upon the recognizance bearing date the 9 day of November, *an.* 41 Eliz. against Sewster, and alledged him to be seised of the said lands *in dominico suo, ut de feodo*, the day of the *scire fac'* brought, which was traversed by the other party. And the truth of the case, being by long pleading disclosed to the court, was this: Sewster 7. *die Novemb.* before the recognizance knowledged, by deed indented for money, had bargained and sold the said land to another, and the deed was inrolled 20 Nov. following. The question was, whether Sewster was upon the whole matter seised in fee the 9 day of November, the deed being not inrolled untill the twentieth of the same November. And it was adjudged *una voce*, that Sewster was not seised in fee of the land the 9 day of November, for that when the deed was inrolled, the bargainee was in judgement of law seised of that land, from the delivery of the deed. And it was resolved, that neither the death

[675]

of the bargainor, nor of the bargainee before inrolment, shall hinder the passing of the estate. And that a release of a stranger to the bargainee before inrolment is good. So as it hold not by relation between the parties by fiction of law; but in point of state as well to them as to strangers also. And that a recovery suffered against the bargainee before inrolment (the deed indented being after within the six moneths inrolled) is good, for that the bargainee was tenant of the freehold in judgement of law at the time

of

of the recovery. And *non refert*, when the deed indented is knowledged, so it be inrolled within the six moneths. And all this was afterwards affirmed for good law by the court of common pleas Trin' 3 Jac. *regis*, upon a speciall verdict given in an *ejectione firmæ* betweene Lellingham plaintife of the demise of Thomas Fitzherbert esquire, and Alsop defendant: and further, it was there resolved, that if the bargainee of land after the bargaine and sale, and before the inrolment doth bargaine and sell the same by deed indented and inrolled to another; and after the first deed is inrolled within the six moneths, the bargaine and sale by the bargainee is good: but there in the principall case, in respect of the speciall manner of the penning of the meane bargaine and sale, the court being divided, *viz.* three judges against two, judgement was given against it. Trin. 3. Jac. in communi banco in eject. firmæ between Lellingham plaintife, and Alsop defendant.

The day of the moneth, and the yeare of our Lord and Saviour Christ, and the yeare of the kings raigne are the usuall dates of deeds. And the day of the moneth by the nones, ides, or kalends is sufficient.

(11) *The custos rotulorum, or justices of the peace, and clerke, taking for the inrolment of every such writing, &c. two shillings, &c.*] A good president, when parliaments appoint new labours, &c. that they would also limit and set downe in certaine what fees shall be taken for the same, as here it is done.

(12) *The clerke of the peace shall sufficiently inroll in parchment, &c.*] Of this somewhat hath been said before.

(13) *Shall deliver them to the custos rotolorum.*] For (as hath been said) he is the keeper of the records and rolls of the sessions of the peace of that county.

Provided alwaies that this act, nor any thing therein contained, extend not to any mannor, lands, tenements, or hereditaments, lying or being within any citie, borough, or towne corporate within this realme, wherein the maiors, recorders, chamberlaines, bailifes, or other officer or officers have authority, or have lawfully used to inroll any evidences (14), deeds, or other writings within their precinct or limits: any thing in this act contained to the contrary notwithstanding.

(14) *In any citie, borough, or towne corporate, wherein the maiors, &c. have authority to inroll evidences, &c.*] Resolved by the opinion of the justices of both benches, that a bargaine and sale for valuable consideration of houses, or lands in London, &c. by word onely is sufficient to passe the same; for that houses and lands in any city, &c. are exempted out of this act: and at the common law such a bargaine and sale by word only raised an use. And the statute of 27 H. 8. cap. 10. doth transferre the use into possession. 6 El. Dyer, 229. in Chilberns case.

When the makers of this act had appropriated the inrolment of all indentures of bargaine and sale to the kings foure courts aforesaid, it was necessary to make a provision for cities, &c. which had authority to inroll, and that there such bargaines and sales should be inrolled. *Sed desunt verba;* for by the words, the mannors, lands, [676]

 tenements,

tenements, and hereditaments are exempted out of the said act, without any provision for inrolment within those cities, &c.

Hill. 20 E. 1. in banco Rot. 100. Somerset. If a deed be shewed in court, or in the custody of the court, and by mischance the seale is broken off, the court shall inroll the deed in court for the availe of the party.

---

[677]

An Exposition upon the Statute of 32 H. 8. Cap. 5. Of Executions.

WHEREAS before this time divers and sundry persons have sued executions, as well upon judgements for them given of their debts or damages, as upon such statutes merchants, statutes of the staple, or recognizances, as have been to them before made, recognized, and knowledged; and thereupon such lands, tenements, and other hereditaments, as were lyable to the same execution, have been by reasonable extent to them delivered in execution for the satisfaction of their said debts and damages, according to the lawes of this realme. Neverthelesse, it hath been oftentimes seen, that such lands, tenements, and hereditaments so delivered, and had in execution, have been recovered, or lawfully devested, taken away or evicted from the possession of the said recoverers, obligees or recognizees, their executors or assignes, before such time as they have been fully satisfied and payed of their debts and damages, without any manner fraud, deceit, covin, collusion, or other default in the said recoverers, obligees, or recognisees, their executors and assignes, by reason whereof the said recoverers, obligees and recognisees have been thereby set cleerly without remedy, by any maner suit of the law, to recover or come by any such part or parcell of their said debts and damages as was behind, and not by them levied or received, before such time as the said lands, tenements, and other hereditaments so by them had in execution, were recovered, lawfully devested, taken or evicted out of and from their possessions, as is aforesaid, to their great hurt and losse, and much seeming to be against equall justice and good conscience.

For reformation whereof, be it enacted by authority of this present parliament, that if hereafter any such lands (2), tenements, or hereditaments, as be, or shall be had and delivered (3) to any person or persons in execution (1), as is aforesaid, upon any just and lawfull title, matter, condition, or cause (4) wherewithall the said lands, tenements, and hereditaments were lyable, tied, and bound, at such time as they were delivered and taken into execution, shall happen to be recovered, lawfully devested, taken, or evicted (5) out of, and from the possession of any such person

person and persons as now have and hold, or hereafter ſhall have and hold the ſame in execution, as is aforeſaid, without any fraud, deceit, covin, colluſion, or other default of the ſaid tenant or tenants by execution, before ſuch time as the ſaid tenants by execution their executors or aſſignes (6) ſhall have fully and wholly levied or received the ſaid whole debt (7) and damages, for the which the ſaid lands, tenements, and other hereditaments were delivered (8) and taken in execution, as is aforeſaid: then every ſuch recoverer, obligee, and recognizee ſhall and may have and purſue a writ of ſcire facias out of the ſame court (9), from whence the ſaid former writ of execution did proceed againſt ſuch perſon or perſons, as the ſaid writ of execution was firſt purſued, [678] their heires, executors, or aſſignes of ſuch lands, tenements, or hereditaments, as were or been then liable or charged to the ſaid execution, retornable into the ſame court at a certaine day, being full forty dayes after the date of the ſame writ.

At which day if the defendant, being lawfully warned, make default, or appeare and doe not ſhew and plead a ſufficient matter or cauſe, other then the acceptance of the ſaid lands, tenements, and hereditaments, by the ſaid former writ of execution, to barre, avoid, or diſcharge the ſaid ſuit for the reſidue of the ſaid debt and damages remaining unlevied, or unreceived by the ſaid former execution: then the lord chancellor, or other ſuch juſtice or juſtices, before whom ſuch writ of ſcire facias ſhall be retornable, ſhall make eftſoones a new writ or writs out of the ſaid former record of judgement, ſtatute merchant, ſtatute ſtaple, or recognizance of like nature and effect, as the ſaid former writ of execution was, for the levying of the reſidue of all ſuch debt and damage, as then ſhall appeare to be unlevied, unſatisfied, or unpayed of the whole ſumme or ſummes in the ſaid former writ of execution contained: any law, cuſtome, or other thing to the contrary hereof, heretofore uſed, in any wiſe notwithſtanding.

(1) That if hereafter any ſuch lands, tenements, or hereditaments, as be or ſhall be had and delivered to any perſon in execution, &c.

See before the ſtatute of W. 2. cap. 18. and the expoſition upon the ſame.

(2) *Such lands.*] This hath relation to the preamble, where there are rehearſed foure kinds of executions of thoſe lands, &c. Firſt, upon judgements: 2. upon ſtatutes merchant: 3. ſtatutes of the ſtaple: 4. recognizances. Theſe recognizances bee of two ſorts; one, uſuall recognizances taken in any of the kings courts of record at Weſtminſter: another, in nature of a ſtatute ſtaple, by the ſtatute of 23 H. 8. cap. 6. This conuſee of the ſtatute ſtaple hereafter in this ſtatute is called obligee, becauſe in them both the ſeale of the party is put, and the [a] tenant by *elegit* upon judgements and recognizances ſhall hold the land, &c. untill he be anſwered his debt without miſes, coſts, &c. But [b] tenant by ſtatute merchant, [c] tenant by ſtatute ſtaple, or by recognizance [d] in nature of a ſtatute ſtaple ſhall hold the land, &c. untill his debt be paid together with miſes; coſts, &c. *Vid.* Regiſt. 151, 152. 289. F.N.B. 131. Flet. lib. 2. cap. 57. lib. intr' Co. 236. Raſt' pl. 542. Dyer 2 Eliz.

To what executions this act extendeth unto.

[a] By the ſtat. of W. 2. cap. 8. for Judgements, and cap. 45. for recognizances.

[b] By the ſtat. of Acton Burnel, 11 E. 1. & 13 E. 1. de mercat. 5 H. 4. cap. 12.

[c] By the ſtat. of 27 E. 3 cap. 9. & 22.

[d] By the ſtat of 23 H. 8. cap. 6.

2 Eliz. 180. b. 37 Hen. 6. 6. 36 H. 6. 2. 2 R. 3. 8. 17. 15 H. 7. 40 E. 3. 28.

(3) *So had and delivered.*] Had, is by *elegit* upon judgements or recognizances, to have the moity in execution.

Delivered, is by *liberate* upon the other three of the whole land, &c. of the conusor; but after the extent in those three cases (of the statutes, or recognizances in nature of a statute) retorned, the conusee may enter without any delivery by the sherife by force of the *liberate*: and he that so entreth without any delivery is within the aide and benefit of this act, which speaketh of delivery.

Lib. 4. fol. 67. Fulwoods case.

(4) *Upon any just and lawfull title, matter, condition or cause.*] That is, upon some former just and lawfull title, &c. before the judgements, statutes, or recognizances.

Lib. 4. fol. 66. Fulwoods case.

(5) *Shall happen to be recovered, devested, taken or evicted.*] By the context of this law, the whole land, &c. had in execution, and the whole interest of the land in execution must be recovered, devested, or evicted for the reasons and causes there expressed.

[679]

Hill. 11 E. 3. coram rege, rot. 93. Norff.

Execution of a recognizance by *elegit* of lands, &c. of Thomas Camoys was had by two merchants; and afterwards by a former statute the same lands were out of the hands of the said merchants delivered to the former conusee, whereupon the two merchants desired to have execution of other lands of the said Thomas Camoys, *et conceditur*.

A man maketh a lease for yeares, rendring a rent, the lessor ousteth the lessee, and bindeth himselfe in a statute, the land is extended, and delivered to the conusee, the lessee re-enters, this is no eviction within this statute: for it appeareth by the preamble, that the conusee must be cleerly without remedy, &c. but here the conusee shall have the rent reserved, and the reversion.

So was it holden Pasch' 12 El. in communi banco.

(6) *Before such time, as the said tenants by execution their executors or assignes,* &c.] Here are administrators, and so through the whole act understood, because they are in equall mischiefe. And likewise and for the same reason, albeit assignees be named in this branch, yet are they implyed throughout this act in branches necessary, where they are not named.

Vid. 46. lib. ass. tit. scire fac' 134.

The assignee of parcell is not within this act, as appeareth by that which hath been said; but if there be severall assignees, and the land is evicted from them all, they are within the letter and remedy of this act, because the whole is evicted from them, and they may have a re-extent for the whole debt, according to the words and meaning of this act.

See the stat. de Mercat. 13 E. 1. Soient liuers al merchant touts les biens del dettor, et touts les terres per reasonable extent a tener jesque a tant que le dett serr' levie plenment.

Which case in 46. lib. ass. because it hath been often mistaken, and mis-applyed by many, we will truly put the same. A. seised of Blacke acre, and White acre in fee, acknowledgeth a statute merchant to J. and infeoffeth B. of White acre, J. sueth execution of Black acre out of the possession of A. the conusor, and of White acre out of the possession of B. A. conveyeth Blacke acre to C. in fee, J. tenant by statute merchant assigneth his interest to D. C. the assignee of A. sueth a *scire fac'* against D. assignee of J. and tendreth the mony that is behind. D. the defendant pleadeth to the writ, for

Notwithstanding by good construction the conusor shall have a scire fac' upon tender of the debt, with mises and costages; for the land was delivered in nature of a gage, though 17 E. 3. 43. b. and 18 E. 3. 11. seeme to the contrary, but in 21 E. 3. tit. scire facias 109. & 47 E. 3. 11. a scire facias was granted. 32 E. 3. scire fac' 101. the assignee of the conusor shall have the scire fac' 6 E. 3. 53. acc'.

that

that C. tenant of the freehold of White acre, whereof execution was also sued of record, is not named in the writ, to whom this suit was as well given, as to the plaintife, judgement of the writ, *et non allocatur*; whereby it appeareth by the rule of the court, that any one feoffee may have a *scire fac'*, and tender * the whole money to the tenant by statute merchant, or to his assignee. Another exception was taken to the writ, for that every *scire fac'* ought to be warranted or grounded upon a record, and this *scire fac'* is not grounded upon the record, but maintained upon a suggestion of tendring of the money, in which case he ought to have a *venire fac'*, and not this writ of *scire fac'*, *et non allocatur*; whereby it appeareth, that partly upon a record, and partly upon a suggestion (no *scire facias* being granted without some suggestion) the *scire fac'* upon this certainty of the tender was maintainable. Lastly, it was excepted against the writ, that it appeared to the court, that the *scire fac'* was brought by the assignee of Blacke acre, against the assignee of tenant by statute merchant, so as each of them, as well of the one part as of the other, plaintife and defendant, were strangers to the record, *et non allocatur*, for that it had been often seen, that this writ did lye as well between strangers, as privies, and the writ of *venire fac'* also to make the conusee, &c. to account, &c. Then doth Belknap of counsell with the defendant put a case upon the statute of Gloc. cap. 3. It is given by statute (saith hee) that if the father alien the right of the mother, that the son and heire of the mother shall not be barred, if he hath not assets by discent, &c. and other lands may after descend to him from his father, that the alienee of the father shall have recovery against him by *scire facias*: but if lands descend to him afterwards from his father, and he alieneth the lands, which he recovered as heire to his mother, the alienee of the father shall not have a *scire fac'* against the alienee of the heire; which opinion is grounded upon these words in the statute, *Donques avera le tenant*, (*id est*, the alienee of the father) *recovery vers luy* (*id est*, the son and heire of the mother) *de la seisin son mere, &c.* And therefore Belknap concludeth, that no *scire fac'* lyeth against the alienee in that case, no more here. Whereunto Thorp chiefe justice answereth, although it be so in the case put by Belknap, it is given by the statute, &c. Wherefore (saith Thorp) will you receive the mony, or no? Belknap, Yes, if he will tender the mises and costages. Kirton, The mises and costages shall be taxed by the court. Thorp, They shall not: for wee cannot know them: and after he tendred a demy marke for mises and costages, and the other said they were not sufficient, and the court held them sufficient. Thorp demanded, if he would receive the money, or no, for mises and costages, as he tendred, otherwise we will (saith he) re-baile to the party his mony. And afterwards he received the same, and the plaintife had execution.

* Nota, hereby the land of the other feoffee shal be discharged, when the whole debt is paid. 2 R. 3. 17. 15 H. 7. 15.

Vi. 17 E. 3. 43. b. 21 E. 3. scire fac' 109. 47 E. 3. 11.

Gloc. 6 E. 1. ca. 3.

See the stat. de Mercat. 13 E. 1. ubi sup.

[680]

These things are necessary to be knowne, for the better understanding of this statute of 32 H. 8.

(7) *Shall have fully and wholly levied or received the said whole debt.*] Although the conusee have received the whole debt by execution upon the statute merchant, statute staple, or recognizance in the nature of a statute staple, yet cannot the conusor enter; for he must hold the land untill he be satisfied, not onely of his debt, but of his costs, damages, labours, and expences: otherwise, it is in case of *elegit*, as hath been said, for there after the debt satisfied, the conusor may enter: for tenant by *elegit* holdeth the land but untill the debt be satisfied.

Vid. lib. 4. fo. 67. in Fulwoods case. 2 R. 3. 8. 17. 15 H. 7. 47 E. 3. fol 11, 12. 44 E. 3. 14, 16.

(8) *For which the ſaid lands were delivered,* &c.] Theſe words are not to be taken literally but according to the meaning of the makers of this law, and ever ſuch conſtruction is to be made, as the party grieved, and in equall miſchiefe may be relieved: and therefore if a ſeigniory conſiſting of fealty and rent be delivered in execution, and after the rent become ſecke by ſurpluſage, and after is evicted, he ſhall have the remedy of this ſtatute: but if a villaine be delivered in execution, and the villaine purchaſe land in fee, and the tenant by execution enter into the perquiſite of the villaine, and after it is evicted, he ſhall have no remedy by this ſtatute, the cauſe is apparent.

(9) *Then every ſuch recoverer, obligee, and recogniſee ſhall and may have a writ of ſcire fac' out of the ſame court.*] If judgement and execution be awarded in the court of common pleas, and in a writ of error the judgement is affirmed in the kings bench, the tenant by execution may upon eviction have a *ſcire fac'* out of the kings bench; for it is the ſame court in equall miſchiefe to the party grieved.

---

[681]

An Expoſition upon the latter Part of the Statute of 32 H. 8. Cap. 28. concerning Diſcontinuances, &c.

AND moreover, for certaine conſiderations, be it enacted, by authority aforeſaid that no fine, feoffment, or other act or acts hereafter to be made, ſuffred, or done by the huſband onely, of any mannors lands, tenements, or hereditaments, being the inheritance or freehold of his wife, during the coverture betweeen them, ſhall in any wiſe be, or make any diſcontinuance thereof, or be prejudiciall or hurtfull to the ſaid wife, or to her heires, or to ſuch as ſhall have right, title, or intereſt to the ſame, by the death of ſuch wife or wives. But that the ſame wife or her heires, and ſuch other to whom ſuch right ſhall appertaine, after her deceaſe, ſhall and may then lawfully enter into all ſuch mannors, lands, tenements, and hereditaments, according to their rights and titles therein: any ſuch fine, feoffment, or other act to the contrary notwithſtanding: fines levied by the huſband and wife (whereunto the ſaid wife is party and privy) onely except.

See lib. 8. fol. 71, 72. &c, Grenelies caſe, Dier, 4 & 5 Ph. & Mar. 162. 2 El'. 191. b. Hawtries caſe. 21 El. 363. b.

Mich. 4 & 5 El. in Scaccario.

We will adde hereunto a notable and a leading caſe upon this part of the act vulgarly and commonly cited by the name of Beaumonts caſe; the truth of which was, that Humfrey Foſter ſeaſed in fee of the ſite of the monaſterie of *Gracedieu int' alia,* gave them to John Beaumont eſquire, and Eliz. his wife, and to the heires of their two bodies begotten, the remainder in fee to the ſaid Jo. Beaumont. *An.* 6 E. 6. John Beaumont levied a fine thereof, with proclamation *come ceo,* &c. to king Ed. 6. his heires and ſucceſſours:

Juſtice Dalyſon 5 Eliz.

king Ed. 6. *anno regni ſui* 7. granted the ſaid ſite &c. by his letters patents to Francis earle of Huntingdon and his heires in fee farme; after-

afterwards John Beaumont died, after whose death, and within five yeares Eliz. entred, inclaiming her estate; the fee farme rent was behind: Henry earle of Huntingdon, sonne and heire of Francis, having the inheritance of Gracedieu &c. was called into the exchequer for the arrerages of the said fee farme, where all the said case being disclosed in pleading, at the last upon open argument, great deliberation and conference, five points were resolved and adjudged:

First, albeit the king is not named in the act, yet he is bound by the act, because it is made to suppresse a wrong, and to give her &c. that right had a more speedy remedy, *viz.* by entry, where by the common law, she &c. was driven to a reall action, and every [a] discontinuance worketh a wrong, and the king being Gods lieutenant * cannot doe wrong, and therefore that the entry of Eliz. was lawfull, &c.

Secondly albeit the words of this act be [being the inheritance or freehold of the wife:] and in this case the lands were as wel the freehold and inheritance of the husband as of the wife, yet for that it was a beneficiall law to suppresse a wrong, and to give the party wronged a speedy remedy, and that it was in equall mischief, it was adjudged to be within this statute: and this point hath been commonly cited in arguments in Westminster-hall, and at moots, &c. by the name of Beaumonts case.

[a] Thirdly, that the fine with proclamations levied by the husband only, was a barre by the statute of 4 H. 7. because the issue in taile must claime as heire to both of them.

Fourthly, that the state of the wife was changed to an estate for life dispunishable of waste, for that the issue in taile by the fine was disabled to inherit; as if the donees had been divorced *causa consanguinitatis, &c.* whereby the issue was disabled to inherit, the donees should have had but an estate for life: but in that case they shall be punishable for waste, because the estate in taile was never perfect, but defeasible by divorce *ab initio*.

Fifthly, that when Elis. entred upon earle Henry into Gracedieu, &c. and defeated the fee farme during her estate, yet the earle having an estate of inheritance remaining in him, the fee farme rent, which was reserved presently by the kings prerogative, was leviable upon his other lands during the estate of Elisabeth; for now upon the matter it is as much in the kings case, as if Elisabeth, being in seison of her estate, the king had granted the inheritance after her estate ended to the earle and his heires, reserving the rent presently: but queen Elisabeth, being acquainted with the equity of the case, was pleased by letters patents under the great seale, which we have seen, to exonerate earle Henry of the arrerages, and of the fee farme it selfe, during the continuance of the estate of the said Elis. that had evicted the land from him: which case we have reported the more at large, for that in the collections of my lord Dyer, written with his own hand, which we have seen, reporteth this case, and maketh a question in these words: *si lentre la feme soit congeable per lestatute, co que le roy nest ly per lestatute,* which was justly omitted out of the print, for that the judgement, as is aforesaid, was given against that private opinion. And it hath been very many times since adjudged in the exchequer, in pleading for the discharge of the debts of Henry earle of Huntingdon, that the entry of the said Elis. was lawfull, divers whereof we have seen.

[a] Vi. li. 11. fo. 72. a. Magd. Colledge case. Pl. com. 246. Seignior Berklyes case acc'.

* 13 E. 4. 8. lib. 1. fol. 44. Alten Woods case acc'

[a] Just. Dalyson an. 5 El. Dyer, 18 El. 351. acc'. Dier 16 El. 362. simil. lib. 9. fol. 139. Beaumonts case.

5 H. 7. 32. by Brian.

[682]

Lib. 9. fol. 139. ubi supra.

7 H. 4. 16. lib. 9. fol. 139. ubi sup.

Otherwise it is in the case of a common person, for he shall be exonerated of the rent during the state evicted, because the rent was reserved out of the whole estate.

An

An Expoſition upon the Statute of 32 H. 8. cap. 38. concerning what Marriages be lawfull, and what not.

SEE the firſt part of the Inſtitutes, ſect. 380. fol. 235. a. Parſons caſe upon this act of 32 H. 8.

For the better underſtanding whereof, and of this ſtatute, the Leviticall degrees are neceſſary to be ſet downe in certaine.

It is to be underſtood, that by the 18 chapter of Leviticus, not onely degrees of kinred and conſanguinity, but degrees of affinity and alliance doe let matrimonie, which may beſt be illuſtrated and expreſſed in this manner:

See theſe degrees truly ſet down in the ſtat. of 25 H. 8. cap. 22. and 28 H. 8. cap. 7.

Of the Mans part.

Degrees of Kinred and Conſanguinity prohibited.			Degrees of Affinity or Alliance prohibited.		
His fathers ſiſter.	His mother.	His mothers ſiſter.	His uncles wife.	His fathers wife.	His fathers wives daughter.
His ſiſter.	*A man may not marry*		His brothers wife.	*A man may not marry*	His wives ſiſter.
	His daughter.			His ſons wife, or his wives daughter.	
	The daughter of his ſon, or daughter.			The daughter of his wives ſon, or daughter.	

Of the Womans part.

Her fathers brother.	Her father.	Her mothers brother.	Her aunts huſband.	Her mothers huſband.	
Her brother	*A woman may not marry*		Her ſiſters huſband.	*A woman may not marry*	Her huſbands brother.
	Her ſon.			Her daughters huſband.	
	The ſon of her ſon, or daughter.			The ſon of her huſbands ſon, or daughter.	

These

These be the Leviticall degrees, which extend as well to the woman as to the man. And herein note, that albeit the marriage of the nephew *cum amita et matertera* is forbidden by the said 18 chapter of Leviticus, and by expresse words the marriage of the uncle with the niece is not thereby prohibited, yet is the same prohibited, *quia eandem habent rationem propinquitatis cum eis qui nominatim prohibentur, et sic de similibus.* [684]

By the preamble of this statute it appeareth, "That by other "prohibitions then Gods law admitted for their lucre by that "court invented, the dispensation whereof they always reserved "to themselves (where there are expressed these examples:) "First, as in kinred and affinity between [a] cousins germans, and "so to the fourth degree. Secondly, [b] carnall knowledge of any "of the same kin or affinity before in such outward degrees." But now by this act all persons are declared to be lawfull to contract matrimony, that be not prohibited by Gods law to marry, and that no reservation or prohibition (Gods law excepted) shall trouble or impeach any marriage without the Leviticall degrees. So as without question, the son of the father, by another wife, and the daughter of the mother, by another husband, and *è converso*, may marry. And now at this day men need not to be at that charge and suit that Roger Donington was, who for that he had committed fornication before marriage, with one that was of kin to his wife in the fourth degree, was driven to sue for a ligitimation of his marriage.

[a] 18 E. 4. 28, 29. 11 H. 4. 76.
[b] 24 H. 8. bastard Br. 44. Vid. 28 H. 8. cap. 7. Pasch. 30 E. 1. coram rege, Chadworths case in the 1 part Instit. ubi supra.

See the statute of 1 and 2 Phil. and Mar. cap. 8. a divorce *propter impedimentum publicæ honestatis et justitiæ.*

Neither after this statute can the husband be afraid to lose his wife, or the wife her husband, nor the heire of them to be bastarded, for that the husband before marriage had been godfather either at baptisme, or confirmation to the cousin of his wife, or that she had been godmother before the marriage to the cousin of her husband, for the divorces *causa* * *compaternitatis et commaternitatis* (which in the act of 1 and 2 Phil. and Mar. is called *cognatio spiritualis*) are by this act taken away; and the divorce *causa professionis* also, and so is the devorce *causa cognationis legalis*, that is to say, *jure adoptionis, et sic de similibus.*

Vid. Conc. Trid. sess. 24. cap. 2. de reform. Bract. li. 4. 298. b. an. 39 E. 3. fol. 31, 32. in assise. Vid. 10 E. 3. 34, 35. * Bract. ubi sup. 1 & 2 Phil. & M. ca. 8. 47 E. 3. fol. 27. 21 H. 7.

Alice de Stircheley took to husband William de Chaddeworth, and after, at her suit, was divorced from him, and the cause of the divorce is expressed in the record. *Et fuit causa divortii eò quòd dictus Willielmus de Chaddeworth carnaliter cognoverat quandam filiam dictæ Aliciæ Stircheley, antequam ipsam desponsavit.*

Pasch. 32 E. 1. coram rege, rot. 83. Nott.

By the Leviticall degrees it is prohibited, that a man shall not uncover the nakednesse of his wife, and of her daughter, and so it is of the rest of the degrees there prohibited.

Levit. cap. 18. ver. 17.

By this act of 32 H. 8. the divorce *causa præcontractus* was taken away, where the marriage was consummate by carnall copulation, &c. but that is repealed, and the divorce allowed by the statute of 2 E. 6. cap. 23. and 1 El. cap. 1.

The residue of the act of 32 H. 8. was repealed by 1 and 2 Phil. and Mar. cap. 8. and revived 1 Elis. cap. 1.

Lib. 4. fol. 29. a. Charles Buntings case, lib. 6. fol. 66. Bracton, lib. 4. fol. 298. b.

But our chiefe aime and endeavour being to set downe in all the parts of the Institutes, how the law at this day standeth, notwithstanding the change and alteration of many statutes, and the repeales of divers, and after repeales of those repeales, and the reviving of statutes repealed, &c. and having mentioned the divorce

causa

causa professionis, it shall be necessary in this place to declare what the law is at this day concerning the marriage of ecclesiasticall persons. And to that end we will report a case resolved, which concerneth not onely the point in question, but another matter of great consequence, which, because the rule and discussing of both points stand in effect upon the same ground of reason, we will relate the whole case:

At the session of parliament holden *anno* 4 *regis Jacobi*, upon a branch of an act made at the first session in the first yeare of his majesties reigne, for continuance and reviving of divers statutes, it was enacted, That an act made in the first yeare of queen Mary, stat. 2. cap. 2. entituled, An act for the repeale of certaine statutes made in the time of king Edw. 6. should stand repealed and void, two doubts were moved: the first concerning the bishops, the
[685] second touching the lawfulnesse of ecclesiasticall persons marriages; the first was divided into two questions: the one, Whether any bishop, made especially since the first day of that first session of parliament, were lawfull or no; the other, Whether the proceedings in the bishops, or other ecclesiasticall courts, being made under the name, stile and seale of the bishops, were warranted by law. And the reason and cause of these two doubts was this: By the statute of *anno* 1 Ed. 6. cap. 2. it was enacted, That bishops should not be elective, as before that time they had been, but donative by the kings letters patents. Secondly, by the said act it is provided, That all summons, citations, and processe in ecclesiasticall courts should be made in the name and stile of the king, and that their processe should be sealed with a seale of the kings armes, &c. And it was strongly urged and enforced, that this act of 1 Ed. 6. was now in force, and consequently, all bishops made (at the least since it became of force) by election, &c. and not by donation, according to the said act of 1 Edw. 6. are unlawfull, and all their processe, proceedings, being in their owne names, stiles and seales (where by the said act they ought to have been in the kings name, and under the kings seale) were all unlawfull, and void. And to prove, that the said act of *anno* 1 Edw. 6. was now in force, they alledged, that this act of 1 Edw. 6. was repealed by the said act of 1 Mar. above mentioned, which act of repeale, being repealed by the said branch of *primo regis Jacobi*, consequently the said act of 1 Edw. 6. was thereby revived: for when an act of repeal is repealed, the first act that was repealed is revived, *remoto impedimento revivifcit statutum*, and herewith agreeth the booke case in 15 Ed. 3. tit' petition, placit' 2. And this is true, and cannot be denied.

The king having understanding hereof, and being informed of the consequents thereof, being matters tending not onely to the infinite prejudice of his subjects in cases of great importance (especially, if any diocesse had no lawfull bishop or ordinary) but to the scandall and impeachment of his majesties justice not onely in those proceedings, but also in administration of justice in certaine cases in his courts of common law at Westminster, commanded his two chiefe justices to consider of the said objections, and to informe him of the true state thereof, that either the scruple conceived might be cleared and satisfied, or the inconvenience (if any were) timely provided for and prevented; who upon diligent consideration had of the said objection, agreed the law to be (as the said case was put) as it had been taken. But upon further

search

ſearch and conſideration had, other manifeſt and direct matters were found to ſatisfie and cleare the ſaid ſcruple and queſtion, which afterwards was agreed and reſolved accordingly by the chiefe baron and other judges then attending in the upper houſe of parliament. For the underſtanding whereof it is to be obſerved, that the ſaid act of 1 Edw. 6. was repealed by three ſeverall acts of parliament, viz. by the ſaid ſtatute of *anno* 1 Mar. in the whole. 2. By the act of 1 and 2 Phil. and Mar. cap. 8. by ſufficient words, as concerning the name, ſtile, and ſeale of their proceſſe, &c. And laſtly, by the ſtatute of 1 Eliſ. cap. 1. the whole act of 1 Edw. 6. is alſo repealed: for *leges poſteriores priores contrarias abrogant.* And as a man that is ſtrongly bounden with three cords or ligaments, albeit one or two of them be untied or cut aſunder, remaines bound, notwithſtanding by and with the ſecond or third, which remaine firme and untouched; ſo a ſtatute repealed by force of three ſeverall acts remaines repealed, ſo long as any of them remaine in force, albeit one or two of them be made void: and therefore although the act of 1 Mar. be repealed by 1 *regis Jacobi*, yet the other two acts remaining in force, the act of *anno primo* E. 6. remaine repealed.

First therefore, as to the name, ſtile, and ſeale, &c. in eccle- 1.
ſiaſticall courts, it is enacted by 1 and 2 Phil. and Mar. cap. 8. in theſe words:

"And the eccleſiaſticall juriſdiction of the archbiſhops, biſhops, "and ordinaries to be in the ſame ſtate for proceſſe of ſutes, "puniſhment of crimes, and execution of cenſures of the church, "with knowledge of cauſes belonging to the ſame, and as large "in thoſe points as the ſaid juriſdiction was in *anno* 20 Hen. 8."

By which clauſe, if the act of repeale of 1 Mar. (now repealed) [686]
had never been made, the act of 1 Ed. 6. as to the name, ſtile, and ſeale in eccleſiaſticall proceedings had been repealed by this latter act of 1 and 2 Phil. and Mar.

But it was objected, that the ſaid act of 1 and 2 Phil. and Mar. 2.
(which is the ſecond cord or ligament) is repealed by the act of 1 Eliſ. cap. 1. To this it was anſwered and reſolved, that this ſecond cord or ligament remains in force: for true it is, that the act of 1 Eliſ repeales the act of 1 and 2 Phil. and Mar. *ſecundum quid*, but not *ſimpliciter*; for the act of 1 Eliſ. doth repeale every branch and article of 1 and 2 Phil. and Mar. other then for ſuch branches as therein be excepted. And afterwards, by another branch of the ſaid act of 1 Eliſ. it is enacted, That all other lawes and ſtatutes repealed, and made void by the ſaid act of 1 and 2 Phil. and Mar. and not in that act ſpecially mentioned and revived, ſhould ſtand, remaine, and be repealed and void, as the ſame were before the making of that act. But the act of 1 Ed. 6. (as it hath been often ſaid) is ſufficiently repealed by the act of 1 and 2 Phil. and Mar. as to the name, ſtile, and ſeale, &c. and the act of 1 Ed. 6. is not ſpecially mentioned and revived by the act of 1 Eliſ. ſo the ſame remaine repealed by the act of 1 and 2 Phil. and Mar.

The third act which clearly repeales and adnulls the act of 1 E. 3.
6. as well for the making and conſtituting of biſhops, as for the name, ſtile and ſeale of proceſſe is the act of 1 Eliſ. cap. 1. for that act doth revive the act of 25 H. 8. cap. 20. and further enacteth, that the ſame ſhall ſtand in full force and effect to all

intents, conſtructions, and purpoſes. By which act of 25 H. 8. it is enacted as followeth:

" And that at every avoidance of any archbiſhoprick, or biſhop- " rick, the king, his heires and ſucceſſors may grant to the prior " and convent, or to the dean and chapter a licence under the " great ſeale, as of old time hath been accuſtomed to proceed to an " election of an archbiſhop or biſhop, with a letter miſſive, con- " taining the name of the perſon which they ſhall elect and chooſe, " &c." And according to this ſtatute revived by *anno* 1 Eliſ. all archbiſhops and biſhops at this day be made, and if they were made according to the act of 1 E. 6. they were unlawfull.

And further it is enacted by the ſaid act of 25 H. 8. " That " every perſon choſen, elected, inveſted, and conſecrated arch- " biſhop or biſhop, according to the forme and effect of this " act, &c. ſhall doe and execute in every thing and things " touching the ſame, as any archbiſhop or biſhop of this realme, " &c. might at any time heretofore doe."

Which latter branch doth extend to all proceſſe and proceedings in eccleſiaſticall courts, and that the ſame ſhall be in ſuch ſort, as the ſame were before the act of 25 H. 8. and before that act, the name, ſtile, and ſeale of their proceſſe, &c. were as now they be.

And the ſaid act of 1 Eliſ. reviving the act of 25 Hen. 8. doth impliedly repeale the act of 1 Ed. 6. which had repealed 25 H. 8. in both the ſaid points: for, as by repealing of a repeale, the firſt act is revived; ſo by reviving of an act repealed the act of repeale is made of no force.

As to the ſecond point, concerning the marriage of eccle- ſiaſticall perſons, it is to be obſerved, that the intention of the act of repeale of *anno* 1 *regis Jacobi*, was to repeale the ſtatutes of 2 Ed. 6. cap. 2. and 5 E. 6. cap. 12. concerning the marriage of eccleſiaſticall perſons, by which ſtat. of 5 E. 6. it is enacted, " That the ma- " trimony of all and every prieſt, and other eccleſiaſticall perſon, " ſhall be adjudged, deemed, and taken, for juſt, true, and lawfull " matrimony, to all intents, conſtructions, and purpoſes, and that " all children borne in any ſuch matrimony ſhall be deemed, and " judged to all intents and purpoſes to be borne in lawfull ma- " trimony, and legitimate, and hereditable to lands, tenements, " and hereditaments, and that there ſhall be tenant by the cur- " teſie, and tenant in dower, &c." But the act of 1 Mar. repeal- ing the ſaid ſtatutes of 1 E. 6. concerning biſhops, as of 2 E. 6. cap. 21. and of 5 E. 6. concerning marriages of eccleſiaſticall perſons, and the ſtatute of 1 *regis Jacobi* repealing generally the ſtatute of 1 Mar. it followeth, that if no other ſtatute had repealed the ſaid act of 1 E. 6. concerning biſhops, but the ſaid act of 1
[687] Mar. then all the ſaid three ſtatutes, and 5 E. 6. had remained in force, when the act of 1 Mar. was repealed; but other acts repealing 1 Edw. 6. as before hath appeared, and no other act re- pealing the acts of 2 and 5 E. 6. concerning marriages, it fol- loweth, that by the repeale of the ſaid act of 1 Mar. the acts of 2 and 5 E. 6. are of force, and that of 1 E. 6. remaine repealed, and is not for the cauſes aboveſaid revived by the ſtatute of 1 *regis Jacobi*.

And it is to be obſerved, that it appeareth in our bookes, that if a deacon or ſecular prieſt had taken wife, the marriage was not

void,

void, but voidable, *causa professionis*, and if either party had died before divorce, their issue had been legitimate, and should have inherited, for that deacons and priests within England were not votaries, that is, had not vowed chastity. But if a monk or a nun had married before the statutes of 32 H. 8. cap. 38. and of 2 E. 6. cap. 21. and this act of 5 E. 6. the marriage had been (as it was then holden) meerly void, for that they had taken a vow of chastity, as it appeareth by our bookes in 5 E. 2. tit' non habilit' 26 19 H. 7. tit' bastard' 33. 21 H. 7. 39. b. for avoiding of which scruple, the said acts of 32 H. 8. 2 E. 6. and 5 E. 6. were made.

See the stat. of 31 H. 8. cap. 6.

There be also other divorces which declare the marriage to be void, as a divorce *causa* [*] *frigiditatis*, where the party hath *perpetuam impotentiam generationis, &c.* And [b] *causa metus, sive duritiæ*, also [c] *causa impubertatis:* these marriages are said to be prohibited by Gods law, otherwise the statute of 32 H. 8. would extend unto them.

Gen. 2. ver. 24. Mat. 19. 5. Ephes. 5. 31. 1 Corin. 7. 2. &c. Mar. 10. 7, 8.

[*] Dyer 2 Elis. 118. b. lib. 5. fol. 98. Buries case. [b] 11 H. 4. 14. rot. parl. 17 H. 6. nu. 15. Isabel Lady Butlers case. [c] 39 E. 3. 32, 33.

An Exposition upon the Statute of 2 E. 6. Cap. 8. Of Offices.

[688]

WHERE many and divers persons holding, or that have holden lands, tenements, or hereditaments, some for terme of yeares, and some by copy of court roll, have been expulsed, and put out of their termes and holds, by reason of inquisitions, or offices founden before eschetours, commissioners, and other, containing tenures of the king in capite, intitling the king to the wardship or custody of such lands or tenements; and sometime intitling the king to the same, upon attainders of treason, felony, or otherwise, by reason that such leases for terme of yeares, or interest by copie of court roll (1) of such persons, have not been found in such inquisitions or offices: after which expulsion or putting out, the said persons have been without remedy, for the obtaining of the said fermes, and holds, during the kings possession therein, and can have no traverse, monstrance de droit, nor other remedy for the same, because their said interest is but a chattell in the law, or customary hold, and no estate of freehold. And also, where any person or persons hath any rent, common, office, fee, or other profit apprender of any estate of freehold, or for yeares, or otherwise out of such lands or tenements, specified in such offices or inquisitions, the said rent, common, office, fee, or profit apprender, not found in the same office or offices, such persons are in like manner without remedy to obtaine, or have the said rent, common, office, fee, or profit

apprender

apprender by any traverſe, or other ſpeedy meane, without great and exceſſe charges, during the kings intereſt therein, by force of ſuch inquiſition or office.

Where and in what caſes before the ſtatutes of 34 E. 3. cap. 14. and 36 Ed. 3. cap. 13. and 8 H. 6 cap. 19. the party grieved by any office might have had his *traverſe*, or *monſtrans de droit* by the common law, and where he was driven to his petition, and how, and in what manner, and in what caſes the ſubject was relieved by those ſtatutes. And where before this ſtatute of 2 E. 6. the party was put to his petition, you may reade in lib. 4. fol. 54, 55. &c. 24 E. 3. 55. untill the end of the caſe, adding thereunto, that Mich. 34 & 35 Eliſ. it was reſolved in the court of wards by the two chiefe juſtices, in the caſe of the counteſſe of Rutland, upon conſideration had of the ſaid acts of 34 E. 3. 36 E. 3. & 8 H. 6. that he in the remainder expectant upon an eſtate taile or freehold, or that hath a drie reverſion expectant upon any eſtate of freehold, without any rent or profit, but onely fealty, ſhall not traverſe a falſe office, finding the dying ſeiſed of ſuch a remainder or reverſion: for theſe ſtatutes give a traverſe, when the lands are ſeiſed by the king, and the party ouſted thereof: and the ſeiſin of tenant for life is the ſeiſin of him in remainder or reverſion. And the judgement cannot be given, *quod manus domini regis amoveantur*. See Stamf. prerog. 13. he in the reverſion may ſue livery, &c. Dyer, 14 Eliſ. 319. Stamf. prerog. 62. a. b.

Lib. 4. fol. 54, 55. &c. Br. travers 55. Stamf. prerog.

(1) *Leaſes for terme of years, or intereſt by copie of court roll*, &c.] Upon theſe words it hath been doubted, whether a tenant by ſtatute merchant, by ſtatute ſtaple, by *elegit*, or executors that have intereſt in lands by deviſe for payment of debts, and the like were within this law, becauſe they are not leſſees for yeares; but the common opinion is, that theſe intereſts are within the purview of this act: for that they are not onely within the ſame miſchiefe, being without remedy, but within the expreſſe reaſon of this law, *viz.* becauſe their ſaid intereſt is but a chattell reall, and all the aboveſaid intereſts are but chattels realls, *et ratio legis eſt anima legis. Lex beneficialis rei conſimili remedium præſtat. Quæcunque intra rationem legis inveniuntur, intra ipſam legem eſſe judicantur.*

See 37. aſſ. p. 11. 4 E. 4. 21.

[689]

29 *H.* 8. *tit. Travers d' office* 50. A termor could not traverſe an office by the common law, but if it were found in the office, he might have a *monſtrans de droit*, and ſo of others that had but chattels realls, 13 E. 4. 8.

7 H. 7. 11. Vid. 9 H. 6. 21.

But *nota*, though there be a double matter of record to entitle the king to a chattell perſonall, as an attainder, and an office, that the perſon attainted was poſſeſſed of a horſe, the office may be traverſed, 34 H. 6. 51. 4 E. 4. 24. 47 E. 3. 26. 13 E. 4. 8. 1 H. 7. fol. becauſe chattels perſonall are *bona peritura*, and cannot abide the delay of a petition. *Vid.* W. 1. cap. 4. that goods wrecked be in ſafety, and kept by the view of the ſherifes, &c. and yet ſuch as be *bona peritura* the ſherife, &c. may ſell them within the yeare.

By the words of the writ of *diem clauſit extremum, mandamus, &c.* the eſcheatour might, according to the common law, ſeiſe, &c. before office: but by the ſtatute of Lincolne, *anno* 29 *E.* 1. *de Eſcheatoribus, Vet. Mag. Chart.* 108. and by *Artic' ſuper Chart. anno* 28 E. 1. cap. 19. the eſcheatour, &c. cannot ſeiſe before office, and yet

yet the words of the writs keep their old forme. Here it appeareth, that the king is intitled by office.

For remedy whereof, be it enacted by authority of this present parliament, that where any such office or inquisition is or shall be founden (2), omitting such titles, interests, or matters, as aforesaid, that in all such cases, every lessee, tenant for terme of yeares, or copiholder, and every such person or persons that have, or shall have any interest to any rent, common, or profit apprender, for terme of yeares, life, or otherwise, out of any of the lands, tenements, or hereditaments contained in such office or inquisition, where the king, his heires or successors is, or shall be entituled, as is aforesaid, to any such lands, tenements, or hereditaments, shall have, hold, enjoy, and perceive all and every their leases and interests for terme of yeares, or by copie of court roll, rents, commons, offices, fees, and profit apprender, in such manner, forme, state, and condition, as they and every of them should, or might have done, in case there had been no such office or inquisition found, and as they should or lawfully might, or ought to have done, in case such lease, interest by copie of court roll, rent, common, office, fee, or profit apprender, had been founden in such office or inquisition: any law, custome, or usage to the contrary heretofore used in such cases, in any wise notwithstanding. And also, where it is or shall be founden for the king, his heires or successors, that the heire or heires of his tenant or tenant is, or shall be within age, where in deed such heire or heires is, or shall be at the same time of full age, or of a more or greater age, then is, or shall be contained within such office. Note this first branch of this beneficiall law.

(2) *Where any such office or inquisition is, or shall be found*, &c.] This hath reference to the preamble, and extendeth not onely to offices in case of wardship by tenure *in capite*, but to offices upon attainders of treason, felony, or otherwise. Wherein the generality of these words [or otherwise] are to be observed.

Be it further enacted by the authority aforesaid, that in every such case, such heire and heires, shall and may at his or their very full age, or after, prosecute a writ of *ætate probanda* (3), and sue his or their liverie, or *ouster le maine*, as his or their cases shall lye, and have the profits of his or their lands, tenements, or hereditaments, from the time of his or their very full age: any such untrue office or inquisition, or any law or custome to the contrary in any wise notwithstanding. Also where one person or moe is or shall be founden heire to the kings tenant by office or inquisition (4), where any other person is, or shall be heire; or if one person or moe be or shall be founden heire by office, or inquisition in one county, and another person or persons is or shall be founden heire to the same person in another county, or if any person be, or shall be untruly founden lunatick, ideot, or dead. [690] The 2. branch.

See 5 E. 4. 3. Stamf. prer. 61. b. 21 R. 2. livery 4. 13 H. 4. 6, 7. Calestens case. 1 H. 7. 3. 14. & 28. Bro. tit. *Office devant Escheator* 27. 40. & *ibid.* 50. Br. tit. *Travers de office* 47. Kelwey, 7 H. 8. fol. 177.

(3) *Or after sue a writ of ætate probanda,* &c.] Or a commission in the nature of an *ætate probanda,* F.N.B. 257. c. d. e. Registr. 294, 295, 296.

See a notable president of an *ætate probanda,* together with the reasons of the jurors. Suff. Hill' 25 E. 1. rot. 14. *coram rege,* Benedict de Blakenhams case.

See Rot. Parl. 40 E. 3. nu. 14, 15. where the heire is found of full age, where in truth he is within age.

(4) *Also where one person or more is, or shall be found heire to the kings tenant by office or inquisition,* &c.] This act is generall, and extendeth as well to offices found *virtute officii* (whereof there was * no interpleader by the common law, because a generall livery could not be sued thereupon: but speciall liveries (now and long since in use) may be sued upon such an office found *virtute officii*) as to offices found *virtute brevis aut commissionis.*

* 30 ass. 28. Kelway, 10 H. 8. fol. 198. b. Stamf. prer. 59. b. 21 H. 7. fol. 35.

The reason wherefore no generall livery could be sued at the common law upon an office found *virtute officii,* was, *Quia vigilantibus, non dormientibus jura subveniunt.* And the office, whereupon livery is to be granted to the heire, is to be upon an office to be found by writ or commission at the suit of the heire, and the escheator may retorne an office *virtute officii* into the court.

Vid. 32 H. 8. cap. 46 for the court of wards. F.N.B. 232, 233. 29. ass. 43. 16 E. 3. liverie 30. 32 E. 3. travers 38. 32. ass. 28. 50. ass. 2. See the jurisdiction of courts, cap. the court of wards.

The 3. branch.

Be it enacted by the authority aforesaid, that every person and persons grieved, or to be grieved by any such office or inquisition, shall and may have his or their traverse to the same, immediately, or after, at his or their pleasure, and proceed to tryall therein, and have like remedie and advantage, as in other cases of traverse upon untrue inquisitions or offices founden: any law, usage, or custome to the contrary in any wise notwithstanding.

See the statute of Marlbridge, ca. 16. and the exposition thereupon. 2 E. 4. 18. 5 E. 4. 3, 4. F.N.B. 262. 12 E. 4. 18. 2 H. 6. 5. 8 Hen. 7. 118. 11 H. 7. 3. *Vide* Dyer 5 Mar. 161, 162. lib. 7. 45. in Kennes case, this act doth not take away any incidents in law: for if one heire traverse the office of another, he first must have an office found for himselfe, as there it is resolved. *Vid.* 36 E. 3. tit. Travers 44. 12 H. 6. travers 45. 5 E. 4. 4. 1 H. 7. 14. 29 ass. 13. 43 ass. p. 20. 32 H. 6. travers 39. 16 E. 4. 4. F.N.B. 262. Stamf. prer. 58. Kennes case, *ubi supra,* the cause of this word [immediately] to make it cleare that before was *vexata quæstio,* so as by this an interpleader, as the case shall require, shall be immediatly.

[691]
The 4. branch.

And where it is or shall be hereafter untruly founden by office or inquisition, that any person or persons attainted, or that shall be attainted of treason, felonie, or premunire, is or shall be seised of any lands, tenements, or hereditaments, at any time of such treason, felonie, or offence committed or done, or any time after, whereunto any other person or persons hath, or shall

ſhall have any juſt title or intereſt of any eſtate of freehold, that then in every ſuch caſe, every perſon and perſons grieved thereby, ſhall have his or their traverſe, or *monſtrans de droit* to the ſame (1) without being driven to any petition of right: and like remedy and reſtitution upon his or their title, found or judged for him or them therein, as hath been accuſtomed and uſed in other caſes of traverſe, although the kings majeſtie, his heires or ſucceſſors be, or ſhall be, in ſuch caſe intitled to any ſuch lands, tenements, or hereditaments, by double matter of record: any law, cuſtome, or uſage to the contrary in any wiſe notwithſtanding.

Lib. 4. fol. 57. b. the reaſon is notably expreſſed, wherefore in theſe caſes at the common law the party grieved was put to his petition. See 49 Ed. 3. 11. 13 H. 4. 7. 10 H. 6. 15. 4 E. 4. 25. 21 E. 4. 2, 3. 4 H. 7. fol. 7. Stamf. prer. 72, 73. 1 E. 5. 8. Pl. com. 486. Rot. parl. 11 H. 6. nu. 29. John Earle of Somerſets caſe, Br. *travers de office* 51. *Vid.* 43. aſſ. p. 28. 33 H. 8. petition Br. 35.

(5) *Shall have his or their traverſe, or monſtrans de droit to the ſame*, &c.] Note, that the traverſe and *monſtrans de droit* are here diſ-junctively divided, and by the ninth branch of this act, the party that ſhall traverſe, muſt ſue out one writ or ſeverall writs of *ſcire facias*, as the caſe ſhall require, and that there ſhall be two writs of ſearch granted upon every traverſe, that ſhall be purſued by vertue or meanes of this act. But *nota*, that proviſo extends onely to traverſes, and not to any *monſtrans de droit* to be purſued by force of this act, either for the ſuing out of writs of *ſcire facias*, or that therein writs of ſearch ſhall be granted, becauſe the *monſtrans de droit* doth confeſſe and avoid the title of the king, and the traverſe denieth it, 14 E. 4. 1, 7. Stamf. prer. 70, 71. ſimile.

And further be it enacted by the authoritie aforeſaid, that where any inquiſition or office is or ſhall be founden (6) by theſe words, or the like, *Quod de quo, vel de quibus* (7) *tenementa prædicta tenentur, jurat' prædict' ignorant:* or elſe founden holden of the king, *per quæ ſervitia ignorant*, or ſuch like; that in ſuch caſe, ſuch tenure ſo uncertainly founden, *de quo, vel de quibus tenementa prædicta tenentur, ignorant*, ſhall not be taken for any immediate tenure of the king; nor ſuch tenure ſo founden of the king, *per quæ ſervitia ignorant*, ſhall not be taken any tenure *in capite*; but in ſuch caſes a *melius inquirendum* to be awarded (8), as hath been accuſtomed in old time; any uſage of latter time to the contrarie notwithſtanding. The 5. branch.

(6) *That where any inquiſition or office is or ſhall be found*, &c.] Upon an office found before the eſcheator, *virtute officii*, there lay no *melius inquirendum* before this act; for the words of the writ be, *per quandam inquiſitionem capt' coram A. eſchaetore noſtro, &c. de mandato noſtro capt'*. F.N.B. 255. Regiſt. fol. But this act is generall, and giveth it when it is found, *virtute officii*. *Vid.* 8. H. 6. cap. 16. Kelwey 199.

(7) *Quod de quo vel de quibus*, &c.] *Vide* 10 H. 4. 2. b. 13 H. 7. 4. 29 Hen. 8. Br. office 58. & 30 H. 8. ibid. 59.

* (8) *But in such cases a melius inquirendum to be awarded*, &c.] *Vide* Dyer, 12 Elis. fol. 291. *Si sur le melius tenure est trove dun common person in certaine, ne besoigne travers.* Dyer 13 Elis. fol. 306. *Si ignoramus soit trove sur le melius, ceo serra prise tenure in capite. Issint fuit resolve* Mich. 33 & 34 Eliz. *per les 2. chiefe justices in le court de gardes.* For this act extends not to the second inquisition upon the melius. And it was then resolved, that he which should traverse such an office, should traverse, that the land was not holden of the king *in capite*; for so much is implyed in the office, Dyer 5 Mar. 161, 162.

Dyer 13 Elis. *ubi supra, si sur le melius soit trove tenure dun roigne ut de manerio, &c. sed per quæ servitia ignorant.* This is a tenure by knight-service, as of the mannor. *Vide pur melius inquirend'* lib. 8. fol. 168. Paris Stoughters case, & 5 Mar. Dyer 155. b. 156. that no *melius inquirendum* is grantable of any office found *de quo vel de quibus, &c.* before this statute.

The 6. branch.

And be it further enacted by the authoritie aforesaid, that where it is or shall be found by any office or inquisition (9), that any lands, tenements, or hereditaments, are, or shall be discended, remained, or common to any heire within age, and in the kings ward, or that ought to be in the kings ward, and that such lands, tenements, or hereditaments are holden of the king immediately, where in deed the same are, or shall be holden of some other common person (10), and not of the king immediately: that in such case, such heire or heires shall and may have their traverse to the same within age, and like remedie and restitution upon his or their title founden or judged for him, or them therein, as hath been accustomed and used in other cases of traverses: any law, usage, or custome to the contrarie in any wise notwithstanding.

(9) *Where it is, or shall be found by any office or inquisition*, &c.] Note the generality of this clause.

(10) *Shall be holden of some other common person*, &c.] The lord might traverse by the common law. 5 Mar. Dyer 161, 162. but the heire could not before this act. *Vide* 1 H. 7. 3.

The 7. branch.

Also where the kings majestie by his prerogative ought to have as well such lands and tenements as be holden of other persons, as holden of himselfe immediately, whereof his tenant holding of him in chiefe, dyeth seised, his heire being within age, untill such time as liverie be sued (11) by such heire, and that the meane lords, of whom the said other lands and tenements of such heire be holden, used to spare the rents (12) due to them for the same lands or tenements holden of them, during the kings possession. And when such heire hath sued his or their liverie they use by distresse, or otherwise to compell the said heire to pay to them the arrerages of such rents, for such time as the said lands, or tenements were in the kings possession

possession by such minoritie, where they should have sued by petition to the kings majestie, to have obtained the same out of the kings hands, if they would have the same which is to the great detriment, losse, and hindrance of such heire and heires. For redresse whereof, be it enacted by the authoritie of this present parliament, that from henceforth such meane lords, during such minoritie shall have, receive, and take the said rents by the hands of such of the kings officers, as shall be appointed to have, receive, and take the issues, revenues, and profits of the same lands and tenements so holden of such meane lords, during the minoritie and nonage of such heire and heires, and until such heire and heires sue his or their liverie, and that such heire and heires, untill such time as he or they shall have sued their liverie, or might conveniently have sued their liverie, shall be thereof clearly discharged. And that such officer or officers, shall upon request made, pay the same to such meane lords (they giving to such officer and officers a sufficient acquittance, or acquittances for the receipt of the same.) And that such payment thereof made with acquittance, or acquittances thereof shewed, shall be to such officers a sufficient discharge against the kings majestie and his heires, upon his or their accompt in that behalfe: any law, usage, or custome heretofore had, or used to the contrary hereof in any wise notwithstanding. [693]

(11) *Untill such time as liverie be sued.*] *Nota*, there be two sorts of liveries, *viz.* liveries in deed, and liveries in law. Of liveries in deed there be two kinds, *viz.* a generall livery, and a speciall livery. For a generall livery an office must be found in every county, an *ætate probanda* found and returned in the chancery; a writ to the lord privie seale, that the heire is of full age: and thereupon a privie seale to the chamberlaine of England to receive his homage, &c. which kind of livery is dangerous, tedious, and chargeable. Vid. 44 E. 3. 12. 12 H. 4. livery 4. 21 R. 2. livery 5. 1 H. 7. 14. E. 4. 18. 7 H. 8. Kelwey 176, 177.

There is also a speciall livery with a pardon much more safe, speedy and beneficiall for the party, and it may be had upon any office found in any one county, and all the rest to come in by certificate, as now the use is without *ætate probanda, &c.* 7 H. 8. Kelwey 177. or without any office at all, and may be made to the heire within age, 21 E. 3. 40. 29 H. 8. livery Br. 56.

By the statute of 33 H. 8. cap. 22. power is given to the master of the wards, surveyor, attorny, and receiver, or three of them, whereof the master or surveyor to be one, to grant a generall or speciall livery. Whereupon some have thought, that speciall liveries became commonly to be granted; but it appeareth by 7 H. 8. *ubi supra*, that it was so commonly used by a good time then past. Dyer, 23 Elis. fol. 377. a speciall livery is not grantable at this day *ex debito justitiæ*.

If the office be traversed, and the king, hanging the traverse, grant livery, &c. the traverse goeth to the ground. Kelw. 2 H. 8. 157. a. b. 1 H. 7. 12. 27. adjudged. See Dyer, 23 Elis. *ubi supra*.

13 H. 4. 6. 7. tit Travers, an office is found, that A. died seised of the mannor of B. and held the same *in capite* by knights-service his

his heire within age; this office is traversed, that A. infeoffed him that traverseth in fee, and traverse the dying seised: whereupon the king taketh issue, and hanging the traverse, it is found by another office, that the said feoffment was by collusion, and after the issue was found against the king; whereupon, by the rule of the court, the party had judgement, and an *amoveas manum*. For the office, found depending the traverse, shall not grieve the party; for so he might be infinitely vexed: but in a *scire fac'* by the king upon the latter office he shall answer, &c. an excellent case for the benefit and speed of them that are driven to traverse. Vid. 11 H. 4. fol. 8. 13 H. 4. tit. travers 16 et 13 H. 4. tit. livery 21.

* 23 H. 8. Br. intrusion 19. 21. 2 H. 6. 57. Kelw. 10 H. 8. 198. 13 H. 4. 3. See Dyer, 12 El. 286. 46 E. 3. grant 50. 34 H. 8. Charter de pardon 54. 29 H. 8. ib. 52. 16 E. 4. fol. 1.

* There be also liveries in law, as by pardons, either by act of parliament, or by charter under the great seale, to the heire of the kings tenant *in capite*, be he within age, or of full age. But where some books say, that a pardon of intrusions to such an heire amounts in law to a livery, it is so to be understood, that in the pardon there be words also, that the heire may enter, &c. for a speciall livery is no other, but that the heire *habeat licentiam ingrediendi, &c.*

[694]

32 H. 8. Br. 62. Stamf. prer. 40. b.

Note, upon every livery the king hath the value of the land for halfe a yeare, but upon an *ouster le mayne* the kings hands be amoved without any profit, &c.

(12) *Used to spare the rents, &c.*] Not onely rents, but reliefes also were due by the common law, 26 H. 8. 8. 24 E. 3. 24. 29 ass. p. 5. 39 E. 3. reliefe 1. Vide Br. tit. Arrerages, pl. 1. & 19. For though there be a kind of suspension of rents, &c. by reason of the kings possession; yet the rents, &c. are due, because the prerogative of the king doth no man wrong, 13 E. 4. 8. &c.

The 8. branch.

Vid. Dier 5 Mar. 155, 156.

Provided alwaies, and it is enacted by the authoritie aforesaid, that this act, or any thing therein contained, shall not in any wise extend to any inquisition or office taken or founden, at any time before the twentieth day of March next coming; nor to hinder, prejudice, or take away the title, interest, or possession of our soveraigne lord the king, or of any other person or persons growne, or commen by vertue, meane, or occasion of any inquisition or office taken, or found before the same day; but that as well our said soveraigne lord the king, as all other person or persons, having any title, interest, or possession by vertue, meane, or occasion of any inquisition or office found before the same day, shall, and may have, hold, and enjoy the same in like manner and forme, as though this act had never been had or made: any thing in the same act to the contrary in any wise notwithstanding.

The 9. branch.

Provided also, and it is enacted by the authoritie aforesaid, that in all such cases, as any person or persons shall be enabled by this act (13) to have any traverse, and shall pursue his or their traverse, that then he or they that shall pursue such traverse, shall sue one writ, or severall writs of *scire facias* (as the case shall require) against all and singular such person and persons, as shall have interest by the king, or by his patentee or patentees, in like manner and form as is requisite upon traverses, or petitions heretofore pursued. And that in every such *scire facias*

the patentees, or other defendants ſhall have like plees and advantages, as they had in any *ſcire facias*, before this time awarded againſt any patentee in any caſe of petition. And alſo, that upon every traverſe that ſhall be purſued by vertue or meane of this act, in ſuch caſe as the partie or parties that ſhall purſue any ſuch traverſe, ſhould, by the order of the common lawes of this realme, have been put to ſue by petition to the king, there ſhall be two writs of ſearch granted in manner and forme, as like writs have been granted upon petitions made to the king.

(13) *Shall be enabled by this act, &c.*] Hereof ſomewhat hath been ſpoken in the fourth branch. *Vid.* 5 E. 4. 3.

Nota, in many caſes two matters of record with neceſſary averrements ſhall amount to an office, but thereupon a *ſcire fac'* is to be granted, wherein the partie may traverſe any of the materiall averrements, &c. 21 aſſ. p. 36. 21 E. 3. liverie. 40 aſſ. 46. 50 aſſ. 2. 2 E. 3. 10. b. but becauſe ſuch records amounting are not within any branch of this act, we will ſpeak no further of them.

Provided alſo, and it is enacted by the authoritie aboveſaid, that if after any judgement ſhalbe given upon any traverſe (9) that ſhalbe tendred, or ſued by vertue or mean of this act, it ſhal appear by any matter of record, that the king hath any other former title, right, or intereſt to the mannors, lands, tenements, or other hereditaments mentioned in the ſame traverſe, that then the ſame title, right, and intereſt ſhall be ſaved to the king, the ſaid traverſe and judgement thereupon given, in any wiſe notwithſtanding. The 10. branch. [695]

(14) *Upon any traverſe.*] This extendeth not to a *monſtrans de droit* to be purſued upon this ſtatute.

This proviſo was added (for that this act gave a traverſe, where none was at the common law, and that it ſhould be judged for them, for whom it was found, &c.) leſt the judgement, being warranted by authority of parliament, ſhould bind any former right the king had; and that appeareth alſo by the concluſion of this branch, *viz.* The ſaid traverſe and judgement thereupon given notwithſtanding: but it ſeemeth to be *abundans cautela*, for the judgement upon a traverſe is, *quod manus domini regis amoveantur, et poſſeſſio reſtituatur* to him that traverſeth *ſalvo jure, &c.* Br. tit. Travers de office 54.

It is to be obſerved, that there be certaine records which intitle the king, that by law are not traverſable; in which caſes, though the king be entituled but by ſingle matter of record, yet the party grieved is put to his petition, and cannot be holpen by traverſe, or *monſtrans de droit*. As taking one example for many: king Henry the fourth recovered in the kings bench in a *quare impedit* againſt the prior of T. the preſentation to a church, and had a writ to the biſhop, and his clerke received, &c. where in truth the prior never knew of the ſuit, nor was ſummoned, attached, or diſtrained by the ſherife; and thereupon the prior moved the court of kings bench to grant a writ, to cauſe to come before them the ſummoners, the pledges, and mainpernors upon the deſtreſſe to be examined in this matter. Mich. 10 H. 4. tit. Travers 51. Fitz. N.B. 99. f. Stamf. prer. 73.

matter. And in this case five points were resolved by Gascoigne chiefe justice, and the court, *viz.* first, that the prior was driven to his petition in nature of a writ of deceit, albeit in this case the king recovered in *auter droit.* 2. That if a common person had recovered, the defendant had been driven to his originall writ out of the chancery, and could not proceed upon any judiciall processe out of this court. 3. That if the conclusion of the petition be, that the king should command the court of kings bench to proceed to the examination, &c. then without any writ out of the chancery, the court may proceed to the examination. 4. But if the petition doth conclude generally, that the king should doe right, then the prior should be driven to his originall out of the chancery. 5. That before such writ be granted, the prior upon a commission out of the chancery, ought to have his right found by enquest.

But seeing our statute extendeth to offices found by writ, commission, or *ex officio*, and not to other records, we will speak no further of them.

3 H. 4. 14. 13 E. 4. 8. 46 E. 3. Travers 17.

Mine advice to such as shall traverse by force of this act, is, that in the inducement to the traverse, they alledge their owne title, (which they ought to doe; for no man shall have the lands out of the kings hands, without making a title) justly and truly: for the attorney generall for the king may either take issue upon the traverse, or by the kings prerogative upon the title of the party, that traverseth at his choice.

17 E. 3. 10. Henry Hills case. 20 E. 4. 11. 14. 21 E. 4. 1. 2. quare imped. 101. 14 H. 7. 21. 15 H. 7. 6.

It is a maxime in law, that whensoever any man is by any office traversable amoved from his possession, that he must traverse the office in the court, where the office is returned. Of houses and lands, which doe lye in livery, and whereof there is manuall occupation, and profit presently taken, the party by finding of the office is out of possession; but of rents, villeins, commons, advowsions, and other inheritances incorporeall which lye in grant, the owner is not out of possession (be they appendant, or in grosse) by the finding of an office; and therefore in any information or action brought by the king for the same, the party may traverse the office in that court, where the information or action is brought for the king.

[696] 29 ass. p. 40. 32 ass. p. 28. 50 ass. 2. Stamf. prer. 54. b.

And in all cases, when the king is not in possession by the office, and he obtaine not possession within the yeare after the office found, then cannot the king seize without a *scire facias.*

We have taken this statute of 2 E. 6. into our consideration, the rather, for that justice Stamford wrote his treatise upon the prerogative (wherein he setteth forth the common law) before this statute of 2 E. 6. by which statute the subject is relieved in many things, which lay heavie upon him, when justice Stamford wrote; our chiefest endeavour being, that it may be knowne how the law standeth at the edition of this second and other parts of the Institutes.

An

An Expoſition upon the Statute of 22 H. 8. Cap. 5. concerning the repairing of decayed Bridges in Highwaies, and by whom.

BE it enacted by the king our ſoveraigne lord, and the lords ſpirituall and temporall, and the commons in this preſent parliament aſſembled, and by authoritie of the ſame, that the juſtices of peace in every ſhire of this realme, franchiſe, citie, or borough, or foure of them at the leaſt, whereof one to be of the quorum, ſhall have power and authoritie to enquire, heare, and determine in the kings generall ſeſſions of peace, of all manner of annoyances of bridges broken in the high-waies, to the damage of the kings liege people, and to make ſuch proceſſe and paines upon every preſentment afore them for the reformation of the ſame, againſt ſuch as owen to be charged for the making or amending of ſuch bridges, as the kings juſtices of his bench uſe commonly to doe, or as it ſhall ſeem by their diſcretions to be neceſſary and convenient for the ſpeedy amendment of ſuch bridges.

And where in many parts of this realme it cannot be knowne and proved what hundred, riding, wapentake, citie, borough, towne, or pariſh, nor what perſon certain, or bodie politick, ought of right to make ſuch bridges decayed, by reaſon whereof ſuch decayed bridges, for lacke of knowledge of ſuch as owen to make them, for the moſt part, lye long without any amendment, to the great annoyance of the kings ſubjects.

For the remedy thereof, be it enacted by authoritie aforeſaid, that in every ſuch caſe the ſaid bridges, if they be without the citie or towne corporate, ſhall be made by the inhabitants of the ſhire (1) or riding, within the which the ſaid bridge decayed ſhall happen to be: and if it be within any citie or towne corporate, then by the inhabitants of every ſuch citie, or towne corporate, wherein ſuch bridges ſhall happen to be. And if part of any ſuch bridges ſo decayed happen to be in one ſhire, riding, citie, or towne corporate, and the other part thereof in another ſhire, riding, city, or towne corporate; or if part be within the limits of any citie, or towne corporate, and part without; or part within one riding, and part within another: that then in every ſuch caſe the inhabitants of the ſhires, ridings, cities, or townes corporate ſhall be charged, and chargeable to amend, make, and repaire ſuch part and portion of ſuch bridges ſo decayed, as ſhall lye and be within the limits of the ſhire, riding, citie, or towne corporate, wherein they be inhabited at the time of the ſame decaies.

And be it further enacted, that in every ſuch caſe, where it cannot be knowne and proved (2) what perſons, lands, tenements,

ments, and bodies politick owen to make and repaire ſuch bridges, that for ſpeedy reformation and amending of ſuch bridges, the juſtices of peace within the ſhires or ridings, wherein ſuch decayed bridges been out of cities and townes corporate; and if it be within cities or towns corporate, then
[698] the juſtices of peace within every ſuch citie, or towne corporate, or foure of the ſaid juſtices at the leaſt, whereof one to be of the quorum, ſhall have power and authority within the limits of their ſeverall commiſſions, and authorities, to call before them the conſtables of every town and pariſh, being within the ſhire, riding, city, or town corporate, as well within liberty, as without, wherein ſuch bridges, or any parcell thereof ſhall happen to be, or elſe two of the moſt honeſt inhabitants within every ſuch towne or pariſh in the ſaid ſhire, riding, city, or towne corporate, by the diſcretion of the ſaid juſtices of peace, or foure of them at the leaſt, whereof one to be of the quorum: and at, and upon the apparances of ſuch conſtables, or inhabitants, the ſaid juſtices of peace, or foure of them (3), whereof one to be of the quorum, with the aſſent of the ſaid conſtables, or inhabitants (4), ſhall have power and authority to taxe, and ſet every inhabitant (5) in any ſuch city, towne or pariſh, within the limits of their commiſſions and authorities, to ſuch reaſonable aid, and ſumme of money, as they ſhall thinke by their diſcretions convenient and ſufficient for the repairing, re-edifying, and amendment of ſuch bridges, and after ſuch taxation made, the ſaid juſtices ſhall cauſe the names and ſummes of every particular perſon ſo by them taxed, to be written (6) in a roll indented (7). And ſhall alſo have power and authority to make two collectors of every hundred, for collection of all ſuch ſummes of money, by them ſet and taxed, which collectors receiving the one part of the ſaid roll indented under the ſeales of the ſaid juſtices, ſhall have power and authoritie to collect and receive all the particular ſummes of money therein contained (8); and to diſtraine every ſuch inhabitant, as ſhall be taxed, and refuſe payment thereof, in his lands, goods, and chattells (9), and to ſell ſuch diſtreſſe, and of the ſale thereof retaine and perceive all the money taxed, and the reſidue (if the diſtreſſe be better) to deliver to the owner thereof (10). And that the ſame juſtices, or foure of them, within the limits of their commiſſions and authorities, ſhall alſo have power and authoritie to name and appoint two ſurveyors, which ſhall ſee every ſuch decayed bridge repaired, and amended from time to time, as often as need ſhall require, to whoſe hands the ſaid collectors ſhall pay the ſaid ſummes of money taxed, and by them received: and that the collectors and ſurveyors, and every of them, and their executors and adminiſtrators, and the executors and adminiſtrators of them, and every of them, from time to time ſhall make a true declaration and accompt to the juſtices of peace of the ſhire, riding, citie, or town corporate, wherein they ſhall be appointed collectors,

lectors or ſurveyors, or to foure of the ſame juſtices, whereof one to be of the quorum, of the receipts, payments, and expences of the ſaid ſummes of money: and if they, or any of them refuſe that to doe, that then the ſame juſtices of peace, or foure of them, from time to time by their diſcretions, ſhall have power and authoritie to make proceſſe againſt the ſaid collectors and ſurveyors, and every of them, their executors and adminiſtrators, and the executors and adminiſtrators of every of them, by attachments under their ſeales returnable at the general ſeſſions of peace: and if they appeare, then to compell them to accompt, as is aforeſaid, or elſe if they, or any of them, refuſe that to doe, then to commit ſuch of them, as ſhall refuſe, [699] to ward, there to remaine without baile or mainpriſe, till the ſaid declaration and accompt be truly made.

And where any bridge or bridges lien in one ſhire or riding, and ſuch perſons inhabitants, bodies politick, lands or tenements, which owen to be charged to the making and amending of ſuch bridges, lien and abiding in another ſhire or riding, or where ſuch bridges been within any citie, or towne corporate, and the perſons inhabitants, bodies politick, lands or tenements, that owen to make or repaire any ſuch bridges, lien and been out of the ſaid cities and townes corporate: be it enacted, that in every ſuch caſe, the juſtices of peace of the ſhire, citie, or towne corporate, within the which ſuch decayed bridges, or any part thereof ſhall happen to be, ſhall have power to enquire, heare, and determine all ſuch annoyances, being within the limits of their commiſſions or authorities. And if the annoyance be preſented, then to make proceſs into every ſhire within this realme againſt ſuch as owen to make, or amend any ſuch bridges ſo preſented before them, to be decayed, to the annoyance and let of the paſſage of the kings ſubjects, and to doe further in every behalfe in every ſuch caſe, as they mought doe by authoritie of this act, in caſe that the perſons or bodies politick, lands or tenements, which owen to be charged to the amending or making of ſuch bridges, or any part thereof, were in the ſame ſhire, riding, citie, or towne corporate, where ſuch annoyance ſhall happen to be. And that all ſherifes and bailifes of liberties and franchiſes, ſhall truly ſerve and execute ſuch proceſſe, as ſhall come to their hands from the ſaid juſtices of peace, afore whom any preſentment ſhall be had for any ſuch annoyance, according to the tenour and effect of the ſaid proceſſe to them directed, without favour, affection or corruption, upon paine to make ſuch fine as ſhall be ſet upon them, or any of them, by the diſcretion of the ſaid juſtices.

Provided alway, that this act, nor any thing therein contained, be not prejudiciall to the liberties of the five ports, or members of the ſame, and for reformation of annoyance of bridges within the ſaid ports and members.

Be it enacted by authoritie of this preſent parliament, that the warden, maiors, and bailiffes elected, and jurates of the ſame ports,

ports, and every of them, have power and authoritie to enquire, heare, and determine all manner of common annoyances of bridges within the ſame ports and members, and to make ſuch proceſſe, paines, taxations, and all other things within the ſame ports and members, as the juſtices of peace may doe in other ſhires, or places out of the ſame ports, by vertue and authoritie of this preſent act in every behalfe.

And be it further enacted by the authoritie aforeſaid, that the juſtices of peace, or foure of them, ſhall have full power and authoritie to allow ſuch reaſonable coſts and charges to the ſaid ſurveyors and collectors, as by their diſcretions ſhall be thought convenient.

For as much that albeit bridges decayed were amended and repaired, according to the tenour of this act, yet neverthleſſe, if ſpeedy remedy for the amendment of the waies next adjoyning to every of the ends of ſuch bridges, ſhould not be had and
[700] made, the kings ſubjects ſhould take little or none availe or commoditie in any parts of this realme by the making of the bridges: in conſideration whereof, be it enacted by the king our ſoveraigne lord, and the lords ſpirituall and temporall, and the commons in this preſent parliament aſſembled, and by the authoritie of the ſame, that ſuch part and portion of the high-waies in every part of this realme, as well within franchiſe, as without, as lye next adjoyning to any ends of any bridges within this realme, diſtant from any of the ſaid ends, by the ſpace of three hundred foot, be made, repaired, and amended as often as need ſhall require. And that the juſtices of the peace in every ſhire of this realme, franchiſe, citie, or borough, or foure of them at the leaſt, whereof one to be of the quorum, within the limits of their commiſſions and authorities, ſhall have power and authoritie to enquire, heare, and determine in the kings generall ſeſſions of peace, all manner of annoyances of and in ſuch high-waies, ſo being and lying next adjoyning to any ends of bridges within this realme, diſtant from any of the ends of ſuch bridges, three hundred foot, and to doe in every thing and things concerning the making, repairing, and amending of ſuch high-waies, and every of them, in as large and ample manner as they might and may doe, to and for the making, repairing, and amending of bridges, by vertue and authoritie of this preſent act.

Before we enter into the expoſition of this act, we will take into conſideration, for a neceſſary introduction thereunto, what the common law was concerning the reparation of decayed * bridges in three points: Firſt, who were to repaire the ſame: 2. what was the remedy for the reparation thereof: 3. before what judges.

* Pons ſignificat omne quod ſuper aquas tranſimus, unde ponticulus.
Nil Tadcaſter habet muſis aut carmine dignum,
Præter magnificè ſtructum ſine flumine pontem.
Vidit et ſcripſit poeta in æſtate.

As

As to the firſt ſome perſons ſpirituall or temporall, incorporate, or not incorporate, are bound to repaire bridges *ratione tenuræ ſuæ terrarum, ſive tenementorum, &c.* ſome *ratione præſcriptionis tantum, ratione tenuræ*, by reaſon that they and thoſe, whoſe eſtate they have in the lands or tenements, are bound in reſpect thereof to repaire the ſame; [a] but they which have lands on the one ſide of the bridge, or on the other, or on both, are not bound of common right to repaire the ſame.

[44 E. 3. 31. 21 E. 4. fol. 46. 5 H. 7. 3. — a 8 H. 7. 5. b.]

[b] If a man, which holdeth an hundred acres of land, ought to repaire a bridge by the tenure of them, if he for example alien twenty acres of them to one, and ten to another, and after one of them is onely upon a preſentment found thereof, diſtrained to repaire this bridge, he ſhall have a ſpeciall writ *de onerando pro rata portione, et ſic de ſimilibus.*

[b Regiſt. 268. a. F.N.B. 235. b. — c 21 E. 4. 38. b. 46. 43 aſſ. 37. 49 E. 3. 5. b. the prior of Markiats caſe. 10 E. 4. 10. a. & b. in ſcir' fac' 19 H. 6. 75. a. b.]

Ratione preſcriptionis tantum, but herein there is a diverſity between bodies politicke or corporate, ſpirituall or temporall, and naturall perſons: for [c] bodies politicke or corporate, ſpirituall or temporall, may be bound by uſage and preſcription only, becauſe they are locall, and have a ſucceſſion perpetuall: but a naturall perſon cannot be bound by act of his anceſter, without a lien, or binding, and aſſets.

[d 10 E. 3. 28, 29. 27 aſſ. pl. 8. 44 E. 3. 31. * Cap. Itineris. M. 13 E. 3. fo. 73, 74. in libro meo, the abbot of S. Auſtins caſe. e Paſch. 10 E. 3. 28, 29. in the Maſt. of Leonards caſe. Vid. Regiſt. 192. 2 E. 3. coron. 147. 14 E. 3. ſtat. 1. cap. 4. where the whole county is amerced.]

[d] *Nota*, if a biſhop or prior, &c. hath at once or twice of almes repaired a bridge, it bindeth not (and yet is evidence againſt him, untill he prove the contrary) but if time out of mind, they and their predeceſſors have repaired it of almes, this ſhall bind them to it. * *De pontibus et calcetis fractis in omnibus tranſitionibus quis ea reparare, et ſuſtentare debet.*

[e] But admit none at all were bounden to the reparation of the bridge, how then? † and by whom ſhould it be repaired by the common law? The anſwer is, that the whole county, that is, the inhabitants of the county or ſhire, wherein the bridge is, ſhall repaire the ſame; for of common right the whole county muſt repaire it, becauſe it is for the common good, and eaſe of the whole county.

† [701]

If a bridge be within a franchiſe, thoſe of the franchiſe are to repaire it. If the bridge be part within a franchiſe, and part within the gildable, ſo much as is within the franchiſe ſhall be repaired by thoſe of the franchiſe; and ſo much as is within the gildable, by thoſe of the gildable. [f] And ſo it is, if it be in two counties, *mutatis mutandis.*

[14 E. 3. tit. Barre 276. the biſhop of Cheſters caſe. — f Regiſt. 154. a. F.N.B. 127. e.]

If a man make a bridge for the common good of all the ſubjects, hee is not bound to repaire it; for no particular man is bound to reparation of bridges by the common law, but *ratione tenuræ*, or *præſcriptionis.*

[8 H. 7. 5.]

As to the ſecond the remedy was, if it were a private bridge: as to a mill which A. was bound to maintaine, over which B. had a paſſage, &c. if the bridge were in decay, B. might have his writ *de ponte reparando.* But if the bridge were for the publicke, &c. the remedy was by preſentment at the ſuit of the king, for avoiding of multiplicity of ſuits.

[Regiſt. 153, 154. F.N.B. 127. d. — g 21 E. 3. 54. 43 aſſ. 37.]

As to the third, this preſentment might be at the common law before the juſtices of the [g] kings bench, or before [h] juſtices in eire, or [i] commiſſioners of oier and terminer, or before the ſherife by commiſſion, or [k] writ in nature of a commiſſion. [l] But as to the ſherife, his power to take inditements, by force of any ſuch writ or

[h 3 E. 3. aſſ. 445. i 27 aſſ. p. 8. 33. aſſ. p. 10. 38. aſſ. p. 15. 22 E. 3. 1. k 14 E. 3. barre 276. l Fitz. N. B. fol. 276. c.]

or commission in the nature of a commission, is taken away by the statute of 28 E. 3. cap. 9. But it may be presented in the [m] turne or leet.

m 29 E. 3. 21.

See the second part of the Institutes, *Mag. Chart. cap.* 15. *Nulla villa nec liber homo distringatur facere pontes, &c. nisi qui ab antiquo et de jure facere consueverunt tempore regis Henrici avi nostri.*

For Pontage, *vid.* the second part of the Institutes, Westmin' 1. cap. 31. W. 2. cap. 25. 3 E. 3. ass. 445. 35 H. 6. 29. b. *per* Fortescue, Pl. Com. 334. 407. *Vide* 13 H. 4. 17. F.N.B. 178. f. Flet. lib. 4. cap. 1. *Vid.* 1 H. 8. cap. 9. 39 El. cap. 24.

Pontage is a toll or contribution for repaire of bridges. See a reasonable taxation therefore 39 Elis. cap. 24. See also of Pontage, lib. 8. fol. 46. b. John Webs case.

5 E. 3. 2. 7 H. 4. 3. &c.

It appeareth in our bookes, that before bridges were made how often defaults were saved, and delayes had *per cretance del ewe*, by encrease of waters.

39 Elis. cap. 24. 43 Elis. cap. 16. 9 H. 5. cap. 12, H. 6. cap. 28. 3 Jac. cap. 24. n Inter leges Canuti regis, ca. 10. & 62.

None can be compelled to make new bridges, where never any were before, but by act of parliament.

[n] The law before the conquest was, *Oppida pontesque posthac instaurantur.* And againe, *Qui pensionem ad oppida pontesve reficiendos denegabit, militiamve subterfugerit, dabit is regi (si Anglus fuerit)* 26. *solidos, &c.*

Now having considered what the common law was concerning the reparation of bridges, we will peruse the parts of this act of 22 H. 8. which may be divided into eight branches.

The first branch. o Just. of peace have power to enquire of nusances, &c. in high-waies, by the statutes of 2 Mar. cap. 8. 5 Elis. cap. 13. 18 Elis. cap. 9.

1. That [o] justices of peace, or any foure or more of them, whereof one to be of the quorum, at the kings generall session of peace, shall have power, and authority (which consisteth in these foure things) first to enquire, heare and determine.

2. Whereof? of all manner nusances of bridges broken in the high-waies, to the damages of the kings liege people. This extendeth only to common bridges in the kings high-waies, where all the kings liege people have, or may have passage, and not to private bridges to mills, or the like. And therefore the inditement upon this statute saith, *Quod* [p] *pons publicus et communis situs in alta regia via super flumen, seu cursum aquæ, &c.*

p Pons à pendendo, quia tanquam in aëre pendet.

3. In what place? In every shire of this realme, franchise, citie, or borough.

[702]

But this is to be understood, *reddendo singula singulis*, that is to say, 1. in every shire or county where there be foure or more justices of peace, whereof one or more is of the quorum. 2. Franchise, where there be foure or more justices of the peace, and one or more of the quorum. 3. Citie, where be foure or more justices of the peace, and one or more of the quorum. 4. Or borough, where there be foure or more justices of the peace, and one or more of the quorum, and where they keep generall sessions of the peace for such franchises, cities, or boroughes; but for want thereof, the justices of peace of the county shall enquire. But if the franchise, citie, or borough be a county of it selfe, and have not foure or more justices of peace, whereof one or more is of the quorum, no other justices of peace of any other shire or county, have any power by this act to enquire of, hear and determine the decay of bridges there, but such decay must be reformed by such remedies (before specified) as the common law did give; therefore it was necessary

to be knowne what the common law was before the making of this statute.

4. Such processe they are to make upon every presentment afore them, for reformation of the same, * against such as owen to be charged for the [a] making or amending of such bridges, as the justices of his majesties bench use commonly to doe, or it shall seem by their discretions to be necessary and convenient for the speedy amendment of such bridges.

* This whole branch, divided into these parts, extendeth only, where such as owen to be charged for making or amending of such bridges are knowne, and presented.

[a] If the whole bridge be decayed, &c. it must be made againe, and re-edified.

Having provided remedy against such as owen to be charged for the making or amending of such bridges, &c. The second and third branches doe provide more speedy remedy, where it cannot be knowne or proved what hundred, riding, wapentake, citie, borough, towne or parish, or what person certaine, or body politicke ought of right to make such bridges decayed, &c. how the same shall be repaired. And these branches doe consist on three parts.

The 2. and 3. branches.

1. That in every such case the said bridges (if they be without city or towne corporate) shall be made by the inhabitants of the shire or * riding, within which the said bridges decayed shall happen to be.

* This was added for Yorkshire, wherein there are ridings.

2. And if they be within a city or towne corporate, then by the inhabitants of every such city or towne corporate.

3. And if part of any bridges so decayed be within shire, riding, citie, or towne corporate, or if part be within the limits of any city, or towne corporate, and part without, or part within one riding, and part within another, that in every such case the inhabitants of the shires, ridings, cities, or townes corporate shall be charged and chargeable to amend, make, and repaire such part and portion of such bridges so decayed, as shall lye and be within the limits of the shire, riding, city, or towne corporate, wherein they be inhabited at the time of such decayes. By this part the law is declared by whom such decayed bridges in any shire, riding, city, or towne corporate ought to be repaired: a necessary clause to be added, for that such decayed bridges may not be within the remedy of the fourth branch: yet the law (who are chargeable) being declared hereby, the remedy shall be by the course of the common law, which before hath been shewed.

(1) *That the inhabitants of the said shires,* &c.] The persons to bee charged by this act are comprehended under this only word [inhabitants;] which word is needfull to be explained, being the largest word of this kind.

See the statute of 23 H. 8. ca. 2. concerning making of gaoles.

First, although a man be dwelling in an house in a forraigne county, riding, city, or towne corporate, yet if he hath lands or tenements in his owne possession and manurance in the county, riding, city, or towne corporate, where the decayed bridge is, he is an inhabitant, both where his person dwelleth, and where he hath lands or tenements in his owne possession within this statute. *Nota, habitatio dicitur ab habendo, quia qui propriis manibus, et sumptibus possidet, et habet, ibi habitare dicitur.*

* Vid. li. 5. fol. 66, 67. Jeffreyes case. ibid. fo. 64. in Clarkes case. Vid. 3. Jac. c. 23.

2. If a man dwelleth in a forraigne shire, riding, city, or towne corporate, and keepeth a house and servants in another shire, riding, city,

city, or town corporate, he is an inhabitant in each ſhire, riding, city, or town corporate within this ſtatute.

3. *Ex vi termini.* Every perſon that dwelleth in any ſhire, riding, city, or towne corporate, though he hath but a perſonall reſidence, yet is he ſaid in law to be an inhabitant, or a dweller there, as ſervants, &c. But this ſtatute extendeth not to them, but to ſuch as be houſholders. And this is gathered by the words of the fourth branch of this act, that giveth the diſtreſſe, *viz.* and to diſtraine every ſuch inhabitant, &c. in his lands, goods, and chattels. And beſides, it were in a manner infinite and impoſſible, to taxe by the next branch of this act every inhabitant, being no houſholder.

4. Every corporation and body politicke reſiding in any county, riding, citie, or towne corporate, or having lands or tenements in any ſhire, riding, city, or towne corporate, *quæ propriis manibus et ſumptibus poſſident et habent*, are ſaid to be inhabitants there within the purview of this ſtatute.

5. An infant that hath houſe or lands by diſcent or purchaſe, is lyable to this publike charge, and ſo is the huſband of a feme covert.

Now the law being declared who were chargeable to repaire decayed bridges, where no perſon, &c. where bound thereunto.

The 4. branch.

The fourth branch, for a more ſpeedy reformation and remedy, provideth and enacteth theſe ſixe things:

1. That in every caſe, where it cannot be knowne and proved what perſons, lands, tenements, and bodies politick owen to make and repaire ſuch bridges, for the ſpeedy reformation and amendment of ſuch bridges, the juſtices of peace within the ſhires or ridings, where ſuch bridges been (being out of cities and townes corporate) and if it be within cities or townes corporate, then the juſtices of peace in every ſuch city or towne corporate, or foure of the ſaid * juſtices at the leaſt, whereof one to be of the quorum, ſhall have power and authority within the limits of their ſeverall commiſſions and [a] authorities, to [b] call before them the conſtables of every towne or pariſh, being within the ſhire, riding, citie, or towne corporate, as well within liberty as without, where ſuch bridges, or any parcell thereof ſhall happen to be, or elſe two of the next honeſt inhabitants within every towne or pariſh in the ſaid ſhire, riding, city, or towne corporate, by the diſcretion of the ſaid juſtices, or foure of them at the leaſt, whereof one to be of the quorum. But it is good policie, that more then foure juſtices, &c. doe take upon them the authority committed to them by any branch of this act: for if there be but foure, if any of them dyeth, or be out of the commiſſion, the ſurviving three have no authority to proceed.

* Theſe words referre as well to the juſtices of the ſhires or ridings, as of the cities or townes corporate.

[a] Juſtices of peace in ſhires and ridings are by commiſſion, in cities and townes corporate for the moſt part by charter; therefore this word [*authorities*] is uſed.

[b] The firſt thing the juſtices are to doe when they are aſſembled, is to call, &c. if they be preſent (as commonly they are) at the generall ſeſſions of peace, or elſe to make warrants to call, &c. before them at a certain day and place, and in thoſe warrants to ſignifie that it is for a taxation of the inhabitants of the whole county, for reparation of ſuch a bridge.

(2) *Where it cannot be knowne or proved,* &c.] By the context and order of this ſtatute, firſt, for inquiry at the generall ſeſſions, who ought to repaire ſuch decayed bridges: and ſecondly of this branch, where it cannot be knowne or proved (that is, at the generall ſeſſions who owen to repaire it.) It hath been gravely adviſed,

[c] advised, that for the better warrant of these foure justices of peace, inquiry should be made by the great inquest for the body of the county at the generall quarter sessions, who ought to repaire it, and if that cannot appeare upon any proofe made, then a presentment to be made, that the bridge is in decay. And to conclude, *et ulterius juratores prædicti præsentant, quod prorsus nescitur quæ personæ, quæ terræ, sive tenementa, aut corpora politica eundem pontem, aut aliquam inde parcellam ex jure, aut antiqua consuetudine reparare debent, aut consueverunt.* And by this meanes, the foure, or more justices of peace, being judges of record, shall be informed of record, that it cannot be knowne or proved, &c. A safe way for these foure or more of the justices; for to charge the subject without just cause, and not warranted by this act, is a great misprision. [704]

c Hereof we have seen a good presidents; and the like for the presentment you may reade in Lambards justice of peace.

2. At the apparance of such constables or inhabitants, the said justices of peace, or foure of them, whereof one to be of the quorum, with the assent of the said constables or inhabitants, shall have power and authority to taxe, and set every inhabitant in such city, towne, or parish, &c. to such reasonable aide and summe of mony, as they shall thinke by their discretions convenient and sufficient, for the repairing, [d] re-edifying, and amendment of such bridges.

d Nota, for re-edifying, or new building.

It is not here mentioned by any expresse words, that these foure or more justices must execute their authority of this act in the generall sessions of the peace, as it was in the first branch. See for this in the last branch.

First by whom, and in what manner taxation shall be made.

(3) *Justices of peace, or foure of them,* &c.] That is, in such cities, or townes corporate, where foure justices, &c. be: for if there be not foure such justices, they are not within the remedy of this branch, but (as hath been said) are left to the remedy at the common law.

(4) *With the assent of the said constables or inhabitants.*] So as neither the justices, without such assent, nor the constables or inhabitants, without the justices, can make any taxation by this act.

(5) *To taxe and set every inhabitant.*] *Unumquemque inhabitantium, i. singulos inhabitantes,* so as every one may be taxed by himself, and each one beare his owne burthen. And the taxation cannot be set upon the hundred, parish, towne, &c. for then one or a few might be distrained for the whole. What inhabitant is here meant, we have touched before.

By these words [every inhabitant] all priviledges of exemptions or discharges whatsoever from contribution, for the reparation of decayed bridges (if any were) are taken away, although the exemption were by act of parliament.

See the second part of the Institutes, Magna Chart. ca. 15.

How the money so taxed shall be collected.

(6) *And after such taxation made, the said justices shall cause the names and summes of every particular person so by them taxed, to be written in a roll indented.*

Note the names and sums of every particular person, so as (as hath been said) the taxation must be severall and particular.

(7) *In a roll indented.*] This is intended of every severall hundred, and they must be inrolled in parchment, and sealed by the said justices, and this to be done presently after the taxation made.

3. (8) *And shall also have power and authoritie to make two collectors of every hundred, for collection of all such summes of money, by them set and taxed, which collectors (viz. of every hundred) receiving the one part of the said roll indented, under the seales of the said justices, shall have power and authoritie, to collect and receive all the particular summes of money * therein contained.*

* By this it appeareth, that the severall ingrossements must be of the severall summes, &c. in every severall hundred, because the collectors be severall of every severall hundred, and these rolls ingrossed are their severall warrants,

4. (9) *And to distraine every such inhabitant, as shall be taxed, and refuse payment thereof, in his lands, goods, and chattells.*] Hereby foure things are to be observed: first (as hath been said) that the taxation must be severall. 2. That the remedy for levying, is by distresse in his lands, goods, and chattels in any place within that hundred, and to sell such distresse. And this the collectors of that hundred may doe by force of this act. 3. That if upon demand the summe be not paid, albeit the inhabitant doe not expresly refuse, it is a refusall in law. 4. Albeit two collectors be appointed, yet one of them, by the command and consent of the other, may distraine and sell; for this is the distresse and sale of them both.

[705]

5. (10) *And if the distresse be better, to deliver to the owner thereof.*] That is, the surplusage upon the sale, above the summe so distrained for, must be delivered to the owner inhabitant.

6. The residue of this branch, concerning the appointment of two surveyors, and the account of them, and of the two collectors, and other things depending on the same, are evident, and need no explanation.

The 7. branch of this act giveth power to the justices to allow reasonable costs and charges to the surveyors and collectors.

* The 5. branch. * The effect of this branch is, that the said justices in every shire, riding, city, or towne corporate, shall make processe respectively into every shire, and other place out of the shire, riding, city, or towne corporate. And that the sherife shall serve the processe, upon paine of such fine as shall be assessed by such justices.

The 6. branch. The sixth branch excepteth the five ports, and provideth remedy, and giveth jurisdiction to the warden, mayors, and bailiffes elect, and jurats of the same ports, to enquire, heare and determine all manner of annoyances of bridges.

The 7. branch. The seventh branch giveth power to the said justices of peace, or foure, or more of them, to allow reasonable costs and charges to the said surveyors and collectors.

The 8. branch. The last branch containeth a law for amendment of high-waies at the end of the bridges, and power given to foure or more justices of peace, whereof one to be of the quorum in every shire, franchise, or borough, to enquire, heare, and determine in the * "kings generall sessions of the peace, all manner of annoyances of and in such high-waies so being and lying, next adjoyning to any ends of bridges within this realm, distant from any ends of such bridges three hundred foot, and to do in every thing and things concerning the making, repairing, and amending of such high-waies, and every of them, in as large and ample maner, as they might and may do to and for the making, repairing, and amending of bridges, by virtue and authority of this present act."

* Nota.

In the kings generall sessions of the peace, &c.] Hereupon it is collected, that seeing the first branch referreth the proceeding con-

cerning

cerning the decay of bridges to the generall ſeſſions of the peace, and the ſecond branch concerning the calling of the conſtables, &c. and this laſt branch referreth the proceeding for the amendment of high-waies at the end of bridges, to the generall ſeſſions of the peace: it is the ſafeſt way, and neareſt to the meaning of the makers of this law (all the parts thereof being conſidered) that the juſtices of peace, where no certain perſon, &c. is knowne, that ought to repaire any decayed bridge, (and the inhabitants of the whole county are generally to be charged) doe proceed as well for the reparation of the bridges, as of the high-waies at the end of thoſe bridges at the generall ſeſſions of the peace, one of them as it were depending upon the other.

The freehold as well of bridges, as of the high-waies, is in him that hath the freehold of the ſoile, but the free paſſage is for all the kings liege people.

See the ſtatutes of 13 Eliſ. cap. 18. 18 El. cap. 18. & 17 23 El. ca. 11. 39 El. cap. 24. &c. concerning bridges.

See the [a] ſtatute of 23 Hen. 8. cap. 2 concerning the new erecting of gaoles, which cannot be done without act of parliament. That act had little effect; for that the juſtices of peace did little or nothing within the time to them preſcribed by that act; yet reade it, for it hath divers good proviſions in it, and divers of them much like to our act.

[a] 23 H. 8. ca. 2. Parliam. 51 E. 3. nu. 68 it appeareth that gaoles were to be repaired at the kings charge.

[706]

A right profitable law was made, *anno* 43 Eliſ. for commiſſioners, to enquire for mis-imployment of lands, tenements, rents, annuities, profits, hereditaments, goods, chattells, money, and ſtockes of money given, limited, appointed, or aſſigned to or for repaire of bridges *(inter alia)* and by their orders to reforme the ſame, which in ſome caſes is a ready and ſpeedy way, and have wrought good effect. And therefore we will in the next place enumerate and explaine the parts and branches of that act, for the better incouragement and inſtruction of the commiſſioners in that behalfe.

43 Eliſ. ca. 4.

A ſpeedy remedy in many caſes.

An Expoſition upon the Statute of 43 Eliſ. Cap. 4. concerning Commiſſioners authorized to enquire of Miſimployment of Lands or Goods given to Hoſpitalls, by their Orders ſhall be reformed.

[707]

WHEREAS lands, tenements, rents, annuities, profits, hereditaments, goods, chattels, money, and ſtockes of money, have been heretofore given, limited, appointed and aſſigned, as well by the queenes moſt excellent majeſtie, and her moſt noble progenitors, as by ſundry other well diſpoſed perſons; ſome for reliefe of aged, impotent, and poore people; ſome for maintenance of ſicke and maimed

fouldiers and mariners, fchooles of learning, free fchooles, and fcholars of univerfities; fome for repaire of bridges, ports, havens, cawfies, churches, fea-bankes, and high-waies; fome for education and preferment of orphans, fome for or towards reliefe, ftocke or maintenance for houfes of correction; fome for marriages of poore maides, fome for fupportation, aide, and help of young tradefmen, handy-crafts-men, and perfons decayed, and others for reliefe or redemption of prifoners or captives, and for aide or eafe of any poore inhabitants, concerning payment of fifteens, fetting out of fouldiers, and other taxes: which lands, tenements, rents, annuities, profits, hereditaments, goods, chattels, money, and ftockes of money, neverthelesse have not been imployed according to the charitable intent of the givers and founders thereof, by reafon of frauds, breaches of truft, and negligence in thofe that fhould pay, deliver, and imploy the fame. For redreffe and remedy whereof, be it enacted by authoritie of this prefent parliament, that it fhall and may be lawfull to and for the lord chancellor, or keeper of the great feale of England for the time being, and for the chancellor of the duchie of Lancafter for the time being, for lands within the county palatine of Lancafter, from time to time, to award commiffions under the great feale of England, or the feele of the county palatine, as the cafe fhall require into all or any part or parts of this realme, refpectively, according to their feverall jurifdictions, as aforefaid, to the bifhop of every feverall dioceffe and his chancellor (in cafe there fhall be any bifhop of that dioceffe, at the time of awarding of the fame commiffions,) and to other perfons of good and found behaviour, authorizing them thereby, or any foure or more of them, to enquire as well by the oaths of 12 lawfull men or more of the county, as by all other good and lawfull waies and meanes of all and fingular fuch gifts, limitations, affignments, and appointments aforefaid, and of the abufes, breaches of trufts, negligences, mis-imployments, not imploying, concealing, defrauding, mis-converting, or mis-government of any lands, tenements, rents, annuities, profits, hereditaments, goods, chattels, money, or ftockes of money, heretofore given, limited, appointed, or affigned, or which hereafter fhall be given, limited, appointed, or affigned, to or for any the charitable and godly
[708] ufes before rehearfed. And after the faid commiffioners, or any foure or more of them (upon calling the parties intereffed in any fuch lands, tenements, rents, annuities, profits, hereditaments, goods, chattels, money, and ftockes of money) fhall make enquiry by the oathes of twelve men or more of the faid county (whereunto the faid parties intereffed fhall and may have, and take their lawfull challenge and challenges) and upon fuch enquiry, hearing, and examining thereof, fet downe fuch orders, judgements, and decrees, as the faid lands, tenements, rents, annuities, profits, goods, chattels, money, and ftockes of money, may be duly and faithfully imployed, to and

for

for ſuch of the charitable uſes and intents before rehearſed, reſpectively, for which they were given, limited, aſſigned, or appointed, by the donors and founders thereof. Which orders, judgements, and decrees, not being contrary or repugnant to the orders, ſtatutes, or decrees of the donors or founders, ſhall by the authoritie of this preſent parliament ſtand firme and good, according to the tenour and purport thereof, and ſhall be executed accordingly, untill the ſame ſhall be undone or altered by the lord chancellour of England, or lord keeper of the great ſeale of England, or the chancellour of the county palatine of Lancaſter, reſpectively within their ſeverall juriſdictions, upon complaint by any party grieved to be made to them.

Provided alwaies, that neither this act, nor any thing therein contained, ſhall in any wiſe extend to any lands, tenements, rents, annuities, profits, goods, chattels, money, or ſtockes of money given, limited, appointed, or aſſigned, or which ſhall be given, limited, appointed or aſſigned to any colledge, hall, or houſe of learning within the univerſities of Oxford or Cambridge, or to the colledges of Weſtminſter, Eaton, or Wincheſter, or any of them, or to any cathedrall or collegiat church within this realme.

And provided alſo, that neither this act, nor any thing therein, ſhall extend to any citie, or towne corporate, or to any the lands, or tenements given to the uſes aforeſaid, within any ſuch citie, or town corporate, where there is a ſpeciall governour or governours appointed to governe or direct ſuch lands, tenements, or things diſpoſed to any the uſes aforeſaid, neither to any colledge, hoſpitall, or free ſchoole, which have ſpeciall viſitors, or governours, or overſeers appointed them by their founders.

Provided alſo, and be it enacted by the authoritie aforeſaid, that neither this act, nor any thing therein contained, ſhall be any way prejudiciall or hurtfull to the juriſdiction of the ordinary, or power of the ordinary, but that he may lawfully in every cauſe execute and perform the ſame, as though this act had never been had or made.

Provided alſo, and be it enacted, that no perſon or perſons that hath or ſhall have any of the ſaid lands, tenements, rents, annuities, profits, hereditaments, goods, chattels, money, or ſtockes of money in his hands or poſſeſſion, or doth or ſhall pretend title thereunto, ſhall be named a commiſſioner or a juror for any the cauſes aforeſaid, or being named, ſhall execute or ſerve in the ſame.

And provided alſo, that no perſon or perſons, which hath purchaſed or obtained, or ſhall purchaſe or obtaine upon valuable conſideration of money or land, any eſtate or intereſt of, [709] in, to, or out of any lands, tenements, rents, annuities, hereditaments, goods, or chattels that have been, or ſhall be given, limited, or appointed to any the charitable uſes above mentioned, without fraud or covin, having no notice of the ſame

charitable uſes, ſhall not be impeached by decrees or orders of commiſſioners above mentioned, for or concerning the ſame his eſtate or intereſt. And yet neverthelesſe, be it enacted that the ſaid commiſſioners, or any foure or more of them, ſhall and may make decrees and orders for recompence to be made by any perſon or perſons, who being put in truſt, or having notice of the charitable uſes above mentioned, hath or ſhall breake the ſame truſt, or defraud the ſame uſes by any conveyance, gift, grant, leaſe, demiſe, releaſe, or converſion whatſoever, and againſt the heires, executors, and adminiſtrators of him, them, or any of them, having aſſets in law or equitie, ſo farre as the ſame aſſets will extend.

Provided alwaies, that this act ſhall not extend to give power or authoritie to any commiſſioners before mentioned, to make any orders, judgements or decrees for or concerning any mannors, lands, tenements, or other hereditaments, aſſured, conveyed, granted, or come unto the queens majeſtie, to the late king Henry the eighth, king Edward the ſixth, or queene Mary, by act of parliament, ſurrender, exchange, relinquiſhment, eſcheat, attainder, conveyance, or otherwiſe. And yet neverthelesſe, be it enacted, that if any ſuch mannors, lands, tenements, or hereditaments, or any of them, or any eſtate, rent, or profit thereof, or out of the ſame, or any part thereof have, or hath been given, granted, limited, appointed, or aſſigned to or for any the charitable uſes before expreſſed at any time ſithence the beginning of her majeſties reigne, that then the ſaid commiſſioners, or any foure or more of them, ſhall and may as concerning the ſame lands, tenements, hereditaments, eſtate, rent, or profit ſo given, limited, appointed or aſſigned, proceed to enquire, and to make orders, judgements and decrees according to the purport and meaning of this act, as before is mentioned: the ſaid laſt mentioned proviſo notwithſtanding.

And be it further enacted, that all orders, judgements and decrees of the ſaid commiſſioners, or of any foure or more of them, ſhall be certified under the ſeales of the ſaid commiſſioners, or any foure or more of them, either into the court of the chancery of England, or into the court of the chancery within the countie palatine of Lancaſter, as the caſe ſhall require reſpectively, according to the ſeverall juriſdictions, within ſuch convenient time as ſhall be limited in the ſaid commiſſions.

And that the ſaid lord chancellor, or lord keeper, and the ſaid chancellor of the dutchy, ſhall and may, within their ſaid ſeverall juriſdictions, take ſuch order for the due execution of all or any of the ſaid judgements, decrees, and orders, as to either of them ſhall ſeem fit and convenient.

And that if after any ſuch certificate or certificates made, any perſon or perſons ſhall find themſelves grieved with any of the ſaid orders, judgements, or decrees, that then it ſhall and may be lawfull to and for them, or any of them to complaine in that behalfe unto the ſaid lord chancellour, or lord keeper, or to the chancellour

chancellour of the ſaid duchie of Lancaſter, according to their ſeverall juriſdictions, for redreſſe therein. And that upon ſuch complaint, the ſaid lord chancellour, or lord keeper, or the ſaid chancellour of the duchy, may, according to their ſaid ſeverall juriſdictions, by ſuch courſe as to their wiſdomes ſhall ſeem meeteſt, the circumſtances of the caſe conſidered, proceed to the examination, hearing and determining thereof: and upon hearing thereof, ſhall and may adnull, diminiſh, alter or enlarge the ſaid orders, judgements and decrees of the ſaid commiſſioners, or any foure or more of them, as to either of them in their ſaid ſeverall juriſdictions ſhall be thought to ſtand with equitie and good conſcience, according to the true intent and meaning of the donors and founders thereof, and ſhall and may taxe and award good coſts of ſuit by their diſcretions, againſt ſuch perſons as they ſhall find to complaine unto them without juſt and ſufficient cauſe of the orders, judgements, and decrees before mentioned, 39 El. 6. 43 El. 9.

Authority is given to the lord chancellour, or lord keeper, and to the chancellour of the dutchy reſpectively, to grant commiſſions under the ſeverall ſeales.

Concerning theſe commiſſions, theſe ſixe things are to be obſerved:

Firſt the number muſt be foure, or more.

2. The commiſſioners to be the biſhop and chancellor of that dioceſſe (if there be a biſhop) and other perſons of good and ſound behaviour.

3. In that commiſſion any foure of them doe ſuffice to make orders and decrees, for therein none is of the quorum.

4. None ſhall be commiſſioners that have any part of the lands, &c. or goods, or chattels, money, or ſtockes in queſtion.

5. The commiſſion is to limit a certaine time, within which the commiſſioners are to order, decree, and certifie.

6. Their authority is to enquire as well by the oath of twelve lawfull men, or more, as by all other good waies and meanes.

Concerning the jurors, or inqueſt of inquiry, theſe two things are to be obſerved:

Firſt, the parties intereſſed may have and take their lawfull challenge and challenges.

2. None that pretend title to any of the lands, &c. goods or chattels, money, or ſtockes in queſtion, ſhall be a juror, &c.

They are to enquire of all and ſingular gifts, limitations, and appointments of any lands, tenements, rents, annuities, profits, hereditaments, goods, chattels, money, and ſtockes of money, for 21. charitable uſes in relieving, maintaining, repairing, educating, preferring, marrying, ſupporting, aiding, helping, redeeming and eaſing.

1. For reliefe of aged, impotent, and poore people, 2. for maintenance of ſicke and maimed ſouldiers, 3. ſchooles of learning, 4. free ſchooles, 5. ſcholars in univerſities, 6. and houſes of correction, 7. for repaire of bridges, 8. of ports or havens, 9. of cawſies, 10. of churches, 11. of ſea-bankes, 12. and of high-waies,

13. for education and preferment of orphans, 14. for marriage of poore maides, 15. for supportation, aide, and help of young trades-men, 16. of handi-crafts men, and 17. of persons decayed, 18. for redemption or reliefe of prisoners or captives, 19. for ease and aide of any poore inhabitants, concerning payment of fifteenes, 20. setting out of souldiers, 21. and other taxes.

[711]

And the commissioners have power also to enquire of these nine things:
1. Of abuses,
2. Breaches of trust,
3. Negligences,
4. Mis-imployments,
5. Not imploying,
6. Concealing,
7. Defrauding,
8. Mis-converting,
9. Mis-government,

of any lands, tenements, &c. rents, &c. goods, money, &c. given to any of the charitable uses aforesaid.

But this act doth not extend to all lands, &c. nor to all goods and chattels, money, or stockes given to any of the charitable uses aforesaid; but certaine are excepted in these eight severall cases, *viz.*

First, of the colledges, halls, or houses of learning in either of the universities.

2. Of the colledge of Westminster.

3. Of the colledge of Eaton.

4. Of the colledge of Winchester.

5. Of any city, or towne corporate, where there is a speciall governour or governours of such lands, &c.

6. Of any colledge, hospitall, or free schoole, which have speciall visitors, or governors, or overseers, appointed to them by their founders.

* So as none but valuable consideration, and no valuable consideration, but for money or land, will serve the turne.

7. Of purchasers, having these three qualities: first, for * valuable consideration of money or land: 2. without fraud or covin: 3. having no notice of the same charitable use. But albeit the commissioners cannot make any decree against any such purchasers, yet may they make decrees for recompence to be made by any person or persons, who being put in trust, or having notice of the charitable uses abovesaid, have or shall breake the said trust, or defraud the same uses by any conveyance, gift, grant, lease, release, or conversion, and against his or their heires, executors and administrators, having assets in law or [a] equity, so farre as the same assets will extend.

[a] Nota, assets in equity, as trusts, confidences, and the like.

8. Of purchasers of lands, tenements, and hereditaments assured, conveyed, or come to queen Elisabeth, Hen. 8. Edw. 6. or queen Mary by act of parliament, surrender, exchange, relinquishment, escheat, attornment, conveyance, or otherwise. But if any such mannors, lands, &c. have since the beginning of queen Elisabeths reigne been given, &c. to any of the charitable uses before expressed, then this act doth extend to the same.

Concerning the certificate of the commissioners, these foure things are to be observed:

First, that they certifie their order and decree respectively, either into the court of the chancery of England, or into the chancery of the county palatine of Lancaster, as the case shall require.

2. That

2. That it ought to be in parchment, under the hands and feals of the commiffioners.

3. It muft be within the time limited in the commiffion.

4. That the lord chancellor, or lord keeper, and the faid chancellor of the duchy fhall and may within their feverall jurifdictions take fuch order for the due execution of all or any of the faid judgements, decrees and orders fo certified, as to either of them fhall feem fit and convenient.

In the remedy for the party grieved with fuch decrees fo certified, thefe five things are to be confidered:

Firft, that he complaine to the lord chancellour, or lord keeper, or to the chancellour of the duchy, according to their feverall jurifdictions for redreffe thereof. And this complaint is to be by bill.

2. Upon fuch complaint, firft, they fhall refpectively by fuch courfe, as to their wifedomes fhall feem meeteft, the circumftance of the cafe confidered, proceed to the examination, hearing, and determining thereof. 2. Upon hearing thereof fhall or may admit the whole (which rarely is done) diminifh (in part) or enlarge (that is, to confirme the former, and to enlarge the fame by adding fomething thereunto) the judgements and decrees fo certified. [712]

3. As fhall be thought to ftand with equity and good confcience.

4. According to the true intent and meaning of the * donors and founders thereof.

* This is the *lapis ductitius*, whereby the commiffioners and chancellors muft inftitute their courfe.

5. And fhall and may taxe and award good cofts of fuit by their difcretions (refpectively) againft fuch perfons as fhall complaine to them refpectively, without juft and fufficient caufe of the orders, judgements, and decrees before mentioned. But this order being given and limited by act of parliament, no cofts (if the order, judgement, or decree be adnulled, diminifhed, or enlarged) ought to be given to the party complaining.

The Expofition of the Statute of 31 Elif. Cap. 12. concerning Sellers of Horfes in * Faires and Markets, &c. [713]

* Forum à ferendo (aut quod fit foris) quia ibidem merces afportari folent: Latinè, Feriæ, quia ibidem merces portantur. Unde *Feires*, or **Faires** Anglicè, & *Foire* Gallicè. Nundinæ à nono die, &c. **Mart** is derived à mercando, of buying and felling, and fo is mercatus alfo. Emporium, Græcè Ἐμπόριον, quia ibi conveniunt Ἔμποροι, i. Mercatores.

BEFORE we enter into the expofition of this ftatute, we will confider, firft, what the common law was before the making of this ftatute, 2. what any acts of parliament have wrought in this cafe, before this act of 31 Elif. 3. we will difcend to the expofition of our faid act of 31 Elif.

As to the firft, the common law did hold it for a point of great policie, and behovefull for the common-wealth, that faires and markets overt fhould be replenifhed, and well furnifhed with all manner

manner of commodities, vendible in faires and markets, for the necessary sustentation and use of the people. And to that end the common law did ordaine (to encourage men thereunto) that all sales and contracts of any thing vendible in faires or markets overt should not be good onely between the parties, but should bind those that right had thereunto. But this rule hath many exceptions.

35 H. 6. 29. Pl. Com. 243. Doct. & Stud. 39. b.

First, it shall not bind the king for any of his goods sold in market overt by any person, but regularly the sale by a stranger in market overt bindeth an infant, a feme covert that hath right either in their owne right, or as executor, or administrator, ideots, *non compos mentis*, men beyond sea, and in prison, that right have to the same.

Lib. 5. fo. 83. b. Lib. int' Rast. 327. 2 & 3 Ph. & Mar. cap. 7. Lib. 5. fo. 83. b. 35 H. 6. 7. simile.

2. Although the faires or markets be overt, yet the sale must be made in a place that is overt and open, not in a backe roome, ware-house, &c. as you may reade, lib. 5. fol. 83. b. case de market overt.

3. Although it be in an open place, yet overt in this case implies apt and sufficient, as not to sell plate openly in a scriveners shop, or the like, but openly in a goldsmiths shop, &c. lib. 5. fol. 83. *ubi supra*.

12 E. 4. 12. b. and all the bookes. Doct. & Stud. 64. b. 33 H. 6. 5. 12 H. 8. 10. b. [a] 14 H. 8. 8 Pl. Com. 46. 18 E. 4. 24. lib. 3. fol. 78. b. in Fermors case, & 83. a. in Windhams case. Doct. & St. f. 39. [b] Vid. the books to the 5. [c] 34 H. 6. 10. & 11.

4. It must be a sale, and not a free gift, without any valuable consideration: for faires and markets were not instituted for gifts, but for sales; therefore gift in this act is to be intended of a gift for valuable consideration, and not a free gift.

[a] 5. If the buyer doth know whose goods they were, and that the seller thereof hath at the most but a wrongfull possession, this shall not bind him that right hath.

[b] 6. If they be sold by covin between two of purpose to barre him that right hath, this barreth not.

[c] 7. If a sale be made of goods by a stranger in a market overt whereby the right of A. is bound, yet if the seller acquireth the goods againe, A. may take them againe, because he was the wrong doer, and he shall not take advantage of his owne wrong.

7 E. 4. 15. 32 H. 6. 1. 18 E. 4. 6. 24. 9 H. 6. 45. [d] 21 H. 7. 40. b. Fineux chiefe justice. Also for the feme covert, vid. Mich. 22 & 23 Elis. coram rege in action sur le case, inter Guibson & Thorpnell, Suff. [e] Dyer 1 Mar. fo. 99. 121.

8. There must be a sale and contract; and therefore a sale to a man of his owne goods in market overt, bindeth not; and likewise a sale in market overt by an infant of such tendernesse of age, as it may appeare to the buyer that he is within age, or by a [d] feme covert, if the buyer know her to be a feme covert (unlesse for such things as she usually trades for, or by the consent of her husband) bindeth not. *Et sic de similibus*.

[e] 9. The contract must be originally and wholly made in the market overt, and * not to have the inception out of the market, and the consummation in the market.

*[714]

Vid. 9 H. 6. 45. 35 H 6. 2 & 3 Ph. & Mar. c. 7. Doct. & St. 39. b.

10. By the common law the property was altered (though some opinions be to the contrary) by sale in market overt, albeit no toll was paid either in respect of the freedome of the faire or market, wherein no toll at all was to be paid, or for that many were discharged of payment of toll, as the king, and some of his subjects by charter, and some by tenure, as ancient demesne, &c. where toll of others was to be taken.

Lib. int' Rast. 327. divisione Feires, &c.

11. The sale must not be in the night, but between the rising of the sun, and the going downe of the same: for he that hath a faire or market, either by grant or prescription, hath power to hold it

per

per unum diem, seu duos, vel tres dies, &c. where *(dies)* is taken for *dies solaris*; for if it should be taken for *dies naturalis*, then might the sale be made at midnight. And yet the sale that is made in the night is good between the parties, but not to bind a stranger that right hath.

12. A. commit a robbery or felony of the goods of B. the officer of the king doth seise the goods (in lawfull manner) to the kings use. B. pursueth his appeale freshly, the kings officer, or any other selleth the goods in market overt; B. pursueth his appeale against A. untill he hath convicted him of the felony, the king shall make him restitution of his goods, notwithstanding the sale in market overt, because of the fresh and diligent suit and pursuit of record, the goods were so protected thereby, and by the kings seisure, that the property of the same, being *tanquam in custodia legis*, cannot be altered by sale in market overt. And by the statute of 21 H. 8. cap. 11. it is enacted, that if any felon be of any money, goods, or chattels, and the said felon be indited, and after arraigned of the same felony, and found guilty, or otherwise attainted, by reason of evidence given by the party so robbed, or owner, or by any other by their procurement, [a] that the party so robbed, or owner shall be restored to his said money, goods, and chattels. And that the justices, &c. have power by this present act to award from time to time writs of restitution, &c. in like manner, [b] as though any such felon were attainted at the suit of the party in appeale.

See Stamf. Pl. Cor. 365. b.

21 H. 8. ca. 11. Nota hoc.

[a] Note these absolute words for restitution, upon the evidence given upon this act, there needeth no fresh suit to be enquired of, as we know by experience.

[b] These words referre only to the manner of the writs of restitution.

So as in this case also the party robbed, or owner shall have restitution, notwithstanding any sale in market overt. See the third part of the Institutes, cap. Restitution. And the reason of the law in this case of restitution is, to incourage the owners to pursue the felons, that they might be condignly punished, *ut pœna ad paucos, metus ad omnes perveniat*. And although in this rare case it may be, that one may lose the horse which he came to *bona fide* in market overt; yet *spoliatus debet ante omnia restitui*. And the old rule, *caveat emptor*, doth hold herein: and when two rights come together, the ancient right is to be preferred.

And it is to be observed, that none of these 12 exceptions are abrogated by any act of parliament, but yet remaine in full force.

As to the second, we are to consider the statute of 2 & 3 Ph. & Mar. cap. 7. entituled, Sellers of horses in faires, markets, &c. which (because horse-stealers may flee farre off in a short space) hath made void the sale of horses in market overt in divers cases. The tenour of which act ensueth:

Forasmuch as stollen horses, mares, and geldings, by theeves and their confederates, be for the most part sold, exchanged, given, or put away in houses, stables, backsides, and other * secret and privie places of markets and faires, and the toll also privily paid for the same, whereby the true owners thereof, being not able to trie the falshood and covin betwixt the buyer and seller of such horse, mare, or gelding, is by the common lawes of this realme without remedy:

2 & 3 Phil. & Mar. cap. 7.

* Hereby the vulgar people were deceived, but in law this changed no property, as before it appeareth, lib. 5. fo. 83. ubi supra.

Be it therefore enacted by the authoritie of this present parliament, that the owner, governour, ruler, fermor, steward, bailiffe,

The 1. branch.

bailiffe, or chiefe keeper of every faire and market overt within this realme, and other * the queenes dominions, shall before the feast of Easter next, and so yearly appoint and limit out a certaine and speciall open place within the towne, place, field, or circuit, where horses, mares, geldings, and colts, have been and shall be used to be sold in any faire or market overt, in which said certaine and open place, as is aforesaid, there shall be by the said ruler or keeper of the said faire or market, put in and appointed one sufficient person or more, to take toll, and keep the same place, from ten of the clocke before noone, untill sun-set of every day of the foresaid faire or market upon pain to lose and forfeit for every default forty shillings.

A certain & speciall place for the horse-faire.

The 2. branch. A sufficient person to take toll, & keep the hors-faire from 10 of the clock before noon, till sunset.

The 3. branch. 1. The toll gatherer to receive the toll between these houres. 2. And shall have presently before him the parties to the bargain at the taking of the toll. 3. And the horse, &c. 4. And shall write in a book the names, sirnames, & dwelling places of the said parties, & the colour, with one speciall marke at the least of every such horse, &c.

And that every toll-gatherer his deputy or deputies, shall, during the time of every the said faires and markets, take their due and lawfull tolls, for every such horse, mare, gelding, or colt, at the said open place to be appointed, as is aforesaid, and betwixt the houres of ten of the clocke in the morning, and the sun-set of the same day, if it be tendered, and not at any other time or place, and shall have presently before him or them at the taking of the same toll the parties to the bargaine, exchange, gift, contract, or putting away of every such horse, mare, gelding, or colt, and also the same horse, mare, gelding, and colt so sold, exchanged, or put away; and shall then write, or cause to be written in a booke to be kept for that purpose, the names, sirnames, and dwelling places of all the said parties, and the colour, with one speciall marke at the least of every such horse, mare, gelding, or colt, on paine to forfeit at and for every default contrary to the tenour hereof forty shillings.

* The 4. branch. The toll-gatherer to deliver the book to the owner, &c. of the faire or market.

* And the said toll-gatherer, or keeper of the said book, shall within one day next after every such faire or market, bring and deliver his said booke to the owner, governour, ruler, steward, bailiffe, or chiefe keeper of the said faire or market, who shall then cause a note to be made of the true number of all horses, mares, geldings, and colts sold at the said market or faire, and shall there subscribe his name, or set his marke thereunto, upon paine to him that shall make default therein to lose and forfeit for every default forty shillings, and also to answer the partie grieved by reason of the same his negligence in every behalfe.

The 5. branch. Sixe points to save the property of the right owner, &c. 1. The horse stolne must be ridden, &c. openly in the faire or market, by the space of an hour, between ten of the clock before noon,

And be it further enacted by the authoritie aforesaid, that the sale, gift, exchange, or putting away after the last day of February now next coming, in any faire or market overt, of any horse, mare, gelding, or colt, that is, or shall be theevishly stollen, or feloniously taken away from any person or persons, shall not alter, take away, nor exchange the propertie of any person or persons to, or from any such horse, mare, gelding, or colt, unlesse the same horse, mare, gelding, or colt, shall be in the time of the said faire or market, wherein the same shall be so sold, given, exchanged, or put away, openly [1] ridden, led, walked, driven, or kept standing, by the space of one houre together

gether at the leaſt, betwixt ten of the clocke in the morning, and the ſun-ſetting, in the open place of the faire or market, wherein horſes are commonly uſed to be ſold, [2] and not within any houſe, yard, backſide, or other privie or ſecret place; [3] and unleſſe all the parties to the bargaine, contract, gift, or exchange, preſent in the ſaid faire or market, ſhall alſo come together, and bring the horſe, mare, gelding, or colt ſo ſold, exchanged, given, or put away to the open place appointed for the toll-taker, or for the book-keeper, where no toll is due, [4] and there enter, or cauſe to be entred their names and dwelling places in manner as is aforeſaid, [5] with the colour or colours, and one ſpeciall marke at the leaſt of every the ſame horſes, mares, geldings, or colts in the toll-takers booke, or in the keepers booke for that purpoſe, whereunto toll is due, as is aforeſaid, [6] and alſo pay him their toll, if they ought to pay any, and if not, then the buyer to give one penny for the entry of their names, and executing the other circumſtances afore rehearſed, to him that ſhall write the ſame in the ſaid booke.

and ſun-ſetting, or elſe no property ſhall be altered or changed. This is in affirmance of the common law.

[716]

The 6. branch. Which is added, for, as hath been aforeſaid, toll is not ever due nor payable by all perſons in faires & markets, to the end that the book-keeper may be equivalent in thoſe caſes to the toll receivers.

And if any horſe, mare, gelding, or colt, that is, or ſhall be theeviſhly ſtollen, or taken away, ſhall after the ſaid laſt day of February next coming be ſold, given, exchanged, or put away in any faire or market, * and not uſed in all points, according to the tenour and intent of this eſtatute, that then the owner of every ſuch horſe, mare, gelding, or colt, ſhall and may by force of this eſtatute ſeiſe, or take againe the ſaid horſe, mare, gelding, or colt, or have an action of detinue or replevin for the ſame, any ſale, gift, exchange, or putting away of any ſuch horſe, mare, gelding, or colt, other then according to this eſtatute in any wiſe notwithſtanding.

The 7. branch. * This maketh void the ſale in faire or market overt, if the horſe be not uſed, &c. in all the ſaid points, according to the tenour and intent of this act. See for theſe points in the 3, 4, 5, & 6. branches.

The 8. branch.

The one halfe of all which forfeitures to be to the king and queens majeſtie, her heires and ſucceſſours, and the other to him or them that will ſue for the ſame before the juſtices of peace, or in any of the king and queenes majeſties ordinary courts of record, by bill, plaint, action of debt, or information; in which ſuits no protection, eſſoine, or wager of law ſhall be allowed.

The penalty to be recovered before juſtices of peace, &c.

The 9. branch.

And be it enacted by the authoritie aforeſaid, that the juſtices of peace of every place and county, as well within liberties, as without, ſhall have authoritie in their ſeſſions within the limits of their authoritie and commiſſion, to enquire, heare, and determine all offences againſt this eſtatute, as they may doe any other matter tryable before them.

Juſtices of peace to heare and determine all offences againſt this ſtatute.

The 10. branch.

Provided alwaies, that in every ſuch faire and market, where any toll is, nor ſhall be due, ne leviable by reaſon of the freedome, liberty, or priviledge of the ſaid faire or market, the keeper or keepers of the booke touching the execution of this preſent act, ſhall take nor exact but one penny upon and for every contract, for his labour in writing the entry concerning the premiſſes, in manner and forme, as is before declared.

The book-keepers fee for his labour in writing the entry of the contract.

But

But ſeeing neither the rules of the common-law, nor the proviſions of this act wrought ſo good effect as was expected, therefore a right profitable additionall law was made *in anno* 31 *reginæ Eliſabethæ*, for the ſaving of the property of horſes, mares, geldings, colts, and fillies, to and for the right owners, which hereafter enſueth:

The cauſes wherefore horſes, &c. are ſo commonly ſtoln.

[717]

* 2 & 3 Phil. & Mar. cap. 7. See 2 E. 3. c. 15. 5 E. 3. c. 3. 27 H. 6. c. 5.

Whereas through the counties of this realme, horſe-ſtealing is growne ſo common, as neither in paſtures or cloſes, nor hardly in ſtables the ſame are to be in ſafety from ſtealing, which enſueth by the ready buying of the ſame by horſe-courſers and others in ſome open faires or markets farre diſtant from the owner, and with ſuch ſpeed as the owner cannot by purſuit poſſibly help the ſame: and * ſundry good ordinances have heretofore been made touching the manner of ſelling and tolling of horſes, mares, geldings, and colts in faires and markets, which have not wrought ſo good effect for the repreſſing or avoiding of horſe-ſtealing, as was expected.

The 1. branch. Nota, for a further remedy, this is an act of addition, conſiſting upon ſix points, for the ſaving of the property of the right owner. [a] A gift, without valuable conſideration in market overt, altereth no property, as before hath been ſaid. This ſtatute reſtraineth the very ſale, and maketh it void, if the act be not purſued, and this firſt branch is in the diſ-junctive, unleſſe either the toll-taker or book-keeper ſhall and will take upon him perfect knowledge, &c. or elſe that he ſo ſelling, or offering to ſell, &c. ſhall bring, &c. one ſufficient and credible perſon, &c. that ſhall avouch, &c. who vulgarly is called a voucher; and this branch extendeth to all ſales of horſes, in market overt, whether the horſe, &c. be ſtolne, or not ſtolne. The 2. branch. That he ſo ſelling, &c. cauſe to be entred the true chriſtian name, and ſirname, myſterie, and place of dwelling, &c. and the very true price and value. See for the 6th point in the ſeventh branch.

Now for a further remedy in that behalfe, be it enacted by the authoritie of this preſent parliament, that no perſon after twenty dayes next after the end of this ſeſſion of parliament, ſhall in any faire or market, ſell, [a] give, exchange, or put away any horſe, mare, gelding, colt, or filly, unleſſe [1] the toll-taker there, or (where no toll is paid) the book-keeper, bailiffe, or chiefe officer of the ſame faire or market, ſhall and will take upon him perfect knowledge of the perſon that ſo ſhall ſell, or offer to ſell, give, or exchange any horſe, mare, gelding, colt, or filly, and of his true chriſten name, ſirname, and place of dwelling or reſiancie, [2] and ſhall enter all the ſame his knowledge into a booke there kept for ſale of horſes, [3] or elſe that he ſo ſelling, or offering to ſell, give, exchange, or put away any horſe, mare, gelding, colt, or filly, ſhall bring unto the toll-taker, or other officer aforeſaid of the ſame faire or market, one ſufficient or credible perſon, that can, ſhall or will teſtifie and declare unto, and before ſuch toll-taker, book-keeper, or other officer, that he knoweth the party that ſo ſelleth, giveth, exchangeth, or putteth away ſuch horſe, mare, gelding, colt, or filly, and his true name, ſirname, myſterie, and dwelling place: [4] and there enter, or cauſe to be entred in the booke of the ſaid toll-taker, or officer, as well the true chriſten name, and ſirname, myſterie, and place of dwelling or reſiancie of him that ſo ſelleth, giveth, exchangeth, or putteth away ſuch horſe, mare, gelding, colt, or filly, as of him that ſo ſhall teſtifie or avouch his knowledge of the ſame perſon, [5] and ſhall alſo cauſe to be entred the very true price or value that he ſhall have for the ſame horſe, mare, gelding, colt, or filly ſo ſold.

And

* And that no person shall take upon him to avouch, testifie, or declare, that he knoweth the party that so shall offer to sell, give, exchange, or put away such horse, mare, gelding, colt, or filly, unlesse he doe indeed truly know the same party, and shall truly declare to the toll-taker, or other officer aforesaid, as well the christen name, sirname, mysterie, and place of dwelling and resiancie of himselfe, as of him, of, and for whom he maketh such testimony and avouchment.

* The 3. branch. No person take upon him to avouch, unlesse he do indeed truly know, &c.

And that no toll-taker, or other person, keeping any booke of entry of sales of horses in faires or markets, shall take or receive any toll, or make entry of any sale, gift, exchange, or putting away of any horse, mare, gelding, colt, or filly, unlesse he knoweth the party that so selleth, giveth, exchangeth, or putteth away any such horse, mare, gelding, colt, or filly, and his true christen name, sirname, mysterie, and place of his dwelling or resiancie, or the party that shall and will testifie and avouch his knowledge of the same person so selling, giving, exchanging, or putting away such horse, mare, gelding, colt, or filly, and his true christen name, sirname, mysterie, and place of dwelling or resiance, and shall make a perfect entry into the said booke of such his knowledge of the person, and of the name, sirname, mysterie, and place of the dwelling or resiancie of the same person, and also the true price, or value that shall be, bona fide, taken or had, for any such horse, mare, gelding, colt, or filly so sold, given, exchanged, or put away, so farre as he can understand the same, and then give to the party so buying, or taking by gift, exchange, or otherwise, such horse, mare, gelding, colt, or filly, requiring and paying two pence for the same, a true and perfect note in writing of all the full contents of the same, subscribed with his hand, on * paine that every person that so shall sell, give, exchange, or put away any horse, mare, gelding, colt, or filly, without being knowne to the toll-taker, or other officer aforesaid, or without bringing such a voucher or witnesse, causing the same to be entred as aforesaid, and every person making any untrue testimony or avouchment in the behalfe aforesaid, and every toll-taker, book-keeper, or other officer of faire or market aforesaid, offending in the premisses contrary to the true meaning aforesaid, shall forfeit for every such default the summe of five pounds; but also that every sale, gift, exchange, or other putting away of any horse, mare, gelding, colt, filly, in faire or market not used in all points according to the true meaning aforesaid, shall be void: the one halfe of all which forfeitures to be to the queenes majestie, her heires and successors and the other halfe to him or them that will sue for the same before the justices of peace, or in any of her majesties ordinary courts of record, by bill, plaint, action of debt, or information, in which no essoin or protection shall be allowed.

The 4. branch. No toll-taker, or book-keeper shall make any entry, &c but upon the disjunctive in the first branch.

[718]

The 5. branch. To give to the party so buying, &c. a true and perfect note in writing, &c. requiring and paying two pence for the same.

* On pain, &c.

To forfeit five pounds.

The penalties to be recovered before justices of peace, &c.

And be it further enacted, that the justices of peace of every place and county, as well within liberties as without, shall have authoritie

The 6 branch. Justices of peace to enquire, heare, and determine.

authoritie in their ſeſſions within the limits of their authoritie and commiſſion, to enquire, heare, and determine all offences againſt this ſtatute, as they may doe any other matter tryable before them.

The 7. branch. Extendeth only to horſes, &c. that are ſtolne. The ſixth point for the ſaving of the property of the right owner. Albeit this act be purſued in all points, yet the ſale in market overt ſhall not take away the property, &c. if the owner, &c. claime within ſix moneths, &c.

And be it further enacted, that if any horſe, mare, gelding, colt, or filly, after twenty dayes next enſuing the end of this ſeſſion of parliament, ſhall be ſtollen, and after ſhall be ſold in open faire or market, and the ſame ſale ſhall be uſed in all points and circumſtances as aforeſaid: that yet neverthleſſe, the ſale of any ſuch horſe, mare, gelding, colt, or filly, within ſix moneths next after the felony done, ſhall not take away the property of the owner from whom the ſame was ſtollen, ſo as claime be made within ſixe moneths by the party from whom the ſame was ſtollen, or by his executors or adminiſtrators, or by any other by any of their appointment, at, or in the towne or pariſh where the ſame horſe, mare, gelding, colt, or filly ſhall be found, before the maior or other head officer of the ſame town or pariſh, if the ſame horſe, mare, gelding, colt, or filly ſhall happen to be found in any towne corporate, or market towne, or elſe before any juſtice of peace of that county neere to the place where ſuch horſe, mare, gelding, colt, or filly ſhall be found, if it be out of towne corporate, or market towne, and ſo as proofe be made within forty daies then next enſuing, by two ſufficient witneſſes to be produced and depoſed before ſuch head officer or juſtice, (* who by vertue of this act ſhall have authority to miniſter an oath in that behalfe) that the property of the ſame horſe, mare, gelding, colt, or filly ſo claimed, was in the party, by, or for whom ſuch claime is made, and was ſtollen from him within ſix moneths next before ſuch claime of any ſuch horſe, gelding, mare, colt, or filly, but that the party from whom the ſaid horſe, mare, gelding, colt, or filly was ſtollen, his executors or adminiſtrators, ſhall and may at all times after notwithſtanding any ſuch ſale or ſales in any faire, or open market thereof made, have propertie and power to have, take againe, and enjoy the ſaid horſe, mare, gelding, colt, or filly, upon payment or readineſſe, or offer to pay to the party that ſhall have the poſſeſſion and intereſt of the ſame horſe, mare, gelding, colt, or filly, if he will receive and accept it, ſo much money as the ſame party ſhall depoſe and ſweare before ſuch head officer, or juſtice of peace (* who, by vertue of this act, ſhall have authoritie to miniſter and give an oath in that behalfe) that hee paid for the ſame bona fide, without fraud or colluſion, any law, ſtatute, or other thing to the contrary thereof in any wiſe notwithſtanding.

Two ſufficient witneſſes.

[719]

* None can examine witneſſes in a new manner, without act of parliament.

Upon payment of ſo much mony as was *bona fide* payed for the ſame.

* No man can give an oath in a new caſe, without act of parliament.

This act is but an act (as hath been ſaid) of addition to the common law, and to the act of 2 & 3 Phil. & Mar. cap. 7. all ſtanding in force, and muſt be purſued.

The 8. branch. Clergy taken from acceſſaries, &c. after.

And be it further enacted by the authoritie aforeſaid, that after twenty daies after the end of this ſeſſion of parliament, not

onely all accessaries before such felony done, but also all accessaries after such felony, shall be deprived and put from all benefit of their clergy, as the principall by statute heretofore made, is, or ought to be.

So as what by the 12 points of the common law, and what by the 12 points of additions by these two statutes the property of horses, &c. are so preserved, as if the owner be of capacity to understand them (being collected together, and explained by our labours) and be vigilant and industrious to pursue the same, it is almost impossible that the property of the horse, &c. either stolne, or not stolne, should be altered by any sale in market overt by him that is *malæ fidei possessor*.

And let the owner or ruler of the faire, the toll-taker, or book-keeper, and the avoucher take heed, that they performe the duty enjoyned to them by this statute, otherwise it will be very penall to them. And hereby good direction is given to courratiers, horse-coursers how they may safely deale. Hippocomi, Mangones equorum.

The Exposition of the Statutes of 39 Elis. Cap. 5. and 21 Jac. Cap. 1. concerning the Erection of Hospitals, and Houses of Correction. [720]

BE it enacted by the authoritie of this present parliament, that all and every person and persons (1) seised of an estate in fee-simple (2), their heires, executors, or assignes (3), at his or their wills and pleasures, shall have full power, strength, licence, and lawfull authoritie at any time during the space of twenty yeares (4) next ensuing, by deed inrolled in the high court of chancerie, to erect (5), found and establish one or more hospitals (6), *measons de dieu*, abiding places, or houses of correction, at his or their will and pleasure, as well for the finding, sustentation and reliefe of the maimed, poore, needy, or impotent people, as to set the poore to worke, to have continuance for ever (7), and from time to time to place therein such head and members, and such number of poore, as to him, his heires and assignes shall seem convenient: and that the same hospitals or houses so founded (8), shall be incorporated, and have perpetuall successions (9) for ever, in fact, deed, and name, and of such head members, and numbers of poore, needy, maimed, or impotent people, as shall be appointed, assigned, limited, or named by the founder or founders, his or their heires, executors or assignes, by any such deed inrolled: and that such hospitall, *meason de dieu*, abiding place, or house of cor- 39 Elis. cap. 5.

correction, and the persons therein placed, shall be incorporated, named, and called by such name as the said founder or founders, his heires, executors or assignes shall so limit, assigne, and appoint: and the same hospitall, *meason de dieu*, abiding place, or house of correction so incorporated and named, shall be a body corporate and politick, and shall by that name of incorporation have full power, authority, and lawfull capacitie and abilitie, to purchase, take, hold, receive, enjoy, and have to them and to their successors for ever, as well goods and cattells, as mannors, lands, tenements, and hereditaments, being freehold, of any person or persons whatsoever. So that the same exceed not the yearly value of two hundred pounds above all charges and reprises, to any one such abiding house, hospitall, *meason de dieu*, or house of correction: and so as the same, or any part thereof be not holden of our soveraigne lady the queene, her heires or successors, immediately in chiefe, or else of our said soveraigne lady the queen, or any other person by knights-service, without licence or writ of *ad quod damnum*, or the statute of mortmain, or any other statute or law to the contrary notwithstanding. And that the same hospitall, *meason de dieu*, abiding place, or house of correction, and the persons so being incorporated, founded and named, shall have full power and lawfull authoritie by the true name of the incorporation thereof, to sue and to be sued, implead and to be impleaded, to answer and to be answered unto, in all manner of courts and places that now are, or hereafter shall be within this realme,
[721] as well temporall as spirituall, in all manner of suits whatsoever, and of what nature and kind soever such suits or actions be or shall be: and that the same hospitall, *meason de dieu*, abiding place, or house of correction, shall have and enjoy for ever such a common seale or seales, as by the said founder or founders, his or their heires, executors or assignes shall be in writing under his or their hand and seale assigned (10), named or appointed: whereby the same corporation shall or may seale any maner of instrument touching the same incorporation, and the lands, tenements, hereditaments, goods, or other things thereto belonging, or in any wise touching or concerning the same. And further shall be ordered, directed, and visited, placed, or upon just cause displaced (11) by such person or persons, bodies politick or corporate, their heires, successors or assignes, as shall be nominated or assigned by the founder or founders thereof, their heires or assignes, according to such rules, statutes, and ordinances, as shall be set forth, made, devised, or established by the said founder or founders, their heires or assignes, in writing under his or their hand and seale, not being repugnant or contrary to the lawes and statutes of this realme, any law, statute, custome, usage, or other thing whatsoever to the contrary in any wise notwithstanding. And that it shall be lawfull unto the founder or founders, his and their heires or assignes, upon the death or removing of any head or member of any

any such corporation, to place one other in the roome of him that dyeth, or is removed successively for ever.

Provided alwaies, that all leases, grants, conveyances, or estates, to be made by any corporation so to be founded as aforesaid, exceeding the number of one and twenty yeares, and that in possession, and whereupon the accustomable yearly rent, or more, by the greater part of twenty yeares next before the making of such lease, shall not be reserved and yearly payable, shall be void: saving to all persons, bodies politick and corporate, their heires and successors (other then the founders and givers, their heires and successors) all such right, title, claime, possession, rents, services, commons, demands, interest, and profits, which they or any of them shall have, or of right ought to have, of, in or to any the lands, tenements, or hereditaments, hereafter to be given, limited or assigned in forme aforesaid, in as ample manner, as if this statute had never been had or made.

Provided also, that this act, or any thing therein contained, shall not extend to enable any person or persons, being within age, women covert without their husbands, or of *non sane memorie*, to make any such corporation, or to endow the same: any thing in this present act to the contrary thereof in any wise notwithstanding.

Provided alwaies, that no such hospitall, *meason de dieu*, abiding place, or house of correction shall be erected, founded, or incorporated by force of this act, unlesse upon the foundation, or erection thereof, the same be endowed for ever with lands, tenements, or hereditaments of the cleare yearly value of ten pounds by the yeare.

Provided also, and be it further enacted, that no such incorporation to be founded by force of this act, shall at any time hereafter doe or suffer to be done (12) any act or thing, whereby, or by meanes whereof any of the lands, tenements, hereditaments, stocke, goods or chattels of such incorporation, or any [722] estate, interest, possession, or property, of, or in the same, or any of them shall be vested or transferred in or to any other whatsoever, contrary to the true meaning of this act: and that such construction shall be made upon this act as shall be most beneficiall and available for the maintenance of the poore, and for repressing and avoiding of all acts and devices to be invented, or put in ure contrary to the true meaning of this act, 21 Jac. 1. made perpetuall.

(1) *That all and every person and persons.*] These words regularly doe extend to any body politick or corporate, but not to such as are restrained by any act of parliament to alien, &c. but doth extend to such bodies politick and corporate as may alien: as maiors and comminalties, bayliffes and burgesses, &c. and the like, and to all other persons whatsoever.

 This

See hereafter the proviso to this effect. See li. 6. fol. 62. b. 22 E. 3. coron. 276. Sed abundans cautela non nocet.

This act enables not persons within age, or feme coverts without their husbands, of *non compos mentis*, or any other persons disabled by law, to found, &c.

This is a very beneficiall law: for the charges of incorporation, and of the licence of mortmaine in these dayes grow so great by one meanes or other, as it hath discouraged many men to undertake these pious and charitable workes, whereas in former times such workes of piety and charity for the poore did ever passe *in forma pauperis*, and so we hope to see it againe.

Whereof the hospitals, &c. must be endowed.

(2) *Seised of any estate in fee-simple, &c.*] First, the mannors, lands, tenements, or hereditaments, whereof the endowment is made, must be of an estate in fee-simple, either absolute, conditionall, or qualified. 2. They must be free-hold. 3. They must be of the cleare yearly value of 10 pounds by the yeare, or more, and not exceeding the yearly value of 200 pounds by the yeare above all charges and reprises. 4. They, or any part thereof must not be holden of the king immediately in chiefe, or of the king, or of any other person by knights-service. But if the first indowment be of the yearly value of 10 pounds or more, and under the yearly value of 200 pounds they may purchase (or any may give to them) mannors, lands, tenements, or hereditaments, having the aforesaid foure qualities, untill they have mannors, lands, tenements, or hereditaments, to the yearly value of 200 pounds, above all charges and reprises by force of this act of parliament, without any licence of mortmaine,

But if they be at the time of the foundation or indowment of the yearly value of 200 pounds, or under, and afterwards they become of greater value by good husbandry, rising of prices, sudden accidents, as by escheat, or otherwise, they shall continue good to be enjoyed by the hospitall, &c. albeit they be above the yearly value of 200 pounds: for the yearly value must be accounted within this statute, as it was at the time of the indowment made. Also goods and chattels (reall or personall) they may take of what value soever.

(3) *Their heires, executors, or assignes.*] That is, when the tenant in fee-simple that hath not time to found himselfe, shall appoint his heires, executors, or assignes to doe the same; and yet if he make no appointment, his heires or assignes may doe it.

(4) *During the space of 20 yeares.*] This act is made perpetuall by the statute of 21 Jac. regis, cap. 1. as more at large shall be shewed when we come to it.

(5) *By deed inrolled in the high court of chancery to erect, &c.*] It cannot be erected by any other instrument, conveyance, or assurance, but by deed inrolled in the chancery. This deed need not be inrolled in the chancery within 6 moneths after the date, but at any time after (but the sooner the safer.) And this deed need not
[723] to be indented, but a deed poll sufficeth. It is good, if the deed bee in paper, but it must bee inrolled in parchment.

(6) *One or more hospitalls, measons de dieu, abiding place, or houses of correction.*] The first three are expressed to be for the finding, sustentation and reliefe of the maimed, poore, needy, or impotent people in the dis-junctive. And the fourth, *viz.* the houses of correction, to set the poore to worke.

(7) To

(7) *To have continuance for ever.*] The founder cannot erect, &c. any of these for yeares, lives, or any other limited time, but for ever.

(8) *And that the same hospitalls, or houses so founded, &c.*] That is, founded by deed inrolled in the chancery.

Fundare is not onely *fundamentum ponere, seu jacere,* but also *firmare, seu stabilire.*

Vid. in le case de Suttons Hospitall, lib. 10. fol. 23. &c.

(9) *Shall be incorporated, and have perpetuall succession, &c.*] And forasmuch as the hospitall, &c. is not properly incorporated, but the persons therein placed, &c. are to be incorporated; therefore it is in the next clause added, And that such hospitall, *meason de dieu,* abiding place, or house of correction, * and the persons therein placed shall be incorporated, named, and called by such name as the said founder or founders, his heires, executors, or assignes shall so (that is, by any such deed inrolled) limit, assigne, and appoint. So as the persons, to be by this act incorporated, must be there placed and named, when the founder giveth them their name of incorporation: for the parliament incorporateth them, and the founder giveth them only their name.

* Note these words.

Now it is necessary, for the better furtherance of these godly and charitable works, to set downe a president warrantable by the said acts. And forasmuch as by this act it must be done by deed (which must have writing, sealing, and delivery) and not by a writing only; it is the surest way to have it by deed indented, between the founder of the one part, and A. B. &c. of the other part, which the founder may seale and deliver to A. B. &c. acknowledge it, and cause it to be inrolled in the chancery: for inrolled it cannot be in any other court.

A president of incorporation by force of this statute.

This indenture made the first day of May, in the first yeare of the reigne of our soveraigne lord king Charles, by the grace of God, &c. between A. B. of B. in the county of C. esquire of the one part, and C. D. E. F. &c. of the other part, witnesseth, that whereas the said A. B. of his charitable affection and disposition hath erected and founded certaine buildings and edifices upon a parcell of ground in the parish of F. in the said county of C. lying between the &c. to be an hospitall, for the finding, sustentation, and reliefe of poore and impotent people, to have continuance for ever. And by these presents the said A. B. doth found, erect, and establish the same for an hospitall of poore and impotent people, to have continuance for ever. And according to the power and authority given to the said A. B. by the statute or statutes in that case provided, the said A. B. doth by these presents limit, assigne, and appoint, that the said hospitall, and the poore and impotent persons therein placed, *viz.* D. E. E. F. F. G. &c. to the number of   shall for ever hereafter be incorporated by the name of the master and brethren of the hospitall of the holy and individed Trinity of F. in the said county of C. And further, the said A. B. doth by these presents name and appoint the said D. E. E. F. F. G. &c. to be present brethren of the said hospitall, and the said D. E. to be present master of the said hospitall, and that by the name of the master and brethren, they shall have full power and authority, and lawfull capacity and ability to purchase, take, hold, receive and enjoy, and have to them, and their successors for ever, as well * goods and chattels, as mannors, lands, tenements, and hereditaments, being free-hold, of any person or persons whatsoever, according

(and abbutell the same.)

* Nota, they may take, without any restraint, goods and chattels, as well reall, personall and mixt, to what value soever.

according to the forme and effects of the statutes in that case made and provided. And that the same hospitall, &c. and the persons so being incorporated, founded and named, shall have full power and lawfull authority by the said name of master and brethren, &c. to sue, and to be sued, implead and be impleaded, to answer and to [724] be answered unto in all manner of courts and places within this realme, as well temporall as spirituall, in all manner of suits whatsoever, and of what nature and kind whatsoever such suits or actions be, or shall be. And the said A. B. doth by these presents assigne, name and appoint, that the said master and brethren, and their successors for ever hereafter shall have a common seale, with a crosse graven therein, and in the circumference thereof, *sigillum hospitalis sanctæ Trinitatis de F.* whereby the said master and brethren, and their successors, shall or may seale any manner of instruments touching the same incorporation, and the lands, tenements and hereditaments, goods, or other things thereto belonging, or in any wise touching or concerning the same. And that it shall be lawfull for the said A. B. during his life, upon the death or removing of the said master, or any of the said brethren, to place one other in the roome of him that dyeth, or is removed. And after the death of the said A. B. it shall be lawfull for the parson of the said towne of F. and the church-wardens of the same for the time being, successively for ever after the decease of the said A. B. upon the death or removing of the master, or any of the brethren of the said hospitall, to place one other in the roome of him that dyed, or is removed, successively for ever. In witnesse whereof, &c.

22 E. 4. tit. Grant 30. li. 10. fol. 30. b. & 32. a. in le case de Suttons hospitall.

And albeit that the onely essentiall point that the founder is to doe in this case is, to appoint and give a name to the corporation, yet by way of illustration we have thought it fit to adde so much as we have done, following the very words and effect of this act. And although that at the common law a corporation may be of an hospitall that is *in potestate* of certaine persons to be governours of the hospitall, and not of the persons placed therein, yet the safest and surest way upon this statute is, first to prepare the hospitall, and to place the poore therein, and to incorporate the persons therein placed. And this we hold by reason of the said words in this act, *viz.* And that such hospitall, &c. and the persons therein placed shall be incorporated, &c.

(10) *Such a common seale or seals, as by the founder or founders, &c. shall be assigned.*] It is necessary to be knowne, who shall be said to be founder or founders, for the better understanding of the clauses subsequent in this act.

Such onely are said to be founder or founders within this act, as are seised of an estate in fee-simple of any mannors, lands, tenements, or hereditaments, having the foure qualities aforesaid, and giveth the same at the first foundation of the hospitall, &c. to the incorporation of the hospitall. For it is a sure rule, that he or they that give the first possessions, is the founder or founders.

38. ass. p. 22. adjudge lib. 3. fol. 74. a. in le case de dean & chap. de Norwich.

But then it is demanded, what if R. S. citizen of London, by his last will and testament do devise, that his executors shall bestow a thousand pounds in purchase of lands, tenements, or hereditaments, and that an hospitall shall thereupon be builded and incorporated for the sustentation and reliefe of poore and impotent people, and dyeth: the executors purchase lands, tenements and hereditaments of the yearly value of threescore pounds, having the said foure qualities,

qualities, and cause the estate to be taken to certaine persons and their heires, and build thereupon an hospitall, and place therein poore and impotent people: in this and the like cases the persons that have the estate in fee-simple in the lands, tenements, and hereditaments, are by the purview of this statute to be founders, and to doe all things that this act doth appoint the founder or founders to doe. But when they name the corporation, it shall be well and worthily done to name the corporation by the name of the master and brethren of the hospitall of the holy and undivided Trinity, founded in F. in the county of C. at the onely costs and charges of the said R. S. or the like; so as the charitable intention of the said R. S. may be had in remembrance, with some just recitall in the beginning of the deed of foundation of the truth of the case.

The next thing that is to be done after the incorporation, is to convey the lands, tenements and hereditaments to the said incorporation, which may be done safely, with greater facility and lesse charge, by bargaine and sale by deed indented and inrolled (according to the statute of 27 H. 8. cap. 16.) between the founder or founders of the one part, and the master and brethren, &c. of the other part, in consideration of five shillings in hand paid by the master of the said hospitall (for himselfe and for his brethren) and of other five shillings in hand paid by the said master and brethren, &c. whereof you may have a president in the tenth booke of my reports in the case of Suttons hospitall, fol. 17. b. & 34. a. *respons al. 9. objection*, which judgement is after allowed and ratified by act of parliament, *anno 4 regis Caroli.* And this bargaine and sale to be a day or two, or some short time after the incorporation. But now let us returne to our act of parliament.

[725]

27 H. 8. ca. 16. See before the exposition of this statute.

Lib. 10. fol. 17. & 34. in the case of Suttons hospitall.

(11) *And further shall be ordered and visited, placed, or upon just cause displaced, &c.*] And forasmuch as nothing can prosper and continue, without good rule and government, the next thing to be done after the lands, &c. be conveyed unto them is, that the founder or founders shall set forth, make, devise and establish in writing under his or their hand and seale (for so it must be by force of this act) such rules, locall statutes and ordinances for the order, direction, visitation, placing, or upon just cause displacing of such master and brethren by such person or persons, bodies politick or corporate, their heirs, successors or assignes, as shall be nominated or assigned by the * founder or founders, the said rules, locall statutes and ordinances being not repugnant or contrary to the lawes and statutes of the realme. And these orders, &c. to containe (amongst many others) two especiall things, *viz.* daily prayer to Almighty God: and that the master and brethren be not idle, but that they and every of them exercise such worke meet for them, as the parson of the parish, and the church-wardens (or such other as the founder shall name) shall appoint or allow of, and to take a weekly account thereof. And these orders, &c. to beare date after the bargaine and sale, and it is good to have them inrolled.

(12) *Provided also, and be it further enacted, that no such corporation to be founded by force of this act, shall at any time hereafter doe, or suffer to be done, &c.*] This clause of restraint in this act is as forcible, and rather more then the restraint by the statute of 13 Elis. cap. 10. And therefore hereby they are disabled as well to make any conveyance to the king, as to any subject, contrary to the true meaning of the act.

* If the founder limit not, who shall visit? The bishop of the diocesse. Vid. 2 H. 5. ca. 1. stat. 1. Vid. 14 Elis. cap. 5. El. cap. 18. 8 ass. p. 29. 31. But if the founder or founders limit who shall visit, such visitor or visitors by force of this act of parliament, shall stand by the statute of 21 Jac. See the statute of 13 El cap. 17.

Peruse well the statute in print in 13 Elis. cap. 17. for the erection and foundation of an hospitall by Robert earle of Leicester, which was the paterne whereby this act was framed. And see the orders and locall statutes made by him, for they were done by good advice, and have had good effect.

---

[726] The Statute of 21 Jac. Regis, Cap. 1. concerning Hospitalls, and Houses of Correction.

WHEREAS in the parliament held in the nine and thirtieth yeare of the reigne of the late queen Elisabeth of happy memory, a good law was made, entituled, An act for erecting of hospitalls, or abiding and working houses for the poore: but the power, licence and authoritie given by the said statute, to erect, found, and establish such houses and abiding places, as are therein mentioned, was confined to the space of twenty yeares then next ensuing, which said time is now expired.

Be it therefore enacted by the authoritie of this present parliament, that the said act, and all things therein contained, shall from henceforth be revived, and made perpetuall to have continuance for ever (1).

And be it also enacted, that all hospitalls, *measons de dieu*, and abiding places for poore, lame, maimed and impotent people, or for houses of correction, at any time since the said twenty yeares expired, erected (2), founded or made, or at any time hereafter to be erected, founded or made, according to the purport of the said statute, shall be incorporated, and have perpetuall succession and capacitie, to have, take and enjoy all other priviledges, benefits, and immunities, to all intents and purposes, according to the provisions, tenour, purport and true meaning of the said act, as if the same had been made, founded, or endowed within the space of twenty yeares next ensuing the said statute, Stat. 43 El. 4.

(1) *That the said act, and all things therein contained, from henceforth be revived, and made perpetuall to have continuance for ever.*]

These words [made perpetuall, and have continuance for ever] have made the said act of 39 Elis. and all things therein contained (at the making thereof but a probationer for 20 yeares long since expired) now by this act perpetuall, and to have continuance for ever.

Nota, *hospitale* an hospitall, is the generall word, & includes *measons de dieu*, & abiding places for the poor, &c. also * houses of correction, as here it appeareth.

(2) *That all hospitals, measons de dieu for the poore, &c. or for * houses of correction, at any time since the said twenty yeares expired, erected, &c.*] Whereas some hospitalls, &c. or houses of correction were founded after the said twenty yeares expired, according to the

the said act, those by this act are incorporated, established and confirmed.

And likewise all hospitalls, &c. and houses of correction hereafter to be erected, &c. according to the purport of the said statute, shall be incorporated, &c. And note, that this branch makes the act of 39 Elis. &c. a perpetuall law.

Vid. 13 Elis. cap. 7. the moity of the forfeiture of bankrupts given to the poore within hospitalls. 13 Elis. cap. 7.

31 Elis. cap. 6. If any which have election, nomination, voice, or assent thereunto of any person to have roome or place in any hospitall, shall have or take any mony, reward or profit, directly or indirectly, or promise of money, reward or profit, that then such roome and place to be void, and another to be preferred to the place by those that have authority to elect, &c. 31 Elis. cap. 6. None that have election, &c. to take reward, &c.

[727]

In 43 Elis. a right profitable law was made, for commissioners to enquire of mis-imployment of lands, tenements, rents, annuities, profits, hereditaments, goods, chattels, money, and stockes of money given or appointed, some for reliefe of aged, impotent, and poore people, and some for reliefe of sicke and maimed souldiers and mariners, or for maintenance of houses of correction (*inter alia*) and by their orders to reforme the same, which act hath wrought very good effect in many cases. 43 Elis. cap. 4. A speedy remedy in many cases.

---

[728]

An Exposition of the Statute of 7 Jac. Regis, Cap. 4. concerning Houses of Correction, and the Government of them.

MANY statutes have been made for the punishment of rogues, vagabonds, and sturdy beggars, but very few to find them worke, and to enforce them thereunto. The principall of that kind is the statute of 39 Elis. ca. 4. which doth enact, that from time to time it shall and may be lawfull to and for the justices of peace of any county or city, assembled at any quarter sessions of the peace within the same county, city, borough, or towne corporate, to set downe order in three things: First, from time to time to erect, or cause to be erected one or more * houses of correction within their severall counties or cities. This first branch is a law perpetuall, and the justices of peace for the time being have power by this act from time to time to erect as many houses of correction, or work-houses, as they shall thinke convenient.

2. For the providing of stockes of money, and all other things necessary for the same. This also is a law perpetuall from time to time, &c. See 43 Elis. ca. 2. & 7 Jac. cap. 4. in the 2. branch.

3. For ruling and governing of the same.

4. For correction and punishment of [a] offenders thither to be committed. These two also are lawes perpetuall, *ut supra*.

5. For the better effecting whereof, they may make such orders as

* Note, these are not only houses of correction, but work-houses also, as hereafter appeareth.

[a] Note the generality of this word.

The life of this businesse consisteth in framing of these orders, & in due execution of the same.

as they shal from time to time thinke convenient, &c. and from time to time to reforme, take, and set down the same.

6. Which orders shall be of force (being warranted by authority of parliament) and be duly performed, and put in execution.

We passe over all the former lawes before this act of 39 Elis. for punishment of rogues, vagabonds, and sturdy beggars, many whereof were repealed by 1 E. 6. cap. 3. and all the rest are repealed by this act of 39 Elis. and will come to the abovesaid act of 7 Jac. This law consisteth upon a short preamble, and the body of the act, which is divided into nine branches.

The preamble.

Whereas heretofore divers good and necessarie lawes and statutes have been made and provided for the erection of houses of correction, for the suppressing and punishing of rogues, vagabonds, and other idle, vagrant, and disorderly persons, which lawes have not wrought so good effect as was expected, as well for that the said houses of correction have not been built according as was intended, as also for that the said statutes have not been duely and severely put in execution, as by the said statutes were appointed.

In this preamble are rehearsed two causes wherefore the former law and statute took not so good effect as was expected: First, for that houses of correction were not built according as was intended, wherein no deficiencie was in the law, but in the justices of peace, which should have ordered the same to be erected. For seeing education of youth, and setting of worke of idle and disorderly persons, are such essentiall parts of the well being of a commonwealth; and the onely meane to compell them to worke (as the law now standeth) is by houses of correction, seeing there hath been a default in the justices of the peace heretofore, and the mischiefe so daily increasing, we hope that the justices of peace, having yet power, will erect more houses of correction (which are also called work-houses) so as we shall have neither beggar (as the law of God commandeth) nor idle person in the common-wealth.

See the third part of the Institutes, cap. Rogues.

[729]

The second cause (which is the cause of causes) is, for that the statutes in that case made and provided were not put in execution, as by the said statutes was appointed.

And this excellent work is without question feasible: for upon the making of the statute of 39 Elis. and a good space after, whilest justices of peace and other officers were diligent and industrious, there was not a rogue to be seen in any part of England, but when justices * and other officers became *tepidi*, or *trepidi*, rogues, &c. swarmed againe.

* 39 Elis. cap. 4.

The 1. branch.

For remedy whereof, be it enacted and established by our soveraign lord the kings majestie, and by the lords spirituall and temporall, and by the commons in this present parliament assembled, and by the authoritie of the same, that all lawes and statutes now in force, made for erecting and building of houses of correction, and for punishing of rogues, vagabonds, and other wandring and idle persons, shall be put in due execution.

The

The firſt branch of the body of this act conſiſteth on two parts: Firſt, that all lawes and ſtatutes made for erecting and building of houſes of correction now in force ſhould be put in due execution; which is ſo enacted, for the incitation and incouragement of juſtices of peace to do their duties in this ſo important a cauſe.

2. For puniſhing of rogues, vagabonds, and ſturdy beggars (for thoſe are the words of the former ſtatute now in force) ſhall be likewiſe put in due execution. Execution is the end and life of the law. 39 Eliſ. ubi ſup.

And be it further enacted and eſtabliſhed by the authority aforeſaid, that before the feaſt of Saint Michael (1) the archangel, which ſhall be in the yeare of our Lord God one thouſand ſixe hundred and eleven, there ſhall be erected, built, or otherwiſe provided (2) within every countie of this realm of England and Wales, where there is not one houſe of correction already built, purchaſed, provided or continued, one or more fit and convenient houſe or houſes of correction, with convenient backſide thereunto adjoyning, together with mills, turns, cards (3), and ſuch like neceſſarie implements, to ſet the ſaid rogues, or ſuch other idle perſons on worke: the ſame houſes to be built, erected or provided in ſome convenient place or towne in every county: which houſes ſhall be purchaſed, conveyed, or aſſured (4) unto ſuch perſon or perſons, as by the juſtices of peace, or the more part of them, in their quarter ſeſſions of the peaee, to be holden within every countie of this realme of England and Wales, upon truſt, to the intent the ſame ſhall be uſed and employed for the keeping, correcting, and ſetting to worke of the ſaid rogues, vagabonds, or ſturdy beggars, and other idle and diſorderly perſons (5). The 2. branch.

(1) *That before the feaſt of Saint Michael, &c.*] This clauſe was to haſten, and upon penalty to inforce juſtices of peace to ſo neceſſary and charitable a worke. * But this clauſe being in the affirmative, taketh not away the perpetuity of the act of 39 Eliſ. for the erection of houſes of correction and work-houſes, from time to time, and at any time hereafter by juſtices of peace. * Nota.

(2) *Shall be erected, built, or otherwiſe provided.*] The ſtatute of 39 El. uſed onely the word [erected,] but that included both the other words of this act, *viz.* [built and provided.] For if they cauſed a houſe already builded, to be provided or purchaſed, and converted the ſame to a houſe of correction, this is an erection of a houſe of correction within the ſtatute of 39 Eliſ. becauſe as to the houſe of correction it was newly erected. [730]

Erectior ſenatus erat noſtris cohortationibus excitatus. Cicero ad Brutum.

(3) *With convenient backſide thereunto adjoyning, together with mills, turnes, cards, &c.* Theſe particulars, and all other neceſſary things appertaing thereunto, are included within the generall words of 39 Eliz. *viz.* [for the providing of ſtockes, and all other things neceſſary for the ſame, &c.] which are generall and large words, and doe include all particulars neceſſary whatſoever.

(4) *Which houſes ſhall be purchaſed, and conveyed, or aſſured, &c.*] This may be done by authority of this act, without licence or offence

ſence of any former law. And theſe may be incorporated by the ſtatute of 39 Eliz. cap. 5. as in the expoſition of that ſtatute appeareth.

The houſe to be imployed to three purpoſes: 1. for the keeping, 2. for the correcting, 3. for the ſetting to worke: ſo as it is not a houſe of correction alone, but of ſafe keeping, and ſetting on worke.

(5) *The ſaid rogues, vagabonds, or ſturdy beggars, and other idle and diſorderly perſons.*] The ſtatute of 39 Eliſ. by particular words did not extend to rogues, vagabonds, and ſturdy beggars, but in generall words, for the puniſhment of offenders thereunto committed. Which generall words are both by the firſt branch of this act explained to be wandring or idle perſons: and many other branches of this act, to idle or diſorderly perſons, and ſpecially by the branch, whereby the authority of the juſtices to commit to the houſe of correction is warranted. All idle or diſorderly perſons may be committed by them to the houſe of correction and workhouſe.

And where all the judges of England did for the good of the common-wealth, and the better inſtruction and direction of juſtices of peace, and for the due execution of the ſaid act of 39 Eliſ. amongſt other things reſolve, that ſuch perſons as be of any pariſh, and have able bodies to worke, and be no wanderers abroad out of the pariſh, though they refuſe to worke at ſuch wages as is taxed (or commonly given) in thoſe parts, are notwithſtanding not to be ſent to their place of birth, or laſt dwelling, by the ſpace of a yeare, but to the houſe of correction, upon conſideration had of both the ſtatutes of the poor and rogues. But if they that have any lawfull meanes to live by, though they be of able bodies, and refuſe to worke, yet are they not to be ſent to the houſe of correction.

But by this ſtatute of 7 Jac. enacted long after the reſolution of the judges, though they have lawfull meanes to live by, yet if they be idle or diſorderly perſons, the juſtices of peace have power to commit them to the houſe of correction, a generall and large power given to them, without exception of any perſon. And their mittimus to the houſe of correction may be more ſafely upon this ſtatute, *quia otioſo et inordinata perſona:* for that he is an * idle and diſorderly perſon, or that he is an idle perſon, or that he is a diſorderly perſon, according to the words of this act, then upon the ſtatute of 39 Eliſ.

* The words in the 5. branch are in the diſjunctive.

The 3. branch.

And be it further enacted by the authoritie aforeſaid, that if the ſaid houſe to be erected, purchaſed, or provided, ſhall not be erected, built, or otherwiſe provided, before the feaſt of S. Michael the archangel, which ſhall be in the yeare, one thouſand ſixe hundred and eleven, next enſuing the laſt day of this preſent ſeſſion of parliament, that then every juſtice of peace within [731] every countie of this realme of England and Wales, where ſuch houſe and backſide ſhall not be erected or provided, ſhall forfeit for his ſaid neglect five pounds of lawfull Engliſh money, the one moietie thereof to be unto him or them that will ſue for the ſame by action of debt, bill, plaint, or information: in which ſuit, no protection, eſſoine, or wager of law ſhall be admitted: and the other moity thereof to be employed and beſtowed

ſtowed towards the erecting, building, procuring or providing the ſaid houſe and backſide, and ſuch neceſſary implements, as aforeſaid.

The penalty of five pounds of every juſtice of peace, if the houſe of correction be not provided within the time of this act of 7 Jac. And how the ſame penalty ſhall be recovered and imployed.

And be it further enacted and eſtabliſhed by the authoritie aforeſaid, that the juſtices of peace of every countie within the realme of England and Wales, at their quarter ſeſſions of the peace, to be holden for their ſeverall counties (next after the erecting, providing or building of the ſaid houſe or houſes, and ſo from time to time) or the moſt part of them ſhall elect, nominate and appoint, at their will and pleaſure, one or more honeſt fit perſon or perſons, to be governour or maſter of the ſaid houſe or houſes ſo to be purchaſed, erected, built or provided: which perſon and perſons ſo choſen by vertue of this preſent act, ſhall have power and authoritie, to ſet ſuch rogues, vagabonds, idle and diſorderly perſons, as ſhall be brought or ſent unto the ſaid houſe to worke and labour (being able) from time to time, for ſuch time, as they ſhall continue and be remaining in the ſaid houſe of correction, and to puniſh the ſaid rogues, vagabonds, idle and diſorderly perſons, by putting fetters or gives upon them, and by moderate whipping of them, and that the ſaid rogues, vagabonds, and idle perſons, during ſuch time as they ſhall continue and remaine in the ſaid houſe of correction, ſhall in no ſort bee chargeable to the countrie for any allowance, either at their bringing in, or going forth, or during the time of their abode there, but ſhall have ſuch and ſo much allowance, as they ſhall deſerve by their owne labour and work. The 4. branch.

By this branch it is enacted, that the juſtices of peace, &c. ſhall elect, &c. one or more fit perſon or perſons, to be governour or maſter of the ſaid houſe or houſes.

Herein alſo are added idle and diſorderly perſons, and power given to the governour or maſter to puniſh them, by putting fetters or gives upon them, and by moderate whipping of them.

Theſe idle and diſorderly perſons ſhall be in no ſort chargeable to the countrie, &c. but ſhall have ſuch allowance as they ſhall deſerve by their owne labour and worke. Nota.

And be it further enacted by the authoritie aforeſaid, that the ſaid juſtices of peace of every countie within every of their ſeverall diviſions, twice in every yeare at the leaſt, and oftner, if there be occaſion, ſhall aſſemble and meet together for the better execution of this ſtatute, and that ſome foure or five daies before their aſſembly and meeting, the ſaid juſtices or the more part of them, ſhall by their warrant command the conſtables and tithingmen The 5. branch.

tithingmen of every hundred, towne, parish, village, and hamlet within their said severall divisions, which shall be assisted with sufficient men of the same places, to make a generall privie search in one night within their said hundreds, townes, villages, and hamlets, for the finding out and apprehending of the said rogues, vagabonds, wandring and idle persons, and that such rogues, vagabonds, wandring and idle persons, as they shall then find and apprehend in the said search, shall by them be brought before the said justices, at their said assembly or meeting, there to be examined of their idle and wandring life, there to be punished, or otherwise by their warrant to be sent or conveyed unto the said house or houses of correction within the said countie, appointed and prefixed, there to be delivered unto the master or governour of the said house, or to his deputie or assignee, to be set to labour and worke; at which daies and times of assembly or meeting, so to be held by the said justices of peace, the constables and tythingmen of every hundred, parish, towne, village and hamlet, shall then appeare in every their severall divisions, before the said justices of peace, at the said assemblies or meetings, and there shall give account and reckoning, upon oath in writing, and under the hand of the minister of every parish, what rogues, vagabonds, and wandring and disorderly persons they have apprehended both in the same search, and also between every such assemblies and meetings, and how many have been by them punished, or otherwise sent unto the houses of correction: which if the said constables or tythingmen shall neglect to performe, as also to convey safely all such rogues, with all other idle or disorderly persons at the charge of the hundred, as by the justices of peace warrants shall be sent unto the houses of correction in the same county, that then they shall forfeit such further fines, paines, and penalties, as by the said justices of peace, or the most part of them, shall be thought fit and convenient, not exceeding the summe of forty shillings for every offence.

The justices of peace within their severall divisions, twice every yeare at the least, and oftener, if there be occasion, shall assemble and meet together, &c.

Generall and privie search shall be made in every hundred, towne, &c.

The constables account of idle or disorderly person, &c. apprehended.

Note this. In this branch these words are specially to be observed, viz. With all other idle or disorderly persons, at the charge of the hundred, as by the justices of peace warrants shall be sent to the houses of correction.

The 6. branch. And for that it is convenient, that the masters or governours of the said houses of correction should have some fit allowance and maintenance for their travell and care to be had in the said service,

ſervice, as alſo for the relieving of ſuch as ſhall happen to be weake and ſicke in their cuſtodie, and that the ſubjects of this realme ſhould in no ſort be overcharged, to raiſe up money for ſtockes to ſet ſuch on worke as ſhall be committed to their cuſtody: be it therefore enacted and eſtabliſhed by the authoritie of this preſent parliament, that the maſters or governours of the ſaid houſes of correction, ſhall have ſuch ſumme of money yearly, as ſhall be thought meet, by the moſt part of the juſtices of peace within the ſaid countie, at the quarter ſeſſions of the peace, the ſame to be paid quarterly before-hand by the treaſurers, appointed by one act made in the three and fortieth yeare [733] of the late queene Eliſabeth, intituled, An Act for the reliefe of the poore, during the time they the ſaid maſters or governours ſhall be imployed in the ſaid ſervice (the ſaid maſter or governour giving ſufficient ſecuritie, for the continuance and performance of the ſaid ſervice) which if the ſaid treaſurer ſhall neglect or refuſe to performe, that then the ſaid maſter or governour of the houſe of correction, ſhall have authoritie by this preſent act, to levie the ſame, or ſo much thereof as ſhall be unpaid, upon the ſaid treaſurers account, in ſuch manner and forme as by the ſaid ſtatute they the ſaid treaſurers are appointed and authorized to levie the weekly ſumme or payment, being to them unpaid.

This branch provideth for fit allowance and maintenance to be made to the maſters or governours of the ſaid houſes, &c. *Dignus operarius mercede.*

Treaſurers appointed by one act made *anno* 43 Eliſ. cap. 2. intituled, For the reliefe of the poor (and falſly intituled in the laſt printed book of ſtatutes, Who ſhall be overſeers for the poore, their office, duty and account) which act of 43 Eliſ. by the right title, being but a probationer, hath been, and yet is continued, as it appeareth by the ſtatute of 4 Car. *regis*, cap. 4.

See 1 Jac. cap. 25. an addition thereunto. 1 Jac. c. 25. 21 Jac. cap. 28.

And becauſe great charge ariſeth upon many places within this realme, by reaſon of baſtardy, beſides the great diſhonour of Almighty God, be it therefore enacted by the authoritie aforeſaid, that every lewd woman, which after this preſent ſeſſion of parliament, ſhall have any baſtard, which may be chargeable to the pariſh, the juſtices of peace ſhall commit ſuch lewd woman unto the houſe of correction, there to be puniſhed, and ſet on worke during the terme of one whole yeare: and if ſhe ſhall eftſoones offend againe, that then to be committed to the ſaid houſe of correction as aforeſaid, and there to remaine untill ſhe can put in good ſureties for her good behaviour, not to offend ſo againe. The 7. branch.

The puniſhment of lewd women having baſtards, &c. That every lewd woman, which ſhall have any baſtard, which may be chargeable to the pariſh, the juſtices of peace may commit her to the See 18 Eliſ. c. 3. and continued to this day, 3 Jac. cap. 4.

the houſe of correction, &c. So as if ſhe will diſcharge the pariſh of the keeping of the baſtard, ſhe cannot be puniſhed by this ſtatute, but by that of 18 Eliſ. cap. 3.

The 8. branch.

And for that many wilfull people, finding that they having children, have ſome hope to have reliefe from the pariſh wherein they dwell, and being able to labour, and thereby to relieve themſelves and their families, doe neverthele ſs run away out of their pariſhes, and leave their families upon the pariſh: for remedy whereof, be it further enacted by this preſent parliament, and the authoritie of the ſame, that all ſuch perſons ſo running away, ſhall be taken and deemed to be incorrigible rogues, and endure the pains of incorrigible rogues: and if either ſuch man or woman being able to work, and ſhall threaten to run away, and leave their families as aforeſaid, the ſame being proved by two ſufficient witneſſes upon oath before two juſtices of peace in that diviſion, that then the ſaid perſon
[734] ſo threatning, ſhall by the ſaid juſtices of peace be ſent to the houſes of correction, (unleſſe he or ſhe can put in ſufficient ſureties for the diſcharge of the pariſh) there to be dealt with and detained as a ſturdy and wandring rogue, and to be delivered at the ſaid aſſembly or meeting, or at the quarter ſeſſions, and not otherwiſe.

This branch conſiſteth upon two parts: firſt, if any man or woman having children, being able to labour, and thereby to relieve their families doe run away out of the pariſhes, and leave their families upon the pariſh, he or ſhe is taken and deemed by authority of this parliament an incorrigible rogue.

2. If any ſuch man or woman, being able to work, ſhall threaten to run away, and leave their families as aforeſaid, the ſame being proved by two ſufficient witneſſes before two juſtices of peace in that diviſion, the ſame perſon ſo threatning, &c. ſhall be ſent to the houſe of correction, as a ſturdy and wandring rogue, &c. unleſſe ſufficient ſurety be found for the diſcharge of the pariſh.

The 9. branch.

And becauſe there ſhall be the more care taken by all ſuch maſters of the houſes of correction, that when the country hath been at trouble and charge, to bring all ſuch diſorderly perſons as aforeſaid to their ſafe keeping, that then they ſhall performe their duties in that behalfe, be it therefore enacted by the authoritie aforeſaid, that if they ſhall not every quarter ſeſſions yeeld a true and lawfull account unto the juſtices of peace, of all ſuch perſons as have been committed to their cuſtody: or if the ſaid perſons committed to their cuſtody, or any of them, ſhall be troubleſome unto the country, by going abroad, or otherwiſe, ſhall eſcape away from the ſaid houſe of correction, before they ſhall be from thence lawfully delivered, that then the ſaid juſtices ſhall ſet downe ſuch fines and penalties upon the ſaid maſter or governours, as the moſt part of them in their quarter ſeſſions ſhall thinke fit and convenient, and all fines and

and penalties not herein before limited, ſhall be paid unto the treaſurer, and accounted for by the treaſurer aforeſaid: this act to have continuance for the ſpace of ſeven yeares, and from thence to the end of the next ſeſſion of parliament after the ſaid ſeven yeares. 3 *Car.* 4. *continued untill the end of the firſt ſeſſion of the next parliament.*

The maſters of the houſes of correction ſhall yeeld a true and lawfull account at every quarter ſeſſions of all ſuch diſorderly perſons as have been committed to their cuſtody.

This act was but a probationer for a certaine time, but it hath been continued: and laſtly, by the ſaid ſtatute of 4 Car. cap. 4.

Thus much have we written for the better and more ſpeedy execution of theſe excellent ſtatutes; and the rather, for that few or none are committed to the common gaole amongſt ſo many malefactors, but they come out worſe then they went in. And few are committed to the houſe of correction, or working houſe, but they come out better.

And where ſome are of opinion, that in particular townes a diſcreet and expert workman may ſet the young and idle people as voluntaries on worke: certainly, the youth on both ſexes hath (in the time of this great negligence) gotten ſuch a * trade of picking theevery, ſtealing of wood, and the like, through idleneſſe, as they will be never brought to worke, unleſſe they be thereunto compelled (and the rather, for that ſome of their parents and maſters have benefit by them) but compelled they may be, and this great worke happily effected, if by the order of the juſtices of peace theſe ſtatutes be put in due execution. See the ſtatute of 43 Eliſ. cap. 2.

* Morem fecerat uſus, *Ovid.* Ars ſit quæ à teneris primum conjungitur annis, *Ovid.*

[735]

We have not gone about to ſpeake of the ſtatute of 39 Eliſ. or other ſtatutes concerning rogues, &c. or the poore, &c. which all the judges of England have upon due conſideration explained, and which are truly rehearſed and imprinted, and ought to be obſerved, other then ſuch as later acts of parliament have altered, whereof ſomewhat hath been ſaid.

Lamb. Juſtice of Peace, lib. 2. page 207.

An Expoſition upon the Statute of 31 Eliſ. Cap. 7. Concerning Cottages and Inmates.

[736]

The 1. branch.

FOR the avoiding of the great inconveniences which are found by experience to grow by the erecting and building of great numbers and multitude of cottages (1), which are daily more and more increaſed in many parts of this realme: be it enacted by the queenes moſt excellent majeſty, and the lords ſpirituall and temporall, and the commons in this preſent parliament aſſembled, and by the authority of the ſame, that after the end of this ſeſſion of parliament, no perſon (2) ſhall within this realme of England, make, build, or erect, or cauſe

to be made, builded, or erected any manner of cottage for habitation or dwelling, nor convert or ordaine any building or housing, made, or hereafter to be made, to be used as a cottage for habitation or dwelling, unlesse the same person doe assigne and lay to the same cottage or building foure acres of ground at the least, to be accounted according to the statute or ordinance *de terris mensurandis*, being his or her owne free-hold and inheritance, lying neere to the said cottage, to be continually occupied and manured therewith, so long as the same cottage shall be inhabited, upon paine that every such offendor shall forfeit to our soveraigne lady the queens majesty, her heires and successors, ten pounds of lawfull mony of England, for every such offence.

1. part Vet. Mag. Chart. 128.

(1) *Cottage.*] Is derived from the Saxon word *cote, unde coterelli* for cottagers, and *cottagium* for a cottage. *Vide* the first part of the Institutes, sect. 1. fol. 5. out of Domesday. And the statute entituled, *Extenta manerii, anno* 4 E. 1. *Item inquirendum est de coterellis, viz. qui cottagia et curtilagia tenent.* And this signification it had by the common law.

(2) *No person,* &c.] This extends as well to persons politicke and incorporate, as to naturall persons whatsoever.

If an ancient cottage had been wholly decayed before this act, it is not lawfull newly to erect the same after the end of our act.

This first branch prohibiteth foure things: first, the new erecting or building of any cottage after the end of this parliament, which was 29 *Martii, anno* 31 Elis. *anno Dom.* 1589.

2. It prohibiteth the conversion or ordaining of any housing or building, made, or hereafter to be made, to be used as a cottage.

3. Albeit the house or building were made before this act, yet if the conversion were after the 29 day of March 1589, it is prohibited by this statute; for in point of conversion the words be (made, or hereafter to be made.)

4. These things are prohibited in this branch, upon paine of forfeiture of ten pounds to the king for every such offence.

The 2. branch.

And be it further enacted by the authority aforesaid, that every person, which after the end of this session of parliament, shall willingly uphold, maintaine, and continue any such cottage hereafter to be erected, converted, or ordained for habitation or dwelling, whereunto four acres of ground, as is aforesaid, shall not be assigned and laid to be used and occupied

[737]

with the same, shall forfeit to our said soveraigne lady the queenes majesty, her heires and successors, forty shillings for every moneth that any such cottage shall be by him or them upholden, maintained, and continued.

Nota, this word [*such*] referreth to the cottages described to be erected or converted after the end of our parliament.

This branch inflicteth punishment upon such as shall willingly uphold, maintaine, and continue any * such cottage after the end of this parliament, either erected, or converted, or ordained, as is aforesaid, for habitation, &c. upon the penalty of forty shillings to the king for every moneth that any such cottage shall be maintained.

So as a cottage is two fold, either newly erected, or builded after our

our ſtatute, or of a houſe built before or after our ſtatute, and converted after our ſtatute to a cottage.

But out of theſe two branches are five exceptions.

By the firſt branch of this act any perſon may either erect a new cottage, or convert an old or a new houſe to a cottage, if he lay to it foure acres of ground at the leaſt, which muſt have theſe foure incidents: firſt, theſe acres muſt be accounted according to the ſtatute or ordinance *de admenſuratione terræ, anno* 35 E. 1. which is after ſixteen foot and an halfe to the pole. 2. Theſe foure acres muſt be his or her freehold and inheritance (for neither grounds holden by copy, or for life or lives, or for any number of yeares will ſerve) and it muſt be freehold either in fee-ſimple, or fee-taile. 3. They muſt lye neere the ſaid cottage. 4. They muſt be continually occupied therewith, ſo long as the cottage ſhall be inhabited.

The 1. exception.

This ſtatute is named in our act, the ſtatute or ordinance *de terris admenſurandis*.

Vid. 35 El. c. 6.

This act extends not to cottages erected, or houſes converted to cottages before the 29 day of March 1589. The ſecond branch maketh this cleare.

The 2. exception.

This act ſhall not extend to any cottage, which ſhall be ordained (that is, converted) or erected to or for habitation or dwelling in any citie, towne corporate, ancient borough, or market towne.

The 3. exception.

Nor to any cottages or buildings erected or converted for the neceſſary habitation of any labourers in any minerall workes, cole-mines, quarries, or delfes of ſtone or ſlate, or about making of brick, tile, lime, or coles; ſo as the ſame cottages or buildings be not above one mile diſtant from the minerall, or other works.

The 4. exception.

Nor to any cottage to be made in three places, *viz.* 1. within a mile of the ſea, 2. upon the ſide of ſuch part of a navigable river, where the * admirall ought to have juriſdiction, ſo long as a ſailer ſhall dwell therein, or ſome perſon of manuell occupation, for the making, furniſhing, or victualling of any ſhip, &c. 3. In any forreſt, chaſe, warren, or parke, ſo long as the under keeper or warrener dwell therein, &c.

The 5. exception.

* See for this the fourth part of the Inſtitutes, ca. of the court of the admiralty.

4. Nor to any cottage * heretofore made, 1. for a common herdman, 2. for a common ſhepherd, &c. (of whom his cottage is called a ſheepcote) ſo long as a common herdman or ſhepherd ſhall therein dwell, 3. for a poore, lame, ſick, aged, or impotent perſon.

* This fourth part needed not: for the body of the act extended to cottages hereafter; but *abundans cautela non nocet.*

Note, this exception extendeth onely to cottages erected or made before this act, by reaſon of theſe words [heretofore made] but none of theſe three can be erected after this ſtatute, for any of theſe three purpoſes, unleſſe there be laid to it foure acres of ground with the foure incidents abovesaid. Lambert Juſtice of Peace, pag. 476. miſtaketh this part, and for heretofore, ſaith hereafter. But by the ſtatute of 43 Eliſ. cap. 2. either the church-wardens and over-ſeers, or the greateſt part of them, by the leave of the lord of the waſte, &c. in writing, under the hand and ſeale of the lord, or by order of the juſtices of peace at their generall quarter ſeſſions, by the leave of the lord, as is aforeſaid, may erect convenient houſes of habitation for poore impotent people, and alſo to place inmates, or more families then one in one cottage or houſe. Firſt, note that this extendeth only to ſuch as be poore and impotent. 2. It extendeth not to any common herdman or ſhepherd, as hath been likewiſe miſtaken.

Nor doth our act extend to any cottage to be made and decreed upon complaint made to juſtices of aſſiſe, or juſtices of peace in [738]

open assises, or quarter sessions of the peace to continue for habitation during the time only of such decree. This last branch extendeth only to cottages made after our statute.

The 3. branch.

Provided also, and be it enacted, that from and after the feast of All Saints next coming, there shall not be any inmate, or more families or housholds then one, dwelling or inhabiting in any one cottage (1), made, or to be made or erected, upon paine that every owner or occupier of any such cottage, placing, or willingly suffering any such inmate, or other family then one, shall forfeit and lose to the lord of the leet, within which such cottage shall be, the summe of ten shillings of lawfull mony of England, for every moneth that any such inmate, or other family then one, shall dwell or inhabit in any one cottage, as aforesaid. And that all and every lord and lords of leet and leets, and their stewards within the precinct of his and their leet and leets, shall have full power and authority within their severall leets, to enquire, and to take presentment by the oath of jurors of all and every offence and offences in this behalfe, and upon such presentment had or made to levie by distresse to the use of the lord of the leet, all such summes of mony as so shall be forfeited: and moreover, that it shall be lawfull for the lord of every such leet where such presentment shall be made, to recover to his own use any such forfeiture, by action of debt in any of the queenes majesties courts of record, wherein no essoine, protection, or wager of law shall be allowed.

See the statute of 43 Elis. ca. 2. ut sup. concerning inmates. *Inquilinus* (derived of *in* & *colo*, to dwell within) is the proper word for an inmate, or undersitter. * Coke lib. Int. 165. b.

(1) *There shall not be any inmate or more families or housholds then one dwelling or inhabiting in any one cottage*, &c.] Inmate. In the statute of 35 Elis. cap. 6. it is said inmate, or under sitter. It is here well explained by these words (or more families in any one cottage.)

Here seven things are to be observed:

1. That no inmate or under-sitter can be within this statute, but in a cottage.

2. This branch concerning inmates extendeth to cottages as well made before this statute, as after.

3. And as well to * cottages having foure acres of ground or more laid to them as is aforesaid, as others that have no ground at all.

4. Upon paine that every owner or occupier of any such cottage, placing, or willingly suffering any such inmate, or other family then one, shall forfeit and lose to the lord of the leet, within which such cottage shall be, the summe of ten shillings for every moneth, &c. This moneth is to be accounted according to the computation of 28 daies.

3 H. 7. 4.

5. And upon such presentment had or made, to levie by distresse, &c. that is, to sell the distresse which he shall take within the precinct of the leet for such forfeiture; and if there be a surplusage over the value of the forfeiture, to deliver it to the owner.

6. This act extendeth as well to inmates in cottages in any city, towne corporate, ancient borough, or market town, as in any other cottage wheresoever. *Vide* Hill. 8 *Jacobi in communi banco*, Rot. 2193. between John Pase plaintife, and Robert Peat defendant in

trespasse, Salop, A justification upon this statute for the penalty for keeping an inmate.

7. Hereby the act giveth election to the lord to take his remedy by action of debt in any of the kings courts of record.

Be it further enacted by the authoritie aforesaid, that all justices of assises, and justices of peace in their open sessions, and every lord within the precinct of his leet, and none others, shall have full power and authority within their several limits and jurisdictions, to enquire of, heare and determine all offences contrary to this present act, as well by indictment, as otherwise by presentment or information, and to award execution for the levying of the severall forfeitures aforesaid, by fieri facias, elegit, capias, or otherwise, as the cause shall require. [739] The 4. branch

In this branch these foure things are to be observed:

1. That these 3. *viz.* justices of assises, justices of peace, and lords of leets and no other judges or justices can enquire, &c. any of the offences against this statute. And therefore the sheriffe in his turn cannot enquire, &c. of any offence against this statute committed within the leet of any lord thereof.

2. That they may enquire, heare, and determine all offences, &c. so as there is a concurrent power in every of these three, and the judgement, &c. of such one of them, as doe first enquire, heare, and determine the same, shall stand; and each of them may enquire of all and every of the offences against this act.

3. As well by inditement, or otherwise by presentment or information. The difference between an inditement and presentment is this, that the inditement is drawne and ingrossed in parchment in forme of law, and delivered to the jurors to be enquired of, &c. And a presentment is properly that which the jurors find and present to the court, without any former inditement delivered to them, which afterward is reduced to a formed inditement. Every inditement which is found by the jurors is presented by them to the court: for the record saith, *juratores præsentant, &c.* when they find an inditement. And therefore every inditement is a presentment, but every presentment is not an inditement.

Offences found in leets, court barons, &c. are commonly called presentments; which was the reason that this act giving jurisdiction to a leet, doth use this word (presentment) in this and the third branch.

4. To award execution by * *fieri facias, elegit, capias,* or otherwise: hereby is greater jurisdiction given to the leet, then it had at the common law; so as the lord of the leet hath by the third branch power to levie the forfeiture due to him by distresse, or by action of debt by the common law; and by this fourth branch, by *fieri facias, elegit,* or *capias.* Co. li. Intrat. 665, 666.

Provided alwaies, that this statute, or any thing therein contained, shall not in any wise be extended to any cottage, which shall be ordained or erected to, or for habitation or dwelling in any city, towne corporate, or ancient borough, or market towne within this realme, nor to any cottages or buildings, which shall be erected, ordained, or converted to, and for the necessary and convenient habitation or dwelling of any workmen, or labourers in

in any minerall workes, cole mines, quarries, or delfes of ftone, or flate, or in or about the making of brick, tile, lime, or coles within this realme; fo as the fame cottages or buildings be not above one mile diftant from the place of the fame minerall or other workes, and fhall be ufed onely for the habitation and dwelling of the faid workmen, nor fhall in any fort prejudice, charge, or impeach any perfon or perfons, for the erecting, maintaining, or continuing of any fuch cottages, as are before in this provifo mentioned and fpecified.

[740] Provided alwaies, that this act fhall not extend to any cottage to be made within a mile of the fea, or upon the fide of fuch part of any navigable river, where the admirall ought to have jurifdiction, fo long as no other perfon fhall therein inhabit; but a failer, or man of manuall occupation, to or for making, furnifhing, or victualling of any fhip or veffell, ufed to ferve on the fea; nor to any cottage to be made in any forreft, chafe, warren, or parke, fo long as no other perfon fhall therein inhabit, but an under-keeper or warrener, for the good keeping of the deere, or other game of warren, nor to any cottage heretofore made, fo long as no other perfon fhall therein inhabit, but a common herdman or fhepherd, for keeping the cattell or fheep of the towne; or a poore lame, fick, aged, or impotent perfon, nor to any cottage to be made, which for any juft refpect upon complaint to the juftice of affife at the affifes, or to the juftices of peace at the quarter feffions, fhall by their order entered in open affifes or quarter feffions, be decreed to continue for habitation, for and during fo long time onely, as by fuch decree fhall be tolerated and limited. Stat. 35 Elif. 6. 43 Elif. 2.

Of thefe provifo's fufficient hath been fpoken before in the fecond branch of this ftatute.

The inconveniences that grow by unlawfull cottages, and inmates in cottages againft this ftatute, as appeare by the preamble, are great, being nefts to hatch idleneffe, the mother of pickings, theeveries, ftealing of wood, &c. tending alfo to the prejudice of lawfull commoners; for that new erected cottages within the memory of man, though they have foure acres of ground, or more laid to them, according to this act, ought not to common in the waftes of the lord; but the greateft inconvenience of all is, the ill breeding and educating of youth, which inconveniences may be eafily helped and remedied by the provifions of this excellent law, if lords of leets and their ftewards would looke to the execution of this act, which we hold the readieft meanes: for albeit the cottage erected, or converted, cannot by any provifion in this ftatute be demolifhed, or pulled downe; yet the execution of the penalty of this act will make it inhabitable, and work the defired effect. And they may alfo be amerced for wrongfull commoning in the court baron.

Cafa à cafu (id eft) ruina, quia ruinæ eft obnoxia.
Domuncula, tugurium à tegendo.

Virg. 2. Eglog. *Pauperis et tuguri congeftum cefpite culmen.*

A Col-

A Collection and Expofition upon the Statutes of Imployments, viz. 14 R. 2. cap. 1. and 2. 2 H. 4. cap. 5. 4 H. 4. cap. 15. 5 H. 4. cap. 9. 6 H. 4. cap. 4. 11 H. 4. cap. 8. 9 H. 5. cap. 9. Stat. 2. 8 H. 6. cap. 24. 27 H. 6. cap. 3. 17 E. 4. cap. 1. 1 H. 7. cap. 2. 3 H. 7. cap. 8.

With their feverall Alterations and Repeales, and Expirations of fome of them; our principall Aime ever being to fet down how the Law ftandeth at this Day.

BEFORE the making of any of thefe ftatutes, we find that merchant-ftrangers found fureties that they fhould not carry out the merchandizes which they brought in. Rot. Vafcon. 18 E. 2. m. 21.

It was ever the policie of this realme to entertaine merchant-ftrangers fairly and freely, having refpect how our merchants were demeaned abroad. See Mag. Charta c. 30. 5 H. 4. c. 7.

In the 18 yeare of E. 1. in the parliament roll it is conteined thus: *Cives London petunt quod alienigenæ mercatores expellantur à civitate, quia ditantur ad depauperationem civium, &c.* Rot. Parliament. 18 E. 1. fol. 4. nu. 55.

Refponfio. Rex intendit quod mercatores extranei funt idonei et utiles magnatibus, &c. et non habet confilium eos expellendi.

There be two kinds of ftatutes concerning imployments, the one where merchandizes, &c. are brought in, the other upon exchange. And firft of the firft..

The ftatutes of 14 R. 2. cap. 1. and 2 H. 4. cap. 5. are altered by the ftatute of 4 H. 4. cap. 15. And therefore we will begin with it.

It is ordained and eftablifhed that all merchant * aliens, ftrangers, and denizens (1), which bring merchandizes into the realme of England, and the fame do fell within the realme, and receive Englifh money (2) for the fame, fhall beftow the fame money upon other merchandizes of England, without carrying of any gold or filver, in coine, plate or maffe out of the faide realme, upon paine of forfeiture of the fame, faving alwaies their reafonable cofts.

* The Parliament Roll hath aliens, which of late hath beene omitted. Vid. 17 E. 4. cap. 1. This act extendeth to the whole merchandizes, and to the whole money, whereas the two former extended but to the halfe. 27 H. 6. cap. 3. further provifion was added, but that ftatute is expired. This act is confirmed by the ftatute of 5 H. 4. cap. 9. vid. 17 E. 4. cap. 1. and 3 H. 7. cap. 8.

There were two notable causes of the making of this act, as it is declared by the statute of 5 H. 4. ca. 9. viz. First, for the better keeping of gold and silver within this realme. Secondly, for the increase of the commodities of the same.

* The former two statutes extended to strangers onely. Nota, the originall is merchant-aliens, strangers and denizens, which doth cleare it.

(1) * *Denizens.*] Here denizens are taken for merchant-aliens, strangers which have obtained letters patents of denizations: and in this case they are derived from *donaison, id est, donatio,* because his freedome is given to him by the king, and were inconvenient if it should extend to naturall borne subjects; and the stranger made denizen is in equall † mischiefe if not in greater, with the meere stranger, and this statute standeth yet in force.

See the first part of the Institutes, s. 198. f. 129. for this word *denizen* † So resolved 7 Eliz. by the Barons.

[742]

This act of 17 E. 4. is confirmed by 3 H. 7. cap. 8.

But the statute of 17 E. 4. cap. 1. extends not to strangers which are made denizens: and therefore such as are so made denizens, are out of the penalty of that statute, but within the penalty of this of 4 Hen. 4. And that act of 17 E. 4. hath altered this act in another point, viz. that either hee may employ the money upon the merchandizes, whereunto 4 H. 4. only extended or other commodities of the realme, or hee may put the same in payment to the kings * liege people within this realme.

* Nota, [liege people,] so as he cannot pay it to a stranger, or he that is made *denizen,* for leige is as much as subject borne. † 1 H. 7. cap 2. 11 H. 7. cap. 14.

Such as are made denizens † by letters patents, or by parliament, or otherwise, shall pay for his merchandize like custome and subsidie, as they ought or should pay afore they were made denizens. See 11 H. 7. cap. 14. and 22 H. 8. cap. 8. See the statute of 1. Eliz. cap. 11.

8 H. 6. cap. 24.

(2) *English money.*] This is intended of all money of gold or silver currant within the realme of England, although it bee not coined within England, By this act he might have received English money either in silver or gold, but by the statute of 8 H. 6. cap. 24. he cannot receive any gold, nor ought to refuse the payment in silver.

See a case upon this Stat. in an information, &c. 10 H. 7. a. b. 9 H. 6. cap. 2.

By the said act of 8 H. 6. no Englishman should sell within this realme, &c. to any merchant alien, &c. any manner of merchandizes but onely for ready payment in hand, or else in merchandizes for merchandizes, to be paid and contented in hand, upon pain of forfeiture of the same; but by the statute of 9 H. 6. ca. 2. at the next parliament libertie was given for clothes onely from six moneths to six moneths next ensuing after such buyings made, without giving any further day of payment, upon paine of forfeiture of the same. This ordinance to endure as long as it shall please the king (3), but for all other merchandizes the statute of 8 H. 6. standeth in force.

10 H. 7. 7. b. Sir William Capels case. 5 E. 6. cap. 7.

(3) *As long as it shall please the king.*] This statute standeth untill the king or some of his successors (for successors are included under the name of king) shall adnull or make the same voide by proclamation under the great seale, which is the meane to make this act voide, and all others of like nature. Like acts are in 6 Hen. 6. cap. 1. 8 Hen. 6. cap. 8. 18 Hen. 6. cap. 13. 5 Ed. 6. cap. 7. &c.

The said act of 4 H. 4. cap. 15. prescribed no time for the employing of the money, but the statute of 5 H. 4. cap. 9. doth bind them to employment within a quarter of a year after their comming into

into this realme: but at the next parliament holden the next yeare, that branch onely for the limitation to a quarter of the yeare is made void and annulled: but the two other branches, viz. for the taking of * sureties by customers and controllers in all the parts of England for due imployment; and concerning money taken by exchange in this realme (whereof more shall be said hereafter) are not repealed by 6 H. 4. 6 H. 4. cap. 4. * A necessary branch to be put in execution.

See the resolution of the barons of the exchequer *anno* 7 Eliz. and entered in the custom-house concerning the statutes of imployments.

The justices of peace have power to heare and determine, all defaults and forfeitures purviewed or inflicted by the statute of 17 E. 4. cap. 1.

The other kind of statutes concerning imployments upon exchange. The second part.

That for every exchange that shall bee made by merchants to the court of Rome, or elsewhere (beyond the seas) that the said merchants bee firmly and surely bound in the chancery, to buy within three moneths after the exchange made merchandizes of the staple, as wooll, leather, woolfells, leade or tinne, butter or cheese, clothes or other commodities of the land, to the value of the sum so exchanged, upon paine of forfeiture of the same. 14 R. 2. cap. 2. It was altered by the statute of 9 H. 5. cap. 9. stat. 2. but that statute is expired, and 14 R. 2. standeth in force.

This statute extendeth to exchanges made by any merchant alien, denizen, or borne subject to foreine parts.

And also that the money delivered by exchange in England be imployed upon the commodities of this realme within the same realme, upon pain of forfeiture of the same money. [743] 5 H. 4. cap. 9.

This act extendeth to money delivered by way of exchange within the realme; and this branch is not repealed by the statute of 6 H. 4. cap. 4.

Anno 23 H. 8. a proclamation was made for observation of the statutes of employments. Holl. Chron. an. 23 H. 8. pag. 297.

An usuall thing when necessary statutes have beene (most commonly for private ends) for a time discontinued, to give all men notice thereof by proclamation, that such statutes for the time to come should bee put in due execution.

This have wee done upon consideration of all the said severall statutes for advancement of trade and traffick, especially of our native commodities, the life of every kingdome, and principally of isles.

The

The Statute of 25 Hen. 8. cap. 15. Concerning Printers, and Binders of Bookes.

BE it enacted, &c. that no person or persons resiant or inhabitant within this realme, &c. shall buy to sell againe any printed bookes, brought from any parts out of the kings obeysance ready bound in boords, leather, or parchment, upon paine to lose and forfeit for every book bound out of the kings obeysance, and brought into this realme, and bought by any person or persons within the same to sell againe contrary to this act, six shillings eight pence.

And be it further enacted by the authority aforesaid, that no person or persons inhabitant or resiant within this realme, &c. shall buy within this realm, of any stranger born out of the kings obedience, other then of denizens, any maner of printed books brought from any the parties beyond the sea, except only by engrosse, and not by retaile: upon pain of forfeiture of 6 s. 8 d. for every book so bought by retaile, contrary to the form and effect of this estatute, the said forfeitures to be alwaies levied of the buyers of any such bookes, contrary to this act: The one halfe of all the said forfeitures to be to the use of our soveraigne lord the king, and the other moitie to be to the party that will seise or sue for the same in any of the kings courts, be it by bill plaint, or information, wherein the defendant shall not be admitted to wage his law, nor no protection, ne essoin shall be unto him allowed.

Provided alway, and be it enacted by the authority beforesaid, that if any of the said printers, or sellers of printed books, inhabited within this realme, at any time hereafter happen in such wise to enhance and encrease the prices of any such printed books in sale or binding, at too high and unreasonable prices, in such wise as complaint be made thereof unto the kings highnesse, or unto the lord chancellor, lord treasurer, or any of the chief justices of the one bench or of the other: that then the same lord chancellor, lord treasurer, and two chief justices, or any two of them, shall have power and authority to enquire thereof, as well by the oaths of twelve honest and discreet persons, as otherwise by due examination by their discretions. And after the same enhaunsing and encreasing of the said prices of the said books and binding shall be so found by the said twelve men, or otherwise by examination of the said lord chancellor, lord treasurer, and justices, or two of them: that then the same lord chancellor, lord treasurer, and justices, or two of them at the least, from time to time, shall have power and authoritie to reform, and redresse such enhaunsing of the prices of printed books, from time to time, by their discretions, and to limit prices as well of the bookes, as for the binding of them: and over

over that the offendor or offendors thereof, being convict by the examination of the same lord chancellor, lord treasurer, and two justices, or two of them, or otherwise, shall lose and forfeit for every booke by them sold, whereof the price shall be enhaunsed, for the booke or binding thereof three shillings four pence, the one halfe thereof shall be to the kings highnesse, and the other halfe unto the parties grieved, that will complaine upon the same, in manner and forme before rehearsed. [745]

To the end, that not onely this second part of the Institutes, but all other bookes of what argument soever, may be sold at reasonable prices, and that the subjects of this realme, being printers, and binders of bookes, may be set on worke, we have thought good in this treatise of statutes to conclude with this statute of 25 H. 8. cap. 15. which consisteth on these three parts: 25 H. 8. cap. 15.

1. That no inhabitant or resiant within this realme shall buy to sell againe any printed bookes brought from any parts out of the kings obeysance ready bound in boords, leather, or parchment.

2. Nor shall buy within this realme of any stranger borne out of the kings obedience, other then of denizens, any manner of printed bookes brought from beyond the seas, except onely by ingrosse, and not by retaile.

3. That the lord chancelor, lord treasurer, and the two chiefe justices, or any two of them shall have power to enquire as well by the oath of twelve men, as otherwise by due examination by their discretion, of the enhaunsing and encreasing of the prices of bookes, or binding of the same, and the same so found, they, or any two of them, from time to time have power to limit prices as well of the bookes, as for the binding of them, as by the said act appeareth.

Which we have thought good to adde, to the end it might be knowne what the law is in these cases; and that if any enhaunsing or encreasing of prices be either of the bookes, or the binding of them, that it may be knowne who may and ought to redresse the same.

The Epilogue.

THUS have we, by the mercifull goodnesse of Almighty God, brought this second part of the Institutes (a large and laborious volume) containing an exposition of Magna Charta, and many other ancient and later statutes, to an end; wherein we could not follow or be guided by any other, for that never any (that we have seen or heard of) have enterprised to publish the like in this kind: and therefore if the piercing eyes of the learned shall find out errors herein, we are not without some kind of excuse. And we desire them to amend and correct those errors, according to the true sense of law, for the which we shall not

not onely give them thankes, but subscribe to the truth, and take it as some recompence for those our manifold and painfull labours herein, which we from the beginning have undertaken for the generall good and profit of the whole realme.

Post varios casus, post tot discrimina rerum.

Nunc sequitur conclusio.

DEO *gloria & gratia.*

Cic. lib. 2. fin. *Jucunda est præteritorum laborum memoria.*

---

[746]

Die Mercurii 12° Maii, 1641.

UPON *debate this day had in the Commons House of Parliament, the said House did then desire and held it fit, that the Heire of Sir* Edward Coke, *should publish in print the Commentary upon* Magna Charta, *the* Plees of the Crowne, *and the* Jurisdiction of Courts, *according to the intention of the said Sir* Edward Coke. *And that none but the Heire of the said Sir* Edward Coke, *or hee that shall be authorised by him, do presume to publish in print any of the foresaid Bookes, or any Copy thereof.*

H. Elsynge Cler. Domus Com.

Die Veneris 3° Junii, 1642.

WHEREAS by an order dated the 12th of May, 1641, this House desired and held fit, that the Heire of Sir *Edward Coke* should publish in print the Commentaries of *Magna Charta*, the *Plees of the Crowne*, and the *Jurisdiction of Courts:* and that none but the said Heire, or his assignes should presume to print the same: and where by another order of this House, dated the seventh of March last, it was ordered, that a bill should be drawn, for the preventing the re-printing of the said bookes for a time certaine to be assigned in the said bill, as by the said severall orders may appeare: according to which last mentioned order a bill was drawne and preferred to this House, and hath been once read: but in respect of the many great and weighty affaires of the kingdome, no further proceedings have been, or as yet can be had therein. It is this day ordered, that, forasmuch as one of the said books *(viz.)* the Comment upon *Magna Charta*

Charta is already printed, and ready to be publiſhed, and the other two alſo ready for the preſſe, that none but the ſaid Heire of Sir *Edward Coke*, or he or they that ſhall be authoriſed by him, doe print or re-print, or cauſe to be printed or re-printed any of the ſaid books, or any part of them, or any of them, before a full yeare after the publiſhing, and putting to ſale of the ſame reſpectively: and that the Maſter and Wardens of the company of Stationers be required to take a ſpeciall care for the due performance of this order; and if any ſhall notwithſtanding preſume to print or re-print, within the time aforeſaid, any of the ſaid books, or any part thereof (other then the ſaid Heire or his aſſignes) that then they certifie their names, to the intent ſome courſe may be taken for the puniſhing of the offendors, as to this Houſe ſhall ſeem meet.

H. Elſynge Cler. Parl. D. Com.

INDEX of Maxims and Rules.

Lex

Maxims and Rules.

Res

Maxims and Rules.

A TABLE

A
TABLE
TO THE
Second Part *of the* Inſtitutes.

A TABLE.

Actions upon the Case.

Actions upon the Statute.

Acquital.

Act of God.

Additions.

Admeasurement of Pasture.

Administrators and Administration.

Admiralty.

A TABLE.

Annum, Diem, & Vastum.

Appeal.

Assets.

Assets

A TABLE.

What

Bastardy.

Bail and Bailable.

Bishops.

Books.

Bridges.

A TABLE.

Bulwarks.

By-laws, *vide* Corporation.

Cambridge.

Canons.

Capite Tenure.

Carriages.

Caſtles, *vide* Bulwarks.

Caſtle Guard.

Certiorari.

Ceſſavit.

Chaſe, *vide* Foreſt.

Challenge.

Chancery and Chancellor.

Regiſter

Charge.

Church.

Cinq-ports.

Clergy.

Clergymen.

Cloth and Clothing.

Coin.

Collusion.

Commissions.

7° &

Where

What

Cottages.

Councells.

Counterplea de voucher, vide Voucher.

County.

County-Court.

Court-Baron.

Court-Christian.

Cai

A TABLE.

Where

Debt

Offices

Homage

11 *H.*

 What

A TABLE.

King's-Bench.

Knight *vide* Nobility.

Knights service.

Laws.

Where

Law Marine.

Law Merchant.

Liberty.

Livery.

London.

Magna Charta.

Mag.

Maintenance and Champerty.

Mannors *vide* Honors.

Merchant and Merchandize.

Market.

Marriage.

Marſhalſea.

Mayhem.

Meſne.

Monopolies.

Judges

Lords

Nonsuit.

Nusans.

Oath.

Office and Officers.

Oppression.

Ordinary.

Ordinary.

Parceners.

Pardon.

Parks *vide* Forests.

Parliament.

Parson.

Petition.

Pleas and Pleading.

A TABLE.

Pledges.

Pope.

Poffeffions.

Prerogative.

Where

Prescription.

Presentation.

Where

Where

Prohibition.

Property.

Purveyor.

Quare impedit.

Quarentine.

Queen.

A TABLE.

Where

Reference.

Relief.

Religion.

Remover de Records.

Rents.

Replevin.

Reftitution.

Refummons.

A TABLE.

Seisure.

Serjeant at Law.

Sheriff.

Socage.

Soldier.

Statutes.

Magna charta edita 9 *H.* 3.

 4. Wast

A TABLE.

Merton edit. 20 *H.* 3.

Marlebridge edit. 52 *H.* 3.

W. 1. edit. 3 *E.* 1.

41. Battle

A TABLE.

Concerning Statutes in general.

Subsidy.

Suit of Court.

Summons.

Summons and Severance.

Suspicion.

Tail.

Tenant

The

Where

Difference

Seperalia brevia de

FINIS.

www.ingramcontent.com/pod-product-compliance
Lightning Source LLC
LaVergne TN
LVHW092115300926
849161LV00002B/138
* 9 7 8 1 5 8 4 7 7 2 0 0 2 *